T0190173

Lecture Notes in Computer Science 12255

More information about this series at http://www.springer.com/series/7407

Osvaldo Gervasi · Beniamino Murgante ·
Sanjay Misra · Chiara Garau ·
Ivan Blečić · David Taniar ·
Bernady O. Apduhan · Ana Maria A. C. Rocha ·
Eufemia Tarantino · Carmelo Maria Torre ·
Yeliz Karaca (Eds.)

Computational Science and Its Applications – ICCSA 2020

20th International Conference
Cagliari, Italy, July 1–4, 2020
Proceedings, Part VII

 Springer

Editors
Osvaldo Gervasi 🆔
University of Perugia
Perugia, Italy

Sanjay Misra 🆔
Chair- Center of ICT/ICE
Covenant University
Ota, Nigeria

Ivan Blečić 🆔
University of Cagliari
Cagliari, Italy

Bernady O. Apduhan
Department of Information Science
Kyushu Sangyo University
Fukuoka, Japan

Eufemia Tarantino 🆔
Polytechnic University of Bari
Bari, Italy

Yeliz Karaca 🆔
Department of Neurology
University of Massachusetts
Medical School
Worcester, MA, USA

Beniamino Murgante 🆔
University of Basilicata
Potenza, Potenza, Italy

Chiara Garau 🆔
University of Cagliari
Cagliari, Italy

David Taniar 🆔
Clayton School of Information Technology
Monash University
Clayton, VIC, Australia

Ana Maria A. C. Rocha 🆔
University of Minho
Braga, Portugal

Carmelo Maria Torre 🆔
Polytechnic University of Bari
Bari, Italy

ISSN 0302-9743   ISSN 1611-3349   (electronic)
Lecture Notes in Computer Science
ISBN 978-3-030-58819-9   ISBN 978-3-030-58820-5   (eBook)
https://doi.org/10.1007/978-3-030-58820-5

LNCS Sublibrary: SL1 – Theoretical Computer Science and General Issues

This Springer imprint is published by the registered company Springer Nature Switzerland AG
The registered company address is: Gewerbestrasse 11, 6330 Cham, Switzerland

Preface

These seven volumes (LNCS volumes 12249–12255) consist of the peer-reviewed papers from the International Conference on Computational Science and Its Applications (ICCSA 2020) which took place from July 1–4, 2020. Initially the conference was planned to be held in Cagliari, Italy, in collaboration with the University of Cagliari, but due to the COVID-19 pandemic it was organized as an online event.

ICCSA 2020 was a successful event in the conference series, previously held in Saint Petersburg, Russia (2019), Melbourne, Australia (2018), Trieste, Italy (2017), Beijing, China (2016), Banff, Canada (2015), Guimaraes, Portugal (2014), Ho Chi Minh City, Vietnam (2013), Salvador, Brazil (2012), Santander, Spain (2011), Fukuoka, Japan (2010), Suwon, South Korea (2009), Perugia, Italy (2008), Kuala Lumpur, Malaysia (2007), Glasgow, UK (2006), Singapore (2005), Assisi, Italy (2004), Montreal, Canada (2003), and (as ICCS) Amsterdam, The Netherlands (2002) and San Francisco, USA (2001).

Computational science is the main pillar of most of the present research, industrial and commercial applications, and plays a unique role in exploiting ICT innovative technologies. The ICCSA conference series has provided a venue for researchers and industry practitioners to discuss new ideas, to share complex problems and their solutions, and to shape new trends in computational science.

Apart from the general track, ICCSA 2020 also included 52 workshops in various areas of computational science, ranging from computational science technologies to specific areas of computational science, such as software engineering, security, machine learning and artificial intelligence, blockchain technologies, and of applications in many fields. We accepted 498 papers, distributed among 6 conference main tracks, which included 52 in workshops and 32 short papers. We would like to express our appreciation to the workshops chairs and co-chairs for their hard work and dedication.

The success of the ICCSA conference series in general, and of ICCSA 2020 in particular, vitaly depends on the support from many people: authors, presenters, participants, keynote speakers, workshop chairs, session chairs, Organizing Committee members, student volunteers, Program Committee members, Advisory Committee members, international liaison chairs, reviewers, and others in various roles. We take this opportunity to wholeheartedly thank them all.

We also wish to thank our publisher, Springer, for their acceptance to publish the proceedings, for sponsoring part of the Best Papers Awards, and for their kind assistance and cooperation during the editing process.

We cordially invite you to visit the ICCSA website http://www.iccsa.org where you can find all the relevant information about this interesting and exciting event.

July 2020

Osvaldo Gervasi
Beniamino Murgante
Sanjay Misra

Welcome to the Online Conference

The COVID-19 pandemic disrupted our plans for ICCSA 2020, as was the case for the scientific community around the world. Hence, we had to promptly regroup and rush to set in place the organization and the underlying infrastructure of the online event.

We chose to build the technological infrastructure using only open source software. In particular, we used Jitsi (`jitsi.org`) for the videoconferencing, Riot (`riot.im`) together with Matrix (`matrix.org`) for chat and asynchronous communication, and Jibri (`github.com/jitsi/jibri`) for live streaming sessions on YouTube.

Six Jitsi servers were set up, one for each parallel session. The participants of the sessions were helped and assisted by eight volunteer students (from the Universities of Cagliari, Florence, Perugia, and Bari), who assured technical support and smooth running of the conference proceedings.

The implementation of the software infrastructure and the technical coordination of the volunteers was carried out by Damiano Perri and Marco Simonetti.

Our warmest thanks go to all the volunteering students, to the technical coordinators, and to the development communities of Jitsi, Jibri, Riot, and Matrix, who made their terrific platforms available as open source software.

Our heartfelt thanks go to the keynote speakers: Yaneer Bar-Yam, Cecilia Ceccarelli, and Vincenzo Piuri and to the guests of the closing keynote panel: Mike Batty, Denise Pumain, and Alexis Tsoukiàs.

A big thank you goes to all the 454 speakers, many of whom showed an enormous collaborative spirit, sometimes participating and presenting in almost prohibitive times of the day, given that the participants of this year's conference come from 52 countries scattered over many time zones of the globe.

Finally, we would like to thank Google for letting us livestream all the events via YouTube. In addition to lightening the load of our Jitsi servers, that will allow us to keep memory and to be able to review the most exciting moments of the conference.

We all hope to meet in our beautiful Cagliari next year, safe from COVID-19, and finally free to meet in person and enjoy the beauty of the ICCSA community in the enchanting Sardinia.

July 2020

Ivan Blečić
Chiara Garau

Organization

ICCSA 2020 was organized by the University of Cagliari (Italy), University of Perugia (Italy), University of Basilicata (Italy), Monash University (Australia), Kyushu Sangyo University (Japan), and University of Minho (Portugal).

Honorary General Chairs

Antonio Laganà	Master-UP, Italy
Norio Shiratori	Chuo University, Japan
Kenneth C. J. Tan	Sardina Systems, UK
Corrado Zoppi	University of Cagliari, Italy

General Chairs

Osvaldo Gervasi	University of Perugia, Italy
Ivan Blečić	University of Cagliari, Italy
David Taniar	Monash University, Australia

Program Committee Chairs

Beniamino Murgante	University of Basilicata, Italy
Bernady O. Apduhan	Kyushu Sangyo University, Japan
Chiara Garau	University of Cagliari, Italy
Ana Maria A. C. Rocha	University of Minho, Portugal

International Advisory Committee

Jemal Abawajy	Deakin University, Australia
Dharma P. Agarwal	University of Cincinnati, USA
Rajkumar Buyya	The University of Melbourne, Australia
Claudia Bauzer Medeiros	University of Campinas, Brazil
Manfred M. Fisher	Vienna University of Economics and Business, Austria
Marina L. Gavrilova	University of Calgary, Canada
Yee Leung	Chinese University of Hong Kong, China

International Liaison Chairs

Giuseppe Borruso	University of Trieste, Italy
Elise De Donker	Western Michigan University, USA
Maria Irene Falcão	University of Minho, Portugal
Robert C. H. Hsu	Chung Hua University, Taiwan

Tai-Hoon Kim	Beijing Jaotong University, China
Vladimir Korkhov	Saint Petersburg University, Russia
Sanjay Misra	Covenant University, Nigeria
Takashi Naka	Kyushu Sangyo University, Japan
Rafael D. C. Santos	National Institute for Space Research, Brazil
Maribel Yasmina Santos	University of Minho, Portugal
Elena Stankova	Saint Petersburg University, Russia

Workshop and Session Organizing Chairs

Beniamino Murgante	University of Basilicata, Italy
Sanjay Misra	Covenant University, Nigeria
Jorge Gustavo Rocha	University of Minho, Portugal

Award Chair

Wenny Rahayu	La Trobe University, Australia

Publicity Committee Chairs

Elmer Dadios	De La Salle University, Philippines
Nataliia Kulabukhova	Saint Petersburg University, Russia
Daisuke Takahashi	Tsukuba University, Japan
Shangwang Wang	Beijing University of Posts and Telecommunications, China

Technology Chairs

Damiano Perri	University of Florence, Italy
Marco Simonetti	University of Florence, Italy

Local Arrangement Chairs

Ivan Blečić	University of Cagliari, Italy
Chiara Garau	University of Cagliari, Italy
Ginevra Balletto	University of Cagliari, Italy
Giuseppe Borruso	University of Trieste, Italy
Michele Campagna	University of Cagliari, Italy
Mauro Coni	University of Cagliari, Italy
Anna Maria Colavitti	University of Cagliari, Italy
Giulia Desogus	University of Cagliari, Italy
Sabrina Lai	University of Cagliari, Italy
Francesca Maltinti	University of Cagliari, Italy
Pasquale Mistretta	University of Cagliari, Italy
Augusto Montisci	University of Cagliari, Italy
Francesco Pinna	University of Cagliari, Italy

Davide Spano	University of Cagliari, Italy
Roberto Tonelli	University of Cagliari, Italy
Giuseppe A. Trunfio	University of Sassari, Italy
Corrado Zoppi	University of Cagliari, Italy

Program Committee

Vera Afreixo	University of Aveiro, Portugal
Filipe Alvelos	University of Minho, Portugal
Hartmut Asche	University of Potsdam, Germany
Ginevra Balletto	University of Cagliari, Italy
Michela Bertolotto	University College Dublin, Ireland
Sandro Bimonte	CEMAGREF, TSCF, France
Rod Blais	University of Calgary, Canada
Ivan Blečić	University of Sassari, Italy
Giuseppe Borruso	University of Trieste, Italy
Ana Cristina Braga	University of Minho, Portugal
Massimo Cafaro	University of Salento, Italy
Yves Caniou	Lyon University, France
José A. Cardoso e Cunha	Universidade Nova de Lisboa, Portugal
Rui Cardoso	University of Beira Interior, Portugal
Leocadio G. Casado	University of Almeria, Spain
Carlo Cattani	University of Salerno, Italy
Mete Celik	Erciyes University, Turkey
Hyunseung Choo	Sungkyunkwan University, South Korea
Min Young Chung	Sungkyunkwan University, South Korea
Florbela Maria da Cruz Domingues Correia	Polytechnic Institute of Viana do Castelo, Portugal
Gilberto Corso Pereira	Federal University of Bahia, Brazil
Alessandro Costantini	INFN, Italy
Carla Dal Sasso Freitas	Universidade Federal do Rio Grande do Sul, Brazil
Pradesh Debba	The Council for Scientific and Industrial Research (CSIR), South Africa
Hendrik Decker	Instituto Tecnológico de Informática, Spain
Frank Devai	London South Bank University, UK
Rodolphe Devillers	Memorial University of Newfoundland, Canada
Joana Matos Dias	University of Coimbra, Portugal
Paolino Di Felice	University of L'Aquila, Italy
Prabu Dorairaj	NetApp, India/USA
M. Irene Falcao	University of Minho, Portugal
Cherry Liu Fang	U.S. DOE Ames Laboratory, USA
Florbela P. Fernandes	Polytechnic Institute of Bragança, Portugal
Jose-Jesus Fernandez	National Centre for Biotechnology, CSIS, Spain
Paula Odete Fernandes	Polytechnic Institute of Bragança, Portugal
Adelaide de Fátima Baptista Valente Freitas	University of Aveiro, Portugal

Manuel Carlos Figueiredo	University of Minho, Portugal
Maria Celia Furtado Rocha	PRODEB–PósCultura, UFBA, Brazil
Chiara Garau	University of Cagliari, Italy
Paulino Jose Garcia Nieto	University of Oviedo, Spain
Jerome Gensel	LSR-IMAG, France
Maria Giaoutzi	National Technical University of Athens, Greece
Arminda Manuela Andrade Pereira Gonçalves	University of Minho, Portugal
Andrzej M. Goscinski	Deakin University, Australia
Sevin Gümgüm	Izmir University of Economics, Turkey
Alex Hagen-Zanker	University of Cambridge, UK
Shanmugasundaram Hariharan	B.S. Abdur Rahman University, India
Eligius M. T. Hendrix	University of Malaga, Spain, and Wageningen University, The Netherlands
Hisamoto Hiyoshi	Gunma University, Japan
Mustafa Inceoglu	EGE University, Turkey
Peter Jimack	University of Leeds, UK
Qun Jin	Waseda University, Japan
Farid Karimipour	Vienna University of Technology, Austria
Baris Kazar	Oracle Corp., USA
Maulana Adhinugraha Kiki	Telkom University, Indonesia
DongSeong Kim	University of Canterbury, New Zealand
Taihoon Kim	Hannam University, South Korea
Ivana Kolingerova	University of West Bohemia, Czech Republic
Nataliia Kulabukhova	Saint Petersburg University, Russia
Vladimir Korkhov	Saint Petersburg University, Russia
Rosa Lasaponara	CNR, Italy
Maurizio Lazzari	CNR, Italy
Cheng Siong Lee	Monash University, Australia
Sangyoun Lee	Yonsei University, South Korea
Jongchan Lee	Kunsan National University, South Korea
Chendong Li	University of Connecticut, USA
Gang Li	Deakin University, Australia
Fang Liu	AMES Laboratories, USA
Xin Liu	University of Calgary, Canada
Andrea Lombardi	University of Perugia, Italy
Savino Longo	University of Bari, Italy
Tinghuai Ma	Nanjing University of Information Science and Technology, China
Ernesto Marcheggiani	Katholieke Universiteit Leuven, Belgium
Antonino Marvuglia	Research Centre Henri Tudor, Luxembourg
Nicola Masini	CNR, Italy
Ilaria Matteucci	CNR, Italy
Eric Medvet	University of Trieste, Italy
Nirvana Meratnia	University of Twente, The Netherlands

Pablo Vanegas	University of Cuenca, Ecuador
Marco Vizzari	University of Perugia, Italy
Varun Vohra	Merck Inc., USA
Koichi Wada	University of Tsukuba, Japan
Krzysztof Walkowiak	Wroclaw University of Technology, Poland
Zequn Wang	Intelligent Automation Inc., USA
Robert Weibel	University of Zurich, Switzerland
Frank Westad	Norwegian University of Science and Technology, Norway
Roland Wismüller	Universität Siegen, Germany
Mudasser Wyne	SOET National University, USA
Chung-Huang Yang	National Kaohsiung Normal University, Taiwan
Xin-She Yang	National Physical Laboratory, UK
Salim Zabir	France Telecom Japan Co., Japan
Haifeng Zhao	University of California, Davis, USA
Fabiana Zollo	University of Venice, Italy
Albert Y. Zomaya	The University of Sydney, Australia

Workshop Organizers

Advanced Transport Tools and Methods (A2TM 2020)

| Massimiliano Petri | University of Pisa, Italy |
| Antonio Pratelli | University of Pisa, Italy |

Advances in Artificial Intelligence Learning Technologies: Blended Learning, STEM, Computational Thinking and Coding (AAILT 2020)

Valentina Franzoni	University of Perugia, Italy
Alfredo Milani	University of Perugia, Italy
Sergio Tasso	University of Perugia, Italy

Workshop on Advancements in Applied Machine Learning and Data Analytics (AAMDA 2020)

Alessandro Costantini	INFN, Italy
Daniele Cesini	INFN, Italy
Davide Salomoni	INFN, Italy
Doina Cristina Duma	INFN, Italy

Advanced Computational Approaches in Artificial Intelligence and Complex Systems Applications (ACAC 2020)

Yeliz Karaca	University of Massachusetts Medical School, USA
Dumitru Baleanu	Çankaya University, Turkey, and Institute of Space Sciences, Romania
Majaz Moonis	University of Massachusetts Medical School, USA
Yu-Dong Zhang	University of Leicester, UK

Affective Computing and Emotion Recognition (ACER-EMORE 2020)

Valentina Franzoni   University of Perugia, Italy
Alfredo Milani   University of Perugia, Italy
Giulio Biondi   University of Florence, Italy

AI Factory and Smart Manufacturing (AIFACTORY 2020)

Jongpil Jeong   Sungkyunkwan University, South Korea

Air Quality Monitoring and Citizen Science for Smart Urban Management. State of the Art And Perspectives (AirQ&CScience 2020)

Grazie Fattoruso   ENEA CR Portici, Italy
Maurizio Pollino   ENEA CR Casaccia, Italy
Saverio De Vito   ENEA CR Portici, Italy

Automatic Landform Classification: Spatial Methods and Applications (ALCSMA 2020)

Maria Danese   CNR-ISPC, Italy
Dario Gioia   CNR-ISPC, Italy

Advances of Modelling Micromobility in Urban Spaces (AMMUS 2020)

Tiziana Campisi   University of Enna KORE, Italy
Giovanni Tesoriere   University of Enna KORE, Italy
Ioannis Politis   Aristotle University of Thessaloniki, Greece
Socrates Basbas   Aristotle University of Thessaloniki, Greece
Sanja Surdonja   University of Rijeka, Croatia
Marko Rencelj   University of Maribor, Slovenia

Advances in Information Systems and Technologies for Emergency Management, Risk Assessment and Mitigation Based on the Resilience Concepts (ASTER 2020)

Maurizio Pollino   ENEA, Italy
Marco Vona   University of Basilicata, Italy
Amedeo Flora   University of Basilicata, Italy
Chiara Iacovino   University of Basilicata, Italy
Beniamino Murgante   University of Basilicata, Italy

Advances in Web Based Learning (AWBL 2020)

Birol Ciloglugil   Ege University, Turkey
Mustafa Murat Inceoglu   Ege University, Turkey

Blockchain and Distributed Ledgers: Technologies and Applications (BDLTA 2020)

Vladimir Korkhov	Saint Petersburg University, Russia
Elena Stankova	Saint Petersburg University, Russia
Nataliia Kulabukhova	Saint Petersburg University, Russia

Bio and Neuro Inspired Computing and Applications (BIONCA 2020)

Nadia Nedjah	State University of Rio de Janeiro, Brazil
Luiza De Macedo Mourelle	State University of Rio de Janeiro, Brazil

Computer Aided Modeling, Simulation and Analysis (CAMSA 2020)

Jie Shen	University of Michigan, USA

Computational and Applied Statistics (CAS 2020)

Ana Cristina Braga	University of Minho, Portugal

Computerized Evidence Based Decision Making (CEBDEM 2020)

Clarice Bleil de Souza	Cardiff University, UK
Valerio Cuttini	University of Pisa, Italy
Federico Cerutti	Cardiff University, UK
Camilla Pezzica	Cardiff University, UK

Computational Geometry and Applications (CGA 2020)

Marina Gavrilova	University of Calgary, Canada

Computational Mathematics, Statistics and Information Management (CMSIM 2020)

Maria Filomena Teodoro	Portuguese Naval Academy, University of Lisbon, Portugal

Computational Optimization and Applications (COA 2020)

Ana Rocha	University of Minho, Portugal
Humberto Rocha	University of Coimbra, Portugal

Computational Astrochemistry (CompAstro 2020)

Marzio Rosi	University of Perugia, Italy
Cecilia Ceccarelli	University of Grenoble, France
Stefano Falcinelli	University of Perugia, Italy
Dimitrios Skouteris	Master-UP, Italy

Cities, Technologies and Planning (CTP 2020)

Beniamino Murgante	University of Basilicata, Italy
Ljiljana Zivkovic	Ministry of Construction, Transport and Infrastructure and Institute of Architecture and Urban & Spatial Planning of Serbia, Serbia
Giuseppe Borruso	University of Trieste, Italy
Malgorzata Hanzl	University of Łódź, Poland

Data Stream Processing and Applications (DASPA 2020)

Raja Chiky	ISEP, France
Rosanna VERDE	University of Campania, Italy
Marcilio De Souto	Orleans University, France

Data Science for Cyber Security (DS4Cyber 2020)

Hongmei Chi	Florida A&M University, USA

Econometric and Multidimensional Evaluation in Urban Environment (EMEUE 2020)

Carmelo Maria Torre	Polytechnic University of Bari, Italy
Pierluigi Morano	Polytechnic University of Bari, Italy
Maria Cerreta	University of Naples, Italy
Paola Perchinunno	University of Bari, Italy
Francesco Tajani	University of Rome, Italy
Simona Panaro	University of Portsmouth, UK
Francesco Scorza	University of Basilicata, Italy

Frontiers in Machine Learning (FIML 2020)

Massimo Bilancia	University of Bari, Italy
Paola Perchinunno	University of Bari, Italy
Pasquale Lops	University of Bari, Italy
Danilo Di Bona	University of Bari, Italy

Future Computing System Technologies and Applications (FiSTA 2020)

Bernady Apduhan	Kyushu Sangyo University, Japan
Rafael Santos	Brazilian National Institute for Space Research, Brazil

Geodesign in Decision Making: Meta Planning and Collaborative Design for Sustainable and Inclusive Development (GDM 2020)

Francesco Scorza	University of Basilicata, Italy
Michele Campagna	University of Cagliari, Italy
Ana Clara Mourao Moura	Federal University of Minas Gerais, Brazil

**Geomatics in Forestry and Agriculture: New Advances
and Perspectives (GeoForAgr 2020)**

Maurizio Pollino	ENEA, Italy
Giuseppe Modica	University of Reggio Calabria, Italy
Marco Vizzari	University of Perugia, Italy

**Geographical Analysis, Urban Modeling, Spatial Statistics
(GEOG-AND-MOD 2020)**

Beniamino Murgante	University of Basilicata, Italy
Giuseppe Borruso	University of Trieste, Italy
Hartmut Asche	University of Potsdam, Germany

Geomatics for Resource Monitoring and Management (GRMM 2020)

Eufemia Tarantino	Polytechnic University of Bari, Italy
Enrico Borgogno Mondino	University of Torino, Italy
Marco Scaioni	Polytechnic University of Milan, Italy
Alessandra Capolupo	Polytechnic University of Bari, Italy

Software Quality (ISSQ 2020)

Sanjay Misra	Covenant University, Nigeria

Collective, Massive and Evolutionary Systems (IWCES 2020)

Alfredo Milani	University of Perugia, Italy
Rajdeep Niyogi	Indian Institute of Technology, Roorkee, India
Alina Elena Baia	University of Florence, Italy

Large Scale Computational Science (LSCS 2020)

Elise De Doncker	Western Michigan University, USA
Fukuko Yuasa	High Energy Accelerator Research Organization (KEK), Japan
Hideo Matsufuru	High Energy Accelerator Research Organization (KEK), Japan

Land Use Monitoring for Sustainability (LUMS 2020)

Carmelo Maria Torre	Polytechnic University of Bari, Italy
Alessandro Bonifazi	Polytechnic University of Bari, Italy
Pasquale Balena	Polytechnic University of Bari, Italy
Massimiliano Bencardino	University of Salerno, Italy
Francesco Tajani	University of Rome, Italy
Pierluigi Morano	Polytechnic University of Bari, Italy
Maria Cerreta	University of Naples, Italy
Giuliano Poli	University of Naples, Italy

Machine Learning for Space and Earth Observation Data (MALSEOD 2020)

Rafael Santos	INPE, Brazil
Karine Ferreira	INPE, Brazil

Building Multi-dimensional Models for Assessing Complex Environmental Systems (MES 2020)

Marta Dell'Ovo	Polytechnic University of Milan, Italy
Vanessa Assumma	Polytechnic University of Torino, Italy
Caterina Caprioli	Polytechnic University of Torino, Italy
Giulia Datola	Polytechnic University of Torino, Italy
Federico dell'Anna	Polytechnic University of Torino, Italy

Ecosystem Services: Nature's Contribution to People in Practice. Assessment Frameworks, Models, Mapping, and Implications (NC2P 2020)

Francesco Scorza	University of Basilicata, Italy
David Cabana	International Marine Center, Italy
Sabrina Lai	University of Cagliari, Italy
Ana Clara Mourao Moura	Federal University of Minas Gerais, Brazil
Corrado Zoppi	University of Cagliari, Italy

Open Knowledge for Socio-economic Development (OKSED 2020)

Luigi Mundula	University of Cagliari, Italy
Flavia Marzano	Link Campus University, Italy
Maria Paradiso	University of Milan, Italy

Scientific Computing Infrastructure (SCI 2020)

Elena Stankova	Saint Petersburg State University, Russia
Vladimir Korkhov	Saint Petersburg State University, Russia
Natalia Kulabukhova	Saint Petersburg State University, Russia

Computational Studies for Energy and Comfort in Buildings (SECoB 2020)

Senhorinha Teixeira	University of Minho, Portugal
Luís Martins	University of Minho, Portugal
Ana Maria Rocha	University of Minho, Portugal

Software Engineering Processes and Applications (SEPA 2020)

Sanjay Misra	Covenant University, Nigeria

Smart Ports - Technologies and Challenges (SmartPorts 2020)

Gianfranco Fancello	University of Cagliari, Italy
Patrizia Serra	University of Cagliari, Italy
Marco Mazzarino	University of Venice, Italy
Luigi Mundula	University of Cagliari, Italy

Ginevra Balletto   University of Cagliari, Italy
Giuseppe Borruso   University of Trieste, Italy

Sustainability Performance Assessment: Models, Approaches and Applications Toward Interdisciplinary and Integrated Solutions (SPA 2020)

Francesco Scorza   University of Basilicata, Italy
Valentin Grecu   Lucian Blaga University, Romania
Jolanta Dvarioniene   Kaunas University of Technology, Lithuania
Sabrina Lai   University of Cagliari, Italy
Iole Cerminara   University of Basilicata, Italy
Corrado Zoppi   University of Cagliari, Italy

Smart and Sustainable Island Communities (SSIC 2020)

Chiara Garau   University of Cagliari, Italy
Anastasia Stratigea   National Technical University of Athens, Greece
Paola Zamperlin   University of Pisa, Italy
Francesco Scorza   University of Basilicata, Italy

Science, Technologies and Policies to Innovate Spatial Planning (STP4P 2020)

Chiara Garau   University of Cagliari, Italy
Daniele La Rosa   University of Catania, Italy
Francesco Scorza   University of Basilicata, Italy
Anna Maria Colavitti   University of Cagliari, Italy
Beniamino Murgante   University of Basilicata, Italy
Paolo La Greca   University of Catania, Italy

New Frontiers for Strategic Urban Planning (StrategicUP 2020)

Luigi Mundula   University of Cagliari, Italy
Ginevra Balletto   University of Cagliari, Italy
Giuseppe Borruso   University of Trieste, Italy
Michele Campagna   University of Cagliari, Italy
Beniamino Murgante   University of Basilicata, Italy

Theoretical and Computational Chemistry and its Applications (TCCMA 2020)

Noelia Faginas-Lago   University of Perugia, Italy
Andrea Lombardi   University of Perugia, Italy

Tools and Techniques in Software Development Process (TTSDP 2020)

Sanjay Misra   Covenant University, Nigeria

Urban Form Studies (UForm 2020)

Malgorzata Hanzl   Łódź University of Technology, Poland

Urban Space Extended Accessibility (USEaccessibility 2020)

Chiara Garau   University of Cagliari, Italy
Francesco Pinna   University of Cagliari, Italy
Beniamino Murgante   University of Basilicata, Italy
Mauro Coni   University of Cagliari, Italy
Francesca Maltinti   University of Cagliari, Italy
Vincenza Torrisi   University of Catania, Italy
Matteo Ignaccolo   University of Catania, Italy

Virtual and Augmented Reality and Applications (VRA 2020)

Osvaldo Gervasi   University of Perugia, Italy
Damiano Perri   University of Perugia, Italy
Marco Simonetti   University of Perugia, Italy
Sergio Tasso   University of Perugia, Italy

Workshop on Advanced and Computational Methods for Earth Science Applications (WACM4ES 2020)

Luca Piroddi   University of Cagliari, Italy
Laura Foddis   University of Cagliari, Italy
Gian Piero Deidda   University of Cagliari, Italy
Augusto Montisci   University of Cagliari, Italy
Gabriele Uras   University of Cagliari, Italy
Giulio Vignoli   University of Cagliari, Italy

Sponsoring Organizations

ICCSA 2020 would not have been possible without tremendous support of many organizations and institutions, for which all organizers and participants of ICCSA 2020 express their sincere gratitude:

Springer International Publishing AG, Germany
(https://www.springer.com)

Computers Open Access Journal
(https://www.mdpi.com/journal/computers)

IEEE Italy Section, Italy
(https://italy.ieeer8.org/)

Centre-North Italy Chapter IEEE GRSS, Italy
(https://cispio.diet.uniroma1.it/marzano/ieee-grs/
index.html)

Italy Section of the Computer Society, Italy
(https://site.ieee.org/italy-cs/)

University of Cagliari, Italy
(https://unica.it/)

University of Perugia, Italy
(https://www.unipg.it)

University of Basilicata, Italy
(http://www.unibas.it)

Monash University, Australia
(https://www.monash.edu/)

Kyushu Sangyo University, Japan
(https://www.kyusan-u.ac.jp/)

University of Minho, Portugal
(https://www.uminho.pt/)

Scientific Association Transport Infrastructures, Italy
(https://www.stradeeautostrade.it/associazioni-e-organizzazioni/asit-associazione-scientifica-infrastrutture-trasporto/)

Regione Sardegna, Italy
(https://regione.sardegna.it/)

Comune di Cagliari, Italy
(https://www.comune.cagliari.it/)

Referees

A. P. Andrade Marina	ISCTE, Instituto Universitário de Lisboa, Portugal
Addesso Paolo	University of Salerno, Italy
Adewumi Adewole	Algonquin College, Canada
Afolabi Adedeji	Covenant University, Nigeria
Afreixo Vera	University of Aveiro, Portugal
Agrawal Smirti	Freelancer, USA
Agrawal Akshat	Amity University Haryana, India
Ahmad Waseem	Federal University of Technology Minna, Nigeria
Akgun Nurten	Bursa Technical University, Turkey
Alam Tauhidul	Louisiana State University Shreveport, USA
Aleixo Sandra M.	CEAUL, Portugal
Alfa Abraham	Federal University of Technology Minna, Nigeria
Alvelos Filipe	University of Minho, Portugal
Alves Alexandra	University of Minho, Portugal
Amato Federico	University of Lausanne, Switzerland
Andrade Marina Alexandra Pedro	ISCTE-IUL, Portugal
Andrianov Sergey	Saint Petersburg State University, Russia
Anelli Angelo	CNR-IGAG, Italy
Anelli Debora	University of Rome, Italy
Annunziata Alfonso	University of Cagliari, Italy
Antognelli Sara	Agricolus, Italy
Aoyama Tatsumi	High Energy Accelerator Research Organization, Japan
Apduhan Bernady	Kyushu Sangyo University, Japan
Ascenzi Daniela	University of Trento, Italy
Asche Harmut	Hasso-Plattner-Institut für Digital Engineering GmbH, Germany
Aslan Burak Galip	Izmir Insitute of Technology, Turkey
Assumma Vanessa	Polytechnic University of Torino, Italy
Astoga Gino	UV, Chile
Atman Uslu Nilüfer	Manisa Celal Bayar University, Turkey
Behera Ranjan Kumar	National Institute of Technology, Rourkela, India
Badsha Shahriar	University of Nevada, USA
Bai Peng	University of Cagliari, Italy
Baia Alina-Elena	University of Perugia, Italy
Balacco Gabriella	Polytechnic University of Bari, Italy
Balci Birim	Celal Bayar University, Turkey
Balena Pasquale	Polytechnic University of Bari, Italy
Balletto Ginevra	University of Cagliari, Italy
Balucani Nadia	University of Perugia, Italy
Bansal Megha	Delhi University, India
Barazzetti Luigi	Polytechnic University of Milan, Italy
Barreto Jeniffer	Istituto Superior Técnico, Portugal
Basbas Socrates	Aristotle University of Thessaloniki, Greece

Berger Katja	Ludwig-Maximilians-Universität München, Germany
Beyene Asrat Mulatu	Addis Ababa Science and Technology University, Ethiopia
Bilancia Massimo	University of Bari Aldo Moro, Italy
Biondi Giulio	University of Firenze, Italy
Blanquer Ignacio	Universitat Politècnica de València, Spain
Bleil de Souza Clarice	Cardiff University, UK
Blečić Ivan	University of Cagliari, Italy
Bogdanov Alexander	Saint Petersburg State University, Russia
Bonifazi Alessandro	Polytechnic University of Bari, Italy
Bontchev Boyan	Sofia University, Bulgaria
Borgogno Mondino Enrico	University of Torino, Italy
Borruso Giuseppe	University of Trieste, Italy
Bouaziz Rahma	Taibah University, Saudi Arabia
Bowles Juliana	University of Saint Andrews, UK
Braga Ana Cristina	University of Minho, Portugal
Brambilla Andrea	Polytechnic University of Milan, Italy
Brito Francisco	University of Minho, Portugal
Buele Jorge	Universidad Tecnológica Indoamérica, Ecuador
Buffoni Andrea	TAGES sc, Italy
Cabana David	International Marine Centre, Italy
Calazan Rogerio	IEAPM, Brazil
Calcina Sergio Vincenzo	University of Cagliari, Italy
Camalan Seda	Atilim University, Turkey
Camarero Alberto	Universidad Politécnica de Madrid, Spain
Campisi Tiziana	University of Enna KORE, Italy
Cannatella Daniele	Delft University of Technology, The Netherlands
Capolupo Alessandra	Polytechnic University of Bari, Italy
Cappucci Sergio	ENEA, Italy
Caprioli Caterina	Polytechnic University of Torino, Italy
Carapau Fernando	Universidade de Evora, Portugal
Carcangiu Sara	University of Cagliari, Italy
Carrasqueira Pedro	INESC Coimbra, Portugal
Caselli Nicolás	PUCV Chile, Chile
Castro de Macedo Jose Nuno	Universidade do Minho, Portugal
Cavallo Carla	University of Naples, Italy
Cerminara Iole	University of Basilicata, Italy
Cerreta Maria	University of Naples, Italy
Cesini Daniele	INFN-CNAF, Italy
Chang Shi-Kuo	University of Pittsburgh, USA
Chetty Girija	University of Canberra, Australia
Chiky Raja	ISEP, France
Chowdhury Dhiman	University of South Carolina, USA
Ciloglugil Birol	Ege University, Turkey
Coletti Cecilia	Università di Chieti-Pescara, Italy

Coni Mauro	University of Cagliari, Italy
Corcoran Padraig	Cardiff University, UK
Cornelio Antonella	Università degli Studi di Brescia, Italy
Correia Aldina	ESTG-PPorto, Portugal
Correia Elisete	University of Trás-os-Montes and Alto Douro, Portugal
Correia Florbela	Polytechnic Institute of Viana do Castelo, Portugal
Costa Lino	Universidade do Minho, Portugal
Costa e Silva Eliana	ESTG-P Porto, Portugal
Costantini Alessandro	INFN, Italy
Crespi Mattia	University of Roma, Italy
Cuca Branka	Polytechnic University of Milano, Italy
De Doncker Elise	Western Michigan University, USA
De Macedo Mourelle Luiza	State University of Rio de Janeiro, Brazil
Daisaka Hiroshi	Hitotsubashi University, Japan
Daldanise Gaia	CNR, Italy
Danese Maria	CNR-ISPC, Italy
Daniele Bartoli	University of Perugia, Italy
Datola Giulia	Polytechnic University of Torino, Italy
De Luca Giandomenico	University of Reggio Calabria, Italy
De Lucia Caterina	University of Foggia, Italy
De Morais Barroca Filho Itamir	Federal University of Rio Grande do Norte, Brazil
De Petris Samuele	University of Torino, Italy
De Sá Alan	Marinha do Brasil, Brazil
De Souto Marcilio	LIFO, University of Orléans, France
De Vito Saverio	ENEA, Italy
De Wilde Pieter	University of Plymouth, UK
Degtyarev Alexander	Saint Petersburg State University, Russia
Dell'Anna Federico	Polytechnic University of Torino, Italy
Dell'Ovo Marta	Polytechnic University of Milano, Italy
Della Mura Fernanda	University of Naples, Italy
Deluka T. Aleksandra	University of Rijeka, Croatia
Demartino Cristoforo	Zhejiang University, China
Dereli Dursun Ahu	Istanbul Commerce University, Turkey
Desogus Giulia	University of Cagliari, Italy
Dettori Marco	University of Sassari, Italy
Devai Frank	London South Bank University, UK
Di Francesco Massimo	University of Cagliari, Italy
Di Liddo Felicia	Polytechnic University of Bari, Italy
Di Paola Gianluigi	University of Molise, Italy
Di Pietro Antonio	ENEA, Italy
Di Pinto Valerio	University of Naples, Italy
Dias Joana	University of Coimbra, Portugal
Dimas Isabel	University of Coimbra, Portugal
Dirvanauskas Darius	Kaunas University of Technology, Lithuania
Djordjevic Aleksandra	University of Belgrade, Serbia

Duma Doina Cristina	INFN-CNAF, Italy
Dumlu Demircioğlu Emine	Yıldız Technical University, Turkey
Dursun Aziz	Virginia Tech University, USA
Dvarioniene Jolanta	Kaunas University of Technology, Lithuania
Errico Maurizio Francesco	University of Enna KORE, Italy
Ezugwu Absalom	University of KwaZulu-Natal, South Africa
Fattoruso Grazia	ENEA, Italy
Faginas-Lago Noelia	University of Perugia, Italy
Falanga Bolognesi Salvatore	ARIESPACE, Italy
Falcinelli Stefano	University of Perugia, Italy
Farias Marcos	National Nuclear Energy Commission, Brazil
Farina Alessandro	University of Pisa, Italy
Feltynowski Marcin	Lodz University of Technology, Poland
Fernandes Florbela	Instituto Politecnico de Bragança, Portugal
Fernandes Paula Odete	Instituto Politécnico de Bragança, Portugal
Fernandez-Sanz Luis	University of Alcala, Spain
Ferreira Ana Cristina	University of Minho, Portugal
Ferreira Fernanda	Porto, Portugal
Fiorini Lorena	University of L'Aquila, Italy
Flora Amedeo	University of Basilicata, Italy
Florez Hector	Universidad Distrital Francisco Jose de Caldas, Colombia
Foddis Maria Laura	University of Cagliari, Italy
Fogli Daniela	University of Brescia, Italy
Fortunelli Martina	Pragma Engineering, Italy
Fragiacomo Massimo	University of L'Aquila, Italy
Franzoni Valentina	Perugia University, Italy
Fusco Giovanni	University of Cote d'Azur, France
Fyrogenis Ioannis	Aristotle University of Thessaloniki, Greece
Gorbachev Yuriy	Coddan Technologies LLC, Russia
Gabrielli Laura	Università Iuav di Venezia, Italy
Gallanos Theodore	Austrian Institute of Technology, Austria
Gamallo Belmonte Pablo	Universitat de Barcelona, Spain
Gankevich Ivan	Saint Petersburg State University, Russia
Garau Chiara	University of Cagliari, Italy
Garcia Para Ernesto	Universidad del Pais Vasco, EHU, Spain
Gargano Riccardo	Universidade de Brasilia, Brazil
Gavrilova Marina	University of Calgary, Canada
Georgiadis Georgios	Aristotle University of Thessaloniki, Greece
Gervasi Osvaldo	University of Perugia, Italy
Giano Salvatore Ivo	University of Basilicata, Italy
Gil Jorge	Chalmers University, Sweden
Gioia Andrea	Polytechnic University of Bari, Italy
Gioia Dario	ISPC-CNT, Italy

Giordano Ludovica	ENEA, Italy
Giorgi Giacomo	University of Perugia, Italy
Giovene di Girasole Eleonora	CNR-IRISS, Italy
Giovinazzi Sonia	ENEA, Italy
Giresini Linda	University of Pisa, Italy
Giuffrida Salvatore	University of Catania, Italy
Golubchikov Oleg	Cardiff University, UK
Gonçalves A. Manuela	University of Minho, Portugal
Gorgoglione Angela	Universidad de la República, Uruguay
Goyal Rinkaj	IPU, Delhi, India
Grishkin Valery	Saint Petersburg State University, Russia
Guerra Eduardo	Free University of Bozen-Bolzano, Italy
Guerrero Abel	University of Guanajuato, Mexico
Gulseven Osman	American University of The Middle East, Kuwait
Gupta Brij	National Institute of Technology, Kurukshetra, India
Guveyi Elcin	Yildiz Teknik University, Turkey
Gülen Kemal Güven	Namk Kemal University, Turkey
Haddad Sandra	Arab Academy for Science, Technology and Maritime Transport, Egypt
Hanzl Malgorzata	Lodz University of Technology, Poland
Hegedus Peter	University of Szeged, Hungary
Hendrix Eligius M. T.	Universidad de Málaga, Spain
Higaki Hiroaki	Tokyo Denki University, Japan
Hossain Syeda Sumbul	Daffodil International University, Bangladesh
Iacovino Chiara	University of Basilicata, Italy
Iakushkin Oleg	Saint Petersburg State University, Russia
Iannuzzo Antonino	ETH Zurich, Switzerland
Idri Ali	University Mohammed V, Morocco
Ignaccolo Matteo	University of Catania, Italy
Ilovan Oana-Ramona	Babeş-Bolyai University, Romania
Isola Federica	University of Cagliari, Italy
Jankovic Marija	CERTH, Greece
Jorge Ana Maria	Instituto Politécnico de Lisboa, Portugal
Kanamori Issaku	RIKEN Center for Computational Science, Japan
Kapenga John	Western Michigan University, USA
Karabulut Korhan	Yasar University, Turkey
Karaca Yeliz	University of Massachusetts Medical School, USA
Karami Ali	University of Guilan, Iran
Kienhofer Frank	WITS, South Africa
Kim Tai-hoon	Beijing Jiaotong University, China
Kimura Shuhei	Tottori University, Japan
Kirillov Denis	Saint Petersburg State University, Russia
Korkhov Vladimir	Saint Petersburg University, Russia
Koszewski Krzysztof	Warsaw University of Technology, Poland
Krzysztofik Sylwia	Lodz University of Technology, Poland

Kulabukhova Nataliia	Saint Petersburg State University, Russia
Kulkarni Shrinivas B.	SDM College of Engineering and Technology, Dharwad, India
Kwiecinski Krystian	Warsaw University of Technology, Poland
Kyvelou Stella	Panteion University of Social and Political Sciences, Greece
Körting Thales	INPE, Brazil
Lal Niranjan	Mody University of Science and Technology, India
Lazzari Maurizio	CNR-ISPC, Italy
Leon Marcelo	Asociacion de Becarios del Ecuador, Ecuador
La Rocca Ludovica	University of Naples, Italy
La Rosa Daniele	University of Catania, Italy
Lai Sabrina	University of Cagliari, Italy
Lalenis Konstantinos	University of Thessaly, Greece
Lannon Simon	Cardiff University, UK
Lasaponara Rosa	CNR, Italy
Lee Chien-Sing	Sunway University, Malaysia
Lemus-Romani José	Pontificia Universidad Católica de Valparaiso, Chile
Leone Federica	University of Cagliari, Italy
Li Yuanxi	Hong Kong Baptist University, China
Locurcio Marco	Polytechnic University of Bari, Italy
Lombardi Andrea	University of Perugia, Italy
Lopez Gayarre Fernando	University of Oviedo, Spain
Lops Pasquale	University of Bari, Italy
Lourenço Vanda	Universidade Nova de Lisboa, Portugal
Luviano José Luís	University of Guanajuato, Mexico
Maltese Antonino	University of Palermo, Italy
Magni Riccardo	Pragma Engineering, Italy
Maheshwari Anil	Carleton University, Canada
Maja Roberto	Polytechnic University of Milano, Italy
Malik Shaveta	Terna Engineering College, India
Maltinti Francesca	University of Cagliari, Italy
Mandado Marcos	University of Vigo, Spain
Manganelli Benedetto	University of Basilicata, Italy
Mangiameli Michele	University of Catania, Italy
Maraschin Clarice	Universidade Federal do Rio Grande do Sul, Brazil
Marigorta Ana Maria	Universidad de Las Palmas de Gran Canaria, Spain
Markov Krassimir	Institute of Electrical Engineering and Informatics, Bulgaria
Martellozzo Federico	University of Firenze, Italy
Marucci Alessandro	University of L'Aquila, Italy
Masini Nicola	IBAM-CNR, Italy
Matsufuru Hideo	High Energy Accelerator Research Organization (KEK), Japan
Matteucci Ilaria	CNR, Italy
Mauro D'Apuzzo	University of Cassino and Southern Lazio, Italy

Mazzarella Chiara	University of Naples, Italy
Mazzarino Marco	University of Venice, Italy
Mazzoni Augusto	University of Roma, Italy
Mele Roberta	University of Naples, Italy
Menezes Raquel	University of Minho, Portugal
Menghini Antonio	Aarhus Geofisica, Italy
Mengoni Paolo	University of Florence, Italy
Merlino Angelo	Università degli Studi Mediterranea, Italy
Milani Alfredo	University of Perugia, Italy
Milic Vladimir	University of Zagreb, Croatia
Millham Richard	Durban University of Technology, South Africa
Mishra B.	University of Szeged, Hungary
Misra Sanjay	Covenant University, Nigeria
Modica Giuseppe	University of Reggio Calabria, Italy
Mohagheghi Mohammadsadegh	Vali-e-Asr University of Rafsanjan, Iran
Molaei Qelichi Mohamad	University of Tehran, Iran
Molinara Mario	University of Cassino and Southern Lazio, Italy
Momo Evelyn Joan	University of Torino, Italy
Monteiro Vitor	University of Minho, Portugal
Montisci Augusto	University of Cagliari, Italy
Morano Pierluigi	Polytechnic University of Bari, Italy
Morganti Alessandro	Polytechnic University of Milano, Italy
Mosca Erica Isa	Polytechnic University of Milan, Italy
Moura Ricardo	CMA-FCT, New University of Lisbon, Portugal
Mourao Maria	Polytechnic Institute of Viana do Castelo, Portugal
Mourão Moura Ana Clara	Federal University of Minas Gerais, Brazil
Mrak Iva	University of Rijeka, Croatia
Murgante Beniamino	University of Basilicata, Italy
Muñoz Mirna	Centro de Investigacion en Matematicas, Mexico
Nedjah Nadia	State University of Rio de Janeiro, Brazil
Nakasato Naohito	University of Aizu, Japan
Natário Isabel Cristina	Universidade Nova de Lisboa, Portugal
Nesticò Antonio	Università degli Studi di Salerno, Italy
Neto Ana Maria	Universidade Federal do ABC, Brazil
Nicolosi Vittorio	University of Rome, Italy
Nikiforiadis Andreas	Aristotle University of Thessaloniki, Greece
Nocera Fabrizio	University of Illinois at Urbana-Champaign, USA
Nocera Silvio	IUAV, Italy
Nogueira Marcelo	Paulista University, Brazil
Nolè Gabriele	CNR, Italy
Nuno Beirao Jose	University of Lisbon, Portugal
Okewu Emma	University of Alcala, Spain
Oluwasefunmi Arogundade	Academy of Mathematics and System Science, China
Oppio Alessandra	Polytechnic University of Milan, Italy
P. Costa M. Fernanda	University of Minho, Portugal

Parisot Olivier	Luxembourg Institute of Science and Technology, Luxembourg
Paddeu Daniela	UWE, UK
Paio Alexandra	ISCTE-Instituto Universitário de Lisboa, Portugal
Palme Massimo	Catholic University of the North, Chile
Panaro Simona	University of Portsmouth, UK
Pancham Jay	Durban University of Technology, South Africa
Pantazis Dimos	University of West Attica, Greece
Papa Enrica	University of Westminster, UK
Pardede Eric	La Trobe University, Australia
Perchinunno Paola	Uniersity of Cagliari, Italy
Perdicoulis Teresa	UTAD, Portugal
Pereira Ana	Polytechnic Institute of Bragança, Portugal
Perri Damiano	University of Perugia, Italy
Petrelli Marco	University of Rome, Italy
Pierri Francesca	University of Perugia, Italy
Piersanti Antonio	ENEA, Italy
Pilogallo Angela	University of Basilicata, Italy
Pinna Francesco	University of Cagliari, Italy
Pinto Telmo	University of Coimbra, Portugal
Piroddi Luca	University of Cagliari, Italy
Poli Giuliano	University of Naples, Italy
Polidoro Maria João	Polytecnic Institute of Porto, Portugal
Polignano Marco	University of Bari, Italy
Politis Ioannis	Aristotle University of Thessaloniki, Greece
Pollino Maurizio	ENEA, Italy
Popoola Segun	Covenant University, Nigeria
Pratelli Antonio	University of Pisa, Italy
Praticò Salvatore	University of Reggio Calabria, Italy
Previtali Mattia	Polytechnic University of Milan, Italy
Puppio Mario Lucio	University of Pisa, Italy
Puttini Ricardo	Universidade de Brasilia, Brazil
Que Zeli	Nanjing Forestry University, China
Queiroz Gilberto	INPE, Brazil
Regalbuto Stefania	University of Naples, Italy
Ravanelli Roberta	University of Roma, Italy
Recanatesi Fabio	University of Tuscia, Italy
Reis Ferreira Gomes Karine	INPE, Brazil
Reis Marco	University of Coimbra, Portugal
Reitano Maria	University of Naples, Italy
Rencelj Marko	University of Maribor, Slovenia
Respondek Jerzy	Silesian University of Technology, Poland
Rimola Albert	Universitat Autònoma de Barcelona, Spain
Rocha Ana	University of Minho, Portugal
Rocha Humberto	University of Coimbra, Portugal
Rocha Maria Celia	UFBA Bahia, Brazil

Rocha Maria Clara	ESTES Coimbra, Portugal
Rocha Miguel	University of Minho, Portugal
Rodriguez Guillermo	UNICEN, Argentina
Rodríguez González Alejandro	Universidad Carlos III de Madrid, Spain
Ronchieri Elisabetta	INFN, Italy
Rosi Marzio	University of Perugia, Italy
Rotondo Francesco	Università Politecnica delle Marche, Italy
Rusci Simone	University of Pisa, Italy
Saganeiti Lucia	University of Basilicata, Italy
Saiu Valeria	University of Cagliari, Italy
Salas Agustin	UPCV, Chile
Salvo Giuseppe	University of Palermo, Italy
Sarvia Filippo	University of Torino, Italy
Santaga Francesco	University of Perugia, Italy
Santangelo Michele	CNR-IRPI, Italy
Santini Francesco	University of Perugia, Italy
Santos Rafael	INPE, Brazil
Santucci Valentino	Università per Stranieri di Perugia, Italy
Saponaro Mirko	Polytechnic University of Bari, Italy
Sarker Iqbal	CUET, Bangladesh
Scaioni Marco	Politecnico Milano, Italy
Scorza Francesco	University of Basilicata, Italy
Scotto di Perta Ester	University of Naples, Italy
Sebillo Monica	University of Salerno, Italy
Sharma Meera	Swami Shraddhanand College, India
Shen Jie	University of Michigan, USA
Shou Huahao	Zhejiang University of Technology, China
Siavvas Miltiadis	Centre of Research and Technology Hellas (CERTH), Greece
Silva Carina	ESTeSL-IPL, Portugal
Silva Joao Carlos	Polytechnic Institute of Cavado and Ave, Portugal
Silva Junior Luneque	Universidade Federal do ABC, Brazil
Silva Ângela	Instituto Politécnico de Viana do Castelo, Portugal
Simonetti Marco	University of Florence, Italy
Situm Zeljko	University of Zagreb, Croatia
Skouteris Dimitrios	Master-Up, Italy
Solano Francesco	Università degli Studi della Tuscia, Italy
Somma Maria	University of Naples, Italy
Sonnessa Alberico	Polytechnic University of Bari, Italy
Sousa Lisete	University of Lisbon, Portugal
Sousa Nelson	University of Algarve, Portugal
Spaeth Benjamin	Cardiff University, UK
Srinivsan M.	Navodaya Institute of Technology, India
Stankova Elena	Saint Petersburg State University, Russia
Stratigea Anastasia	National Technical University of Athens, Greece

Šurdonja Sanja	University of Rijeka, Croatia
Sviatov Kirill	Ulyanovsk State Technical University, Russia
Sánchez de Merás Alfredo	Universitat de Valencia, Spain
Takahashi Daisuke	University of Tsukuba, Japan
Tanaka Kazuaki	Kyushu Institute of Technology, Japan
Taniar David	Monash University, Australia
Tapia McClung Rodrigo	Centro de Investigación en Ciencias de Información Geoespacial, Mexico
Tarantino Eufemia	Polytechnic University of Bari, Italy
Tasso Sergio	University of Perugia, Italy
Teixeira Ana Paula	University of Trás-os-Montes and Alto Douro, Portugal
Teixeira Senhorinha	University of Minho, Portugal
Tengku Izhar Tengku Adil	Universiti Teknologi MARA, Malaysia
Teodoro Maria Filomena	University of Lisbon, Portuguese Naval Academy, Portugal
Tesoriere Giovanni	University of Enna KORE, Italy
Thangeda Amarendar Rao	Botho University, Botswana
Tonbul Gokchan	Atilim University, Turkey
Toraldo Emanuele	Polytechnic University of Milan, Italy
Torre Carmelo Maria	Polytechnic University of Bari, Italy
Torrieri Francesca	University of Naples, Italy
Torrisi Vincenza	University of Catania, Italy
Toscano Domenico	University of Naples, Italy
Totaro Vincenzo	Polytechnic University of Bari, Italy
Trigo Antonio	Instituto Politécnico de Coimbra, Portugal
Trunfio Giuseppe A.	University of Sassari, Italy
Trung Pham	HCMUT, Vietnam
Tsoukalas Dimitrios	Centre of Research and Technology Hellas (CERTH), Greece
Tucci Biagio	CNR, Italy
Tucker Simon	Liverpool John Moores University, UK
Tuñon Iñaki	Universidad de Valencia, Spain
Tyagi Amit Kumar	Vellore Institute of Technology, India
Uchibayashi Toshihiro	Kyushu University, Japan
Ueda Takahiro	Seikei University, Japan
Ugliengo Piero	University of Torino, Italy
Valente Ettore	University of Naples, Italy
Vallverdu Jordi	University Autonoma Barcelona, Spain
Vanelslander Thierry	University of Antwerp, Belgium
Vasyunin Dmitry	T-Systems RUS, Russia
Vazart Fanny	University of Grenoble Alpes, France
Vecchiocattivi Franco	University of Perugia, Italy
Vekeman Jelle	Vrije Universiteit Brussel (VUB), Belgium
Verde Rosanna	Università degli Studi della Campania, Italy
Vermaseren Jos	Nikhef, The Netherlands

Vignoli Giulio	University of Cagliari, Italy
Vizzari Marco	University of Perugia, Italy
Vodyaho Alexander	Saint Petersburg State Electrotechnical University, Russia
Vona Marco	University of Basilicata, Italy
Waluyo Agustinus Borgy	Monash University, Australia
Wen Min	Xi'an Jiaotong-Liverpool University, China
Westad Frank	Norwegian University of Science and Technology, Norway
Yuasa Fukuko	KEK, Japan
Yadav Rekha	KL University, India
Yamu Claudia	University of Groningen, The Netherlands
Yao Fenghui	Tennessee State University, USA
Yañez Manuel	Universidad Autónoma de Madrid, Spain
Yoki Karl	Daegu Catholic University, South Korea
Zamperlin Paola	University of Pisa, Italy
Zekeng Ndadji Milliam Maxime	University of Dschang, Cameroon
Žemlička Michal	Charles University, Czech Republic
Zita Sampaio Alcinia	Technical University of Lisbon, Portugal
Živković Ljiljana	Ministry of Construction, Transport and Infrastructure and Institute of Architecture and Urban & Spatial Planning of Serbia, Serbia
Zoppi Corrado	University of Cagliari, Italy
Zucca Marco	Polytechnic University of Milan, Italy
Zullo Francesco	University of L'Aquila, Italy

Contents – Part VII

International Workshop on Sustainability Performance Assessment: Models, Approaches and Applications toward Interdisciplinary and Integrated Solutions (SPA 2020)

International Workshop on Smart and Sustainable Island Communities (SSIC 2020)

**International Workshop on Tools and Techniques in Software
Development Process (TTSDP 2020)**

International Workshop on Urban Form Studies (UForm 2020)

**International Workshop on Urban Space Extended Accessibility
(USEAccessibility 2020)**

International Workshop on Virtual and Augmented Reality and Applications (VRA 2020)

International Workshop on Advanced and Computational Methods for Earth Science Applications (WACM4ES 2020)

International Workshop on High Performance and Pervasive Computing (WHPPC 2020)

International Workshop on Smart Ports – Technologies and Challenges (SmartPorts 2020)

Use of ICT for More Efficient Port Operations: The Experience of the EASYLOG Project

Patrizia Serra$^{(\boxtimes)}$ ⓘ and Gianfranco Fancello ⓘ

DICAAR – Department of Civil and Environmental Engineering
and Architecture, University of Cagliari, 09123 Cagliari, Italy
pserra@unica.it

Abstract. The 4.0 revolution in the shipping industry is growing fast and ports are requested to constantly innovate and evolve. Ports need to become not only smarter to implement more efficient, sustainable, and safer operations but also interconnected with each other. This paper presents the experience of the Easylog Project – Optimized logistics for ports and intermodal transport – funded under the Interreg IT-FR Maritime 2014–2020 program. Easylog aims to improve the mobility of rolling cargo between Italian and French regions by taking advantage of ICT technologies to increase the performance of intermodal transport chains and the overall quality of the services offered by ports. The project involves five ports in the upper Tyrrhenian area for which it proposes the shared adoption of integrated ICT devices for optimized and secure management of port operations between the operators involved in the cross-border (trans)port chain. The driving idea is to move from a non-integrated and fragmented management and control system of port events and flows to a common and connected ICT system. Easylog may represent a useful case study potentially replicable in many port contexts.

Keywords: Smart ports · Port integration · ICT · Gate automation

1 Introduction

Freight transport is no longer intended as a simple connection service between two areas, but as a key element of the entire logistics process [1]. The insufficient connection among operators and the lack of necessary information along the transport chain are widely believed among the main causes of delays in the shipment of goods, in the operation of ships and the management of port events [2]. In this regard, the desire to develop information and communication technologies (ICT) to support logistics operations and stakeholders' connectivity, has long been evident in the transport sector [3]. Digital-based technologies are now more than ever an element of absolute interest for developing the efficiency of port systems and intermodal chains [4, 5]. In particular, ports as essential gateways in supply chains need to integrate a variety of actors to coordinate traffic flows and related operations [6]. In a port, different operators and service providers must necessarily interact and exchange information and documents with each other. Such information may originate from a variety of sources, both internal (port authorities, port

© Springer Nature Switzerland AG 2020
O. Gervasi et al. (Eds.): ICCSA 2020, LNCS 12255, pp. 3–14, 2020.
https://doi.org/10.1007/978-3-030-58820-5_1

security, customs and inspection bodies, etc.) and external (shipping companies, trucking and logistics companies, shippers, maritime agents, etc.).

The adoption of digital technologies to improve the connectivity of the various stakeholders and the efficiency of operations has now become crucial for many ports. Information systems are recognized to facilitate communication and decision making in ports and enhance efficiency, reliability and security in operations [7]. The enlarging role of cooperation and information sharing, as well as the value of high-quality information for increasing the efficiency of port operations, are both extensively documented; see, for example, the studies by [8, 9]. It is also believed that digital transformation may help ports to compensate constraints related to inadequate infrastructures, capacity limits or accessibility problems [10].

Although with different implementation levels, several ports and stakeholders have now started technological upgrading [11]. However, it seems that to be truly effective, the various actors cannot simply adopt the technologies on their own but must interface with integrated platforms and services that make it easier to interact with the other stakeholders in the network [12]. Several leading ports, such as Hamburg, have already successfully tied multiple individual systems into a single interconnected platform. Furthermore, as supply chains are more integrated and connected, it becomes increasingly clear that stakeholders' connectivity must be guaranteed not only within the single port but also between the various nodes and actors in the transport network [11]. Several challenges characterize the development of shared digital solutions in the (trans)port community. Main problems may typically concern different digital maturity levels between actors, missing standards, and a lack of willingness to participate and share information [10, 13].

This paper describes the experience of developing a common and integrated ICT system for the optimized and secure management of information flows and port operations in five Tyrrhenian ports with different levels of digitalization. The ports analyzed are Bastia, in France, and Livorno, Olbia, Portoferraio and Savona, in Italy. The considered port context shows a lack of systemic vision which hinders the adoption of shared technological solutions along its transport chains. The general objective behind the design of the new system was to contribute to improving the mobility of rolling cargo (Ro-Ro) between the regions of the upper Tyrrhenian area by exploiting ICT technologies to increase the performance of the cross-border chains and the overall quality of services rendered by ports.

The framework of the paper is as follows. Section 2 introduces the application area and the five test ports while Sect. 3 describes the elements of fragmentation existing both in the road haulage sector and in ports which may hinder the adoption of shared ICT systems in the Tyrrhenian area. Section 4 presents the methodology used to design the new integrated IT system for connecting the five ports and illustrates its main features and functionalities. Some final remarks are in Sect. 5.

2   The Test Area

The geographical context of intervention concerns the maritime connections between the ports of 4 Tyrrhenian regions: Corse (France), Liguria (Italy), Sardinia (Italy) and Tuscany (Italy). The ports involved are Bastia, in France, and Livorno, Olbia, Porto-ferraio and Savona – Vado, in Italy. Figure 1 depicts the test area.

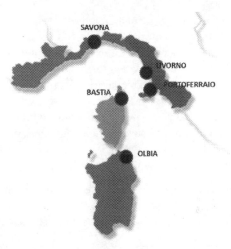

Fig. 1. Test area and ports involved.

The port of Bastia is the main port of Corsica region. It handles nearly 60% of the overall traffic volumes from/to Corsica, passengers and freight combined.

The port of Livorno is classified as a Core Port within the Trans-European Transport Network (TEN-T). It is a complex multipurpose port which handles a variety of goods: containers, Ro-Ro, liquid and solid bulk, new cars, cruises, ferries, forest products, relevant machinery, etc. The port of Livorno is equipped with an advanced Port Community System[1] which allows sharing data and information among a multiplicity of port and logistics actors involved in import and export flows (shippers, hauliers, shipping agents, control bodies, etc.).

The port of Olbia is one of the most important passenger ports in the Tyrrhenian area and a growing Ro-Ro commercial port. From an infrastructural point of view, it is divided into three areas: i) the main area is dedicated to Ro-Pax, Ro-Ro, and cruise traffic; ii) the internal area is reserved for pleasure boats; iii) the industrial area is used for bulk cargo and pure Ro-Ro ships.

The port of Portoferraio is the main port of the Island of Elba. It mainly ensures connection services between the island of Elba and the mainland. It is also a cruise and pleasure port.

---

[1] TPCS - http://tpcs.tpcs.eu/.

The port of Savona – Vado specializes in the fruit sector and consists of an advanced container terminal, a ferry terminal and an oil terminal. Of interest for the study is its ferry terminal, which ensures frequent connections with the Corsica region (up to 3 daily departures during the summer).

3 Background

The fragmentation existing in the Tyrrhenian area, both between the various transport modes and between the various territories, is believed to determine an increase in logistics costs as well as an insufficient integration of the peripheral and island territories in terms of territorial continuity and connection to Trans-European Transport Networks (TEN-T) networks [14]. Particularly, intermodal transport seems to be characterized by a lack of systemic vision on different scales: within the port, between ports, and between the various actors involved. The subjects involved in intermodal transport chains are not only diverse (they may include, a.o., logistics and haulage operators, port operators, port authorities, port security staff, shipping companies, etc.) but also characterized by different and often divergent needs and interests. Broadly speaking:

- port operators need to monitor the vehicles in the port for an optimal yard and berth management;
- port authorities need to monitor port events and supervise the port areas for security purposes;
- logistics and trucking companies need to speed up port operations, check the location of goods and respect delivery times;
- shipping companies want to efficiently manage loading/unloading procedures and related lists.

The road haulage sector is characterized by a strong fragmentation due to the high number of small- and medium-sized companies. As an example, of the 87,361 road haulage companies registered in Italy in 2018, more than 62,000 have less than 5 vehicles [15]. Such small companies can have limited opportunities to invest in innovation (both digital and non-digital), training, and networking. Conversely, larger companies make often use of digital systems for fleet tracking, control of consumption, monitoring of dangerous goods, etc. However, in most cases, such systems are developed in-house and not designed to interact with the other nodes and operators of the logistics chain.

As for the port sector, digitalization levels still differ heavily from port to port. Extensive use of traditional methods of document exchange and manual management of the entire gate-in/gate-out procedure is still predominant in many ports, as well as random or non-optimized management of parking areas. Likewise, automated control systems for the duration of the port stay are rare and so are computerized archives of port accesses, with important limits related to security issues. Starting from early experiments in the late 90s, Port Community Systems (PCS) are spreading in several ports to enable the targeted and secure exchange of information between economic operators and public bodies within the port community [16]. PCSs are intended to optimize, manage and automates port processes, including authorization, administrative and logistical processes, through the single entry of the data and paperless procedures along the logistics chain. The applied systems and procedures vary widely from port to port. In Italy, the Directive "Guidelines to homogenize and organize the PCSs through the National Logistics Platform" 20/03/2018 of the Ministry of Infrastructure and Transport has introduced the obligation for Port System Authorities to migrate their PCSs to the National Logistic Platform - NLP [17]. The NLP is defined as an open and modular hardware and software platform oriented to the management of logistics processes and freight transport which aims at creating the interport network system by allowing the different actors in the logistics chain to be connected, using a common digital language. According to the Directive, Port Authorities that comply with their obligations will be entitled preferential for access to national economic measures for the realization, management and implementation of their Information Technology Services (ITS). Although the change promoted by the Directive is ambitious, to date its level of acceptance in ports is very low and a high level of uncertainty surrounds its practical implementation: most ports are still implementing their own PCSs.

The lack of systemic vision translates into a poor efficiency of the entire cross-border transport chain: the lack or inaccuracy of information produces delays both in the shipment of goods and operation of ships, as well as difficulties in planning, managing and controlling port events. This results in low efficiency of the whole intermodal transport chain and lack of vision of the whole supply chain. Switching from a multitude of uncoordinated port management systems to a common and integrated one seems a necessary evolution for improving intermodal transport chains and the overall quality of the services offered by ports.

4 Methodology to Implement an Integrated ICT Port System

This study aims to design a system that allows the five ports to be connected, using a common digital language and overcoming the poor coordination between subjects. Such a system is designed to meet the following driving objectives:

- optimize the exchange of information in gate-in/gate-out activities to minimize the time required for documentary checks and ensure greater integration between the subjects involved and better plan of port activities;
- increase the security of port operations through the automated management of port gates and the continuous monitoring of port accesses;
- improve the productivity of the whole intermodal chain through the elimination of data input and related errors;
- improve truck-turn-around-times at the terminal by reducing the bottleneck effect of ports.

The development plan of the research consists of 4 main phases:

1. *Cognitive phase*: this phase is aimed at acquiring deep know-how on the port core processes connected to the cross-border exchange of goods in the five test ports (check-in, check-out, disembarkation/embarkation, management of parking areas, security checks) in order to identify critical issues and needs. Although the

processes are known in general, it is essential to detail the analyzes on the use cases of the territories under study. The analyzes allow acquiring knowledge regarding port procedures and associated information flows, ICT systems in use, subjects involved, operational and technological needs.

2. *Design phase*: definition of the functional requirements of the new system in terms of application and information services that respond to the operational needs identified. The new system is designed to be interoperable with the systems already in use in the ports and the new gate automation system.

3. *Implementation phase*: development of the IT architecture of the new system for the optimization of operations and information flows connected to the cross-border transit of goods between the five ports involved, and automation of the access gates at the five test ports.

4. *Experimentation phase*: training to operators for the use of the new system and in situ experimentation at the five ports. The test ports belong, in pairs, to the following traffic corridors: Olbia – Livorno, Bastia – Livorno, Bastia - Savona, Bastia – Portoferraio.

4.1 Cognitive Phase: Identification of Technological Needs

The cognitive analyzes were carried out through interviews with stakeholders and on-site visits at the five test ports. A summary of the state of fact and identified technological needs as emerged from the analyzes are in Table 1. The five ports show very different levels of automation and digitalization. Some of them are already equipped with well-structured PCSs and terminal operating systems (TOS), such as Livorno and Bastia, whereas others lack any IT managing system for rolling cargo.

It is worth noting that the success of integrated IT systems depends heavily on the number of stakeholders who will use it, as well as on their willingness to share information. The biggest challenge is to achieve a common understanding between the different parties involved whereby they agree to adopt such a new system [18].

Considering that parties have different and often divergent roles and interests, to be successful such a system must be able to guarantee the autonomy and benefits of all individual actors on the one hand and the connection between them on the other [19]. In the framework of the study, several workshops were organized in an attempt to establish a good collaboration among the key stakeholders and facilitate the achievement of a common understanding of the proposed system.

Table 1. State of fact and identified technological needs in the 5 ports.

Port	State of fact	Specific needs
Bastia	The Port of Bastia is equipped with a management system called Eris Liner and has a gate-automation system in the North area which detects the plates of the incoming tractors and trailers, their length, and any ADR code. The gate staff checks the travel booking and authorizes access	− extend the gate-automation system to exit gates; − introduce a yard management module to use the port aprons as efficiently as possible

(*continued*)

Table 1. (*continued*)

Port	State of fact	Specific needs
Livorno	The Port of Livorno has a gate-automation system which allows the detection of the vehicles at the port gates. It has advanced digital assets, including the TPCS (Tuscan Port Community System), which constitutes the unique interface towards the port and logistics community. The TPCS is equipped with a "VBS-Vehicle Booking System" module which allows the management of entry and exit reservations of vehicles from the port, to date limited to container traffic	− extend the VBS module to rolling cargo, in order to allow the automatic generation of the loading list, on the basis of: i) booking data received from the VBS, ii) gate-in data received by the gate automation system, iii) gate-in messages sent by the terminal, boarding messages sent by the terminal; − create interfaces for data exchange with the EASYLOG platform, in order to share data of interest for the other ports involved in the experimentation
Olbia	The Port of Olbia is not currently equipped with any telematic support for the management of the physical and information flows relating to Ro-Ro traffic. Access is manned by terminal staff	− introduce a monitoring system for port access, which can allow the control and monitoring of all incoming and outgoing vehicles; − introduce a yard management module
Portoferraio	The Port of Portoferraio is not currently equipped with any telematic support for the management of Ro-Ro traffic	− introduce a system for the control and monitoring of traffic flows for security and compliance reasons with Community indications
Savona	The Port of Savona - Vado has a high level of automation on the container front and no automation on the Ro-Ro side. The access gate of its Ro-Ro terminal is manned by terminal staff. The square is divided into two areas: pre-boarding and boarding. The incoming vehicles are directed to the pre-boarding area, if in possession of a ticket, otherwise they are directed to the ticket office Freight traffic is all accompanied and there is no apron management in terms of parking allocation	− introduce a system for reducing documentary errors and delivery times and facilitating security operations. As for the latter, a computerized data flow that allows correct preventive information (currently the error rate of the lists is 15%) would speed up related operations

Several technological, economic, operational and commercial criticalities emerged during the analysis. Particularly, the main challenges seemed to concern:

- the different availability of input data (from trucking operators, terminal operators, port authorities, shipping companies, etc.);
- the well-known resistance [20] opposed by some stakeholders in the supply chain to share part of the information requested;

- the different operating modes existing in the ports and terminals involved;
- the diverse state of the art and technology in the five ports examined;
- the presence of different trades managed within the sample ports: accompanied and unaccompanied freight traffic, mixed Ro-Pax versus pure Ro-Ro traffic, presence of only residual freight traffic volumes compared to passenger volumes (such as in Portoferraio), etc.

The very different situations, endowments and needs detected in the five ports lead to the need to customize the automation equipment of the gates and the management system on a case-by-case basis, in order to be able to carry out a more adherent and functional experimentation to the individual cases.

4.2   Design Phase: Definition of the Functional Requirements of the New System

The driving principle of the design phase was to build a system that could potentially become a "standard model" for communication between ports, primarily for rolling cargo but with the possibility of further expanding its application to different types of cargo. The basic functionalities of the system have been developed according to the following criteria:

- satisfaction (at least partial) of the needs detected in analyzes and interviews;
- ability to exchange data between the five ports in the network;
- future opening to additional ports currently not included in the test;
- use of open and extensible standards in the future;
- interoperability with the ICT systems already in use in the port, if any;
- interoperability with the new gate automation system;
- need to leave a functioning IT infrastructure even after the end of the project. The infrastructure should not be based on centralized supports, such as central servers or databases, to be maintained by third parties.

The basic modules of the EasyLog system are defined as follows:

- module for managing the pre-arrival notification through ship travel bookings;
- gate-in/gate-out automation module (reading and recording of truck license plates, ADR codes, length, etc.) to identify and record each entity entering or leaving the port area;
- gate management module for security purposes (access to the port is allowed when a ship booking exists);
- yard management module for accompanied and unaccompanied Ro-Ro traffic;
- mobile module by means of personal digital assistants (PDAs) for the management of vehicles in movement in the yard;
- damage control module;
- data exchange module.

Each port in the network can activate one or more of the previous functions. Each function is customized according to what is already in place and the specific local needs. From a technical point of view, the system is designed to ensure input resilience and dataset scalability. The former allows different data input possibilities depending on the hardware environment available in the port while the latter leaves open the possibility of implementing future functionality extensions while maintaining backward compatibility.

The system is designed according to a modular and scalable structure in which the five different port modules dialogue with each other through the so-called Easylog connector (Fig. 2). The Easylog connector is defined centrally and constitutes the heart of the exchange system, intended as a set of rules for data exchange, formatting and availability. Each port has its own customized EasyLog module which can exchange data not only with the different actors in the node (hauliers, port authorities, shipping companies, terminal operators) but also with the other port nodes in the network. Each local module consists of a software component for data processing, storage and exchange, and a hardware component (automated port gate).

As regards the software functionality, the system allows:

- the terminal of destination to know the composition of the incoming cargo in terms of type and number (or linear meters) of vehicles, grouped by ADR class, to timely and properly organize port spaces and activities;
- the ports to reconstruct the origin and destination of the goods starting from the data collected by the automated gates;
- under reasoned requests in case of disputes on damages, to provide the terminal operator with the recorded images of the visible sides of the trailer when accessed to the port, indexed by plate number and access date/time;

The hardware component of each local module coincides with the automated gate for the identification of trucks entering or leaving the port. The developed gates are based on OCR Technology (Optical Character Recognition) that converts visual data to digital data. A truck drives through an OCR access facility, where truck details are captured and stored in the system database. Basic functionality of the Easylog automated gates include:

- reading of the truck license plate;
- reading of any ADR codes;
- detection of vehicle length and capture of images for damages detection;
- management of other passing vehicles (service vehicles, employee vehicles, passenger car traffic, etc.).

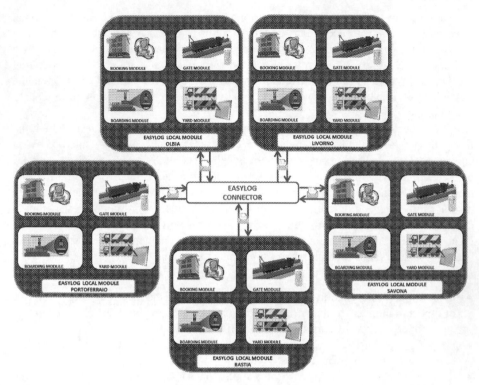

Fig. 2. EasyLog system.

The working principle is that the data (truck license plate, length of the vehicle, etc.) received through the OCR devices are transferred to the Easylog system and matched with the data already in the database.

The variety of situations and needs encountered at the five ports has offered the interesting opportunity to experiment with different systems and automation levels which can meet the needs of a wider range of ports. Depending on the existing local situation, the Easylog gates are implemented according to two levels of automation:

- hard automation – installation, over the entrance and exit gates, of classic physical portals equipped with OCR cameras, entry and exit barriers, sensors, etc.;
- light automation - creation of more flexible and economic "virtual" gates realized by means of PDAs and wearable OCR smart glasses for augmented reality to be used by trained personnel.

The choice of the specific configuration has been dictated by local needs, depending on the availability of physical spaces, integration with current operating procedures, and the economy of operation and installation. The hard configuration has been chosen for the ports of Bastia and Livorno while the light automation for the ports of Olbia, Portoferraio and Savona.

At the time of writing this paper, the implementation of the five gates is underway in the five ports. Both the Easylog system and its automated gates are going to be tested in the coming months to assess their applicability and effectiveness.

5   Conclusion

This paper has presented the experience of the Easylog project which designs and implements an ICT system common to five ports in the Tyrrhenian area for the optimized and secure management of processes and information flows between the operators involved in the cross-border transport chain. The Easylog system is designed according to a modular and scalable structure in which the five local modules dialogue with each other through the so-called Easylog connector. The main innovative aspect proposed by Easylog concerns the systemic implementation of cutting-edge services and tools and their integration and interoperability aimed at activating synergies for the development of a cross-border community of port logistics. The Easylog system, synergistic and integrable with any IT system already in use in ports and with the new gate management system, proposes advanced and integrated technological devices to support both information and operational aspects. The system can allow coordinating the connections between the five ports in the area with the implicitly expected result of improving cross-border mobility and encouraging the development of multimodality between the Tyrrhenian regions, also in order to reduce road congestion by concentrating traffic on maritime routes and to achieve better cohesion between the territories. As a future development of the research, the potential integration of the Easylog system with other platforms will be studied in an effort to embrace a more holistic vision of supply chain digitalization.

Acknowledgements. This research is based upon the EASYLOG Project funded under the Interreg IT-FR Maritime Program 2014–2020[2]. The authors would like to thank Andrea Zoratti for his valuable work within the EASYLOG project.

References

1. Fancello, G., Schintu, A., Serra, P.: An experimental analysis of Mediterranean supply chains through the use of cost KPIs. Transp. Res. Procedia **30**, 137–146 (2018)
2. Fancello, G., Serra, P., Schintu, A., Zoratti, A.: Performance evaluation of a tracking system for intermodal traffic: an experimentation in the Tyrrhenian area. Eur. Transp. **76**(8) (2020)
3. Yang, Y., Zhong, M., Yao, H., Yu, F., Fu, X., Postolache, O.: Internet of Things for smart ports: technologies and challenges. IEEE Instrum. Meas. Mag. **21**(1), 34–43 (2018)
4. Belfkih, A., Duvallet, C., Sadeg, B.: The Internet of Things for smart ports: application to the port of Le Havre. In: International Conference on Intelligent Platform for Smart Port - IPaSPort 2017 (2017)

---

[2] The Easylog project website is available at http://interreg-maritime.eu/web/easylog.

5. Fernández, P., et al.: SmartPort - a platform for sensor data monitoring in a seaport based on FIWARE. Sensors **16**(3), 417 (2016)
6. Baron, M.L., Mathieu, H.: PCS interoperability in Europe: a market for PCS operators? Int. J. Logistics Manag. **24**(1), 117–129 (2013)
7. Heilig, L., Voß, S.: Information systems in seaports: a categorization and overview. Inf. Technol. Manag. **18**(3), 179–201 (2016). https://doi.org/10.1007/s10799-016-0269-1
8. Carlan, V., Sys, C., Vanelslander, T.: How port community systems can contribute to port competitiveness: developing a cost–benefit framework. Res. Transp. Bus. Manage. **19**, 51–64 (2016)
9. Zhao, W., Goodchild, A.V.: The impact of truck arrival information on container terminal rehandling. Transp. Res. Part E: Logistics Transp. Rev. **46**(3), 327–343 (2010)
10. Heilig, L., Schwarze, S., Voß, S.: An analysis of digital transformation in the history and future of modern ports. In: Proceedings of the 50th Hawaii International Conference on System Sciences (HICSS). IEEE (2017)
11. Jović, M., Kavran, N., Aksentijević, S., Tijan, E.: The transition of Croatian seaports into smart ports. In: 42nd International Convention on Information and Communication Technology, Electronics and Microelectronics – MIPRO, pp. 1386–1390. IEEE (2019)
12. Riedl, J., Delenclos, F.X., Rasmussen, A.: To get smart, ports go digital. The Boston Consulting Group (2018). https://www.bcg.com/it-it/publications/2018/to-get-smart-ports-go-digital.aspx. Accessed Mar 2020
13. Van Baalen, P., Zuidwijk, R., Van Nunen, J.: Port inter-organizational information systems: capabilities to service global supply chains. Found. Trends Technol. Inf. Oper. Manag. **2**(2–3), 81–241 (2009)
14. Fancello, G., Serra, P., Mancini, S.: A network design optimization problem for ro-ro freight transport in the Tyrrhenian area. Transp. Probl. **14**(4), 63–75 (2019)
15. Italian register of road hauliers – Ministry of Transport and Infrastructure (2018). https://www.alboautotrasporto.it/web/portale-albo/. Accessed Nov 2019
16. Posti, A., Hakkinen, J., Tapaninen, U.: Promoting information exchange with a port community system–case Finland. Int. Supply Chain Manag. Collab. Pract. **4**, 455–473 (2011)
17. Italian Official Gazette. https://www.gazzettaufficiale.it/eli/id/2018/05/21/18A03440/sg
18. Diaz, M.: Port community system – a key component of the future vision for cargo and port security. Gov. Supply Chain blue papers, Valencia (2003)
19. Tijan, E., Kos, S., Ogrizovic, D.: Disaster recovery and business continuity in port community systems. Multidisciplinary Sci. J. Maritime Res. – POMORSTVO **23**(1), 243–260 (2009)
20. Acciaro, M., Serra, P.: Strategic determinants of terminal operating system choice: an empirical approach using multinomial analysis. Transp. Res. Procedia **3**, 592–601 (2014)

Treatment of Port Wastes According to the Paradigm of the Circular Economy

Paolo Fadda[1] ⓘ, Antonio Viola[2], Michele Carta[3], Debora Secci[3],
Gianfranco Fancello[1] ⓘ, and Patrizia Serra[1(✉)] ⓘ

[1] DICAAR – Department of Civil and Environmental Engineering
and Architecture, University of Cagliari, 09123 Cagliari, Italy
pserra@unica.it
[2] Cagliari, Italy
[3] CENTRALABS - Competence Centre of Sardinia on Transport,
University Campus of Monserrato, 09030 Monserrato, Italy

Abstract. The problem of the presence of waste in the marine environment has recently taken on the dimensions of a complex and global challenge. In an effort to reduce both the economic and environmental costs of managing port waste, many ports are looking for sustainable solutions for marine waste management.

Plasma-assisted gasification (PAG) is an innovative combination of two technologies, namely plasma treatment and gasification, which can be used to efficiently convert carbon-containing wastes to a clean syngas (H2 + CO). The latter can be used to generate electricity directly in gas engines, dual-fuel generators, gas turbines or fuel cells. PAG provides several key benefits which allow removing all the environmental, regulatory and commercial risks typically associated with the potential eco-toxicity of leachable bottom ash produced by incinerators or other thermal processes. PAG does not produce any waste (zero waste), reduces the need for landfilling of waste, and produces a high-value construction material (Plasmarok) which is recognized as a product. All these reasons make PAG a technology capable of optimally solving waste management in ports in line with a circular economy logic.

This study is based upon the IMPATTI-NO Project (Interreg IT-FR Maritime Program 2014–2020) which implements several laboratory applications aimed at the chemical-physical treatment of the non-recyclable waste containing plastics deriving from the collection of beached waste and wastes collected by fishermen's trawls and passenger ships. To demonstrate the effectiveness of PAG for the treatment of port waste, IMPATTI-NO performs experimental tests that simulate PAG pilot plants using artificial samples representative of port waste.

This paper describes the research path developed so far and the preparatory elements that led to the definition of specifications for the sampling and collection of port waste.

Keywords: Circular economy · Marine litter · Port waste · Syn-gas

---

A. Viola—Professional Consultant.

O. Gervasi et al. (Eds.): ICCSA 2020, LNCS 12255, pp. 15–28, 2020.
https://doi.org/10.1007/978-3-030-58820-5_2

1   Introduction

In December 2015, the European Commission adopted the Circular Economy Action Plan, whose priorities include the Plastics Strategy and its life cycle.

In the decades of economic growth that followed the war, plastic began the inexorable rise that would lead it to replace cotton, glass and cardboard as the first-choice material for consumer products. In the early 1950s, thin plastic packaging was introduced, replacing paper to protect food, and within a decade, DuPont had manufactured and sold one billion of these plastic sheets. At the same time, plastic had entered our lives so much that we didn't even realize its presence. And it came everywhere, even into space when you think that in 1969, the flag that Neil Armstrong planted on the moon was made of nylon.

The following year, Coca Cola and Pepsi began replacing their glass bottles with plastic versions produced by Monsanto Chemical and Standard Oil.

Since then, plastic production has soared to 348 million tons in 2017, with European manufacturers (EU28th Norway and Switzerland) contributing 64.4 million tons, 4.4 million more than in 2016. In the world, Europe thus contributes 18.5% to total production, just above the Middle East (17.7%), but a far cry from Asia, which now churns out half of the plastics consumed worldwide (29.4% China alone). In the main target sectors, packaging remains at the top of the list with 39.7% of the 51.2 million tons processed in 2017 in Europe; followed by construction with 19.8%, automotive with 10.1%, the electrical and electronics sector with 6.2%, home and sports and leisure items (4.1%), agriculture (3.4%) applications (16.7%).

Polyolefins are the most used plastics by European processors: all together they reach 49%, between polypropylene (19.3%), low-density polyethylene (17.5%) PE (12.3%). PVC is worth just over 10%, PET accounts for 7%, polyurethanes 7.7%, while for compact and expanded polystyrene it comes to 6.6%.

By focusing on packaging waste, 2016 Official data show a collection of 16.7 million ton, of which 40.8% was mechanically recycled, above the 22.5% expected by the current Packaging and Packaging Waste Directive, but below the 50% expected by the new targets set for 2025, 38.8% was addressed to the thermovalorizers, while 20.3% of the collected packaging has finished in landfill.

Despite the apparent positive balance sheets of plastic waste management, a pitiless estimate by experts leads to say that of the approximately 300 million ton of plastics produced annually worldwide, at least 8–13 million ton are lost at sea every year with an impact that has taken on a level that is no longer sustainable today.

2   The Marine Litter Issues

Solid marine litter (marine litter), defined as any persistent solid material produced by man and abandoned in the marine environment, derives from human activities that take place both on land and at sea. The problem of the presence of waste in the marine environment has recently taken on the dimensions of a complex and global challenge, which is the subject of attention and a cause of widespread concern at all levels.

The main terrestrial activities from which marine litter comes from are the improper disposal of waste in individual homes, the mismanagement of urban waste, the illicit disposal of industrial waste, and the tourist and recreational activities.

From the maritime side there are the loss of fishing gear (lines, nets, lobster pots, etc.) deriving from commercial fishing, the illegal disposal of waste from merchant shipping and passenger ships, pleasure boats, and fish farms.

The most frequently found materials are plastic, rubber, paper, metal, wood, glass that can either float on the surface of the sea and be transported then to the beaches or sink and lie on the seabed. Each of these can, through the mechanical action of the waves and the action of the sun, be reduced and transformed into small sizes. The longer the holding time in the sea, the more fragmentation by natural agents increases and the size of the particles decreases.

Plastics are the most representative components of this marine waste (even over 85%) found along the coasts (beach litter), on the surface of the sea (floating litter) and on the ocean floor (seabed litter). Microplastics are plastic particles ranging in size from a few microns to 500 μ, commonly found in seawater. Microplastics include a very heterogeneous series of particles that vary in size, shape, color, chemical composition and density. They can be divided, according to the source from which they come, into "primary" and "secondary" microplastics [1–3].

The interventions to reduce the pollution problem, although certainly not resolving, may include awareness campaigns on the problem, reuse, recycling, etc.

In the context of the Circular Economy Action Plan, the European Commission adopted the European Plastics Strategy in the Circular Economy Communication on 16 January 2018 [4] with the following main proposed actions:

- make all plastic packaging in the EU recyclable by 2030;
- address the issue of microplastics and oxo-plastics intentionally added in products (cosmetics, paints, detergents, etc.);
- curb the consumption of single-use plastics (through a legislative proposal).

Plastic production was estimated in 2015 to be around 270 million ton, while waste production was estimated to have reached 275 million ton.

A hotly debated issue in the scientific community – and not only – is finding alternatives in the development phase but also eco-friendly solutions for the management of plastic waste.

A first approach is to better manage the disposal phase, which is the end of life of plastic objects. The "Plastic Pollution" study analyzed plastic disposal methods throughout history. According to this study, in the 1980s, 100% of the plastic was dumped, and at that time the risk of dispersion in the environment was quite high. Incineration has taken hold since 1980, but it is only from 2000 onwards that there has been a significant percentage of recycling which now stands at around 20%, which can certainly be improved but not much. Another important aspect to consider is that glass and metals can be recycled indefinitely without losing quality or purity in the processed product while this is not the case for plastic because in the following recycles the plastic worsens its quality. It is important to know that plastics are polymers, i.e., long chains of atoms "arranged in repetitive units often much longer than those found in nature". The longer and stronger these chains, the higher the quality of the plastic; each time the plastic is recycled, the polymer chain gets shorter and its quality decreases. The same piece of plastic can only be recycled 2–3 times before its quality decreases to the point where it can no longer be used.

The most desirable situation would be to convert our traditional linear economic model (make-use-dispose) into a circular economy model.

3   Circular Economy

The most qualified definition of circular economy is that of the Ellen MacArthur Foundation which wrote: "The circular economy is an industrial system that is designed to be regenerative. It replaces the end-of-life concept with restoration, moves towards the use of renewable energy, eliminates the use of toxic chemicals that hinder reuse, and aims to eliminate waste through upstream design of materials, products, systems and even business models" [5].

The circular economy is defined according to three main "actions", namely the so-called Principles of 3R: Reduction, Reuse and Recycle [6].

Figure 1 reports the Waste management hierarchy as suggested by European Commission Directives as reported in European Parliament. Amendments adopted by the European parliament on 14 March 2017 on the proposal for a directive of the European Parliament and of the Council amending directive 2008/98/EC on waste [7].

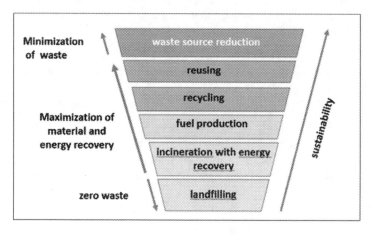

Fig. 1. Waste management hierarchy as suggested by EU Commission Directives

Although the circular economy is often identified with the principle of recycling, it should be stressed that this may be the least sustainable solution compared to the other two principles, both in terms of resource efficiency and profitability [8–10]. Recycling is limited by the complexity of materials such as plastics [11], for example. Some waste materials are recyclable to a certain point or even non-recyclable. Non-recyclable waste can be converted into energy recovery through systems of Waste-to-Energy (WtE) or Waste-to-Products (WtP) by pyrolysis, gasification, plasma gasification or can be dumped [5, 7, 12].

3.1 Waste-to-Energy and Circular Economy

WtE is a broad term that includes various waste treatment processes that generate energy (for example in the form of electricity and/or heat or that produce a fuel derived from waste), each of which has different environmental impacts and a circular economic potential [13, 14]. The main WtE processes identified by the EU Commissions [15] are:

- the co-production of waste in combustion plants and in the production of cement and lime;
- the incineration of waste in dedicated facilities;
- the anaerobic digestion of biodegradable waste;
- the production of solid, liquid or gaseous fuels derived from waste;
- other processes, including indirect incineration following a phase of pyrolysis, gasification, plasma.

Five distinct categories of processes are used as the basis for plasma waste management systems:

- plasma pyrolysis [16];
- plasma combustion (also called plasma incineration or plasma oxidation);
- vitrification of the residue of the thermal process using plasma;
- assisted plasma gasification in two variants [17].

The only technology that at the moment seems to have reached a decent level of industrialization, with better environmental performance than competing technologies based on thermal treatments (combustion or co-combustion or without direct combustion of waste) and without the defects of the more traditional incinerators and gasifiers, is the one that is called plasma assisted gasification, existing in different technological variants, mainly based on the use of "plasma torches" and in very few cases on the use of semi-submerged and submerged arc electrodes.

3.2 Plasma Assisted Gasification

Plasma plants have achieved high levels of reliability, totaling millions of hours of operation (the Westinghouse and Europlasma plants alone exceed 1,000,000 operating hours). The basic principle of this new technology focuses on the molecular dissociation (breakdown in elementary atoms components molecules) of organic waste components (and the fusion of inorganic components) operated at very high temperature within a closed reactor (plasma converter), without combustion and therefore without fumes emission and without ash production (Fig. 2).

An assisted plasma gasification plant is just a syn-gas production plant (a mixture consisting mainly of $CO-H_2$), and it will be the latter's use that will determine the type of waste transformation. Synthesis gas, also known as syn-gas, is a simple blend of carbon monoxide and hydrogen. The Syn-gas can be burned to produce heat and steam, or electricity through the use of boilers, motors and turbines. This gas burns very cleanly with properties very similar to natural gas, albeit with a lower heating value.

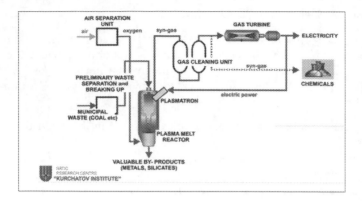

Fig. 2. Plasma assisted gasification process

Alternatively, syn-gas can be processed using catalysts and refined in a variety of liquid fuels and added value products (Fig. 3). Syn-gas can also be used to produce hydrogen and is considered a primary path to a possible hydrogen economy. Syn-gas can be upgraded into synthetic natural gas or used to produce different industrial chemicals. Gasification assisted plasma transforms various raw materials including waste into a synthetic gas instead of producing only heat and electricity. The synthetic gas produced by gasification can be turned into higher-value commercial products such as transport fuels, fertilizers, chemicals and even to replace natural gas.

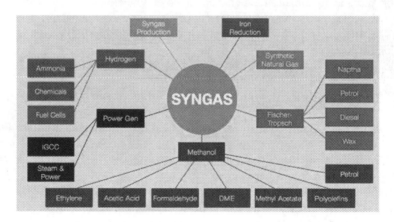

Fig. 3. Alternative use of the syn-gas

Thermochemical conversion of biomass and urban solid waste is being developed as a tool to promote the idea of the energy system without fossil fuels. In urban solid waste management, gasification does not compete with recycling, and also improves recycling programs.

Pre-processing and post-processing must increase the amount of recyclable materials in the circular economy. Since the process is endothermic, the high reaction temperature is provided by an external source of energy consisting of a plasma (ion mixture at 15,000–20,000 °C) activated by a voltaic arc. The result of the process is a synthetic gas purer than methane, predominantly hydrogen and CO with about 1/5 nitrogen and light hydrocarbons (thanks to sophisticated process control, this composition of the synthetic gas remains virtually constant, regardless of the type of waste destroyed: paints, tires, plastics, wood, fabrics, sewage sludge, etc.).

3.3   WtE System Integrated with a Plasma Gasification Thermal Process

In general, the energy exploitation of the syn-gas can be carried out according to two alternatives:

1. the direct combustion of syn-gas as produced (or after mild treatments) in conventional combustion systems placed downstream of the gasifier ("thermal" conversion);
2. the use of syn-gas in unconventional installations, such as internal combustion engines and gas turbines, after thrust purification ("electric" gasification).

In the "thermal" gasification, the syn-gas produced is combusted without undergoing (or after only very gross) purifying treatments aimed at eliminating the dragged powders, tar and other pollutants present (HCl, H_2S, SO_2, etc.), in order to generate electricity through the production of steam. Exhausted fumes must of course be treated downstream from combustion, as is the case in a traditional waste incineration plant. This solution does not differ substantially from the direct combustion of waste in that it takes place in virtually two successive stages without almost continuity. The differentiation becomes almost formal in that it is not possible to physically separate the gasification phase from that of the final combustion of the derived gas, so the treatment is configured as an incineration and as such, rightly, subject to all the requirements and regulations applicable to it.

In the "electric" gasification, the two phases of production of the derived gas and its use in turbine or internal combustion engine to produce electricity are quite distinct. It is this solution that, at present, has greater potential for development, because, on the basis of what has already been experienced with coal and some biomass, the production of a gas fuel destined to be used in a turbine allows the adoption of combined cycles for the production of electricity.

Ultimately, plasma reactors do not determine the combustion of waste but the simultaneous sublimation, pyrolysis, gasification at very high temperature of organic materials (natural or synthetic), the melting of metals and the melting-vitrification of inert materials; they are designed to maximize the conversion of waste in charge to syn-gas, consisting mainly of carbon monoxide and hydrogen, with various alternative uses. They also have several important features:

- they use very limited quantities of air and oxygen (in special cases nitrogen or argon) and operate in a reducing environment, in a closed reactor and in slight depression to avoid uncontrolled gas leaks;

- they do not produce ash or unburnt, while the particulates, dust and sludge from the syn-gas purification are almost always returned to the reactor and vitrified with periodic specific treatment campaigns under controlled process conditions;
- 1 ton of MSW as it is, gasified in plasma reactors, produces between 800 and 1200 Nm^3 of syn-gas (the volume/ton varies according to the quality of the waste and the technological variant of the reactor);
- 1 ton of MSW generates about 180–190 kg of recyclable glass slag (with volumes, if compact and untreated, of just 0.085–0.095 m^3, and density of 1.8–2.2 tons/m^3). The glass slag has proven to be not very leachable. Being an inert, it is recyclable for many uses in the construction sector;
- the syn-gas is purified at high temperature and then also undergoes "quenching" treatments (very rapid reduction of temperature) and further cold purification; the treated gas is used for the production of electricity and steam (combustion in a gas turbine in a combined cycle with a condensation or derivation and condensation steam turbine), and/or for the production of precursors for the chemical industry (methanol, ethanol), and/or for the separation of ultra-pure filtration hydrogen;
- hydrogen from syn-gas can be used in petrochemicals, in the food industry, in buses and electric cars powered by hydrogen fuel cells, in innovative cars with liquid hydrogen or compressed hydrogen gas, in research laboratories and special industrial applications;
- the CO_2 produced is so pure that it can be compressed and reused directly as an additive for carbonated drinks, or returned to the combustion chamber;
- emissions into the atmosphere from possible combustion of the syn-gas in the turbine or boiler are very low due to the fact of burning an already highly purified gas;
- investment costs vary from 1,550 €/(ton annual capacity) for very small mobile units (1,500 ton/y) to be moved to sites to be reclaimed, to 900 €/(ton annual capacity) for medium-small fixed units (30,000 tons/y), at 325 €/(ton annual capacity) for high-size fixed systems (650,000 tons/y) made up of medium or medium-small size reactor batteries;
- the systems are characterized by extremely high flexibility with respect to the charging materials.

4 The Experience of the IMPATTI-NO Project: Verification of a Gasification System with Assisted Plasma on a Pilot Plant

The IMPATTI-NO project, which started in 2018, implements joint action plans for the prevention, reduction and sorting of waste and wastewater in ports. In this context, it aims to identify the best waste and wastewater treatment technologies in port areas. Starting from the characterization of the waste and effluent present in the ports involved, IMPATTI-NO carries out a series of experimental campaigns on multiversatile pilot plants, for the treatment of waste and effluent in four test ports, in order to identify the best technologies to be applied to each one in consideration of the treatment costs and the final economic value of the manufactured product.

4.1   The Phases of the IMPATTI-NO Project

Starting from the analysis of port waste, the chemical-physical characterization of the collected samples is carried out (5–10 kg each):

Chemical characterization:

– immediate analysis (humidity, ash, MV, fixed C);
– elemental analysis (C, H, O, N, Cl, S);
– calorific value (PCS and PCI);
– analysis of the ashes.

Thermogravimetric characterization:

– TGA (thermo-gravimetric analysis) up to 1000 °C in an air atmosphere;
– TGA (thermo-gravimetric analysis) up to 1000 °C in a nitrogen atmosphere.

These characterizations are intended to evaluate the thermal behavior of the plastic material to be used for gasification tests with plasma on a pilot plant. Furthermore, an experimentation is carried out which consists in the treatment by means of assisted gasification with plasma of waste materials of port origin with a high organic content.

The experimentation is divided into 2 phases:

1. syn-gas production by gasification in a rotating drum reactor in an atmosphere enriched with O_2;
2. treatment of the syn-gas produced by the previous gasification phase, in the plasma torch to produce purified gas that can be used in a gas turbine (WtE) or to obtain chemical products (WtP).

The first phase aims to define the optimal conditions of the gasification process and to determine the composition of the syn-gas and any char produced by the gasification phase. These analyzes will aim to identify the appropriate process parameters (heating speed of the incoming material, temperature, atmosphere) of the gasification and the most suitable loading conditions in the system (for example of the materials of the loading system). The pilot gasification plant must be suitably equipped to adapt the incoming atmosphere control system to measure (through thermocouples) the temperature inside the reactor. The syngas produced will pass through a system of condensers which will remove the condensable fraction (water and tar) which will be subjected to chemical analysis. The gasification reactor will be equipped with a differentiated oxygen injection system (enriched air) which, ensuring a high degree of mixing between reagents, allows to achieve faster reaction kinetics and therefore a higher yield in terms of the quality of the syn-gas produced compared to traditional rotating drum reactors.

The second phase of purification of syn-gas through plasma torch treatment has the purpose of determining the composition of the gases produced by this treatment to establish their possible energy use in the turbine. The adoption of the plasma torch technology is the right choice for the reduction of the danger of the syn-gas and for its purification, as it is possible to obtain a very rapid heating of the input syn-gas, a necessary condition for the atomic dissociation of the initial molecules (flash pyrolysis). With this system it is possible to carry out the "flash pyrolysis" at very high temperatures that allow the immediate and complete decomposition of gases and/or liquids into elementary molecules. This technology is particularly suitable for the thermo-destructive disposal of port, urban and special plastic residues.

In particular, the activity involves checking the following parameters:

- reactive kinetics;
- distribution of heat treatment products (and by-products);
- characteristics of syn-gas.

From the results of these tests it will be possible to estimate the treatment costs and the final economic value of the product made. Finally, a technical-economic comparison will be made between the conventional technologies of gasification of plastic waste and the most innovative gasification technology assisted with plasma torches for the purification of syn-gas.

This paper describes the waste collection and sampling process developed within the IMPATTI-NO project.

5   The Waste Sampling Procedure in the IMPATTI-NO Project

In the IMPATTI-NO project, the solid waste accidentally collected by fishermen during normal fishing activities is collected in special containers (e.g. a bin or a big bag), placed on board the boats participating in the fishing-for-litter initiative, and the waste transferred ashore in special structures without any economic burden for the fisherman. This practice has already been operating successfully since 2005 in various marineries, especially in Northern Europe: Scotland, Holland, Belgium, Germany. One of the problems for which this system is not widespread in Italy is the lack of adequate transfer points in the ports and areas where fishing vessels moor, as well as a deficiency in the collection and disposal or recycling processes.

To give the tests carried out on a pilot gasification plant with assisted plasma a certain reproducibility, artificial samples that reproduce the average results of the campaigns carried out by other research groups were built. The protocol used has been developed based on the one created in the Marine Strategy Framework Directive (MSFD Technical Subgroup) by the Marine Waste Technical Group, following a standardized method that allows the comparison between the data collected by anyone who uses it worldwide.

5.1   Preparation of Samples from Marine Waste and from Waste Produced on Board Ships

The sampling involves the preparation of 5 samples, of 5 kg each, in pieces not exceeding 50 mm, coming from waste so diversified by type A, B and C:

- Type A: N°1 sample prepared from beach litter material.

- Type B: N°2 samples prepared from the material collected by fishermen during normal fishing activities and delivered in "demountable bins" (or other containers for waste collection) made available in the ports by the Port Authority:
  - 1 sample free of metal and glass (recyclable) but with all plastics;
  - 1 sample free of metal and glass and recyclable plastics.
- Type C: N°2 samples prepared from non-recyclable dry waste from merchant and civilian ships that operate the separate collection, thus consisting respectively of:
  - N°1 representative sample of the dry non-recyclable waste as it is;
  - N°1 sample consisting only of the non-recyclable plastic present in the dry non-recyclable waste.

Each of these prepared samples is accompanied by a certificate of analysis which reports:

- moisture analysis, Ash, MV, fixed C;
- elementary analysis (C, H, O, N, CI, S);
- heating power (PCS and PCI);
- analysis of the ashes.

5.1.1 Preparation of the Sample of Type a from the Material Collected on the Beaches

In order to obtain from the experimental tests results that have the possibility of being extended to general considerations, it is necessary that the packaged waste samples to be sent to the research institute for subsequent experiments approach a material composed of categories and compositions that respect as much as possible those of an average representative sample of waste collected on the beaches. In the circular economy, only that part of non-recyclable waste must be subjected to the WtE system.

As regards the identification of the recyclable plastic from the total plastic present, samples of plastics are sent to a specialized recycling center to evaluate their recyclability. To facilitate sampling, reference is made, for the identification of the part of the recyclable waste, to the provisions of the Municipalities for separate collection:

- recyclable plastic: plastic bottles (water and drinks), containers for liquids (shampoo, detergents, etc.), yoghurt jars, trays and transparent films for food, polystyrene, saucers, cutlery and plastic glasses, bins of any size, polystyrene for packaging. Toys, basins and chairs are not recyclable.
- recyclable metal: beverage cans (beer, soft drinks, etc.), food cans (peas, tuna, peeled, etc.), metal cables and wires. They are not recyclable: empty cans (shaving foam, hair spray, etc.).
- glass: bottles, jars, jars and containers. They are not recyclable: ceramic and porcelain shards (of plates or cups), mirrors, light bulbs, neon tubes, oven dishes.

Figure 4 summarizes the procedure for packaging the sample.

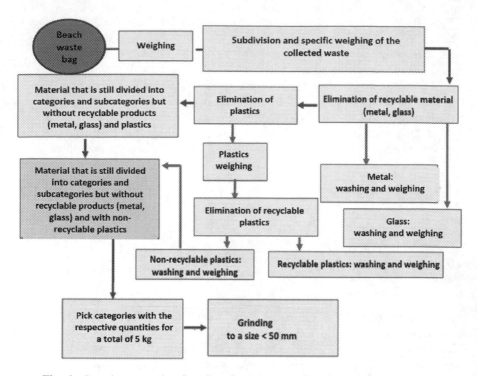

Fig. 4. Sample preparation flowsheet from the material collected on the beaches

5.1.2   Preparation of the Samples of Type B from Material Collected at Sea

The term marine litter is defined as any persistent (durable) solid material produced by man and abandoned in the marine environment. The waste arrives at sea both from land sources (bad individual habits, incorrect management of urban waste, lack of wastewater treatment plants, illicit disposal of industrial waste, floods, etc.) and from marine sources (illegal disposal of the waste produced from passenger ships, merchant ships, platforms). Commercial fishing, mussel farming and fish farming also contribute to the production of solid marine litter when fishing gear (lines, nets, lobster pots, etc.) is accidentally lost or voluntarily disposed of at sea. These solid waste (bottom material), accidentally trapped by nets (especially bottom trawls) during normal fishing activities are collected by fishermen in special containers (e.g. a bin or a big bag) placed on board the boats (at least those participating in the fishing-for-litter initiative), and subsequently transferred to land in special structures (demountable bodies) without any economic burden for the fisherman.

For the preparation of the Type B samples, coming from the material collected by the fishermen at sea and discharged in detachable bins made available in the ports by the Port Authority, reference is made to the products of the different categories (plastic, rubbers, metals, glass, ceramic, concrete, clothes, wood, etc.). The average analytical results of the first experiments obtained by the "Experimental Project Fishing for Litter" are used for preparing the samples.

5.1.3   Preparation of the Samples of Type C from Non-Recyclable Dry Waste from Merchant and Passenger Ships that Carry Out Separate Collection

The samples prepared from the non-recyclable dry waste fraction from merchant and passenger ships that operate the separate collection are made up as follows: the first representative sample of the non-recyclable dry waste as it is (C1), the second sample consisting only of non-recyclable plastic present in the dry non-recyclable waste (C2). Both samples must be ground to a size not exceeding 50 mm.

To obtain a convenient product analysis, it is necessary to take a quantity of dry waste not less than 100 kg. This quantity is placed on a screening surface with 20 mm mesh, in order to separate the smaller materials, which are collected in a special tarpaulin in PE below, and which are subsequently collected in the dedicated container. We then proceed to the manual sorting of the product fractions by placing them in their respective pre-calibrated containers. At the end of this operation, the waste belonging to the different classes is weighed, using a suitable weighing system. To remedy the difference in weight between the sum of the individual fractions and the overall weight of the class previously determined, due to the evaporation of the material during sorting or the loss of small materials, the percentages relating to the individual fractions are referred to their sum once the sorting has been carried out and not at the initial weight. Therefore, the total weight (P_{tot}) of the sample will be given by:

$$P_{tot} = \Sigma \, (product\ fractions\ after\ sorting)$$

In the 5 kg type C1 sample, all the categories are present with the respective % contained in the dry waste non-recyclable as such. The preparation of the 5 kg C2 sample, in which only the non-recyclable plastics are present, is prepared by taking this quantity (5 kg) from the plastic category.

6   Final Remarks

This paper has described the first phases of the IMPATTI-NO project which has the objective of analyzing the costs of collection, transfer and treatment of marine and port wastes, the "economic" benefits resulting from the cleaning of the sea and coasts, and the economic value of the final product of the treatment. The final scope of the project is to identify, within the test area (Upper Tyrrhenian area including Sardinia and Corsica), the most advantageous logistics solution for the treatment of marine litter. The choice of the logistics solution will depend on the volume of waste produced by each port, its location (the census of waste volumes has already been completed within the project), the investment and management costs of the treatment plants, and the location strategy adopted.

The waste sampling phase is currently underway, the study is expected to close in autumn 2021.

Acknowledgements. This research is based upon the IMPATTI-NO Project funded under the Interreg IT-FR Maritime Program 2014–2020.

References

1. Bergmann, M., Gutow, L., Klages, M.: Marine Anthropogenic Litter. Springer, Berlin (2015)
2. Kershaw, P.: Sources, fate and effects of microplastics in the marine environment: a global assessment. Rep. Stud. GESAMP 90, 96 (2015)
3. Derraik, J.G.: The pollution of the marine environment by plastic debris: a review. Marine Pollut. Bull. **44**(9), 842–852 (2002)
4. COM (2018) 28 final: Circular Economy Action Plan, the European Commission adopted the European Plastics Strategy in the Circular Economy Communication on 16 January 2018. https://ec.europa.eu/environment/circular-economy/pdf/plastics-strategy-brochure.pdf
5. ELLEN MACARTHUR FOUNDATION, The new plastics economy – Catalysing action (2017)
6. Zhijun, F., Nailing, Y.: Putting a circular economy into practice in China. Sustain. Sci. **2**(1), 95–101 (2007)
7. COM (2017) 34 final Communication from the Commission to the European Parliament, the Council, the European economic and Social Commettee and the Commettee of the Regions: The role of waste-to-energy in the circular economy
8. Ghisellini, P., Cialani, C., Ulgiati, S.: A review on circular economy: the expected transition to a balanced interplay of environmental and economic systems. J. Cleaner Prod. (2015). https://doi.org/10.1016/j.jclepro.2015.09.007
9. Geissdoerfer, M., Savaget, P., Bocken, N.M.P., Hultink, E.: The circular economy – a new sustainability paradigm? J. Cleaner Prod. **143**, 757–768 (2017). https://doi.org/10.1016/j.jclepro.2016.12.048
10. Kalmykova, Y., Sadagopan, M., Rosado, L.: Circular economy–from review of theories and practices to development of implementation tools. Resour. Conserv. Recycl. **135**, 190–201 (2018)
11. Lazarevic, D., Buclet, N., Brandt, N.: The influence of the waste hierarchy in shaping European waste management: the case of plastic waste. Reg. Dev. Dialogue **31**(2), 124–148 (2010)
12. Malinauskaite, J., Jouhara, H.: The trilemma of waste-to-energy: a multi-purpose solution. Energy Policy **129**, 636–645 (2019)
13. COM (2019) 190 final Report from the Commission to the European Parliament, the Council, The European Economic and Social Committee and the Commettee of the Regions on the implementation of the Circular Economy Action Plan {SWD (2019) 90 final}
14. Themelis, N.J., Vardelle, A.M.: Plasma-assisted waste-to-energy (WTE) process plasma-assisted waste-to-energy process waste-to-energy (WTE) processes: January 2012, Encyclopedia of Sustainability Science and Technology, pp. 8097–8112 (2012). https://doi.org/10.1007/978-1-4419-0851-3_407
15. Saveyn, H., Eder, P., Ramsay, M., Thonier, G., Warren, K., Hestin, M.: Towards a better exploitation of the technical potential of waste-to-energy. EUR 28230 EN (2016). https://doi.org/10.2791/870953
16. Aboughaly, M., Gabbar, H.A., Damideh, V., Hassen, I.: F-ICP thermal plasma for thermoplastic waste pyrolysis process with high conversion yield and tar elimination. Processes **8**(3), 281 (2020)
17. Hinsui, T., Arjharn, W., Pansa Liplap, P.: Plasma assisted gasification of rejected waste from an MTB plant for syngas production. Suranaree J. Sci. Technol. **22**(2), 183–196 (2015)

Processes for Noise Reduction in Urban Port Fronts

Federico Sollai$^{(\boxtimes)}$ ⓘ, Roberto Baccoli ⓘ, Andrea Medda ⓘ,
Gianfranco Fancello ⓘ, Patrizia Serra ⓘ, and Paolo Fadda ⓘ

DICAAR-Department of Civil and Environmental Engineering and Architecture,
University of Cagliari, Cagliari, Italy
federico.sollai@gmail.com, {rbaccoli,a.medda,
fancello,pserra,fadda}@unica.it

Abstract. As part of the LIST-PORT, Report and Decibel Project (Interreg IT-FR Marittimo Programme 2014–2020), which is included in a cluster of initiatives aimed at containing port noise, a synchronized traffic - noise survey campaign involving four ports in as many cities in the upper Tyrrhenian area, is now nearing completion. This paper describes the guidelines on the basis of which the traffic-noise surveys were conducted in the four ports and the types of data collected. In a second step of the study, these data will be used to train the predictive model of the sound pressures generated by traffic in ports, based on neural networks. The database presented in this work is thus the key element for the subsequent implementation of the predictive model which is currently in an advanced phase of development as part of another project in the cluster.

Keywords: Noise reduction · Urban front ports · Artificial neural networks

1 Introduction

Several European waterfront cities are afflicted by through traffic of private and commercial vehicles generated by port activities. Residential areas and susceptible structures such as schools, hospitals, care homes etc. may be exposed, both during the day and at night, to sound pressure levels as high as or sometimes exceeding the critical limits. These values are established by environmental noise regulations for the protection of people and the environment.

The ambitious objective of the projects, named List Port, Report and Decibel, is to develop a procedure/methodology for dynamically generating prediction scenarios for the short-medium term as a function of the noise source distribution and intensity scenarios. To do so, a series of acoustic measurement campaigns was conducted simultaneously with traffic counts in four different ports, whereby all the point and nonpoint sources were monitored. The predicted scenarios can thus be implemented dynamically to define specific noise abatement actions for the benefit of those susceptible areas in port cities that are particularly exposed to acoustic climate fluctuations.

This research was supported by the Interreg IT-FR Marittimo Programme 2014–2020.

© Springer Nature Switzerland AG 2020
O. Gervasi et al. (Eds.): ICCSA 2020, LNCS 12255, pp. 29–39, 2020.
https://doi.org/10.1007/978-3-030-58820-5_3

Lastly, the adaptive learning model, inspired by artificial neural network technology for predicting noise scenarios, is described. Other researchers in [1, 2] investigated the use of a neural network model for traffic noise prediction and also in comparison with statistical methods [3]. The present model is able to correctly estimate the sound pressure level that would be generated at a given point in the presence of an assigned scenario of vehicle traffic composition and layout.

2 The ITS Information Mobility System Driven by a Neural Network Prediction Model

In this paper, we illustrate the results of the experimental campaign and the predictive traffic-noise model, based on artificial intelligence (AI) to be integrated into the Intelligent Transportation System (ITS) system.

The model defined in this research aims to analyze the levels of noise emission generated by certain traffic scenarios. Depending on the levels recorded, the ITS system suggests driving behavior and alternative routes by transmitting info-messages, through variable message signs or mobile device applications (Fig. 1). These strategies are aimed at lowering the levels of noise emission in port cities' waterfronts. The traffic and sound pressure levels constitute the input and output data of the predictive model respectively. The case study concerned the urban waterfront of the port of Olbia, with the intention to extend the methodology to other port environments, such as Piombino, Vado Ligure and Bastia.

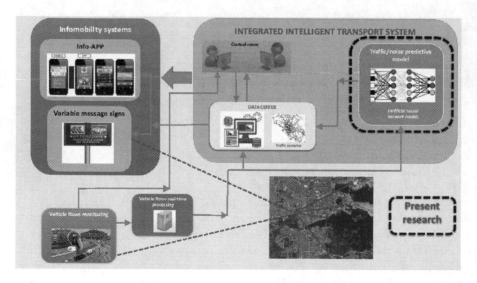

Fig. 1. ITS system diagrams.

The first step consisted in analyzing the existing maps of the city of Olbia, satellite images and the database containing mobility and noise time series analyses. Potential measurement points were then assessed on the basis of their ability to provide a sufficiently comprehensive and representative framework of sound pressure levels, and thus exposure to noise, throughout the commercial port and neighboring area. Figure 2 provides an overview of the area of interest showing the positions of the measuring points for both acoustics and vehicle flows.

Fig. 2. Representation of the area of interest and measuring points.

2.1   Experimental Set-up: Noise and Traffic Measurements

The environmental noise recorded in the *soft* and *peak* periods constitute the database of reference for analyzing the evolution of the waterfront's acoustic climate and for the subsequent implementation of the forecast model.

Measurement campaigns were carried out on March 25–28 (soft period) and on August 23–26, 2019 (peak period).

As for instrumentation and measurement techniques, representation and processing of acoustic data, the current regulatory requirements [4–14] were taken as reference.

In order to build a useful database, average values of acoustic quantities were acquired and stored, with a time base of 100 ms. In particular, sound pressure level trends were stored according to the different frequency weighting curves and the spectrum trends with normalized 1/3 octave bands. Acoustic data was captured in sync with vehicle flow video detection for a period of 72 h. The acquired data was stored in a georeferenced database WGS84 UTM32N.

2.2   The Neural Network Model

One of the most significant scientific results of the research project is the development of a model capable of predicting the sound pressure level that would be generated at a given point of the waterfront for a given vehicle traffic layout in the investigated road sections.

The model is based on the acquisition of noise events, but without necessarily having all sound *patterns* that could occur. To achieve the goal of providing valid, or at least acceptable, predictions, for all possibilities of noise occurrence, starting with partial knowledge of the phenomenon, we implemented a model based on artificial neural networks. This recognition system was chosen because of its ability to generalize the results and thus to associate the correct response even with input signals *never seen* before, or with missing or partially damaged information [15, 16]. Figure 3 depicts a biological neural network and an artificial neural network. These learning models are used with increasing success to solve artificial intelligence problems, such as used in energy [17], building [18], speech recognition [19], etc., where it is necessary to recognize configurations or in general information belonging to a wide universe of accomplishments, both in the discrete and continuous domain.

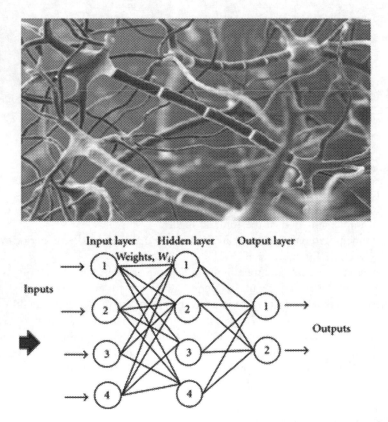

Fig. 3. Representation of a biological neural network (top) and structure of an artificial neural network (bottom).

2.3   Training and Testing Procedure

The development of a learning model based on artificial neural networks starts with a preliminary stage, called training procedure, whereby the network is guided to adapt its internal parameters to the goal of learning a number of instances of noise events related to traffic flows scenario comprising the training set.

Once training is completed, a second phase, namely the testing procedure, is conducted. This is a verification activity and accounts for the learning capacity achieved by the neural network during the training phase.

Learning capacity is measured and evaluated in terms of the network's ability to correctly recognize the largest number of noise event configurations belonging to the training set and also in terms of its ability to extend a valid recognition to cases belonging to the whole test set, i.e. cases that have not been previously included in the training set.

Traffic flows and acoustic measurements recorded during the periods March 25–28, and August 23–26, produced a time series of acoustic data and vehicle traffic. Figure 4 gives an example, both in the time and frequency domain.

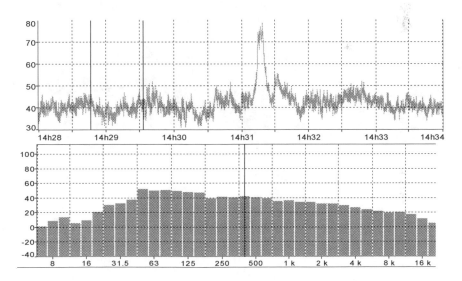

Fig. 4. Leq equivalent level and corresponding spectrum

Figure 5 shows the sound pressure level trend throughout the entire measurement period (March 25 to 28, 2019). We can recognize the typical dynamics that alternate between daytime, evening and nighttime.

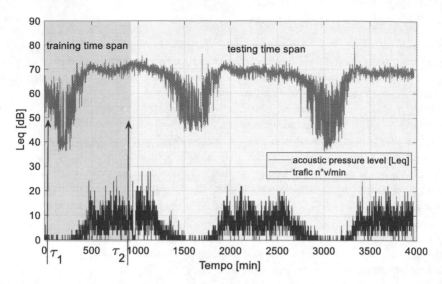

Fig. 5. Trend of vehicle traffic and noise detected. The periods referred to by the data considered for the training and test set are highlighted. Measuring position B.

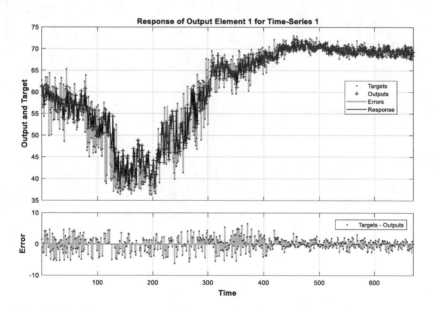

Fig. 6. Experimental trend and prediction of test set noise. Measuring position B.

Figure 6 summarizes the results of a generic network learning process, having used a single training interval containing 800 min.

2.4   Measuring Station C Underpass Exit (August 2019)

To render effective the neural network learning process for estimating the response from the measuring point C, the optimized set of traffic acquisition sections shown in Fig. 7, i.e. Sects. 3A, 3B, 3C, were considered.

Fig. 7. Sound level meter C location and road sections involved

2.5   Results of the Neural Network Applied to Traffic – Noise Prediction

This section presents the results of the neural network model's simulation phase following completion of the training procedure.

Figures 8 and 9 show respectively the performance parameters of the neural network training process and the comparison of the time evolution of sound pressure levels measured experimentally with the neural network model predictions. Each diagram also includes the absolute error between the two trends.

Figure 8 box (a) gives the average quadratic error versus the progress of the training periods; box (b) the output/target regression; box (c) the histogram of errors and frequency distributions in, box (d) the trend of gradient parameters, μ, and the number of validation checks; box (e) the simulated response of the network during training, and box (f) error autocorrelation.

For the sake of brevity, only the network response for a single measurement point (C) is reported. This point is located in via Principe Umberto, above the exit from the underpass. The site is quite complex in terms of the road sections involved and is characterized by different vehicle flow dynamics and sound pressure levels.

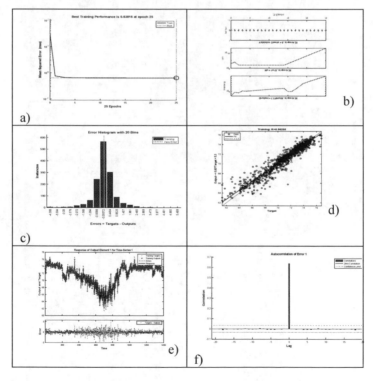

Fig. 8. Diagrams of network performance during the training phase, for C-station (road underpass).

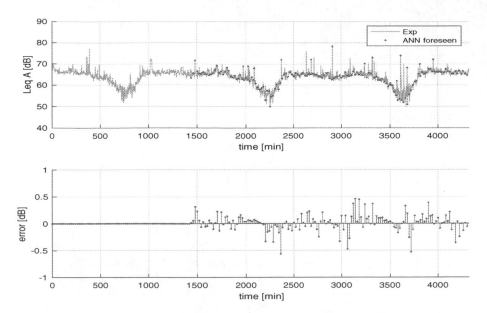

Fig. 9. Top: Leq$_A$ measured experimentally (green) and predicted by the ANN (red pellets). Bottom - difference between calculated and experimental values. Station C peak period August 23–26, 2019 (Color figure online)

2.6 Considerations

As can be seen from the graphs in Fig. 9, the traffic-noise model shows an excellent forecast capacity for the acoustic climate generated by vehicle traffic at the considered points. Neural network model training was based on a time series consisting of the first 1400 min, while the remaining 2600 min were excluded from the training procedure and were therefore reserved for verifying network performance under generalization.

This generalization phase allows one to check whether the network is able to provide correct noise level values only when it receives *"already seen"* traffic configurations or is capable, as is desirable, of extending this ability to recognize brand-new (*"never seen"*) traffic scenarios. As can be observed, the model exhibits excellent generalization ability for all three periods: daytime, evening and nighttime. The absolute error is always below 0.5 dB for the entire "time line" of the measurement campaign. In particular, the following results can be summarized for the measurement station at position C:

Time segment during the training phase: the deviation between the experimental data and the simulated values is near to zero.

Time segment during the test-generalization phase: the deviation between experimental data and simulated values is in all cases below 0.5 dB. Note that excluding nighttime, the error would be confined to values of less than 0.3 dB.

In different environmental, traffic and background noise conditions, for all noise monitoring stations and for the two periods (*soft* and *peak*) the model is able to predict $L_{eq,A}$ values comparable to experimental values, both in quasi-stationary and under highly variable conditions.

3 Conclusions

We have constructed a traffic-noise model based on artificial neural networks for the waterfront of the port city of Olbia. The model is able to predict noise levels in three representative positions along the waterfront with a deviation from the experimental values of less than 0.5 dB. Extensions of the model to the other partner cities involved in the project, are currently being developed. The performance of different models implemented for different cities will be compared so as to identify those elements that can define and characterize a general methodology for implementation in different contexts. The research developed suggests interesting aspects and developments. In fact the results of this first phase are very comforting and provide a good basis on which to develop further studies.

Acknowledgments. The work presented herein has benefited from the support of the Interreg Italia-Francia Marittimo 2014–2020 cooperation program, Call n.2, Project: REPORT (Rumore E Porti), which is gratefully acknowledged.

References

1. Nourani, V., Gökçekuş, H., Umar, I.K., Najafi, H.: An emotional artificial neural network for prediction of vehicular traffic noise. Sci. Total Environ. **707**, 136134 (2020). https://doi.org/10.1016/j.scitotenv.2019.136134. ISSN 0048-9697
2. Bravo-Moncayo, L., Lucio-Naranjo, J., Chávez, M., Pavón-García, I., Garzón, C.: A machine learning approach for traffic-noise annoyance assessment. Appl. Acoust. **156**, 262–270 (2019). https://doi.org/10.1016/j.apacoust.2019.07.010. ISSN 0003-682X
3. Nedic, V., Despotovic, D., Cvetanovic, S., Despotovic, M., Babic, S.: Comparison of classical statistical methods and artificial neural network in traffic noise prediction. Environ. Impact Assess. Rev. **49**, 24–30 (2014). https://doi.org/10.1016/j.eiar.2014.06.004. ISSN 0195-9255
4. Decreto del Ministero Ambiente. Tecniche di rilevamento e misurazione dell'inquinamento acustico (1998)
5. D.P.R. 30 marzo 2004, n. 142 Disposizioni per il contenimento e la prevenzione dell'inquinamento acustico derivante dal traffico veicolare, a norma dell'articolo 11 della L. 26 ottobre 1995, n. 447
6. Decreto Legislativo 19 agosto 2005, n. 194 - Attuazione della direttiva 2002/49/CE relativa alla determinazione e alla gestione del rumore ambientale
7. Decreto Legislativo 17 febbraio 2017, n. 42 Disposizioni in materia di armonizzazione della normativa nazionale in materia di inquinamento acustico
8. ISO 1996-2:2017 Acoustics—Description, measurement and assessment of environmental noise
9. UNI ISO 9613-1,2:2006 Acustica - Attenuazione sonora nella propagazione all'aperto

10. UNI EN ISO 11819-2:2017 – Acustica – Misurazione dell'influenza delle superfici stradali sul rumore da traffico
11. UNI EN 1793-3:1999: Dispositivi per la riduzione del rumore da traffico stradale -
12. UNI 11143-1:2005, "Acustica Metodo per la stima dell'impatto e del clima acustico per tipologia di sorgenti
13. UNI/TS 11387:2010, "Acustica - Linee guida alla mappatura acustica
14. UNI/TR 11326: 2009 Valutazione dell'incertezza nelle misurazioni e nei calcoli di acustica
15. Chen, L., Tang, B., Liu, T., Xiang, H., Sheng, Q., Gong, H.: Modeling traffic noise in a mountainous city using artificial neural networks and gradient correction. Transp. Res. Part D Transp. Environ. **78**, 102196 (2020). https://doi.org/10.1016/j.trd.2019.11.025. ISSN 1361-9209
16. Abiodun, O.I., Jantan, A., Omolara, A.E., Dada, K.V., Mohamed, NA., Arshad, H.: State-of-the-art in artificial neural network applications: a survey. Heliyon **4**(11) (2018). ISSN 2405-8440
17. Roberto, B., Ubaldo, C., Stefano, M., Roberto, I., Elisa, S., Paolo, M.: Graybox and adaptative dynamic neural network identification models to infer the steady state efficiency of solar thermal collectors starting from the transient condition. Solar Energy. **84**(6), 1027–1046 (2010). https://doi.org/10.1016/j.solener.2010.03.011. ISSN 0038-092X
18. Baccoli, R., Di Pilla, L., Frattolillo, A., Mastino, C.C.: An adaptive neural network model for thermal characterization of building components. Energy Procedia **140**, 374–385 (2017). ISSN 1876-6102
19. Mirsamadi, S., Hansen, J.H.L.: Multi-domain adversarial training of neural network acoustic models for distant speech recognition. Speech Commun. **106**, 21–30 (2019). https://doi.org/10.1016/j.specom.2018.10.010. ISSN 0167-6393

Tanger MED SEZs: A Logistic and Industrial Hub in the Western Mediterranean

Massimiliano Bencardino$^{(\boxtimes)}$ (ID) and Vincenzo Esposito

Territorial Development Observatory (OST),
Department of Political and Communication Sciences (POLICOM),
University of Salerno, 84084 Fisciano (SA), Italy
mbencardino@unisa.it

Abstract. This paper aims to investigate the impact of Special Economic Zones within a specific system-based economy, and variations in both individual sectoral specializations and those of the local labour market. There are six Special Economic Zones geographically located within the Tanger-Tétouan-Al Hoceima region in northern Morocco; each zone is centred on specialised production and strictly related to Tanger MED Port Complex, 1 and 2. At the present, they are among the most influential hubs of the Mediterranean and a crucial element of Morocco's economic and commercial development strategy.

The aim of this paper is to demonstrate how the presence of regional SEZs has positively impacted the increase in national FDEs and the increase in company localisations in the area under study.

This research is to be credited equally to both authors, for it is the result of their joint work.

Keywords: Logistic hub · Special Economic Zones · Commercial development strategy

1 Overview

SEZ is a tool with a widespread worldwide application: both for the attraction of foreign direct investment and for the diversification of the industrial sector.

SEZs have been a vastly covered topic in academic literature; both from an economic point of view [1–6] than one of organization of territory [3, 7–9]. The historical evolution of SEZs has been accompanied by several changes [10–12] resulting in a wide variety of tools; these differ on a technical - operational level, and the purpose they are intended for [12].

The following table shows the different types of SEZ used worldwide (Table 1).

The term SEZs is as a generic definition that includes multiple variants of traditional commerce [11]; that is why their institutional definition does not always find convergence within academic literature. International Labour Organization (ILO) defines EPZs as "*industrial zones with special incentives set up to attract foreign investors, in which imported materials undergo some degree of processing before being exported again*" [13]. According to World Bank "*the principles incorporated in the basic concept of a special economic zone include: geographically delimited area,*

© Springer Nature Switzerland AG 2020
O. Gervasi et al. (Eds.): ICCSA 2020, LNCS 12255, pp. 40–50, 2020.
https://doi.org/10.1007/978-3-030-58820-5_4

Table 1. Tipology of SEZs

Tipology	Definition
Free Trade Zone	Commonly known as Commercial Free Zone. Generally located within large ports of entry; it is a duty free, not very large area. It houses facilities for storage and distribution operations in order to facilitate exchange, transfer and re-export of goods
Traditional EPZ	The Export Processing Zones offer incentives and a barrier-free environment. These are preferred locations of export specialised companies and industrial complexes. In these areas, only export-oriented companies are licensed to operate
Hybrid EPZ	These includes non-EPZ companies as well. Thusly, these companies are not exclusively limited to the export market to sell their product
Freeports	They include very large areas that host many businesses: from retail to wholesale. The companies that are part of it enjoy special incentives and benefits
Enterprises Zones	These areas' production is intended exclusively for the domestic market; generally not very extended on the territory, they are closely linked to urban redevelopment
Single Factory EPZ	Individual companies, irrespective of their geographical location within the country, that enjoy particular forms of incentive. Their production is exclusively intended for export markets

usually physically secured (fenced-in); single management/administration; eligibility for benefits based upon physical location within the zone; separate customs area (duty-free benefits) and streamlined producers" [12]. Another definition by World Trade organization is that "*an EPZ refers to one or more areas of a country where barriers to trade are deduced and other incentives are created in order to attract foreign investors. The incentives provided differ in nature and can change over time, but many or most take the form of fiscal measures–tax reductions or exemptions rather than cash*" [14]. These definitions identify SEZs as catalysts for a country's economic growth; that is accomplished through the implementation of a series of policies aimed at achieving short-term static economic benefits (e.g. investment strategies to increase employment) or long-term dynamic economic benefits (e.g. increase of trade openness and international competitiveness of a single country or region) [4]. There are four main reasons why implementing such a tool would be beneficial, especially in developing economies: SEZs could be a support for a wider national economic reform. In a political-economic context, they could be an instrument to abate unemployment rates. These areas could also be used to test new policies and approaches, and to encourage Foreign Direct Investments, in particular in the MENA area [12].

As of 2018 there are 147 economies that over time have implemented this tool (there were 29 in 1975), bringing the number of world SEZs to 5,400 (there were 79 in 1975). Of these, decreased to 5,383 in 2019, 88.64% are located in developing countries; Asia has a leading position with 4,046 (2,645 in South East Asia alone) [15]. Morocco's experience is certainly one of the most deserving of attention; a developing country that over the last twenty years has employed a series of open trade policies that have resulted in some of the highest economic levels in the MENA area. Similarly, in Middle East and North Africa areas, the Dubai government implemented in 1985 the Jebel Ali Free Zone in order to diversify investments in such a way as to disengage from the impact of oil on GPD. They are symbiotically linked to the Jebel Ali port complex launched in 1983, and later with the twin port Port Rashid in 1972. The area currently hosts 3,880 transnational industrial companies, with Europe and the United States as major outlet markets [9]. Between the Atlantic and the Pacific, Panama is worthy of attention for its implementation of SEZs, specifically: Colon Free Zone (launched in 1948) which houses 2,527 companies and 29,786 employed in 2015, Panama-Pacific (launched in 2007) with 251 companies and 2,035 direct jobs in 2015 and the City of Knowledge (launched in 2000) with 75 SMEs and 1,290 workers [3].

2   Modeling of Regional Variables

What emerges, in the specific case of Tanger-Tétouan-Al Hoceima, is an economy that employs, as main strategic levers, an experimental implementation of a structured SEZs scheme: duty free areas, which have tax incentives and simplified administrative procedures. These characteristics are to be considered as functional to the local success of new industrial plants, product and logistics services; over the years, a progressive revitalization of the regional infrastructure fabric has followed. A peculiar case is the very existence of Tanger MED Port Complex focal element of Morocco's economic and commercial development strategy and in a symbiotic and functional relationship with SEZs. Through the systemic use of multiple databases [16–24], this paper has striven to acquire as many detail as possible on the subject, taking into account all the variables that could qualify as consistent for the research.

The purpose of this research: observing a given economic, social and demographic situation before and after the implementation of SEZs in Morocco. The examined time range, in reference to the regional market analysis, covers from 1999 to 2014; the choice of such time frame is to be found in the chronological origin of the implementation of SEZs in Morocco. Tanger Free Zone was the first launched in 1999. Today, it is the first industrial platform in the Tanger-Tétouan-Al Hoceima region and the most important industrial hub in the whole of Morocco. 2014 is the year of the last population census, preceded by that of 2004. The chosen time range, considering an analysis on a national scale and one about the localization regional companies, covers a period of twenty years between 1999 and 2018, the latter being the last available year in the databases at the time of this research.

In particular, the analysis focuses on four elements, both regionally and nationally: 1) economic growth (companies growth for sector and for dimension); 2) trade integration (balance of payments, foreign direct investment); 3) labour market. To better understand the impact of SEZs on local industry and the local labour market, this research will focus on a sample of companies extracted from Orbis database (the companies identified and located in Morocco through the database are 18,202 in total). Companies are categorized by following geographical survey parameters (e.g. sector of membership; company size), financial collection of assets, and time parameters (year of foundation). The variables are analyzed and subsequently matched; this was accomplished using pivot tables in order to identify historical matches in terms of foundation, evolution of sectoral specialization, production, and modification of the local labour market. The six SEZs identified were found in the administrative division of the Tanger-Tétouan-Al Hoceima Region, which includes the following provincial-prefectural scales: 1) Al Hoceima; 2) Chefchaouen; 3) Fahs-Anjra; 4) Larache; 5) Ouezzane; 6) Tanger-Assillah; 7) Tétouan; 8) M'Diq-Finideq with a total of 146 municipalities, of which 86.3% rural and 11.6% urban.

Finally, the 18,202 companies are reclassified by Province and Prefecture, in order to locate them in the region. Out of the entire national sample, the weight of activities located in Tanger-Tétouan-Al Hoceima is 10.4% of the sample, corresponding to 1,900 companies.

3   Tanger MED and the SEZs of Tanger-Tétouan-Al Hoceima

Tanger MED, located on the north coast of the Tanger-Tétouan-Al Hoceima region in Morocco, is now one of the main hubs of the Mediterranean basin. The significant public investment in the expansion and modernization of the entire port complex (Tanger MED 1 was only launched in 2007, while Tanger MED 2 in 2019), alongside the geo-strategic location of the infrastructure (the Strait of Gibraltar) are but few of the elements that have allowed the increases in performance and competitiveness levels. In just over ten years, the complex has indeed become an international model of governance in the global maritime cluster. Morocco, with a population of 33,848,000 in 2014 census, is one of the main emerging economies in MENA, an area strongly characterized by regional heterogeneity, both in terms of growth, commercial openness and institutional capital endowment.

The Moroccan state in 2018 recorded a growth of GDP, at constant prices, of 3%, down from the 4.2% of 2017 [16]. However, it is estimated that product will grow at rates of 3.8% in 2020 and 4.5% in 2024 [25]. Therefore, it is only logical that Morocco endeavors to consolidate on one hand the values of economic and commercial growth (the percentage change in the value of the *Merchandise trade* is 60% between 1999 and 2018), which could benefit from such an investment; on the other hand, connecting population growth to new opportunities arising from the local labour market. In 2018 Morocco, in line with the values of the entire MENA area, has indeed increased its population for an annual rate of 1.25%, given a fertility rate in 2017 of 2.45% [16]. There is no doubt that the localization of the complex also benefits from the centrality of maritime traffic in the AREA of MED (looking at the double track of market penetration, the land and the maritime kind, China's *One Belt Road Initiative* or even the effects of the doubling of the Suez Canal in 2015).

In this strategic view, the port complex is coming closer to the European market, a larger consumer market. It must be also taken into consideration the possible relocating of European companies production departments in the SEZs area. This last point is supported by the existence of a Logistic Duty Free Zone, located at Terminals 1 and 2 of Tanger MED 1; the "Medhub" platform that today hosts numerous companies operating in the value logistics sector. According to data from [26], the entire port complex covers an area of 1,000 ha and consists of four areas with different special-izations. The Tanger MED 1 includes two container terminals TC1 + TC2; their vol-ume capacity of 3 mln TEU, managed by transnational leaders APM Terminals and Eurogate CMA-GMA respectively. A railway connects the Port to the city of Tangier. A hydrocarbon terminal with an annual storage capacity of 15 million tonnes (input/output) of refined products. A Renault vehicle terminal with storage capacity of 1 million vehicles. A terminal dedicated to the management of containerized goods. The global investment of the Tanger MED 1 infrastructure, launched in 2007 (works started in 2003), amounted to 43 billion dirhams, 58% of which were paid by the Agence Spéciale Tanger Mediterranéè (from now on TMSA) and 49% by private investors. TMSA is the result of a public/private partnership established since 2003; an Anonymous company with public prerogatives around which revolve special purpose vehicles related to governance of port, and industrial and service poles. The group, with a social capital allocation of 3,795,079,100 dh, is composed of 87.50% of the "Hassan II Fund for Economic and Social Development"; 12.38% from Etat; 0.12% from the Moroccan investment bank "CDG Capital S.A.". Tanger MED 2 is relatively new, so the actual port operations were launched in 2019, nine years after the start of basic infrastructure works, started in 2010. The total investment amounted to 24 billion dirhams, of which 58.3% was paid by TMSA, the remaining 41.7% paid by privates. The infrastructure includes two container terminals, TC4 and TC3, respectively con-tracted to the APM terminal and Marsa Maroc operators, with a total capacity of 6 million Teu. On the whole, considering the Tanger MED 1 and 2, the potential capacity of the infrastructure reached 9 million TEU, with a storage capacity of 1 million vehicles, 7 million passengers, 700 thousand trucks (Table 2). Furthermore, two other infrastructures make up the extension of the port: "Port Tanger MED Passagers et Rouliers" launched in 2010 and operated by Tanger Med Port Authority and the "Centre d'affaires Tanger Med (Tanger Med Port Center)".

In terms of performance indicators, the investments distribution was very effective and had a considerable impact on the international competitiveness of Moroccan portal economy. In the 2006–2018 range, the country increased its Liner shipping connec-tivity index (LSCI), in a percentage change of +440%, rising the indicator level from 12% of 2006 to 65% in 2018. In terms of international competitiveness, with Chi-nese LSCI set to 100 in 2006, this means that Morocco from 79th position on a global scale raided to 18th in 2018; this growth started since 2007, the year of the launch of anger MED 1. In terms of Container port throughput, expressed in units equivalent to twenty feet (Teu), the percentage change between 2010 and 2018 was 70%, bringing the containerized goods managed by the port from 2,800,000 to the current 4,763,500 Teu [27].

Table 2. Number of arrivals; average size (GT) of vessels, Morocco (UNCATAD, 2018).

Measure	Number of arrivals	Average size (GT) of vessels
Passenger ship	13,929	11,614
Wet bulk	1,576	9,966
Container ship	3,676	39,913
Dry breakbulk	1,988	5,679
Dry bulk	1,351	25,867
Roll-on/roll-off ship	2,281	22,510
Liquefied petroleum gas carriers	332	17,601
All ships	**25,133**	**17,015**

In the same period, 2006–2018, there is also a change in the Liner shipping bilateral connectivity index (from now on LSBCI); in 2018 there is greater bi-lateralization and trade integration with Asian countries: Malaysia, Singapore, South Korea, China. The research identifies four key elements in Tanger MED's development: the strategic location of the port; the ability to attract mega carriers and top-level terminalists; the ability to play a multi-purpose role and thus accommodating every type of ship; the arrangement of a structured Free Zone [28]. The figure (Fig. 1) shows the six SEZs of Tanger-Tétouan-Al Hoceima.

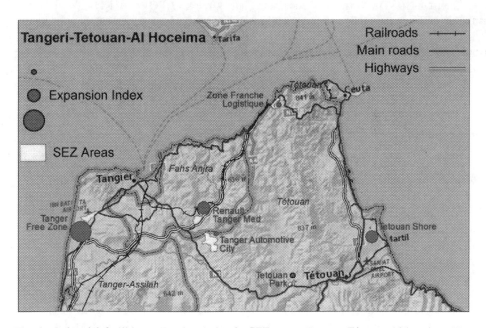

Fig. 1. Industrial facilities expansion index in SEZs ares, Tanger- Tétouan-Al hoceima (Our elaboration from ArcGis source).

The data measured the industrial expansion index within each Free Zone. What emerged is that within the SEZs, an industrial facility equal to 1,162 has an average expansion rate of 3.19%.

In detail, the structured SEZ covers a surface area of 5,000 ha, thus distributed: 1) the industrial platform Tanger Free Zone launched in 1999, a Generalist Free Zone distributed over an area of 400 ha. The area, home to textile, automotive, aerospace and agricultural companies, is 4 km from the region's main airport, Tanger Ibn Battouta, and about 54 km from the Tanger Med complex. It is the main industrial platform of the entire MENA area to date, hosting companies from more than 30 nationalities; it is the 6th Free Zone on a global scale; 2) Tanger Automotive City (TAC) launched in 2012, extended over an area of 800 ha, is an industrial platform specialized in auto-motive industry, 22 km from Tanger Med and 20 km from Tanger Free Zone, next to the Renault Tanger Med Free Zone, founded in 2008 covering a territory of 300 ha. The area is entirely dedicated to administrative location of Renault-Nissan plants; inside models are being made for Lodgy, Sandero, Sandero Stepway, Dokker, Logan MCV. The Free Zone is 7.4 km away from the TAC; 3) Tétouan Park, a logistics and industrial park on an area of 150 ha, currently still under development. Closely connected to the activities of the Tanger Free Zone, the park aims to stimulate industrialization processes (localizing light industry) within the province; 4) Tétouan Shore, launched in 2013, covers an area of 20 ha. The area is entirely dedicated to offshoring activities offering spaces for services related to Information Technology Outsourcing (ITO), Business Processing Outsourcing (BPO) and KPO (Knowledge Process Outsourcing); 5) Commercial Zone of Findeq, launched in 2012, is spread over an area of about 100 ha, designed for wholesale and retail trade development; 6) Logistics MedHub Free Zone, launched in 2008, covering an area of 250 ha behind the terminals of Tanger Med 1, is a unique customs area on the doorstep of the European and African market; it specialises in value logistics activities, distribution to other Moroccan Free Zones, storage, assembly, labelling and quality control.

The table (Table 3) shows the increase in the number of industrial facilities within the northern region. The increase is observed precisely since 1999, year of the launch of Tanger Free Zone platform; there are peaks, in non-cumulative terms, in the cor-responding years of the construction of Tanger MED 1 and the launch of MedHub Free Zone. Between 2003 and 2007, major automotive companies relocated to the area: Lear Automotive Morocco (2003); Delphi Packard Tanger (2007); textiles with Erum Maroc (2003), New Line Fashion (2006); Steelworks with Kaye Aluminium Tanger (2002); to agro-industrial with Maroc-Produits Agro-Alimentaires. A further increase is observed between 2009 and 2011. At this stage, the companies relocating are such as: Sealynx Automotive Morocco (2008); S.N.O.P Tanger (2010); Denso Thermal Systems Mor-occo (2010); Joyson Safety Systems Maroc (2010); Plastic Omnium Auto Inergy Morocco (2010); Procesos Industriales Del Sur Maroc (2010). The sample analysis shows a progressive tertiarization of the regional economy (Fig. 2). By setting to 100 the entire regional sample, the weight of the tertiary sector is 57%; follows the secondary sector with a weight of 39.1%.

Table 3. Company activities classified by foundation year, Tanger-Tétouan-Al Hoceima region. Cumulative values (Orbis sample).

Foundation year	Cumulative values
1970	30
1975	37
1980	58
1985	66
1990	113
1995	183
2000	308
2005	717
2010	1,303
2018	1,900

The sectoral distribution of companies there sited follows the trend measured on the entire national sample where the weight of the service sector is 59%, followed by the manufacturing sector of 36%. It could be assumed that the presence of SEZs in the northern region has attracted services and manufacturing companies mainly. Of the total number of national companies operating in the service sector, the regional weight is 10%; speculatively on the total of secondary sector companies, it is 12%.

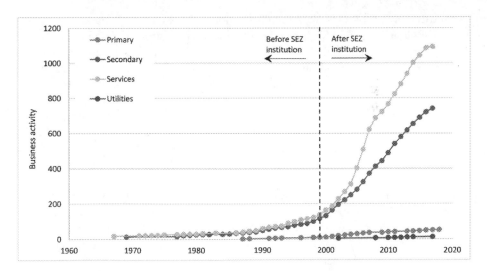

Fig. 2. Sectoral classification of companies in Tanger- Tétouan-Al Hoceima. Cumulative values (Orbis sample).

The location of very large companies was followed by the creation of an industrial ring consisting mainly of medium-sized companies. Indeed, the next figure (Fig. 3) shows the R^2 correlations between the cumulative value of very large and medium size companies, and the correlation between the first and the large companies, respectively at 0.95 and 0.97.

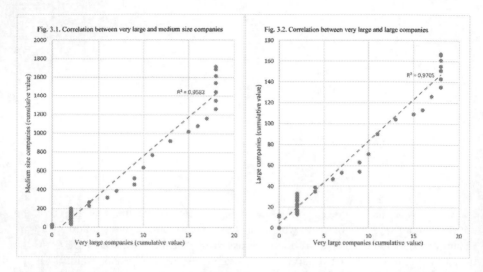

Fig. 3. Correlation between the cumulative value of very large and medium size companies (3.1) and correlation between the first and large companies (3.2)

Morocco is part of those Developing Economies and emerging markets that have made institutionalization of SEZs a competitive leverage instruments; a tool aiming at a more aggressive commercial strategy and at increasing FDI, in order to improve and diversify the pre-existing industrial fabric. The survey of the increase in FDIs in the 1999–2018 time interval finds support in academic literature: in that time range, Morocco increased FDI by 15.42%. In the same period, major infrastructure works have been built to expand and consolidate the port complexes and internal multimodal networks. This is reflected in the trend of gross fixed investment (purchases of plants, machinery, improvements in roads, railways, etc.). Between 1999–2018, the percentage change in gross capital formation was 26%, similar to what happened chronologically regarding FDI.

It should be pointed out that Morocco remains a predominantly importing country; between 1999–2017, importations increased by 62% (especially for petroleum products). However, in the same time frame there is a considerable increase in exports of 48%: 20% textiles; 14% machinery; 11% cars; 6.8% mixed mineral or chemical fertilizers; 4.1% phosphoric acid (2017 data).

4   Conclusions and Research Prospectives

This research provided evidence of the creation of an a industrial ring, both in secondary and tertiary sector. It could be postulated that to very large companies, absent until 1999 in the region, followed a localized growth of medium and large enterprises, connected to both related and support sectors. The increase in the number of activities was observed mainly in tertiary, in the city of Tangier. Hence, the increase in urbanization rate of resident population has been considerable, both nationally and regionally; also, the shift from rural to urban areas, from the primary sector to the industrial sector and services. In absolute terms, the increase in employment showed a greater proportion of industrial sector workers by 10.83% in the 1999–2013 period; on the other hand, a massive 40% in the number of service workers.

Therefore, a seemingly premature tertiarization of the economy can be observed; it is hypothesized that to accompany the surfacing of a stronger industrial fabric, there was an increase in activity in the service sector, which is characterized by a weaker structure in the long run. In the same years, there has been an increase in employment rates, but at the same time an increase of unemployment rates, and a drop in activity rates. The hypothesis is that, given the introduction of SEZs and a still evolving scenario, the regional population has grown rather evidently; much more than the real labour market, where the largest labour force is mainly absorbed by the service sector, would have allowed. In addition, is impossible not to notice that in the same years, at a regional level, there has been an increase in feminization of the labour force, which is to be considered a very positive outcome. At the same time, there is an increase in the proportion of private sector workers relative to the public sector. In the first, the variation was of 27.76%; in the second of −16.58%. This had an effect on employment relations distribution with a 53.44% increase in wage earners between 1999 and 2013.

In conclusion, this paper and the collected data, allowed an analysis of this evolving scenario since the establishment of SEZs in the chosen time frame. The existence of positive correlations between very large companies and industrial rings also emerged. Future studies will cover the comparative analysis between this reference context and other contexts on a global scale.

References

1. Huang, D., Neequaye, E.N., Banahene, J., Van, V.T., Fynn, S.: A comparative analysis of effective free trade zone policies in Ghana: a model from Shanghai free trade zone. Open J. Bus. Manag. 6(4), 900–922 (2018). https://doi.org/10.4236/ojbm.2018.64066
2. Ambroziak, A.A., Hartwell, C.: The impact of investments in special economic zones on regional development: the case of Poland. Reg. Stud. 52(10), 1322–1331 (2018). https://doi.org/10.1080/00343404.2017.1395005
3. Hausmann, R., Obach, J., Santos, M.A.: Special Economic Zones in Panama: Technology spillovers from a labor market perspective. CID Working Papers 326, Center for International Development at Harvard University (2016)
4. Farole, T.: Special Economic Zones in Africa: Comparing Performance and Learning From Global Experiences. World Bank Publications, Washington (2011)

5. Madani, D.: A Review of the Role and Impact of Export Processing Zones. World Bank Publications, Washington (1999)
6. Kusago, T., Tzannatos, Z.: Export Processing Zones: A Review in Need of Update. World Bank Publications, Washington (1998)
7. Kumar, D.: Geographical development of special economic zones (SEZs): a study of Gurgaon district, Haryana. Int. Res. J. Hum. Resour. Soc. Sci. 2(9), 1–11 (2015)
8. Bost, F.: Are economic free zones good for Development? West African Challenges. Technical report, 4, 4–20 (2011)
9. Jacobs, W.: What conditions supply chain strategies of ports? Case Dubai GeoJournal 68, 327–342 (2007). https://doi.org/10.1007/s10708-007-9092-x
10. Lavissière, A., Rodrigue, J.P.: Free ports: towards a network of trade gateways. J. Shipping Trade 2(1), 1–17 (2017). https://doi.org/10.1186/s41072-017-0026-6
11. Meera Bai, M., Udaya, V.K.: Significance of free economic zones: a study from an international perspective. Int. J. Trade Glob. Bus. Perspect. 5(4), 3111–3120 (2016)
12. Akinci, G., Crittle, J.: Special economic zone: performance, lessons learned, and implication for zone development. Foreign Investment Advisory Service (FIAS) occasional paper. Washington, DC: World Bank (2008)
13. ILO: Labour and Social Issues Relating to Export Processing Zones. Technical report, International Labor Organization (ILO), Ginevra (1998)
14. WTO: Exploring the links between subsidies, trade and the WTO. Technical report, World Trade Organization (WTO), Ginevra (2006)
15. UNCTAD: World Investment Report. Special Economic Zones. Technical report, United Nations Conference on Trade and Development (UNCTAD), Ginevra (2019)
16. WORLD BANK, database. https://www.worldbank.org/
17. IMF, database. https://www.imf.org/external/index.htm
18. HCP, database. http://bds.hcp.ma/sectors
19. HCP: Recensement General de la population et de l'habitat de 2004. Caracteristiques demografiques et socio-economiques, Region de Tanger-Tétouan. Technical report, Direction Régionale de Tanger-Tétouan (2006)
20. HCP: Monographie regionale de Tanger-Tétouan-Al Hoceima. Technical report, Direction Régionale de Tanger-Tétouan-Al Hoceima (2018)
21. HCP: Annuaire Statistique du Maroc, Rotaume du Maroc. Technical report (2018)
22. HCP: Activité, employ et chômage 2013. Resultats detailles. Technical report, Direction de la statistique (2013)
23. HCP: Activité, employ et chômage 1999. Resultats detailles. Technical report, Direction de la statistique (1999)
24. ORBIS, database. https://orbis.bvdinfo.com/
25. IMF: World Economic Outlook. April 2019. Technical report, International Monetary Found (2019)
26. TMSA: Rapport Annuel, 2017. Tanger Med. Technical report, Tanger Med Special Agency (2017)
27. UNCTAD, database. https://unctad.org/
28. Berlinguer, A. (ed.): Porti, Retroporti E Zone Economiche Speciali. Giappichelli Editore, Torino (2018)

Smart Marinas. The Case of Metropolitan City of Cagliari

Luigi Mundula[(✉)], Mara Ladu, Ginevra Balletto,
and Alessandra Milesi

DICAAR – Department of Civil and Environmental Engineering
and Architecture, University of Cagliari, Via Marengo 2, Cagliari, Italy
{luigimundula, balletto}@unica.it,
maraladu@hotmail.it, alessandramilesi.unica@gmail.com

Abstract. Nautical tourism market and especially the sector of yachting and marinas is very dynamic. It contributes decisively to the development of local economies of Mediterranean countries and Northern Europe cities. Particularly, marinas (specially designed harbors with moorings for pleasure yachts and small boats) development takes place in coastal areas, which are generally fragile and threatened environments. On one hand marinas are highly desirable for development of recreation and tourism infrastructure, but from the other they are threatened by climate change impacts due to sea level rise. Moreover, marinas are the most complex and highest quality types of port for nautical tourism. They facilitate many nautical tourism activities by providing safe points to access to the water and providing secure locations to store boats. Many marinas also provide additional nautical and ancillary leisure activities and can be visitor attractions in their own right. They also create demand for boating and other tourism products and services and facilitate linkages between nautical and coastal tourism. They have the potential to act as economic hubs for regional development and can catalyze the development of coastal tourism in specific locations. In this perspective, the role of marinas could be reconsidered, transforming them in smart gateway able to push in sustainable way local and regional economy moving the touristic flows from the coastal to the internal areas.

Keywords: Marinas · Nautical tourism · Regional economy · New technologies

1 Introduction

Recent statistical information indicates that tourism is one of the largest and fastest growing industries in the world, and plays an important part in the economic development strategies of many regions. However, the tourism industry can have negative impacts on the environment, such as the loss of natural landscapes, congestion, change or loss of local identity, loss of community employment, and increase of economic

---

This paper is the result of the joint work of the authors. For Italian evaluation purposes Luigi Mundula takes responsibility for sections 1, 2.1 and 3, Mara Ladu for sections 4, Ginevra Balletto for section 2, Luigi Mundula and Alessandra Milesi for section 5.

© Springer Nature Switzerland AG 2020
O. Gervasi et al. (Eds.): ICCSA 2020, LNCS 12255, pp. 51–66, 2020.
https://doi.org/10.1007/978-3-030-58820-5_5

inequalities. These environmental problems can be exacerbated if planning and management are not sustainable. Sustainable tourism development is tourism that fully considers *"current and future economic, social and environmental impacts, addressing the needs of visitors, the industry, the environment and host communities; and maintaining cultural integrity, essential ecological processes, biological diversity and life support systems"* (UNEP and UNWTO 2005).

Marina development takes place in coastal areas, which are generally fragile and threatened environments. On one hand marinas are highly desirable for development of recreation and tourism infrastructure, but from the other they are threatened by climate change impacts due to sea level rise. Moreover, marinas are the most complex and highest quality types of port for nautical tourism. They facilitate many nautical tourism activities by providing safe points to access to the water and providing secure locations to store boats. Many marinas also provide additional nautical and ancillary leisure activities and can be visitor attractions in their own right. They also create demand for boating and other tourism products and services and facilitate linkages between nautical and coastal tourism (Balletto and Casula 2011).

2 Nautical Tourism

Since the addition of tourism to the European Union's competences in 2009 with the Lisbon Treaty, the European Commission has been working to develop a tourism policy, which enhances Europe's broad and competitive tourism industry.

On 20 February 2014, the European Commission adopted the strategy on coastal and marine tourism, where it also recognized the issues signaled by European Boating Industry.

European Boating Industry has been submitting its policy contributions with regards to nautical tourism, given the importance of boating and water based leisure activities (such as water sports) to the wider tourism economy.

Europe boasts close to 70,000 km coastline and 27,000 km of navigable inland waterways. It is a leading destination for boating and water sports enthusiasts from across the world. There are over 4,500 marinas in Europe, which offer 1.75 million berths for a total boat park of 6.3 million vessels. Today, 70% of boat charter takes place in Europe, with a significant part being held in the Mediterranean Sea. These activities represent an important income for coastal and insular economies with boating, water sports and marinas accounting for 180,000 jobs and generating approximately 17 billion euros in revenue per year across Europe.

In its 2012 Communication on Blue Growth the Commission identified coastal and maritime tourism as one of the five sources of new jobs and growth in the Blue Economy[1]. The 2014 Commission Communication "A European strategy for more Growth and jobs in Coastal and Maritime Tourism" (the CMT strategy)[2] proposed

---

[1] Comprising the economic activity of the marine and maritime sectors.

[2] Specifically, related to CMT Strategy actions 5, 6, 9, 10, 11, 12 and 13.

actions to be undertaken at European level, in cooperation with national, regional and local stakeholders, to tackle the needs and challenges of the sector.

Coastal and maritime tourism is a significant sub-sector of both the wider tourism sector and the Blue Economy. It is estimated to employ approximately 3.2 m people and generate €183bn of gross value added (GVA) (Ecorys 2013).

As highlight by Favro (2008), *"nautical tourism is a subsystem in the economic branch of the maritime economy and tourism within overall national economy, with all the characteristics of system and its partial components which are defined as entities, facilities and elements of nautical tourism"*, generating annual revenues of between €20 and €28 billion per year and employing between 200,000 and 234,000 people[3].

The services sector, which includes equipment repair, boat charter, marinas and other services, accounts for around half of this value[4].

There are no official definitions of nautical tourism published by the European Commission or international organizations such as the UN World Tourism Organization (UNWTO). However, the term is not entirely novel. Working definitions have been used in other research. For example: Luković and Gržetić (2007) define nautical tourism as: *"The entirety of multifunctional activities and relations caused by the stay of tourists-boaters in nautical tourism ports or out of them, and by the use of vessels and other objects related to nautical tourism aimed at recreation, sports and entertainment and other needs"*.

There is some debate about whether the adoption of the term 'nautical' should mean that nautical tourism refers only to the activities of 'navigation' (e.g. travelling by boat). However, it is more commonly applied to boating-related activities that occur in the sea; where a boat is any waterborne craft, from a cruise liner to a kayak. It commonly excludes beach-based activities and may include or exclude activities such as surfing. For example, Luković (2012) identified a hierarchical set of nautical tourism activities:

- Main activities: (i) harbors (berths, moorings, marinas) (ii) charters (iii) cruising.
- Secondary activities: diving, surfing, rafting, diving-bells, rowing, fishing, etc.
- Supporting: activity providers and related services; manufacturing industries.

Nautical tourism and maritime tourism (as defined by Ecorys 2013) are broadly similar concepts. For the purpose of this study, nautical tourism is taken to be a subset of maritime tourism as it does not cover cruise ship activities. Nautical tourism is here defined as comprising the following activities in coastal and offshore marine waters:

- Harbor and marina-based/facilitated activities;
- Boating activities (including charter and non-charter) i.e. yachting, dinghy sailing, boat based angling and wildlife watching, other watercraft (e.g. kayaking).

---

[3] There is no comprehensive dataset for nautical tourism activity. The estimated range is from ICF calculations using ICOMIA 2014 data; and Communication from the Commission to the European Parliament calculations using 2011 ICOMIA data (published in COM(2014) 254 final/2 of 13.5.2014).

[4] ICF estimate based on ICOMIA data for 2014.

- Marinas and boating development (including its influence on regional development) and combined nautical and coastal tourism products (henceforth, 'combined products')

Nautical tourism is a phenomenon that in the last three decades has recorded one of the highest development rates known in the European economies. Economic forecasters for tourism development agree that nautical tourism is in its early stages of development and that increasing results are to be expected. From a scientific perspective, nautical tourism development is still not sufficiently represented in the science of tourism even if it contributes to the general development of the economy of any country or any area by fostering growth and development through its regular activities, as well as through horizontally and vertically related activities, such as excursion tourism, diving, photo safaris, servicing, handicrafts and shipbuilding. All these activities contribute to the creation of jobs for residents, in particular, where insular economies are concerned (Jugović et al. 2011).

As far as social aspect of nautical tourism is concerned, its contribution is seen in the transfer of information, knowledge, culture and lifestyle. In this way, nautical tourism has a significant contribution as its foreign boats and yachts and their equipment attract local population, thus promoting the development of ideas, creativity and free thinking. From the viewpoint of the receptive country, nautical tourism represents an important source of foreign exchange yield which is considered a specific form of export (the so-called invisible export). All expenditures of foreign tourism in any country represent a contribution to the balance of payment of the host country.

In this framework, nautical tourism should be considered as a complex system and examined in accordance with the logic of general systems theory (Kovačić 2004) and the principles for the management of integrated complex systems (Favro 2008).

To achieve efficient and maximum results must be guaranteed: manageability of the system; interaction between all the components within the system and between the system and the external components (Favro 2002) - as local services, climate conditions, etc.-; and their joint orientation towards common values and goals.

The above presented characteristics of the system of nautical tourism suggest that nautical tourism is connected with regional economy taking an important place and role.

2.1   The Role of the Marinas in the Nautical Tourism

As highlighted in the previous paragraph, nautical tourism offers enormous development opportunities. In particular, the recreational boating segment is continuously growing. For example looking at the number of megayachts (over 30 m in length) in navigation, the analysis of the data for the last ten years highlights the exponential increase in the world fleet. From 3,906 boats in 2009 it increased to 5,646 in 2019 and the forecast is 5,789 yachts sailing in 2022.

Going into detail, in 2009 there were 2,626 from 30 to 40 m, 1,055 from 40 to 60 m, 183 from 60 to 90 m and 42 over 90 m. In 2019 there are 3,553 by 30–40 m, 1,649 by 40–60 m, 355 by 60–90 m and 89 by more than 90. A growth trend in size that will also be confirmed in 2022, when, according to the forecasts of Redmayne, it will reach 387 boats between 60 and 90 m and even 97 that will exceed 90 m.

Recreational boating is also a sector that has a strong impact on the economy of the area as well as on employment: the multipliers of production and employment are particularly significant and the absolute highest among those of the various sectors of maritime activity.

The Mediterranean is an area extremely affected by recreational boating: in the winter the basin hosts 56% of the yachts, while during the summer the share rises to 70%. Looking at Italy, an ANCE study shows that, considering also the expense of boaters, 1 employed in the sector generates another 6.4 employed; 1 euro spent, activates 4 in the economy. The estimate is that in Italy recreational boating makes a contribution to GDP of 3.35 billion euros: the annual expenditure of boaters is estimated at 5 billion euros, committing overall related activities to more than 120 thousand workers, of whom 27,300 as direct employees.

The main ports for the development of recreational boating are the marinas which, depending on their equipment, determine the development of the sector.

Table 1 illustrates the data on the infrastructural endowments of the Italian regions where recreational boating has a more significant weight. Beyond the figure relating to the numerical consistency of these structures, two indices are presented: the first concerns the ratio between the number of berths and the Km of coastline (density) while the second measures the ratio between the registered recreational boats and the number of berths (crowding) in order to determine the level of infrastructure of the regions in relation to the respective nautical park.

The measurement of these indices is particularly important, since the quantitative (as well as the qualitative) level of recreational infrastructures clearly influences the development of the sector: the scarce or abundant availability of berths can in fact represent an obstacle or an incentive to spread the yachting.

The data in Table 1 show how the docking points for recreational boating are more numerous in Southern Italy, where however the infrastructural facilities for recreational boating highlight significant differences compared to the north of the country. In particular, as of 30/09/2018, the coasts of the Northern Regions offer 73.0 berths per kilometer of coastline to the yachting, compared to the corresponding averages of 28.1 and 13.0 berths calculated respectively for the coasts of the Central Italy and Southern Italy.

The maximum, in the North, is observed in correspondence of Friuli Venezia Giulia (180.8). In the South, however, the minimum of this relationship is found in "Calabria and Basilicata Tirrenica". Looking at the crowding index (number of registered units per 100 berths), there are high values in Lazio, Veneto and Campania, with a maximum of 122.0 for the Lazio coast. Comparing the number of berths with the number of boats registered, it is to note that, with the exception of Lazio, the Italian coastal regions have a number of berths higher than that of the boats registered at the Peripheral Maritime Offices and how, in particular, Puglia, Calabria, Sicily and Sardinia, whose coasts absorb about two thirds of the overall length of the Italian coasts, offer a significantly higher number of docking points than the pleasure craft actually present in the Region; these data also highlight an infrastructural structure, especially in the South, able to meet the high demand for berths for pleasure craft coming, in the summer months, from abroad or from other regions.

Table 1. Statistics on Italian marinas at regional level

Region	n. berths	Density	Crowding	Registered boats
Piemonte e Valle d'Aosta	–	–	–	3756
Lombardia	–	–	–	6811
Trentino Alto Adige	–	–	–	63
Veneto	6887	49,2	93,3	6427
Friuli Venezia Giulia	17001	180,8	23	3918
Liguria	25157	64,7	72,7	18277
Emilia Romagna	5360	43,9	86	4610
Northern Italy	**54405**	**73**	**80,6**	**43862**
Toscana	17550	31,3	57,6	10104
Umbria	–	–	–	237
Marche	5302	28,2	58	3077
Lazio	8356	23	122	10195
Central Italy	**31208**	**28,1**	**75,7**	**23613**
Abruzzo	2751	19,9	31,2	858
Molise	587	16,3	11,4	67
Campania	16190	31,0	93,5	15132
Puglia e Basilicata ionica	13750	13,3	22,3	3066
Calabria e Basilicata tirrenica	5490	6,9	20,4	1118
Sardegna	19948	10,8	21,3	4244
Sicilia	17344	11,8	27,6	4795
Southern Italy	**76060**	**13,0**	**38,5**	**29280**
Italy	**161673**	**21,0**	**59,8**	**96755**

Source: Ministero delle Infrastrutture e dei trasporti "Il Diporto Nautico in Italia 2018"

Analyzing the function of the tourist ports in a wider way, it is necessary to consider the peculiar geo-morphological character of the coasts as a border element and natural passage area - that is, enter or exit - between the marine and terrestrial ecosystem. From the point of view of socio-economic development, the coasts have been anthropized through the port infrastructures that embody the role of transit places and continuous exchanges of populations, people and different know-how, triggering processes of continuous transformation of natural elements and of the built environment but above all of local and supra-local development. The success of seaside towns, which have been able to build empires with the strength of their military and commercial fleets, is the strongest proof of this.

The strong identity of these places of contact between the urban fabric and the water body derives, on the one hand, from the modification of the reference ecosystem, one enters an ecosystem and exits the other, and on the other from being intermodal hub, it passes from the boat (of whatever type it is) to other forms of mobility.

As when a traveler arrives in a city he does not know, he needs to find all the information that can allow him to move easily within it, enjoy its beauty and fuel its economy; so those who arrive in a port should be able to find not only a safe mooring but also all the information, infrastructures and services to visit the territory connected to it.

This function of ports, in particular tourist ones, is not yet fully understood today, with the consequence that these often remain relegated to their role as "shelter places" and "service stations" of boats rather than access doors (gateway) to the territory.

The major problem is the poor communication between the local context (city, village or what else) and the marina. The two entities have to coexist in a restricted area and, from the outset, would appear to have opposing interest and objectives.

- The marina as a business is focused on the economy, productivity, competitiveness, as well as on the market and on business development.
- The city/town/Municipality, together with residents, is more focused on what impact the marina will have on the quality of life, as well as on visual and ecological concerns.

This divergence contributes to a vision of conflict over the physical and functional compatibility of the two opposing sides. Marinas and cities often have conflicting strategies about getting control over the area. The marina industry, looking to build new premises for their activities, can often be to the detriment of the city or local waters. Urban areas generally oppose this expansion due to environmental reasons and insist on the rational use of existing capacity (Robinson 2009). Urban areas are interested in regaining access to the coast by taking abandoned or underutilized areas which can be used for building houses, cultural activities, recreation, swimming and more.

To overcome difficulties arising from the lack of space or from a desire to use space in a different way, it is therefore necessary to implement a concept that will incorporate the marina into the city, making it an integral part of the city and part of a system that works in synergy.

City harbors always contribute to the development of a city and of a territory. This development is in accordance with the pathway determined by the local and broader community. A particular case is that of communal ports because the commercial character of the boatbuilding increasingly being replaced by tourism.

Coastal cities are developing new activities to attract more trade and visitors. These new developments often replace old established businesses, such as boatbuilding and commercial wharfs, that are relocated to a less attractive area. These changes directly give rise to new questions, such as the value of the coastal zone (Bizzarri and La Foresta 2011). This means that the old city ports, harbors and marinas need to find a balance with the expansive demands of nautical tourism that is looking for integrated offer systems. In this view, the established forms of management should be replaced by a way of thinking which should ensure interaction with all the components of the territorial system.

Aiming to ensure sustainable development and achieve optimal regional socio-economic development, the existing classification and categorization of ports of nautical tourism needs to be adapted to established goals and planned results.

Marina should become a meeting point for exchange of experiences, communication with other guests, but also with employees (currently not optimal). Education, i.e. workshops and seminars should provide training of personnel. Nautical tourism should organized into a community. The interest group of people providing professional services in marinas still cannot meet all the needs of leisure mariners. An example of what needs to be provided for leisure mariners is an efficient and prompt mail delivery, because marina is just their temporary address. Marina should have a social and service orientation, not only serve as a physical storage place for vessels.

3   Marinas as Territorial Gateway: A Proposal for an Evaluation Methodology

To calculate the propensity of a marina to be a territorial gateway, two aspects were combined: its introversion, intended as the set of its intrinsic characteristics, and its extroversion, intended as its projection towards the outside.

To calculate introversion, the following indices were considered: physical accessibility and internal services. To calculate the extroversion, the following were taken into consideration: the distance from complementary services outside the marina, virtual accessibility and the quality of virtual accessibility.

Each of the above indices, in turn, is composed of a series of indicators as shown in Table 2.

Table 2. Indicators used to define the "Introvert" and "Extrovert" indices

Introvert (Vi)		Extrovert (Ve)		
Physical Accessibility (PHA)	Internal services (IS)	Distance from complementary services (CS)	Virtual accessibility (VA)	Quality of the virtual accessibility (QVA)
n. of berth (B); Draft (D); Max length (MaxL)	Water; Electricity; WiFi; Fuel; Bath and shower; Laundry; Shipyard; Travel lift; Crane; Boat slide; Swing Lift; Weather service; Parking; Bar/Restaurant/Pizzeria; Sailing school; Diving; Playground; Car rent; Scooter rent; Inflatable boat rent; Bike rent; Surveillance; Mooring assistance; On-board technical and electronic assistance (GPS, depth sounders, air conditioners, etc.).	Supermarket (S); Pharmacy (P); Post office (PO); Bus (B)	Bilingual (Italian - English) (BL); More than 2 languages (ML); Website (WS); Touristic information (TI); Accessibility from different devices (DA); Link to municipality website (LWS)	Touristic information (QTI); User friendly (UF); Quality of accessibility from different devices (QDA); Presence on specialized portal (PSP)

The calculation of the indices was made according to the following criteria.

As regards physical accessibility (PhA), a scale from 0 to 1 has been defined according to the values assumed by the various indicators, as shown in the following Table 3.

Table 3. Score values for the indices of physical accessibility

Berth	Draft	Vessels max length
0–50 = 0,1	0–1 mt = 0,1	0–10 mt = 0,1
51–100 = 0,2	1, 1–2 mt = 0,2	10, 1–20 mt = 0,2
101–150 = 0,3	2, 1–3 mt = 0,3	20, 1–30 mt = 0,3
151–200 = 0,4	3, 1–4 mt = 0,4	30, 1–40 mt = 0,4
210–250 = 0,5	4, 1–5 mt = 0,5	40, 1–50 mt = 0,5
251–300 = 0,6	5, 1–6 mt = 0,6	50, 1–60 mt = 0,6
301–350 = 0,7	6, 1–7 mt = 0,7	60, 1–70 mt = 0,7
351–400 = 0,8	7, 1–8 mt = 0,8	70, 1–80 mt = 0,8
401–450 = 0,9	8, 1–9 mt = 0,9	80, 1–90 mt = 0,9
451–500 = 1	9, 1–10 mt = 1	90, 1–100 mt = 1

The physical accessibility value (PHA) is therefore defined as the average of the values reported in each variable.

$$PhAcc = \frac{B + D + MaxL}{3}$$

The value of internal services (IS) is instead calculated as a percentage, that is, as the number of existing services compared to the total of services identified as relevant.

$$IS = \frac{n.of\ existing\ services}{n.of\ prelevant\ services}$$

As for Distance from complementary services (CS) index, a scale from 0 to 1 has been defined according to the distance of services from the tourist port as shown in the following Table 4.

The value of the Distance from complementary services is therefore defined as the average of the values reported in each variable.

$$LS = \frac{S + P + PO + B}{4}$$

The value of the intangible accessibility (VA) is instead calculated as a percentage, that is, as the number of characteristics present on the websites compared to the total of the characteristics identified as relevant.

Table 4. Score values for the distance from complementary services (CS)

Distance from Complementary services
0–500 mt = 1
501–1000 mt = 0, 9
1001–1500 mt = 0, 8
1501–2000 mt = 0, 7
2001–2500 mt = 0, 6
2501–3000 mt = 0, 5
3001–3500 mt = 0, 4
3501–4000mt = 0, 3
4001–4500mt = 0, 2
4501–5000 mt = 0, 1

$$VA = \frac{n.of\ existing\ characters}{relevant\ characters}$$

As regards the quality of intangible accessibility (QVA), the scores on a scale from 0 to 1 are attributed based on a subjective judgment, except for the presence on the sector portals which is instead calculated as a percentage value (number of portals in which the port appears compared to the total number of reference portals).

The value of the quality of the intangible accessibility is therefore defined as the average of the values reported in each variable.

$$QVA = \frac{QTI + UF + QDA + PSP}{4}$$

The calculation of the introversion (Vi) and extroversion (Ve) values is finally carried out by calculating the average of the values of the various indicators that compose them.

$$Vi = \frac{PHA + S}{2}$$

$$Ve = \frac{BLS + VA + QVA}{3}$$

Finally, the result obtained is normalized through the following formula:

$$x_i norm = \frac{x_i - min}{max - min}$$

The last step is the clustering of marinas according to the indices values (Table 5).

Table 5. Clusters of the marinas

	Extrovert	Introvert	Description
Old way	0–0, 5	0–0, 5	Marinas that have characteristics such as to serve small boats, which have few services and which have a low if not any projection towards the outside in a virtual or physical sense
Potential	0–0, 5	0, 51–1	Marinas that have characteristics such as to serve even large boats, with a good level of services but which have not yet developed an outward projection in a virtual or physical sense
Supporter	0, 51–1	0–0, 5	Marinas that have characteristics such as to serve small boats, which have few services but which have understood that their success passes from a good projection towards the outside both in a virtual and physical sense. Although they cannot, in all likelihood, expand their structural endowments, they constitute an excellent complement to the "gateway" tourist ports
Gateway	0, 5–1	0, 5–1	Tourist ports that have characteristics such as to serve even large boats, with a good level of services and that have developed an outward projection both in a virtual and physical sense

4 The Marinas of the Metropolitan City of Cagliari

With its almost 2000 km of coastline, fine beaches and cliffs, the Sardinia Region remains one of the most beautiful scenarios in the world for those who want to do nautical tourism. Also strong in the presence of several smaller islands, parks, marine reserves and protected areas, this land has no equal in the tourist offer of the Mediterranean.

As shown in Table 1, Sardinia today boasts 31 marinas with 19948 berths offering on the one hand a density significantly lower than the national average with 10.8 berths/km of coastline (Italy figures out for 21), and a number of berths significantly higher than the number of recreational boats registered (that is a crowding index of 21.3, versus an Italian average of 59.8).The latter data reveals the presence of an infrastructure intended to meet the high demand for berths for tourist boats coming in the summer months from abroad or from other regions. A further aspect to highlight concerns the 334 berths over 24 m offered by Sardinia, 10% of Italy. This segment is very important because the expenditure of these units, in Italian waters, was valued at € 209 million (estimate based on a sample of 1,200 units in transit, for an average stay of 3.8 days and with an expense daily average of € 8,900).

In this framework, the case study of the Metropolitan City of Cagliari (CMC) is particularly interesting. In Italy the metropolitan cities are a recent institution, established by the Law 56/2014 (Delrio Law), that represent a new governance level between regions and municipalities replacing, de facto, the Province level. By the way not all the

Province has been replaced by metropolitan cities but only 14[5], and 13 of them (with the exception of Cagliari) are constituted by the same municipalities of the old Province. In the area of the metropolitan city of Cagliari there are eight marinas (Fig. 1).

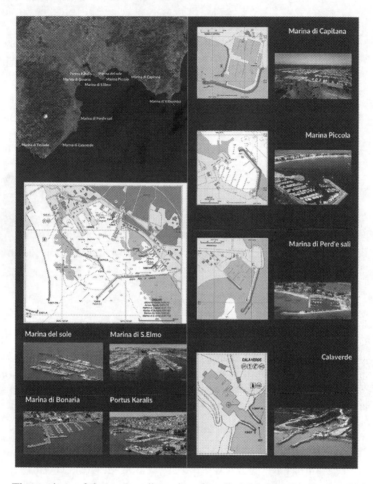

Fig. 1. The marinas of the metropolitan city of cagliari (*elaboration by Luigi Mundula*)

It's to note that three of them (Marina del Sole, Marina di Bonaria, Marina di Sant' Elmo), are very close (just few meter of distance), four of them (Marina del Sole, Marina di Bonaria, Marina di Sant'Elmo and Portus Karalis) are inside the same port (Cagliari port) and five of them (Portus Karalis, Marina del Sole, Marina di Sant'Elmo, Marina di Bonaria, Marina Piccola) are in the same municipality (Cagliari). Nevertheless, these marinas present different characteristics in terms of equipment and services.

---

[5] The Italian Metropolitan Cities are: Bari, Bologna, Catania, Cagliari, Firenze, Genova, Messina, Milano, Napoli, Palermo, Reggio di Calabria, Roma, Torino, Venezia.

Applying the methodology depicted in the previous paragraph to the 8 marinas of the CMC, the final results (Fig. 2) show a polarized situation with three marinas entering in the "gateway" group and five in the "old way" group.

Among the three marinas entering in the "gateway" group (Portus Karalis, Marina di Sant'Elmo and Marina di Capitana), Portus Karalis reach the highest normalized value of the introversion and extroversion indices (Vi, e = 1), followed by Marina di Capitana (Vi = 0.83; Ve = 0.86) and Marina di Sant'Elmo (Vi = 0.55; Ve = 0.95).

The Portus Kalaris thus establishes itself as the most important gateway of the metropolitan area. In fact, although it guarantees a much lower number of berths than those of Marina di Sant'Elmo and Marina di Capitana, Portus Karalis is the only one with characteristics that can accommodate boats of 90 m in length, guaranteeing them a significant offer of services. Moreover, the direct proximity of the infrastructure to the historic urban core of the city of Cagliari and to its main cultural, institutional, administrative, managerial and logistic centers, means that it is possible to reach important external services from this port, located within a buffer less than km. This represents an element of uniqueness compared to all the other ports analyzed. Finally, Portus Karalis presents a good degree of virtual accessibility and quality of the latter. Its presence is confirmed in the main sector portals.

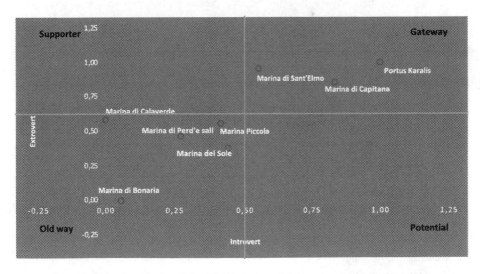

Fig. 2. Cluster analysis of the CMC marinas (*elaboration by Luigi Mundula*)

Among the five Marinas entering the "old way" group (Marina di Bonaria; Marina del Sole; Marina di Perd'e sali; Marina di Calaverde; Marina Piccola) Marina di Bonaria is the one with the lowest values (Vi = 0, 6; Ve = 0). To influence over-whelmingly this result is the absence of internal services (the port offers only water, electricity and fuel), but also the distance greater than 1 km from the main external services and the absence of virtual accessibility. The port is present only on two portals.

Higher values are reached by Marina del Sole (Vi = 0.44; Ve = 38) and Marina di Perd'e sali (Vi = 0.27; Ve = 0.46).

It's to note that two of the "old way" group (Marina di Calaverde and Marina Piccola) are very close to the threshold with the "supporter" group. In fact, the analysis shows that Marina di Calaverde (Vi = 0.00; Ve = 0.58) has a good physical accessibility and a good offer of internal services, although some important external services such as the pharmacy and the post offices are distant about 10 km from the infrastructure. In general, the Port has a good virtual accessibility as well as a good quality of the same. On the other hand, Marina Piccola (Vi = 0.41; Ve = 0.56) guarantees a greater offer of internal services and is about 1 km away from the main external services. It has good virtual accessibility and good quality of the same. Furthermore, it is present in most sector portals.

5 Results and Final Remarks

The results produced by the application of the assessment methodology to the 8 marinas in the Metropolitan City of Cagliari (CMC) form the basis for planning future development policies for smart and sustainable marines, based on innovation and investment in marina infrastructure and boating products, but also on the integration of marinas into regional development planning. It means encourage planning, innovation and investment that supports the sector adjust to, and exploit, changes in consumer demand and broader its role as a hub and catalyst for economic activity. This is expected to benefit the competitiveness and the performance of coastal regions more broadly.

The analysis carried out in the context of this research has highlighted the uneven nature (albeit then polarized into two groups), especially with regard to the quantity and quality of services offered by the CMC tourist ports. Unfortunately, this characteristic unites the whole of Sardinia and more generally the regions that have a potential for development in nautical tourism.

The output, in terms of policy, generated by the results produced, should not necessarily lead to programming a set of measures aimed at transforming each port into a gateway. In a metropolitan context such as the one in question, it could be useful to plan the system of tourist ports by thinking in terms of clusters and networks.

Establish a virtual platform for combined coastal and nautical tourism products to support networking, engagement and information exchange, as well as the provision of a micro-funding facility for SMEs developing combined products can be considered future goals.

The virtual platform will help to address problems created by the fragmented nature of the sector, providing a forum for information sharing, collaboration and partnering. At the same time, support the diversification of tourism products allow to meet a growing area of consumer demand, improving the competitive position of the sector.

Within a network (no longer a node) approach, groups of ports similar in location/context, and function, such as Marina di Bonaria, Marina del sole and Marina di S. Elmo, could constitute a single system based on integrated programming and management, also with reference to the offer of internal and external services. On the other hand, this approach would facilitate the transition of some of the existing infrastructures to the "supporter" level of the main gateways.

As regards the importance of strengthening the link between the tourist ports and the urban and territorial context of reference, one of the main challenges concerns the development of connection and logistics hubs and the promotion of a series of measures to strengthen the public transport service. And alternative and sustainable mobility. In this sense, a virtuous example is provided by the tourist ports of Villasimius and Teulada (which are located just outside the border of the metropolitan city, which since summer 2019 offer some smart services for those arriving by boat. The keywords are three: welcome, technology/innovation and environment/green. The novelties include a smartphone to allow tourists to move more easily and a greater offer of electric vehicles on the quay to improve connections with the coast and the town.

The possibility of using rent electric vehicles allows to think about a welcome that goes beyond the summer. Helping the tourist to get to the heart of the area is a benefit for everyone. The assets to focus on are environmental sustainability and knowledge of the territory, which need an operational tool such as the mobile phone, already equipped with all the information to facilitate the approach with the territory: historical places, places to visit, food and wine excellences, etc.

In this context, the need to establish an association between the managers of the tourist port facilities, which has taken on the consortium form and the name of Sardinia Ports Network, has matured. Established in 2001, among four public entities, today the Sardinia ports network consortium, associates 19 of the main port facilities along the coast of Sardinia and pursues the objective of associating all the tourist ports by raising the standard of services, limiting internal competition, establishing common management platforms and trying to conquer new slices of the yachting market.

In addition, the community project "Odyssea" was presented, which aims to transform marinas from simple parking lots of boats to places of access to the territory. Those who arrive on the island, for example, can immediately immerse themselves in the local culture by tasting the Gallurese soup or the Campidanese malloreddus and discovering the true, sometimes hidden, specificities of the place.

The transformation of the marina into a Marina resort is a cultural leap as well as a technical and technological one. The increase in the number of charters, the presence of foreign boats and crews, the demand for new services as well as climate change are new realities that need to be promptly answered.

An opportunity to be taken in this direction will be the CMC Strategic Plan, currently being defined, which represents an extraordinary opportunity to give a new impulse to the development of smart and sustainable marinas, intended as the main access gates to the metropolitan and island territory.

References

Balletto, G., Casula, S.: La marina turistica di Porto Corallo: da antico scalo commerciale a porto turistico integrato. Portus Plus 1 (2011). http://retedigital.com/wp-content/themes/rete/pdfs/portus_plus/1_2011/Temáticas/La_ciudad_portuaria_contemporánea/02_GinevraBalletto_SalvatoreCasula.pdf. Accessed 05 June 2020

Bizzarri, C., La Foresta, D.: Yachting and Pleasure Crafts in Relation to Local Development and Expansion: Marina di Stabia Case Study, 2nd International Conference on Physical Coastal Processes, Management and Engineering, Coastal Processes. Transactions on Ecology and the Environment 149, 53-61 (2011)

Ecorys Study in support of policy measures for maritime and coastal tourism at EU level: Final Report (2013). https://ec.europa.eu/maritimeaffairs/sites/maritimeaffairs/files/docs/body/study-maritime-and-coastal-tourism_en.pdf. Accessed 03 June 2020

European Commission. Communication from the commission to the European parliament, the council, the European economic and social committee and the committee of the regions Blue growth. Opportunities for marine and maritime sustainable growth (2012)

Favro, S.: Joining of Croatia in the Development of the European Nautical Tourism. First European Yacht Tourism Congress, Rogoznica (2002)

Favro, S., Kovačić, M., Gržetić, Z.: Nautical tourism the basis of the systematic development. Pomorstvo 22(1), 31–51 (2008)

Jugović, A., Kovačić, M., Hadžić, A.: Sustainable development model for nautical tourism ports. Tourism Hospitality Manag. 17(2), 175–186 (2011)

Kovačić, M.: Model organizacije sjevernojadranskih luka nautičkog turizma u funkciji održivog razvoja, magistarski rad, Rijeka (2004)

Luković, T., Gržetić, Z.: Nautičko turističko tržište u teoriji i praksi Hrvatske i europskog dijela Mediterana. Hrvatski hidrografski institut (HHI) Split (2007)

Luković, T.: Nautical Tourism and its Function in the Economic Development of Europe, Visions for Global Tourism Industry - Creating and Sustaining Competitive Strategies, Murat Kasimoglu, InTech (2012). http://www.intechopen.com/books/visions-for-global-tourismindustry-creating-and-sustaining-competitive-strategies/nautical-tourism-in-the-function-of-the-economicdevelopment-of-europe. Accessed 10 June 2020

Ministero delle Infrastrutture e dei trasporti: Il Diporto Nautico in Italia (2018). http://www.mit.gov.it/sites/default/files/media/pubblicazioni/2019–09/Diporto%20Nautico%202018_112%2Bcop.pdf. Accessed 10 June 2020

Robinson, K.: Marinas: The Tourism Aspect of Leisure Boating (2009). http://www.insights.org.uk/articleitem.aspx?title=Marinas:%20The%20Tourism%20Aspect%20of%20Leisure%20Boating. Accessed 01 June 2020

UNEP and UNWTO. Making Tourism More Sustainable - A Guide for Policy Makers. (2005). http://wedocs.unep.org/bitstream/handle/20.500.11822/8741/-Making%20Tourism%20More%20Sustainable_%20A%20Guide%20for%20Policy%20Makers-2005445.pdf?sequence=3&isAllowed=y. Accessed 10 June 2020

Port-City Shared Areas to Improve Freight Transport Sustainability

Nadia Giuffrida[1](✉) , Matteo Ignaccolo[1] , Giuseppe Inturri[2] ,
and Vincenza Torrisi[1](✉)

[1] Department of Civil Engineering and Architecture, University of Catania,
Via S. Sofia 64, 95123 Catania, Italy
{nadia.giuffrida, vtorrisi}@dica.unict.it
[2] Department of Electric, Electronic and Computer Engineering, University
of Catania, Via S. Sofia 64, 95123 Catania, Italy

Abstract. The purpose of this work is to propose a methodological framework to evaluate the reuse of areas located close to the port as "retro-port", in order to reduce the externalities caused by Ro-Ro freight terminal operation and the burden of freight deliveries in urban areas. In this regard, an analysis of the main variables involved in this process is presented, with reference to terminal traffic, terminal capacity, accessibility to the port and freight handling infrastructures. The results of this research constitute the base to support and improve urban logistics activities, rethinking the use of elements and areas that characterize the port and its surroundings. These findings pave the way for further research related to the design and dimensioning of retro-port and the realistic implementation of an urban consolidation centre.

Keywords: Roll-on Roll-off · Urban consolidation centre · Maritime freight transport

1 Introduction

In recent years, maritime transport assumed a relevant role in city planning, moreover in the case of port-cities which are exposed to several externalities due to both operations in the harbour and increase in road transport caused by handling operations in the hinterland [1]. The importance of maritime traffic made that in the past the major industrial areas were installed near the ports, in order to facilitate the transport of raw materials and finished products.

In port-cities, nowadays, such spaces lost their original functions, acquiring a new great potential of transformation due to their closeness to the city and the port and becoming a unique opportunity to redevelop highly degraded or marginal areas: the redesign of these areas with a view to reconciling both the needs of the city and the port represents the opportunity to improve the sustainability of their relationship, making their coexistence possible [2, 3]. This push of sustainable regeneration cannot ignore the logistic needs imposed by the commercial activities of the port, which on the one hand require effective connections with the logistics centres and on the other aim to reduce the terminal operations times to guarantee a rapid delivery of goods in the urban territory.

© Springer Nature Switzerland AG 2020
O. Gervasi et al. (Eds.): ICCSA 2020, LNCS 12255, pp. 67–82, 2020.
https://doi.org/10.1007/978-3-030-58820-5_6

In this context this work frames the possibility of a reuse of large abandoned areas located near the port (with the creation of a so-called *retro-port*) as new shared logistics spaces that allow a reduction of the externalities connected to the maritime transport of goods. The aim of the paper is to provide with a realistic proposal for the regeneration of abandoned areas: a framework for the planning of a retro-port with urban logistic functions. The framework will be designed for a complete planning of the new facility, in the view of realizing a port-based distribution centre. The proposal will be applied to the case study of Catania and its port and in particular of a former industrial cement production plant adjacent to it.

The remainder of the paper is organized as follows. Section 2 will discuss background of the study with the analysis of the related literature. Section 3 will illustrate the different steps of the methodology, including the conceived framework. The framework will be applied to the case study of Catania in Sect. 4. Finally, conclusions will be presented.

2   Ports as Distribution and Logistics Centres

Ports are important and fundamental transport nodes in the supply chain because they play a critical role in the effective and efficient management of product and information flow [4]. The Port Service Quality constitutes a measure of the satisfaction of port customers, shipping lines and cargo owners and it is influenced by several factors. First, the port terminal capacity is the baseline to assess its potentialities. With reference to Ro-Ro terminal capacity, different methods can be found in literature to analyse it [5]. They are generally related to the waiting time over service time (W/S) [6, 7]; berth occupancy rate [8] and total turnaround time [9, 10]; both simulation [11–13] and analytic models can be used to estimate terminal capacity [14, 15]. However, the failure or unreliability of port services may also depend on other factors related to the transport infrastructures to access the port and the presence of additional services that can help to improve port capacity. In fact, ports undertake a variety of activities: loading/unloading cargo by vessels; providing value-added services such as labelling, packaging, cross-docking; acting as warehouse and distribution centres, and others [16]. Shipments located in the port area are considered most valuable by ports, because they are more integrable in the value chain. In this context, the advent of cross-docking represents a successful strategy to improve logistic operations and reduce the storage space needs, with positive and sustainable effects, allowing ship-owners to optimize the use of their assets while the terminal gains from the provision of value-added services. Among the good practices, there are the Ports of Gothenburg [17], Norrköping [18], Newark [19] and Santos [20]. It is possible to use the combination of cross-docking with a warehousing, in order to stage the goods, moving them from supplier to storage to customer practically without any handling except for truck loading [21, 22]. In the case of port cities, the location and construction of a warehouse in an area close to the port is a key element. In this direction, the regeneration of retro-port areas could act on four main aspects [23]: (i) urbanization of abandoned private areas; (ii) new job opportunities; (iii) change from the paradigm "port-city-industrial areas" to the new paradigm "port-city-logistic retro-port" [24]; (iv) opportunity for Public Private Partnership (PPP) actions.

3 Methodology

3.1 Problem Formulation

Ro-Ro transport developed a significant potential, especially in Europe with the concepts of "Short Sea Shipping (SSS)" and "Motorways of the sea" project, created by the European Commission in order to offer an efficient maritime service as a valid alternative to other types of transport systems. To make SSS competitive, times for loading and unloading cargo at terminal must be significantly reduced, considering the frequency of loads arriving at a terminal and the port terminal capacity. An intervention on the logistics chain of sea freight transport can be a fundamental solution to improve the capacity of the terminal itself and, consequently, improve the efficiency of the SSS.

In this view, in case of low capacity of Ro-Ro terminal in port-cities, we propose the use of abandoned areas located close the port in order to (Fig. 1): (i) expand the spaces supplied to the Ro-Ro terminal; (ii) provide the port and the city with a Urban Freight Centre, allowing the dispatchment of the goods with destination (or origin) in the city centre; (iii) reduce the congestion due to freight heavy vehicles that transport goods between the port (urban), the logistics centre (suburban) and in the city centre.

The design of the new retro-port should go along with the study of the port context, according to the following steps:

- analysis of port traffic and terminal capacity,
- analysis of transport infrastructure to access the port,
- analysis of related infrastructures (e.g. freight centre),
- design and dimensioning of retro-port: Ro-Ro terminal and UCC characteristics

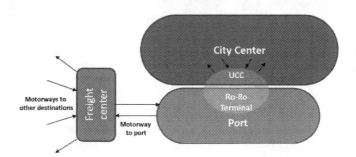

Fig. 1. Framework for the reuse of marginal areas (in green) shared between the port and the city (Source: Our elaboration). (Color figure online)

3.2 Analysis of Port Traffic and Terminal Capacity

The first step to take is the analysis of global port freight traffic, in order to understand the role of Ro-Ro transport within port logistics. If this role is of primary importance, priority policies can be adopted to encourage its operations within the port.

Ro-Ro terminals are characterized by a short stay of the goods in the terminal spaces: dock and yard are connected so that the vehicles that are unloaded from the ship (or should be loaded) can move easily and in a short time; however, the impossibility of stacking the CTUs (Cargo Transport Units) translates into a greater need for space, which is often a weak element of the Ro-Ro terminals. After leaving the yard, vehicles leave the port through the gates, where a series of bureaucratic checks and procedures are provided to allow them to continue towards their destination. The issue of capacity and location on site inside the terminal is one of the most important, as most CTUs arrive before the ship departs. Furthermore, upon arrival of the ships, it takes a certain amount of time to unload the goods, while the CTU waiting for boarding must be parked in a safe area. Conversely, as for the CTUs that disembark from the Ro-Ro ship, they do not immediately leave the terminal and therefore need to be placed in a storage space. For all these reasons, one of the productivity and efficiency indices in Ro-Ro port is precisely the time spent by vehicles inside it: more time means occupied spaces and therefore a general waste of time which translates into economic loss. The frequency of trucks arriving at a terminal (demand) is one of the main criteria for terminal dimensioning: for an existing port, optimization or expansion studies of the terminal area can be carried out in order to increase efficiency. Other variables to be taken into account are the inadequate number of terminal gates and customs control units, the number of vehicles arriving at a terminal, the ship's capacity, the distance between the terminals and bunkering local traffic in relation to the connection of the terminal.

3.3 Analysis of Transport Infrastructure to Access the Port and Intermodal Chain Related Infrastructures

Ports are strategic access "gates" to urban areas and reference territories. Therefore, accessibility is a key concept for urban planning [25–27] and, in particular, for port design and management [28]. According to [29], the concept of accessibility applied to a port has significant potential in determining and explaining its operational, economic and competitiveness performance: a more competitive port should always be associated with a higher level of accessibility.

In the logistic chain of freight transport, the transport network, the geographical constraints, the available modes of transport, times and costs are among the most important criteria for choosing the route to take. Freight accessibility is characterized by the linear transport infrastructures (roads, railways), internal/external to the port system, the port's position in relation to the surrounding area, the main transport nodes and the transport infrastructures with logistic functions. In this context, the port is intended as a node of a transport network: a port is competitive if it has an efficient transport network that allows an easy and quick entry-handle-departure of goods; in addition, intermodality with other modes of transport (roads, railways, inland waterways) must be ensured to guarantee adequate connections with the hinterland.

Several infrastructures can be part of the freight logistic chain involving the Ro-Ro terminal. Examples could be:

- Warehouses: unimodal infrastructures operating as storage facilities (i.e. Warehouse), which do not necessarily involve joint operations.
- Freight/logistic centre: Areas involving integrated operation, such as: filling, emptying, consolidation, handling, stocking and other services by typology of

goods and forwarding of wagons for block trains. In particular, in the case of urban areas Urban Consolidation Centres (UCCs), which are logistic facilities placed in the outskirts of a city [30], play an important role to improve city logistic. In UCCs, freight is consolidated and then distributed to the receivers of goods by a different operator. This type of logistics centre will be the one considered in our study.

- Intermodal Freight Terminal (IFT): or transfer point is a place equipped for the transhipment and storage of Intermodal Transport Units (ITU), connecting different transport modes (e.g. road, rail and waterborne) [31]. They usually include vehicle parking and facilities for loads handling, providing not only transport-related activities but also national and international logistics and distribution.

3.4 Design and Dimensioning of Retro-Port: Ro-Ro Terminal and UCC Characteristics

Ro-Ro Terminal Characteristics

The success of the integration of Ro-Ro traffic into logistical transport chains depends on a optimal design of the Ro-Ro-terminal itself; of course, seaside, terminal and land-side external factors play a relevant role in design criteria.

As in every terminal, it is possible to sub-partition the Ro-Ro terminal spaces in 3 subsystems [32, 33]:

- Berthing and stevedoring area, consisting of: manipulation areas for cargo handling; short-term storage area and traffic lanes for towing-units;
- Storage area for long-term storage of semi-trailers with traffic lanes for towing-units
- Delivery and receipt area, with gates and parking for trucks with semi-trailers

The CTU must complete several steps before reaching its destination [14]: (1) ticket booking and collection; (2) check-in; (3) entering the terminal gateway; (4) border control formalities; (5) custom clearance; (6) waiting at loading site; (7) boarding the ship; (8) transportation phase; (9) disembarkation; (10) queuing at storage site; (11) border control at arrival; (12) custom clearance at arrival; (13) exiting terminal. Considering the three terminal areas, the main optimal operating features of a Ro-Ro terminal can be assumed the following [34]: (i) optimal scheduling of vessels: fixed departure times and appropriate sailing frequencies; (ii) minimum space consumption and obstacles of vehicles cargo handling (e.g. reduced loading and unloading equipment); (iii) effective traffic management inside the terminal (e.g. use of appropriate signage for circulation and parking); (iv) separate internal traffic with dedicated lanes for delivery/pick-up.

UCC Characteristics

The UCC works as an interface between outbound and inbound freight transports, in order to serve a whole city or parts of it, also by offering value-added logistics in terms of more flexible delivery times, stockholding and unpacking larger consignments [35]. According to [36] and [37], UCC represents one of the most studied city logistics initiatives because it has the potentiality to reduce negative effects associated with freight distribution, with both the social and environmental dimension, by giving an alternative to current distribution systems. Furthermore, the integration of intelligent technologies allows to obtain cost-efficient and resource-efficient results, with an impact not only on environmental sustainability targets but also on citizens' wellbeing and financial sustainability [38–40]. The services offered by a UCC can be several: nightly and off-peak deliveries; request delivery time and frequency; stockholding; pre-retail services; ordering processes; waste and return management; etc. Therefore, appropriate ITS systems are required for an optimized management of goods and also physical spaces for their organization and handling. The warehouse constitutes a fundamental component of UCC: it is a logistic structure that allows to adjust the differences between the incoming flows of the goods, i.e. those coming from suppliers or production centres, to the outgoing flows, i.e. the goods that are sent to production and sale.

The benefits the UCCs can provide are linked to two different aspects. The first one is represented by the reduction of negative effects from distribution of goods, because by consolidating goods close to the city, it is possible to have shorter delivery distances and freight vehicles entering in the city with higher load factors, with the direct consequence of the reduction in their number [41–43]. The second one regards benefits aimed at different stakeholders. Authors highlighted the importance of stakeholders' engagement in several ways to structure transport decision-making processes and identify improvement solutions towards sustainability [44–48]. In particular, through the implementation of UCCs, citizens and local can benefit from attaining a more attractive city with fewer freight vehicles [41].

The UCC can be considered an efficient and effective solution to be implemented in an urban area, whether it is able to achieve the following results and implications [49]: (i) Increased cost efficiency of potential customers; (ii) Reliable deliveries; (iii) Reduce number of freight vehicle in urban area; (iv) Reduce freight handling by workers; (v) Provide high customer service; (vi) Generate revenue; (vii) More storage.

Designing a Port-City Shared Space
The constant increase in maritime traffic (and also in the Ro-Ro segment) means that ports must adapt their infrastructure to increasing number, dimensions and speed of vessels; for example, in the case of Ro-Ro terminals, in order to achieve greater time performances, the terminal should be provided with shipborne and dock side ramp systems for loading and unloading processes. One of the major obstacles to these improvements, especially in the case of ports that are located within cities and near the historic centre, is essentially the lack of space. Furthermore, the increase in port traffic also affects the increase in road traffic, affecting the network reliability and with consequent environmental, social and economic externalities [50, 51].

With this in mind, this study proposes the conversion of abandoned areas near the ports with the multiple purpose of: (a) increase the spaces of the port terminals dedicated to the transport of goods; (b) provide the city with an urban logistics centre that will reduce the impact of freight transport on the streets of the city centre.

Based on the characteristics identified in the two previous sections, the new area must therefore have:

- A portion dedicated to the typical port operations of the Ro-Ro terminals and in particular to those that take place far from the seaside area of the terminal (tipically storage, delivery and receipt area);
- A part dedicated to the typical logistics operations of an urban logistics centre and its warehouse (e.g. departure/arrival of unpackaged goods; packaging in load units) (Fig. 2).

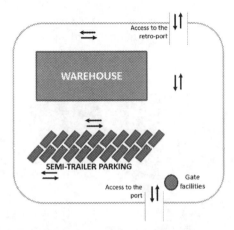

Fig. 2. Framework for the design of a retro-port with Ro-Ro facilities and logistic centre (Source: Our elaboration).

4 Application: A New Retro-Port in Catania as Strategic Asset for City Logistic

4.1 Case Study

Catania is a city located in the south of Italy and it is the second largest city of Sicily, with a population of more than 300.000 inhabitants only in the urban area. Thanks to its strategic position in the region, Catania is the main industrial, logistical and commercial centre of Sicily [52]. The harbour is a fundamental resource for Catania's economy. Located in the centre of the Mediterranean Sea, the Port of Catania, with a total surface of 615,000 m^2 used for goods storage yards, holds a variety of different activities: a tourist and commercial port (with national and international connections provided by major shipping companies) and a transport interchange with rapid connections to motorways, rail services and the airport. Moreover, being an historic Port, it is sited in an area of greatest contact with the city, deeply inserted in the urban context of Catania and specifically in the area of the historic city centre. The unplanned distribution of these heterogeneous functions and activities results in overlapping and intersecting flows of freights/passengers, with the direct consequence of flows that exceed road capacity and the generation of criticalities for vulnerable users [53, 54]. For this reason, it is fundamental to identify the main urban, landscape, architectural and functional components of this area with the aim of resolving the major problems inherent in the commercial activities of the Port while considering the port-city relationship.

The Port of Catania has a total area of about one million square meters, with 470.000 m^2 covered by land areas, 280.000 m^2 dedicated to goods storage and 26 operating docks with an overall length of berths of 4.200 m. It extends in the North-South direction with the entrance of the Port facing south. It is closed to the east by the outer pier *Molo Levante*; to the south it is bordered by the pier *Molo di Mezzogiorno* and by a newly built area called *Nuova Darsena*. The eastern basin is identified as the "new port" and has a polygonal shape, while to the east of it, separated by the *Sporgente Centrale* there is the "old port", mainly used for fishing activities (see Fig. 3, left).

Fig. 3. Terminal Port of Catania (Source: Our elaboration from Google Maps), left; Aerial view of intervention area, right (Color figure online)

In recent years there have been significant developments in containers, Ro-Ro and Ro-Pax ferries volumes, thanks to the location of the Port and its connection with the regional road and motorway network, with the airport and the Bicocca train station and the realization of the *Nuova Darsena*. With its 1.100 m of operational docks, 120.000 m^2 and 5 new berths, *Nuova Darsena* supplies a precious commercial lung for the storage and handling of containers, Ro-Ro and Ro-Ro/pax traffic which has so far occupied the historical part of the port in close contact with the city. With reference to the total tons of goods (i.e. rolling stocks, containers, parcels, dry and liquid bulks), the Sicilian Port has enlivened altogether a volume of more than 2,9 million tons of goods (+3.5 points with respect to the last five years). In this scenario, the Ro-Ro commercial activities positively increased, with 296.990 units of rolling traffic; considering the container sector, it is less developed respect the others, but also increasing thanks to the connections with transhipment hub-ports, with a total movement of 63.179 container units; cruise traffic isn't negligible, reaching a 313.138 passengers (Port Authority, 2019).

One the most relevant factors to consider regarding the Port of Catania is its closeness of the area to the functional and historical heart of the city. The Nuova Darsena is already over-saturated and it is difficult to plan its expansion in urban areas.

For these reasons, with reference to the commercial activities of the Ro-Ro terminal (light blue portion shown in Fig. 3, right), the possibility of having a supporting area would be useful to increase the capacity and improve the effectiveness of these activities. This hypothesis is considered of extreme interest because it would allow flexible delivery times, stockholding and unpacking larger consignments. Furthermore, the proximity to the city centre would allow benefits from different points of view: economic (less travelled kilometres and delivery times), environmental (lower emissions), social (decreasing congestion level in the centre). In this regard, right adjacent to the Ro-Ro terminal area there is a former industrial cement production plant (red portion shown in Fig. 3, right). This abandoned area, called in Italian "Cementeria", could be taken under consideration for a regeneration proposal, through its conversion as a retro-port with urban logistics function. In this regard, next section will provide a more detailed analysis focusing on the relevant characteristics of the Port of Catania (e.g. traffic terminal and related infrastructures) in order to provide a proposal for the design and dimensioning of the retro-port.

4.2 Proposal

Ro-Ro Traffic and Terminal in Catania

The Port of Catania is the first in Sicily as far as the movements of "dry goods" is concerned, thanks to an accurate planning and the use of equipment to work with competitive costs and high productivity.

Ro-Ro is a special type of vessel with special ramps in order to make the loading and the unlading of vehicles and cargo easier and more convenient. Over the years, several technological advancements have taken place in these carrier ships and resultantly, there have emerged into various types of Ro-Ro vessels, e.g. ferries, Ro-Pax, Ro-Con (Rolling Stock + Containers), barges, conventional ships with aft ramp, PCC (Pure Car Carriers) and PCTC (Pure Car and Truck Carriers). Specifically, the latter 2 are characterized by the transport of cars (and heavy construction site vehicles) on ocean routes, transporting an average of 200 trucks, divided on about a dozen internal bridges. Among the Intermodal Loading Units (UTI) most used for the transport of goods between the Mediterranean port (and therefore also for the port of Catania), there are swap bodies and semi-trailers. In particular, about the port commercial activity, it emerged that the Port of Catania is mainly characterized by an increasing Ro-Ro traffic, that is one extra order of magnitude compared to the tons of goods handled through containers. By elaborating the annual statistics collected by the Port Authority of the Eastern Sicily Port System, Fig. 4 shows the different percentage of freight traffic components. From 2014 to 2018, in terms of handled tons, the quantity of liquid bulk and other goods decreased, whereas the container traffic, Ro-Ro and solid bulk increased. Data elaboration (referring to the year 2018) allows to affirm that Ro-Ro constituted the 88.5% of the considered traffic, followed by the 6.5% of containers, 4.9% of solid bulk and the remaining low percentage represented by liquid bulk and other goods.

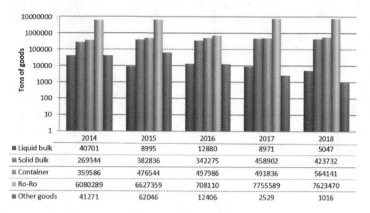

	2014	2015	2016	2017	2018
▩ Liquid bulk	40701	8995	12880	8971	5047
▩ Solid Bulk	269344	382836	342275	458902	423732
▩ Container	359586	476544	497986	491836	564141
▩ Ro-Ro	6080289	6627359	708110	7755589	7623470
▩ Other goods	41271	62046	12406	2529	1016

Fig. 4. Tons of goods for different freight traffic components of Port of Catania, 2014–2018 (Source: Our elaboration from Port Authority data)

An analysis of Ro-Ro terminal capacity has been conducted in a previous study developed by the authors [55], which showed that one of the main critical issue regards the size of the terminal, even though the recent opening of Nuova Darsena. The allowable number of CTUs which can use the storage site depends on several variables, e.g. the time of arrival of the ship at the terminal, the number of CTUs disembarking from each docked ship, the average storage time at a terminal site and the part of CTUs using parking at the terminal. The general intensity of CTUs processed at the gateway was determined by considering the number of gateways of the terminal and the time necessary to realize the entire process of unloading the single CTU. Then, from the application of a Poisson law it was estimated that the reliability of the terminal is insufficient because not all the CTUs can be accepted and that the average queue time outside the gateway is excessive. Even more in detail, the number of CTUs that use the Ro-Ro terminal is 600, and the percentage of CTUs remaining in the terminal following the landing was deemed about 90% of the total, i.e. 540 units. Considering that the Ro-Ro terminal of Catania has 450 spaces for CTUs, it implies that the terminal spaces are not sufficient for handling the current Ro-Ro traffic. These findings demonstrate the necessity of a further area to accommodate growing volumes of Ro-Ro cargo and to improve port operations in the Port of Catania.

Intermodal Chain Related Infrastructures in the Case of Catania
The Port of Catania is characterized by a high "centrality" due to its proximity to nodes of the intermodal network system, such as the central railway station, the freight yard, the dry port, the agri-food market, the airport, the "Circumetnea" urban railway station, Bicocca intermodal railway station, the industrial area and its several logistic companies (see Fig. 5).

Bicocca intermodal station is the main freight station, located inside the industrial area of Catania. This terminal has an area of 32.000 m² , 4 tracks which have a total length of 2000 m and it is serves by rail links to the southern (i.e. Lamezia) and northern Italy (i.e. Milan). The interport of Catania-Bicocca represents a large intermodal complex in the south of the city of Catania. It is divided into two poles about a kilometre and it is divided in two parts: the "Intermodal Pole" located near Bicocca station and the "Logistic Centre" inside the industrial area. The area dedicated to the Logistic Centre occupies about 166.000 m^2, of which approximately 46,000 m^2 belonging to the "Parking Area" functional lot. It provides the allocation of internal and external infrastructures for logistics operations (e.g. warehouses, service building and parking areas for heavy vehicles).

Finally, always located in the industrial area of Catania, there are numerous logistics centres specialized in offering logistics and freight movement services. As emerged from the descriptions of previous infrastructures, these centres have a considerable distance from the city centre and consequently from the port. Therefore, it often happens that the goods arriving at the port are carried out by heavy vehicles in the industrial area. Subsequently, after logistical operations, the goods directed to the city centre are transported back to the port, with obvious economic and environmental disadvantages. Hence, it arises the importance of an area close to the port to be used as a retro-port, supporting commercial operations of the Port of Catania.

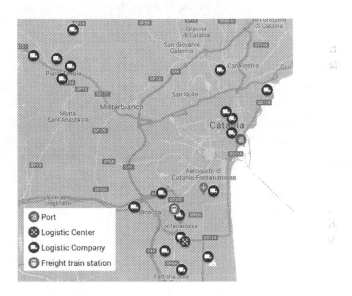

Fig. 5. Map of intermodal chain related infrastructure.

Transport Infrastructure to Access the Port of Catania

The Port of Catania has two main access gates. The first one is located in the northern part and it is intended for the entry of private vehicles and pedestrians; from this gate the port is accessed by an urban arterial road (SS114) which is already very congested, due to the south-north traffic crossing the of the city. The second access is located in the southern part of the port and it is reserved for the entrance of heavy commercial vehicles; in particular, the urban road relating to this access (the same SS114), during the days of departure of the ships, is highly congested because the usual traffic of crossing the city intersects the one related to the commercial vehicles entering/leaving the port. The connection between the port and the interport is guaranteed by the same road 114, which reaches the industrial area of the city, where most of the logistics operators are present. This area is also connected to the city of Catania via the *tangenziale* ring road, a highway that circles the city without crossing it.

Design and Dimensioning of the New Retro-Port

First of all, in order to guarantee an easy connection between the port and the retro-port, the area should be connected directly to the Ro-Ro terminal through either an underpass or an overpass that would cross the arterial road 114, the current only physical separation between the port and the cement plant. Following the integrated scheme in Fig. 4 of the retro-pot, the following minimum characteristics for the new retro-port in Catania emerge: (i) an area dedicated to the parking of semi-trailers that could host at least 90 vehicles more; (ii) a warehouse for city logistics; (iii) an area dedicated to gate controls. The evaluation of the dimension of the facilities' equipment would depend on an estimate of the percentage of Ro-Ro traffic in the port of Catania which, rather than continuing to the usual destinations, would be diverted to the new UCC. Knowing the volume transported in a semi-trailer, the number of rolling stock that arrives in the port per year and the possible working days of the warehouse in a year, the total volume worked per day in the warehouse can be estimated. From this, an average daily warehouse's capacity could be estimated. In the same way, it is possible to calculate the number of ramps needed to allow the semi-trailers to unload the pallets. These could be assessed through assumptions related to the number of hours of work per day and the time required to unload the semi-trailer: in this case, a number of average ramps needed in a day to unload a previously obtained volume of goods can be found.

5 Conclusions

Port city often have to deal with externalities due to port operation and the related traffic congestion [56]; the trend of such issues would inevitably grow together with the constant increase of maritime traffic and the consequent importance of Ro-Ro traffic for freight delivery. In port city, close former industrial zones are often marginal areas; their reuse can be a good opportunity to improve sustainability of port operations. In this paper a framework for the design of a port-city shared space is provided with a twofold aim: improving port operation and enhancing city logistic. The design of the retro-port is based on the evaluation of port's traffic and terminal's capacity, in order to guarantee a good efficiency of terminal operation. It is also proposed to use the new available spaces and the proximity to the city to support urban logistics activities, in order to reduce congestion and externalities caused by heavy vehicles travelling between the port, the logistics centres, and the urban area. The application of the methodology to the Catania case study shows design feasibility and its ability to support port operations during rush hour. Further research should focus on the economic feasibility of the Urban Consolidation Centre and policies related to its organization, both in terms of actors to be involved and entities that should manage its operation.

Acknowledgements. This work has been partially financed by the University of Catania within the project "Piano della Ricerca Dipartimentale 2016–2018" of the Department of Civil Engineering and Architecture and the project "Piano per la Ricerca 2016–2018 - Linea di intervento 2" of the Department of Electric, Electronic and Computer Engineering. The work has been partially financed by the project "THALASSA – Technology and materials for safe low consumption and low life cycle cost vessels and crafts" (unique project code CUP B46C18000720005) under the Italian research programme "PON Ricerca e Innovazione 2014–2020". This study was also supported by the MIUR (Ministry of Education, Universities and Research [Italy]) through a project entitled WEAKI TRANSIT: WEAK-demand areas Innovative TRANsport Shared services for Italian Towns (Project code: 20174ARRHT CUP Code: F74I19001290001), financed with the PRIN 2017 (Research Projects of National Relevance) programme. We authorize the MIUR to reproduce and distribute reprints for Governmental purposes, notwithstanding any copyright notations thereon. Any opinions, findings and conclusions or recommendations expressed in this material are those of the authors, and do not necessarily reflect the views of the MIUR.

References

1. Viana, M., et al.: Impact of maritime transport emissions on coastal air quality in Europe. Atmosph. Environ. **90**, 96–105 (2014)
2. Ignaccolo, M., Inturri, G., Giuffrida, N., Cocuzza, E., Torrisi, V.: Framework for the evaluation of the quality of pedestrian routes for the sustainability of port-city shared areas. In: Coastal Cities and their Sustainable Future III, WIT Transactions on the Built Environment, vol. 188. WIT Press (2019). https://doi.org/10.2495/cc190021. ISSN 1743-3509
3. Ignaccolo, M., Inturri, G., Giuffrida, N., Torrisi, V., Cocuzza, E.: Sustainability of freight transport through an integrated approach: the case of the eastern sicily port system. Transp. Res. Procedia **45**, 177–184 (2020). https://doi.org/10.1016/j.trpro.2020.03.005
4. Yeo, G.T., Thai, V.V., Roh, S.Y.: An analysis of port service quality and customer satisfaction: the case of Korean container ports. Asian J. Shipp. Logist. **31**(4), 437–447 (2015)
5. Morales Fusco, P.: Roll-on/roll-off terminals and truck freight: improving competitiveness in a motorways of the sea context (Doctoral dissertation, Universitat Politècnica de Catalunya) (2016)
6. Fourgeaud, P.: Measuring port performance. The World Bank (2000). http://siteresources.worldbank.org/INTPRAL/Resources/338897-1117630103824/fourgeau.pdf
7. Unctad (United Nations Conference on Trade and Development), 2006. Review of maritime transport, 2006. Geneva, Switzerland: United Nations Publications. (COMPIT 2006), 8–10 May 2003 Oegsteest, The Netherlands (2006)
8. Bassan, S.: Evaluating seaport operation and capacity analysis—preliminary methodology. Marit. Pol. Manage. **34**(1), 3–19 (2007)
9. Ballis, A.: Introducing level-of-service standards for intermodal freight terminals. Transp. Res. Rec. **1873**, 79–88 (2004)
10. Mathonnet, C.: Le project IQ "intermodal quality" une nouvelle approche de la qualité pour les terminaux intermodaux. Transports **400**, 108–116 (2000)
11. Özkan, E.D., Nas, S., Güler, N.: Capacity analysis of RO-RO terminals by using simulation modeling method. Asian J. Shipp. Logist. **32**(3), 139–147 (2016)

12. Keceli, Y., Aksoy, S., Aydogdu, Y.: A simulation model for decision support in Ro-Ro terminal operations. Int. J. Logist. Syst. Manage. **15**(4), 338–358 (2013)
13. Iannone, R., Miranda, S., Prisco, L., Riemma, S., Sarno, D.: Proposal for a flexible discrete event simulation model for assessing the daily operation decisions in a Ro–Ro terminal. Simul. Model. Pract. Theor. **61**, 28–46 (2016)
14. Maksimavičius, R.: Some elements of the Ro-Ro terminals. Transport **19**(2), 75–81 (2004)
15. Malavasi, G., Ricci, S.: The sea-side port capacity: a synthetic evaluation model. WIT Trans. Built Environ. **79**, 471–480 (2005)
16. World Bank. World Bank Seaport Toolkit, 2nd edn. World Bank, Washington USA (2007)
17. Port of Gothenburg. https://www.portofgothenburg.com/news-room/news/construction-of-new-crossdocking-terminal-under-way-at-the-port-of-gothenburg/. Accessed 18 June 2020
18. Port of Norrköping. https://www.scmp.com/article/1329515/nordic-and-baltic-hub-readies-cross-docking-facility-surging-trade. Accessed 18 June 2020
19. Port of Newark. https://glenwaydistribution.com/case-study-cross-docking-storage/. Accessed 18 June 2020
20. Port of Santos. https://www.joc.com/port-news/south-american-ports/port-santos/santos-terminal-turns-cross-docking-protect-market-share-amid-recession_20160705.html. Accessed 18 June 2020
21. Boysen, N., Fliedner, M.: Cross dock scheduling: classification, literature review and research agenda. Omega **38**(6), 413–422 (2010)
22. Schaffer, B.: Implementing a successful crossdocking operation. IIE Solutions **29**(10), 34–36 (1997)
23. Forte, F.: New land values patterns in the space of the Italian metropolitan areas: the case of the logistic retro-port in Naples. Procedia Soc. Behav. Sci. **223**, 503–508 (2016)
24. Delponte, I.: Porto-città-retroporto logistico. In: PORTUS (2007). http://retedigital.com/wp-content/themes/rete/pdfs/portus/Portus_16/Porto-citt%C3%A0-retroporto_logistico.pdf Accessed 25 Apr 2020
25. Giuffrida, N., Ignaccolo, M., Inturri, G., Rofè, Y., Calabrò, G.: Investigating the correlation between transportation social need and accessibility: the case of Catania. Transp. Res. Procedia **27**, 816–823 (2017)
26. Giuffrida, N., Inturri, G., Caprì, S., Spica, S., Ignaccolo, M.: The impact of a bus rapid transit line on spatial accessibility and transport equity: The case of Catania. Transport infrastructure and systems. In: Proceedings of the AIIT International Congress on Transport Infrastructure and Systems, TIS, pp. 753–758 (2017)
27. Ignaccolo, C., Giuffrida, N., Torrisi, V.: The Queensway of New York city. A proposal for sustainable mobility in queens. In: Town and Infrastructure Planning for Safety and Urban Quality, pp. 69–76 (2018). https://doi.org/10.1201/9781351173360-12
28. Ignaccolo, M., Inturri, G., Giuffrida, N., Pira, M.L., Torrisi, V.: Public engagement for designing new transport services: investigating citizen preferences from a multiple criteria perspective. Transp. Res. Procedia **37**, 91–98 (2019). https://doi.org/10.1016/j.trpro.2018.12.170
29. Wang, Y., Cullinane, K.: Measuring container port accessibility: an application of the principal eigenvector method (PEM). Maritime Econ. Logist. **10**(1–2), 75–89 (2008)
30. Browne, M., Sweet, M., Woodburn, A., Allen, J.: Urban Freight Consolidation Centres Final Report (2005)
31. EC. Intermodal freight terminals. In search of efficiency to support intermodality growth (2006). http://www.socool-logistics.eu/www.socoollogistics.eu/socool3/index.php/en/library/doc_download/Intermodal%20Freight%20Terminals%20-%20In%20search%20of%20efficiency%20to%20support%20intermodality%20growth.pdf_%3B%20modification-date%3D_Fri%2C%2014%20Dec%202012%2011_29_13%20%2B0100_%3B%20size%3D1629735%3B. Accessed 23 Apr 2020

32. Stojaković, M., Twrdy, E.: A decision support tool for container terminal optimization within the berth subsystem. Transport **31**(1), 29–40 (2016)
33. Morales-Fusco, P., Saurí, S., Spuch, B.: Quality indicators and capacity calculation for RoRo terminals. Transp. Plann. Technol. **33**(8), 695–717 (2010)
34. Todorov, M.: RoRo Handbook: A Practical Guide to Roll-On Roll-off Cargo Ships, 1st edn. Schiffer publishing, Atglen (2016). ISBN: 978-0-7643-5123-5
35. Janievic, M., Kaminsky, P., Ndiaye, A.B.: Downscaling the consolidation of goods-state of the art and transferability of micro-consolidation initiatives. In: European Transport – Trasporti Europei, pp. 1–23 (2013)
36. Lagorio, A., Pinto, R., Golini, R.: Research in urban logistics: a systematic literature review. Int. J. Phys. Distrib. Logist. Manage. **46**, 908–931 (2016)
37. Gammelegaard, B., Andersen, C.B.G., Aastrup, J.: Value co-creation in the interface between city logistics provider and in-store processes. Transp. Res. Procedia **12**, 787–799 (2016)
38. Torrisi, V., Ignaccolo, M., Inturri, G.: Innovative transport systems to promote sustainable mobility: developing the model architecture of a traffic control and supervisor system. In: Gervasi, O., et al. (eds.) ICCSA 2018. LNCS, vol. 10962, pp. 622–638. Springer, Cham (2018). https://doi.org/10.1007/978-3-319-95168-3_42
39. Torrisi, V., Ignaccolo, M., Inturri, G.: Toward a sustainable mobility through a dynamic real-time traffic monitoring, estimation and forecasting system: the RE.S.E.T. project. In: Town and Infrastructure Planning for Safety and Urban Quality, pp. 241–247 (2018). https://doi.org/10.1201/9781351173360-32
40. Canale, A., Tesoriere, G., Campisi, T.: The MAAS development as a mobility solution based on the individual needs of transport users. In: AIP Conference Proceedings, vol. 2186, no. 1, p. 160005. AIP Publishing LLC, December 2019. https://doi.org/10.1063/1.5138073
41. Browne, M., Woodburn, A., Alle, J.: Evaluating the potential for urban consolidation centres. Eur. Transp. Trasporti Europei **35**, 46–63 (2007)
42. Van Rooijen, T., Quak, H.: Local impacts of a new urban consolidation centre – the case of Binnenstadservice.nl. Procedia Soc. Behav. Sci. **2**, 5967–5979 (2010)
43. Calabrò, G., Torrisi, V., Inturri, G., Ignaccolo, M.: Improving inbound logistic planning for large-scale real-world routing problems: a novel ant-colony simulation-based optimization. Eur. Transp. Res. Rev. **12**(1) (2020). https://doi.org/10.1186/s12544-020-00409-7
44. Ignaccolo, M., Inturri, G., Giuffrida, N., Le Pira, M., Torrisi, V.: Structuring transport decision-making problems through stakeholder engagement: the case of Catania metro accessibility. Transp. Infrastruct. Syst. 919–926 (2017). https://doi.org/10.1201/9781315281896-118
45. Ignaccolo, M., Inturri, G., Giuffrida, N., Le Pira, M., Torrisi, V., Calabrò, G.: A step towards walkable environments: spatial analysis of pedestrian compatibility in an urban context. Eur. Transp. Trasporti Europei **76**(6), 1–12 (2020)
46. Moslem, S., Duleba, S.: Sustainable urban transport development by applying a fuzzy-AHP model: a case study from Mersin, Turkey. Urban Sci. **3**(2), 55 (2019)
47. Campisi, T., Canale, A., Tesoriere, G.: SWOT analysis for the implementation of spaces and pedestrian paths at the street markets of Palermo. In: AIP Conference Proceedings, vol. 2040, no. 1, p. 140003. AIP Publishing LLC, November 2018. https://doi.org/10.1063/1.5079192
48. Campisi, T., Torrisi, V., Ignaccolo, M., Inturri, G., Tesoriere, G.: University propensity assessment to car sharing services using mixed survey data: the Italian case study of Enna city. Transp. Res. Procedia **47**, 433–440 (2020). https://doi.org/10.1016/j.trpro.2020.03.155

49. Quak, H., Tavasszy, L.: Customized solutions for sustainable city logistics: the viability of urban freight consolidation centres. In: van Nunen, J., Huijbregts, P., Rietveld, P. (eds.) Transitions Towards Sustainable Mobility, pp. 213–233. Springer, Heidelberg (2011). https://doi.org/10.1007/978-3-642-21192-8_12

50. Torrisi, V., Ignaccolo, M., Inturri, G., Giuffrida, N.: Combining sensor traffic and simulation data to measure urban road network reliability. In: International Conference on Traffic and Transport Engineering (ICTTE) Proceedings, Belgrade, p. 1004, November 2016

51. Macedo, E., Tomás, R., Fernandes, P., Coelho, M.C., Bandeira, J.M.: Quantifying road traffic emissions embedded in a multi-objective traffic assignment model. Transp. Res. Procedia 47, 648–655 (2020)

52. Ignaccolo, M., Inturri, G., García-Melón, M., Giuffrida, N., Le Pira, M., Torrisi, V.: Combining Analytic Hierarchy Process (AHP) with role-playing games for stakeholder engagement in complex transport decisions. Transp. Res. Procedia 27, 500–507 (2017). https://doi.org/10.1016/j.trpro.2017.12.069

53. Torrisi, V., Ignaccolo, M., Inturri, G.: Estimating travel time reliability in urban areas through a dynamic simulation model. Transp. Res. Procedia 27, 857–864 (2017). https://doi.org/10.1016/j.trpro.2017.12.134

54. Torrisi, V., Ignaccolo, M., Inturri, G.: Analysis of road urban transport network capacity through a dynamic assignment model: validation of different measurement methods. Transp. Res. Procedia 27, 1026–1033 (2017). https://doi.org/10.1016/j.trpro.2017.12.135

55. Ignaccolo, M., Inturri, G., Giuffrida, N., Torrisi, V.: Investigating scenarios for freight traffic in the Eastern Sicily port system. In: Presented at the 18th International Conference on Transport Science - ICTS 2018 - Maritime, Transport And Logistics Science - Conference proceedings, pp. 139–145 (2018). ISBN 978-961-7041-03-3

56. Ignaccolo, M., Inturri, G., Giuffrida, N., Torrisi, V.: A sustainable framework for the analysis of port systems. Eur. Transp. Int. J. Transp. Econ. Eng. Law (78) (2020). Article no. 7. ISSN 1825-3997

Decision-Making for Maritime Networks: Evaluating Corporate and Social Profitability of an Integrated Short Sea Shipping Network in the Upper Tyrrhenian Sea

Gianfranco Fancello[1] , Patrizia Serra[1(✉)] , Michele Carta[2],
Valentina Aramu[1], and Paolo Fadda[1]

[1] DICAAR – Department of Civil and Environmental
Engineering and Architecture, University of Cagliari, 09123 Cagliari, Italy
pserra@unica.it
[2] CENTRALABS - Competence Centre of Sardinia on Transport,
University Campus of Monserrato, 09030 Monserrato, Italy

Abstract. This study applies cost benefit analysis (CBA) approaches to evaluate corporate and social profitability of a coordinated management proposal for a Short Sea Shipping (SSS) network in the upper Tyrrhenian area. The profitability of the maritime network is assessed first for the shipping companies operating therein and then for society as a whole. Corporate profitability analysis reveals a supply system currently over-sized compared to actual demand. The reasons for this must be found in the corporate competition strategies that traditionally characterize the free maritime transport market in the area. Social profitability analysis proves the potential positive impact of services rescheduling and coordination in terms of time savings and emission reduction in port areas and demonstrates the benefits new integrated management policies could yield for achieving higher efficiency and sustainability in SSS Tyrrhenian networks.

Keywords: Short Sea Shipping · Motorways of the sea · Cost benefit analysis · Tyrrhenian area · Ro-Ro maritime services

1 Introduction

European transport policy has long highlighted the importance of short sea shipping (SSS) for reducing road traffic, rebalancing the distribution between modes of transport, and contributing to sustainable development. In the framework of SSS, the European Union promotes the Motorways of the Sea (MoS) initiative whose main purpose is to encourage the modal shift from road to sea and improve the accessibility of peripheral and island regions [1]. One of the main objectives of the EU maritime transport policy concerns the exploitation of the full potential of SSS through the complete implementation of MoS projects [2]. In the last decades, the European Commission has been promoting maritime research and innovation by funding various intermodal and MoS development projects. Particularly, Roll-on Roll-of (Ro-Ro) transport is one of the key options European policy is focusing upon to develop intermodal transport and MoS

© Springer Nature Switzerland AG 2020
O. Gervasi et al. (Eds.): ICCSA 2020, LNCS 12255, pp. 83–95, 2020.
https://doi.org/10.1007/978-3-030-58820-5_7

policies. This paper is based on the outputs of the Go Smart Med project, funded under the Interreg IT-FR Maritime Program 2014–2020. The purpose of the project was to develop intermodal transport in the high-Tyrrhenian area to improve the accessibility of island regions while providing an essential contribution to how existing Ro-Ro shipping services could be streamlined to render them more competitive. The project originated from the analysis of the existing maritime Ro-Ro freight transport system in the area, which revealed the lack of any distinctive pattern for which the available liner services could be considered as a proper maritime network [3]. The various available routes seem to be conceived singularly and sized mainly based on competition struggles between shipping companies rather than to satisfy demand requirements. However, the inter-company competition regime which is typical of the free market does not appear appropriate to benefit from the potential of the Tyrrhenian area. In such contexts, it is believed that new integrated management policies could potentially yield significant benefits for achieving higher global efficiency and competitiveness [4]. In this regard, the Go Smart Med project proposed an alternative governance model to coordinate Ro-Ro connections between the following six ports in the area: Genoa, Leghorn, Cagliari and Palermo, in Italy, and Toulon and Bastia, in France. The proposed governance model was based on an integrated and optimized network scheme for the maritime Ro-Ro freight services currently operating between the six ports. The operating parameters of the new integrated network were determined through an optimization approach based on the integration of timetables and frequencies of the liner services of interest.

This paper aims to evaluate the profitability of the newly optimized system compared to the existing one. The profitability of the optimized network is assessed both for the shipping company and society as a whole.

The paper is organized as follows. Following this introduction, Sect. 2 presents the case study and its peculiarities. Section 3 describes the new integrated network as it was developed by the Go Smart Med project. Section 4 introduces the cost-benefit analysis approach with a brief review of its applications in maritime literature. The numerical application is in Sect. 5. Finally, Sect. 6 concludes the paper.

2   The Case Study

The case study analyzed concerns the Tyrrhenian area and specifically the maritime Ro-Ro connections between the following ports: Cagliari, Genoa, Leghorn and Palermo in Italy, Toulon and Bastia in France. In the Trans European Transport Network (TEN-T), the first four ports are classified as *core* while the last two as *comprehensive*. Table 1 shows the weekly demand matrix for each O/D pair in terms of Ro-Ro units per week. In particular, the O/D pair takes a zero value when direct or combined transport services were not present in the period analyzed. The total weekly demand of the network is estimated at 6,726 Ro-Ro units. At the time of the analysis, the transport offer serving this network counted 16 liner Ro-Ro and Ro-Pax services operated by eight companies. The service frequency and capacity for each O/D pair are listed respectively in Tables 2 and 3. The service capacity is calculated by multiplying the weekly frequency by the average ship capacity. The total weekly capacity is estimated at 12,180 Ro-Ro units. Considering that the weekly demand was estimated at 6,726 Ro-Ro units, the residual capacity of the network amounts to 39%. Table 4 details the surplus capacity for O/D pair. The highest surpluses are on the routes characterized by overlapping services operated by different companies.

Table 1. Average weekly demand (Ro-Ro units/week) - year of reference: 2016

O/D Demand	Bastia	Genoa	Toulon	Cagliari	Leghorn	Palermo
Bastia	–	13	224	0	196	0
Genoa	19	–	0	357	0	867
Toulon	251	0	–	0	0	0
Cagliari	0	426	0	–	849	150
Leghorn	177	0	0	843	–	643
Palermo	0	791	0	246	676	–

Table 2. Weekly frequency (travels/week) - year of reference: 2016

Frequency	Bastia	Genoa	Toulon	Cagliari	Leghorn	Palermo
Bastia	0	1	7	0	10	0
Genoa	1	0	0	5	0	10
Toulon	7	0	0	0	0	0
Cagliari	0	5	0	0	8	4
Leghorn	10	0	0	8	0	3
Palermo	0	10	0	4	3	0

Table 3. Weekly capacity (Ro-Ro units/week) – year of reference: 2016

Capacity	Bastia	Genoa	Toulon	Cagliari	Leghorn	Palermo
Bastia	–	28	315	0	282	0
Genoa	28	–	0	1,018	0	1,684
Toulon	315	0	–	0	0	0
Cagliari	0	1,018	0	–	1,607	475
Leghorn	282	0	0	1,607	–	681
Palermo	0	1,684	0	475	681	–

Table 4. Surplus capacity (Ro-Ro units/week) – year of reference: 2016

Surplus	Bastia	Genoa	Toulon	Cagliari	Leghorn	Palermo
Bastia	–	15	91	0	86	0
Genoa	9	–	0	661	0	817
Toulon	64	0	–	0	0	0
Cagliari	0	592	0	–	758	325
Leghorn	105	0	0	764	–	38
Palermo	0	893	0	229	5	–

Port waiting times and average travel times in the existing network configuration are listed in Tables 5 and 6. To calculate port waiting times it is assumed that the goods to be embarked are available for boarding from 6 p.m. on the day of arrival at the port. The waiting time is thus calculated as the time that elapses from the time the goods arrive by land to the origin port to the time the boarding operations of the first useful departure to the destination port are completed. The total travel time is here defined as the time that elapses from the moment the goods arrive by land at the origin port until the moment they are disembarked at the destination port, it includes the waiting time, the sailing time, the unloading time and the transhipment time, if any. In Table 6, the values in italics refer to the O/D connections for which there is no direct service or an integrated connection service. The relative waiting times for these connections are calculated considering the first useful coincidence between the various combinable services available. The assessment includes the time necessary for the transhipment operations from one vessel to another.

Table 5. Average port waiting time (h)

Waiting time	Bastia	Genoa	Toulon	Cagliari	Leghorn	Palermo
Bastia	–	75.00	8.09	*39.00*	18.45	*42.79*
Genoa	75.00	–	*88.00*	20.71	–	11.97
Toulon	25.68	*113.00*	–	70.86	*36.11*	*52.14*
Cagliari	*35.04*	32.74	*48.57*	–	17.43	31.00
Leghorn	16.26	–	*33.21*	17.43	–	36.35
Palermo	*37.71*	12.84	*51.86*	31.07	30.52	–

Table 6. Average travel time (h)

Travel time	Bastia	Genoa	Toulon	Cagliari	Leghorn	Palermo
Bastia	–	88.00	19.50	*69.71*	25.45	*69.49*
Genoa	88.00	–	*111.00*	55.11	–	42.05
Toulon	38.68	*136.00*	–	106.86	*53.11*	*93.49*
Cagliari	*62.75*	77.83	*85.67*	–	39.43	66.93
Leghorn	23.26	–	*50.21*	39.43	–	58.05
Palermo	*63.86*	41.38	*88.00*	75.07	52.69	–

3 The Project Scenario

The Go Smart Med project has proposed an alternative organization of the transport service along the analyzed network based on the integration of the timetables and frequencies of the existing liner services operating therein. A mixed-integer linear programming model was used to determine the optimal allocation of the demand flows on the network while trying to minimize a multi-objective function composed of a weighted sum of travel times and tariffs. For more details on the analytical formulation of the model, the interested reader can refer to [3]. The model was used to reschedule and coordinate existing services and allowed to determine an optimized network option characterized by lower waiting and travel times than the existing configuration.

Tables 7 and 8 show the average port waiting times and travel times relating to the optimized network configuration. The values in italics refer to the O/D connections involving the combination of two services.

Table 7. Average port waiting time (h) - optimized configuration

Waiting time	Bastia	Genoa	Toulon	Cagliari	Leghorn	Palermo
Bastia	–	75.00	3.00	26.29	18.06	40.43
Genoa	75.00	–	89.00	9.86	–	6.10
Toulon	3.00	89.00	–	17.86	10.57	31.86
Cagliari	17.07	9.86	27.57	–	3.26	13.29
Leghorn	9.51	–	21.71	4.63	–	28.98
Palermo	31.79	6.23	42.29	13.29	30.52	–

Table 8. Average travel time (h) - optimized configuration

Travel time	Bastia	Genoa	Toulon	Cagliari	Leghorn	Palermo
Bastia	–	88.00	16.00	58.00	25.06	68.01
Genoa	88.00	–	112.00	49.33	–	36.38
Toulon	16.00	106.86	–	54.29	28.00	67.78
Cagliari	45.21	55.57	65.71	–	25.26	52.64
Leghorn	16.51	–	40.00	26.63	–	51.67
Palermo	60.64	33.69	81.14	57.29	52.69	–

The potential benefit deriving from reorganizing the maritime transport services in the area clearly emerges when comparing the waiting and travel times related to the existing configuration (Tables 5 and 6) with the optimized ones (Tables 7 and 8). Tables 9 and 10 detail the percentage reduction of waiting time and travel time for each O/D pair. Overall, the optimized network would ensure a 32.7% reduction in waiting time and an 18.7% reduction in travel time.

Although these indicators may demonstrate the greater attractiveness of the transport service rendered by the optimized network, its economic and financial profitability has yet to be verified. The scope of the present application is to assess its corporate and social profitability using cost benefit analysis approaches.

Table 9. Optimized vs existing configuration: waiting time variation (%)

VAR %	Bastia	Genoa	Toulon	Cagliari	Leghorn	Palermo
Bastia	–	0.0%	−88.0%	−32.6%	−2.1%	2.5%
Genoa	0.0%	–	1.1%	−52.4%	–	−49.1%
Toulon	−88.3%	−21.2%	–	−74.8%	−70.7%	−38.9%
Cagliari	−51.3%	−69.9%	−43.2%	–	−81.3%	−57.1%
Leghorn	−41.5%	–	−34.6%	−73.4%	–	−20.3%
Palermo	−15.7%	−51.5%	−18.5%	−57.2%	0.0%	–

Table 10. Optimized vs existing configuration: travel time variation (%)

VAR %	Bastia	Genoa	Toulon	Cagliari	Leghorn	Palermo
Bastia	–	0.0%	−18.0%	−16.8%	−1.5%	2.8%
Genoa	0.0%	–	0.9%	−10.5%	–	−13.5%
Toulon	−58.6%	−21.4%	–	−49.2%	−47.3%	−27.5%
Cagliari	−27.9%	−28.6%	−23.3%	–	−35.9%	−21.3%
Leghorn	−29.0%	–	−20.3%	−32.5%	–	−11.0%
Palermo	−5.0%	−18.6%	−7.8%	−23.7%	0.0%	–

4   Economic and Financial Feasibility Assessment

The economic and financial feasibility assessment of the newly proposed maritime network is aimed at evaluating both the improvement of the maritime transport offer in the area and the reduction of negative externalities that would derive by its entry into service in place of the existing system.

Numerous studies have used and demonstrated the validity of cost-benefit analysis (CBA) to evaluate the cost versus the benefits of alternative project proposals. When evaluating alternative projects, there are two main purposes in using CBA: i) to determine if a given project is justifiable and feasible by figuring out if its benefits outweigh costs; ii) to offer a baseline for comparing project alternatives by determining which one is sounder and more justifiable.

The transport literature shows numerous applications of CBA for assessing transport infrastructure projects, see, for example, the papers by [5] and [6]. CBA has also been applied to numerous studies related to the maritime sector. Among others, the paper by [7] uses CBA to assess the potential benefits resulting from the reduction of the time spent by containers in ports. The study by [8] supports the application of CBA as a useful tool in the evaluation of a better coastal maritime policy in New Zealand. The paper by [9] applies CBA to demonstrate the benefits of MoS compared to road transport in a short sea shipping context. The study by [10] applies CBA to dynamic planning of routes in the Baltic Sea. The work by [11] applies CBA to 74 separate and highly diverse port projects undertaken by private businesses to determine if a traditional CBA was used as part of their decision-making process.

In this application, the profitability of the new prospective network is assessed according to two different viewpoints:

1. that of the shipping companies: analysis of corporate profitability;
2. that of the society as a whole: analysis of social profitability.

The former is a private decision tool that represents the perspective of the shipping company, which evaluates profit as a revenue-cost difference (Eq. 1). The analysis of social profitability reflects the objectives of the entire society, is a tool of public decision and evaluates profit as a benefit-cost difference (Eq. 2). In both approaches, the goal is to maximize profit.

$$maxP = \sum_i P_i = \sum_i (R_i - C_i) \tag{1}$$

$$maxP = \sum_i P_i = \sum_i (B_i - C_i) \tag{2}$$

Let R_i be the operating revenue in year i, C_i the cost in year i, and B_i the benefit in year i.

While in the analysis of corporate profitability the revenue only refers to the company's monetary income, the concept of benefit is wider and may include every resource that can be produced or saved with the project, such as pollution or safety. Although the benefits are not conventionally expressed by monetary values, in the context of CBA, they can be monetized through formulations proposed in the scientific literature.

In this study, the analysis of corporate profitability is carried out on an annual horizon to assess the profitability of the ship owning system based on the difference between revenues and costs in the same reference year. The analysis of social profitability is developed over a 25-year horizon using the discounting of the benefits and costs realized over the period considered and the evaluation of the Net Present Value - NPV (Eq. 3) and the Internal Rate of Return - IRR (Eq. 4). The last two are the reference indicators for evaluating the profitability of investment projects in CBAs.

$$NPV = -I_0 + \sum_{i=0}^{t} \frac{R_i - C_i}{(1+r)^i} \tag{3}$$

$$IRR = r_0 NPV(r_0) = \sum_0^t (R_i - C_i)/(1+r_0)^i = 0 \tag{4}$$

Let R_i be the revenue in year i, C_i the cost in year i, and I_0 the initial investment.

5 Application

5.1 Analysis of Corporate Profitability

Corporate profitability of the system has been assessed from the perspective of the eight shipping companies operating in the network. The analysis represents the point of view not of a specific company but the system of companies as a whole.

Calculation of Benefits. The benefits of the system are represented by operating revenues deriving from the payment of the freight rate by users. The freight rate is assessed for a Ro-Ro unit characterized by an average length of 13 m. The average freight rate for each O/D pair (Table 11) is multiplied by the relative weekly demand (Table 1) to obtain the weekly operating revenue.

Table 12 shows the annual revenue, which is obtained by multiplying the weekly revenue by 52 working weeks. The annual operating revenue is estimated equal to € 209,336,634. Table 13 lists the nautical miles (nm) travelled weekly. They are determined by multiplying the sailing distance between a pair of ports by the weekly frequency of the service. The nautical miles travelled in a year can be calculated by multiplying the weekly miles by the number of working weeks in a year. Considering Ro-Ro units with an average length of 13 linear meters (lm), it is possible to estimate a unitary operating revenue equal to 0.17 €/(lm·nm).

Table 11. Average freight rate (€/Ro-Ro unit)

Freight rate	Bastia	Genoa	Toulon	Cagliari	Leghorn	Palermo
Bastia	–	205	394	–	245	–
Genoa	205	–	–	432	–	955
Toulon	394	–	–	–	–	–
Cagliari	–	432	–	–	481	635
Leghorn	245	–	–	481	–	459
Palermo	–	955	–	635	459	–

Table 12. Annual operating revenue (€/year)

Revenue	Bastia	Genoa	Toulon	Cagliari	Leghorn	Palermo
Bastia	–	143,910	4,775,987	–	2,590,963	–
Genoa	204,795	–	–	8,314,558	–	44,702,978
Toulon	5,345,698	–	–	–	–	–
Cagliari	–	9,916,873	–	–	22,029,775	5,140,151
Leghorn	2,343,103	–	–	21,880,487	–	15,938,883
Palermo	–	40,809,035	–	8,441,903	16,757,534	–

Table 13. Nautical miles travelled weekly (nm/week)

Distance	Bastia	Genoa	Toulon	Cagliari	Leghorn	Palermo
Bastia	–	105	1,246	0	610	0
Genoa	105	–	0	1,745	0	4,270
Toulon	1,246	0	–	0	0	0
Cagliari	0	1,745	0	–	2,352	864
Leghorn	610	0	0	2,352	–	1,065
Palermo	0	4,270	0	864	1,065	–

Calculation of Costs. The total operating cost for the provision of the Ro-Ro service has been calculated using the unitary cost of 173 €/nm defined in the study by [12]. The annual operating cost for each OD pair (Table 14) is calculated by multiplying the nautical miles travelled weekly (Table 13) by the number of working weeks in a year (52) and the unitary cost of 173 €/nm.

The annual operating cost is estimated at 229,009,788 €. Considering annual revenues of 209,336,634 €, it emerges a negative cash flow of 19,673,154 €. This data confirms the oversizing of the transport offer compared to the demand detected. Starting from the existing demand equal to 6,726 Ro-Ro units, a variation range of ±15% was investigated to determine the demand value necessary for the company system to cover the transportation costs incurred. The balance between revenues and costs is achieved with a 9.4% demand increase (Fig. 1).

Table 14. Annual operating cost (€/year)

Cost	Bastia	Genoa	Toulon	Cagliari	Leghorn	Palermo
Bastia	–	980,910	11,640,132	0	5,698,620	0
Genoa	980,910	–	0	16,301,790	0	39,890,340
Toulon	11,640,132	0	–	0	0	0
Cagliari	0	16,301,790	0	–	21,972,384	8,071,488
Leghorn	5,698,620	0	0	21,972,384	–	9,949,230
Palermo	0	39,890,340	0	8,071,488	9,949,230	–

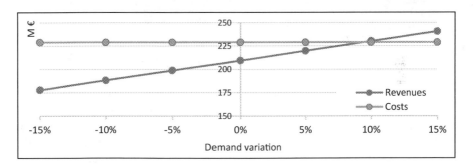

Fig. 1. Point of cancellation of the difference between costs and revenues

5.2   Analysis of Social Profitability

Analysis of social profitability considers a 25-year time horizon and implies hypotheses of variation in demand. A 10% demand increase is assumed in the 25 years, which can be reasonably speculated in the light of the better performance of the transport service offered by the optimized configuration. In this regard, it should be noted that the coordinated scheduling of arrivals and departures at different port nodes allows hauliers to consider several combined connections, which are currently not used, as potential new transport alternatives. The percentage increase in demand over the 25 years is detailed in Appendix 1.

Calculation of Benefits. The benefits considered in this analysis include financial revenues, time savings and the reduction of air pollution in ports.

Financial revenues: they concern the revenue from the transport tariffs paid by users (Table 15). They are valued as the difference between the revenues of the optimized scenario and the existing one.

Time savings: they account for the reduction of travel time which is estimated to occur with the implementation of the new network configuration (Table 10). The value of time (VoT) is assumed equal to 6.82 €/(h·Ro-Ro unit), as assessed by [13]. Time savings are estimated annually at 23,536,919 €.

Pollution reduction: attention should be devoted to port emissions as they directly affect human beings. Reducing the time ships spend in port can thus produce positive effects on air quality and human health. The optimized scenario envisages a 30-minute reduction in the average time spent by ships in port, resulting in better coordination of arrivals and departures. The reduction of air pollution in ports due to shorter hotelling times has been estimated considering the average emissions during the hotelling phase for a ship of gross tonnage of 28.599 tons [14]. The cost associated with air emissions is estimated according to the cost values defined in [15]. Known the reduction in the hotelling time in the optimized configuration, the reduction in the level of port pollution brings a monetary benefit of € 2,673,568 per year.

Table 15. Operating revenues (€)

Year	1	2	3	4	5
Revenue	3,052,308	4,116,892	5,186,798	6,262,054	7,342,687
Year	6	7	8	9	10
Revenue	8,428,722	9,520,188	10,617,111	11,719,519	12,827,439
Year	11	12	13	14	15
Revenue	13,384,168	13,942,290	14,501,807	15,062,722	15,625,040
Year	16	17	18	19	20
Revenue	16,188,764	16,753,897	17,320,443	17,888,405	18,457,787
Year	21	22	23	24	25
Revenue	18,743,190	19,028,949	19,315,066	19,601,540	19,888,373

Calculation of Costs. The costs considered in this CBA include operating costs, investment costs, and costs for the introduction of a tracking system.

Operating costs: operating costs are calculated by multiplying the nautical miles travelled by the unitary operating cost of 173 €/nm introduced in Sect. 5.1. As the service frequencies (and thus the distances travelled) remain unchanged in the two scenarios, the difference in operating costs is zero.

Cost of the new tracking system: the implementation of a tracking system is proposed in the optimized configuration to give users the ability to continuously monitor their goods along the entire transport chain, especially when it includes transhipment operations [16]. The cost of the tracking system is estimated at 19.5 € per Ro-Ro unit. Considering the demand variation in Appendix 1, Table 16 lists the cost of the tracking system year by year.

Investment costs: three start-up cost scenarios attributable to the creation of management and physical infrastructures in the ports considered are hypothesized. The three start-up costs are set as follows: 50 M€ (soft investment), 100 M€ (medium investment) and 200 M€ (hard investment).

Table 16. Annual cost of the tracking system (€)

Year	1	2	3	4	5
Cost	7,193,276	7,229,243	7,265,389	7,301,716	7,338,225
Year	6	7	8	9	10
Cost	7,374,916	7,411,790	7,448,849	7,486,093	7,523,524
Year	11	12	13	14	15
Cost	7,542,333	7,561,189	7,580,092	7,599,042	7,618,039
Year	16	17	18	19	20
Cost	7,637,085	7,656,177	7,675,318	7,694,506	7,713,742
Year	21	22	23	24	25
Cost	7,723,384	7,733,039	7,742,705	7,752,383	7,762,074

The NPV and IRR are calculated for the three hypotheses assuming a 3.5% discount rate. The NPV is positive for all three hypotheses (Table 17), ranging from around 461 M€ (start-up investment cost of 50 M€) to 311 M€ (start-up investment cost of 200 M€).

Table 17. NPV and IRR for the three start-up cost hypotheses

	Hypotheses 1	Hypotheses 2	Hypotheses 3
Start-up Investment (€)	50,000,000	100,000,000	200,000,000
NPV	460,930,812	410,930,812	310,930,812
IRR	48.52%	25.83%	13.43%

6   Conclusions

This paper evaluated the corporate and social profitability of an alternative management proposal for the maritime Ro-Ro freight liner services currently operating between six Tyrrhenian ports. The new network proposal keeps the number of services and their frequencies unchanged compared to the existing transport configuration but proposes their weekly rescheduling in a coordinated and systemic key.

The corporate profitability of the system was assessed from the perspective of the eight shipping companies operating in the network and revealed a negative annual cash flow of around 20 M €, attributable to the strong over-sizing of services currently existing on some routes. The reasons for such an over-sized supply with numerous services overlapping must be found in the corporate competition strategies that traditionally characterize the free maritime transport market. In the current network layout, a 9.4% demand increase would be required for the company system to cover the transportation costs incurred.

The social profitability of the new network scheme was assessed over a 25-year horizon using financial CBA. The analysis proved the positive impact of services rescheduling and coordination in terms of time savings and emission reduction in port areas and demonstrated the greater potential a coordinated network system could offer compared with the single maritime services collectively. Such outcomes can contribute to proving the importance of investigating integrated strategies for improving the quality and sustainability of maritime transport activities in areas such as the Tyrrhenian.

Further developments of this research will concern sensitivity analysis for the CBA discussed and the application of Multi-Criteria methods to widely evaluate corporate profitability and social revenues.

Acknowledgements. This research is based upon the Go Smart Med Project funded under the Interreg IT-FR Maritime Program 2014–2020.

Appendix 1 - Percentage Increase in Demand Over the 25 Years

Year	0	1	2	3	4	5	6
Annual increase (%)	–	1.56	0.500	0.500	0.500	0.500	0.500
Cumulative increase (%)	0	1.56	2.07	2.58	3.10	3.61	4.13
Demand (Ro-Ro units/year)	6,726	6,831	6,865	6,900	6,934	6,969	7,004
Year	7	8	9	10	11	12	13
Annual increase (%)	0.500	0.500	0.500	0.500	0.250	0.250	0.250
Cumulative increase (%)	4.65	5.17	5.70	6.23	6.49	6.76	7.03
Demand (Ro-Ro units/year)	7,039	7,074	7,109	7,145	7,163	7,181	7,199
Year	14	15	16	17	18	19	20
Annual increase (%)	0.250	0.250	0.250	0.250	0.250	0.250	0.250
Cumulative increase (%)	7.29	7.56	7.83	8.10	8.37	8.64	8.91
Demand (Ro-Ro units/year)	7,217	7,235	7,253	7,271	7,289	7,307	7,325
Year	21	22	23	24	25		
Annual increase (%)	0.125	0.125	0.125	0.125	0.125		
Cumulative increase (%)	9.05	9.19	9.32	9.46	9.60		
Demand (Ro-Ro units/year)	7,335	7,344	7,353	7,362	7,371		

References

1. European Parliament resolution on short sea shipping (2004/2161(INI)) OJ C 33E, 2006/02/09, p. 142–146. https://eurlex.europa.eu/legalcontent/EN/TXT/?uri=celex%3A52005IP0086. Accessed 30 Apr 2020
2. Communication from the Commission to the European Parliament, the Council, the European Economic and Social Committee and the Committee of the Regions - Strategic goals and recommendations for the EU's maritime transport policy until 2018, 2009/01/21. https://eur-lex.europa.eu/legal-content/EN/TXT/?uri=celex:52009DC0008. Accessed 30 Apr 2020
3. Fancello, G., Serra, P., Mancini, S.: A network design optimization problem for Ro-Ro freight transport in the Tyrrhenian area. Transp. Prob. 14(4), 63–75 (2019)
4. Fancello, G., Pani, C., Serra, P., Fadda, P.: Port cooperation policies in the mediterranean basin: an experimental approach using cluster analysis. Transp. Res. Procedia 3, 700–709 (2014)
5. Priemus, H., Flyvbjerg, B., Van Wee, B.: Decision-Making on Mega-Projects: Cost-Benefit Analysis, Planning and Innovation. Edward Elgar Publishing, Cheltenham (2008)
6. Jones, H., Moura, F., Domingos, T.: Transport infrastructure project evaluation using cost-benefit analysis. Procedia Soc. Behav. Sci. 111, 400–409 (2014)
7. Vaghi, C., Lucietti, L.: Costs and benefits of speeding up reporting formalities in maritime transport. Transp. Res. Procedia 14, 213–222 (2016)
8. Cavana, R.Y.: Coastal shipping policy in New Zealand: the case for an empirical cost benefit analysis. Marit. Policy Manag. 21(2), 161–172 (1994)
9. Mange, E.: Short sea shipping cost benefit analysis. In: Proceedings of the European Transport Conference, Association for European Transport, Strasbourg, France, pp. 18–20 (2006)
10. Andersson, P., Ivehammar, P.: Dynamic route planning in the baltic sea region–a cost-benefit analysis based on AIS data. Marit. Econ. Logistics 19(4), 631–649 (2017)
11. Giuliano, G., Knatz, G., Hutson, N., Sys, C., Vanelslander, T., Carlan, V.: Decision-making for maritime innovation investments: the significance of cost benefit and cost effectiveness analysis. Research paper 2016-001 (2016)
12. European Commission. Elaboration of the East Mediterranean Motorways of the sea Master Plan. East Mediterranean master plan of the Motorways of the sea. Deliverable 5.2 (2009). https://ec.europa.eu/transport/sites/transport/files/modes/maritime/studies/doc/mos/east_med_deliverable5.pdf
13. Feo, M., Espino, R., Garcia, L.: A stated preference analysis of Spanish freight forwarders modal choice on the south-west Europe Motorway of the sea. Transp. Policy 18(1), 60–67 (2011)
14. Serra, P., Fadda, P., Fancello, G.: Investigating the potential mitigating role of network design measures for reducing the environmental impact of maritime chains: the mediterranean case. Case Stud. Transp. Policy 8(2), 263–280 (2020)
15. Holland, M.: Damages per tonne emission of PM2. 5, NH3, SO2, NOx and VOCs from each EU25 Member State (excluding Cyprus) and surrounding seas. AEA Technology Environment, United Kingdom (2005)
16. Fancello, G., Serra, P., Schintu, A., Zoratti, A.: Performance evaluation of a tracking system for intermodal traffic: an experimentation in the Tyrrhenian area. Eur. Transp. 76(8), 1825–3997 (2020)

On the Automation of Ports and Logistics Chains in the Adriatic Region

Luca Braidotti[1,2(✉)] ⓘ, Marco Mazzarino[3], Maurizio Cociancich[2],
and Vittorio Bucci[1] ⓘ

[1] Department of Engineering and Architecture, University of Trieste,
via A. Valerio 10, 34127 Trieste, Italy
lbraidotti@units.it
[2] TeDIS Program, Sustainable Logistics Unit, Venice International University,
Isola di S. Servolo, 30133 Venice, Italy
[3] Department of Architecture and Arts, Università IUAV di Venezia,
Ca' Tron, Santa Croce 1957, 30135 Venice, Italy

Abstract. Recently, automation is gaining an even more important role in the port and maritime industry. In particular, several technological innovations are changing both the freight and passenger transport sector. The introduction of these technologies in port terminals (smart ports) require involved stakeholders to adapt their asset and organisations in order to improve the economic competitiveness in global markets. The geographical context where new technologies are put in place can also influence their deployment and foreseen impacts. Hence, in order to take the proper decisions at a strategic level and maximize the positive effects in a selected scenario, a feasibility analysis is essential. In the present study, this challenge is addressed for the Adriatic region by proposing a procedure for evaluating and selecting the most promising innovations. Several relevant stakeholders from the selected area are inquired to assess the relevance and deployment difficulties for a set of new technologies dealing with automation in port areas. Then, the impacts on technical operation and labour market are assessed, thus, providing valuable information to support the regional organisations in facing the change and deploying procedures to be potentially replicated in other geographical areas.

Keywords: Automation · Smart ports · Adriatic region · Strategic decisions

1 Introduction

In the last decades, the port and maritime industry has experienced a radical change due to the digital revolution, which is still ongoing. Focusing on port terminals and on the maritime transport chain, digitalisation offers significant opportunities for improvement. Hence, the involved organizations (e.g. port authorities, transport and logistics providers, shipping companies, etc.) should be able to understand the change and gain advantage from its exploitation. Generally, the introduction of innovations can be of two types, e.g., incremental and disruptive. The first one consists of small improvements on existing products and services. Considering the transport sector, characterised

© Springer Nature Switzerland AG 2020
O. Gervasi et al. (Eds.): ICCSA 2020, LNCS 12255, pp. 96–111, 2020.
https://doi.org/10.1007/978-3-030-58820-5_8

by a large set of organisations competing in a global market, incremental innovations are essential to maintain a competitive position. On the other hand, disruptive innovations are the most radical and revolutionary ones [1]. In the first stage, they represent costly solutions which serve a niche in the market. Then, if they reach a wide application becoming a mainstream product, they perform the "disruption", thereby introducing strong changes in processes, procedures or replacing previous state-of-the-art solutions. In this context, automation is one of the main innovation trends applicable to ports and maritime transport chains [2]. Automation enables to perform a process or procedure with minimal human assistance. Automation progresses through the development of technology and its application in order to control and monitor the production and distribution of goods and services, while performing tasks that were previously carried out by humans [3]. Ever since the introduction of automated stacking cranes at the Rotterdam Container Terminal in 1990, automation in ports has firmly progressed [4]. Automation has developed into almost all terminal functions, ranging from sea-side to land-side; from ship-to-shore activities straight across the terminal and including the handling activities related to the land transport modes.

New technologies in this field are now emerging, thus, it is essential to early identify and develop the most promising ones. The present work aims to address this topic in a specific geographical area: the Adriatic region. The main objective is to select the most relevant automation technologies for the area and assess the issues and risks possibly hindering their deployment. The work has been carried out by enquiring experts and relevant stakeholders from the Adriatic region. Eventually, the study aims to guide the regional organisations in the selection and deployment of innovations, fostering the automation of the port terminals and the whole maritime transport chain.

2   Methodology

The present study has been carried out based on the methodology drafted in [2]. It is divided into three main phases: desk research, innovation ranking and impact analyses.

In the first phase, desk research has been carried out to identify the main innovations concerning automation, which might have an impact in the Adriatic Region. In this process, several experts, stakeholders and public authorities have been inquired applying a multidisciplinary approach in order to thoroughly investigate both the passenger and freight transport sectors. Emphasis has been put on different aspects, e.g. automation in port facilities, automation of the logistic chain and development of unmanned technologies and vehicles. All the selected innovations have been collected in a common repository including a brief description of the technology.

In the second phase, a questionnaire has been prepared and submitted to a set of relevant stakeholders from the Adriatic Region. The objective of the questionnaire was to rank the innovations selected in the previous phase by importance and to assess their deployment easiness/difficulty. A five-step scale has been adopted for innovation relevance, namely:

1. not at all relevant;
2. not very relevant;

3. no opinion;
4. relevant;
5. extremely relevant.

The stakeholders have also been required to justify their answers by highlighting the benefits foreseen for each technology. The efforts required for innovation deployment in the Adriatic Region have been defined according to another five-step scale:

1. very difficult to implement;
2. somehow difficult to implement;
3. no opinion;
4. somehow easy to implement;
5. very easy to implement.

Motivations have been required in order to highlight the main obstacles hindering technology deployment in the selected area.

According to the rank coming out from stakeholders' responses, the most promising innovations for the Adriatic area have been selected for more detailed analyses, which have been carried out in the third phase. Here, impact analyses have been conducted focusing on both the impacts on technical operations and on the labour market. The impact analyses have been carried out by consulting experts and they include brief guidelines for the regional stakeholders on how to react and be ready for the change. In the impact analysis, the current scenario is compared with the expected one after the innovation deployment, focusing on the following main aspects:

- Consequences/repercussions: assessment of the expected changes due to innovation deployment;
- Required modifications: assessment of what should be modified to cope with expected changes;
- Potential risks: an assessment of potential risks, e.g., identifying most problematic changes from technical, organizational and stakeholder viewpoints.

Hence, the impact analyses will help stakeholders to rapidly react and face the digital revolution in port and maritime passenger/freight transport, thus, fostering the development of the automation technologies in the Adriatic region.

3 Technologies and Ranking

In the present section, the innovations identified mainly through desk research are briefly presented. Then, the ranking results are provided for both the relevance and deployment easiness/difficulty based on the opinion of several stakeholders of the Adriatic region.

3.1 Selected Technologies

The innovations selected through desk research are hereinafter briefly described. They can be divided into five macro-areas: smart passenger terminals, smart freight terminals, automated warehouses, logistic chain automation and autonomous vehicles.

Automation is expected to be even more applied in the passenger sector in port facilities as well as onboard of large passenger vessels. In the near future, the development of robotics could move the simplest jobs (e.g. cooking, cleaning, serving, etc.) from humans to robots by developing the so-called *Unmanned services.* Seemingly, automation can improve passenger management activities so as to simplify boarding and unboarding operations. In this context, smart sensors (biometrics), Internet of Things (IoT) solutions, computer vision and personal mobile devices can be exploited to develop an Automatic *Digital identification of passengers,* which can reduce the need for manual authentication and identification. Finally, automation can enable costs saving and lower environmental impacts through the adoption of *Automated lighting and air-conditioning systems*. In internal spaces, the lighting system and the load of the conditioning system can be optimised based on the actual number of people detected through sensors, thus, reducing the global energy demand.

In freight terminals, especially container ones, automation can play an even more significant role, simplifying cargo handling and reducing the waste of time and resources. *Unmanned bulk terminals* are already in operation (e.g. in Shanghai) and also *Fully automated container terminals* are in rapid development, integrating several different technologies already available on the market [5]. These ranges from *Remote cranes, Smart connected lift trucks* to *Automatic Stacking Cranes (ASC), Automatic lashing platforms* moving forward fully *Automatic container carriers/truck handling systems*. All these technologies are usually managed by Terminal Operating Systems (TOSs), which play an essential role in the integration of the adopted automated technologies. However, container terminal automation is still at relatively early stage since, currently, only 1% of terminals are fully automated and 2% are semi-automated [6]. Still considering container terminals, other innovative automated systems for container storing and handling are present on the market. Among them, one of the most promising is the *High Bay Storage Systems (BOXBAY)*, where containers are placed in individual racks instead of stacking them on top of each other in order to make each one directly accessible [7]. Technology can also foster the environmental impact reduction in freight terminals. To this end, *Electrified lift solutions* and, in general, electric vehicles inside the port area can be adopted. Moreover, Remotely Piloted Aircraft Systems (RPAS) can be used to measure the emissions of sulphur determining whether a particular vessel is compliant with the rules in force. *RPAS Drones* equipped with a gas sensor, known as a "sniffer", can fly in the ship's plume to estimate the amount of sulphur in its fuel; then, the collected data are forwarded to public authorities for review.

Warehouses are critical nodes in the transportation and logistics processes. Their automation can increase the efficiency of freight logistics substantially [8]. For instance, the *coupling of voice technologies with Warehouse Management System (WMS)* is growing in the number of adoptions, since it increases personnel efficiency during picking operations. The avoidance of looking at monitors and the feeling of listening instructions by a human voice decrease the alienation and foster the speed, allowing the operator to use both hands. In many cases, completely *Unmanned warehouses* are already in place. They exploit autonomous robots capable to move mobile storage racks weighing from 500 to 1500 kg and controlled by the WMS. Finally, the adoption of *Drones connected to the WMS* has been recently proposed [9], especially for periodic inventory procedures. Thanks to drone technology, it is possible to check the consistency of stock more frequently and during the night, when there is no/less activity inside the warehouse.

Among the analysed automation technologies, the most challenging are the ones devoted to improving the automation of the whole logistic chain, which include ports as main nodes but it is extended to a wider port community including shippers, shipping companies, multimodal transport operators etc. [10]. In this context, the first selected solution is *Event data certification* that manages scheduled data validations within a database. Information is added to the database by importing it from third-party technologies or manually, then checked for accuracy and certification. The program generates a checklist for data verification. The data certification is done following a specific certification calendar and the certification activities are created and assigned automatically. Focusing on port operations, the management of vessel arrival and departure times is one of the key factors for port logistics operations as well as for the whole maritime transport chain [11]. Estimation of arrival and departures times are essential for operations planning on all levels and departments. *Estimated Time of Arrival (ETA)* technology allows very accurate predictions of ships' arrival and departure time, thus, increasing the efficiency of all the port operations (berthing, cargo handling) and enabling resource allocation optimisation. In addition, data provided by ETA can also be integrated into third parties applications in order to optimise the other stages of the logistic chain. For instance, transport providers can gain benefit from the introduction of *Deliverables Planning* systems based on machine learning algorithms [12]. In fact, better planning of deliveries based also on real-time and predicted traffic conditions can help to save travel time/cost and improve reliability through the selection of pre-trip and en-route travel routes. For these systems, the quality and the reliability of input data is essential, thus, requiring thrusted external sources. In general, greater benefits can be obtained enhancing the data exchange between all the actors along the transport chain. In fact, the transport of a single good usually involves a large number of different organisations. With automated processes to exchange reliable information, the *maritime transport chain* becomes a network where carriers, ports and freight forwarders are interconnected in the movement of goods. Customers and stakeholders in the port and maritime industry demand more speed, lower cost, more transparency, higher security, lower environmental impact, higher efficiency, which are the main metrics for digital project success. These goals can be achieved by streamlining all these aspects of the transport chain process. Technologies such as blockchain [13] or a distributed electronic ledger system can allow transactions to be verified autonomously by every party involved in cargo transportation. Another promising technology exploits IoT devices [14], which are already present in several parts of the transport chain, either as smart sensors, controllers, embedded devices in cargo manipulation machines and even ship themselves. IoT devices provide the necessary intelligence for improving handling operations and risk mitigation. Hence, the improved automated data exchange along the transport chain can help to face the most critical issues in the transportation industry, such as long paperwork paths, inefficient use of resources and an increasing cargo amount.

Finally, special attention is due to another disruptive innovation that is expected to have a deep impact on port operations and navigation in the next decade: the autonomous vehicles. In the near future, terminals shall be capable to cope with different types of autonomous vehicles. First, *Autonomous vehicles confined in the port area* can be more easily adopted, including cargo handling systems or busses in the freight and passenger sector respectively [15]. Moreover, in case of widespread application of *Autonomous Trucks/Busses* outside the port areas, the terminals shall define specific procedures and processes to deal with them [16]. Eventually, the fast development of autonomous vessels represents the most relevant challenge for port facilities. This concept can be developed with different degrees of automation up to the *Unmanned ships*: a vessel without any crewmember onboard, based on completely automated or remote-controlled systems. *Autonomous vessels for coastal navigation* are already in operation for short repetitive routes, but a wider application in near future is expected, provided that some open issues, mainly legal and regulatory, will be solved [17]. However, the economical benefits (ship's life cycle cost could decrease by minimum 5–22% mainly due to fuel and crew cost reduction [18]) and safety-related benefits (reduction of casualties connected to human error) will certainly lead to a wider application of remote-controlled vessels [19] and finally to fully autonomous ones. From a terminal viewpoint, this can foster the introduction of other collateral technologies such as *Autonomous tugboats* and *Automated mooring systems*, which could be easily interfaced with the autonomous vessels approaching or living the berth.

3.2   Questionnaire Results

The selected innovations have been used to prepare the questionnaire, which has been submitted to regional stakeholders. Responses have been collected from 24 organizations, divided into different categories as shown in Fig. 1. Most of them are port authorities from Italy and Croatia, including the port authorities of Venice, Rijeka, Sibenik and Rovinj.

The ranking results are provided in Table 1. The technologies are ranked by importance I, which is the mean of the stakeholders' judgements based on the five-step scale. In addition, the assessment of deployment difficulty/easiness D is reported along with the standard deviations σ. The colour scale improves the table readability: cells' colour ranges from red to green corresponding to scale values 1 and 5 respectively. The results have also been plotted on a scatter diagram (Fig. 2), providing a more effective graphical representation. It is worth to notice that all the technologies are located in the upper area of the diagram corresponding to high-relevance innovations. This confirms the effectiveness of the selection process carried out during desk research phase. In Fig. 3 a more detailed view is provided of the upper part of the scatter diagram. Numbers in Fig. 3 refer to the ranking (Table 1).

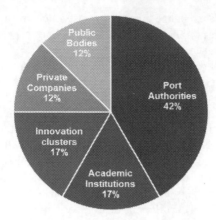

Fig. 1. Stakeholders involved in technologies ranking.

Table 1. Global Rank of innovations

Rank	Innovation	I	σ_I	D	σ_D
1	Maritime transport chain	4.35	0.65	2.70	0.95
2	ETA	4.32	0.76	3.74	0.99
3	Automatic digital identification of passengers	4.21	0.61	2.74	0.85
4	Deliverables Planning	4.21	0.69	3.50	0.90
5	Electrified Lift Solution	4.12	0.83	2.76	0.81
6	Autonomous Trucks/Busses	4.05	0.79	2.43	0.90
7	Automatic container carriers/truck handling systems	4.00	0.69	2.76	0.94
8	Automated Lighting and air-conditioning systems	4.00	0.79	3.44	1.06
9	Smart Connected Lift Trucks	3.93	0.85	3.19	0.88
10	Fully Automated Container Terminal	3.90	0.97	1.95	1.00
11	Unmanned warehouse	3.75	1.04	2.70	0.95
12	Autonomous vessels for coastal navigation	3.68	1.13	2.37	0.81
13	ASC	3.53	0.78	2.65	0.84
14	Unmanned bulk cargo terminal	3.50	0.96	2.18	0.78
15	Unmanned ships/autonomous vessel	3.45	1.20	2.30	0.78
16	Unmanned services	3.41	1.03	2.50	1.17
17	High Bay Storage Systems (BOXBAY)	3.38	0.86	2.94	0.97
18	Autonomous vehicles in port area	3.33	0.94	2.72	0.87
19	WMS with voice integration	3.32	0.86	3.11	1.12
20	Drones for WMS	3.30	1.00	2.70	0.90
21	Remote Cranes	3.26	0.87	3.24	1.03
22	RPAS drones to check ship emissions	3.22	1.23	2.82	0.86
23	Autonomous tugboats	3.19	1.14	1.71	0.76
24	ALP	3.19	0.81	2.80	0.65
25	Automated mooring technologies	3.16	1.18	2.11	0.72
26	Event data certification	2.90	0.92	3.14	0.89

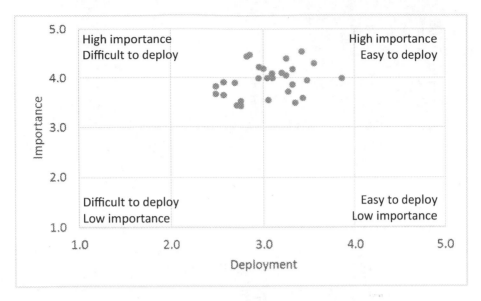

Fig. 2. Importance vs deployment easiness/difficulty

It can be concluded that no clear correlation exists between importance and deployment's easiness/difficulty, since a trend in the scatter diagram does not emerge. Remarkably, groups of innovations having comparable importance can be identified. However, some differences among stakeholders' opinions have led to quite high values of standard deviations related to innovations' importance, thus, partially reducing the significance of the ranking.

According to stakeholders, the most interesting innovations are *Maritime transport chain*, *ETA*, *Automatic digital identification of passengers* and *Deliverables Planning*. It can be noted that all these innovations deal with the automation of the logistics chain in both freight and passenger sectors. Thus, in general, stakeholders from the Adriatic region are strongly interested in such a topic, rather than autonomous vehicles or other automated devices (cranes, lifts, drones, etc.). The inference is confirmed by the group including the least innovations by importance, which are: *RPAS drones to check ship emissions*, *Autonomous tugboats*, *ALP*, *Automated mooring technologies* and, with a quite large gap, *Event data certification*, whose impacts are considered very limited compared to the other options related to transport chain automation.

The results related to innovations' deployment difficulty in the Adriatic Region present a wider spectrum compared to relevance-related ones, while an almost equal level of standard deviations is observed. Hence, deployment easiness/difficulty presents a lower uncertainty on overall stakeholders' preferences. The most easy-to-implement innovation is *ETA*, which largely outdistances the next ones: *Deliverables Planning* and *Automated Lighting and air-conditioning systems*. Hence, *ETA* and *Deliverables Planning* can be considered the most promising innovations among the selected ones in the region, since both show high importance and easy deployment, according to stakeholders.

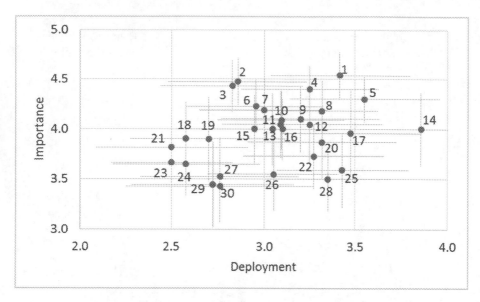

Fig. 3. Detail of importance vs deployment easiness/difficulty; numbers refer to ranking (Table 1); bars refer to a 95% confidence interval

On the other hand, the most difficult-to-deploy technologies are *Fully Automated Container Terminal* and *Autonomous tugboats*, which both require a strong effort to develop dedicated algorithms related to the implementation scenario.

4 Impact Analyses

In the present section, the impact analyses are reported focusing on three of the most important innovations selected for the Adriatic region according to the stakeholders' opinion. As previously stated, the impacts of automation on both technical operations and the labour market are here considered in the freight sector, which has been generally considered by regional stakeholders more relevant than passenger transport.

4.1 Maritime Transport Chain

Global logistics still relies on a huge amount of paperwork. For their operations, the information in such documents has strong influence on the execution speed, the efficiency and the operations planning capability in the transport chain. Anything that can be done to improve the present condition can have a heavy impact on the whole industry. Document digitalization, electronic data exchange, integration of smart sensors, data standardization, visibility and cargo traceability through real-time services like blockchain and other technologies can strongly improve the services in the maritime transport chain. All these technologies have their own benefits, but they can even multiply, if combined in innovative ways, for instance by adopting machine learning and AI-based algorithms on data coming from IoT devices, shared through blockchains with different organisations. Together, they open new opportunities for management, cost reduction and other areas. Innovations for the maritime transport chain does not include just one or single technology, but rather the combination of new services that complement and in some situations supplement existing systems and services. As a consequence, processes will change, having repercussions on both the technical environment and the required human engagement. The main benefits will be lower resources demand, more effective planning, errors reduction and improved transparency. These changes do not necessarily require large modification of existing information systems. This is an advantage since often very large and revolutionary projects would be too expensive and too disruptive for the normal operations, resulting in a difficult integration in the existing logistic chain. Hence, the introduction of innovative technologies in steps should be preferred, e.g. introduce additional services or interfaces capable to speed up, optimize or eliminate time and resource-consuming tasks (in many cases, innovation can replace some part of the process or a legacy technology).

Necessary modifications to implement proposed innovations and new technologies depend on many factors and can range from a relatively small addition to existing management systems in one particular organization to a relatively big shift in management approach. It depends on the maturity and the structure of the existing technical solution and its flexibility in accommodating new data and process modifications. Considering present systems, the biggest issue will be in particular their relatively fixed scope and inability to support a modified process. This should be carefully evaluated when planning the introduction of a new service or solution to better integrate into the maritime transport chain.

Innovative technologies can bring new beneficial opportunities to the maritime transport chain, but also several risks. First, it shall be noted that smaller initiatives and projects might not outlive their pilot stage and become a widespread solution. Most experts agree that innovative technologies (for instance, blockchain) will be successful only with a comprehensive and widespread application [20]. In order to succeed they have to be accepted by all stakeholders involved in the process: shipping lines, terminal operators, manufacturers, banks, insurers, brokers and port authorities. In such a case, the prospects are very promising: documents could be processed in minutes rather than hours or even days. Another open issue is related to the existence of a single or multiple maritime transport networks handling cargo transportation routes. Not all stakeholders might deploy the same technology solutions and platforms. They might adopt different messaging or networks, rising questions about interoperability and/or standardization. Related to this concern is also the choice of closed rather than open chains. Until now, the success of logistics chain solutions was fostered by "permissionless" chains with no central authority granting or prohibiting the access to publicly accessible data. In the maritime industry, this may be a challenge which will have to be addressed. There is also a variety of different languages, laws and organizations involved in moving cargoes, which might lead to a standardisation processes' slowdown.

From a labour market viewpoint, the maritime transportation chain automation will trigger changes in the needs of human resources for supporting modified and new processes. Digitalization of the documents and electronic data exchange will reduce the need for simple manual entry of data and staff necessary to handle these processes. At the same time, innovations in the transport chain will create new job positions with different skill sets. For instance, high demand for skilled people is expected capable to perform advanced resources planning using modern planning tools and to handle intelligent smart devices (e.g. IoT sensors). It is very possible, that the new process will require a reorganization of the work to better exploit its opportunities.

Concerning the risks associated with employees and the labour market, they again depend on the type of innovation applied. Generally, a new skill set will be needed, including specific knowledge of both transportation best practices and particular technology use, representing a challenge for new employments. Another risk is the ability of the organization to re-train the existing personnel in order to utilize the innovative solution regularly and in the proper way. A wrong approach to the change can result in dislike and ultimately the rejection of the new procedures by employees [21]. This issue should be assessed with care during a specific project planning in order to define the appropriate steps and to engage the existing personnel in the change process.

4.2   Vessel ETA

Introduction of advanced estimation of vessel departure and arrival times can improve the port capability of planning berth utilization and optimize all supporting logistic processes, which depend on presence vessels in port. At the same time, the new technology and process will have a beneficial impact on transport resources utilization, including lower waiting time for berthing, cargo loading and unloading. The goal of ETA is to achieve "right on time" management regarding the planning of arrivals, departures and connected services. These estimates are useful for all actors within the port community and transportation chain, being the base for planning their own operations, better exploit available resources and decrease waiting time.

Technology for better estimation of arrival and departure times can be based on metering the progress of transport (arrival) and cargo loading/unloading (departure) processes and comparing the remaining transportation journey or manipulation of cargo towards previously executed (metered) operations. In this way, the estimations can be performed more often and reflect the factors that may change previously calculated estimates. Thus, applying machine learning algorithms, the estimated arrival and departure times will become more accurate and similar to actual times. This approach requires measuring and calculating new estimates, which are then forwarded over common messaging systems to interested parties. On the receiving end, the planning solutions shall be able to process estimates updates, giving to the operators more accurate data for decision and operations' approval. It is preferred that the communication of ETA is compliant to the existing standards, initiatives and project in the maritime sector, like communication and messaging platform MCP (Maritime Connectivity Platform) and IEC 61174:2015 Maritime navigation and radiocommunication equipment and systems. This compliancy can ease the deployment of the ETA and its adoption by a wider number of organisation, which is essential to spread the benefits towards the whole port community.

The main risk for the preparation of estimated arrivals and departures of vessels lays in data accuracy, on which the estimates are based. If the metered data is not reliable, the estimates cannot be accurate and trustworthy. The solution has to be calibrated and monitored to gain adequate accuracy. At the same time, another risk is the overreliance on the estimated arrival and departure times than will be calculated with ETA solution. In case the estimates for any reasons cannot be available or are missing, an alternative source of estimates and verification should be in place to avoid that processes relying on these data are not misled in wrong activities (example: resources reserved and then not used,). Moreover, the methods and standards for estimates calculation might be different from solution to solution, port to port, thus, not immediately comparable. Methods standardization for data collection data and estimation at least in a regional context would be beneficial to mitigate this risk.

Considering the labour market, advanced technologies for the estimation of arrival and departure times are not expected to have strong repercussions on the labour market. Nevertheless, provided that the ETA is reliable and not subject to frequent radical changes, it can improve human resource allocation. Operators will be able to better plan the resources, their utilization and react to external factors that affect changes in departure and arrival times. Finally, as for each technology innovation, the deployment of ETA is expected to increase the demand for specialised personnel capable to maintain and monitor the new systems.

4.3 Deliverables Planning

Deliverables planning solutions can have a strong impact on the efficiency of supply and transport chain enhancing the resources utilization considering the changing conditions during the transportation of the goods. Deliverables planning, providing automatic suggestion or selection of travel routes before the trip and even during the trip, can save costs, decrease the transport time and achieve a smaller environmental impact on the communities affected by the transportation of goods. The proposed solutions can be easily linked to the existing port and maritime information systems, both as sources and targets. The existing operation management solutions can be relatively easy to integrate with new decision planning system, enhancing the data exchange among different organisations within the port community.

The quality of the data provided by a deliverable planning solution depends on the frequency and the reliability of data sources. These may include publicly available data, like traffic conditions, weather data, available transport capacity as well as data available in the transportation management solution, like estimated times of arrivals, number and types of cargo, transportation vehicles. To assemble a successful deliverables planning solution, all this data must be collected, normalized and forwarded to the decision process. This includes developing interfaces for the acquisition of the data from existing sources (e.g. ETA, PCS systems, cargo manifests, etc.) as well as new sources and sensors (location data, transport/stowage capacity monitoring, etc.). Compared to the planning solutions adopted nowadays, innovative deliverables planning can change the suggestions more frequently than today's business practice. Transportation providers will be required to respond to changing requests and adapt their processes. The possibility of frequent delivery changes will have to be verified in the existing operations management systems and processes, in order to assure their response capability to the new requests and still fulfil their service in the supply chain process. New metrics will have to be defined and aligned among interested parties to maximize the potential of changing plans.

The success of Delivery Planning can be achieved only if all the conditions for its usage are met. On the sources side, some routes to a particular port might not be able to provide the required data. This could limit the effectiveness of the whole planning process. Moreover, some legal issues regarding the long-term availability of data could also arise, since a large part of useful data for deliverables planning comes from commercial and closed (not-public) systems. Hence, a solid contractual base is essential to assure the constant availability and quality of data. In addition, too many disruptions in this area can have a significant effect on the results coming from a deliverables planning system. In fact, the new planning tool might not be aligned with the real deadlines/latest time for changes in delivery methods and, thus, might disrupt the whole process. To mitigate such a critical issue, a gradual approach towards desired goals can verify that the newly developed methodology is reliable and has a positive effect. Finally, flexibility (contractual and technical) might also limit the deliverables planning system usability. Transportation providers shall be able to adapt and change plans as results of the system outputs.

Regarding the labour market, the main consequence of the deliverables planning development would be the sensible reduction in the number of people needed to manage the journeys of a fleet of containers and/or semitrailers, but the fewer operative staff that remain employed shall be more skilled and trained. If implemented on a full scale with a real-time traffic information system and an integrated rail/ferry multimodal booking platform, organizations would become more efficient. A full-scale system would allow a single operator to give more than a hundred orders per minute, managing at the same time an exponentially higher number of communications to suppliers and customers than it would have been possible to handle with a traditional email/phone calls method. For this reason, operators will be required to become more managerial and skilful in order to intervene only in out-of-order situations and to monitor the progress of the day-to-day schedule.

Hence, a radical change to the organisation structure is required, including a fully integrated vertical system, allowing the operational base of the organization e.g. drivers, warehouse staff, terminal staff etc. to directly receive real-time instructions from the system controller, while the system controller would need to receive a full set of key monitoring variables in order to be able to tackle potential anomalies and to check the daily progress of the operations.

The main risk for the labour market would be a distorted use of deliverables planning systems by organizations. In particular, these platforms are meant to help operational staff to take decisions on a day-to-day planning and re-routing activity while some organizations may take advantage of the automated process in order to simply reduce staff, to cut internal costs and to make jobs less repetitive. In an extreme scenario, it is even possible to evaluate an AI system running the deliverables planning system alone, without any help or support by human staff. This kind of risk already came out in big companies, where the use of algorithms could become the best solution available on the market for high volumes of traffic. However, for intermodal traffic, considering the high level of involvement of human operators at all stages of the value chain, the regulatory scheme should intervene in order to avoid human-free, AI-run deliverables planning systems, in favour of mixed human + AI ones.

5 Conclusions

In the present study, the most promising technologies regarding automation in the port and maritime industry with regards to the Adriatic region have been identified. The assessment of their relevance and importance showed a clear interest of regional organisations for the innovations in the freight sector, aiming to a more automated maritime transport and logistics chain. In particular, the enhancement of the data collection and exchange systems among the involved parties is identified as a priority, as confirmed by the technologies deemed most relevant: *Maritime transport chain*, *ETA*, and *Deliverables Planning*. These technologies are not considered very difficult to be deployed according to the inquired stakeholders, but require the agreement of a large number of different parties in order to assure the success of an automation project. Hence, future efforts are required in order to build a broader port community committed to the exploitation of new transport chain automation technologies. On the other hand, the infrastructure/vehicle automation in port facilities is neither considered an easy task to be implemented in the Adriatic area nor - according to the stakeholders ranking by relevance - a priority.

The impact analyses carried out on the most promising innovations dealing with maritime logistic chains show the benefits for organizations after their deployment, while providing an assessment of risks and related mitigation measures. In particular, as for automation, the main common risk is related to the reduction in the number of non-specialised jobs. At the same time, the demand for skilled personnel with specific competencies will grow. Hence, it is essential to properly plan re-training activities during the introduction of new technologies to assure their acceptance among the employees.

Our results can be valuable for organisations which are planning automation projects in the selected geographical area. However, more detailed analyses are still required to assure a successful implementation. For instance, Strengths Weaknesses Opportunities and Threats (SWOT) analyses can be the next recommended step to be carried out on the most promising innovations. Moreover, further research aiming to the definition of regional roadmaps to increase port automation is still required and new technologies adoption could be fostered by carrying out pilot projects testing the most promising solutions in a limited environment. In conclusion, the proposed methodology has been here applied in the Adriatic region and it can be easily adopted and replicated in other geographical areas and in other technological contexts to foster the innovation among the local stakeholders and align their priorities.

Acknowledgements. This work was entirely financed by "DigLogs - Digitalising Logistics Process" Interrog Italy-Croatia 2014–2020 project.

References

1. Christensen, C.M.: The Innovator's Dilemma: When New Technologies Cause Great Firms to Fail. Management of Innovation and Change. Harvard Business School Press, Boston (1997)
2. Mazzarino, M., et al.: On the digitalisation processes in the adriatic region. In: Proceedings of the 3rd International Conference of Nautical and Maritime Culture – CNM 2019, Naples, Italy, pp. 180–190 (2019). https://doi.org/10.3233/PMST190019
3. Gupta, A.K., Arora, S.K.: Industrial Automation and Robotics. Laxmi Publications, New Delhi (2009)
4. Zrnić, N., Petković, Z., Bošnjak, S.: Automation of ship-to-shore container cranes: a review of state-of-the-art. FME Trans. **33**(3), 111–121 (2005)
5. Kim, K.H., Günther, H.-O. (eds.): Container Terminals and Cargo Systems. Springer, Heidelberg (2007). https://doi.org/10.1007/978-3-540-49550-5
6. Wang, P., Mileski, J.P., Zeng, Q.: Alignments between strategic content and process structure: the case of container terminal service process automation. Marit. Econ. Logistics **21**, 543–558 (2019)
7. Brinkmann, B.: Operations systems of container terminals: a compendious overview. In: Böse, J. (eds.) Handbook of Terminal Planning. Operations Research/Computer Science Interfaces Series, vol. 49, pp. 25–39. Springer, New York (2011). https://doi.org/10.1007/978-1-4419-8408-1_2
8. Baker, P., Halim, Z.: An exploration of warehouse automation implementations: cost, service and flexibility issues. Supply Chain Manag. Int. J. **12**(2), 12–138 (2007)
9. Xu, L., Kamat, V.R., Menassa, C.: Automatic extraction of 1D barcodes from video scans for drone-assisted inventory management in warehousing applications. Int. J. Logistics Res. Appl. **21**(3), 243–258 (2018)
10. United Nations Conference on Trade and Development: Review of Maritime Transport 2019. United Nations Publications, New York, USA (2019)
11. Jahn, C., Scheidweiler, T.: Port call optimization by estimating ships' time of arrival. In: Freitag, M., Kotzab, H., Pannek, J. (eds.) LDIC 2018. LNL, pp. 172–177. Springer, Cham (2018). https://doi.org/10.1007/978-3-319-74225-0_23
12. Wojtusiak, J., Warden, T., Herzog, O.: The learnable evolution model in agent-based delivery optimization. Memetic Comput. **4**, 165–181 (2012)
13. Loklindt, C., Moeller, M.P., Kinra, A.: How blockchain could be implemented for exchanging documentation in the shipping industry. In: Freitag, M., Kotzab, H., Pannek, J. (eds.) LDIC 2018. LNL, pp. 194–198. Springer, Cham (2018). https://doi.org/10.1007/978-3-319-74225-0_27
14. Muñuzuri, J., Onieva, L., Cortés, P., Guadix, J.: Using IoT data and applications to improve port-based intermodal supply chains. Comput. Ind. Eng. **139** (2020)
15. Bahnes, N., Kechar, B., Haffaf, H.: Co-operation between intelligent autonomous vehicles to enhance container terminal operations. J. Innovation Digit. Ecosys. **3**(1), 22–29 (2016)
16. Flämig, H.: Autonomous vehicles and autonomous driving in freight transport. In: Maurer, M., Gerdes, J.C., Lenz, B., Winner, H. (eds.) Autonomous Driving. LNL, pp. 365–385. Springer, Heidelberg (2016). https://doi.org/10.1007/978-3-662-48847-8_18
17. Hogg, T., Ghosh, S.: Autonomous merchant vessels: examination of factors that impact the effective implementation of unmanned ships. Aust. J. Marit. Ocean Affairs **8**(3), 206–222 (2016)

18. Fiedler, R., Bosse, C., Gehlken, D., Brümmerstedt, K., Burmeister, H.S.: Autonomous Vehicles' Impact On Port Infrastructure Requirements. Fraunhofer Center for Maritime Logistics and Services CML, Hamburg (2019)
19. Ghaderi, H.: Autonomous technologies in short sea shipping: trends, feasibility and implications. Transp. Rev. **39**(1), 152–173 (2019)
20. Gausdal, A.H., Czachorowski, K.V., Solesvik, M.Z.: Applying blockchain technology: evidence from Norwegian companies. Sustainability **10**(6), 1985 (2018)
21. Autor, D.H.: Why are there still so many jobs? The history and future of workplace automation. J. Econ. Perspect. **29**(3), 3–30 (2015)

International Workshop on Sustainability Performance Assessment: Models, Approaches and Applications toward Interdisciplinary and Integrated Solutions (SPA 2020)

Better Deciding Together: Citizens' Trust in Transport and Tourism Public Administration Policies

Francesca Pagliara$^{(\boxtimes)}$ ⑩ and Lucia Russo ⑩

Department of Civil, Architectural and Environmental Engineering,
University of Naples Federico II, Naples, Italy
fpagliar@unina.it, luciarusso993@gmail.com

Abstract. The objective of this manuscript is to understand whether the policies regarding tourism and transport affect positively citizens 'trust in local institutions. A survey was employed to citizens of the metropolitan area of Naples (in Italy), aiming at capturing citizens' perceptions with respect to the positive and negative impacts concerning tourism and transport related policies and the level of their engagement in the institutions 'decisions for a sustainable development.

Keywords: Trust · Stakeholders Engagement · Transport system · Tourism market · Sustainability

1 Introduction

Trust is an important topic in contemporary society and it is essential for social, political, and community relations [1]. Having trust in government initiatives gives legitimacy and authority in decision-making and it is extremely important for good governance, sustainability of the system and democratic consolidation [2, 3]. Therefore, maintaining citizens' trust is an important political objective of any government. Traditionally, it was conceived in a one-to-many relationship rather than in a co-creating process of interaction between politicians and citizens, "shaped" by an exchange of opinions, reciprocal understanding and perceptions. A new vision of trust is born, which is no longer a pre-condition but rather the result of trustworthy behaviors by the involved parties [4, 5]. Indeed, in order to build trust, knowledge and reciprocal benefits from the relationship of the parties are very important [6]. Hall [7] defined trust a glue that holds communities and societies together, when it is absent then collective action is not achievable. Besides, this also means that trust is created when it brings the promised benefits. Empathy is a relevant issue dealt in the literature with reference to inter-cultural issues as well as in hospitality industry [8]. Specifically it refers to the action of being aware of problems, of understanding the needs and of sharing feelings, ideas and experiences.

Public Engagement (PE) or Stakeholders Engagement (SE) is a process which deals with the identification of stakeholder concerns, needs and values in the decision-making process [9]. It is a two-way communication process providing a mechanism for

© Springer Nature Switzerland AG 2020
O. Gervasi et al. (Eds.): ICCSA 2020, LNCS 12255, pp. 115–129, 2020.
https://doi.org/10.1007/978-3-030-58820-5_9

exchanging information and promoting stakeholder interaction with the formal decision-makers. The objective of engagement is to achieve a transparent decision-making process with inputs from stakeholders and their support of the decisions that are taken [10]. Some administrations pay little attention to stakeholder engagement, because politicians believe that they best represent stakeholder interests. This approach is known in the literature as Decide, Announce, Defend (DAD) syndrome [11]. The administration promoting the project Decides with its experts the action to be taken, only later when the choice has been made it Announces it to the public and finally it will Defend the choice from the criticisms. Involving stakeholders in the decision-making process is a rewarding experience, enhancing the decision-making process and the value of what is produced or implemented. Effective engagement can bring about better policy directions, improved local services, possibly new ways to initiate or plan for a particular situation and a better understanding of the local situation by technical experts and community members [12, 13].

Stakeholders can be classified into "primary" and "secondary". In general terms, primary stakeholders can be defined as those with a direct interest, either because they depend on it or they are directly involved in its exploitation in some way. Secondary stakeholders are those with a more indirect interest, such as those involved in institutions or agencies concerned with managing the resource or those who depend, at least partially, on wealth or business generated by the resource [14]. Examples of primary stakeholders are, in transportation planning, institutions/authorities directly responsible for providing transportation services, economic operators (e.g. shop owners), transport operators and transport users; while local communities and unions or business associations belong to the secondary stakeholders group.

Gardner et al. [15] proposed a classification of stakeholders based on two levels of interests and two levels of power (see Fig. 1) and suggested different engagement for the various groups.

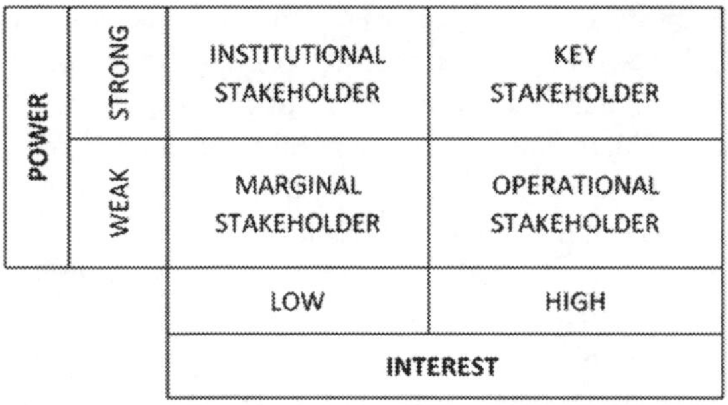

POWER	**STRONG**	INSTITUTIONAL STAKEHOLDER	KEY STAKEHOLDER
	WEAK	MARGINAL STAKEHOLDER	OPERATIONAL STAKEHOLDER
		LOW	HIGH
		INTEREST	

Fig. 1. Stakeholders identification: interest/power matrix. Source: *Gardner et al. (1986)*

It is necessary to keep institutional stakeholders (strong power and low interest) informed. Key stakeholders (strong power and high interest) are the most demanding ones (e.g. mayors or elected officials of areas impacted by projects, unions, etc.) as they have potential for veto rights and should be not only informed but also involved (consulted) on various options and their effects. The marginal stakeholders (weak power and low interest) are the ones requiring the least effort. The last group of operational stakeholders (weak power and high interest) (e.g. transport operators, citizens directly affected, travelers, etc.) could be involved in the process in the listening and information dissemination phases with the appropriate tools as they have the potential to become key stakeholders by empowering themselves, or by being empowered as part of the process management strategy. The objective of this manuscript is to understand whether the policies regarding tourism and transport affect positively citizens 'trust in local institutions. A survey was employed to the citizens of the metropolitan area of Naples (in Italy), aiming at capturing citizens' perceptions with respect to the positive and negative impacts concerning tourism and transport related policies and the level of their engagement in the institutions 'decisions for a sustainable development.

The paper is organized as follows. In Sect. 2 the survey is described. In Sect. 3 the results have been reported and Sect. 4 deals with the conclusions and further perspectives.

2 The Survey

A questionnaire was distributed to the citizens in Campania region, in the South of Italy, with the aim of highlighting the link between the development of tourism and the transport systems policies and the trust that citizens place in the initiatives of the institutions. For all the questions submitted to respondents, a scale with partial semantic autonomy with 5 levels was used, from "I don't trust at all" to "I completely trust" for the first two sections; "In complete disagreement" to "completely agree" for the next four sections. The questionnaire was composed by 6 sections, in the first one it was asked the general level of trust in the municipality of Naples and Campania region administrations. These institutions are responsible for the planning and the developing of the transport and tourism systems initiatives. The second section dealt with the level of trust in the same institutions in the specific context of the transport system and the tourism market development policies. For example, it was asked the level of confidence that citizens placed in the ability of the administrations to do the interests of the community in relation to the development of tourism and transport policies. In the third and fourth sections, the questions asked were useful for evaluating the benefits and the costs related to the transport system and the tourism market policies in the city of Naples. Concerning the benefits, it was asked, for example, how much these two sectors fostered new job opportunities for the local population, how much the transport system could increase the quality of life and how much tourism could encourage investments in territorial development. Regarding the costs, an example of questions to citizens was how much the two sectors contributed to the increase of environmental pollution, how much the transport system could increase user's stress or how much tourism increased the prices of goods and services. In the remaining two sections of the questionnaire, the knowledge of the policies undertaken by the institutions, in the two sectors, and the level of impact perceived in the decisions by the respondents was considered. The number of questionnaires distributed was 1000 and only 463 were received completed. They were submitted to citizens who were at least 18 years old. 51% of the respondents were male, women represented a slightly lower percentage (49%). The age distribution of the sample was as follows 18–24 years (28%), 25–34 years and 55–64 years (20% each), 45–54 years (17%), 35–44 years (10%) and more than 65 years (4%). The sample was on average educated with 94% of respondents with the secondary school, of which 47% of the respondents with at least a university education. The distribution by household income was as follows low income 55.8%, medium income 25.3% and high income 18.9%. 94% of the respondents lived in the metropolitan area of the city of Naples.

3 Results

The results consider as a positive answers "Neither trust them nor distrust them" to "Trust them completely" or "Neither agree nor disagree" to "Strongly agree". The answers to the questionnaire revealed that citizens had little trust in local governments and only 30% of the sample had trust in the municipal administration of Naples and 26% in the Campania region. Referring to the trust in the two sectors under consideration, in the tourism sector the percentage dropped to 27.5% for the municipal administration of Naples and to 23.9% for Campania region, while in the transport system the percentages were lower, i.e. 17.5% for the municipal administration of Naples and 20% for Campania region. The results revealed that men had higher trust in the municipal administration of Naples, while women more in the Campania region administration (see Fig. 2). Concerning the age, young people aged between 18–34 were those who showed less trust in the institutions, the 55–64 years old and those aged more than 65 were those who placed more trust both in the municipal administration of Naples and in the Campania region. Respondents with a low or high income level had less trust in the local administrations while those with a medium income level were the ones who trusted the most. As for the level of education, the results demonstrated that respondents with a master degree had higher trust in the two institutions considered and believed that they were able of doing the interests of the community, those who had the secondary school were those who had the highest trust but did not believe that these interventions met the interests of the community, the three-years graduated respondents were those who placed less trust in the two institutions. The results obtained are shown in the Tables 1 and 2.

Regarding the benefits for the transport system, 65.1% of the respondents believed that the transport system represented a source of job opportunities for the population, 74.2% of the respondents believed that a good transport system could increase the accessibility to the city, tourist attractions and public and private services. About 80% of the respondents believed that interventions in transport system could improve the perception of the quality of life and could also fostered the development of the city as a tourist destination (80% and 83.7% respectively). Within the tourism sector, 85% of the respondents thought that tourism could be a source of job opportunities for the population and local businesses; 80.5% of the respondents declared that tourism could encourage public investment in territorial development, while 83% of them believed

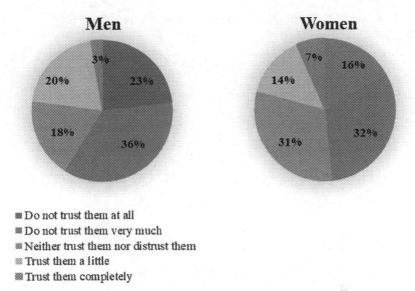

Men   **Women**

■ Do not trust them at all
■ Do not trust them very much
■ Neither trust them nor distrust them
■ Trust them a little
■ Trust them completely

Fig. 2. Trust of men and women in Campania region

that tourism could promote the development of other sectors connected to it, fostering the renewal of sites of interest and cultural heritage.

Concerning the costs deriving from interventions in the transport system, a percentage of respondents believed that it could bring costs for the population in terms of an increase in accident (22.9%), an increase in stress (46.1%) and increase in environmental pollution (42.8%). For the development of tourism policies, 76% of the respondents believed that it could help to preserve the cultural identity of the community. A low number of respondents believed that tourism could bring costs for the population in terms of rising prices of the goods and services (30.7%), increasing traffic (27%), increasing the problem of waste (25.3%) and increasing the environmental pollution (26.7%). A higher percentage of women believed that the development of transport and tourism policies could bring benefits to the local communities, while men believed that these two sectors could increase environmental pollution and that tourism could increase the prices of goods and services. The age groups between 25–34 years and 35–44 years were the ones that most perceived the benefits but also the costs brought by the transport system and the tourism sector. Respondents with a higher level of education believed more in the benefits that these two sectors could bring while those with a low level of education believed that the costs due to the development of the transport system and the tourism sector were high (see Fig. 3). Table 3 shows the impacts of the transport and tourism system policies, Tables 4 and 5 report the benefits and costs that the transport system and the tourism sector could bring.

Table 1. Trust in the municipal administration of the city of Naples

	Trust in general	Transport		Tourism	
		Trust in the development of transport system	Trust in doing the interests of the community	Trust in the development of the tourism sector	Trust in doing the interests of the community
Women	45%	39%	41%	67%	60%
Men	45%	45%	45%	64%	57%
18–24 years	36%	25%	26%	59%	48%
25–34 years	38%	39%	39%	55%	54%
35–44 years	49%	59%	53%	73%	59%
45–54 years	39%	39%	40%	60%	55%
55–64 years	60%	56%	60%	70%	66%
>65 years	53%	53%	74%	79%	63%
Low income	44%	40%	44%	62%	53%
Medium income	53%	48%	49%	69%	64%
High income	42%	41%	40%	69%	65%
Master degree	62%	70%	66%	70%	65%
Three-years degree	52%	61%	48%	61%	58%
High school diploma	57%	64%	60%	64%	56%
Secondary school	48%	67%	44%	67%	48%

As for the development of policies on tourism and the transport system and the impacts they had in the city of Naples, only 23% of the respondents were aware of them. Women believed they knew a little more than men, the age groups with the highest percentage were those aged between 25–34 years for the transport system and 35–44 years for the tourism sector. The age groups with less knowledge were, for the transport sector, the respondents aged between 18–24 years, 35–44 years and more than 65 years. For the tourism sector, instead, the initiatives were less known for respondents aged between 25–34 years, while the effects produced by tourism in the city of Naples were less known to people aged more than 65 (see Fig. 4).

Table 2. Trust in Campania region

	Trust in general	Transport		Tourism	
		Trust in the development of transport system	Trust in doing the interests of the community	Trust in the development of the tourism sector	Trust in doing the interests of the community
Women	50%	45%	40%	69%	62%
Men	40%	51%	46%	57%	55%
18–24 years	42%	37%	36%	60%	54%
25–34 years	35%	41%	41%	58%	50%
35–44 years	53%	57%	51%	61%	63%
45–54 years	39%	49%	40%	58%	60%
55–64 years	57%	60%	52%	71%	64%
>65 years	32%	63%	58%	53%	53%
Low income	42%	49%	40%	61%	55%
Medium income	47%	50%	50%	69%	65%
High income	48%	47%	45%	64%	59%
Master degree	61%	61%	59%	61%	65%
Three-years degree	46%	58%	44%	58%	55%
High school diploma	55%	66%	52%	66%	57%
Secondary school	52%	70%	41%	70%	59%

Respondents with a three-years degree declared that they were aware of the initiatives proposed more than those with a master degree and a secondary school diploma, the only exception was the knowledge of the effects of transport policies which was higher for those interviewed with a secondary school diploma. Concerning the income, for the transport system it was the high-income group which represented the highest percentage, while for the tourism sector the initiatives were better known by citizens with low income. On the contrary, the effects were better known to people with a medium income. Table 6 shows the results.

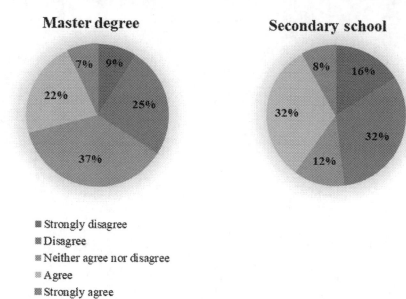

Master degree

Secondary school

- Strongly disagree
- Disagree
- Neither agree nor disagree
- Agree
- Strongly agree

Fig. 3. Perception according to the level of education of how much the policies undertaken in the two sectors increase job opportunities

Finally, only a very small percentage of respondents (5%) believed they had the power of contributing to the decisions concerning the tourism and transport sectors. Men believed they had more influence than women and in particular the age group, that was considered mostly influential, was that of 55–64 years. High-income (see Fig. 5) and low-educated people believed they had more influence on planning decisions. However, the percentages remained very low as shown in the Table 7. Only 46% of the respondents would have been interested in being involved in the planning process.

Summarizing the results explained above, it appears that the sample interviewed has little faith in the policies adopted by local institutions regarding the transport system, this could be a consequence of the low efficiency of public transport in the metropolitan area of Naples. The level of trust in tourism policies, on the other hand, is higher and this can be linked to the increase in tourists that has taken place in the Campania region in the recent years, resulting in many benefits, one of which is the greater economic well-being of workers in the sector.

The population believes that an efficient transport system can bring significant benefits for citizens such as new job opportunities, an increase in the quality of life and greater attraction for tourists. Concerning tourism, it is viewed positively. Indeed most of the respondents believe that it brings greater attention towards the sites of interest and cultural heritage and the development of the sectors connected to it as well as preserving the cultural identity of the city.

Table 3. Impacts of the development of transport and tourism

	Transport			Tourism		
	Source of job opportunities	Creation of opportunities for business	Increase of environmental pollution	Source of job opportunities	Creation of opportunities for business	Increase of environmental pollution
Women	84%	87%	70%	95%	97%	46%
Men	80%	84%	71%	92%	93%	51%
18–24 years	75%	75%	56%	84%	84%	37%
25–34 years	76%	82%	75%	96%	98%	49%
35–44 years	92%	96%	76%	94%	92%	63%
45–54 years	84%	84%	71%	88%	92%	44%
55–64 years	82%	88%	73%	94%	96%	57%
>65 years	84%	84%	63%	95%	84%	42%
Low income	82%	87%	68%	93%	94%	48%
Medium income	84%	84%	69%	98%	98%	45%
High income	83%	84%	77%	94%	94%	55%
Master degree	65%	65%	55%	97%	97%	52%
Three-years degree	58%	55%	58%	94%	95%	52%
High school diploma	56%	57%	52%	92%	94%	44%
Secondary school	48%	59%	56%	93%	96%	63%

The perception of the costs that the two sectors entail is low, men and those with a low level of education are those who have a greater negative perspective. A small percentage of respondents believe that the transport system leads to an increase in road accidents and around 40% consider it a source of stress and environmental pollution. For the tourism sector, few respondents believe that it is the cause of an increase in the prices of goods and services, an increase in traffic and pollution.

Table 4. Benefits and costs of the transport system

| | Transport | | | | | | | |
| | Benefits | | | | | Costs | | |
	More accessibility to services	More accessibility to tourist attractions	Increase of accessibility of the city	Quality of life	Development of the city as a tourist destination	Increase in accidents	Social differences	User stress
Women	90%	90%	94%	93%	95%	45%	57%	65%
Men	85%	90%	90%	89%	93%	44%	57%	63%
18–24 years	78%	79%	84%	78%	80%	26%	46%	48%
25–34 years	86%	87%	90%	93%	95%	42%	53%	74%
35–44 years	88%	92%	92%	86%	96%	63%	69%	69%
45–54 years	84%	91%	87%	92%	90%	51%	58%	64%
55–64 years	93%	97%	93%	92%	99%	57%	60%	63%
>65 years	89%	84%	89%	89%	100%	26%	47%	47%
Low income	90%	92%	93%	90%	93%	43%	58%	63%
Medium income	83%	87%	91%	89%	96%	46%	60%	67%
High income	88%	90%	89%	93%	96%	48%	54%	61%
Master degree	65%	59%	97%	97%	95%	97%	92%	97%
Three-years degree	57%	52%	95%	94%	94%	96%	92%	94%
High school diploma	60%	59%	94%	92%	91%	92%	93%	94%
Secondary school	56%	59%	96%	93%	96%	93%	89%	89%

The knowledge of the policies undertaken in the two sectors is low, few citizens believe that they know the initiatives in the two areas. Respondents with the age over 65 years are the least informed regarding both the transport system and tourism. As for the income, the low-income segment is more informed about tourism policies while the high-income segment is more informed about transport policies. This result is unexpected as it is a common idea that the transport system is more used by low-income people while high-income people are more likely to travel.

Table 5. Benefits and costs of the tourism sector

| | Tourism | | | | | | |
| | Benefits | | | | Costs | | |
	Increase of investment in land development	Encouragement in improvements in the offer of sites of interest	Help to preserve cultural identity	Improvement in the development of sectors connected	Increase of traffic problems	Increase of the waste problem	Increase of prices of goods and services
Women	95%	96%	94%	95%	56%	46%	59%
Men	91%	91%	90%	93%	52%	53%	63%
18–24 years	83%	85%	83%	86%	49%	40%	51%
25–34 years	96%	95%	94%	96%	60%	55%	66%
35–44 years	92%	92%	92%	92%	61%	53%	76%
45–54 years	94%	95%	90%	91%	44%	44%	53%
55–64 years	91%	91%	91%	96%	57%	52%	61%
>65 years	79%	89%	84%	74%	37%	42%	53%
Low income	94%	93%	93%	94%	52%	45%	59%
Medium income	95%	95%	90%	95%	56%	54%	68%
High income	89%	94%	92%	94%	54%	54%	59%
Master degree	95%	97%	92%	97%	55%	53%	61%
Three-years degree	94%	96%	92%	94%	58%	58%	68%
High school diploma	91%	92%	93%	94%	52%	44%	54%
Secondary school	96%	93%	89%	89%	56%	48%	89%

Only a very small percentage (5%) of respondents are aware that they can participate in the decision-making process of both sectors. Higher-income people believe that they can influence decisions as well as those with a low level of education, but this is unusual as it is education that provides greater knowledge and awareness of their role in public administration decision-making processes. The results of the questionnaire show that less than half of the interviewees would still be interested in participating in the decision-making processes of the two sectors analyzed.

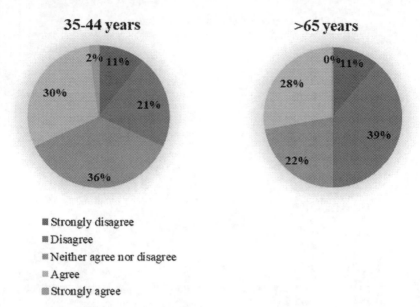

Fig. 4. Knowledge based on the age groups of the effects of tourism in the city of Naples

Table 6. Knowledge of development policies

	Transport		Tourism	
	Knowledge of development initiatives	Knowledge of the effects of transport on the city	Knowledge of development initiatives	Knowledge of the effects of tourism on the city
Women	39%	45%	55%	66%
Men	37%	52%	48%	57%
18–24 years	28%	44%	52%	61%
25–34 years	42%	60%	40%	58%
35–44 years	31%	33%	59%	65%
45–54 years	42%	42%	56%	55%
55–64 years	41%	47%	47%	59%
>65 years	37%	37%	58%	47%
Low income	35%	44%	56%	60%
Medium income	40%	48%	44%	63%
High income	43%	57%	49%	60%

(*continued*)

Table 6. (*continued*)

	Transport		Tourism	
	Knowledge of development initiatives	Knowledge of the effects of transport on the city	Knowledge of development initiatives	Knowledge of the effects of tourism on the city
Master degree	53%	61%	47%	58%
Three-years degree	58%	68%	58%	64%
High school diploma	44%	54%	55%	63%
Secondary school	48%	89%	30%	52%

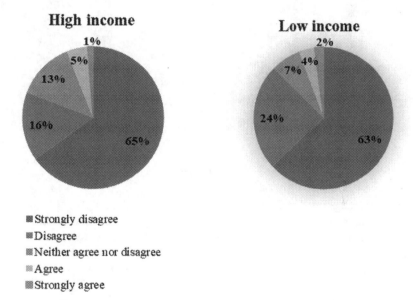

High income

Low income

■ Strongly disagree
■ Disagree
■ Neither agree nor disagree
▥ Agree
▥ Strongly agree

Fig. 5. Perception of the opportunity to participate directly in the planning and development decisions of the transport system based on the income

Table 7. Perception of influence on the planning process

	Transport		Tourism	
	Influence on decisions	Opportunity to participate in planning	Influence on decisions	Opportunity to participate in planning
Women	15%	11%	15%	14%
Men	15%	17%	19%	16%
18–24 years	17%	12%	11%	11%
25–34 years	14%	17%	22%	15%
35–44 years	6%	4%	14%	10%
45–54 years	17%	18%	19%	16%
55–64 years	18%	19%	23%	20%
>65 years	5%	11%	5%	16%
Low income	15%	13%	19%	14%
Medium income	13%	14%	12%	14%
High income	17%	19%	16%	16%
Master degree	50%	58%	14%	11%
Three-years degree	51%	64%	17%	18%
High school diploma	54%	63%	18%	15%
Secondary school	56%	52%	26%	19%

4   Conclusions and Further Perspectives

The results obtained show that citizens' trust in the municipal administration of Naples and the Campania region is greater in relation to the policies undertaken in the tourism sector and the transport system. These two institutions should develop policies and interventions that are well accepted by the population in order to increase the trust that citizens place in them. On the other hand, the lack of trust in the transport and tourism contexts can compromise the trust that citizens place in local governments and lead to a lack of support for the development policies of the transport system and the tourism market. This is because public trust influences citizens' political attitudes and judgments on the acceptability of development projects [16, 17]. Making the decision-making process more accessible and transparent to citizens involves an increase in the knowledge of the two sectors and of the developed policies and this makes the population favorably disposed towards the institutions, moreover the greater the knowledge of the development policies of the two sectors by the residents and the greater the confidence to be able to take part in their development. Residents with greater power in the transport system and in the tourism market looked at development in a positive way. A good development of the transport system and of the tourism market also leads to a better perception of the positive impacts produced by these two sectors and decreases even more the costs that the population believes they involve. For this reason, it is important that local government should be more efficient in promoting initiatives for the development of the transport system and the tourism market.

Further perspectives would consider to carry out a new survey to obtain a larger sample size in order to make the sample more representative of the population. Furthermore, it would be important to have an homogeneity of the respondents 'categories in order not to invalidate the estimates.

References

1. Freitag, M., Bühlmann, M.: Crafting trust: the role of political institutions in a comparative perspective. Comp. Polit. Stud. **42**(12), 1537–1566 (2009)
2. Christensen, T., Lægreid, P.: Trust in government: the relative importance of service satisfaction, political factors, and demography. Public Perform. Manag. Rev. **28**(4), 487–511 (2005)
3. Park, H., Blenkinsopp, J.: The roles of transparency and trust in the relationship between corruption and citizen satisfaction. Int. Rev. Adm. Sci. **77**(2), 254–274 (2011)
4. Pagliara, F., Aria, M., Russo, L., Della Corte, V., Biggiero, L.: Citizens trust in institutions' initiatives on the transportation system. Forthcoming in Paper in Regional Science
5. Pagliara, F., Russo, L., Della Corte, V., Aria, M., Nunkoo, R.: Validating a theoretical model of citizens' trust in tourism development. Forthcoming in Socio-Economic Planning Sciences
6. Nunkoo, R.: Turism development and trust in local government. Tourism Manag. **46**, 623–634 (2015)
7. Hall, C.M.: Tourism and Politics: Policy, Power and Place. Wiley, Chichester (1994)
8. Barlow, J., Maul, D.: Emotional Value: Creating Strong Bonds with Your Customers. Berrett-Koehler Publishers, San Francisco (2000)
9. Pagliara, F., Di Ruocco, I.: How public participation could improve public decisions on rail investments? Reg. Sci. Policy Pract. **10**, 383–403 (2018)
10. Kelly, J., Jones, P., Barta, F., Hossinger, R., Witte, A., Christian, A.: Successful transport decision-making - a project management and stakeholder engagement handbook. Guidemaps consortium (2004)
11. Marincioni, F., Appiotti, F.: The lyon-turin high-speed rail: the public debate and perception of environmental risk in Susa Valley, Italy. Environ. Manag. **43**, 863–875 (2009)
12. Cascetta, E., Pagliara, F.: Public engagement for planning and designing transportation systems. Procedia – Soc. Behav. Sci. **87**, 103–116 (2013)
13. Cascetta, E., Cartenì, A., Pagliara, F., Montanino, M.: A new look at planning and designing transportation systems: a decision-making model based on cognitive rationality, stakeholder engagement and quantitative methods. Transp. Policy **38**, 27–39 (2015)
14. Wheeler, D., Sillanpaa, M.: The stakeholder Corporation. Pittman, London (1997)
15. Gardener, J., Rachlin, R., Sweeny, A.: Handbook of Strategic Planning. Wiley, New York (1986)
16. Bronfman, N.C., Vazquez, E.L., Dorantes, G.: An empirical study for the direct and indirect links between trust in regulatory institutions and acceptability of hazards. Safety Sci. **47**, 686–692 (2009)
17. Easton, D.: A System Analysis of Political Life. Wiley, New York (1965)

Simplified Approach for Liquefaction Risk Assessment of Transportation Systems: Preliminary Outcomes

Mauro D'Apuzzo[1] , Azzurra Evangelisti[1] , Giuseppe Modoni[1] ,
Rose-Line Spacagna[1], Luca Paolella[1], Daniela Santilli[1(✉)],
and Vittorio Nicolosi[2]

[1] University of Cassino and Southern Lazio,
Via G. Di Biasio 43, 03043 Cassino, Italy
{dapuzzo,modoni,rlspacagna,paolella,
daniela.santilli}@unicas.it,
aevangelisti.ing@gmail.com
[2] University of Rome "Tor Vergata", via del Politecnico 1, 00133 Rome, Italy
nicolosi@uniroma2.it

Abstract. In the present study, a strategy to assess liquefaction risk of road infrastructures has been proposed, as combination of liquefaction hazard, infrastructures vulnerability and exposure of transportation network. The proposed methodology includes a capacity analysis of the road network performed on both pre- and post-liquefaction scenarios to evaluate the social cost in terms of delay cost suffered by the transportation system. The approach has been applied to the municipality of Terre del Reno (Italy), that in 2012 suffered a severe seismic sequence that induced extensive liquefaction evidences over the territory. A multi-layer database, on a Geographical Information Systems (GIS) platform, has been created, with the aim to overlap information about subsoil, earthquake intensity, groundwater depth and road network configuration. The Vulnerability of road has been evaluated by the settlements of embankment on liquefied soils and, according to the damage level occurred, a loss of functionality has been assigned. Finally, performing a transportation analysis, the effects on the traffic conditions have been evaluated in terms of Total Delay Cost, suffer by the road users. Preliminary results showed a redistribution of the traffic flows caused by the service loss of crucial road sections due to the liquefaction evidences on the transportation network and the related Total Delay Cost has been quantified.

Keywords: Seismic risk · Liquefaction · Transportation network · Embankments · Serviceability · Social cost

1 Background

The serious consequences of liquefaction induced by earthquakes is worldwide proved by several events as, for example, those occurred in 2010, 2011 and 2016 at Christchurch, in 2011 at Tohoku Oki, in 2012 in Emilia Romagna (Italy) or in 2016 at Kumamoto. The destructive effects could damage all the infrastructure assets of the

© Springer Nature Switzerland AG 2020
O. Gervasi et al. (Eds.): ICCSA 2020, LNCS 12255, pp. 130–145, 2020.
https://doi.org/10.1007/978-3-030-58820-5_10

modern societies as buildings, factories, lifelines, transportation networks, which are directly or indirectly connected to the productive systems. In the past two decades, significant efforts have been performed to develop different methodologies for estimating the potential losses induced by earthquakes but the liquefaction phenomenon has been still considered a side effect, although recently the liquefaction risk assessment have been integrated into national and international standards [e.g. 1, 2]. Among the most recent National and International projects and researches, from the specific viewpoint of Transportation Networks and Infrastructures, deserving of attention are: the European project AllTraIn (All-Hazard Guide for Transport Infrastructure; 2013–2015) and the Italian project STRIT (Tools and Technologies for Risk Management of Transport Infrastructure; 2012–2015) which provide an economic losses estimation performing element analysis, especially bridges and tunnels that are intrinsically considered the most vulnerable of the network [3, 4]. Other European projects, with different approaches and degrees of details, perform analysis at network level considering both natural hazards [5–7] and intentional and exceptional man-made hazards [8, 9]. Seville e Nicholson [10], showed the results of an analysis of the risk of closure of a strategic road section in New Zealand (State Highway 1 which constitutes the major north-south road link). The authors performed a transport analysis at network level, including the assessment of the cost due to: additional travel along the alternative routes, increased accident exposure and loss of user benefit for cancelled trips. As far as seismic risk assessment and mitigation interventions decision-making on transportation systems are concerned, at least the network-level analysis is requested and so far studies have mainly examined the earthquake hazard regarding to bridges, consequently the focus of the researches has been primarily on bridges retrofitting. For example, the seismic risk reduction decision-guidance process proposed within the REDARS 2 (Risks from Earthquake Damage to the Roadway System) Project, would select retrofit sequence that provides the optimum seismic performance of the system, within tentatively hypothesized mitigation strategies (alternative priorities could be

Table 1. Summary of the main research projects/methodologies proposed.

Project/methodology	Hazard		Losses estimation		Transportation analysis
	Natural	Man-made	Element level	Network level	
AllTraIn [3]	Yes	Yes	Yes		
STRIT [4]	Yes		Yes		
HAZUS [5]	Yes			Yes	
SYNER-G [6]	Yes			Yes	Yes
[7]	Yes			Yes	
SecMan [8]		Yes		Yes	
SeRoN [9]		Yes		Yes	Yes
[10]	Yes			Yes	Yes
REDARS 2 [11]	Yes			Yes	Yes
[12]	Yes			Yes	Yes

evaluated in terms of the means and standard deviations of the resulting total costs) [11]. Furthermore, in order to improve the post-earthquake transportation analysis, a more refined methodology has been proposed by Chang [12]. According to the author, it is possible to improve the retrofitting analysis modifying the post-earthquake origin-destination (O/D) matrix respect to the pre-earthquake (static) O/D matrix as an input for traffic flow analysis, in order to take into account the change of traffic pattern after the seismic event and the damage of transportation infrastructures. In particular the trip generation and distribution stages of a traffic analysis are modified to consider the earthquake-induced damage. In the Table 1 are summarized the main features of the aforementioned projects and methodologies.

2   Levels for Road Transportation Network Analysis

With the aim to evaluate the socio-economic impact due to destructive events by means of a risk based analysis, two main approaches can be usually followed to identify the period analysis: *short-term period*, focused on the emergency actions, assuring the accessibility for rescue crews and machines also to smaller and more isolated communities and *long-term period*, which includes the recovery phase needed to perform repair actions for restoring initial conditions of the transportation network.

According to recent literature [6] a systemic analysis of transportation networks, according to the level of assessment of their functionality have been proposed:

- *Vulnerability Analysis*, which, according to a specific post-earthquake scenario, is related to the damage level of each single component of the transportation network (as bridge, tunnel, embankment, etc.);
- *Connectivity Analysis*, which, according to a specific post-earthquake scenario, evaluates the accessibility to specific or strategic areas despite the loss of service of some connections;
- *Capacity Analysis*, which, related to the network capacity to accommodate traffic flows, provides direct and indirect losses due to damage levels occurred of the whole network;
- *Serviceability Analysis*, which, taking into account both direct and indirect impacts on the economic sectors, provides a more realistic estimate of total loss on the long-term period.

In the current economic and social contest, it is worth to be highlighted that, although the objectives in terms of performance and safety of the transportation networks are increasingly ambitious, a marked reduction in investment budgets is observed. In order to cope the limited budget availability, although the *Serviceability Analysis* could return results (in terms of socio-economic losses) more comprehensive than the others, because of the extent and complexity of its input data, it is not carried out. Therefore, the *Capacity Analysis* seems represent a satisfying compromise, while still guaranteeing reliable results in terms of socio-economic impacts related to the traffic flows.

3 Risk Assessment Induced by Liquefaction

Seismic liquefaction may occur when strong earthquake affects loose saturated sand. The pore-water pressure build-up causes a reduction of effective stress that, in critical condition may lead to a considerable loss of shear strength.

The probability of liquefaction occurrence in a soil deposit is mainly due to the combination of several factors, i.e. susceptibility of the soil, depth of groundwater, intensity and duration of the seismic event. While the above factors represent hazard, the presence of infrastructures and the vulnerability of the latter have to be taken into account for risk assessment. In order to formalize the methodology for liquefaction risk assessment, the likelihood of occurrence and the associated uncertainty on earthquake amplitude, ground shaking, liquefaction experiencing, structural response, physical damage, and socio-economic losses have to be quantified and combined. It can be summarized into the synthetic formal definition of *Liquefaction Risk* as the combination of *Hazard*, *Vulnerability* and *Exposure*.

As far as the liquefaction phenomenon is concerned, the seismic event is usually considered the mainly hazard factor combined with the presence of loose granular materials with limited fine content, sufficiently low density and saturation. Hence, the coupling of earthquake and subsoil response induces the demand for the infrastructure at the ground level. According to the proposed methodology, for evaluating the liquefaction hazard, the coupled approach for subsoil and infrastructural responses is proposed. In particular, the formula of Karamitros et al. [13] has been customized to this specific case, comparing the results with an effective stress calculation performed with an advanced numerical model [14]. Generally, according to a specific infrastructure, the vulnerability is its predisposition to suffer a fixed damage state, due to a liquefaction event. In this study, for the definition of the damage state limits for highway embankments, the SYNER-G classification [15] summarized in Table 2 has been adopted:

Table 2. Definition of damage state for highway embankments [15].

Damage	PVG displacement [m]			Description	Serviceability
State	min	max	mean		
Minor	0.02	0.08	0.05	Surface slide of embankment at the top of slope; minor cracks on road surface; minor track displacement	Useful road with speed reduction
Moderate	0.08	0.22	0.15	Deep slide or slump of embankment; medium cracks on road surface and/or settlement; medium track displacement	Partially open during repair works (alternating direction of travel)
Extensive	0.22	0.58	0.40	Extensive slump and slide of embankment; extensive cracks on road surface and/or settlement; extensive tracks displacement	Closed

For completing the *Liquefaction Risk* assessment, the *Exposure* concept for road transportation network, has to be introduced.

4 Road Transportation Network: Exposure and Indirect Losses

As previously mentioned, the probability of occurrence and the associated uncertainty on seismic intensity, ground motion, liquefaction evidences, structural response, physical damage, and socio-economic losses contribute to the seismic liquefaction risk assessment. Indeed, according to a specific transportation network asset, the combination of the Hazard, the Vulnerability and the Exposure defines the risk related to a possible seismic/liquefaction scenario. As far as the liquefaction risk of transport network systems is concerned, the concept of Exposure is expressed as the quantification of the socio-economic damages that a community can suffer, for this reason, it is strongly related to the evaluation of the *Social Costs*, which, in turn, can be defined as all the social and economic *Losses* affecting a community after a catastrophic event and they are usually divided in *direct* and *indirect* losses. The first group consists mainly into repair or replacement cost of the damaged element of the transportation infrastructure and the second one is mainly due to cost derived from temporary reduction or interruption of the transportation network service, which in turn, could implicate losses and missed earnings into others economic sectors. The consequences of loss of serviceability of the transportation networks could depend on the features of the transportation system such as the network configuration, the redundancies, the traffic demand and capacity, the presence, the quantity and the location of critical components (e.g. bridges, tunnels, embankments,...). The impacts on the traffic flows and the trips could affect agriculture, industry and services sectors which use the transportation networks for daily activities. In this study, the indirect losses have been evaluated by means of the *Total Delay Cost, TDC*, as a consequence of loss of serviceability of the transportation networks, within the Capacity Analysis. This approach implies that the travel time is one of the most significant component among the different terms contributing to the *Generalized Transport Cost, GTC*, which is defined as the sum of all the contributes that compose the cost (travel time included) that a generic transport user holds up to perform a specific trip, within a specific analysis area, on a daily basis.

Basing on these premises, the *TDC* can be defined as:

$$TDC = GTC_{post} - GTC_{pre} \tag{1}$$

where:

GTC$_{post}$ is the Generalized Transport Cost in the post - catastrophic scenario;
GTC$_{pre}$ is the Generalized Transport Cost in the pre - catastrophic scenario.

Since the Eq. (1) provides the costs on a daily basis, in order to evaluate the *Overall Social Cost, OSC*, within a specific analysis area, the *TDC* has to be multiplied by the overall amount of days needed to bring back the transportation network to the pre-earthquake event conditions. In order to perform the TDC evaluation, a transportation demand forecasting model, within the analysis area, has to be developed. A brief description is reported below.

4.1   Travel Demand Forecasting Model

The Travel Demand Forecasting Model, TDFM, [16] is one of the most known and used prediction model in Transportation Engineering. The TDFM, historically named four-step travel demand model, is a mathematical four-stage model which, from the entire Origin-Destination (O/D) trip matrix of the analysis area, provides, on an hourly basis, all the trips occurring in a specific analysis area, according to its purpose, time period, origin, destination, path, transport mode and socio-economic role of the user. In particular the TDFM is the ordered combination of four separated sub-models: the traffic emission model, the traffic distribution model, the traffic mode-choice model and the path-choice model. The TDFM can be evaluated by means of the following expression [16]:

$$d_{od}^i(s, h, m, k) = d_o^i(sh) \cdot p^i(d/osh) \cdot p^i(m/oshd) \cdot p^i(k/oshdm) \qquad (2)$$

where:

d_{od}^i (s, h, m, k) is the average number of trips undertaken by class user (cu) i, starting from origin traffic zone o, finishing in the destination traffic zone d, for a specific purpose s, within the time period h, using the transport mode m, and choosing the trip path k;

d_{io} (sh) is the average number of cu i that undertakes a trip from o, for purpose s, within the time period h;

p^i (d/osh) is the fraction of the cu i that travels to d undertaking a trip from o, for purpose s, within the time period h;

p^i (m/oshd) is the fraction of the cu i that uses the transport mode m, undertaking a trip from o, to d, for purpose s, within the time period h;

p^i (k/oshdm) is the fraction of the cu i that chooses the trip path k, undertaking a trip from o, to d, for purpose s, within the time period h, with the transport mode m.

It is worth to be mentioned that, each conurbation and its relative transportation system present peculiarities which deserve ad hoc preliminary evaluations relating to the identification of relevant spatial dimensions of the transportation network. It consists mainly into the definition of the project area (and study area if needed); the subdivision of the defined area into traffic zones (zoning) and the identification of the basic network [16].

5   Case Study

In May 2012, the Emilian Po Valley was struck by an intense seismic activity with two major events occurred respectively May 20th (Mw = 6.1 − hypocentral depth of 6.3 km) and on May 29th (Mw = 5.8 − hypocentral depth of 10.2 km). Widespread liquefaction was observed in areas located near old abandoned watercourses, especially in the municipalities of Sant'Agostino and Mirabello, located along the old riverbed of the Reno River. The village of San Carlo, Municipality of Sant'Agostino, is the most emblematic area for the greatest concentration of liquefaction evidence [17]. The subsoil of San Carlo is the product of a relatively recent geologic history, characterized by an intensive depositional sequence of the Reno river and a very shallow water table. Its urban area and road network are mainly built near the paleo-channel and paleo-levees of the Reno River and consequently the subsoil can be categorized in three main units. Starting from the top, fluvial channel deposits few meters deep are located above a stratum of fine-grained materials (swamps) and Pleistocene alluvial plain. Finally, manmade silty sand layers built to protect the area against flooding (paleo-levees) are positioned along the old riverbed. Due to the fact that Terre del Reno is characterized by the strong presence of trough-traffic, the study and project areas do not coincide. In this case the project area can be identified into San Carlo districts and the dimension of study area (which always includes the first one and encompasses most of the transportation variations' effects) has been defined by the results of the sensitivity analysis: three circular areas with a radius of 20 km, 40 km ad 60 km centred in the project area,

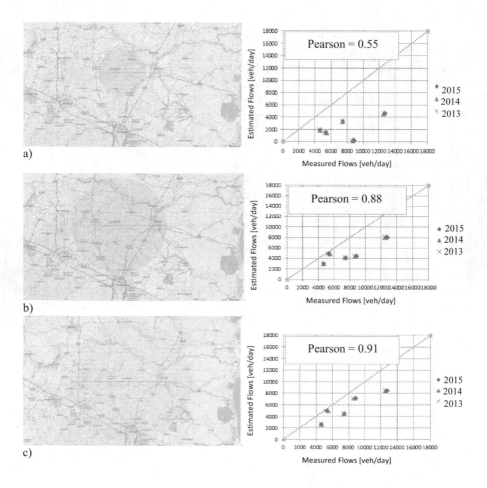

Fig. 1. Sensitivity analysis with study area's radius dimension of a) 20 km; b) 40 km and c) 60 km.

have been used as study areas. A TDFM, for each study areas has been developed and the results has been showed in the following Fig. 1. As shown in the Fig. 1c, the comparison between estimated and measured flows (into three different years: 2013, 2014 and 2015) suggests a size of the study area of at least 60 km of radius.

For this reason, the final version of the TDFM has been developed, calibrated and experimentally validated in a buffer area of 60 km of radius around a rural area located in the district of Terre del Reno. In order to define the model, the following hypotheses have been stated:

- the study area of the model can be considered as a "wide area" (larger than a district but smaller than a regional territorial scale), for this reason the municipal scale has been chosen as zoning size;
- the effects of the seismic events which produce the liquefaction phenomenon are mainly limited to the conurbation of Terre del Reno;
- the trip purpose that can be monetized are usually related to the main home-based trips (home-to-work or/and home-to-study); in this regard, it should be remembered that these types of trip are characterized by the lower rigidity in terms of elasticity of the demand curve respect to other trips purposes;
- home-to-work or/and home-to-study purpose trips are considered prevalent in this mobility scenario, covering more than 80% of the entire mobility, as highlighted by regional traffic studies;
- the daily fluctuation of mobility has been partitioned considering only two sce-narios: a "peak" one that occurs mainly in two time slots (from 7:00 to 9:00 and from 17:00 to 19:00) and an "off-peak" for the rest of the day;
- for the aforementioned reasons, the O/D matrix has been preliminarily developed basing on the commuter mobility data derived by 2011 Census provided by Italian National Institute of Statistics (ISTAT) [18] containing only systematic commuting data and corresponding modal split;
- on a municipal basis, it is assumed that the shelter areas will been located close to the main town center, for this reason, the emission and attraction factors of the traffic zones, in the ex-ante and ex-post earthquake scenarios, have been considered invariant;
- finally, because of the wide analysis area and of the higher incidence of long trips in terms of travel times and paths in the examined traffic scenarios a deterministic approach (all-or-nothing), for the assignment sub-model, has been assumed. As a matter of fact, in this case, path choice mechanisms are characterized by an average low epistemic level (also in view of the possible installation of the temporary directional vertical signs).

Following of the identification of the study area, 31 centroids and relative traffic zones have been pointed out (Fig. 2) and the main traffic supply model has been identified (Fig. 3). However in the project area a more refined road network model taking into account also minor roads has been considered in order to capture traffic deviation scenarios in a more realistic manner.

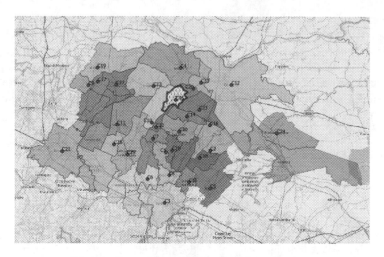

Fig. 2. Centroids and traffic zones identification.

Fig. 3. Identification of the corresponding traffic supply model (main road network).

The Karamitros formula [13] has then been applied to estimate the settlements of the road embankment over the territory of Terre del Reno, thanks to the use of geoinformatics [19], combining seismic hazard with the subsoil and the road network features, spatial databases have been developed, and the results, in terms of the thickness of the liquefiable layer (Fig. 4), the thickness of the overlying crust (Fig. 5) and the embankment height (Fig. 6) have been represented. Finally, according to the specific seismic event of May 20th 2012, the map of the road embankment settlements has been computed and reported in the Fig. 7.

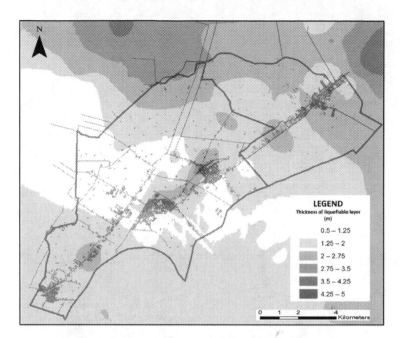

Fig. 4. Map of the thickness of the liquefiable layer.

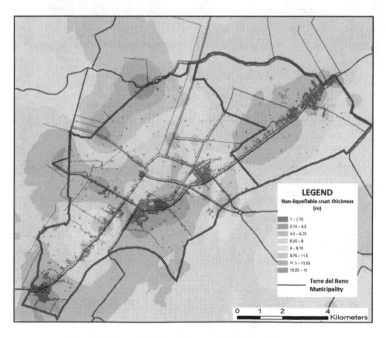

Fig. 5. Map of the thickness of the overlying crust.

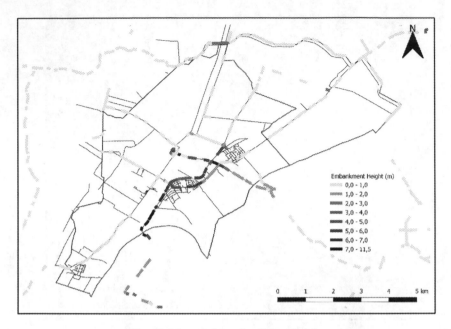

Fig. 6. Map of the embankment height.

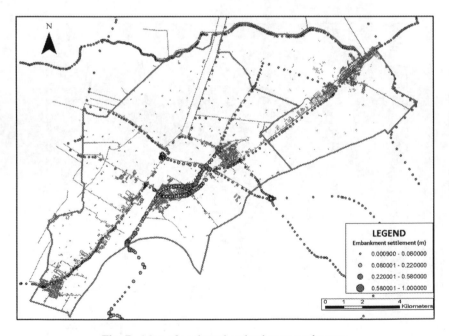

Fig. 7. Map of evaluated embankment settlements.

According to the SYNER-G classification [15] (see Table 2) the evaluation of the damage state limits for highway embankments has been performed and the results, in terms of Serviceability level have been showed in the Fig. 8.

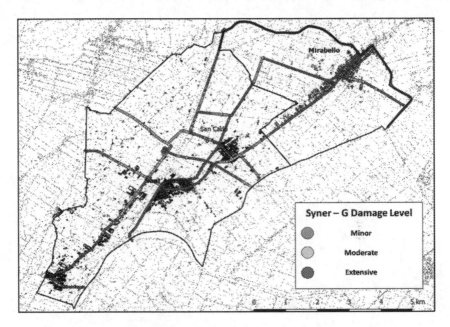

Fig. 8. Map of the embankment damage levels.

Due to the variations of the traffic flows occurring within various time frame during the day and different days in a week, several simulations, with different traffic data characterizing the "peak" periods (early morning and afternoon) and "off-peak" periods have been performed, with the aim to simulate the actual traffic hourly volume on the road network in a typical working day. In this case study, for each scenario (both pre-liquefaction and post-liquefaction), the previous traffic hourly volume values have been assigned according to a "all-or-nothing" conventional rule.

By way of example, the pre and post scenario (related to the specific seismic event of May 20th 2012) within the morning peak period and in the project area, have been reported in the Figs. 9 and 10, respectively. As it can be easily observed from the simulation the disrupt of some road links induced by liquefaction, is responsible for a re-distribution of original traffic flows yielding an increase of travel time and, in turn, of *Social Costs*. For each scenario, the travel times on the whole road network, considering a typical working day and the home-to-work and home-to-study purpose trips, have been evaluated. Comparing the travel times along the road network in the post and pre-liquefaction scenarios, the overall hourly delay suffered by the entire network system, because of the damage occurred (in this case necessarily translates into substantial extensions of travel routes), has been evaluated. Therefore, following the assessment of the hourly delays for both peak and off-peak hours, a daily delay of approximately 16700 min has been calculated.

In the Fig. 11, the cumulative curve of the Delay distributions (i.e. number of road users perceiving a delay lower or at least equal to a defined value), providing an indirect estimate of the cumulated probability associated to a given class of delay within both Peak and Off-Peak hours, has been reported.

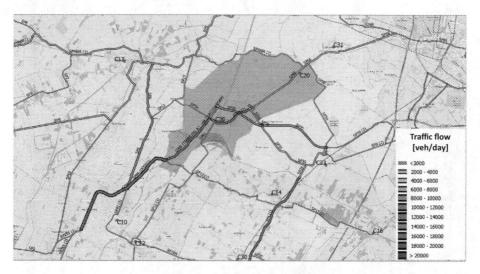

Fig. 9. Daily traffic flow distribution produced by a TDFM in the pre-liquefaction scenario.

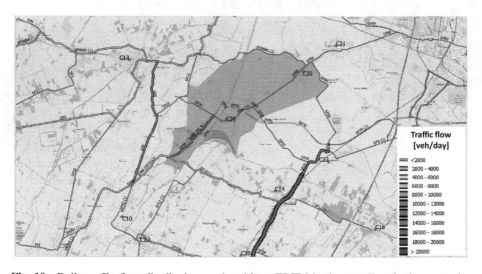

Fig. 10. Daily traffic flow distribution produced by a TDFM in the post-liquefaction scenario.

Finally, according to the travel time cost for heavy and light vehicles, the average transportation generalized cost, have been calculated.

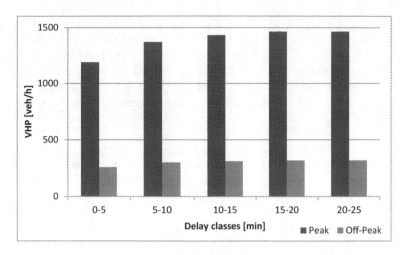

Fig. 11. Cumulative Delay distribution within peak and off-peak hours.

By means of the Eq. 1, the *Total Delay Cost* for each post-scenario have been evaluated and, in order to assess the *Overall Social Cost*, the *Total Delay Cost* should be multiplied by the overall amount of days needed to restore the pre-liquefaction event conditions of transportation network (no variations in travel demand have been considered during the post-liquefaction event period since, as previously stated, the study area is much more larger than the size of the project area and it has been assumed that the prevailing through traffic travelling in the study area will not be dramatically affected by the seismic event).

It is worth to be underlined that the *Overall Social Cost* so far evaluated could be incorporated into a Decision Support Systems within a prioritization scheme that can be developed in order to identify candidate road sections for liquefaction mitigation countermeasures.

6 Conclusion

A seismic liquefaction risk assessment of a road transportation network has been performed: the territorial distribution of hazard, vulnerability and exposure has been estimated and preliminarily evaluations in terms of social cost, have been conducted.

The strategy has been applied on an Italian road system affected by a severe earthquake in 2012: seismic hazard, subsoil features and road network characteristics have been combined in a geo-informatics databases. Then a Capacity Analysis of the road network has been performed, with the aim to evaluate the effects of the loss of functionality due to liquefaction evidences.

Pre- and post-seismic scenarios have been simulated and preliminary outcomes showed a redistribution of the traffic flows, on the road network, caused by the service loss of strategic road sections and preliminary analysis, to evaluate the social effects in terms of Total Delay Cost, have been performed.

The original framework so far developed appears to be a promising screening procedure that can allow to detect, on one hand, liquefaction risk-prone road sections and, on the other, *Overall Social Costs* associated to earthquake-induced road disruptions. It is believed that *Overall Social Costs* can represent an additional factor that can be easily implemented into a prioritization procedure helping Road Managers in identifying vulnerable road sections needing seismic retrofitting interventions against seismic liquefaction scenarios.

Acknowledgement. The authors wish to acknowledge the contribution by the EU funded project LIQUEFACT "Assessment and mitigation of liquefaction potential across Europe: a holistic approach to protect structures/infrastructures for improved resilience to earthquake-induced liquefaction disasters", project ID 700748 funded under the H2020-DRS-2015.

References

1. Ministry of Business, Innovation & Development. Recommendation after the Canterbury Earthquake sequence (2010–2011) (2016)
2. Indirizzi e Criteri per la Microzonazione Sismica. Dipartimento della Protezione Civile (2017): Linee guida per la gestione del territorio in aree interessate da liquefazioni (LQ). Versione 1.0 (2017)
3. All-Hazard Guide for Transport Infrastructure. © Copyright 2013 – 2015. The AllTraIn Consorsium. http://www.alltrain-project.eu/
4. STRIT project Homepage. http://www.stress-scarl.com/it/innovazione/i-progetti-nazionali/strit.html. Accessed 15 Feb 2020
5. Multi-hazard Loss Estimation Methodology Earthquake Model HAZUS®MH MR4 Technical Manual. National Institute of Building Sciences. (NIBS). Washington, DC. (2004). http://www.fema.gov/hazus/
6. Systemic Seismic Vulnerability and Risk Analysis for Buildings, Lifeline Networks and Infrastructures Safety Gain. ISBN: 978-92-79-33135-0 (2014). https://doi.org/10.2788/23242. http://www.vce.at/SYNER-G/files/project/proj-overview.html
7. Molarius, R., et al.: Systemic vulnerability and resilience analysis of electric and transport network failure in cases of extreme winter storms. In: Beer, M., Au, S.-K., Hall, J.W. (Eds.). Vulnerability, Uncertainty, and Risk: Quantification, Mitigation, and Management, pp. 608–617. American Society of Civil Engineers (ASCE), Reston (2014)
8. SECURITY MANUAL FOR EUROPEAN ROAD INFRASTRUCTURE. www.secman-project.eu. Copyright: SecMan Consortium (2013)
9. Deliverable D400: Importance of the structures for the traffic network. © Copyright 2009 – 2012. The SeRoN Consortium (2012)
10. Seville, E., Nicholson, A.: Risk and impact of natural hazards on a road network. J. Transp. Eng. - ASCE **127**(2), 159 (2001). https://doi.org/10.1061/(asce)0733-947x
11. Werner, S.D., et al.: Redars 2 methodology and software for seismic risk analysis of highway systems. Special Report MCEER-06-SP08. Federal Highway Administration (2006)
12. Chang, L.: Transportation system modeling and applications in earthquake engineering. Doctoral Thesis in the Graduate College of the University of Illinois at Urbana-Champaign (2010)
13. Karamitros, D.K., Bouckovalas, G.D., Chaloulos, Y.K.: Seismic settlements of shallow foundations on liquefiable soil with a clay crust. Soil Dyn. Earthq. Eng. **46**, 64–76 (2013)

14. Modoni, G., Spacagna, R.L., Paolella, L., Salvatore, E., Rasulo, A., Martelli, L.: Liquefaction risk assessment: lesson learned from a case study. In: Proceedings of the VI International Conference of Earthquake Geotechnical Engineering, Rome (2019)
15. SYNER-G: typology definition and fragility functions for physical elements at seismic risk (2014). ISBN 978-94-007-7871-9. https://doi.org/10.1007/978-94-007-7872-6
16. Cascetta, E.: Transportation Systems Analysis. Models and Applications, 2nd edn., pp. 1–752. Springer Verlag (2009). https://doi.org/10.1007/978-0-387-75857-2
17. Fioravante, V., et al.: Earthquake geotechnical engineering aspects: the 2012 Emilia Romagna earthquake (Italy). In: Seventh International Conference on Case Histories in Geotechnical Engineering, April 29th–May 4th 2013, Chicago, US (2013)
18. Italian Institute of Statistic (ISTAT). https://www.istat.it/it/archivio/139381. Accessed 16 Feb 2020
19. Spacagna, R.L., Rasulo, A., Modoni, G.: Geostatistical analysis of settlements induced by groundwater extraction. In: Gervasi, O., et al. (eds.) ICCSA 2017. LNCS, vol. 10407, pp. 350–364. Springer, Cham (2017). https://doi.org/10.1007/978-3-319-62401-3_26

Application to a Player Operating in Italy of an AHP Model for the Identification of the Most Advantageous Technical Alternatives in the Management of the Integrated Water Service

Maria Macchiaroli[1]([mail])[iD], Luigi Dolores[1][iD], Vincenzo Pellecchia[2][iD],
Gianluigi De Mare[1][iD], Antonio Nesticò[1][iD], and Gabriella Maselli[1][iD]

[1] University of Salerno, Via Giovanni Paolo II, 132, Fisciano (SA), Italy
{mmacchiaroli,ldolores,gdemare,
anestico,gmaselli}@unisa.it
[2] Ente Idrico Campano, Via A. De Gasperi, 28, Napoli (NA), Italy
vpellecchia@enteidricocampano.it

Abstract. The value of water as a resource has now been recognized on a global scale, albeit with different levels of awareness due to its availability and accessibility. All western countries have regulated the management sector of this resource (Integrated Water System – SII), regarding both its distribution as well as the purification and collection of sewage waste. Italy has also moved towards privatizing its management, proposing a collaborative mechanism between the public regulatory Authority and the private operator. The investments for the maintenance and development of the asset are therefore supported by the private investors. The model proposed in this work is based on the use of AHP to encourage the conciliation of opposing interests and rationalize a rather complex regulatory phase. It facilitates the selection of technical investment alternatives for the improvement of the SII supply standards.

Keywords: Integrated water service · Water infrastructure · Choice of alternatives · Urban water management · AHP · Economic evaluation of projects · Multi-criteria analysis

1 The AHP Model for the Rational Choice of Intervention Alternatives in the Defining of the Intervention Program

1.1 The Regulatory Framework in Italy

As illustrated in a recent study [1], the Water Framework Directive (2000/60/EC) proclaimed by the European Commission describes the problem of water resource management in economic (access to the resource for both civil and business use), social

---

The authors contributed equally to this work.

© Springer Nature Switzerland AG 2020
O. Gervasi et al. (Eds.): ICCSA 2020, LNCS 12255, pp. 146–161, 2020.
https://doi.org/10.1007/978-3-030-58820-5_11

(health standards), and environmental (safety of the water resource) terms. The same Directive introduces the essential principle of *full cost recovery*; it means that the Operator who manages the water service must cover with the applied tariffs all kind of costs, from management and capital costs, to environmental ones [2–5]. Based on this framework, European countries have improved their own management model for Integrated Water Service (SII).

In Italy, a complex regulatory framework characterizes the water service sector; it is the result of a consistent regulatory stratification, which has been accompanied by neither a substantial coordination intervention nor a legislative organisation [6].

The issuing of the Law n. 36/94 (Galli Law) was a historical moment for Italian water legislation, since it defined the meaning of Integrated Water Service (SII) as a set of public services for the *collection*, *supply* and *distribution* of water for civil use, along with *sewerage* and *wastewater* treatment (including industrial uses of the water managed within the same service). The definition was subsequently updated by art. 141 co.2 of Legislative Decree 152/2006 (Consolidated Environmental Text - TUA).

In the years following the issuing of Law n. 36/94, the legislator intervened several times on the matter of local public services and with specific interest on water services, improving the provisions regarding the institutional and organizational set-up of the sector. These interventions included the Legislative Decree of 3 April 2006, n. 152, whose Part III, Sect. 3, organically regulates the water sector, incorporating Law n. 36/1994 and prescribing more precise indications on the tasks and activities belonging to the various institutional interested actors.

To date, the current government is preparing legal hypotheses that could even bring the management of water resources back into the public sphere, thus completely revolutionizing the private sector that was established with the Galli reform. Law n. 36/94 introduced a vertical integration of the aqueduct, sewer and purification activities, along with a functional integration of the existing services. In this way, the legislator wanted to create economies of scale in an industrial management of the entire water service (from caption to wastewater treatment), with the dual aim of encouraging investments in the urban water management sector, while also creating a management capable of self-financing, through reveues so as to cover both the costs induced by the greater demand and the arrears existing in the sewerage and purification sector [7, 8]. The Galli Law also introduced a clear separation between the planning and control functions, assigned by the legislator to the local Authority (EGA – Area Governance Body), and the production and management functions, entrusted to new subjects operating according to a business logic and chosen by the tender.

The reform therefore aimed to introduce forms of competition in the water service sector in order to ensure greater economic efficiency in the production and management of water resources as well as exploit the economies of scale and scope typical of network services. The development of services requires huge financial means that should be obtained through the application of tariffs capable of highlighting both the social opportunity cost of the various uses of the water resource and the opportunity cost of the investments destined for the development of the services.

In synthesis, the Galli reform aimed for a model in which Local Authorities, through the EGA, carried out the main regulatory activities locally. The EGA is reserved the preparation of the Area Plan (PDA), the choice of the form of management, the assigning of the service, the controlling of the Operator's work and the periodic adjustment of the tariffs.

Based on this regulatory context, the relationships between EGA (local Authority) and private operator, regardless of the choice of the form of management of the service, are negotiated through a contract: the management agreement. It is therefore possible to state that the SII is characterized by *a regulation by contract*, combined with regulation factors independently found in a national tariff system (*Regulatory schemes*) and in the functions of the local regulatory body (EGA). Subsequent amendments to the TUA (Consolidated Environmental Text) of 2006 resulted in the repeal of the Galli Law, while the Prime Ministerial Decree of 20 July 2012 defined in art. 1 the functions relating to water services for the Ministry of the Environment and the Protection of the Territory and the Sea (MATTM) and in art. 3 the regulation and control functions transferred to the former AEEGSI (Authority for Electricity, Gas and Water Works), today ARERA (Regulatory Authority for Energy, Networks and Environment), which immediately started reorganizing the service.

1.2 The Intervention Program and a Comparison Between the Technical Intervention Alternatives

ARERA, acting as national Authority in the regulation of water service, with Resolution 585/2012/R/Idr (which incorporates the indications of art.154 c. 4 of Legislative Decree 152/2006) assigned the local Authority (EGA) the task of preparing the proposal of the tariffs that the Operator will apply. This proposal must contain the Intervention Program (PoI) which details the investments that the Operator will have to make within the regulatory four-year period identified by the Authority. This is an instrument with public matrix priority objectives (social, economic and environmental of the community concerned), all borrowed from the PDA (Area plan defined by the EGA) but with careful consideration of the business aims of the Operator, however relevant for the financial sustainability of the management model [9–11]. While the law attributes the responsibility for the tariff proposal to the EGA, the necessarily concerted scope of the tariff construction process is evident, in a close comparison between the public and private operators. These principles are contained in Authority regulatory directives such as 643/2013/R/idr, 664/2015/R/Idr and 917/2017/R/Idr (Technical Quality Regulation - RQTI). ARERA absorbs the European guidelines within the tariff proposal, requesting, for the analysis of intervention programs, the explicit definition and evaluation of investment alternatives in order to solve the critical issues identified in the area of competence. Moreover, the national Authority specifies that the possible alternatives must always be compared at least with the zero option or the do-nothing option.

1.3 The Centrality of the Intervention Program

As mentioned, in the PoI, the local Authority indicates the investments that the Operator must make in the four-year programming period to respond to any emerging needs in the area of competence. In general terms, the needs of the entire ATO (Optimal Territorial Area, a reference territorial dimension introduced by Galli Law in order to achieving adequate management dimensions and creating economies of scale) are listed in the PDA (Area plan defined by the EGA) within a set of critical issues $\{C_A\}$ and described therein with respect to their relevance and the impact they determine. ARERA in the Resolution 3/2014-DSID identified 40 critical issues, classified into 7 thematic areas, to which each EGA had to trace the problems encountered in its area of competence. Subsequently, with the Resolution 2/2016-DSID, the classification of the critical issues was more detailed by presenting 8 *Areas*, 57 *Sub-areas* and 137 critical issues. The EGA remains, however, free to measure them according to its own performance indicators. In recent years, the Authority, with the Resolution 1/2018-DSID, changed the classification of the critical issues again. The current overall classification structure is shown in Fig. 1. There are *Areas* regarding management problems (for example: criticalities referred to the management of the relationship with final users) and others regarding technical problems (for example: problems regarding wastewater treatment). Each *Area* includes several *Sub-Areas* and finally, each of the *Sub-Areas* includes the *critical issues*. For example, the DIS Area – *Critical issues in the distribution* includes the Sub-Areas DIS1 – *Inadequacy of the distribution infrastructures*, DIS2 – *Pressure problems*, etc. Than, the Sub-Area DIS1 presents the critical issues DIS1.1 – *Partial or total absence of the distribution networks*, DIS1.2 – *Inadequate physical conditions of the networks and distribution systems*, etc.

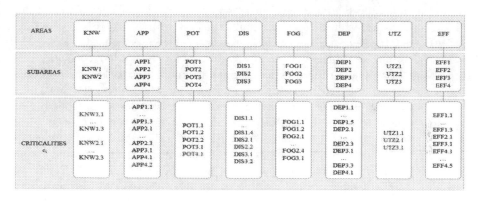

Fig. 1. Complete ramification of the critical issues $\{C\}$ imposed by the Authority. In red, an example of the subset $\{C_T\}$. Source: [1]

In summary, there is a general classification of the critical issues $\{C\}$ carried out by ARERA that is specified for each ATO in a subset $\{C_A\} \in \{C\}$.

The defining of the critical issues c_i in the PDAs often included a descriptive characterization of these, without indicating the parameters that could measure them. This often caused the lack of a clear, evident and shared correspondence between the critical issues and the related indicators. ARERA, with resolution 89/2017/R/Idr, therefore, developed and shared of a series of Pc_i indicators (not imposed, but only suggested) in order to quantification the infrastructural and operational criticalities of the integrated water service. Lastly, with the Resolution 1/2018-DSID, ARERA associated a single or multiple technical quality indicators with most of the critical issues identified. At present, the use of these indicators is not obligatory for the EGAs, but preferable. On the other hand, the use of the RQTI macro-indicators for the measurement of the technical quality standards is mandatory. When the are multiple Operators who manage different part (T) of an ATO, the subset $\{C_A\}$ has to be compared with the specificities of each of these, determining a subset of critical issues $\{C_T\} \in \{C_A\}$ for which coherent and congruous investments will have to be planned. For each criticality of the subset of territorial criticalities ($\forall c_i \in \{C_T\}$), the EGA and the Operator (even if the standard formally attributes this responsibility only to the EGA) will have to agree to identify, with respect to a multiplicity of possible design solutions, the project a_j (action) to be included in the PoI in order to decrease the impact of the criticality c_i. The selection process of the best project solutions a_{Mi} among other investment proposals must be explicit and verifiable in the drafting of the PoI.

1.4   The Hierarchical Analysis Model

The model proposed in the aforementioned study [1] satisfies the selection needs of the project alternatives requested by the national Authority and is based on the use of the AHP methodology in order to comparing alternatives.

The multi-criterion analysis is among the methodologies recommended by ARERA in the Resolution 2/2016-DSID. The choice of the AHP is justified on the basis of the information profile to be processed which, as mentioned, has qualitative and quantitative characteristics, with it requiring a multi-criteria type tool [12–16].

This model innovates the regulatory approach for three reasons.

Firstly, the model outlines an original way of selecting the best project alternatives a_{Mi} to solve the problems of the Service. Second, the model allows to identify project alternatives that may have relevance for more than one criticalities, thus rewarding multi-objective technical solutions. Moreover, it introduces three new criteria, as compared to those proposed by the national Authority, able to define the economic and financial range of the project solutions. The third reason is that the model configures a final hierarchical rout of the interventions selected a_{Mi}, with respect to the needs set out by the EGA in the PDA, capable of guiding the negotiation between the EGA and the Operator currently compulsory between the community interests and business objectives. Among the a_{Mi} defined to resolve the various c_i, some are more oriented in favour of the public operator, while others in favour of the private one. It is obvious that each Operator tends to privilege the investment in those segments (for example, water compared to sewerage) or in those activities (for example, the reduction of losses due to populous agglomerations compared to the construction of a new network branch useful for a small urban fraction) which have a higher and more immediate financial profitability [17–24]. Figure 2 show the logic of the first and second objectives of the hypothesized model. The third goal of the model is incorporated in the implementation of the first two ones. It can be useful to independently represent it, because in the current legislation, there is no reference to similar temporal hierarchization of the interventions to be executed in the PoI. So, this step is completely original with respect to legal indications. However, this study does not explicitly take this into account, postponing it for a later study.

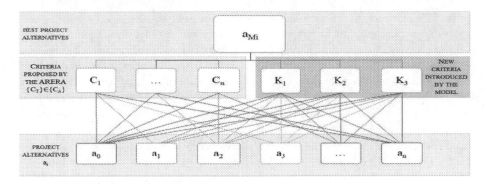

Fig. 2. The proposed model, rationalization in the choice of project alternatives a_{Mi}. Source: [1]

2   Application of the Model to the Case of an Italian Player

The model referred to and schematized in paragraph 1 was subsequently applied to a real case of Intervention Program (PoI) developed by an Operator in southern Italy under the guidance of the Research Group that has produced this article. The company in question has consented to the implementation of the protocol and, within the limits of scientific collaboration applied to a business, was willing to carry out the process as outlined by the Research Group. The Management Company (henceforth Utility) is characterized in reference to the territory served. The implementation of the phases is illustrated in the flow chart of Fig. 3.

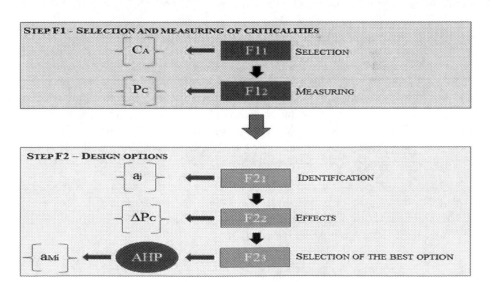

Fig. 3. Flow chart of the logic of the model presented

The discussion ends with the summary of the results obtained.

It is important to highlight how the application results are the result of a demanding mediation between the disciplinary principles responsible for optimizing the process and the stringent business logic of the interlocutor, so that the apparent simplicity of certain solutions and/or determinations also takes place after a complex concertation process between the subjects (operator and research group) with the same purposes (process optimization) but with obviously different cultural backgrounds and evaluation criteria. It should also be noted that the process described ordinarily takes place in symbiosis between the Operator and the EGA, given that the strategic principles to which the Retailer must comply in the implementation phase are contained in the PDA and are concretely declined by the EGA in the concertation phase of the PoI. The EGA is still legally responsible for the intervention program (PoI).

2.1 Management and Infrastructural Characteristics of the Managed Territory

The Utility being analyzed manages the Integrated Water Service of 20 municipalities in the Campania Region, for a total of approximately 118,000 inhabitants and a total area of 677 km^2. From the analysis of the information contained in the PDA, it is also possible to detail the estimated population served by the distribution and sewerage for the different municipalities (the data divided by municipalities, impossible to summarize in this work, can be requested directly from the authors). Overall, the distribution service covers 97% of the total resident population. Whereas, the percentage of the population served by the sewer is lower, reaching around 82%. The purification service is only partially managed by the Utility.

2.2 Application of Phase F1$_1$ – *Selection of the Critical Issues*

Referring to the flow chart of Fig. 3, which sets out the logical-implementation path specific to the model, there is then the operational implementation of each single phase. In order to clarify the phase F1$_1$, the work cannot be separated from the analysis of the critical issues $\{C_A\} \in \{C\}$ that characterize the delivery of the SII in the territory of the entire ATO. These critical issues are identified in the documents prepared by the local Area Governance Body (EGA), relating to the 2012 Update of the 2003 Area Plan drawn up on December 2012. Specifically it is:

– Volume I: Analysis of the current state – Requirements – Resources – Criticalities and Objectives of the Plan – Intervention Plan – Investment Plan;
– Volume II: Investment Plan and Tariff Development;
– Volume III: Description of the interventions.

In addition to the critical issues, the categories of the interventions aimed at solving them are consequently identified in the EGA documents.

The interventions in general deal with the restructuring and reconstruction of existing works (reconstruction of old networks and plants due to age, adaptation and extraordinary maintenance of existing treatment plants and so on); the construction of new works (completion of the water and sewage networks, new purification systems for unused residential areas, interconnections of the water supply networks to guarantee the continuity of the service, etc.); safeguarding the resource emitted from wells and springs.

The planning of the Area Plan selects interventions on the infrastructures of the SII to be paid by each Operator present in the territory. The PoI developed in this article (i.e. the one that the Operator and the Research Group shared in the process that is described here) defines the implementation of the Area Plan according to the indications of Legislative Decree 152/2006, since it includes not only interventions on infrastructures but also interventions aimed at solving critical issues related to management. In the particular case of the Utility in question, for the managed compartments, the criticalities of the SII $\{C_T\} \in \{C_A\}$, were identified through the use of the alphanumeric codes shown in Annex 1 of Resolution 2/2016 – DSID of the Authorities, reclassified for the Municipalities managed. Table 1 lists and defines, by way of example, the critical codes relating to three of the twenty Municipalities.

Table 1. Critical issues identified in the management of the SII pursuant to the Resolution issued by the ARERA 2/2016 – DSID for three municipalities belonging to the territory under the jurisdiction of the utility

ID Municipality	1	4	13
A – Water supply	–	A7.1, A7.4	A7.1, A7.4
B – Distribution	B6.3, B10.2, B1.3, B1.2, B1.1, B4.1, B1.4	B6.3, B10.2, B1.3, B1.2, B1.1, B4.1, B1.4	B6.3, B10.2, B1.3, B1.2, B1.1, B4.1, B1.4
C – Sewerage	C2.1, C2.6, C2.7	C2.1, C2.6, C2.7	C2.1, C2.6, C2.7
D – Depuration	D2.2, D2.3	D2.2, D2.3	D1.1, D2.2, D2.3
K – Knowledge of the infrastructure	K2.1, K3.1	K2.1, K3.1	K2.1, K3.1
M – Management	M1.3, M1.4, M1.5, M3.1	M1.3, M1.4, M1.5, M3.1	M1.3, M1.4, M1.5, M3.1

For example, it is worth noting how for Municipality 1, there are no critical issues in Area A of the water supply; while there are seven critical issues (B1.1, B1.2, B1.3, B1.4, B4.1, B6.3, B10.2) in the distribution segment.

The problems relate to (B1.1) the physical conditions of the pipelines in the distribution networks; (B1.2) the physical conditions of the civil works of the plants; (B1.3) the physical conditions of the mechanical and electromechanical equipment; (B1.4) the failure rate of the pipes; (B4.1) the level of losses along the distribution pipelines; (B6.3) the excessive level of pressures; (B10.2) the malfunction or age of the user metres.

There are also three critical issues (C2.1, C2.6, C2.7) in the sewerage segment (black and mixed networks); two in the treatment plants (D2.2, D2.3) as well as in the knowledge of the infrastructures (K2.1, K3.1); four in the business management segment (M1.3, M1.4, M1.5, M3.1).

The Utility, on the other hand, did not find any critical issues in its management with regards to Areas P (Criticalities in the drinking water plants) and G (Criticalities in the user services).

2.3   Application of Phase F1$_2$ – *Measurement of the Critical Issues*

As illustrated in Fig. 3, step F1$_2$ consists of identifying, for each of the identified critical issues, the Pc$_i$ performance indicator that measures them. The ARERA requires, in particular, for each identified criticality the name of the corresponding performance indicator, the formula underlying the determination, the degree of reliability of the data underlying it and the current level promptly detected/estimated of the indicator that measures the impact of the identified criticality. During the course of this work, for the identification of the performance indicator, reference was constantly made to the indications of the Resolution ARERA 89/2017/R/Idr in cases where the data required for the calculation of Pc$_i$ resulted in the availability of the Utility. If the Operator did not possess the appropriate information to quantify the ARERA indicator, an ad-hoc indicator was developed in accordance with the available datasets [25].

All the indicators useful in the model for the individual criticalities were therefore developed; an example of an indicator is given for Areas A and B.

Area A - Criticalities in the water supply (collection and abstraction pipes).
Criticality A7.1 – Inadequate physical conditions of the pipelines of the supply networks

For the measurement of this criticality, the indicator suggested by the ARERA and adopted in the model is summarized in the following table. The calculation values are also provided (Table 2).

Table 2. Calculation of the performance indicator for the criticality A7.1

Name	Code	Formula	$\sum Li$ (m)	Pc$_{A7.1}$ (years)
Average age of the abstraction pipes	A7.1a	$\sum(Ai*Li)/\sum Li$ where Ai = age from the year of entry into operation of the i-th abstraction pipe section, Li = length of the i-th abstraction pipe section	117.508	50,0

Area B - Critical issues in distribution.
Criticality B1.1 – Inadequate physical conditions of the pipelines of the distribution networks

For the measurement of this criticality, the indicator suggested by the ARERA and adopted in the model is summarized, along with the values obtained, in the following table (Table 3).

Table 3. Calculation of the performance indicator for the criticality B1.1

Name	Code	Formula	$\sum$Li (m)	$Pc_{B1.1}$ (years)
Average age of the pipelines of the distribution networks	B1.1a	$\sum$(Ai*Li)/$\sum$Li where Ai = age from the year of entry into operation of the ith section of distribution network pipelines, Li = length of the i-th section of distribution network pipelines	1.177.925	45,0

2.4 Application of Phase F2₁ – *Identification of the Alternatives*

As part of phase $F2_1$, possible project interventions were outlined aimed at solving the critical issues described in the previous paragraph.

According to the Authority, the aforementioned phase and the subsequent one ($F2_2$) are mainly the prerogative of the Operator. Therefore, following steps $F2_1$ and $F2_2$, the Operator submits to the EGA the proposal relating to the interventions potentially useful for improving the level of impact of the critical issues.

As explicitly requested by the Authority, a set of project options (alternative a_j) for each intervention is identified which also includes the scenario characterized by the absence of the implementation of the intervention (*Alternative 0*). Project solutions can often lead to improvements with respect to more than one of the criticalities. Therefore, in compliance with ARERA terminology, the project solution capable of generating improvements on one or more critical issues will be known as *intervention* hereonin. In order to comply with the ARERA requirements, each intervention is uniquely identified by an identification code (intervention ID), represented by a progressive number from 1 to N (where N is the total number of interventions resulting from the evaluation made).

For each critical issue, the intervention strategies concern:

- *Restoration/Replacement interventions* (R.S.) aimed at the reconstruction of those works which, due to technological obsolescence, age or poor state of maintenance, are no longer able to perform the service for which they are intended;
- *Extraordinary Maintenance Interventions* (M.S.): interventions whose purpose is to keep existing works in a state of efficiency through adequate scheduled mainte-nance, which involves limited substitutions or improvements;

Overall, the Utility offers 11 interventions; for 8 of these (ID 1, 2, 3, 4, 5, 6, 7, 10) it gives 3 project options (including Alternative 0); vice versa, for the remaining three interventions (ID 8, 9 and 11), the Operator is limited to identifying a single supererogatory project alternative to Alternative 0.

Table 4 describes two of the eleven interventions, those with ID 1 and 3. For these there are three technical alternatives (n.TA). The fourth column of Table 4 indicates the critical issues (c_i) that each intervention resolves. Column 5 shows the type of numerical indicator (Pc_i) which describes each criticality; Column 6 shows the unit of measure (UM). Columns 7 and 8 show the values (improving) that the numerical indicator assumes where the first technical alternative (Objective 1 – O1) is applied or the second technical alternative (Objective 2 – O2) is applied. The third alternative is that of not intervening and therefore the performance indicator does not change compared to the initial state.

Table 4. Effects of the alternatives on the identified critical issues

Intervention ID	Description	n. TA	Ci	Pc_i	UM	O1	O2
1	Rehabilitation of the deteriorated water network	3	B1.1	Average age of the pipelines of the distribution networks	years	44,8	45,0
			B1.4	Distribution pipeline breaks	n/100 km/year	62,8	78,1
			B4.1	Percentage of water losses	%	54,6	56,1
3	Adjustment of distribution systems	3	B1.2	Physical condition of the civil works of the plants	%	86,1	95,0
			B1.3	Physical conditions of the mechanical and electromechanical equipment	%	4,9	9,0
			M3.1	Adequate plant rate (safety)	%	2,2	6,6

2.5   Application of Phase $F2_3$ – *Selection of the Preferable Alternative*

After having identified the criticality c_i and measured the relative performance indicator Pc_i (as illustrated in phases $F1_1$ and $F1_2$), during step $F2_1$, the set of solutions a_j relating to the criticality c_i was defined. Finally, with phase $F2_2$, the objective levels of the performance indicators (Oi) that are expected to be achieved with the realization of the alternatives a_j were defined. Phase $F2_3$ of the model involved the application of the AHP methodology [26, 27] to identify the best alternative among the a_j proposed by the Utility. The AHP was applied for interventions, defining the following comparative hierarchy for each of the eleven identified:

- level 1 (general objective of the evaluation), identification for each intervention of the best project alternative a_M;
- level 2, evaluation criteria against which to make the selection;
- level 3, alternatives being compared.

The hierarchy described is presented in the figure below (Fig. 4).

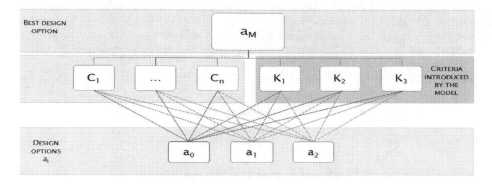

Fig. 4. The AHP hierarchy of the model for each intervention

In this step, the criteria are considered equivalent.

The project alternatives of each individual intervention are compared in pairs with respect to the critical issues for which they are conferred and with respect to the three new criteria introduced by the model. The latter are:

- K_{i1} – Population, i.e. the number of users who benefit from the implementation of the project alternative a_j;
- K_{i2} – Investment cost, intended as the capital cost of the project alternative a_j, with a negative impact on the growth in value of the predictor;
- K_{i3} – Maintenance cost the maintenance cost that the Operator must bear if realizing the alternative a_j.

The Table 5 illustrates the values of the K_{ir} criteria provided by the Operator, and then validated by the Regulator, for the alternatives (including Alternative 0) proposed for two of the eleven Interventions. Having defined all the criteria, both the performance indicators illustrated in step F22 as well as the additional criteria introduced by the proposed model (Ki1, Ki2 and Ki3), the AHP methodology is applied to select the best alternative.

Table 5. Values of the criteria K_{i1}, K_{i2} and K_{i3}

Intervention ID	Alternative a_j	Population K_{i1}	Cost of the intervention K_{i2} (€)	Annual maintenance costs K_{i3} (€)
1	A0	0	0	361.120
	A1	1.419	1.111.200	273.800
	A2	1.408	294.682	340.400
3	A0	0	0	157.350
	A1	15.342	475.000	127.500
	A2	37.275	1.058.000	89.750

The process of comparing the alternatives in pairs with respect to the related criteria is the result of a close consultation between the Regulator and the Utility; concertation that led to the expression of an agreed judgment, representative of a shared position with respect to the different interests.

Using intervention 1 as an example, Fig. 5 illustrates the comparative hierarchy adopted for the implementation of the AHP and the results obtained.

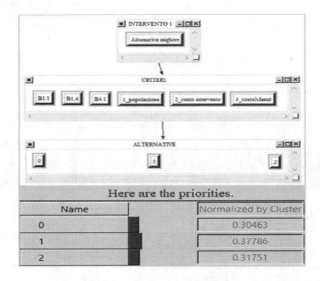

Fig. 5. Comparative hierarchy and results for Intervention 1

It should be highlighted how in this phase the achievement of an agreed judgment is not particularly complex, given that the information framework useful for assuming a critical position is mainly the prerogative of the Operator.

The results obtained are summarized in Table 6, which describes the winning alternatives after the application of the AHP for two interventions as an example.

Table 6. Synthesis of the best alternatives

Intervention ID	Description	Selected alternative and description	Ci
1	Rehabilitation of the deteriorated water network	*Alternative 1*, replacement of a part (approximately 4,600 m) of the portion of the network deemed most critical by the Utility	B1.1
			B1.4
			B4.1
3	Adaptation of Distribution networks	*Alternative 2*, consists of the restoration, both from the point of view of civil works as well as the point of view of electromechanical equipment, of n. 23 plants	B1.2
			B1.3
			M3.1
			A7.4
Tot Investments on the 11 interventions (€)			4.933.113

Finally, the same table gives an indication of the overall cost of the interventions which, for the 2016–2019 four-year period, is equal to approximately € 5,000,000. This is an amount which translates into an investment expenditure of approximately €42/inhabitant.

This value is equal to one third of that recorded by the ARERA in 2017 for the South, which was € 121/inhabitant [28].

The overall incidence of the interventions on the turnover stands at 13.7%, a value which appears, however, entirely in line with Althesys' findings [29] in recent years; from the latter, it is clear that the incidence of investments on the turnover of the main Italian utilities varies between 9.3 and 13.3%; a percentage that grows in inverse proportionality with respect to the size of the Operator.

3   Conclusions

The study describes a model useful for concretely applying the regulatory provisions on tariff regulation for the Integrated Water Service in Italy. It is capable of rationalizing the project choices for investments in the water sector and it is completely in compliance with the Intervention Program as ruled by the ARERA Resolutions 664/2015/R/Idr and 918/2017/R/Idr.

Through the AHP application the model allows to compare the project alternatives with respect to the criteria indicated by the national Authority and the innovative criteria which reconcile both the objectives of economic (population involved in the investment) and financial relevance (investment and maintenance costs).

Moreover, the model allows to reward those project solutions that simultaneously solve more problems, thus reducing intervention times while respecting the principle of maximum cost-effectiveness of the intervention.

Finally, the model can help the consultation between the public and private sectors, by rationalizing the decisive negotiation phase for the temporal scan of investments to be made with the Opertor's funds.

In a forthcoming publication, the model will be implemented on this last step with the aim of highlighting the effects of reconciling complex, often conflicting, objectives.

To date, there are no examples of models with similar characteristics in current specialized bibliography.

References

1. Macchiaroli, M., Pellecchia, V., D'Alpaos, C.: Urban water management in Italy: an innovative model for the selection of water service infrastructures. WSEAS Trans. Environ. Dev. **15**, 463–477 (2019). ISSN/E-ISSN: 1790-5079/2224-3496
2. Nesticò, A., De Mare, G., Frusciante, B., Dolores, L.: Construction costs estimate for civil works. a model for the analysis during the preliminary stage of the project. In: Gervasi, O., et al. (eds.) ICCSA 2017. LNCS, vol. 10408, pp. 89–105. Springer, Cham (2017). https://doi.org/10.1007/978-3-319-62404-4_7

3. Canesi, R., Marella, G.: Residential construction costs: an Italian case study. Int. J. Appl. Eng. Res. **12**(10), 2623–2634 (2017)
4. De Mare, G., Nesticò, A., Macchiaroli, M.: Significant appraisal issues in value estimate of quarries for the public expropriation. Valori e Valutazioni **18**, 17–23 (2017). ISSN: 20362404
5. De Mare, G., Nesticò, A., Macchiaroli, M., Dolores, L.: Market prices and institutional values comparison for tax purposes through GIS instrument. In: Gervasi, O., et al. (eds.) ICCSA 2017. LNCS, vol. 10409, pp. 430–440. Springer, Cham (2017). https://doi.org/10.1007/978-3-319-62407-5_30
6. Mazzei, A.: Manuale operativo per la regolazione del servizio idrico integrato. Franco Angeli, Italy (2017)
7. D'Alpaos, C.: The value of flexibility to switch between water supply sources. Appl. Math. Sci. **6**(125–128), 6381–6401 (2012)
8. D'Alpaos, C.: The privatization of water services in Italy: make or buy, capability and efficiency issues. In: Mondini, G., Fattinnanzi, E., Oppio, A., Bottero, M., Stanghellini, S. (eds.) SIEV 2016. GET, pp. 223–231. Springer, Cham (2018). https://doi.org/10.1007/978-3-319-78271-3_18
9. Tramontana, C., Calabrò, F., Cassalia, G., Rizzuto, M.C.: Economic sustainability in the management of archaeological sites: the case of Bova Marina (Reggio Calabria, Italy). In: Calabrò, F., Della Spina, L., Bevilacqua, C. (eds.) ISHT 2018. SIST, vol. 101, pp. 288–297. Springer, Cham (2019). https://doi.org/10.1007/978-3-319-92102-0_31
10. Antoniucci, V., Marella, G.: The influence of building typology on the economic feasibility of urban developments. Int. J. Appl. Eng. Res. **12**(15), 4946–4954 (2017)
11. Della Spina, L.: Scenarios for a sustainable valorisation of cultural landscape as driver of local development. In: Calabrò, F., Della Spina, L., Bevilacqua, C. (eds.) ISHT 2018. SIST, vol. 100, pp. 113–122. Springer, Cham (2019). https://doi.org/10.1007/978-3-319-92099-3_14
12. Nesticò, A., De Mare, G., Granata, F.: Weak and strong compensation for the prioritization of public investments: multidimensional analysis for pools. Sustainability **7**, 16022–16038 (2015). https://doi.org/10.3390/su71215798
13. Della Spina, L.: Historical cultural heritage: decision making process and reuse scenarios for the enhancement of historic buildings. In: Calabrò, F., Della Spina, L., Bevilacqua, C. (eds.) ISHT 2018. SIST, vol. 101, pp. 442–453. Springer, Cham (2019). https://doi.org/10.1007/978-3-319-92102-0_47
14. Manganelli, B., De Mare, G., Nesticò, A.: Using genetic algorithms in the housing market analysis. In: Gervasi, O., et al. (eds.) ICCSA 2015. LNCS, vol. 9157, pp. 36–45. Springer, Cham (2015). https://doi.org/10.1007/978-3-319-21470-2_3
15. Cassalia, G., Tramontana, C., Calabrò, F.: Evaluation approach to the integrated valorization of territorial resources: the case study of the Tyrrhenian area of the metropolitan city of Reggio Calabria. In: Calabrò, F., Della Spina, L., Bevilacqua, C. (eds.) ISHT 2018. SIST, vol. 101, pp. 3–12. Springer, Cham (2019). https://doi.org/10.1007/978-3-319-92102-0_1
16. Nesticò, A., He, S., De Mare, G., Benintendi, R., Maselli, G.: The ALARP principle in the Cost-Benefit analysis for the acceptability of investment risk. Sustainability **10**(12) (2018). Article no. 4668. https://doi.org/10.3390/su10124668
17. Dolores L., Macchiaroli M., De Mare G.: Sponsorship for the sustainability of historical-architectural heritage: application of a model's original test finalized to maximize the profitability of private investors. Sustainability **9**(10) (2017). Article no. 1750. https://doi.org/10.3390/su9101750
18. Nesticò, A., Maselli, G.: Declining discount rate estimate in the long-term economic evaluation of environmental projects. J. Environ. Account. Manage. **8**(1), 93–110 (2020). https://doi.org/10.5890/JEAM.2020.03.007

19. Dolores, L., Macchiaroli, M., De Mare, G.: A model for defining sponsorship fees in public-private bargaining for the rehabilitation of historical-architectural heritage. In: Calabrò, F., Della Spina, L., Bevilacqua, C. (eds.) ISHT 2018. SIST, vol. 101, pp. 484–492. Springer, Cham (2019). https://doi.org/10.1007/978-3-319-92102-0_51

20. Dolores, L., Macchiaroli, M., De Mare, G.: A dynamic model for the financial sustainability of the restoration sponsorship. Sustainability **12**(4) (2020). Article no. 1694. https://doi.org/10.3390/su12041694

21. Nesticò, A., Maselli, G.: A protocol for the estimate of the social rate of time preference: the case studies of Italy and the USA. J. Econ. Stud. **47**(3), 527–545 (2020). https://doi.org/10.1108/JES-02-2019-0081

22. Nesticò, A., Macchiaroli, M., Pipolo, O.: Historic buildings and energetic requalification a model for the selection of technologically advanced interventions. In: Gervasi, O., et al. (eds.) ICCSA 2015. LNCS, vol. 9157, pp. 61–76. Springer, Cham (2015). https://doi.org/10.1007/978-3-319-21470-2_5

23. Nesticò, A., De Mare, G., Fiore, P., Pipolo, O.: A model for the economic evaluation of energetic requalification projects in buildings. a real case application. In: Murgante, B., et al. (eds.) ICCSA 2014. LNCS, vol. 8580, pp. 563–578. Springer, Cham (2014). https://doi.org/10.1007/978-3-319-09129-7_41

24. Fiore, P., Nesticò, A., Macchiaroli, M.: The energy improvement of monumental buildings. An investigation protocol and case studies. Valori e Valutazioni **16**, 45–55 (2016). ISSN: 2036-2404

25. Alagre, H., et al.: Performance Indicators for Water Supply Services, 3rd edn. IWA Publishing, London (2016)

26. Saaty, T.L.: The Analytic Hierarchy Process. McGraw-Hill, New York (1980)

27. Saaty, T.L.: Decision making with the analytic hierarchy process. Int. J. Serv. Sci. **1**(1), 83–98 (2008)

28. ARERA: Relazione Annuale sullo stato dei servizi e sull'attività svolta, vol. I – Stato dei servizi (2017)

29. Marangoni, A.: Le local italiane e il settore idrico. Gli investimenti e le performance delle imprese. In: Conferenza Nazionale sulla Regolazione dei Servizi Idrici. Althesys, Milano (2013)

Spatial Knowledge in Large-Scale Environments: A Preliminary Planning-Oriented Study

Giulia Mastrodonato and Domenico Camarda[(⊠)]

Polytechnic University of Bari, Bari, Italy
domenico.camarda@poliba.it

Abstract. Strategic planning has recently focused its attention on the elements that characterize the spaces through which the agents move, paying particular attention on the way in which they incorporate them. Spatial environments are currently studied from different perspectives, from the cognitivist point of view they represent knowledge-intensive, significant spatial entities to which human agents need to relate adaptively.

The way in which humans use the surrounding space is influenced by a series of implicit factors, such as perceptions, emotions, sensations. These elements, being often tacit, are difficult to identify although they strongly characterize these spaces. For this reason, these characteristics become basic for effective strategic planning at urban and regional level and for environmental decision-making processes.

This study presents a method for quantitatively measuring the reactions of visitors to scenes they encounter in spaces with an extremely small population. We conducted an experiment that required participants to take photographs of elements that caught their attention in poorly structured rural areas. In this way, the photographed features and the related comments have made it possible to better grasp perceptions, sensations, emotions that can represent crucial spatial variables for structuring and interpreting spaces.

Keywords: Strategic planning · Spatial cognition · Open environments · Spatial variables

1 Introduction

Spatial environments are currently studied from different perspectives. From the cognitive point of view, they represent spatial entities characterized by a high density of knowledge to which human agents need to adaptively relate along their life [33]. These environments present an intrinsic complexity that causes complicated problems in planning and management domains [13]. As a consequence, also the interpretation of the agents' spatial behaviors is difficult to characterize and to simulate within artificial intelligence or cybernetic schemes. With regard to this, it is widely recognized that there is a semantic circularity between AI and cognitive science so that the results of research on robotic artificial intelligence devices are fundamental for understanding spatial changes for human decision-making.

© Springer Nature Switzerland AG 2020
O. Gervasi et al. (Eds.): ICCSA 2020, LNCS 12255, pp. 162–174, 2020.
https://doi.org/10.1007/978-3-030-58820-5_12

In order to simplify the interpretation of the spatial agents' behavior models, it is necessary to recognize and interpret the features of the surrounding space that affect agents both as points of reference for navigation through spaces and in terms of emotions or perceptions.

Although in literature it is difficult to find a clear definition of the concept of cognitive map and of the processes behind their construction, it is generally agreed that they result from the experience with the environment and the expectations people mature with reference to it.

Cognitive maps creation is the result of very complex processes that may involve verbal instructions decoding, reading maps, images, photographs, or whatever else is involved in our experience with the environment. However difficult changing them once learned may be, the comparison with the world, where correspondence with reality is not recognized, can lead to the addition of new elements or to their appropriate correction [2]. Therefore, despite being recognized as providing conceptual basis for wayfinding tasks, cognitive maps are ill-adapted to the surrounding environment.

In more practical terms of structuring a city cognitive map, Lynch [28] laid the foundation for researching in spatial cognition. Relying on a careful study of the maps drawn by people and on the investigation of the route descriptions, he could define some basic elements: landmarks, paths, nodes, edges, districts. Through these elements he defines the legibility as the ease in identifying physical characteristics in the scheme of a city that help create the image of it our mental representation. According to Lynch [28], the construction of such conceptual models is different from person to person and from task to task.

Recognizing the fundamental spatial characteristics is particularly difficult as it is not always possible to distinguish between substantial and ornamental qualities in the humans' perceptions [18]. Borri and Camarda [6] found that the distinction between "substance" and "ornament" or between "content" and "form" is often unclear in spatial analysis. Day & Bartels, [11] Pouget *et al.* [32] argue that the representation space also changes over time in a way that is not always predictable. For these reasons, the recognition of spatial foundations plays a decisive role in strategic planning.

From the above mentioned, spatial knowledge takes on increasingly interdisciplinary connotations by involving psychology, cybernetics, landscape architecture and engineering environments both on micro-scale spaces (buildings or neighborhoods) and in meso-scale spaces (cities as mixed sets of installed spaces and open spaces) [5, 6]. Researches open interesting perspectives on issues related to conceptual, relational and ontological intelligence but also on orientation problems in indoor and outdoor spaces, on the planning of open spaces and on the pleasantness of green areas.

Although at a macro-scale level space research is still limited [14, 33], studies on the configuration of spaces such as deserts, mountains, forests, oceans, are underway. These spatial conditions extremely complex are comparable to a sort of condition preanthropogenic.

In light of the foregoing, we try to study the spatial behavior of agents who move in open and unstructured spaces with extremely small populations, trying to capture the elements that strike their attention. These spaces seem apparently poor compared to urban settlements, so it may be easier to elicit the elements – able to trigger perceptions, sensations, relationships - that influence the user's attention and therefore can be considered as crucial spatial variables.

In particular, we try to analyze the way in which the characterizing features are identified in space during spatial navigation in an open space and to enrich the data information that is gradually acquired. This is also useful in order to identify the elements that can be interpreted as points of reference so that they provide support for navigating such unstructured spaces.

The next chapter provides a research background on spatial cognition, while in chapter three the introduction of the research project structure is presented. Chapter four describes the study we carried out, the methodology adopted and the discussion of some results. The conclusions and an overview of the study outlooks follow.

2   Research Background: An Interdisciplinary Approach

The branch of artificial intelligence focused on spatial cognition pays close attention to the difference between structured and unstructured spaces. The former are characterized by simple geometries - elementary paths, few decisions required, scarcity in terms of furnishings - the latter by numerous articles, composite profiles that require numerous choices to be made or involve unexpected events [10, 16, 23]. Obviously, robots move more easily in poorly structured spaces, being simpler to learn and identify, although recently their behavior is getting closer and closer to human agents' behavior.

Human agents too move more easily in legible spatial layouts that present simple, unidirectional geometries, e.g. a long and empty corridor with doors, windows, skylights lined up. From a logical point of view, they are comparable to a graph arc, with a start point and an end point, without intersections. They require little attention.

Differently it is much more difficult to orientate yourself and navigate through open spaces that offer multiple directions of movement and present a multi-dimensional structure - e.g. a city square - perhaps even more difficult can be the understanding of rural spaces where it is not possible to distinguish the starting/ending points. Although tackle navigation and orientation tasks in spaces with a reduced population is particularly difficult, human agents are able to develop a cognitive map based on the recognition and memorization of points of reference in order to improve the legibility of spaces otherwise incomprehensible [12, 17, 20].

When the information stemming from the surrounding environment is poor, problem arises in identifying the latent variables essential to characterize the space; these variables are extrapolated by human agents to build up the structure of their cognitive map. Knowing that these variables are not easy to identify, the aim of this work is to try to understand, through experimentation on human agents, how these spaces are cognitively modeled.

In fact, it is known that human agents perceive natural elements present in the surrounding environment in a different way and their perception can, in turn, influence the assessments of the surrounding space and human behaviors. A broad body of literature recognizes that some elements of the landscape are preferred by humans; therefore identifying these elements is fundamental for a correct design and management of the environment [25, 40]. On the other hand, preferences are based on the perceptions which are described as a process for understanding sensory information by integrating not only elements present in a scenario but also the unconscious and rapid differences in how space can be used [3, 21, 22].

Understanding how these hostile spaces are interpreted and integrated into the cognitive maps of human agents is also fundamental in shedding light on the navigation strategies they adopt. According to literature in very poor environments, mammals and humans resort to the path integration. The process is triggered thanks to the information coming from our senses through sight, or from our body through proprioception deriving from the movement of the body [23, 24]. Kelly *et al.* [23] claim that in poor environments the absence of external points of reference forces us to refer more to the visual, proprioceptive or kinesthetic flow of information based on perception of the body. Agents assume the initial position and the elements essential to define landmarks. By using this process we are able to construct vectors that are constantly updated along the way [37] in order to provide an estimate of the current position within a larger environment. This continuous updating process for very long paths can result in a demanding cognitive load. Additionally, the absence of significant landmarks significantly worsens spatial orientation because it increases the amount of information to keep in mind.

In this work, we examine the results of experiments conducted with the students of the engineering school of the Polytechnic of Bari. They were asked to walk freely in a rural area and take pictures on what they thought was interesting. Moreover they could add some annotations to tell about their experience. The narration allows them to express the perception of the elements they considered significant. This data is also useful for planners and designers in their decision-making process [19].

This research aimed at identifying which elements characterizing spaces are considered fundamental by users. We tried to do this analyzing the subjects' reactions in order to model the underlying cognitive processes based on the available literature. An attempt has been made to identify a possible correlation between these elements and the perceptions and/or sensations that the agents reported. The resulting data are analyzed in order to trace correlations between the elements present in the protocols collected during the ad hoc experimentation.

3   The Case Study

In 2017, an experiment was carried out with 180 students of the last year of the Urban Planning course at the Polytechnic of Bari were involved. Each student agent freely chose a path in an open rural space. During navigation, they could take pictures of scenarios that attracted their attention. They were also asked to take notes of sensations, perceptions, emotions felt along the way. Route, places of interest and feelings annoted were geo-referenced via smartphone app by each agent, who added his/her profile details on the related online portal.

It has been recently shown that pictures can be used with a high rate of confidence in perceptual studies [19, 21, 35]. The characteristics of the environment are captured through visual experiences, therefore the recognition of elements that have been captured helps understand their experience of space much more than a simple questionnaire. Furthermore, the method offers any participant an immediate and simple way to express the surrounding environment without the need for specific skills [32] allowing, in this way, an immediate identification of essential and latent elements in rural or poorly structured areas.

At present we have carried out a preliminary study, the following analysis refers on a limited sample of 16 out of 180 observations. The statistical work required for the complete analysis of the larger amount of data is currently underway.

Except agent' profile details, the data set is mainly embedded in the kml/ kmz file, from which the quantitative figures are then extracted as strings, texts and graphics (Fig. 1 and 2).

Fig. 1. Example of kmz file: track, photo snapshot and photo locations (Google Earth)

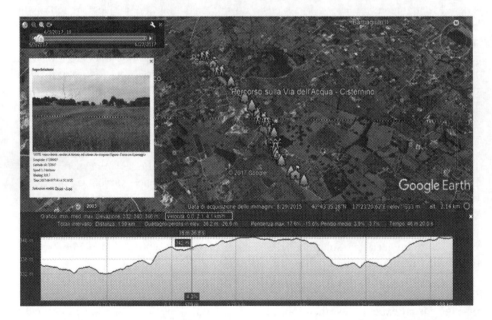

Fig. 2. Example of kmz file: track, levels, snapshot and note locations (icons)

The data mining software Concordance ™ allowed the collection of text annotations in order to calculate the frequencies of word and concept to identify keywords and recognize elements and/or repeats. These are manual ex-post analyzes to aggregate words into conceptual categories [26]. The ordered dataset is reported in Fig. 3, connected to clusters of conceptual categories specified in Fig. 4.

#	ID	Town of residence	Explored location	Residence-location distance (km) LUO	Min altitude (m) ALT	Level difference (m) DIS	Length (km) LUN	Duration TEM	Buildings COS	Fauna FAU	Flora FLO	Natural landscape PAE	Dissipation and pollution INQ	Sensations SEN	Plants and installations TRA	Streets VIE	Abstract features ABS	topology TOP
1	552201	Fasano	Cisternino	12	368,2	44,9	1,6	00:46:20	11	3	11	9	4	8	5	5	14	8
2	553745	Bitritto Puglia	Bitonto	15	81	26,7	2	00:42:00	14	1	1	3	4	3	3	5	5	6
3	555252	TRIGGIANO	Carbonara	3,3	41	15,4	0,835	00:41:00	8	1	2	13	14	10	1	3	10	11
4	555512	Laterza	Laterza	6,6	350	48,4	4,3	00:40:00	7	1	1	11	8	3	1	10	7	1
5	566879	Lucera	Lucera	5	192	19,8	2,82	00:26:00	1	1	4	2	1	1	4	4	3	2
6	566927	Rocchetta S.A. (FG)	Rocchetta	1,6	596	76	1,02	00:12:04	12	1	6	6	3	7	2	4	9	4
7	567428	Altamura	Altamura	6	388	23,4	0,8	00:29:00	1	2	2	5	1	4	1	14	1	2
8	567559	Foggia	Siponto	32	1	3	2,31	00:37:00	7	1	3	2	7	13	5	8	4	10
9	567604	Foggia	Segezia	14	134	208	2	00:45:12	3	1	3	5	6	4	9	11	1	7
10	567637	Martina Franca	Chiancaro	1,5	397	423	2,9	00:51:39	14	2	1	10	3	13	1	3	1	9
11	567658	Manfredonia	Amendola	18	34	39	0,617	00:41:00	1	2	14	9	1	11	2	13	11	5
12	567719	Troia	Troia	0,6	1	1	2,29	00:30:00	1	1	1	5	1	1	2	12	1	5
13	567876	Lucera(FG)	Lucera	5	126	30,4	3,42	00:20:33	11	1	5	11	1	8	1	14	2	6
14	570501	Bari	Torre a mare	12	1	4	1,06	00:13:21	4	1	3	3	1	30	3	11	6	7
15	570643	Foggia	Ordona	17	91	9	1,73	00:36:00	1	1	1	1	1	1	1	4	4	3
16	580072	Colletorto (CB)	Colletorto	0,8	571	775	7,9	01:28:49	8	1	5	1	8	12	8	5	8	6

Fig. 3. The complete database

Buildings	COS	EDILIZIA, BORGO, MASSERIA, CASALE, COSTRUZIONE, URBANI, CONVENTO, FONTANA, PIETRA, PONTE, CHIESA, EDIFICIO, MURETTI, SILOS, TORRE, VILLA, ABBEVERATOIO, ABITATO, CASA, DEPOSITO, FRANTOIO, PAESE, PORTA, POZZO, TORRI, TRULLO, ARCO, ARCO, CAPANNI, CASTELLO, FINESTRE, MANUFATTO, MARMOREE, MONASTERO, SCALA
Fauna	FAU	CAVALLI, INSETTI, ANIMALI, CANI, COLEOTTERO, DOG, FAUNA, VIPERA
Flora	FLO	VEGETAZIONE, ALBERI, PIANTA, FLORA, CIPOLLE, ERBA, FICO, FIORE, FRONDE, MORE, POMODORI, VERDURE
Natural landscape	PAE	CAMPO, GRANO, RURALE, COLTIVAZIONI, TERRA, ULIVI, VIGNA, CAMPAGNA, TORRENTE, VALLE, AMBIENTALE, AMBIENTE, FLUVIALE, INCOLTO, NATURA, PAESAGGIO, AGRICOLO, AGRUMETO, BUCOLICO, FIUMETTO, PARCO, RACCOLTO, ACQUA, AMBIENTE, ARATURA, CANNETO, FILARI, MONTI, PARK, STEPPA, STERPAGLIA
Dissipation and pollution	INQ	RIFIUTI, DEGRADO, ABUSIVISMO, AMIANTO, ECOMOSTRO
Sensations	SEN	ABBAIARE, ABBANDONO, ACCIDENTATO, ACRE, AGEVOLE, APPARIVA, ARIA, ARSO, BELLO, BENESSERE, BREVE, BRUCIATA, CALDO, CALMA, COGNITIVA, COLORI, COMODO, CONFONDE, CONTRASTO, DETURPA, DISMISURA, DISSESTATO, DISTESA, EFFETTO, ESALAZIONI, ESPLORARE, FATICA, GRADEVOLE, IMMAGINE, LIBERTÀ, LUCE, ODORE, ORIENTARMI, PACE, PANORAMA, PERICOLANTE, PERICOLO, PIACEVOLE, RISTORO, RUMORE, SCORCIO, SCORGERE, SECCO, SENSAZIONE, SENSO, SGRADEVOLE, SICUREZZA, SPENSIERATEZZA, SPERANZA, STANCHEZZA, SUGGESTIVO, TORRIDO, TRANQUILLITÀ, VENTICELLO
Plants and installations	TRA	INDUSTRIALE, PALE, EOLICO, ARTIGIANALE, RECINTO, CANCELLO, ACQUEDOTTO, AZIENDA, DIGA, TRATTORE, ANTENNA, PALI, PANNELLI, PISCINA, TRALICCI
Streets	VIE	STRADA, PERCORSO, SENTIERO, ATTRAVERSARE, TRAGITTO, ASFALTO, CAMMINO, STERRATO, RAGGIUNGERE, SEGUIRE, PASSEGGIATA, SALITA, BIVIO, FERROVIA, INCROCIO, SVOLTA, CURVA, RETTILINEO, TRACCIATO, TRAFFICATA, VIAGGIO
Abstract features	ABS	VISTA, FORTUNA, INCOMPIUTI, PRESENZA, TRADIZIONI, IGNOTO, NATURA, QUALITÀ, VISTE, ASSENZA, ANTICO, PROSPETTIVA, OBIETTIVO, ILLUMINAZIONE, INTERNO, PARTI, STATO, TEMPO, APERTO, LONTANANZA,
topology	TOP	CONFINI, LUOGO, POSTO, RECINTO, TERRITORIO, SPAZIO, INGRESSO, INTORNO, LATO, AREA, ORIZZONTE, PUGLIESE, CIGLIO, LUOGHI, PUNTO, QUI, PARTE, TERRENI

Fig. 4. The clusters of conceptual categories (*Italian excerpt*)

The online web portal of the experimentation is reported in Fig. 5, showing the relevant directions and information for respondents to complete their task.

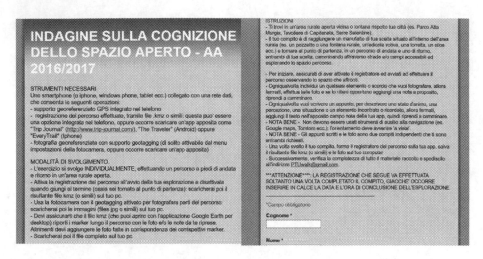

Fig. 5. The web portal of the experimental session (*Italian excerpt*)

The goal of this work, as specified above, is to explore the interconnections between spatial perceptions and/or cognitions of agents and some characterizing elements in the nearby open space.

Regression Statistics	
Multiple R	0,999991784
R Square	0,999983569
Adjusted R Square	0,999753529
Standard Error	0,117466051
Observations	16

ANOVA

	df	SS	MS	F	Significance F
Regression	14	839,7362017	59,98115727	4347,00461	0,01188717
Residual	1	0,013798273	0,013798273		
Total	15	839,75			

	Coefficients	Standard Error	t Stat	P-value
Intercept	25,02714273	0,333871773	74,9603434	0,00849225
LUO	0,269964976	0,006949165	38,8485468	0,0163836
ALT	-0,06864833	0,000777872	-88,2514665	0,00721339
DIS	0,126104067	0,000905269	139,3000343	0,00457006
LUN	1,17971297	0,043601742	27,0565561	0,02351852
TEM	-1,32767152	0,01004726	-132,142648	0,00481758
COS	0,522506398	0,017177803	30,41753346	0,02092183
FAU	19,31984334	0,209791355	92,09075045	0,00691269
FLO	-0,71345684	0,029718375	-24,0072629	0,02650248
PAE	-1,32845931	0,023628667	-56,2223559	0,01132206
INQ	2,703984806	0,043864162	61,64451045	0,01032637
TRA	-0,87958957	0,022028729	-39,9292017	0,01594038
VIE	0,556696904	0,011979752	46,46981903	0,01369753
ABS	1,412044889	0,024395856	57,88052263	0,01099777
TOP	-1,73927257	0,04533949	-38,3610974	0,01659169

Fig. 6. The regression output

At this preliminary stage, a multiple regression analysis was used, as an exploratory approach to investigate on possible relations of mutual dependence among variables, while focusing on multiple independent variables at the same time. The aim was to conduct a thorough and mutually comparative evaluation and discussion, made necessary by the small sample analyzed [9].

Using the multiple regression plug-in of Microsoft Excel (Fig. 6 summarizes statistical outcomes); it is possible to sketch out a formal equation as guideline for subsequent considerations.

$$
\begin{aligned}
Y_{SEN} =\ & 25,02 + 0.27X_{LUO} - 0.06X_{ALT} + 0.126X_{DIS} + 1.179X_{LUN} - 1.32X_{TEM} \\
& + 0.52X_{COS} + 19.31X_{FAU} - 0.71X_{FLO} - 1.33X_{PAE} + 2.70X_{INQ} \\
& - 0.88X_{TRA} + 0.56X_{VIE} + 1.41X_{ABS} - 1.73X_{TOP}
\end{aligned}
$$

Obviously, being an extremely small sample, it is not possible to infer solid evaluations; however interesting trends and suggestions are deduced. Moreover, the general significance acquired ($R2 > 0.99$) does not overshadow the rather low value in many regression coefficients, as well as the little correlation in absolute terms.

The analysis of the data shows an increase in the sensations and perceptions expressed during navigation directly proportional to the quantitative variation of some characteristics. This could be traced back to the fact that the absence of strong environmental characteristics tends to maximize the likelihood of reliance on egocentric reference systems. The approximation of the current position, therefore, is monitored by self-motion generated signals, such as visual, vestibular and proprioception information. In other words, the more information you memorize the easier it is to relocate your position in the cognitive map.

More particularly, expressions of sensation increase with pollution and resource dissipation appearing along the route (INQ: coeff. = +2.70; $p = 0.01$).

Sensation also sharply increases with the presence of animals (FAU: coeff. = +19.31; $p = 0.007$), probably because of their unexpectedly emerging as singularities on the route.

Chenoweth and Gobster [8] found that aesthetic and sensory experiences tend to activate unexpectedly as a result of interaction with natural objects, even following ephemeral events [31]. Furthermore, it has been demonstrated [39] that the environments that include water, vegetation and animals are the most appreciated among the various scenarios photographed taken by subjects moving though natural environments [36].

Yet sensations exhibit mixed correlations with buildings and artificial features, with coefficients fluctuating around zero value. Agents' sensations increase with the perception of buildings ($c = 0.52$, $p = 0.02$) and streets ($c = 0.55$; $p = 0.01$), while decreasing with plants and installations ($c = -0.88$; $p = 0.01$). In particular, this apparently inconsistent result may be connected to a sample bias. The sample is extremely homogeneous since it consists exclusively of engineering students of a planning course. They are particularly sensitive to evaluating buildings and infrastructure as contextual parts of a wider ecological environment. Their background of studies could naturally induce them to give more emphasis to sensations related to events/ transformations of which they feel responsible in terms of design (e.g., houses, farms, streets) and to neglect sensations related to the recognition of features considered out of their competence (plants, installations etc.) [4, 34]. On the other hand, the greater attention paid to buildings and streets in a country setting can also be the result of the fact that in the surrounding environment, they stand out as very visible emergencies and therefore they became a sort of landmark in a territory that otherwise would be too homogeneous. In fact, the literature reports that the recognition of a landmark, reducing the uncertainty of those who navigate, could strengthen the accuracy of the path integration.

It is worthy to note that this underestimation does not seem to limit value judgements: in fact, sensations remain positively correlated with dissipating or polluting elements, which are typically involved with physical transformations. Nassauer [30] refer that "taking care" is a typically western cultural phenomenon, widespread, able to trigger an immediate reaction. Care implies participation in the maintenance of landscapes, which results into a benefit for all. It is also known that the sensations reported often reveal the perceived benefits coming from the surrounding environment but also depend on the individual. Furthermore, the perception of the benefit is not static but can change when new circumstances arise [19].

A further seemingly odd result is the negative correlation with the perception of natural landscape ($c = -1.33$, $p = 0.01$), somehow counterintuitive and difficult to be interpreted. Yet literature suggests that usual environments are poorly perceived by agents continuatively acting in that environment [24, 27]. In this sense, natural landscapes are usual environments for students living with their families in lands still traditionally characterized by rural features Therefore, they may be willing and able to describe landscapes that they know quite well, without deriving particular sensations from them. The opposite may be true as well, because agents may be stimulated to the expression of sensations and emotions, yet without describing perceptions about a landscape inherently known [7, 15]. Quite coherently, the flora element ($c = -0.71$, $p = 0.03$) seems to confirm such interpretation, in broad terms.

Subsequently, other elements define the navigation task from a spatial-temporal, geographic and topographical standpoint. For instance, when considering an increasing distance from the agent's residential place ($c = 0.26$, $p = 0.02$) and particularly an increasing route length ($c = 1.18$, $p = 0.02$), then sensations grow as well. It is also likely that this depends on curiosity or the novelty effect for a new environment and for a more changeable environment [29]. However, an inconsistence arises with an upcoming negative correlation with the time required to cover the route ($c = -1.33$, $p = 0,005$). This apparent incoherence might be overridden if one considers that a longer time can cause some addiction to perceptions, particularly for a short and not very varied route [24, 38]. On the other hand, in terms of orientation, the fact that the recording of perceptions reduces with the approach of the end of the path could be simply due to the fact that having recognized to be towards the end of the path, on the way back, there was no need to memorize new landmarks or reference points. In other words, because the agents recognized the proximity of the starting point, it was no longer necessary to update the path integration vectors. Furthermore, Sugimoto [36] reports that the frequency with which agents take photos tends to decrease gradually due to the greater tiredness of the subjects and an increase in boredom and fatigue. This element should not be overlooked as it allows us to understand changes in perception with broader awareness of the environment acquired by users. In any case, the sensations correlate poorly with the dimensional and topographical aspects to the advantage of the contextual and qualifying ones.

4 Conclusions

According to the literature, the way in which spatial elements are rapidly assessed depends on the operating potentiality of the surrounding environment perceived by users. This is true in terms of aesthetic, environmental, legibility and ease of navigation benefits. Some studies have also clarified the validity of the method of analyzing pictures taken by subjects for identifying and understanding the perceptions of users of open spaces.

This study represents a first step in an attempt to grasp the way in which the elements characterizing the surrounding space are quickly identified. The result of the analysis conducted shows a number of interesting and sometimes intriguing, but not significant enough (at least in some cases) suggestions, due to the reduced number of observations and data. In fact, it is purely a preliminary study, still far from adequate research at this stage. However, the pictures taken and the annotations attached provide first indications of the elements characterizing the open spaces that impact the users.

As a matter of fact, many coefficients show low numerical value, so causing the analyzed variables to limitedly affect the dependent variable – that is, the spatial sensations and perceptions of each agent along the route (SEN).

Moreover, the grouping of textual concepts by categories has been carried out using a raw and hybrid approach that may have caused inaccuracies. In fact, while the frequencies of words have been collected and calculated through data-mining tools, words have been subsequently contextualized and categorized using an ex-post manual analysis by the analyst, intrinsically inaccurate.

Notwithstanding these drawbacks and inaccuracies, the overall analysis is able to provide some interesting, at least qualitative considerations. They seem to suggest that the perception of an open space, broadly lacking the structuring elements typically present in confined urban spaces, is still dependent on some recurring physical and landscape features, able to build a cognition-based latent structuring.

Such suggestions prove to be of particular interest in supporting decisions on the management of open spaces. Also, these suggestions are useful in the processes of identification of environmental resources for sustainable community development, as well as for spatial planning aims. If these open spaces are not perceived positively they will not be used even if available. Therefore, it is essential to investigate the perceptions, needs and preferences of users before making decisions on planning open spaces in order to create natural environments that encourage people to use them more frequently. The contact with natural environments, in fact, represents a moment of psychological restoration for those who live in urban areas. In this perspective, it becomes necessary for planners and designers of outdoor spaces to investigate the perception that people have of the attributes of these spaces and their expectations.

Following the present research stage, it seems important that some particular activities are carried out in the next future, particularly aiming at enhancing the robustness and reliability of the analysis, so as to develop more contextual and useful considerations. Firstly, the analysis needs to be enlarged to the entire sample of 180 observations, and/or complemented/compared with further experimental sessions. A second step will be a necessary attempt to integrate the statistical analysis with a probabilistic approach, using inference techniques. This will be aimed at compensating the statistical errors fatally induced by the multiple regression analysis. Furthermore, the sample made up of students from the Polytechnic was extremely homogeneous, it is necessary to repeat the experimentation with various types of participants and make the sample more numerous and statistically significant. In fact, it is known that people of different ages and social, cultural or economic backgrounds perceive natural landscapes in very different ways [19].

As a longer view, the survey carried out here will be further analyzed and complemented using new ontology-based aggregative approaches, increasing used spatial cognition literature [1]. This effort is oriented to the possible building up of spatial models more suitable to deal with the inherent complexity of open environmental system.

References

1. Barkowsky, T., Knauff, M., Ligozat, G., Montello, D.R. (eds.): Spatial Cognition 2006. LNCS (LNAI), vol. 4387. Springer, Heidelberg (2007). https://doi.org/10.1007/978-3-540-75666-8
2. Barkowsky, T., Freksa, C.: Cognitive requirements on making and interpreting maps. In: Hirtle, S.C., Frank, A.U. (eds.) COSIT 1997. LNCS, vol. 1329, pp. 347–361. Springer, Heidelberg (1997). https://doi.org/10.1007/3-540-63623-4_60
3. Bell, S. (ed.): Landscape, Pattern, Perception and Process. E&FNSpon, New York (1999)
4. Borri, D., Camarda, D.: Visualizing space-based interactions among distributed agents: environmental planning at the inner-city scale. In: Luo, Y. (ed.) CDVE 2006. LNCS, vol. 4101, pp. 182–191. Springer, Heidelberg (2006). https://doi.org/10.1007/11863649_23
5. Borri, D., Camarda, D.: Spatial ontologies in multi-agent environmental planning. In: Yearwood, J., Stranieri, A. (eds.) Technologies for Supporting Reasoning Communities and Collaborative Decision Making: Cooperative Approaches, pp. 272–295. IGI Global Information Science, Hershey (2010)
6. Borri, D., Camarda, D.: Modelling space perception in urban planning: a cognitive ai-based approach. In: Ali, M., Bosse, T., Hindriks, K., Hoogendoorn, M., Jonker, C., Treur, J. (eds.) Contemporary Challenges and Solutions in Applied Artificial Intelligence. Studies in Computational Intelligence, vol. 489. Springer, Heidelberg (2013). https://doi.org/10.1007/978-3-319-00651-2_1
7. Campos, M., Velázquez, A., Verdinelli, G.B., Priego-Santander, Á.G., McCall, M.K., Boada, M.: Rural people's knowledge and perception of landscape: a case study from the mexican pacific coast. Soc. Nat. Resour. 25(8), 759–774 (2012). https://doi.org/10.1080/08941920.2011.606458
8. Chenoweth, R.E., Gobster, P.H.: The nature and ecology of aesthetic experiences in the landscape. Landscape J. 9(1), 1–8 (1990)

9. Cohen, P., West, S., Aiken, L. (eds.): Applied Multiple Regression/Correlation Analysis for the Behavioral Sciences. Psychology Press, New York (2014)
10. Danziger, D., Rafal, R.: The effect of visual signals on spatial decision making. Cognition **110**, 182–197 (2009)
11. Day, S.B., Bartels, D.M.: Representation over time: the effects of temporal distance on similarity. Cognition **106**, 1504–1513 (2008)
12. de Hevia, D.M., Spelke, E.S.: Spontaneous mapping of number and space in adults and young children. Cognition **110**, 198–207 (2009)
13. Denis, M., Loomis, J.M.: Perspectives on human spatial cognition: memory, navigation and environmental learning. Psychol. Res. **71**, 235–239 (2007). https://doi.org/10.1007/s00426-006-0079-x
14. Dolins, F.L., Mitchell, R.W.: Spatial Cognition, Spatial Perception: Mapping the Self and Space. Cambridge University Press, Cambridge (2010)
15. Gantar, D., Golobič, M.: Landscape scenarios: a study of influences on attitudes and actions, a rural landscape. Futures **69**, 1–13 (2015). https://doi.org/10.1016/j.futures.2015.02.002
16. Georgiev A., Allen P.K.: Localization methods for a mobile robot in urban environments. IEEE Trans. Robot. Autom. ({TRO}) **20**, 851–864 (2004)
17. Gero, J.S., Tversky, B. (eds.): Visual and spatial reasoning in design. University of Sydney, Key Centre of Design Computing and Cognition, Sydney (1999)
18. Goodman, N.: The Structure of Appearance. Harvard UP, Cambridge (1951)
19. Hadavi, S., Kaplan, R., Hunter, M.C.R.: Environmental affordances: a practical approach for design of nearby outdoor settings in urban residential areas. Landscape Urban Plann. **134** (2015), 19–32 (2014)
20. Hirtle, S.C.: Neighborhoods and Landmarks. In: Duckham, M., Goodchild, M.F., Worboys, M.F. (eds.) Foundations of Geographic Information Science, pp. 191–230. Taylor & Francis, London (2003)
21. Kaplan, R.: The analysis of perception via preference - a strategy for studying how the environment is experienced. Landscape Plann. **12**(2), 161–176 (1985). http://dx.doi.org/10.1016/0304-3924(85)90058-9
22. Kaplan, S., Kaplan, R. (eds.): Cognition and environment—functioning in anuncertain world. Praeger, New York (1982)
23. Kelly, D.M., Bischof, W.F.: Orienting in virtual environments: how are surface features and environmental geometry weighted in an orientation task? Cognition **109**, 89–104 (2008)
24. Kelly, J.W., McNamara, T.P.: Reference frames during the acquisition and development of spatial memories. Cognition **116**(3), 409–420 (2010)
25. Koun, S.: Quantitative measurement of visitors' reactions to the settings in urban parks: spatial and temporal analysis of photographs. Landscape Urban Plann. **110**(2013), 59–63 (2012)
26. Le Yaouanc, J.M., Saux, E., Claramunt, C.: A semantic and language-based representation of an environmental scene. GeoInformatica **14**(3), 333–352 (2010). https://doi.org/10.1007/s10707-010-0103-6
27. Lipinski, J., Simmering, V.R, Johnson, J.S., Spencer, J.P.: The role of experience in location estimation: target distributions shift location memory biases. Cognition **115**(1), 147–153 (2010)
28. Lynch, K.: The Image of the City. MIT Press, Cambridge (1960)
29. Markwell, K.W.: Dimensions of photography in a nature-based tour. Ann. Tourism Res. **24**, 131–155 (1997). https://doi.org/10.1016/S0160-7383(96)00053-9
30. Nassauer, J.I.: Care and Stewardship—from home to planet. Landscape urban Plann. **100**(4), 321–323 (2011). https://doi.org/10.1016/j.landurbplan.2011.02.022

31. Oku, H., Fukamachi, K.: The differences in scenic perception of forest visitors through their attributes and recreational activity. Landscape Urban Plann. **75**(2006), 34–42 (2004)
32. Pouget, A., Ducom, J.C., Torri, J., Bavelier, D.: Multisensory spatial representations in eye-centered coordinates for reaching. Cognition **83**, B1–B11 (2002)
33. Proulx, M.J., Todorov, O.S., Taylor, A.A., de Sousa, A.A.: Where am I? Who am I? The relation between spatial cognition, social cognition and individual differences in the built environment. Front. Psychol. **7**, 64 (2016). https://doi.org/10.3389/fpsyg.2016.00064
34. Selicato, F., Camarda, D., Cera, M.: Engineering education vs. environmental planning: a case-study in Southern Italy. Plann. Pract. Res **27**(2), 275–291 (2012)
35. Shuttleworth, S.: The use of photographs as an environment presentation medium in landscape studies. J. Environ. Manage. **11**(1), 61–76 (1980)
36. Sugimoto, K.: Analysis of scenic perception and its spatial tendency: using digital cameras, GPS LOGGERS, AND GIS. Proc. Soc. Behav. Sci. **21**(2011), 43–52 (2011)
37. Wang, R.F., Spelke, E.S.: Updating egocentric representation in human navigation. Cognition **77**(3), 215–250 (2000)
38. Weinreb, A.R., Rofè, Y.: Mapping feeling: an approach to the study of emotional response to the built environment and landscape. J. Archit. Plann. Res. **30**(2), 127–145 (2013)
39. Wong, K-K., Domroes, M.: The visual quality of urban park scenes of Kowloon park, Hong Kong: likeability, affective appraisal, and cross-cultural perspectives. Environ. Plann. B Plann. Des. **32**, 617–32 (2005)
40. Zube, E.H., Sell, J.L., Taylor, J.G.: Landscape perception: research, application and theory. Landscape Plann. **9**, 1–33 (1982). https://doi.org/10.1016/0304-3924(82)90009-

Assessing Integration Performance in Coastal and Marine Protected Areas. A Document-Based Approach

Sabrina Lai[(⊠)] and Federica Leone[(⊠)]

Dipartimento di Ingegneria Civile, Ambientale e Architettura (DICAAR),
University of Cagliari, Cagliari, Italy
{sabrinalai,federicaleone}@unica.it

Abstract. Multiple pressures generated by inappropriate uses impact worldwide on coastal areas, the ever-evolving and intrinsically fragile interface where land and sea meet. To contrast such pressures, protected coastal and marine areas have been promoted and established. This adds a further layer of complexity in areas where multiple (often competing and conflicting) uses coexist, each planned and regulated on its own. Hence, integration between planning tools in coastal areas represents a key issue, in particular in the Mediterranean basin, where (in principle) it has been addressed by both legally binding acts and voluntary agreements and charters concerning coastal zone management as well as marine spatial planning. This short contribution aims at proposing a framework that brings together principles from the current legal framework and can be applied to assess the level of integration in relation to planning and management of areas characterized by the coexistence of various nature protection regimes. In other words, this framework, which can easily applied in marine protected areas, allows for evaluating their performance in addressing a key aspect of sustainability.

Keywords: Environmental planning · Marine protected areas · Performance assessment

1 Introduction

Coastal areas, transitional spaces where land and sea meet, interact and impact on each other in ways that are not fully understood yet [20], are affected by environmental degradation due to both the intrinsic fragility of transition areas and conflicting and inadequate uses. In the Mediterranean Sea, around 40 percent of the population lives close to the sea [6]; consequently, high levels of urbanization have posed additional burdens [4] and have increased potential risks deriving from climate change and sea level rise. At the international level, various typologies of protected areas (the most popular of which are Marine Protected Areas (MPAs), covering 4 percent of the Mediterranean Sea [7]) have been established in order to deal with pressures that threaten coastal areas. Moreover, for countries belonging to the European Union (EU), the Habitats Directive (92/43/EEC) mandates that both inland and marine Natura 2000 sites must be established to protect habitats and species that are rare, or threatened with extinction in a given area, or representative of the biogeographic characteristics of that

© Springer Nature Switzerland AG 2020
O. Gervasi et al. (Eds.): ICCSA 2020, LNCS 12255, pp. 175–183, 2020.
https://doi.org/10.1007/978-3-030-58820-5_13

area. Hence, by the end of 2018, marine Natura 2000 sites concerned 9.5 percent of EU seas [5]. If all of the different spatial mechanism through which nature protection is pursued are taken into account, a mere 7.14 percent of the Mediterranean Sea [11] is to be considered as protected.

However, planning and management of coastal and marine protected areas are currently affected by silo mentality and approaches, which often leads to coexistence of several regulatory and planning tools, each pursuing its own objectives, to govern interlinked and interdependent issues in a single territory. Conventional systems of government fail to integrate and coordinate different knowledge, values and interests [2]. It is therefore not surprising that coordination and integration have repeatedly and increasingly been advocated as necessary (among many: [9, 14, 15, 17]) in planning and management of coastal areas. While integrated management-based approaches are regarded as effective tools to mitigate conflicts and to protect ecosystems (e.g., [3, 8]), their implementation in practice is problematic [21]. As a consequence, various frameworks have been proposed in the literature to assess integration levels and extent in coastal areas planning and management. For instance, Portman [13] proposes a two-dimensional framework based on physical characteristics and anthropic uses of environmental systems; others [10, 12] also propose two-dimensional frameworks to evaluate horizontal (across sectors) and vertical (across tiers of government) integration. Smythe and McCann's three-dimensional framework [18] focuses on governance aspects only and comprises interagency integration, stakeholder integration, and knowledge integration. A more complex five-dimension analytical framework is that by Saunders et al. [16], which includes cross-border, policy/sector, knowledge, stakeholder and temporal integration.

It is therefore evident that the various frameworks generally assess integration through the lens of governance (e.g. actors, both stakeholders and institutions, and their roles), and some of them also look at physical or temporal aspects. However, what seems to be missing is the consideration of issues arising due to concurrent compulsory planning tools stemming from different laws and regulations in force that coexist in the same coastal area, in the absence of a comprehensive and integrated planning tool that fulfils the various obligations. Integration in planning in order to solve common problems is strongly advocated by the 2030 Agenda for Sustainable Development, adopted by United Nations Member States in 2015, especially within goal 11 "Make cities and human settlements inclusive, safe, resilient and sustainable" [19]. In particular, target 11A advocates supporting "positive economic, social and environmental links between urban, peri-urban and rural areas by strengthening national and regional development planning", while, according to target 11B, "by 2020, [Nations should] substantially increase the number of cities and human settlements adopting and implementing integrated policies and plans towards inclusion, resource efficiency, mitigation and adaptation to climate change, resilience to disasters [...]".

Hence, in this study, both legally binding and voluntary tools concerning costal and marine areas in the EU are analyzed in order to define a framework aiming at assessing what elements of integration each of them requires and pursues, and how. The framework is next tested on two Mediterranean (Italian) case studies. The methodology, case studies and materials are presented in Sect. 2. After briefly summarizing the main outcomes of this test (Sect. 3), the study concludes by providing some possible explanations for the results, and by addressing the issue of usability of the framework outside EU coastal and marine areas (Sect. 4).

2   Materials and Methods

2.1   Methodology

Six documents concerning management of coastal and marine areas in the Mediterranean, listed in Table 1, have been analyzed.

From the analysis of the above listed documents, the following six types of integration, which constitute as many dimensions of the framework developed in this study, were identified.

Table 1. Legally binding and voluntary agreements ("soft law") concerning marine and coastal areas in the Mediterranean.

Document	Aim	Character
EU Directive 2008/56/EC	To establish a framework for community action in the field of marine environmental policy (Marine Strategy Framework Directive)	Legally binding
EU Directive 2014/89/EU	To establish a framework for maritime spatial planning	Legally binding
ICZM protocol	To promote an Integrated Coastal Zone Management in the Mediterranean area	Legally binding
Bologna charter	To ensure coastal protection and to promote a network of observatories for coastal defense	Voluntary agreement
Barcelona convention	To protect the marine environment, as well as Mediterranean coastal regions	Voluntary agreement
Livorno charter	To promote a marine strategy and blue growth	Voluntary agreement

- Spatial integration (**SI**): are marine and terrestrial areas need regarded as a single, unified system, with special reference to?
- Institutional and administrative integration (**IAI**): do the various tiers of government (local, regional, national) that share competences on coastal and marine areas cooperate and coordinate their actions?
- Functional integration (**FI**): are the various functions performed on (or by) the land-sea interface regarded holistically?
- Socio-economic integration (**SEI**): are different economic activities and social interests, including local communities, NGOs, and the wider civil society involved?
- Environmental integration (**EI**): are environmental effects from terrestrial and maritime activities accounted for?
- Planning integration (**PI**): are other planning tools and policies in force in the coastal zone acknowledged and considered?

The documents listed in Table 1 were scrutinized and sentences in which references (either explicit or implicit) to the above-listed six types of integration were looked for, so as to elicit the understanding of each type of integration emerging from the documents. Table 2 synthesizes the elements of each type of integration that were elicited from each analyzed document.

2.2   Case Studies

To test the framework, two Italian case studies where various natural protected areas have been established under different legal frameworks, and in which a number of compulsory and legally binding regulatory and planning tools are in force, which results in a high level of complexity of their respective governance frameworks. Therefore, the two selected case studies represent a critical case [1] because they represent the most complex Italian examples in terms of overlapping protected areas.

The first case study (in Sardinia) comprises Asinara National Park, the Asinara Island MPA, as well as three Natura 2000 sites (two special protections areas (SPAs), ITB010001 and ITB013011, and one special area of conservation (SAC), ITB010082). The second (in Liguria) comprises Portofino Natural Regional Park, the Portofino MPA, and four Natura 2000 sites (IT1332603, IT1332614, IT1332622, and IT1332674).

2.3   Materials

The following planning and management tools in force in the two selected case studies were analyzed against the framework synthesized in Table 2, to find out evidences of the six integration elements:

- the Plans of the two natural Parks and their Implementation Codes, stemming from, and compliant with, the national law on protected areas. Legally binding and prevailing over any other land use plan or sectoral plan, they aim at preserving natural resources and environmental values by controlling land uses;
- the national Decrees that establish the two MPAs, together with the corresponding regulatory tools; the latter stem from the national law on protected areas, and regulate human activities through a zoning scheme;
- the Natura 2000 Management Plans, together with the general and site-specific conservation measures, compliant with the Habitats Directive and ultimately aimed at guaranteeing that a favorable conservation status is achieved for protected habitats and species.

3   Results

In this section, the main outcomes of the analyses of the documents listed in Sect. 2.3 against the framework presented in Table 2 are summarized.

Table 2. Conceptual framework, synthetically matching types of integration with legally binding acts and voluntary agreements.

	Directive 2008/56/EC	Directive 2014/89/EU	ICZM protocol	Bologna charter	Barcelona convention	Livorno charter
SI	Marine and terrestrial protected areas are to be established	Land-sea interactions are to be accounted for	Marine and terrestrial areas form a single entity	Land, water and living resources must be managed together	–	–
IAI	States having sovereignty or jurisdiction over waters must act in a coordinate way	Trans-boundary cooperation between states bordering marine waters is required	Decisions by public authorities concerning the use of coastal zones must be coordinated	Modeling tools, monitoring systems, and decision support systems must be integrated	States must cooperate against marine pollution (monitoring, data exchange, damage compensation).	Sea and coast surveillance activities must be carried out following unitary standards
FI	–	Competing demands for maritime space require integrated planning and management	All functions relating to environmental, socioeconomic and cultural systems must be integrated	Conservation and use of biological diversity need to be taken into account an must be integrated in whichever tool	–	–
SEI	–	Environmental, economic and social aspects must be taken into account to promote sustainable development of maritime economies	Multiplicity and diversity of activities in coastal zones, as well as their relevant interactions, must be taken into account	Coordination between public and private initiatives which affect the use of the coastal zone is needed	All forms of relevant information (including local knowledge) must be considered, in transparent decision making	Coastal communities are empowered through participation of all involved actors in relation to the marine environment strategy
EI	Environmental considerations are integrated into policy areas and laws impacting on the sea	Healthy marine ecosystems and their multiple services are integrated within planning decisions	The ecosystems approach is applied to coastal planning and management	–	–	–
PI	–	Maritime spatial planning is promoted as a coordinated and integrated approach to achieve coherence between maritime spatial planning and other processes	Competent national, regional and local coastal zone authorities cooperate to strengthen the coherence and effectiveness of coastal strategies, plans and programs	–	–	–

With reference to spatial integration, in the Asinara case the Plan of the Natural Park regards its territory as single, unitary ecosystem where terrestrial and marine areas share common structural and socio-economic features. Some of the spatial conservation tools in force of the area do mention some others (for instance, as regards the zoning scheme, Management Plans refer to the provisions of both the Plan of the Natural Park and the MPA regulation), hence somewhat integrating their provisions, but this acknowledgement is not reciprocal.

In the Portofino case, MPA management tools do not explicitly address spatial integration; however, integrated management of SACs and the Regional Park is promoted by both the Plan of the Natural Park and the SACs conservation measures.

As regards institutional and administrative integration, in the Asinara case no international cooperation or coordination is foreseen, apart for one reference to the Pelagos Sanctuary, an international marine protected area established for the conservation of marine mammals and stretching over Italian, French, and Monaco's waters. However, if lowers tiers of government are considered, various references to inter-institutional coordination appear, for instance, between the regional government and the Porto Torres municipality (to which the island belongs) as regards the implementation of regeneration plans for the built-up areas within the park, or between other institutions in relation to areas bordering the Natural Park. Moreover, the need for institutional cooperation concerning surveillance and control of the area is explicitly acknowledged. To this end, collaboration with the regional government and with universities and research centers is promoted. In the Portofino case, coordination mechanisms to ensure cooperation between the institutions that share competences on the protected areas are foreseen in the various documents here analyzed, particularly in the MPA regulation. As for surveillance and control activities, they represent overarching themes across the management tools; notwithstanding, effective provisions concerning coordination between port authorities and regional administration are only provided in the Natura 2000 sites' conservation measures.

As for functional integration, which looks at how the various functions are regarded, in the Asinara case a vision is set where conservation and use of biodiversity are integrated (e.g. maintenance of fish stocks versus exploitation of nature-based tourism), with prominent importance given to conservation. Apart from that, the issue of co-occurring pressures stemming from users' demands appears to be overlooked. Similarly, in the Portofino case an integrated approach is promoted only in the Natura 2000 sites' conservation measures, whereas the MPA regulation and Plan of the Natural Park take a strictly regulatory approach towards anthropic uses, with the ultimate end of protecting biodiversity.

In relation to socio-economic integration, in the Asinara case participation of local communities and relevant stakeholders is, in principle, promoted by both the Plan of the Natural Park and in the Management Plans of Natura 2000 sites; however, in reality, rather than real participation, consultation and mere information were implemented in the respective plan-making processes. In the Portofino case socio-economic development of the territory is promoted by all of its management tools, each foreseeing and promoting information campaigns in order to disseminate ecological awareness among local communities and interest groups.

Concerning environmental integration, in the Asinara case Management Plans of Natura 2000 sites do address the issue of removing factors that may negatively affect ecosystems, which are regarded as having intrinsic value, regardless of the services that they provide. In the same area, a different approach is taken by the Plan of the Natural Park, which makes use of the ecosystem approach to identify the so-called "landscape-environmental units", i.e., areas sharing common ecological and functional relations and for which the plan provides specific rules. In the Portofino case, all of the tools mention the need to integrate specific objectives and strategies stemming from higher-level laws and directives (e.g. on air and water pollution), with a narrow perspective if compared to Natura 2000 sites' conservation measures, which pursue a much broader normative consistency (in that they do not look only at environmental impacts, but also environmental risks and threats, as well as climate change). All of the Portofino tools refer to the ecosystem approach, and to ecosystem services.

Finally, as regards planning integration, in the Asinara case integration between the various tools in force is explicitly acknowledged in several parts of the Plan of the Natural Park, which also refers to other sectoral planning tools; to the contrary, both Management Plans of Natura 2000 sites and the MPA Regulation do not consider the any other planning tool. In the Portofino case, the Plan of the Natural Park promotes itself as integrating measures and rules established by regional, provincial and local planning, while Natura 2000 conservation measures only pursue integration with the Plan of the Natural Park.

4   Discussion and Conclusions

Integration in coastal areas represents a key aspect of sustainability. Following the 17 Sustainable Development Goals, sustainability should be implemented in practical applications and not only in theoretical global policies and strategies. Practical applications concern various activities such as management of natural resources, mitigation and adaptation to climate change, and so on. Marine and coastal areas are characterized by the coexistence of several regulatory and planning tools that govern a specific aspect concerning human activities. Therefore, coordination and integration have been advocated as necessary in order to deal with problems and practical aspects that should be managed in terms of sustainability.

In this study, we have proposed a six-dimensional framework to assess the level of integration emerging from planning documents in coastal and marine areas characterized by the coexistence of a number of compulsory planning tools. Such framework has been developed by eliciting the way integration is proposed in both legally binding and voluntary agreements in force in the Mediterranean area, and comprises spatial integration, institutional and administrative integration, functional integration, socio-economic integration, environmental integration, and planning integration.

As shown in the introductory section, a number of conceptual frameworks to assess integration have already been proposed. However, the assessment framework here put forward is novel: contrary to what happens in previous studies, whose frameworks develop on the basis of theoretical standpoints and are therefore grounded on a-priori assumptions concerning the ontology of the integration concept, in this work the integration dimensions emerge from the wording of both legally binding documents and soft laws in force in the Mediterranean Sea Basin area, and are not predefined.

Moreover, in order to test the framework, we have examined through its lenses planning and regulatory tools in force in two Mediterranean protected areas where various nature protection regimes overlap. The results of this analysis show that each tool appear to be specifically focused on complying with its own normative framework; hence, all of them are far from contributing to building a truly integrated approach to coastal and marine area management. One possible reason for this has to do with the fact that various categories of protected areas coexist in the hierarchical and multitier Italian institutional arena, where each type of protected area pursues its own mission and needs to comply strictly with the legal act (e.g., a national law, a regional law, or a European directive) upon which its establishment is grounded. For this reason, separate management bodies are often established, which, in the absence of dialogue and of clear mandates for cooperation, may result in parallel, or even competing, managements of the territory.

Since the framework was built on the basis of legal acts, directives and voluntary agreements ratified by countries belonging to the EU concerning integrated management of coastal and marine areas, the method proposed and applied in this study can be replicated in other coastal and marine protected areas in the north Mediterrancan area, while further research is needed to understand to what extent the framework can be useful in non-EU countries in the south Mediterranean region, and what amendments would be required due to the different legal frameworks concerning nature protection and management of coastal and marine protected areas.

References

1. Bryman, A.: Social Research Methods, 4th edn. Oxford University Press, New York (2012)
2. Clarke, B., et al.: Enhancing the knowledge governance interface: coasts, climate and collaboration. Ocean Coast Manage. **86**, 88–99 (2013). https://doi.org/10.1016/j.ocecoaman.2013.02.009
3. Ehler, C.N.: Indicators to measure governance performance in integrated coastal management. Ocean Coast. Manage. **46**, 335–345 (2003). https://doi.org/10.1016/s0964-5691(03)00020-6
4. Engelbert, A., Collet, I.: Coastal regions: People Living Along the Coastline and Integration of NUTS 2010 and Latest Population Grid (2013). https://webgate.ec.europa.eu/maritimeforum/system/files/Sif_coastal%20regions_07Nov2013.pdf. Accessed 26 Apr 2020
5. European Commission: Natura 2000. Key drivers of success for Natura 2000. Nature and Biodiversity Newsletter 2019, n. 45, February 2019. http://ec.europa.eu/environment/nature/info/pubs/docs/nat2000newsl/nat45_en.pdf. Accessed 26 Apr 2020
6. European Environment Agency: Balancing the Future of Europe's Coasts. Knowledge Base for Integrated Management. Report no. 12/2013. Publications Office of the European Union, Luxembourg (2013). https://www.eea.europa.eu/publications/balancing-the-future-of-europes. Accessed 26 Apr 2020
7. Gabrié, C., et al.: The Status of Marine Protected Areas in the Mediterranean Sea, MedPAN and RAC/SPA (2012). http://www.rac-spa.org/sites/default/files/doc_medmpanet/final_docs_regional/5_status_of_marine_protected_areas_in_the_mediterranean_2012.pdf. Accessed 26 Apr 2020

8. Giakoumi, S., et al.: Revisiting "success" and "failure" of marine protected areas: a conservation scientist perspective. Front. Mar. Sci. **5**, 223 (2018). https://doi.org/10.3389/fmars.2018.00223

9. Ioppolo, G., Saija, G., Salomone, R.: From coastal management to environmental management: The sustainable eco-tourism program for the mid-western coast of Sardinia (Italy). Land Use Pol. **31**, 460–471 (2013). https://doi.org/10.1016/j.landusepol.2012.08.010

10. Jones, P.J.S., Lieberknecht, L.M., Qiu, W.: Marine spatial planning in reality: introduction to case studies and discussion of findings. Mar. Policy **71**, 256–264 (2016). https://doi.org/10.1016/j.marpol.2016.04.026

11. MedPAN, UNEP/MAP-RAC/SPA: The 2016 Status of Marine Protected Areas in the Mediterranean. Main Findings (2016). http://d2ouvy59p0dg6k.cloudfront.net/downloads/medpan_forum_mpa_2016___brochure_a4_en_web_1_.pdf. Accessed 26 Apr 2020

12. Olsen, E., Fluharty, D., Hoel, A.H., Hostens, K., Maes, F., Pecceu, E.: Integration at the round table: marine spatial planning in multi-stakeholder settings. PLoS ONE **9**, e109964 (2014). https://doi.org/10.1371/journal.pone.0109964

13. Portman, M.E.: Marine spatial planning: Achieving and evaluating integration. ICES J. Mar. Sci. **68**, 2191–2200 (2011). https://doi.org/10.1093/icesjms/fsr157

14. Portman, M.E., Esteves, L.S., Le, X.Q., Khan, A.Z.: Improving integration for integrated coastal zone management: An eight-country study. Sci. Total Environ. **439**, 194–201 (2012). https://doi.org/10.1016/j.scitotenv.2012.09.016

15. Rochette, J., Billé, R.: ICZM protocols to regional seas conventions: What? Why? How? Mar. Policy **36**, 977–984 (2012). https://doi.org/10.1016/j.marpol.2012.02.014

16. Saunders, F., Gilek, M., Day, J., Hassler, B., McCann, J., Smythe, T.: Examining the role of integration in marine spatial planning: towards an analytical framework to understand challenges in diverse settings. Ocean Coast. Manage. **169**, 1–9 (2019). https://doi.org/10.1016/j.ocecoaman.2018.11.011

17. Shipman, B., Stojanovic, T.: Facts, Fictions, and failures of integrated coastal zone management in Europe. Coast. Manage. **35**, 375–398 (2007). https://doi.org/10.1080/08920750601169659

18. Smythe, T.C., McCann, J.: Achieving integration in marine governance through marine spatial planning: Findings from practice in the United States. Ocean Coast. Manage. **167**, 197–207 (2019). https://doi.org/10.1016/j.ocecoaman.2018.10.006

19. United Nations: Goal 11: Make Cities Inclusive, Safe, Resilient and Sustainable. https://www.un.org/sustainabledevelopment/cities/. Accessed 26 Apr 2020

20. Van Assche, K., Hornidge, A.K., Schlüter, A., Vaidianu, N.: Governance and the coastal condition: Towards new modes of observation, adaptation and integration. Mar. Policy **112**, 1034132 (2020). https://doi.org/10.1016/j.marpol.2019.01.002

21. Walsh, C.: Integration of expertise or collaborative practice? Coastal management and climate adaptation at the Wadden Sea. Ocean Coast. Manage. **167**, 78–86 (2019). https://doi.org/10.1016/j.ocecoaman.2018.10.004

Water Management and Municipal Climate Adaptation Plans: A Preliminary Assessment for Flood Risks Management at Urban Scale

Simone Corrado[1], Benedetta Giannini[1], Luigi Santopietro[1(✉)],
Giuseppe Oliveto[2], and Francesco Scorza[1]

[1] Laboratory of Urban and Regional Systems Engineering (LISUT),
School of Engineering, University of Basilicata, Potenza, Italy
{simone.corrado,francescabenedetta.giannini,
luigi.santopietro}@studenti.unibas.it,
francesco.scorza@unibas.it
[2] Laboratory of Hydraulic Engineering, School of Engineering,
University of Basilicata, Potenza, Italy
giuseppe.oliveto@unibas.it

Abstract. Global Covenant of Mayors for Climate and Energy is the largest movement of local governments committed to going beyond their own national climate and energy objectives, fully in line with the UN Sustainable Development Goals and climate justice principles. Every signatory develops a Sustainable Energy and Climate Action Plan (SECAP) to mitigate climate change. In the Plan for the Protection of European Water Resources, the European Commission expresses the urgency that EU-members focus on environmentally friendly growth and make the resources used more efficient, including water resources, in order to sustainably overcome the current economic and environmental crisis, adapt to climate change and increase the possibility of strengthening the competitiveness and growth of the European water sector. A component of urban systems affected by climate change is the hydrological one. The leading causes affecting hydrological component are floods. The Floods Directive 2007/60/EC establishes a framework on the assessment and management of flood risk, aiming at the reduction of the potential adverse consequences of flooding for human health, the environment, cultural heritage and economic activity. In this work, we propose a first-level framework to identify critical areas for water management in urban contexts. This study involves 13 sub-catchments located in the urban area of the Municipality of Potenza, in Southern Italy. The proposed approach could promote, in the ambit of SECAP (Sustainable Energy Climate Action), the development of mitigation actions and investment sizing for urban water management strategies in critical urban contexts.

Keywords: Urban floods · Storm-water management · Detention tanks · Climate change · SEAP/SECAP · Local climate plans

© Springer Nature Switzerland AG 2020
O. Gervasi et al. (Eds.): ICCSA 2020, LNCS 12255, pp. 184–192, 2020.
https://doi.org/10.1007/978-3-030-58820-5_14

1 Introduction

In urban areas, local flooding might occur as a combined result of heavy rains and poor or insufficient drainage system that is unable to drain out the water discharges efficiently. Traditional road drainage system, typically designed in accordance with local authority regulation, should convey water as quickly as possible far from the surfaces, thereby ensuring clean and safe roads and avoiding potential damages to the structures. However, many roads drainage systems are combined with sewage schemes, the design of which does not require to cope with extreme rain events. The vulnerability of the land, and therefore of the urban area, is primarily attributable to climate change and to a lack of the concept of "limit" in spatial planning. The impermeability of the soil is one of the effects of urbanization that most impact: the reduction of the amount of water infiltration with the consequent reduction of local groundwater recharging; the increase of runoff; the reduction of the time of concentration of a watershed; and the decay of a natural ecosystem because of pollution over-load [1]. Therefore, there is the need to enable a suitable integrated water management both at basin and urban scale [2]. This study involved 13 sub-catchments area located in the urban area of the Municipality of Potenza, in Southern Italy. The catchments area has homogeneous lithological feature, a very deep and moderately silty clay soils characterized by low permeability, while the slopes are mainly weak or moderate, only locally steep, with an average annual precipitation of 697 mm and maximum daily rainfall of 150 mm [3, 4]. The municipal area is densely populated; the percentage of consumed soil, according to the EEA (European Environmental Agency) in the framework of the Copernicus land monitoring service, is 38.01% of the entire territory, and the urban sprawls on the lowest catchment areas near the Basento River with many clustered settlements [5, 6]. Runoff coefficients were evaluated using the Kennessey method, suitable for small hilly watersheds, and subsequently related to the impervious areas of the catchments [7]. Moreover, the morphological analysis of the urban area allows to identify the potential risk areas in which flooding might occur. Lastly, a spatial analytical hierarchy approach allowed to identify priorities areas for taking action. The proposed framework could support, in the ambit of SECAP (Sustainable Energy Climate Action), the development of mitigation measures and investment sizing for urban water management strategies in critical urban contexts.

2 Methodological Approach to Estimate Flooding Areas in Urban Contexts

In this section, in order to support urban planning decision-makers for mitigating the climate change impacts on metropolitan areas and increasing the urban resilience, a first-level assessment procedure for water management strategy is defined. The analytic methodology is addressed with a Geographical Information Systems (GIS), a tool for spatial data analysis and visualization. The basic concept of the methodology is to combine heterogeneous components in view of an integrated territorial management. Firstly, the sealed sinkhole morphology (i.e. water ponding area) has been evaluated – as a potential area of runoff accumulation – by merging the Digital Elevation Model

(DEM) of the urban area with imperviousness data distributed by EEA (European Environmental Agency) in the framework of the Copernicus land monitoring service [8]. The hydrological analysis of the catchments, performed through the GRASS "*r. watershed*" algorithm, also provided the raster map of surface flow accumulation, which has helped to discriminate the sinkholes in categories as shown in Fig. 1.

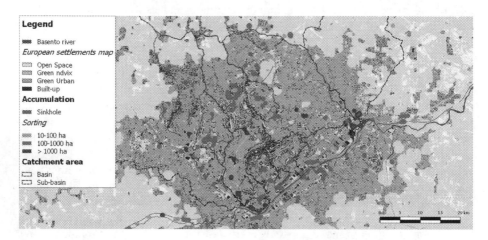

Fig. 1. Map of urban settlements and discriminated sinkholes

Local floods and runoff coefficients are strictly correlated. Here the Kennessey method has been considered to estimate the runoff coefficients [7]. This choice has been justified by the accuracy of this physiographic approach and by its simple adaptability to GIS environment [9]. Specifically, the procedure applied can be summarized as follow:

- Calculation of the Aridity Index using the De Martonne – Gottmann aridity index;
- Study of the areal distribution for the three main parameters: acclivity (i.e. slope), permeability, and vegetational cover of the soil [8];
- multiplication between the percentage areas and coefficients (leading to weighted coefficients) related to acclivity, C_a, permeability, C_p, and vegetational cover of the soil C_v, respectively;
- sum of the three coefficients C_a, C_p, C_v leading to the estimation of the average annual runoff coefficient, R_C, for each sub-catchment.

Table 1 provides estimates of the runoff coefficient for all sub-catchments considered in this study based on the above procedure.

Moreover, in order to identify the hydrological response of each sub-catchments to a rain event, the time of concentration, t_c, has been assessed by the Kirpich's formula which is particularly suitable for very small catchments, as in present case, though developed for agricultural areas [10]. Therefore, in order to identify the potential flood hazard areas and evaluate the priority sites for taking actions, the morphometric and

Table 1. Main characteristics of the sub-catchments considered in this study in terms of area, imperviousness, and run off coefficient.

The main hydrological parameters of the sub-catchments			
Catchment no.	Imperviousness %	Basin area km^2	Runoff coeff.
1	77.8	0.541	0.589
2	85.1	0.166	0.530
3	82.5	0.434	0.590
4	34.2	3.090	0.518
5	59.4	0.416	0.555
6	35.6	4.821	0.547
7	82.5	0.108	0.560
8	44.1	1.791	0.519
9	33.9	0.267	0.559
10	52.9	0.938	0.493
11	53.7	0.141	0.485
12	65.2	0.539	0.514
13	67.1	0.048	0.518

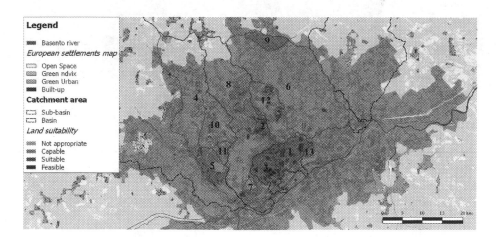

Fig. 2. Land suitability for the sub-catchments considered in this study

hydrological parameters are combined with the distribution map of urban services and infrastructures through a spatial analytical hierarchy approach, thereby achieving a suitability weighted model [11]. Results are shown in Fig. 2.

3 Results and Discussion

The results from the spatial analysis, calculated on seven criteria of land suitability, allow to efficiently evaluating the potentially exposed sites that would require intervention at water management level. The analysis evidences how catchment no.2, no.1, no. 3, in order of importance, require priority measures. Indeed, it is not a coincidence that for these catchments the soil sealing percentages are among the highest recorded in all the sub-catchments analyzed, as it can be observed in Table 2 and Fig. 3.

Table 2. Potentially exposed sites, according to the Floods Directive (2007/60/EC) [12]

Potentially exposed sites, according to the Floods Directive (2007/60/EC)			
Catchment no.	Imperviousness %	Basin area Km^2	Exposed area %
1	**77.8**	0.541	22.2
2	**85.1**	0.166	26.2
3	**82.5**	0.434	33.1

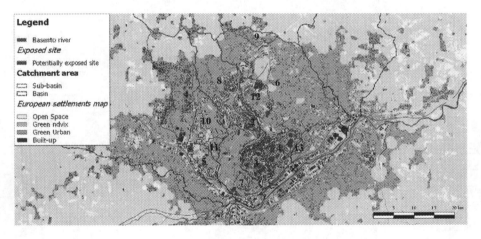

Fig. 3. Identify potentially exposed sites

By making a comparison between catchments with similar geomorphological features, whose the C_a coefficient shows an average of 0.124 and quite limited standard deviation of 0.003, the relationship between imperviousness and runoff coefficient is very tight (Pearson's r equal to 0.93 as shown in Fig. 4). While this is a preliminary flood risk analysis, results look promising for the assessment of potential risk-prone sites in which local flood might be considered likely to occur. Indeed, developed on open source data, this approach results very flexible and can be used as a preliminary tool for urban stormwater management [13].

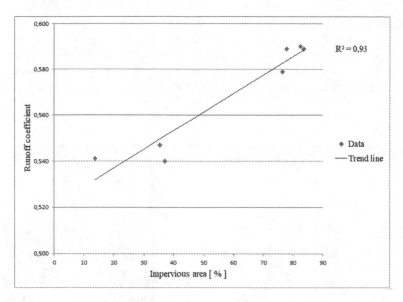

Fig. 4. Runoff coefficient related to impervious area

Hydraulic engineering, in a traditional approach, considers water only as a source of supply for domestic, industrial and agricultural use. Since water is a finite and vulnerable resource, its management and development should be based on a participative approach able to engage stakeholders, urban planners and decision-makers [14–16]. In order to sustainably face the existing crisis of the sector, urban policies for the improvements of water and risks prevention require clear and endorsed strategies and solutions aimed at strengthening the competitiveness and growth in this sector at every level. By including the risk related to climate changes on the whole water integrated cycle, a synergic and integrated approach in the respect of environmental ethics, focused on eco-centric and anthropogenic nature, and social ethics becomes necessary [17, 18].

4   Land Suitability as a Tool for SECAP

The land suitability classification of soil, even at a large scale of detail, might be a useful tool for redirecting investments in the prospective of viewing cities as an adaptive resilient system against the uncertainty of climate change [19, 20]. Previous studies about land suitability gave a general extent of the suitable areas to specific actions planned by SECAP. The support of land suitability can answer to the question "Where is the best location?" and strengthen the place-based approach chosen by the authors. The link between the land suitability and SECAP in a place-based approach could be found in sectors (such as water, agriculture & forestry or environment & biodiversity), that tie actions proposed by SECAP to a territorial dimension.

The proposed framework might be a tool to identify mitigation actions to be developed in the SECAP for Potenza Municipality. These actions, suggested by Charlesworth et al., can be articulated at different scale in: building's stormwater collector tanks, soil permeabilization - such as permeable paving and rain garden, and lastly blue-green infrastructure [21]. They are collected into SECAP template as shown in Fig. 5.

Fig. 5. Adaptation actions for water sector (adapted from SECAP template)

5 Conclusion

The methodological approach suggested in this paper, while not comprehensive, allows to obtain a preliminary scenario that highlights the weaknesses of a territory due to the obsolescence of urban water infrastructures; stormwater is only regarded as a nuisance, not as an opportunity. In the shared perspective of resilient cities, the proposed approach might be useful not also in the defining of appropriate climate changes adaptation strategies for the delineation of SECAP's actions by the decision-makers, but also in the awareness of the citizens to climate change. How tool to develop local climate plans (i.e. SECAP), is a useful and quick framework to find areas more critical and size the investment and actions to urban scale. In order to carry out the research on the Potenza urban area, the methodology described in this work has been developed on the basis of extreme events occurred in the town during the last years. Indeed, the threshold discriminating the sinkholes was chosen on the basis of past experience and of the territorial knowledge. In order to use this framework in different urban contexts, as a potential future development of this study, a potential integration looks at using remote sensing techniques for searching all the feasible areas in which, over the years, an unexpected flood has occurred. However, the identification of these areas by applying passive remote sensing might be hindered by the steady cloudy sky that, after a heavy rainfall, does not allow to clearly acquire images from the soil. In this case, the use of satellite active sensors, such as microwaves, is highly recommended, albeit it is currently a very expensive procedure for the treasury of a small municipality like that one of Potenza. This evaluation can be made after a preliminary careful analysis of intervention conducted on the sub-catchments located in the urban area. In this case, therefore, it would be possible to consider the investment sizing with more accuracy.

In this perspective, future developments are oriented to improve this framework as a support system in order to identify more effective actions for SECAP ensuring positive environmental impacts on multiple matrix [22–24], helping local decision makers, public administrator and stakeholders into decision-making process.

References

1. Shuster, W.D., Bonta, J., Thurston, H., Warnemuende, E., Smith, D.R.: Impacts of impervious surface on watershed hydrology: a review. Urban Water J. **2**, 263–275 (2005)
2. Transforming our world: the 2030 Agenda for Sustainable Development: Sustainable Development Knowledge Platform. https://sustainabledevelopment.un.org/post2015/transformingourworld. Accessed 20 Apr 2020
3. http://www.scia.isprambiente.it/wwwrootscia/Documentazione/rapporto_Valori_normali_def.pdf. Accessed 24 Apr 2020
4. Manfreda, S., Sole, A., De Costanzo, G.: Le Precipiatazioni Estreme in Basilicata, p. 150 (2015)
5. Principali statistiche geografiche sui comuni, https://www.istat.it/it/archivio/156224. Accessed 24 Apr 2020
6. Homepage|Copernicus. https://climate.copernicus.eu/. Accessed 21 Apr 2020
7. Kennessey, B.: Lefolyasi téniezok és retenciok. Vizugy, Koziemények (1930)
8. Status Maps—Copernicus Land Monitoring Service. https://land.copernicus.eu/pan-european/high-resolution-layers/forests/tree-cover-density/status-maps. Accessed 23 Apr 2020
9. Barazzuoli, P., Izzo, S., Micheluccini, M., Salleolini, M.: L'uso della Carta dei Coefficienti di Deflusso nella gestione del territorio. Atti del VI Cong. Har. Ord. Geol., Venezia. pp. 375–382 (1987)
10. Kirpich, Z.P.: Time of concentration of small agricultural watersheds. Civ. Eng. **10**, 362 (1940)
11. Saaty, T.L.: The analytic hierarchy process. Agric. Econ. Rev. **70**. Mcgraw Hill, New York (1980)
12. EUR-Lex - 32007L0060 - EN - EUR-Lex. https://eur-lex.europa.eu/legal-content/EN/ALL/?uri=CELEX:32007L0060. Accessed 22 Apr 2020
13. Scorza, F., Grecu, V.: Assessing sustainability: research directions and relevant issues. In: Gervasi, O., et al. (eds.) ICCSA 2016. LNCS, vol. 9786, pp. 642–647. Springer, Cham (2016). https://doi.org/10.1007/978-3-319-42085-1_55
14. Pontrandolfi, P., Scorza, F.: Sustainable urban regeneration policy making: inclusive participation practice. In: Gervasi, O., et al. (eds.) ICCSA 2016. LNCS, vol. 9788, pp. 552–560. Springer, Cham (2016). https://doi.org/10.1007/978-3-319-42111-7_44

15. Scorza, F., Pontrandolfi, P.: Citizen participation and technologies: the C.A.S.T. architecture. In: Gervasi, O., et al. (eds.) ICCSA 2015. LNCS, vol. 9156, pp. 747–755. Springer, Cham (2015). https://doi.org/10.1007/978-3-319-21407-8_53
16. Murgante, B., Botonico, G., Graziadei, A., Sassano, G., Amato, F., Scorza, F.: Innovation, technologies, participation: new paradigms towards a 2.0 citizenship. Int. J. Electron. Gov. 11, 62–88 (2019). https://doi.org/10.1504/IJEG.2019.098814
17. Rossi, G.: Prospettive etiche nell'uso delle risorse idriche. Bioet. e Cult. 16, 49–75 (2008)
18. Rossi, G.: Ethical Perspectives for Sustainable and Equitable Water Management. (2011)
19. Las Casas, G., Scorza, F., Murgante, B.: New urban agenda and open challenges for urban and regional planning. In: Calabrò, F., Della Spina, L., Bevilacqua, C. (eds.) ISHT 2018. SIST, vol. 100, pp. 282–288. Springer, Cham (2019). https://doi.org/10.1007/978-3-319-92099-3_33
20. Las Casas, G., Scorza, F., Murgante, B.: Razionalità a-priori: una proposta verso una pianificazione antifragile. Sci. Reg. 18, 329–338 (2019). https://doi.org/10.14650/93656
21. Charlesworth, S.M., Booth, C.A.: Sustainable Surface Water Management: A Handbook for SUDS. Wiley, Oxford (2016)
22. Scorza, F., Pilogallo, A., Saganeiti, L., Murgante, B.: Natura 2000 areas and sites of national interest (SNI): measuring (un)Integration between naturalness preservation and environmental remediation policies. Sustainability 12, 2928 (2020). https://doi.org/10.3390/su12072928
23. Scorza, F., Pilogallo, A., Saganeiti, L., Murgante, B., Pontrandolfi, P.: Comparing the territorial performances of Renewable Energy Sources' plants with an integrated Ecosystem Services loss assessment: a case study from the Basilicata region (Italy). Sustain. Cities Soc. 56, 102082 (2020). https://doi.org/10.1016/J.SCS.2020.102082
24. Scorza, F., Saganeiti, L., Pilogallo, A., Murgante, B.: Ghost planning: the inefficiency of energy sector policies in a low population density region. Arch. DI Stud. URBANI E Reg. (2020)

Hybrid Oriented Sustainable Urban Development: A Pattern of Low-Carbon Access to Schools in the City of Potenza

Giovanni Fortunato[(⊠)], Francesco Scorza[iD],
and Beniamino Murgante[iD]

School of Engineering, Laboratory of Urban and Regional Systems Engineering,
University of Basilicata, Viale dell'Ateneo Lucano 10, 85100 Potenza, Italy
giovanni.fortunato88@libero.it, {francesco.scorza,
beniamino.murgante}@unibas.it

Abstract. This study analyzes urban street network of the city of Potenza in Basilicata region to provide input for a sustainable urban mobility-based strategy enabling students to reach schools through the use of low-carbon transport modes' share. The analyses have been carried out by using Place Syntax Analysis in order to identify a network of paths which guarantees pedestrian and bicycle access to schools located in the urban area of Potenza. Within urban space morphology research, combining Space Syntax and GIS-methods, Place Syntax allows to perform analyses of the spatial configuration of streets taking into account both street network layout and the location of spatial opportunities. Urban form (in our analysis, in terms of configurational characteristics) and accessibility to destinations (schools in this study) are essential to increase the share of walking and bicycling as the preferred modes of people's daily travel. The paper shows the potential integration between active transport modes and public transport in the city of Potenza. Ensuring an easy transition between walking, cycling and public transport (e.g. by designing a widespread and direct network of cycle-pedestrian paths to and from the stations) contributes to create a "Hybrid Oriented Sustainable Urban Development" towards low-carbon settlements characterized by a significant reduction in congestion, air pollution and carbon emissions.

Keywords: Urban space morphology · Place syntax analysis · Sustainable urban development · Sustainable urban mobility · Liveable city

1 Introduction

A Sustainable Urban Transport System (SUTS) has three components whose interaction is necessary to ensure sustainable urban development processes: public transport, walking and cycling [1]. A SUTS contributes to create people- and environmental-friendly cities and communities reducing traffic congestion, air pollution and greenhouse gas (GHG) emissions. The United Nations Sustainable Development Goals (SDGs) of the 2030 Agenda recognise that it is possible to improve the cities' quality of life and strengthen their economy by making these mobility modes attractive and

O. Gervasi et al. (Eds.): ICCSA 2020, LNCS 12255, pp. 193–205, 2020.
https://doi.org/10.1007/978-3-030-58820-5_15

competitive [2]. In the next decade, the SDG target 11.2 foresees the need to: "*provide access to safe, affordable, accessible and sustainable transport systems for all, improving road safety*" [2]. Moreover, the New Urban Agenda (NUA) undertakes to promote the realization of: "*safe, sufficient and adequate pedestrian and cycling infrastructure and technology-based innovations in transport and transit systems*" which contributes "*to reduce congestion and pollution while improving efficiency, connectivity, accessibility, health and quality of life*" [3]. Public transport, walking and cycling contribute to achieving liveability, sustainability [4, 5] and health goals in the current difficult context: the urban population will continue to grow [6] and tackling climate change is a relevant concern in the coming years [7].

Within low-carbon city development strategies [8], many cities promote soft transportation modes such as walking and bicycling both as an alternative to the exclusive use of motorized vehicles and as an opportunity for urban space regeneration. Facilitating sustainable urban mobility frees up space in order to create green and public spaces for people. In fact, with an increasing proportion of people living and working in cities, there will be increasing competition for a limited amount of public space [9].

Facilitating sustainable urban mobility also relies on the provision of efficient public transport services. Active and clean mobility modes are well suited for short-distance trips within cities. They can be fostered in association with public transport thus increasing their reach and use on longer journeys according to an intermodal approach. So, it is possible to introduce the concept of "chain mobility". To make active mobility modes competitive transport options, urban development should be based on the location of public transport nodes, so that people can walk and/or cycle to the station [10–12]. Planning for the bicycle further increases the catchment area of the stations.

Better and coordinated transport and urban planning leads to a SUTS where the promotion of bicycling and walking in association with public transport extends the "Transit Oriented Development" (TOD) [13] into a "Hybrid Oriented Sustainable Urban Development" (HOSUD). The latter ensures widespread and sustainable accessibility, guaranteeing adequate levels of usability of urban opportunities to the greatest number of people regardless of origin, income, age and physical ability. As established by the NUA, a sustainable urban mobility-based model should be implemented [3].

Our study focuses on configurational analysis of the street network of the urban area of city of Potenza by using Place Syntax Analysis (PSA), a field of space-morphology research [14]. The city of Potenza is the county seat of the Basilicata region, located in southern Italy with more than 65,000 inhabitants. Several studies show that the city is characterized by urban fragmentation phenomena [9, 15–19].

In particular, this paper shows how it is possible to introduce an urban mobility scheme based on modal integration between the three components of SUTS at the service of schools and students in the Potenza's urban area.

2   Methodology

This study applies Place Syntax theory, its techniques and measures in order to perform a space-morphological analysis. In particular, we use PSA for analyzing syntactic properties of the street network (revealing its structure and hierarchy) of the city of

Potenza as the case study, while taking into account the location of schools as "attraction objects". The street network is the primary spatial structure able to determine the spatial distribution of people's movement potentials and land use. Within urban morphology research, PSA is a quantitative and configurational method which allows to analyze spatial relationships existing between the elements of the built form and to simulate the potential effects both on the single spatial unit (such as street segment) and on the whole system. PSA enriches spatial configuration analysis based on Space Syntax Analysis (SSA) taking into account the location of urban attractions/spatial opportunities within attraction-based network analyses. The use of PSA is motivated by the fact that accessibility connects the two main components of the urban structure: the space-functional component (urban activities, land use) and the space-morphological component (transport network, transportation).

2.1   Place Syntax Analysis (PSA)

Within space morphology research, PSA is a theory which takes into account 'distance' and 'attraction' in urban space modelling [20], including theoretical principles of SSA [21]. "*Space syntax ... is a set of techniques for the representation, quantification, and interpretation of spatial configuration in buildings and settlements*" [22]. The built environment and the mutual relationship between spatial units are analyzed according to a quantitative and configurational method, representing the use of space from a cognitive point of view [23–26].

Unlike the concept of "space" [27], "*'place' simply means a geographically specific space, a location, or a space with a specific content*" [28]. Based on loading "*geographical data for improved predictions of pedestrian movement within space syntax*", PSA is "*an improved tool for accessibility analysis in general*" [28]. In urban modeling, this allows to enrich the knowledge deriving from the syntactic analysis based on how one space is topologically and geometrically connected to all the other spaces of the system. In particular, PSA provides a relevant theoretical and methodological contribution in analysing, understanding and interpreting the relationship between urban space-morphology and the distribution of people's movement in cities [29–32]. In addition, unlike the SSA which only allows the analysis of spatial accessibility of urban spaces, location/attraction-based "*Place syntax analysis can [...] be said to deal with specific spatial accessibility, such as accessibility to different attractions*" [33].

Attraction Betweenness of a node i, $AB(i)^r$ represents the potential "through-movement" of each street network's space unit (node). Using graph theory [34], network Betweenness calculates how often a space unit (street segment) falls on the shortest path between all pairs of spatial units in a system [35]. It is a street network's centrality measure highlighting how important a segment is as a through-road for the network. The AB value depends on location and attributes of the attractions ('spatial opportunities').

$AB(i)^r$ is calculated as follows:

$$AB(i)^r = \sum_{j,k \in G - \{i\}; d[j;k] \leq r} \frac{n_{jk}[i]}{n_{jk}} \cdot W[j] \tag{1}$$

where $n_{jk}[i]$ is the subset of paths which pass through i, with nodes j and k falling within the network radius r (threshold distance) from the node i, n_{jk} is the number of shortest paths from j to k in graph G, $W[j]$ is the weight/attribute characterizing the destination-node j.

Therefore, combining SSA and Geographical Information Systems-GIS (providing spatial analyses and the visualisation of results), the outputs of the AB network centrality analysis depend on the attractiveness of urban destinations (based on their attributes), the number and location of attractions and street network layout (spatial input data). Street segments, with high scores based on attraction points' weights, that control and mediate movement and connections between many other segments have a high AB value.

2.2   Modelling the Place Syntax-Based Street Network's Graph

In our study, we have measured AB value for each of street segments within the urban area of Potenza taking into account the location of schools, i.e. spatial opportunities-attraction objects of the location-based analysis. This quantitative measure makes it possible to identify and classify street segments according to their AB values and to define paths that enable schools to be reached in a sustainable way (walking and bicycling) in Potenza's urban area. Network accessibility to schools is a relevant infrastructure planning parameter for achieving a high rate of sustainable active urban travel modes, such as cycling and walking [36]. To promote them, the AB measure captures the potential distribution of people's movement patterns [37], providing information to be used in the design phase. To perform AB analysis, we have used QGIS-PST tool and chosen different options for "distance mode" and "radius". In particular, we have chosen "angular distance" in the "distance mode" options and set the "radius" based on network "walking distance". Angular distance (measured in degrees) takes into account accumulated angular turns needed to get from origin-point to destination-point in the network. The angular distance of all possible paths between origin-point and destination-point are calculated and the one with the least angular distance is selected as the shortest path [26]. So, paths' angular minimization is a morphological-geometric feature which makes walking and cycling more attractive. "Walking distance" is the metric network distance of the shortest 'walking' path that connects two points through the network. To compute urban street network's syntactic measures and capture "walkable" and "cyclable" centralities, we have set two threshold distances for the analysis: 1,500 m and 3,000 m. These values are compatible with walking and cycling respectively [38]. In our study, we have mapped schools (primary schools, elementary schools, middle schools, high schools) which are in the Potenza's urban area [39, 40]. They are "attraction points", i.e. relevant generators/destinations of systematic daily trips involving a large number of street users. To georeference schools, we used data downloaded from the website of the Italian Ministry of Education[1]. The schools have been weighed up taking into account the number of students.

To capture urban space's configurational properties (focusing on mutual position of the network elements), we have created street network's segment map from the street-centerline map, as GIS vector layer representing the street network. Segment map can be used as spatial network input for the PSA-based analyses revealing urban space's performance. To create a detailed segment map, the GIS-representation of the street network of Potenza has been enriched by using high resolution orthophotos and site-specific surveys. A correct and thorough urban space modelling has a significant impact on the results obtained from the syntactic analysis. Using PST tool, we have considered three geometric features: street-segments, unlinks and attractions. Unlinks represents the intersection points between street segments which should be ignored during the analyses, i.e. bridges, tunnels. With reference to graph theory, PST creates a network graph representation from the segment lines for analysis, where every street segment (the main spatial unit of analysis) is a node and every crossing point provides an edge.

Then, we have post-processed the results by classifying them into classes and producing attraction-based configuration maps (differentiating the network street segments) in order to highlight the spatial distribution of street network's syntactic properties within the urban area of Potenza.

3   Results

In the urban area of the city of Potenza, there are 47 schools with a total number of students equal to 13,232. Specifically, the highest number of students in a school is 1,067 (an high school) while the lowest value is 17 students (a primary school). 80% of schools have less than 435 students while about 4% of them have a student population of more than 800. Most of the schools are located North-West of the Historic Centre (a, Fig. 1) of Potenza, in an area including three districts: "Poggio Tre Galli" (b, Fig. 1), "G Area" and "Study-Centre". They were built between the 1970s and 1980s, have a population of over 6,000 inhabitants (according to Italian National Institute of Statistics (ISTAT) demographic data of 2011) and are characterized by the presence of public services of territorial interest such as the offices of the Basilicata Region. In this area, an experimentation of a bottom–up approach-based participatory process aimed at defining a neighbourhood scale-based regeneration project focused on the promotion of active transport modes have been developed [41–46].

In this area, there is a large part of the city's high schools which also have the highest number of students. The "Verderuolo" district (c, Fig. 1), located North of the Historic Centre, is characterized by the presence of a good number of schools and students. It is served by two railway stations located along the RFI national railway network and the FAL railway network (connecting the Basilicata region and the Puglia region). It is therefore an important interchange railway node in the urban area of

---

[1] Cercalatuascuola.istruzione.it. Available online: http://cercalatuascuola.istruzione.it/cercalatuas cuola/ (accessed on 19 April 2020).

Potenza. Moreover, the "Macchia Romana" district (d, Fig. 1), more recently built and mainly residential (in the North-East), the South-East area including the district of "Bucaletto" (e, Fig. 1) and the South-West area are the most lacking in schools and students.

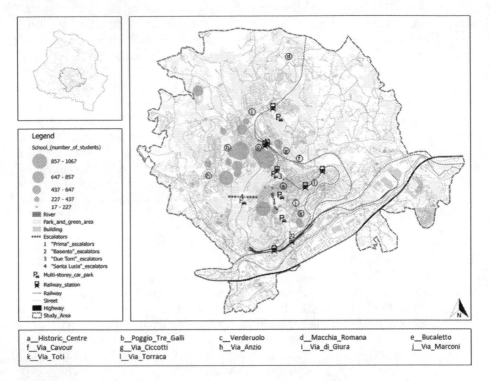

Fig. 1. Potenza's urban area: the location of schools and mobility network infrastructures.

GIS-mapping of schools captures the spatial distribution of schools within the urban area showing the well supplied districts of the city of Potenza. Moreover, in this section, we report the results obtained by applying the AB analyses, where the schools are the "attraction objects" weighed by the number of students. Since all destinations are not counted equally, the attraction analyses provide results depending not only on the location but also on specific quantitative "attractiveness capacity" of schools based on the number of students (Fig. 2).

Considering both the route directness (angular minimization) and the weighed location of schools, streets crossing the "Verderuolo" district (c, Fig. 2) have high AB values setting a threshold radius of 1,500 m as "walking distance" to perform a configurational analysis of the street network compatible with walking. The spatial network analysis at a certain distance highlights the most chosen paths inside the network in dark blue and the least chosen paths in white. The thematic map shows how most of the schools in Potenza, located North of the Historic Centre, are connected by street segments with a high attraction-based network centrality value, i.e. a relevant potential "through-movement". South and near the Historic Centre, it is possible to identify a continuous path connecting the schools in this area (i, Fig. 2) even if the AB value is lower than that of the streets located in the "Poggio Tre Galli" (b, Fig. 2) and "Verderuolo" (c, Fig. 2) districts.

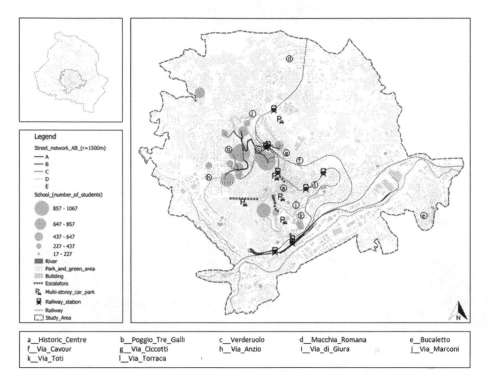

a__Historic_Centre	b__Poggio_Tre_Galli	c__Verderuolo	d__Macchia_Romana	e__Bucaletto
f__Via_Cavour	g__Via_Ciccotti	h__Via_Anzio	i__Via_di_Giura	j__Via_Marconi
k__Via_Toti	l__Via_Torraca			

Fig. 2. Potenza's urban area: Attraction Betweenness(AB)-based analysis of urban street network (r = 1,500 m).

The AB analysis of the urban street network, whose "walking distance" radius is equal to 3,000 m, shows how there are streets which acquire a greater centrality than the scenario described above: Via Cavour (f, Fig. 3), Via Ciccotti (g, Fig. 3), Via Anzio (h, Fig. 3), Via di Giura (i, Fig. 3), Via Marconi (j, Fig. 3), via Toti (k, Fig. 3), Via Torraca (l, Fig. 3). By increasing the radius distance (from 1,500 m to 3,000 m), the network analysis shows the most convenient routes for bicycles and other small electric vehicles, while identifying strategic corridors to sustainably connect adjacent districts [47–54]. As in the previous analysis, a set of streets with a higher potential to be relevant intermediate points (characterized by a greater potential of being used in shortest path within the system) emerges. In this case, the thematic map makes it possible to identify a ring characterized by the street segments with the highest AB values, connecting most of the schools in the urban area of the city of Potenza.

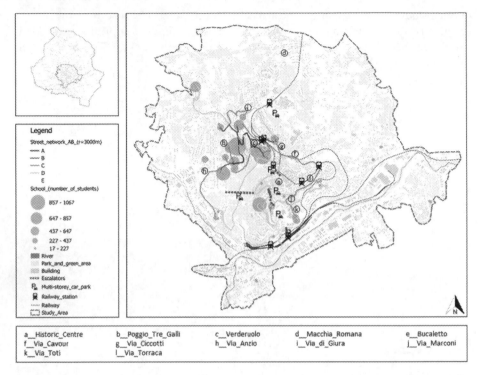

Fig. 3. Potenza's urban area: Attraction Betweenness(AB)-based analysis of urban street network (r = 3,000 m).

4   Conclusions

Results obtained from the attraction-based analyses show how it is possible to promote sustainable (walkable and cyclable) access to schools in the city of Potenza, characterized by a private car-dependant mobility culture. By aiming at the creation of low-carbon settlements, this could be an important incentive for the definition of a new mobility scheme for the whole city, alternative to the current one based almost exclusively on the use of motorized vehicles, in particular the private car. From the thematic maps (providing visualization of spatial distribution of AB analyses' outputs within Potenza's urban street network), it emerges that the concentration of schools in the area North of the Historic Centre of Potenza represents an incentive to promote multimodality for commuting (while reducing private car use). In fact, the streets with the highest AB values (a hierarchy of street network's "walkable" and "cyclable" centralities from space-morphological point of view emerges) are located near a very important railway interchange between the national (RFI) and interregional (FAL) railway lines (Fig. 4). So, project interventions could be defined in order to promote/improve pedestrian and bicycle mobility on the streets leading from the station to schools, covering the first/last parts, i.e. the "last mile", of the daily journey in a sustainable way. Moreover, our methodological approach allow to evaluate the sustainable mobility potential of neighborhoods in the urban area. A spatially integrated routes' network is important for making walking and biking attractive and competitive both for shorter and longer daily trips (in the last case in association with public transit).

Results obtained from the attraction-based syntactic analyses allow to classify the streets segments and select those considered as priority and to be included in a network of urban pedestrian-cycling routes. The two railway lines cross the city of Potenza along the North-South axis: the construction/expansion of interchange car-bus parks near the main vehicular entrances to Potenza, located in the North and especially in the South, and the upgrading of a city rail could contribute to the reduction of motorized vehicle traffic crossing the urban area of Potenza. So, the students coming from the other towns of Basilicata region could take advantage of an intermodal solution (train + walking-bicycling) to reach schools.

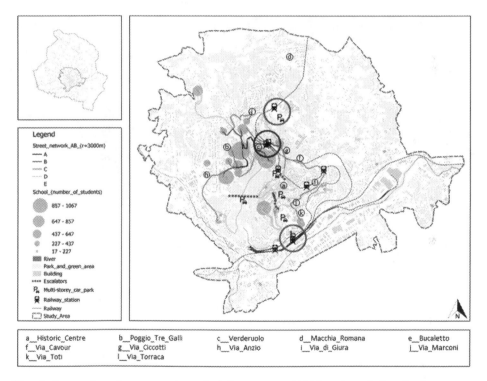

Fig. 4. Potenza's urban area: Attraction Betweenness(AB)-based analysis of urban street network (r = 3,000 m). The car-bus interchange parks are in red circle and railway interchange between the national (RFI) and interregional (FAL) railway lines is in dark red circle. (Color figure online)

The analyses carried out considering as walking distance 3,000 m (Fig. 4) shows how schools and students could benefit from this intermodal solution. In this case, the use of bicycles and, above all, of pedelecs, ebikes would make it easy to cover this distance. Furthermore, the city of Potenza is equipped with 4 mechanized pedestrian mobility systems, escalators and elevators, which allows to implement a sustainable reorganization of urban mobility with advantages for residents and commuters. In fact, the results of attraction-based syntactic analyses could influence policy-makers in the definition of strategies that favour a rational management of urban mobility and sustainable urban development. As a computer techniques-based formal model, the space-morphological analysis (syntactic analysis is a graph theory-based mathematical calculation of configurational properties of street network) should be integrated by detailed traditional site-specific surveys focused on other morphological features for a comprehensive and detailed assessment of the street network.

References

1. UNECE: Sustainable Urban Mobility and Public Transport in UNECE capitals (2015). https://www.unece.org/fileadmin/DAM/trans/doc/2016/itc/ECE-TRANS-245.pdf
2. United Nations: Resolution A/RES/70/1. Transforming our world: the 2030 Agenda for Sustainable Development. Seventieth session of the United Nations General Assembly New York (USA), 25 September 2015, (2015). https://sustainabledevelopment.un.org/post2015/transformingourworld. Accessed 10 Dec 2019
3. United Nations: New Urban Agenda, United Nations, New York (2016). https://www2.habitat3.org/bitcache/99d99fbd0824de50214e99f864459d8081a9be00?vid=591155&disposition=inline&op=view. Accessed 21 Nov 2019
4. Dvarioniene, J., Grecu, V., Lai, S., Scorza, F.: Four perspectives of applied sustainability: research implications and possible integrations. In: Gervasi, O., et al. (eds.) ICCSA 2017. LNCS, vol. 10409, pp. 554–563. Springer, Cham (2017). https://doi.org/10.1007/978-3-319-62407-5_39
5. Scorza, F., Grecu, V.: Assessing sustainability: research directions and relevant issues. In: Gervasi, O., et al. (eds.) ICCSA 2016. LNCS, vol. 9786, pp. 642–647. Springer, Cham (2016). https://doi.org/10.1007/978-3-319-42085-1_55
6. United Nations: State of the World's Cities Report 2012/2013: Prosperity of Cities. United Nations Human Settlements Programme (2012)
7. Staricco, L.: Smart mobility: Opportunità e condizioni. TeMA J. Land Use Mobil. Environ. 6, 341–354 (2013)
8. World Bank: The Low Carbon City Development Program (LCCDP) Guidebook: A Systems Approach to Low Carbon Development in Cities (2013). http://www.bridge.ids.ac.uk/go/home&id=65489&type=Document&langID=1. Accessed 18 Dec 2019
9. Scorza, F., Pilogallo, A., Saganeiti, L., Murgante, B., Pontrandolfi, P.: Comparing the territorial performances of Renewable Energy Sources' plants with an integrated Ecosystem Services loss assessment: a case study from the Basilicata region (Italy). Sustain. Cities Soc. 56, 102082 (2020). https://doi.org/10.1016/j.scs.2020.102082
10. Banister, D.: The sustainable mobility paradigm. Transp. Pol. 15, 73–80 (2008). https://doi.org/10.1016/j.tranpol.2007.10.005
11. Cervero, R., Kockelman, K.: Travel demand and the 3Ds: density, diversity, and design. Transp. Res. Part D Transp. Environ. 2(3), 199–219 (1997). https://doi.org/10.1016/S1361-9209(97)00009-6

12. Ewing, R., Cervero, R.: Travel and the built environment. J. Am. Plann. Assoc. **76**(3), 265–294 (2010). https://doi.org/10.1080/01944361003766766
13. Cervero, R.: Transit-oriented development in the United States: experiences, challenges, and prospects. Report 102. Transit Cooperative Research Program, Washington, DC (2004)
14. Kropf, K.: Aspects of urban form. Urban Morphol. **13**(2), 105–120 (2009). https://doi.org/10.1002/9781118747711.ch3
15. Saganeiti, L., Favale, A., Pilogallo, A., Scorza, F., Murgante, B.: Assessing urban fragmentation at regional scale using sprinkling indexes. Sustainability **10**(9), 3274 (2018). https://doi.org/10.3390/su10093274
16. Saganeiti, L., Pilogallo, A., Scorza, F., Mussuto, G., Murgante, B.: Spatial indicators to evaluate urban fragmentation in Basilicata Region. In: Gervasi, O., et al. (eds.) ICCSA 2018. LNCS, vol. 10964, pp. 100–112. Springer, Cham (2018). https://doi.org/10.1007/978-3-319-95174-4_8
17. Saganeiti, L., Pilogallo, A., Faruolo, G., Scorza, F., Murgante, B.: Territorial fragmentation and renewable energy source plants: which relationship? Sustainability **12**(5), 1828 (2020). https://doi.org/10.3390/su12051828
18. Scorza, F., Pilogallo, A., Saganeiti, L., Murgante, B.: Natura 2000 areas and sites of national interest (SNI): measuring (un) integration between naturalness preservation and environmental remediation policies. Sustainability **12**(7), 2928 (2020). https://doi.org/10.3390/su12072928
19. Scorza, F., Saganeiti, L., Pilogallo, A., Murgante, B.: Ghost planning: the inefficiency of energy sector policies in a low population density region. Arch DI Stud URBANI E Reg. (2020). https://doi.org/10.3280/asur2020-127-s1003
20. Wilson, A.: Complex Spatial Systems: the Modelling Foundations of Urban and Regional Analysis. Prentice Hall, Harlow (2000)
21. Hillier, B., Hanson, J., Peponis, J., Hudson, J., Burdett, R.: Space syntax. A different urban perspective. Architect. J. **30**, 47–63 (1983)
22. Hillier, B., Hanson, J., Graham, H.: Ideas are in things: an application of the space syntax method to discovering house genotypes. Environ. Plann. B Plann. Des. **14**, 363–385 (1987)
23. Kwan, M.: Analysis of human spatial behaviour in a GIS environment: recent developments and future prospects. Geograph. Syst. **2**, 85–90 (2000)
24. Manum, B., Nordström, T.: Integrating bicycle network analysis in urban design; improving bikeability in Trondheim by combining space syntax and GIS-methods using the place syntax tool. In: Kim, Y.O., et al. (eds.) Proceedings of the Ninth International Space Syntax Symposium, vol. 28, pp. 1–14. Sejong University, Seoul (2013)
25. Cutini, V.: When cities lose their tail: sprawl as a configurational matter. In: 12th International Space Syntax Symposium, SSS 2019 (2019)
26. Cutini, V., de Falco, A., Giuliani, F.: Urban grid and seismic prevention: a configurational approach to the emergency management of Italian historic centres. In: 12th International Space Syntax Symposium, SSS 2019 (2019)
27. Jiang, B., Claramunt, C., Batty, M.: Geometric accessibility and geographic information: extending desktop GIS to space syntax. Comput. Environ. Urban Syst. **23**, 127–146 (1999). https://doi.org/10.1016/S0198-9715(99)00017-4
28. Ståhle, A., Marcus, L., KarlstrÄom, A.: Place syntax - geographic accessibility with axial lines in GIS. In: Proceedings of the 5th International Symposium in Space Syntax, Delft (2015)
29. Hillier, B.: Space Is the Machine: A Configurational Theory of Architecture. Cambridge University Press, Cambridge (1996)
30. Hillier, B., Hanson, J.: The Social Logic of Space. Cambridge University Press, Cambridge (1984)

31. Hillier, B., Penn, A., Hanson, J., Grajewski, T., Xu, J.: Natural movement: or, configuration and attraction in urban pedestrian movement. Environ. Plann. B **20**(1), 29–66 (1993)
32. Karlström, A., Mattsson, L.-G.: Place, space syntax and attraction-accessibility. In: Koch, D., Marcus, L., Steen, J. (eds.) Proceedings of the 7th International Space Syntax Symposium. KTH, Stockholm (2009)
33. Marcus, L.: Spatial Capital and How to Measure It: An Outline of an Analytical Theory of the Social Performativity of Urban Form. Istanbul Technical University, Istanbul (2007)
34. March, L., Steadman, P.: The Geometry of Environment. Methuen, London (1974)
35. Freeman, L.C.: A set of measures of centrality based on betweenness. Sociometry **40**(1), 35–41 (1977)
36. Lee, C., Moudon, A.V.: The 3Ds+R: quantifying land use and urban form correlates of walking. Transp. Res. Part D **1**, 204–2015 (2006). https://doi.org/10.1016/j.trd.2006.02.003
37. Berghauser Pont, M., Marcus, L.H.: Connectivity, density and built form: integrating 'Spacemate' with space syntax. In: Conference: ISUF 2015 XXII International Conference: City as Organism, New Visions for Urban Life (2015)
38. Scheiner, J.: Interrelations between travel mode choice and trip distance trends in Germany 1976–2002. J. Transp. Geogr. **18**(1), 75–84 (2010). https://doi.org/10.1016/j.jtrangeo.2009.01.001
39. Las Casas, G., Murgante, B., Scorza, F.: Regional local development strategies benefiting from open data and open tools and an outlook on the renewable energy sources contribution. In: Papa, R., Fistola, R. (eds.) Smart Energy in the Smart City. GET, pp. 275–290. Springer, Cham (2016). https://doi.org/10.1007/978-3-319-31157-9_14
40. Carbone, R., et al.: Using open data and open tools in defining strategies for the enhancement of Basilicata region. In: Gervasi, O., et al. (eds.) ICCSA 2018. LNCS, vol. 10964, pp. 725–733. Springer, Cham (2018). https://doi.org/10.1007/978-3-319-95174-4_55
41. Carbone, R., Saganeiti, L., Scorza, F., Murgante, B.: Increasing the walkability level through a participation process. In: Gervasi, O., et al. (eds.) ICCSA 2018. LNCS, vol. 10964, pp. 113–124. Springer, Cham (2018). https://doi.org/10.1007/978-3-319-95174-4_9
42. Scorza, F., Pontrandolfi, P.: Citizen participation and technologies: the C.A.S.T. architecture. In: Gervasi, O., et al. (eds.) ICCSA 2015. LNCS, vol. 9156, pp. 747–755. Springer, Cham (2015). https://doi.org/10.1007/978-3-319-21407-8_53
43. Murgante, B., Borruso, G.: Smart cities in a smart world. In: Rassia, S.T., Pardalos, P.M. (eds.) Future City Architecture for Optimal Living. SOIA, vol. 102, pp. 13–35. Springer, Cham (2015). https://doi.org/10.1007/978-3-319-15030-7_2
44. Murgante, B., Botonico, G., Graziadei, A., Sassano, G., Amato, F., Scorza, F.: Innovation, technologies, participation: new paradigms towards a 2.0 citizenship. Int. J. Electron. Gov. **11**(1), 62–88 (2019)
45. Scorza, F., Fortunato, G.: Cyclable cities: building feasible scenario through urban space-morphology assessment. J. Urban Plann. Dev. (2020, in printing)
46. Naess, P.: Urban form and travel behavior: experience from a Nordic context. J. Transp. Land Use **5**, 12–45 (2012). http://vbn.aau.dk/files/71021380/Urban_form_and_travel_behavior.pdf
47. Fortunato, G., Sassano, G., Scorza, F., Murgante, B.: Ciclabilità a Potenza: una proposta di intervento per lo sviluppo della mobilità attiva in un contesto urbano acclive. Urbanistica Informazioni **278**(special issue), 109–115 (2018)
48. Fortunato, G., Scorza, F., Murgante, B.: Cyclable city: a territorial assessment procedure for disruptive policy-making on urban mobility. In: Misra, S., et al. (eds.) ICCSA 2019. LNCS, vol. 11624, pp. 291–307. Springer, Cham (2019). https://doi.org/10.1007/978-3-030-24311-1_21

49. Las Casas, G., Scorza, F., Murgante, B.: New urban agenda and open challenges for urban and regional planning. In: Calabrò, F., Della Spina, L., Bevilacqua, C. (eds.) ISHT 2018. SIST, vol. 100, pp. 282–288. Springer, Cham (2019). https://doi.org/10.1007/978-3-319-92099-3_33

50. Las Casas, G., Scorza, F., Murgante, B.: Razionalità a-priori: una proposta verso una pianificazione antifragile. Ital. J. Reg. Sci. 18(2), 329–338 (2019). https://doi.org/10.14650/93656

51. Casas, G.L., Scorza, F.: Sustainable planning: a methodological toolkit. In: Gervasi, O., et al. (eds.) ICCSA 2016. LNCS, vol. 9786, pp. 627–635. Springer, Cham (2016). https://doi.org/10.1007/978-3-319-42085-1_53

52. Las Casas, G., Scorza, F.: A renewed rational approach from liquid society towards antifragile planning. In: Gervasi, O., et al. (eds.) ICCSA 2017. LNCS, vol. 10409, pp. 517–526. Springer, Cham (2017). https://doi.org/10.1007/978-3-319-62407-5_36

53. Curatella, L., et al.: Polycentrism and effective territorial structures: basilicata region case study. In: Bevilacqua, C., Calabrò, F., Della Spina, L. (eds.) New Metropolit. Perspect. NMP 2020. Smart Innovation, Systems and Technologies, vol. 178. Springer, Cham (2021). https://doi.org/10.1007/978-3-030-48279-4_159

54. Fortunato, G., Bonifazi, A., Scorza, F., Murgante, B.: Cycling infrastructures and community based management model for the Lagonegro-Rotonda cycling route: ECO-CICLE perspectives. In: Bevilacqua, C., Calabrò, F., Della Spina, L. (eds.) New Metropolit. Perspect. NMP 2020. Smart Innovation, Systems and Technologies, vol. 178. Springer, Cham (2021). https://doi.org/10.1007/978-3-030-48279-4_160

Green Chemistry, Circular Economy and Sustainable Development: An Operational Perspective to Scale Research Results in SMEs Practices

Iole Cerminara[1] , Lucia Chiummiento[1] , Maria Funicello[1],
Paolo Lupattelli[1] , Patrizia Scafato[1], Francesco Scorza[2(✉)] ,
and Stefano Superchi[1]

[1] University of Basilicata, Science Department,
Viale dell'Ateneo Lucano 10, 85100 Potenza, Italy
iole.cerminara@gmail.com, {lucia.chiummiento,
maria.funicello,paolo.lupattelli,patrizia.scafato,
stedano.superchi}@unibas.it
[2] School of Engineering, Laboratory of Urban and Regional Systems
Engineering (LISUT), University of Basilicata, Viale dell'Ateneo Lucano 10,
85100 Potenza, Italy
francesco.scorza@unibas.it

Abstract. Green Chemistry, Circular Economy and Sustainability are issues at the center of the modern scientific debate and three major trends in the global market. These three subjects are interconnected and interdependent and represent an affordable set of principles bringing innovations in the management of complex processes connected with anthropic use of resources.

Today's world population requires more natural resources be consumed than in previous decades, thus contributing to making primary resources increasingly scarce and with limited access.

Furthermore, an issue that persisted over time to become unsustainable is the waste emergency. It is also linked to the low capacity of operators to recover and re-use scraps of the production processes losing production values and generating environmental pressure.

Companies, whose growth is crucial for the economic system, generate waste in all stages of the production processes; although there is an increasing attention and awareness on the issue of waste, we are still in the early stages of the process that will lead SMEs to zero waste production. If we recognize such attribute as a competitive factor, we can identify in advance a critical innovation demand generated by SMEs operating in low competitive areas which has to be supported with technological transfer inn order to result "green" and effective in the short/medium term.

This paper presents data and defines there critical innovations domain in order to deliver an effective and scalable innovation transfer concerning circular economy thorough the application of green chemistry principles exploiting territorial factors in order to deliver sustainable local production chains.

Keywords: Green chemistry · Circular economy · Sustainable development

© Springer Nature Switzerland AG 2020
O. Gervasi et al. (Eds.): ICCSA 2020, LNCS 12255, pp. 206–213, 2020.
https://doi.org/10.1007/978-3-030-58820-5_16

1   Introduction and Research Position

Green Chemistry, Circular Economy and Sustainability are issues at the center of the modern scientific debate and three major trends in the global market. These three subjects are interconnected and interdependent and represent an affordable set of principles bringing innovations in the management of complex processes connected with anthropic use of resources. The Green Economy discourses is representative of the effort in applying Green Chemistry, Circular Economy and Sustainability thinking on systems innovations defining an attractive framework to deliver more resource efficient, lower carbon, less environmentally damaging, more socially inclusive societies [1].

Global sustainability challenges are closely interconnected yet often separately studied and managed. Systems integration-holistic approaches to integrating various components of coupled human and natural systems is critical to understand socioeconomic and environmental interconnections and to create sustainability solutions [2].

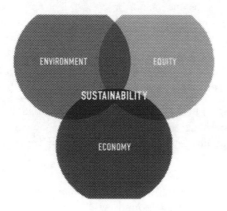

Fig. 1. Sustainability triangle

Today's world population requires more natural resources be consumed than in previous decades, thus contributing to making primary resources increasingly scarce and with limited access (Fig. 1).

Furthermore, an issue that persisted over time to become unsustainable is the waste emergency. It is also linked to the low capacity of operators to re-cover and re-use scraps of the production processes losing production values and generating environmental pressure.

Companies, whose growth is crucial for the economic system, generate waste in all stages of the production processes; although there is an increasing attention and awareness on the issue of waste, we are still in the early stages of the process that will lead SMEs to zero waste production. If we recognize such attribute as a competitive factor, we can identify in advance a critical innovation demand generated by SMEs operating in low competitive areas which has to be supported with technological transfer inn order to result "green" and effective in the short/medium term.

This paper presents a critical proposal oriented to defines three innovations domain in order to deliver an effective and scalable innovation transfer concerning circular economy in peripheral production and manufacturing systems thorough the application of green chemistry principles, exploiting territorial factors in order to deliver sustainable local production chains.

2 "Green" and "Circular": For a Systemic Integration

Green Chemistry (or sustainable chemistry) is a concept orienting the approach of the research and the chemical industry on paths of sustainability. Sustainable development today asks the chemical sciences to play a primary role in the conversion of old technologies into new clean processes and in the design of new products and new eco-compatible processes. Green Chemistry is therefore an area of chemistry and chemical engineering focused on the design of products and processes that minimize the use and generation of dangerous substances and the consequent environmental impact.

"Green chemical" was coined in 1991 by Paul Anastas and refers to a new order of priority in scientific and technological innovation based on general principles aimed at eliminating the use of procedures and substances dangerous [3, 4]. Paul Anastas and John C. Warner published a set of principles to guide the practice of green chemistry [5]. The principles concern these concepts:

- the design of processes to maximize the quantity of matter converted into product and therefore the optimization of the global mass balance so as to minimize waste;
- the use of raw materials and renewable energy sources and therefore the minimization of energy costs, for example by designing processes at room temperature and pressure;
- the use of harmless and safe substances for humans and the environment, therefore the replacement of obsolete compounds with others that maintain their functional efficacy while reducing toxicity towards man and the environment.
- the design of energy efficient processes through, for example, the use, at industrial level, of micro-organisms in enzymatic reactions at ambient temperature and pressure.
- the reduction, through the use of biomimetic processes, of the reaction by-products, present (in different percentages) in all reactions of traditional organic chemistry.

Such principles are scalable and realize a driving framework in order to deliver innovative production approach based on innovation transfer from research to industry. This is the core issue in order to achieve sustainability horizontal principles globally.

It is possible to identify large development share of the green innovation with consequent positive effects in all sectors of primary production and manufacturing, in particular in terms of product technological innovation and eco-innovation processes. Especially if we focus on the contribution of green chemistry as a fundamental link between circular economy and sustainability to guide scientific research and industrial production towards achievable change for a sustainable world.

A transversal market that looks to the development of more sustainable processes/products, from both an environmental and economic point of view, is the goal proposed as a long-term goal by the Green Economy. The growing attention towards sustainable production is also strengthened by legislation, according to what emerged from the latest European measures, increasingly stringent towards criteria of major sustainability [6]. The concept of a green economy has become the new buzz word in sustainability debate translating the effort of decision makers to set their hopes on greening the economy. Particularly after the United Nations Conference on Sustainable Development (or Rio + 20) the "greening" effort applied at political, economical, industrial and cultural domains represents a part of the solutions the last economic crisis [7]. Furthermore, three key issues are highlighted in the global (/local) process of innovation toward sustainability [8]: i) the direction in which innovation and development proceed; ii) the distribution of the costs, benefits, and risks associated with such changes; iii) the diversity of approaches and forms of innovation that contribute to global transitions to sustainability. All this aspects are coupled with the critical issues related to waste management and disposal: hence the great interest in the enhancement of processing by-products.

Especially for those economic systems characterized by a structural peripheric degree, it is difficult to implement effective processes to apply such sustainable production innovations in local SMEs. We directly consider the situation of Basilicata Region (Italy) characterized by a scattered productions in primary sector, weak economic structures, scarce attitude in cooperation among SMEs, low competitivity of local production and a delay in green innovation and sustainable development [9–11].

3   Main Domains for Knowledge and Innovation Transfer

The link between the research activities and small scale production represents the main barrier in order to promote green an circular innovation in practice. It depends on the starting threshold that enterprises perceive in the dialogue with research academics. The threshold could be measured in terms of mutual competences and its integration potential and the need of funds in order to start collaboration and knowledge transfer. Such aspects, combined with small companies structural weaknesses in strategic innovation thinking shape a non-collaboration area between SMEs (the huge microcosmos of productions units) and research and innovations centers.

If we consider the assumption that such barriers doesn't exists a number of applications domain for green chemistry application and sustainable development immediately open: agro-food sector, nutraceutical, primary productions etc.

In all those domains, basic and effective green-chemistry innovations may bring a significant product' and process' improvements with consequent enhancement of competitivity for operators.

Three main innovation demand areas could be identified in order to deliver a systemic green and circular approach for SMEs operating in remote areas:

1. Green Chemistry & Circular Economy
2. Product-territory and local supply chains.
3. Scientific dissemination and training

The first area directly refers to the Green Chemistry & Circular Economy and is based on the provisioning of innovative consulting and experimental research services for qualified companies interested in expanding their market through eco-efficient solutions and products. Using a "green-chemistry" approach, also based on the rediscovery and updating of traditional methods, it implements the recovery of waste products and by-products useful for the production of: bio-materials (textile fibers, insulators and materials for bio-building, bio-plastics), dyes, essences and natural extracts, products for bio-cosmetics.

The second area is oriented to design sustainable and circular "local supply chains" based on "synergies" between companies that, in a specific territory/place, share production processes in terms of raw and second materials supply, waste management, reuse of by-products also for energy purposes. Such agglomeration may offer the opportunity to local operators to raise the required stock in order to access effective technologies and economies reinforcing competitivity.

The third area represents the efforts to be done in the field of scientific dissemination and training. The users/consumers awareness concerning green and circular economy is an huge challenge in order to achieve a shared background knowledge orienting individual and collective behaviors.

4   Final Considerations

According to MIT report [12], companies that engage in a green-innovation process identify the following advantages of choosing the green economy and the principles of sustainability:

1. improvement of the image on the market
2. competitive advantage
3. openings to new markets
4. higher market shares and higher profits
5. reduction of energy costs
6. innovation of the business model and production processes
7. innovation of the products and services offered
8. reduction of costs for raw materials and waste
9. increase in labor productivity
10. less risk

Such benefits are at the basis of the SMEs competitivity and covers structural gaps of organizations operating in peripheral economic system like Basilicata Region one.

Therefore the envisaged schema of innovation transfer connecting research centers and SMEs ecosystem becomes a strategic vision for sustainable development in lagging regions.

The contribution of applied green chemistry is based on the transfer of basic improvement from main stream researches [12–31] to production processes in primary sector.

The analysis proposed by MCKINSEY [32] in the report "Towards the circular economy" is based on the identification of three drivers/factors fundamental for the transition to a circular economy: "Many factors are leading to a change in the consumer and producer habits, making the circular economy increasingly attractive. The growing scarcity of resources together with technological advancement and the development of cities generate a growing awareness that the time is ripe for change:

- scarcity of resources with stringent environmental standards
- advanced technologies generate new opportunities for the transition to a circular model
- growing urbanization is leading to the centralization of flows of consumer goods.

These conditions are also found in peripheral contexts such as that of Basilicata where the growth model of the industry connected with the circular economy exceeds 2% - per year as evidenced by the "Priority Sector Report: Circular Economy, European Commission" (2017).

Most European countries appear to be uniformly growing (e.g. France, United Kingdom, Sweden), falling uniformly (Spain, Portugal, Western Balkan states), or steady (Germany, Poland). Only Belgium, Italy, the Netherlands, Norway and Switzerland show varying situations within the country. In Italy Basilicata has a singular behavior which expresses a favorable tendency for the application of innovation transfer efforts according to the proposed intervention areas. Further researches are needed in order to asses specific case study concerning production sectors and/or selected operators in order to assess to efficiency of applied circular approach in small medium case company located in peripheral areas. Such evaluation could provide reference inn order to assess the propensity for the transition to a circular model by the production system in lagging territories.

References

1. Georgeson, L., Maslin, M., Poessinouw, M.: The global green economy: a review of concepts, definitions, measurement methodologies and their interactions. Geo Geogr. Environ. **4**, e00036 (2017). https://doi.org/10.1002/geo2.36
2. Liu, J., et al.: Systems integration for global sustainability. Science **347**, 6225 (2015). https://doi.org/10.1126/science.1258832
3. Zimmerman, J.B., Anastas, P.T., Erythropel, H.C., Leitner, W.: Designing for a green chemistry future. Science **367**(6476), 397–400 (2020). https://doi.org/10.1126/science.aay3060
4. Scorza, F., Murgante, B., Las Casas, G., Fortino, Y., Pilogallo, A.: Investigating territorial specialization in tourism sector by ecosystem services approach. In: Stratigea, A., Kavroudakis, D. (eds.) Mediterranean Cities and Island Communities. PI, pp. 161–179. Springer, Cham (2019). https://doi.org/10.1007/978-3-319-99444-4_7
5. Anastas, P., Eghbali, N.: Green chemistry: principles and practice. Chem. Soc. Rev. **39**, 301–312 (2010). https://doi.org/10.1039/b918763b
6. EP: REGOLAMENTO (CE) N. 1907/2006 DEL PARLAMENTO EUROPEO E DEL CONSIGLIO. (2006)

7. Bina, O.: The green economy and sustainable development: an uneasy balance? Environ. Plan. C Gov. Policy **31**, 1023–1047 (2013). https://doi.org/10.1068/c1310j
8. Ely, A., Smith, A., Stirling, A., Leach, M., Scoones, I.: Innovation politics post-Rio + 20: hybrid pathways to sustainability. Environ. Plan. C Gov. Policy **31**, 1063–1081 (2013). https://doi.org/10.1068/c12285j
9. Scorza, F., Las Casas, G.B.: Low density region: a spatial interpretation of disparities for the development of a sustainable model supporting rural welfare strategies. PLURIMONDI. 7, (2015)
10. Saganeiti, L., Pilogallo, A., Izzo, C., Piro, R., Scorza, F., Murgante, B.: Development strategies of agro-food sector in basilicata region (Italy): evidence from INNOVAGRO project. In: Misra, S., et al. (eds.) ICCSA 2019. LNCS, vol. 11624, pp. 347–356. Springer, Cham (2019). https://doi.org/10.1007/978-3-030-24311-1_25
11. Scorza, F., Grecu, V.: Assessing sustainability: research directions and relevant issues. In: Gervasi, O., et al. (eds.) ICCSA 2016. LNCS, vol. 9786, pp. 642–647. Springer, Cham (2016). https://doi.org/10.1007/978-3-319-42085-1_55
12. Haanes, K., et al.: Sustainability: the "embracers" seize advantage. MIT Sloan Manag. Rev. **52**(3), 3 (2011)
13. Iuliano, A., Scafato, P., Torchia, R.: Deoxycholic acid-based phosphites as chiral ligands in the enantioselective conjugate addition of dialkylzincs to cyclic enones: preparation of (-)-(R)-muscone. Tetrahedron Asymmetry **15**, 2533–2538 (2004). https://doi.org/10.1016/j.tetasy.2004.07.009
14. Cerminara, I., D'Alessio, L., D'Auria, M., Funicello, M., Guarnaccio, A.: 5-substituted benzothiophenes: synthesis, mechanism, and kinetic studies. Helv. Chim. Acta **99**, 384–392 (2016). https://doi.org/10.1002/hlca.201500285
15. Funicello, M., Cerminara, I.: heterocycles for alzheimer disease: 4- and 5-substituted benzothiophenes as starting scaffold in the construction of potential new inhibitors of bace 1. Med. Chem. **6**, 377–384 (2016). https://doi.org/10.4172/2161-0444.1000373
16. Lamorte, D., et al.: Future in the past: azorella glabra wedd. as a source of new natural compounds with antiproliferative and cytotoxic activity on multiple myeloma cells. Int. J. Mol. Sci. **19**(11), 3348 (2018). https://doi.org/10.3390/ijms19113348
17. Faraone, I., et al.: Antioxidant activity and phytochemical characterization of senecio clivicolus wedd. Molecules **23**, 10–2497 (2018). https://doi.org/10.3390/molecules23102497
18. Bonini, C., Chiummiento, L., Funicello, M.: Preparation of chiral 1,3 skipped anti- and syn-tetrols via highly enantioselective biocatalytic resolution. Tetrahedron Asymmetry **12**, 2755–2760 (2001). https://doi.org/10.1016/S0957-4166(01)00467-0
19. Bernini, R., et al.: Synthesis and evaluation of the antioxidant activity of lipophilic phenethyl trifluoroacetate esters by in vitro ABTS, DPPH and in cell-culture DCF assays. Molecules **23**(1), 208 (2018). https://doi.org/10.3390/molecules23010208
20. Lupattelli, P., Chiummiento, L., Funicello, M., Tramutola, F., Marmo, A., Gliubizzi, N., Tofani, D.: A mild access to chiral syn 1,2-diaryl glycols by stereoselective ring opening of ortho substituted trans 2,3-diaryl-oxiranes using Amberlyst 15 in H2O/THF system. Tetrahedron **71**, 5662–5668 (2015). https://doi.org/10.1016/j.tet.2015.06.039
21. Bovicelli, P., Lupattelli, P., Mincione, E.: Regio- and stereoselective epoxidation of steroidal 1,4-diene 3-ones by dimethyldioxirane: a new access to a-norsteroids and to a class of estrogen synthetase inhibitors. J. Org. Chem. **59**(15), 4304–4307 (1994). https://doi.org/10.1021/jo00094a050
22. Cacciari, I., et al.: Isotactic polypropylene biodegradation by a microbial community: physicochemical characterization of metabolites produced. Appl. Environ. Microbiol. **59**, 3695–3700 (1993). https://doi.org/10.1128/aem.59.11.3695-3700.1993

23. Iole, C., Luciano, D., Maria, F., Francesco, S.: La chimica in versi e musica. Diagnosis for the conservation and valorization of cultural heritage. Atti del quinto convegno internazionale, Napoli 11-12 dicembre 2014, pp. 247–254. Aracne, Ariccia (RM) (2014)
24. Superchi, S., Scafato, P., Gorecki, M., Pescitelli, G.: Absolute configuration determination by quantum mechanical calculation of chiroptical spectra: basics and applications to fungal metabolites. Curr. Med. Chem. **25**(2), 287–320 (2017). https://doi.org/10.2174/0929867324666170310112009
25. Lattmann, E., et al.: Synthesis and evaluation of 5-arylated 2(5 H)-furanones and 2-arylated pyridazin-3(2 H)-ones as anti-cancer agents. J. Pharm. Pharmacol. **55**, 1259–1265 (2003). https://doi.org/10.1211/0022357021756
26. Cimmino, A., Masi, M., Evidente, M., Superchi, S., Evidente, A.: Fungal phytotoxins with potential herbicidal activity: chemical and biological characterization. Nat. Prod. Rep. **32**(2), 1629–1659 (2015). https://doi.org/10.1039/c5np00081e
27. Pisani, L., Superchi, S., D'Elia, A., Scafato, P., Rosini, C.: Synthetic approach toward cis-disubstituted γ- and δ-lactones through enantioselective dialkylzinc addition to aldehydes: application to the synthesis of optically active flavors and fragrances. Tetrahedron **68**, 5779–5784 (2012). https://doi.org/10.1016/j.tet.2012.05.028
28. Superchi, S., Marchitiello, V., Pisani, L., Scafato, P.: Asymmetric addition of dimethylzinc to alkylidenmalonates mediated by phosphorous ligands: a new synthetic route to floral fragrances. Chirality **23**, 761–767 (2011). https://doi.org/10.1002/chir.20987
29. Superchi, S., Nardiello, M., Donnoli, M.I., Scafato, P., Menicagli, R., Rosini, C.: Enantioselective synthesis of the fragrance trans-magnolione under asymmetric phase transfer catalysis. Comptes Rendus Chim. **8**, 867–874 (2005). https://doi.org/10.1016/j.crci.2005.02.017
30. Superchi, S., et al.: Synthesis and toxicity to mammalian cells of the carrot dihydroiso-coumarins. Chem. Res. Toxicol. **6**, 46–49 (1993). https://doi.org/10.1021/tx00031a007
31. Cerminara, I., Chiummiento, L., Funicello, M., Guarnaccio, A., Lupattelli, P.: Heterocycles in peptidomimetics and pseudopeptides: design and synthesis. Pharmaceuticals **5**, 297–316 (2012). https://doi.org/10.3390/ph5030297
32. MCKINSEY: Towards the circular economy. Economic and business rationale for an accelerated transition (2013)

The Design of an Urban Atlas to Spread Information Concerning the Growth of Anthropic Settlements in Basilicata Region

Giuseppe Faruolo, Luigi Santopietro[✉], Lucia Saganeiti,
Angela Pilogallo, Francesco Scorza, and Beniamino Murgante

School of Engineering, Laboratory of Urban and Regional
Systems Engineering (LISUT), University of Basilicata,
Viale Dell'Ateneo Lucano 10, 85100 Potenza, Italy
giuseppe.far88@gmail.com,
luigi.santopietro@studenti.unibas.it,
{lucia.saganeiti,angela.pilogallo,francesco.scorza,
beniamino.murgante}@unibas.it

Abstract. Social, demographic and economics transformations occurred in Basilicata Region (Italy) since 1950's, have been developed transformations not always linked to effective and sustainable urban planning tools. A general research gap regards the tools for assessing such effectiveness of planning. In this work we describe the preliminary design of a thematic Atlas presenting Basilicata Region results achieved in previous researches concerning urban growth and consequently land use changes. On the bases of a territorial information system developed by LISUT research group we analyzed urban growth since 1950 comparing it with recent phenomena of RES (renewable energy sources) plants settlement occurred since 2000. Such spatial information, evaluated through fragmentation indexes, are compared with socio-economic data at municipal scale. The results are a comprehensive picture of local settlement development trends that allows to communicate evidences of current planning system including urban planning tools, sectorial planning (operating at regional scale), public investments program evidences. The Atlas will be published for Basilicata Region area (Italy) as a model in order to analyze and compare other European Regions.

Keywords: RES · Fragmentation · Sprinkling

1 Introduction

Urban expansion produces heavy externalities on environmental components of the territory, we may affirm that the nature, the intensity and the extension of such impacts strongly depends on the quality of urban and territorial plans and their implementation process. These phenomena produce land consumption, in terms of the loss of natural or agricultural land in favor of anthropic settlement. In recent decades, in urban and rural areas, urban expansion has generated a strong fragmentation of the landscape. Often city boundaries are unrecognizable, dispersion of settlement generate urban areas

© Springer Nature Switzerland AG 2020
O. Gervasi et al. (Eds.): ICCSA 2020, LNCS 12255, pp. 214–225, 2020.
https://doi.org/10.1007/978-3-030-58820-5_17

where unsustainable criticalities in terms of urban services develop continuously and consequent quality of life declines. Sprawl and sprinkling phenomena are two ways of urban expansion. A shared definition of sprawl phenomenon is given by many authors [1–4] as *"the spreading of urban developments (such as houses and shopping centers) on undeveloped land near a city"* (Merriam Webster) [5], while sprinkling phenomenon can be defined as, "a small quantity distributed in drops or scattered particles" [6]. Each phenomenon gives as result fragmentation, that in Italy is mainly expressed by the sprinkling. The spatial configuration of sprinkling is connected to a scattered and pulverized settlement of buildings and concerning the case of Basilicata Region, this phenomenon is empathized by the installation of RES plants.

This research lays the groundwork for a careful evaluation of the settlement stock and effects that the spread of RES has generated. We should assume that the spread of RES technology installations (particularly on portions of natural and semi-natural territory) cannot be considered as a win-win process [7, 8]. In fact, there is a significant system of values (even economic and potentially speculative) linked to such transformations in which the achievement of collective (we could say global) energy sustainability goals corresponds to the development of an economy guaranteed by public income that leads to the consumption of environmental resources (soil, landscape, ecosystems).

The complexity of arguments and analysis related to soil consumption (or land take) [9–11], have to be simplified in order to make it accessible not only to expert users, but mainly for citizens and decision makers in order to gain effective communication and to reinforce the awareness concerning externalities on environmental and landscape values [12, 13].

An Atlas could represent an effective tool in order to show spatial analysis and research results concerning this complex domain connected with settlements typologies and dynamics at local scale through simple and reliable indicators showing current trends.

In this sense a set of simple indicators has been adopted to present, in the Atlas, the results of the assessment concerning territorial fragmentation due to anthropogenic settlement. The methodology suggested by the authors, combine the detail location of the RES plants with the evolution of settlement respect to the evolution of the population.

In this way, the Atlas may cover a structural information gap that does not enable the decision makers, stakeholders interested in the process, or citizens to understand and know the changes taking place.

2   Previous Research Results Towards a Comprehensive Communication Box

LISUT research group widely applied in urban development research field [8, 14–19]. The main case study area is the Basilicata region. These studies, on one side, considered specific research question, on the other side allowed to develop a wide informative asset related to "settlement stock" in Basilicata. Such information, through Atlas project, will be valued to provide expressive interpretative tools allowing to identify relationship between settlements system and main territorial planning issues in Basilicata region. Among actual emerging arguments: management of natural risks, protection/enhancement of natural and ecosystem resources [20], management of productive industrial sites and remediation policies of decommissioned industrial sites.

2.1   Study Area

Basilicata Region is located in the South of Italy (Fig. 1). It covers about 10.000 Km^2, and it has a population of 562.869 inhabitants (ISTAT [21], 2019). Only between years 2018-19 the population is decreased by 4249 inhabitants (ISTAT [21], 2019), while, according to ISPRA report 2019 [22] there was an important transformation from rural to sub-urban areas or urban areas, in the period 2016–2018, with an increment about 1, 48% of new urban areas. In addition, since 2010, a large part of the territory has been affected by the installation of RES plants, and at the end of 2017, the number of RES plants was 2122, including wind turbines and photovoltaic fields with a total power output of over 1000 MW.

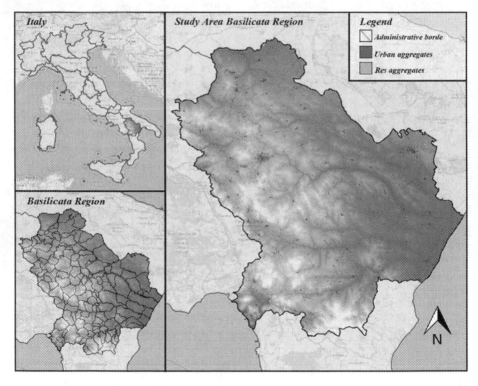

Fig. 1. Basilicata region study area

Starting from the data and results deriving from researches developed at regional scale by Saganeiti et al. [7, 8, 15], the Atlas has the objective to organize information in order to make it expressive at a different scale: the Municipal scale. Using the methodology described above, into the Urban Atlas the fundamental step is the calibration of the grid. In fact, there was a research about the best size of the grid cell to choose, applying SPX index. Testing different values of step length for the grid, the value of 250 m has been chosen because is the more appropriate to describe the fragmentation. Smaller grid resolutions (below 250 m as example 50 m) have been excluded because they are not able to describe properly fragmentation at municipal scale, and are not useful to draw up indicators for the Urban Atlas (see Fig. 2).

Using a grid cell with a step length of 250 m, the SPX index is computed for every municipality of Basilicata Region, considering the evolution of settlement respect to the evolution of the population and the growing of RES plants. In this way, the information is collected into an information database to municipal scale, which forms the Urban Atlas.

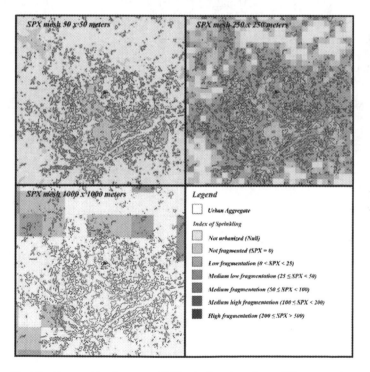

Fig. 2. Comparison between SPX calculated on three different meshes

2.2   Urban Settlements Growth

The urban settlements growth baseline is related to Saganeiti et al. [15]. The buildings are classified for five temporal phases and characterized for their intended use (residential or other use). For each municipality of the region, for the five times phases, were calculated two indices: population density D_p and total amount of residential buildings per hectare D_b. Only for residential buildings, D_b is calculated. In Table 1 the results are collected for whole region and for each of the considered periods.

Table 1. Variation of population and buildings in the Basilicata region over time.

Year	Population (No.)	Residential buildings [B_R] (n)	D_p (Inhabitants/ha)	D_b (B_R/ha)
1950	627,586	117,687	0.63	0.12
1989	610,186	238,603	0.61	0.24
1998	597,468	269,019	0.60	0.27
2006	591,338	285,072	0.59	0.28
2013	578,391	297,810	0.58	0.30
2017	570,365	311,494	0.57	0.31

Observing data between 1950 and 2017, in 108 of 131 municipalities a decreasing of population not matches a corresponding decreasing urban expansion, on the contrary there was a positive trend. In most municipalities, the expansion of housing is not proportionate to demographic change This result is useful to Atlas because remarks that the development of settlements was not related to a real housing need Table 2.

Table 2. Areas [he] occupied by different typology of buildings in the six time phases considered.

Year	Agricultural buildings	Public buildings	Commercial buildings	Industrial buildings	Residential buildings
1950	150	49	0,9	28	1469
1989	3540	3538	3389	287	7079
1998	4057	4047	3884	476	8110
2006	4344	4343	4297	611	8687
2013	4578	4577	4439	655	9153
2017	4578	4577	4441	669	9272

2.3   Mapping of RES Plants in Basilicata Region

Starting from study area, we move on to the characterization of the process of construction of the space dataset of the plants with reference to the sources used and the territorialization procedures. Therefore, is proposed an exemplification for the formation of the territorial units to assess the areas interested by the installation process of RES plants. Through essential geo-processes, the areas of influence of individual installations and territorial aggregates are obtained, to which a descriptive function of the effects in terms of territorial fragmentation is attributed. Based on these preliminary elaborations, the main fragmentation indices proposed in the literature for RES implants were calculated. The results were compared with those relating to the evaluation of the settlement system already developed in previous research works [14, 15].

2.4 A Comprehensive Picture for the Basilicata Region

Starting from 1950's, the population of Basilicata Region has gradually decreased. Instead, from 1990 to date there is a change in trend between urban aggregates and population (Table 3). From 2006, a significant increase of soil consumption has been given by RES surfaces (see Fig. 3). SPX index has been computed for different areas of grid cell of 0.025 km^2. SPX index has been computed in two different steps: first the SPX is computed for Basilicata Region, then SPX is clipped for every Municipality boundary, to eliminate local errors due to the Municipality boundary.

Table 3. Population, Aggregates buildings surface (**Abs**), Aggregates surface RES Area (**AsA RES**)

Year	Population (No.)	Abs (he)	AsA RES (he)
1950	627,586	3328	–
1989	610,186	10475	–
1998	597,468	12758	
2006	591,338	14492	565
2013	578,391	15530	866
2017	570,365	15908	1719

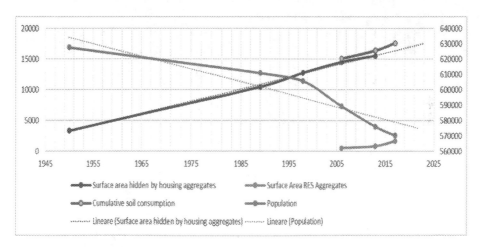

Fig. 3. Correlation between population, surface area hidden by housing aggregates, surface area RES aggregates and cumulative soil consumption

3   Data Processing for Urban Atlas

The data processed, present for each Municipality multiple elaboration. The elaborations were carried out for the years 1950, 1989, 1998, 2006, 2013, 2017, they are:

1. Evolution of the buildings and urban aggregates;
2. Evolution of RES plants for the years 2006, 2013 and 2017;
3. The table showing territorial surface occupied by building stock for usage categories;
4. The graphs that compare the building stock with the evolution of RES installations, compared to the evolution of the population;
5. Sprinkling index with mesh 250 x 250 m, of the building stock combined with RES plants.

In the following figures are presented, as prototypes, some elaborations drawn up for the municipality of Avigliano.

In Fig. 4, is represented the evolution of urban aggregates from 1989 to 2013, where it is possible note the continuous increase of the same at the expense of land consumption, with zooms on some areas of interest, where this phenomenon has occurred more.

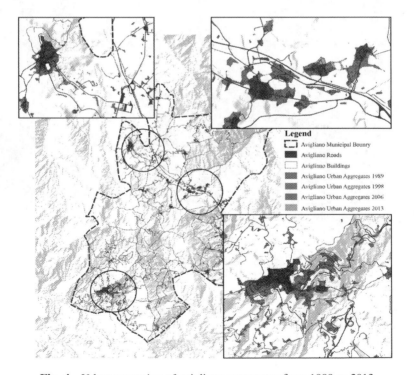

Fig. 4. Urban expansion of avigliano aggregates from 1989 to 2013

In Fig. 5, the evolution of the urban aggregates from 1950 to 2013, with the aggregates of wind turbines and photovoltaic plants (representing RES plants expansion) from 2006 to 2017.

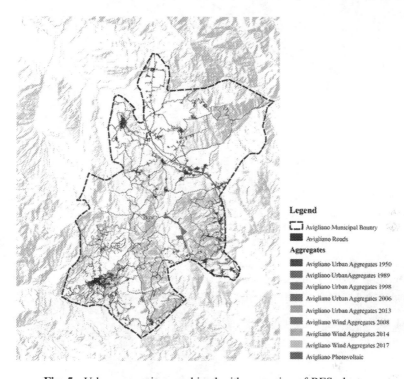

Fig. 5. Urban expansion combined with expansion of RES plants

For each municipality, there is a summary table showing data concerning surfaces occupied by building stock divided per building use categories (see Table 4), while in a graph (see Fig. 6) are compared building stock with the evolution of RES installations, related to evolution of population

Table 4. Areas [he] occupied by different typology of buildings in the six time phases considered for Avigliano municipality.

Year	Agricultural buildings	Public buildings	Commercial buildings	Industrial buildings	Residential buildings
1950	3.02	1.27	0.33	0.96	25.06
1989	9.06	1.94	0.33	7.31	50.52
1998	11.08	2.52	0.33	32.60	55.67
2006	12.63	2.52	0.33	41.75	58.91
2013	13.15	2.53	0.33	43.15	63.20
2017	14.08	3.03	0.41	60.68	85.29

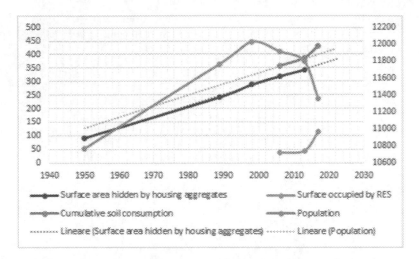

Fig. 6. Correlation between population, surface area hidden by housing aggregates, surface area RES aggregates and cumulative soil consumption for avigliano municipality

In Fig. 7, is represented urban fragmentation, through the sprinkling index. In this case the urban fragmentation is related to 2013, where it is possible notice an important fragmentation in different parts of the territory, due to the increase sometimes of urban aggregates, but more and more frequently from the evolution of RES plants.

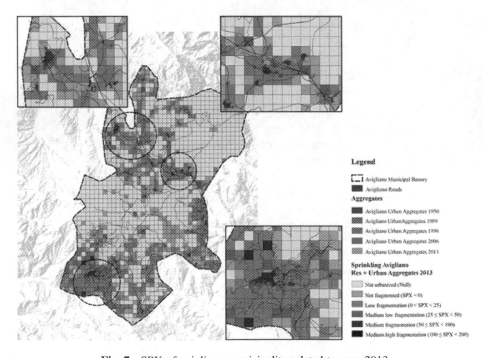

Fig. 7. SPX of avigliano municipality related to year 2013

4   Conclusions

The Atlas lays the foundation for develop sustainable policies in territorial planning and engagement of public and private actors [13, 23–25]. Fully in the line with the goals of New Urban Agenda [26], the Atlas provides guidelines to a rational use of soil resource [27, 28].

Computing carried out, showed what is the status actually of the fragmentation and it's a framework exportable to other case study to improve the methodology. An interesting future perspective is a comparison between two different scenarios: the first business as usual and the second planning actions to achieve the reduction of fragmentation or compaction of the urban areas.

Atlas can help to understand how RES have contributed to the transformation of urban system with inevitable consequences on the landscape. The use of Urban Atlas can be related to different aspects:

- To be a tool for local administrators, helping them to know the status and the evolution of land consumption or land use;
- Define regulatory frameworks having Regional value, with the aim to achieve the (ambitious) goal of zero land consumption;
- As base-line to monitoring land consumption (or land use) and to planning in several sectors (energy, landscape, environment...)

Concerning the spatial evaluations included as basic data in this work, future research development perspective concerns the improvement of the methodology with the fragmentation caused by infrastructures in the region, not valued in this work.

Future perspectives are oriented to realize a web-based platform where users are able to visualize and retrieve data available structured in a GIS model. The idea is dissemination of the data through a free consulting services in order to allow the majority of potential users (not only expert users) to take advantages from the Atlas. The technological tools we are oriented to adopt is a web gis portal including OCS standards for maps and geodata sharing on the internet.

Therefore the aim is to structure a GIS model in a co-design view [29] as help desk to decision making (public administration) with two specific functions:

- Territorial planning and knowledge of developments of urban fragmentation, in order to reduce or mitigate the effects of urban expansion,
- Planning actions aimed to increase urban fragmentation, supporting decisions undertaken by stakeholders or public administration.

In addition, considering or not a web platform as a dissemination tool, the data collected into the Atlas has to be updated both in terms more accurate time steps and in terms of multi-scale resolution.

References

1. Herold, M., Couclelis, H., Clarke, K.C.: The role of spatial metrics in the analysis and modeling of urban land use change. Comput. Environ. Urban Syst. **29**, 369–399 (2005)
2. Galster, G., Hanson, R., Ratcliffe, M.R., Wolman, H., Coleman, S., Freihage, J.: Wrestling sprawl to the ground: defining and measuring an elusive concept. Hous. Policy Debate. **12**, 681–717 (2001)
3. Hasse, J.E., Lathrop, R.G.: Land resource impact indicators of urban sprawl. Appl. Geogr. **23**, 159–175 (2003)
4. Jaeger, J.A.G.: Landscape division, splitting index, and effective mesh size: new measures of landscape fragmentation. Landsc. Ecol. **15**, 115–130 (2000)
5. Urban Sprawl| Definition of Urban Sprawl by Merriam-Webster, https://www.merriam-webster.com/dictionary/urban sprawl, Accessed 04 May 2020
6. Romano, B., Zullo, F., Ciabò, S., Fiorini, L., Marucci, A.: Geografie e modelli di 50 anni di consumo di suolo in Italia. Sci. e Ric. **6**, 17–28 (2015)
7. Saganeiti, L., Pilogallo, A., Faruolo, G., Scorza, F., Murgante, B.: Territorial fragmentation and renewable energy source plants: which relationship? Sustain. **12**, 1828 (2020). https://doi.org/10.3390/su12051828
8. Saganeiti, L., Pilogallo, A., Faruolo, G., Scorza, F., Murgante, B.: Energy landscape fragmentation: basilicata region (Italy) study case. In: Misra, S., et al. (eds.) ICCSA 2019. LNCS, vol. 11621, pp. 692–700. Springer, Cham (2019). https://doi.org/10.1007/978-3-030-24302-9_50
9. Scorza, F., Pilogallo, A., Saganeiti, L., Murgante, B.: Natura 2000 areas and sites of national interest (sni): measuring (un) integration between naturalness preservation and environmental remediation policies. Sustain. **12**, 2928 (2020). https://doi.org/10.3390/su12072928
10. Scorza, F., Saganeiti, L., Pilogallo, A., Murgante, B.: GHOST PLANNING: The Inefficiency of Energy Sector Policies in a Low Population Density Region. Arch. DI Stud, URBANI E Reg (2020)
11. Scorza, F., Pilogallo, A., Saganeiti, L., Murgante, B.: Comparing the territorial performances of renewable energy sources' plants with an integrated ecosystem services loss assessment: a case study from the basilicata region (Italy). Sustain. Cities Soc. **56**, 102052 (2020). https://doi.org/10.1016/j.scs.2020.102082
12. Murgante, B., Botonico, G., Graziadei, A., Sassano, G., Amato, F., Scorza, F.: Innovation, technologies, participation: new paradigms towards a 2.0 citizenship. Int. J. Electron. Gov. **11**, 62–88 (2019). https://doi.org/10.1504/IJEG.2019.098814
13. Pontrandolfi, P., Scorza, F.: Sustainable urban regeneration policy making: inclusive participation practice. In: Gervasi, O., et al. (eds.) ICCSA 2016. LNCS, vol. 9788, pp. 552–560. Springer, Cham (2016). https://doi.org/10.1007/978-3-319-42111-7_44
14. Saganeiti, L., Pilogallo, A., Scorza, F., Mussuto, G., Murgante, B.: Spatial indicators to evaluate urban fragmentation in basilicata region. In: Gervasi, O., et al. (eds.) ICCSA 2018. LNCS, vol. 10964, pp. 100–112. Springer, Cham (2018). https://doi.org/10.1007/978-3-319-95174-4_8
15. Saganeiti, L., Favale, A., Pilogallo, A., Scorza, F., Murgante, B.: Assessing urban fragmentation at regional scale using sprinkling indexes. Sustain. **10**(9), 3274 (2018). https://doi.org/10.3390/su10093274
16. Amato, F., Martellozzo, F., Nolè, G., Murgante, B.: Preserving cultural heritage by supporting landscape planning with quantitative predictions of soil consumption. J. Cult. Herit. **23**, 44–54 (2017)

17. Martellozzo, F., Amato, F., Murgante, B., Clarke, K.C.: Modelling the impact of urban growth on agriculture and natural land in Italy to 2030. Appl. Geogr. **91**, 156–167 (2018)
18. Amato, F., Maimone, B.A., Martellozzo, F., Nolè, G., Murgante, B.: The effects of urban policies on the development of urban areas. Sustainability. **8**, 297 (2016)
19. Di Palma, F., Amato, F., Nolè, G., Martellozzo, F., Murgante, B.: A SMAP supervised classification of landsat images for urban sprawl evaluation. ISPRS Int. J. Geo-Inf. **5**, 109 (2016)
20. Lai, S., Zoppi, C.: The influence of natura 2000 sites on land-taking processes at the regional level: an empirical analysis concerning sardinia (Italy). Sustain. **9**, 259 (2017). https://doi.org/10.3390/su9020259
21. Istat.it, https://www.istat.it/, Accessed 28 April 2020
22. SNPA, R.: Consumo di suolo, dinamiche territoriali e servizi ecosistemici. (2019)
23. Dvarioniene, J., Grecu, V., Lai, S., Scorza, F.: Four perspectives of applied sustainability: research implications and possible integrations. In: Gervasi, O., et al. (eds.) ICCSA 2017. LNCS, vol. 10409, pp. 554–563. Springer, Cham (2017). https://doi.org/10.1007/978-3-319-62407-5_39
24. Scorza, F., Grecu, V.: Assessing sustainability: research directions and relevant issues. In: Gervasi, O., et al. (eds.) ICCSA 2016. LNCS, vol. 9786, pp. 642–647. Springer, Cham (2016). https://doi.org/10.1007/978-3-319-42085-1_55
25. Scorza, F., Pontrandolfi, P.: Citizen participation and technologies: the c.a.s.t. architecture. In: Gervasi, O., et al. (eds.) ICCSA 2015. LNCS, vol. 9156, pp. 747–755. Springer, Cham (2015). https://doi.org/10.1007/978-3-319-21407-8_53
26. The New Urban Agenda - Habitat III, http://habitat3.org/the-new-urban-agenda/, Accessed 19 March 2020
27. Las Casas, G., Scorza, F., Murgante, B.: New urban agenda and open challenges for urban and regional planning. In: Calabrò, F., Della Spina, L., Bevilacqua, C. (eds.) ISHT 2018. SIST, vol. 100, pp. 282–288. Springer, Cham (2019). https://doi.org/10.1007/978-3-319-92099-3_33
28. Las Casas, G., Scorza, F., Murgante, B.: Razionalità a-priori: una proposta verso una pianificazione antifragile. Reg. Sci. **18**(2), 329–338 (2017). https://doi.org/10.14650/93656
29. Moura, A.C.M., Campagna, M.: Co-design: digital tools for knowledge-building and decision-making in planning and design. Disegnarecon **11**(20), 1–3 (2018)

A Place-Based Approach for the SECAP of Potenza Municipality: The Case of Green Spaces System

Luigi Santopietro[✉] and Francesco Scorza

School of Engineering, Laboratory of Urban and Regional Systems
Engineering (LISUT), University of Basilicata, Viale dell'Ateneo Lucano 10,
85100 Potenza, Italy
luigi.santopietro@studenti.unibas.it,
francesco.scorza@unibas.it

Abstract. Action Plans for Energy and Sustainable Climate (SECAP) represent an operational dimension of urban planning that organizes investments and urban transformation processes outside the traditional urban planning instruments. In this work, a methodological approach for SECAP development is discussed in order to reinforce the links between energy and climate objectives and actions of the SECAP with the territorial dimension assessed through systems and targets from the very beginning of the planning process. This methodology takes into account an analytical/cognitive approach of the application context based on energy-consumption data, morpho-climatic parameters, and environmental data generally available for all municipalities. It produces Systemic interpretation useful to support the decision-making process and the monitoring of SECAP implementation enhancement of a territorial approach in SECAP development leads to the clear identification of the intervention targets and the selection of site-specific actions accompanied by an adequate system of indicators. This represents an innovation proposal in the framework of the NewCOM approach. The application to case study of Potenza Municipality is a component of a wider process of developing the SECAP. It shows how methodological approach suggested, can be considered as a tool to support decisions making and monitoring of actions to be included in the plan.

Keywords: SEAP/SECAP · Local climate plans · Urban green spaces

1 Introduction

The Covenant of Mayors (COM) actually is the world's largest movement for local climate and energy actions [1]. Fully in line with the UN Sustainable Development Goals and climate justice principles [2], the Covenant of Mayors will tackle three key issues: climate change mitigation, adaptation to the adverse effects of climate change and universal access to secure, clean and affordable energy. Every signatory, who join COM, shares a common view in terms of the decarbonization of territories, strengthening capacity to adapt to unavoidable climate change impacts. In Italy at this moment, the most adopted strategic energy plan at Municipal level is SECAP. These plans, with

© Springer Nature Switzerland AG 2020
O. Gervasi et al. (Eds.): ICCSA 2020, LNCS 12255, pp. 226–234, 2020.
https://doi.org/10.1007/978-3-030-58820-5_18

a bottom-up process, are structured on a numbers of local scale actions, policies and transformations directed to improve the performance of the territorial systems addressing energy efficiency objectives and interested in climate change mitigation/adaptation processes.

The SECAP development process, is based on a very synthetic table of contents and, in the perspectives of the authors, could reveal several weaknesses in the comprehensive structure linking objectives to actions and indicators. The SECAP structure proposes holistic reasoning for the adaptation and mitigation of climate change. With respect to climate mitigation, local governments are guided to relate to all emission sources either direct or due to combustion of fuel within the territory, or indirect, related to the production of energy consumed in the territory and produced elsewhere. Key components for mitigation action are the "residential", "tertiary", "municipal/public" and "transport" sector. With regard to climate adaptation, the territorial components more vulnerable are: "buildings", "transportation", "energy", "water", "waste", "land management", "environment & biodiversity", "agriculture & forestry", "health", "civil protection & emergency", "tourism" and "other". The methodology proposed by the New Covenant of Mayors is based on planning to integrate climate and energy actions in which local stakeholders can play an active role. At the time of the drafting of SECAP, reducing the selection of actions to the mere verification of correspondence between the proposed sectors and the activities appears to be a weak process from a territorial point of view, as it does not highlight the relationship of actions with the context and therefore does not promote future monitoring actions and the assessment of the relationship between SECAP and urban planning instruments. Therefore, the methodological proposal developed in this work, after the analytical/cognitive insights on the individual territorial components related to the sectors proposed by SECAP, is oriented to develop a reasoning "by systems". In other words, the sectoral breakdown of SECAP is overcome by promoting an integrated reading of these components into 5 systems to which multiple sectors are identified according to a relational scheme (see Fig. 1).

Every system identified is related to a background map, that represents the minimal process of knowledge. Every map is a result of GIS processing. The resulting elaborations allow to fill out the SECAP worksheet, adding to what is already provided by the SECAP methodology, analytical/cognitive insights on the individual territorial components (see Fig. 2). In this approach, "territorial targets", i.e. real elements of the territory, are proposed to locate the interventions envisaged by SECAP. This is an innovative element since neither SEAP (Sustainable Energy and Action Plan), nor subsequently SECAP, in their proposals provided for a spatialization of interventions and therefore a direct correlation between what was envisaged by the intervention and the consequent territorial transformation.

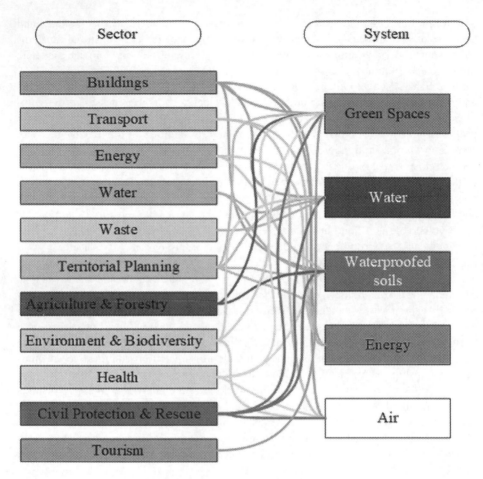

Fig. 1. Relationship between sectors and system identified

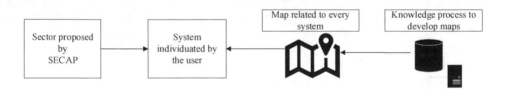

Fig. 2. Relationship between system individuated by the user and process to develop maps

2   A Placed Based Approach

In the last decades, European Programs gave a push to a sustainable urban planning and transition towards low-carbon economy. As remarked by Scorza et al. [3–7], the planning of the actions and the transformation provided need three fundamental features:

- A hierarchical and flexible system of objectives, achieved by the actions. The objectives are organized in overall objectives and several sub-objectives able to achieve the overall objective;
- A place-based approach, with definition of "territorial target" that are physical objects present on the territory where implement the actions provided by the objectives. These territorial targets are at same time targets and results of the developments of the provided actions.
- A research of specific indicators of the actions progress, with an assessment process based on the protection of the principles of equity, efficiency and irreproducible resource conservation;

At this moment, SECAP can be considered as urban planning tool at municipal or urban scale, able to develop sustainable transformation supported by a participative process [4, 5, 8]. An application of this methodological approach, is related to the SECAP of Potenza Municipality next to be realized. The authors suggest as example, the knowledge process and development of the actions for the green spaces system in Potenza Municipality.

3   The Case Study of Potenza Municipality SECAP: Green Spaces System

The National Plan to Climate Change (PNACC) [9] provides for increase of green infrastructure to reduce effects of heat islands, heavy rainfall and flood in urban settlements. The urban green is a theme that is part of the production structure of the ecosystem services that nature provides us (from the natural purification of the water we drink or the air we breathe, to the urban park or the landscape alpine for walking) through natural capital (understood as the entire stock of natural assets – living organisms, air, water, soil and geological resources – that help to provide valuable goods and services, direct or indirect, for man and which are necessary for the survival of the environment in which it lives) [10]. The specific note of green spaces (especially urban green spaces), in this context, is that it represents a natural capital – able to provide several essential ecosystem services of proximity. In this way, the first step is the knowledge of the green available to find the more critical areas where take action. The data are collected consulting the Regional Geoportal of Basilicata Region (RSDI) [11], Urban Planning Regulations of Potenza Municipality [12] and orthophotos. Identifying the green spaces, they are distinguished between the green spaces inside and outside of urban boundary. The green spaces are classified according to several usage class, as following:

- City parks;
- Green space (flower-bids or green spaces between buildings);
- City parks and sub-urban parks in planning;
- Urban garden
- Rural areas, i.e. green spaces outside the urban boundary classified as forest and shrub and/or herbaceous vegetation associations by CLC [13].

In Table 1 are shown the data collected, classified by typology and extension.

Table 1. Typology of green spaces and related area

Typology	Area [he]	% on the area of urban environment
City parks	57	1.96
Green space	9	0.03
City parks and sub-urban parks in planning	116	4.01
Urban garden	2	0.06
Rural areas	14681	5.09

A synthetic map collecting several typologies of green spaces is shown in Fig. 3.

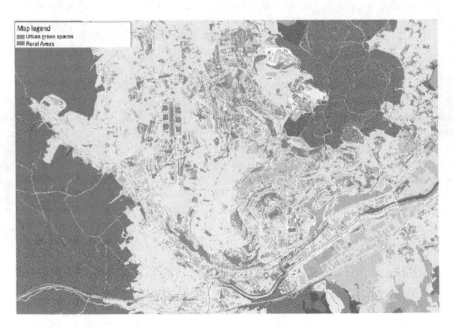

Map legend
Urban green spaces
Rural Areas

Fig. 3. Green spaces map

An overall scheme of possible actions for green system is shown in Fig. 4. Every action is related to several territorial targets to achieve the overall objective and it's overcome the connection one-by-one between territorial target and actions.

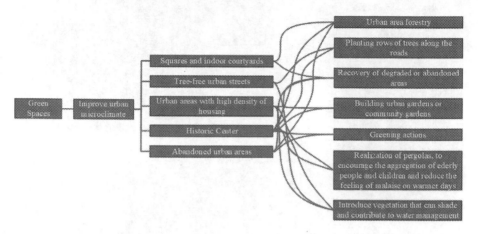

Fig. 4. Logical scheme for definition of actions

3.1   A Proposal of Actions for Green Spaces of "Risorgimento" District

Potenza Municipality, according to the annual leaderboard of Legambiente (an environmental organization [14]), for the year 2018 is the fourth of "greenest city" [15] in Italy for inhabitants per square meter. The green areas not always are accessible to the people for different reasons: areas with high slope, abandoned or degraded green areas, and green areas without a specific intended use so able to became green spaces to restore to citizen. An example in the city could be Risorgimento district.

Risorgimento is one of districts related to the expansion of Potenza Municipality between years 1946–1970. In this district, the green available over the years was left to itself and has lost its function as meeting place or improving the quality of urban life. Starting from the actions proposed for the green spaces system, has been chosen some of the actions to engage in the district as recovery of abandoned degraded areas or planting trees along the roads to improve urban microclimate (see Fig. 5).

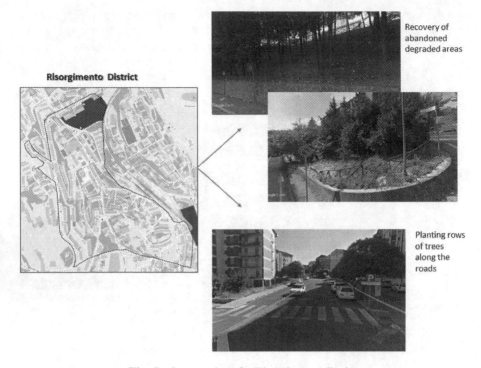

Fig. 5. Some actions for Risorgimento district

4 Conclusion

The work highlighted two potential issues in relation to the use of SECAP as planning tools for the transition of cities to "low carbon" and "climate responsive" scenarios:

- A sector-by-sector "watertight" approach, which sees the definition of actions exclusively related to the sector, as it is convenient to identify systems on which to carry out analytical/cognitive insights on the individual territorial components related to the sectors proposed by the SECAP, and to arrive at intersystemic synthesis for the selection of actions,
- The definition of territorial targets, an innovative element proposed within the SECAP. Territorial targets represent real elements of the territory on which the planned actions are implemented. This approach allows a spatial definition of the planned interventions, which will allow administrators and stakeholders to be able to manage, plan and monitor interventions.

This innovative approach to SECAP can be strengthened through participatory planning, involving local citizen, stakeholders and decision makers to role an active part in the process. A key factor to achieve results in green structure planning is based on participation of citizen, local administrator and stakeholders, also to link urban and rural landscapes. In this way a best practice is Ronneby, southern Sweden [16], that show how 'connoisseurs' (local associations) across the Municipality can help green structure planning for identifying the most important places, routes, and landmarks strengthening the relations between people and their everyday landscape at a municipal level.

In conclusion, the future developments that this work suggests are linked to the deepening of the techniques and methods proposed on further case studies, to the definition of flexible tools in the management of data and information necessary to build scenarios for climate adaptation to different scales, to effectively address the challenges that climate-change calls us to undertake. The objectives of this process are contained in the main address documents on sustainable urban development [17], which refers to a renewed urban planning oriented to the rationality of the government processes of the city and the territory [8, 18, 19].

References

1. Covenant of Mayors - Home, https://www.covenantofmayors.eu/en/, Accessed 13 March 2020
2. Transforming our world: the 2030 Agenda for Sustainable Development.:. Sustainable Development Knowledge Platform, https://sustainabledevelopment.un.org/post2015/transformingourworld, Accessed 20 April 2020
3. Scorza, F., Las Casas, G.: Un approccio "contex based" e "valutazione integrata" per il futuro della programmazione operativa regionale in Europa. Presented at the January 1 (2009)
4. Pontrandolfi, P., Scorza, F.: Sustainable urban regeneration policy making: inclusive participation practice. In: Gervasi, O., et al. (eds.) ICCSA 2016. LNCS, vol. 9788, pp. 552–560. Springer, Cham (2016). https://doi.org/10.1007/978-3-319-42111-7_44
5. Scorza, F., Pontrandolfi, P.: Citizen participation and technologies: the C.A.S.T. architecture. In: Gervasi, O., et al. (eds.) ICCSA 2015. LNCS, vol. 9156, pp. 747–755. Springer, Cham (2015). https://doi.org/10.1007/978-3-319-21407-8_53
6. Scorza, F., Grecu, V.: Assessing sustainability: research directions and relevant issues. In: Gervasi, O., et al. (eds.) ICCSA 2016. LNCS, vol. 9786, pp. 642–647. Springer, Cham (2016). https://doi.org/10.1007/978-3-319-42085-1_55
7. Dvarioniene, J., Grecu, V., Lai, S., Scorza, F.: Four perspectives of applied sustainability: research implications and possible integrations. In: Gervasi, O., et al. (eds.) ICCSA 2017. LNCS, vol. 10409, pp. 554–563. Springer, Cham (2017). https://doi.org/10.1007/978-3-319-62407-5_39
8. Casas, G.L., Scorza, F.: Sustainable planning: a methodological toolkit. In: Gervasi, O., et al. (eds.) ICCSA 2016. LNCS, vol. 9786, pp. 627–635. Springer, Cham (2016). https://doi.org/10.1007/978-3-319-42085-1_53
9. Piano Nazionale di Adattamento ai Cambiamenti Climatici - PNACC, https://www.minambiente.it/sites/default/files/archivio_immagini/adattamenti_climatici/documento_pnacc_luglio_2017.pdf. Accessed 09 May 2020
10. Scorza, F., Pilogallo, A., Saganeiti, L., Murgante, B.: Natura 2000 areas and sites of national interest (SNI): measuring (un)integration between naturalness preservation and environmental remediation policies. Sustainability. **12**, 2928 (2020). https://doi.org/10.3390/su12072928
11. RSDI – Geoportale Basilicata, https://rsdi.regione.basilicata.it/, Accessed 09 May 2020

12. Regolamento urbanistico| Comune di Potenza, http://www.comune.potenza.it/?cat=464, Accessed 09 May 2020
13. Home :: Corine Land Cover classes, https://land.copernicus.eu/user-corner/technical-library/corine-land-cover-nomenclature-guidelines/html, Accessed 09 May 2020
14. Home ⋆ Legambiente, https://www.legambiente.it/, Accessed 12 June 2020
15. Le città più verdi d'Italia - Il Sole 24 Ore, https://lab24.ilsole24ore.com/ecosistema-urbano/indexT.php, Accessed 12 June 2020
16. Mellqvist, H., Kristensen, L., Konijnendijk van den Bosch, C.: Participatory green structure planning for linking urban and rural landscapes – examples from a swedish municipality. Nord. J. Archit. Res. **28**(3), 71–96 (2016)
17. About the Sustainable Development Goals - United Nations Sustainable Development, https://www.un.org/sustainabledevelopment/sustainable-development-goals/. Accessed 13 March 2020
18. Las Casas, G., Scorza, F., Murgante, B.: New urban agenda and open challenges for urban and regional planning. In: Calabrò, F., Della Spina, L., Bevilacqua, C. (eds.) ISHT 2018. SIST, vol. 100, pp. 282–288. Springer, Cham (2019). https://doi.org/10.1007/978-3-319-92099-3_33
19. Las Casas, G., Scorza, F., Murgante, B.: Razionalità a-priori: Una proposta verso una pianificazione antifragile. Sci. Reg. **18**, 329–338 (2019). https://doi.org/10.14650/93656

International Workshop on Smart and Sustainable Island Communities (SSIC 2020)

Leveraging Underwater Cultural Heritage (UCH) Potential for Smart and Sustainable Development in Mediterranean Islands

Dionisia Koutsi$^{(\boxtimes)}$ and Anastasia Stratigea

Department of Geography and Regional Planning,
School of Rural and Surveying Engineering,
National Technical University of Athens, Athens, Greece
koutsi.dionisia@gmail.com, stratige@central.ntua.gr

Abstract. Martial incidents during wars (World War I and II), but also ship-ping fatalities through centuries along the densely populated commercial routes of the Mediterranean Sea have resulted in significant submerged remnants, falling into the Underwater Cultural Heritage (UCH) corps. A large part of this heritage is located in the neighborhood of insular territories. Preservation and sustainable exploitation of this UCH in the Mediterranean presents an important opportunity for both keeping alive the European identity for future generations, and tracking alternative, heritage-led future development trails for remote peripheral and lagging-behind island communities. The paper explores the context of UCH in the Mediterranean and elaborates on the value attached to Information and Communication Technologies (ICT) for reaping this opportu-nity by means of surveying, geolocating, preserving, sustainably exploiting and marketing this heritage. Based on this exploration, but also on the authors' experience from a specific (U)CH-related cultural planning endeavor, conducted in Leros Island Greece, ICT and non-ICT related barriers for planning heritage-led future trails of insular regions are delineated.

Keywords: (Underwater) Cultural Heritage · Insular territories · Mediterranean Region · Cultural governance · Sustainable development · Cultural/battlefield tourism

1   Introduction

Cultural Heritage (CH) in the 21st century is grasped as a valuable resource and a quadruple bottom line for coping with environmental, social and economic as well as climate change challenges [1]. The realization of the exceptional role and value of CH and its importance in the way to sustainability has guided efforts of contemporary societies towards the: preservation of tangible and intangible cultural resources as a means for keeping track with historical evidence and roots of the past; and their exploitation in a sustainable, resilient as well as value - and human-centric way for reaching qualitative and heritage-led enduring developmental trails of the future. These efforts go hand in hand with policy orientation and a range of related documents,

The original version of this chapter was revised: the name of Dionisia Koutsi was corrected. The correction to this chapter is available at https://doi.org/10.1007/978-3-030-58820-5_72

addressing *multiple objectives of glocal (global-local) nature*. Among these objectives fall the preservation and protection of CH as well as its promotion for peace and intercultural dialogue building within and beyond national borders [2], but also objectives such as heritage-led local development and sustainable cultural tourism, social cohesion and sense of belonging, quality of life and attractiveness of cities and regions, to name a few [3].

Sustainable exploitation of CH has, among others, given rise to the *experience-based cultural tourism paradigm* [4]. This constitutes nowadays a quite noticeable and dynamic trend in the evolving tourism market (the supply side) in response to demand-driven signs for new, meaningful and authentic tourist experiences, roughly presented as a combination of four *'e'* words, namely *e*ntertainment, *e*xcitement, *e*ducation and *e*xperience of tourists [4]. Cultural tourism constitutes currently a major segment in many destinations (counts for over 39% of cultural tourism arrivals in 2014), as pointed out by UNWTO [5] and an essential feature of tourist destinations' profiles [6]; while also a factor of decisive influence in travelers' destination preferences.

A particular type of *cultural tourism form*, recently receiving much attention in terms of both attractiveness to visitors all around the world and concerns as to the CH preservation and sustainable exploitation, refers to the *battlefield tourism*, i.e. tourism linked to places in which historical martial events have occurred. *Battlefield tourism* is considered as a variant of *"Dark Tourism"*; and implies tourist activities strongly linked to death and/or war disaster-related sites [7]. Destinations falling into the *"Dark"* category are nowadays proliferating in the global tourist realm; and are also varying in content, taking forms such as battlefield scenes, concentration camps, sites of major human disasters, to name a few.

In the rapidly evolving tourism market, an outstanding and steadily growing tourism niche is *maritime battlefield tourism* [3], i.e. visiting and exploration of *sea-related battlefield scenes*. Properly and respectfully addressing this type of tourism in a specific destination presents a new challenge for planners and decision makers with regard to the protection and preservation as well as the value-based and sustainable exploitation of related *Underwater Cultural Heritage* (UCH) for cultural, recreational, educational and diving tourism purposes [8], and its smooth co-existence with other maritime activities.

At this stage, it is useful to clarify the very essence of UCH, being defined as a *non-renewable resource* comprising a set of *tangible and intangible* heritage items that are linked to past or present human activities in the sea [9]. More specifically, UCH is understood as the archaeological heritage which is in, or has been removed from, an underwater environment; and includes submerged sites and structures, wreck sites, and wreckage and their archaeological and natural context [10]. UCH, in this respect, may refer to remnants of human settlements and civilizations in the sea, such as sites of archaeological interest or sunk martial equipment, ancient harbors and ship or plane wrecks, to name a few; and encounters to approximately 3 million worldwide [11]. It is perceived as a *capsule in time*, delivering important historical and other kinds of information about the past. When associated with human loss, as in case of UCH from World War (WW) I or II (e.g. ship and plane wrecks), UCH is also considered as a site of remembrance; and a site that bears witness to significant instances of the European history, being thus part of the Europe's identity and historical trajectory.

A resounding example of areas exhibiting a large potential as maritime battlefield tourism destinations are many *insular regions* in the Mediterranean Sea. This is due to the UCH evidence lying on their coastal and surrounding maritime areas, being the outcome of their role as important WW I and II scenes. However, despite their cultural but also natural richness and diversity, islands in general and a large number of Mediterranean islands in particular are perceived as disadvantaged, fragmented and isolated areas, and distinct examples of lagging behind spatial entities at the European scale [8, 12]. This is due to a range of inadequacies, briefly summarized under the term *"insularity"* [12] and mainly relating to: the location of islands in the state's periphery; the confined geographical space and resource availability; the declining population pattern marked by aged, of low educational profile and digitally illiterate inhabitants; the lack of economies of scale, delimiting potential of local economy; the geographical fragmentation, associated with insufficient infrastructure provision for serving population's basic needs.

Insularity, however, can also be perceived as a *comparative advantage* of insular territories, broadening their attractiveness as peaceful and qualitative, authentic and experience-based cultural tourism destinations. The usually exceptional cultural profile of such regions comprises an *amalgam of tangible and mostly intangible, land and underwater, natural and cultural elements*, a legacy that is backed to the ancient but also recent history; and is the outcome of the enduring interaction of local culture and society with externally imposed events (war occupation and involvement, location as nodes in the Mediterranean historical merchant sea routes, etc.). Land CH and particularly the largely underexploited UCH can leverage sustainable development trails and remove isolation by building up competitive and attractive (U)CH-based *narratives* and respective *brands* and place them as niches in the rapidly specializing tourism market.

Along these lines, the *goal* of this article is to open up an intriguing new theme for planners, i.e. (U)CH and manifest its role for paving smart and sustainable, heritage-led development of less-privileged insular territories in the Mediterranean. Towards this end, in Sect. 2, a review of the current policy and legal considerations of UCH management is carried out, delineating the decision-making environment; Sect. 3 provides evidence as to the UCH wealth of the Mediterranean and its potential for coastal and insular communities; in Sect. 4 the convergence of ICT and (U)CH management is sketched, elucidating also ICT and non-ICT enabled barriers applying to (U)CH planning endeavors in insular regions; while finally in Sect. 5 some conclusions are drawn.

2 Legislative and Policy Considerations of UCH Management

UCH preservation and sustainable exploitation is a rather *"wicked"* planning problem [13], fraught with difficulties and new challenges for planners and policy makers. These are mainly emanating from the: specific attributes of the UCH surrounding environment raising, among others, *jurisdictional issues* and *risks* that threaten UCH to loss, e.g. climate change impacts; multiple, occasionally controversial guidance, of *institutional actors* (from national to global) having a 'say' as to the UCH preservation and exploitation, revealing the necessity for *UCH governance*; *multi- and interdisciplinary nature* of this heritage, incorporating environmental, cultural, historical, social, economic and technological dimensions; value attached to UCH at different value systems; need to approach UCH in conjunction with land CH for embedding this to the wider spatial and cultural context and creating added value, especially in remote insular communities [13].

UCH policy decisions need, among others, to be in alignment with complex, *legislative considerations on a global scale*, as these are expressed by international Conventions with reference to both the surrounding environment of UCH, i.e. the sea, and the UCH per se. These considerations are, at present, predominantly demarcated by the [13]:

- *1982 United Nations Convention on the Law of the Sea* [14]: The most comprehensive international legal document, exclusively dealing with maritime issues [15]. It elucidates aspects of nations' rights and responsibilities as to the use of world's oceans and seas, thus indirectly conditioning policies for UCH protection. It disentangles the meanings of warships and their sovereign immunity on high seas. However, it deals exclusively with tangible underwater heritage, leaving aside the equally important intangible UCH dimension.
- *1992 European Convention on the Protection of the Archaeological Heritage* (Valetta or Malta Convention) [16]: It mainly addresses issues such as the protection of archaeological heritage as a source of the European identity and a resource of historical/scientific glow, and the consideration of archaeological interests in spatial planning endeavours, to name a few.
- *1996 Charter on the Protection and Management of Underwater Cultural Heritage* [10]: A supplement of the ICOMOS Protection and Management of Archaeological Heritage of 1990. It outlines the fundamental principles for UCH conservation. It addresses a variety of issues such as research objectives; investigation, documentation and material conservation; management and maintenance of a UCH site. It fosters public awareness for grasping the value of UCH and its preservation.
- 2001 *UNESCO Convention on the Protection of Underwater Cultural Heritage* [17]: A bedrock for the preservation of sunken heritage, providing location-specific guidelines to interesting member states. It constitutes the international protection framework for UCH *older than 100 years*. It sheds light on the essence of UCH and the types that are given cultural importance. It also clarifies the rights of flag states to excavate and preserve these vessels beyond their territorial waters. It goes beyond the UNCLOS Convention in order for the rights/duties of the coastal state and/or flag nation to be set out, according to the sunken UCH location.
- *Convention for the Safeguarding of the Intangible Cultural Heritage* [18]. Recognition of the value of intangible CH as a vehicle for building identity and social cohesion, providing communities with a sense of continuity, while promoting respect for cultural diversity and human creativity.

Legislative considerations with regard to UCH protection and management are complemented by a range of recent European policy directions. These, although depicting a *sectoral* (e.g. tourism, culture) or *spatial* (e.g. blue growth and marine spatial planning) orientation, they enhance opportunities for UCH sustainable exploitation and management. To start with, the sectors of tourism and culture or more precisely the *'tourism and culture complex'* has been placed as an important pillar of the Regional Innovation Strategy for Smart Specialization (RIS3); and a locomotive for urban and regional development at the European Union (EU) level. In support of this complex, a bundle of policy guidelines is established at this level. With regard to tourism, the main corps relate to the "Agenda for a Sustainable and Competitive European Tourism" [19] and the "Europe, the World's No 1 Tourist Destination—A New Political Framework for Tourism in Europe" [20]. These are further reinforced by culture-specific policy directions, mostly articulated during the last decade. Such directions incorporate the: "Europe 2020" Strategy [21]; "Convention on the Value of Cultural Heritage for Society" or Faro Convention [22]; "European Agenda for Culture in a Globalization World" [23]; "Communication towards an Integrated Approach to Cultural Heritage for Europe" [24]; and the recent Work Plan for Culture 2019–2022 [25]. The importance of *public participation* is fully addressed in these documents, while the role of *culture* for public empowerment and social cohesion as well as for leveraging local development endeavors is also appreciated.

A further step forward for UCH management relates to the EU *Blue Growth Strategy* [26], stressing the importance of emerging sea-related economic opportunities. This strategy is complemented by dedicated spatial planning tools, namely the *Marine Spatial Planning* (MSP) [27] and the *Integrated Coastal Zone Management* (ICZM) [28] for effectively handling the spatial aspects of these opportunities. Blue Growth Strategy and related spatial planning tools bring on board new perspectives for the sustainable exploitation of maritime resources, including UCH. They also imply new obligations for planners, i.e. the imperative to place UCH within the framework of MSP and ICZM, in order for conflicting to UCH maritime uses to be properly handled. Finally, they also introduce new, highly supportive to UCH preservation and management concepts, such as *'territorial governance'*, *'consultation'* and *'public participation'*, *'place-based approach'*, and *'ecosystem-approach'*.

3   The Mediterranean Sea – a Densely UCH Populated Region

Mediterranean is one of the most important *"theatres"* of great, land and maritime, martial events of WWI and particularly WWII in Europe [29]. The strategic geographical position at the crossroad of three continents has rendered this region a pivotal war operations' scene; and a main sea transport route for raw materials and troops during WWI and II [30]. Commercial activity in the Mediterranean sea routes, shipping fatalities, war occupations, but also martial activity of WW I and II have left their 'signs' in the Mediterranean, in the form of both *land remains* (e.g. batteries and military installations) and *sunken remnants* (e.g. ship and plane wrecks) that are dated back to the ancient but also the recent history. These remains are largely unknown to the wider public and not fully explored and documented, constituting thus parts of *'a story yet largely untold'* [13:20]. They also are highly valued by local communities, being in many cases inseparable parts of this story, and distinct elements of the European identity and history, while attracting also interest as World Cultural Heritage sites.

Scattered throughout the whole Mediterranean Sea, UCH is a finite, irreplaceable and quite fragile part of CH. Its value varies, based on the causes of submerging, the wrecks' location and depth, their type (warships, aircraft, submarines, cargo, etc.), nationality, bonds to local communities, linkages to human losses, etc. [13, 31]. Speaking of WWI and especially WWII ship and plane wrecks, while abundant in the Mediterranean Sea, they are partially explored, with the majority of them lacking information as to the exact location and depth, current status and specific characteristics [8, 32]. Furthermore, their exact *number* is still unknown. It is worth noticing that 1,061 shipwrecks are reported as being sunk during WWII in the Aegean Sea, Greece; 500 of which were under a Greek flag [32].

In the Mediterranean Region there are few, albeit quite important, *WWI UCH* sites, closely related to famous naval battles [33], well-documented, and sustainably exploited as diving tourism destinations. Additionally, *WWII*, as the most geographically widespread military conflict the world has ever seen, has left a vast number of sunken military UCH [13]. A large share of these UCH remnants is located in the Mediterranean waters, scattered around the shores of Croatia, southern France, Greece, Italy, Malta, and North Africa; and witnessing important naval warfare under the *'Mediterranean Theater'*.

Promoting and protecting UCH in general and historical ship & plane wrecks in particular seems to gain importance as a lever for tracking and preserving European historical paths and identity; and tracing heritage-led local development of remote and isolated coastal and insular regions. The latter can be achieved by means of *cultural* and most importantly *diving tourism*, where entertainment UCH-related activities constitute a 'vehicle' for educating people in past failures and providing access to historical evidence. Cultural and diving tourism is also expected to have an economic counterpart, emanating from the rating of diving tourism as the second most attractive tourist sport activity worldwide [34]. As distinguished examples of diving tourism destinations in Europe can be mentioned sites located in the *French coastline*, featuring numerous restored wrecks (Le Donator Wreck-Fig. 1), diving parks and underwater protected areas; diving destinations in *Spain* and in particular at the *Mendes Islands*; submerged WWII battleships in *Malta* (Fig. 2) [35]; UCH in *Croatia*, where 400 submerged and 100 sites are listed as protected CH, to name a few.

As opposed to the above successful examples, the majority of wrecks in the Mediterranean and even worldwide do not receive that kind of attention. In fact, less than 10% of the globally submerged shipwrecks have been surveyed or visited by divers [11]. In the UCH wealthy Mediterranean Region in particular, heritage-led development prospects seem to be rather fragmented and immature. Same holds for UCH in the *Greek territory*, encompassing outstanding ancient but also wars' shipwrecks, such as the one located in Antikythera island [36]; the 58 shipwrecks recently discovered in the neighborhood of Fournoi island [37] being the *shipwreck capital of the world*, as noticed by Koutsouflakis and Campbell, marine archaeologists working on the field; the Destroyer 'Queen Olga' in Leros island [8]. These, although perceived as the largest shipwrecks in the Mediterranean, remain unexplored, unexploited and, most importantly, *unprotected*. The lack of reliable and accurate data, the 'silo' approach adopted by archaeologists [13], and the lack of MSP [3] appear as major constraints, preventing their sustainable exploitation.

Fig. 1. Le Donator" wreck in France, Source: [38]

Fig. 2. The Blenheim Bomber in the Maltese Archipelago Source: [35]

4 ICT-Enabled Management of UCH in Mediterranean Insular Communities: A Conditionally Win-Win Marriage

In this section, the potential of ICT for UCH management is roughly presented; while are also explored ICT and non-ICT related barriers appearing in the context of heritage-led (U)CH developmental planning endeavors in insular regions.

4.1 Tracking ICT Potential for Unfolding UCH Narratives in the Mediterranean

In the current, globally wired, environment, cities and regions are challenged to constantly deliver better, creative, innovative and qualitative products and services by making use of the Internet and ICT-enabled developments. These developments have also opened up new opportunities for remote and disadvantaged insular communities enabling them, under certain conditions, to enter the rapidly changing geography of cultural tourism destinations and the evolving cultural tourism market; and establish own niche markets, based on their distinguishable cultural assets. The role of technology though is not exhausted in simply marketing insular regions as cultural tourism destinations. On the contrary, it is traced to all the way from surveying, identification, exploration and visualization, as well as documentation and preservation of cultural assets, including UCH, to the process of place- and culture-based narrative building as well as commodification of narrative aspects into experience-based cultural products for destination marketing purposes (Fig. 3). A short discussion of the role of technology in each of these stages is following, having at its heart the UCH context.

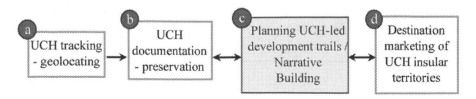

Fig. 3. ICT-enabled stages for promoting insular regions as UCH destinations

Tracking UCH is a complex task, mainly due to the lack of adequate knowledge as to its exact location within a largely unexplored environment, the marine one. Same holds for its documentation and preservation, taking into account the surrounding environment of a UCH site and the preservation obstacles this entails.

Speaking of the *Mediterranean Region*, despite the large number of sunken vessels located in its seabed, their exact location is yet unknown. Geo-locating UCH deposits is a first step in order for documentation, preservation and monitoring, risk assessment and sustainable exploitation of UCH sites to be advanced. This can nowadays be supported by state-of-the-art developments in *underwater technology*, which are capable of conducting UCH survey, identification, navigation, excavation, meticulously documentation, restoration and conservation [13]; while hull-mounted multi-beam sonar can provide high-resolution seafloor maps down to 90 m, thus enabling survey of UCH sunken in deeper waters. Moreover, high-quality UCH mapping and extensive photographical documentation is supported by various options and systems available, such as 3D LiDAR underwater laser systems, remotely operated vehicles (ROV) [39], remotely controlled underwater robots, high-resolution acoustic sensors, like the synthetic aperture sonar (SAS) technology [40]. Underwater technology developments can be of substantial help for UCH tracking, surveying, documenting and monitoring, while they can also steer content creation for visualization and marketing purposes, bringing UCH much closer to interested audience for recreational purposes.

CH in general and UCH in particular, apart from major *economic drivers* for local development by linking traditions and historical paths to creativity and entrepreneurship, they are also by many grasped as the *nexus* between individuals and society [41], promoting social cohesion. In order this to be achieved, there is a need for a broader understanding by planners and decision makers of: its inseparable tangible and intangible attributes and their role for delivering a sense of identity and continuity [18]; its nature as a non-renewable resource; the social, economic, environmental and cultural implications of planning interventions for society; and the principal role that communities, as custodians of (U)CH and those having a profound connection with a certain (U)CH site, can play. This understanding goes hand in hand with the concept of *public archaeology* [42], stressing the importance of *community engagement* for awareness raising as well as empowering and engaging the public in addressing UCH preservation and sustainable exploitation concerns. Public engagement in (U)CH management is already early highlighted in the 2001 UNESCO Convention (Rule 35 of the Annexes). It is further stressed by the Shanghai Charter in 2002, recognizing (U)CH insights of local communities as irreplaceable; and placing them as equals in decision-making processes questioning the way this heritage should be perceived and interpreted, valued and managed, as well as conveyed to others. Community engagement as the current paradigm in planning endeavors is not just useful, it is rather indispensable when (U)CH is concerned. This especially holds true in planning exercises that have as a spatial reference battlegrounds and/or places where historical events have occurred. Localized knowledge or voices of local people, who witnessed or even were part of these events is crucial for building meaningful and respectful cultural narratives as well as respective policies for preserving and promoting these places as cultural tourism destinations. This implies the adoption of *participatory decision-making models* in order for the multi-actor interests, values, expectations etc. to be fully embraced in (U)CH management.

Participatory or community-based planning endeavors for the sustainable exploitation of UCH place effort in identifying the peculiar meanings endowing tangible UCH elements, such as a ship or a plane wreck, i.e. integrating the UCH intangible dimension; and properly embedding these meanings in the planning process and outcomes. Furthermore, an *integrated approach* of tangible and intangible UCH elements, but also of maritime and land remains of historical events, such as WWI and II at a certain location, can broaden understanding and value of (U)CH in the planning process; and support cultural empowerment and awareness, responsibility and ownership of this heritage by local communities. It can also encourage engagement in *co-creating* place- and human-centric, value-respectful (U)CH-based narratives, which successfully integrate past into present for the current and future generations. Finally, it can support the *collective construction* of UCH-based cultural tourism products, embracing different perspectives and forms of local knowledge and enriching visitors' experience.

Currently, ICT and their applications have led to a *methodological revolution* of urban and regional planning approaches [43] and the digitalization of various stages of the planning process, giving rise to *e-planning*. This, among others, integrates spatial planning approaches and visualization techniques, while provides new potential for managing and visualizing, in meaningful for the local population ways, large spatial data sets [44]. ICT and their applications have also enabled the establishment of digital interaction among decision makers, planners and local communities, thus promoting *e-participation* and enriching the corps of planning knowledge through *crowdsourcing* remarkable and multidimensional local experiential knowledge. e-Planning and e-Participation have furthermore advocated the concept of *cultural governance*, giving rise to a range of ICT-enabled interaction means, such as online questionnaires or the more sophisticated Public Participatory Geographic Information Systems (PPGIS). The latter incorporates a range of mapping and participation techniques, ranging from ground mapping to participatory interpretation of remote sensing images, crowdsourcing online maps and data, networking, communication and partnerships' building [45]. E-Planning and e-Participation have been further popularized by the advent of *social networks*, presenting an exponentially growing e-interaction mean and a great chance for endorsing e-planning exercises. In case of *remote insular communities*, the aforementioned developments offer powerful tools for *removing insularity bottlenecks* in multiple ways, enabling also potential application of e-planning and e-participation approaches for widening e-engagement of local communities in planning UCH sustainable exploitation and management. They support also the use of visual media in the form of *maps and images*, accompanied with textual description, as an important *substitute of face-to-face interaction* in participatory planning endeavors.

Of importance is also the role of ICT in *marketing* insular communities as culturally-rich and peaceful destinations, by promoting in an integrated way, land and underwater CH. ICT have had a traditionally pervasive role in the tourist sector, a notably data-intensive industry. This role is nowadays further intensified, giving birth to the concept of *smart destinations* (SDs), i.e. places where the tourism sector is built upon a variety of harmonically interwoven cutting-edge technological applications and exploitation of big data. These applications serve the establishment of bridges between demand and supply, the attainment of more informed decision-making at the destination level, the effective place-branding and marketing, to name a few. They also contribute to a better understanding of tourists' behavior, needs and choice influential factors; while attempting to promote destinations as innovative, modern places that make efforts to offer ICT-enabled visitors' experiences. Technological advances, such as Virtual Reality (VR) technologies, Augmented Reality (AR) models, three-dimensional (3D) reconstruction techniques or dedicated mobile phone applications at the service of visitors are perceived as powerful (U)CH marketing tools for coping with strong competition among destinations. They support attractiveness and act as an *accelerator* of newcomers' engagement and inclusiveness at a certain destination [41], both considered as issues of crucial importance for bolstering insular regions as synonymous of *seamless and accessible (U)CH experience-based personalized outputs*.

4.2 Barriers Identified in Planning (U)CH-Led Local Development in Insular Communities – Lessons Learnt from the Leros Case Study

Small Greek islands have played a major role during the WWI and especially WWII events, serving as grounds for martial operations and surveillance. As such, they were placed at the epicenter of important war incidents, leaving aside a rich historical heritage in the form of *sunken* and, in several cases, *land remnants*. Leros Island in the Aegean Sea represents a distinct example of WWII remembrance, evidenced by combined land and underwater remains. The island's trajectory throughout its history was marked by various occupations and martial activities. As the battleground of the famous *'Battle of Leros'* during WWII (1943), several important *ship and plane wrecks* rest in peace in Lakki Bay, while 14 non-protected wrecks (Fig. 4) are also scattered in the seabed around the island's coasts, all rendering the island as a whole an *immense UCH park*. The longstanding Italian occupation of Leros, being the biggest Italian aero-naval base in southeastern Mediterranean, has also left important *land remains* as inseparable parts of the Leros WWII narrative.

The authors of this paper have conducted a *participatory e-planning exercise* in an effort to sketch promising future pathways of Leros Island by coping, in an integrated way, with land and maritime WWII remains, coupled with elements of the island's natural heritage [see 8]. *Social networks* were used as a mean for engaging Leros community in this endeavor. Two spatially distinct and challenging future scenarios of Leros and related policy packages for local prosperity were communicated to Leros community through a Web-GIS (*Scenario A "From a 'Soul-House' to a place of Multiple-Opportunity"* and *Scenario B "Leros - An Open Museum of the European Cultural Heritage"*); and opinions, visions, attitudes, expectations etc. were gathered by local population for further improving and finalizing planning outcomes.

JUNKERS JU 52, sunk in the Battle of Leros

ARADO 196, German hydroplane

Destroyer 'Queen Olga', sunk the Battle of Leros

Fig. 4. WWII sunken remnants in Leros island, Source: [46]

Based on the previously described potential of ICT for unfolding WWI and II narratives in Mediterranean insular regions and the experience gained from the aforementioned e-planning exercise in Leros island, a number of ICT and non-ICT related *bottlenecks* are identified (Fig. 5) that restrain efforts in all four ICT-enabled stages for promoting insular regions as UCH destinations (Fig. 3). It should be noted here that discussion in the following leaves aside institutional and legislative barriers, emanating from lack of UCH governance at the global/national level as well as inconsistencies noticed between national laws and international conventions. On the contrary, it mainly focuses on *barriers applying at the local level* and more specifically on evidenced-based results emerging in a (U)CH-related cultural planning exercise in a specific insular territory, namely Leros, Greece.

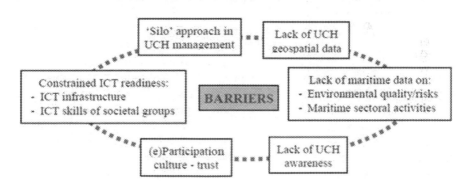

Fig. 5. ICT and non-ICT related barriers weakening effectiveness of planning endeavors towards (U)CH-led development in insular regions

To start with, a main obstacle is the *'silo' approach* so far prevailing in UCH management that places marine archaeologists as the main protagonists of such a task. This approach lacks a broader UCH management view, while largely ignores UCH potential as a valuable resource and a lever for delivering social cohesion and new economic opportunities. It also deprives UCH management from a fundamental first step, being its *interpretation* [47], which calls for widening the viewpoints and valuing of UCH as well as strengthening the very essence of its management, i.e., imparting values and meanings this carries to society and future generations, and acting as a catalyst for social cohesion and identity building. Shift from a 'silo' to a more integrated, multi- and interdisciplinary, approach of UCH will fertilize ground for unfolding planning initiatives targeting UCH-led local development.

An important constraint is also the lack of *UCH geospatial data availability*, a critical aspect and the ground of any planning exercise. A comprehensive effort towards establishing a database that incorporates combined UCH geospatial and historical information, as well as documentation of already known UCH does not really exist; nor exists also a systematic effort towards the identification of historically known, but not yet geolocated UCH. A good example of this gap comes from Greece, where despite the abundance of information on UCH from a variety of sources, e.g. articles, books, international websites, oral stories and scuba divers' community, a spatial database, presenting in an integrated way available UCH data is lacking [32]. This partially emanates from the fragmented and uncoordinated efforts of various research groups engaged in the field. Current progress in geoinformatics but also in underwater technology seem promising developments for filling this gap for already known UCH; while they can support surveying of the yet spatially unidentified UCH. Linked to this gap is also the lack of *maritime data*, useful for making inferences as to the status and quality as well as carrying capacity of the surrounding environment of UCH and potential risks that may harm its status. This is a critical issue for UCH preservation especially in the Mediterranean, a highly vulnerable region to climate change, with unpredictable impacts on UCH condition and stability. Lack of *MSP studies* constitute also an important *gap* in the sense that incompatible to UCH maritime uses can threaten its status and preservation concerns.

Identifying, quantifying, and geographically locating UCH assets sets the ground for building up strategies and effective policies targeting societal, cultural and economic prosperity gains. Of great help in this respect is the enhancement of spatial data management and visualization potential in a GIS environment, coupled with Web developments that allow interactive Web-based GIS exploitation as a bidirectional interactive tool [48]. This, in conjunction with the potential offered by the advent of Web 2.0, enabling access to planning information and processes by a wide spectrum of actors through a variety of effective digital communication channels and visualization techniques, can broaden access to information and thus create new perspectives for participation and more *inclusive procedures in UCH management* to the benefit of both UCH and local communities. This was, to a certain extent, proven by the Leros participatory e-planning exercise, conducted by the authors of this work. However, this exercise has also unveiled a range of *barriers* in such a perspective, probably common in most remote insular regions. These relate to the lack of *awareness* as to the value of UCH for achieving social cohesion and local economic prosperity objectives, aspects that could constitute an attractive motive for population in less privileged regions for actively engaging in UCH preservation and responsible management and acting as safeguards of this heritage. Additionally, the aging population of island regions and the usually low level of its educational profile, coupled with the lack of *participatory culture* and *trust* to ICT-enabled interaction, are important obstacles. Finally, a major barrier is the lack of *ICT skills* that largely impede local population to become part of an e-planning exercise and e-participation and to fully grasp relevant planning information, conveyed through a Web-GIS and distributed through various electronic means. This is critical, taking into account insularity and respective isolation this introduces, and the power of ICT-enabled interaction to remove insularity constraints; and is largely proven in Leros e-planning exercise. Despite all aforementioned difficulties however, all present in the Leros e-planning endeavor, it is worth noting the eagerness of local population of this remote island to overcome isolation and become part of initiatives targeting more inclusive, qualitative and heritage-led future development trails, with special reference to sustainable management of UCH.

5 Conclusions

Perpetual interest of humans through time in exploring the sea and using it as a main route for commercial purposes and cultural exchanges, but also as the ground of fatal martial events of the past, such as WWI and II, has left in the bottom of the world oceans, Mediterranean as well, more historical artefacts than all the museums of the world combined [49]. This justifies the worth for: shedding light on the abundant number of underwater historical heritage, laying largely unexplored and unprotected in the bottom of the seas; and taking steps for preserving and sustainably exploiting it to the benefit of the society as a whole. Speaking of the Mediterranean, preservation and sustainable management of WWI and II UCH is a two-sided coin, serving endurance of European identity, memory, and cultural heritage for future generations on the one side; and leveraging future cultural tourism trails of lagging behind and disadvantaged insular areas on the other [13]. The latter is further invigorated by the reviving interest in cultural and diving tourism as a remarkable *cultural turn* of contemporary travellers for satisfying *e*ntertainment, *e*xcitement, *e*ducation and *e*xperience objectives in a certain destination.

The Mediterranean Region, with its extended *coastal and insular territories* and the impressive, in terms of number and value, WWI and II UCH is a distinguishable, rather underexplored, example in such a context, and a challenging UCH-related narrative yet largely untold. Land and especially underwater CH can constitute a *key driver* for future development of such territories, especially for fragmented and remote insular communities, endowed with UCH and other land-related cultural and natural resources. However, viability and durability of future development of islands as storehouses of exquisite natural and cultural resources is fraught with a range of difficulties. ICT-enabled developments for effectively dealing with insularity drawbacks in general and sustainable exploitation of UCH resources in particular is a promising perspective in island territories. The latter seems that can be further enhanced by the currently favourable decision environment, which encourages blue growth development directions; facilitates well planned distribution of maritime uses for synergies' creation; and promotes community empowerment and engagement in decision-making processes. Based on these developments, but also the rapidly evolving cultural and diving tourism trends and the competitive advantages of coastal and insular regions by means of cultural richness and diversity as well as global reach, future chances towards sustainable exploitation of (WWI and II) UCH for local developmental objectives can become a remarkable trend.

References

1. Pita da Costa, D.: Mapping of cultural heritage actions in European union policies, programmes and activities. Interpr. Eur. Newslett. **3**, 21 (2017)
2. Montalto, V., Tacao Moura, C., Panella, F., Alberti, V., Becker, W., Saisana, M.: The cultural and creative cities monitor. 2019 edn. Publications Office of the European Union, Luxembourg (2019). https://doi.org/10.2760/257371
3. Koutsi, D., Stratigea, A.: Integrated maritime policy and management of underwater cultural heritage. In: Defner, A., Skagianis, P., Rodakinias, P., Psatha, E. (eds.) 3rd National Conference of Urban and Regional Planning and Regional Development, pp. 565–577. University of Thessaly, Volos (2018). (In Greek)
4. Stratigea, A., Katsoni, V.: A strategic policy scenario analysis framework for the sustainable tourist development of peripheral small island areas - the case of Lefkada-Greece island. Eur. J. Fut. Res. **3**(5), 1–17 (2015). https://doi.org/10.1007/s40309-015-0063-z
5. UNWTO: Tourism and culture synergies. UNWTO Publications, Madrid (2018). ISBN 978-92-844-1896-1
6. Katsoni, V., Stratigea, A. (eds.): Tourism and Culture in the Age of Innovation. SPBE. Springer, Cham (2016). https://doi.org/10.1007/978-3-319-27528-4. ISBN 2198-7246
7. Kunwar, R.R., Karki, N.: A Study of dark (disaster) tourism in reconstructed Barpak, Nepal. Gaze J. Tourism Hospit. **11**(1), 140–180 (2020). https://doi.org/10.3126/gaze.v11i1.26637
8. Koutsi, D., Stratigea, A.: Unburying hidden land and maritime cultural potential of small islands in the mediterranean for tracking heritage-led local development paths. Heritage **2**(1), 938–966 (2019). https://doi.org/10.3390/heritage2010062
9. Forrest, C.: Defining underwater cultural heritage. Int. J. Naut. Archaeol. **31**, 3–11 (2001). https://doi.org/10.1006/ijna.2002.1022
10. ICOMOS: Chapter on the protection and management of underwater cultural heritage. In: 11th ICOMOS General Assembly, Sofia (1996)
11. Bennett, J.: Less Than 1 percent of the world's shipwrecks have been explored. Popular mechanics (2016). https://www.popularmechanics.com/science/a19000/less-than-one-percent-worlds-shipwrecks-explored/. Accessed 5 Jan 2020
12. Spilanis, J.: European Island and Political Cohesion. Gutenberg, Athens (2012). ISBN 978-960-01-1544-4 (In Greek)
13. Argyropoulos, V., Stratigea, A.: Sustainable management of underwater cultural heritage: the route from discovery to engagement—open issues in the mediterranean. Heritage **2**(2), 1588–1613 (2019). https://doi.org/10.3390/heritage2020098
14. UNCLOS: United Nations convention on the law of the sea. United Nations, New York (1982)
15. Alegret, J.L., Carbonell, E.: Introduction. In: Tejero, J.L.A., Camós, E.C., (eds.) Revisiting the Coast: New Practices in Maritime Heritage, vol. 11, pp. 7–20. Documenta Universitaria, Girona (2014)
16. Forrest, C.: Culturally and environmentally sensitive sunken warships. Aust. N. Z. Marit. Law J. **26**, 80–88 (2012)

17. UNESCO. Convention on the protection of the underwater cultural heritage. In: General Conference of UNESCO. UNESCO, Paris (2001)
18. UNESCO: Basic texts of the 2003 convention for the safeguarding of the intangible cultural heritage, 5th edn. UNESCO, Paris (2018). CLT-2018/WS/15, CLD-1918.18
19. COM. 621 final: Agenda for a sustainable and competitive European tourism. Commission of the European communities. Brussels, 19 October 2007 (2007)
20. COM. 352 final: Europe, the world's no 1 tourist destination—A new political framework for tourism in Europe. European Commission, Brussels, Brussels, 30 June 2010 (2010)
21. COM. 2020: EUROPE 2020 - A strategy for smart, sustainable and inclusive growth. European Commission, Brussels, 3 March 2010 (2010)
22. Council of Europe: Framework convention on the value of cultural heritage for society. Council of Europe Treaty Series-No. 199 (2005). https://rm.coe.int/1680083746
23. COM. 242 final: European Agenda for Culture in a Globalizing World. Commission of the European Communities, Brussels, 10 May 2007 (2007)
24. COM. 477 final: Towards an integrated approach to cultural heritage for Europe, European Commission, Brussels, 22 July 2014 (2014)
25. Council of European Union: Council conclusions on the work plan for Culture 2019–2022. Off. J. Eur. Union, C 460/12, 21 December 2018 (2018)
26. SWD. 128 final: Report on the Blue Growth Strategy - Towards more Sustainable Growth and Jobs in the Blue Economy, European Commission, Brussels, 31 Mar 2017 (2017)
27. Directive 2014/89/EU: Establishing a Framework for Maritime Spatial Planning. European Parliament and European Council. Off. J. Eur. Union, L **257**, 135–145 (2014)
28. COM. 308 final: Report to the European Parliament and the Council: An Evaluation of Integrated Coastal Zone Management (ICZM) in Europe, Commission of the European Communities, Brussels, 7 June 2007 (2007)
29. Porch, D.: The Path to Victory: The Mediterranean Theater in World War II. Farrar, Straus and Giroux, New York (2004)
30. Miller, M.B.: Sea transport and supply—1914–1918 (2016). https://encyclopedia.1914-1918-online.net/article/sea_transport_and_supply. Accessed 7 Feb 2020
31. Koutsi, D.: Integrated management of land and underwater cultural resources as a pillar for the development of isolated insular islands. Master's Thesis, National Technical University of Athens, Athens (2018)
32. Papadimitriou, K.: Shipwrecks during world war II - thematic mapping of the Pagasitic area – Pelion. In: 15th National Cartography Conference on the Cartography of the Crisis. Cartographic Scientific Society of Greece, Thessaloniki (2018)
33. Timmermans, D., Guerin, U., da Silva, A.R.: Heritage for Peace and Reconciliation, Safeguarding the Underwater Cultural Heritage of the First World War. UNESCO, Paris (2015). https://doi.org/10.1016/0301-4207(78)90050-8
34. Garrod, B., Gössling, S.: New Frontiers in Marine Tourism: Diving Experiences, Sustainability, Management. Routledge, London (2008). https://doi.org/10.1016/b978-0-08-045357-6.50004-8
35. Hood, C.: In Depth, Malta's wrecks (2019). http://divemagazine.co.uk/travel/6189-malta-wrecks. Accessed 15 Jan 2020
36. Sample, I.: Antikythera shipwreck Yields Bronze Arm – and hints at spectacular haul of statues. The Guardian (2017). https://www.theguardian.com/science/2017/oct/04/antikythera-shipwreck-yields-new-treasures-and-hints-of-priceless-classical-statues. Accessed 19 Jan 2020
37. Whelan, E.: Shipping blackspot: Largest find of shipwrecks in the Mediterranean intensifies. ancient origins (2018). https://www.ancient-origins.net/news-history-archaeology/mediterranean-shipwrecks-0010835. Accessed 9 Jan 2020

38. Hyères Tourisme. Le Donator wreck diving spot. https://www.hyeres-tourism.co.uk/fauna-flora-parks-garden/le-donator-wreck/. Accessed 15 Jan 2020
39. Lickliter-Mundon, M., et al.: Identification of a deep-water B-29 WWII Aircraft via ROV telepresence survey. J. Marit. Archaeol. **13**, 167–189 (2018). https://doi.org/10.1007/s11457-018-9200-8
40. Argyropoulos, V., Giannoulaki, M., Charalambous, D.: Conservation of Underwater Metallic Shipwrecks and Their Finds From the Aegean. Dionicos, Athens (2015). (in Greek)
41. Duxbury, N., Baltà, J., Hosagrahar, J., Pascual, J.: Culture in urban development policies: an agenda for local governments. In: UNESCO (ed.) Culture: Urban Future–Global Report on Culture for Sustainable Urban Development, pp. 204–211. UNESCO, Paris (2016)
42. Moshenska, G.: Introduction: public archaeology as practice and scholarship where archaeology meets the world. In: Moshenska, G. (ed.) Key Concepts in Public Archaeology. UCL Press, London (2017). https://doi.org/10.2307/j.ctt1vxm8r7
43. Silva, C.N.: The e-planning paradigm – theory, methods and tools: an overview. In: Silva, C. N. (ed.) E-planning – ICTs for Urban Development and Monitoring, pp. 1–14. Information Science Reference, New York (2010). ISBN 978-1-61520-929-3
44. Panagiotopoulou, M., Somarakis, G., Stratigea, A.: Smartening up participatory cultural tourism planning in historical city centers. J. Urban Technol. 1–24 (2018). https://doi.org/10.1080/10630732.2018.1528540
45. IRMCo: PPGIS practical guide. Mare Nostrum Project: Bridging the implementation gap in coastal management around the Mediterranean. ENPI CBC MED Project – I-A_1.3_093 (2015)
46. Collings, P.: Leros shipwrecks. Leros active (2008). http://lerosactive.com/main/images/2014-LEROSACTIVE-EBOOK.pdf. Accessed 30 Dec 2019
47. Nutley, D.M.: Look outwards, reach inwards, pass it on: the three tenures of underwater cultural heritage interpretation. In: Jameson, J.H., Scott-Ireton, D.A. (eds.) Out of the Blue, pp. 33–51. Springer, Boston (2007). https://doi.org/10.1007/978-0-387-47862-3_3
48. Hansen, H.S., Prosperi, D.: Citizen participation and internet GIS-Some recent advances. Comput. Environ. Urban **29**, 617–629 (2005). https://doi.org/10.1016/j.compenvurbsys.2005.07.001
49. Snyder, K.: Saving the oceans, one person at a time, Clipperton project (2017). http://www.clippertonproject.com/oceans-have-more-historical-artifacts-than-all-museums-combined/. Accessed 20 Jan 2020

Polycentrism and Insularity Metrics for In-Land Areas

Laura Curatella and Francesco Scorza[(✉)]

School of Engineering, Laboratory of Urban and Regional Systems Engineering,
10, Viale dell'Ateneo Lucano, 85100 Potenza, Italy
lauracu8@gmail.com, francesco.scorza@unibas.it

Abstract. The aim of polycentrism, as a policy, is to promote balanced territorial development between urban centres and its hinterland by creating functional integration. In this view, polycentric urban systems are a mean to achieve
a more efficient and more sustainable territorial organization than single-centric
systems and small dispersed settlements. At regional/local level, an operational
objective could be to move from one or two dominant regional centres (polarization) to a network of small and medium-sized centres providing regional
services. This process has to be finalized through strategic alliances between
cities, particularly where critical mass is lacking, and rural partnerships urban
exploring common potential and joint development projects.

The idea is to deliver a territorial schema to organize the connection of cities,
metropolitan regions and their hinterland through infrastructures and effective
services supply distribution. The negative part of this schema represents the
territorial insularity effect: it is the case of those in-land areas, considered as the
extreme periphery of the polycentric structure, that are not connected, in facts,
with any center belonging to the top-level hierarchy adopted in the model.

The study for the identification of territorial structures in Basilicata was
carried out through the analysis of various variables: the demographic structure,
the infrastructure endowment and organizational models that condition the territorial accessibility. In Basilicata three levels of polycentric hierarchy have been
identified, according to different levels of concentration of high and medium-
level functions. The insularity effect had been mapped. The calculations reveal a
large gap between the outermost and the innermost centres of the Region (referring to their geographical position).

Keywords: Polycentrism · Monocentrism · Territorial balance · Territorial
islands · Marginality

1 Introduction

Detecting "insularity effect" in inland areas deals with the operative identification of
marginal and remote territorial portions where an adequate level of quality of live and
equitable distribution of opportunities if far to be ensured to local inhabitants.

Our approach goes in the direction to adopt quantitative analytics used for the
Polycentric territorial organization in order to define targets and metrics characterizing
territorial insularity in a specific context: Basilicata region.

© Springer Nature Switzerland AG 2020
O. Gervasi et al. (Eds.): ICCSA 2020, LNCS 12255, pp. 253–261, 2020.
https://doi.org/10.1007/978-3-030-58820-5_20

Defining a polycentric territorial model [1–3] means organizing spatial data and information that includes mechanisms that, at the local scale, determine the organization of demand and consequently the provision of services and facilities.

It seeks to interpret the dynamics of settlement, infrastructure and organizational changes that condition territorial accessibility and that lead citizens to self-define residence and systematic displacements according to criteria of optimization of the use of the space and the territory.

The rules and criteria which contribute to the definition of the settlement model are useful in the planning of sustainable forms of territorial development: a substantial and particularly critical exercise in the management of the territories so called to (i.e., low settlement density) in which rules and standards defined for the organization of large metropolitan aggregates lose their effectiveness. Additionally, the "in-land island" goes absolutely out of any standard classification in services and infrastructures supply/availability or "standard costs" estimation for public endowment.

These considerations are at the origin of the research question that underlies this work: identify "insularity effect areas" through the analysis of the polycentric territorial organizational model of Basilicata region (Italy).

It is the case of Basilicata region, one of the regions with the lowest population density of Italy (56,3 inhabitants/kmq), affected by a development delay that results from a secular infrastructural deficit [4, 5].

In this work, two main information components are considered for the definition of poly centric geographies of spatial planning organized on a four-level hierarchy of the Lucanian centres: the demographic structure of the population and the provision of services and equipment. The first refers to the Istat data, the second comes from a work of recollection and mapping of detail of the current offer of public and private services that together determine different levels of territorial endowment. Assessing accessibility in terms of the time needed to travel to centres providing primary services has been decisive for the definition of the geographies highlighted in the research.

This spatial pattern was then compared with a planned dimension which takes into account the evolution of the demand for services and equipment by 2050 according to the current demographic growth rates of ISTAT (in reality of depopulation) for each municipality in Basilicata. The map of insularity effects comes as the complementary geography of the polycentric regional structure. This result opens to a more structured research and analytical investigation about the issues of sustainable and inclusive development that should be completely reconsidered for those territories. The regional government, but also the national government, should act in order to define concrete actions overcoming the standardized governance models that are actually applied to development programs both in EU cohesion framework and extraordinary national development planning tools ("il Piano per il Sud" [6]).

2 The Demographic Structure of Basilicata

Basilicata region is characterized by a high degree of structural backwardness that originates from troubled historical events and difficult geographical conditions. Demographic structure is characterized by a historical trend towards depopulation as a result of migratory processes [7].

The Basilicata described by the data on the demographic structure of population recorded through the last Censuses is characterized by the negative demographic trend, the ageing of the population, the decrease of young people and the increase of foreigners [8]. The demographic analysis provides an image of the region which is characterized by a remarkable polarization in a few centers in the face of the excessive emptiness of the internal areas that favors the intensification of regional gaps. The interpretation of the dynamics of depopulation that has affected the regional territory, in fact, makes a differentiated analysis at territorial level appropriate because it arises from different demographic trends. Strong areas are identified where there are significant increases in population that coincide with the provincial capitals and the municipalities of the hinterland, which accommodate part of the surplus population of the capitals and originate a form of suburbanization. To these areas are added other centers attractors of the region such as for example the Vulture for the presence of the settlement FCA. Sata of Melfi and its related, the Ionian belt for the development of intensive agriculture and tourist attractiveness and, In more recent times, even some centres in the Val d'Agri which, thanks to the large-scale start of oil mining, show an appreciable demographic vitality. The rest of the region, which mostly coincides with the mountain area, is characterized by a significant demographic decline with significant population losses. The negative dynamics are determined by the conformation and the natural characteristics of the territory, by the complex morphology, by a limited coastal development, from particular altimetric characteristics that hinder the development of the productive system rendering more burdensome and less profitable the economic activities and they emphasize the chronic deficiencies is in terms of infrastructural endowment of the territory. These factors contribute to increasing the phenomenon of the abandonment of territories with the relative consequence of the weakening of the socioeconomic system. It is in these areas that the problem of the ageing of the population and the gradual depopulation of the municipalities is most felt.

The latter is not compensated by the increase in foreign immigration that only partially corrects the decline of the regional population. Demographic ageing, in line with global dynamics, is a phenomenon that is as important in the region as it is now widespread. The increase in the elderly population is due to the combined effect of different demographic trends due both to the considerable progress made in the economic, social and health sectors which, by fostering scientific progress, have led to an increase in life expectancy, both the decline in fertility that led to a contraction of births. This is a great achievement, but it necessarily has major economic, social and cultural implications. The social and economic variations associated with the ageing of the population are likely to have significant repercussions in many sectors, with an impact, inter alia, on the size of the working population, on health care, on social protection and social security issues. This territorial weakness is matched by the provision of services to the fragmented population [9–12] (Fig. 1).

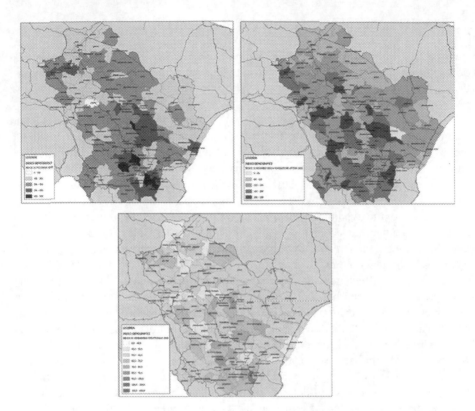

Fig. 1. Some of the demographic indices concerning the Basilicata region are given. They are, respectively: old age index, structural dependency index and turnover index of the working population. The data were updated to 2018.

3 Methodology

The provision of services and equipment is a parameter against which to assess the quality of life in a specific territory also through comparison (benchmark) with reference realities. Other part can be understood as an assessment of deficit, or lack of minimum requirements for the provision of services and equipment in relation to the urban functions exercised by each territorial unit. Using open source data available online, reworked through GIS systems, has defined a map of the services of the territory related to the entire region (including over 17,000 instances) [13]. Ten macrocategories have been defined: trade, culture, education and training, sport and leisure, tourism, general services, public services, financial services, security (Fig. 2).

This paper highlights a very discouraging condition: in principle, we can say that few municipalities in Basilicata really stand out for their equipment and services and are represented, in most cases, from the two provincial capitals and from Melfi and Policoro. To these are added the municipalities of Lagonegro and Lauria.

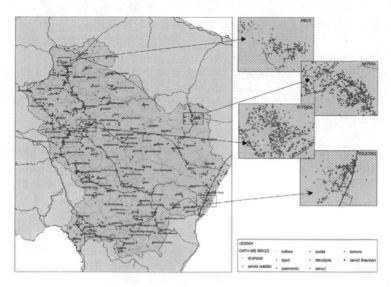

Fig. 2. Map of Basilicata services.

Exploiting the information derived from georeferencing and statistical maps, the analysis has been deepened by means of advanced spatial analysis techniques, such as the Kernel Density Estimation (KDE) [14].

These methodologies allow to study the polarization and the density of economic activities and not in the territory, analyzing the interconnection between them. What has emerged is that the activities are not evenly distributed and are greatly affected by the distribution of the population on the territory. In the most densely populated municipalities, there is a greater concentration of services and also their greater diversification, while the number of services is extremely small in the least populated municipalities.

The kernel density has thus enabled us to identify areas where the values of service and equipment concentration are significant and which represent a greater liveliness in economic terms. These areas are represented by the two regional capitals, the Vulture-Melfese, the Lagonegrese and the Ionian area.

In the more central areas of the Region, where the population is lower and the endowment index is very low, the activity concentration is minimal.

These data were then analyzed on the basis of ACP techniques and territorial classifications to balance levels of supply and demand in relation to territorial accessibility parameters that led us to the definition of a polycentric model for Basilicata [15].

The purpose of the analysis in main components is to reduce the more or less high number of variables describing a set of data to a smaller number of latent variables, limiting as much as possible the loss of information. This happens through a linear transformation of the variables that projects the original ones into a new Cartesian system in which the new variable with the greatest variance is projected on the first axis, the new variable, depending on the dimensions of the variance, on the second axis and so on.

The reduction of complexity is limited to analyzing the main new variables. The 131 municipalities of Basilicata were evaluated by taking into account 192 variables related to information on population structure, labor and business systems and the provision of services and equipment. This information base describes the socio-demographic structure to which we refer for the proposal of territorial organizational models oriented to balance the demand for services. The variables related to the presence of services, organized on two levels of very detailed classification, describe the side of the offer of services and therefore the territorial endowment. The link between demand and supply of services, although at the basis of any reflection of polycentric organization of the territory, is particularly weak in the analytical deter-mination especially in contexts of low settlement density. Formalized rules for large urban aggregations have no validity in fragmented contexts where the presence of population is weak and declining (weak demand) and where generic services such as retail businesses or small artisans have a value beyond the mere offering of functions and opportunities. Rather, they represent a form of protection of the territory and at the same time an essential element to ensure minimum standards of quality of life for residents.

To the definition of the hierarchy of the centers has been placed side by side the analysis of the territorial accessibility expressed in terms of times of distance that a resident citizen must carry out for the fruition of present services on the territory [16]. [17] The calculation of isochrons is the basis for calculating the population actually falling within the polygons defined by the curves. It is therefore of fundamental importance for a precise identification of the user that gravitates within the defined basins, take into account the census sections and the corresponding population, referring to the last census (Fig. 3).

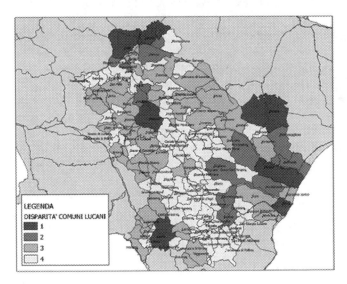

Fig. 3. It represents the inequality and heterogeneity of the municipalities of Basilicata. Data on the services and equipment of each municipality and its population were taken into account.

The following table proposes the polycentric model for Basilicata obtained through the application of the geo-statistical techniques mentioned above [18].

To the centralities of first, second and third levels, correspond isochrone of accessibility to 45 min that demonstrate as wide part of the regional territory is external to areas of proximity. This results in costs for the population which are often unsustainable and in internal and external migration which weakens local demand and contributes to the marginalization of the territory [19] (Fig. 4).

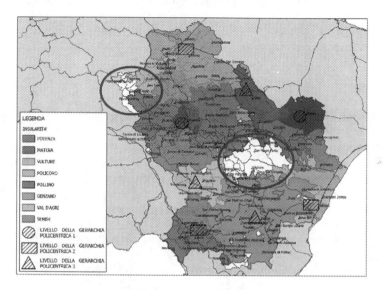

Fig. 4. Insularity map.

The areas defined by 45-min isocrones are wider areas where higher level services are available. These areas, despite their extension, cannot cover the entire territory of Lucania. The municipalities of Garaguso, Mauro Forte, Salandra, Stigliano, Cirigliano, Gorgoglione, Guardia Perticara, Pescopagano and Castelgrande remain outside. For the areas defined by the isocrone at 45 min the area of Potenza is the largest with an area of 2680 km^2 and the most populated with about 175900 inhabitants. Unlike what one would expect the second area for both extension and number of inhabitants is Genzano, center of third level, which with an area of 2233 km^2 encloses 1181815 inhabitants. The area of Matera has an extension of 1494 km^2 with a population.

From the map it can be noted that some municipalities, circled in red, are located outside the isochrone at 45 min and this makes them marginal and peripheral areas not connected with the main municipalities of the Region.

4   Conclusion

If we compare the results obtained and the set of territorial development policies in Basilicata, emerge a geography substantially different form the regional maps that can be found in the main regional development planning documents currently in force in Basilicata (of all the ERDF OP 2014-2020).

Basilicata Region is characterized by structural gaps among municipalities: those located in the hinterland of the territorial arrangements highlighted, which enjoying the presence of services and equipment are in a more favorable position compared to those of the hinterland, difficult to connect and sometimes without basic services.

In the perspective of this paper such gaps has to be considered as a form od insularity effect. It is representative of a new development perspective: island pay a gap of connections and accessibility and therefore needs extraordinary tools supporting territorial development.

This preliminary research basically provides a case study application of statistical and geo-statistical tools in order to map insularity effects in inland areas, further development has to consider the sustainability threshold analysis for those territories in order to deliver proposals and operative tools to adopt "smart" [20] approach in planning ad development. Main issues regards: urban quality [21]; effective planning tools [22]; Ecosystem Services and their provisioning [23]; cultural heritage exploitation [24]; citizens participation [25] and inclusion.

References

1. Contato, A.: Policentrismo reticolare. Teorie, approcci e modelli per lo sviluppo territoriale. Franco Angeli Editore (2019)
2. Clementi, A., Dematteis, G.: Le forme del territorio. Temi ed immagini del mutamento. Laterza (1996)
3. Dematteis, G.: Da aree metropolitane a rete. Tendenze recenti dell'urbanizzazione italiana ed europea. In: Quaderni di scienze storiche (1997)
4. Las Casas, G., Scorza, F., Murgante, B.: Conflicts and sustainable planning: peculiar instances coming from val d'agri structural inter-municipal plan. In: Papa, R., Fistola, R., Gargiulo, C. (eds.) Smart Planning: Sustainability and Mobility in the Age of Change. GET, pp. 163–177. Springer, Cham (2018). https://doi.org/10.1007/978-3-319-77682-8_10
5. Las Casas, G., Lombardo, S., Murgante, B., Pontrandolfi, P., Scorza, F.: Open data for territorial specialization assessment territorial specialization in attracting local development funds: an assessment. Procedure based on open data and open tools. J. L. Use Mobil. Environ. (2014). https://doi.org/10.6092/1970-9870/2557
6. Provenzano G.: Piano Sud 2030, sviluppo e coesione per l'Italia (2020)
7. Comitato Regionale per la programmazione economica della Basilicata.: Schema di sviluppo regionale per la Basilicata, quinquennio 1966/1970 (1967)
8. Scardaccione, G., Scorza, F., Casas, G.L., Murgante, B.: Spatial autocorrelation analysis for the evaluation of migration flows: the Italian case. In: Taniar, D., Gervasi, O., Murgante, B., Pardede, E., Apduhan, Bernady O. (eds.) ICCSA 2010. LNCS, vol. 6016, pp. 62–76. Springer, Heidelberg (2010). https://doi.org/10.1007/978-3-642-12156-2_5

9. Scorza, F., Pilogallo, A., Saganeiti, L., Murgante, B., Pontrandolfi, P.: Comparing the territorial performances of renewable energy sources' plants with an integrated ecosystem services loss assessment: A case study from the Basilicata region (Italy). Sustain. Cities Soc. **56**, 102082 (2020)

10. Di Fazio, S., Modica, G.: Historic rural landscapes: sustainable planning strategies and action criteria. The Italian experience in the global and European context. Sustainability **10**, 3834 (2018)

11. Morano, P., Tajani, F.: Saving soil and financial feasibility. A model to support the public-private partnerships in the regeneration of abandoned areas. Land Use Pol. **73**, 40–48 (2018)

12. Tajani, F., Morano, P.: Concession and lease or sale? A model for the enhancement of public properties in disuse or underutilized. WSEAS Trans. Bus. Econ. **11**, 787–800 (2014). Article no. 74

13. Carbone, R., et al.: Using open data and open tools in defining strategies for the enhancement of Basilicata Region. In: Gervasi, O., et al. (eds.) ICCSA 2018. LNCS, vol. 10964, pp. 725–733. Springer, Cham (2018). https://doi.org/10.1007/978-3-319-95174-4_55

14. Cecchini, A., Plaisant, A.: Analisi e modelli per la pianificazione. Teoria e pratica: lo stato dell'arte. Francoangeli/ Facoltà di Architettura di Alghero (2005)

15. O' Sullivan, D., Unwin, D.: Geographic Information Analysis (2002)

16. Fortunato, G., Scorza, F., Murgante, B.: Cyclable city: a territorial assessment procedure for disruptive policy-making on urban mobility. In: Misra, S., et al. (eds.) ICCSA 2019. LNCS, vol. 11624, pp. 291–307. Springer, Cham (2019). https://doi.org/10.1007/978-3-030-24311-1_21

17. Fortunato, G., Sassano, G., Scorza, F., Murgante, B.: Ciclabilità a Potenza: una proposta di intervento per lo sviluppo della mobilità attiva in un contesto urbano acclive. Urban. Inf. 109–115 (2018)

18. Pontrandolfi, P., Cartolano, A.: The role of intermediate territories for new sustainable planning and governance approaches. criteria and requirements for determining multi-municipal dimension: South Italy case. In: Gervasi, O., et al. (eds.) ICCSA 2018. LNCS, vol. 10964, pp. 744–762. Springer, Cham (2018). https://doi.org/10.1007/978-3-319-95174-4_57

19. Curatella, L.: La struttura policentrica del sistema insediativo lucano: un modello territoriale calibrato sulla dotazione di servizi ed attrezzature. Master thesis in Architectural Engineering, UNIBAS (2020)

20. Murgante, B., Borruso, G.: Smart cities in a smart world. In: Rassia, S.T., Pardalos, P.M. (eds.) Future City Architecture for Optimal Living. SOIA, vol. 102, pp. 13–35. Springer, Cham (2015). https://doi.org/10.1007/978-3-319-15030-7_2

21. Garau, C., Pavan, V.M.: Evaluating urban quality: indicators and assessment tools for smart sustainable cities. Sustainability **10**, 575 (2018). https://doi.org/10.3390/su10030575

22. Scorza, F., Saganeiti, L., Pilogallo, A., Murgante, B.: Ghost planning: the inefficiency of energy sector policies in a low population density region. Archivio Di Studi Urbani e Regionali (ASUR) (2020)

23. Scorza, F., Murgante, B., Las Casas, G., Fortino, Y., Pilogallo, A.: Investigating territorial specialization in tourism sector by ecosystem services approach. In: Stratigea, A., Kavroudakis, D. (eds.) Mediterranean Cities and Island Communities. PI, pp. 161–179. Springer, Cham (2019). https://doi.org/10.1007/978-3-319-99444-4_7

24. Garau, C.: Smart paths for advanced management of cultural heritage. Reg. Stud. Reg. Sci. **1**, 286–293 (2014). https://doi.org/10.1080/21681376.2014.973439

25. Somarakis, G., Stratigea, A.: Public involvement in taking legislative action as to the spatial development of the tourist sector in Greece—the "OpenGov" platform experience. Future Internet **6**, 735–759 (2014). https://doi.org/10.3390/fi6040735

A Service Network Design Problem for Freight Transportation in Port Cities

Massimo Di Francesco$^{(\boxtimes)}$ (iD), Dennis Incollu, Claudia Porcu, and Simone Zanda

Department of Mathematics and Computer Science, University of Cagliari,
09124 Cagliari, Italy
{mdifrance,simone.zanda}@unica.it
d.incollu@gmail.com,claudia.porcu92@gmail.com

Abstract. This paper investigates a service network design problem, which is motivated by the case of freight transportation in a port city. We describe the novel features of this problem, which are based on the possible (but still unexploited) knowledge on the composition of the disaggregated loads in containers and semitrailers entering the port. In this problem, the transportation requests of these loads are highly customized and have different delivery costs. We must determine the paths of vehicles and loads, which result in costs paid by carriers and customers, as well as external costs for the city itself. The resulting network design problem is faced from the holistic viewpoint of a possible mobility manager, which must minimize the overall system costs. We present a mixed integer linear programming model (MILP) for this problem. Since it is very difficult to solve by standard MILP solvers, we present a Tabu Search algorithm exploiting the specific problem features. The computational experiments show to what extent this problem can be tackled by a general purpose mixed-integer programming solver and the Tabu Search algorithm.

Keywords: Network design problems · City logistics · Tabu Search

1 Introduction

Freight transportation is a fundamental element enabling several economic and social activities in urban areas (for example, stores and offices need to be supplied, items need to be delivered at home and citizens must get rid of garbage). It is a crucial link between suppliers and customers and involves several stakeholders (e.g. carriers, depots, shippers, receivers, etc.). However, freight transportation generates nuisances in urban areas. Freight vehicles compete with vehicles transporting people for the capacities of streets and contribute to congestion and related issues (e.g. emissions, pollution and noise). Clearly, these nuisances impact the lives of people in cities, the productivity of the firms in urban areas,

Supported by *Fondazione di Sardegna* through the project *Algorithms for Approximation with Applications*.

O. Gervasi et al. (Eds.): ICCSA 2020, LNCS 12255, pp. 262–277, 2020.
https://doi.org/10.1007/978-3-030-58820-5_21

as well as the efficiency of the same freight transportation services. These problems are expected to continue growing, owing to logistics practices based on low inventories and time delivery, particularly in the domain of business-to-customer electronic commerce. Moreover, the problems are amplified by the increasing urbanization: in 2014, 54% of the world population lived in urban areas this percentage is expected to increase up to 66% until 2050 [1].

Freight transportation in urban areas has been subject to a significant amount of research [2,3]. The general objective is to decrease the impact of freight transportation on city living conditions without penalizing social and economic activities. More specifically, the goal is to reduce the number and the dimensions of freight vehicles and increase the efficiency of their movements. The key idea is to stop considering each shipment, firm, and vehicle individually and start viewing individual stakeholders as parts of an integrated logistics system, which must be optimized. The term "City Logistics" has been adopted to denote the need for an optimized consolidation of loads of different shippers in the vehicles of different carriers for the coordination of the freight transportation activities within the city [4]. City Logistics plans must be arranged by local/national authorities to make decisions and evaluate policies in order to regulate urban freight flows. Sometimes these plans are made by urban mobility managers, who need to be supported by optimization-based methods.

The research on these methods is based on the representation of cities as holistic systems, where consolidation and coordination activities are performed at facilities organized into a hierarchical two-echelon structure and two facility types: major terminals, which are located at the city limits, and satellite facilities, which are smaller redistribution points in the city where the goods are transshipped into smaller vehicles for the final distribution [5]. Particular vehicle fleets are dedicated to each echelon. However, this network topology does not apply to port cities, in which the port represents a very major terminal located in the city centre [6]. This paper investigates this variant, which often arises in island territories.

The port represents the main entrance for freight entering and leaving islands. In these areas freight transportation is necessarily intermodal (or multimodal), as goods are moved from their origin to their destination by a sequence of at least two transportation modes [7]. To improve the efficiency of the whole distribution process, loads (e.g. pallets) are consolidated in containers (or semi-trailers) for long-haul maritime transportation, while taking advantage of the efficiency of local pick-up and delivery operations by truck for the last-mile distribution. Carriers may either provide a customized service, where the overall container is dedicated exclusively to a particular customer (full-load service), or operate on the basis of consolidation (less-than-truckload service), where each container moves freight for different customers with possibly different origins and destinations.

In this problem the destinations of the loads in containers are supposed to be located in the city surrounding the port (i.e. if the destinations are out of the city, containers are moved out of the city and are not of interest for the urban mobility manager (e.g. [8]); we also neglect the freight flows originating from the city, as most islands are import dominant). Containers cannot be opened in the port, because it aims to quickly remove containers from docks to create room for containers arriving shortly from the seaside and the landside. The destinations in the city cannot be typically joined by vehicles carrying containers, because they cannot enter many streets or this is disallowed by local regulations, to reduce congestion and pollutant emissions.

To deal with this problem, a special two-echelon distribution structure needs to be adopted. In the first echelon, containers are moved by vehicles from the port to intermediate facilities called satellites, where loads are unpacked from containers and packed into smaller and, possibly, environment-friendly vehicles (the activity of satellites is also called cross-docking [9]). In the second echelon, loads are moved from satellites to their destinations by the smaller vehicles. To our knowledge, a similar distribution scheme was investigated in studies on dry ports, which are facilities *directly connected to one or more seaports with high-capacity transport means, where customers can drop and pick up their standardized units as if directly at a seaport* [10]. Dry ports can act as special satellites to alleviate congestion in the hinterland of maritime harbours [11].

Typically containers are *a priori* assigned to satellites according to existing contracts regardless of the destinations of their loads. Clearly, this *modus operandi* is often inefficient, as "better" satellites can be selected if one knows the destinations of the loads in containers. For example, a mobility manager could determine the "average" destination of the loads in a container and select the closest satellite to this artificial destination. More important, the precise composition of the loads in each container can be derived from data on transportation requests, but it is still almost unexploited for the planning of freight transportation in maritime cities. Nevertheless, the potential of technological developments in data sharing represents viable perspectives to deal with such inefficiencies effectively.

This paper investigates the service network design problem for freight transportation in the second echelon of a port city. More precisely, we assume that containers are already assigned to satellites according to predefined (and, possibly, cost-effective) policies and focus on inbound containers filled with loads to be delivered within the city. The objective is to support a mobility manager in the construction of a transportation plan to serve the freight demand by the vehicles of several consolidation-based carriers, while operating at the same time in an efficient and profitable manner. This service network design problem aims to determine the routes of vehicles and the itineraries of each load from the satellite to the final destination.

This paper aims to introduce readers without a background in Operations Research (but research interests in ICT, urban planning and logistics) to explore its potential in approaching this challenging problem. First, the problem is mathematically described by a mixed integer programming model (MILP), in which the legs of paths of vehicles and loads are represented by boolean or integer decision variables. They must be determined, such that all customers are served with their loads by the available vehicles and the overall system costs are minimized. These costs are described by a linear function of the decision variables and the objective is to minimize this function. The need to serve customers by the available vehicles is enforced by linear constraints in the decision variables. Therefore, the service network design problem is presented as a constrained optimization problem (or MILP model), which can be solved (i.e. to determine decision variables) by algorithms.

Several MILP solvers do incorporate exact optimization algorithms, which aim to determine the least-cost problem solution (in this problem the least-cost paths for vehicles and loads). However, service network design problems are very difficult to solve, because in the worst case the computational time increases exponentially with the size of the instance (these problems are said to be $\mathcal{NP} - hard$, which means that it is very unlikely to solve them in polynomial time). Therefore, the exact algorithms of MILP solvers are expected to solve only small problem instances of our service network design problem, i.e. they cannot be useful for mobility managers in dealing with City Logistics. Nevertheless, in this paper we investigate which instances of this new problem are in the grasp of a standard MILP solver.

In order to solve larger problem instances, we propose an algorithm which determines the paths of vehicles and loads, even if the overall system costs are not guaranteed to be minimized. This algorithm is a metaheuristic in the class of Tabu Search methods. It is based on a sequence of local changes to the paths of vehicles and loads and adopts specific memories (the so-called Tabu Lists), to avoid solutions already visited during the search. Two variants of Tabu Search are presented: in the first variant, the algorithm visits only the set of feasible solutions (i.e. the set of paths of vehicles and loads that satisfy all the constraints). In order to improve the solutions, we investigate an algorithmic variant in which the temporary visits of infeasible solutions is allowed and penalized to reestablish their feasibility (i.e. the ability to satisfy all the constraints). Some computational experiments are reported, to discuss the effectiveness of the MILP solver and that of the Tabu Search algorithms.

This paper is organized as follows. In Sect. 2 we describe this service network design problem and illustrate the MILP model for this problem. In Sect. 3 we describe the Tabu Search algorithm. In Sect. 4 we report the experimentation of the MILP solver and the Tabu Search algorithms. We list conclusions and research perspectives in Sect. 5.

2   Problem Setting and Modeling

Consider a fleet of inbound containers in a satellite. Each container is filled with loads (or pallets), which have different destinations (or customers) in the city. Each final customer is associated with a known demand of the loads packed in containers. The transportation service is highly customized, as different costs are paid by customers for the transportation of loads to each destination. As a result, each demand can be seen as a different commodity, which can be identified by its destination. A fleet of vehicles is available in the satellite to serve the transportation requests. They are heterogeneous in terms of transportation capacity and routing cost per unitary distance. Moreover, we assume that the overall fleet of vehicles provides a sufficient transportation capacity to serve all the requests of customers.

In this problem setting, the routes of vehicles are supposed to be open, i.e. they are not required to return to the satellite after servicing the last customer in the route. Moreover, splitting is allowed for all destinations of the second tier, i.e. the loads requested by each customer can be provided by several vehicles.

The problem can be described by the following MILP formulation. Let s be a satellite, K the set of customers and V the set of vehicles. Consider a directed graph $G = (N, A)$, where the set N of nodes is defined as $\{s\} \cup K$ and the set A of arcs consists of all possible links from the satellite or a customer to any other customer: $A = \{(i, j) : i \in s \cup K, j \in K, i \neq j\}$. If vehicle $v \in V$ moves along arc $(i, j) \in A$, a routing cost $c^v(i, j)$ is paid. In the simplest setting, this cost is paid by the carrier, but it can also incorporate external costs paid by the city due to the movement of this vehicle. If vehicle $v \in V$ moves the loads with destination $k \in K$ from node $i \in N$ to node $j \in N$, a unitary transportation cost $f_k^v(i, j)$ is paid by customer $k \in K$ for this transportation service. Let d_k be the number of loads requested by customer $k \in K$ and u_v the maximum number of loads carried by vehicle $v \in V$.

The following quantities (or decision variables) must be determined:

$y_k^v(i, j)$: it represents the number of loads with destination $k \in K$ shipped along arc $(i, j) \in A$ by vehicle $v \in V$;

$x^v(i, j)$: it takes value 1 if vehicle $v \in V$ traverses arc $(i, j) \in A$, 0 otherwise.

According to the former notation, the following objective function is minimized: $z = \sum_{v \in V} \sum_{(i,j) \in A} \left(c^v(i, j) x^v(i, j) + \sum_{k \in K} f_k^v(i, j) y_k^v(i, j) \right)$. It accounts for the overall system costs from the viewpoint of mobility managers. The first term represents the costs generated by the movement of each vehicle along each traversed arc. It can incorporate not only the routing costs of carriers, but also the costs for the city (even if their quantification is beyond the scope of this paper). The second term represents the overall costs generated by each load traversing specific arcs by specific vehicles. It accounts for the costs of shippers, but it can also be used by mobility managers to penalize the transportation of specific commodities on specific arcs by specific vehicles.

Decision variables must satisfy the following constraints:

- All loads with destination $k \in K$ must leave the satellite; this constraint is enforced as follows: $\sum_{v \in V} \sum_{j \in N-s} y_k^v(s, j) = d_k, \ \forall k \in K$;
- Each destination $k \in K$ must receive its own pallets; this constraint is imposed as follows: $\sum_{v \in V} \sum_{i:(i,k) \in A} y_k^v(i, k) = d_k, \ \forall k \in K$;
- The loads with destination $k \in K$ traverse any customer $k' \in K$ visited before $k \in K$; this constraint is formulated as follows:
  $\sum_{i:(i,k') \in A} y_k^v(i, k') - \sum_{i:(k',i) \in A} y_k^v(k', i) = 0, \ \forall v \in V, \ \forall k', k \in K, k' \neq k$;
- Each vehicle is used at most once; this constraint is formulated as follows:
  $\sum_{i \in K} x^v(s, i) \leq 1, \ \forall v \in V$;

– If a vehicle joins a customer, it leaves and moves toward the next customer, or it terminates the service, if the last customer in the route has been served; this constraint is enforced as follows:
$$\sum_{i:(i,k)\in A} x^v(i,k) \geq \sum_{l:(k,l)\in A} x^v(k,l) \ , \ \forall v \in V \ , \ \forall k \in K;$$
– The total demand of the customers assigned to the route of vehicle $v \in V$ does not exceed its capacity u_v in each arc; this constraint is imposed as follows:
$$\sum_{k \in K} y_k^v(i,j) \leq u_v x^v(i,j) \ , \ \forall v \in V \ , \ (i,j) \in A.$$

A feasible solution for this problem consists in a collection of paths of vehicles and loads from the satellite to a subset of customers. The total demand of the customers in the path of a vehicle is not larger than the capacity of the vehicle.

To the best of our knowledge, this problem has not been addressed yet, even if some similar problems were investigated in the literature on routing. Tavakkoli-Moghaddam et al. [12] investigated a vehicle routing problems with splits and heterogeneous fleets, but they ignored the customer-dependent transportation costs. Cattaruzza et al. [14] investigated a multi-commodity vehicle routing problem without splits to minimize the number of vehicles. Archetti et al. [13] adopted a path-based model to investigate the routing costs of vehicles capable of carrying any set of commodities, but ignored transportation costs.

3   Tabu Search

Approximate solution techniques (or heuristics) have been broadly used for solving combinatorial optimization problems. The most popular ones are based on Local Search (LS) improvement techniques: starting from an initial feasible solution, it is progressively improved by applying a series of local modifications (or moves). At each iteration, LS switches to an improving feasible solution, such that the difference between the previous and the new solution is one move. The LS terminates when it encounters a local optimum with respect to the considered transformations, but this local optimum is often a solution of low or moderate quality. Tabu Search (TS) allows LS methods to overcome local optima: TS continues LS whenever a local optimum is visited by allowing non-improving moves and preventing cycling back to previously visited solutions by memories (or tabu lists), which record the recent history of the search. The basic elements of any LS or TS algorithm are the search space and its neighborhood structure. The search space is the space of all possible solutions that can be visited during the search. The neighborhood of the current solution is the set of solutions obtained by applying a single move to it [15].

In the following subsections we present a TS algorithm tailored to our service network design problem. For the sake of clarity, we first introduce the simplest variant, in which the search space is the set of feasible paths. It is called *Basic Tabu Search* and denoted by TS_B. Next, we present a variant in which the visit of infeasible solutions is temporarily allowed and penalized. It is called *Tabu Search with Penalties* and denoted by TS_P.

3.1   Basic Tabu Search

Several initial solutions are built by two ordered lists of pallets for each destination and vehicles available in the satellite. The first initial solution is determined as follows. Starting from the top of the list of pallets, all pallets of the first destination are assigned to the first vehicle, if it has sufficient capacity, else a part of the pallets are assigned to the second vehicle. Next, the pallets of the second destination are assigned to the first available vehicle in the list and so on. The other initial solutions are built by the same procedure after a random reordering of the two former lists.

For each initial solution, the following tabu search steps are performed. The search space is the set of feasible solutions to the problem. Therefore, each point in the search space corresponds to a set of loads carried in each segment of a route performed by a vehicle. Two types of non-tabu moves are considered:

1-0 Exchange (or customer relocate): a part or the totality of the loads (or pallets) for a destination are moved at each iteration from the current position in a route. The pallets for the selected destination are inserted in the same route or in another route with sufficient residual capacity. We evaluate all possible *0-1 exchange* moves and select the move resulting in the minimum overall cost in the next iteration.

1-1 Exchange (or customer exchange): all pallets for two destinations are swapped at each iteration from their current positions, which can be in the same route or in two different routes. The vehicles involved in this move are required to have sufficient residual capacity. We evaluate all possible *1-1 exchange* moves and select the move resulting in the minimum overall cost in the next iteration.

In Fig. 1 the caption (v_1, v_2, n_1, n_2, p) describes the *1-0 exchange* move of p pallets with destination n_2 from vehicle v_2 to vehicle v_1, which will serve n_2 after n_1. In the left side of the figure, the current solution is reported; in the right side, we show the solution after the local move. The following cases can occur:

case (a) One pallet for node D is moved to route v_1 and delivered after node A. Thus, in the LS one must remove arc (A, B) and add arcs (A, D) and (D, B) in route v_1. If all pallets for node D are removed from route v_2, in the LS one also needs to remove arcs (C, D) and (D, E) and add arc (C, E) in route v_2.

case (b) Two pallets for node E are moved to route v_1 and delivered after node A. Thus, in the LS one must remove arc (A, B) and add arcs (A, E) and (E, B) in route v_1. If all pallets for node E are removed from route v_2, in the LS one also needs to remove arcs (C, D) and (D, E) and add arc (C, E) in route v_2.

case (c) One pallet for node D is moved to route v_1 and delivered after node B. Thus, in the LS one must add arcs (B, D) at the end of route v_1. If all pallets for node D are removed from route v_2, in the LS one also needs to remove arcs (C, D) and (D, E) and add arc (C, E) in route v_2.

case (d) Two pallets for node E are moved to route v_1 and delivered after node B. Thus, in the LS one must add arcs (B, E) at the end of route v_1. If all pallets for node E are removed from route v_2, in the LS one also needs to remove arc (D, E) in route v_2.

If a customer is served by two different routes at the current iteration, a *1-0 exchange* move between these routes may lead to unsplit the service to this customer in the next iteration.

In Fig. 2 the caption (v_1, v_2, n_1, n_2) describes a *1-1 exchange* move, in which all pallets in vehicle v_2 for customer n_2 are swapped with all pallets in route v_1 for customer n_1. In the left side of the figure, the current solution is reported; in the right side, we show the solution after the local move. The following cases can occur:

case (a) Customer D in route v_2 is swapped with customer A in route v_1. Thus, in route v_2 one must remove arcs (C, D) and (D, E) and add arcs (C, A) and (A, F). In route v_1 one must remove arcs (s, A) and (A, B) and add arcs (s, D) and (D, B).

case (b) Customer E in route v_2 is swapped with customer B in route v_1. Thus, in route v_2 one must remove arc (D, E) and add arc (D, B). In route v_1 one must remove arc (A, B) and add arc (A, E).

case (c) Customer E in route v_2 is swapped with customer A in route v_1. Thus, in route v_2 one must remove arc (D, E) and add arc (D, A). In route v_1 one must remove arcs (s, A) and (A, B) and add arcs (s, E) and (E, B).

case (d) Customer D in route v_2 is swapped with customer B in route v_1. Thus, in route v_2 one must remove arcs (C, D) and (D, E), and add arcs (C, B) and (B, E). In route v_1 one must remove arc (A, B) and add arc (A, D).

If a customer is served by two different routes at the current iteration, a *1-1 exchange* move may result in the double occurrence of a customer in a route. Since it is clearly uneconomical to serve a customer twice in the same route, an additional move is performed to reach this customer only once in the route.

The following notation is introduced to present the TS algorithm:

- α is the number of initial solutions;
- S_j^0 is the jth initial solution;
- t_{run} is the running time of the TS algorithm;
- t_{max} is the maximum running time of the TS algorithm;
- S_j is the current solution built from S_j^0;
- $z(S_j)$ is the value of solution S_j;
- S_j^* is the best current solution derived from S_j^0;
- z_j^* is the value of solution S_j^* built from S_j^0;
- it is the number of iterations without any improvement;
- it_{max} is the maximum number of iterations without any improvement;
- $N(S_j)$ is the overall neighborhood of S_j (i.e. the set of solutions obtained both tabu and non-tabu moves to S_j);
- $\overline{N}(S_j)$ is the subset of $N(S_j)$ containing the solutions obtained by applying only non-tabu moves to S_j;

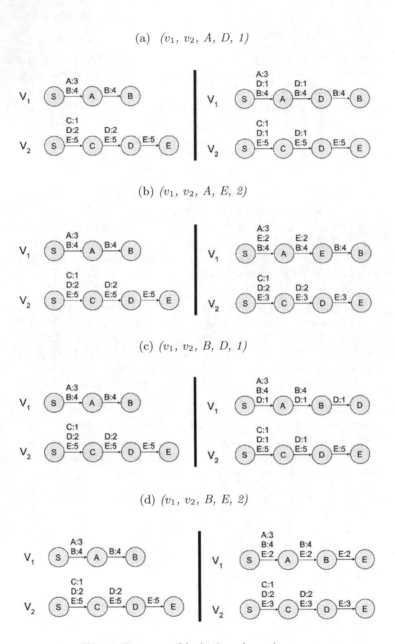

Fig. 1. Four possible (*1-0 exchange*) moves

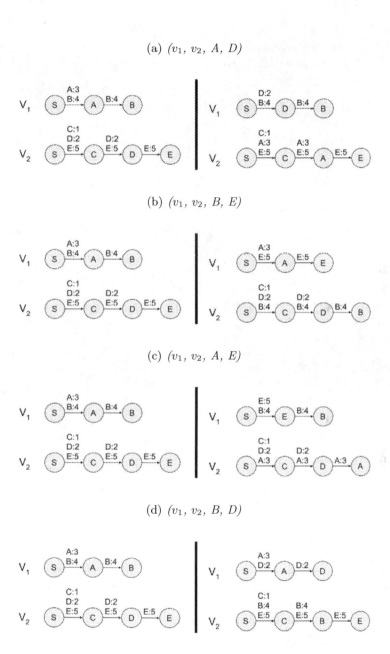

Fig. 2. Four possible (*1-1 exchange*) moves

– T: the Tabu List;

This is the template of the Tabu Search algorithm:

Construct α initial solutions $S_1^0...S_\alpha^0$; $j = 1$;

while $j \leq \alpha$ *and* $t_{run} \leq t_{max}$ **do**

{

    set $S_j \leftarrow S_j^0$, $z_j^* \leftarrow z(S_j^0)$, $S_j^* \leftarrow S_j^0$, $T \leftarrow \emptyset$, $it = 0$;

    while $it \leq it_{max}$ **do**

    {

        select S_j in $argmin_{S_j' \in \overline{N}(S_j)}[z(S_j')]$;

        if $z(S_j) < z_j^*$ **then**

        {

            $z_j^* \leftarrow z(S_j)$; $S_j^* \leftarrow S_j$;

        }

        else

        {

            it=it+1;

        }

        record tabu for the current move in T;

        delete the oldest entries from T;

    }

    $j = j + 1$; update t_{run};

}

return S_k^* such that $z_k^* = min_{j=1,...,\alpha} z*j$;

Algorithm 1: Tabu Search

The stopping criteria of the overall algorithm are the maximum running time t_{max} and the conclusion of the Tabu Search steps for all initial solutions. For a given initial solution, the non-tabu moves are made until the number of iterations without any improvement is lower or equal to it_{max}. The algorithm returns the best solution among those determined from all initial solutions.

Two parameters need to be calibrated according to the former scheme of the algorithm: α and it_{max}. Moreover, the tabu tenure β is set to be equal to it_{max}. Moreover, a parameter denoted by γ is adopted to control the size of the neighbourhood. When it is set to *AND*, the neighbourhood contains all solutions obtained by applying both *1-0 exchange* and *1-1 exchange* moves to the current solution. When it is set to *OR*, the neighbourhood contains all solutions obtained by applying a *1-0 exchange* move in an iteration, a *1-1 exchange* move in the next iteration and so on.

3.2   Tabu Search with Penalties

In this problem, the former definition of the search space may restrict the search too much and lead to low-quality solutions. More precisely, the route capacity may be too tight to allow effective LS search moves between two different routes. Therefore, we relax the capacity constraint and create a larger search space that can be visited according to the moves described in the former section. Hence, the capacity constraint is dropped from the search space definition and weighted penalties for constraint violation are added to the objective. Clearly, this raises the issue of finding suitable weights for the constraint violation. The issue is faced by the calibration of two parameters:

- δ: it is the penalty (in percentage) to apply to the total cost of the infeasible solutions;
- ϵ: it is the percent increase in the capacity of vehicles.

4   Experimentation

The objectives of this section are twofold. The first objective is to show to what extent the problem can be solved by an off-the-shelf MILP solver. The second objective is to investigate the effectiveness of former variants of the Tabu Search for solving the problem. All tests have been implemented in Python and solved by the MILP solver Cplex 12.9 running with default parameters, except a maximum running time of 1 h and a required relative gap of 1e-4 (i.e. 0.01%). The experiments were performed on a 64 Gigabyte Ubuntu 16.04.6 LTS virtual machine running on a physical computer Cisco UCS B480 M5 Intel Xeon Gold 6136 3.00 GHz 12-core CPU equipped with 1 Terabyte of DDR4 RAM and 10 Terabytes SAS Hard drives.

The outcomes are reported in Table 1 and 2. All tables are divided into three groups of columns denoted by PROBLEM DATA, MILP and a variant of the Tabu Search algorithm: TS_B for the Basic Tabu Search in Table 1 and TS_P for the Tabu Search with penalties in Table 2. Since the problem is new, we generate several instances for the experimentation. The columns under PROBLEM DATA and MILP are identical in both tables. They report the name of the problem instance, the number of destinations ($|K|$), the number of vehicles ($|V|$), the overall number of pallets requested by all destinations ($\sum_{k \in K} d_k$) and the available transportation capacity ($\sum_{v \in V} u_v$). For example, instance P_1 has 6 customers, 2 vehicles, 70 pallets to be delivered and an overall transportation capacity of 80 pallets.

The group of columns denoted by MILP reports some outcomes on the solutions obtained by Cplex. More precisely, we indicate the time spent by Cplex to determine the best solution (t_{best}), the overall execution time (t_{exe}) and the relative optimality gap between the best solution and the lower bound (gap). For example, instance P_5 was solved to optimality after 2304, 2 seconds, it was solved to optimality, but the best solution was already determined after 244, 12 seconds. Therefore, the MILP solver determined this solution in a few minutes, but it took about 2000 additional seconds to prove its optimality. Cplex optimally solved all instances with less than 17 customers. In the range between 20 and 50 customers, one typically obtains a feasible solution without proving its optimality. Moreover, it is not possible to obtain a feasible solution for instances with more than 60 customers in one hour (these solutions are denoted by "UNSOLVED" in the tables). Therefore different solution methods must be adopted for the largest instances of this problem. Hence, it is of interest to evaluate if they can be solved by the Tabu Search and evaluate its computational effectiveness.

The following configurations of the *Basic Tabu Search* were tested:

1. $\alpha = 20$, $\beta = 10$, $\gamma = OR$;
2. $\alpha = 50$, $\beta = 5$, $\gamma = OR$;
3. $\alpha = 50$, $\beta = 5$, $\gamma = AND$;
4. $\alpha = 10$, $\beta = 30$, $\gamma = OR$;
5. $\alpha = 20$, $\beta = 10$, $\gamma = AND$.

Each instance was run in the server according to each configuration for one hour (i.e. t_{max} was also set to 1 hour). In Table 1 we denote by gap_{avg} the average relative gap between these configurations and the best solution determined by the MILP solver. Moreover, gap_{best} is the best gap among all configurations and $cnfg_{best}$ is the index of the best configuration according to the former list. For example, in problem P_2, the best configuration is the third in the former list.

Table 1. Computational experiments on the Basic Tabu Search

PROBLEM DATA					MILP			TS_B		
Instance	$\lvert K\rvert$	$\lvert V\rvert$	$\sum_{k\in K} d_k$	$\sum_{v\in V} u_v$	t_{best}	t_{exe}	gap_{opt}	gap_{avg}	gap_{best}	$cnfg_{best}$
P_1	006	2	70	80	0,18	0,04	0,00	0,00	0,00	all
P_2	009	4	78	80	34,81	34,81	0,00	2,08	0,99	3
P_3	010	8	113	120	87,40	820,13	0,00	3,58	2,65	2
P_4	015	2	117	120	150,42	212,15	0,00	0,18	0,00	3
P_5	016	3	176	195	244,12	2304,2	0,00	4,96	4,29	2
P_6	017	2	181	200	83,5	185,56	0,00	3,28	3,03	2
P_7	019	3	212	250	630	3600	1,81	1,47	0,82	3
P_8	020	3	202	210	1756,58	3600	6,10	5,34	1,96	3
P_9	030	4	389	400	520,69	1057,23	0,00	41,20	28,55	2
P_{10}	040	4	370	375	2100	3600	19,21	38,41	29,79	2
P_{11}	050	3	533	550	2400	3600	22,69	33,04	12,76	2
P_{12}	060	3	649	675	UNSOLVED			SOLVED		2
P_{13}	070	4	806	810	UNSOLVED			SOLVED		2
P_{14}	080	2	804	850	UNSOLVED			SOLVED		2
P_{15}	090	4	914	925	UNSOLVED			SOLVED		2
P_{16}	100	6	1030	1050	UNSOLVED			SOLVED		2

Generally speaking, the *Basic Tabu Search* can solve all instances within one hour. As for the largest instances, we cannot compute any gap, as no comparison is possible with respect to the MILP solver. Nevertheless, we denote these solutions by the string "SOLVED", to point out the ability to determinate feasible solutions. The best calibrations are those denoted by 2 and 3. Therefore, the number of initial solutions is the most beneficial parameter for the quality of final solutions.

The outcomes exhibit near optimal gaps w.r.t the MILP solver in the case of small instances. Clearly, some gaps become clearly high in the case of medium instances (e.g. in instances P_9, P_{10} and P_{11}) and they need to be decreased. In what follows, we investigate if some improvement is obtained by the *Tabu Search with Penalties*. The following configurations of TS_P were investigated:

a. $\delta = 25\%$, $\epsilon = 25\%$;
b. $\delta = 10\%$, $\epsilon = 25\%$;
c. $\delta = 25\%$, $\epsilon = 10\%$;
d. $\delta = 10\%$, $\epsilon = 10\%$;
e. $\delta = 5\%$, $\epsilon = 10\%$;
f. $\delta = 5\%$, $\epsilon = 5\%$.

These configurations were combined with those on TS_B and result in 30 calibrations. They are denoted by a pair of indices, each taken from the list of configurations. For example, configuration $2f$ means $\alpha = 50$, $\beta = 5$, $\gamma = OR$, $\delta = 5\%$, $\epsilon = 5\%$. The best calibration is reported in column $cnfg_{best}$.

Table 2. Computational experiments on the Tabu Search with penalties

PROBLEM DATA					MILP			TS_P			
Instance	$|K|$	$|V|$	$\sum_{k \in K} d_k$	$\sum_{v \in V} u_v$	t_{best}	t_{exe}	gap_{opt}	gap_{avg}	gap_{best}	$cnfg_{best}$
P_1	006	2	70	80	0,18	0,04	0,00	0,00	0,00	all
P_2	009	4	78	80	34,81	34,81	0,00	4,47	0,97	2f
P_3	010	8	113	120	87,40	820,13	0,00	7,58	1,08	5d
P_4	015	2	117	120	150,42	212,15	0,00	1,31	0,00	1d, 2e, 3c, 3d, 3e, 5a
P_5	016	3	176	195	244,12	2304,2	0,00	9,22	3,50	1f
P_6	017	2	181	200	83,5	185,56	0,00	6,36	0,93	2b
P_7	019	3	212	250	630	3600	1,81	6,65	0,80	2a, 4b
P_8	020	3	202	210	1756,58	3600	6,10	4,63	0,00	1e, 2e, 4c
P_9	030	4	389	400	520,69	1057,23	0,00	57,05	25,98	3f
P_{10}	040	4	370	375	2100	3600	19,21	49,30	29,74	2f
P_{11}	050	3	533	550	2400	3600	22,69	34,12	3,75	3f
P_{12}	060	3	649	675	UNSOLVED			SOLVED			5f
P_{13}	070	4	806	810	UNSOLVED			SOLVED			4f
P_{14}	080	2	804	850	UNSOLVED			SOLVED			1f
P_{15}	090	4	914	925	UNSOLVED			SOLVED			3f
P_{16}	100	6	1030	1050	UNSOLVED			SOLVED			2f

The outcomes show that TS_P can improve the gaps w.r.t TS_B, even if some room for improvement does exist in the solutions of medium sized instances. Moreover, the best outcomes are obtained in the case $\delta = 5\%$ and $\epsilon = 5\%$, which means that limited violated capacities and low penalization costs are typically recommended. In both tables, the execution of the Tabu Search algorithm is stopped by the number α of initial solutions in instances $P_1, ..., P_8$ (i.e. a local optimum is joined for $\beta = it_{max}$ times for each initial solution). The execution of the other instances is stopped by t_{max}.

5   Conclusions

The efficient management of the freight flows is one of the key pillars for sustainable growth of cities. Urban mobility managers must adopt smart transport solutions within the framework of the City Logistics to meet the biggest challenges that cities are facing today (e.g. traffic and congestion). Generally speaking, ICT tools must be developed to overcome socio-economic problems and must be coupled with Operations Research methods to optimize the operations.

In this paper we investigated a problem motivated by the missing implementation of ICT tools, that can share knowledge on disaggregated loads in containers (or semi-trailers) entering a port city. This knowledge can be exploited to determine the intermediate facilities (or satellites) where containers can be cross-docked, in order to start the last-mile distribution of these loads toward their final destinations.

We aimed to determine the paths of vehicles from a selected satellite to the destinations, as well as the paths of the loads carried by these vehicles. Since the transportation requests are highly customized, the problem was described as a service network design problem, in which each request is a commodity. This characteristic allows to evaluate the tradeoffs between the costs of vehicles and those generated by the volumes of the different loads moved by vehicles. The added value of this paper is the explicit consideration of the last costs, which are typically ignored by planning tools based on Vehicle Routing Problems. The information on the flows of each commodity can be adopted by urban mobility managers to support the decision processes on planning or improving facilities, the definition of new transportation services and the allocation of (human and material) resources to tasks [16].

The objective of this paper was the minimization the overall costs faced by carriers, customers and cities, while satisfying all the transportation requests by the available vehicles. The problem was faced by Operations Research methods. First, a Mixed Integer Linear Programming Model was formulated for this problem. Next, a Tabu Search metaheuristic was presented as a solution method to solve larger problem instances.

The research in the field is in progress. The concept of granularity will be investigated to reduce the size of the neighborhood and, thus, increase the number of initial solutions in the Tabu Search algorithm. Moreover, we will present a full city-logistics model, which will also incorporate decisions on the selection of vehicles and satellites. Finally, it will be worth comparing the outcomes of this paper with respect to the current *modus operandi* of mobility managers.

References

1. United Nations: World urbanization prospects, the 2014 revision. Technical report, United Nations, Department of Economic and Social Affairs, Population Division, New York, USA (2014)

2. Bektas, T., Crainic, T.G., Van Woensel, T.: From managing urban freight to smart city logistics networks. In: Gakis, K., Pardalos, P. (eds.) Networks Design and Optimization for Smart Cities (Series on Computers and Operations Research), vol. 8, pp. 143–188. World Scientific Publishing, Singapore (2017)

3. Savelsbergh, M., Van Woensel, T.: City logistics: challenges and opportunities. Transp. Sci. **50**(2), 579–590 (2016)

4. Crainic, T.G., Ricciardi, N., Storchi, G.: Models for evaluating and planning city logistics systems. Transp. Sci. **43**(4), 432–454 (2009)

5. Paddeu, D.: Sustainable solutions for urban freight transport and logistics: an analysis of urban consolidation centers. In: Zeimpekis, V., Aktas, E., Bourlakis, M., Minis, I. (eds.) Sustainable Freight Transport. ORSIS, vol. 63, pp. 121–137. Springer, Cham (2018). https://doi.org/10.1007/978-3-319-62917-9_8

6. Ignaccolo, M., Inturri, G., Giuffrida, N., Torrisi, V., Cocuzza, E.: Sustainability of freight transport through an integrated approach: the case of the eastern sicily port system. Transp. Res. Proc. **45**, 177–184 (2020)

7. Crainic, T.G., Kim, K.H.: Intermodal transportation. In: Henderson, S.G., Nelson, B.L. (eds.) Handbooks in Operations Research and Management Science, vol. 14, pp. 467–537. Elsevier, Amsterdam (2007)

8. Calabrò, G., Torrisi, V., Inturri, G., Ignaccolo, M.: Improving inbound logistic planning for large-scale real-world routing problems: a novel ant-colony simulation-based optimization. Eur. Transp. Res. Rev. **12**, 1–11 (2020). https://doi.org/10.1186/s12544-020-00409-7

9. Wen, M., Larsen, J., Clausen, J., Cordeau, J.F., Laporte, G.: Vehicle routing with cross-docking. J. Oper. Res. Soc. **60**(12), 1708–1718 (2009). https://doi.org/10.1057/jors.2008.108

10. Roso, V., Woxenius, J., Lumsden, K.: The dry port concept: connecting container seaports with the hinterland. J. Transp. Geogr. **17**(5), 338–345 (2009)

11. Crainic, T.G., Dell'Olmo, P., Ricciardi, N., Sgalambro, A.: Modeling dry-port-based freight distribution planning. Transp. Res. Part C Emerg. Technol. **55**, 518–534 (2015)

12. Tavakkoli-Moghaddam, R., Safaei, N., Kah, M.M.O., Rabbani, M.: A new capacitated vehicle routing problem with split service for minimizing fleet cost by simulated annealing. J. Franklin Inst. **344**(5), 406–425 (2007)

13. Archetti, C., Campbell, A.M., Speranza, M.G.: Multicommodity vs. single-commodity routing. Transp. Sci. **50**(2), 461–472 (2016)

14. Cattaruzza, D., Absi, N., Feillet, D., Vigo, D.: An iterated local search for the multi-commodity multi-trip vehicle routing problem with time windows. Comput. Oper. Res. **51**, 257–267 (2014)

15. Gendreau, M.: An introduction to tabu search. In: Glover, F., Laguna, M. (eds.) Handbbok of Metaheuristics, pp. 37–54. Springer, Boston (2003). https://doi.org/10.1007/0-306-48056-5_2

16. Crainic, T.G.: Service network design in freight transportation. Eur. J. Oper. Res. **122**(2), 272–288 (2000)

Tracing Sustainable Island Complexes in Response to Insularity Dilemmas _ Methodological Considerations

Yiota Theodora(✉) (iD)

Department of Urban and Regional Planning, School of Architecture, National Technical University of Athens (NTUA), Patission 42, 10682 Athens, Greece
ptheodora@arch.ntua.gr

Abstract. In an era of globalization, multidimensional crisis, as well as climate and demographic changes, intense consideration is placed on the identification of development patterns and their spatial counterparts that would alleviate the newly emerging inequalities among regions; and allow sustainability and resilience objectives of their ecosystems to be reached. Insular regions and small islands in particular are critical spatial entities in this respect, as lagging behind regions confronted with a range of contemporary risks and challenges. These raise concerns for spatial planning and policies that are capable of dealing with their geographical specificities. However, issues of conceptual clarification and methodological approach regarding as to the insularity phenomenon remain rather open at the official planning scene. The problem lies in the lack of a multi-factorial assessment of islands' dynamics and determination of their area of influence or their dependence on powerful insular/mainland territories. Focusing on the Aegean insular territory, it is investigated whether, and under what conditions, isolation or relinquishment of small islands can be prevented, and smart sustainable development can be ensured. The answer is sought in the leveraging of their competitive advantages as a ground for endogenous development and their organic inclusion in broader spatial, sectoral, and social networks of supralocal/supranational reach.

Keywords: Territorial planning and sustainable development · Blue economy and maritime spatial planning · Natural- cultural heritage · Fragmented insular regions · Small islands · Collaborative networks and smart communities

1 Framing the Discussion

In the territorial cohesion policy of the European Union (EU) emphasis is placed on the development of regions suffering from environmental downgrading, demographic alteration, and severe economic recession (The Treaty of Lisbon, 2017). This category (Article 174 TFEU) includes islands/insular regions, i.e. disadvantaged areas compared to mainland due to their location and their geographical, geopolitical, spatio-functional and socio-economic particularities [1, 2], facing multiple and severe impacts that are established by: a) exacerbation of unemployment and migration phenomena (demographic decline) at *local level*; b) aggravation of intra-/interregional disparities at

© Springer Nature Switzerland AG 2020
O. Gervasi et al. (Eds.): ICCSA 2020, LNCS 12255, pp. 278–293, 2020.
https://doi.org/10.1007/978-3-030-58820-5_22

national level, affecting geostrategic stability of countries; and c) intensification of problems during the socio-economic integration process at *supranational level*, hampering the achievement of territorial - social cohesion in the European area.

Island regions are thus confronted with a multitude of *risks and challenges*, raising issues of resource preservation, spatial management, and territorial planning. *Smaller islands* find themselves in a more disadvantageous position, given the inherent (often insurmountable) incompatibilities of their local production base with the quite demanding requirements of the globalised economy, being rather unprepared to venture the necessary qualitative changes assuring long-term development. Problems are intensified in fragmented insular regions where there is a considerable number of *small islands*, mostly of low density, suffering from shortage of key infrastructures. Due to the aforementioned particularities, the Greek insular space with the numerous small, remote/frontier islands presents interest for research and experimentation [1–5].

Unfortunately, despite the increasing research interest and awareness-raising of local governments, agencies and communities, at the EU level there has been no firmly articulated position on the development of insular territories. There is no EU insular law, nor regime or particular status for islands in European law, also no specific funds for islands, except for outmost regions (OR)[1], although islands are confronted with crucial structural and socio-economic handicaps restraining their development. The only exception applies to the Trans-European Networks - an intention that remains still open. As for secondary law, provisions for OR can be permanent [6], whereas provisions for (non-OR) islands may only provide for limited derogations. One such case is small Aegean islands [7], as there are no clearly determined criteria for their selection in the developmental process [8]. Hence, intra-/interregional disparities are enhanced preventing territorial - social cohesion across the geographical levels of the EU [9].

In Greece - a country with the 10th largest coastline worldwide on which the majority of its settlements/cities and a multitude of islands can be found, covering 19% of its territory - the lack of an overall *insular developmental policy* creates numerous problems. Indeed, despite the fact that almost all insular regions (except for Crete) constitute insular complexes (*archipelagos*), many *small islands* have not really been recipients of development efforts due to their satellite relationship with larger islands and/or mainland areas. The reason is that there is no such *developmental policy* for Greek islands and insular regions. It has been more than a decade now that, a *Special Plan for Coastal - Insular Space* was formulated in the country without being instituted.

Currently, crucial issues of: a) conceptual clarification (i.e. *insular region, small island, insularity, peripherality*), b) research methodology regarding the *insularity phenomenon*, and c) *evaluation* and *typological classification* of islands, remain open at the level of official planning. At the EU level the definition of *island regions* remains also controversial, while the definition of an *island* is not as straight-forward as it seems [8] due to the diversity/differentiation of the EU islands in terms of: a) *size* (area,

---

[1] This category includes: The Azores, Madeira, the Canary Islands, Martinique, Guadeloupe, Reunion, French Guinea (is not an island), Saint-Barthelemy and Saint Martin. Numerous provisions may concern areas such as customs and trade policies, fiscal policy, free zones, agriculture and fisheries, state aid and conditions of access to structural funds [8].

population) as well as building and population density, b) *centrality* of location (geopolitical weight/networking extent), c) *level of development*, which relates to different objectives under the structural funds, d) differences in the *territorial organisation* (network of settlements, land uses), *administrative structure* (system of central/decentralised administration) and *degree of autonomy* of islands and island regions. These are highly critical aspects as they can influence the integration process of *insular regions* (i.e. islands, complexes, regions) into *territorial development policies* and support incentive strategies. At the same time, concepts such as *insularity* and *peripherality* remain rather vague, hindering the prioritisation of interventions and allocation of funding. An equally important hindrance for understanding and addressing the insularity phenomenon is the absence of a holistic, properly documented *methodological approach* in order to assess its multiple dimensions and enable its mapping. Thus, although a fairly extensive and scientifically valid discussion has been elaborated at *theoretical level*, there has been no consensus at the EU level on the principles and guidelines for such a *methodology* to date. As a result, this makes it difficult to resolve issues related to the territorial - social cohesion in insular Member States [10]; while focusing on the Greek case - a top island state worldwide - it is indeed an oxymoron that the above *conceptual - methodological issues* remain unanswered.

In the context of the above discussion, the question arises as to whether, and under what conditions, the *isolation* or *abandonment* of *small islands* can be reversed, and the *smart sustainable development* of their *local communities* can be ensured, being the focus of this work.

2   Research Question and Spatial Reference

Experience has shown that qualitative natural - cultural attributes is the only comparative advantage that *small islands' economies* can have; and specialising in them can be a way out for their development. In this sense, the response to the development of *small islands* could lie in the optimal use of local natural, cultural and human resources [11–13]. However, in a context of intense competition and networking, such an objective can only be achieved through the organic integration of *small islands* into broader spatial, sectoral, and social networks (of a similar or complementary nature) of supralocal/supranational reach. This approach entails the risk that *small islands* may pay the price for their development with environmental degradation and alteration of their *local identity*. Therefore, any attempt to network them with other more powerful islands must be ventured on the basis of *endogenous development*, respecting the *carrying capacity* and *sensitivity* of their ecosystems, and aiming to meet the *real needs* of the local population. How easily can this be achieved in countries with a strongly multi-island character, such as Greece? Given the territorial fragmentation, what mechanisms could avert the abandonment of *smaller islands* and allow them to evolve from *satellites* to *reference hubs* of strong *island entities*? These are questions that cause consideration and division in the absence of a *national insular policy*.

Following the evolution of the Greek *insularity phenomenon*, for realizing its multiplicity and complexity, it becomes clear that the successful integration of *smaller islands* into potential *insular complexes* (network structure) requires thorough knowledge of their problems and prospects. This is where the problem lies.

Given the circumstances, and acknowledging the importance of adopting a rather *polycentric territorial organisation pattern* at the national level, this article seeks to restore the question of island development to public debate, and re-launch the discussion on the role of *small islands*. Recognising that the island dynamics is not always linked to *size* (area, population), *place in the administrative hierarchy* or *power of economic performance* (such as GDP), it is attempted to highlight other equally important *dimensions or criteria* (i.e. geographical, geopolitical, spatio-functional, environmental, socio-economic) from which new *key performance indicators* (KPIs) could emerge. Thus, a more elaborated approach would enable a comprehensive follow up/evaluation of the Greek *insularity phenomenon*. The missing element from the study of islands is a *thematic database* that would allow ongoing update and multiplex correlation of its data. This should be a multifactorial *pool of criteria* to help drawing conclusions about the level of development of islands and the type of risks and challenges they face. This *pool* could be used as a *tool* to: a) assess the current dynamics of (small) islands and their evolutionary trends; b) highlight and rank local needs/priorities; and c) perform a typological classification of (small) islands and determine the type and importance of their spatio-functional networking among them and with the mainland. Therefore, the proposed *pool* could serve as a *policy instrument* for the Greek insular territory based on three main principles: a) equitable consideration of dynamic and less dynamic islands with comparative advantages; b) consolidation of the necessary correlations between continental and island regions; c) establishment of permanent close links between *territorial - maritime planning* and *sectoral policies*.

In this rationale, the article aims at determining *regional criteria*, which could be embedded into this multidimensional *pool of criteria* and used the proposed *methodology* to: a) identify *small islands* and understand their developmental prospects; b) map the immediate and broader space where *small islands* interact (Greek maritime space, (inter) regional spatial entities, six nautical mile zones); and c) *typologically classify* them with a view to highlighting those that could play a key role in potential *insular complexes-poles*. The contribution of the proposal is considered significant, as its broad logic allows to be applied at all spatial levels (national, intra-/(inter-) regional, local) or at special categories of space (e.g. coastal, mountainous) [14]. Setting the Greek maritime space as the spatial level of reference, the interest is placed on *smaller islands*, with an emphasis on the *frontier Aegean islands*. The latter constitute a fragile environment, demonstrating the need for prioritisation and the criticality of establishing specific support strategies at the level of *national insular policy* [1]. Key reasons are: a) the geopolitical weight of the islands; b) the highly fragmented nature of *insular regions* with a vast variety of *islands* and *island complexes* where all types of island economies converge; c) the unfathomable concentration of many small, low-density islands of exceptional natural-cultural value, showing trends of continuous and steady decline in the permanent population, coupled with the development of tourism; d) the coexistence of islands functioning autonomously, or as satellites of adjacent islands, or as parts of broader island groups, or developing relations with neighbouring countries (often stronger than those developing with the mainland of Greece).

3 Research Methodology

The scope of the article is approached by two mutually reinforcing levels of research (A and B) (Fig. 1), aiming at working as a basis to feed the debate as to the identification of *insular complexes* in the Aegean, where *small frontier islands* will play a key role. *Level (A)* deals with the study of the specific characteristics of *island regions* and their management/planning. The focus is on *concepts and typologies* of insular areas as well as *contemporary approaches* for *insular development*. *Level (B)* is dedicated to Greece and it is implemented in two *stages*. Having identified the deficit of a *national insular policy*, the *first stage* aims at formulating a proposal on the assessment of *small islands* based on *regional criteria*, and at *typologically classifying* them in such a manner so that potential *insular entities* in the outermost Aegean area to be highlighted. The *second stage* presents the findings in a way as to re-open the discussion of how these *entities* could act as new *development poles* of national importance, where *small islands* would take on the role of *reference hubs*. More specifically:

- *Phase A* attempts to establish a *pool of assessment criteria*, falling into *seven main themes*, namely: (i) *geographical location*, indicating the islands' centrality/geopolitical significance (central, remote, outermost); (ii) *locus*, highlighting environmental/territorial characteristics (e.g. geomorphology, climate, residential network, density); (iii) *nature - culture*, identifying specificities of high local value (history, cultural heritage, protected areas); (iv) *population* (size, social structure); (v) *local economy and production sectors* (primary, secondary, tertiary, economic specialisation); (vi) *accessibility and networking* (transport/communications networks); and (vii) *services and infrastructures of supralocal reach* (administrative, technical, social). These are deliberately selected and can assess the competitiveness of *small islands* in the national/international arena. The *geographical location* coupled with *locus* features bring out significant specificities for the islands' political/economic weight. The *population size* indicates islands' dynamics, especially when correlated with *locus* and *local economy and production sectors*. A competitiveness criterion is also the existence of high-quality *services and infrastructures of supralocal reach*, especially in the fields of administration, education, health care and culture. *In case of small islands, it is highly important to strengthen their centrality and take on board the criteria of nature - culture and accessibility - networking*. The division of the proposed themes into subsections highlights the qualitative differentiation of the criteria, and showcases their quantitative importance. Selection of criteria has also taken into account their capacity to generate measurement indicators.
- In the *Phase B*, the criteria that fit the scale and specificities of *small frontier islands* are selected from the *pool* emerging in the *first phase*, in order to proceed to their *typological classification*. This is attempted by successively implementing two *investigation procedures*, the results of which are illustrated per successive *phase*. The first *investigation procedure* pertain to the generation of three tables (Tables 1, 2 and 3), in the form of checklists, listing from the selected *pool of criteria* what exists - and what does not exist - on each island, and to what extent. More specifically, Tables 1 and 2 *allow for observations regarding the centrality and*

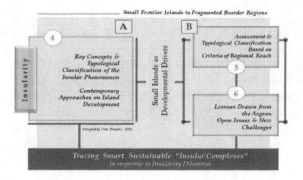

Fig. 1. The Main Levels of Investigation (designed by Yiota Theodora, 2020)

infrastructure of small frontier islands, while Table 3 *illustrates island assessment criteria.* The second *procedure* is implemented in two *stages,* namely: <u>*Assessment A*</u>- assessment of quality criteria; and <u>*Assessment B*</u> - consideration of the quantitative differentiation of qualitative criteria. This *last phase* is concluded with *the identification of potential insular complexes in frontier areas of the Aegean Sea* (Sect. 5).

It should be noted that, in the context of the ongoing investigation: a) in the absence of an official definition of *small island,* the selection criteria are an area of <96 km² and a permanent population of <8,000 inhabitants. In addition, islands must constitute municipalities; b) *frontier islands* are considered to be those bordering another country on at least one side; c) *small islands* were mapped at national level to ensure the follow up of their development prospects in close correlation with their immediate and broader environment. The themes of the maps are in line with the proposed *assessment criteria.* Emphasis is placed on *locus, nature - culture, population, local economy - production sectors* (tourism), and *accessibility - networking*; d) the identification of potential strong *insular complexes* is attempted at the *frontier area* of the Aegean (at the borders with Turkey). In particular, *small frontier islands* of the north-east and southern Aegean *island regions* (the Dodecanese) are selected; and e) official data from national, European and international bodies were used to draw up tables and maps.

4   Insularity and Smart Sustainable Development in an Era of Network Organization

In this section, key *concepts and typological classifications* of insular areas are briefly presented while *contemporary approaches* on island development are highlighted.

4.1   Key Concepts and Typological Classifications of the Insular Phenomenon

At the *theoretical level,* an interesting discussion is developing on whether *islands* are a structural spatial entity for the implementation of regional analysis and policy. The problem is that, thus far case studies have mostly tackled *island states* or *tropical islands* of the oceans and much less *island regions* of the EU. This creates certain gaps in terms of: a) *conceptual definitions - approaches* to anthropological and socio-economic theories regarding the development and sustainability of *islands* and *island regions*; and b) establishment of *methodologies* for research and assessment of their characteristics/problems. Unfortunately, *island regions*, which are under the administration of a largely continental state (most island states of the EU), does not seem so far to have been as elaborated to the extent that it should have been. The same holds true in case of *small islands*, which are missing from census and economic analyses, unless they are considered sufficiently *"large"* to be included in reviews/ inspections of EU regional policy. Such findings are of exceptional importance for Greece as an *island country*.

The literature is rife with *approaches* relating to the *insular phenomenon* and the *typological classification* of island regions. *Island* is defined as any small part of land provided that: a) is surrounded by water (regardless of whether it is in a river, lake or sea); b) has been naturally created; c) protrudes from the surface of the water and is not covered during the tide; and d) it can support housing and economic activity, a condition that could differentiate an *island* from an islet or rocky islet. *Island complex* means a group of *islands* belonging to a single geographical area, without necessarily developing interdependencies. *Island region* implies a large island or a group of islands with similar natural and socio-economic features and problems. At the EU level, Structural and Cohesion Funds Article 52 of EC Regulation No 1083/2006, *islands* are defined as *Island Member States eligible under the cohesion funds and other islands except those on which the capital of a Member State is situated or which have a fixed linked to the mainland* [15]. This definition is based on the following criteria: a) minimum surface area of 1 km^2; b) minimum distance between the *island* and the mainland of 1 km; c) resident population $\geq 50,000$ inhabitants; and d) no fixed link (bridge, tunnel, dyke) between the *island* and the mainland. *Island regions* have been defined by the European Commission as regions in which a substantial part of their population lives on islands or a large fraction or their territory is islands. *Island regions* account for 53 NUTS 3 in the EU, all with different degrees of *insularity*, with some of them completely insular (100% of the region's population lives on islands). In this case the NUTS 3 region can correspond to one *island* (Sicily, Sardinia) or the NUTS 3 is an *archipelago* (e.g. the Greek Archipelago Regions, and the Azores) [8]. Diverse views are also developed on the *typological classification* of *island regions*, highlighting different aspects depending on whether the criteria are physical (area, physical characteristics) or anthropogenic (e.g. population, density, level of development, administrative structure); whether they focus on quantitative or qualitative characteristics; and whether they are simple or complex. Two factors causing problems in the *classification* of *islands* are the: a) almost exclusive use of the area or the population, as the *size* is not always linked to the competitiveness of an *island*; and b) adoption of a single criterion (especially population size). Thus, estimates/classifications using concepts such as *small, large, saturated, developed, dynamic, vulnerable* island raise doubts about their reliability and common understanding, hence the effectiveness of their use in developmental policy-making.

In such circumstances of broader ambiguity, two critical, equally unclear concepts to the monitoring/assessment of the *island phenomenon* are *insularity* and *peripherality*. *Insularity* reflects the degree of isolation of an *island* resulting from its location in relation to the nearest continental land. Its assessment parameters are *distance, intensity* and *size of flows*, and *population distribution* weighted by potential economic capacity. *Peripherality* - one of the most widely used concepts in terms of *island development* - is traditionally related to the: a) *distance* from central developed areas; b) degree of *accessibility*; and c) dynamics of the *collaboration relationships* through developing networks for the flow of goods, people, capital, as well as the level of development of each of these networks and the degree to which they are depended on decisions taken in other more central areas of insular or mainland space. It is usually measured by the average travel time index, i.e. average travel time to a main centre of economic activity of the EU by a means of transport or by a composite indicator derived from economic (per capita GDP) and geographical (distance) indicators [16].

4.2   Development of Islands and Island Regions

Insular areas constitute special *spatial category* due to their particular features, which become reasons for geographical and socio-economic isolation and for increasing inequalities at a local or regional level. These features are also encountered in *spatial entities* within developed areas. However, in *insular areas* their concentration/potency are far greater, particularly in instances of *small/remote islands*. In such vulnerable loci, there are many factors which should be evaluated as part of *developmental policy* and counted during the *planning process*, namely: a) *spatial factors* that concern geographical position and the features of their natural/manmade environment; b) *demographic factors* (e.g. ageing population, limited dynamic, seasonal variation in population); c) *economic factors* linked mainly to supply and demand, high production cost and small market, insufficient work force skills, deficient investments and seasonal activities (e.g. tourism); d) *social factors*, mainly related to insufficient technical/societal infrastructures and services. In fact, every *island*, no matter how small, requires a full set of infrastructures and services, necessary for its development. However much of this might not be justified by its population size. No *island* can depend on the infrastructures of a developed neighbouring area, particularly when said *island* is isolated [1].

In the case of EU, diversity of insular regions sets special conditions. This diversity is mainly expressed through the: a) high concentration of population on a few *islands* and a very large number of less populated *islands*; b) population from 50 to 5,000,000; c) surface from 1 km^2 to over 25,000 km^2; d) distance from the mainland from less than 1 km to 1,450 km (e.g. Azores); e) service sector is pivotal for the development of *islands* especially tourism; f) economic growth capacity of *islands* is usually limited due to the small size of local markets and the distance to larger mainland markets, especially for less populated *islands*; and g) distinct natural and cultural environment [8]. Indubitably, *islands* are exceptionally fragile environments of multi-factorial *peripheralisation*, which renders them vulnerable. The territorial multiple dispersion of *insular territories*, the heterogeneity of their segments (size and dynamics) and the differences in the relationships among them (i.e. kinds, quality, frequency of flows and networks) as well as the extent of their dependence on the continental space, in conjunction with the variety of inherent weaknesses/developmental prospects compose a field where crucial matters that should be dealt with co-exist. *The development of these peculiar insular regions must necessitate a special methodology for research and spatial regulation and allow for the simultaneous approach of general and special matters.*

Various approaches have been set out to address the specificities of the *insular territory* and develop its parts. On a *theoretical level*, the *classical regional development theory* applied to island regions ranges between the dependency principle of the *centre-periphery model* (Myrdal) and the *neoclassical theory of comparative advantage*. In *classical theory*, *island* underdevelopment is interpreted by the predominance of backwash over spread effects. The *neoclassical theory* found fertile ground in the interpretation of the underdevelopment of *small spatial entities*, such as *islands*, whereby the degree of resource scarcity or abundance has ultimately determined their dynamics. In the context of the two theories, the debate on *regional policy* tends to be structured around three positions, namely: a) *top-down* development in the form of centralised policies focusing on the introduction of capital and technology in a region and aiming at the development of infrastructure and investment attraction; b) *endogenous* or *bottom-up* development, based on decentralisation, local decision-making and new job creation, while focusing on leveraging their *competitive advantages*; and c) establishment of strong *networks for cooperation & exchange of experience* among regions with shared problems, in line with the logic of *endogenous development*. At the EU level, the last two positions are supported for the planning of spatial (territorial and maritime) and sectoral (e.g. rural, tourism, environmental, energy, transport) policies, with a view to increasing competitiveness in *declining island regions*, and restructuring the most problematic ones. After 1990, this discussion has been enriched with variations of previous *concepts*, such as *sustainable development* and *smart growth*, which underscore the protection of the natural - cultural environment as well as the use of human resources and new technology [17–22]. Despite weaknesses, the contribution of all views has strengthened the debate through the introduction of critical parameters that need to be considered in the *economic analysis - planning* of *island regions* [23].

5 Evaluation and Typological Classification Based on Criteria of Regional Reach _ the Aegean Small Frontier Islands

Greece is among the countries with the largest number of islands in the world. The multi-island structure coupled with the fragmentation of its *insular regions* make the Greek *insular phenomenon* quite unique. The Greek *islands* belong administratively to four purely *island regions* (three are located in the EU's external borders) and eight continental regions with insular sections (*Kallikrates*, Law 3852/2010). Of the purely *island regions*, the South Aegean (i.e. Cyclades and Dodecanese *archipelagos*) comes first comprising the largest number of *islands*, 34.38% of the total island territories and 26% of the country's total coastline, followed by Crete (12.44%), the Ionian Islands

(9.65%) and the Northern Aegean (4.49%). Of the continental regions, Attica has the largest island Sect. (16.12% of its region), Epirus the smallest (0.04%) and Western Macedonia none at all. According to a synthetic assessment of demographic and socio-economic indicators, Crete and the South Aegean region are the most dynamic *island regions* with a favourable sectoral structure and positive local factors. They are followed by the Ionian Islands and the Northern Aegean regions, which have a weak or unfavourable sectoral structure and negative local factors, with the declining trends having reversed after 2001.The *frontier island regions* of the North and South Aegean (research spatial scope) are characterised by: a) lack of agricultural reorientation with strong trends of sectoral reorganisation and professional specialisation (as per case), b) weaknesses in the secondary and tertiary sectors, tourism monoculture trends, and c) infrastructure deficiencies (productive, technical, social). Specifically for *small islands*, the contacted research identified 32 cases in seven of the country's thirteen regions. Their share in the total Greek insular area and national territory is 6.97% and 1.14%, respectively. Of the 32 *small islands*, 16 belong to *frontier island regions* (i.e. Northern Aegean: 3; South Aegean (Dodecanese): 10; Crete: 1; Ionian Islands: 2) with the 14 of those located in the outermost parts of the Aegean (border with Turkey). (Fig. 2)

In the absence of a reliable system for the *evaluation* and *typological classification* of *island regions* at national level, the aim is to introduce a different dimension to the monitoring and assessment of island dynamics. Emphasis is placed on the correlation of quantitative and qualitative variables based on a multi-dimensional approach which takes into account regional criteria capable of capturing the nature, number and intensity of the islands' relations with each other, and with mainland regions, thereby highlighting the sustainability of their local communities. The proposal, which is theoretically based on the concepts of *polycentric development and network spatial organisation*, consists of a specific scientific approach which, without eliminating quantitative data, or the quantitative dimension of qualitative variables, uses them in a subsequent *phase* to complement the picture resulting from the assessment of the qualitative variables and the way they are combined. The proposal has research interest since it demonstrates in practice that *spatial entities* increasingly take the form of *island combinations* (dipoles, polypoles) rather than autonomous *islands*. This trend necessitates the identification of *hub islands* and their interconnections (*axes-flows*).

To evaluate the dynamics and perform a *typological classification* of *small frontier islands*, subsets of seven proposed criteria sets (Sect. 3) are selected on the basis of their suitability for the scale of these islands. The thematic subsets are: (i) *geographical location*: cross-border character (distance from neighbouring country); (ii) *locus*: area (km^2), number of settlements, density (inhabitants/km^2); (iii) *nature - culture*: historic/remembrance sites, natural-cultural heritage features, protected areas; (iv) *population*: permanent population (1991, 2001, 2011), % population change; (v) *local economy - production sectors*: % change in economic activity by sector (2001–2011), % change in beds (2009–2019); (vi) *accessibility - networking*: Multi-modal Hub (MH: port and airport); (vii) *supralocal services - infrastructure*: in sectors of administration (A), military (M), healthcare (H), education (E), culture (C), and other (o). Three thematic tables are organised to best monitor the process. The islands are presented by *region/ regional unit* (from north to south), and by *size*, starting with the smallest in area. Specifically, Table 1 combines criteria from the thematic of

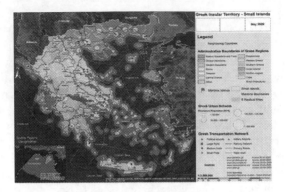

Fig. 2. Greek Insular Territory - Small Islands (Source: Sotiris Piperis, May 2020)

(i) *geographical location*, (ii) *locus*, (iii) *nature-culture*, and (vii) *services - infras-tructures of supralocal reach*; while Table 2 reflects (v) *local economy and production sectors* and (vi) *accessibility -networking* criteria. Both tables provide data on administrative structure, population, area, density (population/area) and urban structure (number of settlements). Table 3 (being a product of a synthesis of Tables 1 and 2) illustrates the *island assessment criteria* divided into *six themes*: (i) *geographical location*, (ii) *locus*, (iii) *nature -culture*, (iv) *population*, (vi) *accessibility - networking*, and (vii) *services and infrastructures of regional reach*. The criteria for *area* (<5, 25–50, 50–96), *population* (500 < 500–1,500, 1,500–3,500, 3,500 >), *density* (20< , 20–50, >50), and *supralocal infrastructures-services* (1–2, 3–4, >5) are divided into cat-egories (Fig. 3).

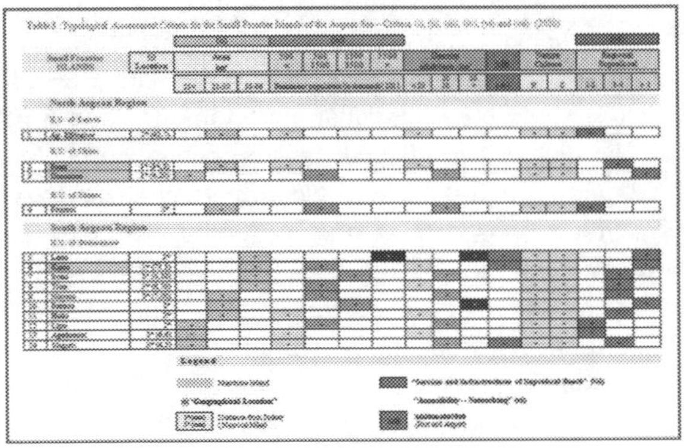

Fig. 3. Typological Assessment Criteria for the Aegean Small Frontier Islands

Because sufficient size is desirable, but it is the hub function of *islands* that is most interesting, the information from Table 3 is evaluated in two *phases*:

- In the *first phase*, emphasis is on the *centrality* of location. Interest is thus basically focused on whether the following three subsets are present: (iii) *nature - culture* (historic/remembrance site, maritime island, quality of natural-cultural heritage), (vi) *accessibility - networking* [(MH), connection with Turkey and neighbouring island of administrative dependence (seat of regional unit/prefecture)], and (vii) *services and infrastructures of supralocal reach*.
- In the *second phase*, the size of the *centrality* is also of interest. Therefore, account is taken of the (iv) *population* sub-groups (500< , 500–1,500, 1,500>), and the quantitative differentiation of the qualitative criteria: (i) *geopolitical location* [distance from Turkey: 1* (max), 2*, 3* (min)], (vi) *accessibility - networking* [(MH), connection with Turkey and frequency of connection to the neighbouring *island* of administrative dependence (seat of regional unit/prefecture): 1–2, 3–5, 6–7 per week), and (vii) number of *services and infrastructures of supralocal reach* (1–2, 3–4, 5>).

The findings drawn from the *assessment* and *typological classification* of the *Aegean small frontier islands* are summarized below in such a way as to re-think their contribution to the creation of new dynamic *insular entities - poles* of supranational reach.

6 Building Sustainable Island Complexes in the Aegean Sea _ The Small Frontier Islands as a Key Factor

The assessment of *small frontier islands* delivered a first impression of their dynamics/perspectives, which was subsequently enriched with their *typological classification*. This has brought to the fore those *islands* that, according to the proposed *criteria*, could serve as *hubs* in the potential *insular entities*. With regard to the developmental impression of the *islands*, the following are noted per criterion:

- They are all *frontier islands*. However, some are more remote due to their location (long distance from Greek mainland, short distance from Turkey) or more isolated [geographical or actual distance (networks and frequency of connections to neighbouring islands)]. This raises issues of security, priorities and perspectives; Ag. Efstratios, Psara, Agathonisi and Lipsi are in a more unfavourable position, whilst Leros (Kalymnos), Halki and Symi (Rhodes) and Oinousses (Chios) in more favourable. Patmos and Megisti, despite their geographic distance from dynamic *islands*, are not considered isolated, due to good transport networking;
- 71.42% of *small islands* have an area <50 km^2. The most remote islands are Oinousses (4th smallest, 18 km^2) Agathonisi (2nd smallest, 14 km^2), Nisyros and Megisti (the smallest, 12 km^2). The islands with the largest area are Leros and Kasos, both multimodal hubs, with negative % change in the primary sector, positive in the tertiary and considerable unemployment rate;
- All islands have a rich natural-cultural heritage on land and at sea (marine archaeology, underwater caves, shipwrecks) and belong to the Natura 2000 network of protected areas. Psara, Kasos and Oinousses are *maritime islands*, i.e. they have a significant maritime history and a strong orientation to the shipping/shipbuilding

sectors. Among remembrance islands are the first two heroic loci and Ag. Efstratios (exile island), while Patmos is well known for its religious character;

- Leros is by far the *island* with the largest population, followed by the smaller (in area) Patmos and Symi islands. The majority of *islands* (78.57%) have population <1500 inhabitants. Ag. Efstratios, Psara, Agathonisi, Halki, Megisti have a population <500 inhabitants. In period '01-'11, 50% of the *islands* demonstrated an increase in permanent population, with the most important noted in Halki and Nisyros. Population decline is observed in five *islands*, with Ag. Efstratios rating first (−12%), followed by Psara and Oinousses (which in period '91-'01 had a spectacular increase of >40%, as did Tilos and Megisti). 85.71% of *islands* are equally divided between the low (<20 inhabitants/ km^2) and medium density (20–50 inhabitants/km^2) categories. Leros (105.56 inhabitants/ km^2), Patmos (67.71 inhabitants/km^2), Lipsi (46.47 inhabitants/km^2), Oinousses (45.89 inhabitants/km^2), Megisti (41.0 inhabitants/km^2), Symi (39.84 inhabitants/ km^2), and Fournoi (31.71 inhabitants/km^2) have the highest density. It is clear that a *density problem* is encountered not only in *islands* with the largest area and population (Leros), but also in the medium-sized i*slands* (25–50 km^2) with a population of 500–1,500 inhabitants (Fournoi, Nisyros), or a population of 1,500–3,500 inhabitants (Patmos), as well as in smaller *islands* (<24 km^2) with a population of 500–1,500 inhabitants (Oinousses, Lipsi), and even in the smallest ones with a population of <500 inhabitants (Megisti). Agathonisi belongs to the category of very small, low density islands (<24 km^2, <500 inhabitants), while among the low density islands (25–50 km^2, 500–1,000 inhabitants) are Tilos and Kasos;
- The highest unemployment rates (>50%) in period '01-'11 were noted in Halki, Psara, Leros, Ag. Efstratios, Kasos and Agathonisi; Oinousses have been an exception (60% reduction in unemployment). The largest % decrease in the primary sector has been recorded in Fournoi, Ag. Efstratios and Patmos, while the largest increase in Megisti and Nisyros. Oinousses and Megisti have a positive % change in the secondary sector, while Psara and Tilos have a negative one. A positive % change in the tertiary sector is seen in Agathonisi, Lipsi, Psara, Symi and Kasos. In the tourism sector (index: % change in beds '09-'19), the largest positive change is found in Psara (46%), Tilos (37%), Halki (16%) and Megisti (9%) and the largest negative in Kasos (−27%);
- Multimodal transport hubs (i.e. port and airport) are Leros, Kasos, and Megisti. The first two belong to the islands with the largest areas, while Megisti to those with the smallest area (<24 km^2). Kasos (a *low-density island*) has the shortest flight duration (Karpathos). All *islands* have heliport to serve in case of an emergency. The best networked *islands* with their neighbouring island of administrative dependence (seat of regional unit/prefecture) are Oinousses (Chios), Leros and Lipsi (Kalymnos) with a daily connection; followed by Symi (Rhodes) and Ag. Efstratios (Limnos) with 5–6 days/week; Psara (Chios), Agathonisi (Kalymnos), Halki/ Megisti (Rhodes) with 2 days/week; and Fournoi (Ikaria) with 1 day/week. Leros, Symi and Megisti have connections to Turkey and Oinousses and Patmos only during the summer. For better assessing islands' networking the following (at a next *stage*) will be studied per *island*: type (direct, transit), spatial reach (local, (inter) regional, national), seasonality, frequency and quality of connections;

- All *islands* have a town hall, while only Patmos and Leros have Healthcare centres of supralocal reach. Oinousses (*Merchant Marine Academy, Maritime Lyceum*) and Patmos (*Patmiada Ecclesiastical School*) have education infrastructure of supralocal reach. The highest concentration of cultural infrastructures is found in Oinousses, Patmos, Leros and Kasos, while only limited is in Ag. Efstratios, Fournoi, Agathonisi and Lipsi.

With regard to the *centrality* and degree of networking of *small frontier islands*, two ranking assessments emerged from the proposed *typological classification*. Islands are noted from north to south. In <u>Assessment A</u>, based on the *qualitative approach* of the proposed criteria (i.e. what exists and what doesn't exist on each island), *small islands* are divided into three categories, namely of: a) *major importance* Ag. Efstratios, Psara, Oinousses, Patmos, Leros, Symi, Megisti, b) *medium importance* Nisyros, Halki, Kasos, c) *minor importance* Fournoi, Agathonisi, Lipsi, Tilos. The ranking changes when *population* and the *quantitative differentiation* of the *quality criteria* are taken into consideration in <u>Assessment B</u>. Thus, the following categories of *small islands* emerge: a) *national/interregional reach* Patmos, Leros and Symi (>1,500 inhabitants, infrastructures >5), b) *regional reach* Oinousses, Fournoi, Nisyros, Tilos, Kasos (500–1,500 inhabitants, infrastructures 3–4), and c) *local reach* Ag. Efstratios, Psara, Agathonisi, Lipsi, Halki, Megisti (<500 inhabitants, infrastructures 1–2) (Fig. 4).

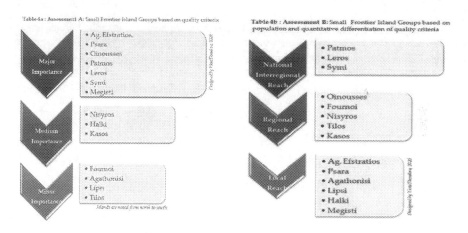

Fig. 4. SmallAegean Frontier Island Groups from the Typological Classification

In an effort to compare the results of the two rankings, it becomes evident that when the *population size* is taken into account, changes in the ranking may emerge, confirming the dominance of the *"largest" small islands*. However, the dynamics of an *island* is not necessarily related to the *size* of its population or area [(Leros, Oinousses (MH, infrastructure >5)], but rather to its *density* [Kasos (MH, infrastructure >5), Megisti (MH, infrastructure >3)] coupled with *accessibility and networking* (Oinousses, Megisti < 24 km² and MH) and the existence of *supralocal infrastructure* [(Leros

(>5), Patmos (>5), Oinousses (>5)]. Therefore, the value of this proposal is more relevant for *small islands* belonging to the middle and small categories of area and population, for which the results regarding their importance are different, due to their natural and cultural wealth, good networking and the existence of infrastructures of supralocal reach (Oinousses, Megisti).

Concluding the search trail, *small frontier islands* that are particularly dynamic and could the first to play a key role in the formation of dynamic *insular complexes* in the Aegean (from north to south) are Oinousses, Psara, Patmos, Leros, Tilos, Symi and Halki. By strengthening their already strong networking with the neighbouring large and *smaller islands* of the broader region, they could act as a catalyst for the creation of three powerful *potential networks*, thus helping to reduce inter-regional disparities and strengthen Greece's position globally. Through the networking of *larger/smaller islands* as part of an overall *insular policy*, three new dynamic *developmental complexes-poles* could arise, namely: (I) Chios - Oinousses - Psara; (II) Patmos - Leros -Kalimnos - Kos; and (III) Rhodes - Simi - Halki - Tilos. To determine the nature and role of these new *entities* at a national level, it would be necessary to be investigated at lower levels of *planning* in order to set up the appropriate *research - demarcation methodology*. Steps are taken to this direction and initial results are expected shortly.

References

1. Theodora, Y.: Aegean sea - challenges and dilemmas in management and planning for local development in fragmented insular regions. Heritage **2**(3), 1762–1784 (2019). https://doi.org/10.3390/heritage2030108. Accessed 08 Apr 2020
2. Stratigea, A., Leka, A., Nicolaides, C.: Small and medium-sized cities and insular communities in the mediterranean: coping with sustainability challenges in the smart city context. In: Stratigea, A., Kyriakides, E., Nicolaides, C. (eds.) Smart Cities in the Mediterranean. PI, pp. 3–29. Springer, Cham (2017). https://doi.org/10.1007/978-3-319-54558-5_1
3. Gaetano, A.: Manifesto for European islands: a proposal from the insular regions intergroup of the European committee of regions. In: The European Committee of the Regions 1994–2019, December 2019
4. Greenhill, L.: Maritime spatial planning for islands. draft workshop briefing paper, European Commission, European MSP Platform (2018)
5. Coccossis, H.: Sustainable development, landscape conservation and tourism in the small islands of Greece. In: Dieterich, M., van der Straaten, J. (eds.) Cultural Landscapes and land Uses, pp. 1–12. Kluwer Academic Publishers, Netherlands (2003)
6. Council Regulation (EC) No 247/2006 of 30 January 2006 laying down specific measures for agriculture in the outermost regions of the Union (2006)
7. Council Regulation (EC) No 615/2008 of 23 June 2008 amending Regulation (EC) No 1405/2006 laying down specific measures for agriculture in favour of the smaller Aegean islands and amending Regulation (EC) No 1782/2003 establishing common rules for direct support schemes under the common agricultural policy and establishing certain support schemes for farmers (2008)
8. Freitas, T.: Environmental sustainability of EU islands. In: Briefing Library, Library of the European Parliament 2010/06/07 (2010)

9. Lierop, C.: Towards a renewed territorial agenda for the EU. In EPRS/European Parliament Research Service, PE649.355-March (2020)
10. Spilanis, J.: European Island and Political Cohesion. Gutenberg Publications, Athens (2012). ISBN 978-960-01-1544-4. (in Greek)
11. Theodora, Y.: Cultural heritage as a means for local development in mediterranean historic cities - the need for an urban policy. Heritage 3(2), 152–175 (2020). https://doi.org/10.3390/heritage3020010. Accessed 08 Apr 2020
12. Argyropoulos, V., Stratigea, A.: Linking WWI and II underwater cultural heritage to sustainable development in the mediterranean: an integrated participatory strategic planning approach. In: International Conference in Management of Accessible Underwater, Cultural and Natural Heritage Sites: Dive in Blue Growth, 16–18 October, Athens, Greece (2019). Accessed 05 Dec 2019
13. Koutsi, D., Stratigea, A.: Unburying hidden land and maritime cultural potential of small islands in the mediterranean for tracking heritage - led local development paths - case study Leros-Greece. Heritage 2(1), 938–966 (2019). https://doi.org/10.3390/heritage2010062. Accessed 06 Nov 2019
14. Theodora, Y., Loukakis, P.: Typology of Greek cities on spatial criteria of regional gravity. Aeihoros, University of Thessaly, Volos, Greece, vol. 7, pp. 128–157, (2007). (in Greek)
15. Council Regulation (EC) No 1083/2006 laying down general provisions on the European Regional Development Fund, the European Social Fund and the Cohesion Fund and repealing regulation (EE) No. 1260/1999 (2006)
16. Dommen, E., Philippe H., (eds.): States, Microstates, and islands. Croom Helm Ltd. Pub., Kent (1985)
17. Theodora, Y.: Knowledge as a parameter in the theories of spatial development; Scientific Volume in honor of Professor Emeritus P. Loukakis, pp. 241–285, Gutenberg Publications, Athens (2009). ISBN 978-960-87470-1-2. (in Greek)
18. Scholaert, Fr., Margaras, V., Pape, M., Wilson, A., Kloecker, C.A.: The blue economy. overview and EU framework. In-Depth Analysis. In: EPRS/European parliament Research Service, PE646. 152-January (2020)
19. Territorial Agenda 2030: A future for all places (Draft Version, Dec 2019) (2019). www.territorialagenda.eu. Accessed 08 Apr 2020
20. Islands Commission of the CPMR: The Final Declaration adopted by its members. In: 36th Annual General Meeting, 19–20 May, Rhodes, South Aegean, Greece (2016)
21. Eskelinen, H.: Peripheries in a network economy. In: Proceedings of the European Summer Institute in Regional Science: European Integration and Peripheral Areas, Spetses Island, Greece (1995)
22. Kyvelou, S.: From Spatial Planning to Spatial Management: The Concepts of Strategic Spatial Planning and Territorial Cohesion in Europe. KRITIKI Publications, Athens (2010). ISBN 978-960-218-671-8. (in Greek)
23. Interreg Mediterranean Blue Islands. https://blueislands.interreg-med.eu/. Accessed 08 Apr 2020

Reticular Systems to Identify Aggregation and Attraction Potentials in Island Contexts. The Case Study of Sardinia (Italy)

Chiara Garau$^{(\boxtimes)}$ ⓘ, Giulia Desogus ⓘ, Federica Banchiero ⓘ,
and Pasquale Mistretta ⓘ

Department of Civil and Environmental
Engineering and Architecture (DICAAR),
University of Cagliari, 09129 Cagliari, Italy
cgarau@unica.it

Abstract. The purpose of the article is to evaluate territorial hierarchies, internal to an island context, through the theory of central places. To this end, the authors want to demonstrate how some key points of these theories are still relevant all the more if applied to geographically closed contexts, such as an island. Starting from these premises, this paper begins with a literature revision on the most important theories on central places with particular reference to the theories closest to contemporary world. Therefore, the authors study the attraction and aggregation potential of the Sardinian case study, defined by the most suitable localization theories for studying island contexts. This allowed not only to study the analysis of flows through a territorial-hierarchical model, under the theoretical assumptions of the Central Places Theories (CPTs), but also to develop a model and a reticular system on several levels, starting from the population data. This paper shows a first phase of a wider research and provides a bibliographic framework to understand how the theories of central places are still suitable for studying a closed system like an island.

Keywords: Central Places Theories · Reticular system · Analysis of flows · Territorial-hierarchical model · Smart island · Sardinia

1 Introduction

Nowadays, the urbanization process is increasing significantly, by changing the size and the spatial distribution of population in cities and, for that reason, outlining a clear distinction between major and minor polarities [1], in which the irregular development of the territory is evident especially in geographically closed contexts such as islands. In fact, the islands are characterized by an irregular urban structure that presents in the coastal areas the hubs of major urban, economic and social development and the

---

This paper is the result of the joint work of the authors. In particular, paragraphs 3, and 4 have been jointly written by all authors. Giulia Desogus has written paragraph 1. Chiara Garau has written paragraph 2. Pasquale Mistretta has written paragraph 5.

© Springer Nature Switzerland AG 2020
O. Gervasi et al. (Eds.): ICCSA 2020, LNCS 12255, pp. 294–308, 2020.
https://doi.org/10.1007/978-3-030-58820-5_23

centers with the least progress in the internal areas. This topic related to the study of the central theories has a long history and among the different models that have attempted to describe the evolution of an urban structure, that one of Christaller [2–5] (with the appropriate precautions in relation to the contemporaneity of tools and of data analysis) remains the most authoritative one. The authors therefore considered appropriate to conduct a comparative study of the evolution of central places theories, starting from the theoretical apparatus, to then deepen the analysis on island contexts, where, for obvious geomorphological reasons, the problem appears more evident. In this regard, before tackling the aforementioned historical excursus, it is fundamental to understand what is meant by an insular context. The European Union defines an island as a system surrounded by the sea which must be "a minimum surface of 1 km^2, a minimum distance between the island and the mainland of 1 km, a resident population of more than 50 inhabitants, no fixed link (for example, a bridge, a tunnel, or a dyke) between the island(s) and the mainland" [6]. This identifies the island with a precise border within which there is its own geographical and urban structure. This typicality leads to reasoning on two issues that by definition are common to all the islands. The first issue concerns the structural problems typical of an island context [7, 8]. As the European Union argues, all island regions have the problem of insularity facing much greater difficulties in achieving an average level of socio-economic development in the European Union [8–11]. The second issue concerns the lack of homogeneity between coastal and inland areas, even more evident in an island context [12–14], especially in those contexts in which (as in Sicily and Sardinia for Italy) the same islands are considered for their development, comparable as extension to non-island regions.

These aspects of insularity are strongly linked not only to the functionality of urban settlements, but also to their interconnections within the island and to the urban effect derived from the concentration and location of activities in the area.

These reasons lead the authors to reflect on smart governance capable of balancing this closed system, with problems related to insularity and lack of place-based homogeneity. In particular, the authors consider those contexts within the islands, subject to a gravitational dynamic with respect to the different (large, medium and small) centralities, by identifying as internal areas "a network of municipalities or groups of municipalities [...] around which gravitate areas characterized by different levels of the spatial periphery" [15: 1].

The central places theory (CPT) with its subsequent evolutions and proper integrations will be presented in the following paragraph and it appears to be the most significant theory to analyze this, because the theme of island development, especially in terms of smart urban planning in a regional geographical area, must be developed through synthesis of organizational mechanisms between major cities, suburbs, inland areas and rural areas [16, 17]. Subsequently, the theoretical apparatus will be applied to the island context of Sardinia (Italy). Sardinia appears to be a significant case study, because its geographic extension and conformation allows the territory to be divided into subsystems with which the large gap between inland and coastal areas can be analyzed.

This research makes possible to identify urban strategic polarities not only for having a new and widespread awareness of the internal areas of the island contexts, but also for developing and better planning a complete framework, by considering all multipolar interconnections of the considered island.

2 State of the Art on Regional and Urban Growth: Central Places Theories and its Evolution

The central places theories (CPTs) appear to be applied in its beginnings, mainly to economic geography and, although they were applied to contexts far from the contemporary, it seems useful to make a historical excursus to trace the theories still applicable and effective today. Over the course of time, these theories have dealt with how territorial features changed, analyzing in detail how territorial imbalances are produced as a result of central hubs [18].

The most important and pioneering theoretical insights about the central places theories - aimed at an analysis of urban systems with correlations on regional growth - were provided by Weber (1909) with his classical theory of industrial location [19]; by Christaller [20] with its theory of central places; by Zipf with his rank-size rule [21].

The basic element constituted by Christaller's theory considers the city (in its tertiary function as producer of service goods) as the central point of the territory and it influences its nearby cities and the number of inhabitants distributed in the territory. The areas of influence, associated with the tertiary functions, overlap each other, creating interrelated regions (nodal regions) determining urban systems consisting of agglomerations and dominant centers or dominated areas, through the so-called hubs formation [18]. This is defined by Christaller as a hierarchical process, in which there is an automatic association between the urban center and the area of influence from the center. Lösch [22] took Christaller's empirical observations more systemically and regionally, but his model was based on industrial production (Christaller's system was based on the production of services).

However, Christaller's and Lösch's models did not address three very important issues: (a) an analysis on the consumer demand side was not present; (b) the function of costs in relation to location was not considered and, for this reason, they did not consider the cost of urban land and the spatial variability of the price and productivity of the productive factors; (c) the different productions were aggregated on the territory without an interdependence mechanism on the side of possible complementarity effects in the demand, and on that of possible input - output links in the offer. In a nutshell, in the founders' formulation, the model of central locations creates, from an analytical point of view, a hierarchy of cities without cities, where the city appears to be a concentration of residential activities, a large labor market and an efficient way of organizing of social production.

Around the 1950s, numerous applications around the world began, starting from an approach on territorial hierarchies of the input-output type [23–26] to the problem of planning transport, the use of gravitational models.

In the sixties, Izard published Methods of Regional Analysis which represents a fundamental text for probabilistic analysis at regional level. After him a large production of urban models developed. The most important contributions are Wingo [27], Alonso [28] and Lowry [29]. They dealt with the problem by following the line of probabilistic techniques thanks not only to statistics and mathematical theories, but also to the concept of entropy and related complex models.

Richardson, in 1975 [30], conducts spatial analyses following the kinetic theory of gases on the line of probabilistic techniques and on the concept of entropy and lays the theoretical foundations for representing reality through complex models.

The seventies also saw the evolution of management models to represent the territory. he first multi-objective and multi-criteria models are due to Van Delft and Nijkamp [31]. The analogy with the structure of a regional or urban economy also lies in the diversification of the products. The variety of a regional context can be "considered as a strategy to protect regional income from sudden sector-specific asymmetric shocks" [32, p. 53].

As suggested by Philip McCann and Frank van Oort [33], the main concept behind these premises is that urban and regional growth, manifested as innovations, propagates from a main hub of growth (or a main city) to nearby towns and cities of a lower order. Innovations, knowledge and know-how once generated in a particular central location should propagate across regions from one location to neighbors. However, this leads to two possible spillovers associated with growth pole theory: backward connections and forward connections. The first effects are associated with services into the cities that provide input to urban activities, attracting people in the main hub. The second ones are related to urban activities that use the results of new activities, or expand existing activities. However, this can lead to unexpected effects, such as when the growth pole attracts so much people and cumulative growth that it drains the surrounding areas. This therefore leads to a further polarization of urban growth, limiting growth elsewhere [34]. More recently, this theoretical framework has been applied in different studies of urban and regional growth [35, 36]; of agglomeration and innovation [37] and of employment growth and resilience [38].

These studies therefore argue that there is an urban product cycle concept in which urban activities are more easily developed in different metropolitan areas (the main hubs) with a diversified industrial structure and a diversified skills base, while in the end the mature urban activities or products are decentralized towards the hinterland or the peripheral areas (the secondary hubs).

However, the authors consider essential to insert an additional factor that reads and interprets the development of the urban systems (and their internal hierarchization) through the analysis of the (migratory, permanent, commuting, etc.) flows between the various towns or cities (or hubs) of the urban system itself. Each town (city) or hub is characterized by its own attraction potential which expresses the proximity of the population of that city to that ones of the other centers of the entire urban system.

These factors, together with the identification of the territorial hierarchies, can still constitute a key interpretative efficacy of the analysis of urban systems, obviously with operational and scientific tools suitable for the contemporary.

In fact, the territorial-hierarchical phenomenon, topic that has been widely studied, can interpret (and therefore predict) the spatial distribution and size of the main hubs that constitute the urban system, aimed at regional and territorial growth. However, the territorial-hierarchical model does not take into consideration the evolution (or involution) of the intermediate centers [39]. This phenomenon analyzes the trends of main urban aggregates where the structure of the territory itself is organized through diversified specializations according to variable hierarchies. There is no single focal hub, but different hubs that spread, thanks also to the multidirectional movement of goods and people.

The theoretical set of flow analysis and the necessary adjustment of the line linked to the identification of territorial-hierarchical model lead the authors to a new methodological and empirical hypothesis of the Central Place Theories, applied to the context under study in Sardinia. All this with the awareness that in recent decades, the digital revolution made great strides leading to the cancellation of space, distances, a space-time dissociation with consequences on lifestyle, work, etc., which can also be transferred to the city, upsetting traditional policies and consolidated hierarchies.

3 The CPTs with the Territorial-Hierarchical Model Applied in Sardinia (Italy): The First Step in Empirical Research

The review of the literature has revealed a significant consideration linked to CPTs integrated with the analysis of flows and territorial-hierarchical model for reading and controlling the gravitation phenomenon. In fact, it can be useful to strategic planning for proposing balanced scenarios between compatibility and diseconomies in the organization of the system and in the functions that the urbanized area can develop.

In particular, CTPs with the territorial-hierarchical model allows a reading of the territory through nuclei of different entities. From their aggregation, they form a reticular distribution capable, on the one hand, of analyzing the attraction potential of each individual nucleus and, on the other, of highlighting the aggregation potential of the different nuclei.

From the literature review and from the following analyzes, the authors conceive the aggregation potential as the capacity of several centers (strong, medium or small) to associate. This association is given not only by geographic, infrastructural (proximity, few impediments, mobility, etc.) and economic factors (primary and secondary services, work, etc.) but also by social ones (culture, language or dialects, etc.). The attraction potential, however, is established by the attractive force of a hub (almost always a strong urban cores) which, through tangible elements (roads, transport, rental of services, etc.) and intangible ones (governance, social policy, etc.) dynamics.) attracts a smaller center, which in turn, connected with the strong urban cores, can attract even smaller centers. This chain effect is what allows to revitalize the internal areas of an island.

Indeed, this is particularly important for island contexts because, both the attraction and aggregation potential, are bound by a specific limit that allows a specific study of the territory. The analysis of flows for obtaining an analysis of a reticular system will be applied in the context under study in the following paragraph.

With these premises, the authors want to understand if it is possible to give an urban response to the gaps that exist between the different hubs of the island contexts considering the attraction and aggregation of the nuclei of a particularly emblematic context, such as the island of Sardinia. In addition, Sardinia is not only an island system, but it is also particularly emblematic as a case study for three reasons.

The first is to be a Mediterranean island: Sardinia is at the center of the Mediterranean Basin [40] and, with an area of 23,813 km^2, it is also one of the largest islands in the area of the same basin. This allows to have common characteristics with other Mediterranean islands and therefore to be able to replicate the study.

The second reason is to be a particularly sensitive context. In the European programming 2014–2020 [41: 4–35], Sardinia belongs (together with Abruzzo and Molise) to the Italian regions with great difficulty in economic and social development.

The third motivation concerns the geography of places. The Sardinia region is inside the National Strategy for the Italian internal Areas (NSIA, in Italian: *Strategia Nazionale per le Aree Interne Italiana*—SNAI). In NSIA, the peculiarities of the territory are seen as a fundamental potential to contrast the phenomenon of depopulation and promote the economic and social development [42, 43]. In addition, SNAI describes the Italian territories not only with a strong gap between inland and coastal areas, but also with a polycentric articulation that allows the territory to be divided into historical subsystems (large, medium, small urban systems; and internal areas). To obtain the nuclei and their potential of attraction and aggregation, the authors first consider the historical regions of Sardinia and the Regional Landscape Plan (RLP) that allow a first schematic of the area (Fig. 1).

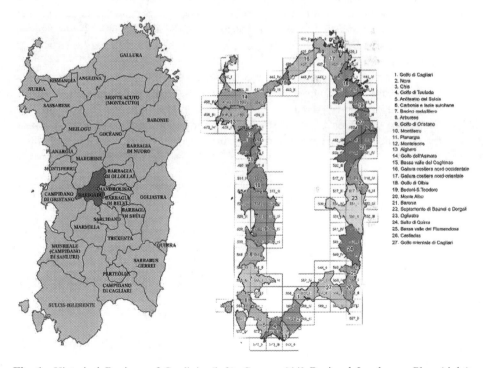

Fig. 1. Historical Regions of Sardinia (left). Source: [44] Regional Landscape Plan (right). Source: [45]

The Historical Regions of Sardinia are territorial groupings defined in 1952 which divided the island into administrative districts deriving from the Kingdom of Sardinia [46, 47] and the Regional Landscape Plan (RLP) is the legislative framework in Sardinia which guides and coordinates planning and sustainable development of the island in the coastal areas [48].

In other words, Historical Regions are a first aggregation of the territory which represent the functional dependencies between municipalities, so the strength with which municipalities attract [43]. As mentioned above, the RLP (Regional Landscape Plan) coordinates and plans sustainable development only on the coasts of the island. In fact, the RLP protects and enhances only the territories bordering the sea which by their nature are stronger in terms of economy, demography and services.

These two planning tools allow to think about the aggregation and attraction of the Municipalities of Sardinia. In fact, the Historical Regions summarize the aggregation potential between Municipalities, still valid today, and the RLP shows which are the centers of greatest attraction.

The main component analysis highlighted by Garau et al. [49] shows how the homogeneity of the groupings and the territorial-hierarchy in Sardinia are still directly deriving from the Sardinian historical regions, underlining the concept of their potential aggregation.

Instead, the RLP defines the coastal areas that are the most economically developed and those with the greatest number of services, namely, those areas that have a greater attraction force than the inland areas. Considering these factors, the authors analyze the relationships existing between different nuclei of Sardinia to have a general framework of development on a territorial scale.

Table 1 shows the different aggregations and centers of attraction through the CPTs with the territorial-hierarchical model, applied through the study of Historical Regions and the RLP. Subsequently, for each aggregation, the population is analyzed with Istat 2020 data [50]. These data are subsequently inserted in Fig. 2 and Fig. 3, where respectively a) the attraction centers and b) the attraction centers with the municipalities attracted appear.

Table 1. Aggregations, attraction hubs and population

Aggregations	Attraction centers	N° Municipalities attracted to each attraction center	Population divided into centers of attraction	Total population involved in the aggregations
Aggregation 1	Cagliari + Metropolitan area	49	539,095	600,305
	Isili	16	22,555	
	Senorbì-Muravera	18	38,655	
Aggregation 2	Iglesias-Carbonia	14	104,346	185,160
	Sanluri	24	80,814	
Aggregation 3	Lanusei-Tortolì	19	48,816	48,816
Aggregation 4	Olbia	23	138,293	175,936
	Siniscola	8	37,643	

(*continued*)

Table 1. (*continued*)

Aggregations	Attraction centers	N° Municipalities attracted to each attraction center	Population divided into centers of attraction	Total population involved in the aggregations
Aggregation 5	Sassari	16	238,601	282,223
	Ozieri	4	43,622	
Aggregation 6	Oristano	8	134,423	171,088
	Macomer-Bosa	20	36,665	
Aggregation 7	Nuoro	16	85,975	102,875
	Sorgono	12	16,900	

The analysis of the data (Table 1 and Figs. 2 and 3) shows seven aggregations given by the study of both the Historical Regions and the RLP. The seven aggregations (Table 1 first column), derive from the choice of 18 centers of attraction (Fig. 3, Table 1 second column) which historically perform mainly administrative functions defined by being provincial capitals or intermediate reference offices between the inner territory and the coastlines.

The municipalities attracted (Fig. 3, Table 1 third column) are the smaller centers which are geographically and economically connected to the centers of attraction.

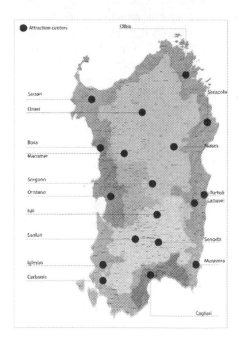

Fig. 2. Attraction centers - Leading municipalities

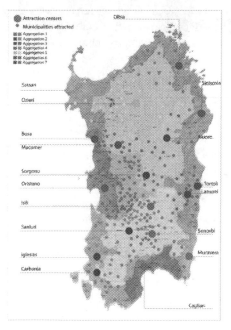

Fig. 3. Centers of attraction with the municipalities attracted

The number of municipalities attracted therefore depends on social dynamics that have strengthened over time through the construction of mobility networks, shared primary and secondary services, commuting and daily commuting. It is therefore clear that a center of attraction with a strong social impact for the whole island (for example Cagliari which attracts 49 surrounding municipalities) attracts more municipalities than a center which has a lesser impact than the regional system (for example Olbia which attracts 23 municipalities). Subsequently, the population was first divided into attraction centers (Table 1 column 4) and then total by aggregations (Table 1 column 5), to understand what the effective aggregating force is for each pole. This study was carried out for all 377 municipalities in Sardinia, however only 247 municipalities strongly attracted to attraction centers were taken into consideration. The 130 remaining municipalities, which will be treated in subsequent analyzes, are the border areas between aggregations, namely, those that are connected marginally with two or more aggregation centers.

4   Results on the Sardinian Reticular System Through the CPTs with the Flows Analysis and the Territorial-Hierarchical Model

The study conducted analysed the Territorial-hierarchical Model applied in Sardinia, highlighting, through the population variable, how the municipalities of the island have different social aggregations that distinguish today's urban structure. This paragraph wants to weigh these aggregations to insert them in different attraction levels through the CPTs analysis, the analysis of flows and Territorial-hierarchical Model. Indeed, confirming the authors' choice to take urban cores from the historically main centers, the analysis of the aggregations shows an organic system composed of the set of subsystems identified by the population that is able to achieve adequate territorial development conditions through strong nuclei of attraction. To achieve this goal, the CPTs with the territorial-hierarchical model is used with the analysis of flows. In fact, the different territorial hierarchies of the aggregations create a reticular system of the territory that allows the comparison between coastal centers and inland areas. On the basis of a bibliographic research on intra-regional aggregations [51–54], that the authors have not included in this article for space reasons, the territory was divided into different attraction/aggregation levels (Table 2).

Table 2 shows the hierarchy of the aggregations described above (Table 1). These aggregations do not all have the same weight in the regional system because the aggregation centers, that compose them, have a different level of attraction. For example, aggregation 4 composed of Olbia which attracts 23 municipalities (Strong Urban Core: intensity 2) and Siniscola which attracts 8 municipalities (Medium Urban Core: intensity 1) has a greater weight than aggregation 2 with Iglesias -Carbonia which attracts 14 municipalities (Medium Urban Core: intensity 1) and Sanluri which attracts 24 municipalities (Medium Urban Core: intensity 2). This is because the centers of attraction within the aggregation have lower attraction intensities. In addition, the 23 municipalities attracted to Olbia with a resident population of 138,293 inhabitants. are

Table 2. Aggregations, Attraction centers, Levels

Aggregations	Attraction centers	Levels
Aggregation 1	Cagliari + Area metropolitana	Strong Urban Core: intensity 1
	Isili	Medium Urban Core: intensity 1
	Senorbì-Muravera	Medium Urban Core: intensity 2
Aggregation 2	Iglesias-Carbonia	Medium Urban Core: intensity 1
	Sanluri	Medium Urban Core: intensity 2
Aggregation 3	Lanusei-Tortolì	Medium Urban Core: intensity 2
Aggregation 4	Olbia	Strong Urban Core: intensity 2
	Siniscola	Medium Urban Core: intensity 1
Aggregation 5	Sassari	Strong Urban Core: intensity 2
	Ozieri	Medium Urban Core: intensity 1
Aggregation 6	Oristano	Strong Urban Core: intensity 3
	Macomer-Bosa	Medium Urban Core: intensity 2
Aggregation 7	Nuoro	Strong Urban Core: intensity 3
	Sorgono	Medium Urban Core: intensity 1

much more significant than the 24 municipalities attracted to Sanluri which have a resident population of only 80,814 inhabitants.

Consequently, the levels shown in Table 2 are decisive not only by the number of municipalities attracted but also by the number of resident population.

In some aggregations, the leading municipalities are more than one so both the number of leading municipalities and the total population is greater than the average of the level to which they belong. For example, Senorbì-Muravera have a total of 18 towed municipalities and a total population of 38,655 inhab. Instead, Isili alone has 16 attracted municipalities and a population of 22,555 inhab.

Figure 4 shows these aggregations and the reticular system, allowing to have a reading of the territory from the coastal areas to the internal areas with the main key points of aggregation and attraction. In addition, Fig. 4 shows the analysis of the flows or the movement of the population from one municipality to another for work and study reasons.

Figure 4 shows 7 aggregations (red lines), each of which inside has municipalities with different levels of attraction (red and green circles). The black lines show the attraction that these municipalities exercise in the surrounding municipalities deduced from the analysis of flows, the population that attracts each individual center and urban hierarchization.

A strong centralization is visible on Cagliari, Olbia, Sassari and Oristano and subsequently on Nuoro which, although it has a minimum number of attracted municipalities, joins and involves a part of Sardinia that would otherwise be isolated and free of exchanges between municipalities.

This analysis shows that the Sardinian island system is strongly centered on the coastal areas and that the permeability between coastal and inner areas is still difficult. In this context, in fact, action should be taken on the potential of the resources located,

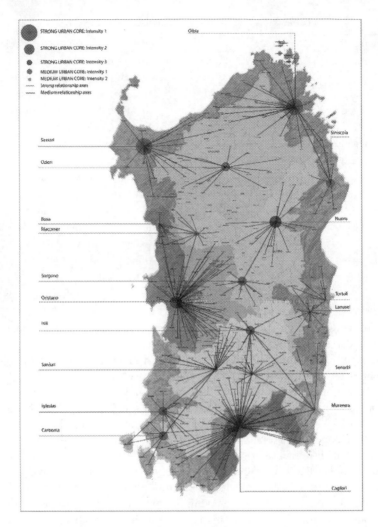

Fig. 4. Aggregations map (Color figure online)

on the daily trips that take place for study or work reasons and on the degree of employment that a municipality can offer.

5   Conclusions and Developments on Future Research

Starting from the theoretical assumptions of the CPTs, the research first outlines a territorial hierarchical model applied to Sardinia. Subsequently, through this model we study a reticular system that expands throughout the region. This is analyzed through the population variable that allows to study the analysis of flows to form a territorial-hierarchical model, repeatable in other contexts.

The proposed research therefore outlines a socio-territorial framework through the attraction and aggregation potential determined through two theories of central places based on flows analysis and the territorial-hierarchical model. This has led to the development of a reticular system that has made possible to understand both the dynamics existing between coastal areas and inland areas (Figs. 2 and 3). In addition, it was possible to delineate how these aggregated areas below certain levels can be a springboard for a most important economic and social system by concentrating the effects on an area of semicircular attraction, considering that the other half falls on the sea (Fig. 4). In addition, the assessment of the scenarios, which open up to the development of Sardinia in this article, is correlated with the consistency of the population of the entire island and the structural balance between the various geographical/economic areas. The results of the research, therefore, highlight a system formed by centers of attraction at different levels of attraction in the island system, and by common attractions that must be compared with the strongest centralities.

These analyzes would allow local politics to confirm or modify the settlement structures and the typology of services to be spread in the territory and to evaluate the size and typology of the propulsive places in the whole island to decide on the actions to be taken for the functional organization of the regional system. The main goal is to identify the main hubs in order to direct regional strategies in a targeted way towards smart urbanism [55, 56].

In other words, these aggregations (Fig. 4) can allow to evaluate important changes in the redistribution of primary activities and also the smaller municipalities can develop attractive affects to add to those that already characterize the centers of strong attraction described in this paper. Only with the analysis of the flows and with the construction of a hierarchical territorial model, which lead to the examination of direct effects on the regional reality, it was possible to measure the real size of the areas of gravitation and, therefore, to reason on the influence they exert towards other nearby cities and those further away with reference to growth and the effects, positive or negative, on development. Aggregations between strong urban hubs and medium urban hubs and their direct and indirect effects are important for the study and analysis of a closed system, such as islands. This is particularly important because in island contexts, which by their nature have a limited number of centers, the relationships between them must be strategically defined to allow for a homogeneous development between coastal and inland centers.

However, it is important to underline that, in order to have a complete framework on the urban dimension and on the articulation in the territory of the whole island, the data on the population must be crossed with those on mobility, geography, services and commuting, as determining and preparatory factors for intervening on the reorganization of the production system and on the interlocution between the internal and the coastal areas. This study allowed to make an initial reasoning for two types of future studies: 1) the possibility, through these aggregations, to study other sectors, for example to analyze tourism or cultural heritage for each aggregation would allow to have a much broader picture of the same aggregations; 2) the same analysis could be replicated not only on island contexts but also on non-island territories where the territorial hierarchy could go beyond the region.

Acknowledgments. This study was supported by the project "Urban Polarities in the Cities of Newcastle (UK) and Cagliari (Italy) for monitoring the central and attractive effects of the city-territory", founded by the programme "Bando 2019 Mobilità Giovani Ricercatori (MGR)", financed by the Autonomous Region of Sardinia (under the Regional Law of 7 August 2007, n. 7 "Promotion of Scientific Research and Technological Innovation in Sardinia"). This study was also supported by the MIUR (Ministry of Education, Universities and Research [Italy]) through a project entitled WEAKI TRANSIT: WEAK-demand areas Innovative TRANsport Shared services for Italian Towns (Project protocol: 20174ARRHT_004; CUP Code: F74I19001290001), financed with the PRIN 2017 (Research Projects of National Relevance) programme. We authorize the MIUR to reproduce and distribute reprints for Governmental purposes, notwithstanding any copyright notations thereon. Any opinions, findings and conclusions or recommendations expressed in this material are those of the authors, and do not necessarily reflect the views of the MIUR.

References

1. ONU World Urbanization Prospects. World Urbanization Prospects: The 2018 Revision (2018). https://population.un.org/wup/Publications/Files/WUP2018-KeyFacts.pdf
2. Berry, B.J.I., Baskin, C.W., Christaller, W.: Central places in Southern Germany. Econ. Geogr. **43**, 275–276 (1967). https://doi.org/10.2307/143299
3. Getis, A., Getis, J.: Christaller's central place. Theory J. Geog. (1966). https://doi.org/10.1080/00221346608982415
4. Van Meeteren. M., Poorthuis, A.: Christaller and "big data": recalibrating central place theory via the geoweb. Urban Geogr. **39**, 122–148 (2018). https://doi.org/10.1080/02723638.2017.1298017
5. Brown, S.: Christaller knew my father: recycling central place theory. J. Macromarket. **15**, 60–72 (1995). https://doi.org/10.1177/027614679501500107
6. Eurostat. https://ec.europa.eu/eurostat/statisticsexplained/index.php?title=Territorial_typologies_manual__island_regions#Classes_for_the_typology_and_their_conditions
7. Garau, C., Desogus, G.: A preliminary survey fora smart framework for the island contexts. In: 2nd IFAU International Forum on Architecture and Urbanism, pp. 596–703. Gangemi Editore, Italia (2018). ISBN 9788849236675
8. Access to European Union Law. Gazzetta ufficiale Comunità Europee (2000/C268/09) (2018). https://eur-lex.europa.eu/legal-content/IT/TXT/?uri=OJ%3AC%3A2000%3A268%3ATOC
9. Territories with specific geographical features. https://ec.europa.eu/regional_policy/sources/docgener/work/2009_02_geographical.pdf
10. Analysis of the island regions and outermost regions of the European Union. https://ec.europa.eu/regional_policy/sources/docgener/studies/pdf/ilesrup/islands_part1_summary_en.pdf
11. Territorial typologies manual - island regions. https://ec.europa.eu/eurostat/statistics-explained/index.php?title=Territorial_typologies_manual__island_regions#Classes_for_the_typology_and_their_conditions
12. Novembre, C.: Le aree interne della sicilia tra problemi di sviluppo e ricomposizione territorial. Riv. Geogr. Ital. **122**, 235–253 (2015). ISSN 0035-6697
13. Andriotis, K.: Researching the development gap between the hinterland and the coast evidence from the island of Crete. Tour. Manag. **27**, 629–639 (2006). https://doi.org/10.1016/j.tourman.2005.02.005

14. Core, B.: Spatial dynamics of Mediterranean coastal regions. J. Coast. Conserv. **5**, 105–112 (1999). https://doi.org/10.1007/BF02802747
15. Internal Areas: Which Territories Are We Talking About? Explanatory Note on the Method of Classifying Areas. http://old2018.agenziacoesione.gov.it/opencms/export/sites/dps/it/documentazione/Aree_interne/Nota_metodologica_Aree_interne.pdf
16. Mulligan, G.F., Partridge, M.D., Carruthers, J.I.: Central place theory and its reemergence in regional science. Ann. Reg. Sci. **48**, 405–431 (2012). https://doi.org/10.1007/s00168-011-0496-7
17. Doran, D., Fox, A.: Operationalizing central place and central flow theory with mobile phone data. Annal. Data Sci. **3**, 1–24 (2015). https://doi.org/10.1007/s40745-015-0066-4
18. Scandurra, E.: Tecniche urbanistiche per la pianificazione del territorio. Editore Città Studi, Milano (1992)
19. Weber, A.: Theory of the Location of Industries, Chicago. Chicago University Press, Chicago (1909)
20. Christaller, W.: Central Places in Southern Germany. Prentice Hall, Englewood Cliffs (1933). Trans. C.W. Baskin, repr. 1966
21. Zipf deepened and applied the rank-size rule with appropriate weightings in 1949. Previously it was discovered by Auerbach in 1913 and subsequently modified and refined by Lotka in 1924. Zipf identifies a regularity of behavior in the distribution of the centers of a system, but "does not recognize an automatic association between the development of service activities and the demographic dimension of the center" (Scandurra, 1992; p. 69). In summary, in its simplest formulation, it provides statistical growth methods, where the urban centers of an area have a population inversely proportional to the position they occupy in a decreasing ranking by population: thus, the second city by number of inhabitants it should have a population equal to half that of the most populous city; the third city, a population equal to a third and so on. In these terms, the rule actually finds a very partial application, and therefore attempts have been made to make it more realistic by introducing forms of weighting of values
22. Lösch, A.: The Economics of Location. Yale University Press, New Haven (1954)
23. Harris, C.D.: The nature of cities and urban geography in the last half century. Urban Geogr. **18**, 15–35 (1997). https://doi.org/10.2747/0272-3638.18.1.15
24. Smailes, A.E.: The Geography of Towns. Aldine, Chicago (1966)
25. Brush, J.E.: The hierarchy of central places in southwestern wisconsin. Geogr. Rev. **43**, 380–402 (1953). https://doi.org/10.2307/211754
26. Isard, W.: Location and Space-economy. A General Theory Relating to Industrial Location, Market Areas, Land Use. Trade and Urban Structure. MIT Press, Cambridge (1956)
27. Wingo Jr, L..: Transportation and Urban Land, Resources for the Future. D.C., Washington (1961)
28. Alonso, W.: Location and Land Use. Harvard University Press, Cambridge (1964)
29. Lowry, I.S.: A Model of Metropolis. Rand Corporation, Santa Monica (1964)
30. Richardson, H.W.: Discontinuous densities, urban spatial structure and growth: a new approach. Land Econ. **51**, 305–315 (1975). https://doi.org/10.2307/3144948
31. Van Delft, A., Nijkamp, P.: A multi-objective decision model for regional development, environmental quality control and industrial land use. Pap. Reg. Sci. Assoc. **36**, 35–57 (1976). https://doi.org/10.1007/BF01944374
32. Torre, A., Wallet, F. (eds.): Regional Development and Proximity Relations. Edward Elgar Publishing, Cheltenham (2014)
33. McCann, P., Van Oort, F.: Theories of agglomeration and regional economic growth: a historical review. In: Handbook of Regional Growth and Development Theories. Edward Elgar Publishing (2019)

34. Richardson, H.W.: Regional and Urban Economics. Dryden Press, Hinsdale (1978)
35. Hewings, G.J.: Regional Industrial Analysis and Development. Routledge, Kondon (2017)
36. Galster, G.: Why shrinking cities are not mirror images of growing cities: a research agenda of six testable propositions. Urban Aff. Rev. 55(1), 355–372 (2019)
37. Carlino, G., Kerr, W.R.: Agglomeration and innovation. In: Duranton, G., Henderson, J.V., Strange, W.C. (eds) Handbook of Regional and Urban Economics, pp. 349–404. Elsevier, Amsterdam (2015). https://doi.org/10.3386/w20367
38. Eriksson, R., Hane-Weijman, E.: How do regional economies respond to crises? The geography of job creation and destruction in Sweden (1990–2010). Eur. Urban Reg. Stud. 24, 87–103 (2017). https://doi.org/10.1177/0969776415604016
39. Indovina, E.: La metropolizzazione del territorio Nuove gerarchie territoriali. Economia e società regionale, 3–4 (2003)
40. European Atlas of the Seas. https://ec.europa.eu/maritimeaffairs/atlas_en
41. European Structural and Investment Funds Regulations 2014–2020 (2015). https://ec.europa.eu/regional_policy/en/information/legislation/regulations/
42. State of Implementation of the Public Preliminary Investigation State-Regions/Autonomous Provinces.   http://old2018.agenziacoesione.gov.it/it/arint/Stato_di_attuazione/stato_di_attuazione.html
43. Autonomous Region of Sardinia, Resolution n. 6/13 of 10.2.2015. http://www.regione.sardegna.it/documenti/1_274_20150211164206.pdf
44. La mia Sardegna. https://www.lamiasardegna.it/sardegna-regioni.htm
45. Regione Autonoma della Sardegna. Sardegna Territorio. http://www.sardegnaterritorio.it/j/v/1123?s=6&v=9&c=7426&na=1&n=10
46. Baldacci, O.: La casa rurale in Sardegna. Olschki, Firenze (2012)
47. Gulli, L.: Pasquale Mistretta. Storia e attualità di un percorso critic. Documenti di urbanistica. CUEC, Cagliari (2011)
48. Garau, C., Pavan, V.: Regional cultural heritage: new vision for preservation in Sardinia (Italy). J. Landscape Stud. 3, 127–138 (2010)
49. Garau, C., Desogus, D., Coni, M.: Fostering and planning a smart governance strategy for evaluating the urban polarities of the Sardinian Island (Italy). Sustainability 11, 4962 (2019). https://doi.org/10.3390/su11184962
50. Statistiche Istat. http://dati.istat.it/
51. AA.VV: Agriregionieuropa (2013). https://iris.unito.it/retrieve/handle/2318/141401/23224/agriregionieuropa_n34.pdf#page=102
52. Forte, P.: Aggregazioni Pubbliche locali. Franco Angeli, Milano (2011)
53. Lupo, S.: Tra centro e periferia. Sui modi dell'aggregazione politica nel Mezzogiorno contemporaneo. Meridiana 2, 13–50 (1988)
54. Brunetta, G., Morandi, C.: Polarità commerciali e trasformazioni territoriali. Un approccio interregionale. Alinea, Firenze (2009)
55. Azzari, M., Garau, C., Nesi, P., Paolucci, M., Zamperlin, P.: Smart city governance strategies to better move towards a smart urbanism. In: Gervasi, O., et al. (eds.) ICCSA 2018. LNCS, vol. 10962, pp. 639–653. Springer, Cham (2018). https://doi.org/10.1007/978-3-319-95168-3_43
56. Dembski, F., Wössner, U., Letzgus, M., Ruddat, M., Yamu, C.: Urban digital twins for smart cities and citizens: the case study of Herrenberg, Germany. Sustainability 12(6), 2307 (2020)

Structural and Thermal Retrofitting of Masonry Walls: The Case of a School in Vittoria (RG)

Flavio Stochino$^{(\boxtimes)}$ ⓘ, Mauro Sassu ⓘ, and Fausto Mistretta ⓘ

Department of Civil, Environmental Engineering and Architecture,
University of Cagliari, 09123 Cagliari, Italy
fstochino@unica.it

Abstract. Sustainability awareness of buildings life-cycle represents one of the most important engineering challenge. This is more important in developed country like Italy in which buildings age and importance can be huge. Consequently, the whole life-cycle of constructions should be analyzed and assessed during the design of retrofitting interventions. This works reports on the application of an integrated approach to evaluate structural and thermal retrofitting strategies for masonry walls. Ecological (equivalent CO_2) and economic costs of each examined retrofitting solution are evaluated and compared. In this way the structural and thermal capacity of the masonry walls is represented by an iso-cost mapping. The environmental demand considering both thermal and seismic load of the construction site is represented by an equivalent function that is used to find the optimal retrofitting solution for each considered cost.

In this case study the masonry walls of a school located in Vittoria (RG - Italy) are considered. Six retrofitting techniques are described and the comparison between ecological and economical cost allowed to highlight the characteristics of the different interventions and the best retrofitting strategy.

Keywords: Masonry · Retrofitting · CO_2 equivalent · Structural engineering

1 Introduction

Masonry constructions represents a large part of traditional European buildings. Most of them were built in absence of seismic codes and thermal requirements. For this reason, the needs of integrated retrofitting interventions to fulfill current standards requirements is often patent.

In addition, the sustainability awareness of buildings life cycle has grown in the last years and re-use of construction demolition waste is becoming a common approach to reduce the construction environmental impact [1–3]. It is then necessary to design the retrofitting, considering how much energy will be spent for the refurbishment and how much the thermal and structural performance of the construction will be changed.

The literature devoted to structural retrofitting is wide. A general approach to this theme is presented in [4]. In the latter paper the problem of associating a cost to each different retrofitting procedure is discussed with a cost-benefit analysis to compare alternative choices in order to optimize the refurbishments.

© Springer Nature Switzerland AG 2020
O. Gervasi et al. (Eds.): ICCSA 2020, LNCS 12255, pp. 309–320, 2020.
https://doi.org/10.1007/978-3-030-58820-5_24

Surface treatment of masonry panels represents a quite common retrofitting technique: reinforced plaster [5], ferrocement [6], and shotcrete sprayed [7, 8].

An interesting evolution of this set of techniques is the application of Fiber Reinforced Polymers FRP nets on the masonry wall [9–12]. A recent trend is the use of Fiber Reinforced Cementitious Matrix (FRCM), for example: basalt textile coupled to different inorganic matrices see [13].

Also grout and epoxy injection represent an interesting retrofitting method. With this approach it is possible to restore the original integrity of the cracked or damaged masonry wall, see [14, 15].

Finally, external reinforcements represent useful retrofitting techniques for masonry: steel plates, tubes, grids are directly applied to the masonry to improve the lateral in and out of plane resistance of the wall. The introduction of horizontal connectors (diaton) to avoid masonry walls out-of-plane displacements [16–18].

The whole set of interventions aimed at reducing its energy needs can defined as "energy retrofitting". In this paper the focus is on the improvement of the thermal insulation of masonry buildings. A State-of-Art review for the energy retrofitting methods applied to existing buildings can be found in [19]. The improvement of thermal insulation and waterproofing properties of masonry walls is described in [20, 21]. Examples of masonry walls with high thermal insulation properties are in [22, 23].

Building thermal performances are strictly linked to sustainability considerations. Indeed, the construction sector is responsible for a significant part of the primary energy consumption and for a large part of the greenhouse gas (GHG) emissions all over the world, see [24, 25].

Sustainable refurbishment of existing buildings is promoted by the political strategies of several European countries. Actually, it is often required by political decision makers to consider the seismic and the energetic demands in a given area with a multicriteria analysis. The aim is to take into account both structural and energy needs of building in an integrated way. Unfortunately, there is not an international standard method for this kind of analysis.

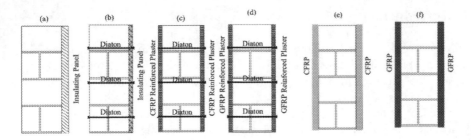

Fig. 1. Retrofitting strategies.

The authors recently published a proposal [26, 27] for a synthetic performance parameter considering both structural and thermal issues. Calvi et al. [28] presented the idea of a common indicator for both structural and energy performances with a cost/benefit analysis characterizing different retrofitting strategies.

Instead, this works reports on the application to a real case study of the integrated approach to evaluate structural and thermal retrofitting strategies for masonry walls introduced in [27]. Ecological (equivalent CO_2) and economic costs of each examined retrofitting solution are evaluated and compared. In this way, the structural and thermal capacity of the masonry walls is represented by an iso-cost mapping. The environmental demand, considering both thermal and seismic load of the construction site, is represented by an equivalent function to find the optimal retrofitting solution for each considered cost.

The paper is organized as follows: the retrofitting scenarios are discussed in Sect. 2. The iso-cost capacity curves are calculated in Sect. 3. Section 4 presents local demands and a design criterion. The main results are in Sect. 5 and finally, in Sect. 6, some conclusive remarks are drawn.

2 Retrofitting Strategies

In order to explain the proposed method a set of six emblematic retrofitting scenarios are presented in Fig. 1. Intervention (a) consists in applying single insulating polystyrene panel, characterized by a thermal conductance $\lambda = 0.04$ W/mK, on traditional plaster through adhesive glue. Clearly, it does not increase the strength, while it strongly improves the thermal performance. In case (b), both thermal resistance and structural strength have been improved using a polystyrene panel with lime plaster and transverse steel connectors (diaton). Intervention (c) is characterized by the application to both side of the wall panel of a CFRP (Carbon Fiber Reinforced Polymers) reinforced plaster, thermal conductance $\lambda = 0.08$ W/mK. Transverse connectors are present also in this case. The CFRP is characterized by a tensile strength f_{fRp} equal to 2.8 GPa and an elastic modulus E_{frp} of 350 GPa. Similarly, a GFRP (Glass Fiber Reinforced Polymers) reinforced plaster is applied to both side of the wall panel in addition to transverse connectors in case (d). The GFRP characteristics are: tensile strength f_{fRp} equal to 1.0 GPa and elastic modulus E_{frp} equal to 45 GPa. Finally, a net of CFRP and GFRP is respectively applied on both sides of the wall panel in case (e) and (f). In these last cases, thermal resistance is not appreciably increased due to the lack of any insulation layer, thus only the structural resistance is enhanced.

Table 1. Existing masonry characteristics, $f_{M,k}$ is the compressive strength, τ_0 is the shear strength, E is the longitudinal elastic modulus, G is the shear elastic modulus, λ is the thermal conductance.

E [N/mm^2]	$f_{M,k}$ [N/mm^2]	τ_0 [N/mm^2]	λ [W/mK]
2000	4.9	0.07	1.4

3 Capacity Iso-Cost Curves

The relative variation of a generic performance parameter ΔC is defined by the ratio of the performance variation between its value before (C_0) and after the retrofitting (C_1) and the initial value C_0:

$$\Delta C = (C_1 - C_0)/C_0 \tag{1}$$

Thus, for each wall panel is possible to calculate the relative increment of structural resistance referring to bending moment ΔM:

$$\Delta M = (M_1 - M_0)/M_0 \tag{2}$$

or shear force ΔV:

$$\Delta V = (V_1 - V_0)/V_0 \tag{3}$$

and the relative variation in the thermal resistance ΔR obtained after retrofitting:

$$\Delta R = (R_1 - R_0)/R_0 \tag{4}$$

In the following, the variation of ΔM, ΔV and ΔR is considered for a single 1×1 m wall panel. The masonry characteristics adopted for the numerical analysis are presented in Table 1. These are the characteristics of the emblematic case study of the school in Vittoria (Ragusa – Italy) made of 70 cm thick stone blocks.

The resistant bending moment of FRP retrofitted masonry is calculated by the methods presented in [29]. The equilibrium conditions of the wall cross sections yield to the definition of the neutral axis and of bending moment capacity. The shear force strength V of the wall panel is assessed following the methods presented in [30]. Considering the contribution of the masonry and of the possible FRP reinforcement, the resistant shear value is obtained considering an equivalent truss approach: more details can be found in [27].

Thermal insulation resistance has been assessed by a layer-wise approach:

$$R = \sum s_i/\lambda_i \tag{5}$$

where λ_i and s_i are the thermal conductance and the thickness of the i-th layer of the panel, see [31].

Table 2. Adopted materials costs.

Material	Spec. ecological cost	Spec. economic cost
CFRP web	77700 kgCO$_2$/m^3	650000 €/m^3
GFRP web	520 kgCO$_2$/m^3	344000 €/m^3
Polystirene panel	138 kgCO$_2$/m^3	1517 €/m^3
Diatons	0.25 kgCO$_2$/m^2	80 €/m^2
CFRP reinf. plaster	1096 kgCO$_2$/m^3	17133 €/m^3
GFRP reinf. plaster	734 kgCO$_2$/m^3	10767 €/m^3

The thickness of the retrofitting layers strongly modifies the economic cost of the six interventions. In order to obtain a general economic cost relationship between ΔM and ΔR, six different cost varying between 100 €/m^2 and 350 €/m^2 have been taken into account. In the construction cost both supply and manpower have been considered, see Table 2. These values have been obtained from the Italian public works market. In this way, six points define each cost scenario. These points represent retrofitting conditions in which the economic cost is the same. Then, a hyperbolic regression curve has been found to fit these data, see Fig. 2:

$$\Delta R(\alpha_1 - \Delta M) = \alpha_0 \tag{6}$$

where the numerical parameters (α_0, α_1) are determined by least squares approach.

The cost regression lines have been found for the ΔR - ΔV plane, see Fig. 3. As expected, CFRP reinforced plaster retrofitting scenario (c) obtained the best structural performance while scenario (a) yields to the most effective thermal performance.

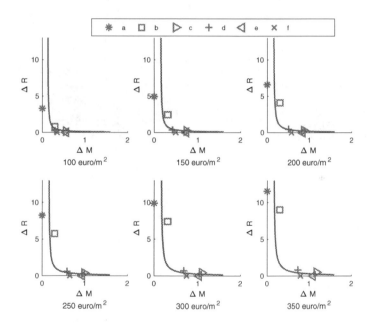

Fig. 2. Capacity regression functions ΔR - ΔM corresponding to six different budgets per square meter for the six retrofitting scenarios (a–f).

Now, it is interesting to see the problem no longer from an economic cost but from an ecological one. Given that carbon footprint can be defined as the total set of greenhouse gas emissions during the life cycle of a building, the ecological cost of each retrofitting intervention can be expressed as equivalent kg of CO_2 necessary for constructing the single 1×1 m masonry panel. Clearly, this computation does not assess the life cycle carbon footprint of a complete building, but it is focused only on the masonry component and the construction stage. The detailed kg CO_2 equivalent is reported in Table 2 and has been taken from [32–34].

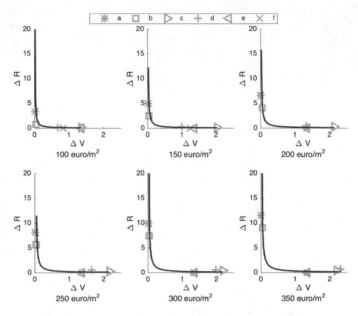

Fig. 3. Capacity regression functions ΔR - ΔV corresponding to six different budgets per square meter for the six retrofitting scenarios (a–f).

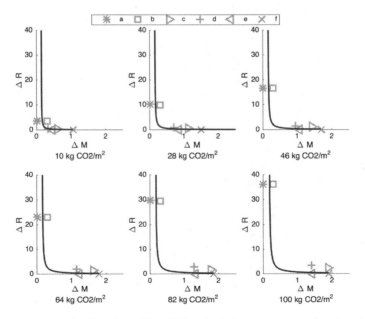

Fig. 4. Capacity regression functions ΔR - ΔM for six different scenarios of Carbon footprint in terms of CO_2 equivalent for the six retrofitting scenarios (a–f).

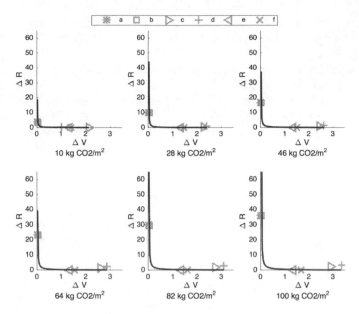

Fig. 5. Capacity regression functions ΔR - ΔV for six different scenarios of Carbon footprint in terms of CO_2 equivalent for the six retrofitting scenarios (a–f).

In this way, a set of hyperbolic regression curves, see Eq. (6) has been calculated for six scenarios characterized by a fixed mass of CO_2 equivalent. Figure 4 presents the ΔR - ΔM results and Fig. 5 the ΔR - ΔV one.

Figures 2, 3, 4 and 5 presents the iso-cost performance curves as an integrated capacity measure for the retrofitting interventions.

4   Local Demands

The retrofitting performance analysis should be based on the specific site of the building location. Indeed, there are zones in which the seismic risk is critical in comparison to the thermal conditions and vice versa. Considering the Italian example, the seismic demand is commonly expressed throughout the peak ground acceleration (PGA), see [35]. Furthermore, the thermal demand is measured throughout the Degree Day (DD) [36]

$$c_R = PGA_i/PGA_M \tag{7}$$

$$c_U = DD_i/DD_M \tag{8}$$

where PGA_M denotes the maximum PGA of Italy and PGA_i represents the peak ground acceleration for the considered i-th location of the building. Similarly, DD_M is the maximum Degree Day value for the same area and DD_i is the corresponding value for the considered i-th location.

c_R and c_U represent the "weights" of the structural and energy demands in that area. Italy is divided into 107 districts, assigning conventionally to each of them the values of PGA_i and DD_i.

In this work the assumed location is Vittoria (RG) in Sicily with c_R equal to 0.368 and c_u equal to 0.187.

A possible criterion to infer both thermal and structural demands for the design of masonry panel retrofitting intervention is represented by Eqs. (9, 10) considering respectively the ΔR - ΔM performance plane and the ΔR - ΔV plane.

$$\Delta R = \alpha\, c_R/c_U \Delta M \tag{9}$$

$$\Delta R = \alpha\, c_R/c_U \Delta V \tag{10}$$

Where α is a tuning parameter that can be assigned by the political decision-makers. Indeed, modifying α, it is possible to encourage thermal retrofitting interventions or structural ones.

5   Results

Based on the above-mentioned location (Vittoria, Ragusa) the criterions expressed in Eqs. (9, 10) and the economic (Figs. 6, 7) or ecological (Figs. 8, 9) cost regression line can be plot on the ΔR - ΔM plane or on the ΔR - ΔV plane. These Figures represent a synthetic way to evaluate the integrated retrofitting. Each crossing between a retrofitting criterion (Eqs. (9, 10)) and a cost regression curve represents an optimal retrofitting solution.

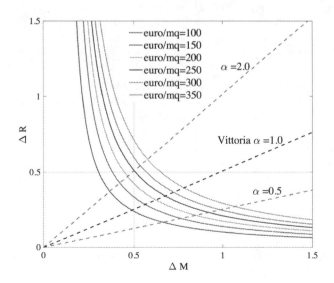

Fig. 6. Retrofitting strategy considering economic costs for plane ΔR - ΔM.

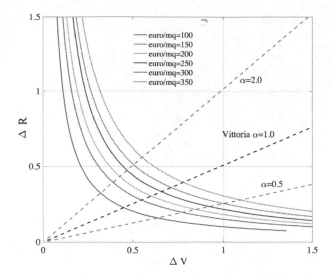

Fig. 7. Retrofitting strategy considering economic costs for plane ΔR - ΔV.

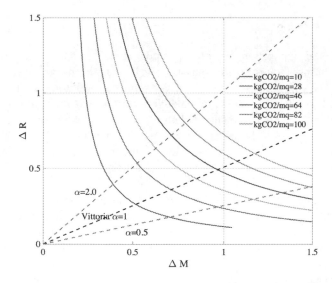

Fig. 8. Retrofitting strategy considering ecologic costs for plane ΔR - ΔM.

It is interesting to highlight that varying the α parameter (the so called "political parameter") it is possible to modify the results of the above described optimization of the retrofitting interventions, to fulfil different political strategies.

It is also important to underline that Figs. 6, 7, 8 and 9 can compare the ecological and economic cost of the same performance improvement. For example, in the given case an improvement of $\Delta R = \Delta R = 0.5$ corresponds to 300 €/m^2 and in an equivalent way to 26 kgCO$_2$/m^2. This information can be of primary importance to plan a sustainable retrofitting of urban areas and infrastructures.

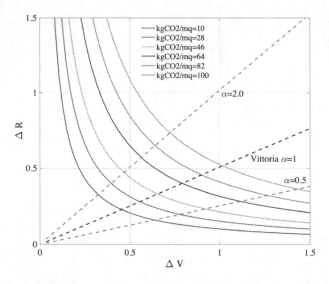

Fig. 9. Retrofitting strategy considering ecologic costs for plane ΔR - ΔV.

6   Conclusions

In this paper the application of an integrated approach to evaluate structural and thermal retrofitting strategies for masonry walls has been presented. Ecological (equivalent CO_2) and economic costs of each examined retrofitting solution have been evaluated and compared. Six representative retrofitting interventions have been parameterized by the improvement of thermal resistance, bending moment and the shear structural strength. The economic and ecological costs of the retrofitting have been evaluated to map the capacity of the retrofitting interventions in the structural and thermal framework. The local site demand has been accounted with specific parameters based on the seismic and the thermal characteristics of the zone.

The main results presented by Figs. 6, 7, 8 and 9 are a synthetic view of the possible alternative masonry building retrofitting strategies. In this way given a fixed cost (economic or ecological) it is possible to find the best solution.

Thus, in order to establish an urban redevelopment plan, this approach can give to the political decision makers an effective and synthetic view to manage both economic and environmental aspects. Indeed, the retrofitting strategy can be extended to the territorial scale similarly to what has been done for the thermal case in China [37].

Further developments of this approach are expected considering other constructive components. Indeed, an extension of this approach to existing concrete and steel frames (see [38, 39]) can be useful and effective.

Funding Statement. The support of the Autonomous Region of Sardinia under grant P.O.R. SARDEGNA 2014–2020, CCI: 2014 - IT05SFOP021, Project: Retrofitting, rehabilitation and requalification of the historical cultural architectural 506 heritage (R3-PAS), and of ReLuis DPC – Department of Civil Protection, project: ReLUIS-DPC 2019-2021 -WP5 – Rapid, low-impact and integrated retrofit interventions are acknowledged.

References

1. López Gayarre, F., Suárez González, J., Blanco Viñuela, R., López-Colina Pérez, C., Serrano López, M.A.: Use of recycled mixed aggregates in floor blocks manufacturing. J. Clean. Prod. **167**, 713–722 (2018)
2. Francesconi, L., Pani, L., Stochino, F.: Punching shear strength of reinforced recycled concrete slabs. Constr. Build. Mater. **127**, 248–263 (2016)
3. Sassu, M., Giresini, L., Bonannini, E., Puppio, M.L.: On the use of vibro-compressed units with bio-natural aggregate. Buildings **6**(3), 40 (2016)
4. Calvi, G.M.: Choices and criteria for seismic strengthening. J. Earthquake Eng. **17**, 769–802 (2013)
5. Yardim, Y., Lalaj, O.: Shear strengthening of unreinforced masonry wall with different fiber reinforced mortar jacketing. Constr. Build. Mater. **102**, 149–154 (2016)
6. El-Diasity, M., Okail, H., Kamal, O., Said, M.: Structural performance of confined masonry walls retrofitted using ferrocement and GFRP under in-plane cyclic loading. Eng. Struct. **94**, 54–69 (2015)
7. Shabdin, M., Attari, N.K.A., Zargaran, M.: Experimental study on seismic behavior of Un-Reinforced Masonry (URM) brick walls strengthened with shotcrete. Bull. Earthq. Eng. **16**(9), 3931–3956 (2018). https://doi.org/10.1007/s10518-018-0340-x
8. Lin, Y., Lawley, D., Wotherspoon, L., Ingham, J.M.: Out-of-plane testing of unreinforced masonry walls strengthened using ECC shotcrete. Structures **7**, 33–42 (2016)
9. Malena, M., Focacci, F., Carloni, C., De Felice, G.: The effect of the shape of the cohesive material law on the stress transfer at the FRP-masonry interface. Compos. Part B Eng. **110**, 368–380 (2017)
10. Ramirez, R., Maljaee, H., Ghiassi, B., Lourenço, P.B., Oliveira, D.V.: Bond behavior degradation between FRP and masonry under aggressive environmental conditions. Mech. Adv. Mater. Struct. **26**, 6–14 (2018)
11. D'Altri, A.M., Carloni, C., de Miranda, S., Castellazzi, G.: Numerical modeling of FRP strips bonded to a masonry substrate. Compos. Struct. **200**, 420–433 (2018)
12. Oskouei, A.V., Jafari, A., Bazli, M., Ghahri, R.: Effect of different retrofitting techniques on in-plane behavior of masonry wallettes. Constr. Build. Mater. **169**, 578–590 (2018)
13. Barducci, S., Alecci, V., De Stefano, M., Misseri, G., Rovero, L., Stipo, G.: Experimental and analytical investigations on bond behavior of Basalt-FRCM systems. J. Compos. Constr. **24**(1), 04019055 (2020)
14. Wang, M., et al.: In-plane cyclic tests of seismic retrofits of rubble-stone masonry walls. Bull. Earthq. Eng. **16**(5), 1941–1959 (2017). https://doi.org/10.1007/s10518-017-0262-z
15. Al-Jaberi, Z., Myers, J.J., El Gawady, M.A.: Out-of-plane flexural behavior of reinforced masonry walls strengthened with near-surface-mounted fiber-reinforced polymer. ACI Struct. J. **115**(4), 997–1010 (2018)
16. Solarino, F., Oliveira, D., Giresini, L.: Wall-to-horizontal diaphragm connections in historical buildings: a state-of-the-art review. Eng. Struct. **199**, 109559 (2019)
17. Giresini, L., Solarino, F., Paganelli, O., Oliveira, D.V., Froli, M.: One-sided rocking analysis of corner mechanisms in masonry structures: Influence of geometry, energy dissipation, boundary conditions. Soil Dyn. Earthq. Eng. **123**, 357–370 (2019)
18. Casapulla, C., Giresini, L., Argiento, L.U., Maione, A.: Non-linear static and dynamic analysis of rocking masonry corners using rigid macro-block modelling. Int. J. Struct. Stabil. Dyn. **19**(11), 1950137 (2019)
19. Ma, Z., Cooper, P., Daly, D., Ledo, L.: Existing building retrofits: methodology and state-of-the-art. Energy Build. **55**, 889–902 (2012)

20. Al-Homoud, M.S.: Performance characteristics and practical applications of common building thermal insulation materials. Build. Environ. **40**, 353–366 (2005)
21. Jelle, B.P.: Traditional, state-of-the-art and future thermal building insulation materials and solutions—properties, requirements and possibilities. Energy Build. **43**, 2549–2563 (2011)
22. Al-Jabri, K.S., Hago, A.W., Al-Nuaimi, A.S., Al-Saidy, A.H.: Concrete blocks for thermal insulation in hot climate. Cement Concr. Res. **35**, 1472–1479 (2005)
23. Lin, M.W., Berman, J.B., Khoshbakht, M., Feickert, C.A., Abatan, A.O.: Modeling of moisture migration in an FRP reinforced masonry structure. Build. Environ. **41**(5), 646–656 (2006)
24. Lanza, C.: A stochastic formulation to assess building performances in terms of environmental impact. Ph.D. thesis (2018)
25. Börjesson, P., Gustavsson, L.: Greenhouse gas balances in building construction: wood versus concrete from life-cycle and forest land-use perspectives. Energy Policy **28**(9), 575–588 (2000)
26. Sassu, M., Stochino, F., Mistretta, F.: Assessment method for combined structural and energy retrofitting in masonry buildings. Buildings **7**(3), 71 (2017)
27. Mistretta, F., Stochino, F., Sassu, M.: Structural and thermal retrofitting of masonry walls: An integrated cost-analysis approach for the Italian context. Build. Environ. **155**, 127–136 (2019)
28. Calvi, G.M., Sousa, L., Ruggeri, C.: Energy efficiency and seismic resilience: a common approach. In: Gardoni, P., LaFave, J.M.M. (eds.) Multi-Hazard Approaches to Civil Infrastructure Engineering, pp. 165–208. Springer, Cham (2016). https://doi.org/10.1007/978-3-319-29713-2_9
29. Valluzzi, M.R., Valdemarca, M., Modena, C.: Behavior of brick masonry vaults strengthened by FRP laminates. J. Compos. Constr. ASCE **5**(3), 163–169 (2001)
30. CNR, D 200/R1/2012. Guide for the design and construction of externally bonded FRP systems for strengthening existing structures. Advisory committee on technical recommendation for construction of national research council, Rome, Italy (2014)
31. UNI EN ISO 6946: Building components and building elements - Thermal resistance and thermal transmittance - Calculation methods (2018)
32. Duflou, J.R., Deng, Y., Van Acker, K., Dewulf, W.: Do fiber-reinforced polymer composites provide environmentally benign alternatives? A life-cycle-assessment-based study. MRS Bull. **37**(4), 374–382 (2012)
33. Takahashi, J., et al.: Life cycle assessment of ultra lightweight vehicles using CFRP. In: 5th International Conference on EcoBalance, Tsukuba, Japan, 7–9 Nov 2002, pp. 1–4 (2002)
34. Zhou, H.: The Comparative Life Cycle Assessment of Structural Retrofit Techniques. Arizona State University. SSEBE-CESEM-2013-CPR-009 (2013)
35. Italian Institute of Geophysics and Volcanology, Map of seismic hazard. https://www.ingv.it
36. Italian Technical Norm on Energy Regulations. http://www.gazzettaufficiale.it/eli/id/1993/10/14/093G0451/sg
37. Wang, J.S., Demartino, C., Xiao, Y., Li, Y.Y.: Thermal insulation performance of bamboo- and wood-based shear walls in light-frame buildings. Energy Build. **168**, 167–179 (2018)
38. Sassu, M., Puppio, M.L., Mannari, E.: Seismic reinforcement of a R.C. school structure with strength irregularities throughout external bracing walls. Buildings **7**(3), 58 (2017)
39. De Falco, A., Froli, M., Giresini, L., Puppio, M.L., Sassu, M.: A proposal for the consolidation of a R.C. social housing by means of external hybrid steel-glass frameworks Appl. Mech. Mater. **638–640**, 3–8 (2014)

Beyond the Infrastructure. Sustainable Landscape Regeneration Through Greenways: Towards Project Guidelines for the Sardinia Island (Italy)

Valeria Saiu[✉] [iD] and Francesco Pinna [iD]

University of Cagliari, 09124 Cagliari, Italy
{v.saiu, fpinna}@unica.it

Abstract. In the context of the challenges posed by development models based on overconsumption of natural resources, the paradigm of sustainability defines a new orientation for territorial planning and design. In this regard, greenways play a key role, contributing to safeguard the environment, rehabilitate the fragmented habitats, connect urban and rural areas, revitalize peripheral and degraded areas, and balancing economic growth needs with equal distribution of opportunities and resources. However, the prevailing technical and sectoral approach with which these issues are still addressed – reflecting the fragmentation of instruments and expertises involved in the territorial project – hinder the intervention's long-term effectiveness. Starting from the critical analysis of the most significant experiences of greenways, this paper highlights the prevailing strategies and actions, in order to build a catalog of good practices transferable to the Sardinian regional context. Sardinia, in fact, represents a potential laboratory for the study of an innovative approach to sustainable territorial regeneration, conceived as an opportunity for local development starting from the networking of the resources – environmental, cultural, economic and social – that compose its complex landscape palimpsest.

Keywords: Sustainable urbanism · Landscape regeneration · Green infrastructures · Greenways · Active mobility

1 Introduction

In the context of policies aimed at the sustainable development of the urban environment, the Greenways project is gaining great interest from national Governments and local Administrations. The greenways, in fact, represent a potentially "low cost" strategy to promote environmental protection and the socio-economic valorization of the territory. Moreover, the Region of Sardinia (Italy) is showing a growing commitment in the implementation of soft mobility networks. In December 2018, the Regional Plan for Cycling Mobility of Sardinia was approved. This Plan provides for the construction of a cycle network of over 2,000 km, developed on 52 itineraries covering the whole island. The Region sees in these systems the opportunity to develop integrated projects capable to transform the project of a mere infrastructure into a landscape

© Springer Nature Switzerland AG 2020
O. Gervasi et al. (Eds.): ICCSA 2020, LNCS 12255, pp. 321–336, 2020.
https://doi.org/10.1007/978-3-030-58820-5_25

project. This objective appears particularly relevant in relation to the opportunities offered by the great variety of landscapes and of the natural and anthropic elements that favor the territorial connectivity: the network of forsaken railway routes, the system of rural roads and flat and mountain paths, but also the dense hydrographic network, can be part of a capillary network of paths with which to make accessible the conspicuous regional heritage – historical, archaeological and environmental – still scarcely valued. In this context, authors have been developed a study aimed to build a system of guidelines for the design of greenways in Sardinia. The work was carried out by the University of Cagliari in collaboration with several offices of the Sardinia Region, responsible for the management of local authorities and finance, public works, transport, state property and heritage, hydraulic works.

As emerged in the interdisciplinary working groups organized by the regional administration, the realization of this project implies the construction of programming, planning and design tools capable to build a holistic vision of the territory, overcoming sectoral approaches. In particular, the plurality of constraints on the environmental, architectural and archaeological heritage, and the numerous levels and regulatory instruments still represent today a strong limit to the effectiveness of public action. The lack of a direction able to guide the work of the various public offices, linking the various involved figures, in fact, translates into a sectoral and vertical approach that tends to fragment knowledge and skills at the expense of an integrated territorial project, essential for the realization of these complex infrastructures.

These are some of the problems that were analyzed during the research work, briefly presented in this text, which, starting from the study of the most interesting international experiences, led to the development of a system of guidelines, aimed to summarize applicable strategies and objectives in the regional context. In this way, an operating framework has been defined which is useful to provide a common reference for all actors – technicians, administrators, citizens, economic subjects, etc. – involved in various capacities in the planning, and to put the existing sectoral initiatives online. From a more specifically operational point of view, through the guidelines it is possible to highlight the potential that the greenways project can have in terms of feasibility and economic enhancement of the territory. On the one hand, in fact, this project appears strategic and transversal to many European Community policies – in particular with regard to territorial cohesion, biodiversity conservation, soil conservation, fight against climate change [1–4] – allowing to intercept important European funding for various sectors. On the other hand, it allows developing new local economies, by re-centralizing peripheral territories.

This paper is divided into three main sections. The first present a literature review on greenways that provides the conceptual framework in which this study is conducted, focusing on the complexities of the concept and on the multiple application potentialities, particularly with regard to the economic and social value (Sect. 2); the second section describes the transition from the conceptual framework to field application: through nine selected case studies, we have highlighted the main programmatic points and design actions, useful for identifying a set of guidelines (Sect. 3); at last the third section proposes the application of the concepts and design guidelines, described in the previous sections, to an demonstration project in Sardinia (Sect. 4).

2 Greenways: From Infrastructure to Landscape

Despite the wide use of the term, there is no clear definition of Greenway [5]. This concept, in fact, has assumed and still assumes multiple meanings, in relation to the different context – political, economic, socio-cultural – where it is applied from time to time. Very often, moreover, this term has been used as a mere synonym of a green path or cycle path, severely limiting the design potential inherent in the articulated and complex conception of the territorial network that substantiates the Greenway concept. In the Italian context, this is the case of Law 11/01/2018, n.2 *"Disposizioni per lo sviluppodellamobilità in bicicletta e la realizzazionedella rete nazionale di percorribilitàciclistica"* (Orders for the development of bicycle mobility and the creation of the national cycling network). It defines as "green bike path" or "green-way" *a track or cycle path on which motorized traffic is not allowed* (art. 2).

Compared to this partial and reductive concept, the definition adopted in 1998 by the Italian Greenways Association is still current today and represents an important reference [6]. Indeed, it effectively summarizes the most significant characteristics of the Greenways, underlining the idea of "system" and "connection" between different territories. This idea was already present in the concepts of Greenbelt (green belt) and Parkway (park road) developed between the late nineteenth and early twentieth century, respectively in Europe and America thanks to the work of E. Howard [7] and F.L. Olmsted [8], as well as "multifunctionality". This takes up the definition of Ahern [9] and leads the greenways to be configured as territorial networks designed for multiple purposes: ecological, recreational, cultural, aesthetic or other, compatible with sustainable land use. In fact, the concept of greenway develops in parallel with a new sensibility for the environment and the increasingly widespread adoption of the principles of sustainable development in urban and territorial policies [10–17].

This sensibility fits within an integrated and holistic vision of spatial planning that definitively shifts the attention from the single element to the system. In this perspective, the networking of local resources [18] through the design of new multifunctional ways that exploit the advantages derived from the connections between spaces [11, 19, 20], represents a key action for the efficient management of complex territories such as contemporary ones. The concept of greenway as "linear multifunctional green areas" sanctions the transition from the route project to the landscape project, intended as an interpretative and operational tool in the dynamics of territorial transformation, following the definition introduced by the European Landscape Convention adopted on 20 October 2000 in Florence (Italy) [21].

2.1 Building New Human-Nature Interactions: The Social Value of Greenways

There is a large literature on the social and cultural benefits derived from nature [22–25]. The search for a new relationship between mankind and nature and the abandonment of an constraining approach to environmental protection has led to the interpretation of ecosystem goods and services as potential support elements for human well-being [26–34] or, vice versa, as elements potentially negative for the quality of life, so much to configure them as "ecosystem disservices" [35–37]. This aspect shows as places are intertwined with ecological and social networks, and as the flows and inter-changes between natural processes and human decisions are crucial for the quality of the living environment [38]. Green infrastructures, in fact, are configured not only as elements capable to promote the conservation and protection of biodiversity [39, 40], ensuring the right to environment healthiness, but as a collective resource to promote the socio-economic development of the territory and to improve social exchanges [41–43]. For this reason, the greenways project represents an opportunity – as well as for the protection, for the enhancement of green areas – to connect existing public spaces and to create new ones. They are "devices" for the development of places which contribute to the creation of new identities through the recognition and re-signification of environmental and cultural historical values. In this context, the components of "everyday life" play a decisive role for the success of a project that intends to integrate environment, economy, society and therefore culture as fundamental aspects in the planning and design processes of the landscape. In fact, new cultural and social values can be assigned to these. An example of this approach is the Greenway of the Battle of Pavia (Italia), an itinerary of about 26 km that connects different "everyday landscapes" – the agricultural reality of farmed fields divided by a network of historical irrigation ditches; the urban-agricultural reality, marked by the presence of disordered urbanization and numerous unfarmed land; the consolidated urban reality, the city of Pavia; the fluvial reality of Ticino and other waterways – whose protection, recovery and development rotate around the historical event.

In accordance with this vision, greenways are configured as potentials cultural and ecological landscape corridors [44]. Many studies, in fact, highlight the social value of greenways, considered as an instrument of cultural landscape design [45], expression of cultural values linked to biodiversity [46] able to improve community attachment [47]. As Little claims «to make a greenway is to make a community» [48]. It is indicative of this that the wide adhesion to the greenways project by public administrations and local populations that have formed various forms of associations to promote their spread. Created in 1998, the European Greenways Association (1998) brings together over 50 associations, active in several EU Countries.

3 Recompose Landscapes Through the Greenway Project: A Design and Regulatory Approach

The greenway planning, design and implementation process allows to operate on different levels, giving to the landscape three main functions: (1) Structural, a guide for the transformations; (2) Ecological, the guarantor of the correct environ-mental functioning (e.g. reduction of air and water pollution, improvement of micro-climatic conditions, mitigation of the impacts of human activities); (3) Socio-relational, the connector of services, resources and soft mobility forms.

The design of these complex landscape networks, therefore, plays a decisive role in the contemporary project, especially within the policies of sustainable regeneration of the territory. Through the greenways, in fact, strategic elements for the urban growth control, the soil consumption and degradation, and the consequently landscape fragmentation can be introduced. For this reason, they are particularly useful for deal with problems of degrading and degraded areas, and more in general of territorial contexts in which the landscape re-composition – carried out starting from the anthropic and environmental resources of the territory enhancement – allows to attribute new economic and social uses and meanings also to the residual patches. In this context, we need to know what relationships exist or can be established between fragmented landscapes and environmental corridors [49, 50]. To this end, it can learn to recognize the main elements that compose the territory – existing resources and constraints – in order to establish new spatial and functional relationships between different areas. An issue already highlighted in Seventies by G. Angus Hills, Philip H. Lewis and Ian L. McHarg [see: 51] who were among the first to claim that the project (and optimal locations) should derive from the spatial overlapping of multiple thematic maps, elaborated through the recognition of the different resources of the territory.

3.1 Towards Decision and Design Guidelines: The Case Study Analysis

The considerations set out in the previous paragraphs summarize central themes and issues related to the greenways project. In order to verify how these theoretical concepts are applied and transferred into planning strategies and design principles – useful for coding a replicable model of good practices – some of the most interesting experiences put in place so far have been selected (Fig. 1, Table 1).

The selected projects allow to analyze a wide range of significant projects which refer to different contexts such as United States, Canada, Belgium, France, United Kingdom and Italy. These projects include networks located within internal to densely urbanized areas (1, 4, 5), between urban and rural areas (2, 3) and within dispersed settlements (6–9). The latter scenario characterizes Italian projects that aim at the protection, safeguard, and enhancement of environment and historical-cultural resources, which are recognized as useful devices to reduce the fragmentation caused by the widespread construction of infrastructures and settlements. The Italian greenways, in fact, are not configured as single routes, but rather as complex connectivity structures. The choice of these case studies is based on the fact that these are completed or ongoing projects for which studies and data exist, useful to document objectives, actions and results in a sufficiently exhaustive way.

The analysis of the selected case studies allows to summarize in seven points the main objectives pursued and the results obtained by almost all the projects (Table 2):

1. Re-assemble Landscapes. The project originates from resources and critical elements of territory, conceived as a driver for development strategies, aimed at establishing new links between natural and cultural heritage, promoting to this end the reuse of existing infrastructures (e.g. disused railway lines, river towpaths, urban and rural paths);

2. Promote Soft Mobility. The project discourages the use of private cars and promotes transit and non-motorized transports that use only the "human energy" such as walking and cycling, encouraging public intermodal and multi-modal transport services;

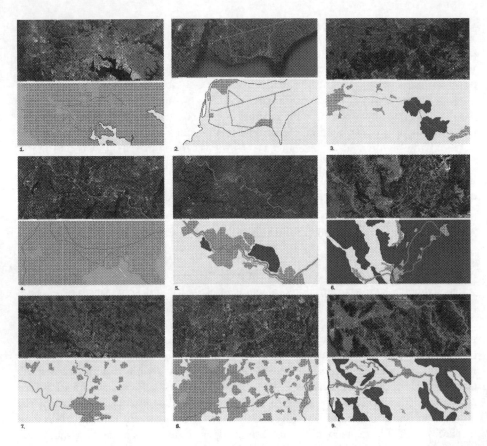

Fig. 1. The nine selected case studies: (1) Baltimore Greenway Trails Network; (2) Chrysler Canada Greenway; (3) Vèloroutes & Voies Vertes (Chambery); (5) Greenways and Quiet roads (Bristol-Bath); (6) Greenway of Nera; (7) Battle of Pavia Greenway; (8) Greenway of Martesana; (9) Greenway of Arno.

Table 1. Data from nine selected case studies.

Project	Location	Path length	Infrastructures	Involved actors	Fundings
P1. Baltimore Greenway Trails Network	Baltimora, Maryland	56 km	Urban and rural paths	Municipality, Citizen Associations	State
P2. Chrysler Canada Greenway	Essex County, Canada	50 km	Disused railway network	Conservation Authorities	Donations

(*continued*)

Table 1. (*continued*)

Project	Location	Path length	Infrastructures	Involved actors	Fundings
P3. Reseau Autonome des Voies Lentes (RAVeL)	Wallonie, Belgium	19 km	Disused railway network, canal and river towpaths, country roads	Regions, Municipalities, Local Associations, Minister for Public Works	EU, State
P4. Vèloroutes & Voies Vertes	Chambery, France	45 km	Disused railway network, canal and river towpaths, country and forestry roads	Minister for Land Planning and Environment, Minister for Transport, Minister for Youth and Sport, Associations	EU, State
P5. Greenways and Quiet roads	Bristol-Bath, Great Britain	20 km	Disused railway network, canal and river towpaths, forestry roads, urban parks	Minister for Transport and Health, Associations, government organizations of citizens	State, Private, Tourism Companies
P6. Greenway of Nera	Umbria, Italy	180 km	Canal and river towpaths, forestry roads, urban parks	Region, Provinces, Municipalities	EU
P7. Battle of Pavia Greenway	Pavia, Italia	26 km	Canal and river towpaths, forestry roads, urban parks	Region, Provinces, Municipalities	Regional
P8. Greenway of Martesana	Lombardia, Italy	35 km	Canal and river towpaths, forestry roads, urban parks	Provinces, Municipalities Milan's local public transport company, Associations	State, Local Associations
P9. Greenway of Arno	Toscana, Italy	350 km	Canal and river towpaths, forestry roads, urban parks	State "Genio Civile", Region, Provinces, Municipalities	EU, State, Local Administrations, Private

3. Improve Environmental Quality. The project safeguards natural habitats and their biodiversity and contributes to create new ecosystems through the connection between diversified natural environments and the facilitation of fauna movements;

4. Enhance the Historical-Cultural Heritage. The project makes accessible the historical and cultural heritage, promoting its protection and enhancement, and increasing the sense of identity and community;

5. Include Different Social Categories. The project encourages multiple soft travel modes in relation to different types of users (pedestrians, cyclists, etc.), facilitating movements of people with reduced motor skills, compatibly with the territory morphology.

6. Promote Social Participation. The project promotes a bottom-up approach based on participation processes and encourages public-private partnerships, in order to respond to the needs of all the actors involved.

Table 2. Case studies: consistency with the identified objectives.

Case study	Project objectives						
	1.	2.	3.	4.	5.	6.	7.
P1.	x	x	x	x	x	–	x
P2.	x	x	x	x	x	–	–
P3.	x	x	x	x	x	x	x
P4.	x	x	x	x	x	–	x
P5.	x	x	x	x	x	–	x
P6.	x	x	x	x	x	x	x
P7.	x	x	x	x	x	x	x
P8.	x	x	x	x	x	x	x
P9.	x	x	x	x	x	x	x

7. Know and Make Known the Territory. The project must become part of the collective imagination. To this end, it is necessary to promote large-scale dissemination and information initiatives, aimed at a broad audience, such as websites, educational and didactic projects.

Starting from these points, a series of successful actions, which are believed to be replicable in other contexts and in particular in the Sardinian Region, have been highlighted. These actions were divided into three categories according to the three main dimensions of the sustainable project: social well-being, environmental protection and economic development (Table 3).

Table 3. Project actions.

1. Social well-being	2. Environmental protection	3. Economic development
1.1. Encourage the active involvement of all interested parties in planning and design processes	2.1. Safeguard and enhance environmental resources	3.1. Improve the local tourism economy through the relaunch of the traditional economic resources
1.2. Promote educational paths, awareness campaigns and cultural events	2.2 Define new uses of space according to resources, limits and constraints of different ecosystems	3.2 Equip the territory in order to guarantee services for its optimal use
1.3. Design accessible paths for different users, with regard to people with reduced motor ability	2.3 Decrease investments in new buildings and infrastructures, in favor of the reuse of unused or underused spaces and settlement structures	3.3. Promote specific local economic activities, strengthening traditional materials and products
1.4. Create safe connections between places of interest and places of everyday life (home-school-work)	2.4 Ameliorate the quality of the peripheral areas, improving their environmental value	3.4. Promote local private entrepreneurship at the service of public interest
1.5. Create new public spaces and recreational areas in order to enhance the sense of community, and the sense of belonging to the place	2.5 Secure the territory, improving risk management	3.5. Narrate the territory, using different media and languages

Table 4 summarizes the schedule of project actions, assigning to each one a "weight" calculated on the basis of the sampling frequencies. The table highlights how some actions are very common, while others are less used because they respond to critical issues for specific the territory.

Table 4. Evaluation of the frequency of the identified project actions.

Sustainability goal	Project actions				
1. Social well-being	**1.1**	**1.2**	**1.3**	**1.4**	**1.5**
	+8	+9	+9	+9	+6
2. Environmental protection	**2.1**	**2.2**	**2.3**	**2.4**	**2.5**
	+9	+9	+9	+8	+6
3. Economic development	**3.1**	**3.2**	**3.3**	**3.4**	**3.5**
	+5	+8	+4	+3	+6

4 Greenways in Sardinia

The operating framework previously described, allows us to identify a series of key actions for the construction of greenways network in the Sardinia Island (Italy). In this context, it is important to consider that the regional cycle mobility network is currently being planned and in part it has already been completed (Deliberazione N. 6/22 of 31.1.2017) through a project that foresees the reuse of disused infrastructure networks, especially railway routes.

In fact, the Sardinia Region is investing huge resources to encourage the development of bicycle mobility. The Regional Plan for Cycling Mobility defines a coordinated set of complementary and integrated measures, interventions and activities aimed to promote and to make available a new way of knowing and experiencing Sardinia, with a strong ecological and environmental connotation [52]. Another characteristic of this Plan is that the cycle mobility system is strongly integrated with all other modes of transport and includes actions and interventions aimed at promoting and spreading slow mobility. This network will also represent an important tool of tourist attraction and, consequently, the driving force of a new production system with effects directly visible on the territory [53].

The plan that defines the network of the connections between urban centers and between the main transport exchange nodes (e.g. bus and train stations, ports, airports), could be empowered through others existing paths that characterized the landscapes crossed. In particular, the green and blue infrastructures, described in the previous paragraphs, can therefore be connected to this network, in order to allow a complete use of environmental and historical-cultural assets that connote internal areas, and which are located very far from the regional cycling network.

From this point of view, the reuse of State property, which is in a state of neglect and degradation, is fundamental. On the one hand, these public goods constitute a resource for the network, because they allow it to be equipped with the services, useful to guarantee its full use. On the other, the greenway network creates necessary conditions for their recovery and reuse.

The hydrographic network, which is part of the state property, is characterized by a high degree of capillarity which can be particularly useful for defining privileged access lines to the territory. The dense network of waterways and canals, in fact, guarantees not only the enjoyment of pleasant paths but the effective territorial protection. The water courses, in fact, can be understood as: (1) Structuring axes, systems for reorganization through which to connect different landscapes; (2) Development axes, systems for territorial transformation useful for orienting decision/making processes and the dynamics of local economic development; (3) Discovery axes, systems for the promotion of an articulated and sustainable territorial fruition.

The analysis of the small and main river paths, carried out with the support of the regional databases, allows us to identify the potential landscape elements of a greenway, in order to configure an integrated project at regional scale.

4.1 A Project Hypothesis for the Sulcis Area: The Four Possible Scenarios

In order to verify the applicability of the theoretical and operational considerations made in the previous paragraphs, we propose an explorative project in Sardinia. To that end, we have analyzed and mapped the hydrographic network in order to identify all possible paths that could be part of the greenways network. In a second step, using the GIS tools, we verify the connections between these routes and the points of environmental, historical and archaeological interest, and their connections with the Regional Cycling Mobility Plan. Finally, among all these paths we have selected the most representative for the purpose of this study, because it allows applying the proposed methodological approach at an appropriate scale.

The identified area is located in the Sulcis area of Sardinia, in a territory characterized at the same time by a landscape of great environmental quality and by a complex settlement system, linked to the mining history of the area. The crisis of mining activity, in fact, is one of the main factors of degradation and land abandonment. In this context, the project of greenways represents an opportunity to activate the redevelopment of large areas of the territory. In particular, we propose a greenway that connects the city of Carbonia – the largest foundation city in Sardinia emblem of industrial modernization of the island – with the coast, along the Rio San Milano. The path length is about 8 km and develops mainly along the pre-existing dirt roads, trying to minimize the conflict with vehicular traffic. The greenway crosses different territories: urban areas, countryside, dispersed settlements and scattered buildings, of recent and historical origin. A heterogeneous and articulated set of landscapes which at present which at present is scarcely used and therefore risks being degraded and abandoned. The proposal adopts a strategic approach based on three key actions (Fig. 2):

a) *Connect*: provide users with a wide range of mobility options, alternatives to vehicular transport, through a network of paths that guarantee the safe mobility of pedestrians and cyclists;

b) *Re-sew*: contrast the fragmented status of the territory by connecting different areas and elements, and reduce the soil consumption dynamics through the promotion of the reuse of the existing building stock, with particular regard to degraded and abandoned heritage;

c) *Develop*: enhance policies aiming to increase the environmental and historical/cultural safeguard and development, in order to create new local economic and recreational opportunities.

These actions were applied in four project scenarios that allow showing the flexibility of greenways networks able to adapt to various place. Through these scenarios it is possible to demonstrate the applicability of the greenways project in different territorial contexts, whose peculiarities allow to explore many complementary themes and scales. The potential for landscape regeneration offered by greenways, in fact, is expressed precisely in the possibility to activate an integrated project, fielding a complex of different intersectoral actions, strictly coherent and interconnected, which converge towards a common target of territory development. The four scenarios are briefly described below.

Scenario 1: Urban and Peri-Urban Areas. The greenway starts from the Carbonia intermodal station that connects 24 municipalities. This area is the main interchange node between rail and road transport, from which it develops the cycle path that connects the intermodal station to the city center. This place constitutes a strategic node because the station assumes the role of gateway to the territory and to the greenway. Through the greenway project is possible to strengthen the connections to the internal and coastal areas and consequently favor the activation of territorial regeneration processes. In particular we planned the transformation of some abandoned areas into urban parks the provision of some essential services, such as parking areas for bikes, cycle workshops, bike sharing, etc.

Scenario 2: Agricultural Contexts. In this scenario, the greenway crosses fragmented and abandoned agricultural territories. The proposal encourages the shared use of land, also through diversified forms of local economic development. Among these a widespread agricultural market would allow those who travel to the greenway paths to appreciate the typical productions, encouraging the local economy. Further-more, in order to hand down the agricultural tradition to future generations, the commercial areas could be flanked by spaces dedicated to educational laboratories. In this context, some architectures of the historical agricultural landscape are particularly suitable for hosting these functions. Among these the "medaus" and the "furriadroxius", micro residential and productive settlements dating back to 18th century, that by their scattered and widespread nature, are particularly suitable to become new reception centers, for hospitality and tourism services.

Scenario 3: Historical Sites. The third scenario includes the archaeological site of Locci Santus, one of the most important necropolises of the Sulcis, dating back to the Neolithic age (c 3,000 BC), consisting of 13 burials in Domus de Janas. Through the greenways it allows to highlight how it is possible to make historical and cultural heritage accessible, in order to promote the protection of the existing heritage and increase the sense of belonging of the communities. Following these principles, in addition to safeguarding and managing the asset, it was considered important to realize a service area for full use of the site. As in other contexts, the new network of soft mobility becomes a way to rediscover and enhance the history of places.

Scenario 4: Coastal Areas. The path traced by the greenway ends on the coast, near an area with a strong environmental value but poorly equipped with services and infrastructures. Here the project provides new recreational areas, structures and services for fishing activities, some of which to be built inside the new pier that allows to ex-tend the greenway to the sea. Despite their simplicity, these interventions can be of great importance to incentivize new forms of local economies.

Fig. 2. The four project scenarios: views and maps of intervention areas.

According to the Sect. 3.1, Table 5 summarizes the project actions which can be included in each of the four scenarios presented.

Table 5. Scheme of the actions applied to the definition of each design scenario.

Sustainability goal	Project actions				
1. Social well-being	**1.1**	**1.2**	**1.3**	**1.4**	**1.5**
	S1, S2 S3, S4	S1, S2 S3, S4	S1, S2 S3, S4	S1	S1, S2 S3, S4
2. Environmental protection	**2.1**	**2.2**	**2.3**	**2.4**	**2.5**
	S1, S2 S3, S4	S1, S2 S3, S4	S1, S2	S1	S1, S2 S4
3. Economic development	**3.1**	**3.2**	**3.3**	**3.4**	**3.5**
	S2, S4	S1, S2 S3, S4	S2, S3, S4	S1, S2 S3, S4	S1, S2 S3, S4

5 Discussion and Conclusions

As shown by the literature and case studies examined, the promotion of territorial and urban regeneration strategies through the creation of green systems is now shared by researchers and administrators of many cities. In fact, they see these infrastructures as an important opportunity for sustainable transformation of their territory. In this context, the greenways allow to overcome the binding and sectoral approach characterizing the planning and design logics, and to configure a strategic "tool" useful to simultaneously pursue multiple objectives. Among these, it emerges the promotion of active mobility, the safe-guard of the biodiversity and ecosystem services, the revitalization of local economies, the enhancement of the historical and cultural identity of the territory and the construction of new spaces of social relationship, all capable to promote a new sense of belonging to places and to strengthen the sense of community.

It follows that the greenways project is a complex project that must be built starting from the in-depth knowledge of the characteristics of the territory, the needs and aspirations of the local community and the market analyzes exclusively oriented to generate profit. In fact, the greenways projects require the active involvement of all the potential actors concerned in the project: public administrations, economic operators, associations and individual citizens. For this reason, consistently with the concept of landscape defined by the European Convention of the Council of Europe in 2000, the greenways take on the function of "landscape infrastructures" to try to establish a new balance between population and environment. Beyond these theoretical reflections, the study is propaedeutic to the development of a system of guidelines for the planning and design of a system of greenways in the Sardinian regional territory. In fact, the comparison between case studies has been useful to define recurring themes, objectives and actions allowing to outline a shared strategic framework. In this common frame, it is possible to develop multiple design variations which adhere to the specific features of each different territories, making each project unique. The proposed project exploration addresses the case of the territory of the Sardinia Region, where a greenways project has not yet been undertaken. The article builds a synthetic picture, trying to identify the strategies and the carried-out projects, which, put to system, can contribute to the construction of a system of greenways for Sardinia. Among these, the regional cycle network project is the first strong framework to which a second network could join, made up of more capillary pedestrian paths. As said, the regional hydrographic network could represent suitable reinforcement for this purpose. In this way, the greenways network construction would offer an opportunity to promote the places active protection not reached through the cycle network and the river rods themselves. The presented scenarios are not intended to create solutions. Through the heterogeneity, and therefore the richness, of the landscape, the scenarios show the potentiality of this project which, as underlined several times, will have to be built starting from the knowledge of the ecological and environmental, socio-economic and historical-cultural characteristics of the territory. A potential development of this work is the creation of guide-lines, useful to support the public decision makers in decision-making processes. It is not a question to give strict indications but to guide the project, evaluating the locational, formal and technological choices through a multiscale and multidisciplinary approach. This method will also allow to share and clearly communicate the reasons of the choices, activating a participatory design process which is crucial for the project outcome. Finally, the guide-lines, as well as for the project, could give indications for the implementation and management of the interventions, that are two critical phases requiring a careful planning of the activities.

Acknowledgments. This work was carried out in collaboration with the technical offices of the Autonomous Region of Sardinia, in particular with the General Directorate for Local Authorities and Finance – State Property and Heritage Service, as part of the curricular training and orientation internship agreement, established between the General Directorate for Local Authorities and Finance, the University of Cagliari – Master of Science in Architecture, and the General Directorate for Public Works, Territorial Service of Cagliari Hydraulic Works (STOICA). The case study data presented in this article were collected by M. Mallus and C. Porcu under the coordination of the authors [54].

References

1. European Commission: The multifunctionality of Green Infrastructure. https://ec.europa.eu/environment/nature/ecosystems/docs/Green_Infrastructure.pdf. Accessed 27 Jan 2020
2. European Commission: The Forms and the Functions of the Green Infrastructures. https://ec.europa.eu/environment/nature/ecosystems/benefits/index_en.htm. Accessed 27 Jan 2020
3. European Environment Agency: Green Infrastructure and Territorial Cohesion. The Concept of Green Infrastructure and its Integration into Policies Using Monitoring Systems. https://www.eea.europa.eu/publications/green-infrastructure-and-territorial-cohesion. Accessed 27 Jan 2020
4. European Environment Agency, Signals 2019 - Land and soil in Europe: Why we need to use these vital and finite resources sustainably. https://www.eea.europa.eu/publications/eea-signals-2019-land. Accessed 27 Jan 2020
5. Flink, C.A., Sears, R.M.: Greenway: a Guide to Planning. Design and Development. Island Press, Washington, D.C (1993)
6. AssociazioneItaliana Greenway: Greenways: Concept and Definitions. http://www.greenways.it/definizioni.php. Accessed 27 Jan 2020
7. Howard, E.: To-Morrow: The Peaceful Path to Social Reform. Swan Sonnenschein & Co., London (1898)
8. Eisemann, T.S.: Frederick law olmsted, green infrastructure, and the evolving city. J. Plan. Hist. **12**(4), 287–311 (2013)
9. Ahern, J.F.: Greenways as a planning strategy. Landsc. Urban Plan. **33**, 131–155 (1995)
10. Lyle, J.T.: Regenerative Design for Sustainable Development. Wiley, New York (1994)
11. Ahern, J.F.: Greenways as a planning strategy. In: Fabos, J., Ahern, J. (eds.) Greenways: the Beginning of an International Movement, pp. 131–155. Elsevier, Amsterdam (1996)
12. Turner, T.: Landscape Planning and Environmental Impact Design. UCL Press, London (1998)
13. Fabos, J.G., Allan, J.J., Ryan, R.L.: Understanding opportunities and challenges for collaborative greenway planning in New England. Landsc. Urban Plan. **76**(1–4), 172–191 (2006)
14. Steadman, P.: The Evolution of Designs. Biological Analogy in Architecture and the Applied Arts, A revised edition. Routledge, New York (2008). (Original edition printed in 1979 by the Syndics of Cambridge University Press)

15. Sharma, A.: Decoding the genotype of greenway design thinking and practice: a steadmanian frame for systematic understanding, synthesis and tracking multidisciplinary discourse. J. Des. Res. **13**(2), 150–166 (2015)

16. Palmisano, G.O., Govindan, K., Loisi, R.V., Sasso, P.D., Roma, R.: Greenways for rural sustainable development: an integration between geographic information systems and group analytic hierarchy process. Land Use Policy **50**, 429–440 (2016)

17. Culligan, P.J.: Green infrastructure and urban sustainability: a discussion of recent advances and future challenges based on multiyear observations in New York City. Sci. Technol. Built Environ. **25**(9), 1113–1120 (2019)

18. Gambino, R.: Oltre la insostenibile periferia. In: Camagni, R. (ed.) La pianificazione sostenibile delle aree periurbane. Il Mulino, Bologna, pp. 179–203 (1999)

19. Checkland, P.: Systems Thinking. Systems Practice. Wiley, Chichester (1989)

20. Zonneveld, W.: Conceptvorming in de Ruimtelijke Planning. Patronenen Processes (vol. 1) and Encyclopedie van Planconcepten (vol. 2). PlanoloaischeStudues 9, Universiteit van Amsterdam, Amsterdam, Netherlands (1991)

21. Council of Europe: The European Landscape Convention. https://www.coe.int/en/web/landscape. Accessed 27 Jan 2020

22. Bull, J., et al.: Strengths, weaknesses, opportunities and threats: a SWOT analysis of the ecosystem services framework. Ecosyst. Serv.s **17**, 99–111 (2016)

23. Chan, K.M.A., et al.: Where are cultural and social in ecosystem services? A framework for constructive engagement. BioScience **62**(8), 744–756 (2012)

24. Daniel, T.C., et al.: Contributions of cultural services to the ecosystem services agenda. Proc. Natl. Acad. Sci. **109**(23), 8812–8819 (2012)

25. Larson, R., Keith, S.J., Fernandez, M., Hallo, J.C., Shafer, C.S.: Ecosystem services and urban greenways: what's the public's perspective? Ecosyst. Serv. **22**, 111–116 (2016)

26. Ehrlich, P.R., Ehrlich, A.H.: Extinction: The Causes and Consequences of the Disappearance of Species. Random House, New York (1981)

27. Ehrlich, P.R., Ehrlich, A.H.: Extinction, substitution, and ecosystem services. Bioscience **33**(4), 248–254 (1983)

28. Odum, E.P.: Ecology and our Endangered Life-Support Systems. Sinuaer Associates, Sunderland (1989)

29. Folke, C., Hammer, M., Jansson, A.M.: The life-support value of ecosystems: a case study of the Baltic Sea Region. Ecol. Econ. **3**, 123–137 (1991)

30. De Groot, R.S., Wilson, M.A., Boumans, R.M.J.: A typology for the classification, description and valuation of ecosystem functions, goods and services. Ecol. Econ. **41**, 393–408 (2002)

31. Daily, G.C. (ed.): Nature's Services: Societal Dependence on Natural Ecosystems. Island Press, Washington D.C. (1997)

32. Costanza, R., d'Arge, R., de Groot, R., Farber, S., Grasso, M., Hannon, B., et al.: The value of the world's ecosystem services and natural capital. Nature **387**, 253–260 (1997)

33. de Groot, R.S.: Functions of nature: evaluation of nature in environmental planning, management and decision making. Wolters-Noordhoff BV, Groningen (1992)

34. Fisher, B., Turner, R.K.: Ecosystem services: classification for valuation. Biol. Cons. **141**, 1167–1169 (2008)

35. Lyytimaki, J., Petersen, L.K., Normander, B., Bezàk, P.: Nature as a nuisance? Ecosystem services and disservices urban lifestyle. Environ. Sci. **5**, 161–172 (2008)

36. Lyytimaki, J., Sipilä, M.: Hopping on one leg. The challenge of ecosystem disservices for urban green management. Urban For Urban Green 8(4), 309–315 (2009)

37. Escobedo, F.J., Kroeger, T., Wagner, J.E.: Urban forests and pollution mitigation: analyzing ecosystem services and disservices. Environ. Pollut. **159**, 2078–2087 (2011)

38. Malcevschi, S.: Appunti di viaggio nell'interregno. Parole-chiave per non soccombere. StreetLib (2015)
39. Bryant, M.M.: Urban landscape conservation and the role of ecological greenways at local and metropolitan scales. Landsc. Urban Plan. **76**, 23–44 (2006)
40. Ahern, J.: Urban landscape sustainability and resilience: the promise and challenges of integrating ecology with urban planning and design. Landscape Ecol. **28**, 1203–1212 (2013)
41. Lindesy, G., Maraj, M., Kuan, S.: Access, equity, and urban greenways: an exploratory investigation. Prof. Geogr. **53**(3), 332–346 (2001)
42. Larson, L.R., Keith, S.J., Fernandez, M., Hallo, J.C., Shafer, C.S., Jennings, V.: Ecosystem services and urban greenways: what's the public's perspective? Ecosyst. Serv. **22**, 111–116 (2011)
43. Paneerchelvam, P.T., Maruthaveeran, S., Maulan, S., Shukor, S.F.A.: The use and associated constraints of urban greenway from a socioecological perspective: a systematic review. Urban For. Urban Green. **47**, 1–20 (2020)
44. Xu, H., Plieninger, T., Primdahl, J.: A systematic comparison of cultural and ecological landscape corridors in Europe. Land **8**(3), 1–32 (2019)
45. Ryan, R.L., Eisenman, T.S.: Building connections to the minute man national historic park: greenway planning and cultural landscape design. In: Proceedings of the Fábos Conference on Landscape and Greenway Planning, vol. 6, no. 1, Art. 25 (2019)
46. Clark, N.E., Lovell, R., Wheeler, B.W., Higgins, S.L., Depledge, M.H., Norris, K.: Biodiversity, cultural pathways, and human health: a framework. Trends Ecol. Evol. **29**(4), 198–204 (2014)
47. Arneberger, A., Eder, R.: The influence of green space on community attachment of urban and suburban residents. Urban For. Urban Green. **11**(1), 41–49 (2012)
48. Little, C.: Greenways for American. Johns Hopkins University Press, Baltimore (1990)
49. Dunning, J.B., Borgella, R., Clements, K., Meffe, G.K.: Patch isolation, corridor effects, and colonization by a resident sparrow in a managed pine woodland. Conserv. Biol. **9**, 542–550 (1995)
50. Henein, K., Merriam, G.: The elements of connectivity where corridor quality is variable. Landsc. Ecol. **4**(2–3), 157–170 (1990)
51. Belknap, R.K., Furtado, J.G.: Three approaches to environment resource analyses. In: Angus Hills, G., Lewis, P.H., McHarg, I.L. (eds.) The Conservation Foundation, Washington DC (1967)
52. Meloni, I., Saba, C., Scappini, B., Zucca, V.: Improving regional accessibility through planning a comprehensive cycle network: the case of Sardinia (Italy). In: Gargiulo, C., Zoppi, C. (eds.) Planning, Nature and Ecosystem Services, pp. 859–868. FedOAPress, Napoli (2019)
53. Regione Autonoma della Sardegna: Rete ciclabile della Sardegna. https://www.sardegnaciclabile.it/. Accessed 27 Jan 2020
54. Mallus, M., Porcu, C.: Greenway guidelines. Master's Thesis, University of Cagliari, Faculty of Engineering and Architecture, Cagliari (Italy) (2017)

Accessibility Improvements and Place-Based Organization in the Island of Sardinia (Italy)

Mauro Coni[(⊠)] , Chiara Garau , Francesca Maltinti ,
and Francesco Pinna

Department of Civil and Environmental Engineering and Architecture
(DICAAR), University of Cagliari, via Marengo 2, 09123 Cagliari, Italy
mconi@unica.it

Abstract. The poor transport system in Sardinia, particularly in the inner areas, affects the social-economic development and the determinants of the productive activities. After illustrating the specificities of these areas in terms of transport accessibility, orography, and the relationship between populations, a new territorial organization is proposed, integrating the new tendencies in mobility. The development of the transport system of these marginal areas plays a key role in future scenarios. In the paper, some analysis highlights the infrastructural weaknesses and the limited accessibility of the inner areas and its negative effects on the local economy. These can be overcome fixing reference hubs, with the function of supplying services and connecting most developed and rich territories located in the coastal areas. On a regional basis, the reference hubs would accomplish the task of a firm, efficient link with the mainland, while the minor hubs would have the function of spreading the urban impact throughout the territory. The strategy matches with the improvement in land accessibility, with vast intervention on the inner road system, and with the creation of a system of strong links with the main urban settlements of the island and with the regional and national transport network. A further strategy is maximizing the integration among infrastructural systems, productive structures, agricultural areas, services, and residential centers, with the perspective of promoting the tourist and environmental vocation of Sardinia. Finally, a new criteria for the infrastructures, integration of the different transport modes with the main transport terminals, is proposed.

Keywords: Accessibility · Place-based organization · Sardinia transport system · Smart and sustainable Island

1 Introduction

In recent decades, urban growth has manifested an important concern, due to the prediction that over 70% of the world's population will live in urban areas by 2050 [1]. In addition, the urban context is characterized by a higher concentration of highly

---

This paper is the result of the joint work of the authors. In particular, the abstract, paragraphs 3, 4, and 5 have been jointly written by all authors. Chiara Garau has written the introduction, Mauro Coni has written the conclusions.

O. Gervasi et al. (Eds.): ICCSA 2020, LNCS 12255, pp. 337–352, 2020.
https://doi.org/10.1007/978-3-030-58820-5_26

qualify human capital is related with positive externalities, such as density efficiency, employment growth, income and innovation [2]. All elements are essential to recognize and spread the urban development and are also functional characteristics of the transport system that support the mobility [3–5], also considering innovative transport systems and technologies to promote sustainable mobility [6, 7]. However, the transport system sector can play a fundamental role in increasing development even in polycentric areas, by implementing the accessibility and mobility between urban and rural areas [8]. In fact, "polycentric development can create critical mass by combining the efforts of urban centres, while delivering more balanced development between regions and more cooperative and functional urban-rural linkages" [9, p. 2]. It is an approach that can enhance accessibility of distant areas and generating opportunities to satisfy people's needs [10]. This process has been highly irregular throughout the Italian territory, mainly influenced by the degree of development of transport [11].

Many areas register depopulation phenomena, and at the same time, the territories are scattered and strongly polycentric with a potential for attraction and resources not expressed. The Technical Committee of the "Inner Areas" of Italian Regions drafted a report relating to the National Strategy of Internal Areas, to develop the local economy through local production chains and supporting primary services to the needs of the population [12]. This document defines a better plan for them by considering multi-polar interconnections [13].

In particular, the disadvantage of South's Italy, but also of the major Italian islands (Sicily and Sardinia) is its mountainous territory, and the limited and inadequate transport system [14, 15]. In this regard, according to [16–19] stakeholder engagement in complex transport decisions results fundamental to investigate users' preferences and design new transport services.

Sardinia has the same amount of flat land as the South, but almost two-thirds of its area is on hilly with high altitude, and its altitude distribution is quite unbalanced. Sardinia is also a closed system and for this reason, the mobility sector is easier to study, by considering the different polarities.

The territory organization is not structured as "networks" according to criteria of decentralization and specialization of production and services; these processes are not allowed by the low articulation of the economic structure and related functions that favor the extreme fragmentation in small villages, towns, cities (377 municipalities over 24,100 km^2).

In the past fifty years, the most important in the evolution of Sardinia's economy, the population of the inner areas was characterized by the combined effects of the four following trends, which have weakened the economic-productive structure:

1) a decrease in the population, because of the emigration and the negative balance of demography;
2) population structure and aging;
3) the transfer between population decrease areas and those with an increase, which expand to include the neighborhood centers;
4) a progressive shifting of the population from higher to lower altitudes and coastal areas.

The depopulated territories are nearly always the inner areas of the high hills and mountains, while the growing areas are mostly the coastal areas (tourist economy) and those immediately gravitating around the industrial poles and principal towns (manufacture and commerce).

Starting from these assumptions, the authors intend to propose some practical suggestions for the infrastructures, by integrating the different transport modes with the main transport terminals. The paper is divided into six sections. Section two presents some reference data of demographic change in Europe and on road network infrastructure. The third section discusses the main objectives for introducing a new Transportation Plan in Sardinia. The fourth and the fifth sections present the results obtained in Sardinia, by considering the accessibility. Finally, the conclusions section summarises the fundamental findings of the study, by underlining the implications of the research, and by giving practical suggestions for their implementation.

2 Some Reference Data on Demographic Changes and on Road Network Infrastructure

Demographic changes have various consequences for European territories [20]. Rural and inland areas are experiencing a significant population decline, exacerbating the economic decline. This situation, common in Europe, is a problem faced by the regions and which unfortunately increases the gap between rural and urban areas and affects the social, economic, and territorial cohesion of the EU. Figure 1 shows the average annual population change.

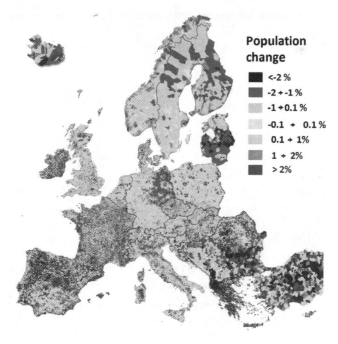

Fig. 1. The average annual population change in Europe 2019 [20].

However, at the same time, the high concentration of people in urban metropolitan hubs creates many negative consequences, such as pollution, life quality, road congestion, the impact on the pre-existing natural environment, and the tragic road accidents [21]. The mobility phenomenon means also to observe circulation as it appears exteriorly, by identifying the diverse and multiple economic and existential causes of mobility. The first two factors to be considered are 1) the capabilities of the available infrastructural systems, and 2) the correct use of resource-saving technologies.

Italy has a road network infrastructure of about 492,000 km with a territorial density of about 1.63 km/km^2, which is more than the European average (1.23 km/km^2) though it has a higher vehicle density, about 78 vehicles per km, compared to the 53 vehicles per km in Europe e and the 28 vehicles per km of the USA [15, 22]. An immediate consideration is that Italy needs a different distribution of passenger and goods transport without necessarily having to develop, rather than adapt, the Italian road network in order to develop road transport. Figure 2 shows the distribution of the total road network in Europe and Italian regions, underlining the actual situation (the region of Sardina is in black).

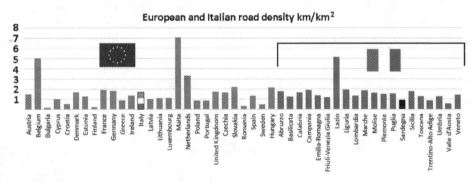

Fig. 2. Density of the total road network in Europe and Italian regions (km/km^2) (Graph based on available data in [15, 20]

In addition, about the 50% of the ordinary roads shows clear signs of a need to be adapted to conform to new design criteria, and those more dangerous accidents have been found to happen on ordinary roads [15]. The 50% of the Italian roads defined "mediocre" are in the South and islands and these roads represent only a third of the total road network. Nevertheless, only 2‰ of the total economic resources were allotted for maintenance. In a nutshell, protection of the present state of the asset is an important priority. It is also important to underline that the expansion of the infrastructural communication network (particularly in the Sardinian road network) has not responded to the different territorial needs. The new roads were often a consequence of the sectorial needs and demands, rather than as a result of a general regional plan.

There is an absolute necessity of rationalizing the system of transport infrastructures that should be adapted to the socio-economic reality of the territory and its development corridors [23, 24], in order to ensure adequate traffic conditions, limiting congestion and saturation of road capacity and ensuring adequate travel time reliability of transport services [25–27]. All this, however, respecting, safeguarding and valorizing particular historical-environmental features, promoting and guaranteeing conditions of widespread accessibility and paying attention to all mobility levels [28–30] as well as agreeing with complex economic planning.

Over time, the Italian regional and local administrations have prepared many General and Provincial Transportation Plans. These plans contain a preliminary knowledge of the general characteristics of the land, populations, economic and service activities, the transport system and in particular of the road network.

In Sardinia the main regional tool of transportation and transport system is the General Transportation Plan (approved by Regional Government in 2008) and its main objective is a comprehensive transportation system oriented towards sustainable forms of transport, the shortcomings of which have contributed to the success of road transport.

However, in a society characterized by ever-increasing mobility, the road network is one of the weak links in the productive chain of the island of Sardinia and damage the competitiveness of the local enterprise and the social texture of the territory.

Considering the existing situations, plan, programs, choices, objectives, and to the general lines of the planning tools, the authors propose the following suggestions:

a) adaptation and restructuring of the transportation system;
b) creation or transformation of new sustainable communication infrastructures.

The principal objective in planning the transport system, and in particular the road network, is that of reducing the economic cost of transport, and of improving the serviceability and safety of the road network so as to increase land accessibility.

These premises serve to understand the needs and objectives to be pursued in redesigning the transport system, especially considering the Sardinian case study.

3   Objectives for a New Sardinia Transportation Plan Considering the Road Network

In general, the General Transportation Plan deals with different aspects: mobility of people, the generalized cost of transport, the reduction of impacts on the environment and the increase in job opportunities.

However, the authors in this paper deal only with the road sector, by analyzing how it can change social and economic structures.

The objectives of the transport system in Sardinia must be based on the consideration that its territory is characterized by a marked organization of "poles" of productive activity and services. The indications that could be reached, therefore, regard communication infrastructures not strictly referred to provincial territories of competence. In areas of a low settlement density, the availability of jobs, of social and cultural exchange of a higher level, and access to services on a regional scale, is almost always concentrated in a few "poles". On the one hand, this situation of unbalance is the main reason for trips towards "strong" areas, and on the other, it is difficult to change except at the price of oversizing some of the services, thus supporting diseconomies. Thus, the accessibility in certain areas is made possible and therefore facilitated through the creation of opportunities for enjoyment, economic and socio-cultural activities that tend to be located in specific areas. So, the presence of an adequate transport system causes structural conditions for the creation of a more homogeneous territorial distribution of employment and service opportunities.

The main objective in the transportation planning of the various territorial systems is to design an organic transport system capable of creating conditions of accessibility in the function of improving the economic conditions and the general living conditions of its inhabitants.

The Sardinia Transportation Plan identifies eight prevalent gravitation centers. Therefore, the authors with the found data and information, intend to determine whether the same territorial organization is to be confirmed in the future or whether, without prejudice to the functions localized in these centers, a role could realistically be found in the provincial and regional territory. This hub can be a gravitational point for other centers with a district effect concerning education, health and other services of an administrative nature. The main issue is understanding the correspondence between the existing road network and the demand generated by i) present and future forms of settlement; ii) changes in the productive organization; iii) the necessity of guaranteeing adequate road support to tourism, for example. The intervention on the road network is not neutral for the structure of the phenomena that it meets.

The dislocation of settlements (human, productive, and services), the mobility system, and the general function of an area are strongly conditioned by the type of internal and external road structures that support them.

The processes of population concentration, abandonment of inner areas and development of tourist activities will extend to the whole of the next decade: Sardinia is still in the early phases of industrialization, where according to a behavior model observed in other regions, economic development accompanies processes of territorial concentration. The Sardinia economic development will be characterized by the same trend as in the past and dragged by the development of already formed "strong" areas is forecast. The demand for land accessibility derives from the people mobility the needs of the productive world. Tue external road structures can support all of this.

A significant consideration is to be given to: i) demographic evolution; ii) demand and supply of access to primary and specialized services; iii) the accessibility opportunity of the territory and iv) development of economic resources, by considering also the protection of areas with environmental and landscape value.

These different requirements express the general need for requalification and re-equilibrium in the utilization of the resources of a territory where a few "strong" areas tend to affect the development of surrounding areas, and therefore where the opposition between "poles of development" and deep layers of emarginated territory prevails. The strategic objective proposed in planning a new transport system is a land re-equilibrium, that recognizes the high-risk level deriving from the abandonment and marginalization of large portions of territory. Moreover, it should be rearranged and rationalize the "strong" axes network and the "poles," but that should also contribute to reconstruct and reinforce the weak areas, by considering planning tools, urban and transport processes and strategic spatial planning [31–33].

Obviously, a simple intervention on the road system is not able to manage and solve rebalancing problems. The possible solutions are combined with adequate land policies and real activities i) for the location of civil services, business services and production and ii) for the environment and urban planning in general. However, a set of capillary works on the internal road network and a robust connection system with the main urban settlements may play a fundamental role in the re-utilization of these territories and their recovery towards economic development based on the valorization of natural, cultural, handicraft and agricultural resources.

Authors suggest the following activities to bring into consideration:

- the removal of the severe difficulties experienced by these areas in the utilization of the primary social and economic services concentrated in a small number of "poles";
- the creation of efficient intermediate hubs capable of determining a road structure that works as a frame of reference for the minor settlements as an alternative to the Provinces;
- the creation of a network of tourist itineraries involving not only to the main tourist areas but also the surrounding ones with minor cultural goods, in order to support the unique local environmental and cultural resources.

But before showing the results of the research in detail, it is important to frame the concept of accessibility and how this concept can be applied for Sardinia.

4 Land Accessibility: The Case Study of Sardinia

The term accessibility, intended as "facility of access" to a specific place, is define as the measure "to which land-use and transport systems enable groups of individuals to reach activities or destinations by means of a combination of transport modes" [34, p. 115]. The accessibility does not consider the presence in the neighborhood of residences, services or workplaces convenient for facilitating access in order to satisfy a concrete trip demand.

A different interpretation of accessibility is not necessary for the traditional procedure for the transport system layout. The sizing and choice of transport alternatives follow the analysis and forecast of the demand for mobility and, after adequate consideration of both demand and supply, the accessibility can be guaranteed to the users who wish to go from a point A to a Point B or to different centers. In this way, if the demand is either impossible or difficult to quantify, a reasoned choice of works on the transport system is prevented. The actual system imposes to proceed following a general logic (of guaranteeing communication among all centers, functionally distinguishing ways of communication, adjusting the characteristics of the infrastructures along main itineraries, and so on).

In Sardinia, this logic is applied through the analysis on the 377 municipalities of the travel times allowed by the current road network. The area that can be reached at a certain moment increases as the movement is greater and less expensive.

Two distinct cases are represented in Fig. 3: Cagliari is on the plain and has many highways with few curves and high travel speeds. Seui is in the mountains and has a narrow winding road with very low speeds. In the first case, the area that can be reached in an hour (within the blue area) is much larger. Furthermore, Seui is in a much more central position, but has longer travel times to more distant centers (more intense red areas) and for large portions of territory (larger red surface).

The direct distance from coastal areas to Seui is only 30.5 km, but the real road distance is 75 km traveled in $1^{h}.30^{m}$. Seui registers in the last decade a depopulation of 11.69% and, at the same time Tortolì (the closest coastal center) increase of 3.1% their population.

Infrastructural support appears very inadequate to sustain the socio-economic development trends of the different regions of Sardinia. Generally, the elaborated analyses shows that land accessibility, and, therefore, the quality of life are compromised not only by the lack of appropriate infrastructures but also by the geometric and layout characteristics of the road network.

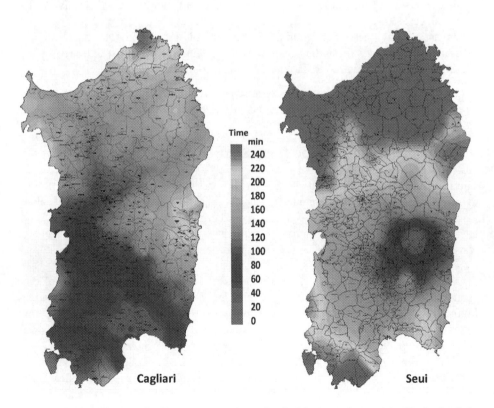

Fig. 3. The isochronous distribution comparison: Cagliari is the main municipality in Sardinia (on the left) on the south coast; Seui is a small village (on the right).

Distance in traveling time is judged as the most representative parameter to describe the state of road accessibility and Fig. 4 shows la distribution of time for five different situations.

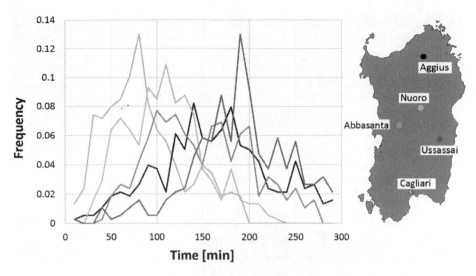

Fig. 4. The distribution of time from one municipality and the other 376 ones.

Furthermore, Fig. 5 shows the distribution of the average time to reach the other 376 municipalities. Namely, the municipality located in the blue area has excellent accessibility conditions unlike those in the red area. The commercial speeds on the whole road network as a function of the geometric and layout characteristics and the entity of traffic flow were measured preliminarily. The distances in traveling time for each provincial territory and the whole regional territory were measured for the primarily residential, productive, and services settlements and to other hubs that may be defined as having a "pole function", such that they can be assigned land re-equilibrium functions.

The following municipalities are considered as hubs:

- Metropolitan City of Cagliari: Cagliari;
- Province of South Sardinia: Carbonia, Dolianova, Guspini, Iglesias, Muravera, San Gavino, Sanluri, Sant'Andrea Frius, Sant'Antioco, Senorbì, Silius, Villacidro, and Villasor;
- Province of Nuoro: Nuoro, Bosa, Isili, Lanusei, Macomer, Siniscola, Sorgono, and Tortolì;
- Province of Oristano: Oristano, Abbasanta/Ghilarza, Ales, Arborea, Cuglieri, Samugheo, and Santulussurgiu;
- province of Sassari: Sassari, Alghero, Olbia, Ozieri, Portotorres, and Tempio.

As residential, productive, and services settlements and external transport hubs at the regional level, following municipalities are considered: Cagliari, Iglesias, Macomer, Nuoro, Olbia (for Olbia and Golfo Aranci), Oristano, Sassari (for Alghero, Portotorres and Sassari) and Tortolì. The analysis shows the deficiencies of the road network in the different regions of the provincial and regional territory. Accessibility conditions depend on the quality of the geometric and layout characteristics, and therefore on the serviceability levels of the road networks of the different regions.

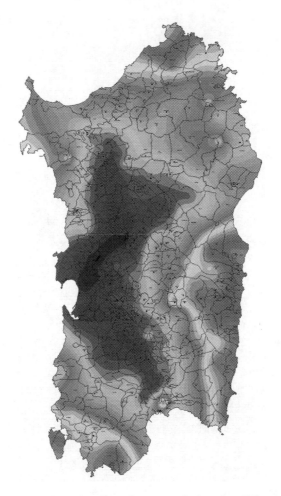

Fig. 5. The distribution of average time to reach the other 376 municipalities.

Particularly deficient are the road networks serving the Flumini region (between Iglesias and Guspini) and the Sarrabus-Gerrei region in the province of South Sardegna; the Barbagia d'Ogliastra and the Barbagia of Sarcidano regions in the province of Nuoro; in the regions in the province of Oristano with Ales, Cuglieri, Samugheo and Santulussurgiu as "hubs" of reference; and in Anglona, Goceano and mountain Gallura in the province of Sassari. Land accessibility is different and better in areas served by "type A - particular destination" roads such as the S.S. 131 - 131 DCN main roads, or roads serving the Industrial Development Areas and Industrialisation Nuclei.

To those factors, it is also necessary to consider also the correlation between depopulation and accessibility. For the region of Sardinia, this correlation is significant, equal to 0.696 using an exponential trend line (Fig. 6).

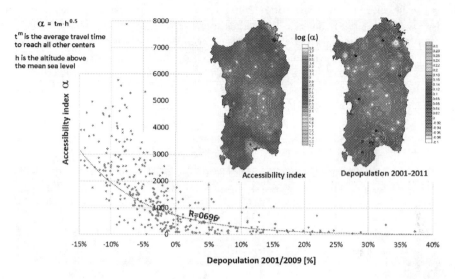

Fig. 6. A good correlation (R = 0.696) was found between depopulation and accessibility index

5   Results: Proposal of a Method of Intervention for the Insular Context of Sardinia

The analyses proposed on the transport system in Sardinia have shown that, according to technical characteristics, internal and external relations impose a general adjustment of the communication infrastructures, mainly through an improvement of the layout characteristics.

Historically, the study of the growth dynamics of many economic systems has shown that investments in the transportation sector often are a decisive factor in the formation of capital. In the south of Italy and islands, despite many works had been guided, often they remain unfinished for decades. The conclusion is that investment in transport represents a necessary, though not sufficient, condition for the development of a specific geographic area. A critical structural transformations is needed in order to create, or change, the transport network, but it is necessary a good coordination for investments aimed at stimulating growth.

A consequence of this approach is that specific traditional procedures aimed at assessing the appropriateness of investment projects, for example, in the road sector, do not respond to the objective of promoting balanced growth. On the contrary, in some cases, the creation of large-scale works were done, using resources that could have been invested in more urgent projects for development.

Therefore, it is important to abandon the purely sectorial vision of the problem of road planning and transport planning in general; this could only be done by introducing what we can call "development benefits" in the analysis.

This category of benefits should be determined as the result of global investment, or better, of the entire productive effort, and not as an effect of partial investments, such as roads. From these brief remarks, it emerges that the planning and layout of transport systems must no longer (or better not only) be confronted sectorial, but in the general view of the process of economic development within which the works are done. The layout of a road or a railway does not have a separate configuration but is an integral part of land planning.

Each transport component plays a role corresponding to its own technical and economic peculiarities, and all the components, organized hierarchically, concur to define the territorial layout that is functional to the pre-established socioeconomic layout. All this determines the mobility of people and is fundamental for understanding the processes underway. Figure 7 shows some characteristics in terms of attracted and generated trips.

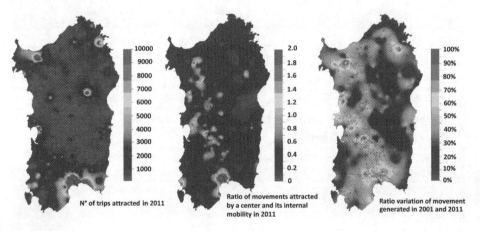

Fig. 7. Some characteristics of mobility in Sardinia: the number of total trips attracted by each hub (on the left), the ratio of trips attracted by a hub and its internal mobility and, variation of movements between 2001 and 2011 (on the right).

Another inspiring concept is that the transport system must be used to control the localization of activities on the territory, which is the crucial point not only of town-planning and territorial problems but also of traffic and circulation problems. In order to assess the territorial layout that can be associated with intervention in transport, connectivity is of fundamental importance, at least for the following reasons:

- the increase in the connectivity of the transport network is the fundamental condition for supporting the formation of a more territorial network structure, in view of a better extension of development;

- some of the main impediments and constraints to the extension of development are related to variations in connectivity due to the unequal development of transport.

The layout of a transportation system should be founded on the following main options:

- an adequate exploration of the possibilities of requalifying the intercity road communication network with investments aimed at relieving congested areas by offering a better distribution of the values of accessibility and connectivity;
- a check of the hypotheses of improvement of the connection between minor urban systems and "strong" areas, through efficient local transport services in terms of service reliability and intensity.

Considering the organization of urban areas, the authors suggest the following guidelines:

- a detailed study of the possibility of promoting the mobility shift from private to public transport, while checking the attainable thresholds and town-planning implications;
- an exploration of the possibilities and implications of organization strategies of the primary railway hubs serving regional and metropolitan mobility, both in terms of the distribution of accessibility values that could promote evolution towards a net structure of settlement patterns, and in terms of management models;
- an integrated holistic approach that brings people's needs back to the center of projects [35].

Finally, productive sectors require a transport system that should respond to high levels of efficiency, safety, and speed, in order to operate efficiently and in a competitive way. Occasional, spontaneous, partial responses to such needs have not led to a transportation system with modern, technological, and organizational characteristics so far, and are very unlikely to do so in the future. The crucial intervention in the sector, relating to both the functioning, reorganization, and renewal of the existing transport supply as well as improving it, should be planned, defined, and proposed according to a new way of organizing the system of decisions in transport.

This allows that intervention and the corresponding expense a) are consistent at all levels, b) concern expense needs arising from reliable forecasts of demands of a growing economic system, and c) are done most opportunely according to a scheme of priorities. Unacceptable expense delays or useless anticipations are avoid, by integrating among different modes, by globalizing the expense wasted today, and by optimizing the resources. The choice of priorities must occur, therefore, based on a uniform method that can examine not only economic but also social and environmental aspects.

6 Conclusions and Remarks

The paper presented wanted to underline how the traditional planning and design procedures don't work if in the preparation of plans for areas of a low population density is partially characterized by the presence of medium-large urban concentrations. In fact, in such a case, also owing to insufficiently defined scenarios of socio-economic development, the future demand for transport is not easily foreseen and for this reason, sizing a communication system can be a challenging task.

It is, therefore, not the entity of the demand, that may be binding for choices, but more articulated considerations related to the level of the quality of life, the safety and care of the territory, the environmental protection and enhancing local products and culture.

An essential component is the availability of job opportunities, higher-level services, and the possibility of social relationships. It is clear the importance of connecting the inner areas to coastal ones, where commerce and tourism offer jobs, better incomes, services, and social relationships.

In order to make the "poles" entirely available for the population of marginal areas, it is essential to make them accessible, that is, to make the trip to reach them cheap, fast, safe, and comfortable. Namely, it is crucial to improve their accessibility. Accessibility and quality of life thus establish an inseparable couple in low population density areas: accessibility may become reliable support in the definition of priorities of intervention on the transport system.

Acknowledgments. This study was supported by the MIUR (Ministry of Education, Universities and Research [Italy]) through a project entitled WEAKI TRANSIT: WEAK-demand areas Innovative TRANsport Shared services for Italian Towns (Project protocol: 20174ARRHT_004; CUP Code: F74I19001290001), financed with the PRIN 2017 (Research Projects of National Relevance) program. We authorize the MIUR to reproduce and distribute reprints for Governmental purposes, notwithstanding any copyright notations thereon. Any opinions, findings, and conclusions or recommendations expressed in this material are those of the authors and do not necessarily reflect the views of the MIUR. This study was supported by the project "Urban Polarities in the Cities of Newcastle (UK) and Cagliari (Italy) for monitoring the central and attractive effects of the city-territory", founded by the programme "Bando 2019 Mobilità Giovani Ricercatori (MGR)", financed by the Autonomous Region of Sardinia (under the Regional Law of 7 August 2007, n. 7 "Promotion of Scientific Research and Technological Innovation in Sardinia"). This work also has been partially supported by the MIUR within the Smart City framework (project: PON04a2_00381 "CAGLIARI2020"). The authors are grateful for the CTM SpA, which made its data available for this study. The views expressed herein are those of the authors and are not necessarily those of the Italian bus operator.

References

1. United Nations. World Population Prospects - Population Division - United Nations (2019). https://population.un.org/wpp/
2. Faggian, A., Modrego, F., McCann, P.: Human capital and regional development. In: Handbook of Regional Growth and Development Theories. Edward Elgar Publishing (2019)
3. Glaeser, E.L.: Reinventing Boston: 1630–2003. J. Econ. Geogr. **5**, 119–153 (2005)
4. Carlino, G.A., Chatterjee, S., Hunt, R.M.: Urban density and the rate of invention. J. Urban Econ. **61**, 389–419 (2007)
5. Cattaneo, M., Malighetti, P., Paleari, S., Redondi, R.: Evolution of long-distance students' mobility: the role of the air transport service in Italy. Transp. Res. Part A Policy Pract. **93**, 66–82. http://hdl.handle.net/10446/77425

6. Torrisi, V., Ignaccolo, M., Inturri, G.: Innovative transport systems to promote sustainable mobility: developing the model architecture of a traffic control and supervisor system. In: Gervasi, O., et al. (eds.) ICCSA 2018. LNCS, vol. 10962, pp. 622–638. Springer, Cham (2018). https://doi.org/10.1007/978-3-319-95168-3_42

7. Torrisi, V., Ignaccolo, M., Inturri, G.: Toward a sustainable mobility through a dynamic real-time traffic monitoring, estimation and forecasting system: The RE.S.E.T. project. In: Town and Infrastructure Planning for Safety and Urban Quality - Proceedings of the 23rd International Conference on Living and Walking in Cities, LWC 2017, pp. 241–247 (2018). https://doi.org/10.1201/9781351173360-32

8. Garmendia, M., Ureña, J.M., Coronado, J.M.: Long-distance trips in a sparsely populated region: the impact of high-speed infrastructures. J. Transp. Geogr. **19**, 537–551 (2011)

9. European Spatial Planning Observation Network – ESPON. Governance, planning and financial tools in support of polycentric development. Working paper. ESPON, Luxembourg (2018)

10. Henke, I., Cartenì, A., Molitierno, C., Errico, A.: Decision-making in the transport sector: a sustainable evaluation method for road infrastructure. Sustainability **12**(3), 764 (2020)

11. Coni, M., Maltinti, F., Portas, S., Pinna, F., Annunziata, F.: White Paper SIIV. Italian Road Network Critical Issue. In: Angeli, F. (ed.) SIIV (Italian Society of Transport Infrastructures) (2002). http://people.unica.it/mauroconi/files/2011/10/coni47full.pdf

12. National Strategy for Internal Areas, Department for Planning and Coordination of Economic Policy. http://www.programmazioneeconomica.gov.it/2019/05/23/strategia-nazionale-delle-aree-interne/. Accessed 30 Apr 2020

13. Garau, C., Desogus, G., Coni, M.: Fostering and planning a smart governance strategy for evaluating the urban polarities of the sardinian island (Italy). Sustainability **11**(18), 4962 (2019). https://doi.org/10.3390/su11184962

14. Coni, M., Pinna, F., Annunziata, F.: The transport system in the land organization of the inner regions of Sardinia. In: Proceedings of International Conference "The role of infrastructures for development of the Mediterranean island", Iraklion, Crete (1997). http://people.unica.it/mauroconi/files/2011/10/coni24full.pdf

15. Passarelli, D., Foresta, S., Fazia, C.: The role of transport system in the implementation of the strategy for the inland areas. Procedia Soc. Behav. Sci. **223**, 520–527 (2016)

16. Ignaccolo, M., Inturri, G., García-Melón, M., Giuffrida, N., Le Pira, M., Torrisi, V.: Combining Analytic Hierarchy Process (AHP) with role-playing games for stakeholder engagement in complex transport decisions. Transp. Res. Procedia **27**, 500–507 (2017). https://doi.org/10.1016/j.trpro.2017.12.069

17. Ignaccolo, M., Inturri, G., Giuffrida, N., Pira, M.L., Torrisi, V.: Public engagement for designing new transport services: investigating citizen preferences from a multiple criteria perspective. Transp. Res. Procedia **37**, 91–98 (2019). https://doi.org/10.1016/j.trpro.2018.12.170

18. Campisi, T., Torrisi, V., Ignaccolo, M., Inturri, G., Tesoriere, G.: University propensity assessment to car sharing services using mixed survey data: the Italian case study of Enna city. Transp. Res. Procedia **47**, 433–440 (2020). https://doi.org/10.1016/j.trpro.2020.03.155

19. Ignaccolo, M., Inturri, G., Giuffrida, N., Le Pira, M., Torrisi, V.: Structuring transport decision-making problems through stakeholder engagement: The case of Catania metro accessibility. Transp. Infrastruct. Syst. 919–926 (2017). https://doi.org/10.1201/9781315281896-118

20. European Commission. "Demographic trends in EU regions", EU regional and urban development (2019). https://ec.europa.eu/regional_policy/en/newsroom/news/2019/01/31-01-2019-demographic-trends-in-eu-regions

21. Wey, W.M.: Constructing urban dynamic transportation planning strategies for improving quality of life and urban sustainability under emerging growth management principles. Sustain. Cities Soc. **44**, 275–290 (2019)

22. Nicodème, C., Diamandouros, K., Diez, J., Durso, C., Arampidou, K., Nuri, A.K.: ERF Road Statistics Yearbook 2017. European Road Federation (2017). http://www.erf.be/wp-content/uploads/2018/01/Road_statistics_2017.pdf

23. Calabrò, G., Torrisi, V., Inturri, G., Ignaccolo, M.: Improving inbound logistic planning for large-scale real-world routing problems: a novel ant-colony simulation-based optimization. Eur. Transp. Res. Rev. **12**(1) (2020). https://doi.org/10.1186/s12544-020-00409-7

24. Ignaccolo, M., Inturri, G., Giuffrida, N., Torrisi, V., Cocuzza, E.: Sustainability of freight transport through an integrated approach: the case of the eastern sicily port system. Transp. Res. Procedia **45**, 177–184 (2020). https://doi.org/10.1016/j.trpro.2020.03.005

25. Torrisi, V., Ignaccolo, M., Inturri, G.: Estimating travel time reliability in urban areas through a dynamic simulation model. Transp. Res. Procedia **27**, 857–864 (2017). https://doi.org/10.1016/j.trpro.2017.12.134

26. Torrisi, V., Ignaccolo, M., Inturri, G., Giuffrida, N.: Combining sensor traffic and simulation data to measure urban road network reliability. In: International Conference on Traffic and Transport Engineering (ICTTE) Proceedings, Belgrade, p. 1004, November 2016

27. Torrisi, V., Ignaccolo, M., Inturri, G.: Analysis of road urban transport network capacity through a dynamic assignment model: validation of different measurement methods. Transp. Res. Procedia **27**, 1026–1033 (2017). https://doi.org/10.1016/j.trpro.2017.12.135

28. Ignaccolo, M., Inturri, G., Giuffrida, N., Le Pira, M., Torrisi, V., Calabrò, G.: A step towards walkable environments: spatial analysis of pedestrian compatibility in an urban context. Eur. Transp. Trasporti Europei **76**(6), 1–12 (2020)

29. Ignaccolo, C., Giuffrida, N., Torrisi, V.: The queensway of New York city. A proposal for sustainable mobility in queens. Town Infrastruct. Plan. Saf. Urban Qual. 69–76 (2018). https://doi.org/10.1201/9781351173360-12

30. Ignaccolo, M., Inturri, G., Cocuzza, E., Giuffrida, N., Torrisi, V.: Framework for the evaluation of the quality of pedestrian routes for the sustainability of port-city shared areas. In: Coastal Cities and Their Sustainable Future III. WIT Transactions on The Built Environment, vol. 188. WIT Press (2019). https://doi.org/10.2495/cc190021. ISSN 1743-3509

31. Yamu, C.: It is simply complex(ity) modeling and simulation in the light of decision-making, emergent structures and a world of non-linearity. disP Plan. Rev. **50**(4), 43–53 (2014)

32. Abis, E., Garau, C.: An assessment of the effectiveness of strategic spatial planning: a study of Sardinian municipalities. Eur. Plan. Stud. **24**(1), 139–162 (2016)

33. Ignaccolo, M., Inturri, G., Giuffrida, N., Torrisi, V.: A sustainable framework for the analysis of port systems. Int. J. Transp. Econ. Eng. Law (78) (2020). European Transport

34. Moreno-Monroy, A.I., Lovelace, R., Ramos, F.R.: Public transport and school location impacts on educational inequalities: insights from São Paulo. J. Transp. Geogr. **67**, 110–118 (2018)

35. Coni, M., Garau, C., Pinna, F.: How has Cagliari changed its citizens in smart citizens? Exploring the influence of ITS technology on urban social interactions. In: Gervasi, O., et al. (eds.) ICCSA 2018. LNCS, vol. 10962, pp. 573–588. Springer, Cham (2018). https://doi.org/10.1007/978-3-319-95168-3_39

Sustainability of the Timber Supply Chain on the Island of Sardinia

Giovanna Concu[✉]

Department of Civil and Environmental Engineering and Architecture,
University of Cagliari, Cagliari, Italy
gconcu@unica.it

Abstract. This paper illustrates the potential of using wood as a structural material in terms of sustainable construction and analyses the opportunities offered by the plant of production processes based on the use of locally-grown wood to the end of promoting the development of sustainable economies in narrow and interconnected communities like those of the islands. In detail, the convenience of planting in Sardinia a supply chain for manufacturing structural laminated timber elements made of locally-grown maritime pine is addressed, also by referring to the results of a research activity devoted to this purpose.

Keywords: Timber buildings · Circular economy in Islands · Local supply chain

1 Introduction

The issue of sustainability is now a paradigm that informs all human activities. It is closely linked to the concept of development, in the sense that currently the only conceivable development is the sustainable one. In fact, in an era such as the contemporary one, in which anthropic processes are marked by the depletion of raw materials, by the increase in polluting emissions and by the increase in waste, it has become a mandatory requirement, as well as a moral duty, the attention to development models oriented to environmental, economic and social improvement.

The concept of sustainable development was made explicit, for the first time, in a document presented by G.H. Brundtland in a meeting of the World Commission on Environment and Development [1]. The document, better known as the Brundtland Report, Our Common Future, highlighted the need to implement a strategy capable of integrating the needs of development and the environment. This strategy was defined with the term *sustainable development*, whose precise definition was as follows: development is sustainable if it meets the needs of the present without compromising the ability of future generations to meet their own needs. This definition contained a new concept relating to sustainable development, able to reconcile aspects such as expectations of social well-being, economic growth, maintenance of natural resources, and respect for the environment. To guarantee all this, it is necessary to fulfil ethical principles and moral responsibility, touching on fundamental elements for eco-sustainability such as maintaining existing resources and the planet's environmental balance.

© Springer Nature Switzerland AG 2020
O. Gervasi et al. (Eds.): ICCSA 2020, LNCS 12255, pp. 353–367, 2020.
https://doi.org/10.1007/978-3-030-58820-5_27

Sustainability is therefore a multifaceted concept, both as regards the needs to be satisfied and the capacities to be guaranteed over time and as regards the capitals to be protected and enhanced, such as in particular the environmental and human-social ones.

Sustainable development revolves around four key concepts (Fig. 1):

- environmental sustainability, understood as the protection and enhancement of natural capital, that is the maintenance of the quality and renewability of natural resources;
- economic sustainability, understood as protection and enhancement of economic capital, i.e. guarantee of income and work for the population;
- social sustainability, understood as protection and enhancement of human-social capital, that is guarantee of well-being (safety, health, education, etc.) equally distributed among the population;
- institutional sustainability, understood as protection and enhancement of human-social, economic and environmental capital through the guarantee of conditions of democracy, stability and participation.

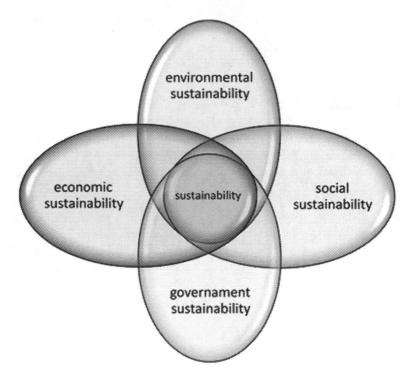

Fig. 1. Sustainability pillars.

A key point of sustainability is the idea of a limit to the exploitation of a resource or capital, but it is possible or necessary to admit that the stocks of capital at stake (environmental, economic and human-social) can be considered interchangeable with each other, for example admitting that a reduction in environmental capital can be counterbalanced by an increase in human-social capital, and vice versa.

In the context of sustainable development, it is necessary to highlight the role of the construction sector. Currently, this sector is globally responsible on average for over 35% of the consumption of raw materials, soil, water and energy and for over 30% of pollution and the production of waste. The buildings built in the second half of the last century and in the first decade of this century are characterized by the enormous consumption of energy and natural resources, so that the consumption of natural resources, the production of a considerable amount of waste, and the pollution of air and water are the largest undesirable effects related to the construction industry. The construction sector expands at a rate of around 2 billion of square meters per year, producing pollution and consumption of resources to create buildings which in turn require energy to be habitable and comfortable.

To promote the effective reduction of the impact of the construction sector, a synergic action is needed both on the production front (supply of raw materials, saving of energy resources, waste management) and on the design front (construction techniques, energy saving, maintenance and renovation).

The need for sustainability is further amplified in territories such as the islands, which are often particularly vulnerable to climate changes and over-dependent on fossil fuels and energy imports. As stated by the European Commission [2] many of European islands are small isolated systems and have small markets, are more vulnerable to the effects of the anthropic impact and must produce a considerable effort to implement policies and practices to reverse it. Therefore, it is essential that the islands manage their resources in a sustainable way, to become increasingly efficient, self-sufficient and be able to protect their environmental heritage.

The now unavoidable need to produce in a sustainable way is finding in the circular economy paradigm a strong conceptual key that can become the real driver of a process of change of epochal importance. In fact, an economy model is placed at the centre which, starting from the awareness of the finite nature of resources, reduces or eliminates waste, differentiates the sources of supply of materials, recovers and recycles the materials, makes consumer products as durable as possible maximizing their use value. The cradle to cradle approach of the circular economy involves all phases, from design to production, distribution, use and possible reuse, and then ends with the recycling and recovery of raw materials thus making the whole process sustainable and interconnected. It therefore clearly differs from the traditional paradigm of the linear economy in which raw materials, through the application of energy and work, are processed with the sole objective of obtaining marketable products, dealing waste of production secondarily and conceiving it as end of use products (Fig. 2).

One of the aspects on which to intervene to make the construction sector sustainable is therefore the use of construction materials that are themselves sustainable, such as for example materials of natural origin. Among these, wood is one of the most effective materials in terms of environmental sustainability because of its natural eco-compatibility, mechanical and building physic performance, ease to install.

In light of the foregoing considerations, this paper illustrates the potential of using wood as a structural material in terms of sustainable construction, also analysing the opportunities offered by the plant of local supply chains that allow implementing production processes based on the use of locally-grown wood, promoting the development of sustainable economies in narrow and interconnected communities like those of the islands.

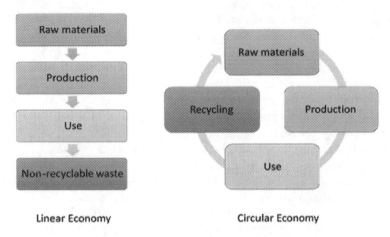

Fig. 2. Linear economy vs Circular economy

2 Timber Buildings and Sustainability

Timber in construction has a series of advantages linked to the origin and intrinsic characteristics of the material itself. Aspects such as the renewability of the raw material, which requires only land, water and sun to develop, and the positive effect on the environment, linked above all to the ability to sequester carbon dioxide from the atmosphere and store it for proportional times to the life of the material itself, make it one of the most suitable building materials to meet the current requirements of eco-compatibility and sustainability, as it minimizes the environmental impact at all levels as it is recyclable, renewable, biodegradable, and free of toxic contents [3]. Starting from the assumption that the reduction of climate-changing emissions (carbon dioxide and other greenhouse gases) and the expansion of carbon reservoirs, the term carbon reservoir meaning any stored form of carbon dioxide, are the two possible approaches to mitigate actual climate changes, wood allows both roads to be travelled [4, 5]. Due to photosynthesis, a tree stores large amounts of carbon dioxide in the wood. It is estimated that 1 cubic meter of wood stores approximately 1 ton of carbon dioxide, which continues to be stored into the material throughout its life, even when the wood undergoes the processes that make it a product, for example, for the building industry. Therefore, the use of wood in construction generates two advantages: on the one hand, the gradual replacement of the most energy-intensive and polluting building materials with timber reduces the climate changing emissions associated with the production and management of these materials; on the other hand, the management of forests aimed at the use of wood in industrial sectors such as buildings involves the continuous renewal of the forest itself with an increase in the capacity to extract carbon dioxide from the environment and with significant added value with respect to firewood, landscape improvement, reduction of hydrogeological hazard [6].

In terms of economic sustainability, the high ratio between timber mechanical performance and weight, combined with the possibility of dry connections and achieving high levels of prefabrication, allows to significantly reduce construction times and storage spaces for materials on site, to facilitate handling, transport and assembly operations and to reduce the size of the foundation structures. All these aspects favourably affect the abatement and minimization of costs, as well as the environmental impact. There are numerous studies aimed at evaluating, through LCA approaches, the environmental impact of timber constructions in relation to other materials, especially concrete and steel, with reference to the consumption of raw materials and primary energy, to the production of carbon dioxide and in general to the emission of greenhouse gases in all phases of the useful life of the material [7–18]. The general result is the lower level of environmental impact of timber, especially considering the carbon dioxide storage capacity of the wood. Assuming that the trend in the construction sector does not vary, only 0.5% of new buildings will be built with timber by 2050. If wood production increases, this could be pushed up to 10% in a conservative scenario and could involve the storage of around 10 M tons of carbon dioxide per year. Assuming that the use of cement and steel in construction continues and assuming an increase in the surface area per person, the cumulative emissions due to these building materials could reach up to 1/5 of the carbon dioxide emissions balance up to 2050. Shifting towards timber buildings can reduce cumulative greenhouse gas emissions from steel and cement production by at least half. This may not seem like much compared to the current amount of around 11,000 M tonnes of carbon dioxide emissions per year, but the move to timber would make a difference in achieving climate stabilization goals [19]. In addition, wood contributes to environmental comfort due to its low conductivity, high thermal inertia, and natural hygroscopicity. Natural materials such as wood or cork are already comfortable at room temperature, while those like stone or cement are perceived as comfortable only at higher surface temperatures. In this regard, it is interesting to note that there are several studies concerning the link between the use of wood in locations and the psychophysical well-being of the occupants. Some of these studies point out that nature stimulates the reward brain system by reducing stress and consequently cortisol levels, heart rate and blood pressure, with a better immune system response [20], and the use of wood inside a building has clear physiological and psychological benefits that mimic the effect of spending time outdoors in contact with nature [21]. Other studies highlight that offices with wooden interiors convey sensations of innovation, energy and comfort. This results in increased worker happiness, decreased stress and reduced sick leaving with a 15% increase in productivity [22]. There is a connection between architecture, materials and health; there is indicative evidence that wood used in hospital settings can have effects on improving healing processes and other results such as shorter length of stay [23].

3   Timber in Architecture

Wood is the oldest of building materials. In the past the great availability of material, the ease of manufacturing and handling, the renewability and some others specific qualities, have made it the most widespread construction material. This spread has seen a halt since the nineteenth century, especially in some countries such as Italy where reinforced concrete and steel have monopolized the attention of researchers, technicians and consequently the market. The reasons for this downgrading of wood in construction are due to various cultural, economic and environmental factors. These include natural degradability, combustibility, shape and size restrictions dependent on the starting tree and the general mistrust of a natural material that has innate defects that affect its mechanical performance, in spite of the large number of works carried out in the past which have demonstrated remarkable strength and durability. In Italy for example, although belonging to the construction tradition of this country especially for floors and roofs, for a long time since the post-war period wood has been relegated to a secondary role in construction, being used mainly in the context of the recovery of historical or rural buildings or for provisional uses, being effectively excluded from the list of materials of engineering interest, similarly to what happened to masonry.

In recent decades, however, there has been a notable revival of wood in structural uses, thanks above all to the introduction of laminated timber, an industrial product that reconciles the great qualities of wood such as naturalness and sustainability with the reliability and high performance of a material industrially manufactured. In fact, laminated timber allows the most defective and unreliable parts to be discarded and provides for a certified production control that includes repeated mechanical tests; this allows to overcome the defects of solid wood, such as lower reliability due to uncertainty about the content of defects and the variability of physical characteristics over time, as well as the limits of use linked to the natural dimensions of the elements. The production virtually does not limit the size and shape of the structural elements, which can be made with high precision thanks to the numerical control machines, conferring ample freedom to architectural forms.

Besides that, timber buildings guarantee considerable mechanical performance and high durability, even in case of response to seismic actions, so that, also from a structural point of view, timber constructions are excellent competitors even for the most modern structures in reinforced concrete or steel. Timber is characterized by good mechanical strength both in tension and in compression, so it can be used for the manufacturing of elements prone to bending such as beams, compressed like the pillars, stretched like tie rods, without the need to combine it with other materials, unlike concrete and masonry.

3.1   Cross Laminated Timber

Among the various timber construction typologies, it is worth mentioning the CLT (Cross Laminated Timber) technology, which consists in the production of flat structural elements made by gluing layers of boards mutually oriented at 90° (Fig. 3). This arrangement in crossed layers mitigates the typical effects of anisotropy of the wood and gives the structural element the possibility of being used as a load-bearing element both for floors and roofs and for vertical walls. The positive effect of the cross lamination on the mechanical performance makes it is also possible to use wood species with non-high mechanical characteristics, favouring the exploitation of local species, even with modest basic mechanical performance, other than those coming from central Europe traditionally treated for the manufacturing of laminated elements [24].

CLT is particularly suitable for advanced prefabrication, allowing all parts to be made off-site, and reserving for the construction site almost exclusively the connections and finishing.

Fig. 3. Glue laminated timber (left) and cross laminated timber (right)

3.2   Building Information Modeling

Currently, the request for buildings or infrastructures is strictly connected to specific needs, such as accurate design, speed of construction, energy efficiency, ease of management and maintenance, and durability. In the rapidly evolving global construction market, clear and precise rules are needed to help all actors of the construction supply chain to adapt skills to change and to innovate successfully.

The importance of Building Information Modeling (BIM) in this context is widely recognized. BIM is a process that permits to create and manage information about a building throughout its life cycle. It is witnessing an increasing diffusion in the construction market because it leads to considerable savings in realization times and building management costs. BIM also allows interchange of data for interoperability between various computer applications for the most varied purposes and uses (management, monitoring, performance calculation) [25].

As will be illustrated in the next section, the global timber construction market is rapidly growing and technologically evolving, but this still does not match with a growth in sector interoperability. The technological development of the last few years has led to an increase in the speed, precision and efficiency of the production plants for prefabricated timber elements. However, two important differences still remain compared to other strictly industrial products [26]:

1) the behavior of the wood depends on the environmental conditions in which the construction arises, and this must be taken into account by any standardization process;

2) the timber construction industry is very fragmented, made up of many small companies that produce highly specialized components and services, very often focused on particular territorial areas.

These two aspects can be greatly improved by the diffusion of BIM methodologies capable of optimizing the design, production and management of wooden structures. In fact, the growth and optimization potential offered by BIM is remarkable, especially as regards to prefabricated building systems, such as CLT and other timber building systems. The development of BIM in the structural timber sector would allow to obtain various advantages in terms of design flexibility, prefabrication process, management of construction, use and maintenance phases.

4 Timber Market in Italy

The wood sector in Italy is worth about 1.6% of the gross national product, involves about 15% of companies and generates a turnover greater than 30 billion euros, of which about two thirds are relating to the wood-furniture sector. The timber construction sector is growing and today the turnover of construction companies exceeds 720 million euros, marking a + 5% compared to 2017 [27]. The number of timber houses is growing, currently corresponding to about 7% of residential construction, with CLT constructions representing about 50%. Italy is currently the fourth European manufacturer of prefabricated timber buildings, with positive exports, highlighting a market aimed towards excellence and resilient to the crisis of the building sector. In addition to these considerations, it is interesting to note that in Italy the forestry area corresponds to over 35% of the total territory.

Despite the positive market trend and the availability of raw materials, Italy is the EU country with the lowest degree of self-sufficiency in the supply of wood raw material (<1/3 of needs). The dependence from abroad is such as to result in a highly unfavorable trade balance for the wood products sector (logs and sawn, veneer, panels, semi-finished products and components for furniture and construction) which is counterbalanced only thanks to the Italian furniture industry and the significant added value generated by this sector. The level of extraction of Italian forests is one of the lowest in the EU with an annual share of less than 25% of the increase, compared to 65% of the European average. In general, the supply of Italian timber is quantitatively low, generally characterized by a lack of quantitative and qualitative homogeneity and, overall, not addressed towards adequate economic and technological enhancement [28].

With reference to the situation on the island of Sardinia, although the constructions entirely made of wood do not belong to Sardinian building tradition, focused above all on the use of masonry for vertical load-bearing structures and on the use of wood limited to floors and roofs, the timber buildings market of the island is following the national trend, marking a continuous growth also evidenced by the large number of companies involved in the marketing and installation of timber prefabricated buildings (Fig. 4). To this must be added the fact that Sardinia has a forestry area between 40% and 60% of the total, the main wood species being oaks, other broadleaves such as eucalyptus, and conifers such as stone pine, Aleppo pine, Corsican pine, maritime pine

Fig. 4. Sardinian wooden structures: traditional truss (upper left), common roof (upper right) and modern CLT building (down)

and radiate pine [6]. Despite these aspects, in line with the national trend the wood used for prefabricated buildings in Sardinia is almost 100% imported.

5 Timber Supply Chain in the Island of Sardinia

Sardinia, as emerges from the document related to the Smart Specialization Strategy S3 [29] is characterized by an economic and productive system of modest competitiveness and with little propensity for innovation. This connotation also involves the building sector, which is affected by historical problems connected to insularity, employment difficulties, lack of economic resources, as well as the contingent and more general economic-productive crisis. The crisis in the building sector has serious repercussions on the entire supply chain of the construction industry, investing companies, producers, artisans and traders. Moreover, Sardinian building sector, one of the least eco-efficient in Europe, is responsible for 30% of the region's total energy consumption and 25% of carbon dioxide emissions into the atmosphere. Then the awareness emerges that the reversal of the negative trend that invests the building sector can effectively combine with the policies aimed at stimulating energy efficiency and the use of natural materials in the sector, which have now become a necessity and no longer just an intellectual or ideological choice. The use of local resources by the building industry, moreover of natural origin such as wood, as well as meeting the needs of green building, is revealed as a real chance of development that would directly invest the building sector and consequently the employment, environmental, social and cultural context. This choice of circular economy in the building sector is also the best path towards the sustainable development of the islands. The islands in fact have a greater fragility with respect to the effects of the anthropic impact and must produce a considerable effort to put in place systems of resilience, so it is essential that there are more and more circular systems to effectively exploit islands natural resources [2].

On the basis of the framework described above, a research activity, funded by the Sardinian local administration and still ongoing, has been launched in Sardinia aimed at verifying the possibility of using local wood as structural timber. The research involves an experimental agenda carried out on locally-grown maritime pine (Pinus Pinaster), which is a widely spread and relatively fast growing conifer available in Sardinia, in the rest of Italy and also in several Mediterranean regions. This Sardinian species has never been considered as a structural material before this research started.

Sardinian maritime pine is generally characterized by medium-low quality due to the presence of defects (knots, clusters of knots, resin pockets, grain deviation etc.), so the research has proposed to verify its performance when used in CLT elements with and without natural fibers reinforcement.

The research activity has been divided into several phases, such as:

- identification of the areas from which to take the material;
- selection and cutting of plants;
- cutting of logs in boards;
- drying;
- laboratory experimental tests on boards (Fig. 5) in order to define a grading rule for this material (i.e. attribution to the material of a performance profile containing the mechanical, elastic and physical properties as a function of the defects);
- manufacturing of CLT structural elements in the laboratory (Fig. 6);
- mechanical tests on the structural elements (Fig. 7);
- study and implementation of numerical models;
- extrapolation of design formulas.

Very briefly, the main results achieved so far have shown that [6, 24, 30–35]:

- the mechanical performance of the CLT elements is comparable with that of similar elements already on the market;
- the CLT elements reinforced with natural fibers allow, with the same mechanical performance, a reduction in thickness, with consequent economic and dimension advantages;
- it is possible to implement a supply chain process aimed at the manufacturing of laminated timber elements based on Sardinian maritime pine.

Fig. 5. Boards testing

Fig. 6. Manufacturing of CLT structural elements

Fig. 7. Mechanical tests

A further step in the direction of improving sustainability of Sardinian building sector is taking place through a further research line concerning the development of eco-sustainable building solutions for energy-efficient walls and floors. This research aims to study the energy performance of CLT Sardinian maritime pine elements conjugated with layers of thermo-acoustic insulation made with local and natural materials, such as cork, sheep's wool, etc. [36]. In addition, it will be of interest to study the possibility of using in the construction industry the other Sardinian wood species, in order to make the development of the production chain of timber elements economically more advantageous and make these elements more competitive on the global market.

6 Discussion

The research conducted so far has allowed, as well as to formulate the conclusions illustrated in the previous section, to simulate the entire supply chain process for the manufacturing of CLT elements in Sardinian maritime pine, allowing the detection and analysis of the inherent critical issues.

The study has highlighted that the use of locally produced wood can allow to reduce the energy consumption linked to import wood from abroad, a factor particularly important for island regions such as Sardinia, and at the same time can allow to create employment in areas often economically depressed. The potential of the studied structural products is high. The timber market is in fact continuously expanding, in Europe and in Italy, given the considerable possibilities of use, the performance characteristics and the progress of technology. The use of timber allows the construction of buildings that meet the requirements for energy efficiency and environmental sustainability.

The development of timber structural products based on local wood can allow:

- the reduction of the costs of timber structures, thanks to the possibility of producing them on site rather than importing them from afar, thus promoting the sustainable construction sector in Sardinia with great environmental advantages;
- an increase in the demand for structural timber, with a consequent further increase in the Sardinian forestry area and with important environmental, tourist and hydrogeological protection advantages - as already underlined, the forestry potential of Sardinia is significant, being currently the fourth Italian region by extension of the forestry surface;
- the creation of new jobs in the timber chain, such as activities related to forest maintenance, new plants for the production of sawn wood (sawmills) and manufacture of structural components (prefabrication workshops), new specialized assembly companies, currently almost absent in Sardinia, with important repercussions in terms of employment in the Sardinian territory and a significant social function to reduce unemployment and abandonment of depressed areas;
- certification of the construction quality in all phases of the process (materials, production, installation).

7   Conclusions

The potential of using wood as a structural material in terms of sustainable construction has been analyzed and discussed. In detail, the opportunities offered by the plant in Sardinia of a supply chain for manufacturing structural laminated timber elements made of locally-grown wood has been addressed, also by referring to the results of a research activity devoted to this purpose.

Beside the specific scientific goals of the research, the collateral results and the positive effects of the supply chain can be summarized in the promotion of an industrial, occupational and social growth determined by the use of local resources and the innovative and transversal use of traditional products, all in terms of all-round sustainability.

What has been discussed appears even more significant if considered with a view to optimizing the strategies to be implemented in the islands in order to respond to the challenges currently imposed by the pillars of sustainability.

References

1. Brundtland, G.H.: Our Common Future: Report of the World Commission on Environment and Development. Geneva: UN-Dokument A/42/427 (1987)
2. Clean energy for EU islands, https://ec.europa.eu/energy/en/topics/energy-strategy-and-energy-union/clean-energy-eu-islands. Accessed 26 Apr 2020
3. Buchanan, A.H., Honey, B.G.: Energy and carbon dioxide implications of building construction. Energ. Build. **20**(3), 205–217 (1994)
4. Hildebrandt, J., Hagemann, N., Thrän, D.: The contribution of wood based construction materials for leveraging a low carbon building sector in Europe. Sustain. Cities Soc. **34**, 405–418 (2017)
5. Ramage, M.H., et al.: The wood from the trees: the use of timber in construction. Renew. Sustain. Energ. Rev. **68**, 333–359 (2017)
6. Fragiacomo, M., Riu, R., Scotti, R.: Can structural timber foster short procurement chains within mediterranean forests? a research case in Sardinia. South-east Euro. For. **6**(1), 107–117 (2015)
7. BoKrjesson, P., Gustavsson, L.: Greenhouse gas balances in building construction: wood versus concrete from life-cycle and forest land-use perspectives. Energ. Policy **28**, 575–588 (2000)
8. Gustavsson, L., Sathre, R.: Variability in energy and carbon dioxide balances of wood and concrete building materials. Build. Environ. **41**, 940–951 (2006)
9. Hafner, A., Schafer, S.: Comparative LCA study of different timber and mineral buildings and calculation method for substitution factors on building level. J. Clean. Prod. **167**, 630–642 (2017)
10. Lu, H.R., El Hanandeh, A., Benoit, P.G.: A comparative life cycle study of alternative materials for Australian multi-storey apartment building frame constructions: environmental and economic perspective. J. Cleaner Prod. **166**, 458–473 (2017)
11. Gerilla, G.P., Teknomo, K., Hokao, K.: An environmental assessment of wood and steel reinforced concrete housing construction. Build. Environ. **42**, 2778–2784 (2007)
12. Hill, C.A.S., Dibdiakova, J.: The environmental impact of wood compared to other building materials. Int. Wood Prod. J. **7**(4), 215–219 (2016)

13. Hassan, O., Johansson, C.: Glued laminated timber and steel beams: a comparative study of structural design, economic and environmental consequences. J. Eng. Des. Technol. **16**(3), 398–417 (2018)
14. Anejo, J.A.: Impact of concrete, steel and timber on the environment: a review. Int. J. Technol. Enhancements Emerg. Eng. Res. **2**(7), 2347–4289 (2014)
15. Ede, A.N., Adebayo, S.O., Ugwu, E.I., Emenike, C.: Life cycle assessment of environmental impacts of using concrete or timber to construct a duplex residential building. IOSR J. Mech. Civil Eng. **11**(2), 62–72 (2014)
16. Liu, Y., Guo, H., Sun, C., Chang, W.-S.: Assessing cross laminated timber (CLT) as an alternative material for mid-rise residential buildings in cold regions in China—a life-cycle assessment approach. Sustainability **8**, 1047 (2016)
17. Sandanayake, M., Lokuge, W., Zhang, G., Setunge, S., Thushar, Q.: Greenhouse gas emissions during timber and concrete building construction—a scenario based comparative case study. Sustain. Cities Soc. **38**, 91–97 (2018)
18. Lyslo Skullestad, J., Bohne, R.A., Lohne, J.: High-rise timber buildings as a climate change mitigation measure - a comparative LCA of structural system alternatives. Energ. Procedia **96**, 112–123 (2016)
19. Potsdam Institute for Climate Impact Research (PIK), Buildings can become a global CO2 sink if made out of wood instead of cement and steel, ScienceDaily, 27 January 2020. https://www.sciencedaily.com/releases/2020/01/200127134828.htm. Accessed 17 Jun 2020
20. Selhub, E.M., Logan, A.C.: Your Brain on Nature. Harper Collins (2014)
21. Housing, Health, Humanity. Planet Ark's Make It Wood Program (2014), https://makeitwood.org/documents/doc-1253-wood–housing–health–humanity-report-2015-03-00-final.pdf. Accessed 26 Apr 2020
22. Ball, R.D., Killerby, S.K., Ridoutt, B.G.: First impressions of organisations and the qualities connoted by wood in interior design. For. Prod. J. **52**(10), 30 (2002)
23. Cronhjort, Y.: Project Wood2New (2015). https://doi.org/10.13140/rg.2.1.4002.7923. Accessed 26 Apr 2020
24. Concu, G., De Nicolo, B., Fragiacomo, M., Trulli, N., Valdes, M.: Grading of maritime pine from Sardinia (Italy) for use in cross-laminated timber. Proc. Inst. Civil Eng. Constr. Mater. **171**(1), 11–21 (2018)
25. Sacks, R., Eastmann, C., Lee, G., Teicholz, P.: BIM handbook: a guide to building information modeling for owners, designers, engineers, contractors, and facility managers, 3rd edn. John Wiley & Sons Inc, Hoboken (2018)
26. Rudella, E.: BIM for prefabricated wooden structures: interoperability between modeling, structural analysis and industrial production. MSc. Thesis, University of Padova, a.a. 2017–2018 (in Italian)
27. 4° Rapporto Case ed Edifici in Legno, Federlegnoarredo (2019) (in Italian)
28. Il legno massiccio, materiale per un'edilizia sostenibile. Assolegno – FederlegnoArredo (2014) (in Italian). https://www.federlegnoarredo.it/ContentsFiles/Il%20Legno%20Massiccio%20-%20Materiale%20per%20un%20Edilizia%20Sostenibile.pdf. Accessed 26 Apr 2020
29. Sardegna Programmazione, Smart Specialization Strategy S3 (in Italian). http://www.sardegnapro-grammazione.it/index.php?xsl=1384&s=278012&v=2&c=12950. Accessed 26 Apr 2020
30. Giaccu, G.F., Meloni, D., Concu, G., Valdes, M.: Consideration on dynamic identification of wood composite panels using a cantilever vibration method. In: Proceeding World Conference on Timber Engineering. Seoul, Rep. of Korea (2018)

31. Meloni, D., Concu, G., Valdes, M., Giaccu, G.F.: FEM models for elastic parameters identifications of cross laminated maritime pine panels. In: Proceeding of World Conference on Timber Engineering, Seoul, Rep. of Korea (2018)
32. Concu, G., Fragiacomo, M., Trulli, N., Valdes, M.: Non-destructive assessment of gluing in cross-laminated timber panels. WIT Trans. Ecol. Environ. **226**, 559–569 (2017). Sustainable Development and Planning IX
33. Concu, G., De Nicolo, B., Riu, R., Trulli, N., Valdès, M., Fragiacomo M.: Sonic testing on cross laminated timber panels. In: Proceeding of the 6th International Conference on Structural Engineering, Mechanics and Computation - Insights and Innovations in Structural Engineering, Mechanics and Computation, Cape Town, South Africa (2016)
34. Valdes, M., Giaccu, G.F., Meloni, D., Concu, G.: Reinforcement of maritime pine cross-laminated timber panels by means of natural flax fibers. Constr. Build. Mater. **233**, 117741 (2020)
35. Mastino, C.C., Concu, G., Baccoli, R., Frattolillo, A., Di Bella, A.: Methods for acoustic classification in buildings: an example of application of BIM procedures on wooden buildings. In: Proceeding of the 48th International Congress and Exhibition on Noise Control Engineering. Madrid, Spain, vol. 259, pp. 7018–7029 (2019)
36. Concu, G., Pani, L.: Buildings materials, sustainability and circular economy. research projects in the island of Sardinia. In: Monteiro, J., et al. (eds.) INCREaSE 2019, pp. 935–949. Springer, Cham (2020). https://doi.org/10.1007/978-3-030-30938-1_73

The Role of Parent Concrete in Recycled Aggregate Concrete

Luisa Pani⬤, Lorena Francesconi⬤, James Rombi⬤,
Flavio Stochino$^{(\boxtimes)}$⬤, and Fausto Mistretta⬤

Department of Civil, Environmental Engineering and Architecture,
University of Cagliari, 09123 Cagliari, Italy
fstochino@unica.it

Abstract. A current promising way towards sustainable construction is the concrete construction and demolition waste recycling. Indeed, the use of recycled concrete aggregates instead of natural aggregates promotes the natural resources conservation and reduces the environmental impact of concrete. This paper presents the results of an experimental investigation on the mechanical properties of concretes with recycled aggregates obtained from two different parent concretes, belonging to the structure of old Cagliari football stadium. The main target of this work is to verify the effectiveness of adopting concrete debris as recycled aggregates in the new structural concrete. The influence of parent concrete on the characteristics of coarse recycled aggregates and of new structural concrete with these aggregates are investigated. Modulus of elasticity, compressive strength, splitting tensile strength of recycled concretes have been assessed and discussed in order to highlight the role of parent concrete.

Keywords: Reinforced concrete · Environmental impact · Recycled aggregate · Sustainability

1 Introduction

The deterioration of natural resources is partially due to concrete constructions techniques. Thus, concrete construction and demolition waste (C&DW) recycling aimed at producing recycled concrete aggregates, can be a very promising strategy to reduce the important impact on the environment. Actually, the use of recycled aggregates instead of Natural Aggregates (NA) for new concrete structures promotes natural resources preservation and reduces landfill disposal.

The Italian Ministry of the Environment, Land and Sea protection, has published the National Action Plan on Green Public Procurement, see [1]. This document, in agreement with the European Commission guidelines, defines the Minimum Environmental Criteria for the assignment of design and work services for new buildings, retrofitting, maintenance, energy requalification and management of construction sites. These criteria give highlight to the environmental aspects of each construction contract, with the aim of recycling and reusing a large part of non-hazardous C&DW. The need of applied research on the use of recycled aggregates of concrete in structural concretes is patent.

© Springer Nature Switzerland AG 2020
O. Gervasi et al. (Eds.): ICCSA 2020, LNCS 12255, pp. 368–378, 2020.
https://doi.org/10.1007/978-3-030-58820-5_28

Furthermore, it is important to know if the new concrete chemical, physical and mechanical characteristics are influenced by the parent concrete.

Available experimental data on concrete made with Recycled concrete Aggregate (RA) are variable [2–6] claim that the quality of RA mostly depends on the quality of parent concrete. Even if some results are contradictory, some general conclusions can be drawn about the effects of coarse RA. Recycled concrete with low to medium compressive strength can be easily obtained irrespective of the specific quality of parent concrete [7–11]. Instead, in [12] the quality of parent concrete is considered more significative in a weak concrete than in a stronger one. Indeed, according to these authors the strength of concrete depends on both the coarse aggregate and cement.

Actually, the adhered cement mortar quality strongly influences the physical properties of RA. In [8, 13] it is shown that the quantity of adhered mortar increases with the decrease of the recycled aggregate size. Actually, the production process of recycled aggregates (see [14]) has a key role on the final performance because it can strongly modify the amount of adhered mortar. The latter one allows RA to have a lower density and higher water absorption, compared to natural one. Moreover, the presence of potentially unhydrated cement on the surface of RA can further affect the concrete properties [15] and the crack propagation characteristics [16–18].

Compressive strength, splitting tensile strength and modulus of elasticity of concrete with RA were found to decrease with the increase of the aggregates replacement percentage: [19–21]. Instead flexural strength and modulus of elasticity of concrete containing RA are similar to concrete made with natural aggregates according to [22].

In this context additional experimental tests are of paramount relevance.

Fig. 1. View of old Cagliari football stadium.

This paper reports on the experimental tests developed at University of Cagliari aimed at evaluating the mechanical performance of concrete with coarse RA obtained by crushing structural concrete with low compressive strength ($R_{ck} \leq 20$ MPa). The RA derive from concrete structures (cantilever beams and foundations) of the old football stadium located in Cagliari (Sardinia, Italy, built in 1968) see Fig. 1.

Beams with cantilevers and foundation blocks are the concrete structures chosen for the preliminary analysis (see orange elements in Fig. 2).

At first, the parent concrete mechanical performance was tested. Part of cantilever beams and foundations have been demolished and crushed separately, to obtain two types of coarse RA with size 4–16 mm. Using three different replacement percentages (30%, 50% and 80%) of NA with RA a set of six concrete mixes with RA has been produced. For comparison purposes an additional mix of conventional concrete with only natural aggregates was also produced.

This paper is organized as follows. After this introduction Sect. 2 presents the quality of parent concrete while Sect. 3 describes the characteristics of RA. In Sect. 4 the mechanical characteristics of the obtained concrete mixes are shown. Finally, some conclusive remarks are drawn in Sect. 5.

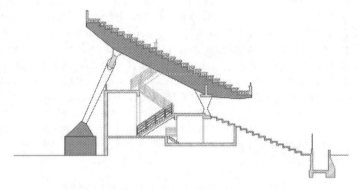

Fig. 2. Transversal cross section of old football stadium reinforced concrete structures. The analyzed structures are highlighted in orange. (Color figure online)

2   Parent Concrete

In the first phase of the research, the integrity and mechanical behavior of Cagliari RC football stadium were analyzed. The concrete structures chosen for the preliminary analysis are the cantilever beams and the foundation blocks. A total of 12 cored specimens were collected from both the foundation and the beams, respectively named C. Found. and C. Beam. A preliminary visual inspection performed on the cored specimens did not highlight any abnormalities. In Table 1 the test results on cored specimens and average values of parent concrete are reported.

Table 1. Mechanical characteristics of Parent Concrete.

C. Found.	1	2	3	4	5	6	Average value
R_c (MPa)	26.8	32.2	24.7	–	–	–	27.9
f_{ct} (MPa)	–	–	–	2.04	1.83	2.28	2.05
E_c (MPa)	24470	27751	23785	–	–	–	25335
C. Beam	1	2	3	4	5	6	Average value
R_c (MPa)	22.2	22.1	18.7	–	–	–	21.0
f_{ct} (MPa)	–	–	–	1.50	1.58	1.40	1.49
E_c (MPa)	19774	18537	15845	–	–	–	18042

The experimental data show that the beams and foundations were made with two types of concrete characterized by different mechanical properties and composition. The mechanical behavior of the foundation is better than that of the beam. Moreover, definite compositional differences between the two materials are confirmed from petrographic analyses on thin sections. The samples are characterized by the presence of several types of aggregates, embedded in a fine cement matrix, which may be distinguished both by mineralogical composition and by size distribution. Polarized light microscopy analyses performed on sample labelled C. Found revealed, in the fine cement matrix, the presence of a coarse fraction entirely made of centimetric angular fragments of micritic (cryptocrystalline) limestone. This component contrasts with a very varied siliciclastic fine-grained (millimetric to sub-millimetric) fraction, made of granite and metamorphic rock fragments, with quartz and feldspar free crystals; all the fragments are sharp-edged. Analyses on sample C. Beam indicate a more homogeneous siliciclastic com-position, with a millimetric-centimetric fraction prevalently made of angular fragments of granite rocks with various types of metamorphic rocks (quartzites to metavolcanics), and a fine-grained, sub-millimetric fraction consisting of the same materials associated to free crystals of quartz, feldspars and biotite.

3   Recycled Aggregated

Two types of RA have been produced, called respectively Recycled Aggregate Foundation (RA_F), obtained from crushed foundation blocks, and Recycled Aggregate Beam (RA_B), obtained from crushed cantilever beams, both with size 4–16 mm.

The two types of RA were subjected to all the tests complying with UNI EN 12620: 2008 [23] and UNI 8520-1: 2015 [24]. In Table 2 the results are shown and in Fig. 3 RA size distribution is reported.

The analysis carried out showed that RA, even if obtained by crushing two different concretes, have very similar characteristics. In Table 2 it can be observed that only four parameters (Shape Index, Percentage of fines, Content of acid-soluble sulfate, Content of water-soluble sulfates) are slightly different.

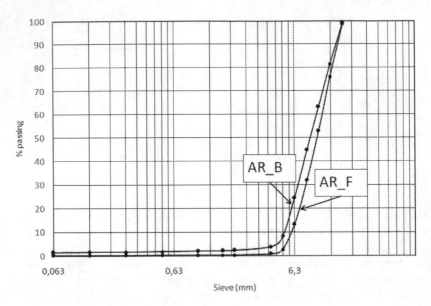

Fig. 3. RA size distribution.

Table 2. Characteristics of RA.

Requirements		RA_Foundation	RA_Beam
Requirements		RA_Foundation	RA_Beam
Geometrical	Aggregate sizes	4/16	4/16
	Grading	GC 90/15, GT 17.5	GC 90/15, GT 17.5
	Shape Index	59	34
	Flakiness Index	4	4
	Shell content of coarse aggregate	Absent	Absent
	Fines content	0.15%	0.59%
Physical	Resistance to fragmentation of coarse aggregate	39	39
	Saturated surface-dried particle density	2.39	2.38
	Bulk density	1.23	1.14
	Voids%	45	49
	Water absorption	7.0	6.7
	Classification of the coarse recycled aggregates constituents:		
	X	0	0
	Rc %	74	78
	Ru %	27	22
	Rb = Ra = Rg %	0	0
Chemical	Content of water-soluble chloride salts	0.005%	0.005%
	Content of acid-soluble chloride salts	0.325%	0.325%
	Content of acid-soluble sulphate	0.43%	0.26%
	Content of Total Sulfur	<0.1%	<0.1%
	Content of water-soluble sulphates	0.148%	0.068%

3.1 Residual Mortar Content in Recycled Concrete Aggregates

In RA the adhered cement mortar to the original natural aggregate particles influences significantly physical properties, workability and mechanical performances of recycled concrete.

The determination of the Residual Mortar Content (RMC) has critical importance to better estimate the properties of concrete incorporating RA. However, there is currently no standard method for the RMC determination.

The method used in this research, proposed by [25], consists in submitting representative samples of RA to daily freezing and thawing cycles in a solution of sodium sulphate. The RMC obtained in RA_F and RA_B, divided into two fraction sizes (retained 4 mm and 10 mm sieve), is shown in Table 3. The test shows that RMC is significantly similar for RA_F and RA_B.

Table 3. Residual mortar content (%).

	Sieve retained 4 mm	Sieve retained 10 mm
RA_Found.	55.81	45.82%
RA_Beams	49.67%	45.65%

4 Mechanical Characteristics of Concrete

CEM II/A-LL 42.5 R was used in all concrete mixes. Both NA and coarse RA were used. Crushed natural granite was used as the natural aggregate. Two type of recycled aggregates (RA_F and RA_B) were used. Natural sand was used as the fine aggregate in all concrete mixes. A superplasticizer based on polycarboxylate was used in all the concrete mixtures. Recycled concrete mixes were produced using different replacement percentages (30%, 50% and 80%) of coarse RA in place of coarse NA. Six recycled concrete mixes were produced, using separately the two types of coarse RA. In comparison an additional mix of Normal Concrete (NC) with only NA was produced.

In Table 4 the proportions for each mix produced are shown. The mix of recycled concrete was designated to include type of coarse RA and aggregate replacement ratio. For example, the designation RC_F 30% represents a mix containing RA_F with replacement percentage 30% and RC_B 80% represents a mix containing RA_B with replacement percentage 80%. Each mix is characterized by water to cement ratio equal to 0.463, and an average density of 2283 kg/m^3.

Compressive and splitting tensile strength and secant modulus of elasticity in compression tests were performed according to UNI EN 12390-3: 2019 [26], UNI EN 12390-6: 2010 [27] and UNI EN 12390-13: 2013 [28], respectively. The compressive strength test for each mix was determined at 14 and 28 days, while splitting tensile strength and modulus of elasticity were determined at 28 days. In Figs. 4, 5, 6 and 7 the results of tests are reported.

Table 4. Aggregates proportion for different concrete mixes.

	Fine NA (kg/m^3)	Coarse NA (kg/m^3)	Coarse RA_F (kg/m^3)	Coarse RA_B (kg/m^3)	Additive (kg/m^3)
NC	847.49	880.06	–	–	2.91
RC_B 30%	821.80	616.04	–	263.69	3.31
RC_B 50%	802.97	440.03	–	440.27	3.31
RC_B 80%	778.15	176.01	–	703.96	4.00
RC_F 30%	821.80	616.04	263.69	–	3.31
RC_F 50%	802.97	440.03	440.27	–	4.00
RC_F 80%	778.15	176.01	703.96	–	4.00

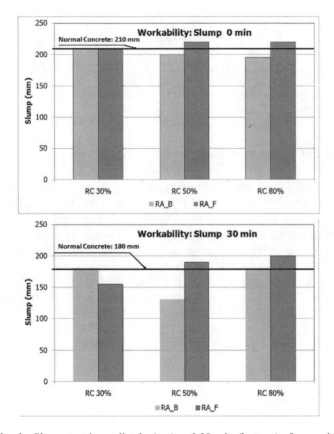

Fig. 4. Slump test immediately (top) and 30 min (bottom) after casting.

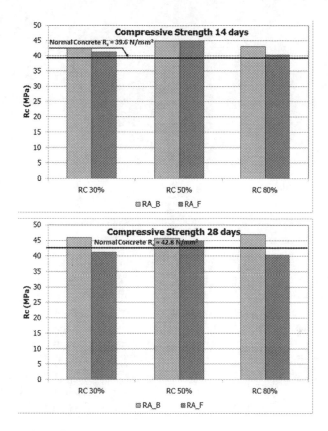

Fig. 5. Average values of concrete compressive strength at 28 (bottom) and 14 days (top) after casting.

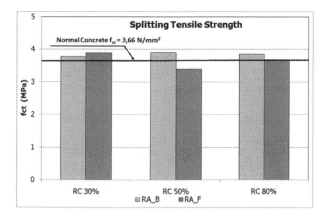

Fig. 6. Concrete splitting tensile strength average values.

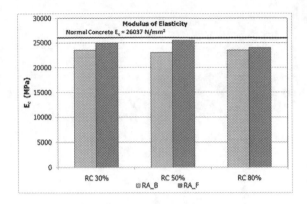

Fig. 7. Concrete modulus of elasticity average values.

The results of the average compressive strength at 14 and 28 days (Fig. 5) show optimal performance even when the percentage of coarse RA reaches 80%. It should also be noted that the compressive strength of recycled concrete does not appear to be influenced by the parent concrete. Rather it results that, in some cases, the compressive strength of recycled concrete is higher than NC. Splitting tensile strength (Fig. 6) is greater or equal for all recycled concrete, compared to NC. This result was expected and can be explained by the greater roughness of RA that produces an increase in tensile strength of concrete. The secant modulus of elasticity in compression (Fig. 7) appears slightly lower (limited to a maximum of 10%) for recycled concrete compared to NC. This result was expected and mainly due to the adherent mortar [29].

5 Conclusions

This experimental campaign shows that the mechanical properties of recycled concrete are not affected by the mechanical characteristics of the parent concrete. Furthermore, it is possible to obtain structural concrete even when the percentage of replacement of coarse RA reaches 80%. This data is very important because it proves the presence of RA does not necessarily lead to a reduction in the performance of the new concrete casted with them. Actually, the design mix of concrete with recycled aggregates plays a fundamental role.

Further developments of this research are expected considering also the durability properties of these materials and their application to real scale structural elements like columns or beams: [30–32].

It is clear that the use of this kind of concrete can reduce the building impact on the environment and creating new opportunities for the construction companies with beneficial results for all the society. For example: the processing scraps of precast concrete can be successfully used as recycled aggregates.

Finally, given that the transportation costs of these materials it is always a key variable for all economic analysis, they can be useful also in case of the retrofitting of existing structures and infrastructures, see [33, 34]. In particular when the environmental impact of the retrofitting intervention is taken into account (see [35, 36]) the use of recycled aggregates can reduce the equivalent CO_2 cost of that intervention.

Funding Statement. Authors would like to acknowledge Sardegna Ricerche for the financial support of project: Materials for Sustainable Building and Infrastructure - Recycled Aggregates (MEISAR). POR FESR 2014/2020 - ASSE PRIORITARIO I "RICERCA SCIENTIFICA, SVILUPPO TECNOLOGICO E INNOVAZIONE.

References

1. Italian Minister for the environment and protection of land and sea. DM 11/10/17 - Minimum environmental criteria for design services and works for the new construction, renovation and maintenance of public buildings (2017). (in Italian)
2. Pacheco, J., de Brito, J., Chastre, C., Evangelista, L.: Experimental investigation on the variability of the main mechanical properties of concrete produced with coarse recycled concrete aggregates. Constr. Build. Mater. **201**, 110–120 (2019)
3. Francesconi, L., Pani, L., Stochino, F.: Punching shear strength of reinforced recycled concrete slabs. Constr. Build. Mater. **127**, 248–263 (2016)
4. Koenders, E.A., Pepe, M., Martinelli, E.: Compressive strength and hydration processes of concrete with recycled aggregates. Cem. Concr. Res. **56**, 203–212 (2014)
5. Padmini, A.K., Ramamurthy, D.K., Mathews, M.S.: Influence of parent concrete on the properties of recycled aggregate concrete. Constr. Build. Mater. **23**, 829–836 (2009)
6. Kou, S.C., Poon, C.S.: Effect of the quality of parent concrete on the properties of high performance recycled aggregate concrete. Constr. Build. Mater. **77**, 501–508 (2015)
7. Ajdukiewicz, A., Kliszczewicz, A.: Influence of recycled aggregates on mechanical properties of HS/HPC. Cem. Concr. Compos. **24**, 269–279 (2002)
8. Etxeberria, M., Marı, A.R., Vazquez, E.: Recycled aggregate concrete as structural material. Mater. Struct. **40**, 529–541 (2007)
9. Rahal, K.N.: Mechanical properties of concrete with recycled coarse aggregate. Build. Environ. **42**(1), 407–415 (2007)
10. González-Fonteboa, B., Martínez-Abella, F.: Concretes with aggregates from demolition waste and silica fume. Materials and mechanical properties. Build. Environ. **43**(4), 429–437 (2008)
11. Pani, L., Francesconi, L., Rombi, J., Naitza, S., Balletto, G., Mei, G.: Recycled aggregates, mechanical properties and environmental sustainability. In: Planning, Nature and Ecosystem Services, INPUT aCAdemy 2019, pp. 431–442 (2019)
12. Tabsh, S.W., Abdelfatah, A.S.: Influence of recycled concrete aggregates on strength properties of concrete. Constr. Build. Mater. **23**, 1163–1167 (2009)
13. De Juan, M.S., Gutiérrez, P.A.: Study on the influence of attached mortar content on the properties of recycled concrete aggregate. Constr. Build. Mater. **23**(2), 872–877 (2009)
14. Pepe, M., Toledo Filho, R.D., Koenders, E.A., Martinelli, E.: Alternative processing procedures for recycled aggregates in structural concrete. Constr. Build. Mater. **69**, 124–132 (2014)
15. Katz, A.: Properties of concrete made with recycled aggregate from partially hydrated old concrete. Cem. Concr. Res. **33**(5), 703–711 (2003)
16. Li, W., Long, C., Tam, V.W., Poon, C.S., Duan, W.H.: Effects of nanoparticles on failure process and micro-structural properties of recycled aggregate concrete. Constr. Build. Mater. **142**, 42–50 (2017)

17. Li, W., Luo, Z., Sun, Z., Hu, Y., Duan, W.H.: Numerical modelling of plastic–damage response and crack propagation in RAC under uniaxial loading. Mag. Concr. Res. **70**(9), 459–472 (2018)
18. Stochino, F., Pani, L., Francesconi, L., Mistretta, F.: Cracking of reinforced recycled concrete slabs. Int. J. Struct. Glass Adv. Mater. Res. **1**(1), 3–9 (2017)
19. Silva, R.V., de Brito, J., Dhir, R.K.: The influence of the use of recycled aggregates on the compressive strength of concrete: a review. Eur. J. Environ. Civ. Eng. **19**(7), 825–849 (2015)
20. Silva, R.V., de Brito, J., Dhir, R.K.: Tensile strength behaviour of recycled aggregate concrete. Constr. Build. Mater. **83**, 108–118 (2015)
21. Silva, R.V., de Brito, J., Dhir, R.K.: Establishing a relationship between modulus of elasticity and compressive strength of recycled aggregate concrete. J. Clean. Prod. **112**(4), 2171–2186 (2016)
22. Limbachiya, M.C., Leelawat, T., Dhir, R.K.: Use of recycled concrete aggregate in high-strength concrete. Mater. Struct. **33**, 574–580 (2000)
23. UNI EN 12620: Aggregates for concrete (2008)
24. UNI 8520-1: Aggregates for concrete. Additional provisions for the application of EN 12620 Part 1: Designation and conformity criteria (2015)
25. Abbas, A., Fathifazl, G., Isgor, O.B., Razaqpur, A.G., Fournier, B., Foo, S.: Proposed method for determining the residual mortar content of recycled concrete aggregates. J. ASTM Int. **5**(1), 1–12 (2007)
26. UNI EN 12390-3: Testing hardened concrete. Part 3: Compressive strength of test specimens (2019)
27. UNI EN 12390-6: Tests on hardened concrete - Part 6: Splitting tensile strength of the specimens (2010)
28. UNI EN 12390-13: Test on hardened concrete - Part 13: Determination of the secant modulus of elasticity in compression (2013)
29. Salem, R.M., Burdette, E.G.: Role of chemical and mineral admixtures on physical properties and frost-resistance of recycled aggregate concrete. ACI Mater. J. **95**(5), 558–563 (1998)
30. Xu, J.J., Chen, Z.P., Zhao, X.Y., Demartino, C., Ozbakkaloglu, T., Xue, J.Y.: Seismic performance of circular recycled aggregate concrete-filled steel tubular columns: FEM modelling and sensitivity analysis. Thin Walled Struct. **141**, 509–525 (2019)
31. Xu, J.J., Chen, Z.P., Ozbakkaloglu, T., Zhao, X.-Y., Demartino, C.: A critical assessment of the compressive behavior of reinforced recycled aggregate concrete columns. Eng. Struct. **161**, 161–175 (2018)
32. Xu, J.J., Chen, Z.P., Xiao, Y., Demartino, C., Wang, J.H.: Recycled Aggregate Concrete in FRP- confined columns: a review of experimental results. Compos. Struct. **174**, 277–291 (2017)
33. Stochino, F., Fadda, M.L., Mistretta, F.: Assessment of RC Bridges integrity by means of low-cost investigations. Frattura ed Integrità Strutturale **46**, 216–225 (2018)
34. Stochino, F., Fadda, M.L., Mistretta, F.: Low cost condition assessment method for existing RC bridges. Eng. Fail. Anal. **86**, 56–71 (2018)
35. Sassu, M., Stochino, F., Mistretta, F.: Assessment method for combined structural and energy retrofitting in masonry buildings. Buildings **7**(3), 71 (2017)
36. Mistretta, F., Stochino, F., Sassu, M.: Structural and thermal retrofitting of masonry walls: an integrated cost-analysis approach for the Italian context. Build. Environ. **155**, 127–136 (2019)

International Workshop on Science, Technologies and Policies to Innovate Spatial Planning (STP4P 2020)

Green Infrastructure and Private Property: The Crucial Relationship for the Sustainable Future of Cities

Daniele La Rosa[(⊠)] and Riccardo Privitera

Department of Civil Engineering and Architecture,
University of Catania, Via S. Sofia 64, 95125 Catania, Italy
dlarosa@darc.unict.it

Abstract. Over the past decades, intense urbanization processes have generated built environments with a low energy efficiency and a severe lack of green spaces. These represent the main providers of ecosystem services in cities, especially for the regulation of local microclimate. Despite their importance, the implementation of a green infrastructure from public administrations often faces the lack of economic resources to acquire and manage the land to be used as new green spaces.

This article investigates the suitability of open spaces located in private residential areas to be components of a green infrastructure through a trees planting strategy. A high-res GIS Land Cover analysis models the potential of private residential areas to host new greenery by comparing the actual availability of open spaces near residential buildings and the mutual position between buildings and new trees. The method is tested in a portion of the Metropolitan Area of Catania (Italy).

Results for private residential areas, which represents a relevant percentage of the built environment, show that the implementation of the Green Infrastructure depends on the configurations of buildings and open spaces, and is limited by the actual room of open space around residential buildings. The work allows identifying different scenarios and alternatives for a Green Infrastructure to better balance public and private costs and generated benefits.

Keywords: Green infrastructure · Land cover · Energy saving · Private property · Urban planning

1 Introduction

Cities are widely considered as the places where behavioral, economic, and technological interventions for climate change adaptation and mitigation have the best potential to be implemented and scaled up (van der Heijden 2019; IPCC 2018). Cities can also be considered as key victims of climate change, as it is in cities that the effects of climate change will be experienced most severely by humans (Tyler and Moench 2012). Seeking to utilise their climate mitigation and adaptation potential, cities have developed as sites of innovative and experimental governance to spur on climate actions (Martinico et al. 2013; Rosenzweig et al. 2018).

In urban contexts, natural ecosystems are increasingly used to provide solutions to many urban issues and improve the overall sustainability of urban environments

© Springer Nature Switzerland AG 2020
O. Gervasi et al. (Eds.): ICCSA 2020, LNCS 12255, pp. 381–392, 2020.
https://doi.org/10.1007/978-3-030-58820-5_29

(Cohen-Shacham et al. 2016). These nature-based solutions provide sustainable, cost-effective, multi-purpose, and flexible alternatives for various planning objectives and are able to enhance significantly the resilience of cities.

Among Nature-based solutions, Green Infrastructure (GI) is a 'natural, semi-natural and artificial network of multifunctional ecological systems within, around and between urban areas, at all spatial scales (Nesshöver et al. 2017). This definition emphasizes the holistic ecosystem vision of urban environments (including the abiotic, biotic and cultural functions) and claims for multi-scale approaches able to take into account the scale-dependent relationships of ecological processes occurring in cities, with particular reference to the human health and well-being of residents.

Among the services provided by GI, climate regulation is of utmost importance in cities, where the microclimatic benefits of urban vegetation can contribute to the mitigation of the urban heat island effect. Vegetation contributes to regulate the urban temperature through three main actions: shading the built environment, modifying the airflow around it and directly lowering the outdoor air temperature through evapo-transpiration processes (Hwang et al. 2017).

Climate regulation potential of vegetation has relevant positive impacts on the energy demand of buildings, as demonstrated by a growing body of research and experimental measurements (Simpson and McPherson 1998; Konarska et al. 2015) and confirmed in different climate conditions and type of buildings (Laband and Sopho-cleus 2009; Palme et al. 2017).

Shade effect by trees reduces the amount of solar energy a building absorbs and therefore reduces the energy required for cooling. Vegetation also cools the air around buildings and this has an indirect effect on the need of energy for cooling the inner parts of buildings. If looked at city or district level, effects of vegetation can generate relevant electrical energy savings (Simpson 1998; Wang et al. 2019) with energy performances that can be further increased by the evapotranspiration effect (Hsieh et al. 2018). The positive effect depends on the multiple different configurations among urban environments, land-use configurations, and micro-climate conditions (Calcerano and Martinelli 2016).

Different approaches and models have been developed for evaluating the potentiality of trees on cooling energy reduction, but limited research has focused on the different relations between buildings and trees in the urban environment (Farhadi et al. 2019; Wang et al. 2019). This is a crucial issue, in instances when the availability of open spaces for planting trees is limited and when the feasibility of planning and design alternatives for GI must deal with the private property.

Indeed, planting trees and other forms of greenery requires availability of suitable open spaces located just in the surrounding of the buildings. These kind of open spaces can be found in private setback yards, reduced in size and characterised by different land cover types such lawns, shrubs, bare soil, impervious surfaces and trees as well. The actual chance to implement a public and accessible GI is strongly affected by the private asset of landownership and the limited physical and geometrical features of the open spaces close to the buildings.

In this article we evaluate the potential of open spaces located in private residential areas to host new trees to be planted and which can become new components of a local GI aimed at i) providing local temperature cooling effects resulting in a considerable decrease of energy demand of adjacent buildings and ii) implementing public and accessible green spaces for the neighboring community.

2 Study Area, Materials and Method

2.1 Study Area and Materials

We have tested the methodology presented in a portion of the municipality of Aci Castello, a small municipality located within the metropolitan area of Catania (Italy), the largest in Sicily. The location of the test area is shown in Fig. 1.

2.2 Land Cover Analysis

A land cover map was derived by a pixel-based, supervised classification of high resolution (0.25 m) regional aerial photograph, done with ERDAS Imagine. The following land cover categories were used: Trees and Shrubs, Grass, Bare soil, Building, Impervious surface. These represent typical categories for urban and peri-urban contexts, as well as for the tested area (La Rosa and Wiesmann 2013; Myant et al. 2011). Maximum likelihood classification algorithm was used.

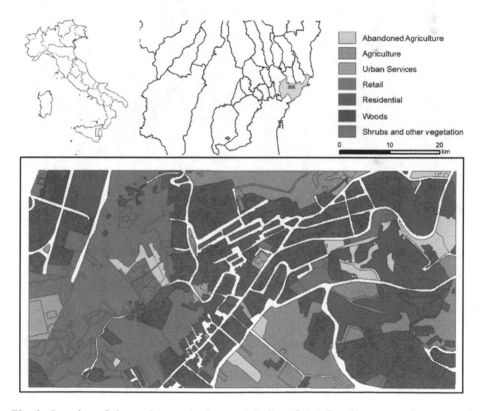

Fig. 1. Location of the study area in the municipality of Aci Castello, metropolitan area of Catania (Italy)

For the training step, a small-block sampling procedure was chosen. A total of 30 polygons of different sizes and shapes were sampled, with all pixels within each polygon belonging to the same land cover category. The sample data set contains around 11,000 pixels, which is a sufficient number according to existing heuristic rules for multiband images (Congalton and Green 2009).

2.3   Distance Analysis

In the second step, two distance rasters were derived from the residential buildings extracted from regional topographic maps (at the scale of 1: 10,000). Residential buildings were then divided into two main categories following a morphological analysis and representative of the most common type in the area (Privitera and La Rosa 2018): detached, semi-detached and terraced houses (usually with available private open spaces) and multi-storey buildings (with shared open spaces) (Fig. 2).

Fig. 2. Example of the morphological categories for residential buildings: detached house (left) and multi-storey buildings (right)

The distance raster allowed to identify those areas ranging from 5 to 8 m from the buildings, where the shading effects of trees can maximise its cooling effect and energy savings potential on the buildings (Palme et al. 2019; Privitera et al. submitted). These areas thus represent optimal places where new trees can be planted.

The Land Cover map was then overlaid with the distance raster, to select the land covers present in the distance range 5–8 m only. Trees and Shrubs were excluded from the land cover categories to be extracted, as it would make no sense to plant new trees where trees or shrubs are present already.

3   Results

3.1   Land Cover Mapping

Table 1 reports the accuracy matrix after the supervised classification, with an overall accuracy of 88%, while Table 2 shows the distribution of the different categories for the two morphological buildings categories.

Figure 3 shows the produced Land Cover map for the study area. In general, Bare soil is the most critical category because of its spectral similarity to other impervious surfaces and their limited extent in the study area. Best accuracies were obtained by the classification of Trees and Shrubs and Grass (the most frequent).

Table 1. Accuracy table for the land cover categories.

	Trees & Shrubs	Grass	Bare soil	Building	Impervious	Shadows	ROWS TOT	Producer accuracy %
Trees and Shrubs	370	10	5	2	10	5	**402**	0.92
Grass	13	211	2	3	2	4	**235**	0.91
Bare soil	2	1	44	4	4	2	**57**	0.79
Building	2	2	1	309	20	5	**339**	0.88
Impervious	7	3	3	30	270	5	**318**	0.86
Shadows	7	4	1	5	7	60	**84**	0.74
COLUMNS TOT	**401**	**231**	**56**	**353**	**313**	**81**	1435	
User accuracy %	0.92	0.90	0.77	0.91	0.85	0.71		**0.88**

Table 2. Shares of Land Cover categories in the study area

Land cover category	%
Buildings	23.6%
Bare soil	7.2%
Impervious	22.6%
Trees and Shrubs	34.6%
Grass	0.9%
Shadows	11.2%

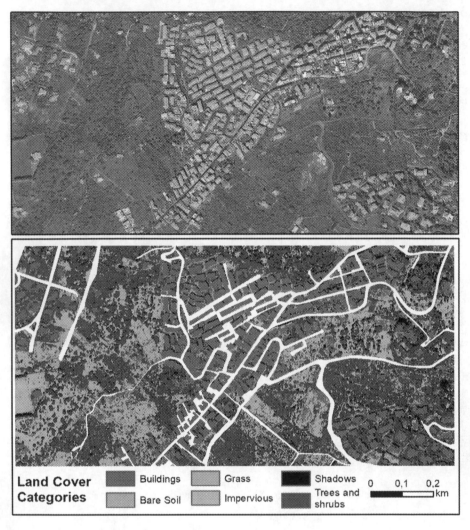

Fig. 3. Aerial photo and land cover map after the supervised classification

3.2   Distance Analysis

Figure 4 and 5 are the result of the intersection between the distance raster and the Land Cover map of Fig. 3. They map the different categories of permeable land covers located at a distance ranging between 5 and 8 m from detached/semi-detached and terraced houses and multi-storey buildings respectively.

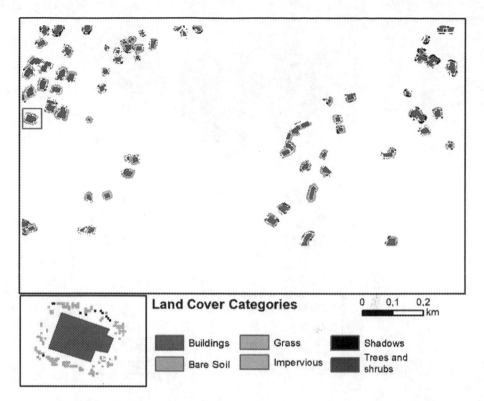

Fig. 4. Land cover categories within the distance range 5–8 m for detached/semi-detached and terraced houses

Table 3 shows the extent of each category of land cover (not including Trees and Shrubs) in the distance range for the 2 types of buildings considered. A first evidence from this analysis is the high difference of the shares of the land cover categories that are located within the distance range. For multi-storey buildings, the most frequent category is given by impervious category and this represents an indication of a highly urbanised residential built environment, where different types impervious surfaces can be present (terraces, internal roads, parking areas, etc.). For detached/semi-detached and terraced buildings, a lower extent of land covers can be found, mainly because there is a good presence of Trees and Shrubs at the distance range considered. This is a typical feature of low density urban environment, also for Italian metropolitan contexts (La Rosa and Wiesmann 2013), where set-back yards often include different types of green and permeable covers. Overall, grass is the category most frequently found.

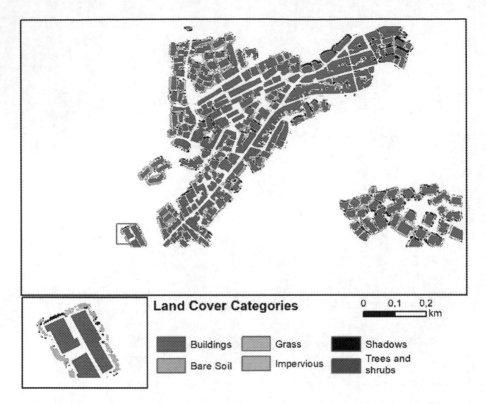

Fig. 5. Land cover categories within the distance range 5–8 m for multistorey buildings

Table 3. Shares of available land cover at the distance range 5–8 m for detached/semi-detached and terraced houses and multistorey buildings

	Area (m^2)	Area (m^2)
	Detached/semi-detached and terraced houses	Multi-storey buildings
Bare soil	1607	2063
Impervious	6157	12508
Grass	2717	1442
Shadows	1278	10789
Total	**11.759**	**26.802**

4 Policies and Planning Implications

A strategy of planting street trees for shading buildings and reducing their energy demand should be included in a wider strategy aimed at designing larger and accessible public green spaces equipped with pathways, bike lanes, playgrounds, benches to be enjoyed by local residents. Nevertheless, the complexity and variety of different types of urban environment with fragmented and scattered patches of greenery could hamper the implementation of a new public GI.

In this paper we focused on two morphological types of residential areas: multi-storey apartment buildings and detached/semi-detached and terraced houses. Within both of these private assets, the implementation of GI must deal with land acquisition of those private plots where GI could be designed. Effectively, land acquisition strongly influences the economic feasibility of the implementation of GI, as direct public acquisitions of land are often economically unsustainable for local administration and face resistance from private landowners (Bengston et al. 2004). The issue of economic feasibility for managing public intervention and providing accessible public green spaces could be addressed through the Transfer of Development Rights (TDR) approach (Brabec and Smith 2002). In this approach, landowners can transfer the assigned rights to develop one parcel of land to another one, which could be located in different part of the municipality. As a consequence, the parcel from which the development rights are being transferred can no longer be developed and private landowners will get economic incentives or compensation from selling their developing rights.

According to this approach, local policy makers can identify the portions of private land parcels to be acquired for the GI and propose to the private landowners different economic incentives/compensation according to the specific morphological and property assets of urban fabric.

Multi-storey apartment buildings and tower blocks compounds are often characterised by large number of private landowners sharing the same common spaces or setback yards such as walkways, park plots and green spaces. In such a multiple property asset any potential intervention for improving the quality of buildings and other facilities is often affected and limited by the single landowner ability to pay and contribute to the overall urban transformation. In these cases, the most suitable economic incentive could be to monetise the gained development rights and provide a cash flow to adopt specific measures to improve the conditions of the multi-storey apartments buildings, including energy/seismic/aesthetic retrofitting interventions. As a consequence, open spaces acquired by public administrations (i.e. the municipality) thanks to Transfer of Development Right approach could be turned into new components of the public GI.

Differently, detached/semi-detached and terraced houses are characterised by private assets of landownership and usually include green back yards. In this case the most effective economic incentives could be to assign development rights to strips of private land parcels for increasing the square footage or height of existing buildings within the same parcel. Single private landowners could be also restored through tailored Tax Credits for collecting the earned revenues from the development rights and channeling it into a tax credit fund for local tax bills and other fiscal duties (Tapp 2019). In urban districts characterised by detached/semi-detached and terraced houses, the demand for green spaces from residents could be lower than the one of more compact district, where residents do not have private yards or garden. For this reason, the land strips acquired by the municipality in detached/semi-detached and terraced houses could be used not to implement new public green spaces, but rather to design new connecting cycling and pedestrian tracks, therefore improving the accessibility to other urban gardens and green areas.

Results from the application of the methodology presented, show that the actual implementation of GI according to the above proposed mechanisms and policies is highly dependent on the physical configurations of the open spaces where the GI can be implemented. The actual configuration of land covers represents a fundamental information to understand if and where new forms of greenery (trees above all) can be planted and if the planting could be suitable according to the current land cover situation and how much can the planting costs be.

Results of our analysis showed a different possibilities of GI implementation for the two types of morphological categories considered. For the category of multi-storey apartment buildings, which are present in the more central and compact parts of the urban context, a good extent of open spaces around residential buildings is available. However, these spaces are characterised by impervious land cover, and this will make the planting of new trees more complicated and costly. On the other hand, for the category of detached/semi-detached and terraced houses, the available spaces for planting trees is more limited in extent. However, the plantation could be more feasible and less expensive, as it will involve mostly permeable land covers (i.e. bare soils or grass).

5   Conclusions

The relationship between GI and energy is crucial for the sustainable future of the cities. The importance of nature-based solutions in providing urban climate regulation and, more specifically, the potential of vegetation to deliver positive impacts on the energy demand of buildings are increasingly being demonstrated in cities.

This study analysed the complex relation between open spaces and buildings within private compounds of highly dense multi-storey apartments and low-density urban fringes made of detached/semi-detached and terraced houses. The paper explored the morphological relation between buildings and land covers, spatially identifying the opportunities and limitations for planning a new GI around residential buildings through a high resolution land cover analysis. The limited data required for this analysis also allows its easy replicability of the method to other urban and metropolitan areas.

The complex relation among different land covers in the built environment requires a better understanding of the morphological features and the different property assets to develop feasible and effective policies aimed at implementing GI while reducing the energy demand of cities. This is even more important for cities where greenery is lacking or where the access to green spaces is low or unequal in the different districts of the city.

To this end, comprehensive planning policies should be based on an assessment of the economic viability of public investment and related public benefits (such as provision of ecosystem services) as well as private costs (loss of private/shared open spaces, parking plots, view blocking, cleaning costs and storm drains obstructing due to the falling leaves and bird droppings) and benefits (building energy savings, gained development credits, etc.). Such policies should also be tailored to different parts of the urban environment and take into account the different possibilities and limitation offered by private open spaces around residential buildings. This would allow identifying different scenarios and alternatives of a Green Infrastructure to better balance public and private costs and generated benefits.

References

Congalton, R.G., Green, K.: Assessing the Accuracy of Remotely Sensed Data: Principles and Practices. CRC Press, Boca Raton (2009)

La Rosa, D., Wiesmann, D.: Land cover and impervious surface extraction using parametric and non-parametric algorithms from the open-source software R: an application to sustainable urban planning in Sicily. GIScience Remote Sens. **50**(2), 231–250 (2013)

Myint, S.W., Gober, P., Brazel, A., Grossman-Clarke, S., Weng, Q.: Per-pixel vs. object-based classification of urban land cover extraction using high spatial resolution imagery. Remote Sens. Environ. **115**(5), 1145–1161 (2011)

Bengston, D.N., Fletcher, J.O., Nelson, K.C.: Public policies for managing urban growth and protecting open space: policy instruments and lessons learned in the United States. Landscape Urban Plann. **69**, 271–286 (2004)

Brabec, E., Smith, C.: Agricultural land fragmentation: the spatial effects of three land protection strategies in the eastern United States. Landscape Urban Plann. **58**, 255–268 (2002)

Calcerano, F., Martinelli, L.: Numerical optimisation through dynamic simulation of the position of trees around a stand-alone building to reduce cooling energy consumption. Energy Build. **112**, 234–243 (2016)

Cohen-Shacham, E., Walters, G., Janzen, C., Maginnis, S.: Nature-based Solutions to address global societal challenges. IUCN, Gland Switzerland (2016)

Farhadi, H., Faizi, M., Sanaieian, H.: Mitigating the urban heat island in a residential area in Tehran: investigating the role of vegetation, materials, and orientation of buildings. Sustain. Cities Soc. **46**, 101448 (2019)

Hsieh, C.M., Li, J.J., Zhang, L., Schwegler, B.: Effects of tree shading and transpiration on building cooling energy use. Energy Build. **159**, 382–397 (2018)

Hwang, W.H., Wiseman, P.E., Thomas, V.A.: Enhancing the energy conservation benefits of shade trees in dense residential developments using an alternative tree placement strategy. Landscape Urban Plann. **158**, 62–74 (2017)

IPCC: Global warming of 1.5 °C. Intergovernmental Panel on Climate Change, Incheon (2018)

Konarska, J., et al.: Transpiration of urban trees and its cooling effect in a high latitude city. Int. J. Biometeorol. **60**(1), 159–172 (2015). https://doi.org/10.1007/s00484-015-1014-x

Laband, D., Sophocleus, V.: An experimental analysis of the impact of tree shade on electricity consumption. Arboric. Urban Forest. **35**, 197–202 (2009)

Martinico, F., La Rosa, D., Privitera, R.: Il ruolo delle aree non urbanizzate nei contesti metropolitani: scenari di adattamento ai cambiamenti climatici. Territorio **66**, 92–100 (2013)

Nesshöver, C., et al.: The science, policy and practice of nature-based solutions: an interdisciplinary perspective. Sci. Total Environ. **579**, 1215–1227 (2017)

Palme, M., Inostroza, L., Villacreses, G., Lobato, A., Carrasco, C.: From urban climate to energy consumption. Enhancing building performance simulation by considering the urban heat island effect. Energy Build. **145**, 107–120 (2017)

Palme, M., La Rosa, D., Privitera, R., Chiesa, G.: Evaluating the potential energy savings of an urban green infrastructure through environmental simulation. In: Corrado, V., Fabrizio, A., Gasparella, A., Patuzzi, F. (eds.) Proceedings of Building Simulation 2019 Conference, IBPSA. https://doi.org/10.26868/25222708.2019.210698

Privitera, R., Evola, G., La Rosa, D., Costanzo, V.: Green infrastructure to reduce the energy demand of cities. In: Palme, M., Salvati, A. (eds.) Urban Microclimate Simulation for Comfort and Energy Studies. Springer, Heidelberg (submitted)

Rosenzweig, C., Solecki, W., Romero-Lankao, P., Mehrotra, S., Dhakal, S., Ali Ibrahim, S.: Climate Change and Cities: Second Assessment Report of the Urban Climate Change Research Network. Cambridge University Press, Cambridge (2018)

Simpson, J.R.: Urban forest impacts on regional cooling and heating energy use: Sacramento County case study. J. Arboric. **24**(4), 201–214 (1998)

Simpson, J.R., McPherson, E.G.: Simulation of tree shade impacts on residential energy use for space conditioning in Sacramento. Atmos. Environ. **32**, 69–74 (1998)

Tapp, R.: Layers of finance: Historic tax credits and the fiscal geographies of urban redevelopment. Geoforum **105**, 13–22 (2019)

Tyler, S., Moench, S.: A framework for urban climate resilience. Climate Dev. **4**(4), 311–326 (2012)

van der Heijden, J.: Studying urban climate governance: where to begin, what to look for, and how to make a meaningful contribution to scholarship and practice. Earth Syst. Gov. **1** (100005), 1–10 (2019)

Wang, Y., Ni, Z., Chen, S., Xia, B.: Microclimate regulation and energy saving potential from different urban green infrastructures in a subtropical city. J. Clean. Prod. **226**, 913–927 (2019)

A Big Data Platform for Smart and Sustainable Cities: Environmental Monitoring Case Studies in Europe

Chiara Garau[1] ⓘ, Paolo Nesi[2] ⓘ, Irene Paoli[2] ⓘ,
Michela Paolucci[2] ⓘ, and Paola Zamperlin[3(✉)] ⓘ

[1] Department of Civil and Environmental Engineering and Architecture
(DICAAR), University of Cagliari, 09129 Cagliari, Italy
cgarau@unica.it
[2] Department of Information Engineering with its DISIT Lab,
University of Florence, 09129 Florence, Italy
{paolo.nesi,irene.paoli,michela.paolucci}@unifi.it
[3] Department of Civilisations and Forms of Knowledge (CFS),
University of Pisa, 50126 Pisa, Italy
paola.zamperlin@unipi.it

Abstract. One of the most challenging aspects of the actual smart city trend is to keep under control the environmental parameters with the aim of general sustainability. The impact of daily activities of humans in the city is presently very evident. The geographical and social characteristics of the cities may react and facilitate the sustainability as well as may really influence how the city may be more or less resilient to certain pollution production. After investigating the theoretical concept of Smart Sustainable City (SSC), this paper reported the work performed in supporting the aforementioned trend and analysis in three European cities (Florence, Helsinki and Cagliari) that despite having different characteristics for population and density, have some similarities, such as geomorphic aspects. In addition, two of them present a relevant port (Helsinki and Cagliari), two of them have similar urban complexity, such as traffic (Florence and Helsinki). The work presented has exploited Snap4City big data for smart city infrastructure and has been developed in the context of Snap4City, Trafair, and GHOST projects. The results have shown that critical aspects have been identified over time for pollution issues, in particular with PM10 and NOX.

Keywords: Smart Sustainable Cities · City dashboard · Snap4city · Big data · IoT · IoE · Florence · Helsinki · Cagliari

1 Introduction

Over the years, the "smart city" label has begun to no longer be considered sufficient to encompass all the possible implications related to the new idea of the city [1, 2]. On the one hand, scientific studies introduced the concept of "smart and sustainable cities" [3] so as not to lose the connotation of sustainability in the broader terminology of smart cities even when not explicitly referred to, and on the other hand, literature divided the

© Springer Nature Switzerland AG 2020
O. Gervasi et al. (Eds.): ICCSA 2020, LNCS 12255, pp. 393–406, 2020.
https://doi.org/10.1007/978-3-030-58820-5_30

smart city paradigm into eras: "smart city 1.0", "smart city 2.0" [4, 5] and, only recently, scholarships started to perceive the "smart city 3.0" [6].

The smart sustainable city that belongs to the "smart city 3.0" era is, therefore, an innovative and human-centred city that tries to achieve the fusion of two urban development strategies with a greater respect for the environment: on the one hand, the achievement of sustainability "with respect to environment, operations, functions, services, designs, and policies" [7, p. 11]; on the other hand, the pursuit of smartness with the potential of ICT in order to provide the technological infrastructures, solutions, and approaches needed for improving the quality of life, with big data analytics and context-aware computing and in light of the goals of sustainable development [8–10, p. 11–13].

As a consequence of these premises, the development of a city, or of a highly urbanized region, today more than ever, must go hand in hand with the improvement of technologies for the acquisition, management, analysis and display of information. These technologies allow real-time and constant monitoring of all urban areas in which human activities take place, by implying a smart governance of the considered context [11]. If the extended urban system is considered as a complex organic system that behaves like an articulated sentient organism, it is possible to identify some crucial hubs for its correct functioning that concern the sources (internal and external to the system), the acquisition systems, information processing and response management processes [12]. In this regard, this article reports three examples in Europe, in particular three cities at different levels of maturity of the identification and smartification process (Florence, Helsinki and Cagliari) where this process is launched through the big data platform Snap4City. To this end, the authors begin with a theoretical framework on what is meant by smart sustainable cities of the future. Subsequently, the article focuses on the data aggregation phase which includes the monitoring of environmental variables, in order to identify problems and possible operational solutions for the optimal government of the cities under study. In fact, today environmental issues appear even more of fundamental importance as they reflect wider implications not only for long-term approaches and strategies to public health, but also for a smart management and for a smart city governance, in order to better shape together the smart sustainable cities of the future.

2   The Future of Smart Sustainable Cities Considering the "Deep Ecology" Paradigm, IoT, and Big Data

Modern cities have a significant role in strategic sustainable development, in fact, according to estimates, the intense urbanization of the last few years will led about two thirds of the world's population to live in urban areas in 2050 [13], with imaginable repercussions on social and spatial issues ranging from land use modification to the management of natural resources, waste and pollution, without neglecting the effects still not determinable on climate change. These issues are clearly reflected in the Sustainable Development Goals (SGDs) of the United Nations' 2030 Agenda for Sustainable Development, which entails, among other things, making cities more sustainable, resilient, and safe (UN, 2015) [14].

Currently, therefore, all those involved in the monitoring and management of cities in a smart and sustainable way and considering the "smart city 3.0" era must face problems inherent in transforming them into sustainable cities and in this effort, fortunately, the growing availability of technologies, tools and data offers a high potential for solutions to many of the challenges in a direction that respects the environment and living beings. In relation to environmental data, their analysis allows to read the city to its ecological component, closely connected to the people and the different subsystems of the city [15, 16].

The intent of the paper is in particular, to focus on smart environment management through the so-called "deep ecology" which, according to Vinod Kumar [15] considers, through basic principles, the environment, not exclusively that one of "living plants and animals, or the paradigmatic thought of the word "environment", but basically the world around us, the place in which we live" [15, p. 10]. In relation to environmental data under the "deep ecology" paradigm, their analysis allows to read the city to its ecological component, closely connected to the people and the different subsystems of the city. In addition, the data availability alone is not a sufficient condition for the provision of smart services. It is necessary to adopt an ontology-based approach, namely an approach based on the formal and explicit specification of a conceptualization, which allows the representation and semantic interoperability of geospatial data and related processes. This is because "the lack of explicit semantics inhibits the dynamic selection of those geoprocessing data, services and workflows needed for processing geospatial information and discovering knowledge in a data-rich distributed environment" [17, p. 37]. The integration of semantic information makes location-based services smart and truly capable of improving a smart city. The amount of information available today is such that the problems related to the quality and meaning of it must already be addressed in the design of an architecture to support the smart city. Namely, first of all, the reference scenarios must be well defined to analyse the specific needs of citizens and analyse their behaviour and the actions that contribute to reaching them. Within these scenarios, georeferenced information is crucial for obtaining a context-sensitive description and an analysis of emerging local practices.

Furthermore, considering the georeferred or in any case positional nature of the sensor measurements, it is important to consider the area dependence of the measurements, even if in the case of big data [18], the large size of the dataset allows to limit the problems of the area nature by treating the choices of aggregation of data at different territorial levels to check for critical issues.

The analysis of big data amplifies the interpretative capacities of cities as sentient organisms with new meanings and, since it is the prerequisite for the creation of more in-depth knowledge bases, it facilitates the adoption of targeted and smart solutions, also in relation to environmental problems, traffic, health and their interconnections [11, 12]. In this new flow, sensors act as inputs for big data applications, together with all the information of geospatial, political and social context. The combination of IoT and analytics through big data is rapidly changing the way cities themselves operate and the dynamics through which they can be monitored and managed also regarding decision-making processes in the various sectors of urban planning, in accordance with the principles of social, economic and environmental sustainability. An example is given by the optimization of energy distribution, with monitoring of consumption or interruption peaks, or by the management of mobility, by monitoring traffic in real time or by mitigating environmental risks. In concrete terms, in a context of smart and sustainable cities, the analysis of big data involves the implementation of very sophisticated software applications and databases managed by machines with very high computing power, such as to transform raw data flows into knowledge useful for urban planning and design.

Technologies are nowadays so invasive that they permeate objects, structures, infrastructures, ecosystems and living beings, so much so that expressions such as the Internet of Things (IoT) [19] or the Internet of Everything (IoE). They are referring to a physical environment on which an Internet infrastructure support data collection device, including RFID, NFC, GPS, infrared sensors, laser scanner, etc. Taking advantage of this expansion of global connectivity, the growth in data traffic, which was already quadruple between 2011 and 2016, shows no sign of decreasing [20], thanks also to the production of sensors low cost and the enhancement of wireless communication networks and Web technologies.

It can therefore be easily understood that the IoT, in an approach oriented to constant monitoring to improve air quality, can represent a decisive component for urban development within the ICT infrastructure of sustainable smart cities, due to its great potential to promote environmental sustainability.

Empirical examples of what is described in this paragraph will be shown in the next paragraph through the description of the three case studies.

3   Empirical Examples of IoT and IoE in the Case Studies of Florence, Helsinki and Cagliari

The integration among physical (material) and digital (immaterial) entities is increasingly widespread, namely the data describing a smart and sustainable city come from different sources and providers, that usually are available under different standards and communication protocols, realized with distinct technologies of IoT Devices.

Moreover, they are related to all the variety of areas describing a city. Thus, they describe transport and traffic systems, mobility of goods and people, land use and land cover, environmental factors, resources and energy consumption, waste, home automation and building automation, etc. This scenario from one hand, has made possible the birth of a whole new class of applications and services, from the other the use of Big Data analysis is necessary to manage a so huge variety of dataset. The use of Big Data platforms, applied in such context and having a mature experimentation level, can be considered a key factor in promoting environmental sustainability.

In this regard, the authors describe three empirical case studies: Florence, Helsinki and Cagliari. In these cities the Snap4city Big Data Platform, has been applied. The Snap4City methodology starts with the work related to the analysis of the context and the study of the goals to be reached to make the city smart and sustainable, enabling Living Lab Support and co-working. This analysis is finalized to determine which are the main relevant aspects they continuously want to monitor basing and the available resources. The next step involves the analysis of the available data coming from the different city providers that operate and collaborate with the municipalities to provide them public or private services. Then the datasets must be ingested in the Big Data Platform, according to the objectives outlined in the first phase. Only after an efficient data gathering and data aggregation activity, it is possible to proceed with data analytic processes for the production of smart services. For example, by means of computing predictions, anomaly detection, Key Performance Indicators (KPI) monitoring, heat-maps interpolation, and studying a large set of derived data: trajectories, hot Point of Interest, origin and destination matrices, etc. The final phase, no less important, involves the exploitation of the results obtained through the creation of ad hoc visu-alization tools, such as mobile applications for citizens and dashboards for decision makers. These highly complex tools can also work as actuators and are able to manage any type of event from the most classic maps enriched with the Points of Interest, through comparative graphs for the management of heatmaps that are updated in real time.

In the City of Florence were made the first experiments in various contexts related to many different areas of interest such as Mobility, Environment and Pollution, Industry 4.0, Energy, Social Media, Emergency Management, Healthiness.

The City of Helsinki realized an experimentation based on the Snap4City platform, in the following domains: environment, citizen awareness, dashboard, mobile app for a number of different categories of users: citizens, tourists, and city officers. The city of Cagliari has experimented the Snap4city platform mainly to take advantages and monitor the aspects connected to the fields of tourism, culture and mobility, as appears in Fig. 1, in which a search on the TPL (Local Public Transport) timetables around a point is visible.

The comparative analysis among the three cities is realized in this paper on the environmental aspects. The study of pollution levels in urban areas, is one of the most strategic topics when it is talked about a smart and sustainable city under the "smart city 3.0" era, because it is strictly connected with the health of the city, allowing long-term approaches and strategies also in managing and designing their future. In addition, cities have an interest in understanding how much pollution affects the quality of the air that citizens breath in order to properly regulate urban mobility and give to all the awareness that they are living in a city that is increasingly technological and oriented towards focusing on citizens' health and thus quality of life. The air quality in a city is primarily related to the production of pollution coming from the vehicles running in the city [21].

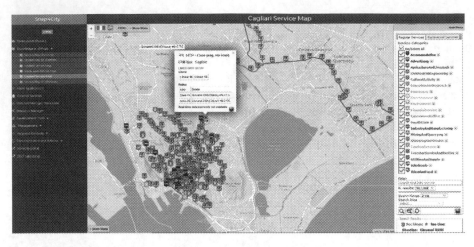

Fig. 1. Public Transport Lines in Cagliari: routes, stops, timetables around a point with a radius of 2 km

The three cities, as can be seen in Table 1, are different both demographically and territorially.

Table 1. Inhabitants, surface and density of the 3 cities under study

City	Inhabitants	Surface (km^2)	Density (inhab./km^2)
Helsinki	648.650	213,8	3.033,91
Florence	378.917	102,41	3.700
Cagliari	154.227	85,01	1.814,22

4   The Big Data Platform Snap4City for the Case Studies

Each city is faced with its own specific problems, due to its geographical location, geomorphology or its history and culture that make it unique. Although digital and technology-based approaches are often considered in the literature as a universal solution. When replicating a model in different cities or geographical areas, it is necessary to take into account individual specificities and therefore develop strategies that can draw inspiration from other contexts but are as unique and specific as the city itself [22].

Demonstrating how the fabric of smart and sustainable cities is somehow interwoven with electronic fibers, sewn together with integrated real-time detection and measurement devices, communication networks and advanced information processing systems, we bring here Snap4City, as a scalable *Smart aNalytic APplication builder for sentient Cities* [23].

Snap4city has been created to provide many online tools and guidelines to involve all different kinds of organizations (e.g., Research Centres and Universities, small business, large industries, public administrations and local governments) and citizens (e.g., city operators, resource operators, companies, tech providers, category Associations, corporations, research groups, advertisers, city users, community builders). Snap4city is GDPR (General Data Protection Regulation of the European Commission) compliant, it ingests and manages large set of datasets and provides a set of smart city APIs to access the data that can be publicly available or private (the Application Program Interface, APIs in this case are available only for the people having the permission on the data - e.g., using the registration to the platform, [24, 25]).

The Snap4City Big Data Architecture has been created to as a smart city infrastructure and it is actually applied in many Italian (Firenze, Cagliari, Pisa, Livorno, Prato, Lonato, etc.) and European cities (Helsinki, Antwerp, Santiago De Compostela) and their surrounding geographical area (such as in Italy the region of Tuscany, Sardinia and Lombardia but also Belgium and Finland) [11].

The Snap4City solution provides methods and tools to quickly create a wide range of smart city applications by leveraging heterogeneous data. It enables services for stakeholders through IoT/IoE, provides Big Data analytics and technologies, provides Smart Living Labs for enabling in co-working activities all the different people involved in a Sentient city (city decision-makers, researchers, stakeholders, citizens).

Moreover, it is capable to show in advanced Dashboards information, services, applications and dashboards sharing environments for differentiated users and developers, urban operators and decision makers, serving the city [26, 27].

As anticipated, the reference scenario for comparing the three cities Florence, Helsinki and Cagliari relates to the real-time analysis of the major polluting factors in the context of a Smart City and the estimation of pollution levels for the next 48 h, exploiting the potential of the Snap4City platform (Table 2). There main work phases that must be addressed to reach the final goal are: i) Data analysis; ii) Data ingestion; iii) Data analytic and development/application/comparison of predicting algorithms and related Visualization.

Phase I – Data analysis. In Table 1 the details related to the available raw data for each city. The data considered are related to pollution, weather and weather predictions and comes from different providers. All the data founded are Open Data, excluding those on pollution in Helsinki, coming from Forum Virium activities and in which we have a specific agreement in the context of Snap4City, Select4City PCP of the European Commission. All the data is ingested in a periodical modality, each data with the frequency reported in the table, excluding those related to Cagliari. The Ingestion phase in the City of Cagliari is under development. Moreover, we pose a (*) when data is provided both in a dynamic modality for every day and as a prediction.

Phase II – Data ingestion. In this phase a set of data gathering processes are created (one for each dataset), that can be IoT Applications, based on NodeRED or ETL (Extract Transform and Load) processes based on Spoon, [16, 18, 20]. The static data (sensor position, city, type of data, unit measures, frequency of update, etc.) are semantically aggregated, in compliance with the KM4City multi-domains ontology [33] and the dynamic data are automatically updated thanks to the fact that each IoT App or ETL runs basing on the frequency update of the related dataset, as reported in the above table.

Table 2. Data analysis among Florence, Helsinki, Cagliari.

City	Data category	Provider	Frequency of update	Type of pollutants	# of sensors
Florence	Pollution	Arpat [28] validated data (from experts)	daily (related to the previous day)	NO2, CO, H2S, C6H6, O3	6
	Pollution	Arpat instrumental data (non-validated)	hourly	NO2, CO, H2S, C6H6, O3	6
	Pollution	CNR C calibrated data	5 min	CO, CO2, NO, O3, PM10, PM2.5,	10
	Weather	CNR	5 min	Humidity, temperature	10
	Weather	OpenWeather [29]	hourly and prediction (*) for next 3 days	humidity*, temperature*, pressure*, wind speed and direction*, rain, temp_max*, temp_min*, snow, clouds*, weather description (e.g. clear sky), seaLevel Pressure*, sunrise and sunset, ground level pressure*	2
Helsinki	Pollution	Finnish meteorological Institute - ENFUSER [30]	hourly	NO, NO2, SO2, PM10, PM2.5, O3, AQI,	5
	Pollution	Forum Virium project, giving sensors to citizens	5 min	NO, NO2, SO2, O3, PM10, PM2.5	20
	Pollution predictions	ENFUSER	For the next 24 h (prediction for every hour)	NO2, O3, AQI [31], PM10, PM2.5	30 heatmaps
	Weather	OpenWeather [29]	hourly and prediction for next 3 days	Same as Florence	3
Cagliari	Pollution	SardegnaAmbiente [32] validated data (experts)	Daily (related to the previous day)	CO, NO2, SO2, O3, PM10, PM2.5, C6H6	8
	Pollution	SardegnaAmbiente instrumental data (non-validated)	hourly	CO, NO2, SO2, O3, PM10, PM2.5, C6H6	8
	Weather	OpenWeather [29]	hourly and prediction for next 3 days	Same as Florence	8

Phase III – Data analytic and development/application/comparison of predicting algorithms. In order to have a complete picture of the pollution situation in a smart city, it is necessary to start from the air quality data analyzing the level of the several pollution aspects have to be assessed measuring, for example: SO2, NO, NO2, O3, CO, CO2, PM10, PM2.5, etc., but also considering the weather conditions and weather forecasts, and traffic data. This makes it possible to monitor pollution in two different levels: to have the current state but also to elaborate, thanks to the use of predictive methods, the future state of pollutant levels.

Florence:

- Algorithms to estimate heatmaps for each pollutant. The frequency in which the interpolation is estimated depends on the data frequency, thus the algorithms run every hour on PM10, PM2.5, NO2, CO, humidity, air temperature.
- Algorithms to obtain the European Air Quality Index, EAQI, based on the European Environment Agency guidelines [34]. The EAQI takes into account for air quality assessment about PM10, PM2.5, NO2, O3, and SO2 considering the worst cases among the values of those measures according to a formula. The resulting index from 1 to 5 (good, fair, moderate, poor and very poor) indicate the quality of air.

Helsinki:

- Algorithms to estimate heatmaps for each pollutant. The frequency in which the interpolation is estimated depends on the data frequency, thus the algorithms run every hour on PM10, PM2.5, NO2, AQI, humidity, air temperature.
- Algorithms to obtain the European Air Quality Index, EAQI, based on the European Environment Agency guidelines, as described for the city of Florence.
- Visualization of the ENFUSER Open Data AQI heatmaps. The Finnish Air Quality Index is a hourly index which describes the air quality today, based on hourly values and updated every hour. The index takes into account the concentrations of sulphur dioxide (SO_2), nitrogen dioxide (NO_2), respirable particles (PM_{10}), fine particles ($PM_{2.5}$), ozone (O_3) carbon monoxide (CO), and the Total Reduced Sulphur compounds (TRS). The air quality index in use in Finland is developed and maintained by the Helsinki Region Environmental Services Authority HSY and the National Institute for Health and Welfare THL.
- Visualization of the ENFUSER Open Data heatmap: hourly previsions for the next 24 h on AQI, PM10, PM2.5 on NO2, O3, AQI, PM10, PM2.5.

Heatmaps are computed using a bilinear interpolation (Akima method, [40, 41]). Interpolated maps are delimited by external sensors and the value are estimated inside the external sensors area (triangulation). The bivariate interpolation method consists of five procedures: (1) triangulation (i.e., partitioning into a number of triangles) of the x-y plane; (2) selection of several data points that are closest to each data point (sensor) and are used for estimating the partial derivatives; (3) organization of the output with respect to triangle numbers; (4) estimation of partial derivatives at each data point; and (5) punctual interpolation at each output point. The z value of the function at point of coordinates (x, y) in a triangle is interpolated by a bivariate fifth-degree polynomial in x and y. The algorithm has been implemented as an R script, that is put in execution periodically on the Snap4City Infrastructure.

In Fig. 2, the hourly heatmaps related to the cities of Helsinki and Florence are compared. Moreover, a set of heatmap controls is available and useful to go back and forth in time as method to compare the status of pollutants and weather data not only today but also in the past (and in future in case of the ENFUSER data). While in Fig. 3, is available the comparison, which once again connects the cities of Helsinki and Florence. This model makes predictions on the next 48 h at two level (3 and 6 m) on NOx, also in this case the heatmap controls allow the user to scroll through time and display heatmaps both in past and future. It as possible to view a video showing the next 24 h. Looking at Fig. 3, the NO2 heatmaps are shown.

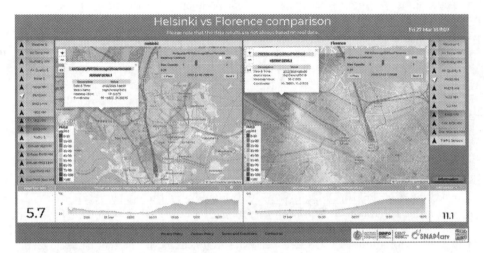

Fig. 2. Snap4City Dashboard comparing Helsinki and Florence: PM10 heatmaps [35].

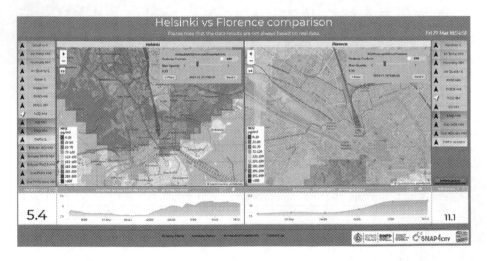

Fig. 3. Snap4City. Prediction of NO2 presence on Helsinki and Florence.

In order to make a comparison on the three different European, for each city two sensors have been selected (from the Air quality monitoring stations) covering a downtown position and a peripherical position. In Table 3, for each sensor are reported the Annual Means related to PM10, PM2.5, NOX, EAQI. NOx is a generic term for the nitrogen oxides that are most relevant for air pollution, produced from combustion, namely nitric oxide (NO) and nitrogen dioxide (NO2). For the city of Cagliari on the NO2, is available. Moreover, only for the city of Cagliari, the data are not already ingested in the Snap4City Platform and comes directly from the provider (SardegnaAmbiente) and are related to 2018. The other means comes from data on Snap4City.

Table 3 Comparison among Florence, Helsinki, Cagliari on Annual Means related to PM2.5, PM10, NOX, AQI/EAQI, considering that regarding Cagliari, for EAQI (*) only a qualitative evaluation is available in the Sardegna Ambiente Portal.

Sensor name	Mean annual PM10	Mean annual PM2.5	Mean annual NOX	Mean annual EAQI
Florence Gramsci – downtown	27.52	15.59	97.03	2.43 (Moderate)
Florence Airport - periphery	21.07	21.89	64.59	2.67 (Moderate)
Helsinki station - downtown	19.34	6.83	21.62	1.64 (Fair)
Helsinki Länsisatama 4 in Jätkäsaari periphery	no measures	4.62	15.21	1.73 (Fair)
Cagliari Cencal - Periphery	30.16	18.68	28.51 (NO2)	Fair (*)
Cagliari Cenmol - downtown	27.63	11.48	13.44 (NO2)	Fair (*)

5   Discussions and Conclusions

Smart and sustainable cities of the future represent a techno-urban innovation that triggered transformative processes that are developed due to the growing infiltration of sensors and of the enhancement of connectivity in urban systems with the consequent production of data, services, functions and projects [36, 37].

As with any transformation process in sustainable smart cities, it is necessary to establish road maps that take into account virtuous experiences and are able to make continuous improvements in urban contexts where they operate, always starting from the verification of the starting conditions, that is, having awareness the degree of maturity and the city's willingness to change.

The integration of IoT and big data will undoubtedly have significant short- and long-term effects in the creation of increasingly smart sustainable cities, even if open challenges for the analysis and management of big data must not be overlooked, including all the related implications. to ownership and privacy, to the integration of databases between different urban domains, data sharing, in addition to the usual long-standing questions regarding uncertainty, incompleteness, accuracy and quality of data.

This paper reported the work performed in supporting this trend and analysis in three cities in Europe, which are from certain point of views are similar: Florence, Helsinki and Cagliari, for geomorphic aspects and for population. Two of them present a relevant port, two of them have similar population and traffic, etc. The results have shown that critical aspects have been identified for PM10 and NOX over time.

The Snap4city architecture, quickly described in this paper, through experimentation conducted in different urban areas, highlights a paradigm shift, since it does not adopt an approach simply driven by technology but more specifically driven by data. Big data, open data, sensors, IoT, IoE for monitoring, controlling and managing urban developments, resources, urban infrastructure, energy consumption, traffic congestion, waste, pollution, risks and people, are the tools for governance and urban planning, for which the expected changes are a consequence of a decision-making process based on the data [38, 39]. The work presented has exploited Snap4City bigdata for smart city infrastructure and has been developed in the context of Snap4City, TRAFAIR, and GHOST projects.

Acknowledgments. This study was also supported by the MIUR (Ministry of Education, Universities and Research [Italy]) through a project entitled WEAKI TRANSIT: WEAK-demand areas Innovative TRANsport Shared services for Italian Towns (Project code: 20174ARRHT; CUP Code: F74119001290001), financed with the PRIN 2017 (Research Projects of National Relevance) programme. We authorize the MIUR to reproduce and distribute reprints for Governmental purposes, notwithstanding any copyright notations thereon. Any opinions, findings and conclusions or recommendations expressed in this material are those of the authors, and do not necessarily reflect the views of the MIUR. In addition, the authors would like to thank the European Union's Horizon 2020 research and innovation program for funding the "Select4Cities" PCP project (within which the Snap4City framework has been supported) under grant agreement No 688196, and also all the companies and partners involved. Snap4City and Km4City are open technologies and research of DISIT Lab https://www.snap4city.org. The authors would like also to thank the TRAFAIR CEF project of the EC with grant AGREEMENT No INEA/CEF/ICT/A2017/1566782 also all the companies and partners involved.

References and Notes

1. This paper is the result of the joint work of the authors. In particular, 'Abstract' was written jointly by the authors. Chiara Garau wrote the 'Introduction'. Paola Zamperlin wrote the 'The Future of Smart Sustainable Cities Considering the "Deep Ecology" Paradigm, IoT, and Big data'. Irene Paoli wrote 'The Big Data Platform Snap4City for the Case Studies'. Michela Paolucci wrote 'Empirical Examples of IoT and IoE in the Case studies of Florence, Helsinki and Cagliari'. Paolo Nesi wrote 'Conclusions'

2. Ahvenniemi, H., Huovila, A., Pinto-Seppä, I., Airaksinen, M.: What are the differences between sustainable and smart cities? Cities **60**, 234–245 (2017)

3. Janik, A., Ryszko, A., Szafraniec, M.: Scientific landscape of smart and sustainable cities literature: a bibliometric analysis. Sustainability **12**(3), 779 (2020)

4. Garau, C., Desogus, G., Zamperlin, P.: Governing technology-based urbanism: technocratic governance or progressive planning? In: Willis, K.S., Aurigi, A., (eds.) The Routledge Companion to Smart Cities (2020)
5. Cellina, F., Castri, R., Simão, J.V., Granato, P.: Co-creating app-based policy measures for mobility behavior change: a trigger for novel governance practices at the urban level. Sustain. Cities Soc. **53**, 101911 (2020)
6. Sahib, U.: Smart Dubai: sensing Dubai smart city for smart environment management. In: Vinod Kumar, T.M. (ed.) Smart Environment for Smart Cities. ACHS, pp. 437–489. Springer, Singapore (2020). https://doi.org/10.1007/978-981-13-6822-6_12
7. Bibri, S.E.: Smart Sustainable Cities of the Future. TUBS. Springer, Cham (2018). https://doi.org/10.1007/978-3-319-73981-6
8. Al-Nasrawi, S., Adams, C., El-Zaart, A.: A conceptual multidimensional model for assessing smart sustainable cities. J. Inf. Syst. Technol. Manag. **12**(3), 541–558 (2015)
9. Bibri, S.E., Krogstie, J.: Smart sustainable cities of the future: an extensive interdisciplinary literature review. Sustain. Cities Soc. **31**, 183–212 (2017)
10. Bibri, S.E.: Smart Sustainable Cities of the Future. TUBS. Springer, Cham (2018). https://doi.org/10.1007/978-3-319-73981-6
11. Azzari, M., Garau, C., Nesi, P., Paolucci, M., Zamperlin, P.: Smart city governance strategies to better move towards a smart urbanism. In: Gervasi, O., et al. (eds.) ICCSA 2018. LNCS, vol. 10962, pp. 639–653. Springer, Cham (2018). https://doi.org/10.1007/978-3-319-95168-3_43
12. Garau, C., Zamperlin, P., Balletto, G.: Reconsidering the Geddesian concepts of community and space through the paradigm of smart cities. Sustainability **8**(10), 985 (2016)
13. United Nations. World urbanization prospects: the 2018 revision (2018)
14. United Nations. Transforming our world: The 2030 agenda for sustainable development. New York, NY (2015). https://sustainabledevelopment.un.org/post2015/transformingour world
15. Vinod Kumar, T.M. (ed.): Smart Environment for Smart Cities. ACHS. Springer, Singapore (2020). https://doi.org/10.1007/978-981-13-6822-6
16. Macy, J.: Mutual Causality in Buddhism and General Systems Theory. State University of New York Press, Albany (1991)
17. Yue, P., Gong, J., Di, L., et al.: Integrating semantic web technologies and geospatial catalog services for geospatial information discovery and processing in cyberinfrastructure. Geoinformatica **15**, 273 (2013). https://doi.org/10.1007/s10707-009-0096-1
18. The term big data means the availability and proliferation of large quantities of data characterized by heterogeneity, complexity, temporality, modifiability and their use in disparate application domains. By convention and for brevity it is usual to refer to the well-known 5 V, that is velocity, volume, value, variety, and veracity. (to which later validity and volatility were added). Due to these characteristics, the computational and analytical capabilities of standard software applications and conventional database infrastructures are no longer sufficient for the processing and management of big data. The data acquired by sensors are analyzed through data-mining and machine learning techniques in order to build descriptive and predictive models to support decisions
19. The IoT actually constitutes an increasingly sophisticated network of sensors (i.e. electronic devices that react to certain physical inputs and return a digital signal) that affects almost every type of everyday object: roads, railways, bridges, roads, buildings, water systems, electricity networks, vehicles, appliances, goods, machines, animals, plants, soil and air, including people themselves. In essence, the connectivity achieved by the IoT involves living beings, objects and places and is destined to grow

20. Index, Cisco Global Cloud. Forecast and Methodology, 2012–2017, Cisco Systems. Inc., San Jose, CA, USA (2014)
21. Bellini, P., Bilotta, S., Nesi, P., Paolucci, M., Soderi, M.: WiP: traffic flow reconstruction from scattered data. In: Proceedings of 2018 IEEE International Conference on Smart Computing (SMARTCOMP), pp. 264–266 (2018). https://doi.org/10.1109/SMARTCOMP. 2018.00052. https://ieeexplore.ieee.org/document/8421365
22. Verrest, H., Pfeffer, K.: Elaborating the urbanism in smart urbanism: distilling relevant dimensions for a comprehensive analysis of Smart City approaches. Inf. Commun. Soc. 1–15 (2018)
23. https://www.snap4city.org
24. Bellini, P., Nesi, P., Paolucci, M., Zaza, I.: Smart city architecture for data ingestion and analytics: processes and solutions. In: IEEE 4th International Conference on Big Data Computing Service and Applications, BigDataService, pp. 7–144 (2018). https://doi.org/10. 1109/BigDataService.2018.00028
25. Badii, C., et al.: Snap4City: a scalable IOT/IOE platform for developing smart city applications. In: Proceedings - IEEE SmartWorld (2018). https://doi.org/10.1109/SmartWor ld.2018.00353
26. Badii, C., Bellini, P., Cenni, D., Difino, A., Paolucci, M., Nesi, P.: User engagement engine for smart city strategies. In: IEEE International Conference on Smart Computing, SMARTCOMP (2017). https://doi.org/10.1109/SMARTCOMP.2017.7947059
27. Badii, C., Bellini, P., Difino, A., Nesi, P., Pantaleo, G., Paolucci, M.: Microservices suite for smart city applications. Sensors - Switzerland (2019). https://doi.org/10.3390/s19214798
28. Agenzia Regionale per la Protezione Ambientale della Toscana – Regional Agency for the Environmental Protection of Tuscany. http://www.arpat.toscana.it/
29. Consiglio Nazionale delle Ricerche - National Research Council. http://www.fi.ibimet.cnr.it/
30. Finnish Metereological Institute – ENFUSER. https://en.ilmatieteenlaitos.fi/
31. Air Quality Index - AQI
32. Sardegna Ambiente – regione Autonome della Sardegna. https://portal.sardegnasira.it
33. KM4City multi-ontology. https://www.km4city.org/
34. European Air Quality Index, EAQI. http://airindex.eea.europa.eu/. https://www.eea.europa.eu/
35. https://www.snap4city.org/dashboardSmartCity/view/index.php?iddasboard=MTc0MQ==
36. Dembski, F., Wössner, U., Letzgus, M., Ruddat, M., Yamu, C.: Urban digital twins for smart cities and citizens: the case study of Herrenberg, Germany. Sustainability 12(6), 2307 (2020)
37. Mannaro, K., Baralla, G., Garau, C.: A goal-oriented framework for analyzing and modeling city dashboards in smart cities. In: Bisello, A., Vettorato, D., Laconte, P., Costa, S. (eds.) SSPCR 2017. GET, pp. 179–195. Springer, Cham (2018). https://doi.org/10.1007/978-3-319-75774-2_13
38. Acuto, M., Steenmans, K., Iwaszuk, E., Ortega-Garza, L.: Informing urban governance? Boundary-spanning organisations and the ecosystem of urban data. Area 51(1), 94–103 (2019)
39. Po, L., et al.: TRAFAIR: understanding traffic flow to improve air quality. In: 5th IEEE International Smart Cities Conference, ISC2 2019. October 2019, Article number 9071661, pp. 36–43 (2019)
40. Akima, H.: A method of bivariate interpolation and smooth surface fitting for values given at irregularly distributed points, vol. 75, no. 70. US Department of Commerce, Office of Telecommunications (1975)
41. Badii, C., et al.: Real-time automatic air pollution services from IOT data network. In: Proceedings of IEEE Symposium on Computers and Communications (ISCC), MOCS track, 10th Workshop on Management of Cloud and Smart City System, 2020 July 7th, Rennes, France (2020)

Challenges and Opportunities for the Historic Urban Landscape Planning. The Sardinia Region Case Study

Anna Maria Colavitti$^{(\boxtimes)}$ (ID), Alessio Floris (ID), and Sergio Serra (ID)

Università di Cagliari, 09122 Cagliari, CA, Italy
amcolavt@unica.it

Abstract. The 2011 UNESCO Recommendation defines the Historic Urban Landscape (HUL) as a stratification of historical, cultural and natural values, which broadens the notion of "historic centre" to include the social, environmental and economic components of the urban and geographical context.

Italian urban planning has so far adopted a conservative and binding approach to the protection and valorisation of historic settlements. Regulatory planning tools have often failed to combine the protection of physical heritage with the general improvement of urban quality and socio-economic conditions. The limitations of traditional planning can be identified in the difficulty to interpret the urban complexity and in the lack of projects and actions monitoring. The paper investigates the critical issues arising from the application of the traditional planning models for the historic centre, focusing on the case study of the Sardinia Region. The objective of the study is to identify some fields of innovation in the use of planning tools, that take into consideration the characteristics of local contexts and the needs of communities, as recommended by UNESCO. New technologies can contribute to a regularly updated knowledge framework and to the involvement of private actors in regeneration projects. The study shows that the continuous evolution of socio-economic conditions in cities requires open and flexible decision-making based on the principles of sustainability, social inclusion and innovation. The conclusions highlight the need for a review of approaches and tools to give more dynamism and effectiveness to the planning process, including the integration of innovative methods and technologies.

Keywords: Historic Urban Landscape · Urban planning · Regeneration

1 Policies for the Recovery of the Historic Centres in Italy

1.1 The Theoretical Debate and the Evolution of the Regulatory Framework

In the second half of the Nineteenth century the rapid urban growth, determined by the new needs of the industrial civilization, has made increasingly marked the gap between the historical city and the new developments. The inadequate protection policies has fostered processes of abandonment, shift to the service sector and radical change in

© Springer Nature Switzerland AG 2020
O. Gervasi et al. (Eds.): ICCSA 2020, LNCS 12255, pp. 407–421, 2020.
https://doi.org/10.1007/978-3-030-58820-5_31

physical and social characters, excepted to some rural contexts where the urban structure keeps unaltered until the Second World War [1].

In the 1930s there was an intense debate on the values of the pre-industrial city and the need to extend protection from monumental architecture to the whole urban areas with historical value [2, 3].

In Italy, the identification of "Zone A" by the General Plan (PRG) contributed to protect an area limited by a physical boundary, in which the multiple components and different characteristics of the historical landscape are lost [4, 5]. Since the 1960s, the topic of safeguarding the historical heritage has been widely established in the European countries. The uniqueness of the Italian contribution is characterized by a constant permeability and conflict between innovation and conservation, in search of appropriate functions in order to ensure the preservation and the strengthening of the sense of community [6–9].

The overcoming of the notion of the historic centre as a "monolithic monument" to be entirely preserved in favour of a new vision of economic asset, in terms of financial and social values, feeds new experimentations in the field of urban renewal [10, 11].

The policies for the conservation of historic centre, understood as carriers of economic, cultural and social values, require an evaluation and redefinition of the role that it assumes in the current urban and territorial situation [12]. This vision is sometimes in contrast with some conservationist positions, which put historical and artistic values before those of the socio-economic context, rejecting any intervention other than integral conservation. The policies of integral protection put at risk the permanence of the productive and commercial activities or of the residence itself, as well as being ineffective due to the difficult to verify the respect of the regulations [13, 14]. Severe restrictions and constraints, even in the presence of a building heritage of low value, can lead to physical degradation and abandonment, for example non-compliance with the rules and unauthorized interventions. In 2011, the UNESCO General Conference adopted the Recommendation on Historic Urban Landscape (HUL), an innovative and dynamic approach to HUL management, which Member States can implement on a voluntary basis. The overall management of the city must be based on the recognition of a stratification and interconnection of natural and cultural, material and immaterial, inter-national and local values present in any city. In fact, the term Historic Urban Landscape refers to a stratification of historical, cultural and natural values, which goes beyond the notion of "historic centre" to include the wider urban and geographical context. The singularity of the city is not only linked to its natural characteristics, the built environment (historical and contemporary) and spatial organization, but also to social and cultural practices, economic processes and intangible heritage.

The intervention in the historical settlements was initially guided by plans designed to govern urban expansion processes, gradually renewed with specific tools, such as the Recovery Plan (L.457/1978) and the Integrated Program of Intervention (L.179/1992), which became part of the ordinary planning activities. The Recovery Plan acts within the recovery areas, not necessarily historical, identified in the General Plan, in order to rehabilitee, reconstruct and preserve the existing heritage in degraded conditions [15]. Often the results have been disappointing, failing to involve the private operator without economic incentives [16].

The Integrated Program of Intervention overcomes some of the limits of the Recovery Plan thanks to the strong autonomy of design and content, also for the location of the interventions, acting in derogation of the urban plans in force. They fall into the category of consensual urban planning, characterized by greater flexibility in reaching agreements between public and private, even in the absence of an overall and strategic urban design [17, 18].

The UNESCO Recommendation of 2011 recognizes the need for an inclusive approach to interpret the complex system of values, not only architectural monuments, which constitute the identity and character of the urban context. It proposes a comprehensive and integrated approach for the identification, assessment, conservation and sustainable management of historic urban landscapes in order to address the new challenges brought by rapid social and economic change. Regulatory systems should reflect local conditions and help to protect the integrity and authenticity of urban heritage, by monitoring and managing processes to improve the quality of life and space. Documentation and mapping of cultural and natural features and social and environmental heritage support decision-making [19–21].

The HUL approach implies the use of traditional and innovative instruments according to the characteristics of the local contexts and the needs of the communities. In this direction, it is fundamental the provision of participation practices and civic commitment in the involvement of a multitude of subjects able to support the process of identification of key values and definition of objectives, strategies and actions to safeguard heritage and promote local development [22, 23]. They also facilitate mediation and negotiation between conflicting interests and groups, promoting the development of local entrepreneurship and associations to support the economic and productive sectors with private public partnership and financial instruments [21, 24].

In this direction, the paper assesses whether the evolution of the urban planning practice and the regulatory framework in Italy has incorporated these theoretical and methodological innovations. In particular, the role of landscape planning in the recovery of the historic centres and the effectiveness of the implementation methods through municipal urban planning are analysed. A specific focus on the Sardinia Region case study allows to reflect on the need to combine the experimentation of new tools, including information technology, with the revision of the structure of municipal planning to adapt to the new demands of contemporary urban environment.

1.2   Landscape Planning and Historic Centres

The theoretical and regulative innovations, introduced on the national context, had a significant impact at regional level, in particular within the landscape plans that contain provisions for intervention in historic centres. Five regional planning instruments with a landscape value are currently in force in Italy: after the Regional Landscape Plan (RLP) for the coastal areas of Sardinia in 2006, a decade is expected to pass, in 2015, for the approval of the RLP of Puglia Region and the Territorial Plan with a value of PPR of Tuscany Region, until the most recent PPR of Piedmont Region in 2017 and Friuli Venezia Giulia Region in 2018.

The RLP of Friuli Venezia Giulia interprets the landscape areas according to the hydro-geomorphological, ecosystemic and environmental characteristics and the settlement and infra-structural systems. The plan identifies the historical centres of considerable interest for landscape purposes and the identity settlement aspects through the recognition of "morphotypes", understood as the result of the interaction of natural, anthropic and identity factors, which can be typified or recognized in different contexts. The abacus of morphotypes constitutes the regulatory framework for landscape areas in order to address territorial and urban planning towards compatible development directions.

The Territorial Plan (PIT) of the Region of Tuscany recognizes the settlement structure of historical-territorial and identity value, which includes the cities, the minor settlements and the relative infrastructural, industrial and technological systems. The preservation of the polycentric and identity character of the settlements passes through a strategy of protection and enhancement of the historical centres and the surrounding area, identified in the local plans, in order to ensure the permanence of the historical values and architectural features. The landscape context is represented by the area strongly connected on the morphological, perceptual, identity and historically functional level, generally consisting of the area next to the historic core for a belt of 300 m from the perimeter of "Zone A". In this context, actions are planned to safeguard the perceptual value and the historical and cultural heritage of the settlement, also protecting the agricultural destination and the hydraulic and agricultural systems of the areas of pertinence. The plan hopes for the permanence of the inhabitants and the strengthening of the role of the settled communities, evaluating the direct and indirect transformations induced by the tourist flows.

The RLP of the Region of Piedmont protects the components of historical and cultural interest, which are the key elements of historical and documentary value and of the regional cultural identity, also identified in a precise way in the complementary Regional Territorial Plan (RTP). The historic centres, qualified as consolidated urban areas, fall into the morphological and settlement components (major centres, minor centres and external settlements). The local plans define the perimeter of the historical centres, including areas on board and free spaces to safeguard the fundamental relationships with the landscape context. The detailed regulatory framework aims at the conservation and enhancement of the original morphology, the aspects of interaction between historical and territorial systems at the local scale, the specificity of the structures, the types and built fabrics, the elements of perceptual landscape value. Areas to be requalified, to be subject to a recovery plan, can be identified in order to ensure the coherence of the interventions with the original aggregative patterns, the alignments, the relationships between full and empty spaces, the orientation of the roofs, the materials and the typical colours of the place.

In the RLP of Apulia Region the historical fabrics fall within the cultural and settlement components and consist of the portion of the urban centers that goes from the foundation nucleus to the compact urbanization of the first half of the twentieth century. The historical settlement resources, consisting of the historical centres and nuclei or the complex of elements that constitute the natural productive and infrastructural completion and the recognizable traces of the historical organization of the territory, are understood in the double value of the constitutive elements of the settlement system and of significant parts of the cultural heritage to be protected. The local plans ensure the conservation and enhancement of integrated territorial systems, the result of long-term territorialisation processes, identifying the qualities to be preserved and the specific problems to be faced for the protection, redevelopment and enhancement of the consolidated city. The municipal planning system provides for a General Urban Plan (PUG), divided into a programmatic and operational component, to be implemented through the use of detailed plans or integrated programs of public, private or mixed initiatives. The structural part of the plan analyses urban and rural contexts, including the structural invariants of a historical and cultural nature, identifying the morphological characteristics of settlement resources through a reading of the models and values deposited by the process of anthropic stratification. It identifies the "urban contexts to be protected", defining the perimeter of the settlements constituting the cultural heritage and deserving of protection, the peculiar elements and the potential for qualification and development, the transformation processes underway as well as any factors of abandonment and social, environmental and building degradation.

2 Protection and Valorisation of Historic Centres in Sardinia

2.1 The Regional Landscape Plan and the Municipal Urban Planning

In Sardinia, the Regional Landscape Plan (RLP) of 2006 has allowed a deep revision of the planning processes of historical fabrics, with a view to an innovative openness to transformation for contemporary use, respecting the preeminence of values and the identity character of the context, even in the case of minor buildings, often subject to degradation, destruction or misrepresentation, given the lack of interpretative awareness of the value frameworks contained therein. The RLP guarantees the protection of areas characterized by historical settlements, including the development matrices of the centers of ancient origins and early foundation deductible from the reading of historical cartography, as well as modern and contemporary original centers, including specialized nuclei of work and spread settlement (Art.51 RLP), defining specific prescriptions and guidelines, to be taken into account when adapting local urban plans. The municipalities verify the perimeters of the centers of ancient origins and early foundation, through an analysis of the building fabric and factors attesting its "historicity" [25]. The subsequent drafting of the Detailed Plan for the Historic Centre requires further investigation of the many physical and socio-cultural aspects of the historical settlement. It classifies the existing buildings on the basis of their period of origin, the traditional historical character or the existing compatibility with the context in the case of recent construction, expressing a judgement of historical landscape value that translates into a different degree of transformability and a specific regulation for the interventions.

The preservation of the historical stratification of the settlement and the valorisation of the traces that testify its historical origin, are guaranteed through a set of interventions to protect the specificity of each historic centre, enhancing the separation between adjacent districts and promoting the recognition of the margins. Some urban portions have been profoundly altered in recent times by replacement or obvious transformation interventions that have influenced the perception of the identity elements, the typological and construction features, the land layout and the organization of the blocks. For these areas, the RLP promotes building and urban restructuring interventions, preferring the use of public-private partnerships, for the replacement of incongruous and incompatible parts and the requalification of public spaces in order to recover the original urban layout and the historically recognizable morphological characteristics.

The planning of new construction is allowed for any functional completions and additions of new volumes, in accordance with the characteristics of the historical background and the context. In the case of undeveloped areas, the appropriateness of allocating them for public purposes is evaluated. The design of the interventions is based on criteria and rules taken from the Abacus of the building typologies, aimed at interpreting the specific spatial relationships of the historical building type, in order to avoid the so-called "typological degradation" caused by the inclusion of incompatible settlement models in historical contexts.

In order to restore high levels of landscape value to the environmental, cultural and historical context, it is necessary to eliminate or mitigate the incongruous, legitimately authorized artefacts and works with negative aesthetic value or in disharmony with the context, which can cause a loss in terms of identity and quality of places. In some cases, such incongruities can be removed by the renovation of the building, in others it is necessary to totally replace the building after demolition. The plan cannot impose the demolition of a legitimate building, even if it is incompatible with the historical landscape context, but it can define restrictive measures for the building transformation, limiting the interventions to "extraordinary maintenance" only. In some cases, voluntary demolition by private individuals is encouraged, allowing the reconstruction of the existing volume, in a compatible way in terms of construction characteristics, heights, shadows and positioning in the lot. This plan strategy clashes with the lack of consensus of private owners, considering the low economic convenience.

A strict regulation can lead to the maintenance of the status quo, not only in the possible demolition and reconstruction in compatible forms, but also in the ordinary building maintenance, which results in an increase in the conditions of degradation.

2.2 Regional Rewards and Incentives for the Rehabilitation of Historic Centres

The Sardinia Region grants subsidies for the recovery, redevelopment and reuse of buildings in historic centres and minor settlements (L.R.29/1998) intended for residential use or economic activities. Further incentives have been allocated from Community funds: the European project called LAB.net, funded under the 2004 Interreg IIIA Programme, which aims to enhance the historical and architectural heritage of cross-border territories and to protect the local identity, the countryside and the natural environment of several municipalities and provinces in Sardinia, Corsica and Tuscany; the 2006 CIVIS call for proposals, which promotes the creation of cooperation networks of minor centres for the requalification, recovery and reuse of the settlements, the strengthening of public services in order to deal with the depopulation of internal areas; the 2008 Biddas call for proposals, which financed "network programmes" to consolidate the process of valorisation of historical buildings through Integrated Programs (IP) and Urban Redevelopment Interventions (URI).

The Region of Sardinia also promotes the use of integrated urban programs that provide for the recovery and enhancement of buildings in the historic centers of the inner areas, offered at a symbolic price (L.R.8/2015).

This regulatory framework includes the initiative "Houses for 1 euro", which aims to deal with the depopulation of smaller towns in the inner areas of the island, already experienced in Campania, Sicily, Lazio, Tuscany and Abruzzo. The mechanism is based on the presence of unused properties in conditions of physical deterioration such as to make it difficult for private owners to place them on the market for rent or sale. These are often properties acquired by inheritance, with a fragmented ownership that makes it difficult to adopt decisions on the property use, subjected to heavy taxation. The initiative is remarkable but cannot be considered a strong strategy for the redevelopment of historic centres. It can only be adopted in the presence of low real estate prices that would encourage the owner to give up the income that could be gained from its sale, but at the same time adequate to make the investment profitable for the buyer. With these levels of income the operation will be attractive only for amateurs, excluding an economic convenience such as to activate a mechanism of self-promotion of the initiative in the real estate market. Its action will be limited to stimulate the local market, with a merely promotional role and positive impacts of an economic rather than of urban nature.

The regional legislation is contradictory because, despite promoting the protection of the historical landscape, it provides for the allocation of incentives for the extension of buildings without historical value and incompatible with the context even within the historical centers, as an exception to the RLP and local planning (L.R. 4/2009, L.R. 8/2015). The increase in volume, even if limited to a building without no historical value, could have negative consequences for the whole historical context, altering the relationship between full and empty spaces and the harmonious development of the facades. In line with the national context, it seems to prevail the idea of being able to act in derogation of urban planning instruments for any intervention that has the character of priority or urgency, attributing less importance to the urban scale of interventions than to the building one [25–27].

3 The Effectiveness of the Plan for the Historic Centre Between Traditional Approaches and Perspectives for Innovation

3.1 Limitation of Traditional Planning for Historic Centres

Sardinia is an example of a strictly conservative approach that requires a detailed plan to be drawn up for the historic centre, in order to make possible any transformation project, even minor building renovation. Direct intervention is allowed only for maintenance and restoration works, leaving the definition of other transformations to the detailed plan. The conventional recovery plans, linked to a concept of public planning, have proved to be ineffective in the regeneration of the historical fabric, despite the excellent results achieved in the analysis of the settlement features and characteristics, in the definition of the degree of conservation and transformability, in the protection of the preserved historical values with development restrictions.

However, the detailed plan provides a picture of the current state of an urban environment which, even if detailed and accurate, refers to a given time, often outdated at the end of the adoption procedure. The ineffectiveness of the plan, in addition, is usually due to the lack of agreement of the local community, because of the inadequate participation and sharing of choices made by the political decision-makers. It is also essential to be able to monitor the state of urban areas and their evolution, to facilitate the appraisal of the projects proposals and to improve the management skills and procedures. The procedures for adapting municipal urban plans to the regional landscape plan are excessively complex and time-consuming, discouraging any initiative to update or revise planning choices.

The decision-making phase is necessarily developed on a multidimensional level, integrating aspects of economic, social, cultural and environmental nature. Therefore it is necessary to build an adequate cognitive framework that, in relation to the characteristics of the context, is a prerequisite for the implementation of the objectives identified and the consequent control of the results.

The planning tools, at different levels, show a clear difficulty in the interpretation of the reality that is complex and summarize it within a knowledge framework that is periodically updated according to the changing socio-economic conditions. The structure, availability and quality of data are considered a basic condition for a correct definition and management of policies and actions. The choices concerning the regeneration, preservation and enhancement of the historical urban landscapes accordingly depend on a deepening of knowledge, in a process that involves the architectural aspects of the heritage but also and especially the background in which they are located, in order to guarantee their integrity and authenticity [28]. The awareness of the need to capture a complex and dynamic process that is difficult to define in terms of time rather than a static phenomenon, is fundamental. The continuous changes affecting an urban area, even more so if historical, require a constant acquisition and monitoring of data [29]. According to the increasingly use of advanced tools thanks to the new technologies, it can be said with conviction that the planning model, based on the deterministic and functionalistic paradigm, has exhausted its effectiveness, revealing the need for flexible and dynamic tools that allow the monitoring over time of the made choices.

It is important and strategic to evaluate the effects of the planning choices, at a spatial and administrative level, in particular when they are not in line with the expectations of the plan [30]. This monitoring activities should be carried out both on the plan and on the real context, through tools that describe the effectiveness in relation to the actions implemented, the financial resources involved and the objectives achieved [31].

Theoretically, monitoring and assessment activities are now well established and often integrated within the urban planning practices and legislation, at national and local level. There are many fields of application and aims: from the energy field to mobility, risk management and ecological and environmental issues.

However, these instruments have not a real impact at the level of evaluation of the transformations to which a given urban system is subjected, especially concerning historical contexts and their specific features and values.

For example, the Strategic Environmental Assessment (SEA), aimed at the management of complex plans and programmes, mainly oriented to the assessment of environmental issues, cannot be considered an effective tool in this direction.

The need for a monitoring and updating activity to support the implementation of the detailed plan is even clearer due to the different types of urban and architectural transformations coordinated by the instrument, based on the ex-ante analysis of the settlement. The different degree of transformability, attributed to each existing building and area, is characterised by strict and static regulation that need to be adapted and updated following the implementation of the plan actions.

An example of monitoring of urban and architectural transformations in Sardinia is provided for by Regional Law no. 8 of 23 April 2015, which requires municipalities to register the use of development rights bonus [32], but is limited to a simple census of authorized volume increases, providing information on the location of the buildings subject to intervention and the extent of volumes involved. There is a lack in the control of the impact of the interventions from the landscape point of view, compared to the proceedings of changes in the urban environment that can affect the landscape quality.

3.2 Innovative Approaches and New Technologies

The integration of new methodologies and digital tools in urban planning has facilitated the analysis of urban phenomena, with the consequence of putting the planning process in close relation with socio-economic trends, of significantly increasing the opportunity for local administrations to have control of the territory, of incorporating urban design and local finances [33].

The use of increasingly advanced analysis methods, thanks to the introduction of new digital technologies, has allowed high levels of restitution of existing heritage through the acquisition of data from stereoscopic photographic images, the use of laser scanner systems and the use of photogrammetry and software for the management of the next phases of elaboration [34].

The need to operate with scales of representation extended from the territory to the built environment has fostered the use of technologies to report, analyze and evidence the complex stratification of urban areas and their constitutive components.

On the basis of these needs, the Geographical Information Systems (GIS) has become an essential tool for the management of projects at the territorial and local scale, in line with the emerging of the contemporary concept of urban planning as a continuous and systematic activity [35–37].

The flexibility of GIS is particularly effective in the management of the cultural heritage, in its multiple forms and relations with the territory [28].

Despite the progressive evolution of its potentialities in terms of interaction, interpretation and detail, GIS are tools intended principally for the management of spatial elements characterized by a mainly "horizontal" distribution.

This attitude is not totally satisfactory, due to the complexity required by some urban planning tools, such as the detailed plan for the historical centre, where it is necessary to manage and regulate landscape aspects at the territorial scale, but at the same time at the architectural and building detail, involving the specific elements that contribute to the definition of the built environment [38].

In this regard, the development of new technologies such as Building Information Modelling (BIM), defined by international standards as the shared digital representation of the physical and functional characteristics of every building object, constitute a reliable basis for decision making [39].

The softwares based on this paradigm allow to represent building structures through semantic and queryable digital models, consisting of parametric elements, useful for the management of the single components of buildings [40, 41].

More recently we have seen an evolution of this approach, the Historic Building Information Modelling (HBIM), with a perspective aimed directly at interventions on the existing heritage which, declining the key concepts of BIM, allows to introduce procedures to generate three dimensional models of historical buildings [42, 43].

The HBIM is a specific solution that is developed through interactive parametric objects, which are geometrically constructed on the basis of handbooks and conventions, with the aim of creating models able to represent the heritage according to its historical-cultural values [44]. The development of new methodologies, which are able to collect the factors that contribute to the structure of a cultural and historical landscape, is therefore useful for the construction of a cognitive framework that is not just a technical elaboration, but a media by which to spread the knowledge of the cultural heritage, improving its accessibility [34].

The local community, in fact, is an essential component of the territorial area, which is required to preserve the sense of belonging and identity, weakened over time by the ongoing process of globalization. The tissue of historical buildings, as an asset of cultural heritage, must be considered an "investment", a repository of values and memories, able to dialogue with the specificity and identity of places [45–47].

The roads to be followed cannot be standardised and homologated, without taking into account the specific characteristics of the different territorial situations. Effective action and strategies for historical settlements in metropolitan areas cannot be applied to smaller centres located in the inner areas, which are characterised by a low population density, a weak economic and social structure, a lack of collective services and therefore a progressive demographic decrease.

Each local community must pursue policies that are specific to its own context and based on the enhancement of its typicality and identity values, arresting the loss of territorial resources. As a result, it is also necessary to rethink the ways in which private-sector involvement in the regeneration policies of historic city centres can be achieved, not only in terms of economic resources, but also in the elaboration of common strategies that, on the one hand, guarantee the economic sustainability of interventions and, on the other, intercept the needs of the local community.

The development of new media has facilitated the creation of new "public spaces", making it possible to connect an increasing number of individuals able to share information and multimedia data, using tools characterized by a remarkable promptness and flexibility of use [48]. In this perspective, the development of softwares and digital platforms is now widespread and very common, thanks to which public authorities can make their data available, at the same time supporting the strategic decisions and guidelines on the governance of the territory.

Digital participatory platforms are a specific civic technology tool structured to promote social inclusion, which allows the production of user generated content, including analytics, mapping, classification and data management functions [48].

There are several cases in which the use of these methods and tools has contributed to the development of virtuous planning processes aimed at involving public and private actors, both internationally [49, 50] and nationally [51, 52]. With such instruments it is possible to facilitate the inclusion in the planning processes, thanks to the sharing of information and the opportunity to interact with them through public communication interfaces, in a principle of subsidiarity that is coordinated by the public administrations [53].

4 Conclusions

In general, landscape planning emphasizes the identity value of historical settlements and recognizes their fundamental role within territorial systems. While the conservative approach is still the guiding principle of the planning directives, it is nevertheless clear the attempt to introduce objectives for the valorisation and regeneration of the existing city, which often do not correspond to concrete actions.

The implementation practice used for the historic centres of large cities cannot be applied in the same way to smaller historic centres, which in Italy represent a more widespread cultural and economic heritage than centres of greater importance. In few cases the emphasis is placed on the protection of the intangible components that constitute the identity of historical urban contexts and a fundamental resource to be exploited for the recovery of the territory and the activation of widespread urban regeneration processes. The redevelopment of the historic centre is part of a wider strategy to sew up the different parts of the urban settlement, from the consolidated city to the recent expansions. The recognition of a system of settlement values is indispensable for the construction of regulations able to compose an overall urban planning project for the existing city and the territory of reference. The recovery plan is often an interesting tool for the detailed study of fabrics but it is not very effective from an operational point of view. In some realities it would perhaps be desirable to overcome the implementation phase through the integration of the general instrument, in the different structural and operational components, to remedy the technical and economic difficulties linked to the drafting of a further planning act and to allow direct interventions of urban transformation, according to well-defined criteria and time horizons. The preservation of the historical fabric is enriched over time with new meanings pursuing the protection of the urban historical identity and conceiving the urban redevelopment project as an integration of conservation and innovation, in full respect of the sense of memory of the place. The historic centre is also a dynamic and changing entity in time that needs to be constantly updated as the political, social and economic conditions change [54]. The digital revolution has inevitably influenced urban spaces, which are structured through their physical dimension but at the same time permeated by information flows, in line with the well-established paradigm of the Smart City. Historic centres are not excluded from this process, due to the recognition of everything that contributes to the composition of the territorial capital, the sum of material and immaterial factors, in which current and traditional themes such as sustainability, community and landscape quality are combined [55]. The sharing of choices requires concertation operations between the public and private sectors, in order to transform the plan into a complex protocol for the definition of a series of programme contracts between public bodies and local actors. Even in detailed planning, the contribution of the private sector, as expressed in the plan observations, can take on a proactive character, a hypothesis already tested for integrated programmes [56]. The use of information and communication technologies can contribute to the implementation of open processes with a view to accessibility and transparency, enabling administrations to interact with all levels of society [57].

The potential offered by technological innovation can contribute to a more effective management of the planning process, starting from the construction phase of the knowledge framework, also making it possible to control its implementation and monitor its subsequent developments, constantly integrating the instrument over time on the basis of the changes and dynamics taking place.

Technological innovation can contribute to increasing the effectiveness of planning only if it is part of a process of reviewing the form of the plan in order to overcome the static nature and rigidity of the knowledge and regulatory framework.

References

1. Cervellati, P.L.: La città bella. Il recupero dell'ambiente urbano. Società editrice Il Mulino, Bologna (1991)
2. Gabellini, P.: Un progetto urbanistico per la città storica. In: Evangelisti, F., Orlandi, P., Piccinini, M. (eds.) La città storica contemporanea. Edisai Editore, Ferrara (2008)
3. Siravo, F.: Ideazione e applicazione delle discipline di conservazione. In: Benevolo, L. (eds.) Il Nuovo Manuale di Urbanistica. Pratica dell'urbanistica. Mancosu, Roma (2007)
4. Gasparrini, C.: La costruzione del piano. Strategie, regole e progetti per la Città storica. Urbanistica 116, 93–108 (2001)
5. Giambruno, M.C.: Per una storia del restauro urbano. Piani, strumenti e progetti per i Centri storici. Città Studi edizioni, Novara (2007)
6. Aristone, O., Palazzo, A.L.: Città storiche. Interventi per il riuso. Il Sole 24 Ore, Milano (2000)
7. Bandarin, F., Van Oers, R.: The Historic Urban Landscape. Managing Heritage in an Urban Century. Wiley Blackwell, Oxford (2012)
8. Bonfantini, B.G.: Planning the historic centres in Italy: for a critical outline. Planum. J. Urbanism 2/2012, 1–19 (2012)
9. Gabrielli, B.: Il recupero della città esistente. Saggi 1968–1992. Etas libri, Milano (1993)

10. Mazzoleni, C.: Dalla salvaguardia del centro storico alla riqualificazione della città esistente. Trent'anni di dibattito dell'ANCSA. Archivio di studi urbani e regionali n. 40 (1991)
11. Tallon, A.: Urban Regeneration in the UK. Rontledge, London and New York (2010)
12. Wallach, R.: L'ambiente costruito storico. La conservazione come trasformazione. Gangemi Editore, Roma (2000)
13. Indovina, F., Savino, M.: I vantaggi dell'integrazione tra città storica e città moderna. In: La ciutat històrica dins la ciutat. d'humanitats, Girona (1997)
14. Savino, M.: L'intervento nei centri storici in una complessa realtà territoriale e normativa. In: Savino, M. (eds.) Pianificazione alla prova nel Mezzogiorno. Franco Angeli editore, Milano (2005)
15. Indovina, F.: Governare la città con l'urbanistica. Guida agli strumenti di pianificazione urbana e del territorio. Maggioli editore, Santarcangelo di Romagna (2006)
16. Karrer, F., Moscato, M., Ricci, M., Segnalini, O.: Il rinnovo urbano. Programmi integrati, di riqualificazione e di recupero urbano: valutazioni e prospettive. Carocci editore, Roma (1998)
17. Indovina, F. (eds.): Il territorio derivato. Franco Angeli, Milano (2004)
18. Urbani, P.: La riconversione urbana: dallo straordinario all'ordinario. Problemi aperti nell'urbanistica consensuale. Archivio di studi urbani e regionali n. 70 (2001)
19. UNESCO: Managing Historic Cities, World Heritage Papers No. 27, Paris (2010). http://whc.unesco.org/en/series/27. Accessed 08 May 2020
20. UNESCO: Recommendation on the Historic Urban Landscape, 10 November2011. http://whc.unesco.org/en/activities/638. Accessed 08 May 2020
21. UNESCO: New life for historic cities: The historic urban landscape approach explained (2013).http://whc.unesco.org/en/activities/727. Accessed 08 May 2020
22. Ripp, M., Rodwell, D.: Governance in UNESCO world heritage sites: reframing the role of management plans as a tool to improve community engagement. In: Makuvaza, S. (ed.) Aspects of Management Planning for Cultural World Heritage Sites, pp. 241–253. Springer, Cham (2018). https://doi.org/10.1007/978-3-319-69856-4_18
23. Rodwell, D.: The historic urban landscape and the geography of urban heritage. Hist. Environ.: Policy Pract. 9(3–4), 180–206 (2018). https://doi.org/10.1080/17567505.2018. 1517140
24. UNESCO: The HUL guidebook. Managing heritage in dynamic and constantly changing urban environments. A practical guide to UNESCO's Recommendation on the Historic Urban Landscape (2016). http://historicurbanlandscape.com/themes/196/userfiles/download/2016/6/7/wirey5prpznidqx.pdf. Accessed 08 May 2020
25. Colavitti, A.M., Serra, S.: Il piano particolareggiato per il recupero del centro storico di Cagliari. Prime considerazioni critiche alla proposta di piano. In: Archivio di Studi Urbani e Regionali, vol. 107, pp. 74–106 (2013)
26. Colavitti, A.M., Serra, S.: La pianificazione dei centri storici in Sardegna: la sostituzione del tessuto edilizio incongruo per la riqualificazione del paesaggio urbano storico. In: Valori e valutazioni, vol. 19, pp. 79–89 (2017)
27. Lazzarotti, R.: Piani casa e centri storici: declinazioni regionali dell'intesa stato-regioni. Urbanistica n. 141 (2010)
28. Centofanti, M.: Integrated software systems in architectural and urban heritage conservation, protection and exploitation. In: Moscati, A., Sgariglia, S. (eds.) Sistemi Informativi Integrati per la tutela, la conservazione e la valorizzazione del Patrimonio Architettonico Urbano - Architettura, Urbanistica, Ambiente, pp. 320. Gangemi Editore, Roma (2010). ISBN 9788849218602

29. Cundari, C.: Il rilievo urbano per sistemi complessi. Un nuovo protocollo per un sistema informativo di documentazione e gestione della città. Edizioni Kappa, Roma (2015). ISBN 978-88-7890-668-6

30. Curto, R., Brigato, M.V., Coscia, C., Fregonara, E.: Valutazioni per strategie disviluppo turistico sostenibile nell'iglesiente. Territorio **69**, 123–133 (2014). https://doi.org/10.3280/TR2014-069018

31. Laniado, E., Cappiello, A., Cellina, F., Cerioli, R.: Un approccio metodologico e un Sistema di Supporto alle decisioni per la pianificazione territorial: il Progetto SFIDA. In: Cecchini, A., Plaisant, A. (eds.) Analisi e modelli per la pianificazione. Teoria e pratica: lo stato dell'arte, Franco Angeli, pp. 304–315 (2005). ISBN 9788846470959

32. Regione Autonoma della Sardegna (RAS): Legge regionale 23 aprile 2015, n. 8 Norme per la semplifi cazione e il riordino di disposizioni in materia urbanistica ed edilizia e per il miglioramento del patrimonio edilizio. Published in BURAS n. 19 of 30 April 2015 (2015)

33. Stanghellini: Come rendere efficace la pianificazione? Urbanistica Informazioni n. 140, pp. 3–4 (1995)

34. Amoruso, G.: Handbook of Research on Visual Computing and Emerging Geometrical Design Tools (2 volumi), pp. 1–924. IGI Global, Hershey (2016). ISBN 9781522500308

35. Camagni, R.: I fondamenti delle politiche di sviluppo regionale e di pianificazione urbana. In: Mazzola, F., Maggioni, M.A. (eds.) Crescita regionale ed urbana nel mercato globale. Modelli, politiche, processi di valutazione, Milano, Franco Angeli, pp. 177–199 (2001). ISBN 9788846432377

36. Giannopoulou, M., Vavatsikos, A.P., Lykostratis, K., Roukouni, A.: Using GIS to record and analyse historical urban areas. TeMA – J. Land Use Mobility Environ. (2014). https://doi.org/10.6092/1970-9870/2525

37. Lazzari, M., Patriziano, M.S., Aliano, G.A.: GIS assessment and planning of conservation priorities of historical centers through quantitative methods of vulnerability analysis: an example from southern Italy. In: Murgante, B., et al. (eds.) ICCSA 2014. LNCS, vol. 8580, pp. 677–692. Springer, Cham (2014). https://doi.org/10.1007/978-3-319-09129-7_49

38. Carta, E., Scanu, S.: Fotogrammetria, GIS e BIM per la gestione del Piano Particolareggiato di un Centro Storico della Sardegna, in Atti della 22a Conferenza Nazionale ASITA 2018, Federazione italiana delle Associazioni Scientifiche per le Informazioni Territoriali e Ambientali, 27–29 Novembre, Bolzano (2018). ISBN 978-88-941232-1-0

39. ISO Standard, ISO 29481-1:2010(E): Building Information Modeling - Information Delivery Manual - Part 1: Methodology and Format (2010)

40. Eastman, T., Sacks, L.: BIM Handbook — a guide to building information modeling for owners, managers, designers, engineers and contractors, Aufl, 2, Wiley, Hoboken (2011)

41. Volk, R., Stengel, J., Schultmann, F.: Building Information Modeling (BIM) for existing buildings. Literature review and future needs. Autom. Constr. **38**, 109–127 (2014). https://doi.org/10.1016/j.autcon.2013.10.023

42. Murphy, M., McGovern, E., Pavia, S.: Historic building information modelling (HBIM). Struct. Surv. **27**(4), 311–327 (2009). https://doi.org/10.1108/02630800910985108

43. Murphy, M., Govern, E.M., Pavia, S.: Historic building information modelling. Adding intelligence to laser and image based surveys of European classical architecture. ISPRS J. Photogrammetry Remote Sens. (2013). ISSN 0924-2716

44. Dore, C., Murphy, M.: Historic building information modeling (HBIM). In: Brusaporci, S. (eds.) Handbook of Research on Emerging Digital Tools for Architectural Surveying, Modeling, and Representation, pp. 239–279. IGI Global, Hershey (2015). https://doi.org/10.4018/978-1-4666-8379-2

45. Carta, M.: L'armatura culturale del territorio: il patrimonio culturale come matrice di di identità e strumento di sviluppo. FrancoAngeli, Milano (2006)

46. Colavitti, A.M. (ed.): Urban Heritage Management. Planning with History. The Urban Book Series. Springer, Cham (2018). https://doi.org/10.1007/978-3-319-72338-9_5
47. Colavitti, A.M., Floris, A., Serra, S.: Dalla conservazione alla rigenerazione dei centri storici. Alcune riflessioni sul contesto sardo. Atti della XI Giornata di Studi INU, Napoli, 14/12/2018. Urbanistica Informazioni, 278, pp. 61–66 (2018)
48. Falco, E., Klenhans, R.: Digital participatory platforms for coproduction in urban development: a systematic review. Int. J. E-Plann. Res. 7(3) (2018). https://doi.org/10.4018/ijepr.2018070105
49. Desouza, K.C., Bhagwatwar, A.: Technology-enabled participatory platforms for civic engagement: the case of U.S. Cities. J. Urban Technol. 21(4), 25–50 (2014). https://doi.org/10.1080/10630732.2014.954898
50. de Hoop, E., Smith, A., Boon, W., Macrorie, R., Marvin, S., Raven, R.: Smart urbanism in barcelona. A knowledge-politics perspective. In: Jensen, J.S., Cashmore, M., Spath, P. (eds.) The Politics of Urban Sustainability Transitions. Knowledge, Power and Governance. Routledge, New York (2019). ISBN 9781138479654
51. De Filippi, F., Coscia, C., Guido, R.: How technologies can enhance open policy making and citizen-responsive urban planning: MiraMap - a governing tool for the Mirafiori Sud District in Turin (Italy). Int. J. E-Plann. Res. (IJEPR) 6(1) (2017). https://doi.org/10.4018/ijepr.2017010102
52. De Blasio, E., Selva, D.: Le piattaforme di partecipazione tra tecnologia e governance: i modelli di sviluppo in Italia, Spagna e Regno Unito. Rivista Italiana di Politiche Pubbliche Rivista quadrimestrale 3/2019, 349–382 (2019). https://doi.org/10.1483/95209
53. Schulze-Wolf, T.: Internet based participation: emerging from a local planning tool to a federal participation-system. In: Schrank, M., Popovich, V., Benedikt, J. (eds.) "REAL CORP 007: To Plan Is Not Enough: Strategies, Plans, Concepts, Projects and their successful implementation in Urban, Regional and Real Estate Development" - Proceedings of 12th International Conference on Urban Planning and Spatial Development in the Information Society, Vienna(2007)
54. Gabrielli, B., Gastaldi, F.: Politiche "integrate" di recupero dei centri storici: riflessioni generali e considerazioni sul caso Genova. In: Deplano, G. (ed.) Politiche e strumenti per il recupero urbano. Edicom Edizioni, Udine, Monfalcone (2004)
55. Viviani, S.: Progetti integrati per le città storiche nell'era digitale. In: Urbanistica Informazioni, no. 275–276, pp. 7–8 (2017). ISSN 0932-5005
56. Piroddi, E.: Il piano regolatore: velocità e senso. Urbanistica Informazioni no 140, pp. 8–9 (1995)
57. Björn-Sören, G., Bailur, S. (eds.): Closing the Feedback Loop, Can Technology Bridge the Accountability Gap? World Bank (2014). https://doi.org/10.1596/978-1-4648-0191-4

A Literature Review on Walkability and its Theoretical Framework. Emerging Perspectives for Research Developments

Alfonso Annunziata(ID) and Chiara Garau(✉)(ID)

Department of Civil and Environmental Engineering and Architecture
(DICAAR), University of Cagliari, 09129 Cagliari, Italy
annunziata.alfonso@yahoo.it, cgarau@unica.it

Abstract. Urbanization identifies the contemporary city as the crucible of human condition. This tendency elicits the issue of the ways in which the built environment affects human behaviour. In particular, walking emerges as a central topic. Walking, in fact, is conceptualized as a vector for engaging with the world, and as a conduit to physical activity, social contact and optional practices. Consequently, a vast body of literature exists, related to the concept of walkability. The latter can be defined as the built environment potential to affect people's propensity to walk to different destinations and for different purposes. This study, through a comprehensive literature review investigates four concepts: capability; affordance; configuration and Urban ethics. These concepts embody four central dimensions of the research on walkability: arguments for investigating walkability; conceptualization of person-environment transactions; methodologies and ethical implications. The aim of this study, thus, is to individuate the theoretical framework for a precise understanding of the impact of the built environment on human behaviour and to underline perspectives for the further development of the research on walkability.

Keywords: Walkability · Capability · Affordance · Space syntax · Urban ethics

1 Introduction

Increasingly people live in an artificial environment superimposed to the natural environment. By 2050, this second nature will be constituted for almost 75% of the world population by urban areas [1]. Urbanization thus emerges as a vital force affecting human well-being in the next future and determines the primacy of the city in defining the human condition for the majority of humanity [2].

The political, social, and environmental aspects of urbanization constitute thus a central issue for research in different disciplines. The ways in which the attributes of the built environment (BE) affect human behaviour are a central issue within the disciplinary areas of urban studies and urban planning. In particular, walkability, defined as the

---

This paper is the result of the joint work of the authors. 'Abstract' 'Introduction' 'Methodology' and 'Results' were written jointly by the authors. Chiara Garau wrote the 'State of the art on walkability' and 'Conclusions'. Alfonso Annunziata wrote the 'Theoretical framework'.

© Springer Nature Switzerland AG 2020
O. Gervasi et al. (Eds.): ICCSA 2020, LNCS 12255, pp. 422–437, 2020.
https://doi.org/10.1007/978-3-030-58820-5_32

potential of the BE to afford walking, emerges as a central topic. Walking, in fact, entails an embodied basis for engaging with one's material environment [3] and a multi-dimensional category of behaviour, including an utilitarian component – e.g. walking as a form of transportation – and a recreative and social component – walking as a vector to physical activity, or as a pre-condition for social interactions [4–6]. This study aims to investigate, via a literature review, the concepts of capability, affordance, configuration and urban ethics, within the context of walkability. Capability refers to the ability of a person to achieve a state or condition deemed as valuable [7]. Affordances refer to the functional, emotional, and social opportunities and constraints incorporated into a setting in relation to a specific category of individuals [8, 9]. Configuration refers to topological relations among elements within a structure and urban ethics entail the ethical and moral implications of urbanization and of urban processes [10].

These concepts are emerging as central for framing and understanding four distinct dimensions of the discourse on walkability: i] capability refers to the conceptualization of outcomes on well-being of environmental opportunities for walking for different purposes and to different destination; ii] affordances incorporate a conceptualization of person-environment transactions; iii] the notion of configuration relates to the indi-viduation of environmental co-relates of walkability and definition of indicators and techniques for their assessment; and iv] urban ethics underlines Consequences of walkability on inter-subjective relations, identities and norms within the contemporary city. Consequently, the objective of this study is twofold: on the one hand the objective is to define a consistent theoretical framework for understanding the relations between the built environment and the outdoor practices of the urban populations. On the other hand, the focus of this paper is to underline potential perspectives for the future development of the research on walkability.

The paper is structured into six sections: after the introduction, a review of the literature on walkability is presented. The third section describes the methodological framework and the fourth section introduced the concepts of capability, affordance, configuration and urban ethics. The results obtained from the literature review are then discussed. Finally, conclusions reassume the fundamental findings of the study and outlines the objectives of its development.

2   State of the Art on Walkability

Walkability can be defined as a measure of the physical environment potential to enable walking, as a predictive indicator of active travel and physical activity [11], or as an indicator of the usability of the built environment to people [12] who walk to different destinations and for different purposes [4, 5, 13, 14].

Walking is conceptualized, in fact, as a multi-dimensional behavioural category that includes an utilitarian dimension - walking as a necessary activity - a leisure dimension - walking as an optional and recreational activity per se or as a conduit to physical activity - and a social dimension, thus related to walking as a vector to interactions among individuals [6, 15]. A vast consensus exists, about the beneficial effects of walking. In particular, walking is associated to improved physical and mental health, to better perceived well-being and to quality of life, to health-economic effects, and sociability [16]. In Ferdman's words, Walking, as an embodied mobility mode, is conducive to multiple types of objective goods, including walking as knowing, walking as creativity, walking as sociability and walking as achievement [17].

As a consequence, an association between built environment, every-day practices and health outcomes is recognized particularly with respect to the areas of obesity, cardio-vascular and chronic diseases, autonomy, local economic development, independence of the elderly and social connectedness [12, 16, 17].

The existing literature correlates walkability to attributes of both the social and physical environment. Environmental correlates include contextual factors, such as access to transit, network configuration and land-use patterns and intrinsic factors, such as width and slope of pedestrian paths, condition of surfaces, street furniture, priority of pedestrian movement.

Different approaches to the relation between built environment and outdoor practices result in different definitions and categorizations of environmental correlates of walkability [4, 18]. Web-based tools focus on quantitative macroscale indicators, such as intersection density, population density, and distance from amenities; questionnaires report pedestrians' perceptions and preferences related to significant spatial and social properties of the urban space [20]. Audit tools are based on qualitative evaluation of urban design microscale aspects of route segments. Lastly, Multi-criteria analysis model conceptualizes walkability in terms of both inherent and endowed characters of the built environment. More precisely, the 3Ds layout [19], operationalizes walkability in terms of density, diversity, and design. Ewing et al. [20] propose a 5-dimension layout, adding the categories of distance to transit and destination accessibility. Alternative layouts include attractiveness, safety, comfort and accessibility [21]; use and fruition, health and wellbeing, appearance, management, environment, and safety and security [22]. Furthermore, The 5Cs layout relates walkability to connectedness, conviviality, convenience, comfort and conspicuousness [23]. Moura et al. [24] added the further dimensions of commitment and coexistence. This 7C's layout is then adapted by Garau et al. [18, 25], to structure a methodological framework for the analysis of built-environment factors conducive to children's independent outdoor activities. Despite the relevance of walkability-related methodological frameworks for supporting decision-making processes, significant limits emerge from the existing literature. Firstly, despite the fact that arguments for improving walkability refer to human well-being, a comprehensive conceptualization of the latter is rarely considered. Furthermore, the ethical issues emerging from the discourse on walkability, and related to the category of conflict, are neither recognized or exhaustively investigated. Secondly Moura et al. [24] and Battista and Manaugh [26] Underline limits in accounting for the effects of individual characteristics, including age, gender, abilities, needs and purposes and contextual socio-economic factors, on people's perceptions of the public space. Lastly, the existing measures of walkability marginally account for the effect of the topology of spatial structures on patterns of natural movement, co-presence and co-awareness. Prospects of addressing these criticalities are embodied in the concepts of capability, affordance, urban ethics and configuration, which are comprehensively analysed in the subsequent sections.

3 Methodology

This study investigates to what extent the existing literature on walkability recognizes the research prospects embodied in the concepts of capability, affordance, configuration and urban ethics. This study is articulated in two parts. Firstly, a theoretical framework is established by discussing the concepts of capability, affordance, configuration and urban ethics. Then a review of the literature on walkability is conducted and a set of indicators is measured to determine the centrality of each concept within the existing literature.

Indicators include number of results found (Na), number of citations (Nc), average citations per item (Ac), Number of citing articles (Nca) and h-index. The latter is expressed as an integer value, h, measuring the number of articles cited at least h times. Moreover, the distribution across disciplinary areas of articles and of citing articles is assessed, by measuring the number of items per WoS category. These indicators are relevant for measuring the general impact of topics and articles.

Table 1. Queries utilized for the research of Articles on walkability included into the Web of Science Database

	Query
1	TS = ("walkab*" AND ("built environment" OR "neighborhood*" OR "street*")) AND Document type: Article; Time-span: 2011–2020
2	TS = ("walkab*" AND ("built environment" OR "neighborhood*" OR "street*")) Refined by: WoS Categories: (Transportation OR Environmental Sciences OR Engineering Multidisciplinary OR Environmental Studies OR Urban Studies OR Geography OR Regional Urban Planning OR Transportation Science Technology OR Engineering Civil OR Green Sustainable Science Technology OR Economics OR Engineering Environmental OR Architecture) AND Document type: Article; Time-span: 2011–2020
3	TS = ("walkab*" AND ("built environment" OR "neighborhood*" OR "street*")) Refined by: WoS Categories: (#2) AND Topic: ("capabilit*" OR "capacit*") AND Document type: Article; Time-span: 2011–2020
4	TS = ("walkab*" AND ("built environment" OR "neighborhood*" OR "street*")) Refined by: WoS Categories: (#2) AND Topic: ("affordanc*") AND Document type: Article; Time-span: 2011–2020
5	TS = ("walkab*" AND ("built environment" OR "neighborhood*" OR "street*")) Refined by: WoS Categories: (#2) AND Topic: ("space syntax") AND Document type: Article; Time-span: 2011–2020
6	TS = ("walkab*" AND ("built environment" OR "neighborhood*" OR "street*")) Refined by: WoS Categories: (#2) AND Topic: ("ethic*" OR "gentrif*" OR "inequalit*") AND Document type: Article; Time-span: 2011–2020

The literature review is articulated on six stage. Primarily, a set of articles on walkability is selected within the Web of Science (WoS) database, through a query containing the terms 'walkability', 'built environment', 'street' and 'neighbourhood', and considering the interval 2011–2020 as time span. Then, the indicators Na, Nc, Ac,

Nca and h-index are measured, and the distribution of items across WoS categories is determined. The set of articles is then refined by considering documents related to the disciplines of urban planning, according to WoS categories (see Table 1). The indicators Na, Nc, Ac, Nca and h-index are calculated with respect to the refined set of articles. In stage 3 the set of documents resulting from step 2 is refined through the query "topic: 'capacity' OR 'capability'" and the indicators Na, Nc, Ac, Nca and h-index are determined. The articles are then analysed to investigate two factors: definition of capability and its positioning within a theoretical model relating built environment attributes, walking behaviour and well-being.

In stage 4 the set of documents identified in stage 2 is refined through the query "topic: 'affordance'" and the indicators of impact and frequency are measured. Then, the articles are analysed to investigate conceptualizations of affordance and of its positioning within a model of interactions among individuals and the built environment.

In stage 5, the set of documents resulting from step two is refined according to the query "topic = 'space syntax'". The term space syntax refers to a complex of techniques and models for investigating the relation between topological properties of a spatial structure and patterns of human behaviours. Space-syntax is herein considered as instrumental to assess the centrality of the concept of configuration within the literature. The resulting set of articles is then analysed to measure the Na, Nc, Ac, Nca and h-index indicators. Afterwards, a thorough review of the articles is conducted according to four criteria: i) conceptualization of walking; ii) representation of the spatial structure; iii) Configurational properties considered; iv) relation of the configurational independent variable(s) with walking. Lastly the refined set from stage 2 is queried to identify a sub-set of documents containing the terms "ethics", "inequality" and "gentrification" and the Na, Nc, Ac, Nca and h-index indicators are measured. The articles are then analysed to identify ethical issues related to walkability and to identify the type and direction of the relation between walkability and the observed ethical issues. In the sub-sequent section a comprehensive definition of the concepts of capability, affordance, configuration and Urban ethics is presented.

4   Theoretical Framework: Capability, Affordance, Configuration and Urban Ethics

The relevance of walking with respect to people's well-being can be re-conceptualised through the capability approach. In Sen's words [7], capability can be defined as the ability of an individual to achieve a specific functioning, hence a state or condition, deemed as valuable. Sen intends the concept of capability also as the alternative combinations of functions, from which the person can choose one set. In this sense the concept of capability, while accounting for achievements, incorporates the intrinsic significance, in terms of an individual's well-being, of freedom and of the act of choosing per se [27].

Martha Nussbaum, [28] points to the incompleteness of Sen's framework. In particular, Nussbaum builds on the Aristotelian analysis of the human good, to underline the necessity to individuate a list of capabilities central to human good living. According to Nussbaum, the central capabilities include: life; bodily health; bodily integrity; affiliation; practical reason; play; senses, imagination, and thought; emotions; connection to nature and other species; control over one's environment [28]. Furthermore, the concept of capability implies the availability of different opportunities, as a condition that shapes the alternative combinations of functions constituting the capability set. This opportunity dimension is the focus of the research on the assessment of the walkability of public open spaces.

In this respect the concept of affordance [8, 29] emerges as a central category. Affordances are defined as the functional, emotional and social opportunities and constraints incorporated into a setting in relation to a specific individual or to a specific category of individuals. Thus, the concept of affordance is relational, situational and dynamic [30, 31]. It is relational since it refers to a set of relations among the attributes of the environment and the corporality of the individual. Hence, the concept of affordance overcomes the subject-object dichotomy. It is situational, Since the actualization of opportunities is situated in space and time. Moreover, it is dynamic, since processes of perception-action affect both the environment and individual abilities, thus determining new or reshaped patterns of affordances. Thus, affordances are instrumental to a conceptualization of opportunities for individual-environment transactions that accounts for individual characteristics and contextual factors.

Finally, the accessibility component of walkability is related to the configuration of the urban layout [12]. Configuration can be defined as the set of relationships among parts, all of which interdepend in a global structure. Distance is the fundamental relation determining the structure of a spatial layout. Within the space syntax theory, three conceptualizations of distance are utilized [32]: metric, which refers to the distance in metres between the centre of an origin segment and the centre of a destination segment; topological, which defines distance as the number of syntactic steps in a graph needed to move from a space to the other; and geometrical, which conceptualizes distance in terms of angular changes of direction along the path between an origin space and a destination space. These conceptualizations of distance are applied to two different forms of representing a spatial system: the axial map is a representation of a spatial system as the set of the fewest and longest lines that intersect all the convex spaces within the system. The segment map represents a spatial system as the set of sections of axial lines lying between two consecutive intersections. Two configurational properties capture the movement dimension of accessibility [33]. Integration is referred to as the normalised distance of an origin space to all other spaces in a system; integration hence describes the to-movement potential of a space [34]. Choice is defined as the probability that a space is comprised in the shortest routes from all spaces to all other spaces. Thus, choice measures the through movement of a space [32].

Furthermore, integration, and choice, can be measured at different radii from an origin space, to focus the analysis of configurational variables on specific forms of movement. For instance, radii ranging from 400 to 800 m are relevant for the analysis of patterns of natural pedestrian movement. Furthermore, Pedestrian movement, determines patterns of co-presence and co-awareness, which constitute an opportunity for social interaction. Co-presence, in fact, is defined as the group of people who may not know each other, that are present at the same time in a space that they share and use. Co-awareness, on the other side, identifies a group of people using a space, who are aware of each other [10]. A further relevant property is intelligibility, which refers to the co-relation between local and global properties. Intelligibility indexes the degree to which the number of connections from a line to adjacent spaces is a reliable indicator of the importance of that line in the whole system [35].

Finally, a further research direction concerns the position of walkability, particularly from the point of view of marginalized groups of users, within urban ethics [2, 36, 37]. Ethics can be mobilized through spatial design and planning for advancing social justice, diversity, sustainability via the project of the contemporary city and of its spaces [2]. In particular the discourse on the Just city [38], underlines the need to emphasise equity as a central objective of urban planning. The idea of the 'ethical city' underlines the centrality of ethics for the development of attractive, competitive, resilient and sustainable cities. Moreover, Mitchell [39] and Soja [40] claim for an urban realm more responsive to the needs of the diverse urban populations, and in particular of the most disadvantaged users. Within this perspective tendencies towards Gentrification as a "process of displacement of one group of residents with another of higher social status, entailing new patterns of social segregation" emerge as a central issue [41].

These concepts constitute the premises of a theoretical model encompassed in a methodology for the assessment of the public space with respect to walkability. Within this model walkability is determined by the environmental factors that, in relation with the characteristics of the user, produce accessibility and the functional, social, emotional affordances of a setting. Walkability in turn, affects people's well-being, by shaping their capability set. Within this perspective, walkability, as an opportunity for achieving central capabilities, acquires an ethical significance. The results from the analysis of the impact of the proposed concepts on the existing literature on walkability, and a set of hypotheses for the future development of the research on this topic are presented in the following sections.

5   Results

The analysis of the existing literature on walkability reveals that the concepts of capability, affordance, configuration and urban ethics are still largely unexplored. More precisely, the concept of affordance has the least impact and centrality within the existing literature on walkability, while urban ethics and configuration present higher centrality and represent increasingly studied aspects of the walkability issue (see Table 2). In particular, the research through the WoS database, reveal the existence of 1385 articles, published during the interval 2011–2020, referring to 'walkability', 'built environment', 'street' and 'neighbourhood'. These articles have been cited 18122 times (Nc = 18122), within 7638 articles, excluding self-citing articles. These values result in an average number of citations per item equal to 13.08, and in an h-index equal to 56. With respect to the distribution of items across WoS categories, 633 articles belong with the disciplinary field 'Public environmental occupational health'(45.7%) 186 with the research area 'transportation' (13.4%), 145 with the research area 'environmental science' (10.5%), 144 with both the categories 'environmental studies' and 'urban studies' (10.4%).

Table 2 Measures of Centrality of the concepts of capability, affordance, configuration and Urban ethics, within the literature on walkability. Indicators include Number of articles (Na), Number of citing Articles (Nca), Number of citations (Nc), Average Citations per item (Ac) h-index, most frequent category (MFC) and most frequent category for citing articles (MFCca).

	Query #1	Query #2	Query #3	Query #4	Query #5	Query #6
	Walkability (general)	Walkability (Refined)	Capability	Affordance	Configuration	Urban ethics
(Na)	1385	618	14	1	18	31
(Nca)	7638	3102	111	–	178	215
(Nc)	18122	5334	114	–	200	256
(Ac)	13,08	8,63	8,14	–	11,11	8,26
h-index	56	34	5	–	8	9
MFC	Public Occ environmental health (633)	Transportation (186)	Urban Studies (7)	Environmental studies	Urban Studies (7)	Public Occ environmental health (11)
MFCca	Public Occ envir. health (2514)	Public Occ envir. health (746)	Envir. Science (35)	–	Envir. Studies (51)	Urban Studies (71)

The refined set, determined through query #2 (see Table 1) includes 618 articles, cited 5334 times within 3102 articles, determining an average number of citations per item of 8,63 and an h-index of 34, thus inferior than the Ac and h-index measured for the set determined via the query #1.

Furthermore, 14 articles included in the sub-set including 633 results identified via the query #2, refer to capability or capacities. Items within this sub-set are cited 114 times, within 111 different articles, and are characterized by an average number of citations per item of 8.14 and an h-index equal to 5. An in-depth review of items within this sub-set reveals that only four articles refer to capacity or capability as the ability of an individual to achieve a specific state deemed as valuable (See Table 3). More precisely, capacity is conceptualized by Ferdman [17] as a potential that manifests itself in things that are intrinsically valuable and therefore objectively good, thus resembling Nussbaum's definition of fundamental capabilities [28]. On the other hand, Gadd [42] defines capacity as a quality of an actor, thus referring either to a potential of a material element or to capabilities of individuals. Lastly, capabilities, are defined by Blecic et al. [4] and Annunziata et al. [43] as valuable states of being that a person has effective access to, thus resembling Sen's original definition. Within this framework, walkability is conceptualized as a potential of the built environment, resulting from different morphological and social factors, that embodies an external opportunity for the individual to achieve capabilities.

As for the concept of affordance, only one article recognizes its relevance within the context of walkability [27]. The concept of affordance is herein utilized to conceptualize the emotional, social and functional opportunities embodied in the built environment that determine the usefulness of public open spaces. Usefulness, and walkability, are in turn conceptualized as a dimension of external opportunity that shapes the capability set of the individuals, thus affecting their well-being.

Table 3. Conceptualization of Capability in the existing literature on walkability

Title	Definition of capability	Capability-walkability relation
Blecic, Ivan, et al. [4]	Person's capabilities are valuable states of being that a person has effective access to	W. as external conditions affecting the capability set
Dovey, Kim, Pafka, Elek [14]	Capacity as a potential of the BE; Capacity as capability	W. is a set of capacities embodied in urban morphologies. W. as an external condition for achieving capabilities
Ferdman, Avigail [17]	A potential that manifests itself in things that are intrinsically valuable and objectively good	W. as an external condition for development and exercise of capabilities

Within the refined set resulting from query #2, only 18 articles refer to configurational properties measured via Space Syntax. Items within this sub-set are cited 200 times within 178 different articles, with an average number of citations per item of 11.11 and an h-index of 8. These articles, nonetheless refer to different aspects of the spatial structure of the city, and individuate different relations between configurational variables and walking. More precisely, the configurational properties analysed include Control, axial integration (within a topological radius of 3) [44], Segment integration (within a metric radius of 1000 m) [45], Intelligibility, Angular segment Integration (within a topological radius of 3) [46], Topological segment Integration (within a metric radius of 1000 m), Segment angular choice (within metric radii equal to 200 and 3000 m) [47]; The relation between configurational properties and walkability or walking behaviours is positive for measures of angular integration and angular choice, measured within radii ranging from 100 to 2000 m [48, 49], while a negative relation is observed for Control, Local axial integration (r = 3) and Segment integration (r = 1000 m), with respect to walking as optional activity [44, 45] (see Table 4).

Lastly, 31 articles contain the terms ("ethic*" or "gentrif*" or "inequalit*"). These articles are cited 256 times within 215 different documents, excluding self-citing articles. The sub-set is thus characterised by an average number of citations per item equal to 8.26 and by an h-index of 9. An in-depth analysis of the sub-set of the 12 most cited articles, underlines a relevant ethical perspective within the research on walkability, focused on the issue of social inequalities engendered by urban policies. In particular, the distributive asymmetry embodied in policies of urban renewal aimed at structuring dense, walkable, transit-accessible neighbourhoods, engenders an increase in house and land values, resulting in gentrification pressures, issues of affordability, and decrease in inclusiveness and social diversity [52–54]. Moreover, walkability is positively associated with the socio-economic status of neighbourhoods, and with health outcomes by Su et al. [55]. Their research underlines that, in the city of Shenzen, China, neighbourhoods with significant concentration of rental properties, unemployment, individuals with low level of education, and Children, are characterized by low level of walkability, resulting in a greater incidence of cardiopathy and hypertension in the population.

Table 4. Conceptualization of configuration in the existing literature on walkability

Title	Conceptualization of walking	Topological property	Relation to walking
Koohsari, M. Javad, et al. [44]	Walking as optional activity	Control; Local axial integration (r = 3)	(−) Control; Local axial integration (r = 3) to walking
Koohsari, M. Javad, et al. [45]	Walking as optional activity	Segment integration (R = 1000)	(−) Segment integration (R = 1000) to walking
Lamíquiz, Patxi J., and Jorge López-Domínguez [46]	Walking as transport	Connectivity; Axial integration (r = 3, 5, n); Intelligibility	(+) Axial Integration r = 5, 3, n to walking
Su, Shiliang, et al. [47]	Walking as transport; Walking as vector to PA	Segment integration (r = 5, n); Segment mean depth (r = n)	(+) IWI - Integrated Walkability Index, to walking
Dhanani, Ashley, Lusine Tarkhanyan, and Laura Vaughan [49]	Walking as active transport	Segment angular integration (200 < R < 3000); Segment angular choice (200 < R < 3000);	(+) Segment angular integration (400 < R < 2000) to pedestrian densities. (+) Segment angular choice (R = 2000) to ped densities; Segm. Ang. integration R = 2000 > Segm. Ang. choice (R = 2000)
Koohsari, Mohammad Javad, et al. [50]	Walking as physical activity	Topological segment Integration (R = 1000)	(+) Topological segment Integration (R = 1000) to walking
Bielik, Martin, et al. [48]	Walking as transport	Segment Angular Choice (100 < R < 2000)	(+) (R600) to Actual ped movement; (+) to AWA
Ozbil, Ayse, et al. [51]	total walking	Angular segment Integration (R = n);	(+) Directional reach to natural movement

Lastly, Zandieh et al. [56] observe heterogeneous associations of walkability factors to socio-economic factors measured at the neighbourhood scale and to levels of walking, conceptualized as a vector to physical activity and, thus, to healthy aging. In particular, residential density, land-use mix, street connectivity, and retail density are positively associated to levels of area deprivation and negatively associated to walking levels. On the contrary, land-use intensity, referred to green areas and recreation centres and measured by land area, is negatively associated to levels of area deprivation and positively related to walking levels. These studies emphasise that spatial inequalities in built environment correlates of walkability, exacerbated by policies of urban renewal, tend to manifest and reproduce inequalities in access to spatial, social and financial capital. This tendency results in increasing social injustice, particularly with respect to achievement and exercise of the foundational human capabilities related to life, bodily health, bodily integrity, affiliation and control over one's environment (see Table 5).

Table 5 Urban Ethics in the existing literature on walkability and association to walkability. (+) indexes a positive association of the independent environmental variable with ethically relevant variables. (−) indexes a negative association

Title	Ethical issue considered	Relation with walkability
Quastel, Noah, Moos, Markus, Lynch, Nicholas [52]	Gentrification	(+) Densification to gentrification and affordability issues; (+) walkability, density, proximity to transit, and increasing social status
Gose, Maria, et al. [57]	Inequality	(+) SES and BE factors to Weight status among children. (−) walkability to BMI-SDS.
Talen, Emily, Menozzi, Sunny, Schaefer, Chloe [53]	Gentrification, affordability, inclusiveness, social diversity	(+) Walkability to less affordability, less social diversity, inclusiveness and to processes of gentrification
Su, Shiliang, Pi, Jianhua, Xie, Huan, Cai, Zhongliang, Weng, Min [55]	Social inequalities	(+) Walkability to SES and health outcomes. (−) walk score to No house property, unemployment, Less educated, Blue-collars, and Children
Immergluck, Dan, Balan, Tharunya [54]	Social inequalities; gentrification	(+) walkability, and density to higher land and housing costs and gentrification pressures;
Su, Shiliang, Zhou, Hao, Xu, Mengya, Ru, Hu, Wang, Wen, Weng, Min [47]	Social Inequalities	(+) Walkability to Socio-economic conditions. (+) IWI – ind. of walkability – to proportion of uneducated, of blue collar, of people with undergraduate degree and above
Zandieh, Razieh, Flacke, Johannes, Martinez, Javier, Jones, Phil, van Maarseveen, Martin [56]	Social Inequalities	(+) residential density, land-use mix, street connectivity, and retail density to levels of area deprivation; (−) to walking levels. (−) land-use intensity (green areas and recreation centres) to levels of area deprivation; (+) to walking levels
Koschinsky, Julia, Talen, Emily, Alfonzo, Mariela, Lee, Sungduck [58]	Social Inequalities	(+) Walkability factors (safety, connectivity, signs of neglect) to income

In the sub-sequent section research perspective comprehensive related to capability, affordance, configuration and urban ethics are outlined.

6 Conclusions

The proposed research outlines a perspective for the development of the research on walkability, building on the concepts of capability, affordance, configuration and urban ethics. These concepts are marginally considered by the existing literature on walkability, within the context of transportation, urban and regional planning. The proposed literature review emphasizes that these concepts are instrumental to overcome limits of existing approaches to the operationalization of walkability. These limits relate to four dimensions: i) conceptualization of well-being; ii) consideration of the relational and situational character of the actualization of opportunities embodied in the BE; iii) Assessment of the effects of the configuration of spatial layouts on patterns of movement; iv) ethical implications of spatial inequalities in the distribution of environmental correlates of walkability.

These findings embody relevant indications for the development of the research on walkability. Future stages of this study will focus on the definition of a methodological framework for the assessment of the built environment from the point of view of walkability. According to the findings of this literature review, the framework for walkability will take into consideration three aspects: i) the operationalization of the concept of affordance via the utilization of techniques of consensus building and Public Participatory GIS tools for the selection and weighting of indicators, according to the characteristics of different stakeholders; ii) The integration of multi-criteria analysis and Space Syntax techniques for increasing the validity and relevance of the measure of walkability [59]; iii) definition of indicators for measuring aspects of social inequalities at different stages of the planning process: firstly, for assessing the correlation between levels of walkability and levels of area deprivation; secondly for monitoring policies of urban renewal with respect to the arising of social injustice and pressures for gentrification.

As a result, the objective is the construction of a framework that supports decision-making processes within urban and territorial planning practices, in two ways: first, in the identification of criticalities embodied in the spatial, material and socio-economic structures of the city; and, secondly, by monitoring variations in patterns of spatial practices and social inequalities, engendered by interventions of urban renewal and regeneration. In this respect, the framework for walkability will be able to orient the design and planning processes towards the construction of meaningful, imageable, inclusive public spaces, respondent to the needs of different stakeholders, by doing good strategies for new smart cities paradigm [60].

Acknowledgments. This study was supported by the project "Space Syntax and Multicriteria Analysis for the Measurement of Walkability in the Build Environment", founded by the programme "Bando 2019 Mobilità Giovani Ricercatori (MGR)", financed by the Autonomous Region of Sardinia (under the Regional Law of 7 August 2007, n. 7 "Promotion of Scientific Research and Technological Innovation in Sardinia"). This study was also supported by the MIUR) through the project "WEAKI TRANSIT: WEAK-demand areas Innovative TRANsport Shared services for Italian Towns (Project protocol: 20174ARRHT_004; CUP Code: F74I19001290001), financed with the PRIN 2017 (Research Projects of National Relevance) programme. We authorize the MIUR to reproduce and distribute reprints for Governmental purposes, notwithstanding any copyright notations thereon. Any opinions, findings and conclusions or recommendations expressed in this material are those of the authors, and do not necessarily reflect the views of the MIUR.

References

1. OECD: The Metropolitan Century (2015). https://www.oecd-ilibrary.org/content/publication/9789264228733-en. Accessed 12 Jan 2020
2. Chang, J.: Urban Ethics in the Anthropocene. The Moral Dimensions of Six Emerging Conditions in Contemporary Urbanism, 1st edn. Palgrave Macmillan, Singapore, Singapore; VII, 172 p. (2019)
3. Rybråten, S., Skår, M., Nordh, H.: The phenomenon of walking: diverse and dynamic. Landscape Res. **44**(1), 62–74 (2019)
4. Blečić, I., Cecchini, A., Congiu, T., Fancello, F., Fancello, G., Trunfio, G.A.: Walkability explorer: application to a case-study. In: Gervasi, O., et al. (eds.) ICCSA 2015. LNCS, vol. 9157, pp. 758–770. Springer, Cham (2015). https://doi.org/10.1007/978-3-319-21470-2_55
5. Careri, F.: Walkscapes, G. Einaudi, Torino (2006)
6. Gehl, J.: Cities for People. Island Press, New York (2013)
7. Sen, A.: Capability and well-being. In: Nussbaum, M., Sen, A. (eds.) The Quality of Life, pp. 30–53. Clarendon Press, Oxford (1993)
8. Gibson, J.J.: The Theory of Affordances. The Ecological Approach to Visual Perception. Houghton Mifflin, Boston (1979)
9. Heft, H.: Affordances of children's environments: a functional approach to environmental description. Children's Environ. Q. **5**(3), 29–37 (1988)
10. Hillier, B.: Space is the machine: a configurational theory of architecture. Space Syntax, University College of London, London (2007)
11. Frank, L.D., Sallis, J.F., Conway, T.L., Chapman, J.E., Saelens, B.E., Bachman, W.: Many pathways from land use to health: associations between neighborhood walkability and active transportation, body mass index, and air quality. J. Am. Plann. Assoc. **72**(1), 75–87 (2006)
12. Frank, L.D., Andresen, M.A., Schmid, T.L.: Obesity relationships with community design, physical activity, and time spent in cars. Am. J. Prev. Med. **27**(2), 87–96 (2004)
13. Saelens, B.E., Handy, S.L.: Built environment correlates of walking: a review. Med. Sci. Sports Exerc. **40**(7), 550–566 (2008)
14. Dovey, K., Pafka, E.: What is walkability? The urban DMA. Urban Stud. **57**(1), 93–108 (2020)
15. Giles-Corti, B., Timperio, A., Bull, F., Pikora, T.: Understanding physical activity environmental correlates: increased specificity for ecological models. Exerc. Sport Sci. Rev. **33**(4), 175–181 (2005)
16. Credit, K., Mack, E.: Place-making and performance: the impact of walkable built environments on business performance in Phoenix and Boston. Environ. Plann. B: Urban Anal. City Sci. **46**(2), 264–285 (2017)
17. Ferdman, A.: Walking and its contribution to objective well-being. J. Plann. Educ. Res. (2019). https://doi.org/10.1177/0739456X19875195
18. Garau, C., Annunziata, A., Coni, M.: A methodological framework for assessing practicability of the urban space: the survey on conditions of practicable environments (SCOPE) procedure applied in the case study of Cagliari (Italy). Sustainability **10**(11), 4189 (2019)

19. Cervero, R., Kockelman, K.: Travel demand and the 3Ds: density, diversity, and design. Transp. Res. Part D Transport Environ. **2**(3), 199–219 (1997)
20. Ewing, R., Connors, M.B., Goates, J.P., Hajrasouliha, A., Neckerman, K., Nelson, A.C.: Validating urban design measures, (13-1662) (2013) .
21. Talavera-Garcia, R., Soria-Lara, J.A.: Q-PLOS, developing an alternative walking index. A method based on urban design quality. Cities **45**, 7–17 (2015)
22. Garau, C., Pavan, V.M.: Evaluating urban quality: indicators and assessment tools for smart sustainable cities. Sustainability **10**(3), 575 (2018)
23. Gardner, K., Johnson, T., Buchan, K., Pharaoh, T.: Developing a pedestrian strategy for London. In: Transport Policy and its Implementation. Proceedings of Seminar B held at the 24th European Transport Forum, Brunel University, England (P402) (1996)
24. Moura, F., Cambra, P., Gonçalves, A.B.: Measuring walkability for distinct pedestrian groups with a participatory assessment method: a case study in Lisbon. Landscape Urban Plann. **157**, 282–296 (2017)
25. Garau, C., Annunziata, A., Vale, D.: Smart city governance and children's rights: perspectives and findings from literature on natural elements influencing children's activities within public spaces. In: Misra, S., et al. (eds.) ICCSA 2019. LNCS, vol. 11624, pp. 152–168. Springer, Cham (2019). https://doi.org/10.1007/978-3-030-24311-1_11
26. Battista, G.A., Manaugh, K.: Stores and mores: toward socializing walkability. J. Transp. Geogr. **67**, 53–60 (2018)
27. Garau, C., Annunziata, A.: Smart city governance and children's agency: an assessment of the green infrastructure impact on children's activities in Cagliari (Italy) with the tool "opportunities for children in urban spaces (OCUS)". Sustainability **11**(18), 4848 (2019)
28. Nussbaum, M.C.: Creating Capabilities. Harvard University Press, Cambridge (2011)
29. Kyttä, M.: Affordances of children's environments in the context of cities, small towns, suburbs and rural villages in Finland and Belarus. J. Environ. Psychol. **22**(1), 109–123 (2002)
30. Kyttä, M., Oliver, M., Ikeda, E., Ahmadi, E., Omiya, I., Laatikainen, T.: Children as urbanites: mapping the affordances and behavior settings of urban environments for Finnish and Japanese children. Children's Geogr. **16**(3), 319–332 (2018)
31. Raymond, C.M., Giusti, M., Barthel, S.: An embodied perspective on the co-production of cultural ecosystem services: toward embodied ecosystems. J. Environ. Plann. Manag. **61**(5–6), 778–799 (2018)
32. Hillier, B.: Spatial sustainability in cities: organic patterns and sustainable forms. Royal Institute of Technology (KTH) (2009)
33. van Nes, A., Yamu, C.: Space Syntax: a method to measure urban space related to social, economic and cognitive factors. In: Poplin, A., Devisch, O., de Roo G. (eds.) The Virtual and the Real in Planning and Urban Design, pp. 136–150. Routledge (2017)
34. Hillier, B., Iida, S.: Network effects and psychological effects: a theory of urban movement. In: Proceedings of the 5th International Symposium on Space Syntax, pp. 553–564. TU Delft, Delft (2005)
35. Hillier, B., Burdett, R., Peponis, J., Penn, A.: Creating life: or, does architecture determine anything? Architect. Comport./Architect. Behav. **3**(3), 233–250 (1986)
36. Hidayati, I., Yamu, C., Tan, W.: The emergence of mobility inequality in greater Jakarta, Indonesia: a socio-spatial analysis of path dependencies in transport-land use policies. Sustainability **11**(18), 5115 (2019)
37. Yamu, C., van Nes, A.: Fractal urban models and their potential for sustainable mobility: a spatio-syntactic analysis. In: Proceedings of the 12th International Space Syntax Symposium Beijing, pp. 415.01–415.13 (2019)

38. Fainstein, S.S.: The just city. Int. J. Urban Sci. **18**(1), 1–18 (2014)
39. Mitchell, D.: The Right to the City: Social Justice and the Fight for Public Space. Guilford Press, New York (2003)
40. Soja, E.W.: Seeking spatial justice. (16) University of Minnesota Press, Minneapolis (2013)
41. Warde, A.: Gentrification as consumption: issues of class and gender. Environ. Plan. D. 1 **9** (2), 223–232 (1991)
42. Gadd, K.J.: Street children's lives and actor-networks. Children's Geogr. **14**(3), 295–309 (2016)
43. Annunziata, A., Garau, C.: Smart city governance for child-friendly cities. Impacts of green and blue infrastructures on children's independent activities. In: Planning, Nature and Ecosystem Services. FedOAPress, pp. 524–538 (2019)
44. Koohsari, M.J., Karakiewicz, J.A., Kaczynski, A.T.: Public open space and walking: the role of proximity, perceptual qualities of the surrounding built environment, and street configuration. Environ. Behav. **45**(6), 706–736 (2012)
45. Koohsari, M.J., Kaczynski, A.T., Giles-Corti, B., Karakiewicz, J.A.: Effects of access to public open spaces on walking: is proximity enough? Landscape Urban Plann. **117**, 92–99 (2012)
46. Lamíquiz, P.J., López-Domínguez, J.: Effects of built environment on walking at the neighbourhood scale. A new role for street networks by modelling their configurational accessibility? Transp. Res. Part A: Policy Pract. **74**, 148–163 (2015)
47. Su, S., Zhou, H., Xu, M., Ru, H., Wang, W., Weng, M.: Auditing street walkability and associated social inequalities for planning implications. J. Transp. Geogr. **74**, 62–76 (2019)
48. Bielik, M., König, R., Schneider, S., Varoudis, T.: Measuring the impact of street network configuration on the accessibility to people and walking attractors. Netw. Spatial Econ. **18**, 1–20 (2018). https://doi.org/10.1007/s11067-018-9426-x
49. Dhanani, A., Tarkhanyan, L., Vaughan, L.: Estimating pedestrian demand for active transport evaluation and planning. Transp. Res. Part A: Policy Pract. **103**, 54–69 (2017)
50. Koohsari, M.J., Oka, K., Shibata, A., Liao, Y., Hanibuchi, T., Owen, N.: Associations of neighbourhood walkability indices with weight gain. Int. J. Behav. Nutr. Phys. Activity **15** (1), 33 (2018)
51. Ozbil, A., Gurleyen, T., Yesiltepe, D., Zunbuloglu, E.: Comparative associations of street network design, streetscape attributes and land-use characteristics on pedestrian flows in peripheral neighbourhoods. Int. J. Environ. Res. Public Health **16**(10), 1846 (2019)
52. Quastel, N., Moos, M., Lynch, N.: Sustainability-as-density and the return of the social: the case of vancouver, British Columbia. Urban Geogr. **33**(7), 1055–1084 (2012)
53. Talen, E., Menozzi, S., Schaefer, C.: What is a "great neighborhood"? An analysis of APA's top-rated places. J. Am. Plann. Assoc. **81**(2), 121–141 (2015)
54. Immergluck, D., Balan, T.: Sustainable for whom? Green urban development, environmental gentrification, and the Atlanta Beltline. Urban Geogr. **39**(4), 546–562 (2018)
55. Su, S., Pi, J., Xie, H., Cai, Z., Weng, M.: Community deprivation, walkability, and public health: highlighting the social inequalities in land use planning for health promotion. Land Use Policy **67**, 315–326 (2017)
56. Zandieh, R., Flacke, J., Martinez, J., Jones, P., Van Maarseveen, M.: Do inequalities in neighborhood walkability drive disparities in older adults' outdoor walking? Int. J. Environ. Res. Public Health **14**(7), 740 (2017)

57. Gose, M., Plachta-Danielzik, S., Willié, B., Johannsen, M., Landsberg, B., Müller, M.J.: Longitudinal influences of neighbourhood built and social environment on children's weight status. Int. J. Environ. Res. Public Health **10**(10), 5083–5096 (2013)
58. Koschinsky, J., Talen, E., Alfonzo, M., Lee, S.: How walkable is Walker's paradise? Environ. Plann. B: Urban Anal. City Sci. **44**(2), 343–363 (2016)
59. Garau, C., Annunziata, A., Yamu, C.: A walkability assessment tool coupling multi-criteria analysis and space syntax: the case study of Iglesias, Italy. Eur. Plann. Stud. 1–23 (2020)
60. Azzari, M., Garau, C., Nesi, P., Paolucci, M., Zamperlin, P.: Smart city governance strategies to better move towards a smart urbanism. In: Gervasi, O., et al. (eds.) ICCSA 2018. LNCS, vol. 10962, pp. 639–653. Springer, Cham (2018). https://doi.org/10.1007/978-3-319-95168-3_43

International Workshop on New Frontiers for Strategic Urban Planning (StrategicUP 2020)

Cohesion Policies in Italian Metropolitan Cities. Evaluation and Challenges

Ginevra Balletto, Luigi Mundula[✉], Alessandra Milesi,
and Mara Ladu

DICAAR - Department of Civil Environmental Engineering and Architecture,
University of Cagliari, Cagliari, Italy
{balletto,luigimundula}@unica.it,
alessandra.milesi@gmail.com, maraladu@hotmail.it

Abstract. The 2014–2020 European programming is coming to an end with numerous critical issues that will have to be resolved by 2023, both with reference to spending power and with reference to performance evaluation. The European institutions are currently in the process of drafting the new Cohesion Policy 2021–2027, which will respond to the difficulties encountered in the previous programming through three key rules: simplicity, flexibility, efficiency and transparent administrative processes. The ambition of the new programming is to make the countries of the European Union smart, sustainable and increasingly inclusive economies. Three priorities that mutually reinforce each other to help achieve high levels of employment, productivity and social cohesion in the Member States. In this context, the present study intends to evaluate the "smart specialization" (S3 strategy) deriving from the 11 thematic objectives (or sectors of intervention), in particular that of the "environment", in the 2007–2013 and 2014–2020 periods, through the Local Indicators of Spatial Association (LISA), thus identifying areas of intelligent specialization.

Keywords: Cohesion policies · Metropolitan cities · Smart specialization · Environment

1 Introduction

The profound economic and social transformations in Italy make the spatial governance increasingly complex [1, 2]. The new challenges imposed by the globalized market, new technologies, demographic flows and balances, climate change, etc. require integrated and negotiated planning strategies between public and private actors, as well as connected with ongoing technological innovation processes [3]. The future of planning, in fact, requires developing relationships between realistic and sustainable public - private

---

The paper is the result of the shared reflections, research and work of the authors involved. However, Ginevra Balletto realized paragraph 1, Mara Ladu realized paragraph 2, Ginevra Balletto and Alessandra Milesi realized paragraph 3, Ginevra Balletto and Luigi Mundula realized paragraph 4 - extrapolated from previous research with Murgante et al (2020), Luigi Mundula realized paragraph 5, LISA Maps have been drawn up by Giuseppe Borruso.

O. Gervasi et al. (Eds.): ICCSA 2020, LNCS 12255, pp. 441–455, 2020.
https://doi.org/10.1007/978-3-030-58820-5_33

actors [4]. In Italy, the multiple interpretations and articulations of its internal space have been many and have been mainly referred to the principles of economic geography [5, 6]. In fact, as early as the 1960s and 1970s, efforts were being made to find the 'optimal size of the territory', and not the 'efficient size', which is closely related to the functional urban characteristics and spatial organization [7]. The search for the urban and territorial dimension, although it is an ancient phenomenon, has been in the last 50 years in Italy that there have been the main changes to the structures, the result of demographic, economic and environmental changes. In particular, the Urban Planning and Environmental Planning Plans have always acted through the concept of "limit" beyond which, following any possible variation, the "advantage" decreases or the "risk" of the agglomeration increases. Also, to overcome this old concept of 'limit' with the reform of the Italian intermediate bodies through Law 56/2014 (Delrio law), a new intermediate level of Governance of a large area compared to the Region has been introduced [8]. The aim is to "focus on the development of the metropolitan area; promotion and integrated management of services, infrastructures and communication networks of interest to the metropolitan city: institutional relations relating to its level, including those with European cities and metropolitan areas." (L. 56/2014, art. 2). Among the functions of the metropolitan city there is the adoption and annual update of the three-year Strategic Plan of the metropolitan area, which addresses the exercise of the functions of the Municipalities (L. 56/2014, art. 44). The participation flexibility approach typical of Strategic Planning with respect to traditional urban planning (based on the limit), is in fact better able to favor the construction of a vision of development through the enhancement and systematization of the contribution of the multiple actors, both public and private individuals, thus providing effective coordination of all actions towards common and shared objectives [9].

It is no coincidence that Strategic Planning (SP) constitutes one of the most important innovations in urban and territorial governance that emerged in the last twenty years [10].

However, this importance is the result of an international evolutionary process, which we can group into three main phases (Fig. 1):

1. **First generation**. The SP were related to urban infrastructure and macro-uses. Born from the English but also French experience of the 1960s and 1970s, to identify large strategic infrastructures and relevant macro-decisions on land use. The fundamental areas of the SP referred to the identification of urbanizing territories, the areas of agricultural and landscape protection, in the context of defining the network of large transport infrastructures and the localization of metropolitan functions;

2. **Second generation**. The SP of mixed type of a corporate nature. Born in some cities of North America and later in Europe in the 1980s, they were characterized by the application to territorial planning of methods, languages and analogies drawn from the planning of large corporations. They presented a relevant context analysis and a long-term vision and the role of leadership. These SPs established themselves in a context of profound change in urban dynamics on the occasion of the information technology paradigm, the growing economic globalization and competition between cities;

3. **Third generation**. The SP as a shared vision through networks of synergies, complementarity and active citizenship. Born around the 90s with the aim of the sustainable city in relation to its physical growth, the main economic changes and its metabolism.
4. **Fourth generation.** The SP as a search for the balance of competitiveness objectives with those of environmental quality and social cohesion, in response to socioeconomic and environmental changes. Born in the 2000s, in the transition from smart city to smart region understood as a cluster of municipalities united by a long-term development and innovation perspective.

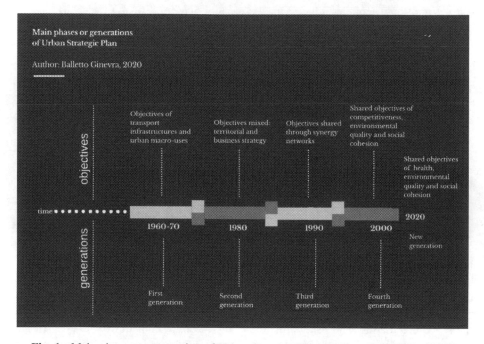

Fig. 1. Main phases or generation of Urban Strategic Plan (Author: G. Balletto, 2020)

In addition, the recent international health emergency has highlighted the need to re-evaluate and remodel the strategic objectives to guarantee primarily the health and well-being of the communities [11]. In response to these challenges, in recent years various 'recipes' have been indicated by urban development experts who have found syntheses in definitions such as: green cities, livable cities, digital cities, intelligent cities, knowledge cities. Furthermore, according to the results of the Triennale di Milano - UrbanPromo 2016 [12], it can be summarized how all these definitions are substantially attributable to three main groups: sustainable cities, resilient cities and smart cities. These three ideas of cities with three distinct conceptual approaches, which although strongly interrelated and complementary in their ability to respond to major global challenges, have only recently started to be considered jointly [33]. Furthermore, the recent health emergency has highlighted the need to approach according to an ecological paradigm referred to overlapping-integration, understood as the necessary complementarity between cities: sustainable, resilient and smart [13].

In this framework, the contribution aims to evaluate the spatial autocorrelation with the LISA method in reference to the two programming cycles of the European Structural Funds, with particular reference to the 'Environment' sector. It is in fact the 'Environment' sector with all its applications, which guarantees the pre-health conditions of its communities both in ordinary and extraordinary conditions [14]. In addition, the choice of the LISA method referring to Italian provinces and metropolitan cities allows to evaluate the autocorrelation of cohesion policies. However, it should be remembered that through an institutional act some old 'provinces' have been transformed into 'metropolitan cities'. More a semantic variation than a reorganization of the urban system through a real geographical and planning evaluation [15]. In this Italian geographical and administrative context, the article is developed in the following paragraphs.

– Paragraph 1 - Introduction is dedicated to the framing of the research topic;
– Paragraph 2 - Materials - explores the challenges of the Metropolitan Strategic Plan to govern the development of contemporary urban systems;
– Paragraph 3 - Method - describes in detail the LISA method adopted to develop this research;
– Paragraph 4 - Results - highlights the main results obtained from the study;
– Paragraph 5 - Final remarks - is dedicated to the final considerations.

2 Materials

In the face of the multitude of changes that have taken place over the past 30 years, both natural and anthropic, the strategic plan therefore seems to respond effectively to the new economic and social demand that was no longer answered in classic planning.

The Strategic Plan is in fact oriented towards integrating socio-economic actions rather than regulating land use. Furthermore, the recent administrative structure of the Italian metropolitan cities together with the idea of complementarity of the sustainable city, resilient city and Smart city [33], require a renewed systematic approach, where objectives and actions are no longer the sum of the individual components, but the deep integration of them. In this sense, strategic planning captures the speed of transformations and the complexities of urban development. The reticular strategic plan approach of sharing and co planning policies, based on relational networks, participation and negotiation, allows to interpret the contemporary complexity [16].

The SP is not prescriptive-binding but voluntary referred to smart governance. In fact, the network underlying strategic planning is something different and qualitatively superior to the individual actions of the urban plan, instead attributable to zoning with geometric forms referring to land use. In this sense, strategic planning processes have received increasing attention from Italian metropolitan cities in recent years, as a suitable method for developing new forms of urban and territorial governance [17]. The status of the strategic planning situation referred to the 14 Italian metropolitan cities is shown below. The Fig. 2 highlights how the Strategic Planning was concluded in

Northern Italy and how the Center - South is still lacking. However, all cities have initiated the Strategic Plan procedure represented in Fig. 3 where their respective missions and visions are represented.

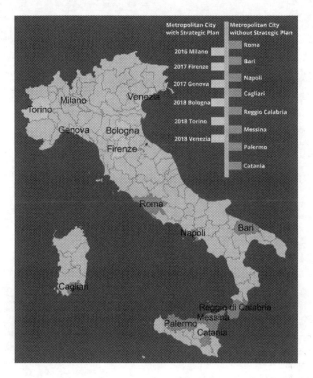

Fig. 2. Italy, metropolitan city and approved or ongoing strategic plans (2020). Author: A Milesi (2020)

Within this scenario, cohesion policies were investigated, with particular reference to those relating to the environment, which include interventions on the distribution, waste treatment and management. Risk prevention interventions, which include the construction of defense works for inhabited centers, production sites and infrastructures, as well as the prevention of coastal erosion and hydrogeological instability, interventions to combat climate change, the promotion of biodiversity and nature protection (including the European Natura 2000 network). The environment also constitutes the transversal and prevalent sector on which all the other intervention sectors are grafted. In fact, planners and geographers converge on the need for an ecological approach to ensure a more balanced urban development, in response to the right to the city within the framework of the 2030 Agenda objectives (Fig. 4).

MC	Mission	Vision
Bari	- Promoting participatory and federated development models in an innovative and "smart" way that join the different Municipalities of the metropolitan area and stimulate the energies of young people, creativity and entrepreneurship.	- "European-level "smart area" with a specialization in the ICT, energy efficiency and sustainable mobility sectors. - Pole of excellence in agro-food, mechatronics and in the chemical-pharmaceutical sector, strongly attractive for productive investments. - Tourist center of national importance, which enhances the landscape, the typical local features and the recognisability of the Puglia brand.
Bologna	- Being a logistic, productive and research hub for the Northern Italy. - Building a highly integrated network of Municipalities connected by state-of-the-art infrastructures - the "Greater Bologna" - which surpasses the traditional polycentric development model and has high homogeneous service standards for citizens, businesses and hospitality.	- Center of industrial and service excellence in the automation / machinery, health and agri-food sector. - Pole of attraction and growth of SMEs, internationalized and competitive, with a widespread entrepreneurial culture throughout the metropolitan area. - Reference fair center of Emilia Romagna.
Cagliari	- Being a cohesive metropolitan area open to the outside, strongly attractive to talents, businesses and life settlements, capable of being a driving force for growth for the entire Region, through a development model that focuses on the quality of life, widespread well-being and innovative high-level services for residents' needs.	- Center of the digital new economy (ICT, Internet Service Provision) and integrated ecosystem of start-ups, innovative companies and large players. - Research hub for: health technologies (biomedicine and neuroscience), digital and computer science. - Advanced center of the industry of the sea industry. - High level tourism destination that leverages on local products of excellence.
Catania	- Building a metropolitan area that grows through integration with the surrounding territories, with a aggregation and specialization model. - Being the relationship hub for the Mediterranean ("open" city), capable of enhancing the welcome and inclusiveness in terms of opportunities for economic development and social and institutional innovation.	- Widespread "Startup city", able to accelerate entrepreneurship and investments (especially in microelectronics, biomedical and agrifood). - Center of reference for sustainable construction. - Tourist attraction that integrates agri-food, cultural and landscape offerings and intercepts international cruise flows. - Laboratory for testing good practices for P.A. in Italy.
Firenze	- Being the "cradle" of luxury brands and the reference area where to live the humanistic dimension in a contemporary key through the enhancement of environmental sustainability and new technologies at the service of quality of life.	- high-quality manufacturing and craftsmanship center, based on the Fashion and chemical-pharmaceutical system. - reference destination for international tourism, through an integrated offer system in the metropolitan area for cultural and natural-landscape assets.
Genova	- Being the port of the Northern Mediterranean and the gateway to Northern Italy and southern Europe. - Promoting a growth model that combines economic development and sustainability with a widespread "area quality" and a strong sense of belonging to the Community.	- Port hub developed in all supply chains connected to it. - center of high-tech industries where to invent new products and services. - Pole for the accumulation of skills and solutions in the field of soil protection and hydrogeological risk mitigation. - tourist territory with a multi-product offer that leverages quality of life, climate and personal services.
Messina	- Being the Metropolitan City of the Strait - gateway to entrance to Sicily - integrated with Reggio Calabria according to a complementarity paradigm and with a diffuse and polycentric development model in the territory.	- International reference destination for sea-nature and art tourism, with supra-metropolitan offer (Strait area). - Industrial center with relaunch of the shipbuilding industry and expansion of the agri-food sector. - Laboratory for testing new energy technologies.
Milano	- Being a European reference center competitive, welcoming and attractive of investment and talent and a socio-economic laboratory of modern capitalism capable of driving the development of the country, acting according to a system logic with the rest of Italy.	- Hub of the knowledge economy and laboratory of experimentation of its organization in an industrial key (places, spaces, work models, etc.) - Center of excellence in the health supply chains, life sciences and the welfare system.
Napoli	- Being an integrated and multipolar networking urban area, with a unifying identity capable of enhancing the autonomy and specificity of its Municipalities	- Industrial hub with a "brain intensive" model, high innovation rate guide chains (aerospace, biotech and automation), and traditional excellence (textiles, goldsmiths and agrifood). - Tourist destination, among the first in the world, for tourism of "mass of excellence". - Center of the sea economy.
Palermo	- Being a metropolitan area made of interconnected places that promotes sustainability and balance in the development and processes of social innovation, lifestyles and land use patterns.	- Production area with a vocation on the advanced service sector and tourism. - Center for shipbuilding and ship repairs. - Administrative and political center.
Reggio Calabria	- Being the Metropolitan City of the Strait, integrated with Messina to promote co-development initiatives in the reference territories.	- Entrepreneurship and innovation laboratory, starting from the sustainable construction, agro-food and innovative industries sectors. - Logistics and transformation center. - City of tourism and art integrated into the main international circuits. - University training center, with strong attractiveness in the Mediterranean basin.
Roma Capitale	- Being a metropolitan area of global reach, the heart of Italy and national values. - Create an integrated system that promotes metropolitan citizenship and an urban development model according to principles of sustainability, polycentrism and quality of life.	
Torino	- Being the Metropolitan City of "being able to do", catalyst of talents, knowledge and strategic investments, able to reinvent itself thanks to the multiple vocations of the territory and capable of combining manufacturing tradition with technological innovation. - Being a metropolitan European area modern, dynamic, multicultural, inclusive with a participatory governance.	- Industrial and innovation hub, home to production centers of excellence (automotive, mechatronics, aerospace, biotech and smart solutions and ICT). - University city of international scope with strong collaboration between research and businesses. - National reference center for health services and technologies.
Venezia	- Enhance its specialty as a city of water, with the role of logistic, productive and cultural center of the North-East, crossroads of traffic to Northern Europe and the East, connecting in its development on these axes the other vast areas of its water catchment area. - Retrieving the ancient tradition of City-State, neutral, highly inclusive, respectful and a factor of development for its many communities, at the service of the economic recovery of the entire country.	

Fig. 3. Italy, strategic metropolitan plans: vision and mission (2020)

Eligibility of regions for cohesion funds, by NUTS 2 regions, for the programming period 2014-2020
(% of EU-27 average, based on GDP per inhabitant in PPS)

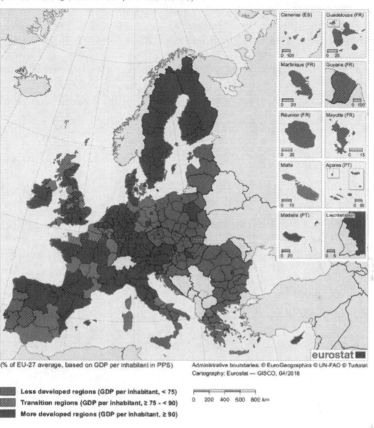

(% of EU-27 average, based on GDP per inhabitant in PPS)   Administrative boundaries: © EuroGeographics © UN-FAO © Turkstat
Cartography: Eurostat — GISCO, 04/2018

■ Less developed regions (GDP per inhabitant, < 75)
■ Transition regions (GDP per inhabitant, ≥ 75 - < 90)   0 200 400 600 800 km
■ More developed regions (GDP per inhabitant, ≥ 90)

Note: GDP per inhabitant (in PPS) over the period 2007–09 was used as the basis for the allocation of structural funds for 2014–20; as such, calculations relating to regional eligibility were based on the NUTS 2006 classification and with reference to the EU-27 average. The EU-28 regions in this publication are delineated on the basis of the NUTS 2013 classification and as a result there are regions where regional eligibility does not follow the new NUTS boundaries: Chemnitz (DED4) and Merseyside (UKD7) are partly eligible as transition regions and partly as more developed regions; Vzhodna Slovenija (SI03) is mostly eligible as a less developed region and partly as a more developed region.
Source: European Commission, Directorate-General for Regional and Urban Policy

Fig. 4. Eligibility of regions for cohesion funds, by NUTS 2 regions, for programming period 2014–2020 [18].

3   Methods

Cohesion policies, referring to spatial units that are generally contiguous in geographical terms, can benefit of a vast set of spatial analytical techniques to evaluate their local and proximity effects. In such sense, evaluating the so-called spatial autocorrelation of some kind of data or indicator to a set of contiguous geographical units, can be useful for evaluating local effects and clusters in terms of attribute and geographical data. Area units in fact can mutually influence themselves in geographical terms and in terms of the data referred to such units. In geographical analytical terms, it is the capability of analyzing locational and attribute information at the same time [19]. It is recalled by Tobler [20] as "nearby things are more related than distant things", apparently an intuitive approach [21], although only recently rediscovered [22].

In analytical terms, spatial autocorrelation can be defined as follows [23]:

$$SAC = \frac{\sum_i^N \sum_j^N c_{ij} w_{ij}}{\sum_i^N \sum_j^N w_{ij}} \tag{3}$$

Where:

1. i and j are two objects;
2. N is the number of objects;
3. c_{ij} is a degree of similarity of attributes i and j;
4. w_{ij} is a degree of similarity of location i and j;

From the general formula two indices derive as the Geary C Ratio [24] and the Moran Index I [25].

Defining x_i as the value of object i attribute; if $c_{ij} = (x_i - x_j)^2$, Geary C Ratio can be defined as follows:

$$c = \frac{(N-1)\left(\sum_i \sum_j w_{ij}(x_i - x_j)^2\right)}{2\left(\sum_i \sum_j w_{ij}\right)\sum_i(x_i - \bar{x})^2} \tag{4}$$

If $c_{ij} = (x_i - \bar{x})(x_j - \bar{x})$, Moran Index I can be defined as follows:

$$I = \frac{N \sum_i \sum_j w_{ij}(x_i - \bar{x})(x_j - \bar{x})}{\sum_i \sum_j w_{ij}) \sum_i(x_i - \bar{x})^2} \tag{5}$$

As recalled and applied recently in several Italian contexts [11, 14, 26], these indices are quite similar, differing by the cross-product term in the numerator, calculated using the deviations from the mean in Moran, while directly computed in Geary.

The main message coming from the indices is highlighting the presence - or absence - of spatial autocorrelation at a global level in the overall distribution, while the local presence of autocorrelation can be highlighted by the LISA (Local Indicators of Spatial Association), or, as after Anselin [27, 28], a local Moran index, as the sum of all local indices is proportional to the value of the Moran one:

$$\sum_i I_i = \gamma * I$$

The index is calculated as follows:

$$I_i = \frac{(X_i - \bar{X})}{S_X^2} \sum_{j=1}^N (w_{ij}(X_j - \bar{X})) \tag{6}$$

The index allows assessing for each location assess the similarity of each observation with its neighbors, and five combinations can be obtained from its application:

- Hot spots: areas with high values of the phenomenon and a high level of similarity with its surroundings (high-high H-H);
- Cold spots, as areas with low values of the phenomenon and a low level of similarity with its surroundings (low-low L-L);
- Potentially spatial outliers, with high values of the phenomenon and a low level of similarity with its surroundings (high-low H-L);
- Potentially spatial outliers, with low values of the phenomenon and a high level of similarity with its surroundings (low-high L-H);
- Lack of significant autocorrelation.

The interesting characteristic of LISA is in providing an effective measure of the degree of relative spatial association between each territorial unit and its neighboring elements, thereby highlighting the type of spatial concentration and clustering. An important element to be considered in the above-mentioned equations, related The neighborhood property is analyzed by means of the parameter weight, w_{ij}, [29] whose values indicate the presence, or absence, of neighboring spatial units to a given one. A spatial weight matrix is realized, with w_{ij} assuming values of 0 in cases in which i and j are not neighbors, or 1 when i and j are neighbors. Neighborhood is computed in terms of contiguity such as, in the case of areal units, sharing a common border of non-zero length [30].

4 Results

The evaluations of the elaborations of data collected by the present research, according to a geographic and territorial planning approach that refers to the provincial/metropolitan city scale, allows authors to obtain some important results, which will also be developed in future steps. In particular, the autocorrelation of the total public cost and of the per capita total public cost of the first programming cycle (2007–13) (Fig. 5) as well as of the second cycle (2014–20) in the 'environment' sector (Fig. 6) highlights the following spatial autocorrelation:

- In the first and second programming cycle, the total public cost is found in a portion of the South (Province of Naples and then, from 2016, metropolitan city of Naples and contiguous provinces; Province of Palermo and then metropolitan city of Palermo (2016), Province of Messina and then the metropolitan city of Messina and contiguous provinces), but in the second programming cycle there is less auto-correlation than in the first;
- The total public cost and the per capita total public cost of both the first and second programming cycle is always found in the south; a high-low autocorrelation of the metropolitan city of Florence emerges in the north.

A confirm is represented in Figs. 5 and 6.

The cost of cohesion policies is autocorrelated in Southern Italy, whether because of the lower GDP of the south compared to that of the north, in line with the assessment of Fig. 4, or because of the lack of a Cohesion Fund (CF).

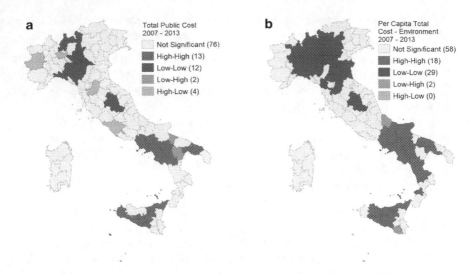

Fig. 5. Lisa Map: a) Total Public Cost 2007–2013; b) and Per capita Total Public Cost 2007–13

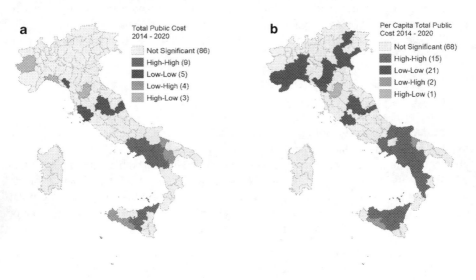

Fig. 6. Lisa Map: a) Total Public Cost 2014–2020; b) Per capita Total Public Cost 2014–20

Furthermore, the analysis of the total public cost and the per capita public cost of the 'Environment' sector related to the first programming cycle (2007–13) (Fig. 7) and to the second (2014–20) (Fig. 8), highlighted the following autocorrelations:

– In both the first and second programming cycles, the public 'environment' cost can be found in a portion of the south (metropolitan city of Naples and contiguous provinces up to the Adriatic border). However, a less autocorrelation can be observed in the second cycle than in the first, while other autocorrelations emerge. In particular, a high-low autocorrelation in the metropolitan cities of Milan, Genoa, Venice and Florence.

– The per capita 'Environment' public cost of the first and second programming
   cycles is always found in the south, including a large part of Sardinia with the
   exception of the metropolitan city of Cagliari, while high-low autocorrelations
   emerge in the metropolitan cities of Venice and Genoa in the north.

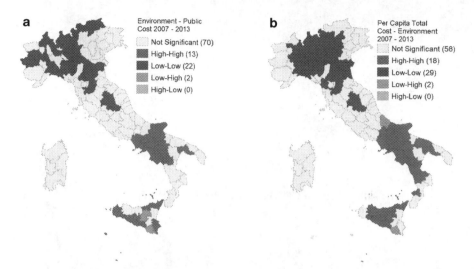

Fig. 7. Lisa Map: a) Environment – Public Cost 2007–2013; b) Public Cost Per capita 2007–
2013

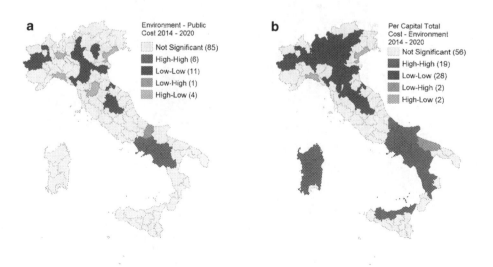

Fig. 8. Lisa Map: a) Environment – Total Public Cost 2014–2020; b) Public Cost per capita
2014–2020

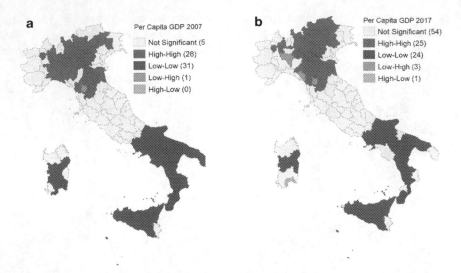

Fig. 9. LISA Map: a) GDP Per capita 2007, b) GDP Per capita 2017

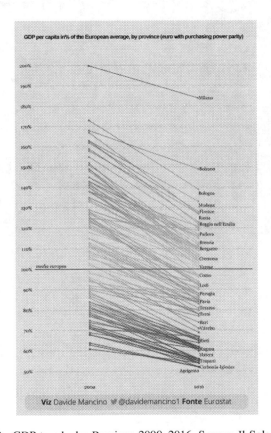

Fig. 10. GDP trend - by Province 2000–2016. Source: Il Sole 24 ore.

Authors then proceeded to evaluate the GDP indicator recognized at the basis of cohesion policies (by province/metropolitan city; 2007–17) through the autocorrelation method (Fig. 9), which led to make the following consideration:

– The GDP has positive autocorrelations in the north. However, the same decreased from 2007 to 2017 in terms of extension and moved to the east side.

This decrease is in line with the trend of the Italian average GDP which saw a significant decrease between 2000–2016, also in northern Italy (Fig. 10). Besides, it is in line with the European GDP that sees an increase in the Eastern EU countries [31, 32].

5   Final Remarks

The analysis through the spatial autocorrelation by means of LISA has highlighted how in the absence of the European Cohesion Fund for Italy, the Cohesion policies, and in particular of the - environment sector - have had a spatial autocorrelation in southern Italy and that in the last 2014–20 cycle a gradual autocorrelation occurred in northern Italy. This is partly related to progressive decrease in GDP that interested all of Italy without excluding the North. In this context, which allows the North of Italy to see an interest in the direction - Environment - of cohesion policies compared to the past, it is possible to recognize the result of the combination of multiple factors, including the increasingly urgent renewal of the ecological approach of urban and territorial planning. Furthermore, the recent health emergency from Covid-19 highlighted such need. Also following this emergency, or rather its results on the national economy, the Cohesion Fund in Italy will also be re-evaluated, which has the reduction of economic and social disparities and the promotion of sustainable development as its main purpose. In this sense, through the assessment of the sector - Environment - we have in fact investigated the Italian trend over time and some phenomena have been encountered, such as the gradual autocorrelation of total and per capita expenditure in the northern provinces. This highlights how Italy also presents a dual role towards the EU, a country divided in two areas: North and South, with relative differences in GDP which are the consequence of a generalized socio-economic crisis with consequent and its implications on the environment. The environmental emergency highlighted some aspects that require maximum attention both for economic recovery and for social cohesion.

References

1. Gaeta, L., Rivolin, U.J., Mazza, L.: Governo del territorio e pianificazione spaziale, 2nd edn. Città studi edizioni, Torino (2018)
2. Picozza, E., Police, A., Primerano, G.A., Rota, R., Spena, A.: Le politiche di programmazione per la resilienza dei sistemi infrastrutturali: economia circolare, governo del territorio e sostenibilità energetica. Giappichelli Editore, Torino (2019)
3. Testoni, C.: Towards Smart City. Amministrazione Pubblica e città di media dimensione: strategie di governance per uno sviluppo intelligente sostenibile e inclusivo del territorio. FrancoAngeli, Milano (2016)

4. Voghera, A., Regis, D.: Progetti per sistemi territoriali in trasformazione (2020)
5. Zilli, S., Dini, F.: Introduzione a Territori amministrati: regioni, città metropolitane, aree vaste e la nuova geografia politica dell'Italia. In: Fuschi, M. (a cura di), Barriere/Barriers, Società di studi geografici. Memorie geografiche NS 16, pp. 449–452 (2018)
6. Cusimano, G.: Alla ricerca di nuovi spazi e di nuovi ordini territoriali. Geotema **57**, 3–7 (2018)
7. Benassi, F., Mantuano, M., Martini, A., Pintaldi, F., et al.: Le dinamiche occupazionali in Italia alla luce di classificazioni non standard di geografie funzionali. Economia E Società Regionale **1**, 121–140 (2019)
8. Vetritto, G.: L'Italia da rammendare. Legge Delrio e ridisegno del sistema delle autonomie. Rivista giuridica del Mezzogiorno **30**(1), 153–172 (2016)
9. Corrado, F., Durbiano, E.: La Città Metropolitana in Italia: nuovi spazi di dialogo e relazione tra città e montagna. J. Alpine Research| Revue de géographie alpine 106-2 (2018)
10. Longo, A., Cicirello, L.: Città metropolitane e pianificazione di area vasta. Prospettive di governo territoriale per la gestione delle metamorfosi urbane. FrancoAngeli, Milano (2016)
11. Murgante, B., Borruso, G., Balletto, G., Castiglia, P., Dettori, M.: Why Italy first? Health, geographical and planning aspects of the Covid-19 outbreak. Sustainability **12**(12), 5064 (2020). https://www.mdpi.com/2071-1050/12/12/5064/htm
12. Talia, M. (a cura di): Un nuovo ciclo della pianificazione urbanistica tra tattica e strategia. In: International Proceedings, 11 November 2016, Urbanpromo, XIII ed. Progetto Paese, triennale di Milano, Planum Pubblisher (2016). http://media.planum.bedita.net/7a/72/Tra_Tattica_e_Strategia_Atti_Conferenza_Talia_a_cura_di_Urbanpromo_2016_Planum_Publisher.pdf
13. Bertin, M., Maragno, D., Musco, F.: Pianificare l'adattamento al cambiamento climatico come gestione di una macro-emergenza locale. Territorio **89**, 138–144 (2019)
14. Murgante, B., Balletto, G., Borruso, G., Las Casas, G., Paolo, C., Marco, D.: Geographical analyses of Covid-19's spreading contagion in the challenge of global health risks. TeMA-J. Land Use Mobility Environ. 283–304 (2020). Special Issue. Covid-19 vs City-20
15. Sbetti, F.: Le città metropolitane al lavoro, in Urbanistica Dossier, Città Metropolitane. Nuove geografie nuove istituzioni, Inu Edizioni, Roma, pp. 7–8 (2015)
16. Balletto, G., Ladu, M., Milesi, A., Mundula, L.: Riflessioni sulla pianificazione strategica della Città Metropolitana di Cagliari, tra attuazione della riforma degli enti intermedi, zone interne ed aspetti sanitari urbani. Urbanistica Informazioni, 287 e 288 s.i, sessione speciale, 102–105 (2019)
17. Vetritto, G.: La "lentissima fondazione" delle Autorità metropolitane. Argomenti **2**(1), 68–94 (2019)
18. EUROSTAT. ec.europa.eu/eurostat/statistics-explained/index.php?title=File:Eligibility_of_regions_for_cohesion_funds_based_on_gross_domestic_product_(GDP)_per_inhabitant_(in_PPS),_by_NUTS_2_regions,_for_the_programming_period_2014–2020_(%25_of_EU-27_average)_RYB17.png&direction=next&oldid=338331#filelinks. Accessed 27 June 2020
19. Goodchild, M.F.: Spatial Autocorrelation, Concepts and Techniques in Modern Geography. Geo Books, Norwich (1986)
20. Tobler, W.R.: A computer movie simulating urban growth in the detroit region. Econ. Geogr. **46**, 234 (1970)
21. Tobler, W.: On the first law of geography: a reply. Ann. Assoc. Am. Geogr. **94**, 304–310 (2004)
22. Sui, D.Z.: Tobler's first law of geography: a big idea for a small world? Ann. Assoc. Am. Geogr. **94**, 269–277 (2004)
23. Lee, J., Wong, D.W.S., David, W.-S.: GIS and Statistical Analysis with ArcView. Wiley, Hoboken (2000). ISBN 0471348740

24. Geary, R.C.: The contiguity ratio and statistical mapping. Inc. Stat. **5**, 11 (1954)
25. Moran, P.A.P.: The interpretation of statistical maps. J. R. Stat. Soc. Ser. B **10**, 243–251 (1948)
26. Murgante, B., Borruso, G.: Analyzing migration phenomena with spatial autocorrelation techniques. In: Murgante, B., et al. (eds.) ICCSA 2012. LNCS, vol. 7334, pp. 670–685. Springer, Heidelberg (2012). https://doi.org/10.1007/978-3-642-31075-1_50
27. Anselin, L.: Spatial Econometrics: Methods and Models. Springer, Dordrecht (1988). https://doi.org/10.1007/978-94-015-7799-1. ISBN 978-90-481-8311-1
28. Anselin, L.: Local indicators of spatial association—LISA. Geogr. Anal. **27**, 93–115 (1995)
29. Cliff, A.D., Ord, J.K.: The problem of spatial autocorrelation. In: Scott, A.J. (ed.) Studies in Regional Science, pp. 25–55. Pion, London (1969)
30. O'Sullivan, D., Unwin, D.J.: Geographic Information Analysis: Second Edition. Wiley, Hoboken (2010). ISBN 9780470288573
31. https://www.indexmundi.com/.   https://www.indexmundi.com/map/?v=67&r=eu&l=it. Accessed 25 June 2020
32. https://ec.europa.eu/.   https://ec.europa.eu/eurostat/statistics-explained/index.php?title=Archive:Pil_a_livello_regionale&oldid=263943. Accessed 25 June 2020
33. Mundula, L., Auci, S.: Smartness, sustainability and resilience: are they related? In: Monteiro, J., et al. (eds.) INCREaSE 2019. LNCS, pp. 568–586. Springer, Cham (2020). https://doi.org/10.1007/978-3-030-30938-1_44

Environmental Dimension into Strategic Planning. The Case of Metropolitan City of Cagliari

Maria Elena Palumbo[1], Luigi Mundula[2(✉)], Ginevra Balletto[2], Erika Bazzato[1], and Michela Marignani[1]

[1] DISVA - Department of Life Sciences and Environment, University of Cagliari, 09100 Cagliari, Italy
{mariae.palumbo,marignani}@unica.it,
erika.bazzato@hotmail.com
[2] DICAAR - Department of Civil and Environmental Engineering and Architecture, University of Cagliari, 09100 Cagliari, Italy
{luigimundula,balletto}@unica.it

Abstract. Global changes in the Anthropocene are unprecedented in history. They are closely linked to the use of the soil, the sea and the exploitation of natural resources and in turn determine important changes in the values and socio-cultural behavior of entire populations. In this context, the focus on the environmental dimension is the main way to govern the city and territory. In this sense, the environmental assets through the criterion of participation in decision-making processes, the identification and assessment of reasonable plan/program alternatives through the construction of forecast scenarios related to the evolution of the state of the environment constitutes the spatial planning paradigm, from the municipal level implementation strategy and the metropolitan level strategic one. Although in fact all Italian metropolitan cities are oriented towards adopting strategic and sustainable development models, capable of fighting the consumption of soil and natural resources in general, these have not always correspondence in an approach that specific environmental assessments part of the plan process and therefore functional for future governance choices. In this context, the objective of this work is to describe the case of the metropolitan city of Cagliari highlighting how the environmental dynamic and assets should be considered into its (actually in defining phase) strategic plan.

Keywords: Ecosystem services · Strategic planning · Metropolitan cities · Climate change

This paper is the result of the joint work of the authors. For Italian evaluation purposes Maria Elena Palumbo takes responsibility for Sect. 3.1, Luigi Mundula for Sects. 2 and 4, Ginevra Balletto for Sect. 1, Erika Bazzato for Sect. 3.2 and Michela Marignani for Sect. 3.3.

O. Gervasi et al. (Eds.): ICCSA 2020, LNCS 12255, pp. 456–471, 2020.
https://doi.org/10.1007/978-3-030-58820-5_34

1   A New Season for the Strategic Planning in Italy

The "strategic" adjective has become commonly used in the language of territorial planning, even if, as often happens, it is not always used with the appropriate level of precision and/or awareness and is now applied in a variety of experiences in an easy way [11].

The origin of the term must be sought in military science and is often linked to the term tactics; a strategy is a long-term action plan used to set up and coordinate actions aimed at achieving a predetermined goal or objective, while by tactics we mean a targeted action aimed at the short term, at a specific and specific episode, a segment of that wider goal which is the field of strategy; in short, the strategy is war, the tactic is the single battle. To win a war (strategy) you can also order a retreat or lose a battle (tactic).

Strategic planning then entered predominantly within the private sector to define the competitive strategies of companies in the markets, aimed at achieving precise business objectives through short-term measures and actions. Strategic business planning is now a consolidated practice and is a basic technique taught in business administration and business administration schools and in recent years it has gradually spread also in the non-profit sector and in the public sector [12].

In many European cities, between the 80s and 90s, strategic planning was included among the tools for territorial and urban planning to experiment with new methods and procedures that would go beyond traditional urban planning tools. A little later, with the new millennium, the territorial strategic planning tools also made their appearance in Italy.

Starting from the early 2000s, in fact, we witness the first Italian experiences of Strategic Planning, both in the urban/administrative sphere and in the disciplinary and transdisciplinary scientific sphere [13]. In those years, the Italian network of strategic cities (which included the pioneering cities of Turin, Florence, Pesaro, Trento, Piacenza and Verona, was quickly established, which was later joined by Venice, Perugia, La Spezia, Naples and the Province of Trento) with the aim of exchanging experiences and good practices, examining the main unresolved political and organizational issues and connecting with the most important experiences realized in the European panorama.

Apart from some pioneering experience, it was practice that imposed a new and relevant reflective approach on theory, especially in the urban field, which viewed the new tool with skepticism, tending to give it a minimalist, pejorative and misleading interpretation. In response to the traditional "plan crisis", strategic planning provides a rational and viable response, allowing to get out of the contrast between cognitive limits and implementation rigidities of regulatory-totalising planning and irresponsibility in terms of interest collective of purely derogatory practices.

However, if at the beginning the strategic territorial planning had a mere voluntaristic nature, it is only recently that in Italy it has become mandatory, even if only for metropolitan cities with the Law 56/2014 (Delrio Law). This Law defined also the metropolitan cities as a new governance level between regions and municipalities replacing, de facto, the Province level. By the way not all the Province has been replaced by metropolitan cities but only 14[1], and 13 of them (with the exception of Cagliari) are constituted by the same municipalities of the old Province.

2 Resilience, Sustainability and Smartness as the Fulcrum of Strategic Planning Action

In defining their strategic plans, the Italian metropolitan cities have stepped up and started setting their own agendas on the base on sustainability, resilience or smartness concepts focusing in different ways on them.

It's to note that in the last years these concepts have been coupled by researchers and institutions generating crossing paradigms, i.e. incorporating sustainability in smart city approaches for developing a more complex smart sustainable urban model.

The increasing awareness about environmental and sustainability issues related to urban growth and technological transformation is at the basis of the Smart Sustainable Cities concept [14]. The cities which has to face climate change as well as other challenges as concentration of population within an urban area, have become to use this concept widely since mid-2010s [15, 16]. With smart sustainable city, it is described a city "that is supported by a pervasive presence and massive use of advanced ICT, which, in connection with various urban domains and systems and how these intricately interrelate, enables cities to become more sustainable and to provide citizens with a better quality of life" [16]. The new technology, based on the Internet of Things (IoT) [17], allows citizens to be always connected through several devices. The real-time data may provide the opportunity of real-time feedback which may support real-time citizens' decisions in light of sustainable choices. The smart sustainable city allows decoupling high quality of life and economic growth from resource consumption and environmental impact [18].

Moreover, sustainability has been closely associated with the concept of resilience [19], since this last term "is often used to describe characteristic features of a system that are related to sustainability" [20].

Verma and Raghubanshi [21] distinguishing among three aspects, economic, social and environmental, underline how these have resulted in the development of Sustainable Development Goals [22]. These goals allow both developing and developed Nations to reach sustainable development through a holistic approach. In particular, Sustainable Development Goal 11 vows to "Make cities and human settlements inclusive, safe, resilient and sustainable".

However, there are some authors [23] which disapprove this connection considering resilience as just a label. To be sustainable, cities and urban areas must be ready to face shocks and stresses which undoubtedly sooner or later will occur and will modify the state and the operating ways. In other words, they must be resilient [24]. Coherently with this approach, Beatley and Newman [25] propose the term of Biophilic City. The idea is that to make cities greener, more natural or, in their words, more

---

[1] The Italian metropolitan cities are: Bari, Bologna, Catania, Cagliari, Firenze, Genova, Messina, Milano, Napoli, Palermo, Reggio di Calabria, Roma, Torino, Venezia.

biophilic, it is important to make them more resilient. This target can be reached in a direct way when investments in green infrastructure – i.e. a strategically planned network of natural and semi-natural areas with other environmental features designed and managed to deliver a wide range of ecosystem services' in both rural and urban settings [26] – achieve resilience outcomes; or in an indirect way when actions or projects stimulate green and healthy behaviors that in turn serves to enhance the resilience of a city and of individuals.

Over the past decade and from a political point of view, urban resilience concept has emerged as one of the core principles of sustainable urban development widely acknowledged among various agreements such as the 2030 Agenda for Sustainable Development with its dedicated goal on cities—SDG 11, the Paris Agreement on climate change and the Sendai Framework for Disaster Risk Reduction.

It is worth to note that the urban resilience issue has also been associated with the smart city concept [27]. In fact, both concepts "are operationalized on the basis of similar or even the same systems, having similar trajectories of development and similar dilemmas to be solved" [28]. Moreover, these notions aim at improving sustainability and increase the quality of life, although follow different paths. Even if some international organizations or networks as well as a wide number of cities are fostering integrated projects and strategies for building up smarter and more resilient cities, a theoretical framework is still missing.

3   The Metropolitan City of Cagliari (MCC)

In this framework the Metropolitan city of Cagliari started the definition process of its strategic plan in the 2019. The process is articulated in three main phases:

1. *Collecting*: data collection according to an objective approach (desk analysis) and a subjective one (participatory diagnosis);
2. *Frameworking*: identification of the vision, formulation of the objectives and identification of the actions necessary to achieve the objectives;
3. *Assessment and monitoring*: construction of indicators that allow to verify the implementation of the plan and the achievement of the objectives.

Actually, the first phase is concluded and the second one is ongoing. The results of the first phase highlight the central role of the environmental aspect in order to define the strategic pathway.

3.1   Environmental Factors Shaping the MCC

The areas occupied by the Metropolitan City of Cagliari is characterized by a high heterogeneity of the environmental mosaic, as a consequence of a wide variability of the physical, geomorphological, pedological-vegetational and historical-cultural elements.

Geology, Geomorphology and Hydrography
From a geological point of view, the territory of the Metropolitan City falls into three large geological areas:

- Campidano, an area whose geological structure consists of a series of geological formations from the Oligocene up to the recent Quaternary, such as terraced ancient floods, clay soils and recent soils of reclaimed marsh areas. From a geomorphological point of view, this area is characterized by landscape with "conoids", typical in the western sectors of Campidano, or "plains" modified by agricultural activities
- Linas-Sulcis, consisting of three large homogeneous units: the valley area of Cixerri and the foothills. The sedimentation phases can be distinguished in: a pre-Pliocene sedimentation related to the opening of the great tectonic structure known as "Fossa Sarda" and a Plio-Quaternary sedimentation related to the opening of the Campidano graben; the volcanic reliefs; metamorphites and Paleozoic intrusions;
- Sulcis and gulf coasts, with a geo-structural conformation derived from a series of ancient orogenesis, extensional or compressional tectonic phases, volcanic activity and erosion and sedimentation phases over time. Characterized by hills and predominantly rounded forms, this area represents a small portion of the southern sector of the large Oligo-Miocene tectonic structure known as "Fossa Sarda".

The urban area of Cagliari shows a hilly morphology connected to coastal morphological systems by a complex hydrography. The coastal system shows an articulated system of lagoons, ponds, marshes and salt marshes separated from the sea by coastal cords. Dynamics are strongly influenced by intense anthropization, which, by reducing its runoff, has strongly compromised the drainage network of the coastal areal, fundamental for the maintenance of the coastal ponds system.

From a hydrographic point of view, the Metropolitan City of Cagliari falls into the Flumendosa-Campidano-Cixerri sub-basin, which extends for almost 6000 km^2. The main rivers are "Flumini Mannu", major tributary of the pond of Santa Gilla, and "Rio Cixerri", once a tributary of the Flumini Mannu, then artificially separated near the S. Gilla lagoon. The intense urbanization has drastically reduced the recharge potential of the aquifers. The strong contamination also prevents their use for drinking purposes. Further damage derives from the excessive drainage activity near the coasts, which caused the rise of waters with a high salinity.

Climate and Natural and Semi-natural Vegetation

The territory of the metropolitan area is characterised by the Mediterranean macrobioclimate, falling within a upper or lower mesomediterranean and thermomediterranean phytoclimatic belt [1]. Potential vegetation ranges from areas of scrublands and coastal scrub to areas of thermo-xerophilous woods and thermophilic holm oaks, especially in areas belonging to the districts of "Sette Fratelli" and "Monti del Sulcis".

The vegetation is mainly composed of matorral of evergreen oaks, *Olea europaea* and *Pistacia lentiscus* formations, garrigues and silicic mesomediterranean scrub vegetation [2]. The territory has a high heterogeneity, with 40 different land use coverages [3]. More than half of the territory (52.3%) is represented by wooded areas and semi-natural environments; 31.9% of the area is occupied by agricultural areas, while 10.2% is occupied by artificial surfaces, mainly residential urban areas or industrial, commercial and infrastructural areas. The remaining territory is occupied by an important system of wetlands (3.3%) and water bodies (2.3%).

Coastal Wetland Ecosystem

Coastal wetlands are characterized by a delicate balance linked to the supply of solid materials from water courses: the deposition of sediments shapes the mouth of the rivers and constitute a determining agent in the drainage of the hydrographic-lagoon-sea basin. The functional role of hydraulic regulation of the territory depends on this dynamic equilibrium, that appears particularly relevant during the flood waves following the extreme meteoric events.

The resilience of coastal wetlands is therefore strictly connected to continental contributions which, due to morphological alterations and/or pollution of the areas further upstream of the river basin, may present poor water quality, or be unavailable during the summer period.

The consequences of these phenomena can have a negative impact on the ecology of these environments, specifically on the components of biodiversity of ecosystems (flora and fauna), but also on lagoon production, resulting in fluctuating returns, negatively influencing the ecosystem services provided by the wetlands. In particular, the wetlands of Cagliari are subject to a condition of "urban encirclement" or the tendency to weld of the urban centers of the MCC (Fig. 1), which progressively leads to reducing the residual physical and functional corridors of communication between the wetlands and their feeding basins [4]. These vulnerabilities, added to the future instability caused by climate change, represent a great challenge for the management of coastal wetlands.

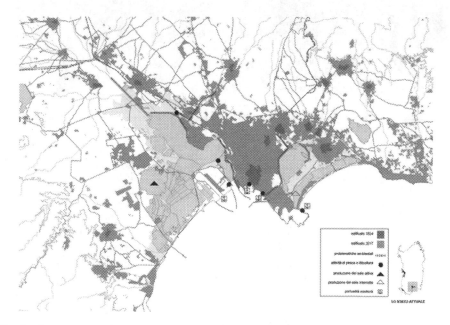

Fig. 1. Current state of the building in the wetland system of the city of Cagliari (*DICAAR-DISVA-CRENOS Interdepartmental research University of Cagliari*)

3.2   Threats and Vulnerability

Climate and Land Use Change
According to the National Climate Change Adaptation Strategy, in the coming decades the impacts resulting from climate change in the European Mediterranean region will be particularly negative and, combined with the effects of anthropogenic pressures on natural resources, it will make this area one of the most vulnerable in Europe. The future climate projections, included in the Regional Strategy of Adaptation to Climate Change of the Sardinia Region (reference period 1981–2010) and performed according to two scenarios, show for MCC an expected increase in the average temperature which varies between +1 °C and +2 °C in the period 2021–2050 (Fig. 2).

As regards rainfall, the projections show an increase in the annual values for the municipalities of the Metropolitan City in the first scenario, and a significant reduction in the second scenario, particularly marked in the municipalities of the eastern arch (Fig. 2). A general slight increase in the number of days with more intense rainfall is also expected, which suggests a future scenario in which rainfall could be concentrated in a limited number of intense events.

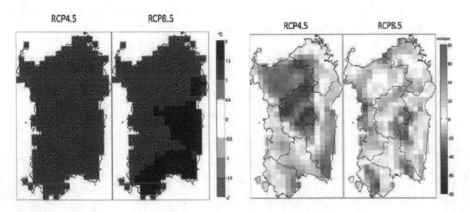

Fig. 2. Anomalies [°C] of the average temperature (left) and anomalies [mm/year] of the AP indicator for the period 2021–2050 (right). (Regional Strategy for Adaptation to Climate Change)

The main vulnerabilities related to the natural landscape are directly or indirectly related to anthropic activities, influencing hydrogeological processes and altering the ecological connections of the territory, through alterations and changes in land use which lead to habitat loss and environmental fragmentation, with a special intensification on coastal areas [5].

Fragmentation and Conservation Status of the Landscape
Landscape level metrics and specific metrics show an overall medium-low degree of environmental fragmentation in the metropolitan area [6]; only 2 municipal territories, out of a total of 17, have a high degree of fragmentation (Fig. 4). The ILC Landscape

Conservation Status Index [6, 7] calculated for the metropolitan area shows an overall conservation status with a high value (ILC = 0.63), except for only one municipality with a low conservation status (0 < ILC ≤ 0.2) [6].

The analysis of the degree of fragmentation and the state of conservation of the administrative units of the MCC [6] allows to identify the municipal territories that present the most critical conditions and, at the same time, to highlight the territories that would need the implementation of strategies aimed at the protection and/or restoration of natural and semi-natural habitats. By framing the state of conservation and fragmentation of the municipal territories belonging to the MCC within the system of protected natural areas, it is possible to highlight and locate the inconsistencies existing between ecological emergencies and current distribution of the areas subject to conservation actions (Fig. 4).

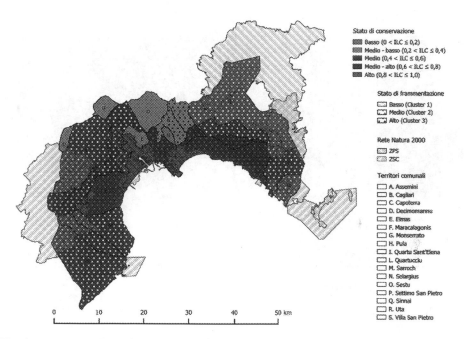

Fig. 3. Protected areas and the Natura 2000 network in relation to the state of conservation and degree of fragmentation of the Metropolitan City of Cagliari. (elaboration of Maria Elena Palumbo)

Hydrogeological Risk

The concept of flood risk pursuant to art. 6 of Legislative Decree n. 49/2010 is linked to the contextual analysis of Flood Hazard (H) and Potential Damage (D). Flood hazard is based on modeling referring to flood events, floods, linked to different return times. The potential damage is based on the analysis of the elements at risk present in the territory and their respective vulnerability.

The planning tools adopted or approved by the Sardinia Region (PAI, PSFF, studies pursuant to art. 8 paragraph 2 of the NA of the PAI) identify 3 hazard classes and increasing probability of occurrence and four classes of potential damage to people, to the socio-economic system and to non-monetizable assets. The Flood Risk map is the results of the overlaying of the Hydraulic Hazard map and the Potential Damage map. In accordance with the operational guidelines prepared by the Italian Ministry of the Environment (MATTM), the Flood Risk identifies four classes of increasing risk degree, ranging from R1 no risk (yellow) to R4 very high risk (red).

Only 4% of the entire territory is subject to very high hydrogeological risk (Fig. 3); this area is mainly concentrated in the territory of the municipalities of Elmas and Cagliari. A complete study of the network is missing: in this context, a lack of coordination between the different levels of constraint and study of the individual branches of the basin represent a major threat.

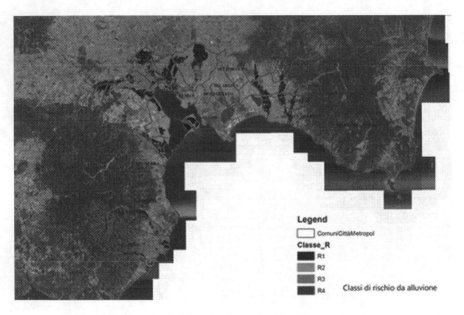

Fig. 4. Flood risk map of MCC (Color figure online)

Drought and Wild Fires

The following indicators can be used to map the vulnerability to fire and drought risk as developed in the project Life "Master Adapt" (https://masteradapt.eu/?lang=en):

- exposure indicators, used to identify the main categories of activities and services exposed to fires and droughts, including the percentage of industrial and residential areas that could be mainly affected by fires and droughts;
- sensitivity indicators, which indicate how much the potential impact of climate change will be greater for each category of environmental typology involved;

- indicators of adaptive capacity, calculated considering the level of education, the economic resources available per capita, the people employed in the agricultural and forestry sectors, the people employed to manage the risk of fires and the presence of fire risk plans, as well as projects o plans relating to adaptation to climate change for each municipality;
- global vulnerability indicators, derived from the aggregation of the normalized values of the global sensitivity index and the global adaptive capacity index.

As regards fires, there is a general low level of sensitivity in almost all the metropolitan area, because of the presence of vast irrigated lands and green urban areas. The adaptation capacity for the area is medium, therefore the global vulnerability index is classified at medium level (class 3).

As regards the drought, an average sensitivity to drought is reported for the area, apart from the municipalities of Sinnai and Villa San Pietro with a medium-high sensitivity level. The municipality of Cagliari reported a sensitivity class of 2. The global vulnerability index is therefore classified at a medium and medium-high level with classes 3 and 4 (Fig. 5).

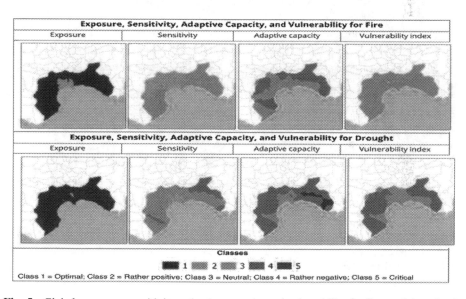

Fig. 5. Global exposure, sensitivity, adaptive capacity and vulnerability for fires and droughts in the MCC. (Life Project "Master Adapt")

Climate projections indicate a marked future heating for the MCC, with an increase in the minimum, maximum and average temperature (from +1.3 °C to −3.6 °C, depending on the CPR scenario and the future period considered). It is also expected a sharp increase in hot extremes (summer days, consecutive dry days, etc.) and a decrease in cold extremes. A slight general reduction in total rainfall is also expected, which could exacerbate fires and drought.

Heat Waves

To map the vulnerability related to heat wave risk as developed in the project Life "Master Adapt" (https://masteradapt.eu/?lang=en) the following indicators can be used:

- exposure indicators, considering the population density, which determines the "Urban Heat Island" effect;
- sensitivity indicators, considering heat related diseases and deaths, two categories in direct relation with the intensity peaks of the urban heat islands (UHI), therefore representative for studying the sensitivity of the heat waves;
- indicators of adaptive capacity to cope with heat waves, considering the level of education, the economic resources available per capita, the unemployment percentage and the number of medical points and projects related to climate change.
- global vulnerability indicators, derived from the aggregation of the normalized values of the global sensitivity index and the global adaptive capacity index.

The global heat wave vulnerability index, however, reports a higher class for the hinterland of Cagliari. Climate projections indicate an increase in extreme temperatures, especially on tropical nights (21–61 days) and on summer days (22–53 days). This could lead to a greater vulnerability for heat waves, in particular for the municipality of Cagliari (Fig. 6).

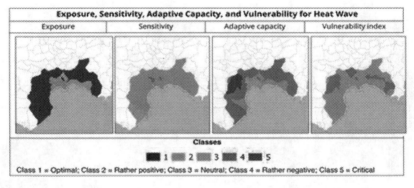

Fig. 6. Global exposure, sensitivity, adaptive capacity and vulnerability for heat waves in the MCC. (Life Project "Master Adapt")

3.3   The Main Environmental Assets to Build the Strategic Plan on

The strong characterization of the Metropolitan City of Cagliari highlights how the environment should be at the center of the targets of the strategic plan. In particular, there are some assets to be considered as main reference: coastal wetlands, protected areas and hills system.

Coastal Wetlands

The wetlands of Cagliari constitute a single environmental macrosystem consisting on the western side of the Santa Gilla lagoon, Macchiareddu salt pans and Capoterra pond, which, together with the Molentargius-Saline system, located symmetrically east of the city, complete the belt of wetlands of the city. In the overall view of the Metropolitan City, the pond of Nora or Sant'Efisio, in the municipality of Pula, is also included.

The wetland system of Cagliari is one of the most important wetlands in Italy and in the Mediterranean basin: it represents a highly complex system, affected by strong alterations and multifaceted environmental dynamics given by the overlaps between natural habitats, production systems, infrastructure and ecological systems.

The wetlands of the MCC, with the traditional fishing, salt cultivation, combined with activities for recreational, tourist and cultural purposes (visits to the park and salt marshes, birdwatching, fish tourism, sport fishing etc.), represent a social, cultural and economic wealth, closely linked to the MCC natural capital. This natural capital (e.g. the landscape and the biodiversity therein) structured in communities rich in highly specialized species, with functions related to resilience and resistance to drastic environmental variations, represent a reservoir for ecosystem goods and services [8].

The coastal wetlands system of Cagliari (Santa Gilla lagoon, Macchiareddu salt marshes and Capoterra pond) are characterized by different levels of exploitation for production, settlement and infrastructure. In addition to traditional fishing and water-culture activities, salt extraction and agricultural activities, industrial structures and plants coexist with some areas of urban functions (service areas, infrastructures, purification and green areas). public). In the same area we find concentrated the strategic large infrastructures of Porto Canale, the International Airport, railway and road network and the industrial area of Macchiareddu and Elmas, for which the lagoon represents both a point connection and separation (Fig. 1).

Terrestrial Protected Areas and Green Infrastructures

The MCC territory hosts several types of protected areas s.l., such as permanent oases of fauna protection and capture, IPA areas (Important Plant Areas), IBA areas (Important Bird Areas), Ramsar areas ("Stagno di Santa Gilla" and "Stagno di Molentargius"), Regional Natural Parks (Molentargius-Saline Regional Nature Park and Gutturu Mannu Regional Nature Park) and Natura 2000 Network sites. The latter is represented by 12 Special Conservation Zones (SACs) and 4 Special Protection Zones (SPAs), falling totally or at least in part within the MCC. The area belonging to the Natura 2000 network amounts approximately to 52,000 ha of SAC areas, of which more than 31,000 ha fall entirely within the territory of the MCC and approximately 49,000 ha of SPA areas, of which about 18,000 ha fall entirely within the MCC.

Protected areas can be considered as core areas of the green infrastructure, showing a great potential to create a network for the protection of the natural capital of MCC [9, 10].

The Calcareous Hills of Cagliari

According to some scholars, the name of Cagliari (*Krly*) derives from a "*particular geophysical condition: the imposing masses of bare and craggy limestone rocks of the current castle and of Mount S. Elia, bleached ... are the most characteristic and suggestive*, Emidio De Felice". Cagliari, therefore, is simply the place of the white hills.

These biotopes therefore represent a characterizing and identifying element of the territory, but they also have a naturalistic and environmental relevance. In fact, Capo S. Elia Promontory and the calcareous hills rise in the southern part of the Campidano plain, the only limestones emergencies of south-eastern Sardinia, places where, in some cases, high levels of biodiversity are preserved. In the last 50 years, the development of the city has profoundly changed these sites and in the near future a further alteration of the environments is expected with a strong compromise of naturalistic values.

The promontory of Capo Sant'Elia consists of reliefs aligned according to the SE-NO direction. Cala Mosca divides the promontory into two parts, one higher in the east (136 m) and one in the west, called Sant'Ignazio (94 m). The promontory of Sant'Elia to the south is joined to the other hills by flood lands of the Pleistocene. The hills of Cagliari are emergencies set on the terminal part of the Campidano plain, partly eroded by the quarries and compromised by the building development, they are distributed along two alignments with direction NNO-SSE and include the hill of S. Michele, the hill of mount Claro, the hill of Tuvixeddu - Tuvumannu, mount Is Mirrionis, the hill of Castello, the hill of Monte Urpino, the hill of Mount Mixi, the hill of Bonaria and the hill of San Bartolomeo.

Where natural vegetation is still present, the hills retain high values of naturalness in the urban area, representing unique reservoirs for biodiversity. For example, the garrigues present in these territories are recognized as of particular botanical interest: in addition to the presence of Sardinian endemics (*Genista corsica* (Loisel.) DC., *Helichrysum italicum* (Roth) G.Don subsp. *tyrrhenicum* (Bacch., Brullo & Giusso) Herrando, JMBlanco, L.Sáez & Galbany), these plant communities are characterized by having plant species that have a Mediterranean-Eastern gravitation (*Satureja thymbra* L., *Thymbra capitata* (L.) Cav., *Poterium spinosum* L.) which differentiates them from other plant communities in Sardinia that generally show a Western-Mediterranean floristic contingent. In particular, the Promontory of Sant'Elia (Cagliari) is the only place where *Poterium spinosum* is present in Sardinia and represents the western limit of distribution of the species at a global level (Natura 2000, habitat 5420: *Sarcopoterium spinosum* phryganas), while on Colle San Michele we can find a widespread population of *Satureja thymbra*.

On the other hills of Cagliari, in the remaining fragments of natural vegetation, the garrigue vegetation appears floristically depleted compared to that of Capo Sant'Elia. For these reasons, the Promontory of Capo Sant'Elia and the system of the hills of Cagliari still characterized by the presence of spontaneous vegetation are of strategic importance for the preservation of urban diversity. These elements, closely correlated with the human settlement, could identify some of the nodes of the green infrastructure of the MCC, to be developed for the conservation of biodiversity and its sustainable use in the urban area.

4   Conclusions

The Metropolitan City of Cagliari is characterized by an important amount of environmental assets but at the same time presents a high degree of vulnerability due to internal characteristics but also to external pressures, due primarily to climate change, to which it is subjected. The definition of a medium-long term development perspective must necessarily deal with this situation and must include within its development vision the integration of the principles of sustainability, resilience and smartness.

The smartness pursues sustainability through creating a digitally-enabled environment which promotes a more efficient use of energy consumptions and a more effective management of networks. The more a city is innovative, the more information and communication technologies is used improving the quality of life and the sustainable development. Uncertain events such as weather and climate negative events at urban level, together with a growing population which increases the urban sprawl phenomenon, feature the need of creating and maintaining prosperous social, economic and ecological systems through sustainable urban systems [29]. Moreover, the capability of a city planner to develop a strategic approach that adopts a wide and long-term vision may contribute to make a city more resilient and less vulnerable. Climate resilience as well as a digital environment may contribute to support strategies for reducing vulnerability and achieving sustainability. In fact, the more information and data are available from multiple sources in a smart city context the more it may facilitate the knowledge of potential climate-related risks and damages. This may increase urban resilience due to a more conscious planning and decision-making process in reducing urban vulnerability. Finally, technology may contribute to better planning and managing a resilient city through the improvement of city's adaptive capacity and the implement of city's mitigation strategies [30].

As a consequence, these three definitions provide a common paradigm of future urban development and structure. The city's evolution aims at increasing the quality of life and reducing vulnerability following a sustainable path of development in the near future as well as guaranteeing further progress in the future. This new paradigm for a sustainable, digital, and less vulnerable city may be defined as "bright city" [31], where combined actions are implemented in order to maximize city's efficiency and management efficacy and without increasing negative externalities and long-distance conflicts [32].

References

1. Canu, S., Rosati, L., Fiori, M., Motroni, A., Filigheddu, R., Farris, E.: Bioclimate map of Sardinia (Italy). J. Maps **11**(5), 711–718 (2014)
2. ISPRA, Istituto Superiore per la Protezione e la Ricerca Ambientale: Gli habitat in Carta della Natura (Schede descrittive degli habitat per la cartografia alla scala 1:50.000). Manuali e Linee Guida 49/2009, Roma (2009)
3. RAS, Carta dell'uso del suolo. Sardegna Geoportale. http://www.sardegnageoportale.it/index.php?xsl=2420&s=40&v=9&c=14480&es=6603&na=1&n=100&esp=1&tb=14401. Accessed 20 May 2017. Accessed 01 June 2020
4. De Martis, G., Mulas, B., Malavasi, V., Marignani, M.: Can artificial ecosystems enhance local biodiversity? The case of a constructed wetland in a mediterranean urban context. Environ. Manag. **57**(5), 1088–1097 (2016). https://doi.org/10.1007/s00267-016-0668-4
5. Marignani, M., et al.: Identification and prioritization of areas with high environmental risk in mediterranean coastal areas: a flexible approach. Sci. Total Environ. **590–591**, 566–578 (2017)
6. Bazzato, E., Marignani, M.: Landscape and species integration for a nature-based planning of a mediterranean functional urban area. In: Gargiulo, C., Zoppi, C. (eds.) Planning, Nature and Ecosystem Services, pp. 630–639. FedOAPress, Naples (2019)

7. Pizzolotto, R., Brandmayr, P.: An index to evaluate landscape conservation state based on land-use pattern analysis and geographic information system techniques. Coenoses **11**, 37–44 (1996)
8. Millennium Ecosystem Assessment (Program): Ecosystems and human well-being. Island Press, Washington, D.C. (2005)
9. Blasi, C., et al.: The concept of land ecological network and its design using a land unit approach. Plant Biosyst. **142**(3), 540–549 (2008)
10. Capotorti, G., et al.: Do National Parks play an active role in conserving the natural capital of Italy? Plant Biosyst. **146**(2), 258–265 (2012)
11. Martinelli, F.: La pianificazione strategica in Italia e in Europa - Metodologie ed esiti a confronto. Milano, Franco Angeli (2005)
12. Stanghellini, S., Bonifaci, P.: La pianificazione strategica. http://www.iuav.it/Ateneo1/docenti/architettu/docenti-st/Stefano-St/archivio-p/Corso-di-P/02a_Pianificazione-strategica–2014-15-.pdf
13. Camagni, R.: Cinque tesi a proposito di pianificazione strategica urbana. In: Pianificazione strategica per la governance del territorio – Modelli e soluzioni per garantire la sostenibilità e la realizzazione efficace del piano strategico del territorio. Lattanzio Group Srl, Milano (2006)
14. Höjer, M., Wangel, J.: Smart sustainable cities: definition and challenges. In: Hilty, L.M., Aebischer, B. (eds.) ICT Innovations for Sustainability. AISC, vol. 310, pp. 333–349. Springer, Cham (2015). https://doi.org/10.1007/978-3-319-09228-7_20
15. Al-Nasrawi, S., Adams, C., El-Zaart, A.: A conceptual multidimensional model for assessing smart sustainable cities. J. Inf. Syst. Technol. Manag. **12**(3), 541–558 (2015)
16. Bibri, S.E., Krogstie, J.: Smart sustainable cities of the future: an extensive interdisciplinary literature review. Sustain. Cities Soc. **31**, 183–212 (2017)
17. ITU: Shaping smarter and more sustainable cities. Striving for sustainable development goals. ITU, Geneva (2016)
18. Addanki, S.C., Venkataraman, H.: Greening the economy: a review of urban sustainability measures for developing new cities. Sustain. Cities Soc. **32**, 1–8 (2017)
19. Folke, C., Carpenter, S., Elmqvist, T., Gunderson, L., Holling, C.S., Walker, B.: Resilience and sustainable development: building adaptive capacity in a world of transformations. AMBIO: J. Hum. Environ. **31**(5), 437–441 (2002)
20. Carpenter, S., Walker, B., Anderies, J.M., Abel, N.: From metaphor to measurement: resilience of what to what? Ecosystems **4**(8), 765–781 (2001)
21. Verma, P., Raghubanshi, A.S.: Urban sustainability indicators: challenges and opportunities. Ecol. Ind. **93**, 282–291 (2018)
22. United Nations: Transforming our world: The 2030 Agenda for sustainable development. New York, (2015). https://www.un.org/pga/wp-content/uploads/sites/3/2015/08/120815_outcome-document-of-Summit-for-adoption-ofthe-post-2015-development-agenda.pdf. Accessed 12 May 2020
23. Timon, M.: The rise of resilience: linking resilience and sustainability in city planning. Urban ecology at The New School in New York City, New York (2014)
24. Pierce, J.C., Budd, W.W., Lovrich Jr., N.P.: Resilience and sustainability in US urban areas. Environ. Polit. **20**(4), 566–584 (2011)
25. Beatley, T., Newman, P.: Biophilic cities are sustainable, resilient cities. Sustainability **5**(8), 3328–3345 (2013)
26. EU EC: Infrastrutture verdi – Rafforzare il capitale naturale in EU. Comunicazione della Commissione al Parlamento europeo, al Consiglio al CESE e al Comitato delle Regioni, COM (2013) 249 final (2013)

27. Arafah, Y., Winarso, H., Suroso, D.S.A.: Towards smart and resilient city: a conceptual model. IOP Conf. Ser.: Earth Environ. Sci. **158**(1), 1–20 (2018)
28. Baron, M.: Do we need smart cities for resilience. J. Econ. Manag. **10**, 32–46 (2012)
29. Papa, R., Galderisi, A., VigoMajello, M.C., Saretta, E.: Smart and resilient cities. A systemic approach for developing cross-sectoral strategies in the face of climate change, TeMA. J. Land Use Mobility Environ. **8**(1), 19–49 (2015)
30. Buzási, A., Csete, M.S.: Adaptive planning for reducing negative impacts of climate change in case of hungarian cities. In: Stratigea, A., Kyriakides, E., Nicolaides, C. (eds.) Smart Cities in the Mediterranean. PI, pp. 205–223. Springer, Cham (2017). https://doi.org/10.1007/978-3-319-54558-5_10
31. Mundula, L., Auci, S.: Smartness, sustainability and resilience: are they related? In: Monteiro, J., et al. (eds.) INCREaSE 2019, pp. 568–586. Springer, Cham (2020). https://doi.org/10.1007/978-3-030-30938-1_44
32. Borruso, G., Balletto G.: Materiali tecnologici, risorse e conflitti. La sfida per la smart city. Conflitti, Edizioni Edicusano (2020)

Public Real Estate Assets and the Metropolitan Strategic Plan in Italy. The Two Cases of Milan and Cagliari

Mara Ladu[1], Ginevra Balletto[1], Alessandra Milesi[1],
Luigi Mundula[1(✉)], and Giuseppe Borruso[2]

[1] DICAAR - Department of Civil and Environmental Engineering
and Architecture, University of Cagliari, Cagliari, Italy
maraladu@hotmail.it, {balletto,
luigimundula}@unica.it, alessandra.milesi@gmail.com
[2] DEAMS - Department of Economics, Business, Mathematics and Statistics
Sciences "Bruno de Finetti", University of Trieste, 34127 Trieste, Italy
giuseppe.borruso@deams.units.it

Abstract. The process of economic transition from the old to the new economy produces significant effects also on cities and territories. The change in the production cycles has led to numerous and significant phenomena of delocalization and consequent abandonment of buildings and infrastructures, according to the markets. In Italy, starting from the 70 s, the divestment of industrial areas and the more recent Federalism Law have increased the interest on reuse of public properties as an act proper to municipal urban planning. However, the public real estate management (PREM) and the choice of new urban functions to be assigned represents a difficult challenge still today, at all levels of government, including that of the Metropolitan Cities (MCs), established by the Delrio Law.

MCs, which define development strategies in a medium-term period through the Metropolitan Strategic Plan (SP), represent a great opportunity to integrate PREM and public policies objectives. Within this framework, the aim of the present study is to evaluate meaning and roles recognized to the public assets in the SP drawn up by the Metropolitan City of Milan (MCM) - Lombardy Region - and in the ongoing SP of the Metropolitan City of Cagliari (MCC) - Sardinia Region. The qualitative and quantitative analysis of the two case studies allows authors to make considerations on the multiple roles that public real estate can play in the context of strategic planning to pursue sustainable development of territories.

Keywords: Public real estate management · Metropolitan strategic plan · Sustainable development

This study was supported by the research grant for the project "Investigating the relationships between knowledge-building and design and decision-making in spatial planning with geodesign" funded by Fondazione di Sardegna (2018).
This paper is the result of the joint work of the authors. In particular: paragraph 1, has been written by Ladu M.; para. 2 by Milesi A.; para. 3 by Balletto G. and Borruso G.; para. 3.1 by Ladu M.; para. 3.2 by Balletto G.; para. 4 by Ladu M.; para. 5 by Mundula L.

© Springer Nature Switzerland AG 2020
O. Gervasi et al. (Eds.): ICCSA 2020, LNCS 12255, pp. 472–486, 2020.
https://doi.org/10.1007/978-3-030-58820-5_35

1   Introduction

Public real estate management (PREM) is an important issue at the core of the political agendas of national and local governments [1, 2]. It has progressively acquired a significant role in implementing the theories of New Public Management (NPM) and Public Governance (PG), which have introduced important principles for a comprehensive restructuring of the public administration system, including those of efficiency, transparency, responsibility and decentralization [3, 4]. At the same time, a new awareness has grown about the environmental, economic and social benefits generated by an efficient management of public real estate assets (buildings and areas), capable of promoting the transition towards sustainable development models [5]. As a matter of fact, the reuse of this asset, which often represents a significant component of the existing city [6], both in quantitative and in qualitative terms, is a precondition for pursuing the ideal of "compact city" that grows mainly through the regeneration of derelict or abandoned sites [7], thus limiting soil consumption [8]. Furthermore, effective PREM allows a reduction in public expenditure, an increase in economic opportunities for the subjects directly or indirectly involved in the process (private investors or citizens) [9] and social benefits for the local community, especially in terms of public services and urban facilities [10, 11], two factors that improve the quality of life and the attractiveness of the urban context.

In Italy, the political debate on PREM has been characterized by different approaches [12]. Policies of economic-financial nature, aimed at reducing costs and consolidating the state budget, have alternated with more sustainable approaches aimed at recognizing the public asset as an extraordinary resource to support local community development. The Federalism Law (2013) which allows to transfer State-owned assets to all those Local Authorities that request them, as well as the various initiatives and projects launched by the State Property Agency to promote the knowledge, management and enhancement of the state properties are the first manifestation of this renewed approach [13].

However, several problems can be found at the local level, both in terms of knowledge and planning. Despite the Legislative Decree no. 33 of 14 March 2013, art. 30, which asks public administrations to publish information concerning the real estate owned and held and the related management policies adopted, not all the Italian municipalities have built up a comprehensive knowledge framework to support efficient long-term PREM. Significant delays are also found in the technological tools, which often does not allow to frame the real estate data within a more complex set of public policies and performance indicators of the city [14–16]. Furthermore, the specificity of the public asset has not always been recognized in the local plans for a long time and municipalities have rarely developed strategies to plan and manage the real estate assets within an urban vision for the future [17]. Only in recent decades the divestment phenomena that invest a significant number of buildings and sites in the city has required the introduction of new knowledge and planning tools also at the local level. Several municipalities have drawn up Charts, Masterplans and Strategic Projects to pursue a vision for the "city of tomorrow" based on the recognition of the values and potential of the "public city", understood as a complex system of buildings, open spaces and green areas belonging to different public bodies and institutions [18, 19].

Nowadays, PREM is an important issue at all levels of government, including that of the Metropolitan Cities (MCs), a new government body established by the Delrio Law (No. 56/2014). MCs, which define development strategies in a medium-term period through the Metropolitan Strategic Plan (SP), represent a great opportunity to integrate PREM and public policies objectives of environmental, economic and social nature [20]. Within this conceptual framework, the aim of the present research is to evaluate meaning and roles recognized to the public assets in the SP drawn up by the Metropolitan City of Milan (MCM) - Lombardy Region - and in the ongoing SP of the Metropolitan City of Cagliari (MCC) - Sardinia Region (see Fig. 1).

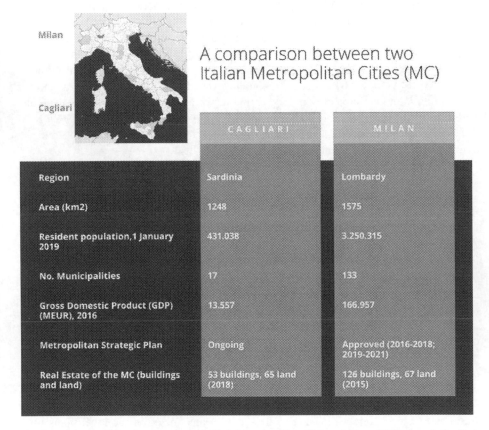

A comparison between two Italian Metropolitan Cities (MC)

	CAGLIARI	MILAN
Region	Sardinia	Lombardy
Area (km2)	1248	1575
Resident population, 1 January 2019	431.038	3.250.315
No. Municipalities	17	133
Gross Domestic Product (GDP) (MEUR), 2016	13.557	166.957
Metropolitan Strategic Plan	Ongoing	Approved (2016-2018; 2019-2021)
Real Estate of the MC (buildings and land)	53 buildings, 65 land (2018)	126 buildings, 67 land (2015)

Fig. 1. A comparison between two Italian Metropolitan Cities: Milan (MCM) and Cagliari (MCC).

As a matter of fact, the two MCs, characterized by very different geographic, social [21] and economic [22] situations, adopt specific approaches in planning their public real estate assets [23, 24]. The comparison was carried out through a qualitative-quantitative analysis to evaluate projects and actions concerning public properties introduced by the SP of the MCM and the results obtained from the participatory strategic planning promoted by the MCC to collect weakness and opportunities of the "public city" to be considered in the ongoing SP.

After illustrating the objectives that Italian legislation assigns to the SP (paragraph 2), the contribution explores the two experiences of strategic planning carried out by the MCM (paragraph 3.1) and by the MCC (paragraph 3.2). The results of the comparison between the two case studies (paragraph 4) led the authors to make considerations on the multiple roles that public real estate can play in the context of strategic planning to pursue sustainable development of territories in the new political-administrative geography of the country (paragraph 5).

2 Material: The Objectives of the Metropolitan Strategic Plan

The Metropolitan level represents the scale which we must refer from 2014 to plan a large part of Italian territory in all of its variables including the public real estate asset. The institution of the MC, defined by Law No. 56/2014, represents an intermediate level of Governance of vast area Governance compared to the region level, elected not directly by the citizens, but by the representatives of the Municipalities that com-pose it. Except for the case of Cagliari, the borders of the other 13 metropolitan cities coincide with those of the former provinces. Its aims are to take care of the devel-opement of the metropolitan area, to promote the integrated management of services, infrastructures and communication networks of interest of the metropolitan city.

In addition to the functions already attributed to the provinces, the metropolitan city is assigned new functions including that of having a three-year metropolitan strategic plan to be updated every year. It constitutes an act of direction for the Public Body and for the exercise of the functions of the municipalities and the unions of municipalities included within the aforementioned territory. (L. 56/2014, art.44). Strategic planning, born as a voluntary act, with the Law No. 54/2014 becomes a mandatory act for the Italian metropolitan cities, putting in the foreground a shared vision of the development of the territory.

The "three-years strategic plan of the metropolitan territory" represents, therefore, a programmatic document that outlines the "Metropolitan city vocation" (L. 54/2014 art. 1, c. 44, lett. e) and indicates the main lines of the development for a determinate territory, answering more effectively about an economic and social question, com-pared to the traditional territorial planning.

As established in all of the Metropolitan city Statute, the Strategic Plan "defines the programming guidelines general, sectoral and transversal objectives of development in the medium and long term for the metropolitan area, identifying the priorities of intervention, the resources needed to their pursuit, the timing and method of implementation, methods and tools for monitoring".

3 Method: A Comparison Between Experiences of Metropolitan Strategic Planning

As part of a broader research focused on new opportunities for the public real estate management and planning at the scale of the Italian metropolitan cities[1], the present paper aims to compare the two experiences of metropolitan strategic planning carried out by the metropolitan cities of Milan (MCM) and Cagliari (MCC). The MCM has been selected as a case study as one of the first in Italy to have adopted the Metropolitan Strategic Plan (SP). On the other hand, the MCC has been taken as a field of investigation as the authors of the present study, involved in the drafting of the SP, have completed important phases that allow to understand the future approach of the new public body toward the public real estate portfolio, which differs from that adopted by the MCM in some aspects.[2]

The research methodology adopted consists in a qualitative-quantitative analysis based on word cloud maps to evaluate the set of projects and actions on public properties introduced by the SP of the MCM, and the results of the participatory planning process carried out by MCC to highlight opportunities and weaknesses of the "public city" that the new government body will have to consider in the drafting of the SP. In more detail, the present study assigns a decreasing weight (W) to projects and actions adopted by the MCM and to opportunities and weaknesses emerged during the public consultation in the MCC based on their strategic value for the metropolitan territory: aspects concerning the territorial governance ($W = 1$), general public policies ($W = 0.5$) and more specific public measures ($W = 0.25$).

3.1   The Role of the Public Real Estate Assets in the SP of the MCM

The MCM, established by Law No. 54/2014, from 1 January 2015 has replaced the existing province of Milan, coinciding perfectly with its borders. It covers an area of approximately 1,575 sq km and includes 133 municipalities, with a population that exceeds 3 million inhabitants [25]. It was the first Italian Metropolitan City to draw-up a three-years strategic plan of the metropolitan area (2016–2018) [26], definitively approved with Council resolution of May 12, 2016.

The Plan is the result of an inclusive process that lasted about a year, which involved the main stakeholders of the territory with the aim of planning actions in the short term and defining long-term future scenarios for a "real metropolis, possible

---

[1] This paper is part of the research work carried out by Mara Ladu for the research scholarship entitled "The role of the public real estate for the governance of the Metropolitan City of Cagliari", under the supervision of prof. Ginevra Balletto.

[2] The Metropolitan City of Cagliari launched a call to draw up the Strategic Plan in 2018. It was won by the Temporary Business Association (ATI), constituted by Lattanzio Advisory and Lattanzio Communication in 2019. The authors of the present study are taking part in the activities of the interdisciplinary working group set up ad hoc by the aforementioned companies. Particularly, Professor Luigi Mundula as project leader, Professor Ginevra Balletto as head of the "City and territory" working group, Arch. Mara Ladu and Eng. Alessandra Milesi as collaborators of the research group.

metropolis". The Ideas Map [27] (September 2015), a document that guided the drafting of the SP, identified six development strategies for the area, which can be summarized as follows (see Fig. 2):

– Agile and high-performing (innovation and simplification of public administration);
– Creative and innovative (promotion of new economic activities and new employment);
– Attractive and open to the world (enhancement and attraction of resources and talents);
– Smart and sustainable (territorial and environmental transformations);
– Fast and integrated (integration of infrastructure and mobility services of people and data);
– Cohesive and collaborative (inter-municipal cooperation for proximity services).

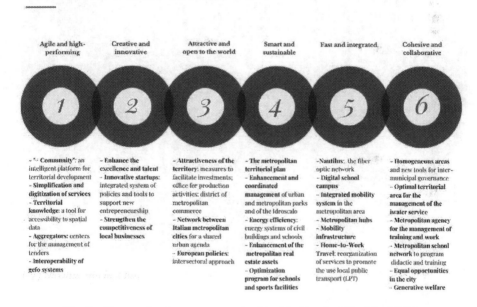

Fig. 2. The six development strategies identified by the SP of the MCM.

These strategies are configured as "design platforms" within which the Metropolitan city is called to develop policies, projects and partnerships by a dynamic and incremental process. At the same time, they are the starting point to develop territorial based projects and political agendas according to the vocations of the different contexts, involving local actors, primarily the Municipalities, in a cooperative form.

According to Law 56/2014, art. 47, the metropolitan city is responsible for the public properties, personnel and resources of the former Province. In the SP, the efficient PREM is a prerogative for a comprehensive reorganization of the public administration, which is at the core of the idea of an "agile and performing" city to be implemented by streamlining the authorization procedures, investing in the digitization processes, ensuring greater transparency. However, it is the strategy for an "intelligent and sustainable" city that introduces specific actions for the public asset (buildings and land) (see Fig. 3). The present study assigns a decreasing weight (W) to each project and action adopted by the SP according to their strategic value for the metropolitan territory.

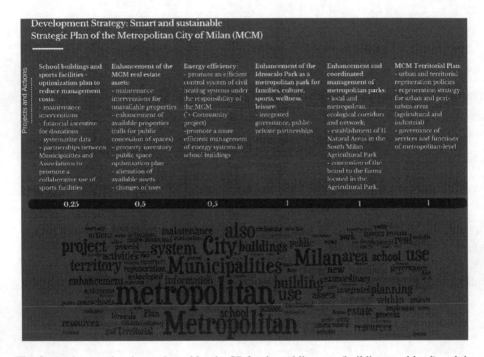

Fig. 3. Projects and actions adopted by the SP for the public asset (buildings and land) and the specific weight (W) assigned according to their strategic value for the metropolitan territory.

In this sense, urban and territorial regeneration policies and the governance of supra-local services and facilities that will be defined in the future Metropolitan Spatial Plan are considered decisive for the development of the entire metropolitan city (W = 1). The same level of importance has been recognized for actions relating to the enhancement and coordinated management of the parks in order to create a network of ecological corridors on a local and metropolitan scale, as well as to the valorization of the Idroscalo, to be understood as a new metropolitan centrality with cultural, sport, wellness and leisure activities. On the other hand, the present study attributes a minor weight (W = 0.5) to the set of measures aimed at improving the energy efficiency of public and private buildings and to the enhancement policies of the real estate assets owned by MCM (unavailable and available assets). The enhancement policies consist in the promotion of calls for the concession or the alienation of the public asset, in the definition of different uses for spaces, in the policy of maximizing economic return from property leased to ensure adequate level of maintenance, in the rationalization and efficient space utilization. Considering that in the case of the MCM the real estate assets consist of about 190 buildings, 180 of which are school buildings, the SP introduces specific actions to optimize and contain public spending through a better use of school buildings and related sports facilities. The first aim is to update existing agreements, especially as regards school gyms, in order to propose new forms of management in collaboration with municipalities and local associations. Considering that the school buildings and the related sports facilities represent only a part of the total real estate portfolio of the MCM - although very consistent -, the research assigns a minor weight to these actions (W = 0,25).

The analysis highlights that the SP mainly focuses on the public real estate assets owned by the MCM which contributes significantly to pursuing the idea of "intelligent and sustainable city". In particular, the energy efficiency of public and private buildings contributes to reducing emissions and therefore to safeguarding the territory and the environment. More generally, the reuse of the underutilized buildings and the urban regeneration process are intended as priority actions to reduce land consumption and improve the quality of the urban environment.

These principles have been confirmed in the current SP for the three-year period 2019–2021 [28]. The update of the previous SP frames the metropolitan city development strategies into six policy fields (Simplification and digitization; Intermunicipal management, support for municipalities and European policies; Economic development, training and work; Territorial planning, metropolitan welfare and urban regeneration; Environmental sustainability and parks; Infrastructure and mobility system) according to the objectives and targets of the 2030 Agenda and to the Italian National Strategy for the Sustainable Development (SNSvS) [29]. Urban regeneration strategies are implemented through the enhancement of the public asset, especially that owned by MCM, as well as through redevelopment projects of underutilized spaces capable of promoting economic, cultural and social innovation, thus better responding to the community needs.

3.2 The Role of the "Public City" in the Ongoing SP of the MCC

The drafting phase of the SP of the MCC, established in 2016, has started in September 2019. To date, the construction of the knowledge framework has been completed through a desk analysis and a participatory diagnosis which involved both the mayors and stakeholders of the interested area during dedicated meetings, and the local community through the administration of questionnaires.

The participatory process "Towards a shared future" [30] aimed at drafting the SP consisted of three days of confrontation with the main stakeholders of the territory (February 19–21, 2020), at a time when still no cases of Covid-19 had been registered in Italy. The three days were organized into 6 Thematic Tables dedicated to key issues for the development of the metropolitan area: Resilience and environmental vulnerability of the territory; Research, technology and business; Tourism, economic, productive and service activities; Transport and sustainable mobility; Health, social cohesion and quality of life; Urban fabric (see Fig. 4). Each Table included three sub-tables to which the guests took part according to their personal skills and interests.

Thematic table
Strategic Plan of Metropolitan City of Cagliari

Resilience and environmental vulnerability of the territory	Research, technology and business	Tourism, economic, productive and service activities	Transports and sustainable mobility	Health, social cohesion and quality of life	Urban fabric
1	2	3	4	5	6
-Wetlands, natural areas, urban parks - Hydrogeological risk, heat islands, sea level rise, coastal erosion, desertification risk - Ecological networks and eco-systemic services	- Technology transfer and research: role of research centers as a driving force for development - Digital transformation and 4.0 enterprise: broadband network, 5G - Circular economy: renewable sources, energy efficiency of buildings, smart grids, waste	- Agrifood: agriculture, fishing - Industry, trade, crafts - Material and immaterial cultural heritage: historical-archaeological emergencies, events and festivals, typical products	- Large hubs and logistics - Road infrastructure and public transport - Soft and innovative mobility: walkability, cycling; car sharing	- Health promotion, leisure, lifestyle, sport - Social vulnerability: Volunteering, immigration, poverty, security, work, disability - Offer of socio-sanitary and educational services	- The public city: public spaces, urban voids, spaces for sports - The private city: private, social and cooperative housing stock - Enclaves: military, ethnic, religious

Fig. 4. The 6 Thematic Tables and the related sub-tables organized as part of the participatory process aimed at drafting the SP of the MCC. Elaboration by G. Balletto 2020.

The activity of the working groups was organized in two phases: in the first, participants were asked to evaluate opportunity and weakness of the proposed topic; in the second, after a collective discussion, each working group identified general and specific objectives up to develop some project proposals.

The public real estate theme was mainly analyzed by the Thematic Table dedicated to the "Urban Fabric", which focused on the concepts of "public city", private city and military enclaves. The stakeholders understood the public city as a system of public buildings, open spaces, green areas and mobility infrastructures (Ladu, 2018) which assumes a predominant role in contemporary lifestyles (pre-Covid-19) characterized by a reduction of the private sphere and a growing propensity towards the use of collective, public or semi-public spaces.

The list of opportunity and weakness emerged during the discussion led authors to develop a mixed assessment, where the qualitative aspects were highlighted through keyword maps and the attribution of a decreasing weight (W) according to their relevance and strategic value for the metropolitan territory (see Fig. 5).

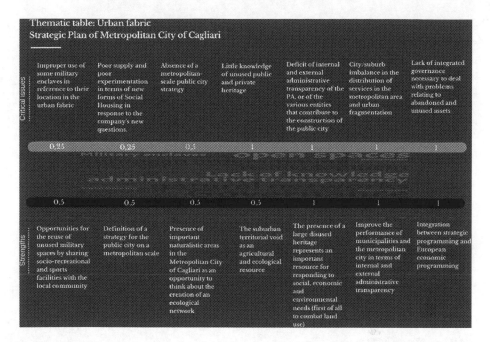

Fig. 5. The main outcomes produced by the thematic table dedicated to the urban fabric. elaborated by Balletto G., Milesi A. and Ladu M., 2020.

The main outcomes produced by the Thematic Table dedicated to the Urban Fabric show how the public assets can represent a significant resource to pursue the sustainable development objectives. The establishment of the new government body of the MCC is recognized as a great opportunity to:

– improve local and supra-local governance through an approach capable of integrating strategic planning and European economic policies;
– improve the administrative transparency on a local and supralocal scale;
– integrate the PREM issue within more general public policies objectives of social, economic and environmental nature;
– define a strategy for the public city on a metropolitan scale.

More specifically, the public asset (buildings and areas) represents an opportunity to improve the provision of socio-recreational and sports facilities, also through new forms of shared management between municipalities, institutions, private investors and citizens. At the same time, virgin land owned by public or private subjects represent an opportunity to increase the agricultural and ecological footprint, thus limiting soil consumption. This principle, recognized worldwide even before the current pandemic, nowadays assumes even greater weight because, as assessed by Murgante B. et al. (2020) [31, 32], the Covid 19 has spread mainly in urban contexts with higher land consumption.

In general, it is possible to say that in the case of the MCC, the public asset represents a cross-cutting theme. As a matter of fact, the Table dedicated to "Research,

Technology and Business", in discussing the circular economy issue, recognized specific objectives that the MCC should face to guarantee sustainable development of the territory, including: the drafting of a Metropolitan Spatial Plan to identify territories to be safeguarded, renewed, transformed; the adoption of monitoring tools to ensure constant assessment of the energy levels of existing buildings; the promotion of public policies to improve the energy efficiency of the building stock and to provide available public spaces to support start-up's activities.

Moreover, in light of the results produced by the other Thematic Tables, in the SP the public real estate assets will play an important role in pursuing the protection of the natural and built environment and its transformations, as well as in increasing efficiency and competitiveness in the sign of digital transformation.

Within this perspective, the ongoing Strategic Agenda defines the main objectives of the SP and the respective actions that the MCC should implement in the future.

These considerations are in line with the new challenges imposed by the contingent moment, which requires to adopt an interdisciplinary ecological qualitative-quantitative approach. Nowadays, even more than in the past, the strategic planning should be understood as an upgradeable and implementable process to govern effectively in ordinary and extraordinary conditions.

4   Results

The present study investigated the issue of public real estate management (PREM) in Italy, a topic that is gradually playing a central role in the civil, political and disciplinary debate. Following the establishment of the Metropolitan Cities (MCs) as a new government body, PREM need to be tackled on a metropolitan scale, going beyond municipal administrative boundaries. Indeed, the MC represents an opportunity to manage the public asset as a resource to pursue the territorial development objectives expressed by the Metropolitan Strategic Plan (SP).

Starting from these assumptions, the research set up a comparison between the two strategic planning experiences carried on by the Metropolitan cities of Milan (MCM) and Cagliari (MCC). A research methodology based on a qualitative-quantitative analysis has been developed to evaluate both the meaning attributed to the public real estate and the role assigned in pursuing the most complex government aims.

As regard the first aspect, the MCM intended the public asset mainly as the property owned by the new public body of the Metropolitan City, introducing different projects and actions depending on whether it is available or unavailable. Furthermore, considering that the majority of MCM's real estate portfolio mainly consists of school buildings, the SP introduces specific actions for this category. On the other hand, the MCC addressed the issue of public real estate assets from a broader perspective, as manifested during the participatory process for drafting the SP. Indeed, the main stakeholders called to the "Urban fabric" thematic table considered the public city as a system of built buildings and related services, open spaces, green areas and mobility infrastructures. Therefore, the working group did not focus only on the property owned by the Metropolitan City but, more generally, on the entire public asset present in the metropolitan area, owned by different public bodies and institutions. The military asset has been recognized as a specific category of the public real estate, demonstrating its significant weight in the metropolitan context and, more generally, in the regional territory, in qualitative and quantitative terms.

The results obtained from the participatory process lead to define guidelines on the entire real estate portfolio present in the metropolitan area, also in order to support and coordinate the action of individual municipalities on their assets within a shared management and enhancement strategy.

As for the second aspect considered by the present research, it's possible to assert that both the cities assign a transversal role to the public real estate assets to pursue development strategies. Particularly, the MCM's SP recognizes:

- efficient management of the public asset among the actions necessary to pursue the idea of "Agile and performing" city;
- the energy efficiency of private and public buildings (in particular school buildings) and the enhancement of the real estate assets owned by the Metropolitan City as fundamental actions to pursue the strategy for a "Smart and sustainable" city;
- the enhancement and coordinated management of metropolitan parks as an opportunity to build ecological corridors on a local and metropolitan scale, thus pursuing the strategy for a "Smart and sustainable" city.

At the same time, the stakeholders involved in the participatory planning process of the MCC have recognized that:

- effective management of the public asset (buildings and areas) allows to improve the performance levels of the PA, to answer the demand for social housing, to increase and diversify the provision of socio-recreational and sports facilities through new collaborative management forms between institutions, private investors and citizens, but also to support start-up at an early stage, providing available public spaces;
- the energy efficiency of the public real estate assets is fundamental to reduce the emissions and to promote a circular economy model;
- effective management of the extra-urban territorial void, public or private, allows to strengthen the agricultural and ecological footprint, thus limiting the further consumption of virgin soils.

5   Conclusions

The comparison carried out by the present research work allows authors to make some considerations on the approaches adopted by the two metropolitan cities of Milan (MCM) and Cagliari (MCC).

First of all, even if the Law assigns the Metropolitan City (MC) the task of managing the real estate assets owned by the entity, the choice to consider the public asset as a whole, as the MCC is doing in drafting its metropolitan strategic plan (SP), can represent a great opportunity. As a matter of fact, a comprehensive knowledge of the public asset in qualitative and quantitative terms, of its intrinsic and extrinsic characteristics, is a precondition for guaranteeing efficient management and defining future uses for spaces. In particular, the knowledge framework supports the MC not only in implementing rationalization, enhancement or alienation policies, but also in planning a balanced provision of public services and urban facilities throughout the metropolitan territory, especially as regards those of supra-local rank. Furthermore, a strategy for the entire real estate portfolio on a metropolitan scale stimulates and guides the process of knowledge and management of public properties also at the local level. For this reason, the MCC understand the entire "public city" as a set of buildings, open spaces, green areas and infrastructures for mobility.

The analyzes conducted also show that the SP can constitute a great opportunity to integrate the objectives of public real estate asset management and those of the more complex set of public policies. The two MCs examined have attributed to the public asset a strategic role in pursuing future development objectives, in line with the principles of the Urban Agenda for the EU (Pact of Amsterdam) [33] which recognize urban regeneration as a transversal action in guiding the transition towards sustainable development models. It is within this renewed cultural perspective that strategic planning in Italy should consider the public real estate assets, thus maximizing its potential to support the development of the territories.

References

1. Kaganova, O., Telgarsky, J.: Management of capital assets by local governments: an assessment and benchmarking survey. Int. J. Strateg. Property Manage. 22(2), 143–156 (2018)
2. Migliore, A.: Valorisation of public real estate from strategies selection to the proposal of a procedural model for enhancement (2019)
3. Kaganova, O.: Managing Government Property Assets: International Experiences. The Urban Institute, Washington, D.C. (2006)
4. Marona, B., van den Beemt, A.: Impact of public management theory on municipal real estate management in Netherlands and Poland. European Real Estate Society (ERES), 317 (2018)
5. UNGA (United Nations General Assembly): Transforming our world: the 2030 Agenda for Sustainable Development. Resolution adopted by the General Assembly on 25 September 2015. A/RES/70/1 (2015)
6. Kaw, J.K., Lee, H., Wahba, S.: The Hidden Wealth Of Cities Creating, Financing, and Managing Public Spaces. International bank for Reconstruction and Development. The World Bank, Washington (2020)
7. Lehmann, S.: Understanding and quantifying urban density toward more sustainable city form. In: D'Acci, L. (ed.) The Mathematics of Urban Morphology. MSSET, pp. 547–556. Springer, Cham (2019). https://doi.org/10.1007/978-3-030-12381-9_30
8. Loures, L.C.: Introductory chapter: land-use planning and land-use change as catalysts of sustainable development. In: Loures, L.C. (ed.) Land Use-Assessing the Past Envisioning the Future. IntechOpen, London (2019)
9. Ladu, M.: Pratiche innovative di riuso del patrimonio immobiliare pubblico per una città inclusiva. In: AA. VV. Atti della XXII Conferenza Nazionale SIU. L'Urbanistica italiana di fronte all'Agenda 2030. Portare territori e comunità sulla strada della sostenibilità e della resilienza, Matera-Bari 6–7–8 giugno 2019, pp. 512–516. Planum Publisher, Roma Milano (2020)

10. Ladu, M., Bernardini, S.: Opportunities and challenges of social innovation practices in Urban development and public real estate management. Italy as a case study. In: Bevilacqua, C., Calabrò, F., Della Spina, L. (eds.) NMP 2020. SIST, vol. 178, pp. 1012–1022. Springer, Cham (2021). https://doi.org/10.1007/978-3-030-48279-4_95

11. Balletto, G., Milesi, A., Fenu, N., Borruso, G., Mundula, L.: Military training areas as semicommons: the territorial valorization of Quirra (Sardinia) from easements to ecosystem services. Sustainability **12**(2), 622 (2020)

12. Falanga, C., Cuzzola, E., Nasso, I.: La dismissione del patrimonio immobiliare pubblico. Guida pratica per gli enti locali. Maggioli Editore, Rimini (2013)

13. Agenzia del Demanio Homepage. https://www.agenziademanio.it/opencms/it/

14. Ladu, M.: Forthcoming: the role of city dashboards in managing public real estate in Italy. Proposals for a conceptual framework. J. Urban Planning Dev. https://doi.org/10.1061/(ASCE)UP.1943-5444.0000622

15. Ladu, M., Borruso, G., Balletto, G.: Il ruolo delle piattaforme digitali nei processi di valorizzazione del patrimonio immobiliare pubblico. In Atti della XXIII Conferenza Nazionale ASITA, Trieste, 12–14 November 2019, pp. 587–594. ASITA (2019)

16. Balletto, G., Milesi, A., Ladu, M., Borruso, G.: A dashboard for supporting slow tourism in green infrastructures. a methodological proposal in Sardinia (Italy). Sustainability **12**(9), 3579 (2020)

17. Manzo, R.: Immobili pubblici e rigenerazione della città. In: Tronconi, O. (ed.) La valorizzazione del patrimonio immobiliare pubblico, pp. 71–78. Franco Angeli, Milano (2015)

18. Abis, E., Ladu, M.: Il paesaggio della città pubblica. Il patrimonio immobiliare e il sistema del verde nella città storica. In: Abis, E. (eds.) Paesaggio storico urbano. Progetto e qualità per il castello di Cagliari, pp. 266–299. Gangemi, Roma (2015)

19. Ladu, M.: La "città pubblica" nel nuovo piano. Strumenti strategici per rigenerare la componente pubblica del paesaggio urbano. Urbanistica Informazioni 278, s.i, sessione speciale 05, 65–69 (2018b)

20. Balletto, G., Ladu, M., Milesi, A., Mundula, L.: Riflessioni sulla pianificazione strategica della Città Metropolitana di Cagliari, tra attuazione della riforma degli enti intermedi, zone interne ed aspetti sanitari urbani. Urbanistica Informazioni 287 and 288, s.i, sessione speciale (2020). In corso di pubblicazione

21. ISTAT Demo-Geodemo. http://demo.istat.it/pop2019/index.html

22. Il Sole 24 ore. https://www.infodata.ilsole24ore.com/2019/11/16/scopri-pil-pro-capite-delle-tua-provincia-misura-la-tua

23. Metropolitan City of Cagliari (MCC). https://www.cittametropolitanacagliari.it/web/cmdca/patrimonio-immobiliare

24. Metropolitan City of Milan (MCM). http://www.cittametropolitana.mi.it/portale/amministrazione-trasparente/beni_immobili_gestione_patrimonio/

25. Metropolitan City of Milan. http://www.cittametropolitana.milano.it/portale/

26. Metropolitan City of Milan (MCM): Milano metropoli reale, metropoli possibile. Piano strategico triennale del territorio metropolitano (2016–2018). Atti n. 94317/1.19/2016/7, Allegato 1 (2016). http://www.cittametropolitana.mi.it/export/sites/default/PSM_2016_2018/doc/Piano-strategico-della-Citta-metropolitana-di-Milano.pdf

27. Metropolitan City of Milan (MCM): Milano metropoli reale, metropoli possibile. Mappa delle idee/Settembre 2015 (2015). http://www.cittametropolitana.mi.it/export/sites/default/PSM_2016_2018/doc/Piano_strategico_metropolitano-Mappa_delle_idee.pdf

28. Metropolitan City of Milan (MCM): Milano metropolitana al futuro. Piano strategico triennale del territorio metropolitano. Aggiornamento (2019–2021). Allegato 1 (2019). http://www.cittametropolitana.mi.it/export/sites/default/Piano_Strategico_2019_2021/doc/Piano-strategico-2019_2021.pdf

29. Directive of the President of the Council of Ministers March 16, 2018: Indirizzi per l'attuazione dell'Agenda 2030 delle Nazioni Unite e della Strategia nazionale per lo sviluppo sostenibile (SNSvS)

30. Metropolitan City of Cagliari (MCC). https://www.cittametropolitanacagliari.it/web/cmdca/-/a-2

31. Murgante, B., Borruso, G., Balletto, G., Castiglia, P., Dettori, M.: Why Italy first? health, geographical and planning aspects of the covid-19 outbreak. Sustainability **12**(12), 5064 (2020)

32. Murgante, B., Balletto, G., Borruso, G., Las Casas, G., Paolo, C., Marco, D.: Geographical analyses of Covid-19's spreading contagion in the challenge of global health risks. TeMA-J. Land Use, Mob. Environ. 283–304 (2020)

33. European Union (EU): Pact of Amsterdam (2016). https://ec.europa.eu/regional_policy/sources/policy/themes/urban-development/agenda/pact-of-amsterdam.pdf

International Workshop on Theoretical and Computational Chemistry and Its Applications (TCCMA 2020)

Carbon Capture and Separation from $CO_2/N_2/$ H_2O Gaseous Mixtures in Bilayer Graphtriyne: A Molecular Dynamics Study

Noelia Faginas-Lago[1]([✉]) [iD],
Yusuf Bramastya Apriliyanto[2] [iD], and Andrea Lombardi[1] [iD]

[1] Dipartimento di Chimica, Biologia e Biotecnologie,
Università degli Studi di Perugia, Via Elce di Sotto 8, 06123 Perugia, Italy
noelia.faginaslago@unipg.it
[2] Department of Chemistry, IPB University,
Jl Tanjung Kampus IPB Dramaga, 16680 Bogor, Indonesia

Abstract. Molecular dynamics simulations have been performed for CO_2 capture and separation from $CO_2/N_2/H_2O$ gaseous mixtures in bilayer graphtriyne. The gas uptake capacity, permeability as well as selectivity of the layers were simulated based on an improved formulation of force fields tested on accurate *ab initio* calculations on specific systems for mixture separation in post-combustion process. The effect of pressure and temperature on the separation performances of graphtriyne layers was investigated. Compared with the single layer graphtriyne, bilayer graphtriyne can adsorb more molecules with relatively good selectivity, due to the action of the interlayer region as an adsorption site. The interlayer adsorption selectivity of CO_2/N_2 and CO_2/H_2O at a temperature of 333 K and a pressure of 4 atm have been found to be equal to about 20.23 and 1.85, respectively. We also observed that the bilayer graphtriyne membrane has high CO_2 and H_2O permeances compared to N_2, with permeance selectivity ranging from 4.8 to 6.5. Moreover, we found that permeation and adsorption depend on the applied temperature; at high temperatures, permeation and adsorption tend to decrease for all molecules.

Keywords: MD simulations · Graphynes · Carbon capture and separation · Selectivity

1 Introduction

Gas adsorption by porous materials as a phenomenon to ground technologies aimed at reducing greenhouse gas emissions has actively been investigated in the past few years [1–3]. All of these efforts are eventually directed to mitigate possible anthropic contributions to climate change and global warming. Among the greenhouse gases, CO_2 is the most abundant and is regularly released into the atmosphere [4]. Therefore, post-combustion CO_2 capture and separation are important to control the CO_2 emission mainly produced from fossil fuels combustion. Major advantages of porous materials over the traditional aqueous chemical absorbent are in terms of its simplicity, recovery and low implementation costs [5]. Carbon-based materials bearing intrinsic pores

© Springer Nature Switzerland AG 2020
O. Gervasi et al. (Eds.): ICCSA 2020, LNCS 12255, pp. 489–501, 2020.
https://doi.org/10.1007/978-3-030-58820-5_36

currently emerge as potential solid adsorbent candidates for CO_2 capture [6–8]. Unlike other porous materials (e.g. MOFs and polymers), carbon-based materials are hydrophobic, chemically inert and thermally stable. Thanks to their exceptional properties, carbon-based materials are not susceptible to heat and water vapour, which is a characteristic of post-combustion flue gas. Moreover, compared with MOFs and zeolites, carbon-based materials are constructed from lightweight elements linked by strong covalent bonds producing low density and robust structures [9–13]. Therefore, carbon-based materials are economically suitable and viable for post combustion CO_2 capture and separation.

Instead of only capture CO_2 molecules by surface adsorption, two-dimensional carbon-based membranes provide a unique properties harnessed from a combination of surface adsorption and their intrinsic pores acting as molecular sieving to separate CO_2 from other gaseous mixtures [14, 15]. Graphene, a class of carbon-based materials, have been attracting much attention in recent years. It is a single atom thick planar membrane with remarkable properties [16–18]. Surface functionalization by introducing holes or attaching different organic groups is commonly performed in order to modify graphene to meet the requirements for a specific application. For gas adsorption and separation, nano-porous graphene is reported as a promising porous membrane material based on carbon [19, 20]. However, a major drawback of nano-porous graphene is the tendency to form aggregates that limits its gas uptake capacity. Moreover, practically, it is difficult to control the pore size and the homogeneity of their distribution. Analogous with the graphene, γ-graphynes are single atomic layers belonging to the class of carbon allotropes. The carbon atoms in γ-graphynes are arranged as a function of the C-C triple bonds bridging two adjacent hexagons. Possessing similar properties with graphene, γ-graphynes have uniformly distributed and adjustable pores [21–23]. In addition, with lower dispersion forces and therefore a reduced tendency to form aggregates, γ-graphynes are suited for gas capture and separation [24, 25].

Since synthesis and characterization techniques of graphynes are still actively being developed [26–29], computer modelling and simulations play an important role in the material development and evaluation of their performance for gas capture and separation [30, 31]. Recent studies reported that graphtriyne (a form of graphynes, in which each benzene ring is connected to each of six others through a chain composed by three acetylenic bonds), showed a strong physisorption of CO_2 over N_2 and H_2O molecules [32, 33]. It is also reported that the adsorption energy of CO_2 can be enhanced by introducing a new layer of graphtriyne over an existing graphtriyne membrane and so on. The multi-layered graphtriyne systems introduce interlayer spaces that can confine CO_2 molecules trough strong attractive forces. These interlayer spaces can be exploited as new adsorption sites thus the uptake capacity of CO_2 can be increased [34]. In this work, a study of the performance of bilayer graphtriyne membrane for CO_2 capture and separation is evaluated using extended molecular dynamics (MD) simulations. A wide range of relevant conditions in post combustion involving a gaseous mixture of $CO_2/N_2/H_2O$ has been applied in the molecular simulations.

2   Methods

For modelling the intermolecular interactions, the total potential energy of the system is split into electrostatic and non-electrostatic contributions. The total potential energy represents the sum of the intermolecular potential energy between any interacting pair in the system involving CO_2, N_2, H_2O and graphtriyne layers. The electrostatic contribution is calculated using a standard Coulombic summation, by assigning point charges to the interacting molecules. Meanwhile, the non-electrostatic term is expressed using the Improved Lennard-Jones (ILJ) potential [35], as follows:

$$V_{tot}(r) = \sum_{i,j}^{n} \frac{q_i q_j}{r_{ij}} + \sum_{i}^{n} V_{ILJ}(r_i)$$

where

$$V_{ILJ}(r_i) = \varepsilon \left[\frac{m}{n(r) - m} \left(\frac{r_0}{r} \right)^{n(r)} - \frac{n(r)}{n(r) - m} \left(\frac{r_0}{r} \right)^{m} \right]$$

with

$$n(r) = \beta + 4.0 \left(\frac{r}{r_0} \right)^2$$

As can be seen from the above equations, the ILJ potential requires four parameters (r_0, ε, m and β) to be specified. The r_0 and ε are pair specific parameters representing the equilibrium distance and the depth of the potential well, respectively. The m parameter takes the value of 6 for describing interactions between neutral molecules, while the dimensionless β is a parameter that can be adjusted following the hardness of the interaction. The β parameter also corrects the dependence of the interaction on the internuclear distance, improving the potential function at the asymptotic region. The ILJ function so formulated versatile improves the energy profile at equilibrium distance and at short and long range compared to the traditional Lennard-Jones (LJ) function. For a full account of the advantages of the ILJ function see Refs [36–42] and references therein. All of the ILJ parameters used in this report were improved and tested in comparison with high level *ab initio* calculations as reported in the Ref [34]. Figure 1 shows molecular models that represent the gas molecules. These molecular models along with their point charge distributions are adopted from Ref [41–45], where di- and quadrupole moments of the molecules have been considered.

The MD simulations were performed in a simulation box with dimension $72.210 \times 62.523 \times 280.0$ Å^3. The $CO_2/N_2/H_2O$ gaseous mixture with equal fractions of CO_2, N_2 and H_2O molecules was generated randomly distributing the molecules inside the simulation box. A bilayered-graphtriyne membrane with a dimension of 72.210×62.523 Å^2 was placed in the middle of the box (see Fig. 2). The molecular structure of graphtriyne used for the MD simulations is presented in Fig. 3. The graphtriyne structure were optimized by means of periodic density functional theory

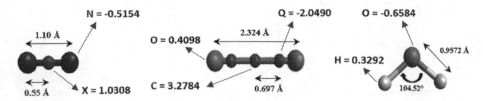

N = -0.5154

1.10 Å

0.55 Å   X = 1.0308

O = 0.4098

Q = -2.0490   O = -0.6584

2.324 Å

C = 3.2784   0.697 Å

H = 0.3292

0.9572 Å

104.52°

Fig. 1. The models used to represent nitrogen, carbon dioxide and water molecules along with their point charges (e). Q is a point charge representing the C–O bond of CO_2 while X is a point charge representing the N–N bond of N_2.

(DFT) [33]. Seven different amounts of gas molecules have been loaded into the box for the simulations, to investigate the influence of pressure to the gaseous mixtures. The amount of gas molecules inside the box was directly proportional to the initial gas pressure, according to the Peng-Robinson equation of state [46]. In order to mimic post-combustion conditions, four different temperatures (i.e. 333, 353, 373 and 400 K) were considered with initial pressures at relatively low pressure, below 5.5 atm.

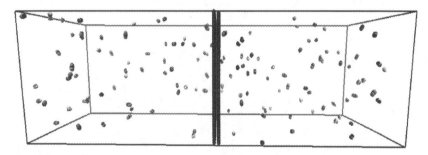

Fig. 2. A snapshot of the simulation box loaded with $CO_2/N_2/H_2O$ mixtures. The graphytriyne is represented by cyan layers located at the centre of simulation box. The cyan and red molecules are CO_2, the blue molecules are N_2, while H_2O is represented by red and white molecules. (Color figure online)

The cut-off distances for the ILJ and electrostatic interactions were set to 15 Å, and the Ewald sum method was applied for the calculation of the electrostatic interactions. The graphtriyne layers were considered as a frozen framework and the gas molecules were treated as rigid bodies. Each simulation was performed for 5.5 ns after a 0.5 ns equilibration period with a fixed time step of 1 fs. The statistical data and trajectory were collected at every 2 ps. The gas molecules could cross the layers multiple times in both directions during the simulation. The number of permeation events was then monitored along calculating the z-density and the radial distribution function profiles. All the MD simulations were performed by using DL_POLY package [47] in the canonical (NVT) ensemble employing the Nose-Hoover algorithm to maintain the applied temperatures. Periodic boundary conditions were implemented in x, y and z directions. The graphical representations and the molecular trajectories were processed by using the VMD program [48].

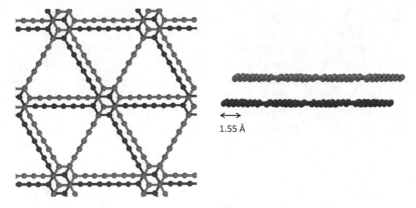

Fig. 3. Top and side views of the bilayer graphtriyne structure. According to the structure predicted by the periodic DFT optimization, one of the carbon sheets is shifted of 1.55 Å with respect to the other sheet [33].

3   Results and Discussions

3.1   Gas Permeability

Production runs of each system were started after 0.5 ns equilibration time. The energy and temperature convergence were checked as an indication of the equilibrated system. The number of permeation events occurred during the production runs was counted and plotted as a function of the simulation time. The slope of this plot is an estimation of the gas permeation rate measured in units of molecules ps^{-1}. Left panel of Fig. 4 shows the permeation events as a function of time for a system simulated at 3.18 atm and 333 K. It can be seen that CO_2 has a higher permeation rate than H_2O and N_2. The high permeation rate of CO_2 can be verified by looking at the radial distribution function profiles that are presented in the right panel of Fig. 4. CO_2 has the largest and highest peaks meaning that CO_2 is more likely to be located near the C atoms of graphtriyne. Consequently, CO_2 molecules have the highest probability to permeate the graphtriyne layers. N_2 has the lowest permeation due to small number of N_2 molecules found near the layers.

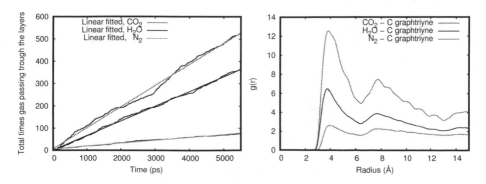

Fig. 4. Permeation events (left) and radial distribution functions (right) at 3.18 atm and 333 K.

Furthermore, knowing the permeation rate, the gas permeance can be calculated by dividing it by the corresponding pressure and area of the graphtriyne layers. The gas permeances were reported in gas permeance unit (GPU) (1 GPU = 3.35×10^{-10} mol m^{-2} s^{-1} Pa^{-1}). In order to widen the applied conditions, we also performed MD simulations at seven different pressures and four different temperatures. The results are reported in Fig. 5. Figure 5, left panel, shows that N_2 permeances are slightly affected by the pressures. On the other hand, CO_2 and H_2O permeances tend to decrease as the pressure increases. From these data, the average of gas permeances were calculated and then plotted as a function of temperature (Fig. 5, right panel). It was observed that the average of gas permeance for all gas decreases with the increasing of temperature. This phenomenon is indeed related to their kinetic energy as the temperature varies. The higher is the kinetic energy, the higher is the velocity of molecules to compete with attraction forces of the layers. A high temperature decreases gas permeance by minimizing attraction effects to steer gas molecules toward the graphtriyne layers. The gas permeation reported in Fig. 5 is in a good agreement with the potential energy curves reported by Bartolomei and co-workers [33], where well depths increase according to the sequence N_2, H_2O, CO_2 (highest value). Although CO_2 has a deeper potential well than H_2O, the average gas permeances for CO_2 and H_2O are comparable. This fact is closely related with the stereoselective requirement for CO_2 to pass through the layers as already discussed in Ref [34]. Nevertheless, by including also the deviation into our consideration (Fig. 5), we can say that CO_2 still has the highest gas permeance. For the case of N_2, low N_2 permeance at all temperatures indicates that attraction force of the graphtriyne layers to N_2 is too weak compared to that of CO_2 and H_2O.

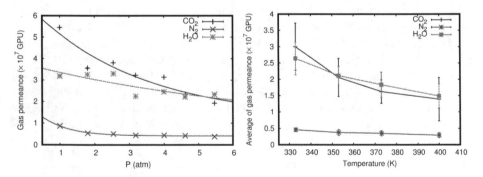

Fig. 5. Gas permeance at 333 K (left panel) and average of gas permeance as a function of temperature (right panel).

Although the data presented in Fig. 5 follow a similar trend as reported in the Ref [34], the gas permeances in this report are relatively lower (ranging from 0.6 to 3.0×10^7 GPU and 0.3 to 0.6×10^7 GPU for CO_2 and N_2 respectively). Low values of gas permeances are caused by more competitions existing between the $CO_2/N_2/H_2O$ gaseous mixtures when interacting with graphtriyne. Moreover, the temperatures applied in this report are also higher. Furthermore, by comparing the average of gas permeances obtained for all type of systems, we calculated permeance selectivities and plotted the values as function of temperature (Fig. 6). In general, temperature slightly affects the permeance selectivity of all pairs. Permeance selectivity values of H_2O/N_2 overlap with those of CO_2/N_2 by having similar values ranging from 4.8 to 6.5. On the other hand, H_2O/CO_2 selectivity is around 1 which implies that the bilayer graphtriyne membrane is not selective for CO_2–H_2O separation. Although the permeance selectivities are lower than CO_2/N_2 selectivity reported by Liu *et al.* [15] (about 100, with CO_2 permeance = 2.8×10^5 GPU) for nanoporous graphene at 300 K and by Schrier [12] (about 60, with CO_2 permeance = 3×10^5 GPU) for Porous Graphene-E-Stilbene-1 (PG-ES1) at 325 K, the CO_2 permeances for bilayer graphtriyne (ranging from 0.6 to 3.0×10^7 GPU) are two order of magnitudes higher. Nevertheless, the CO_2/N_2 permeance selectivities are comparable to those reported by Wu and co-workers [17] for fluorine modified nano-porous graphene at 300 K (ranging from 4 to 11). It is already known that trade-off issue between selectivity and permeability is a drawback of membrane based-materials. However, its simplicity and efficiency make membrane-based technology still widely used for gas separation [18].

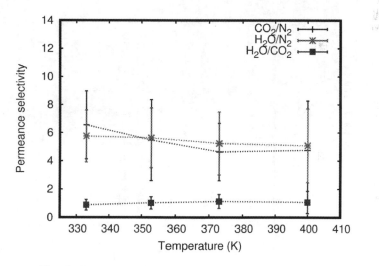

Fig. 6. Permeance selectivity as a function of temperature.

3.2 Gas Adsorption

In addition to the radial distribution functions reported in Fig. 4, the stronger attraction for CO_2 than H_2O and N_2 is also reflected in the z-density profiles presented in Fig. 7. The z-density is a plot of the mean number density of gas along the z-axis, where the z-axis is perpendicular with the graphtriyne layers. The highest peaks of CO_2 indicate that graphtriyne layers exhibit strong adsorption of CO_2, especially inside the interlayer region. The z-density profiles also present sharp peaks outside the layers at a distance of around 3.4 Å from the surface for all gas molecules. Figure 7 also shows that the interlayer region is selective for CO_2 uptake and separation from the $CO_2/H_2O/N_2$

gaseous mixture. For instance, at 333 K and 4 atm, we obtained interlayer adsorption selectivity of CO_2/N_2 and CO_2/H_2O about 20.23 and 1.85 respectively. High and broad peaks of CO_2 presented in Fig. 7 correspond to the deep and wide of CO_2 potential well, meaning a strong long ranged attractions. Therefore, compared with the single layer, the bilayer graphriyne membrane adsorbs more molecules facilitated by their interlayer pores [32]. As already discussed before, the permeation events are closely related to the adsorption of gas over the surfaces of membrane. The more gas is adsorbed over the surfaces, the more probable is the gas to cross the layers. However, the amount of adsorbed molecules in the interlayer region also can diminish the gas permeance by saturating the pores and blocking other molecules to cross the membrane. This phenomenon happens for the case of CO_2, where the attraction forces are very strong in the interlayer region. Beside the stereodynamic requirement of CO_2 to cross the layers, permeation events of CO_2 were also inhibited by other CO_2 molecules that occupied the intermolecular pores. Consequently, the average of CO_2 permeances are relatively low and comparable with those of H_2O (Fig. 5, right panel) even though a lot of CO_2 molecules were adsorbed at the surfaces of graphtriyne.

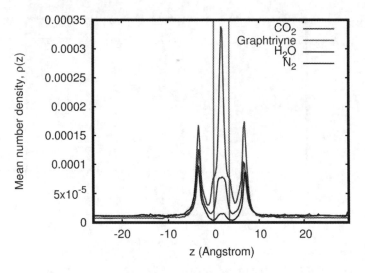

Fig. 7. Z-density profiles simulated at 1.8 atm and 353 K.

We also calculated the total gas uptakes by integrating the z-density profiles at the adsorption region. The adsorption region is the area under the z-density peaks, in which located in the range of 6.9 Å from the surface of graphtriyne including the area between the layers presented in the z-density profiles. The gas uptakes at 333 K for all applied pressures were presented in the left panel of Fig. 8 as adsorption isotherms. It can be seen that the gas uptake is linearly proportional to the initial pressure; the higher is the initial pressure, the higher is the gas uptake value. The linear trend has been expected since the MD simulations are conducted at low pressures regimes, where the gas molecules have not saturate the adsorption sites. Furthermore, by calculating the slope of adsorption isotherms, we estimated the adsorption coefficient of each systems. The adsorption coefficients for all molecules are reported in the right panel of Fig. 8 as a function of temperature. Figure 8 shows that CO_2 has the highest gas uptakes and adsorption coefficients among gas molecules. The adsorption coefficients decrease as the increasing of temperature for all gas molecules. It can be expected that gas physisorption is relatively ineffective at high temperatures. Weak attraction of N_2 is manifested by the fact that N_2 has the lowest adsorption coefficients (about 0.02 to 0.04 mmol g^{-1} atm^{-1}). Low uptake of N_2 caused low permeance values of N_2 as presented in Fig. 5.

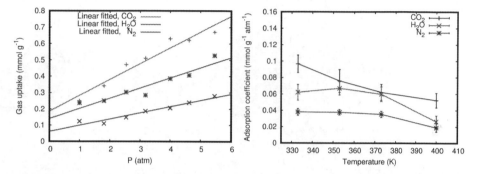

Fig. 8. Adsorption isotherm profiles at 333 K (left panel) and adsorption coefficient as a function of temperature (right panel).

Adsorption selectivity of graphtriyne layers were reported in term of total adsorption selectivity. The total adsorption refers to the sum of the interlayer adsorption and the surface adsorption. The total adsorption selectivity $S_{ads}^{A/B}$ were calculated as the following,

$$S_{ads}^{A/B} = \frac{n_{A(ads)}}{n_{A(free)}} \times \frac{n_{B(free)}}{n_{B(ads)}}$$

$n_{A(ads)}$ and $n_{B(ads)}$ are the numbers of adsorbed molecules A and B, while $n_{A(free)}$ and $n_{B(free)}$ are the numbers of free molecules A and B, respectively. The total adsorption selectivity for all systems are provided in Table 1. In general, total adsorption selectivity of all gas pairs decreases as the increasing of pressure and temperature. Table 1 shows that bilayer graphtriyne exhibits relatively high CO_2/N_2 total adsorption selectivity especially at low pressure and temperature. The CO_2/N_2 selectivities reported in Table 1 are higher than those reported in our previous report for the single layer system [32]. We obtained CO_2/N_2 total adsorption selectivities at 373 K for bilayer system ranging from 2.3 to 5.2, while in the previous work for single layer system are in the range of 1.3 to 2.4 at the same temperature. However, the bilayer graphtriyne is not selective enough for CO_2/H_2O adsorption with total selectivity values ranging from 1 to 2 for all applied temperatures. It has been reported that competitive adsorption between water vapour and CO_2 on the same adsorption sites of various materials is observed in post-combustion CO_2 capture and separation [5, 30]. In most cases, H_2O interferences are minimized by condensing the water molecules or by modifying the adsorbent materials to have more hydrophobic surfaces. Nevertheless, doubling the graphtriyne layer can enhance the amount of adsorbed molecules and the selectivity by providing new adsorption sites in the interlayer pores.

Table 1. Total adsorption selectivity of $CO_2/N_2/H_2O$ gaseous mixture

Temperature (K)	Gas	Total adsorption selectivity						
		1.00 atm	1.80 atm	2.54 atm	3.18 atm	4.00 atm	4.62 atm	5.47 atm
333	CO_2/N_2	3.43	4.58	4.67	3.67	4.14	3.26	2.90
	H_2O/N_2	3.00	2.84	2.40	1.65	2.10	1.86	2.12
	CO_2/H_2O	1.14	1.62	1.95	2.22	1.97	1.75	1.37
353	CO_2/N_2	3.19	4.24	3.64	4.19	2.79	2.78	2.60
	H_2O/N_2	2.45	1.69	2.08	2.06	1.88	1.93	1.99
	CO_2/H_2O	1.30	2.51	1.75	2.03	1.48	1.44	1.31
373	CO_2/N_2	5.16	3.04	3.40	2.67	2.62	2.62	2.33
	H_2O/N_2	0.81	3.12	2.05	1.42	2.04	1.59	1.84
	CO_2/H_2O	6.35	0.97	1.65	1.88	1.28	1.65	1.26
400	CO_2/N_2	1.08	3.96	3.12	2.26	2.68	2.54	2.36
	H_2O/N_2	1.87	2.00	1.65	1.57	1.75	1.54	1.57
	CO_2/H_2O	0.58	1.98	1.89	1.44	1.53	1.66	1.50

4   Conclusions

Bilayer graphtriyne has been investigated for the purpose of CO_2 capture and separation materials. The gas uptake capacity and permeability of the layers were simulated computationally employing $CO_2/H_2O/N_2$ gaseous mixture systems in wide range of conditions. Extensive MD simulations were performed based on an improved formulation of force fields. Compared to generic force fields, our formulation was tested on accurate *ab initio* calculations on specific systems for mixture separation and gas capture in post-combustion process. Therefore, a quantitative description of the interactions and realistic results were obtained for the dynamics under considered systems. We observed that the bilayer graphtriyne membrane has high CO_2 and H_2O permeances compared to N_2 with relatively good selectivity (from 4.8 to 6.5). Adsorbed CO_2 molecules lower the CO_2 permeance by occupying the interlayer pores and preventing permeation events. As a result, CO_2 has permeance values similar to H_2O, despite the CO_2 adsorption is more favourable than that of other molecules. High CO_2 uptake capacity and selectivity were founded in the interlayer region. The interlayer adsorption selectivity of CO_2/N_2 and CO_2/H_2O are about 20.23 and 1.85, respectively at 333 K and 4 atm. The layers are not selective enough for CO_2/H_2O capture and separation as also reported for other materials. Nevertheless, in post-combustion application, competitive CO_2/H_2O adsorption can be reduced by condensing H_2O prior interacting the flue gas with the graphtriyne layers. In addition, we also investigated the effect of temperature to the gas uptake capacity, permeability and selectivity. As the temperature increases; the gas uptake, adsorption coefficient and gas permeance decrease for all gas molecules. Among carbon-based materials, bilayer graphtriyne can be considered as an alternative membrane with its potential properties for mixture separation that offers fast and efficient separation of different molecular species.

Acknowledgements. YBA thanks to the LCPQ - Université de Toulouse III for allocated computing time. NF-L, AL thank MIUR and the University of Perugia for the financial support of the AMIS project through the "Dipartimenti di Eccellenza" programme. N. F.-L. also acknowledges the Fondo Ricerca di Base 2017 (RICBASE2017BALUCANI) del Dipartimento di Chimica, Biologia e Biotecnologie della Università di Perugia for financial support. A. L. acknowledges financial support from MIUR PRIN 2015 (contract 2015F59J3R 002) and the OU Super-computing Center for Education & Research (OSCER) at the University of Oklahoma, for allocated computing time.

References

1. Bui, M., et al.: Carbon capture and storage (CCS): the way forward. Energy Environ. Sci. **11**, 1062–1176 (2018)
2. Huck, J.M., et al.: Evaluating different classes of porous materials for carbon capture. Energy Environ. Sci. **7**, 4132–4146 (2014)
3. Li, J.R., et al.: Porous materials with pre-designed single-molecule traps for CO_2 selective adsorption. Nat. Commun. **4**, 1538 (2013)
4. World Resources Institute (WRI): Climate Analysis Indicators Tool (CAIT): WRI's climate data explorer (2020). http://cait.wri.org. Accessed February 2020
5. Smit, B.: Carbon capture and storage: introductory lecture. Faraday Discuss. **192**, 9–25 (2016)
6. Srinivas, G., Krungleviciute, V., Guo, Z.X., Yildrim, T.: Exceptional CO_2 capture in a hieararchically porous carbon with simultaneous high surface area and pore volume. Energy Environ. Sci. **7**, 335–342 (2014)
7. Ganesan, A., Shaijumon, M.M.: Activated graphene-derived porous carbon with exceptional gas adsorption properties. Microporous Mesoporous Mater. **220**, 21–27 (2016)
8. Ghosh, S., Sevilla, M., Fuertes, A.B., Andreoli, E., Ho, J., Barron, A.R.: Defining a performance map of porous carbon sorbents for high-pressure carbon dioxide uptake and carbon dioxide-methane selectivity. J. Mater. Chem. A **4**, 14739–14751 (2016)
9. Kim, J., Lin, L.C., Swisher, J.A., Haranczyk, M., Smit, B.: Predicting large CO_2 adsorption in aluminosilicate zeolites for postcombustion carbon dioxide capture. J. Am. Chem. Soc. **134**, 18940–18943 (2012)
10. Lin, L.C., et al.: Understanding CO2 dynamics in metal-organic frameworks with open metal sites. Angew. Chem. **125**, 4506–4509 (2013)
11. Queen, W.L., et al.: Comprehensive study of carbon dioxide adsorption in the metal-organic frameworks M2 (dobdc) (M = Mg, Mn, Fe Co, Ni, Cu, Zn). Chem. Sci. **5**, 4569–4581 (2014)
12. Schrier, J.: Carbon dioxide separation with a two-dimensional polymer membrane. ACS Appl. Mater. Interfaces **4**, 3745–3752 (2012)

13. Xiang, Z., et al.: Systematic tuning and multifunctionalization of covalent organic polymers for enhanced carbon capture. J. Am. Chem. Soc. **137**, 13301–13307 (2015)
14. Koenig, S.P., Wang, L., Pellegrino, J., Bunch, S.: Selective molecular sieving trough porous graphene. Nat. Nanotechnol. **7**, 728–732 (2012)
15. Liu, H., Dai, S., Jiang, D.: Insights into CO_2/N_2 separation trough nanoporous graphene from molecular dynamics. Nanoscale **5**, 9984–9987 (2013)
16. Vekeman, J., Cuesta, I.G., Faginas-Lago, N., Wilson, J., Sánchez-Marín, J., de Merás, A.S.: Potential models for the simulation of methane adsorption on graphene: development and CCSD (T) benchmarks. Phys. Chem. Chem. Phys. **20**, 25518–25530 (2018)
17. Wu, T., et al.: Fluorine-modified porous graphene as membrane for CO_2/N_2 separation: molecular dynamic and first-principles simulations. J. Phys. Chem. C **118**, 7369–7376 (2014)
18. Du, H., Li, J., Zhang, J., Su, G., Li, X., Zhao, Y.: Separation of hydrogen and nitrogen gases with porous graphene membrane. J. Phys. Chem. C **115**, 23261–23266 (2011)
19. Tao, Y., et al.: Tunable hydrogen separation in porous graphene membrane: first-principle and molecular dynamic simulation. ACS Appl. Mater. Interfaces **6**, 8048–8058 (2014)
20. Ambrosetti, A., Silvestrelli, P.L.: Gas separation in nanoporous graphene from first principle calculations. J. Phys. Chem. C **118**, 19172–19179 (2014)
21. James, A., et al.: Graphynes: indispensable nanoporous architectures in carbon flatland. RSC Adv. **8**, 22998–23018 (2018)
22. Bartolomei, M., et al.: Penetration barrier of water through graphynes' pores: first-principles predictions and force field optimization. J. Phys. Chem. Lett. **5**, 751–755 (2014)
23. Lin, S., Buehler, M.J.: Mechanics and molecular filtration performance of graphyne nanoweb membranes for selective water purification. Nanoscale **5**, 11801–11807 (2013)
24. Meng, Z., et al.: Graphdiyne as a high-efficiency membrane for separating oxygen from harmful gases: a first-principles study. ACS Appl. Mater. Interfaces **8**, 28166–28170 (2016)
25. Bartolomei, M., Carmona-Novillo, E., Giorgi, G.: First principles investigation of hydrogen physical adsorption on graphynes' layers. Carbon **95**, 1076–1081 (2015)
26. Zhou, J., et al.: Synthesis of graphdiyne nanowalls using acetylenic coupling reaction. J. Am. Chem. Soc. **137**, 7596–7599 (2015)
27. Gao, X., et al.: Ultrathin graphdiyne film on graphene through solution-phase Van Der Waals epitaxy. Sci. Adv. **4**, eaat6378 (2018)
28. Sakamoto, R., et al.: A pyrazine-incorporated graphdiyne nanofilm as a metal-free electrocatalyst for the hydrogen evolution reaction. J. Mater. Chem. A **6**, 22189–22194 (2018)
29. Bao, H., Wang, L., Li, C., Luo, J.: Structural characterization and identification of graphdiyne and graphdiyne-based materials. ACS Appl. Mater. Interfaces. **11**, 2717–2729 (2018)
30. Joos, L., Huck, J.M., Speybroeck, V.V., Smit, B.: Cutting the cost of carbon capture: a case for carbon capture and utilization. Faraday Discuss. **192**, 391–414 (2016)
31. Braun, E., et al.: High-throughput computational screening of nanoporous adsorbents for CO_2 capture from natural gas. Mol. Syst. Des. Eng. **1**, 175–188 (2016)
32. Faginas-Lago, N., Apriliyanto, Y.B., Lombardi, A.: Molecular simulations of $CO_2/N_2/H_2O$ gaseous mixture separation in graphtriyne membrane. In: Misra, S., et al. (eds.) ICCSA 2019. LNCS, vol. 11624, pp. 374–387. Springer, Cham (2019). https://doi.org/10.1007/978-3-030-24311-1_27
33. Bartolomei, M., Giorgi, G.: A novel nanoporous graphite based on graphynes: first-principles structure and carbon dioxide preferential physisorption. ACS Appl. Mater. Interfaces. **8**, 27996–28003 (2016)

34. Apriliyanto, Y.B., et al.: Nanostructure selectivity for molecular adsorption and separation: the case of graphyne layers. J. Phys. Chem. C **122**, 16195–16208 (2018)

35. Pirani, F., Brizi, S., Roncaratti, L.F., Casavecchia, P., Cappelletti, D., Vecchiocattivi, F.: Beyond the Lennard-Jones model: a simple and accurate potential function probed by high resolution scattering data useful for molecular dynamics simulations. Phys. Chem. Chem. Phys. **10**, 5489–5503 (2008)

36. Lago, N.F., Larrañaga, F.H., Albertí, M.: On the suitability of the ILJ function to match different formulations of the electrostatic potential for water-water interactions. Eur. Phys. J. D **55**, 75–85 (2009). https://doi.org/10.1140/epjd/e2009-00215-5

37. Faginas-Lago, N., Yeni, D., Huarte, F., Wang, Y., Alcamí, M., Martin, F.: Adsorption of hydrogen molecules on carbon nanotubes using quantum chemistry and molecular dynamics. J. Phys. Chem. A **120**, 6451–6458 (2016)

38. Faginas-Lago, N., Lombardi, A., Albertí, M., Grossi, G.: Accurate analytic intermolecular potential for the simulation of Na^+ and K^+ ion hydration in liquid water. J. Mol. Liq. **204**, 192–197 (2015)

39. Albertí, M., Lago, N.: Competitive solvation of K^+ by C_6H_6 and H_2O in the K^+-$(C_6H_6)_n$-$(H_2O)_m$ (n = 1–4; m = 1–6) aggregates. Eur. Phys. J. D **67**, 73 (2013). https://doi.org/10.1140/epjd/e2013-30753-x

40. Albertí, M., Faginas Lago, N., Pirani, F.: Ar solvation shells in K^+–HFBz: from cluster rearrangement to solvation dynamics. J. Phys. Chem. A **115**(40), 10871–10879 (2011)

41. Albertí, M., Aguilar, A., Cappelletti, D., Laganà, A., Pirani, F.: On the development of an effective model potential to describe water interaction in neutral and ionic clusters. Int. J. Mass Spectrom. **280**, 50–56 (2009)

42. Lombardi, A., Palazzetti, F.: A comparison of interatomic potentials for rare gas nanoaggregates. J. Mol. Struct. THEOCHEM **852**, 22–29 (2008)

43. Albertí, M., Pirani, F., Lagana, A.: Carbon dioxide clathrate hydrates: selective role of intermolecular interactions and action of the SDS catalyst. J. Phys. Chem. A **117**, 6991–7000 (2013)

44. Lombardi, A., Pirani, F., Laganà, A., Bartolomei, M.: Energy transfer dynamics and kinetics of elementary processes (promoted) by gas-phase CO_2-N_2 collisions: selectivity control by the anisotropy of the interaction. J. Comput. Chem. **37**, 1463–1475 (2016)

45. Bartolomei, M., Pirani, F., Laganà, A., Lombardi, A.: A full dimensional grid empowered simulation of the CO_2 + CO_2 processes. J. Comput. Chem. **33**, 1806–1819 (2012)

46. Elliott, J.R., Lira, C.T.: Introductory Chemical Engineering Thermodynamics, 2nd edn. Prentice Hall, New Jersey (2012)

47. Smith, W., Yong, C., Rodger, P.: DL_POLY: application to molecular simulation. Mol. Simul. **28**, 385–471 (2002)

48. Humphrey, W., Dalke, A., Schulten, K.V.M.D.: Visual molecular dynamics. J. Mol. Graph. **14**, 33–38 (1996)

Formamide Dehydration and Condensation on Acidic Montmorillonite: Mechanistic Insights from *Ab-Initio* Periodic Simulations

Stefano Pantaleone[1,2(✉)] ⓘ, Albert Rimola[3] ⓘ,
Javier Navarro-Ruiz[3,4] ⓘ, Pierre Mignon[5] ⓘ, Mariona Sodupe[3] ⓘ,
Piero Ugliengo[1] ⓘ, and Nadia Balucani[2,6,7] ⓘ

[1] Dipartimento di Chimica and Nanostructured Interfaces and Surfaces (NIS),
Università degli Studi di Torino, Via P. Giuria 7, 10125 Turin, Italy
stefano.pantaleone@unito.it
[2] Dipartimento di Chimica, Biologia e Biotecnologie, Università degli Studi di
Perugia, Via Elce di Sotto 8, 06123 Perugia, Italy
[3] Departament de Química, Universitat Autònoma de Barcelona,
08193 Bellaterra, Catalonia, Spain
[4] Institute of Chemical Research of Catalonia, ICIQ, and the Barcelona Institute
of Science and Technology, BIST, Av. Països Catalans 16, 43007 Tarragona,
Spain
[5] Institut Lumière Matière, UMR 5306, Université Claude Bernard Lyon 1,
CNRS, Université de Lyon, 69622 Villeurbanne Cedex, France
[6] Osservatorio Astrofisico di Arcetri, Largo E. Fermi 5, 50125 Florence, Italy
[7] Univ. Grenoble Alpes, Institut de Planétologie et Astrophysique de Grenoble
(IPAG), 38000 Grenoble, France

Abstract. Formamide (NH_2CHO) is a molecule of extraordinary relevance as
prebiotic precursor of many biological building blocks. Its dehydration reaction,
which could take place during the Archean Era, leads to the production of HCN,
the fundamental brick of DNA/RNA nitrogenous bases. Mineral surfaces could
have played a crucial role in activating biological processes which in gas phase
would have too high activation barriers to occur, thus allowing the event cas-
cade, which finally led to the formation of biological macromolecules. In the
present work we studied the dehydration process of formamide ($NH_2CHO \rightarrow$
$HCN + H_2O$) as catalyzed by a surface of acid montmorillonite. In this surface,
a silicon atom has been substituted by an aluminium one, thus generating a
negative charge that is compensated by an acidic proton on the top of the
surface. This proton should, in principle, help the formamide dehydration.
However, our results indicate that this particular acidic surface does not exert an
efficient catalytic behavior in the decomposition of formamide.

Keywords: Montmorillonite · Formamide · Prebiotic chemistry · DFT

Electronic supplementary material The online version of this chapter (https://doi.org/10.1007/
978-3-030-58820-5_37) contains supplementary material, which is available to authorized users.

1 Introduction

The interaction of various materials with biomolecules is a topic of extraordinary relevance due to its broad application in many fields of science [1]: biomedicine [2], nanotechnology [3–5], water-cleaning [6, 7]. Among others, mineral surfaces are also important in the field of prebiotic chemistry. As advocated by Bernal [8], their role in the prebiotic world could have been:

- act as scaffold where small monomers of biomolecules (nitrogenous bases, amino acids, and even their precursors) concentrate because of their favorable interactions with the surfaces;
- protect them from stress-induced processes: organic molecules in general are reactive to thermal heating and UV-photons;
- promote their polymerization, until the formation of small oligomers essential for life generation.

One of the molecules which captured the attention of the scientific community is formamide (NH_2CHO), because it is the precursor of many other molecules of biological interest [9]. In particular, in the present paper, the interest is focused on its dehydration process, which leads to the production of HCN and H_2O. It has been demonstrated by Oró that the polymerization of HCN leads to nitrogenous base of adenine ($C_5H_5N_5$) [10, 11], and, accordingly, it can be a potential reservoir of nitrogenous bases.

Saladino and coworkers studied the decomposition of formamide catalyzed by many mineral surfaces in several environmental conditions [9, 12–21]. As a general trend they showed that high temperatures are needed to obtain at least purine ($C_5H_4N_4$), and that, depending on the nature of the catalyst, the production of the other nitrogenous bases can also be achieved.

Among the several mineral surfaces, montmorillonite plays an important role because it is capable to decompose formamide through the production of DNA/RNA oligomers [17, 22–27].

From a computational point of view many works available in literature have assessed Bernal's hypothesis, investigating mineral surfaces both as scaffold for biomolecules [28–32], and as promoters of chemical reactions among adsorbates [33–36]. In recent studies, the interactions of dry and wet DNA bases with montmorillonite has been analyzed using molecular dynamics simulations [28–30, 37], also proving that nitrogenous bases adsorb with a dimer-like structure, which seems to be prone to form a phosphodiester bond, the first hot spot for a subsequent polymerization. However, a detailed mechanism of the complex process starting from the formamide decomposition to obtain HCN, the subsequent HCN polymerization to form nitrogenous bases, and their reaction with phosphates and sugars to lead to a DNA nucleotide is still missing in the literature.

Therefore, in the present work we study the first step of this process, namely, the dehydration reaction of formamide (in competition with a possible condensation reaction) in the gas phase and once adsorbed on montmorillonite by means of periodic quantum simulations.

2 Computational Details

2.1 Methods

Periodic DFT calculations, as implemented in the Vienna Ab-initio Simulation Package, VASP [38–41], were carried out to compute equilibrium structures and energies. All calculations were performed with the Perdew-Burke-Ernzerhof (PBE) functional [42], with the Grimme's D3 empirical correction for dispersion [43]. The projector-augmented wave (PAW) pseudopotentials [44] describing the ionic cores and a plane wave basis set for the valence electrons were adopted. The energy cutoff was set to 500 eV. The self-consistent field (SCF) iterative procedure was converged to a tolerance in total energy of $\Delta E = 10^{-5}$ eV. The tolerance on gradients for geometry optimization was set to 0.01 eV/Å for each atom in each direction. For transition state optimization, the DIMER method [45–48] was used, and in some difficult cases the climbing image–nudged elastic band (CI-NEB) method [49–53] was used. The k-points mesh was set to (1,1,1) both for molecular and periodic calculations: *i.e.* the unit cell of montmorillonite was large enough that the calculation in the Γ point returned energies already converged.

Visualization and manipulation of computed structures were done with the MOLDRAW package [54]. Figures were rendered with the POVRAY program [55] using MOLDRAW to build up the input file.

2.2 Surface Model

The surface model used in this work was created from a single layer of pristine montmorillonite $((Na,Ca)_{0.33}(Al,Mg)_2(Si_4O_{10})(OH)_2 \cdot nH_2O)$, consisting of two layers of tetrahedral silica interplayed by a layer of octahedral alumina (see Supplementary Material, SM, Figure S1). The cell parameters used are a = 15.48 Å, b = 17.93 Å, c = 25.00 Å, $\alpha = 91.18°$, $\beta = 100.46°$, $\gamma = 89.64°$. Such a large supercell ensures that no interaction among adsorbate of neighboring cells occurs, while the non-periodic cell parameter (c) warrants that there is enough vacuum space among fictitious replicas of the surface. A substitution of Si^{4+} with Al^{3+} was done to generate a negative charge which is saturated by a proton (see Fig. 1) [30].

3 Results

As a first step, some calculations have been done both on the formamide in the gas phase (in its protonated state) and adsorbed on the surface, in order to evaluate a good starting structure to study reactivity. In the gas phase this is straightforward as only two possible isomers exist: the H atom protonating the carbonyl O can be in CIS or TRANS

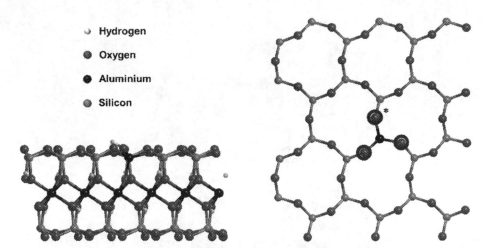

Fig. 1. PBE-D3 optimized geometries of the acidic montmorillonite. Lateral (left) and top (right) views. Green circles correspond to the possible sites to be saturated with a proton. The one marked with the asterisk is the most stable one. (Color figure online)

with respect to the H bound to the C atom (see Figure S2). Calculations show that the CIS isomer (RD_G of Fig. 2) is the most stable one ($\Delta E = 3$ kJ mol^{-1}). Moreover, it is also ready to receive the H from the amino group, the first step for dehydration (TS1_G in Fig. 2).

On the surface a more careful conformational exploration was required as formamide can adsorb in several stable adsorption modes. Five different starting positions were explored (see Figure S3) and, finally, we started with the reactivity pathway from the most stable structure (see R_MNT of Fig. 3).

3.1 Dehydration

For the sake of comparison between the dehydration reaction in the gas-phase and on the acidic montmorillonite surface, the gas phase reaction has been performed accounting for a protonated formamide.

Figures 2 shows the reaction profile of the dehydration process of formamide in the gas phase. Its decomposition is analogous as for a neutral formamide molecule which has been already discussed in details in a previous paper of some of us [56]. In this case, just one proton transfer is needed to obtain a water molecule. However, there is still a high barrier to be overcome which can be lowered by a proper catalyst. The acidic montmorillonite surface is capable to both accept and donate protons and, accordingly, is a good candidate to help the dehydration reaction of formamide.

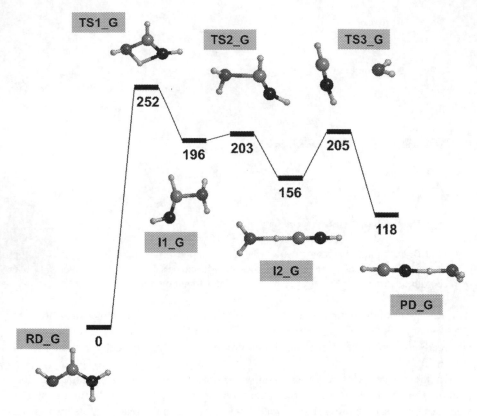

Fig. 2. PBE-D3 potential energy surface of the dehydration reaction of protonated formamide. Hydrogen in white, carbon in grey, nitrogen in blue, oxygen in red. Energy units are in kJ mol^{-1}. (Color figure online)

Figure 3 shows the reaction profile of the dehydration process of formamide catalysed by acidic montmorillonite. As one can see, montmorillonite does not exert an efficient catalytic role in this process, the highest barrier in the gas phase (252 kJ mol^{-1}, see Fig. 2 TS1_G) modestly decreases on the surface (204 kJ mol^{-1}, see Fig. 3 TS1_MNT), probably due to some stabilizing effects of the H-bond between the four-member ring in the transition state and the acidic surface proton. In both cases the activation barrier is very high, due to the presence of a strained four-member ring in the transition state. Moreover, the reaction on montmorillonite presents another important barrier, the isomerization of HNC to give HCN (see Fig. 3, TS4_MNT). From a thermodynamic point of view, both the processes are endothermic. These results are in line with the experimental results showing that formamide starts its decomposition only at high temperatures (160 °C) [16, 17].

3.2 Condensation

Figure 4 shows the condensation between two formamide molecules both in gas phase (left) and on the acidic montmorillonite (right). Also in this case the reactions involve high-energy transition states, and hence that the surface does not seem to help the process at all. In this case the reaction involves only one step with the nucleophilic attack of the nitrogen of neutral formamide to the carbon of protonated formamide, and, in a concerted fashion, the proton transfer of the amidic hydrogen of neutral formamide to the protonated oxygen to form water. Both in gas phase and on the surface the transition state involves a strained four-member ring (see TS_G and TS_MNT in Fig. 4) which strongly destabilizes the structure.

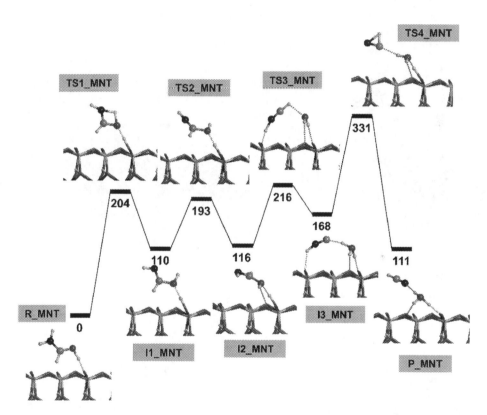

Fig. 3. PBE-D3 potential energy surface of the dehydration reaction of formamide on the acidic montmorillonite surface. Hydrogen in white, carbon in grey, nitrogen in blue, oxygen in red, silicon in yellow. Energy units are in kJ mol^{-1}. (Color figure online)

Therefore, from a kinetic standpoint, if in gas phase the two processes (i.e., dehydration vs condensation) are competitive (252 *vs* 249 kJ mol^{-1}), on the surface dehydration is less energetic than condensation (204 *vs* 242 kJ mol^{-1}).

In contrast, from a thermodynamic standpoint, condensation is more favorable than dehydration, both in the gas phase and on the surface. It is important to notice that the condensation process leads to products where some favorable interaction of the newly formed molecules is missing (see PC_G and PC_MNT in Fig. 4). Therefore, we rearranged the products in order to maximize those interactions (in these case H-bonds and dispersive forces) which stabilize the structure.

4 Discussion and Conclusion

In this work, the formamide decomposition *vs* condensation reactions are discussed both in the gas phase and on an acidic model of montmorillonite. As formamide is a very stable molecule, its decomposition in the prebiotic era is thought to be due to stressing environmental conditions: thermal [57–59] and light shocks [59–61], or surface-catalyzed processes [17, 19]. In the present paper we study the formamide dehydration *vs* its condensation on an acidic model of montmorillonite [30].

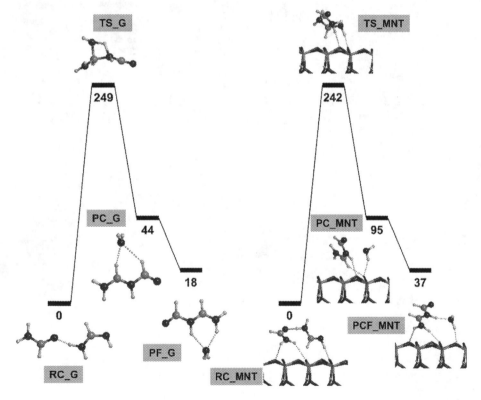

Fig. 4. PBE-D3 potential energy surfaces of the condensation reaction between two formamide molecules in the gas phase (left) and on the acidic montmorillonite surface (right). Hydrogen in white, carbon in grey, nitrogen in blue, oxygen in red, silicon in yellow. Energy units are in kJ mol^{-1}. (Color figure online)

Results show that the basal plane of acidic montmorillonite apparently does not exert a remarkable catalytic effect for any of these two processes. A slight decrease of the activation barrier for the dehydration channel (compared to the gas-phase process) is observed, while regarding the condensation, the surface does not play any catalytic role.

According to the results, we can conclude that the basal plane of acidic montmorillonite is not a suitable mineral surface that allows us to explain the catalytic activity of minerals in formamide decomposition. A plausible possibility could be that adsorption and reactivity take place at clay edges, where the chemistry (and so the reactivity) should be completely different, as silanol groups and Mg/Fe coordinated water molecules are present in the outermost layer of the surface [37].

References

1. Patwardhan, S.V., Patwardhan, G., Perry, C.C.: Interactions of biomolecules with inorganic materials: principles, applications and future prospects. J. Mater. Chem. **17**, 2875 (2007)
2. Roco, M.C.: Nanotechnology: convergence with modern biology and medicine. Curr. Opin. Biotechnol. **14**, 337–346 (2003)
3. Ghadiri, M., Chrzanowski, W., Rohanizadeh, R.: Biomedical applications of cationic clay minerals. RSC Adv. **5**, 29467–29481 (2015)
4. Mahon, E., Salvati, A., Baldelli Bombelli, F., Lynch, I., Dawson, K.A.: Designing the nanoparticle-biomolecule interface for "targeting and therapeutic delivery". J. Control. Release **161**, 164–174 (2012)
5. Tamerler, C., Sarikaya, M.: Molecular biomimetics: nanotechnology and bionanotechnology using genetically engineered peptides. Philos. Trans. R. Soc. A Math. Phys. Eng. Sci. **367**, 1705–1726 (2009)
6. Unuabonah, E.I., Günter, C., Weber, J., Lubahn, S., Taubert, A.: Hybrid clay: a new highly efficient adsorbent for water treatment. ACS Sustain. Chem. Eng. **1**, 966–973 (2013)
7. Liu, L., Yang, L.Q., Liang, H.W., Cong, H.P., Jiang, J., Yu, S.H.: Bio-inspired fabrication of hierarchical feooh nanostructure array films at the air-water interface, their hydrophobicity and application for water treatment. ACS Nano **7**, 1368–1378 (2013)
8. Bernal, J.D.: The physical basis of life. Proc. Phys. Soc. B. **62**, 597–618 (1949)
9. Saladino, R., Crestini, C., Ciciriello, F., Costanzo, G., Di Mauro, E.: Formamide chemistry and the origin of informational polymers. Chem. Biodivers. **4**, 694–720 (2007)
10. Orò, J.: Synthesis of adenine from ammonium cyanide. Biochem. Bioph. Res. Co. **2**, 407–412 (1960)
11. Orò, J.: Mechanism of synthesis of adenine from hydrogen cyanide under possible primitive earth conditions. Nature **4794**, 1193–1194 (1961). https://doi.org/10.1038/1911193a0
12. Saladino, R., Crestini, C., Neri, V., Ciciriello, F., Costanzo, G., Di Mauro, E.: Origin of informational polymers: the concurrent roles of formamide and phosphates. ChemBioChem **7**, 1707–1714 (2006)
13. Saladino, R., Crestini, C., Pino, S., Costanzo, G., Di Mauro, E.: Formamide and the origin of life. Phys. Life Rev. **9**, 84–104 (2012)
14. Saladino, R., Crestini, C., Costanzo, G., Negri, R., Di Mauro, E.: A Possible prebiotic synthesis of purine, adenine, cytosine, and 4(3H)-Pyrimidinone from formamide: implications for the origin of life. Bioorgan. Med. Chem. **9**, 1249–1253 (2001)

15. Saladino, R., Crestini, C., Di Mauro, E.: Advances in the prebiotic synthesis of nucleic acids bases: implications for the origin of life. Curr. Org. Chem. **8**, 1425–1443 (2004)

16. Costanzo, G., Saladino, R., Crestini, C., Ciciriello, F., Di Mauro, E.: Formamide as the main building block in the origin of nucleic acids. Evol. Bio. **7**, S1 (2007)

17. Saladino, R., Crestini, C., Ciambecchini, U., Ciciriello, F., Costanzo, G., Di Mauro, E.: Synthesis and degradation of nucleobases and nucleic acids by formamide in the presence of montmorillonites. ChemBioChem **5**, 1558–1566 (2004)

18. Saladino, R., Botta, G., Delfino, M., Di Mauro, E.: Meteorites as catalysts for prebiotic chemistry. Chem. Eur. J. **19**, 16916–16922 (2013)

19. Saladino, R., Ciambecchini, U., Crestini, C., Costanzo, G., Negri, R., Di Mauro, E.: One-pot TiO2-catalyzed synthesis of nucleic bases and acyclonucleosides from formamide: implications for the origin of life. ChemBioChem **4**, 514–521 (2003)

20. Saladino, R., et al.: Synthesis and degradation of nucleic acid components by formamide and cosmic dust analogues. ChemBioChem **6**, 1368–1374 (2005)

21. Rotelli, L., et al.: The key role of meteorites in the formation of relevant prebiotic molecules in a formamide/water environment. Sci. Rep. **6**, 38888 (2016)

22. Ferris, J.P.: Mineral calalysis and prebiotic synthesis: montmorillonite-catalysed formation of RNA. Elements **1**, 145–149 (2005)

23. Wang, K.J., Ferris, J.P.: Catalysis and selectivity in prebiotic synthesis: Initiation of the formation of oligo(U)s on montmorillonite clay by adenosine-5′- methylphosphate. Orig. Life Evol. Biosph. **35**, 187–212 (2005). https://doi.org/10.1007/s11084-005-0657-8

24. Ferris, J.P.: Mineral catalysis and prebiotic synthesis : formation of RNA. Orig. Life **1**, 145–150 (2005)

25. Huang, W., Ferris, J.P.: One-step, regioselective synthesis of up to 50-mers of RNA oligomers by montmorillonite catalysis. J. Am. Chem. Soc. **128**, 8914–8919 (2006)

26. Miyakawa, S., Ferris, J.P.: Sequence- and regioselectivity in the montmorillonite-catalyzed synthesis of RNA. J. Am. Chem. Soc. **125**, 8202–8208 (2003)

27. Ferris, J.P.: Sequence- and regio-selectivity in the montmorillonite-catalyzed synthesis of RNA. Orig. Life Evol. Biosph. **30**, 411–422 (2000). https://doi.org/10.1023/A:1006767019897

28. Mignon, P., Ugliengo, P., Sodupe, M.: Theoretical study of the adsorption of RNA/NA bases on the external surfaces of Na + -Montmorillonite. J. Phys. Chem. C **113**, 13741–13749 (2009)

29. Mignon, P., Sodupe, M.: Structural behaviors of cytosine into the hydrated interlayer of Na +-montmorillonite clay: an ab initio molecular dynamics study. J. Phys. Chem. C. **117**, 26179–26189 (2013)

30. Mignon, P., Sodupe, M.: Theoretical study of the adsorption of DNA bases on the acidic external surface of montmorillonite. Phys. Chem. Chem. Phys. **14**, 945–954 (2012)

31. Pantaleone, S., Rimola, A., Sodupe, M.: Canonical, Deprotonated, or Zwitterionic? A computational study on amino acid interaction with the TiO2 (101) anatase surface. J. Phys. Chem. C. **121**, 14156–14165 (2017)

32. Rimola, A., Costa, D., Sodupe, M., Lambert, J.-F., Ugliengo, P.: Silica surface features and their role in the adsorption of biomolecules: computational modeling and experiments. Chem. Rev. **113**, 4216–4313 (2013)

33. Pantaleone, S., Ugliengo, P., Sodupe, M., Rimola, A.: When the surface matters: prebiotic peptide-bond formation on the TiO2 (101) anatase surface through periodic DFT-D2 simulations. Chem. Eur. J. **24**, 16292–16301 (2018)

34. Rimola, A., Fabbiani, M., Sodupe, M., Ugliengo, P., Martra, G.: How does silica catalyze the amide bond formation under dry conditions? Role of specific surface silanol pairs. ACS Catal. **8**, 4558–4568 (2018)

35. Rimola, A., Tosoni, S., Sodupe, M., Ugliengo, P.: Does silica surface catalyse peptide bond formation? New insights from first-principles calculations. ChemPhysChem **7**, 157–163 (2006)

36. Rimola, A., Sodupe, M., Ugliengo, P.: Aluminosilicate surfaces as promoters for peptide bond formation: an assessment of Bernal's hypothesis by ab initio methods. J. Am. Chem. Soc. **129**, 8333–8344 (2007)

37. Mignon, P., Navarro-Ruiz, J., Rimola, A., Sodupe, M.: Nucleobase stacking at clay edges, a favorable interaction for RNA/DNA oligomerization. ACS Earth Sp. Chem. **3**, 1023–1033 (2019)

38. Kresse, G., Hafner, J.: Ab initio molecular dynamcis for liquid metals. Phys. Rev. B. **47**, 558 (1993)

39. Kresse, G., Furthmüller, J., Hafner, J.: Ab initio molecular-dynamics simulation of the liquid-metal–amorphous-semiconductor transition in germanium. Phys. Rev. B. **6**, 558–561 (1996)

40. Kresse, G., Furthmüller, J.: Efficient iterative schemes for ab initio total-energy calculations using a plane-wave basis set. Phys. Rev. B - Condens. Matter Mater. Phys. **54**, 11169–11186 (1996)

41. Kresse, G., Furthmüller, J.: Efficiency of ab-initio total energy calculations for metals and semiconductors using a plane-wave basis set. Comput. Mater. Sci. **6**, 15–50 (1996)

42. Perdew, J.P., Burke, K., Ernzerhof, M.: Generalized gradient approximation made simple. Phys. Rev. Lett. **77**, 3865–3868 (1996)

43. Grimme, S., Antony, J., Ehrlich, S., Krieg, H.: A consistent and accurate ab initio parametrization of density functional dispersion correction (DFT-D) for the 94 elements H-Pu. J. Chem. Phys. **132**, 154104 (2010)

44. Kresse, G., Joubert, D.: From ultrasoft pseudopotentials to the projector augmented - wave method. Phys. Rev. B. **59**, 1758–1775 (1999)

45. Henkelman, G., Jónsson, H.: A dimer method for finding saddle points on high dimensional potential surfaces using only first derivatives. J. Chem. Phys. **111**, 7010–7022 (1999). https://doi.org/10.1063/1.480097

46. Heyden, A., Bell, A.T., Keil, F.J.: Efficient methods for finding transition states in chemical reactions: Comparison of improved dimer method and partitioned rational function optimization method. J. Chem. Phys. **123**, 224010 (2005). https://doi.org/10.1063/1.2104507

47. Kästner, J., Sherwood, P.: Superlinearly converging dimer method for transition state search. J. Chem. Phys. **128**, 014106 (2008). https://doi.org/10.1063/1.2815812

48. Xiao, P., Sheppard, D., Rogal, J., Henkelman, G.: Solid-state dimer method for calculating solid-solid phase transitions. J. Chem. Phys. **140**, 174104 (2014). https://doi.org/10.1063/1.4873437

49. Henkelman, G., Jónsson, H.: Improved tangent estimate in the nudged elastic band method for finding minimum energy paths and saddle points. J. Chem. Phys. **113**, 9978–9985 (2000). https://doi.org/10.1063/1.1323224

50. Henkelman, G., Uberuaga, B.P., Jónsson, H.: Climbing image nudged elastic band method for finding saddle points and minimum energy paths. J. Chem. Phys. **113**, 9901–9904 (2000). https://doi.org/10.1063/1.1329672

51. Sheppard, D., Terrell, R., Henkelman, G.: Optimization methods for finding minimum energy paths. J. Chem. Phys. **128**, 134106 (2008). https://doi.org/10.1063/1.2841941

52. Sheppard, D., Xiao, P., Chemelewski, W., Johnson, D.D., Henkelman, G.: A generalized solid-state nudged elastic band method. J. Chem. Phys. **136**, 074103 (2012). https://doi.org/10.1063/1.3684549

53. Sheppard, D., Henkelman, G.: Paths to which the nudged elastic band converges. J. Comput. Chem. **32**, 1769–1771 (2011). https://doi.org/10.1002/jcc
54. Ugliengo, P., Viterbo, D., Chiari, G.: MOLDRAW: molecular graphics on a personal computer. Zeitschrift fur Krist. - New Cryst. Struct. **207**, 9–23 (1993)
55. POV-Ray: The persistence of vision Raytracer. http://www.povray.org/
56. Pantaleone, S., Salvini, C., Zamirri, L., Signorile, M., Bonino, F., Ugliengo, P.: A quantum mechanical study of dehydrationvs.decarbonylation of formamide catalysed by amorphous silica surfaces. Phys. Chem. Chem. Phys. **22**, 8353–8363 (2020). https://doi.org/10.1039/d0cp00572j
57. Kakumoto, T., Saito, K., Imamura, A.: Thermal decomposition of formamide: Shock tube experiments and ab initio calculations. J. Phys. Chem. **89**, 2286–2291 (1985)
58. Cataldo, F., Lilla, E., Ursini, O., Angelini, G.: TGA-FT-IR study of pyrolysis of poly (hydrogen cyanide) synthesized from thermal decomposition of formamide. Implications in cometary emissions. J. Anal. Appl. Pyrolysis. **87**, 34–44 (2010)
59. Ferus, M., Kubelík, P., Civiš, S.: Laser spark formamide decomposition studied by FT-IR spectroscopy. J. Phys. Chem. A **115**, 12132–12141 (2011)
60. Ferus, M., Michalčíková, R., Shestivská, V., Šponer, J., Šponer, J.E., Civiš, S.: High-energy chemistry of formamide: a simpler way for nucleobase formation. J. Phys. Chem. A **118**, 719–736 (2014)
61. Ferus, M., et al.: High-energy chemistry of formamide: a unified mechanism of nucleobase formation. Proc. Natl. Acad. Sci. U.S.A. **112**, 657–662 (2015)

Gas Adsorption on Graphtriyne Membrane: Impact of the Induction Interaction Term on the Computational Cost

Emília Valença Ferreira de Aragão[1,2]([✉]) [ID], Noelia Faginas-Lago[1] [ID], Yusuf Bramastya Apriliyanto[3] [ID], and Andrea Lombardi[1] [ID]

[1] Dipartimento di Chimica, Biologia e Biotecnologie, Università degli Studi di Perugia, 06123 Perugia, Italy
emilia.dearagao@studenti.unipg.it,
{noelia.faginaslago,andrea.lombardi}@unipg.it
[2] Master-up srl, Via Sicilia 41, 06128 Perugia, Italy
emilia.dearagao@master-up.it
[3] Department of Chemistry, Bogor Agricultural University, Jl Tanjung Kampus IPB Dramaga, 16680 Bogor, Indonesia

Abstract. Graphynes are a family of porous carbon allotropes that are viewed as ideal 2D nanofilters. In this present work, the authors have modified the Improved Lennard-Jones (ILJ) semi-empirical potential used in the previous works by adding the induction term (iind) to define the full interaction. The evaluation of the computational cost was done comparing ILJ vs ILJ-iind and analyzing the adsorption of 1 gas (CO_2) and a small mixture of gases containing CO_2, N_2 and H_2O. The computational time of the different calculations is compared and possible improvements of the potential models are discussed.

Keywords: Molecular dynamics · Empirical potential energy surface · Gaseous separation · Graphtriyne membrane · DL_POLY software

1 Introduction

Recent reports have shown that the concentration of CO_2 in the atmosphere has risen a lot the last few decades [1]. This trend is seen as a consequence of large-scale human activity, whether it involves energy production or manufacturing materials (cement, iron, steel, etc) [2]. The excess of CO_2 in the atmosphere causes many problems, such as the more frequent apparition of toxic blue green algae in lakes during hot seasons and the rising of global temperatures [3]. This is why it is urgent to investigate strategies that can be implemented in order to, if not lower the CO_2 in the atmosphere, at least change the evolution trend and keep the CO_2 concentration at the current level. There are two main ways to do it: either capturing CO_2 in the open air or in the place where it is produced

© Springer Nature Switzerland AG 2020
O. Gervasi et al. (Eds.): ICCSA 2020, LNCS 12255, pp. 513–525, 2020.
https://doi.org/10.1007/978-3-030-58820-5_38

(and later, the captured CO_2 can be converted into methane and other fuels [4–6]). The second approach is generally seen as more efficient and energetically cheaper than the first, but there are some constraints: the flue gas is a mixture of water, carbon dioxide, oxygen and nitrogen molecules [7]. One way to selectively capture CO_2 in flue gas is through the adsorption using porous materials [8–11]. The advantage of this method is that it is relatively cheaper and simpler to implement on existing power plants [2]. In the last few years, a range of porous materials have been evaluated in their ability to selectively capture CO_2: a) nanoporous carbons [12–14], b) zeolites and zeolitic imidazolate frameworks (ZIFs) [15,16], c) metal-organic frameworks (MOFs) [17], d) porous polymer networks (PPNs) or covalent organic frameworks/polymers (COFs/COPs) [18,19], and e) a slurry made of solid adsorbents in a liquid absorbent [20]. In particular, carbon-based membranes have desirable physicochemical properties (e.g. hydrophobic, chemically inert and thermally stable) and are economically suitable and viable for carbon capture and sequestration (CCS) [21,22]. In contrast, MOFs show permeability and good selectivity, but they are not resistant in the presence of water vapor nor in high temperature, which are usually the conditions of CO_2 combustion. What makes both of these classes effective for gas separation is their permeability and their selectivity. In addition, the thinner a membrane is, the more it is permeable, which makes single-layer membranes interesting objects of study in this context [23].

In CCS the range of options of applicable materials is vast, so it is impossible to do the synthesis, the characterization and the evaluation of the ability to selectively capture CO_2 for all of the candidates [24–26]. This is why a preliminary investigation with computational modelling and simulation is crucial for narrowing the selection of molecules. Molecular Dynamics (MD) simulations are a theoretical chemistry method for analyzing the movement of atoms and molecules using potential functions. It can be employed to investigate the structural rearrangement of pure solvents, mixed solutions and combustion processes. [27–32]. In MD, a set of potential functions is called a force field. Currently, a number of options for force fields are available in MD software, such as UFF [33] and AMBER [34]. However, both these force fields are limited in use: when studying a particular system, those force fields do not always have appropriate parameters to describe it since they are too generic. Therefore, the researcher interested in a particular system has to develop or modify parts of the force field, choosing better potential energy functions. The choice of the modifications must be based on experimental and theoretical data available from the literature or prior quantum chemical computations. While the parameterization of force fields is not a simple task, it is crucial for describing a system correctly. Recently, a number of force fields have been developed for evaluating the adsorption of gas molecules on different porous materials like zeolites [35], MOFs [36,37], graphene and its derivatives [38–40] and other polymeric materials [21]. These force fields are used to describe molecular interactions between the gases and the porous layer in a quantitative manner, aiming to give predictions of the adsorption dynamics and transport properties of the gases.

The authors of this paper have been recently involved in the study of γ-graphynes using MD tools, in particular the development of force fields related to gas adsorption in that class of carbon allotropes. [41–45]. γ-graphynes are atomic monolayers where the carbon atoms are arranged in a way that two adjacent hexagons are connected through C-C triple bonds. As nanoporous materials, γ-graphynes are interesting candidates for CCS. It has been reported in the literature that the pores are uniformly distributed and adjustable [46] and that they are not prone to form aggregates due to low dispersion forces. In this work, simulations were performed involving a form of γ-graphyne called graphtriyne and a mixture of $CO_2/N_2/H_2O$ in an attempt to reproduce the chemical environment of flue gases. A challenge the authors have been facing is the considerable increase of the computational time by many times because of a choice made in the potential function to represent the interaction between the gases. In this report, a discussion is hold on how this problem is being confronted.

In the next section of the present work, methods and construction of the present potential energy function are outlined. In Sect. 3 a discussion about the improvements of the code is hold and in Sect. 4 the paper brings up concluding remarks.

2   Methods

The MD simulations were performed in simulation boxes with dimensions 72.210 Å x 62.523 Å x 280.0 Å. Inside each box, a graphtriyne membrane with dimensions 72.210 Å x 62.523 Å was placed. The membrane structure was taken from Ref. [47], and had been previously optimized through periodic DFT calculations. Simulations were performed uniquely at the temperature of 333 K. Part of the simulations were performed with only CO_2 molecules, while the other part involved a $CO_2/N_2/H_2O$ gaseous mixture. This mixture was composed of an equal number of moles of all molecules. For the nitrogen and the carbon dioxide molecules, models taking into account the quadrupole moment were employed. Those models were a three-charge-site N_2 model [48] and a five-charge-site CO_2 model [49]. As for the water molecule, a model taken from Ref. [50] was used. In this model, the charge is distributed in a way that corresponds to the dipole moment of water in the gas phase (1.85 D) [51]. All the details of the geometries of those molecules are shown in Fig. 1. For the MD simulation, the membranes were set as a frozen framework while the gas molecules were set as rigid bodies. The gas molecules were randomly distributed with equal amount into each region of the box. Figure 2 shows the relative sizes of the gas molecules, the graphtryine membrane and the simulation box in a qualitative way.

In a MD simulation, defining correctly the intermolecular forces at play is important for obtaining accurate results. In this system, the intermolecular forces of interest are those between gas molecules and between the gas molecules and the graphtriyne membrane. The intermolecular interaction energy is decomposed in terms of molecule-molecule pair contribution, which are electrostatic and non-electrostatic contributions. The non-electrostatic contributions are measured by

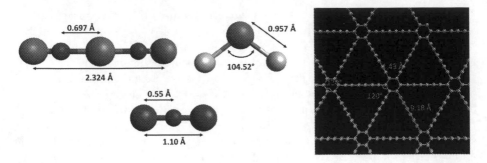

Fig. 1. Structural details of the model representation of carbon dioxide, water and nitrogen molecules and graphtryine membrane. Bond lengths are shown in Å and water's bond angle is displayed in degrees.

taking into consideration the strength of induced dipoles and the average molecular sizes. This can be done by assigning a value of polarizability to the both interacting centers, as shown in Fig. 1. Here, the intermolecular forces were expressed using the Improved Lennard-Jones (ILJ) potential [52–60].

$$V_{ILJ}(r) = \varepsilon \left[\frac{m}{n(r) - m} \left(\frac{r_0}{r} \right)^{n(r)} - \frac{n(r)}{n(r) - m} \left(\frac{r_0}{r} \right)^{m} \right] \tag{1}$$

In Eq. 1, ε, r_0 and m are parameters specific to the molecular pair involved, and r is the distance between the two interacting centers of the same molecular pair. In particular, m assumes the value of 6 for neutral-neutral pairs, 4 for ion-neutral pair and 1 for ion-ion pairs. The first term of the Eq. 1 represents the dependence of the repulsion in function of r, while the second term is the dependence of the long-range attraction in function of r. To modulate the decline of the repulsion and the strength of the attraction in Eq. 1, the $n(r)$ term is employed (Eq. 2).

$$n(r) = \beta + 4.0 \left(\frac{r}{r_0} \right)^2 \tag{2}$$

In Eq. 2, β is a factor that modulates the hardness of the interacting pair [61,62]. This newly introduced parameter is what makes ILJ potential (Eq. 1) able to indirectly take into account some effects of atom clustering, induction and charge transfer and to improve the Lennard-Jones function in the asymptotic region. Nevertheless, while ILJ improves the description of the present system, other effects should be included in the intermolecular potential for enhancing the model of the system. Bearing in mind that charge transfer and induction effects may be important in the interaction between H_2O and CO_2 and N_2 a careful separate characterization of each contribution was performed. Charge transfer effects in the perturbative limit were taken into account indirectly by lowering the value of β as discussed, for instance, in ref. [42]. In addition, induction due to the permanent water dipole was estimated and incorporated explicitly using the following semiempirical asymptotic expression (in meV)

$$V_{ind}(r) = -2140 \sum_{i=1}^{3} \left(\frac{3\cos^2\gamma + 1}{2R_{OW-X_i}} \right) \alpha_i \tag{3}$$

which is applicable because of the small dimension of water with respect to the related intermolecular distances. In Eq. 3, the left coefficient -2140 (that incorporates the square of the water dipole moment value) is given in meV·$\mathring{A}^3$, X_i refers each to the C, N or to the O atoms of CO_2 and N_2, α_i is the polarizability (in $\mathring{A}^3$) associated with them, R_{OW-X_i} is the distance vector between the oxygen atom from the water molecule and C, N or O atoms of CO_2 and N_2 and γ is the angle formed by the R_{OW-X_i} vector and the dipole moment of H_2O.

In the present system, the ILJ potential and the electrostatic interactions cutoff distance was set to 15 Å. The electrostatic interactions were calculated using the Ewald method, present in the DL_POLY 2 code [63]. All molecular dynamics calculations were performed using the DL_POLY 2. The system was studied in the canonical NVT ensemble using the Nose-Hoover thermostat and periodic boundary conditions in all directions. At first, two simulations with only CO_2 were run with using ILJ and ILJ coupled with induction. Both lasted 5.5 ns after 0.5 ns of equilibration period with a time step of 1 fs. It was observed that the simulation with ILJ and induction took about 10 times longer than the calculation where only the ILJ potential was involved. Then eight shorter calculations were run in order to analyze why the simulations with ILJ and induction were many times longer than the simulations employing only the ILJ potential. They all lasted 600 fs after 50 fs of equilibration period and a time step of 1 fs. Half of those calculations involved the box containing only CO_2 and the other part was done in the system with the gas mixture. The simulations were performed before and after a modification in one particular routine.

3   Computational Results

As stated in the introduction, the aim of this work is to compare the time for the different simulations. Table 1 reports the original simulation time before any modification was done to the code. At first the calculations were run with the gas mixture, and it was observed that the total CPU time of the simulation with the ILJ and the induction took about five times longer than the simulation with only the ILJ potential. Then calculations were run with only CO_2 and they were a little bit shorter compared to the ones with the gas mixture, but the simulations with ILJ+induction were still five times longer than with only ILJ. There are no other differences in both ILJ and ILJ+induction options in the code besides the inclusion of the induction part in the latter. This modification was done in a subroutine of the DL_POLY2 code that calculates all the interatomic forces using the verlet neighbour list and is written in the forces_modules.f file. The *forces* subroutine of DL_POLY2 is a piece of code that calls other subroutines to calculate the intermolecular forces for each atom of the system. The subroutines subsequently called by *forces* change if one is using ILJ or ILJ+induction. If the calculation involves only the ILJ potential, the *ewald1* subroutine is called. If the

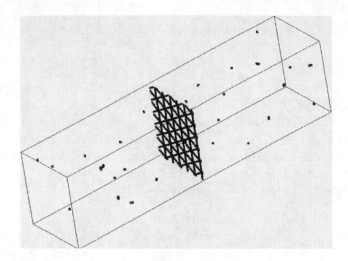

Fig. 2. A screenshot of a simulation box with gaseous mixture of CO_2, N_2 and H_2O. The layer in the middle of the box is the graphtriyne membrane.

simulation involves ILJ+induction, then the *ewaldm1* and *induct* subroutines are called. Both *ewaldm1* and *induct* were written by members of the authors group in order to take the induction into account and are situated in ewald_module.f and coulomb_module.f respectively.

In Table 1, the time is about the same for every simulation when it starts to go through *forces*. After the ewald module is called, the time of the ILJ+induction simulations is already 3.9 times higher than the time at the ILJ simulations. Between the ewald module and the coulomb module other subroutines are called, but there is not much difference in the CPU time. The *induct* subroutine is only used in ILJ+induction simulations and because of it the CPU time becomes five longer than the ILJ simulation. The *forces* subroutine is called for each of the 600 steps of the simulation. The last two lines in Table 1 report that there is not a significant time difference between leaving the forces module at the last step and the end of the simulation. Evidence points to something inside *ewaldm1* and *induct* subroutines that makes the simulation take more time. At the moment this paper is being written, the *ewaldm1* routine is still being analysed. So discussions of the modifications in this subroutine will be left for the future.

The *induct* subroutine was analysed for both the cases with CO_2 and the gas mixture. As said before, the *forces* module is called in every step of the simulation, so 600 times. However, the *induct* subroutine is not called only once in the Forces module. In fact, *induct* is run for every single atom (including pseudoatoms) in the system at every step of the simulation. In the calculation with only CO_2, there are 909 atoms in total, so *induct* is called 545400 times in the simulation. As for the calculation with the gas mixture, the total number of atoms is 972 and the *induct* subroutine is called 583200 times. Calling that sub-

Table 1. Original CPU time for 600 steps

	Simulation with only CO_2		Simulation with $CO_2/H_2O/N_2$	
	ILJ	ILJ +induction	ILJ	ILJ +induction
CPU time at beginning of *forces* subroutine (s)	0.006	0.006	0.007	0.008
CPU time after call of *ewald1/ ewaldm1* subroutine (s)	0.085	0.331	0.097	0.377
CPU time before the first *induct* subroutine call cycle (s)	0.085	0.331	0.097	0.377
CPU time after the last *induct* subroutine call cycle (s)	0.085	0.419	0.097	0.469
CPU time at end of *forces* subroutine after 600 steps(s)	48.881	243.959	56.093	279.606
Total CPU time (s)	48.909	243.987	56.154	279.667

routine one or ten times has reported no difference in the time of the simulation, since this piece of code contains only loops and arithmetic operations. However, when such subroutine is called hundreds of thousands of times in a simulation, it begins to heavily impact in the full CPU time. Moreover, a further analysis of the coulomb module has shown that calling the routine for most of the atoms in the system is useless: there are if statements inside *induct* that only applies to carbon and oxygen atoms of CO_2, oxygen atoms of water and nitrogen atoms of N_2. The proposed solution for turning this task less time consuming was to modify the *forces* subroutine in order to only call *induct* when treating those particular atoms. In the code, if statements were written to make the call of *induct* conditional: *if* the atom being treated at the moment was O from H_2O or C from CO_2, the *induct* subroutine was called. *Else if* the atom was O from CO_2 or N from N_2, the *induct* subroutine was called. No *else* statement was made.

Table 2 reports the result of this change in the code. Calculations were run again for ILJ and ILJ+induction, with CO_2 and the gas mixture. There were some fluctuations in the simulation times, but the most important is to look at the values of the CPU time after the last *induct* call cycle. The difference with it and the CPU time before the *induct* subroutine is less than 0.01 s in both CO_2 and the gas mixture simulations. Total CPU time for ILJ+induction is now around 4 times the Total CPU time of ILJ simulations. When running longer calculations with ILJ+induction, for instance a simulation with 6 million steps, it is expected that the modification made on *induct* will contribute to spare days of computer time.

In this work, the simulation running time of 600 fs is not long enough for estimating the improvement in the forces results. A simulation on the order of nanoseconds or millions steps is more adequate. In the current version of the code, a simulation of 6 million steps lasts around 20 days when using

ILJ+induction, and some technical problems have happened to the cluster during the calculation. Further improvements are needed to be made to the code in order to have a faster running simulation using ILJ+induction, therefore the discussion on the improvement of the forces results will be made in future works.

Table 2. CPU time for 600 steps after modification in the *Forces* module

	Simulation with only CO_2		Simulation with $CO_2/H_2O/N_2$	
	ILJ	ILJ +induction	ILJ	ILJ +induction
CPU time at beginning of *forces* subroutine (s)	0.006	0.006	0.008	0.007
CPU time after call of *ewald1/ ewaldm1* subroutine (s)	0.086	0.321	0.098	0.379
CPU time before the first *induct* subroutine call cycle (s)	0.086	0.321	0.098	0.379
CPU time after the last *induct* subroutine call cycle (s)	0.086	0.326	0.098	0.386
CPU time at end of *forces* subroutine after 600 steps(s)	49.123	194.896	57.396	236.203
Total CPU time (s)	49.154	194.927	57.470	236.265

4   Conclusions

A small modification in part of the code has had a considerable impact on the total simulation time. Future modifications in the *ewaldm1* subroutine are expected to diminish CPU time even further for calculations with ILJ and induction potentials. While the time will not be the same as simulations with only the ILJ potential, there is at least hope that it will not be 5 or 10 times longer. That way, future simulations with even larger quantities of gas in the box will be possible, and the system will be described better than in simulations with only ILJ.

Acknowledgements. This project has received funding from the European Union's Horizon 2020 research and innovation programme under the Marie Skłodowska Curie grant agreement No 811312 for the project "Astro-Chemical Origins" (ACO). E. V. F. A thanks the Herla Project (http://hscw.herla.unipg.it) - Università degli Studi di Perugia for allocated computing time. N. F.-L and A. L. thanks MIUR and the University of Perugia for the financial support of the AMIS project through the "Dipartimenti di Eccellenza" programme. N. F.-L and A. L. also acknowledges the Fondo Ricerca di Base 2017 (RICBASE2017BALUCANI) del Dipartimento di Chimica, Biologia e Biotecnologie della Università di Perugia for financial support. A. L. acknowledges financial support from MIUR PRIN 2015 (contract 2015F59J3R 002).

References

1. United States Environmental Protection Agency (US EPA): Climate Change Indicators in the United States: Global Greenhouse Gas Emissions (2016). http://www.epa.gov/climate-indicators. Accessed Feb 2019
2. Smit, B.: Carbon capture and storage: introductory lecture. Faraday Discuss. **192**, 9–25 (2016). https://doi.org/10.1039/C6FD00148C
3. World Resources Institute (WRI): Climate Analysis Indicators Tool (CAIT) 2.0: WRI's climate data explorer. http://cait.wri.org. Accessed 28 Feb 2019
4. Falcinelli, S., et al.: Methane production by CO_2 hydrogenation reaction with and without solid phase catalysis. Fuel **209**, 802–811 (2017). https://doi.org/10.1016/j.fuel.2017.07.109
5. Heijkers, S., Martini, L.M., Dilecce, G., Tosi, P., Bogaerts, A.: Nanosecond pulsed discharge for CO_2 conversion: kinetic modeling to elucidate the chemistry and improve the performance. J. Phys. Chem. C **123**(19), 12104–12116 (2019). https://doi.org/10.1021/acs.jpcc.9b01543
6. Falcinelli, S.: Fuel production from waste CO_2 using renewable energies. Catal. Today **348**, 95–101 (2020). https://doi.org/10.1016/j.cattod.2019.08.041
7. Song, C., et al.: Tri-reforming of methane over Ni catalysts for CO_2 conversion to Syngas with desired H_2/CO ratios using flue gas of power plants without CO_2 separation. In: Carbon Dioxide Utilization for Global Sustainability, Studies in Surface Science and Catalysis, vol. 153, pp. 315–322. Elsevier (2004). https://doi.org/10.1016/S0167-2991(04)80270-2
8. Huck, J.M., et al.: Evaluating different classes of porous materials for carbon capture. Energy Environ. Sci. **7**, 4132–4146 (2014). https://doi.org/10.1039/C4EE02636E
9. Bui, M., et al.: Carbon capture and storage (CCS): the way forward. Energy Environ. Sci. **11**, 1062–1176 (2018). https://doi.org/10.1039/C7EE02342A
10. Li, J.R., et al.: Porous materials with pre-designed single-molecule traps for CO_2 selective adsorption. Nat. Commun. **4**, 1538 (2014). https://doi.org/10.1038/ncomms2552
11. Celiberto, R., et al.: Atomic and molecular data for spacecraft re-entry plasmas. Plasma Sources Sci. Technol. **25**(3), 033004 (2016)
12. Srinivas, G., Krungleviciute, V., Guo, Z.X., Yildirim, T.: Exceptional CO_2 capture in a hierarchically porous carbon with simultaneous high surface area and pore volume. Energy Environ. Sci. **7**, 335–342 (2014). https://doi.org/10.1039/C3EE42918K
13. Ganesan, A., Shaijumon, M.: Activated graphene-derived porous carbon with exceptional gas adsorption properties. Microporous Mesoporous Mater. **220**, 21–27 (2015). https://doi.org/10.1016/j.micromeso.2015.08.021
14. Ghosh, S., Sevilla, M., Fuertes, A.B., Andreoli, E., Ho, J., Barron, A.R.: Defining a performance map of porous carbon sorbents for high-pressure carbon dioxide uptake and carbon dioxide-methane selectivity. J. Mater. Chem. A **4**, 14739–14751 (2016). https://doi.org/10.1039/C6TA04936B
15. Kim, J., Lin, L.C., Swisher, J.A., Haranczyk, M., Smit, B.: Predicting large CO_2 adsorption in aluminosilicate zeolites for postcombustion carbon dioxide capture. J. Am. Chem. Soc. **134**(46), 18940–18943 (2012). https://doi.org/10.1021/ja309818u
16. Liu, B., Smit, B.: Molecular simulation studies of separation of CO_2/N_2, CO_2/CH_4, and CH_4/N_2 by ZIFs. J. Phys. Chem. C **114**(18), 8515–8522 (2010). https://doi.org/10.1021/jp101531m

17. Lin, L.C., et al.: Understanding CO_2 dynamics in metal-organic frameworks with open metal sites. Angew. Chem. Int. Ed. **52**(16), 4410–4413 (2013). https://doi.org/10.1002/anie.201300446
18. Schrier, J.: Carbon dioxide separation with a two-dimensional polymer membrane. ACS Appl. Mater. Interfaces **4**(7), 3745–3752 (2012). https://doi.org/10.1021/am300867d
19. Xiang, Z., et al.: Systematic tuning and multifunctionalization of covalent organic polymers for enhanced carbon capture. J. Am. Chem. Soc. **137**(41), 13301–13307 (2015). https://doi.org/10.1021/jacs.5b06266
20. Liu, H., et al.: A hybrid absorption-adsorption method to efficiently capture carbon. Nat. Commun. **5**, 5147 (2014). https://doi.org/10.1038/ncomms6147
21. DuBay, K.H., Hall, M.L., Hughes, T.F., Wu, C., Reichman, D.R., Friesner, R.A.: Accurate force field development for modeling conjugated polymers. J. Chem. Theory Comput. **8**(11), 4556–4569 (2012). https://doi.org/10.1021/ct300175w
22. Bartolomei, M., Carmona-Novillo, E., Giorgi, G.: First principles investigation of hydrogen physical adsorption on graphynes' layers. Carbon **95**, 1076–1081 (2015). https://doi.org/10.1016/j.carbon.2015.08.118
23. Du, H., Li, J., Zhang, J., Su, G., Li, X., Zhao, Y.: Separation of hydrogen and nitrogen gases with porous graphene membrane. J. Phys. Chem. C **115**(47), 23261–23266 (2011). https://doi.org/10.1021/jp206258u
24. Lombardi, A., Lago, N.F., Laganà, A., Pirani, F., Falcinelli, S.: A bond-bond portable approach to intermolecular interactions: simulations for n-methylacetamide and carbon dioxide dimers. In: Murgante, B., et al. (eds.) ICCSA 2012. LNCS, vol. 7333, pp. 387–400. Springer, Heidelberg (2012). https://doi.org/10.1007/978-3-642-31125-3_30
25. Lombardi, A., Faginas-Lago, N., Pacifici, L., Costantini, A.: Modeling of energy transfer from vibrationally excited CO_2 molecules: cross sections and probabilities for kinetic modeling of atmospheres, flows, and plasmas. J. Phys. Chem. A **117**(45), 11430–11440 (2013). https://doi.org/10.1021/jp408522m
26. Falcinelli, S., et al.: Modeling the intermolecular interactions and characterization of the dynamics of collisional autoionization processes. In: Murgante, B., et al. (eds.) ICCSA 2013. LNCS, vol. 7971, pp. 69–83. Springer, Heidelberg (2013). https://doi.org/10.1007/978-3-642-39637-3_6
27. Faginas-Lago, N., Laganà, A., Gargano, R., Barreto, P.: On the semiclassical initial value calculation of thermal rate coefficients for the N + N_2 reaction. J. Chem. Phys. **125**(11), 114311 (2006). https://doi.org/10.1063/1.2345363
28. Laganà, A., Faginas-Lago, N., Rampino, S., Huarte-Larrañaga, F., García, E.: Thermal rate coefficients in collinear versus bent transition state reactions: the N + N_2 case study. Phys. Scr. **78**(5), 058116 (2008). https://doi.org/10.1088/0031-8949/78/05/058116
29. Rampino, S., Faginas-Lago, N., Laganà, A., Huarte-Larrañaga, F.: An extension of the grid empowered molecular simulator to quantum reactive scattering. J. Comput. Chem. **33**(6), 708–714 (2012). https://doi.org/10.1002/jcc.22878
30. Laganà, A., Crocchianti, S., Faginas-Lago, N., Pacifici, L., Ferraro, G.: A nonorthogonal coordinate approach to atom-diatom parallel reactive scattering calculations. Collect. Czech. Chem. Commun. **68**(2), 307–330 (2003). https://doi.org/10.1135/cccc20030307
31. Faginas-Lago, N., Lombardi, A., Pacifici, L., Costantini, A.: Design and implementation of a Grid application for direct calculations of reactive rates. Comput. Theor. Chem. **1022**, 103–107 (2013). https://doi.org/10.1016/j.comptc.2013.08.014

32. Lombardi, A., Faginas-Lago, N., Laganà, A.: Grid calculation tools for massive applications of collision dynamics simulations: carbon dioxide energy transfer. In: Murgante, B., et al. (eds.) ICCSA 2014. LNCS, vol. 8579, pp. 627–639. Springer, Cham (2014). https://doi.org/10.1007/978-3-319-09144-0_43

33. Rappe, A.K., Casewit, C.J., Colwell, K.S., Goddard, W.A., Skiff, W.M.: UFF, a full periodic table force field for molecular mechanics and molecular dynamics simulations. J. Am. Chem. Soc. **114**(25), 10024–10035 (1992). https://doi.org/10.1021/ja00051a040

34. Pearlman, D., et al.: AMBER. A package of computer-programs for applying molecular mechanics, normal-mode analysis, molecular-dynamics and free-energy calculations to simulate the structural and energetic properties of molecules. Compute. Phys. Commun. **91**, 1–41 (1995). https://doi.org/10.1016/0010-4655(95)00041-D

35. Lim, J.R., Yang, C.T., Kim, J., Lin, L.C.: Transferability of CO_2 force fields for prediction of adsorption properties in all-silica zeolites. J. Phys. Chem. C **122**(20), 10892–10903 (2018). https://doi.org/10.1021/acs.jpcc.8b02208

36. Boyd, P.G., Moosavi, S.M., Witman, M., Smit, B.: Force-field prediction of materials properties in metal-organic frameworks. J. Phys. Chem. Lett. **8**(2), 357–363 (2017). https://doi.org/10.1021/acs.jpclett.6b02532

37. Lin, L.C., Lee, K., Gagliardi, L., Neaton, J.B., Smit, B.: Force-field development from electronic structure calculations with periodic boundary conditions: applications to gaseous adsorption and transport in metal-organic frameworks. J. Chem. Theory Comput. **10**(4), 1477–1488 (2014). https://doi.org/10.1021/ct500094w

38. Vekeman, J., García Cuesta, I., Faginas-Lago, N., Wilson, J., Sánchez-Marín, J., Sánchez de Merás, A.: Potential models for the simulation of methane adsorption on graphene: development and CCSD(T) benchmarks. Phys. Chem. Chem. Phys. (18), 25518–25530 (2018). https://doi.org/10.1039/C8CP03652G

39. Lombardi, A., Faginas-Lago, N., Pacifici, L., Grossi, G.: Energy transfer upon collision of selectively excited CO_2 molecules: state-to-state cross sections and probabilities for modeling of atmospheres and gaseous flows. J. Chem. Phys. **143**(3), 034307 (2015). https://doi.org/10.1063/1.4926880

40. Faginas-Lago, N., Albertí, M., Costantini, A., Laganà, A., Lombardi, A., Pacifici, L.: An innovative synergistic grid approach to the computational study of protein aggregation mechanisms. J. Mol. Model. **20**(7), 1–9 (2014). https://doi.org/10.1007/s00894-014-2226-4

41. Faginas-Lago, N., Huarte-Larrañaga, F., Laganà, A.: Full dimensional quantum versus semiclassical reactivity for the bent transition state reaction N + N_2. Chem. Phys. Lett. **464**(4–6), 249–255 (2008). https://doi.org/10.1016/j.cplett.2008.09.008

42. Apriliyanto, Y.B., et al.: Nanostructure selectivity for molecular adsorption and separation: the case of graphyne layers. J. Phys. Chem. C **122**(28), 16195–16208 (2018). https://doi.org/10.1021/acs.jpcc.8b04960

43. Faginas-Lago, N., Yeni, D., Huarte, F., Wang, Y., Alcamí, M., Martin, F.: Adsorption of hydrogen molecules on carbon nanotubes using quantum chemistry and molecular dynamics. J. Phys. Chem. A **120**(32), 6451–6458 (2016). https://doi.org/10.1021/acs.jpca.5b12574

44. Yeamin, M.B., Faginas-Lago, N., Albertí, M., García Cuesta, I., Sánchez-Marín, J., Sánchez de Merás, A.: Multi-scale theoretical investigation of molecular hydrogen adsorption over graphene: coronene as a case study. RSC Adv. **4**, 54447–54453 (2014). https://doi.org/10.1039/C4RA08487J

45. Faginas-Lago, N., Apriliyanto, Y.B., Lombardi, A.: Molecular simulations of $CO_2/N_2/H_2O$ gaseous mixture separation in graphtriyne membrane. In: Misra, S., et al. (eds.) ICCSA 2019. LNCS, vol. 11624, pp. 374–387. Springer, Cham (2019). https://doi.org/10.1007/978-3-030-24311-1_27

46. James, A., et al.: Graphynes: indispensable nanoporous architectures in carbon flatland. RSC Adv. **8**, 22998–23018 (2018). https://doi.org/10.1039/C8RA03715A

47. Bartolomei, M., Giorgi, G.: A novel nanoporous graphite based on graphynes: first-principles structure and carbon dioxide preferential physisorption. ACS Appl. Mater. Interfaces **8**(41), 27996–28003 (2016). https://doi.org/10.1021/acsami.6b08743

48. Lombardi, A., Pirani, F., Laganà, A., Bartolomei, M.: Energy transfer dynamics and kinetics of elementary processes (promoted) by gas-phase CO_2-N_2 collisions: selectivity control by the anisotropy of the interaction. J. Comput. Chem. **37**(16), 1463–1475 (2016). https://doi.org/10.1002/jcc.24359

49. Bartolomei, M., Pirani, F., Laganà, A., Lombardi, A.: A full dimensional grid empowered simulation of the CO_2 + CO_2 processes. J. Comput. Chem. **33**(22), 1806–1819 (2012). https://doi.org/10.1002/jcc.23010

50. Albertí, M., Aguilar, A., Cappelletti, D., Laganà, A., Pirani, F.: On the development of an effective model potential to describe water interaction in neutral and ionic clusters. Int. J. Mass Spectrom. **280**, 50–56 (2009). https://doi.org/10.1016/j.ijms.2008.07.018

51. Albertí, M., Pirani, F., Laganà, A.: Carbon dioxide clathrate hydrates: selective role of intermolecular interactions and action of the SDS catalyst. J. Phys. Chem. A **117**(32), 6991–7000 (2013). https://doi.org/10.1021/jp3126158

52. Pirani, P., Brizi, S., Roncaratti, L., Casavecchia, P., Cappelletti, D., Vecchiocattivi, F.: Beyond the lennard-jones model: a simple and accurate potential function probed by high resolution scattering data useful for molecular dynamics simulations. Phys. Chem. Chem. Phys. **10**, 5489–5503 (2008). https://doi.org/10.1039/B808524B

53. Lombardi, A., Laganà, A., Pirani, F., Palazzetti, F., Lago, N.F.: Carbon oxides in gas flows and earth and planetary atmospheres: state-to-state simulations of energy transfer and dissociation reactions. In: Murgante, B., et al. (eds.) ICCSA 2013. LNCS, vol. 7972, pp. 17–31. Springer, Heidelberg (2013). https://doi.org/10.1007/978-3-642-39643-4_2

54. Lago, N.F., Albertí, M., Laganà, A., Lombardi, A., Pacifici, L., Costantini, A.: The molecular stirrer catalytic effect in methane ice formation. In: Murgante, B., et al. (eds.) ICCSA 2014. LNCS, vol. 8579, pp. 585–600. Springer, Cham (2014). https://doi.org/10.1007/978-3-319-09144-0_40

55. Faginas Lago, N., Albertí, M., Lombardi, A., Pirani, F.: A force field for acetone: the transition from small clusters to liquid phase investigated by molecular dynamics simulations. Theoret. Chem. Acc. **135**(7), 1–9 (2016). https://doi.org/10.1007/s00214-016-1914-9

56. Faginas-Lago, N., Albertí, M., Laganà, A., Lombardi, A.: Ion-water cluster molecular dynamics using a semiempirical intermolecular potential. In: Gervasi, O., et al. (eds.) ICCSA 2015. LNCS, vol. 9156, pp. 355–370. Springer, Cham (2015). https://doi.org/10.1007/978-3-319-21407-8_26

57. Lago, N.F., Albertí, M., Laganà, A., Lombardi, A.: Water $(H_2O)_m$ or Benzene $(C_6H_6)_n$ Aggregates to Solvate the K^+? In: Murgante, B., et al. (eds.) ICCSA 2013. LNCS, vol. 7971, pp. 1–15. Springer, Heidelberg (2013). https://doi.org/10.1007/978-3-642-39637-3_1

58. Faginas-Lago, N., Lombardi, A., Albertí, M., Grossi, G.: Accurate analytic inter-molecular potential for the simulation of Na^+ and K^+ ion hydration in liquid water. J. Mol. Liq. **204**, 192–197 (2015). https://doi.org/10.1016/j.molliq.2015.01.029

59. Lombardi, A., Faginas-Lago, N., Gaia, G., Federico, P., Aquilanti, V.: Collisional energy exchange in CO_2–N_2 gaseous mixtures. In: Gervasi, O., et al. (eds.) ICCSA 2016. LNCS, vol. 9786, pp. 246–257. Springer, Cham (2016). https://doi.org/10.1007/978-3-319-42085-1_19

60. Albertí, M., Faginas-Lago, N.: Ion size influence on the Ar solvation shells of $M^+C_6F_6$ clusters (M = Na, K, Rb, Cs). J. Phys. Chem. A **116**(12), 3094–3102 (2012). https://doi.org/10.1021/jp300156k

61. Pirani, F., Albertí, M., Castro, A., Moix Teixidor, M., Cappelletti, D.: Atom-bond pairwise additive representation for intermolecular potential energy surfaces. Chem. Phys. Lett. **394**(1–3), 37–44 (2004). https://doi.org/10.1016/j.cplett.2004.06.100

62. Pacifici, L., Verdicchio, M., Faginas-Lago, N., Lombardi, A., Costantini, A.: A high-level ab initio study of the $N_2 + N_2$ reaction channel. J. Comput. Chem. **34**(31), 2668–2676 (2013). https://doi.org/10.1002/jcc.23415

63. Smith, W., Yong, C., Rodger, P.: DL_POLY: application to molecularsimulation. Mol. Simul. **28**(5), 385–471 (2002).https://doi.org/10.1080/08927020290018769. http://www.cse.clrc.ac.uk/ccg/software/DL_POLY/index.shtm

Improvements to the G-Lorep Federation of Learning Object Repositories

Federico Sabbatini, Sergio Tasso$^{(\boxtimes)}$, Simonetta Pallottelli, and Osvaldo Gervasi

Department of Mathematics and Computer Science,
University of Perugia, via Vanvitelli 1, 06123 Perugia, Italy
federicosabbatini96@gmail.com,
{sergio.tasso,simonetta.pallottelli,osvaldo.gervasi}@unipg.it

Abstract. The G-Lorep project of the European Chemistry Thematic Network (ECTN), based on a federation of distributed repositories of Molecular Science Learning Objects, leverages at present a "hybrid" centralized/distributed architecture in which the central node hosts a shared database. The shared database deals only with the task of managing metadata in order to synchronize the information made available to the federation members at regular time intervals. To avoid security problems and reach a better code updating, the project has been migrated from *Drupal* CMS to *Laravel* framework. All modules have been written from the start, also a REST API server used as interface to the shared database is implemented and related performances are evaluated.

Keywords: Cloud · Distributed systems · Learning objects · Repositories · Security · Synchronization

1 Introduction

G-Lorep [1] is a technology aimed at facilitating the sharing of *Learning Objects* (LOs) among distributed repositories (whose typical scheme is illustrated in Fig. 1). For this reason G-Lorep leverages the assembling of a federation of repositories among the members of a scientific community wishing to share their LOs and to offer them to other community members for further development. Each federate in its domain has the same web application with its own local database in order to make users feel, even visually, to be using the same environment even when they are operating on a different federate.

The network structure adopted by G-Lorep is hybrid. This permits each website to work stand-alone like (with no need to communicate with the other servers) and to use a central database to get information on the LOs made available on the network. Accordingly, each federate can contact autonomously the central node whose tasks are only to distribute metadata and to allow each member of the federation to update the learning objects through a simple operation of synchronization occurring at regular time intervals [2]. In particular, when an "update" request is received, the member refreshes its own database adding the

O. Gervasi et al. (Eds.): ICCSA 2020, LNCS 12255, pp. 526–537, 2020.
https://doi.org/10.1007/978-3-030-58820-5_39

new data received, creating an image of the LO equal to the original one and providing a link to the federate of origin [3,4].

In the G-Lorep initial implementation the central node was placed on a server physically located inside the University of Perugia. This, while guaranteeing a more direct control of the system, was reducing its fault tolerance in the case of Internet communication break-up causing miscommunication among the federates. An additional weakness of the initial implementation was the impossibility of guaranteeing that good practices of security (like the adoption of *HTTPS*, the automatic updating of *Drupal* [13] and Linux, the configuring of *SSH* and Firewall) would be adopted.

Accordingly, the paper focuses on the full restyling of the G-Lorep obtained by migrating from *Drupal* CMS to *Laravel* [12] framework as discussed in Sect. 2 where the new G-Lorep federate implementation is described and Sect. 3 where the new approach to shared database through a REST API server is detailed. In Sect. 4 is described how G-Lorep will be distributed through a interactive script that installs *Docker* [14] images, finally in Sect. 5 some conclusions are drawn and some directions of related future work are outlined.

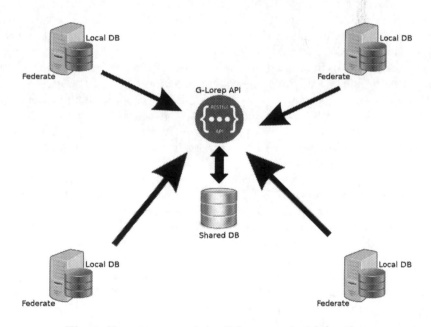

Fig. 1. New structure of the G-Lorep project federation

2   G-Lorep Migration to *Laravel*

2.1   How G-Lorep Was Structured

The distribution of the old version of G-Lorep was structured in three main components:

- the shared database which aims to store only metadata of each learning object;
- the *php_socket_io* located in each federate machine whose task is performing the synchronization between his host and the shared database;
- the latest *Drupal* 7 version with installed modules created to manipulate learning objects.

In each of these components there are security problems if we have a look to the future. *Drupal* 7 will be abandoned in november 2021, so this can cause some entry points for future attacks; furthermore actually there is not an automatic update system, so each webmaster should perform updates of his/her own platform; moreover it is easy to think *Drupal* being a really famous CMS put it at the center of interests of attackers that mass hacking websites created with CMS exploiting feature that often are not used. In the case of G-Lorep the unique functions used are modules and user management. Looking in this way there are no vantages in keeping updated G-Lorep project over this platform. So it has been decided to migrate the system to *Laravel*, one of the most famous PHP frameworks. It permits to easily maintain the code, keeping it more safe, because it will be harder to become a target of attackers. Furthermore, adding new features taking advantage of powerful functions of *Laravel* will be easier. During this migration new features have been implemented and they will be described in the next subsection.

If an attacker gains access to a federate, the *php_socket_io* daemon and shared database can be a security issue. The daemon can be considered like a client of the shared database, in fact it allows the direct access to the database and normally, via its software permits, each federate can manipulate its own learning objects over the shared database. But if an attacker edits the deamon or steals database credentials, he/she can full manipulate the shared database, and this is a serious problem. Taking advantage of the cronjob system directly managed via *Laravel* and creating a RESTFUL API server that acts like an interface to the shared database one can protect the central node from malicious attackers. This synchronization system will be described in the next section.

2.2   The New G-Lorep

The principal difference between old and new G-Lorep it's its structure. In *Drupal* modules it is needed to handle all parts of platform from scratch, from the database to the query functions, from the data manipulation to their visualization via HTML. In *Laravel* these phases are well separated following the MVC (**M**odel **V**iew **C**ontroller) pattern (Fig. 2).

Migrations and Models are the main features of *Laravel*. With migrations one can create, drop and alter existing tables of a database without writing SQL commands. Models work like an interface to the database, using them you can build customized queries which can be performed many times. For example an automatic `join` between two or more tables can be handled just calling a specific function declared in one of their classes. Furthermore *Laravel* has many predefined functions like `TableName::find($id)`, which returns a single row filtered by its primary key (in pure PHP is needed to write full SQL query, then run that, finally extract the first row from the returned array if its result is not null) or `TableName::firstOrCreate`, which returns a record matching specific conditions, and if it does not exist it will be created than returned.

In G-Lorep a massive usage of these features have been adopted to perform `joins` between a table containing the list of IDs of all learning objects (and others information) and relative table, that can be local learning objects or other federate learning objects. Furthermore, adding future features to the G-Lorep project will be really easy because using Migrations and Models it is just needed to edit their functions instead of navigating full website code searching where to apply modifications.

Routes and Middlewares keep coding funny and at the same time secure. Using routes you can communicate to a server. When a client is visiting a certain specific URL, the server must be up and running. Building structured routes is easy, because you can create groups to aggregate them, for example all URIs like `/learning_object/edit`, `/learning_object/show` and `/learning_object/new` can be merged into a group called `/learning_object/` and `edit`, `show` and `new` can be treated like its children; it is just like a switch that distributes packages between hosts of a network instead of linking each device directly to the router.

With middlewares, rules (and other operations) to access a certain route are described and applied without efforts. For example a programmer can forget to check if a user is logged or not to let him/her access a certain resource. Using middleware the rule is matched before the function is called, in this way the programmer does not need to bother himself/herself checking anything. Definitively middlewares can be applied to whole groups, for example can be created a middleware that checks if a visitor is a logged user to the whole group `/your_profile/` inheriting it to its children `show` and `edit` too.

In G-Lorep a huge usage of a middleware which checks if a user is logged as author has been adopted because many functions related to learning objects like downloading of attachments or creation of new LOs are permitted only to authorized users.

Controllers are the *heart* of *Laravel* because functions are written inside them. They are called via routes, then a specified function is executed; with a function you can run queries via Models or Eloquent query builder of *Laravel*, then they return results like JSON, HTML, or better **views**. Using the `with()` function a controller can pass not only results of queries, but any kind of variable like informative messages to the called view. Then the view will have the variable declared by itself without the need to call any other function.

Views are returned from controller, they are pieces of HTML (and PHP code). In *Laravel* they are written using *Blade* templates. *Blade* is the simple, yet powerful templating engine provided with *Laravel*. Unlike other popular PHP templating engines, *Blade* does not restrict the programmer from using plain PHP code in the views. In fact, all *Blade* views are compiled into plain PHP code and cached until they are modified, meaning *Blade* adds essentially zero overhead to the application. In this way you can add generated variable from controller into the HTML without writing PHP code or worry about Cross Site Scripting (XSS) attacks. Moreover other PHP, JavaScript or HTML files can be incorporated into a view just using few characters, indeed you can print information, error or warning messages to the user without writing the code every time. A programmer can create and import a different *Blade* file containing code checking if a passed variable through controller is set and in that case it prints nice looking HTML messages.

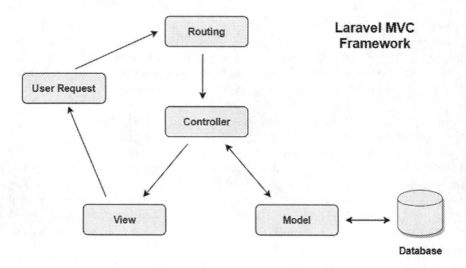

Fig. 2. *Laravel* model view controller representation

2.3   New Features in G-Lorep

During the migration many features have been directly implemented in the new platform. These features are added to the existing ones of the old version. In the old version of G-Lorep learning objects are stored following standards of Learning Object Metadata (IEEE LOM), but in this version many information are automatically compiled. For example, in the old version through writing title and description of a LO you could already obtain a relative suggested category based on provided terms thanks to *Taxonomy Assistant* [5]. In the new version this mechanism has been improved to make it more accurate (Fig. 3). Moreover it has been used to automatically suggest synonyms words for the description and keywords to obtaining a best cataloging of the learning object that joins the already existing differentiation by category [6].

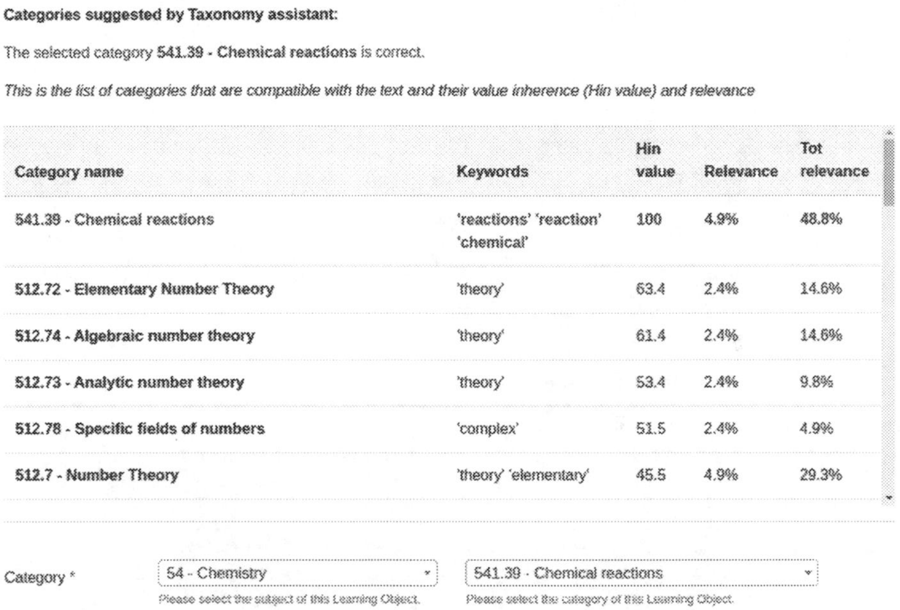

Categories suggested by Taxonomy assistant:

The selected category **541.39 - Chemical reactions** is correct.

This is the list of categories that are compatible with the text and their value inherence (Hin value) and relevance

Category name	Keywords	Hin value	Relevance	Tot relevance
541.39 - Chemical reactions	'reactions' 'reaction' 'chemical'	100	4.9%	48.8%
512.72 - Elementary Number Theory	'theory'	63.4	2.4%	14.6%
512.74 - Algebraic number theory	'theory'	61.4	2.4%	14.6%
512.73 - Analytic number theory	'theory'	53.4	2.4%	9.8%
512.78 - Specific fields of numbers	'complex'	51.5	2.4%	4.9%
512.7 - Number Theory	'theory' 'elementary'	45.5	4.9%	29.3%

Category * | 54 - Chemistry ▾ | | 541.39 - Chemical reactions ▾ |

Please select the subject of this Learning Object.   Please select the category of this Learning Object.

Fig. 3. New layout of *Taxonomy Assistant*

Computer Science. G-Lorep was initially designed to catalogue only Chemical learning objects, later it was extended to manage learning objects of other scientific subjects too, so Mathematics categories were added to the platform. From now on it will include Computer Science, too.

Management of Attachments. In G-Lorep *Drupal* version, if someone knew the structure of the website he/she could download attachments without the need to authenticate himself/herself. In the new version files are provided via a function instead of directly provide their URL. Furthermore files are renamed with a secret random string keeping them safe from being downloaded without using the required function, that is protected via the middleware for the authentication and authorization. In this way files are inaccessible and can be downloaded only from authorized logged users calling a certain route with a middleware.

Links as Attachment. Before the migrations you could not directly include a link as attachment. For example, if an author would like to add a not listed YouTube video as LO, he/she should have to create a `txt` file, write inside the YouTube link, then add this file as attachment to the object. Later a reader of that learning object should open the attachment in a tab of the browser, than copy and paste the link in a new tab. It was just a workaround to accomplish that, but now it is directly implemented permitting to give a name to a certain URL, too.

New Management of Keywords. As explained before, keywords are now automatically generated. A user can create a learning object adding suggested keywords or typing new ones by himself/herself. Most used are directly showed like a popup in the input box. Thanks to this feature, now keywords are effectively used, and the search engine has been improved adding a research via keywords, in addition to the already existent search via category, title, description, authors and other metadata.

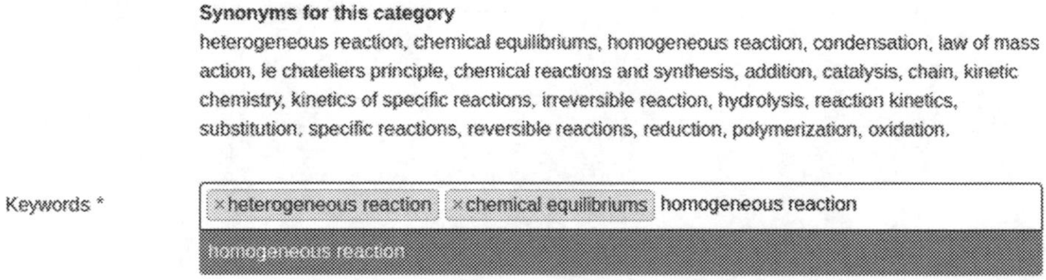

Synonyms for this category
heterogeneous reaction, chemical equilibriums, homogeneous reaction, condensation, law of mass action, le chateliers principle, chemical reactions and synthesis, addition, catalysis, chain, kinetic chemistry, kinetics of specific reactions, irreversible reaction, hydrolysis, reaction kinetics, substitution, specific reactions, reversible reactions, reduction, polymerization, oxidation.

Keywords *   ×heterogeneous reaction   ×chemical equilibriums   homogeneous reaction

homogeneous reaction

Fig. 4. New management of keywords

Visible Statistics for All Users. Now statistics of usage of learning objects, like views of the single LO or clicks and downloads of their attachments are fully logged and showed to users. Thanks to this feature tabs can be added in the learning object feed that shows the most interacted objects ordering them by views or interactions to their attachments.

Multilingual. A system that manages localization of the federate has been provided in the new platform. Now a client can select the wished language for the navigation of the website. This also allows to keep the editing of texts easy, because there is no need for a programmer to search the view or the controller that uses a certain text (maybe it has more occurrences too) and edit it, just apply modifications to localization files is now required.

Maintaining G-Lorep Updated into All the Federation. Finally, with this last but not least feature all federates website can be kept updated without concerning each webmaster to manually update it. It is just necessary debugging a new version into a development environment, then the updating to the new version of G-Lorep will be automatically propagated to all the networks of federation without paying attention to eventual incompatibility between security updates and installed modules for managing learning objects like in the old G-Lorep based on *Drupal.*

3 The New Architecture of G-Lorep Synchronization

At regular interval of time a synchronization between each federate and shared database is performed. Using this hybrid approach, if the shared database goes down only the synchronization between federates is compromised, still permitting the navigation of every single federate, visualization of foreign LOs of previous synchronizations will be still accessible. Similarly if a federate goes offline only the access to its attachments and the synchronization between its learning objects and the rest of federation is temporary compromised. Then when the server comes again up the synchronization will be performed and attachments will be again accessible.

3.1 The Central Node Architecture

In the first version of G-Lorep the shared database was located in a virtual machine inside the Department of Mathematics and Computer Science of University of Perugia. Last year the shared database migrated into the Cloud taking advantage of *PaaS* services like *Amazon RDS* [1]. This solution permitted to reach a great level of resiliency and availability and a good level of security (thanking the whitelist of authorized IP addresses and the infrastructure of Amazon), because the safety of the service was full managed by third parties. As said in the previous section, however despite it keeps the central node secure from external attacks, it does not protect it from authorized hacked federates, permitting in this way malicious queries.

The solutions was creating a RESTFUL API server that acts like an interface to the shared database. In this way the only authorized host accessing to the database is the one owning the API, then each federate needs to contact the central node asking for new learning objects or sending its own updated tables.

Access to the RESTFUL API server is permitted only to authenticated federate behind a white-listed IP address, using an architecture of this type permits to add a additional security layer because it is not possible anymore run customized queries.

The central node is written in Python3 using *Flask* [15] as framework to manage routes, then *SQLAlchemy* [16] is used to perform queries.

Flask has been choosen because it is a lightweight WSGI web application framework. It is designed to make getting started quick and easy, with the ability to scale up to complex applications. It is not a great solution for websites because using it standalone it does not permit to manage layouts, but in the G-Lorep case only JSON requests and responses are required, furthermore only few routes are needed to upload and download learning objects composed by metadata, information about attachments and eventually the relation tables between learning objects. So *Flask* represented for G-Lorep a great solution, easy to code and to maintain.

SQLAlchemy is the Python SQL toolkit and Object Relational Mapper that gives application developers the full power and flexibility of SQL. It provides a full suite of well known enterprise-level persistence patterns, designed for efficient and high-performing database access, adapted into a simple and Pythonic domain language; it is used by famous organizations like OpenStack Project. Like *Laravel* it allows to use models to create table and perform queries, so it represented a great opportunity to write clearer code without the need to write pure SQL.

The approach to the shared database is quite similar to the last version: the federate sends new or updated learning objects to the server; the server checks if the ID of a certain learning object is already in the database and if a record is returned it is deleted, then each learning object is added to the shared database keeping trace of which federate sent it. Deleting then adding updated learning objects instead of directly update them permits to assign them a new incremental ID by the central node to each received learning object. In this way a federate in the synchronization phase just needs to ask the G-Lorep synchronizer to return learning objects having the ID bigger than the received ID of the latest synchronization. A similar approach could be reached using timestamps, but sometimes it can happen that databases or web servers are in different timezones, and often they are not set to use the Unix timestamp. In this way the timestamp is not used for the synchronization of the federation, avoiding problems of this type.

3.2   The Federate Synchronization Architecture

The federate synchronization architecture is easy to understand (Fig. 5):

- when a new LO is created or an old one is edited, the timestamp of that LO inside the local database is updated
- at regular intervals of time the cronjob of each federate runs sending metadata of learning objects to the central node. These metadata have the timestamp greater than the one of the last synchronization
- the central node saves learning objects and adds the ID of the authenticated federate who sent those LOs to the metadata
- if LOs are successfully stored the federate updates the timestamp of the last synchronization
- the local node checks the biggest ID among the foreign LOs received in the previous synchronization and it asks the central node for a list of LOs having the ID bigger than that number
- the central node sends requested metadata of LOs owned by different federates
- finally the received data are saved and showed inside of the federate website.

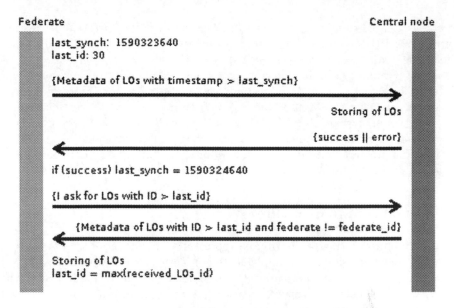

Fig. 5. The federate synchronization architecture

4   Distribution of G-Lorep

This version of G-Lorep has been studied to be easy to install but at the same time easy to customize.

The provided script automatically installs `Docker` and `Docker-compose`, then adds the current user to the `docker` group. After reloading, the privileges of the user latest version of project is downloaded and unpacked in the home directory, then configurations file for Docker-compose are created. A Docker image of G-Lorep is created starting from the official `php-fpm-alpine` with installed dependencies like PHP extensions and composer, this G-Lorep Docker image is the *PHP-FPM* server.

Through `mysql:5.7` and `nginx:alpine` images database and web server are installed, and through Docker-compose are managed to work together, in particular the installed Nginx will use the G-Lorep container as `fastcgi_pass`. *FastCGI* is a PHP protocol used by the web server; in the initialization phase the web server using *FastCGI* creates a process, then when a request arrives the server send the request to this created process, the *FastCGI* process then execs PHP code and returns the output (generally in HTML or JSON) to the web server which in turn will send it to the client, in this way the number of PHP process is optimized because only in the startup phase processes are created. *PHP-FPM* (**F**astCGI **P**rocess **M**anager) is a more recent alternative `version` of *FastCGI*, it implements additive functionality useful to websites with high traffic. *PHP-FPM* works similar to *PHP FastCGI* and it is focused on process optimization too, the main difference is that with *PHP FastCGI* the process is created directly from the web server, instead with *PHP-FPM* a different service is created to manage by itself PHP executions. *PHP-FPM* creates *pools* for replying PHP requests and generated process are *childs* of the Process Manager which can be separately managed from the web server. The use of this approach permits to obtain a better service high-availability because processes restart will impact only FPM pools and not the web server anymore.

Finally the user will be prompted to optionally install a SSL certificate provided by Let's Encrypt and *HTTPS* is automatically activated. Let's Encrypt is a free, automated, and open certificate authority (CA) provided by the Internet Security Research Group (ISRG), run for the public's benefit. It permits to create or update automatically in few seconds secure and free certificates.

5   Conclusion and Future Work

The G-Lorep federation of distributed repositories, previously based on *Drupal* CMS, has been redesigned and implemented on *Laravel* framework. As explained above, there are many advantages in this new version. In fact, in addition to the security aspects, new user features have been introduced and the federation itself has been equipped with a more efficient synchronization mechanism.

For years, the G-Lorep federation's organization of distributed repositories has been suitable to create, assemble, store and retrieve Chemistry Learning Objects in a cooperative way [7–10]. Now, it can also open up to two other areas such as Mathematics and Computer Science, even making use of a future general G-Lorep located in the Cloud, where everyone can insert their own learning objects regardless of their institution of origin [11].

Acknowledgements. The authors acknowledge ECTN (VEC standing committee) and the EC2E2N 2 LLP project for stimulating debates and providing partial financial support.

References

1. Tasso, S., Pallottelli, S., Gervasi, O., Sabbatini, F., Franzoni, V., Laganà, A.: Cloud and local servers for a federation of molecular science learning object repositories. In: Misra, S., et al. (eds.) ICCSA 2019. LNCS, vol. 11624, pp. 359–373. Springer, Cham (2019). https://doi.org/10.1007/978-3-030-24311-1_26
2. Tasso, S., Pallottelli, S., Gervasi, O., Tanase, R., Rui, M.: Synchronized content and metadata management in a federation of distributed repositories of chemical learning objects. In: Gervasi, O., et al. (eds.) ICCSA 2017. LNCS, vol. 10406, pp. 14–28. Springer, Cham (2017). https://doi.org/10.1007/978-3-319-62398-6_2
3. Tasso, S., Pallottelli, S., Bastianini, R., Lagana, A.: Federation of distributed and collaborative repositories and its application on science learning objects. In: Murgante, B., Gervasi, O., Iglesias, A., Taniar, D., Apduhan, B.O. (eds.) ICCSA 2011. LNCS, vol. 6784, pp. 466–478. Springer, Heidelberg (2011). https://doi.org/10.1007/978-3-642-21931-3_36

4. Tasso, S., Pallottelli, S., Rui, M., Laganá, A.: Learning objects efficient handling in a federation of science distributed repositories. In: Murgante, B., et al. (eds.) ICCSA 2014. LNCS, vol. 8579, pp. 615–626. Springer, Cham (2014). https://doi.org/10.1007/978-3-319-09144-0_42

5. Tasso, S., Pallottelli, S., Ferroni, M., Bastianini, R., Laganà, A.: Taxonomy management in a federation of distributed repositories: a chemistry use case. In: Murgante, B., et al. (eds.) ICCSA 2012. LNCS, vol. 7333, pp. 358–370. Springer, Heidelberg (2012). https://doi.org/10.1007/978-3-642-31125-3_28

6. Pallottelli, S., Tasso, S., Rui, M., Laganà, A., Kozaris, I.: Exchange of learning objects between a learning management system and a federation of science distributed repositories. In: Gervasi, O., et al. (eds.) ICCSA 2015. LNCS, vol. 9156, pp. 371–383. Springer, Cham (2015). https://doi.org/10.1007/978-3-319-21407-8_27

7. Tasso, S., Pallottelli, S., Laganà, A.: Mobile device access to collaborative distributed repositories of chemistry learning objects. In: Gervasi, O., et al. (eds.) ICCSA 2016. LNCS, vol. 9786, pp. 443–454. Springer, Cham (2016). https://doi.org/10.1007/978-3-319-42085-1_34

8. Tasso, S., Pallottelli, S., Gervasi, O., Rui, M., Laganà, A.: Sharing learning objects between learning platforms and repositories. In: Gervasi, O., et al. (eds.) ICCSA 2018. LNCS, vol. 10963, pp. 804–816. Springer, Cham (2018). https://doi.org/10.1007/978-3-319-95171-3_62

9. Franzoni, V., Tasso, S., Pallottelli, S., Perri, D.: Sharing linkable learning objects with the use of metadata and a taxonomy assistant for categorization. In: Misra, S., et al. (eds.) ICCSA 2019. LNCS, vol. 11620, pp. 336–348. Springer, Cham (2019). https://doi.org/10.1007/978-3-030-24296-1_28

10. Laganà, A., Gervasi, O., Tasso, S., Perri, D., Franciosa, F.: The ECTN virtual education community prosumer model for promoting and assessing chemical knowledge. In: Gervasi, O., et al. (eds.) ICCSA 2018. LNCS, vol. 10964, pp. 533–548. Springer, Cham (2018). https://doi.org/10.1007/978-3-319-95174-4_42

11. Laganà, A., Terstyanszky, G., Krüger, J.: Open molecular science for the open science cloud. In: Gervasi, O., et al. (eds.) ICCSA 2017. LNCS, vol. 10406, pp. 29–43. Springer, Cham (2017). https://doi.org/10.1007/978-3-319-62398-6_3

12. Laravel.: https://laravel.com/. Accessed May 2020

13. Drupal.: https://www.drupal.org/. Accessed May 2020

14. Docker.: https://www.docker.com/. Accessed May 2020

15. Flask.: https://flask.palletsprojects.com/en/1.1.x/. Accessed May 2020

16. SQLAlchemy.: https://www.sqlalchemy.org/. Accessed May 2020

Classification of Shapes and Deformations of Large Systems by Invariant Coordinates

Lombardi Andrea$^{(\boxtimes)}$ and Noelia Faginas-Lago

Dipartimento di Chimica, Biologia e Biotecnologie,
Università di Perugia, Perugia, Italy
ebiu2005@gmail.com, noelia.faginaslago@unipg.it
http://www.chm.unipg.it/

Abstract. The use of hyperspherical coordinates is widespread in reactive scattering studies, allowing for a symmetric representation of the quantum dynamics of reactive processes. Indeed, among the variants of hyperspherical coordinates, the so called "symmetric" ones are "democratic" with respect to the asymptotic channels and so are the corresponding basis sets, since basis functions can be symmetrized with respect to particle exchange, acting on just a reduced subset of coordinates. Applications to scattering problems are limited to few-atom systems, due to computational cost. An extension of the representation to many-body classical dynamics is possible and has been proposed in a series of papers, where different aspects have been investigated. Here we recall the possibility of defining shape coordinates invariant with respect to the remaining degrees of freedom, which are suitable for systematic classification of structures of clusters and large biomolecules. The definition of shape parameters and to provide examples of their application are the purposes of the present paper.

Keywords: Hyperspherical coordinates · Intermolecular interactions · Atomic clusters · Global minimum · Isomers · Shape coordinates

1 Introduction

The hyperspherical approach to molecular dynamics is well suited for quantum reactive scattering calculations and has been extensively adopted during the last decades, when efforts have been dedicated to the definition of sets of hyperspherical functions [1–3] for three and four-body collision dynamics (see e.g. [4–9]). The Hamiltonian in "symmetric" hyperspherical coordinates is invariant with respect to the possible product arrangements, typical of multi-channel processes, and for such reason the hyperspherical one is largely preferable with respect to other approaches. A further benefit of the use of hyperspherical coordinates is that the hyperspherical basis functions, conveniently chosen, can be used to represent the intermolecular and intramolecular interactions [10–36].

© Springer Nature Switzerland AG 2020
O. Gervasi et al. (Eds.): ICCSA 2020, LNCS 12255, pp. 538–548, 2020.
https://doi.org/10.1007/978-3-030-58820-5_40

The use of hyperspherical method is not restricted to quantum dynamics, where it is limited to systems of three or four atoms, but can be extended to classical dynamics, to simulate large molecules and atomic and molecular clusters, liquids and solids, taking advantage of the reduced computational cost of classical trajectories (see e.g. [37]).

The hyperspherical coordinates separate the degrees of freedom into homogeneous sets of variables, each contributing separately to the kinetic energy, and these are shape deformation coordinates, ordinary rotations and kinematic rotations angles [6,38–42]. The corresponding kinetic energy terms are defined in the classical mechanics framework by the hyperangular momenta appearing in the Hamilton function, which, apart from some purely quantum extra-terms, not present in classical mechanics, can be put into correspondence with the quantum Hamiltonian operator. Although classical equations of motion could in principle be obtained and integrated in hyperspherical form, integration in Cartesian coordinates is much more convenient. A procedure based on matrix transformations of the set of position vectors has been developed, which allows for the evaluation of the energy terms appearing in the Hyperspherical Hamilton function as a function of time [6,39].

It is relevant for us that the hyperspherical separation scheme of the degrees of freedom introduce ordinary rotations and rotations in the kinematic space, under the action of which the global shape of the system in the three-dimensional physical space is invariant, meaning that the remaining three degrees of freedom must be themselves invariant with respect to both kinds of rotations. This "invariance" approach to classical dynamics of molecules and clusters has been investigated in previous papers [38,43–48].

Here, we consider the use of invariant hyperspherical shape parameters for the classification of local and global minimum energy structures of atomic and molecular clusters.

2   Theoretical Background

The hyperspherical coordinates are defined for an N-particle system starting from the corresponding set of $N-1$ Jacobi vectors $\mathbf{Q}_\alpha$, with $\alpha = 1, \cdots, N-1$, a combinations of the radial vectors of the particles in the center of mass reference frame, the latter denoted by $\mathbf{r}_\alpha$ [38]. A "canonical" sequential generation of such vectors is as follows: take the vector which connects particles 1 and 2, then the one connecting the center of mass of the pair to the third particle, and so on, up to the $(N-1)$th vector, which connects the center of mass of the first $N-1$ particles to the Nth particle. The coefficients of the combination depends on the particle masses, see Sect. 2.1 for details. The next step consists in the definition of an hyperradius ρ as the modulus of a vector of dimension $3N-3$, spanning the configuration space of the system. The Cartesian components of the hyperradial vector, is given by the ordered sequence of the Jacobi vector components, which can be expressed as a function of the hyperradius itself and $3N-4$ "hyperangles", which define the hyperspherical coordinate system. There are in principle many alternatives for the choice of the a angular variables, but the most interesting for us is the one who leads to the so called Symmetric hyperspherical representation. In algebraic terms, this is the result of a matrix transformation, the *singular value decomposition*, operating on a properly constructed position matrix. The procedure to generate hyperspherical coordinates is described in the following section.

2.1   Hyperspherical Coordinates for Atomic and Molecular Aggregates

An appropriate mathematical tool for the representation of N-center systems is the *singular value decomposition* [49], a matrix decomposition theorem that can be applied to any given set of N vectors arranged column-wise to form a $3 \times N$ position matrix.

Let us suppose we have a collection of $N \geq 2$ particles with masses $m_1, \cdots, m_N$ and positions identified by a set of radii vectors in the center of mass reference frame, $\mathbf{r_1}, \cdots, \mathbf{r_N}$. Mass *scaled* radii vectors $\mathbf{q}_\alpha = (m_\alpha/M)^{1/2}\mathbf{r}_\alpha$ ($1 \leq \alpha \leq N$), can be obtained, where $M = \sum_\alpha^N m_\alpha$ is the total mass of the system.

A $3 \times N$ position matrix denoted by Z containing column-wise the components of the mass scaled vectors, can be generated, as follows:

$$Z = \begin{pmatrix} q_{1,1} & q_{1,2} & \cdots & q_{1,N} \\ q_{2,1} & q_{2,2} & \cdots & q_{2,N} \\ q_{3,1} & q_{3,2} & \cdots & q_{3,N} \end{pmatrix}. \tag{1}$$

The coordinate frame can be rotated, by the action of an orthogonal matrix R^t (transpose of a matrix $R \in O(3)$) on the position matrix Z by left-multiplication. An orthogonal matrix $K \in O(N)$ acting in the position matrix by right-multiplication instead rotates the coordinate frame in the so called *kinematic space* [5,39], $Z' = ZK$.

It is possible to identify a subset of K matrices having the following form (see last column):

$$K = \begin{pmatrix} k_{1,1} & k_{1,2} & \cdots & (m_1/M)^{1/2} \\ k_{2,1} & k_{2,2} & \cdots & (m_2/M)^{1/2} \\ \cdots & \cdots & \cdots & \cdots \\ k_{N,1} & k_{N,2} & \cdots & (m_N/M)^{1/2} \end{pmatrix} \tag{2}$$

and its application to the Z matrix generates a subset of all the possible Cartesian frames. Remarkably, the elements of the last column of such Z matrices are identically zero, due to the relation $\sum_\alpha^N m_\alpha^{1/2}\mathbf{q}_\alpha = 0$, valid for the mass scaled vectors and that has the physical meaning of separating the motion of the center of mass, so reducing the number of necessary degrees of freedom to $3N - 3$. This smaller matrix Z is called *reduced position matrix*.

The sets of $(N - 1)$ Jacobi and related vectors invariably form reduced matrices. The Jacobi vectors are obtained as a linear combinations of the N Cartesian particle position vectors, with coefficients being a function of the particle masses [50,51]. Different Jacobi vector sets are possible, corresponding to the different particle coupling schemes, a representation of the reactive channels of the system; the sets are smoothly connected by coordinate transformation in the kinematic space.

The *singular value decomposition* theorem applied to the $3 \times n$ position matrix Z (where $n = N$ or $n = N - 1$) gives a product of three matrices:

$$Z = R \Xi K^t \tag{3}$$

where $R \in O(3)$ and $K \in O(n)$ are 3×3 and $3 \times n$ orthogonal matrices, respectively. The elements of the $3 \times n$ matrix Ξ are zeroes, with the possible exception of the diagonal entries, $\Xi_{11} = \xi_1, \Xi_{22} = \xi_2, \Xi_{33} = \xi_3$, which are subjected to the inequality $\xi_1 \geq \xi_2 \geq \xi_3 \geq 0$.

The values ξ_i, $(i = 1, 2, 3)$ are called the *singular values* of the matrix Z and are uniquely determined, although the factors R and K in Eq. 3 are not. If $N \leq 3$ and Z is the full $3 \times N$ position matrix, then the smallest singular value ξ_3 is necessarily zero. The singular values are connected to the hyperradius as follows [38,39]:

$$\xi_1^2 + \xi_2^2 + \xi_3^2 = \rho^2. \tag{4}$$

The ξ's are invariant under both ordinary rotations in the physical space and kinematic rotations [5,6,39,52], a property that can be exploited in molecular dynamics [38,53–56] and in the study of the minimum energy structures of N-particle aggregates.

In the case $n = N - 1 = 3$, the matrix Z represent four particles or four center systems. In this special case, the two matrices R and K cannot be chosen to be *special orthogonal* ($R \in SO(3)$ and $K \in SO(n)$), but are required to be just orthogonal matrices ($O(3)$). Under such circumstances, if the determinant of Z is lower than zero, its sign depends on the sign of the product of the ξ's, and so one has $\xi_3 \leq 0$. This fact is directly connected to the mirror image and chirality sign of the system [43,57,58].

The previous matrix transformation has the effect of partitioning the $3N - 3$ degrees of freedom into three distinct sets of coordinates: three angles, parametrizing the rotation matrix R and accounting for spatial rotations, $3N - 9$ angles, parametrizing the rotation matrix K, accounting for rotations in the kinematic space, and 3 ξ's, the invariant quantities which are related to the hyperradius, being the only quantities with units of length.

2.2   Hyperradius and Invariant Deformation Indexes

The singular values (ξ_1, ξ_2, ξ_3) are invariant under the action of kinematic and ordinary rotations [59] and are related to the moments of inertia of the system, as follows:

$$\frac{I_1}{M} = \xi_2^2 + \xi_3^2$$

$$\frac{I_2}{M} = \xi_1^2 + \xi_3^2 \tag{5}$$

$$\frac{I_3}{M} = \xi_1^2 + \xi_2^2$$

where I_1, I_2 and I_3 are the moments of inertia in the principal axis reference frame. From Eq. 4 one obtains:

$$I_1 + I_2 + I_3 = 2M\rho^2. \tag{6}$$

It is clear how the relative values of the ξ's determine whether the system is an asymmetric, symmetric or a spherical rotor. Spherical top configurations are those for which $\xi_1 = \xi_2 = \xi_3$, prolate tops those for which $\xi_3 = \xi_2 < \xi_1$, while oblate tops occur when $\xi_1 = \xi_2 > \xi_3$.

It is convenient to parametrize the ξ's in terms of the hyperradius and two angles θ and ϕ as follows:

$$\xi_1 = \rho \sin \theta \cos \phi$$

$$\xi_2 = \rho \sin \theta \sin \phi \tag{7}$$

$$\xi_2 = \rho \cos \theta$$

Parameters measuring the deviation from the spherical top shapes, can be introduced by two following *deformation indexes* [38]:

$$\xi_+ = \frac{\xi_2^2 - \xi_3^2}{\rho^2}, \quad \xi_+ \geq 0 \tag{8}$$

which is zero for prolate top configurations, and

$$\xi_- = \frac{\xi_2^2 - \xi_1^2}{\rho^2}, \quad \xi_- \leq 0 \tag{9}$$

which is zero for oblate top configurations. By definition, when both indexes are zero, one has a spherical rotor.

2.3   Deformation Indexes of Atomic and Molecular Clusters

Being the deformation indexes rotationally invariant (in the sense illustrated in the previous sections) they can naturally be used to classify global structures of large molecular systems, looking for patterns and regularities in the global an local minimum energy structures. As an example of application, we consider sets of global and local minima of simple Lennard-Jones clusters. To calculate the indexes, one needs the values of the invariant ξ's for each cluster structure. A direct way to get them is to use the following relation coming from Eq. 3:

$$ZZ^t = R\Xi\Xi^t R^t \tag{10}$$

where the product $\Xi\Xi^t$ is 3×3 square diagonal matrix, whose entries are the squares of the ξ's. The diagonal entries are just the eigenvalues of the matrix product ZZ^t involving the position matrix. Using the Cartesian components of the mass scaled atomic position vectors (see Sect. 2.1), one has to calculate the ZZ^t matrix and diagonalize it, numerically, or by using the well known Cardano's formula for the characteristic equation [38].

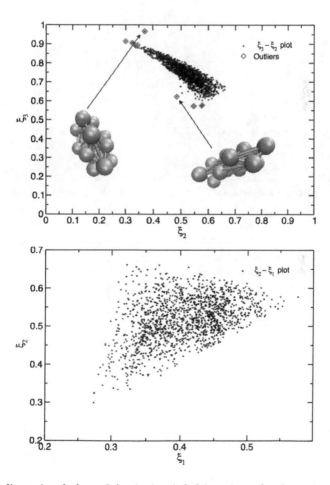

Fig. 1. Two-dimensional plots of the ξ_i, $i = 1, 2, 3$ invariants for the entire set of global and local minima of a 13-atom Lennard-Jones (LJ) 12-6 cluster. (See Ref. [38] for a 12-atom cluster). Structures have been obtained from the database [60]

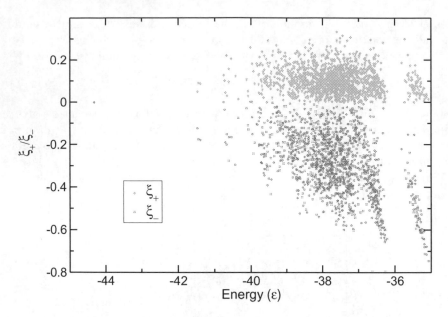

Fig. 2. Plot of the ξ_+ and ξ_+ deformation indexes as a function of energy, for the global and minimum energy structures of a 13-atom Lennard-Jones cluster.

The series of local minimum structures, are those freely available at the Cambridge Cluster Database [60], for the 13-atom Lennard-Jones cluster. In Fig. 1, the invariant ξ's of Sect. 2.2 for the LJ cluster minima are reported in two panels where ξ_3-ξ_2 plots (upper panel) and ξ_2-ξ_3 plots (lower panels) are represented. Note that the allowed values are restricted to a partial subspace. Some outliers, corresponding to very deformed structure are indicated.

In Fig. 2 the deformation indexes ξ_+ and ξ_- are shown for the same minimum energy structures, as a function of energy in terms of the Lennard-Jones well dept ϵ. The trend shows marked oscillations, interrupted by the occurrence of spherical top configurations, where strong deviations from the spherical top configuration occur. Some energy gaps can be noticed, where no minima are present.

3   Conclusions

In this paper we outlined some aspects of the hyperspherical coordinate approach to structure and dynamics, that can be applied in a classical mechanics framework to large molecules and clusters. It has been shown the possible use of rotationally invariant quantities and deformation indexes to classify structures and identify outlying geometries, which makes hyperspherical invariants a perspective tool for systematic classification of minimum energy structures of clusters and biomolecules.

Acknowledgments. The authors acknowledge financial support from MIUR PRIN 2010–2011 (contract 2010ERFKXL_002) and from "Fondazione Cassa di Risparmio di Perugia (Codice Progetto: 2015.0331.021 Ricerca Scientifica e Tecnologica)". Thanks are due to the Dipartimento di Chimica, Biologia e Biotecnologie dell'Università di Perugia (FRB, Fondo per la Ricerca di Base 2017) and to the MIUR and the University of Perugia for the financial support of the AMIS project through the program "Dipartimenti di Eccellenza". A. L. acknowledges financial support from MIUR PRIN 2015 (contract 2015F59J3R_002). A.L. thanks the OU Supercomputing Center for Education & Research (OSCER) at the University of Oklahoma, for allocated computing time.

References

1. Zhao, B., Guo, H.: State-to-state quantum reactive scattering in four-atom systems. WIREs Comput. Mol. Sci. **7**, e1301 (2017)
2. Skouteris, D., Castillo, J., Manolopoulos, D.E.: Abc: a quantum reactive scattering program. Comput. Phys. Comm. **133**, 128–135 (2000)
3. Lepetit, B., Launay, J.M.: Quantum-mechanical study of the reaction $He+H_2^+ \rightarrow HeH^+ + H$ with hyperspherical coordinates. J. Chem. Phys. **95**, 5159–5168 (1991)
4. Aquilanti, V., Beddoni, A., Cavalli, S., Lombardi, A., Littlejohn, R.: Collective hyperspherical coordinates for polyatomic molecules and clusters. Mol. Phys. **98**(21), 1763–1770 (2000)
5. Aquilanti, V., Beddoni, A., Lombardi, A., Littlejohn, R.: Hyperspherical harmonics for polyatomic systems: basis set for kinematic rotations. Int. J. Quantum Chem. **89**(4), 277–291 (2002)
6. Aquilanti, V., Lombardi, A., Littlejohn, R.: Hyperspherical harmonics for polyatomic systems: basis set for collective motions. Theor. Chem. Acc. **111**(2–6), 400–406 (2004)
7. Kuppermann, A.: Quantum reaction dynamics and hyperspherical harmonics. Isr. J. Chem. **43**, 229 (2003)
8. De Fazio, D., Cavalli, S., Aquilanti, V.: Benchmark quantum mechanical calculations of vibrationally resolved cross sections and rate constants on ab initio potential energy surfaces for the F + HD reaction: comparisons with experiments. J. Phys. Chem. A **120**, 5288–5299 (2016)
9. Aquilanti, V., Cavalli, S.: The quantum-mechanical hamiltonian for tetraatomic systems insymmetric hyperspherical coordinates. J. Chem. Soc., Faraday Trans. **93**, 801–809 (1997)
10. Lombardi, A., Laganà, A., Pirani, F., Palazzetti, F., Faginas-Lago, N.: Carbon oxides in gas flows and earth and planetary atmospheres: state-to-state simulations of energy transfer and dissociation reactions. In: Murgante, B., Misra, S., Carlini, M., Torre, C., Nguyen, H.Q., Taniar, D., Apduhan, B., Gervasi, O. (eds.) Computational Science and Its Applications - ICCSA 2013. Lecture Notes in Computer Science, vol. 7972, pp. 17–31. Springer, Berlin Heidelberg (2013). https://doi.org/10.1007/978-3-642-39643-4_2
11. Lago, N.F., Albertí, M., Laganà, A., Lombardi, A.: Water $(H_2O)_m$ or benzene $(C_6H_6)_n$ aggregates to solvate the K^+. In: Murgante, B., et al. (eds.) ICCSA 2013. LNCS, vol. 7971, pp. 1–15. Springer, Heidelberg (2013). https://doi.org/10.1007/978-3-642-39637-3_1

12. Faginas-Lago, N., Albertí, M., Costantini, A., Laganá, A., Lombardi, A., Pacifici, L.: An innovative synergistic grid approach to the computational study of protein aggregation mechanisms. J. Mol. Model. **20**(7), 2226 (2014)
13. Faginas-Lago, N., Yeni, D., Huarte, F., Alcamì, M., Martin, F.: Adsorption of hydrogen molecules on carbon nanotubes using quantum chemistry and molecular dynamics. J. Phys. Chem. A **120**, 6451–6458 (2016)
14. Faginas-Lago, N., Lombardi, A., Albertí, M., Grossi, G.: Accurate analytic intermolecular potential for the simulation of Na^+ and K^+ ion hydration in liquid water. J. Mol. Liq. **204**, 192–197 (2015)
15. Albertí, M., Faginas Lago, N.: Competitive solvation of K^+ by C_6H_6 and H_2O in the K^+-$(C_6h_6)_n$-$(H_2O)_m$ (n = 1–4; m = 1–6) aggregates. Eur. Phys. J. D **67**, 73 (2013)
16. Albertí, M., Faginas Lago, N.: Ion size influence on the ar solvation shells of M^+-C_6F_6 clusters (m = na, k, rb, cs). J. Phys. Chem. A **116**, 3094–3102 (2012)
17. Albertí, M., Faginas Lago, N., Pirani, F.: Ar solvation shells in K^+-HFBz: From cluster rearrangement to solvation dynamics. J. Phys. Chem. A **115**, 10871–10879 (2011)
18. Lago, N.F., Albertí, M., Laganà, A., Lombardi, A., Pacifici, L., Costantini, A.: The molecular stirrer catalytic effect in methane ice formation. In: Murgante, B., et al. (eds.) ICCSA 2014. LNCS, vol. 8579, pp. 585–600. Springer, Cham (2014). https://doi.org/10.1007/978-3-319-09144-0_40
19. Faginas-Lago, N., Huarte Larrañaga, F., Albertí, M.: On the suitability of the ilj function to match different formulations of the electrostatic potential for water-water interactions. Eur. Phys. J. D **55**(1), 75 (2009)
20. Bartolomei, M., Pirani, F., Laganà, A., Lombardi, A.: A full dimensional grid empowered simulation of the CO_2+ CO_2 processes. J. Comp. Chem. **33**, 1806 (2012)
21. Lombardi, A., Faginas-Lago, N., Laganà, A., Pirani, F., Falcinelli, S.: A bond-bond portable approach to intermolecular interactions: Simulations for n-methylacetamide and carbon dioxide dimers. In: Murgante, B., et al. (eds.) Computational Science and Its Applications - ICCSA 2012. Lecture Notes in Computer Science, vol. 7333, pp. 387–400. Springer, Berlin Heidelberg (2012). https://doi.org/10.1007/978-3-642-31125-3_30
22. Albertí, M., Faginas-Lago, N., Laganà, A., Pirani, F.: A portable intermolecular potential for molecular dynamics studies of nma-nma and nma-H_2O aggregates. Phys. Chem. Chem. Phys. **13**(18), 8422–8432 (2011)
23. Albertí, M., Faginas-Lago, N., Pirani, F.: Benzene water interaction: from gaseous dimers to solvated aggregates. Chem. Phys. **399**, 232 (2012)
24. Falcinelli, S., Rosi, M., Candori, P., Vecchiocattivi, F., Bartocci, A., Lombardi, A., Faginas-Lago, N., Pirani, F.: Modeling the intermolecular interactions and characterization of the dynamics of collisional autoionization processes. In: Murgante, B., et al. (eds.) Computational Science and Its Applications - ICCSA 2013. Lecture Notes in Computer Science, vol. 7971, pp. 69–83. Springer, Berlin Heidelberg (2013). https://doi.org/10.1007/978-3-642-39637-3_6
25. Lombardi, A., Faginas-Lago, N., Pacifici, L., Costantini, A.: Modeling of energy transfer from vibrationally excited CO_2 molecules: cross sections and probabilities for kinetic modeling of atmospheres, flows, and plasmas. J. Phys. Chem. A **117**(45), 11430–11440 (2013)

26. Lombardi, A., Pirani, F., Laganà, A., Bartolomei, M.: Energy transfer dynamics and kinetics of elementary processes (promoted) by gas-phase CO_2-N_2 collisions: selectivity control by the anisotropy of the interaction. J. Comp. Chem. **37**, 1463–1475 (2016)

27. Pacifici, L., Verdicchio, M., Faginas-Lago, N., Lombardi, A., Costantini, A.: A high-level ab initio study of the n2 + n2 reaction channel. J. Comput. Chem. **34**(31), 2668–2676 (2013)

28. Lombardi, A., Faginas-Lago, N., Pacifici, L., Grossi, G.: Energy transfer upon collision of selectively excited CO_2 molecules: state-to-state cross sections and probabilities for modeling of atmospheres and gaseous flows. J. Chem. Phys. **143**, 034307 (2015)

29. Celiberto, R., et al.: Atomic and molecular data for spacecraft re-entry plasmas. Plasma Sources Sci. Technol. **25**(3), 033004 (2016)

30. Faginas-Lago, N., Lombardi, A., Albertí, M.: Aqueous n-methylacetamide: new analytic potentials and a molecular dynamics study. J. Mol. Liq. **224**, 792–800 (2016)

31. Palazzetti, F., Munusamy, E., Lombardi, A., Grossi, G., Aquilanti, V.: Spherical and hyperspherical representation of potential energy surfaces for intermolecular interactions. Int. J. Quantum Chem. **111**(2), 318–332 (2011)

32. Lombardi, A., Palazzetti, F.: A comparison of interatomic potentials for rare gas nanoaggregates. J. Mol. Struc-THEOCHEM **852**(1–3), 22–29 (2008)

33. Barreto, P.R., Albernaz, A.F., Palazzetti, F., Lombardi, A., Grossi, G., Aquilanti, V.: Hyperspherical representation of potential energy surfaces: intermolecular interactions in tetra-atomic and penta-atomic systems. Phys. Scr. **84**(2), 028111 (2011)

34. Barreto, P.R., et al.: Potential energy surfaces for interactions of H^2O with H_2, N_2 and O_2: a hyperspherical harmonics representation, and a minimal model for the H_2O-rare-gas-atom systems. Comput. Theor. Chem. **990**, 53–61 (2012)

35. Lombardi, A., Pirani, F., Bartolomei, M., Coletti, C., Laganà, A.: A full dimensional potential energy function and the calculation of the state-specific properties of the CO+ N_2 inelastic processes within an Open Molecular Science Cloud perspective. Front. Chem. **7**, 309 (2019)

36. Faginas Lago, N., Lombardi, A., Vekeman, J., Rosi, M., et al.: Molecular dynamics of CH_4/N_2 mixtures on a flexible graphene layer: adsorption and selectivity case study. Front. Chem. **7**, 386 (2019)

37. Nakamura, M., et al.: Dynamical, spectroscopic and computational imaging of bond breaking in photodissociation: roaming and role of conical intersections. Faraday Discuss. **177**, 77–98 (2015)

38. Aquilanti, V., Lombardi, A., Yurtsever, E.: Global view of classical clusters: the hyperspherical approach to structure and dynamics. Phys. Chem. Chem. Phys. **4**(20), 5040–5051 (2002)

39. Sevryuk, M.B., Lombardi, A., Aquilanti, V.: Hyperangular momenta and energy partitions in multidimensional many-particle classical mechanics: the invariance approach to cluster dynamics. Phys. Rev. A **72**(3), 033201 (2005)

40. Castro Palacio, J., Velazquez Abad, L., Lombardi, A., Aquilanti, V., Rubayo Soneira, J.: Normal and hyperspherical mode analysis of no-doped kr crystals upon rydberg excitation of the impurity. J. Chem. Phys. **126**(17), 174701 (2007)

41. Lombardi, A., Palazzetti, F., Aquilanti, V.: Molecular dynamics of chiral molecules in hyperspherical coordinates. In: Misra, S., et al. (eds.) ICCSA 2019. LNCS, vol. 11624, pp. 413–427. Springer, Cham (2019). https://doi.org/10.1007/978-3-030-24311-1_30

42. Lombardi, A., Palazzetti, F., Sevryuk, M.B.: Hyperspherical coordinates and energy partitions for reactive processes and clusters. In: AIP Conference Proceedings. Volume 2186, p. 030014. AIP Publishing LLC (2019)

43. Lombardi, A., Palazzetti, F.: Chirality in molecular collision dynamics. J. Condens. Matter Phys. **30**(6), 063003 (2018)

44. Lombardi, A., Palazzetti, F., Peroncelli, L., Grossi, G., Aquilanti, V., Sevryuk, M.: Few-body quantum and many-body classical hyperspherical approaches to reactions and to cluster dynamics. Theor. Chem. Acc. **117**(5–6), 709–721 (2007)

45. Aquilanti, V., Grossi, G., Lombardi, A., Maciel, G.S., Palazzetti, F.: Aligned molecular collisions and a stereodynamical mechanism for selective chirality. Rend. Fis. Acc. Lincei **22**, 125–135 (2011)

46. Lombardi, A., Faginas-Lago, N., Aquilanti, V.: The invariance approach to structure and dynamics: classical hyperspherical coordinates. In: Misra, S., et al. (eds.) ICCSA 2019. LNCS, vol. 11624, pp. 428–438. Springer, Cham (2019). https://doi.org/10.1007/978-3-030-24311-1_31

47. Caglioti, C., Dos Santos, R.F., Lombardi, A., Palazzetti, F., Aquilanti, V.: Screens displaying structural properties of aminoacids in polypeptide chains: alanine as a case study. In: Misra, S., et al. (eds.) ICCSA 2019. LNCS, vol. 11624, pp. 439–449. Springer, Cham (2019). https://doi.org/10.1007/978-3-030-24311-1_32

48. Caglioti, C., Ferreira, R.d.S., Palazzetti, F., Lombardi, A., Aquilanti, V.: Screen representation of structural properties of alanine in polypeptide chains. In: AIP Conference Proceedings. Volume 2186, p. 030015, AIP Publishing LLC (2019)

49. Horn, R.A., Johnson, C.R.: Matrix Analysis, 2nd edn. University Press, Cambridge (1990)

50. Gatti, F., Lung, C.: Vector parametrization of the n-atom problem in quantum mechanics. i. jacobi vectors. J. Chem. Phys. **108**(21), 8804–8820 (1998)

51. Aquilanti, V., Lombardi, A., Yurtsever, E.: Global view of classical clusters: the hyperspherical approach to structure and dynamics. Phys. Chem. Chem. Phys. **4**, 5040–5051 (2002)

52. Aquilanti, V., Lombardi, A., Sevryuk, M.B.: Phase-space invariants for aggregates of particles: hyperangular momenta and partitions of the classical kinetic energy. J. Chem. Phys. **121**, 5579 (2004)

53. Aquilanti, V., Carmona Novillo, E., Garcia, E., Lombardi, A., Sevryuk, M.B., Yurtsever, E.: Invariant energy partitions in chemical reactions and cluster dynamics simulations. Comput. Mat. Sci. **35**, 187–191 (2006)

54. Aquilanti, V., Lombardi, A., Sevryuk, M.B., Yurtsever, E.: Phase-space invariants as indicators of the critical behavior of nanoaggregates. Phys. Rev. Lett. **93**, 113402 (2004)

55. Calvo, F., Gadea, X., Lombardi, A., Aquilanti, V.: Isomerization dynamics and thermodynamics of ionic argon clusters. J. Chem. Phys. **125**, 114307 (2006)

56. Lombardi, A., Aquilanti, V., Yurtsever, E., Sevryuk, M.B.: Specific heats of clusters near a phase transition: energy partitions among internal modes. Chem. Phys. Lett. **30**, 424–428 (2006)

57. Lombardi, A., Maciel, G.S., Palazzetti, F., Grossi, G., Aquilanti, V.: Alignment and chirality in gaseous flows. J. Vacuum Soc. Japan **53**(11), 645–653 (2010)

58. Palazzetti, F., et al.: Aligned molecules: chirality discrimination in photodissociation and in molecular dynamics. Rendiconti Lincei **24**(3), 299–308 (2013)

59. Littlejohn, R.G., Mitchell, A., Aquilanti, V.: Quantum dynamics of kinematic invariants in tetra-and polyatomic systems. Phys. Chem. Chem. Phys. **1**, 1259–1264 (1999)

60. Wales, D.G., et al.: The Cambridge Cluster Database (2001)

Binary Classification of Proteins by a Machine Learning Approach

Damiano Perri[1]([✉])(iD), Marco Simonetti[1](iD), Andrea Lombardi[2](iD),
Noelia Faginas-Lago[2](iD), and Osvaldo Gervasi[3](iD)

[1] Department of Mathematics and Computer Science, University of Florence,
Florence, Italy
damiano.perri@gmail.com

[2] Department of Chemistry, Biology and Biotechnology, University of Perugia,
Perugia, Italy

[3] Department of Mathematics and Computer Science, University of Perugia,
Perugia, Italy

Abstract. In this work we present a system based on a Deep Learning approach, by using a Convolutional Neural Network, capable of classifying protein chains of amino acids based on the protein description contained in the Protein Data Bank. Each protein is fully described in its chemical-physical-geometric properties in a file in XML format. The aim of the work is to design a prototypical Deep Learning machinery for the collection and management of a huge amount of data and to validate it through its application to the classification of a sequences of amino acids. We envisage applying the described approach to more general classification problems in biomolecules, related to structural properties and similarities.

Keywords: Machine Learning · Computational chemistry · Protein Data Bank

1 Introduction

Proteins in Nature exhibit a very complicate relationship between their complex structures, with considerable differences from a chemical, physical and geometric point of view and their biological functions. The theoretical and computational study of proteins structure and function, as well as of nucleic acids, lipid membranes and other biosystems, is mainly carried on by Molecular Dynamics (MD) simulations, grounded upon classical mechanics and Force Fields. MD is used to sample the system phase space and to capture the relevant dynamical processes of proteins across different timescales. Simulations can be carried out at different levels of details. These can be atomistic simulations, where each atom is followed in detail, or can be based on coarse grained models, where group of atoms are replaced by pseudo-atoms and a reduced number of degrees of freedom allows to model biological phenomena accessing much longer time scales.

© Springer Nature Switzerland AG 2020
O. Gervasi et al. (Eds.): ICCSA 2020, LNCS 12255, pp. 549–558, 2020.
https://doi.org/10.1007/978-3-030-58820-5_41

In spite of continuous progress and increasing availability of High Performance Computing resources, many aspects in the dynamics and structure modelling still remain problematic, due to the inherent computational complexity of proteins and other biomolecules. These are related to (i) very high computational demand and sampling limitations and ii) limited force field accuracy, (iii) search for main stable structure and reactive or isomerization pathways, (iv) multiscale nature of dynamics.

In the last few years, the recourse to Machine Learning (ML) applications has become widespread in molecular dynamics. Particularly, approaches based on a variant of ML called deep neural networks [1,2] are becoming broadly popular. These can be applied to the many classification problems that, generally speaking, occur in the theoretical and computational modelling of proteins and other biomolecules. The growing amount of both experimental and theoretical data, available in databases and repositories, makes it increasingly feasible an efficient training of neural networks.

In this work, we have posed the basic problem of classifying as "real" a protein given its amino acid sequence, using a Deep Learning approach.

The choice of the network to process the sequences fell on Convolutional Neural Network (CNN). A choice in some ways less obvious than a Recurrent Neural Network (RNN) [3], given the nature and form of the data to be processed, but one that has revealed to be able to return results that are quite satisfactory.

In addition, CNNs can be easily implemented even on hardware that is not particularly performing, with the advantage of enabling to use the model developed on a plurality of platforms [4] and even on dedicated boards [5]. The cnn are mainly used for image analysis, they allow to extract features that are then used to correctly classify objects, people or things [6,7]. In this article we explain our approach to the problem using CNN 1D, i.e. one-dimensional.

The data set to train our network was taken from The Protein Data Bank (PDB) [8], that is a free access archive containing 3D structure data of proteins and nucleic acids.

2   The Architecture of the System

The system must be able to correctly classify a sequence of amino acids, telling whether it represents a "possible" real protein. To get to this, we decided to use a less conventional approach, but which seemed to us very promising, based on a CNN, a kind of networks particularly appreciated in the recognition of images and characteristics from two-dimensional and three-dimensional objects.

2.1   Data Extraction and Processing

Our work was developed entirely in Python working in the development environment provided by Google, called Colab. We divided the problem into a set of sub-problems. First of all we downloaded all the protein database provided by Protein Data Bank. The dataset is downloadable in two different formats:

PDB and XML. Between the two formats the information content is the same, the only difference being only the data format to store with the information. The PDB database is composed of hundreds of thousands of proteins all entirely described by single files in different formats: our choice has been placed on an open format like XML because it is much easier to be read and analyzed through the libraries made available by Python. The first problem we had to solve was related to the size of the dataset. In total there are 160,797 files in "xml.gz" compressed format for a total size of 57.6 GB. Once extracted the archive takes up more than 2 TB of disk space due to the huge amount of data it contains. First we created a script that solves the problem of rearranging the dataset in order to be conveniently handled by our tools. In practice, it outputs a single compressed file in which the proteins are arranged as a list. Each protein in the list is represented by a sequence of amino acids. In this way we were able to obtain a single file named "dataset.csv.gz" with a size of 7 GB, where just the relevant information was extracted, ready to be used for the next steps. Each single protein was entirely mapped and unequivocally encoded as a very precise sequence of numbers, consisting of a dictionary of type "amino acid's name: positive integer number".

A first analysis of the data showed that the amino acids present in the dataset were 52, but only a part of them (23), was really present in the whole set of proteins examined, containing 105,123 instances.

In addition, the sequences had variable lengths (defined as the number of amino acids in the chain) for the various molecules, with a distribution which is shown in the table below:

Length of molecules' sequences		
Chain length (interval)	Number of molecules	Number of molecules %
1 .. 9	96	0.09
10 .. 99	3,149	3.00
100 .. 999	83,526	79.46
1,000 .. 1,500	9,107	8.66
1,501 .. 9,999	9,117	8.67
10,000 .. 99,999	127	0.12
100,000 .. 1,000,000	1	0.00

Since the sequence to be fed to the network must have a predetermined fixed length, we have chosen to consider only those proteins with a length of less than 1,500, which make up about 91.21% of the entire set of sequences.

Since a protein in its constitutive unfolded sequence can be passed from left to right or vice versa, the dataset has been "augmented", by inserting the same sequences of proteins already present, but reversed. This allowed to obtain a dataset of real proteins with double size respect of the original one.

The second step for the preparation of the dataset was the generation of the fake samples (FALSE samples), in equal number to the real samples (TRUE samples).

Initially, trivial cases were inserted, as whole sequences of length 1,500 of the same amino acid repeated more times, obtaining 23 new false proteins. Subsequently, the generation level became more sophisticated: in each true protein, a fragment at a random position of the protein sequence was replaced by another one, giving place to a sequence mutation; each new fragment had a random length between 5 and 7% of the entire protein sequence length and contained amino acids randomly taken from the dictionary of all possible amino acids in our real cases (Fig. 1).

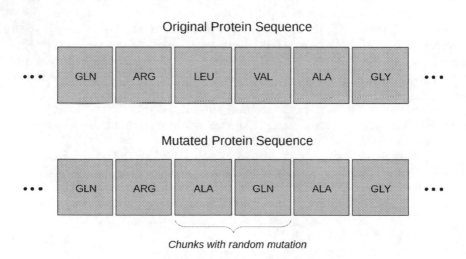

Fig. 1. False chunks in sequence

2.2   Model Construction and Validation

During the working phases we tested several networks built with different parameters and layers. A simple model and at the same time satisfactory for the quality of the results, was the one represented in Fig. 2 and Fig. 3, characterized as follows:

- Embedding Layer: to create the weight matrix and to index it, according to the inputs which should be lists of positive integers (encoded amino acids)
- Convolution Layer: these are our first two layers that define a feature detector with a kernel equal to 3.
- Pooling Layer: with a size of the max pooling windows of 5.
- Convolution Layer: another layer that define a feature detector with a kernel equal to 5 to refine outcomes.

- MaxPooling Layer: to reduce the complexity of the output and prevent over-fitting of the data.
- The final dense layer: this is a fully connected layer with SIGMOID activation; this layer will reduce the vector dimensions to a binary vector since we have 2 classes that we want to predict.

The model is extremely light, using a total of only 13,988 parameters.

```
Layer (type)                    Output Shape              Param #
=================================================================
embedding (Embedding)           (None, 1500, 3)           195

conv1d (Conv1D)                 (None, 1498, 32)          320

conv1d_1 (Conv1D)               (None, 1496, 32)          3104

max_pooling1d (MaxPooling1D)    (None, 299, 32)           0

conv1d_2 (Conv1D)               (None, 295, 64)           10304

global_max_pooling1d (Global    (None, 64)                0

dense (Dense)                   (None, 1)                 65
=================================================================
Total params: 13,988
Trainable params: 13,988
Non-trainable params: 0
```

Fig. 2. Structure of the network model

In the section where the model is compiled we have chosen the "binary crossentropy" [9,10] as a feedback signal for learning the weight tensors to be minimized, as an optimizer to rule the gradient descent the "Adadelta optimizer" [11], with a fixed learning-rate equal to 1.0 and rho equal to 0.95, and as our metric the accuracy of the model.

The network was let to iterate on the training data (306,812 samples) in mini-batches of 50 samples for 50 epochs.

In addition, we have inserted checkpoints to the simulation, so that we can save the best weight configuration of the model.

2.3   Analysis of Results

The results obtained are very encouraging, having achieved a score of 95.6% on the accuracy of the tests.

In Fig. 4 and Fig. 5 it is shown the plot the loss and accuracy of the model, as a function of the various periods (epochs) of the simulation.

Despite the presence of sudden and rare spikes in the graphs, essentially due to a temporary displacement of the trajectory from the set of solutions by

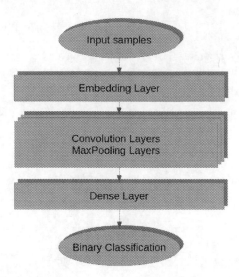

Fig. 3. Flow Diagram of the network model

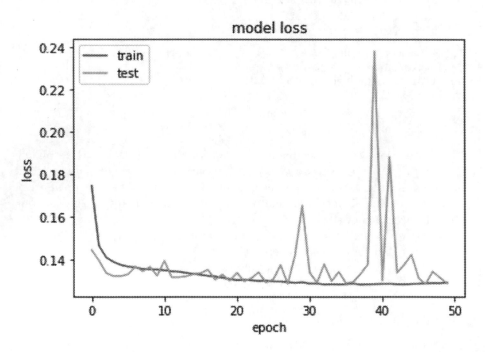

Fig. 4. Loss and validation loss for the model

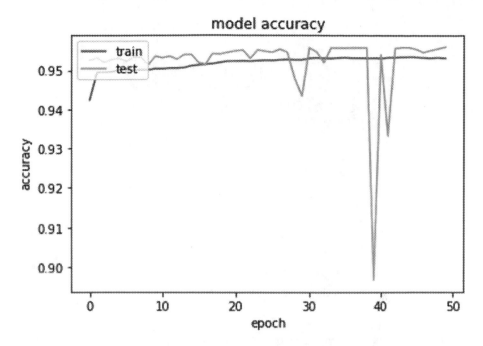

Fig. 5. Accuracy and validation accuracy for the model

		Predicted Labels	
		True	False
True Labels	True	34,912	3,226
	False	140	38,142

Fig. 6. Confusion matrix of results

the search algorithm, it can be seen that asymptotically there is a converging attractor around which our model is stationed.

The Confusion Matrix [12] indicates that the model is well performing, while highlighting rooms for improvement, especially in the phase of choosing the optimizer and modulating the hyper-parameters, see Fig. 6 and Fig. 7.

The apparent high number of "true negatives" depends on the phenomenon of training data padding, necessary for neural networks of this type, which require input sequences of a predetermined length.

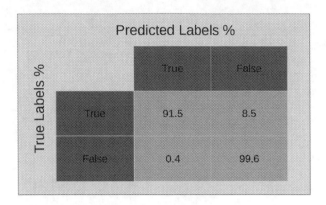

Fig. 7. Confusion matrix of results (%)

3   Further Development of the CNN Approach to Proteins as a Tool for Chemical Modelling

A further development of this work is to extend the Deep Learning model to the analysis of more subtle properties of the aminoacid sequences of the proteins and, above all, to classification of properties of the protein molecular structure and energy. General possible relationships between sequence, structure and function of proteins are of particular interest.

There is no obvious way how to proceed towards the objective of feeding the CNN with different kind of protein properties, but next work clearly would imply at least an adaptation or even a reshaping of the CNN input layer, while the preparatory phase of the organization of data can be retained.

We can now anticipate, without going into details, some of the possible ways to simply make next moves, according to some directions as follows:

- adding more view to the statistical analysis of sequences, recasting the learning as directed also by occurrence and recurrence of single aminoacids in the protein sequences and at which position
- adding to the sequences, here represented as a series of integer numbers, some physically meaningful parameter, such as deformation indexes [13] for the aminoacids in the chain or order parameters such as the number of hydrogen bonding interactions
- adding to the sequences parameters describing the global minimum energy structure corresponding to the protein native status, looking for patterns and regularities.

4 Conclusions and Future Works

Despite the very promising results shown by the simulations, we believe that there is considerable room for improvement both in the selection of the system's hyper-parameters and in the preparation and management of the data needed to learn the machine.

Our idea is to continue to explore the possibility of using CNN rather than RNN, as we consider it advantageous to use light models that can be easily implemented on machines with more modest hardware equipment.

Furthermore, it is important to limit the use of training data padding to decrease the number of "true negatives": a working hypothesis could be the segmentation of the sequences, hypotheses on which we are currently working.

Acknowledgments. A.L. and N.F.L. thank the Dipartimento di Chimica, Biologia e Biotecnologie dell'Università di Perugia (FRB, Fondo per la Ricerca di Base 2017) and the Italian MIUR and the University of Perugia for the financial support of the AMIS project through the program "Dipartimenti di Eccellenza". A. L. acknowledges financial support from MIUR PRIN 2015 (contract 2015F59J3R_002). A.L. thanks the OU Supercomputing Center for Education & Research (OSCER) at the University of Oklahoma, for allocated computing time.

References

1. LeCun, Y., Bengio, Y., Hinton, G.: Deep learning. Nature **521**, 436–444 (2015)
2. Schmidhuber, J.: Deep learning in neural networks: an overview. Neural Netw. **61**, 85–117 (2015)
3. Liu, X.: Deep recurrent neural network for protein function prediction from sequence (2017). arXiv: 1701.08318 [q-bio.QM]
4. Sze, V., et al.: Hardware for machine learning: challenges and opportunities. In: IEEE Custom Integrated Circuits Conference (CICC), pp. 1–8. IEEE (2017)
5. Zhang, C., et al.: Optimizing FPGA-based accelerator design for deep convolutional neural networks. In: Proceedings of the 2015 ACM/SIGDA International Symposium on Field-Programmable Gate Arrays, pp. 161–170 (2015)
6. Biondi, G., Franzoni, V., Gervasi, O., Perri, D.: An approach for improving automatic mouth emotion recognition. In: Misra, S., et al. (eds.) ICCSA 2019. LNCS, vol. 11619, pp. 649–664. Springer, Cham (2019). https://doi.org/10.1007/978-3-030-24289-3_48
7. Perri, D., Sylos Labini, P., Gervasi, O., Tasso, S., Vella, F.: Towards a learning-based performance modeling for accelerating deep neural networks. In: Misra, S., et al. (eds.) ICCSA 2019. LNCS, vol. 11619, pp. 665–676. Springer, Cham (2019). https://doi.org/10.1007/978-3-030-24289-3_49
8. Berman, H.M., et al.: The protein data bank. Nucleic Acids Res. **28**, 235–242 (2000). http://www.rcsb.org/
9. Rubinstein, R.Y., Kroese, D.P.: The Cross-entropy Method: A Unified Approach to Combinatorial Optimization, Monte-Carlo Simulation and Machine Learning. Springer, New York (2013)
10. De Boer, P.-T., et al.: A tutorial on the cross-entropy method. Ann. Oper. Res. **134**(1), 19–67 (2005). https://doi.org/10.1007/s10479-005-5724-z

11. Zeiler, M.D.: ADADELTA: an adaptive learning rate method. arXiv preprint arXiv:1212.5701 (2012)
12. Visa, S., et al.: Confusion matrix-based feature selection. MAICS **710**, 120–127 (2011)
13. Aquilanti, V., Lombardi, A., Yurtsever, E.: Global view of classical clusters: the hyperspherical approach to structure and dynamics. Phys. Chem. Chem. Phys. **4**, 5040–5051 (2002)

International Workshop on Tools and Techniques in Software Development Process (TTSDP 2020)

Evolution and Progress of Women's Participation in the Ecuadorian Policy Period 2009–2019

Marcelo León[1](✉), Wladimir Sosa[1](✉), Angélica Guamán[1](✉),
Rodrigo Rivera[1](✉), and Mireya Serrano[2](✉)

[1] Universidad Nacional de Loja, Loja, Ecuador
marcelo.leon@unileon.es, wladimirsj.93@gmail.com,
guamangie@gmail.com, bryan.rivera@unl.edu.ec
[2] Asociación de Becarios del Ecuador ABREC, Loja, Ecuador
mireserranob@gmail.com

Abstract. This paper analyses the evolution of women's political participation in Ecuador in the last decade, 2009–2019. This is highly important since it helps to develop an international and regional retrospective on equal political participation. When measuring the political participation of Ecuadorian women, official data from the National Electoral Council-Ecuador was used, as well as, other state databases. The results of this research indicate that, firstly, there has been a substantial change in the participation of Ecuadorian women's policy over time, and in the legislation and its application. Secondly, there is a notable gender disparity. Male are mostly seen as candidates for political position such as Mayors, Governors, or Presidents. This reflects cultural marked aspects in the Ecuadorian society. Thirdly, the country is deficient in its vertical parity policy, and does not have a horizontal parity. And finally, this paper shows that the political participation of women in Ecuador depends on the region.

Keywords: Political participation · Women · Ecuador · Equality · Gender

1 Introduction

The end of the 20th and the initial years of the 21th century was a period of time marked by a sustained economic growth; nonetheless, Latin America and other regions have low equality levels and not strong indicators of well-being [26]. Countries have been under a process of growth and expansion of the economic variables of the countries [16], however, this have not been translated in a better access to income-generating opportunities [22, 27], or access to information [10–13], or in other non-economic conditions such as self-esteem [23, 24], or better life conditions to people [30], such as health and education [21, 24]. If these economic problems have not been solved or partially solved, is less probable that gender gaps are reduced. Nonetheless, it has also been argued that the scenario for women and minorities groups, regarding employment and the general situation have been improving in the last decades [30].

Roles of women and men have been changed in the last decades at the worldwide level, as well as in particular regions. There has been an evolution in the dimensions of

© Springer Nature Switzerland AG 2020
O. Gervasi et al. (Eds.): ICCSA 2020, LNCS 12255, pp. 561–573, 2020.
https://doi.org/10.1007/978-3-030-58820-5_42

the role of women into the social, economic and political aspects of the society [26]. It is also important to mention that women and men have different positions at the society, and different resource access, where not only roles, but also necessities are different. This differentiation is helpful to understand how to achieve long term emancipation for women [24].

In the field of the politics, this has not been an exception. Men have dominated the field of politics. They have been those with the power to make decisions and develop unequal normative systems and parameters that have normalized gender inequalities [2, 3, 21, 27]. It was not until the 20th century that women got the right to active and passive suffrage, thus, the right to vote and be elected [17]. Not surprisingly, women access to politics is weak [30], they have been always excluded from politics [17], and are not well represented in high level positions [30]. Hence, this group have to fight to be nominated for politics positions, and if they are considered, they are allocated in lower prestige positions [8, 18]. In fact, between 1980s and the first decade of the 21st century, there were only seven female presidents democratically elected, 20% of women were able to be part of the parliamentary seats, and up to 22 percent of elected municipal council representatives [9].

One of the greatest achievements of the women's movement, in several countries, was to debate about gender. By itself, gender equality is an important objective [30]. Indisputable, if women win votes that are directly related with a traditional norms evolution [17] and the greater the emphasis on gender equality, the greater the link with a cultural change process associated with democratization [17]. However, even in these cases, gender inequality is still present. For instance, in Africa since the 80 s the proportion of women having cabinet positions has increase, but women are still not assigned to the strategically policy areas like military force, foreign affairs, or economics, or the "masculine" ones [18]. Additionally, if we compare men and women, women tend to think that men are more like qualified to run for office and are more politically ambitious [20].

The present study gathers some data about the women participation in Ecuador. The first section refers to a review of the literature about the political women participation at a regional and national scale, which serves as a theoretical basis for this document. The second section analyses the electoral context in Ecuador in the past decades. While the third section explains the statistical analysis through excel and stata. Finally, the fourth section details the results and the main conclusions.

2   Regional Vision of Women's Political Participation

Over the years, equal political participation has evolved in Latin America and the Caribbean, as reported in 2015, by the United Nations Entity for Gender Equality and the Empowerment of Women (UNWOMEN). There have been important meetings where equal participation has been promoted, and this has helped to boost the presence of women in the political regional arena [9]. In the last years, it has been common to find women Ministers and high female authorities signing international agreements [30]. Regarding the regional meetings, there are several examples. The first one is the I Conference of the International Year of Women, held in Mexico in 1975, where a continuous and systematized process began, promoting the creation and articulation of institutions and organizations that seek the women equal participation [28, 30].

There has been a systematic leadership lead by the Economic Commission for Latin America and the Caribbean (ECLAC). This institution has been promoting the inclusion of women in the politics at the IV World Conference of Women, held in 1995 in Beijing, China. In later regional conferences, the presence of senior female helped to sensitize about the important role of equality in both public policy and policy maker. Finally, the X Regional Conference of Women held in Quito in 2007 has been one of the most important conference, because it was where a consensus regards the regional agreements on women's equal political rights were achieved.

Nonetheless, the number of women with positions in the executive branch and in parliament has stagnated worldwide, and has only experienced some marginal improvements since 2015. According to data from the Inter-Parliamentary Union shows than in 2018, only 30.7% of representatives in the region are women, and they have lower or single chambers, as mentioned by Krook and O'Brien [18]. At the regional level, the three countries with the highest rates of female participation are: Cuba with a 53.2%, followed by Bolivia with 53.1%, and Mexico with 48.2%; while the countries with the lowest values are: Nicaragua with 45.6%, Costa Rica with 45.6%, and finally Ecuador with 34%, as we can see on Fig. 1.

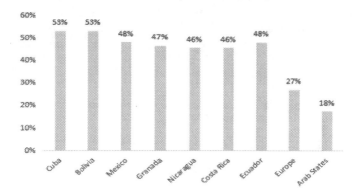

Fig. 1. Female participation.

3   The Political Participation of Women in Ecuador

The year of 1928 was a historically date for Ecuador; under the presidency of Isidro Ayora, women obtained the right to vote being a remarkable milestone in politics and in the public bodies for women. Matilde Hidalgo Navarro de Procel was the precursor in 1929; and Ecuador became the first country in Latin America that granted the vote to women. It was not until 1967 where the woman's right to vote was optional, and mandatory for lawyer's women [28].

Even with those regional milestones, Ecuador has the lowest rate of women participation in the region. Actually, this is also confirmed by the National Electoral Council (CNE), which states that from 2002 to 2014, participation of women in election process is lower than men participation [5]. As a result, four legal reforms have been promoted by women's movements in Ecuador directly influencing in the improvement of women's participation in Ecuadorian politics [7]. Those reforms are going to be mention chronologically.

First, the Labour Protection Act of 1997. This policy established a minimum quota of 20 women in the multi-personal lists of November 30, 1998, for the elections at national and provincial deputies. Second, the Constitutional Reform of 1998 states an equitable participation of men and women in electoral processes (article 102). The 1998 constitution introduces equal opportunities despite gender. It establishes a minimum percentage of women political participation, which ranges from 30% to a cap of 50%. Finally, the 2008 Constitution approved by referendum in the same year, in its article 116, establishes principles of proportionality, equality of vote, equity, parity and alternation between women and men, or what can be called as horizontal parity [ASAMBLEA]. This document also indicates that in Ecuador, the candidate's selection must be developing in internal democratic processes, where equal participation between men and women has to be guaranteed [6].

As seen in Fig. 2, there has been an increase of women participation from 1995 to 2015, which can be directly related with the Ecuadorian reforms established. At 90s, women participation was almost null; on the following decade, women participation in politics have increased, but still women have not been well represented. It is only since 2010, where the numbers of women participation in politics have been close to reach the suggested Ecuadorian quote.

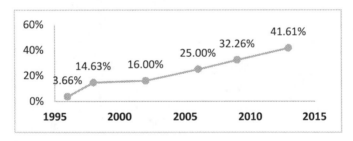

Fig. 2. Evolution of the percentage of participation of women in Ecuadorian politics. **Source:** [1]

It is also important to refer to vertical and horizontal parity. Vertical parity proposes gender parity in the number of delegations, and party bodies. In other words, vertical parity focuses on numerical parity specifically at the stage of the nomination of candidates on the lists. While, horizontal parity is used to refer where not only numerical parity is important. Here the alternation in the nomination of candidates, demanding that women also enter the first places [4].

3.1 Historical Background: Women Participation in Jurisdictional and National Elections from 2002–2008

In Ecuador, information related to the elections processes, are officially presented by the National Electoral Council (CNE). This data helps to analyses the compliance with the legal participation quotas, regarding the equal opportunities principle. For example, if we analyse women participation in the seven electoral processes from 2002 to 2014, it is possible to identify that the highest disparity occurred in General Elections of 2002, where approximately men candidates were twice that female candidates (61% of men compared to 39% of women). In contrast, the more equal elections happened in 2007, regarding the election of Constituent Assembly Members, with a 48.8% presence of women leading candidates.

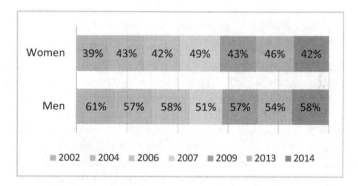

Fig. 3. Historical elections participation: 2002–2014. **Source:** CNE 2016

As seen in Fig. 3, regarding women participation in these seven elections processes, it can be identified that the average of women participation is 43%, and that each new voting process have a higher participation from 2002 to 2007, and a slowly decrease between 2009 and 2014. There is a high probability that these participation values are the result of reform policy implemented in the 2000, regarding candidate's participation.

However, this increase in women participation in elections does not have a direct relationship with women elected authorities. For instance, in 2002, only 21% of the elected authorities were women from the 39% participating. By 2004, the percentage of elected women increased about 8%, but it and fallen again to 23% in 2006.

It is only in the Constituent Assembly elections (2007), where women have a 49% of participation and 35% of election. This is the unique electoral process, where a high percentage of women were elected. Nevertheless, this election was a highly important one since representatives elected where part of the decision-making process to elaborate the new Constitution of the Republic of Ecuador in 2008.

Therefore, it is identified that there is no gender equity for electoral process participation between 2002 and 2014, even when the trend tends to converge on 2007. Also, There is still a big gap to achieve gender equity, even when the trend have a progressively reduction between men and women, as we can see on Fig. 4.

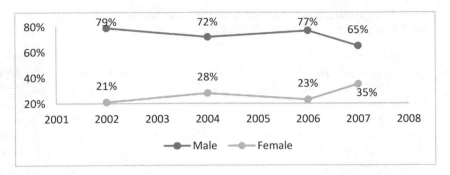

Fig. 4. Evolution of women participation in Ecuadorian politics, expressed in percentages.
Source: [CNE16; CNE19]

3.2   Historical Background: Women Participation in Jurisdictional and National Elections from 2008–2019

The Montecristi Constitution approved in 2008, in its article 95 established that the participation of citizens is guaranteed, both at the individual or collective scenarios, and every process of decision-making, planning and management of public affairs, it is guided among other equality principles [5]. In fact, in the general and sectional elections in 2009, 44% were women from a total of 39.580 people among the different political positions. The difference in participation between men and women was low. From that total, there was space only for 5.640 political representatives. And not surprisingly, numbers for men where higher that numbers for women, 75% versus 23%, respectively. Lowest percentages for women election are related with President - Vicepresident and Mayor Positions. This confirms again previous studies who mentioned that even with a higher participation of women in the political arena; they are still not elected for influential positions [18, 27] (Table 1).

Table 1. Participation of women in the general and sectional elections of 2009, expressed in percentage.

Elections of 2009			
Candidates		Elected authorities	
Parameter	% women	Parameter	% women
Mayors	57%	Mayors	6%
National Assembly Members	48%	National Assembly Members	40%
Provincial and foreign assembly members	47%	Provincial and foreign assembly members	31%
Rural Councillors	44%	Rural Councillors	25%
Urban councillors	47%	Urban councillors	31%
Vowels Parish Boards	43%	Vowels Parish Boards	22%
Andean parliamentarians	43%	Andean parliamentarians	60%
Prefects and vice prefects	13%	Prefects and vice prefects	9%
President and Vice President	25%	President and Vice President	0%
Total participation	**44%**	**Total participation**	23%

Source: [5]

In the general elections held in 2013, 2.071 candidates were available for the different dignities, from which 54% were men and 46% women. In this electoral process there was a minimal difference in participation between men and women. In this case, from the 203 dignities elected, 38% of the 46% women participated were elected.

It is important to note that all the Andean parliamentarians participated obtained the votes increasing their power access to Latin America opportunities; nevertheless their presence in this political decision making scenario has never equalled men [15] (Table 2).

Table 2. Participation of women in the general elections of 2013 (%).

Elections of 2013			
Candidates		Elected authorities	
Parameter	% women	Parameter	% women
National Assembly Members	50%	National Assembly Members	47%
Constituents by constituency	46%	Constituents by constituency	44%
Provincial and foreign assembly members	47%	Provincial and foreign assembly members	34%
Andean parliamentarians	40%	Andean parliamentarians	40%
President and Vice President	0%	President and Vice President	0%
Total participation	46%	Total participation	38%

Source: [5]

In the sectional elections of 2014, 26.911 candidates presented for the different dignities from which 44% were women. There is also a minimal difference between the participation between men and women. In this process only 26% of the 5.628 dignities elected where women.

In this election, the category of Mayors and Prefects and Vice prefects are the most influential and powerful ones. One is focused on the county level and the other one at the province level, respectively. In both cases, the difference in the percentage of women participating versus women, elected is the 5%, which is also the lower percentage difference between a candidate and elected authorities. This can be the result of the increase in education and work experience in women; the more educated and experienced women are the lower the gap difference between women and men profiles [15] (Table 3).

In the 2017 general elections, 26.911 candidates participated in the election process. From this number of candidates 46% were women. In this specific electoral process, there is a small difference between the participation of men and women. As in 2014, elections, there are 5.628 available elected positions, where 38% of that total were women.

Table 3. Women participation women in the sectional elections of 2014.

Elections of 2014			
Candidates		Elected authorities	
Parameter	% women	Parameter	% women
Mayors	12%	Mayors	7%
Rural Councillors	88%	Rural Councillors	25%
Urban councillors	45%	Urban councillors	34%
Vowels Parish Boards	43%	Vowels Parish Boards	25%
Prefects and vice prefects	14%	Prefects and vice prefects	9%
Total participation	44%	Total participation	26%

Source: [5]

As seen in Table 4, the highest percentage of women electoral participation is for National Assembly members at national and provincial positions. And there was a small percentage, in fact, the lowest one, for women participation for President and Vice president Positions. Regarding the elected authorities, the highest percentage is for Andean parliamentarians with a 60%, followed by the National Assembly Members with a 53%. Even when the numbers show that women are being represented, it is highly probable that the individual characteristics of the female candidates do not matter to the electorate, because parties are more important. Voters will choose those candidates in the parties that they believe have a great probability to win [20].

Table 4. Women participation in the 2017 general elections.

Elections of 2017			
Candidates		Elected authorities	
Parameter	% women	Parameter	% women
National Assembly Members	48%	National Assembly Members	53%
Constituents by constituency	45%	Constituents by constituency	44%
Provincial and foreign assembly members	47%	Provincial and foreign assembly members	31%
Andean parliamentarians	45%	Andean parliamentarians	60%
President and Vice President	13%	President and Vice President	0%
Total participation	46%	Total participation	38%

Elaboration: Research team.
Source: [7, 8]

The last election happened on 2019 and it was for sectional elections. 41.517 candidates run for the different sectional dignities, from where 43% were women. However, percentages show that women participation is less than the 50%, and the lowers percentages are for Mayors (14%) and Prefects (18%). As historical, men are significantly more likely than women to be recruited to run for high level positions [21].

As in the other cases, the percentage of elected women is less than the 50%. From the total of 5.607 dignities elected only 27% were women. Most of women were elected as urban councillors (33%) and Vowels in Parish boards (27%), and percentages of election is almost the same as in 2013, 2014 and 2017 elections. Despite of the years, women elections for the jurisdictional positions remain equal (Table 5).

Table 5. Women participation in the sectional elections of 2019, expressed in percentage.

Elections of 2019			
Candidates		Candidates	
Parameter	% women	Parameter	% women
Mayors	14%	Mayors	8%
Rural Councillors	43%	Rural Councillors*	26%
Urban councillors	46%	Urban councillors*	33%
Vowels Parish Boards	44%	Vowels Parish Boards	27%
Prefects and vice prefects	18%	Prefects and vice prefects	17%
Total participation	43%	Total participation	27%

Source: [5]

Note: Data provided until March 31, in the Los Ríos province the results are not yet available for the repetition of the electoral process.

3.3 Women Participation for General and Sectional Dignities Between 2009 and 2017

In this part of the research, women participation in general election between 2009 and 2017 is analysed regarding the horizontal and vertical parity. Figures were made using a statistical program.

It is important to mention that in general elections there are 7 positions available, being the president and vice president the most influential or important positions, followed by the National Assemblies. In the sectional elections, there are 5 categories: Mayors, Rural councillors, Urban councillors, Prefect and vice prefect and vowels of parish boards in sectional elections, where mayors and prefects and vice prefects are the most influential ones.

Women maintain a relative parity in the participation with a range of 40% and 53%, except for the dignity of President and Vice President where women participation is not representative, as seen in Fig. 5.

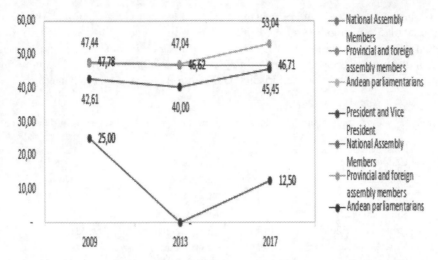

Fig. 5. Women's candidacy for general elections in the period 2009–2017. **Source:** [5]

In the case of the elected authorities since 2009, the average of participation is 45%; however, women have not been able to win the highest cabinet positions, such as President (Fig. 6).

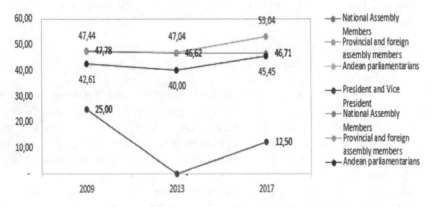

Fig. 6. Women elected in general elections during the period 2009–2017. **Source:** [5]

In the case of women participation for sectional authorities, it is evident that female participation has been considered mostly to occupy lower cabinet positions. There is a low participation for Mayor or Prefect. Even when the women participation is low for power and influential positions, there have an average participation of 61%, which can be considered relative gender parity (Fig. 7).

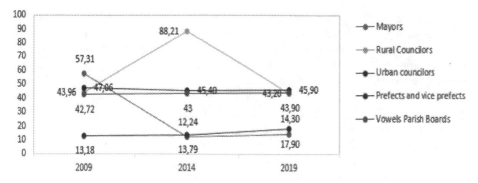

Fig. 7. Women's Candidacies for sectional elections 2009–2019. **Source:** [5]

In the case of the elected authorities since 2009, an average participation of 20 spaces is in the urban councils, which obtain greater preference from the citizens to exercise the position. Mayor's positions, on the other hand, even when they have a high level of influence on the society, have the lower women candidatures. Numbers have not changed from 2009 to 2019, they are around 5 candidacies. Same scenario happens for the Prefects and vice prefect's positions, where historically numbers are less than 15 positions. Hence, horizontal parity is not achieved (Fig. 8).

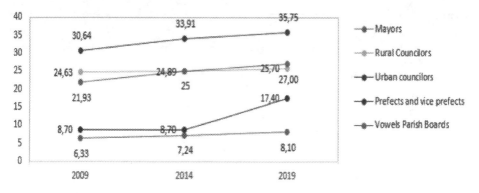

Fig. 8. Women's candidacies for sectional elections 2009–2019. **Source:** [5]

4   Conclusions

Currently, equal participation is a development goal set by international organizations and adapted by the different development plans and national legislatures of each country. Over time, the necessary policies have been implementing to ensure and guarantee the participation of women's policy in the country.

At the public sector, women's participation has gotten important achievements. The principles of equal opportunities are established, in the run for different dignities of popular election. However, despite this equal opportunities scenario proposed, in general and sectional elections, the vote of citizens in the exercise of democracy shows a strong preference of the electors for male candidates to occupy the dignities as mayor's offices, prefectures, or president positions, conditioning reflected by cultural aspects and trust issues. In other words, women participation in election have increase for the lower cabinet position as we can see on sectional elections from 2014 to 2019, but the number of women elected is still low. It was only on 2017 that elected women achieved the cap proposed in the normative. A few percentage of women have been nominated for high political positions such as President, Vice president, Mayors or Prefecture, but only a few have been elected for this elections.

In the way of the equal participation of women in Ecuadorian politics, many substantial changes have been seen for equity; nevertheless, Ecuador has a vertical parity and does not have a horizontal parity, to face problems such as the heading of male lists, or so that in the unipersonal positions there is no mandatory parity.

As a result of this research, the team group suggest that in order to achieve equal participation of women in Ecuadorian politics, we have to move from a vertical to horizontal parity, where beyond equal access opportunities established in the normative documents of the country, application of those norms could help to significantly reduce the equity gap in Ecuador. Undoubtedly, some improvements have occurred in women participation; but still, there are topics and maybe normative documents that have to be elaborated in order to comply with the gender equality principles.

References

1. Constitution of the Republic of Ecuador. https://www.gob.ec/sites/default/files/regulations/2018-09/Constituci%C3%B3n.pdf
2. Badillo, S.: Affirmative actions such as the development of women's Right to Political Participation. Undergraduate thesis, Central University of Ecuador (2015)
3. Bareiro, L., Soto, L.: The hour of substantive equality. Political participation of women in Latin America and the Hispanic Caribbean. Technical report, ONU Women (2015)
4. Benavides, T.: The effect of vertical and horizontal parity mechanisms on political representation in Costa Rica: the case of the 2018 legislative elections. J. Derecho Electoral **27**, 1659–2069 (2019)
5. National Electoral Council. http://cne.gob.ec/es/estadisticas/publicaciones/category/877-publicaciones
6. National Electoral Council. https://app03.cne.gob.ec/EstadisticaCNE/Ambito/Index.aspx
7. Del Campo, E., Magdaleno, E.: Legislative advances of positive action in Bolivia, Ecuador and Peru. In: Women and Citizen Scenarios. FLACSO, Quito (2008)
8. Escobar-Lemmon, M., Michelle, M., Taylor-Robinson, M.: Women ministers in Latin American government. Am. J. Polit. Sci. **49**, 829–844 (2005)
9. Fernández, A.: Gender quotas and female political representation in Mexico and Latin America. Argumentos **24**, 247–2774 (2011)
10. Fletschner, D., Mesbah, D.: Gender disparity in access to information: do spouses share what they know? World Dev., 1422–1433 (2011)
11. Florez, H., Sánchez, M., Villalobos, J.: A catalog of automated analysis methods for enterprise models. SpringerPlus **5**(1), 1–24 (2016). https://doi.org/10.1186/s40064-016-2032-9

12. Florez, H., Sánchez, M.E., Villalobos, J.: Embracing imperfection in enterprise architecture models. In: PoEM (Short Papers), pp. 8–17, November 2013
13. Florez, H., Sánchez, M., Villalobos, J.: iArchiMate: a tool for managing imperfection in enterprise models. In: 2014 IEEE 18th International Enterprise Distributed Object Computing Conference Workshops and Demonstrations, pp. 201–210. IEEE, 1 September 2014
14. Fox, R., Lawless, J.: If only they'd ask: gender, recruitment, and political ambition. J. Polit. **72**, 310–326 (2010)
15. Hunt, M., Piscopo, J.: Women in politics in Latin America and the Caribbean. Working paper, Social Science Research Council (2014)
16. International Labour Organization (ILO): Model of Global Employment Trends. International Labour Organization, Geneva (2007)
17. Inglehart, R., Norris, P., Welzel, C.: Gender equality and democracy. Comp. Soc. **1**, 235–264 (2002)
18. Krook, M., O'Brien, D.: All the president's men? The appointment of female cabinet ministers worldwide. J. Polit. **74**, 840–855 (2012)
19. Lawless, J., Fox, R.: It Still Takes a Candidate: Why Women Don't Run for Office. Cambridge University Press, New York (2010)
20. Mackay, F., Kenny, M., Chappell, L.: New institutionalism through a gender lens: towards a feminine institutionalism? Int. Polit. Sci. Rev. **31** (2010)
21. Mendez, O., Florez, H.: Applying the flipped classroom model using a VLE for foreign languages learning. In: Florez, H., Diaz, C., Chavarriaga, J. (eds.) ICAI 2018. CCIS, vol. 942, pp. 215–227. Springer, Cham (2018). https://doi.org/10.1007/978-3-030-01535-0_16
22. Milazzo, A., Goldstein, M.: Governance and Women's Economic and Political Participation: Power Inequalities, Formal Constraints and Norms. Oxford Press, Oxford (2019)
23. Morante, A., del Pilar Villamil, M., Florez, H.: Framework for supporting the creation of marketing strategies. Int. Inf. Inst. (Tokyo) Inf. **20**(10A), 7371–7378 (2017)
24. Moser, C.: Gender Planning and Development. Theory, Practice and Training. Red entre mujeres and Flora Tristán ediciones, Lima (1995)
25. United Nations: Women's rights are human rights. United Nations Publication, Naciones Unidas Derechos Humanos (2014)
26. Ñopo, H.: New Century Old Disparities. Gender and Ethnic Earnings Gaps in Latin America and the Caribbean. IDB, Washington (2012)
27. Paes de Barros, R., Ferreira, G., Molinas Vega, J., Saavedra Chanduvi, J.: Measuring Inequality of Opportunities in Latin America and the Caribbean. World Bank, Washington (2009)
28. Sosa-Buchholz, X.: Women, public sphere and populism in Brazil, Argentina and Ecuador, 1870–1960. Procesos **27**, 81–105 (2008)
29. Unión Interparlamentaria. https://www.ipu.org/
30. World Bank: Gender Equality and Development. World Development Report 2012, Washington (2011)
31. Zuluaga, I.: Economic Development Principles. ECOE Ediciones, Bogotá (2008)

International Workshop on Urban Form Studies (UForm 2020)

Finding Centrality: Developing GIS-Based Analytical Tools for Active and Human-Oriented Centres

Yannis Paraskevopoulos[(✉)] and Yorgos N. Photis

National Technical University of Athens,
Heroon Polytechneiou 9, Athens 15780, Greece
parask.yannis@gmail.com

Abstract. Integrated urban-transport planning should exploit not only conventional methodologies, which are crucial for identifying the already established local centres of the city (*places with people*), but also multi-dimensional methodologies for identifying the vibrant places of the city that can facilitate the centrality needs of citizens and provide access to urban vitality, functionality, and liveability (*places for people*). In this article, we conceptualise and quantitatively define these two types of centres, as *Active Centres (AC)* and *Human-oriented Centres (HoC)*, respectively. Accordingly, two distinct methodological tools (available as python scripts and ArcGIS toolboxes in a public repository) are introduced for identifying **Active** (*where-it-is*) and **Human-oriented** (*where-it-should be*) centres. Active Centres are identified based on the functional density of the study area, while Human-oriented centres are found based on the density and diversity of typological criteria, considered essential for liveable centres. To this end, the aim of this work is two-fold. On the one hand, to formulate a comprehensive methodology for identifying different types of centrality and on the other to develop a GIS-based analytical toolkit which can assist evidence-based planning and support decision making towards sustainable urban form, active mobility, and human-scale public places. The proposed methodology and tools have been implemented and evaluated while effectively identifying the Active and Human-oriented Centres of an Athenian suburb, Greece.

Keywords: Centrality · Urban centres · Space syntax · Spatial analysis · Urban planning

1 Introduction

City constitutes the place where all kinds and classes of people are mixed so as to produce a common, though constantly changing and ephemeral life, forcing this heterogeneous ensemble to interact [1]. The essential feature of urbanity is, therefore, concentration and co-existence [2] and the local centres that emerge in a city are at the core of this process. These "*activity nodes*" [3, p. 166] beyond their role in city's functionality, act as meeting points for citizens, where practices of encounter and exchange (economic, social etc.) take place, where "*you can go to see people, and to be*

© Springer Nature Switzerland AG 2020
O. Gervasi et al. (Eds.): ICCSA 2020, LNCS 12255, pp. 577–592, 2020.
https://doi.org/10.1007/978-3-030-58820-5_43

seen (...), the place where people with a shared way of life gather together to rub shoulders and confirm their communities" (p. 169). Therefore, a centre in order to be meaningfully successful should be functional for its residents but also vibrant, attractive and accessible for all its users. It should promote active street life, animation in the street, dense and diverse human activity and movement -especially walking- and in summary to create what Jacobs [4] called "*intricate sidewalk ballet*" (p. 50) of people walking around neighbourhoods, at different times for different purposes.

There are numerous theoretical approaches framing the notion and the different aspects of centrality [3–5]. However, relevant analytical methods describe and define a city's centrality by focusing on the distribution and density of limited urban features such as population groups, jobs and retail activity [6]. Despite their strength in locating established local centres, these conventional approaches fail to explore and reveal the complex nature of centrality as a phenomenon. The main reason for that is because functional, vibrant and accessible centres cannot be captured through a limited number of the urban environment's characteristics.

In this paper, we conceptualize these two types of centres, as **Active** and **Human-oriented**, develop detailed methodologies for exploring them and provide GIS-based analytical tools to identify them. Therefore, the research questions of this paper are the following:

RQ1. How to quantitatively define and evaluate the magnitude of the Active Centres of a city?

RQ2. How to quantitatively define and evaluate the completeness of the Human-oriented Centres of a city?

RQ3. Can we develop semi-automated GIS-based analytical tools which can support the identification of these two types of centres?

In order to address these questions, we set a two-fold focus. First, to introduce methodologies for identifying Active Centres (AC) and Human-oriented Centres (HoC) and subsequently, to develop GIS-based analytical tools for implementing these methodologies. Supplemental material (python scripts and ArcGIS Pro toolboxes) has been made available in a public repository[1], along with all maps and figures of this article[2].

2   Background and Conceptual Framework

2.1   Theoretical Background and Relevant Work

Centrality clusters can be understood as descriptions of phenomena or as abstractions or symbols for a certain function in a larger context (the neighbourhood or the city or the region) The concept of 'centre' within architecture and urban design is rather different from its more precise definition within physics: it is ambiguous; both in a

---

[1] https://doi.org/10.6084/m9.figshare.11973951.v1, https://doi.org/10.6084/m9.figshare.11973933.v1,
   https://doi.org/10.6084/m9.figshare.11974059.v1, https://doi.org/10.6084/m9.figshare.11973996.v1.

[2] https://doi.org/10.6084/m9.figshare.11973642.v1.

symbolic sense and in that it should be perceived as a centre in terms of their urban surroundings [7]. Consequently, centrality and the local centres that emerge in a city have been researched by numerous approaches, both theoretical and analytical. The former frame the notion of centrality and the different aspects of a vibrant and liveable centre while the latter mostly quantify centrality based on individual urban characteristics.

However, the majority of the analytical approaches identifying urban centres derive from a geographical or configurational perspective, and exploit limited, if not just one, dimensions of urbanity. To this end, geographical approaches generally utilise functional pattern, population density and job density (e.g. [8, 9]) whereas, configurational research focuses mostly on network centrality, as conceptualised by Space Syntax [10], in order to predict human activity in urban space and verify the emergence of centrality clusters (e.g. [11–13]). Hence, most empirical studies of the urban structure and consequently the developed methodologies suffer from the limitation of focusing on single attributes when quantifying centrality. What is more, the available geoprocessing tools for analysing urban centres, are either geographical (e.g. Metropolitan Form Analysis Toolbox for ArcGIS [9]) or configurational (e.g. Space Syntax Toolkit [14] and Place Syntax Tool [15] for QGis/MapInfo), and in either case uni-dimensional. In addition, these GIS-based analytical tools despite their success in identifying the existing centrality pattern of a city, meaning the already established local centres, fail to quantify the various urban elements that contribute to liveable, vibrant and functional central areas.

On the other hand, theoretical approaches put forward a combination of spatio-functional urban elements for defining the meaningful centres of the city [3–5]. Meaning the public places that are integrated in city's everyday life and can facilitate citizens' centrality needs. In particular, urban features such as pubic open spaces, commercial activities and network centrality have been highlighted as fundamental to vibrant centrality clusters [4, 12, 16, 17]. Moreover, activities beyond retail, such as places of work, education, public/municipal services etc., have been singled out as unique sources of urban viability and functionality [3, 6]. Evidently, such multidimensional approaches have not been significantly researched under a quantitative scope. Lately, there has been an increasing interest in terms of studies, research and publications towards the identification of urban centres as multi-dimensional phenomena [18–20] none of which is combined with GIS-based analytical tools and/or toolkits.

2.2 Conceptual Framework

As presented in previous sections of this work, local centres that emerge in a city constitute one of its most elemental component and therefore should be at the epicentre of any planning process [16]. To this end, we argue that any integrated urban planning strategy should take into account both the already established local centres of the city (*places-with-people*), and the centres of the city that have the ability to facilitate everyday practices of human co-existence, (*places-for-people*). Accordingly, we provide conceptual and quantitative definitions of the former as '*Active Centres*' (AC) a term derived from the work of Vaughan et al. [6] and the latter as '*Human-oriented Centres*' (HoC) based on the work of Jacobs and Gehl [4, 5].

Active Centres (AC)

AC refer to the already established urban centres with dense people's presence, the existing pattern of centrality regardless of any additional criteria towards urban vitality, functionality and liveability. Founded on the relevant approach introduced by Vaughan et al. [6] we define AC as the places of the cities with significant functional density. Meaning the density of non-residential uses, which corresponds with a variety of human activities and therefore attract dense people's presence [8, 18, 19, 21] (Fig. 1).

Fig. 1. Conceptualization of Active Centres (AC)

The critical advantage of the proposed approach, is that it builds upon the latest relevant research [19, 20] which challenges the retail-centric view for identifying centrality clusters and proposes that the sources of centrality are embedded in the diverse socio-economic and cultural activities that take place beyond the high street's shopping hub. Namely, the utilisation of functional density constitutes the suitable proxy for identifying the AC of the city, since it encompasses this wide variety of activities. It should be noted that in this paper, the term 'non-residential uses' includes any and all build-use/land-use that is not a residence, that attract/generate human activity.

Human-oriented Centres (HoC)

We define HoC as the central places of the city that are suitable to facilitate meaningful centrality (*where-it-should be*). As places integrated in the everyday life of citizens that satisfy their *centrality needs* for entertainment, communal activities, work etc.; as 'human nodes' where practices of co-existence can manifest without any restrictions in access and finally as places where the physical form of the city and network centrality, in particular, can provide the opportunity of human encounter and urban vibrancy [4, 11]. In other words, we define this type of centrality as 'Human-Oriented' and 'Human-oriented Centres' as places for people, *and* as places with people [5]. Therefore, in order to define HoC, we utilise five typological criteria that derive from three different components of centrality (Functional Centrality, Network Centrality, and Accessible Centrality).

We introduce these three centrality components to create a more comprehensive understanding of the needs that a HoC should facilitate. 'Functional Centrality' refers to the different urban functions (commercial activities, public services, places of work etc.) and to what degree they are facilitated by the central areas of the city. 'Network Centrality' quantifies "*natural movement*" [11], as the intrinsic property of urban grid itself to form human activity and to unearth "*natural*" centralities. 'Accessible Centrality' refers to a fundamental element of human-oriented centralities, which is the meaningful open access to the places of human co-existence and interaction. Consequently, the proposed centrality criteria are defined as follows (Fig. 2):

1. '*Public open places of accessible co-existence (POPoAC)*' criterion refer to the Public Open Spaces of the city, formal and informal, which contribute to liveable and sustainable centralities as they provide a public meeting place with social meaning and open access.
2. '*Places of everyday retail and entertainment (PoERE)*' criterion refer to commercial activities such as markets, cafes, entertainment and other activities that facilitate the citizens' everyday needs for retail and recreation.
3. '*Places of communal activities (PoCA)*' criterion refer to the wide spectrum of activities beyond commercial that facilitate the everyday needs of residents, such as education, health facilities, religion, and municipal/public services. Their presence is essential for the '*place identity*' of a centre, especially a local one, and is what makes a city functional, competent and self-sufficient.

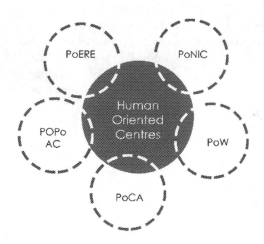

Fig. 2. Conceptualization of Human-oriented Centres (HoC)

4. '*Places of work (PoW)*' criterion refer to the urban functions providing jobs to citizens such as professional workshops, offices etc. These functions contribute to local economy not only as places of work but also as nodes of human activity creating movement at overlapping scales [6]

5. *'Places of network-driven intrinsic co-presence (PoNIC)'* criterion is essential for a human-scale centre as it refers to the ability of the urban grid to shape human activity and attract dense pedestrian movement. Specifically, we utilise the space syntax measure of local angular betweenness (also known as angular choice)[3] with a walkable radius (i.e. 600 m) which is found to be instrumental in detecting major pedestrian through-movement paths in a city [22].

3   Methodology and Methods

In order to provide the conceptual and analytical tools for identifying different typologies of urban centres, namely, AC and HoC, spatial analysis and geoprocessing tools are utilised and corresponding methodological workflows are developed. Kernel Density Estimation (KDE) is used for the elemental task of measuring the density of the features of interest for each methodology (land-use for AC and typological criteria for HoC). KDE uses the density within a range (window) of each observation to represent the value at the centre of the window [23, pp. 68–71]. KDE is not only a widely adopted tool for calculating the density of events, but is also considered ideal in a substantial amount of relevant research, regarding the identification and analysis of centrality clusters [8, 9, 24] since it has the comparative advantage of estimating the density of nearby objects to represent the property at the middle location. In this respect, KDE captures the very essence of location as reflected by densities of nearby Features of Interest. Ultimately, such an approach stresses the notion that it is not the place itself, in terms of X, Y coordinates that make it central and explain its setting but rather its surroundings [24]. Hence, KDE is not only utilized in order to for the analysis to be performed at a unified spatial reference unit level but also a prerequisite of accurately capturing the true dimensions and geographical extent of centres.

In such a framework, the radius and cell size of KDE, effectively signify the anticipated radius and (minimum) size of the identified centre, respectively, and thus shall be representative of the study area. Therefore, Centrality Cell size and Centrality radius are automatically estimated inside the developed tools as relative measures, representative of the study area. Specifically, based on the statistics of the study area's street segments, its average street-length is automatically calculated (*Mean_-Street_Length*) and subsequently the Centrality Radius is automatically set as three typical street segments. Respectively, the minimum (accepted) cluster size is automatically set as two typical urban blocks, after has been automatically estimated (*Mean_Block_Area*).

---

[3] **Angular Betweenness** (also known as Angular choice) is calculated by counting the number of times each street segment falls on the 'shortest path' (in terms of angular deviation) between all pairs of segments within a selected distance (termed 'radius') [22].

Table 1. Calculation of representative values for the various centre characteristics

Centre attribute	Representative value	Calculation
Centrality radius	3 typical street segments	3 × Mean_Street_Length
Centrality (min) size	2 typical urban block	2 × Mean_Block_Area

Table 1 depicts the study case-specific characteristics that are automatically cal-culated based on the urban blocks and the street segments of the study area.

3.1   Identifying Active Centres (AC)

This section describes the methodology for identifying the AC of a study area and their magnitude. The next figure (Fig. 3) demonstrates the 4-step methodological framework for constructing this workflow. The first step refers to the automatic calculation of the study area-specific Centrality radius and Centrality (min) size, as extensively explained in the previous section. The second-step concerns the estimation of non-residential density with the previously calculated radius and size which are representative for the study area. Subsequently, the cut-off Active Centrality Thresholds are automatically calculated based on the density statistics of the study area in order to single out the AC and their different magnitude (see Table 2). Finally, the delineation of the AC is implemented by reclassifying the *Functional Density Raster* (created in step-2) based on the *Active Centrality Thresholds* (estimated in step-3).

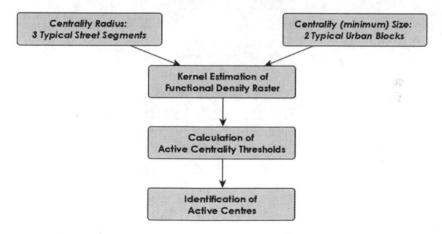

Fig. 3. Methodological steps for identifying AC and their magnitude

Table 2. Thresholds for identifying active centres and evaluating their magnitude

Centrality magnitude	Active centrality threshold (Functional_Density>)
Neighborhood centre	MEAN + 1 × STD
In-between centre	MEAN + 2 × STD
City centre	MEAN + 4 × STD

The only initial prerequisite data for implementing this methodology are the Features of Interest (Non-residential Uses) as lines or points; the Study Area as a single polygon feature; the Urban Blocks as polygons feature and the Street Segments as lines feature.

3.2   Identifying Human-Oriented Centres (HoC)

One of the primary objectives of this paper is to propose a method for identifying HoC, as places with people, *and* places for people. The proposed methodological framework for identifying HoC can be seen in the following figure (Fig. 4).

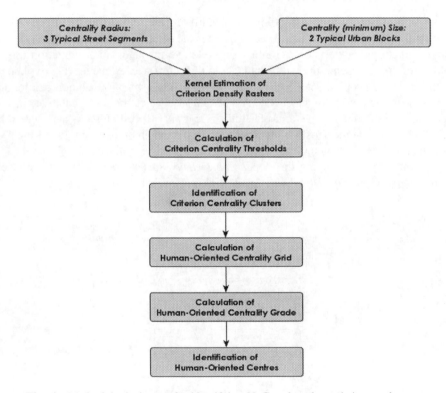

Fig. 4. Methodological steps for identifying HoC and evaluate their completeness

In order to identify and evaluate HoC, we introduce the *'Centrality Grade'* metric based on the proposed typological criteria, which have been extensively analysed in Sect. 2.2. To determine whether any of the above mentioned centrality criteria is met, firstly, its spatial density is calculated and the norm of $Density > Mean + 1STD$ is implemented as a suitable cut-off threshold, and shown in Table 3. The introduced *'Centrality Grade'* assesses both the functional and configurational/network properties of the study area, along with its accessibility, to designate areas where urban characteristics that make a place meaningfully central coexist. Its implementation results are shown in Table 4.

Ultimately to identify the HoC of the study area, a Centrality Grade cut-off threshold is set (***Centrality Grade*** $\geq$ ***2/5***), meaning that if an area has two criteria or more, is deemed as 'HoC'. Subsequently, if several adjacent polygons pass the above cut-off *Centrality Grade threshold*, then these neighbouring polygons are grouped together to form joint centres, as has been also done by relevant analytical tools [9]. Then, a *Geometry cut-off threshold* is implemented ensuring that all identified HoC are larger than two urban blocks.

Table 3. The typological criteria forming the Centrality Grade

Centrality component	Centrality criterion	Criterion threshold (Kernel Density>)
Accessible centrality	1. POPoAC	Mean + 1 STD
Functional centrality	2. PoERE	Mean + 1 STD
	3. PoCA	Mean + 1 STD
	4. PoW	Mean + 1 STD
Network centrality	5. PoNIC	Mean + 1 STD

Table 4. The conceptual explanation of Centrality Grade

Centrality Grade	Description	Criteria (n/5)	Criteria (0–1)
A	Excellent	5/5	1
B	Very good	4/5	0.8
C	Good	3/5	0.6
D	Sufficient	2/5	0.4
E	Fail (some more work is required)	1/5	0.2
F	Fail (considerable further work is required)	0/5	0

The above table (Table 3 and Table 4) depict the suggested typological criteria forming the Centrality Grade and the explanation of the introduced Centrality Grade.

4   Implementation and Results

4.1   Study Area and Data Sources

Our proposed methodological approach and the developed GIS-based analytical tools were both utilized in order to define and evaluate the designed and evident based centralities of an Athenian suburb, namely, the Alimos municipality, Attika, Greece. Alimos is a coastal suburb of Athens located 8 km southeast of the Athens city centre. The municipality has an area of almost 6 km^2 and according to the 2011 census has a population of 41,720.

Data used in this research are either confidentially provided and/or commercially distributed and therefore cannot be publically shared. Data regarding Non-Residential Uses (point feature dataset) contain detailed information about all land-uses and build-uses of the study area, gathered by in-situ surveys in 2015, and are confidentially granted by an urban planning firm ('Polis L.P'). Datasets regarding urban blocks (polygon feature dataset with geometry attributes) and streets segments (line feature dataset with geometry attributes) come from the Hellenic Statistical Authority and refer to the latest census available (2011).

However, the primary aim of this paper is to introduce reproducible GIS-based analytical tools and these have been published as python scripts and ArcGIS Pro toolboxes in a public repository under these DOIs https://doi.org/10.6084/m9.figshare. 11973951.v1 and https://doi.org/10.6084/m9.figshare.11973933.v1. Finally, the software used for this paper is documented below: ArcGIS Pro 2.4.3; DepthmapX 0.30, DepthmapXnet 0.35, Space Syntax Toolkit (Qgis 2.16.3 plugin), and Microsoft Excel 2013.

4.2   Identification of Active Centres (AC)

In order to locate the AC of the study area the GIS-based analytical tools described in the previous chapter are implemented and the result can be seen in Fig. 5. The density of human activity, in the form of city's non-residential uses, is estimated with the Kernel Density Estimation (KDE) method, as described in previous Sects. 2.2 and 3.1. A semi-automated workflow is introduced for the identification of AC, consisted of two spatial models, constructed as geoprocessing tools. Thereafter, all spatial models and geoprocessing tools created for this workflow are available as ArcGIS Pro toolbox and python scripts in a public repository (https://doi.org/10.6084/m9.figshare.11973951.v1). Furthermore, due to lack of space, visualizations of all spatial models and geoprocessing tools of this workflow can be also found online (https://doi.org/10.6084/m9. figshare.11974059.v1).

Fig. 5. Identified AC of the study area

In Fig. 5 the identified AC of Alimos are depicted. The result of the proposed workflow is successful since has recognized the central areas of Alimos as mentioned in the "Operational Program of the Municipality of Alimos 2015–2019" [25]. More specifically, it has identified as 'City Centre' the traditional costal centre in the south of Alimos while the northeast commercial centre in 'Upper Alimos' has been identified as 'In-between Centre'.

4.3   Identification of Human-oriented Centres (HoC)

The second objective of this paper is to propose a semi-automated workflow for identifying HoC and the result is shown in Fig. 7. To this end a 'Centrality Grade' is proposed based on multiple typological criteria (mapped in Fig. 6) referring to functional centrality, network centrality and accessible centrality, as analysed in the previous Sects. 2.2 and 3.2. All spatial models and geoprocessing tools created for this workflow are also available as ArcGIS Pro toolbox and python scripts under the following DOI (https://doi.org/10.6084/m9.figshare.11973933.v1) as well as their visualisations (https://doi.org/10.6084/m9.figshare.11973996.v1).

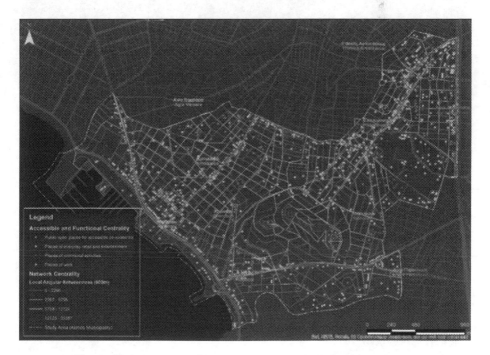

Fig. 6. The geography of the selected HoC Criteria for the study area

As can be seen on Fig. 7 five HoC of various size and 'Centrality Grade', ranging from 40286 to 502173 m^2 and from 0.4 to 0.6 grade, respectively. The traditional coastal centre of the municipality has been identified as HoC along with two other satellite HoC, while the 'Upper Alimos' market has also been identified as an extensive HoC. Finally, an independent HoC cluster has emerged in Lofos Pani. Tellingly, the proposed workflow has successfully identified the meaningfully central areas of Alimos, by promoting areas with diverse human activity, network centrality (PoNIC) and Open Public Spaces (POPoAC) rather than exclusively retail-centric areas of intense mono-functional activity. This is why the traditional coastal centre of Alimos is graded as 'Fairly Good' (for its most part with 0.4 or 0.6, namely mean_centrality_grade = 0.47), due to its limited multifunctionality and absence of local network Centrality (PoNIC).

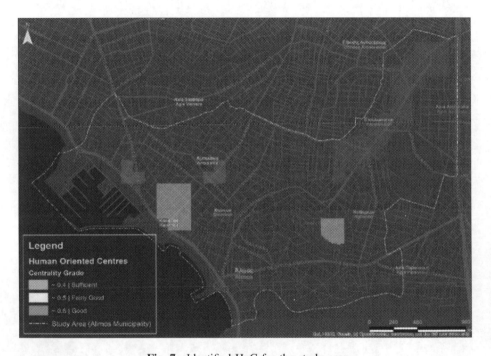

Fig. 7. Identified HoC for the study area

On the contrary, the more recent northeast centre of 'Upper Alimos' scores substantially higher in all of its extent and is graded as 'Good' (for its most part 0.6 or 0.8, namely mean_centrality_grade = 0.62) since it demonstrates both dense and diverse functional (PoERE, PoCE, PoW), accessible (POPoAC) and network centrality (PoNIC).

5   Conclusions

The local urban centre is the spatial setting of human interaction, co-existence and exchange (social, economic etc.) in the city and therefore authorities, experts and citizens should focus on the different types of centralities that emerge in a city. However, planning authorities have been overly focused on the established centres of the city while disregarding the centrality clusters that can function as the vibrant human nodes of the city. In this paper we presented a methodological approach along with metrics and tools for defining and measuring different types of city centralities. The introduced metrics have been developed as GIS-based analytical tools accessible and mainly addressed to non-expert users in the fields of urban planning, transportation planning, urban geography etc. We argue that our work fills and bridges this gap by incorporating the multi-dimensional definitions provided by theoretical approaches into an analytical/quantitative framework, in order to identify both the existing centrality pattern of the city (*where-it-is*) and the central areas of the city that have the potential to be functional, vibrant, accessible and liveable (*where-it-should be*).

In essence, this research explores two different types of centres: Active Centres (*places with people*) and Human-oriented Centres (*places for people*). Furthermore, we developed detailed methodologies for exploring these two types of centre, and also provide easy-to-use GIS-based analytical tools to identify them. For addressing the first question posed by this research (*RQ1. How to quantitatively define the Active Centres of a city, and evaluate their magnitude?*), a comprehensive methodology was introduced that successfully located the AC of the study area, as the centrality clusters characterised by dense human activity, and also assessed their magnitude and significance for the study area. Regarding the second question (*RQ2. How to quantitatively define Human-oriented Centres of a city, and evaluate their completeness?*), a novel methodology was proposed based on the density and diversity of selected typological criteria corresponding with the significant (co)presence of accessible public open spaces, commercial activities, communal activities, places of work and local network centrality. Finally, the third research question (*How to create semi-automated GIS-based analytical tools for identifying these two types of centres?*) was addressed by two distinct computational workflows which constitute comprehensive and easy-to-use GIS-based analytical tools/spatial models, for identifying the AC and HoC of any study area and also evaluate their magnitude and completeness, respectively.

Reproducibility is a key focus of this work and this is why the spatial models of this publications are available in a public repository[4] as python scripts and ArcGIS Pro toolboxes. Another, important objective of this research is the applicability of the introduced analytical tools. To this end the only initial prerequisite data for implementing the developed geoprocessing tools are the features of interest (with attributes regarding the presence of the selected typological criteria, if any) and the fundamental elements of the urban form, meaning the urban blocks and street segments (with geometry attributes). The former describes the different types of centrality in a city while the latter describe the physical form and the scale of the city, properties essential

---

[4] https://doi.org/10.6084/m9.figshare.11973951.v1, https://doi.org/10.6084/m9.figshare.11973933.v1.

for estimating representative and study case-specific dimensions of the centrality cluster (centre radius and minimum centre size).

The findings of this research indicate that the presented methodological frameworks and the accompanied GIS-enabled analytical tools are successful in identifying Active and Human-oriented Centres of the selected study area (Alimos, Athens, Greece). Regarding the AC-identification tool, the proposed workflow has been successful in locating the central areas of Alimos and recognizing their importance and magnitude, as described by the Operational Program of the Municipality of Alimos that was published in 2015 [25]. A significant advantage of the geoprocessing tools regarding AC-identification, is the use of Non-Residential Uses which is an excellent proxy for quantifying human activity, compared to other urban features commonly used by similar tools (e.g. job density in Metropolitan Form Analysis toolbox [9]). The methodological tool introduced for HoC-identification generates a Human-oriented Centrality Grid that describes the centrality of the entire study area and has accomplished to recognize the places with high functional diversity, network centrality and public open spaces, thus high functionality and active street life. Furthermore, it integrates a multidimensional definition of centrality not only into a methodological framework but also into a GIS-based analytical tool More specifically, the presented research and associated findings can be used as references to better understanding the dynamic phenomenon of centrality, and its different typologies. Moreover, the analytical tools presented in this paper regarding the identification and analysis of AC and HoC could be integrated into a decision-support system in order to inform evidence-based planning towards sustainable urban form, sustainable mobility, and liveable public space.

While the research detailed in this article has illustrated meaningful insights, the highly complex phenomenon of centrality and its different facets cannot be entirely analysed in one single study. The issues of human activity, movement and centrality in general, have been effectively repositioned in the age of the Fourth Industrial Revolution. Since, digital technology and especially smartphones enable a completely different definition of the urban space, and create a digital (urban) form which interconnects with the physical environment to produce an augmented network (digital and physical) with a new "*topology*" of paths, movements and activities. The integration of this conceptual element into a novel definition and metric of centrality is an interesting future work, that could substantially expand the presented research, possibly by including social media check-ins as a sixth criterion for measuring HoC. Furthermore, in-situ surveys (interviews and/or questionnaires) could substantially benefit this research by providing insight about public perceptions and desires towards shared public space and local centres. Regarding the more technical part, future work should ensure the development of the introduced computational workflows into fully automated GIS-based analytical tools. Another limitation of the introduced analytical tools is that are compatible with a commercial GIS software (ArcGIS Pro 2.4.3) and future work should ensure the construction of an equivalent open-source workflow, namely developing an GIS-based analytical tool for Active and Human-oriented Centres in an open-source environment (e.g. as a Qgis plugin). Finally, it should be abundantly clear that the introduced analytical tools are not so much constructed as "*global*" geoprocessing tools for identifying centralities, rather than the semi-automated, reproducible tools for identifying and evaluating centres (Active and Human-oriented) as defined in this article. Therefore, the developed spatial models cannot fully adapt to a different centrality approach (e.g. with fewer criteria or with a different format), but this could be an interesting future advancement of this work.

Acknowledgements. This paper constitutes the latest findings of research conducted at the National Technical University of Athens since 2018 [26, 27] and the authors would like to thank Dr. Maria Pigaki for her contribution to the early stages of this project.

References

1. Harvey, D.: Rebel Cities: From the Right to the City to the Urban Revolution, 1st edn. Verso, London (2012)
2. Lefebvre, H.: The Right to the City. In: Kofman, E., Lebas, E. (eds.) Writings on Cities, pp. 63–182. Blackwell, Oxford (1968, 1996)
3. Alexander, C., Ishikawa, S., Silverstein, M.: A Pattern Language: Towns, Buildings, Construction. Oxford University Press, Oxford (1977)
4. Jacobs, J.: The Death and Life of Great American Cities. Random House, New York (1961)
5. Gehl, J.: Cities for People. Island Press, London (2010)
6. Vaughan, L., Jones, C.E., Griffiths, S., Haklay, M.: The spatial signature of suburban town centres. J. Space Syntax **1**(1), 77–91 (2010)
7. Allen, S.: Points + Lines: Diagrams and Projects for the City. Princeton Architectural Press, New York (1999)
8. Borruso, G., Porceddu, A.: A tale of two cities: density analysis of CBD on two midsize urban areas in northeastern Italy. In: Murgante, B., Borruso, G., Lapucci, A. (eds.) Geocomputation and Urban Planning. SCI, vol. 176, pp. 37–56. Springer, Heidelberg (2009). https://doi.org/10.1007/978-3-540-89930-3_3
9. Sevtsuk, A., Amindarbari, R.: Measuring growth and change in metropolitan form: progress report on urban form and land use measures. City Form Lab, Singapore (2012)
10. Hillier, B., Hanson, J.: The Social Logic of Space. Cambridge University Press, Cambridge (1984)
11. Hillier, B., Penn, A., Hanson, J., Grajewski, T., Xu, J.: Natural movement: or configuration and attraction in urban pedestrian movement. Environ. Plan. B: Plan. Des. **20**(1), 29–66 (1993)
12. Hillier, B.: Centrality as a process: accounting for attraction inequalities in deformed grids. Urban Des. Int. **4**, 107–127 (1999). https://doi.org/10.1057/udi.1999.19
13. Yang, T., Li, M., Shen, Z.: Between morphology and function: how syntactic centers of the Beijing city are defined. J. Urban Manag. **4**, 125–134 (2015)
14. Gil, J., Varoudis, T., Karimi, K., Penn, A.: The space syntax toolkit: integrating depthmapX and exploratory spatial analysis workflows in QGIS. In: Karimi, K., Vaughan, L., Sailer, K., Palaiologou, G., Bolton, T. (eds.) Proceedings of the 10th International Space Syntax Symposium (SSS 2010). Space Syntax Laboratory, The Bartlett School of Architecture, UCL, London (2015)
15. Ståhle, A., Marcus, L., Karlström, A.: Place syntax: geographic accessibility with axial lines in GIS. In: Van Nes, A. (ed.) Proceedings of the 5th Space Syntax Symposium, Amsterdam, Netherlands. Techne Press, TU Delft (2005)
16. Whyte, W.: City: Rediscovering the Center. University of Pennsylvania Press, Philadelpheia (1988)

17. Pinto, A.J., Brandão, A.L.: A multi-scale approach of public space networks in the scattered city. Urban Des. Int. **20**(3), 175–194 (2015). https://doi.org/10.1057/udi.2015.4

18. Shen, Y., Karimi, K.: Urban evolution as a spatio-functional interaction process: the case of central Shanghai. J. Urban Des. **23**(1), 42–70 (2017)

19. Li, J., Long, Y., Dang, A.: Live-Work-Play Centers of Chinese cities: identification and temporal evolution with emerging data. Comput. Environ. Urban Syst. (2018)

20. Zhong, C., Schlapfer, M.M., Muller Arisona, S., Batty, M., Ratti, C., Schmitt, G.: Revealing centrality in the spatial structure of cities from human activity patterns. Urban Stud. **54**(2), 437–455 (2015)

21. Ozbil, A., Peponis, J., Stone, B.: Understanding the link between street connectivity, land use and pedestrian flows. Urban Des. Int. **2**(16), 125–141 (2011). https://doi.org/10.1057/udi.2011.2

22. Al_Sayed, K., Turner, A., Hillier, B., Iida, S., Penn, A.: Space Syntax Methodology, 4th edn. Bartlett School of Architecture, UCL, London (2014)

23. O'Sullivan, D., Unwin, D.: Geographic Information Analysis, 2nd edn. Wiley, Hoboken (2010)

24. Porta, S., Latora, V., Wang, F.: Street centrality and densities of retail and services in Bologna, Italy. Environ. Plan. B **36**, 450–465 (2009)

25. Alimos Municipality: Strategic Planning: Operational Program of the Municipality of Alimos 2015–2019. Alimos Municipality, Alimos (2015)

26. Paraskevopoulos, Y., Pigaki, M.: Combinatorial syntactic analysis of suburban centralities: application of methodology framework for identification, typological analysis and evaluation of activity centres in Alimos, Attica, Greece. In: Proceedings of the 11th ICHGS, Athens, Greece. Govostis Publishers (2018)

27. Paraskevopoulos, Y., Photis, Y.N.: A methodological framework for identifying and evaluating centralities with space syntax and land-use pattern analysis in a GIS environment. In: Charalambous, N., Cömert, N.Z., Hoşkara, Ş. (eds.) Proceedings of CyNUM 2018. Urban Morphology in South-Eastern Mediterranean Cities: Challenges and Opportunities, Nicosia, Cyprus, CyNUM 2018, pp. 36–45 (2018)

Assessing Morphological Resilience. Methodological Challenges for Metropolitan Areas

Giovanni Fusco[1](✉) and Alessandro Venerandi[2]

[1] Université Côte d'Azur, CNRS, ESPACE, Nice, France
giovanni.fusco@univ-cotedazur.fr
[2] Université Côte d'Azur, ESPACE, Nice, France
alessandro.venerandi@univ-cotedazur.fr

Abstract. Morphological resilience to urban change is the capacity of the form of the physical city to adapt to everchanging social, economic, and technical contexts. It echoes the theory of general resilience in ecology and is not linked to catastrophic events. Complexity theory informs principles of resilient systems that can be applied to urban form. This paper shows how morphological resilience can be assessed in a wide metropolitan area using geoprocessing protocols and available geospatial information. More specifically, a two-step methodology is proposed and tested on the French Riviera. First, spatial units of analysis are identified based on the interconnectedness of the street network, which is a major morphological component in itself. Next, a set of morpho-functional quantitative indicators of resilience is computed for such spatial units, accounting for both internal structure and integration within the wider metropolitan area. Thirteen indicators are selected to describe five different proxies of morphological resilience: diversity, connectivity, redundancy, modularity and efficiency. The paper also presents the preliminary results of morphological resilience assessment in the French Riviera. Urban central areas on the coast generally show more resilient characteristics, while more contrasted patterns emerge in the hinterland.

Keywords: Morphological resilience · Urban form · Geoprocessing · French Riviera

1 Introduction

The form of the physical city is at the centre of the planning effort and of urban policies by local authorities. When urban expansion attains the size of a whole metropolitan area, local authorities must manage a great variety of urban forms and identify the most appropriate policies for their conservation and/or transformation. In France, for example, master plans have to be established at the metropolitan level, encompassing thus several municipalities and very diverse urban and suburban contexts. In their founding analyses, these plans have to tackle landscape, architectural, environmental and socioeconomic issues related to urban form.

© Springer Nature Switzerland AG 2020
O. Gervasi et al. (Eds.): ICCSA 2020, LNCS 12255, pp. 593–609, 2020.
https://doi.org/10.1007/978-3-030-58820-5_44

The context of the present debate in planning is increasingly the uncertainty of urban and metropolitan futures [4]. Well established paradigms of urban development are questioned by the much needed adaptation to a post-carbon society, to socioeconomic and technical changes, to the integration of new metropolitan functions and, at the same time, to changes in lifestyles and to an increased demand for a sense of place. In this context, new issues arise for metropolitan authorities and for planners and urban geographers supporting them. Which urban forms within a vast metropolitan area are more able to adapt to unknown future socio-technical changes? Which forms are intrinsically fragile because they have been optimized only for a given function and are thus not able to cope with change?

In this very context, Feliciotti [10] and Fusco [13] recently proposed the concept of morphological resilience. If cities cannot foresee their future, we can, as of now, assess the potential resilience (or fragility) of their physical forms and prepare them to the challenges of uncertain futures. Researchers at ESPACE have proposed such an assessment to the planning department of the metropolitan authority Nice-Côte d'Azur, in France, within the POPSU Métropoles national program. Assessing the properties of urban forms in a large metropolitan area inevitably implies the use of appropriate geoprocessing algorithms on available geospatial information. This paper thus relates the operationalization of the concept of morphological resilience at the metropolitan scale and the preliminary outcomes obtained in the French Riviera.

The paper is structured as follows. Section 2 provides the theoretical and methodological bases of morphological resilience and its multidimensional nature. Section 3 presents in more detail the methodology for the assessment of morphological resilience and the case study of the French Riviera metropolitan area. Preliminary results are also mapped and briefly presented. Section 4 concludes with a discussion on the proposed methodology and on its future developments.

2   Morphological Resilience

2.1   Theoretical Bases

Urban morphological resilience is the ability of the city's physical forms to adapt and transform in the presence of urban change, without requiring heavy operations, such as the destruction and reconstruction of entire neighbourhoods. It is the capacity of the physical city to avoid obsolescence (often even early obsolescence) through self-organized processes of adaptation to change. We are not dealing here with resilience to catastrophic events, being them natural (flooding, earthquake, etc.) or anthropogenic (terrorist attack, industrial accident, etc.). This kind of resilience of urban form has already been studied by a rich scientific literature [1, 8, 9, 25]. Rather, we are concerned with the potential adaptability and transformability (or, conversely, with the potential fragility) of the present forms of the physical city when confronted with future socioeconomic and technical changes that urban societies constantly produce endogenously [17, 33, 37], for example, in lifestyles, work organization, and use of technology, in the urban space. Recent works on the concept of resilience [2, 33] or even on urban resilience [26] fail to recognize the existence of a specific domain of research on morphological resilience, above all when disconnected from disaster risk reduction.

From a theoretical point of view, urban morphological resilience is rooted in complexity theory [28–30] and in the theory of general resilience of ecosystems first proposed by Holling [16] and later extended to social-ecological systems [6, 12, 17].

Inspired by previous works in ecology and, in particular, by the ones focusing on the structure and functioning of ecosystems, Mehaffy and Salingaros [27] lay down the founding principles of the theory of resilient urban forms. They identify several physical features characterizing resilience, such as interconnectedness of streets, redundant path types (echoing the high interconnectedness and redundancy of trophic chains in ecosystems), and organic/fine-meshed street networks with small blocks (like the ones of medieval towns or the first planned European and North American cities, such as Turin, Barcelona and Philadelphia) as opposed to tree-like street networks or grids with big blocks. Mehaffy and Salingaros also suggest that resilient urban forms should have a great diversity of activities, building types, functions and populations. Contrary to what was prescribed by functionalist urban planning [24], they consider functional and morphological diversity, across different urban scales, a fundamental aspect of resilience in face of unknown urban change. Fragility, on the other hand, is considered to be linked to the sectorization of urban space, typical of modernist/functionalist zoning, (e.g., CBD, residential neighbourhoods, shopping centres, etc.). Accepting diversity and redundancy thus entails renouncing to optimization (e.g., of form with respect to function, of results with respect to means, etc.). Resilient urban form is not optimized for a given function, but it is redundant and its program is open, thus ensuring greater levels of adaptability in face of possible future functional requirements.

As mentioned above, resilience in urban form should apply to a variety of scales, from the macro-form of the whole metropolitan area, to the finer fabrics of each district and the details of urban design at the micro-scale. Great importance has also been recently attributed to the scale of the single plot [7], as it seems to provide a local, autonomous, and fast response to change. Large urban projects, conceived as a whole, for example with buildings laying above the street on a single concrete slab, are typically fragile urban forms, where incremental adaptation through small additions/transformations is very difficult to achieve. As a result, these projects are often doomed to complete demolition and reconstruction, a sort of admission of failure of non-resilient urbanism. Even in resilient urban forms, urban change often implies a pivot scale of response, but tight trans-scalar relations articulate response at all scales. We can thus think of a level of more autonomous response by individual actors at the finest scale (the plot, the building), whereas change of the morphological infrastructure (the street network, the whole plot system) or the building of large facilities need more coordination among urban actors.

2.2 Operationalizing Morphological Resilience

A full conceptualization of morphological resilience goes beyond the scope of this paper. The aforementioned delimitation of scope and concepts is nevertheless needed to tackle the challenging task of operationalizing urban resilience [26]. In this respect, Feliciotti et al. [11] re-interpreted the resilience proxies of social-ecological systems [6] through the lens of urban morphology. Resilience is a property of complex systems that cannot be directly measured. Analysts must thus resort to resilience proxies, i.e. context-based attributes indirectly inferable to resilience on the bases of resilience theory. Proxies are operational as they are ascertainable through observation. Feliciotti et al. [11] thus identify five resilience proxies for urban form: diversity, connectivity, redundancy, modularity and efficiency. The diversity contributing to morphological resilience is both functional and typo-morphological. Diversity contributes to system adaptability by providing a multiplicity of options in face of change. Connectivity eases flows (of people, goods, services, information, etc.) within a system and across systems. High connectivity tends to be positive for morphological resilience, although interstices of less-connected fragments can be accommodated within a highly connected whole. Redundancy contributes to morphological resilience by offering a multiplicity of choices that ensure the functioning of the system even when change is happening. Modularity is the degree to which a system's components are made up of identifiable smaller components or parts which can be combined to create larger wholes. High modularity, at different scales, ensures the possibility of piecemeal transformation of urban form at the right scale. Efficiency is a controversial proxy, instead. It is not the optimization of form with respect to a given functional program at a given scale. In a complex system, efficiency requires more structural complexity at each and every scale [34]. Form is thus efficient when it shows a scale-free structure, described by a power-law distribution [19, 35], with many small elements, some intermediate and very few large ones.

For each of the proxies mentioned above, Feliciotti [10] then identifies a set of appropriate measurable indicators. More specifically, she proposes two metrics of diversity, 17 of connectivity, two of redundancy, one of modularity, and one of efficiency. Plot heterogeneity is, for example, a metric of diversity and quantifies to what extent plot sizes are different in a spatial unit. Node degree corresponds to the number of street segments connected to each intersection and measures connectivity. Meshedness indicates to what extent the street network in a spatial unit is more similar to a tree-like structure or a grid and is proposed as a measure of redundancy. Feliciotti also uses these metrics to perform a resilience assessment of the different configurations taken by Gorbals, a neighbourhood in Glasgow (UK), throughout the XX century. This work is a fundamental step forward in the operationalization of morphological resilience. However, it shows some limitations: it focuses on one neighbourhood only rather than on a larger study area; it proposes an unbalanced number of indicators for each resilience proxy; finally, it relies on a fixed spatial unit of analysis, even though resilience has multi-scalar properties. In the next section, we propose a methodology that takes inspiration by Feliciotti's work but that, at the same time, tries to overcome some of its limitations. Details of such a methodology are presented next.

3 Morphological Resilience in Metropolitan Areas

The main challenge of the present work is to extend the assessment of morphological resilience to a whole metropolitan area. Morphometric and morpho-functional indicators for each resilience proxy must be calculated through geoprocessing algorithms applicable to easily accessible geographical databases. Before that, though, appropriate spatial units of analysis must be determined. A brief presentation of the study area and of available data sources will guide these fundamental methodological steps.

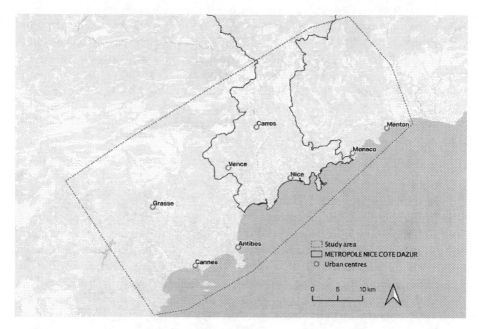

Fig. 1. The French Riviera Metropolitan area and the Metropolitan authority Nice-Côte d'Azur.

3.1   The French Riviera

The case study of the analysis is the French Riviera (Fig. 1), an emerging metropolitan area located in Southern France. With a population of more than one million inhabitants over 1,500 km^2 [15], this space is characterized by very different urban forms that grew together to form a large conurbation stretching from the French-Italian border (to the east) to the Esterel mountains (closing the bay of Cannes to the west). Such an extensive conurbation developed around the coastal cities of, from east to west, Menton, Monaco, Nice, Antibes and Cannes. Fusco and Araldi [14] reported the existence of nine different types of urban fabric in the French Riviera: old cities and villages, traditionally planned urban fabrics with adjoining buildings, discontinuous and irregular fabrics with houses and buildings, modernist discontinuous fabrics, connective artificial fabrics, two different types of suburban fabrics and two different types of scarcely developed landscapes. These fabrics make up different morphological regions: some are more homogeneous, while others are more mixed (e.g., they are characterized by the co-presence of two or three different fabrics).

The perimeter of the study area does not correspond to any administrative boundary. Although this space forms a unique urban entity, it is in fact fragmented in several local governments, and an independent country (i.e., the Principality of Monaco). More than half of its population is nevertheless located in the metropolitan authority of Nice Côte d'Azur (NCA), our partner within the above mentioned POPSU project.

Several geographic databases are available for the French Riviera. The TOPO Database by IGN (the French national cartographic agency) provides a vector representation of buildings, plots and streets with metric precision for the whole of France. Similar data are available on OpenStreetMap for many cities in the world. Urban functions (retail, services, jobs, population counts) are obtained from the database of the local Chamber of Commerce and the household mobility survey. National census and/or local authorities can supply similar data in other world cities.

The methodology presented in this work mainly consists of two steps. The first is the definition of the spatial unit of analysis. The second is the computation of a set of 13 quantitative indicators for such units, describing the five proxies of morphological resilience. We present both next.

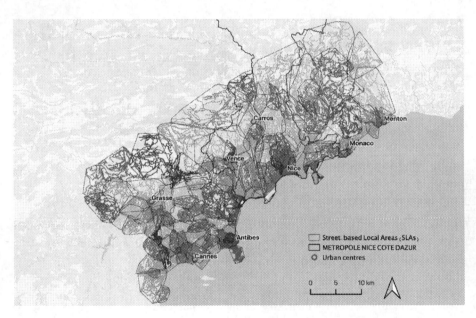

Fig. 2. Partitioning of the French Riviera in Street-based Local Areas (SLAs). Colours are randomly assigned and serve only to make SLAs distinguishable. (Color figure online)

3.2   Street-Based Local Areas

The first methodological issue to be addressed is the definition of appropriate spatial units for the analysis. The spatial extent of the assessment is ultimately the whole metropolitan area, making a distinction between its central part (the NCA metropolitan authority) and its eastern (Menton, Monaco, locally named "Riviera") and western (Cannes, Grasse and Antibes) neighbours. Nevertheless, to assess morphological resilience at such a large scale, we first have to identify coherent subspaces of intermediate size to evaluate resilience properties at a more local level. At the same time, these units must be big enough to have meaningful assessments of their internal structure. Inter-scalar relationships are fundamental to understand resilience properties. Most of these depend on the links between the micro-scale of plots, buildings and streets and the meso-scale of the spatial units of analysis. Scaling up, relationship between these units and the whole of the metropolitan area also participate to the resilience assessment. The street network is a fundamental component of urban form. It coordinates the organization of plots and buildings at the micro level, but also creates the necessary connections within the morphological system at greater scales. We thus decided to identify intermediate morphological units based on the interconnectedness of the street network. Using the Louvain algorithm of modularity optimization within large networks [3], we thus identified 145 morphological basins, maximizing internal street interconnectedness while minimizing external links. This way of partitioning urban space based on the morphology of the street network has already been applied by Law [23] on the city of London. Law designates the resulting spatial units as Street Local Areas (SLAs). SLAs within the French Riviera typically include between 500 and 800 junction-to-junction street segments. They correspond to urban or suburban districts larger than single neighbourhoods or villages. In the suburbs, they typically include the immediate periphery around village cores. Their limits identify synapses within the street network, i.e. strategic connective segments within the metropolitan area. 52 SLAs fall totally or partially within the administrative area of NCA. A map of the 145 SLAs identified in the French Riviera is presented in Fig. 2. Having defined the basic unit of analysis, we will present next the specific morphometrics for each resilience proxy.

3.3 Diversity

Diversity is a fundamental factor for resilience. Both typo-morphological and morpho-functional diversity can be measured for each SLA. Functional diversity is evaluated above all through its primary functional mix, i.e. jobs to residents ratio. The evaluation of this index needs careful attention. Bedroom communities, highly specialized CBDs and commercial areas are all characterized by greater fragility. Ideally, each SLA should have values of jobs to residents ratio similar to the average for the whole metropolitan area. Values smaller than the average tend to be associated with residential areas. Conversely, values greater than the average could at first sight be associated with greater local resilience (as long as jobs are also linked to the presence of other urban functions). Nevertheless, the interconnection among the different SLAs within a whole metropolitan area implies that these above-average values correspond to below-average values elsewhere, hence reducing morpho-functional resilience at the scale of the metropolitan area. For these reasons, the index is calculated as the absolute difference of the jobs to residents ratio from the metropolitan average. The more the SLA differs from the metropolitan average, the more it contributes to morpho-functional fragility.

A second indicator measuring functional diversity focuses on retail and services. The local chamber of commerce identifies 22 different categories of retail and services. Their diversity is a direct contribution to the vitality of the district. We propose to compute such diversity through the Gini-Simpson index [22], which measures the probability that two elements randomly chosen within a given SLA are different. Its minimum is zero (in SLAs with only one type of retail or service) its maximum is $1 - (1/k)^2$, where k is the number of different categories (in our case study, these are 22).

The third indicator measures typo-morphological diversity of the buildings within each SLA. As Perez et al. [31] showed for Osaka (Japan) and Marseille (France), a small number of quantitative descriptors can be used to identify types of buildings within a vast metropolitan area. We thus used the very same indicators (i.e., building footprint surface, height, contiguity, convexity index, elongation index and special-ization) plus a seventh descriptor (i.e., presence of lightweight extensions, such as verandas, balconies, porches, adjoining sheds, etc.) to cluster the buildings of the French Riviera in types, through a Naive Bayes classifier. After having binned the indicators like in [31], we obtained nine broad types of buildings:

– Type 1. Small compact low-rise detached/semidetached houses or garages.
– Type 2. Detached/semidetached articulated houses with extensions.
– Type 3. Mainly detached articulated small buildings/large villas with extensions.
– Type 4. Small compact adjoining mid-rise buildings and townhouses.
– Type 5. Mid-sized mid-rise relatively compact adjoining buildings.
– Type 6. Mid-sized elongated tall free-standing residential buildings.
– Type 7. Big high-rise articulated and elongated free-standing buildings.
– Type 8. Specialized low-rise compact buildings (sometimes light construction).
– Type 9. Large specialized mid-rise articulated buildings.

The 390 000 buildings of the study area were weighted by their footprint area in the clustering algorithm. The optimum number of clusters was determined through a random walk in parameter space under a few constraints (minimum average cluster purity of 90%, maximum of 20 clusters, minimum cluster content of 4% of building footprint area). The contingency table fit of the selected clustering solution is 58.03%, indicating that the clustering variable accounts for more than half of the information content of the seven original indicators. The diversity of building types is then com-puted through the implementation of Gini-Simpson index on these nine building classes, in each SLA. Greater values are associated with more morphological resilience, since the presence of different building types allows more flexibility for future func-tional needs.

Figure 3 shows the Gini-Simpson diversity indexes calculated for the 22 categories of retail and services and the 9 building types, respectively. By visually inspecting the map, we observe that traditional central areas on the coast have relatively greater values of functional diversity, but not necessarily of typo-morphological diversity. The centre of Cannes is an exception and shows lower than expected functional diversity but higher than expected typo-morphological diversity. The hinterland shows smaller values, both in typo-morphological and functional diversity, with few exceptions for the latter.

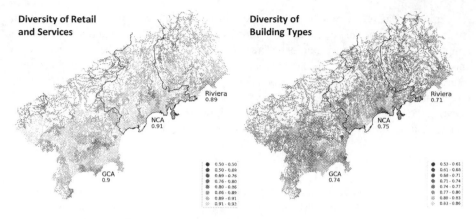

Fig. 3. Gini-Simpson diversity indexes in the SLAs of the French Riviera.

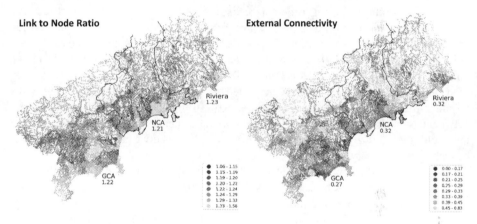

Fig. 4. Street-network connectivity for the SLAs of the French Riviera.

3.4   Connectivity

Highly connected systems are more resilient than poorly connected ones [27]. As far as urban form is concerned, connectivity is mainly linked to its street network. This can be described, at the level of SLAs, by classical measures of graph theory: Connected Node Ratio (i.e., the ratio between the number of intersections that are not cul-de-sac and the total number of intersections in each SLA) and Link to Node Ratio (i.e., ratio between the number of links and the number of intersections in each SLA). The spatial units also need to be well connected with the rest of the metropolitan area to ensure resilience at greater scales (and this even though they were identified by minimizing external interconnectedness). We thus measured the External Connectivity of each SLA by computing the ratio between the number of external connections and the square root of the total number of connections in each SLA (which is indicative of the linear dimension of the spatial unit, hence of its perimeter).

Figure 4 illustrates two of these street-network connectivity indicators. Link to Node Ratio is greater in coastal urban centres. However, the study area does not show a simple coast to hinterland gradient. The smallest values tend to be associated with suburban developments in the close hinterland, especially in the western section of the metropolitan area. Many of such areas are also characterised by low values of outward connections, making them particularly fragile in terms of connectivity. Several peripheral areas in the further hinterland and in the eastern section of the Riviera compensate low Link to Node Ratios with more outward connections.

3.5   Redundancy

Redundancy contributes to morphological resilience by offering a multiplicity of choices that ensure functionality in case change happens. In our methodology, this aspect is investigated in terms of urban mobility in two ways: redundancy of paths and multimodality of the transport system. The former is essential both for short-range pedestrian trips and for mid-to-long-range car travel. As already highlighted by Jacobs [18], the possibility of using different paths for daily trips spreads pedestrian and vehicular flows in the city, increases opportunities for services and retail, and avoids charge overload on few axes only [35]. Redundancy of paths is computed through 2 indicators. Path Redundancy assumes that having several streets with good levels of through-movement in each SLA is beneficial. This indicator is computed in two steps. First betweenness centrality [32] is computed for each street in each SLA. Then, we calculate the percentage of streets in the top 50% of the cumulative distribution of the betweenness values within the SLA. The more segments are needed to attain this threshold, the more resilient the path system is because betweenness centrality is not concentrated in a very small set of street segments.

The second indicator is the Constraint Score of the Path System, i.e. Burt's index [5], which measures to what extents the connections that each street segment establishes with its neighbours are limited within clusters of mutually interconnected segments. SLAs with smaller constraint values tend to have more connections beyond a highly cohesive pool of mutually interconnected segments. This condition can thus be considered positive for morphological resilience. Figure 5 (left) shows that this is usually the case for finely meshed SLAs on the coast (e.g., the city centres of Nice and Antibes) and in the hinterland (e.g., Grasse). Greater values are associated with more fragile areas, for example, the SLAs located in many suburban developments of the close hinterland of the western section of the Riviera.

A different aspect of redundancy is the ability of the network to offer modal alternatives for mid- and long-range trips. The presence of cycle paths, bus routes and high-performance transit service (i.e., light-rail lines and metropolitan railways) were thus considered. Different infrastructures are not independent but operate as multiplex networks working in synergy [36]. The multi-modality potential of the transportation network, named in this work Redundancy of Transport Modes, was computed as the average number of modal options available on the streets of each SLA. To determine the number of modes in each street, we first created buffers around each transport entry point, 300 m around bus stops and cycle lanes and 600 m around LRT/railway stations. We then intersected these buffers with each street and added 1 every time a buffer

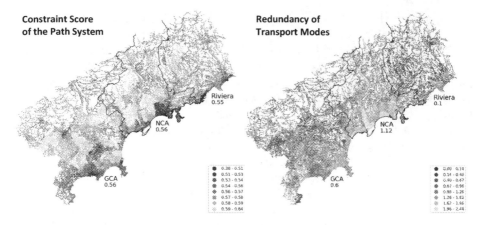

Fig. 5. Redundancy of the mobility system within SLAs of the French Riviera.

corresponding to a new transport mode was found. The minimum value of 0 is associated with areas of car dependence, where private motorized transport is the only available option. The maximum value of 3 is associated with streets with all types of transport modes (i.e., car, buses, cycle lanes, and LRT/railways stations). Figure 5 (right) shows that coastal areas, especially within the NCA perimeter, are characterized by higher redundancy of transport modes, with the exception of the capes. Along with areas in key north-to-south valleys, they benefit from the presence of transportation corridors including roads with dedicated bus lanes, railways and bicycle routes. Most of the hinterland has few alternatives to the car, but this is not the case within the NCA perimeter.

3.6 Modularity

Modularity is the degree to which a system's components are made up of identifiable smaller components or parts which can be combined to create larger wholes. High modularity, at different scales, ensures the possibility of piecemeal transformation of urban form at the right scale. Our methodology requires to measure modularity through two indicators, focusing on the plot system and built-fabric.

The plot is the basic component at which scale interventions on urban form are usually carried out. Small plots are easier to be changed/repurposed than larger ones, thus allowing easier bottom-up transformations/adaptations at smaller costs. We propose Plot Granularity as first indicator of modularity. It is computed as the average number of plots per hectare of plots served by the street network. By considering only plots served by street segments, we avoid penalizing SLAs characterized by the presence of undeveloped land. The highest levels of Plot Granularity were found in the coastal cities (Fig. 6, left). A coast-to-hinterland gradient seemed also present, although SLAs representing capes seemed not to follow such a trend.

For what concerned the modularity of the built fabric, the aim was to detect the existence of identifiable modules at different scales, using a geometric sequence of spacing between built-up components. To do so, building footprints were subsequently dilated to test whether they could melt in larger structures (i.e., modules) or stayed isolated. This process was performed for the following thresholds: 0 m, 1 m, 2 m, 4 m, 8 m, 16 m, 32 m, 64 m. We then calculated the percentage of built-up components lost at each threshold. Greater percentages at any given dilation indicate that its specific distance is active in structuring built-up modules at SLA level. More precisely, the distance characterising the modules is twice the value of the dilation threshold. The 64 m dilation, corresponds thus to modules separated by more than 128 m. The 0 m dilation accounts for the adjoining relations among buildings. This distance is particularly active in continuous built-up fabrics and inactive in discontinuous fabrics of free-standing buildings. The Built-Fabric Modularity indicator thus corresponds to the sum of the percentages of building footprints lost at each of the thresholds mentioned above. The highest values (i.e., between 390 and 447) are associated with the traditional fabric of the coastal cities and the city town of Grasse, in the hinterland. On average, more than 50% of built-up components are lost at each of the eight dilation thresholds in these areas. Once again, a coast-to-hinterland gradient can be observed (except for Grasse). In SLAs with the smallest values of Built-Fabric Modularity, losses with more than 50% of built-up components happened rarely (i.e., only for one to three thresholds), meaning that such SLAs show less nested scales in structure of built-up modules.

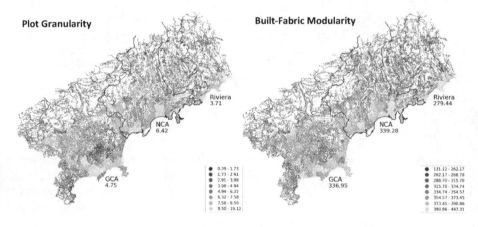

Fig. 6. Morphological modularity in the SLAs of the French Riviera.

3.7 Efficiency

Resilient urban form must respect the principles of self-organized complex structures, which proved particularly resilient in natural processes [21, 27]. Efficiency of urban form could thus be measured in terms of degree of self-organized complexity. We propose to measure the morphological efficiency of the built-up fabric and plot system, in each SLA, through the Head/Tail index [19, 20]. The higher the values of such index, the more the empirical distributions of building footprints and plot sizes resemble a power-law distribution. This is a statistical behaviour associated with the self-organization of the morphological system [35], corresponding to the presence of large numbers of small elements, several of intermediate size, and very few of big and huge size. In this respect, efficiency is not the contrary of redundancy, but the characteristic of a morphological system to offer all possible dimensional scales, in the way a self-organized system would. Figure 7 shows the Head/Tail indexes of self-organized complexity for plots (Efficiency of the Plot System) and building footprints (Efficiency of the Built-up Fabric), respectively. The two maps show relevant differences. Overall, the plot system shows more complexity levels than the built-up fabric, with most SLAs having 5 to 6 levels of nested complexity and no SLA falling lower than 3. No spatial patterns emerge in this map since small and great values are present everywhere in the metropolitan area under exam. The relative complexity and self-organisation of the plot system is likely to be due to many centuries of both rural and urban history, with the noticeable exceptions of large residential subdivisions in the coastal area. By comparison, the built-up system shows less self-organized complexity and, above all, much more spatial heterogeneity. The coastal cities have the highest levels of complexity (6 or 7), but important sectors of the close hinterland present just 1 or 2 levels of power-law distribution, hinting at processes of control and standardisation of the built-up fabric.

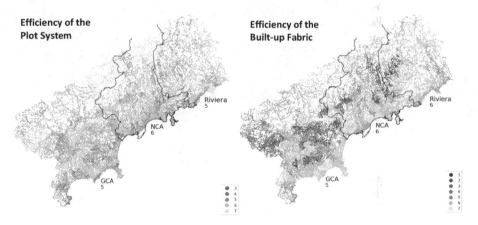

Fig. 7. Efficiency of the morphological system in the SLAs of the French Riviera.

4 Conclusion

4.1 Assessing the Methodological Proposal

The main goal of this paper was to show how morphological resilience could be assessed in a wide metropolitan area using geoprocessing protocols and available geospatial information. More specifically, we proposed a methodology based on two steps. The first consists in the implementation of the Louvain algorithm of modularity optimization, which identifies spatial units of analysis, the Street-Based Local Areas (i.e., SLAs), through the evaluation of the interconnectedness of the street network of the study area under exam. The second step consists in computing a set of morpho-functional indicators of resilience describing five different proxies of diversity, connectivity, redundancy, modularity and efficiency.

Table 1 summarises the indicators that were used to quantify the five different dimensions of morphological resilience in each SLA of the metropolitan area under exam. It is a compact set of 13 quantitative indicators, computable from geospatial information, easily available for the case study and for other world cities.

One main specificity of the proposed assessment is the absence of recognized thresholds for the evaluation of proxy indicators. Table 1 only specifies, on a theoretical basis, whether the indicators are positively or negatively associated with morphological resilience. It is thus only possible to assess their relative performances across the SLAs of a metropolitan area. Possible redundancies among indicators do not constitute an issue, since the assessment is based on the evaluation of proxies and not of individual indicators. At the same time, proxies are not completely independent. Path Redundancy, for example, is linked to the connectivity of the street network and Diversity of Building Types is affected by the Efficiency of the Plot System and of the Built-up Fabric. By construction, proxies are different complementary dimensions of urban morphological resilience.

Table 1. List of resilience indicators for urban form.

Resilience proxy	Indicator	Evaluation
Diversity	Primary Functional Mix (Absolute Difference of Jobs/Residents Ratio from Metropolitan Average)	–
	Diversity of Retail and Services (Gini-Simpson Index)	+
	Diversity of Building Types (Gini-Simpson Index)	+
Connectivity	Street Internal Connectivity (Connected Node Ratio)	+
	Street Internal Connectivity (Links to Node Ratio)	+
	External Connectivity (External Links/square root number of connections)	+
Redundancy	Path Redundancy (Share of street segments concentrating half of point-to-point minimal paths)	+
	Constrain Score of the Path System (Burt Index)	–
	Redundancy of Transport Modes (average number of modal alternatives to the car available in each street)	+
Modularity	Plot Granularity (average number of plots per hectare served by the street network)	+
	Built-Fabric Modularity (% of loss of built-up elements at 0–1–2–4–8–16–32–64 m dilations)	+
Efficiency	Structural Efficiency of the Plot System (Head/Tail Index)	+
	Structural Efficiency of the Built-up Fabric (Head/Tail Index)	+

The proposed methodology was tested on the French Riviera, a large metropolitan area in southern France. The Louvain algorithm of modularity optimization identified a total of 145 SLAs, corresponding to urban or suburban districts larger than single neighbourhoods or villages. Partial assessments carried out through the different indicators revealed that the most resilient SLAs are located in urban areas on the coast

(Monaco, Nice, Antibes, Cannes), with only one case located inland (the city of Grasse). These SLAs all share similar characteristics as they offer functional diversity, but not necessarily the highest Diversity of Building Types. Furthermore, they tend to be well connected internally, but also with respect to the surrounding SLAs and offer redundant paths. Finally, their plots and buildings show self-organized complexity. SLAs with lower levels of resilience tend to be inland and mainly characterised by residential areas served by non-redundant/tree-like street networks, and uniform plot and building sizes. While the findings outlined above are location specific, the methodology is replicable and can thus be applied to assess resilience levels in different study areas.

4.2   Future Work

The quantitative indicators proposed in this paper allow a first protocol-based analysis of complementary aspects of morphological resilience in a large metropolitan area. However, they still offer a fragmented appraisal of morphological resilience. The most important perspective for our methodology is thus the development of a third step of the analysis. This will consist in a synthetic multi-dimensional assessment of morphological resilience integrating the five proxies of diversity, connectivity, redundancy, modularity, and efficiency. The absence of recognized thresholds and reference levels, already pointed out for the indicators, will be an important issue for this overall assessment. The multi-scalar aspect of morphological resilience can also be further investigated. The proposed methodology relies on a technique for the identification of spatial units of analysis that can be utilised in study areas of different sizes. However, such an eventuality was not tested in this work. Future work might thus apply the proposed methodology to smaller sub-spaces of the study area.

A more in-depth analysis of the outcome of the resilience assessment in the French Riviera, integrating multi-dimensionality and change of scale, will deserve a dedicated paper. Possible sub-spaces of analysis can be the morphological regions identified by Fusco and Araldi [14] in the French Riviera.

Finally, future research endeavours should consider coupling morphological resilience with other aspects of urban resilience, more closely related to human and social capital in urban areas (governance networks, socio-economic dynamics) or to urban functions (mobility, material and energy flows) as proposed by Meerow et al. [26].

Acknowledgements.   This research was carried out thanks to a research grant of the POPSU-Métropole program of the PUCA (Plan Urbanisme Construction Architecture) French governmental agency.

References

1. Abshirini, A., Koch, D.: Resilience, space syntax and spatial interfaces: the case of river cities. ITU A|Z **14**(1), 25–41 (2017)
2. Alexander, D.: Resilience and disaster risk reduction: an etymological journey. Nat. Hazards Earth Syst. Sci. **13**(11), 2707–2716 (2013)

3. Blondel, V., Guillaume, J., Lambiotte, R., Lefebvre, E.: Fast unfolding of communities in large networks. J. Stat. Mech: Theory Exp. **10**, P10008 (2008)
4. Bunting, T., Filion, P. (eds.): Canadian Cities in Transition – Local Through Global Perspectives. Oxford University Press, Oxford (2006)
5. Burt, R.: Structural holes and good ideas. Am. J. Soc. **110**(2), 349–399 (2004)
6. Carpenter, S.R., Westley, F., Turner, M.G.: Surrogates for resilience of social-ecological systems. Ecosystems **8**(8), 941–944 (2005). https://doi.org/10.1007/s10021-005-0170-y
7. Cozzolino, S.: The (anti) adaptive neighbourhoods. Embracing complexity and distribution of design control in the ordinary built environment. Environ. Plan. B: Urban Anal. City Sci. **47**(2), 203–219 (2020)
8. Cutini V.: The city when it trembles. Earthquake destructions, post-earthquake reconstruction and grid configuration. In: Kim, Y.O., Park, H.T., Seo, K.W. (eds.) Proceedings of the 9th International Space Syntax Symposium. Sejong University, Seoul (2013)
9. Cutini, V., Di Pinto, V.: On the slopes of Vesuvius: configuration as a thread between hazard and opportunity. In: 10th Space Syntax Symposium Proceedings, vol. 66, pp. 1–13. UCL, London (2015)
10. Feliciotti, A.: Resilience and urban design: a systems approach to the study of resilience in urban form. Ph.D. thesis, Strathclyde University, Glasgow (2018)
11. Feliciotti, A., Romice, O., Porta, S.: Design for change: five proxies for resilience in the urban form. Open House Int. **41**(4), 23–30 (2016)
12. Folke, C.: Resilience: the emergence of a perspective for social-ecological systems analyses. Glob. Environ. Change **16**(3), 253–267 (2006)
13. Fusco, G.: Ville, complexité, incertitude. Enjeux de connaissance pour le géographe et l'urbaniste. Habilitation à Diriger des Recherches en Géographie, Université Côte d'Azur, Nice (2018). https://hal.archives-ouvertes.fr/tel-01968002
14. Fusco, G., Araldi, A.: The nine forms of the French Riviera: classifying urban fabrics from the pedestrian perspective. In: Proceedings of the 24th ISUF International Conference: City and Territory in the Globalization Age, Ed. Universitat Politècnica de València, pp. 1313–1325 (2017)
15. Fusco, G., Scarella, F.: Recompositions territoriales en Provence-Alpes-Côte d'Azur. Analyse croisée par les mobilités quotidiennes et résidentielles. Cybergeo **656** (2013). http://cybergeo.revues.org/26080
16. Holling, C.S.: Resilience and stability of ecological systems. Ann. Rev. Ecol. Evol. Syst. **4**, 1–23 (1973)
17. Holling, C.S., Sanderson, S.: Dynamics of (dis)harmony in ecological and social systems. In: Hanna, S., et al. (eds.) Rights to Nature: Ecological, Economic, Cultural, and Political Principles of Institutions for the Environment, pp. 57–86. Island Press, Washington (1996)
18. Jacobs, J.: The Death and Life of Great American Cities. Random House, New York (1961)
19. Jiang, B.: Head/tail breaks: a new classification scheme for data with a heavy-tailed distribution. Prof. Geogr. **65**(3), 482–494 (2013)
20. Jiang, B.: Head/tail breaks for visualization of city structure and dynamics. Cities **43**, 69–77 (2015)
21. Jiang, B.: Living structure down to earth and up to heaven: Christopher Alexander. Urban Sci. **3**(3), 96 (2019). https://doi.org/10.3390/urbansci3030096
22. Jost, L.: Entropy and diversity. Oikos **113**(2), 363–375 (2006)
23. Law, S.: Defining street-based local area and measuring its effect on house price using a hedonic price approach: the case study of Metropolitan London. Cities **60**, 166–179 (2017)
24. Le Corbusier: La Charte d'Athènes. Editions de Minuit, Paris (1957)

25. Lhomme, S.: Les réseaux techniques comme vecteur de propagation des risques en milieu urbain. Une contribution théorique et pratique à l'analyse de la résilience urbaine. Thèse de doctorat en géographie, Université Paris-Diderot, Paris (2012)
26. Meerow, S., Newell, J., Stults, M.: Defining urban resilience: a review. Landsc. Urban Plan. **147**, 38–49 (2016)
27. Mehaffy, M., Salingaros, N.: Towards Resilient Architectures I: Biology Lessons. Metropolismag.com, March 2013. http://www.resilience.org/stories/2013-03-25/toward-resilient-architectures-i-biology-lessons/
28. Morin, E.: Introduction à la pensée complexe. Seuil, Paris (1990)
29. Morin, E.: La Méthode, 6 vols. Seuil, Paris (2006). (Collection Opus)
30. Morin, E.: La complexité humaine. Champs Flammarion, Paris (1994)
31. Perez, J., Fusco, G., Araldi, A., Fuse, T.: Identifying building typologies and their spatial patterns in the metropolitan areas of Marseille and Osaka. Asia-Pacific J. Reg. Sci. **4**(2020), 193–217 (2019). https://doi.org/10.1007/s41685-019-00127-6
32. Porta, S., Crucitti, P., Latora, V.: The network analysis of urban streets: a primal approach. Environ. Plann. B: Plann. Des. **33**(5), 705–725 (2006)
33. Reghezza-Zitt, M., et al.: What resilience is not: uses and abuses. CyberGeo **2012**(621), 1–23 (2012)
34. Salat, S., Bourdic, L.: Urban complexity, efficiency and resilience. In: Morvaj, Z. (ed.) Energy Efficiency - A Bridge to Low Carbon Economy. IntechOpen (2012). https://www.intechopen.com/books/energy-efficiency-a-bridge-to-low-carbon-economy/urban-complexity-efficiency-and-resilience
35. Salingaros, N.: Principles of Urban Structure. Techne Press, Delft (2005)
36. Strano, E., Shai, S., Dobson, S., Barthelemy, M.: Multiplex networks in metropolitan areas: generic features and local effects. J. Roy. Soc. Interface **12**, 20150651 (2015)
37. Voiron, Ch., Dutozia, J.: Anticiper et simuler les dynamiques de changement pour diagnostiquer et améliorer la résilience du système territorial urbain. Risques Urbains **1**, 1–17 (2017)

International Workshop on Urban Space Extended Accessibility (USEAccessibility 2020)

"Sustainable Urban Mobility Plans": Key Concepts and a Critical Revision on SUMPs Guidelines

Vincenza Torrisi[1]([✉]) [ID], Chiara Garau[2]([✉]) [ID], Matteo Ignaccolo[1] [ID], and Giuseppe Inturri[3] [ID]

[1] Department of Civil Engineering and Architecture (DICAR), University of Catania, 95125 Catania, Italy
vtorrisi@dica.unict.it

[2] Department of Civil and Environmental Engineering and Architecture (DICAAR), University of Cagliari, 09129 Cagliari, Italy
cgarau@unica.it

[3] Department of Electric, Electronic and Computer Engineering (DIEEI), University of Catania, 95125 Catania, Italy

Abstract. Cities play a fundamental role not only in the growth processes under the sustainability paradigm, but also as a driving-force behind economy and they constitute places of connectivity and innovation. More than two thirds of the European population live in urban areas and this percentage is continuously growing. Therefore, cities are fundamental hubs of the transport system, since most journeys start or end within urban areas. The direct consequence is that many of the negative transport externalities, such as congestion, road accidents and pollution, have the greatest impacts in these contexts. The European Commission emphasized integrated planning at all mobility level to enhance new forms of sustainable urban mobility, in order to reduce externalities associated with transport sector. In this view, the aim of this paper is to analyze the European guidelines for the development and the implementation of Sustainable Urban Mobility Plan (SUMP) and the corresponding Italian guidelines for the preparation of so-called "Piani Urbani della Mobilità Sostenibile" (PUMS). A comparative evaluation is proposed to emphasize the new paradigm of sustainable transport planning and highlight critical evidence between the European legal tools and their transposition at national level, also in the light of their recent updates. The results of this analysis lay the basis for the critical assessment of best practices and the review of related SUMP, in order to identify the key elements to assist traffic planners and managers in their decision-making procedures for the identification of successful strategies and the implementation of effective actions towards sustainable mobility.

Notes. This paper is the result of the joint work of the authors. 'Abstract' 'Urban Mobility and Transport Sector: Statistic Evidences' and 'Theoretical and legal framework: from the European to the Italian perspective' with subparagraphs were written jointly by Vincenza Torrisi and Chiara Garau. Vincenza Torrisi wrote the 'Discussion and conclusions'. Chiara Garau wrote the "Introduction"; Matteo Ignaccolo and Giuseppe Inturri coordinated the research.

© Springer Nature Switzerland AG 2020
O. Gervasi et al. (Eds.): ICCSA 2020, LNCS 12255, pp. 613–628, 2020.
https://doi.org/10.1007/978-3-030-58820-5_45

Keywords: PUMS · Transport planning · Urban sustainability · Smart and sustainable mobility

1   Introduction

In recent years, the scientific and technical interest in managing cities with principles of sustainable urban mobility grown significantly, not only because the technological innovations offer effective and possible real time solutions, but also because the transport sector continues to cause negative externalities (such as traffic congestion, climate-altering gases, etc.) in local contexts, which are no longer negligible.

However, the city governance, or more generally the governance of a territory, based on the principles of sustainable urban mobility, is a complex duty because of political and technical conflicts (which inevitably emerge in a multifaceted socio-technical framework) and it can be helped by considering adequate strategies and measures, also investigating citizen preferences and stakeholder engagement [1, 2]. These include, for example, effective solutions for public transport and accessibility [3, 4], adaptive transport services [5], adequate infrastructures [6, 7], technological devices for managing traffic [8–10], advanced automation techniques for raising peoples well-being and advanced intelligent transport system solutions [11–13], in order to satisfy the mobility needs of residents and, more in general, of the city users [14].

In Europe these issues are particularly felt starting from 1987 with the sustainable development concept - introduced by the Brundtland report [15] - and with several EU formal directives and regulations, focusing on the development of sustainable urban transport [16]. According to the traditional planning tool, strategies were defined and applied for enhancing urban mobility in cities over a medium/long-term period and the Italian transport planning was regulated by the Urban Mobility Plans - UMPs - (from Italian *Piani Urbani della Mobilità* – PUM), oriented by a cost-benefit approach.

Today, the concept of sustainability (or a sustainable city or sustainable urban development) is part of the broader concept of smart and sustainable cities [17–19]. In particular, Höjer and Wangel [19] rewrite the Brundtland definition, by considering a Smart Sustainable City a place "that meets the needs of its present inhabitants without compromising the ability for other people or future generations to meet their needs, and thus, does not exceed local or planetary environmental limitations, and where this is supported by ICT" [19; pag. 10]. However, in this context, the authors particularly consider the transport sector.

The sustainability concept introduces long-term goals for passenger and freight transport and environmental protection and considers a new human-centred approach, the UMPs have adapted to the new paradigm, becoming the Sustainable Urban Mobility Plans - SUMPs (from Italian: *Piani Urbani della Mobilità Sostenibile* - PUMS). The addition of the letter "S" of Sustainability is prominent for the future of our Communities, which is linked not only to the challenge of reducing emissions in the atmosphere, but it regards a wide-ranging viewing with also economic and social issues. It is an opportunity to reflect on habits and tangible actions to promote sustainable development, as evidenced in [20–21]. In fact, the PUMS is no longer focused on the concept of "mobility", as the realization of infrastructures, but is pursues the "sustainability", by proposing a human-centered approach that places the individual and his needs at the center of the project and not the physical infrastructures that derive from it.

The sustainability concept under the paradigm of smart and sustainable cities is inserted in specific strategic documents [22, 23] and the adoption of a SUMP in a particular context is supported by the definition of guidelines deriving by several projects and initiatives (e.g. CIVITAS, ELTISplus).

Considering this, the SUMPs highlight the importance of citizens' quality of life, proposing the integration of passenger and freight transport demands [24–27].

So, a SUMP can be considered as "a strategic plan designed to satisfy the mobility needs of people and businesses in cities and their surroundings for a better quality of life. It builds on existing planning practices and takes due consideration of integration, participation, and evaluation principles" [28, pag. 9].

In Italy, with the M.D. 4/08/2017, the SUMP is mandatory only for metropolitan cities, large area entities and single and aggregate municipalities with more than 100,000 inhabitants. However, it remains a useful tool for other typologies of cities for accessing different types of funding for mobility sector. Some examples are the Sustainable Urban Mobility Plan in European countries are, Hungary, France for its guidelines [29] and Portugal and Czech Republic for the way of monitoring and evaluation. In Italy, some best practices are Bologna, engaged in the drafting of the first metropolitan plan and the city of Padua which pays more attention to urban logistic [30].

Based on these premises, this paper proposes a critical analysis of European and Italian Guidelines for the drafting of SUMP, also in the light of the recent revisions and updates, emphasizing the new paradigm of sustainable transport planning. The paper is structured in four section: the first one introduces the principals of smart and sustainable mobility explaining the role of SUMP; the second section provides some statistic evidences about transport sector and shows the differences between the traditional and sustainable transport planning; the third section analysis the theoretical and legal framework from the European to the Italian perspective; the final section gives a critical review of SUMP Guidelines through a discussion and provides main conclusions and further research of the work.

2   Urban Mobility and Transport Sector: Statistic Evidences

Before starting to analyse the comparison between the (European and Italian) mobility plans, the authors believe it is necessary to focus on the evident problems that concern the transport sector in relation to the urban area.

In 2017, considering the transport and storage services sector, the Gross Value Added (GVA) accounted for about the 5% of the total GVA in EU-28. Figure 1 includes the GVA of companies whose main activity is the provision of transport (and transport-related) services and that own account transport operations are not included. The transport and storage services sector (including postal and courier activities) employed around 11.7 million persons, representing 5.3% of the total workforce. The percentage division between the various transport modes is as follows: 52% in land transport (road, rail and pipelines); 3% in water transport (sea and inland waterways), 4% in air transport and 27% in warehousing and supporting and transport activities (such as cargo handling, storage and warehousing) and the remaining 15% in postal and courier activities. Moreover, about the 13% of the total private household consumption was committed to purchasing transport-related items: around a third of the entire sum was used to purchase vehicles, around half was spent on the operation of personal transport equipment (e.g. to buy fuel for the vehicles) and the rest was spent for transport services (e.g. bus, train, plane tickets).

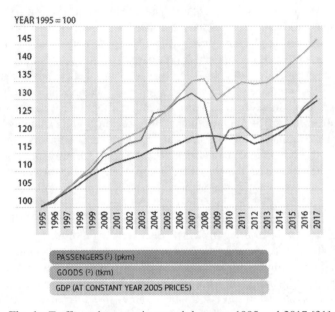

Fig. 1. Traffic and economic growth between 1995 and 2017 [31]

As regards the goods transport, for the year 2017, it was estimated to amount to 3731 billion of ton-kilometre (tkm) moved. Figure 1 shows the trend of goods, by considering only the European air and sea transport excluding the transport activities between the EU and the rest of the world. Goods transport by road represents the highest percentage (more than 50% of this total), followed by maritime transport (about 31%), by rail (11%) and the rest by inland waterways and oil pipelines. With reference to passenger transport, is was estimated an amount of 69133 billion of passenger-kilometre (pkm) with an average of around 13505 km per person. Passenger cars accounted for 70.9% of these total, powered two-wheelers for 1.8%, buses & coaches for 7.4%, railways for 6.8% and tram and metro for 1.6%. Intra-EU air and intra-EU maritime transport contributed for 11.2% and 0.4% respectively [31].

To face these issues, the promotion of smart and sustainable approaches, indicated in the previously paragraph, may represent the solution. However, in relation to transport and mobility sectors, a city cannot be considered smart if it is not sustainable, in which all priorities, strategies and actions are coordinated in an integrated system of several projects and intentions all aimed at sustainability [32–34]. The outcomes are addressed at improving the efficiency, the effectiveness and the environmental sustainability of cities.

This significant awareness of the sustainability concept under the paradigm of smart and sustainable cities has changed also the transport planning. In a nutshell, Table 1 shows the main differences (nine) between the traditional and the sustainable transport planning.

Table 1. Differences between the traditional transport planning and the sustainable transport planning (Source: Authors elaboration starting from [32])

	Traditional Transport Planning (TTP)	Sustainable Transport Planning (STP)
1	Planning for sectors	Integrated planning
2	Mobility	Accessibility
3	Motorized mobility	Soft Mobility
4	Street as movement artery	Street as a public space
5	Cost-benefits analysis	Multi-criteria analysis
6	Ownership	Sharing
7	Increasing supply	Demand management
8	Hight speed	Low speed
9	Segregation	Users integration

Therefore, two generations of transport plans are distinguished in Table 1 and the nine differences concern:

1) The transport planning in general. With TTP, the transport planning was for sectors without dialogue with other planning tools. Instead, STP becomes integrated according to the logic of TOD (Transit Oriented Development). Namely, transport and territory must influence each other for having an efficient transport system [35];
2) The shift from Mobility (planning for cars) to Accessibility (planning for people, considering their movements) [36];
3) The STP is focalized on any non-motorized transport (human powered mobility) [37, 38];
4) The STP considers the streets and the squares in a more complex way: they are spaces for social interaction [39];
5) Cost-benefit analysis of TTP is in contrast with multi-criteria analysis of STP. The multi-criteria analysis also takes into account intangible costs (e.g. environmental cost) [40–42];
6) Ownership of the vehicle of TTP is in contrast with the vehicle sharing of STP [43];
7) Increasing the roads supply of TTP is in contrast with the managing of the demand of STP (for example, regulation of rush hour flows with congestion charge policies; optimize urban logistics) [44–46];

8) With the STP, great importance is given to the movement of the pedestrian, and therefore to the low speeds of the vehicles [47];

9) With the TTP the traffic components are clearly separated. Instead, the STP promotes the integration of road users (pedestrians and cars), in more accessible and sustainable contexts [48, 49].

From an operational point of view, the European Commission (EC) agrees to move in that direction and it is required long-term decisions on the basis of strategic plans [50]. Therefore, the SUMP, from Italian "Piano Urbano della Mobilità Sostenibile" (PUMS), is a strategic planning tool with a time horizon of medium-long term (10 years). It develops a new vision of urban mobility, as a "system of mobility", (preferably referring to a metropolitan city area), by proposing the achievement of environmental, social and economic sustainability objectives. In order to achieve them, the SUMP provides the definition of actions aimed at improving the effectiveness and efficiency of the mobility system and its integration with the urban and territorial planning and development.

3 Theoretical and Legal Framework: From the European to the Italian Perspective

In the EU context, attention to the urban scale has been growing through funding programs (e.g. CIVITAS), Horizon 2020 research projects, the construction of a European network (SUMP conference), and other several initiatives to boost sustainability. As regards the establishment of the right goals and the identification of strategies and actions for sustainable transport planning, the European Commission has launched a series of research and demonstration projects with the aim of promoting SUMPs. The European Guidelines for the development and implementation of these plans have been developed in 2014 within the European project Eltis and implemented at national level with a ministerial decree in 2017. Considering these regulatory tools, the methodological and operational contents of the SUMP and PUMS are similar, otherwise the procedural steps that characterize them are articulated and grouped in a different way. In addition, both guidelines have recently been revised and updated in order to better clarify the planning steps, also through numerous examples of cities and the inclusion of further insights. Based on this premise, this section presents a critical analysis of the European and Italian Guidelines in order to highlight the critical evidence and the differences between the two planning contexts and to identify the key elements to promote effective strategies and actions towards sustainable mobility.

3.1 European Guidelines for SUMP

The adoption of SUMP has been encouraged and recommended by the Commission's Action Plan on Urban Mobility [31]. The next year (June 2010), the EU Council also expressed its consensus, encouraging the development of incentives, such as the assistance of experts and the information exchange, for the creation of new SUMP. The subsequent 2011 White Paper [51] proposed that the drafting of SUMP might be a mandatory requirement for cities with a population of over 100,000 inhabitants, and that the allocation of regional and cohesion funds might be made conditional on the submission and auditing of such legal instruments.

The starting point is represented by the Community Guidelines "Developing and Implementing a Sustainable Urban Mobility Plan" [52], developed by Eltis and approved in 2014 by the EU General Directorate for Mobility and Transport. This document highlighted the assessment of SUMP implementation and the results deriving through the realization of measures envisaged by the Plan [53–55].

The link between the SUMP and sustainability can be found from a social, economic and environmental point of view. The SUMP focuses on environmental aspects considering the pollution deriving from the transport sector and the consequent need to reduce CO_2 emissions, noise and congestion and to improve air quality. Moreover, the SUMP aims at decreasing the private motorization rate, by promoting the use of public transport and encouraging soft mobility (i.e. walking and cycling). With reference to the social aspect, the key concepts of the PUMS consist in a greater accessibility and safety of urban areas, thus making cities more attractive and improving the citizens quality of life. Finally, as regards the economic aspect, the SUMP considers a multi-criteria approach, in order to improve the efficiency and cost-effectiveness associated to the transport of persons and goods, and at the same time taking into consideration a broader view social benefit.

Figure 2 shows a comparison between the two SUMP cycles, representing the complex planning process, respectively for the first edition of the European Guidelines (2014) and for the second edition published last year, in 2019.

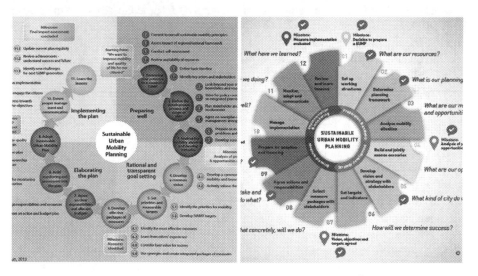

Fig. 2. SUMP cycle for the 1st edition of Guidelines (left) and the 2nd edition (right) [52]

The new SUMP cycle includes 4 consecutive phases that characterize the entire development of the plan. The articulation of the phases and their main contents are described in a concise but effective way in the following table (Table 2):

Table 2. Description of phases for the development of SUMP, according to the 2nd edition of Guidelines (Source: Authors elaboration starting from [53])

Phases	Description	Main contents and scope
Phase 1	Preparation and analysis	- Definition of geographical limits of intervention, considering the area of influence - Recognition of the planning tools - Identification of data (eventually available) for the reconstruction of the state of affairs
Phase 2	Development of strategies	- Definition of the vision, strategies, objectives, targets and indicators, based on the cognitive framework and the analysis of critical issues
Phase 3	Planning of actions	- Exploration of possible measures to be assessed and finalized in the plan
Phase 4	Implementation and monitoring	- Management of the plan implementation through the effective enactment of actions - Monitoring and review of the Plan according to the obtained results

This second edition of Guidelines is completed by 17 Topic Guides and Practitioner Briefings which investigate particular issues related to urban mobility, providing detailed indications and practical information that can support city administrations to develop even more effective SUMP.

3.2   Italian Guidelines for PUMS

Regarding the country Italy, the legislation has been transposed at national level through the ministerial decree of 4 August 2017 [56]. With this decree, the Ministry of Infrastructure and Transport has identified the guidelines for PUMS, with the aim of promoting the homogeneous and coordinated application of guidelines for the drafting of these plans, throughout the national territory. According to [57], to access state funding for the construction of new interventions regarding rapid mass transport (i.e. metropolitan railway systems, metro and trams), metropolitan cities must present three administrative tools: (i) Feasibility Projects; (ii) Report of consistency of proposed projects with the objectives of [41]; (iii) PUMS. Cities must proceed with the definition of their own PUMS, using the guidelines adopted with [56], recently updated by the M. D. 28/08/2019.

In line with the Annex I of [56], the different procedural steps for the drafting and approval of PUMS, reported are showed in Fig. 3:

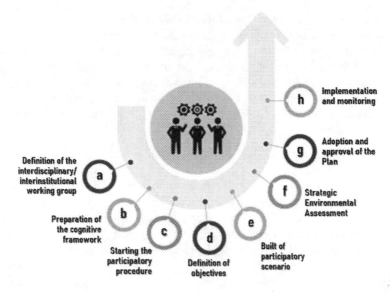

Fig. 3. Procedural steps for the drafting and approval of PUMS (Source: Authors elaboration starting from [40])

(a) Definition of the Interdisciplinary/Interinstitutional Working Group. The plan should be drafted by acquiring the knowledge of different disciplines from the various institutional actors involved in the planning process. Therefore, it is advisable the collaboration between various sectors within the municipal administration (i.e. urban planning, mobility, environment, tourism, municipal police, economic activities, etc.). The creation of the *interdisciplinary* working group also takes into consideration the possibility of appointing external technicians with consolidated experience, to identify the actions with the related economic and environmental costs and to manage the participation processes. Among the important factors, it emerges the presence of a mobility manager [58] in the working group and, at the *interinstitutional* level, the involvement of conurbations and neighboring municipalities within a local public transport service is provided.

(b) Preparation of the Cognitive Framework. This step involves the collection of data from different sources to provide all useful information to characterize the area and identify its critical issues. In this regard, the cognitive framework should contain information concerning the regulatory, planning and programmatic tools both at regional and local level and a territorial and socio-economic explanation of the Plan area. In addition, it should include a description regarding the transport demand and supply (with a focus on ITS systems for information, regulation and traffic control) and their interaction. Finally, it identifies the critical issues and impacts in terms of degree of accessibility, congestion, incidents and environmental pollution, including a SWOT (strengths and weaknesses, opportunities and threats) analysis.

(c) **Starting the Participatory Procedure.** In this context, the participatory process takes on a particularly important role. It already begins in the previous procedural step with the identification of critical issues highlighted by citizens and stakeholders and contributes to the subsequent definition of the objectives of the Plan. However, the selection of approaches and techniques for introducing this procedure it is delegated to the administrations, on the basis of what it considers most appropriate in relation to the territorial characteristics and available resources and by considering also the most innovative techniques, such as VGI [59].

(d) **Definition of Objectives.** This is a fundamental procedural step because the outline of strategies and actions for the scenario construction derives from a clear identification of the objectives. Specifically, macro-objectives are identified in response to the general interests of the efficacy and efficiency of mobility and the social, economic and environmental sustainability of the system. They are associated with the results and the relative target values to be achieved within 10 years. Then there are specific objectives with a lower hierarchical level, functional to the achievement of macro-objectives. In relation to them, a biennial monitoring activity through defined indicators is crucial to evaluate their achievement and confirm their relevance

(e) **Build of the Participatory Scenario.** The starting point for the construction depends on the strategies and actions identified following the previous steps. Then, follows the definition of different alternative scenarios compared with the Reference Scenario (RS) (i.e. configured if the PUMS strategies are not implemented). From a comparative evaluation of the alternative scenarios, through ex-ante indicators, the Plan Scenario (PS) is identified, including the list of priority interventions and a time schedule of its implementation in the short term (e.g. 5 years) and long term (10 years). To define the effectiveness of these interventions, it is important to indicate a costs estimation and possible financial coverage, highlighting the available resources in the municipal budget.

(f) **Strategic Environmental Assessment.** This evaluation, (from Italian Valutazione Ambientale Strategica - VAS) accompanies the entire planning process until its approval. Indeed, according to [57], being the PUMS a strategic plan and considering that it may have a significant impact on the environment, its eligibility for the VAS procedure must be evaluated in order to guarantee a high level of environmental protection and promote a Sustainable Development.

(g) **Adoption and Approval of the Plan.** These two actions follow a well-defined procedure, which envisages a first phase of adoption of the Plan; then its publication for 30 days in order to collect any observations; finally, subsequent approval of the plan.

(h) **Implementation and Monitoring.** To evaluate the pursuit of the objectives and the effectiveness and efficiency of the actions and interventions identified in the Plan, the monitoring activity is considered indispensable. Its periodicity, through a biennial report analyzing the state of implementation of the PUMS, allows a possible critical reconsideration of the interventions and revision of the targets to be achieved. For this purpose, it is appropriate the definition of a system of indicators and realize their ex-ante and ex-post comparison. In this step, the participation is also expected to ensure the progressive achievement of the objectives and to identify any issues that hinder the regular implementation of the Plan.

4 Discussion and Conclusions

The hitherto given work consisted in a comparative analysis between the traditional transport planning and the new paradigm of sustainable urban and transport planning by considering the sustainable development, in the context of the smart cities paradigm.

In addition, the paper provided an analysis of the European and Italian guidelines for the development and the implementation of SUMP, in order to highlight the main contents and the critical evidence of these legal tools and their transposition at national level, also in the light of recent revisions and updates.

By analysing the structure of SUMP (and PUMS at the national level) with its relative contents, it emerges that the main principles on which these plans are based are the following [52]:

- develop the Plan taking into account the functional urban area, which in some cases may extend beyond the administrative boundaries of the municipality;
- cooperate across institutional boundaries, in accordance with what is described in the first point;
- involve citizens and stakeholders in the preparation of the Plan;
- evaluate the current and future performance deriving from the identification of strategies and the implementation of actions, by using indicators;
- define a long-term vision, so as to have a clear implementation plan;
- promote the inter-modality and intra-modality through actions that aims to integrate all transport modes;
- provide the monitoring and evaluation phases of the Plan, which are fundamental for assessing its actual effectiveness and for identifying any corrective actions;
- ensure a quality plan, that leads to tangible benefits.

The previous European Guidelines drawn up in 2014 represented a determined "turning point" in the debate on urban mobility planning, constituting a fundamental methodological reference for city initiatives and anticipating approaches and operational guidelines. The second edition of 2019 Guidelines considers the novelties of a rapidly evolving sector and new challenges, arising from extensive consultations with stakeholders and expert contributions. Moreover, thanks to this, a series of new thematic guides have been produced, in order to further encourage the development and implementation of SUMPs with content related to the new urban logistics, the electrification, the role of ITS, the road security, the harmonization of approaches between climate and energy policies, the financial aspects and funds for actions, etc.

Going into more detail, the main changes compared to the first edition of the Guidelines essentially concern a different articulation of the phases of the Plan, as highlighted in the previous section. The SUMP cycle is completely updated and more balanced. There is a clear separation of the strategic planning phase (1st and 2nd phase) and the operational one (3rd and 4th phase), often having different time horizons: the strategic objectives have a medium-long term time horizon, while the measures can be updated more frequently. This allows a greater formal balance of the process, reporting a division of the SUMP cycle into four phases with three steps each, always ending with the achievement of a milestone. Furthermore, there is an additional focus on sectors of particular interest (e.g. accessibility, health, social inclusion, road safety), accompanied by numerous examples of cities and various insights.

Likewise, at the national level there was an evolution which have seen the update of these guidelines by the Ministry of Infrastructure and Transport in 2019. One of the main differences on rewriting this document concerns significant changes to the result indicators, in particular those associated with the macro-objectives, which are more detailed than the initial formulation. In addition, some terms and conditions have been changed relating to the compliance with the Guidelines by institutions, i.e. municipalities with more than one hundred thousand inhabitants have the requirement for the drafting of PUMS as an essential condition for accessing state funding in new interventions for rapid mass transport (i.e. metropolitan railways, metro, trams). This obligation was previously envisaged only for Metropolitan cities. Therefore, the aspect linked to financial funding meant that many municipalities decided to invest in the drafting of PUMS. In this vision, it is significant to observe the state of the art in Italy about the elaboration and implementation of PUMS. From the database provided by the National Observatory of PUMS is emerges that 164 cities have (or are working to have) their own Plan. Specifically, considering the data updated in February 2020, the approved plans are 36, while those adopted are 35; the remaining part (i.e. 93) are drafting Plans. These last are classified "in drafting" when the plan has officially started, by drafting the address lines or publishing the notice for its assignment; or even when the drafting has ended but the plan has not yet been adopted.

The results of this analysis lay the basis for the critical assessment of best practices and the review of related SUMP, in order to identify the key elements to assist traffic planners and managers in their decision-making procedures for the identification of successful strategies and the implementation of effective actions towards sustainable mobility.

Acknowledgments. This work has been partially financed by the University of Catania within the project "Piano della Ricerca Dipartimentale 2016-2018" of the Department of Civil Engineering and Architecture and the project "Piano per la Ricerca 2016-2018 - Linea di intervento 2" of the Department of Electric, Electronic and Computer Engineering. This study was also supported by the MIUR (Ministry of Education, Universities and Research [Italy]) through a project entitled WEAKI TRANSIT: WEAK-demand areas Innovative TRANsport Shared services for Italian Towns (Project code: 20174ARRHT; CUP Codes: E44I17000050001, F74I19001290001), financed with the PRIN 2017 (Research Projects of National Relevance) programme. We authorize the MIUR to reproduce and distribute reprints for Governmental purposes, notwithstanding any copyright notations thereon. Any opinions, findings and conclusions or recommendations expressed in this material are those of the authors, and do not necessarily reflect the views of the MIUR.

References

1. Ignaccolo, M., Inturri, G., Giuffrida, N., Le Pira, M., Torrisi, V.: Public engagement for designing new transport services: investigating citizen preferences from a multiple critera perspective. Transp. Res. Procedia **37**, 91–98 (2019). https://doi.org/10.1016/j.trpro.2018.12.170

2. Ignaccolo, M., Inturri, G., Giuffrida, N., Le Pira, M., Torrisi, V.: Structuring transport decision-making problems through stakeholder engagement: The case of Catania metro accessibility. Transp. Infrastruct. Syst. pp. 919–926 (2017). https://doi.org/10.1201/9781315281896-118

3. Curtis, C., Scheurer, J.: Planning for Public Transport Accessibility: An International Sourcebook. Routledge, London (2016)

4. Caggiani, L., Camporeale, R., Dimitrijević, B., Vidović, M.: An approach to modeling bike-sharing systems based on spatial equity concept. Transp. Res. Procedia 45, 185–192 (2020)

5. Canale, A., Tesoriere, G., Campisi, T.: The MAAS development as a mobility solution based on the individual needs of transport users. In: AIP Conference Proceedings, vol. 2186, no. 1, p. 160005. AIP Publishing LLC, December 2019. https://doi.org/10.1063/1.5138073

6. Campisi, T., Acampa, G., Marino, G., Tesoriere, G.: Cycling master plans in Italy: The I-BIM feasibility tool for cost and safety assessments. Sustainability 12(11), 4723 (2020). https://doi.org/10.3390/su12114723

7. Caggiani, L., Camporeale, R., Binetti, M., Ottomanelli, M.: An urban bikeway network design model for inclusive and equitable transport policies. Transp. Res. procedia 37, 59–66 (2019)

8. Torrisi, V., Ignaccolo, M., Inturri, G.: Estimating travel time reliability in urban areas through a dynamic simulation model. Transp. Res. Procedia 27, 857–864 (2017). https://doi.org/10.1016/j.trpro.2017.12.134

9. Torrisi, V., Ignaccolo, M., Inturri, G.: Innovative transport systems to promote sustainable mobility: developing the model architecture of a traffic control and supervisor system. In: Gervasi, O., et al. (eds.) ICCSA 2018. LNCS, vol. 10962, pp. 622–638. Springer, Cham (2018). https://doi.org/10.1007/978-3-319-95168-3_42

10. Torrisi, V., Ignaccolo, M., Inturri, G., Giuffrida, N.: Combining sensor traffic and simulation data to measure urban road network reliability. In: International Conference on Traffic and Transport Engineering (ICTTE) Proceedings, Belgrade, p. 1004, November 2016

11. Singh, B., Gupta, A.: Recent trends in intelligent transportation systems: a review. J. Transp. Lit. 9(2), 30–34 (2015)

12. Torrisi V., Ignaccolo M., Inturri G.: Toward a sustainable mobility through a dynamic real-time traffic monitoring, estimation and forecasting system: The RE.S.E.T. project. In: Town and Infrastructure Planning for Safety and Urban Quality - Proceedings of the 23rd International Conference on Living and Walking in Cities, LWC 2017, pp. 241–250 (2018). https://doi.org/10.1201/9781351173360-32

13. Bandeira, J.M., et al.: Exploring the potential of web based information of business popularity for supporting sustainable traffic management. Transp. Telecommun. J. 21(1), 47–60 (2020)

14. Bezerra, B.S., dos Santos, A.L.L., Delmonico, D.V.: Unfolding barriers for urban mobility plan in small and medium municipalities–a case study in Brazil. Transp. Res. Part A Policy Pract. 132, 808–822 (2020)

15. Brundtland, G.H.: Our Common Future: The World Commission on Environment and Development. Oxford University Press, Oxford (1987)

16. European Commission, White Paper. La politica europea dei trasporti fino al 2010: il momento delle scelte (2001)

17. Garau, C., Pavan, V.M.: Evaluating urban quality: indicators and assessment tools for smart sustainable cities. Sustainability 10(3), 575 (2018)

18. Pinna, F., Masala, F., Garau, C.: Urban policies and mobility trends in Italian smart cities. Sustainability 9(4), 494 (2017)

19. Höjer, M., Wangel, J.: Smart Sustainable Cities: Definition and Challenges. In: Hilty, L., Aebischer, B. (eds.) ICT Innovations for Sustainability. Advances in Intelligent Systems and Computing, vol. 310, pp. 333–349. Springer, Cham (2015). https://doi.org/10.1007/978-3-319-09228-7_20

20. Dembski, F., Wössner, U., Letzgus, M., Ruddat, M., Yamu, C.: Urban digital twins for smart cities and citizens: The case study of Herrenberg, Germany. Sustainability 12(6), 2307 (2020)

21. Campisi, T., Canale, A., Tesoriere, G.: SWOT analysis for the implementation of spaces and pedestrian paths at the street markets of Palermo. In: AIP Conference Proceedings, vol. 2040, no. 1, p. 140003. AIP Publishing LLC, November 2018. https://doi.org/10.1063/1.5079192

22. Tesoriere, G., Campisi, T., Canale, A., Severino, A.: The effects of urban traffic noise on children at kindergarten and primary school: a case study in Enna. In: AIP Conference Proceedings, vol. 2040, no. 1, p. 140005. AIP Publishing LLC, November 2018. https://doi.org/10.1063/1.5079194

23. Kiba-Janiak, M.: Urban freight transport in city strategic planning. Res. Trans. Busin. Manag. 24, 4–16 (2017)

24. Lindenau, M., Böhler-Baedeker, S.: Citizen and stakeholder involvement: a precondition for sustainable urban mobility. Trans. Res. Procedia 4, 347–360 (2014)

25. Louro, A., da Costa, N.M., da Costa, E.M.: Sustainable urban mobility policies as a path to healthy cities—the case study of LMA, Portugal. Sustainability 11, 2929 (2019)

26. Okraszewska, R., Romanowska, A., Wołek, M., Oskarbski, J., Birr, K., Jamroz, K.: Integration of a multilevel transport system model into sustainable urban mobility planning. Sustainability 10, 479 (2018)

27. European Commission: 2nd edition of Guidelines for developing and implementing a sustainable urban mobility plan (2019)

28. Ignaccolo M., Inturri G., Giuffrida N., Torrisi V.: A sustainable framework for the analysis of port systems. Eur. Trans. Int. J. Transp. Econ. Eng. Law (78), 7 (2020). ISSN 1825-3997

29. Rupprech Consult: The status of SUMPs in EU Member States (2017). http://www.rupprecht-consult.eu/uploads/tx_rupprecht/SUMPs-Up___PROSPERITY-SUMP-Status-in-EU-Report.pdf. Accessed 24 Apr 2020

30. Molinaro, W.: How Italian metropolitan cities are dealing with the issue of climate change? TeMA – J. Land Use Mobility Environ. 13(1), 55–80 (2020). https://doi.org/10.6092/1970-9870/6606

31. European Commission DG Energy and Transport: Action Plan on Urban Mobility. DGTREN, Brussels (2009)

32. Marshall: The challenge of sustainable transport and Banister, 2008. "The sustainable mobility paradigm" (2001)

33. Fichera, A., Marrasso, E., Sasso, M., Volpe, R.: Energy, environmental and economic performance of an urban community hybrid distributed energy system. Energies 13(10), 2545 (2020)

34. Fichera, A., Frasca, M., Palermo, V., Volpe, R.: An optimization tool for the assessment of urban energy scenarios. Energy 156, 418–429 (2018)

35. Appleyard, B.S., Frost, A.R., Allen, C.: Are all transit stations equal and equitable? Calculating sustainability, livability, health, & equity performance of smart growth & transit-oriented-development (TOD). J. Transp. Health 14, 100584 (2019)

36. Rossetti, S., Tiboni, M., Vetturi, D., Calderòn, E.J.: Pedestrian mobility and accessibility planning: some remarks towards the implementation of travel time maps. CSE-City Safety Energy (1), 67–78 (2015)

37. La Rocca, R.A.: Soft mobility and urban transformation. TeMA J. Land Use Mobility Environ. **2** (2009). ISSN 1970-9870 Vol 3 - SP - March 2010

38. Coni, M., Garau, C., Pinna, F.: How has Cagliari changed its citizens in smart citizens? Exploring the influence of ITS technology on urban social interactions. In: Gervasi, O., et al. (eds.) ICCSA 2018. LNCS, vol. 10962, pp. 573–588. Springer, Cham (2018). https://doi.org/10.1007/978-3-319-95168-3_39

39. Ignaccolo, C., Giuffrida, N., Torrisi, V.: The queensway of New York city. A proposal for sustainable mobility in queens. In: Town and Infrastructure Planning for Safety and Urban Quality, pp. 69–76 (2018). https://doi.org/10.1201/9781351173360-12

40. Ignaccolo, M., Inturri, G., García-Melón, M., Giuffrida, N., Le Pira, M., Torrisi, V.: Combining analytic hierarchy process (AHP) with role-playing games for stakeholder engagement in complex transport decisions. Transp. Res. Procedia **27**, 500–507 (2017). https://doi.org/10.1016/j.trpro.2017.12.069

41. Campisi, T., Torrisi, V., Ignaccolo, M., Inturri, G., Tesoriere, G.: University propensity assessment to car sharing services using mixed survey data: the Italian case study of Enna city. Transp. Res. Procedia **47**, 433–444 (2020). https://doi.org/10.1016/j.trpro.2020.03.155

42. Moslem, S., Duleba, S.: Sustainable urban transport development by applying a Fuzzy-AHP model: a case study from Mersin, Turkey. Urban Sci. **3**(2), 55 (2019)

43. Fernandes, P., et al.: Integrating road traffic externalities through a sustainability indicator. Sci. Total Environ. **691**, 483–498 (2019)

44. Torrisi, V., Ignaccolo, M., Inturri, G.: Analysis of road urban transport network capacity through a dynamic assignment model: validation of different measurement methods. Transp. Res. Procedia **27**, 1026–1033 (2017). https://doi.org/10.1016/j.trpro.2017.12.135

45. Tira, M., Tiboni, M., Rossetti, S., De Robertis, M.: "Smart" planning to enhance nonmotorised and safe mobility in today's cities. In: Papa, R., Fistola, R., Gargiulo, C. (eds.) Smart Planning: Sustainability and Mobility in the Age of Change. GET, pp. 201–213. Springer, Cham (2018). https://doi.org/10.1007/978-3-319-77682-8_12

46. Calabrò, G., Torrisi, V., Inturri, G., Ignaccolo, M.: Improving inbound logistic planning for large-scale real-world routing problems: a novel ant-colony simulation-based optimization. Eur. Transp. Res. Rev. **12**(1) (2020). https://doi.org/10.1186/s12544-020-00409-7

47. Ignaccolo, M., Inturri, G., Giuffrida, N., Torrisi, V., Cocuzza, E.: Sustainability of freight transport through an integrated approach: the case of the Eastern Sicily Port system. Transp. Res. Procedia **45**, 177–184 (2020). https://doi.org/10.1016/j.trpro.2020.03.005

48. Ignaccolo, M., Inturri, G., Cocuzza, E., Giuffrida, N., Torrisi, V.: Framework for the evaluation of the quality of pedestrian routes for the sustainability of port–city shared areas. In: Coastal Cities and their Sustainable Future III, vol. 188, p. 11 (2019)

49. Kiba-Janiak, M., Witkowski, J.: Sustainable urban mobility plans: how do they work? Sustainability **11**(17), 4605 (2019)

50. Ignaccolo, M., Inturri, G., Giuffrida, N., Le Pira, M., Torrisi, V., Calabrò, G.: A step towards walkable environments: spatial analysis of pedestrian compatibility in an urban context. Eur. Transp. Trasporti Europei **76**(6), 1–12 (2020)

51. European Commission: White book Verso un sistema dei trasporti competitivo e sostenibile (2011)

52. ELTIS. http://www.eltis.org/mobility-plans/project-partners/civitas-sumps. Accessed 10 Jan 2019

53. de Oliveira Cavalcanti, C., Limont, M., Dziedzic, M., Fernandes, V.: Sustainability of urban mobility projects in the Curitiba metropolitan region. Land Use Policy **60**, 395–402 (2017)

54. Diez, J.M., Lopez-Lambas, M.E., Gonzalo, H., Rojo, M., Garcia-Martinez, A.: Methodology for assessing the cost of sustainable urban mobility plans (SUMPs). The case of the city of Burgos. J. Trans. Geogr. **68**, 22–30 (2018)

55. Zope, R., Vasudevan, N., Arkatkar, S.S., Joshi, G.: Benchmarking: a tool for evaluation and monitoring sustainability of urban transport system in metropolitan cities of India. Sustain. Cit. Soc. **45**, 48–58 (2019)

56. Ministerial Decree: Individuazione delle linee guida per i piani urbani di mobilità sostenibile, ai sensi dell'articolo 3, comma 7, del decreto legislativo 16 dicembre 2016, n. 257, 4 August 2017

57. D.E.F.: Documento di Economia e Finanzia, Annex. Connettere l'Italia, fabbisogni e progetti di infrastrutture (2017)

58. Interministerial decree: «Mobilità sostenibile nelle aree urbane» and law n. 340/2000 27 March 1998

59. Maciel de Brito Soares, I., Yamu, C., Weitkamp, G.: Space syntax and volunteered geographic information for university campus planning and design: Evidence from the Netherlands, Zernike Campus Groningen. In: Proceedings of the 12th International Space Syntax Symposium, Beijing, pp. 134.1–134.15. (2019)

60. Ministerial Decree 152/2006: Norme in materia ambientale. Artt. 6, 7, 12

The Growing Urban Accessibility: A Model to Measure the Car Sharing Effectiveness Based on Parking Distances

Tiziana Campisi[1](✉) ⓘ, Matteo Ignaccolo[2] ⓘ, Giuseppe Inturri[3] ⓘ,
Giovanni Tesoriere[1] ⓘ, and Vincenza Torrisi[2](✉) ⓘ

[1] University of Enna Kore, Cittadella Universitaria, Enna, Italy
tiziana.campisi@unikore.it
[2] Department of Civil Engineering and Architecture, University of Catania,
Via Santa Sofia 64, 95125 Catania, Italy
vtorrisi@dica.unict.it
[3] Department of Electric, Electronic and Computer Engineering (DIEEI),
University of Catania, 95125 Catania, Italy

Abstract. The spread and development of shared mobility makes it possible to offer users various forms of shared service that promote a sustainable approach. The choice of transport mode often depends on the distance travelled and the motivation for the journey. Among the conditions and variables that most influence the propensity to use a shared transport mode, the distance between the users' places of origin or destination and the parking areas covered plays an important role, especially in the case of station-based type. The common system that has become more and more widespread in Italy is car sharing, with its various forms (i.e. station-based, free-floating, electric vehicles) that allow the use of reserved parking spaces or shared with other circulating vehicles. In urban areas, people generally tend to walk the first and last mile or use micro-mobility, while for longer distances they tend to use private or shared motor vehicles. Starting from this premise, this thesis provides a methodology for evaluating the effectiveness of car sharing by measuring the probability of using it based on parking distance. The proposed model is based on the estimation of O/D matrices with associated distance levels and the calculation of a probability index derived from several distance combinations. This research lays the foundation for a deeper analysis, which includes model calibration for different common mobility solutions and the evaluation of user probability in relation to implemented common mobility systems in several case studies.

Keywords: Propensity to car sharing · Parking distance · O/D matrix · User perception

This paper is the result of the joint work of the authors. 'Abstract' 'Introduction' 'Methodology' and 'Results' were written jointly by the authors. TC focused on the state of the art. VT designed the methodological approach and discussion. Supervision and research funding GI, MI, GT.

O. Gervasi et al. (Eds.): ICCSA 2020, LNCS 12255, pp. 629–644, 2020.
https://doi.org/10.1007/978-3-030-58820-5_46

1   Introduction

Urban and infrastructure planning have effects on the entire national system. Several strategies and actions are essential to optimize the use of transport networks, improving different aspects, such as urban logistics, public transport system and intermodality, urban spaces and interactions between different traffic components, all in the vision of sustainability [1–3]. The design and construction of new transport systems change the urban layout and spaces. This has a profound effect on the functional layout of the city by changing the accessibility, times and land uses.

The sustainable city development aims to reduce the use of private means by promoting both slow mobility and means-sharing strategies [4–7]. This type of mobility is often identified as a socio-economic phenomenon that correlates the supply and demand of transport [8]. This concept was developed from traditional to innovative system and it was described by the authors, by highlighting the increase of the use of sensors, digital platforms, the interactivity and community cooperation collaboration and finally by the flexibility of the service [9–11].

Four different parameters generally had described the mobility with private car such as accessibility, availability, continuity and versatility. The spread of integrated mobility has provided a good opportunity to redefine the city map and to consider a new mobility management. The widespread change in the preference for shared use of the medium at the expense of private medium use is associated with an increase in efficiency in resource consumption, emissions and social inclusion.

Among the negative externalities associated to the high levels of motorization rate and traffic congestion there are the oversaturation of road capacity and unreliability of travel times [12, 13]. According to [14], the implementation of shared mobility will make it possible to eliminate road congestion, reduce CO_2 emissions by about 30% and cut the need for public parking by 95%. Furthermore, it has been shown that shared mobility guarantees greater social justice by eliminating or reducing the problems associated with home schooling and home health facilities.

The future structure of this transport resource involves the implementation of the concept of mobility as a service (MaaS) and thus the creation of a platform that is optimally linked to the other modes of transport, with the choice of vehicle being essentially determined by the needs of the users [15–17].

The parameters that describe this utility include the definition of transport capacity and unused capacity. The former is considered as an estimate of the number of passengers transported per day/month/year. The second, however, which is largely related to the MaaS, correlates with a more general concept of the industrial sector and the examination of when a machine/vehicle produces less than it could. As a result, the fixed and general costs integrated into the unit cost of the product tend to carry more weight than if the machine could fill its remaining capacity. Residual capacity is typical for ridesharing such as carpooling and vanpooling, but also for some of the on-demand facility that offer the possibility to share the vehicle for the same itinerary. In the case of the bike, scooter and micromobility, there is only one seat used by those booking this transport mode, instead the remaining capacity is linked to the number of free seats on board. The choice is often linked to the measurement of distances: these concern both the distances to be covered during the journey (short, medium and long distance) and the distances to reach the car park from the starting point of the movement.

With regard to its development, the aim of this research is to describe a methodology to define the probability of using car sharing when the distance between the origin of the movement and the car park where the shared car can be collected is changed. In the second paragraph, attention was paid to the development of car sharing and its effects; in the third paragraph, the evaluation methodology based on a probability calculation was described; and finally, discussions were held on the potential of the methodology and future research developments.

2   The Development of Car-Sharing and its Implication

Car Sharing is an urban mobility service consisting in renting a car owned or owned by third parties so that users can use a vehicle on reservation for a limited period of time, paying for the use. Its development depends on the purpose of the move and on the infrastructure of the cities where it is implemented as described below.

2.1   The Benefits of Car Sharing Development

From an economic point of view, a Car-Sharing user does not have to bear the fixed costs that a car entails by refraining from buying and using a private car. These costs are additional to the purchase and insurance. In addition, there are costs defined as variables, such as maintenance, the purchase of winter tires and vehicle cleaning. It can be observed that costs are incurred not only when the car is moving, but also when it is stationary, i.e. when it is in a garage or in a public parking lot, very often for a fee. Moreover, it is necessary to take into account the costs that have the greatest influence on the ownership of a car, namely the cost of fuel, which is certainly not a small expense in the case of a petrol or diesel car.

Car sharing makes it possible to reduce these costs. In some cases, the km tariff is activated only after a certain number of kilometers has been exceeded, in other cases it is possible to choose a daily tariff. In general, in order to ensure the spread of joint mobility, companies agree with local administrations on the location of stands and relative areas (e.g. ticket offices). As far as time and space management is concerned, Car-Sharing customers can also easily gain access in areas with limited traffic volume that are inaccessible to private drivers. Moreover, the problem of parking costs does not exist, as cars can be parked in any parking space, including the blue stripes, provided that this is obviously in the area where it operates. However, reducing costs must also be understood in the sense of reducing environmental pollution. The continuous use and the consequent reduction in the number of vehicles in circulation leads to a drastic reduction in CO_2 emissions into the atmosphere [18–20].

Car sharing is a system that is often seen as an alternative to public transport (not flexible) and to the taxi (more expensive) than your own car. Apart from the economic aspect, users who want to use it take other aspects into account. The system is often judged on cleanliness (critical aspect, especially if a previous user has transported animals there), the presence of safety systems and the availability of essential accessories such as Bluetooth and the navigator.

2.2 Different Business Model of Car Sharing

Car Sharing, born in Switzerland on the initiative of some private individuals motivated by ecological ideals, then moved away from the original idea of timeshare to progressively arrive at an organization of the offer according to commercial and entrepreneurial criteria.

Four different emerging models are identified in:

- Free floating within an operating area;
- Free-floating with swimming pool stations;
- Return, based on the area of residence;
- Round trip, based on the pool station;
- Peer-to-peer and community schemes.

Currently, it is going through a phase of full development, especially in the countries of Northern Europe, where it has managed to consolidate an image of quality and reliability and the operators in the sector have reached a good level of professionalism. The favourable condition for this development lies mainly in the current rigidity of the vehicle market, which offers ample choice for those who want to buy a vehicle, but grant few alternatives, economic and functional, to those who use it occasionally. Car Sharing is aimed at the latter category of motorists: the choice opportunities guaranteed by the composition of the car fleet and the ability to move without incurring the inconvenience and fixed costs associated with owning the car represent a valid alternative to purchasing.

Paying attention to shared model and the type of vehicle power, it is possible to guarantee a reduction of environmental impacts in terms of CO_2. The specific configuration cannot be assimilated to traditional forms of car rental, which represent the ideal solution for long and protracted journeys over time. The vehicles that make up the Car Sharing fleet are in fact positioned on several parking areas, located near the residences or at the stops and public transport stations (in city centers they can be also made in garages, private spaces, condominium courtyards or directly on the street). The use of vehicles is reserved for members of the organization only and is allowed even for limited periods of one hour. The member can book and pick up the vehicle requested from the nearest parking area at any time of day or night. The return of the vehicle usually takes place in the departure parking area, but in the most advanced systems it is possible to leave the vehicle in a different equipped area.

The overall cost for the member is made up of a fixed cost and a variable cost linked to the use of this facility. The fixed cost includes a non-refundable entry fee, which the member pays one-time membership fees, a refundable deposit and a subscription fee to be paid annually or monthly to join the association. The variable cost, linked to the use of the vehicles, includes a mileage and an hourly quota, which can vary according to the vehicle class, the time of use and any additional resource requested (for example, the home delivery of the vehicle).

Regarding the geographical dispersion of car sharing organizations, there is not a uniform distribution in Europe, according to [21, 22]. In Eastern Europe, the lowest number of car sharing organizations was detected (8%), the services are on average the younger ones and also the freer buoyancy systems of the round-trip systems are active there. Northern and Southern Europe have an almost equal share in the total number of car sharing organizations, respectively 15% and 18%. However, there are many differences for the average age of organizations and the car the category of sharing to which they belong most. The organizations in Southern Europe are among the youngest and are mostly aimed at a free-floating system with an operating area compared to organizations in other parts of Europe. In Northern Europe, peer-to-peer fill car sharing has a strong position.

The shared mobility provides for adequate planning or a review of its implementation in order to promote total accessibility, for the purpose of accessibility which can be both physical and cognitive [23, 24]. In addition, the implementation of car sharing in urban and it cannot support the strategies of the public system in order to guarantee an optimal use of resources for the creation of overall present and future value in local communities, mitigating the economic-social and environmental impacts.

2.3   Italian Car Sharing and Statistical Values

In accordance with [25, 26] in 2018 there were one million and 860 thousand subscribers to car sharing services in Italy, of which 90% subscribed to free-floating. From a geographical point of view, a prevalence of the north over the center-south is confirmed, where almost 60% of the entire Italian sharing mobility offer is available, for a total of 271 Italian municipalities with at least one system accessible to 2018.If on the one hand the fleet of shared vehicles present on Italian roads slows down, mainly due to the exit from the market of some free-floating bike-sharing that arrived only a year ago, on the other the movements continue in a trend of positive growth. The common national user is male with 66% of members and on average in the age group between 30 and 39 years.

The user of electric Carsharing is younger, of which 2 out of 3 users are between 18 and 29 years old. Rentals that are on average shorter in terms of km travelled for free-floating (6.8 km/rental) than station-based (30.8 km/rental), but for both types of service, more on weekdays that is from Monday to Friday (66% and 78% of the total respectively). On a national level, the kilometers travelled by carpooling total 88.9 million in 2018. The free-floating sector, with 80 million km, doubled those travelled in 2015, while the station-based sector total a plus 12 in 2018% compared to the previous year, for an absolute value slightly lower than the maximum recorded in 2016. In Italy in 2018, 7.4% of those who move share their car with their study or work colleagues.

Car sharing is widespread above all in urban areas: 10.8% of people up to 34 years of age have used it in municipalities in the centers of metropolitan areas (against 1.5% of the national total); among the major users of car sharing students (11.9%) and employees (11.1%). Among the reasons that induce citizens to choose car sharing over their own car there is ease of parking, while the benefit compared to public transport is given by flexibility. Therefore, it is possible to affirm that the success of car sharing is not registered as uniform at national and European level. This criticality can be addressed by investigating user characteristics and infrastructure and parking through surveys and interviews. The variables that influence its implementation are manifold and this work highlights how the distance between origin and destination and origin and stall where picking up the vehicle can sometimes be fundamental in travel choices.

3 Methodology

The methodology presented in this study in based on a structured procedure to evaluate the probability of using a shared mobility service based on the infrastructural characteristics related to the service itself. In particular, in applying the proposed methodological framework it is possible to assess the potential use resulting from the implementation of a station-based car sharing service in an urban area, by relating the location of parking spaces (reserved and not) and points of origins and destinations of daily trips. The overall procedure consists of three steps and is summarized in Fig. 1.

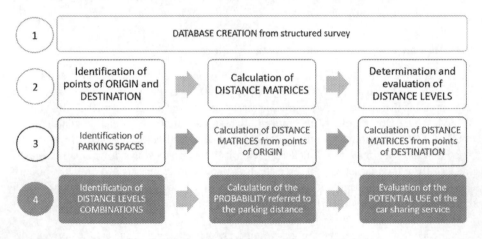

Fig. 1. Methodological framework (own setup)

3.1 Structured Survey for Database Creation

The acquisition of data relating to the transport demand has been acquired for years through surveys and the administration of online and paper questionnaires. Through these methods it is possible not only to collect socio-economic data but also the users' attitudes related to mobility and citizens preferences [27–31].

In literature many authors show preparatory or a posteriori analyses to the implementation of car sharing services, obtained through surveys. In accordance with [32, 33] it is possible to outline the characteristics of the most frequent car sharing users through descriptive statistics of the survey on the Internet and qualitative analyses of the results of the focus groups (both verified with respect to the previous literature) and from this emerges a behaviour of social activists, environmental protectors, innovators, economists or practical travellers. Therefore, car sharing companies and their partners could presumably increase their membership by targeting individuals and others with certain demographic characteristics.

The survey approach is also useful in order to evaluate the best choice of type of service to be implemented. According to [34] the survey data allow to compare the user groups and the usage patterns of a self-floating and station-based car sharing service, both operating in the city of Basel, Switzerland. These results suggest that the schemes actually attract different groups of users and are also used differently, changing the city size, from small towns to megacities. According to [35] making a comparison with the taxi service and obtaining as a result that car sharing tends to thrive in environments where the large population has experience with driving and car ownership. Analysis of the Shanghai-based survey showed that those interested in car sharing were younger, more likely to be educated, had longer journeys and owned fewer cars than those without interest in car sharing.

3.2   O/D Matrices and Distance Levels

The second step is primarily based on the identification of the main points of origin and destination of journeys. The motivations connected to a single trip can derive from different reasons: e.g. it is possible to consider regular movements from places of residence to the workplace and to the school or occasional ones as leisure trips. Depending of the motivation, the users' needs linked to the transport system change in terms of travel time reliability, flexibility of departure or arrival times, need for a private vehicle, etc. These factors are also strongly influenced by the context of analysis and by the transport supply present in the considered study area. Therefore, the previous phase described as the database creation, through a structured survey, constitute a fundamental support for identifying the points of origin and destination. Table 1 shows some examples of O/D points classified into different categories (i.e. residential; transport; public services; health; education; leisure; tourism) according to the list of Points of Interest (POIs) provided by HERE Navteq (2020).

Table 1. Subset of categories for the identification of points of origin and destination (Source: HERE Navteq, 2020)

Category	Point of O/D
Residential	Residence or domicile
Transport	Airport; taxi station; bus station; metro station; railway station; port; car rental; park & ride; sharing mobility parking area; open parking area; garage station
Public services	Post office; bank; insurance; police station; government office
Health	Hospital/policlinic; medical center; pharmacy
Education	School; college; university; library
Leisure	Gym; cinema; pub; disco; supermarket/shopping area; green area; historical monuments; museum; restaurant; theatre
Tourism	Hotels and B&B; tourist office; ATM; cash point; tourist attractions

After the identification of the points of origin and destination and their categorization, it is necessary to evaluate the distances between them. The calculation of these distances can be carried out considering different approaches. The most immediate is represented by the identification of the O/D distance as the crow flies between origins and destinations. However, when the orography of the terrain is particularly variable it is possible that this simplifying hypothesis could lead to too excessive approximations. Thus, in this case it is better to consider the real road-distance instead of the Euclidean one. Often, this distance is made to coincide with the shortest path. All the way, in congested urban contexts it may be useful to take into account travel times as well as only distances, as it may happen that longer routes have shorter travel times.

Then, once this identification is complete, it is possible to define the O/D matrices, in terms of distances or travel times. Afterwards, it is necessary to evaluate the values of these matrices, in order to immediately understand which movements can be subject to the use of a vehicle and which ones will certainly be accomplished by walking, given the short distance. In this regard, in the case of the considered shared mobility service, i.e. car-sharing, five distance levels are identified on the basis of an increasing range of distances, as reported in the following Table 2.

Table 2. Distance levels determination for O/D matrices

Level	O/D distance [m]	Walking	Micromobility	Bike	Car/Bus
1	$D_{o/d} < 500$	++	+	+	− −
2	$500 < D_{o/d} < 1000$	+	++	++	±
3	$1000 < D_{o/d} < 2000$	±	+	++	+
4	$2000 < D_{o/d} < 4000$	−	±	±	++
5	$D_{o/d} > 4000$	− −	−	±	++

The values relating to the O/D distances (in meters) shown in the table above, specifically refer to the car sharing service provided in an urban area. It would be possible to hypothetically associate these levels with other specific shared transport modes (e.g. bike sharing; scooter sharing, etc.), by recalibrating the values of these distances. Indeed, relying on these levels, it is possible to categorize each element of the distance matrices: in the case of distances less than 500 m, it is probable that the trips will be made by walking (see "++" in Table 2), therefore these connections will not be considered in the subsequent analysis; distances between 500 m and 1 km still fall within the walking range or even better by using bike or micromobility; while for greater distances a bike or motorized vehicle (i.e. car or bus) is almost certainly necessary.

3.3   Distance Matrices from Car Parks and Distance Levels

In the third step, a similar calculation of the distance matrices must be done considering, instead, the location of the car parks with respect to the points of origin and destination, identified in the previous step. The considered quantities are represented by the schematization of distances in Fig. 2. The respective distances between origin and car parking $D_{o/p}$ and between destination and car parking $D_{p/d}$ are assumed to be covered by walking (dashed line sections), while the distance between the two parking lots will be traveled by the car sharing vehicle (double continuous line section).

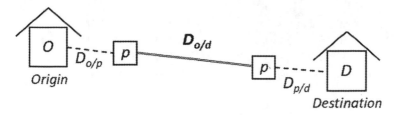

Fig. 2. Schematization of car parking distances (own setup)

In this case, the distance levels L_i (for origin-parking distance) and L_j (for parking-destination distance), with $i, j = 1, 2, 3$, are related to walking distances.

The identified levels are three, as shown in Table 3: the first occurs when the distances from the parking area are less than 500 m, which is an absolutely compatible with the pedestrian mode; the second one is and intermediate level, whit a distance between 500 and 1000 m, so it is still possible walking but it starts to get onerous; and finally the third level for distances greater than one kilometer, for which it will no longer be convenient walking to reach the parking lot and use the shared car.

Table 3. Distance levels determination for distance matrices from car parks

Level	$D_{o/p}$, $D_{p/d}$ distance [m]	Walking
L_1	$D_{o/p} < 500$ V $D_{p/d} < 500$	+
L_2	$500 < D_{o/p} < 1000$ V $500 < D_{p/d} < 1000$	±
L_3	$D_{o/p} > 1000$ V $D_{p/d} > 1000$	−

Through the evaluation of the distances, it is possible to trace the need to place other parking stalls or reallocate existing ones in order to induce the users to use it minimizing the distances that link the presence of each stall at the various points of origin and destination. This hypothesis starts from the idea that each user starts to experience discomfort in moving on foot for a distance greater than 500 m.

3.4   Distance Levels Combinations and Probability Estimation

In the last step, the probabilities associated with the potential use of car sharing are determined, based on the simultaneous distance between the car park and the points of origin and destination, respectively. Different combinations of distance levels are considered both for the total distance of the trip $D_{o/d}$ and for the partial distances of origin and destination with respect to the parking $D_{o/p}$ and $D_{p/d}$, as resumed in Table 4:

Table 4. Probabilities of potential use of station-based car sharing

Hyp.	Parking distance [m]	Total travel distance [m]	Probability P_{ij}
1	–	$D_{o/d} < 500$	Not considered
2	$D_{o/p} < 500$ and $D_{d/p} < 500$	$500 < D_{o/d} < 1000$	Medium
	$D_{o/p} < 500$ and $500 < D_{d/p} < 1000$	$500 < D_{o/d} < 1000$	Low
	$500 < D_{o/p} < 1000$ and $D_{d/p} < 500$	$500 < D_{o/d} < 1000$	Low
	$500 < D_{o/p} < 1000$ and $500 < D_{d/p} < 1000$	$500 < D_{o/d} < 1000$	Very low
	$D_{o/p} < 500$ and $D_{d/p} > 1000$	$500 < D_{o/d} < 1000$	Null
	$D_{o/p} > 1000$ and $D_{d/p} < 500$	$500 < D_{o/d} < 1000$	Null
	$500 < D_{o/p} < 1000$ and $D_{d/p} > 1000$	$500 < D_{o/d} < 1000$	Null
	$D_{o/p} > 1000$ and $500 < D_{d/p} < 1000$	$500 < D_{o/d} < 1000$	Null
	$D_{o/p} > 1000$ and $D_{d/p} > 1000$	$500 < D_{o/d} < 1000$	Null
3	$D_{o/p} < 500$ and $D_{d/p} < 500$	$D_{o/d} > 1000$	Very high
	$D_{o/p} < 500$ and $500 < D_{d/p} < 1000$	$D_{o/d} > 1000$	High
	$500 < D_{o/p} < 1000$ and $D_{d/p} < 500$	$D_{o/d} > 1000$	High
	$500 < D_{o/p} < 1000$ and $500 < D_{d/p} < 1000$	$D_{o/d} > 1000$	Medium
	$D_{o/p} < 500$ and $D_{d/p} > 1000$	$D_{o/d} > 1000$	Null
	$D_{o/p} > 1000$ and $D_{d/p} < 500$	$D_{o/d} > 1000$	Null
	$500 < D_{o/p} < 1000$ and $D_{d/p} > 1000$	$D_{o/d} > 1000$	Null
	$D_{o/p} > 1000$ and $500 < D_{d/p} < 1000$	$D_{o/d} > 1000$	Null
	$D_{o/p} > 1000$ and $D_{d/p} > 1000$	$D_{o/d} > 1000$	Null

By crossing the data of the distance matrices calculated in the second and in the third steps, it is possible to estimate the associated probability matrices P_{csO} and P_{csD} referred to each area of origin O and destination D. From these probabilities, it is possible to evaluate P_{ij}, that estimates the potential use of the station-based car sharing, related to each O/D pair, depending on the infrastructural characteristics deriving from the location of the parking areas (Eq. 1):

$$P_{csO} * P_{csD} = P_{ij} \tag{1}$$

Specifically, three different hypotheses have been identified. The first refers to trips less than 500 m and for which a probability of using car sharing is assumed to be zero since the distance can be made by walking. On the other hand, the second and the third hypothesis refer respectively to trips between 500 m and 1 km and more than 1 km. In these cases, it is plausible to think about the use of a motorized vehicle, and obviously, at equal distance from the car park, the probabilities of using car sharing are higher in the case of the third hypothesis. Finally, for distances to the parking areas higher than one kilometre, it is difficult to think of a potential use of car sharing and, therefore, the associated probability is zero.

Figure 3 shows a schematization of an O/D pair and the possible combinations by considering the total number n of parking lots associated to the point of origin and the total number m of parking lots associated to the point of destination.

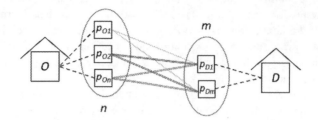

Fig. 3. Schematization of probability combinations (own setup)

Accordingly, the probability P_{cs} associated to the potential use of car sharing to move from the origin O to the destination D depends both on the distance $D_{o/d}$ between them and also on the presence of car parks and more specifically on the distances $D_{o/p}$ and $D_{p/d}$ that these car parks have with respect to the departure and arrival point of the trip. Therefore, this probability P_{cs} can be estimated through the following equation (Eq. 2):

$$P_{cs} = \sum_{i=1;j=1}^{3} n_{Li(r,f,p)} * m_{Lj(r,f,p)} * P_{ij(r,f,p)} \qquad (2)$$

where:

- n_{Li} is the number of car parks with a variable distance L_i from the point of origin, depending on the value assumed by subscript i in accordance with the levels identified in Table 3;
- m_{Lj} is the number of car parks with a variable distance L_j from the point of destination, depending on the value assumed by subscript j in accordance with the levels identified in Table 3;
- P_{ij} is the probability of using the car sharing service associated with the single combination ij of car parks, in accordance with the probability combinations identified in Table 4;
- the three subscripts r, f, p refer to the type of parking. Specifically, r stands for "reserved"; f stands for "free" and p stands for "paid". The associated probability is variable depending on the considered type of parking, in fact reserved car parks will have a greater weight in terms of probability because these are parking areas specifically dedicated to the car sharing service.

4 Discussion and Conclusions

The analyzes carried out in the context of this work show that car sharing is an innovative mobility service that guarantees performance comparable to that of a private car in terms of reliability, comfort and flexibility. The car-sharing formula is particularly advantageous for users who occasionally use the car for their journeys and who can count on more convenient transport alternatives at the same time. The economic benefits for those who give up possession of the car to join the car sharing scheme are considerable, as it is possible to use the car when needed without having to bear the fixed costs associated with its ownership.

It distribution is entrusted to both companies and local administrations. Among the main features of car sharing that qualify the offer and satisfy the needs of users that are not met by other mobility systems are two in particular, namely the possibility of using the vehicles for limited periods and distances at any time of day and the ease of its access. At present, the efforts of undertakings are directed towards achieving and maintaining a high level of efficiency, productivity and quality of service:

- to increase market share;
- to spread on a wider geographical scale, keeping at the same time a dense network of stations in the area;
- to modernize the dispensing process with the introduction of new solutions technology;
- to orientate the service to customer needs and expectations;
- to establish partnership relationships with other operators in the transport sector in order to offer its customers integrated facilities with an excellent relationship quality price.

Although the operators of the sector agree that the strategies for the development of new shared mode should leverage the market, there is no doubt that the introduction of political measures to support the start-up process and relative dissemination is of utmost importance. Furthermore, in order to implement an effective shared transport system that reflects the demand it is fundamental a thorough knowledge of the study area and the characteristics of the potential users. In this sense, the urban planning must be integrated at all mobility levels, paying particular attention not only to the possibility of implementing shared transport utilities within a city, but also outlining the infrastructures and spaces dedicated to (e.g. the parking locations in the case of station-based car sharing). Moreover, it must consider the community as a decision support, using specific tools and procedures (i.e. debates or questionnaires or interviews) to acquire data of preference. In fact, it allows to highlight the benefits and critical issues related to the context in which its is implemented.

The last decade has been characterized by the maximum diffusion of the use of car sharing with its different business models, offering an ad-hoc utility in accordance to the type of user (e.g. tourist, worker, student, etc.). Therefore, as previously highlighted, during its development (i.e. planning and implementation) by companies, it is necessary to establish active collaboration with the community (democratic participation).

The current transport supply is very wide, with the diffusion of various shared transport modes. In Italy, the car sharing is not evenly spread within the national territory and this often derives from the usability of a service that is not well tailored to the transport demand. Even in some of these cases, the car sharing facility threatens to cease in the short term.

Several parameters tend to influence the definition of transport in charge of sharing. In particular, the planning and location of reserved parking areas for the users represent a pillar of the car sharing system. The possibility of having a determined parking space, with an optimal location respect to the points of departure and arrival of the trip, implies two important consequences: from a strictly individual point of view, it allows to save time and from an overall point of view, the average travelled mileage and the impact of air emissions are reduced. For this reason, the identification of parking areas must be the result of an in-depth analysis of the city territory, which takes into consideration socio-economic and transport indicators with reference to the inhabitants' transport mobility behaviour.

Generally, the parking areas of the car sharing can contain a variable number of stalls between 2 and 5, depending on the number of potential users, and in accordance with the objective of integrated mobility, they are located in correspondence of intermodal exchange nodes or attracting poles (e.g. shopping centers). The methodology presented in this work considers as the main variable the distance between the points of origin and destination linked to daily trips in urban areas and the location of car parking, in order to evaluate the potential use of car sharing. The research brings forward interesting evidence from both a methodological and operational point of view, by defining an estimation method of the effectiveness of car sharing, that can be also applied as a planning support tool.

The diffusion of a well-modulated utility based on the characteristics of the user offers direct benefits in terms of better accessibility in the cities where the it is implemented, as well as other benefits from an environmental, social and economic point of view. In this respect, this thesis lays the groundwork for further research, based on the development of a composite estimation methodology, focusing on the combination with other specific variables (i.e. the type of parking and the type of power supply of the vehicle; the existing traffic supply in the study area; variables characterizing the user and his willingness to pay), in order to evaluate the probability of users in relation to implemented shared mobility systems in several case studies.

Acknowledgments. This work has been partially financed by the University of Catania within the project "Piano della Ricerca Dipartimentale 2016-2018" of the Department of Civil Engineering and Architecture and the project "Piano per la Ricerca 2016–2018 - Linea di intervento 2" of the Department of Electric, Electronic and Computer Engineering. This study was also supported by the MIUR (Ministry of Education, Universities and Research [Italy]) through a project entitled WEAKI TRANSIT: WEAK-demand areas Innovative TRANsport Shared services for Italian Towns (Project code: CUP Code: F74I19001290001), financed with the PRIN 2017 (Research Projects of National Relevance) programme. We authorize the MIUR to reproduce and distribute reprints for Governmental purposes, notwithstanding any copyright notations thereon. Any opinions, findings and conclusions or recommendations expressed in this material are those of the authors, and do not necessarily reflect the views of the MIUR.

References

1. Calabrò, G., Torrisi, V., Inturri, G., Ignaccolo, M.: Improving inbound logistic planning for large-scale real-world routing problems: a novel ant-colony simulation-based optimization. Eur. Trans. Res. Rev. **12**(1) (2020). https://doi.org/10.1186/s12544-020-00409-7
2. Ignaccolo, M., Inturri, G., Giuffrida, N., Torrisi, V., Cocuzza, E.: Sustainability of freight transport through an integrated approach: the case of the eastern sicily port system. Transp. Res. Procedia **45**, 177–184 (2020). https://doi.org/10.1016/j.trpro.2020.03.005
3. Ignaccolo, M., Inturri, G., Giuffrida, N., Torrisi, V.: A sustainable framework for the analysis of port systems. Eur. Trans. Int. J. Transp. Econ. Eng. Law (78) (2020). Paper no. 7. ISSN 1825-3997
4. Ignaccolo, C., Giuffrida, N., Torrisi, V.: The queensway of New York city. A proposal for sustainable mobility in queens. In: Town and Infrastructure Planning for Safety and Urban Quality: Proceedings of the XXIII International Conference on Living and Walking in Cities (LWC 2017), 15–16 June 2017, Brescia, Italy, p. 69. CRC Press, July 2018. https://doi.org/10.1201/9781351173360-12
5. Ignaccolo, M., Inturri, G., Giuffrida, N., Le Pira, M., Torrisi, V., Calabrò, G.: A step towards walkable environments: spatial analysis of pedestrian compatibility in an urban context. Eur. Trans.\Trasporti Europei **76**(6), 1–12 (2020)
6. Ignaccolo, M., Inturri, G., Cocuzza, E., Giuffrida, N., Torrisi, V.: Framework for the evaluation of the quality of pedestrian routes for the sustainability of port-city shared areas. In: Coastal Cities and Their Sustainable Future III. WIT Transactions on The Built Environment, vol. 188. WIT Press (2019). ISSN 1743-3509. https://doi.org/10.2495/cc190021
7. Campisi, T., Canale, A., Tesoriere, G.: SWOT analysis for the implementation of spaces and pedestrian paths at the street markets of Palermo. In: AIP Conference Proceedings, vol. 2040, no. 1, p. 140003. AIP Publishing LLC, November 2018. https://doi.org/10.1063/1.5079192
8. Shaheen, S., Cohen, A.: Shared ride services in North America: definitions, impacts, and the future of pooling. Transp. Rev. **39**(4), 427–442 (2019)
9. Torrisi, V., Ignaccolo, M., Inturri, G.: Innovative transport systems to promote sustainable mobility: developing the model architecture of a traffic control and supervisor system. In: Gervasi, O., et al. (eds.) ICCSA 2018. LNCS, vol. 10962, pp. 622–638. Springer, Cham (2018). https://doi.org/10.1007/978-3-319-95168-3_42
10. Torrisi V., Ignaccolo M., Inturri G.: Toward a sustainable mobility through a dynamic real-time traffic monitoring, estimation and forecasting system: The RE.S.E.T. project. In: Town and Infrastructure Planning for Safety and Urban Quality - Proceedings of the 23rd International Conference on Living and Walking in Cities, LWC 2017, pp. 241–250 (2018). https://doi.org/10.1201/9781351173360-32
11. Torrisi, V., Ignaccolo, M., Inturri, G., Giuffrida, N.: Combining sensor traffic and simulation data to measure urban road network reliability. In: Proceedings International Conference on Traffic and Transport Engineering (ICTTE), Belgrade, p. 1004, November 2016
12. Torrisi, V., Ignaccolo, M., Inturri, G.: Analysis of road urban transport network capacity through a dynamic assignment model: validation of different measurement methods. Transp. Res. Procedia **27**, 1026–1033 (2017). https://doi.org/10.1016/j.trpro.2017.12.135
13. Torrisi, V., Ignaccolo, M., Inturri, G.: Estimating travel time reliability in urban areas through a dynamic simulation model. Transp. Res. Procedia **27**, 857–864 (2017). https://doi.org/10.1016/j.trpro.2017.12.134
14. Nishimura, A.: A Study on New Mobility Services and Sustainable Urban Development (2019)

15. Canale, A., Tesoriere, G., Campisi, T.: The MAAS development as a mobility solution based on the individual needs of transport users. In: AIP Conference Proceedings, vol. 2186, no. 1, p. 160005. AIP Publishing LLC, December 2019

16. Pangbourne, K., Stead, D., Mladenović, M., Milakis, D.: The case of mobility as a service: A critical reflection on challenges for urban transport and mobility governance. Governance of the smart mobility transition, pp. 33–48 (2018)

17. Azzari, M., Garau, C., Nesi, P., Paolucci, M., Zamperlin, P.: Smart city governance strategies to better move towards a smart urbanism. In: Gervasi, O., et al. (eds.) ICCSA 2018. LNCS, vol. 10962, pp. 639–653. Springer, Cham (2018). https://doi.org/10.1007/978-3-319-95168-3_43

18. Macedo, E., Tomás, R., Fernandes, P., Coelho, M.C., Bandeira, J.M.: Quantifying road traffic emissions embedded in a multi-objective traffic assignment model. Transp. Res. Procedia 47, 648–655 (2020)

19. Fernandes, P., Macedo, E., Bahmankhah, B., Tomas, R.F., Bandeira, J.M., Coelho, M.C.: Are internally observable vehicle data good predictors of vehicle emissions? Transp. Res. Part D Transp. Environ. 77, 252–270 (2019)

20. Fichera, A., Fortuna, L., Frasca, M., Volpe, R.: Integration of complex networks for urban energy mapping. Int. J. Heat Tech. 33(4), 181–184 (2015)

21. Birdsall, M.: Carsharing in a sharing economy. Inst. Transp. Eng. ITE J. 84(4), 37 (2014)

22. Firnkorn, J., Müller, M.: Free-floating electric carsharing-fleets in smart cities: the dawning of a post-private car era in urban environments? Environ. Sci. Policy 45, 30–40 (2015)

23. Camporeale, R., Caggiani, L., Fonzone, A., Ottomanelli, M.: Study of the accessibility inequalities of cordon-based pricing strategies using a multimodal Theil index. Transp. Plann. Technol. 42(5), 498–514 (2019)

24. Camporeale, R., Caggiani, L., Fonzone, A., Ottomanelli, M.: Better for everyone: an approach to multimodal network design considering equity. Transp. Res. Procedia 19, 303–315 (2016)

25. Viegas, J., Martinez, L., Crist, P., Masterson, S.: Shared Mobility: Innovation for Liveable Cities. In: International Transport Forum's Corporate Partnership Board, pp. 1–56 (2016)

26. Santos, G.: Sustainability and shared mobility models. Sustainability 10(9), 3194 (2018)

27. Ignaccolo, M., Inturri, G., Giuffrida, N., Le Pira, M., Torrisi, V.: Public engagement for designing new transport services: investigating citizen preferences from a multiple criteria perspective. Transp. Res. Procedia 37, 91–98 (2019). https://doi.org/10.1016/j.trpro.2018.12.170

28. Ignaccolo, M., Inturri, G., García-Melón, M., Giuffrida, N., Le Pira, M., Torrisi, V.: Combining Analytic Hierarchy Process (AHP) with role-playing games for stakeholder engagement in complex transport decisions. Transp. Res. Procedia 27, 500–507 (2017). https://doi.org/10.1016/j.trpro.2017.12.069

29. Ignaccolo, M., Inturri, G., Giuffrida, N., Le Pira, M., Torrisi, V.: Structuring transport decision-making problems through stakeholder engagement: the case of Catania metro accessibility. Transp. Infrastruct. Syst. 919–926 (2017). https://doi.org/10.1201/9781315281896-118

30. Campisi, T., Akgün, N., Ticali, D., Tesoriere, G.: Exploring public opinion on personal mobility vehicle use: a case study in Palermo, Italy. Sustainability 12(13), 5460 (2020). https://doi.org/10.3390/su12135460

31. Moslem, S., Campisi, T., Szmelter-Jarosz, A., Duleba, S., Nahiduzzaman, K.M., Tesoriere, G.: Best–worst method for modelling mobility choice after COVID-19: evidence from Italy. Sustainability 12(17), 6824 (2020). https://doi.org/10.3390/su12176824

32. Burkhardt, J.E., Millard-Ball, A.: Who is attracted to carsharing? Transp. Res. Record 1986 (1), 98–105 (2006)

33. Campisi, T., Torrisi, V., Ignaccolo, M., Inturri, G., Tesoriere, G.: University propensity assessment to car sharing services using mixed survey data: the Italian case study of Enna city. Transp. Res. Procedia **47**, 433–440 (2020). https://doi.org/10.1016/j.trpro.2020.03.155
34. Becker, H., Ciari, F., Axhausen, K.W.: Comparing car-sharing schemes in Switzerland: user groups and usage patterns. Transp. Res. Part A Policy Pract. **97**, 17–29 (2017)
35. Wang, M., Martin, E.W., Shaheen, S.A.: Carsharing in Shanghai, China: analysis of behavioral response to local survey and potential competition. Transp. Res. Rec. **2319**(1), 86–95 (2012)

An Exploratory Step to Evaluate the Pedestrian Flow in Urban Environment

Mauro D'Apuzzo[1] , Daniela Santilli[1(✉)] , Azzurra Evangelisti[1] ,
Vincenzo Pelagalli[1] , Orlando Montanaro[1] , and Vittorio Nicolosi[2]

[1] Department of Civil and Mechanical Engineering DICEM,
University of Cassino and Southern Lazio, Cassino, Italy
{dapuzzo,daniela.santilli}@unicas.it,
aevangelisti.ing@gmail.com
[2] Department of Enterprise Engineering "Mario Lucertini",
University of Rome "Tor Vergata", Rome, Italy
nicolosi@uniroma2.it

Abstract. The pedestrian accounts for part of the road safety problem in most developed countries. Pedestrian accidents are thus an urgent issue for safety improvement, particularly in urban area. Furthermore, recent sustainable mobility oriented policies are boosting walking in urban areas. In order to cope with this increase in pedestrian flows, European municipal authorities, responsible for road safety, traffic management and mobility, need reliable engineering methods to plan urban road safety and protect vulnerable users.

Road safety management systems are usually developed to identify hazardous sites and to find suitable countermeasures. Risk exposure assessment is required to identify sites with high accident potential. This assessment requires the knowledge, on one side, of the known vehicular flows and, on the other, of the pedestrian flows, which are not normally known to road operators.

In this paper a methodology to develop and calibrate forecasting model aimed at evaluating pedestrian exposure is presented. The model is based on original approach that integrates the Space Syntax modelling framework with pedestrian mobility aspects and a calibration procedure was proposed that use counts on a limited number of roads. Preliminary results derived from a case study in an urban environment seem promising and confirm the model's good ability to predict pedestrian flows.

Keywords: Urban pedestrian exposure · Space syntax · Hybrid approach

1 Introduction

In recent years, several countries have been looking for solutions to reduce environmental pollution (noise and air) in urban environment; sustainable mobility has therefore become an effective measure to reduce traffic pollution. Within this framework, multimodal transport alternatives that are more environmental-friendly such as public transports services, electric vehicles, cycling and walking are constantly promoted to replace the use of the private internal combustion vehicles.

© Springer Nature Switzerland AG 2020
O. Gervasi et al. (Eds.): ICCSA 2020, LNCS 12255, pp. 645–657, 2020.
https://doi.org/10.1007/978-3-030-58820-5_47

However, it has to be acknowledged that pedestrians in cities often conflict with other traffic components because the infrastructure is often not properly designed.

In this connection, in Italy, as well in other countries, vehicle-pedestrian collision data are routinely collected through law enforcement reports. These reports are often of limited value because of poor information on collisions with minor damage, on accident location, and, above all, on pedestrian exposure. Furthermore, the evaluation of pedestrian exposure is not a simple task since several studies have shown that pedestrian activity is affected by the network connectivity and other variables such as population, land use, purpose of travel, travel mode, etc. [3, 14, 16].

To correctly design the road infrastructure, it is necessary to evaluate the risk that, in road traffic, is a function of three factors: the first is the exposure (the amount of movement or travel within the system by different users or a given population density), the second is the underlying probability of a crash, given a particular exposure and the third is the probability of injury, given a crash. Exposure is defined as the percentage of pedestrians in contact with potentially harmful vehicular traffic [20]. Under simplified assumptions, at intersection level, risk can be evaluated as the annual number of vehicle-pedestrian collisions divided by the product of annual pedestrian and vehicle volumes estimated at a given intersection [13, 17].

In order to assess this risk, it is necessary to describe pedestrian mobility and therefore to know the extent of the flows and to model their distribution on the road network.

Pedestrian mobility can be reconstructed by estimating the number of people who, based on their choices, move over a period of time mainly for work, study, shopping or other purpose according to the distribution of pedestrian trip "attractors" located within a proximity area. Numerous theories have been proposed to analyze pedestrian mobility such as: stochastic model [2], transition matrix model [6, 15], queuing models [10, 19], route choice model [10] and others. Most of these models are used to describe critical situations (emergency exits, emergency evacuations, etc.), but due to the complex formulations they are difficult to be applied in real contexts. Path selection models such those used within the Space Syntax framework using a graphical "proximity" algorithm seem to offer an effective trade-off between complexity and easiness to implement, in order to estimate pedestrian movement potentials.

In this work a new methodology based on Space Syntax framework was used to estimate pedestrian exposure. The methodology has been calibrated by means of pedestrian counts on a limited number of urban roads within a case study.

2 Space Syntax

Space Syntax is based on a series of theories and techniques for the analysis of the spatial configuration of road networks and buildings, and of the interactions that coexist with each other. It was conceived by Bill Hillier, Professor of the Bartlett School of Architecture, University College London (UCL), in the late 1970s. Space Syntax was created to help urban planners to simulate the likely social effects (intended as human behavior and business development) generated by their projects; in fact he defines it as: "*Space syntax ... is a set of techniques for the representation, quantification, and interpretation of spatial configuration in buildings and settlements.*" [8].

According to this approach, the pedestrian movements are influenced by the configuration of the network. The configurational approach assumes that the urban space, as it is structured, influences both the settlement processes and the movement on roads and spaces [9].

Space Syntax is able to perform analysis considering both an arbitrary closed space or one-dimensional structures. For the estimation of pedestrian flows, the axial analysis technique is usually preferred where the two-dimensional urban space is reduced in a one-dimensional system. In fact, the road network is schematized with a network made up of linear segments. Once a line (road) has been selected, as starting point, this line will intersect other n lines, which are numbered according to how many changes of direction separate it from the starting line. The hypothesis is that the observer moves according to visual perception, preferring linear paths not related to visual variations because travel seems shorter [21].

All movements estimated by Space Syntax are defined by Hiller as natural movements [8]. The latter are the relationship between the configuration of the network and each other element of the road system. In many cases the displacements are not only generated by the network configuration but can also be influenced by other attractors.

The main morphological parameters of Space Syntax are: connectivity, depth and integration. Connectivity represents the number of lines that directly intersect a particular axial line. Depth is defined as the minimum number of changes of direction to reach any other segment of the network from the origin [1]. This parameter cannot be used to compare the layout of the roads in different cities, as it is influenced by the total number of nodes in the system. Different road layouts can be evaluated by means of the integration parameter representing how well the initial segment is integrated into the global system, where higher integration means greater connection to the network.

The type of analysis that takes into account the geometric, topological and angular characteristics of the network, producing the best results in terms of traffic flow forecasting is the *Angular Segment Analysis with Metric Radius, (ASAMR)*. This analysis is based on the calculation of the angular depth of each section in relation to the other sections of the network, setting a buffer with finite metric radius within which the connections between the sections are evaluated [1]. The angular variation represents the "cost" of the move. According to Hillier [9], in fact, the ability of the road user to plan the most convenient route from point A to point B is linked to his perception of the distance to travel. This distance is unconsciously evaluated on the basis of tortuosity (expressed as angular variation). The user is willing to travel more road, "spending less" in terms of tortuosity (Fig. 1).

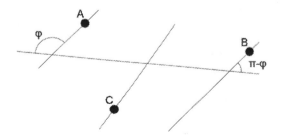

Fig. 1. Angular variation between the sections of the network

All this is evaluated within a buffer with a variable metric radius depending on the purpose of the analysis. For the evaluation of pedestrian flows in an urban center, a radius of 400 m is usually assumed (according to the impedance functions [12]), corresponding to a typical 5 min trip on foot. With this restriction, the system will calculate the angular turns of all sections within 400 m of the current section; path deviations beyond this radius will not be calculated. Therefore the system will identify only local relationships between elements within 400 m from each of the segments. The analysis returns among the many configurational parameters of the network, Integration (INT) and Choice (CH), which contain an intrinsic meaning relating to the probability of each road segment of being chosen or not in the different possible paths from an Origin to a Destination. Integration represents a good indicator of how each of the segments can be a highly desired destination by users; while Choice indicates the probability that each segment can be chosen by pedestrians as the shortest route.

Integration has been correlated with pedestrian flows, in different contexts [5, 7, 18]. However till now, poor correlation coefficients ranging between 0.2 and 0.4 have been obtained. Since the pure configurational approach does not seems to entirely capture the nature of urban pedestrian activities, it was proposed to use an "hybrid" approach that integrates the configurational analysis performed within the Space Syntax approach with the land use and pedestrian trip behavior in order to obtain better forecasts.

3   Description of Procedure

The analysis conducted in this study can be divided into two phases.

In the first, the road and pedestrian network was derived, creating the spatial relationship of contiguity between the census sections and the sections of the road system. The values of the population (obtained from Italian National Institute of Statistics, ISTAT, Databases) in the census sections were attributed as an average to the sections of the network through the proximity approach. This approach correlates the characteristics of each of the network centroids (i.e. the central point of each road segments) with the surrounding ones, according to a sequence of buffers with increasing radius. The radii of the buffers range from 100 to 1600 m and are chosen on the basis of an impedance function [12] that describes the propensity/probability to travel (expressed in term of a dimensionless parameter, k) of pedestrians as the distance to travel varies.

A typical impedance function is shown below, with a table reporting the k values as a function of the pedestrian travel distance assumed by the buffers (Fig. 2 and Table 1).

For each network centroid, a weight *Pprox* is obtained; this is assessed at an increasing distance from the single centroid, taking into account the actual propensity of users to move as their distance from it increases. The aim is to define a *weight factor*, expressed in term of attractiveness of pedestrian flows as a function of the average of the population living in the specific circular crown area for each road segments.

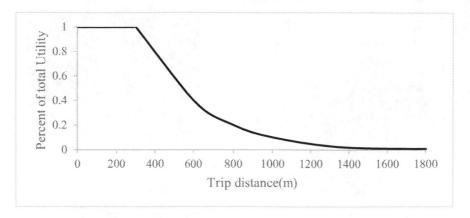

Fig. 2. Impedance function for pedestrian movement

Table 1. Table of mean k values for each circular crown

Distance (m)	k
0	1.00
100	1.00
300	1.00
600	0.40
800	0.20
1000	0.10
1300	0.03
1600	0.01

In the second phase, configurational analysis within the Space Syntax framework is carried out and a comparison is performed with corresponding pedestrian counts for each road segment. In detail, "weighted" and "unweighted" analysis are carried out to evaluate the effectiveness of the new "hybrid" approach with that provided by a conventional configurational analysis in predicting the pedestrian flows in a real urban context.

4   The Simulations and the Case Study

In order to calibrate and validate the model, the city of Cassino (FR) was analyzed. This municipality of Lazio region has about 36000 inhabitants (Figs. 3 and 4).

The study area examines only the city center. The socio-demographic data necessary for the analysis can be obtained from the ISTAT website on the census sections (about 60) of the analysis area. The idea behind this study was to use the population that insists on each road segment as weights. This stems from the consideration that although an area of the road network can be geometrically and topologically "attractive", well connected and integrated, it will be affected by quantitatively different pedestrian flows depending on the resident population.

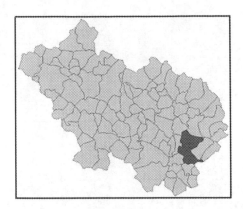

Fig. 3. The position of the municipality of Cassino in the province of Frosinone is shown in red (Color figure online)

Fig. 4. Aerophotogrammetry of Cassino center, with the study area highlighted in red (Color figure online)

Once the network was defined, the Space Syntax model was calibrated, attributing, to each road section, a weight connected to the population residing in the various census sections whose population was assumed, under conventional simplifying assumptions, concentrated in their center of gravity or "census section centroid".

4.1   Collection of Pedestrian Exposure Data

Before proceeding with the simulations, some counts were made on some of the main road sections or those characterized by the presence of attractors. For the identification of pedestrian flows, it was decided to proceed with a visual survey conducted by one or more operators by means of video. A moving observer approach for pedestrian count was adopted as investigation technique. According to this approach, videos were made, by different software, from inside a vehicle moving on the route to be examined (Fig. 5).

Fig. 5. Layout example of video cameras positioning in the moving observer survey

The advantage was that the human operator has the able to discriminate between different pedestrian activities (standing, moving or crossing) according to different directions, although longer times to process the data can be expected.

To determine the route, the areas of major pedestrian attraction were taken into account. Two itineraries have been created (one for the weekday and one for a pre-holiday day), both with the same starting and ending points (Figs. 6 and 7).

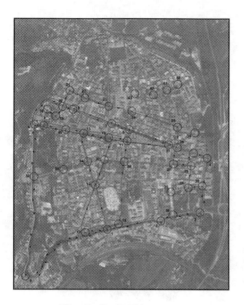

Fig. 6. Pre-holiday route   **Fig. 7.** Weekday route

Experimental campaign was carried out in the peak-hour period within the day: on weekdays the following three observation periods have been considered: from 8.00 to 9.00, from 12.00 to 14.00 and in the evening from 18.00 to 19.00.

As for the pre-holiday day, three observation periods were investigated in the morning (8.00–9.00, 9.00–10.00, 10.00–11.00) to highlight pedestrian activity near the market areas and one in the evening (20.00–21.00) in areas close to temporary pedestrian zones.

Following the video processing, the number and position of pedestrians was obtained in the different investigation periods (Fig. 8).

Fig. 8. Example video processing

4.2   Results from Configurational Analysis

Following the analyzes carried out by means of Space Syntax, different results were obtained if weight was used or not. In Fig. 9 a contour map of the road network showing the Integration parameter level provided by the simple configurational analysis via the ASAMR approach was conveniently depicted. This parameter was chosen because according to most of scientific literature, it seems to be the one exhibiting the highest correlation with pedestrian movements actually observed on the network [4, 9].

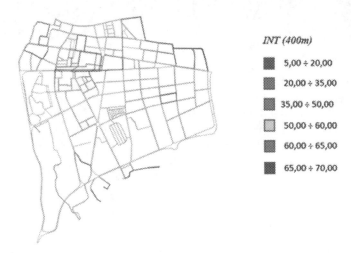

Fig. 9. Result of the configurational analysis (not weighed) on the Cassino network

Segment Analysis – Unweighted

It has to be highlighted that the simple configurational analysis (unweighted) depicted in the Fig. 9 refers only to the geometric and topological characteristics of the network.

The area of the center, with sections more interconnected to each other, was the one in which highest values of Integration were reached. As it can be observed, Integration values decrease moving away from Central Business Distric (CBD) to peripheral areas with less connectivity.

Segment Analysis – Prox Weight

Unlike the previous analysis, the combined effect determined by the population geographical distribution and by the pedestrian willingness to move has been taken into account by the hybrid approach employing the Prox-weighted analysis (Fig. 10). The central area continues to have high Integration values (10,000–12,000), due to the connectivity of the sections, however high values were observed near the railway station and the eastern limit of the study area. In these areas, in fact, there was a larger resident population, which necessarily generates a greater amount of daily movements.

INT (Pprox)

◼ 1500 ÷ 3500
◼ 3500 ÷ 5500
◼ 5500 ÷ 8500
◻ 8500 ÷ 9500
◼ 9500 ÷ 10500
◼ 10500 ÷ 14500

Fig. 10. Result of the weighted configurational analysis on the Cassino network

4.3   Comparison Between Real and Forecast Data

The data obtained from the Space Syntax forecast model were compared with the pedestrian counts collected in several weekday and pre-holiday days according to the aforementioned analysis periods (Figs. 11 and 12).

The graphs show that the only "unweighted" morphological model derived with a 400 m long metric radius, has fairly good correlation coefficients ranging between around 0.6 and 0.7. While by taking into account the proximity weight, the model returns somehow higher R^2 values, especially for working day pedestrian movements.

In the unweighted scenarios, the outlier points were identified, to understand the reason for these anomalies. These are linked to a large number of pedestrians in some areas of the network characterized by the presence of bus stops, a high concentration of commercial establishments or the presence of schools/universities (Fig. 13).

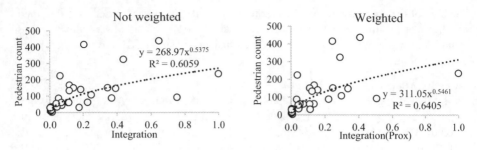

Fig. 11. Pedestrian count versus Integration on the weekday

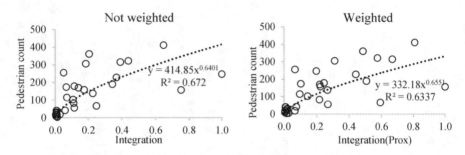

Fig. 12. Pedestrian count versus Integration on the pre-holiday day

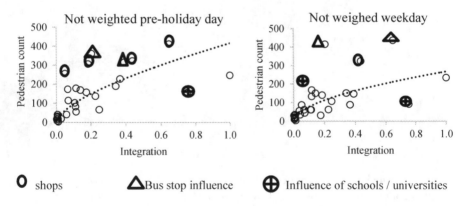

Fig. 13. Pedestrian count versus Integration diagrams with highlighted outliers

By observing these points, it can be argued that the presence of singular "attractors" may be not consistent with the configurational analysis theory and therefore the significant influence of these elements on the pedestrian mobility needs to be separately evaluated. Therefore, the points related to the presence of singular attractors such as educational institutions and bus stops were excluded providing higher R^2 values (Figs. 14 and 15).

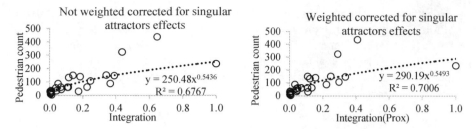

Fig. 14. Pedestrian count versus Integration diagrams without singular pedestrian attractors on the weekday

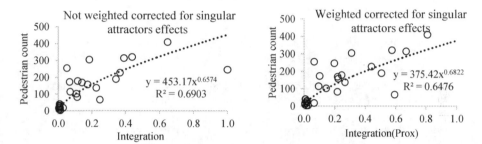

Fig. 15. Pedestrian count versus Integration diagrams without singular pedestrian attractors on the pre-holiday day

It should be noted that by removing the data referring to the singular attractors, results with the "hybrid" approach employing a proximity weight provides fairly satisfactory correlation in the working day scenarios. While in the pre-holiday scenario the values of the correlation coefficient seem slightly lower if compared with those provided by the conventional (unweighted) configurational approach.

It is believed that this may be due to a different walking aptitude in terms impedance function in the pre-holiday scenario for Cassino inhabitants.

5   Conclusions

In this work an original hybrid approach employing a configurational analysis combined with land use and pedestrian mobility aptitude has been proposed and calibrated by means of an experimental pedestrian count campaign carried out in the downtown of Cassino. The ultimate aim of the study is to develop a pedestrian exposure prediction methodology that can help road manager to identify prone-risk area for vulnerable users. Further improvements are expected concerning:

- the increase of the pedestrian counts to improve statistical significance;
- the experimental validation of the proposed methodological approach;
- the extension of the proposed methodology to different urban contexts.

Nonetheless, preliminary results obtained seem somehow promising and allow us to affirm that the hybrid approach developed can provide a satisfactory estimate of pedestrian movements compared to that obtained so far in the scientific literature.

It is believed that the evaluation of the pedestrian movements may constitute a valid support for the study of accident related to vulnerable users in the urban area.

References

1. Al Sayed, K.: Space Syntax Methodology. Bartlett School of Architecture, UCL: London, UK (2018)
2. Ashford, N.M.: Stochastic modelling of passenger and baggage. Traffic Eng. Control **17**, 207–210 (1976)
3. Cervero, R.A.: Travel choices in pedestrian versus automobile oriented neighborhoods. Working Paper 644, University of California at Berkeley, Berkeley, CA (1995)
4. Cutini, V.: Spazio urbano e movimento pedonale. Uno studio sull'ipotesi configurazionale. Cybergeo Eur. J. Geogr. (1999)
5. Dai, W.: A configurational exploration of pedestrian and cyclist movements: using Hangzhou as a case study, China. In: Proceedings of the Ninth International Space Syntax Symposium (2013)
6. Helbing, D.P.: Self-organizing pedestrian movement. Environ. Plann. B: Plann. Des. **28**, 361–383 (2001)
7. Hillier, B., Penn, A.: Natural movement: or configuration and attraction in urban pedestrian movement. Environ. Plann. B: Plann. Des. **20**, 29–66 (1993)
8. Hillier, B., Hanson, J.: Ideas are in things: an application of the space syntax method to descovering house genotypes. Environ. Plann. B: Plann. Des. **14**, 363–385 (1987)
9. Hillier, B.: Network effects and psychological effects: a theory of urban movement. In: International Conference on Spatial Information Theory, pp. 475–490 (2005)
10. Hoogendoorn, S.P.: Pedestrian route-choice and activity scheduling theoryand models. Transp. Res. Part B. **38**, 169–190 (2004)
11. ISTAT. Atti del 9° Censimento generale dell'industria e dei servizi e Censimento delle istituzioni non profit, 5 - Le sezioni di censimento (2015)
12. Kuzmyak, J.R., Walters, J.: NCHRP Report 770 - Estimating Bicycling and Walking for Planning and Project Development: A Guidebook (2014)
13. Jacobsen, P.: Safety in numbers: more walkers and bicyclists, safer walking and bicycling. Injury Prev. **9**, 205–209 (2003)
14. Kitamura, R.M.: A micro-analysis of land use and travel in five neighborhoods in the San Francisco Bay Area. Transportation **24**, 125–158 (1997). https://doi.org/10.1023/A:1017959825565
15. Kurose, S.: A method for identifying accessibility properties of pedestrian shopping networks. J. Retail. Consum. Serv. **2**(2), 111–118 (1995)
16. Landis, B.O.: The Roadside Pedestrian Environment: Toward A Comprehensive Level of Service. Paper 990570, TRB, National Research Council, Washington, D.C. (1999)
17. Leden, L.: Pedestrian risk decrease with pedestrian flow. A case study based on data from signalized intersections in Hamilton. Ontario. Accid. Anal. Prev. **34**, 457–464 (2002)

18. Lerman, Y., Rofè, Y.: Using space syntax to model pedestrian movement in urban transportation planning. Geogr. Anal. **46**, 392–410 (2014)
19. Løvås, G.G.: Modeling and simulation of pedestrian traffic flow. Transp. Res. Part B: Methodol. **28**(6), 429–443 (1994)
20. Raford, N.: Space syntax: an innovative pedestrian volume modeling tool for pedestrian safety. In: Annual Meeting of the Transportation Review Board, Paper 04-2977 (2003)
21. Southworth, M.: The evolving metropolis: studies of community, neighborhood, and street form at the urban edge. J. Am. Plann. Assoc. **59**, 271–287 (1993)

On-Board Comfort of Different Age Passengers and Bus-Lane Characteristics

Mauro Coni[1]([⊠]) [iD], Francesca Maltinti[1] [iD], Francesco Pinna[1] [iD],
Nicoletta Rassu[1] [iD], Chiara Garau[1] [iD], Benedetto Barabino[2] [iD],
and Giulio Maternini[2] [iD]

[1] Department of Civil and Environmental Engineering and Architecture
(DICAAR), University of Cagliari, via Marengo 2, 09123 Cagliari, Italy
mconi@unica.it
[2] Department of Civil, Environmental, Architectural Engineering
and Mathematics (DICATAM), University of Brescia,
via Branze 43, 25123 Brescia, Italy

Abstract. Onboard bus comfort significantly depends on the bus lanes characteristics, such as horizontal curvature, pavement roughness, longitudinal, and transversal slope. A literature review shows a statistical relationship between acceleration level and passenger features, such as age and gender. A large number of onboard interviews have been collected and correlated to bus-lane geometry parameters, to evaluate the vibrational comfort of different passengers. Passenger's judgments are related to the lateral, longitudinal, and vertical shake. At the same time, a geometric investigation on bus-lane corridors, traveled during interviews, in the city of Cagliari in Italy allowed to extract infrastructure parameters in terms of numbers and density of turns, horizontal curvature radius, speed design, and acceleration variance. The paper analyzed the correlation between some geometric and cinematics road parameters that may affect the comfort and the different passenger's judgments on the three acceleration components by age classes and hourly day. The results generally show weak correlations between the selected parameters and passenger judgments. Conversely, travel speeds have significant correlation values. There is a moderate inverse correlation between the vibrational level and the age of the passengers. The younger age groups tend to have more severe judgments, attributable to their higher demand for comfort. The presence of preferential lanes increases the onboard comfort quality in terms of speed regularity, without private cars interferences.

Keywords: Bus comfort · Bus-lane · Vibrational level · Road geometric

1 Introduction

Passenger's onboard comfort (OBC) and satisfaction are critical factors of a bus-service quality and one of the best strategies to increase the bus users [1–3]. For these reasons, in recent years, the OBC of passengers in the public means of transportation received considerable attention in order to define appropriate parameters, efficient measurement systems, and procedures.

© Springer Nature Switzerland AG 2020
O. Gervasi et al. (Eds.): ICCSA 2020, LNCS 12255, pp. 658–672, 2020.
https://doi.org/10.1007/978-3-030-58820-5_48

The comfort level depends on several aspects related to vehicle and road characteristics, degree of crowding, traffic condition, internal microclimate, driver's behavior [1, 3–6]. Most of the investigations on OBC study the physical measurements of vibrations, and several studies [1, 2, 4] consider the subjective perception of the users. Also, many researchers investigated the correlation between judgment collected by the onboard questionnaire (qualitative and subjective) and contextual measurements of vibration (quantitative and objective) [1, 6–9]. The effect of whole-body vibration on balance, mobility and falls in older adults are well known and systematically reviewed in the literature [10, 11]. However, no specific studies are available on the bus passengers by age. Several studies [12–15] propose an innovative approach that allows the simultaneous measurement of subjective and objective of the OBC. The subjective measurements of the OBCL is an expensive activity due to time-consuming surveys and personal interviews. Thus, light and automatic vibrational collecting systems are desirable [1]. For these reasons, many recent studies involve the capability of the smartphones to gather acceleration values (longitudinal, lateral, and vertical accelerations), speed over the time with at the frequency of 1.0 Hz [1, 4, 12–14]. At the same time, the device can record instantaneous geographical coordinate (latitude, longitude, and altitude) from the global positioning system (GPS). However, many authors [17–21] pointed out how the automatic construction of a digital map is a considerable challenge, related to positioning errors, GPS noise and variability of speed, and the complexity of roads and urban streets. Therefore, many approaches are available to increase trajectory precision and consistency, classifiable into three categories [22–24]. In the "point clustering" method [17, 25], raw data are clustered in many ways (i.e., k-means clustering) to create a street segmentation. The "incremental track insertion" [18, 19] and [27] generates a road alignment by incrementally inserting trajectory data into an initially empty diagram. In the "intersection linking" method [20, 21], the intersection nodes of the road trajectory are detected and linked together.

Fig. 1. The 25 of the 36 bus routes investigated in Cagliari.

In this paper, the point clustering of digital data from GPS operates in the key-point from the topographic survey and DEM (Digital Elevation Model) of the bus-lane based. Moreover, the polyline of the bus-lane axis has been segmented every 10 m evaluating for each point curvature radius, tortuosity, acceleration variance, and velocity diagrams.

The objective of this paper is to investigate the correlation between geometric and cinematics road parameters that may affect the comfort of passengers as well as the passenger's judgments of three acceleration components and class ages. The experimental investigation involves the public transportation network in the city of Cagliari (Italy) as shown in Fig. 1. During three weeks in July 2019, 755 questionnaires were collected in 198 bus rides, covering 25 of the 36 active lines in Cagliari. This study is essential for public transport companies needing to improve and certificate the service quality on routes according to European norms [28], also using ITS technologies, increasing modal shift, and urban social interactions [29, 30].

2   Data and Methodology

The structure of the research follows four levels: 1) data type, 2) data collection tools onboard, 3) bus-lane geometry and cinematic, and 4) data analysis (Fig. 2).

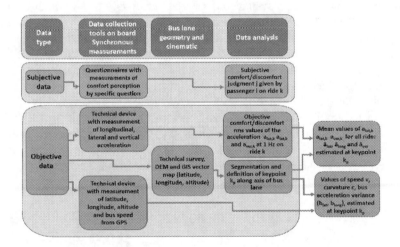

Fig. 2. The 4-level framework of the research.

Data Type

The study comprises two types of data: 1) "subjective data" regarding passengers' judgments on board comfort and, 2) "objective data" concerning vibration parameters, on ride k, along the route. The first assumption of the research considers the on-board comfort level as a function of passenger shaking, mainly due to the driver's behavior (braking, slowing down, accelerations and steering) and bus-lane characteristics (turns, pavements roughness, slope).

Data Collection Tools on Board

Two types of instruments have been used to collect the data. The subjective data were gathered through an on-board questionnaire, administered to passengers, in order to estimate their perception of the comfort level. In July 2019, during the periodical quality survey collected by CTM. (the local public transport company) 8 new questions were submitted to passengers: 1) position during the interview; 2) position related to the direction of the travel; 3), 4) and 5) expected driving style for a) braking/acceleration; b) horizontal curves; c) vertical vibration; 6), 7) and 8) perceived driving style for a) braking/acceleration; b) horizontal curves; c) vertical vibration.

A total of 755 questionnaires were collected.

Several studies revealed the different roles of expectation for comfort perception evaluation [31]. The expectation is a factor associated with the environment, and it is strongly affected by the cultural/experience background of the passengers. For this reason, expectation and perception judgments were collected. Objective data refers to the kinematic parameters on ride k, which were measured through technical devices, in the longitudinal, lateral, and vertical directions at low frequencies. In general, frequencies ≤ 3 Hz depends by the vehicle age, materials and seats, road pavement roughness and bus engine and mechanic characteristics, whereas frequencies ≤ 2 Hz mainly depend on the bus weight, length, suspension type, traffic density, speed distribution, bus-route geometric characteristics and driving behavior [31–33].

Four operators with smartphones collected objective data with the Android system, during each entire ride, concurrently with the passenger's interview. The smartphone's GPS device and 3-axis accelerometer MEMS provide geographical position (lat, long, alt), GTM time, accelerations (a_{lat}, a_{long} and a_{vert}) at the frequency of 1.0 Hz. A specific app (Torque) recorded the data of the several parameters a_{long} the bus ride k. Figure 3 shows some objective data record.

n.ord	Line-ride code	GPS Time	Longitude	Latitude	GPS Speed (Meters/second)	Altitude	G(x)	G(y)	G(z)	Bus number
1	1_OB_1	Fri Jul 26 13:13:07 GMT+02:00 2019	9.131383241	39.23754713	0.00	60.44	-0.68	1.85	9.40	344
2	1_OB_1	Fri Jul 26 13:13:08 GMT+02:00 2019	9.131383241	39.23754713	0.00	60.52	-0.21	1.24	8.95	344
3	1_OB_1	Fri Jul 26 13:13:09 GMT+02:00 2019	9.131383241	39.23754713	0.00	60.62	-0.47	1.22	9.67	344
4	1_OB_1	Fri Jul 26 13:13:10 GMT+02:00 2019	9.131499221	39.23752446	1.20	60.62	0.10	0.29	9.43	344
5	1_OB_1	Fri Jul 26 13:13:11 GMT+02:00 2019	9.131494824	39.23751886	2.11	60.64	-0.14	0.81	9.59	344
6	1_OB_1	Fri Jul 26 13:13:12 GMT+02:00 2019	9.131507066	39.23750344	2.63	60.64	-0.96	2.08	9.09	344

Fig. 3. Objective data record.

The smartphone's location inside the bus and its orientations affect the recorded vibrational level. All the smartphones were in the seat close to the driver, on a horizontal plane, and in longitudinal orientation (see Fig. 4).

Fig. 4. Smartphone and bus coordinates systems.

Bus-Lane Geometry and Cinematic

The automatic polylines are drawable directly from the GPS data for each ride and show high variability related to noise and positioning errors. The mean value of the measured accelerations and speeds were associated with a key-point p in the real trajectory to enhance the trajectory precision and consistency between different rides. Figure 5 shows the GPS data-position compared to the real bus path.

The real trajectory was assumed the axis of the bus lane, derived from an official map database, DEM, and the topographic survey. The segmentation of the axis' polyline, every 10 m, allows extracting each key-point coordinates. The values of the GPS measured parameters (v, a_{lat}, a_{long}, a_{vert}) were averaged in the circular area of radius 10 m and assigned to the central key-point p.

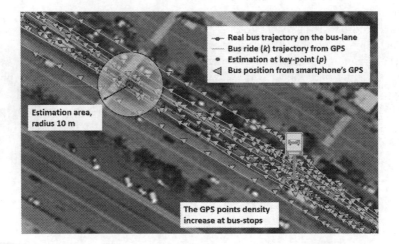

Fig. 5. Objective data position. The real bus trajectory and GPS data.

At key-point p, several parameters have also been calculated: curvature radius R; cornering speed limit v_l; tortuosity t; longitudinal speed v; lateral, longitudinal and vertical acceleration and lateral jerk (variation of acceleration over the time).

Data Analysis

The fourth level of the research concerns the data analysis in order to evaluate the onboard comfort and bus-lane ride quality. First, the subjective and objective raw data have been gathered concurrently, and each questionnaire has been associated with smartphone measurements. During the interview, each passenger u rates the different aspects of the onboard comfort of ride k with average judgment j, from 1 to 10. For instance, the question on the satisfactions against braking/acceleration was formulated as follows: "On a scale from 1 to 10, how satisfied are you with the acceleration and braking of the bus operator concerning this route?". The judgments have been elaborated considering different characteristics: age, gender, profession, position during the interview, driving style for braking acceleration, curves and vertical oscillation, educational qualification, and trip time. The mean, the median, the mode, the standard deviation, and the coefficient of variation have been calculated for the subjective judgments:

Mean: $$\bar{x} = \frac{\sum x_i}{n}$$

Median: central data value. The data are sorted in ascending order, and the middle value is detected to obtain the median.

Mode: the value that occurs most frequently.

Standard deviation: $$s = \sqrt{\frac{\sqrt{(x_i - \bar{x})^2}}{(n-1)}}$$

Variance: $$s^2 = \frac{(x_i - \bar{x})^2}{(n-1)}$$

Coefficient of variation: $$V = \frac{s}{\bar{x}}$$

For the processing of the accelerometer data from MEMS, the authors compute the RMSWA (Root Mean Square) of the weighted accelerations in m/s^2 according to International Standard ISO 2631 [34] at the frequency of 1.0 Hz, by the following expression:

$$RMSa_{lat,j} = \sqrt{\frac{\sum_{d=1}^{n_j}\left(a_{lat,j,d}\right)^2}{n_j}} \quad \forall j = 1,\ldots j$$

$$RMSa_{long,j} = \sqrt{\frac{\sum_{d=1}^{n_j}\left(a_{long,j,d}\right)^2}{n_j}} \quad \forall j = 1,\ldots j$$

$$RMSa_{vert,j} = \sqrt{\frac{\sum_{d=1}^{n_j}\left(a_{vert,j,d}\right)^2}{n_j}} \quad \forall j = 1,\ldots j$$

$$RMSWA_j = \sqrt{\left[\left(k_{lat}RMSWAa_{lat,j}\right)^2 + \left(k_{long}RMSWAa_{long,j}\right)^2 + \left(k_{vert}RMSWAa_{vert,j}\right)^2\right]} \quad \forall j = 1,\ldots J$$

where:

- d: index of the observation;
- n_j: total number of samples of a_{lat}, a_{long} and a_{vert} associated with judgment j;
- $a_{lat,j}$, $a_{long,j}$, and $a_{vert,j}$: transversal, longitudinal and vertical components of the accelerations for each judgment j;
- k_{lat}, k_{long}, and k_{vert} are the weight factors that reflect the importance of the acceleration along the x, y, and z axes, respectively.
- $RMSa_{lat,j}$, $RMSa_{long,j}$, and $RMSa_{vert,j}$: root mean square value of the accelerations along the transversal x, longitudinal y and vertical z axes for the judgment j;
- $RMSWAj$: root mean square of the weighted accelerations for the judgment j;

Some simplifications on the frequency range and the method of measurement are assumed. Unlike ISO 2631 (frequency range from 0.1 Hz–80.0 Hz), the authors consider only 1.0 Hz frequency, since the main annoyance to the transport passengers is between 0.5 and 5 Hz [32, 35]. Also, the maximum sensitivity of the human body for horizontal acceleration occurs at 1.0 Hz, and other frequencies are less relevant.

Finally, the following equations and procedures were used to calculate the kinematic parameters of the bus lane axis in the key-points.

Longitudinal Speed v at key-point p is estimated as a mean of GPS positioning data in a circular area of radius 10 m around key-point.

Acceleration at key-point p. The same procedure described above has been applied to lateral, longitudinal, and vertical accelerations.

Lateral Jerk. The variation of acceleration over time.

Curvature Radius R. To determine the radius of curvature, triplets of key-points p were considered in sequence. The radius of the circle circumscribed to this triplet is given by $R = \frac{abc}{4S}$ while a, b and c are the sides of the triangle and S its area, according to the following expressions:

$$a = \sqrt{\left(x_{p-1} - x_p\right)^2 + \left(y_{p-1} - y_p\right)^2}$$

$$b = \sqrt{\left(x_p - x_{p+1}\right)^2 + \left(y_p - y_{p+1}\right)^2}$$

$$c = \sqrt{\left(x_{p-1} - x_{p+1}\right)^2 + \left(y_{p-1} - y_{p+1}\right)^2}$$

$$S = \sqrt{sp(sp - a)(sp - b)(sp - c)} \text{ where } S = \frac{a+b+c}{2}$$

Tortuosity. The tortuosity has practical relevance in many aspects of transportation: for road design, cost of the journey, passengers' comfort, accessibility and, fuel consumption. It can be defined as the rate between real length (L) of the path and the distance of the ends (D), as shown in Fig. 6. If the lane is defined as a poly-line connecting key-point p, the total length L is the sum of each segment.

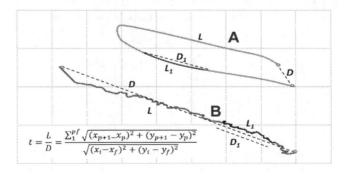

$$t = \frac{L}{D} = \frac{\sum_1^{pf} \sqrt{(x_{p+1} - x_p)^2 + (y_{p+1} - y_p)^2}}{\sqrt{(x_i - x_f)^2 + (y_i - y_f)^2}}$$

Fig. 6. Local and global tortuosity of a pathline.

Cornering Speed Limit. The two main hazards of excessive cornering are tire slip and rollover [36, 37]. Before the cornering, the speed limit can be evaluated by the equation: $v_{Lim} = \sqrt{gR(f_t + tag\beta)}$ m/s or $V_{Lim} = \sqrt{127R(f_t + tag\beta)}$ km/h.

A precautionary values of the skid coefficient f_t of 0.15 and transverse slope *tag* $\beta = 0$ are assumed.

Lateral Jerk (acceleration variation over time). It is necessary to limit the maximum jerk to avoid vehicle passengers' losing control over body movements and, to allow muscles to adapt to tension changes during sudden acceleration.

However, high jerk values are uncomfortable. The roads are designed to limit the jerk at $0.4 \div 1.4$ m/s^3 as a maximum as a function of the speed, which has been assumed $c = 50.4/V$ according to Italian Regulation DM 6792/2001 (c [m/s] and V [km/h]).

3   Results

The survey saw a total of 130.1 h of accelerometric recordings on buses, which covered 2,393.9 km with an average travel speed of 18.4 km/h. The peak speeds are 87.8 km/h, and for 25.3% of the time, the bus was stopped (mostly at the bus stop and traffic light). Figure 7 shows the distribution of travel speeds.

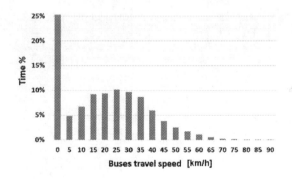

Fig. 7. Distribution of travel speeds.

Some observations concern the objective acceleration values linked to the subjective judgments (Fig. 8). The lateral accelerations a_x has values between -12.2 and 12.7 m/s^2, the longitudinal accelerations a_y between -4.0 and 10.5 m/s^2, and the vertical accelerations a_z between -10.2 and 21.0 m/s^2. Interestingly, the longitudinal accelerations are concentrated in the range between -4 and $+4$ m/s^2. A plausible interpretation is that they are linked to the characteristics of the bus braking system, which automatically introduces gradual braking (Fig. 8).

Figure 9 shows the trend of the geometric and kinematic parameters estimated along route 1OB, which was selected as an example.

The correlation matrix among all the analyzed variables shows that the parameters are generally not correlated with each other, with some exceptions (Fig. 10).

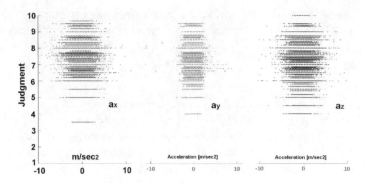

Fig. 8. Acceleration range as a function of judgments.

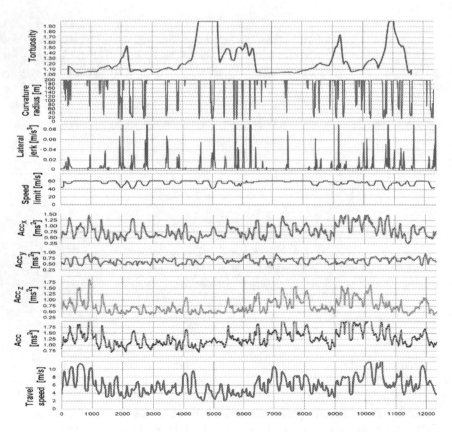

Fig. 9. Geometric and kinematic parameters estimated along the Line 1OB.

They concern the accelerations with the travel speed, the kickback with a radius of curvature. Perhaps high trivial correlations mutually abated among the three components of accelerations.

	ax m/s2	ay m/s2	az m/s2	a m/s2	speed m/s	tortuosity	curvature radius m	lateral jerk m/s3	cornering speed limit m/s	Judgment Jx	Judgment Jy	Judgment Jz
ax m/s2	100%											
ay m/s2	-18.5%	100%				symmetric						
az m/s2	79.0%	-17.8%	100%									
a m/s2	92.3%	-0.8%	93.2%	100%								
speed m/s	55.8%	-11.8%	72.4%	67.1%	100%							
tortuosity	-4.8%	11.2%	-18.7%	-10.2%	-24.1%	100%						
curvature radius m	-20.3%	4.5%	10.4%	-4.3%	18.9%	-17.2%	100%					
lateral jerk m/s3	5.1%	-1.7%	-6.6%	-1.3%	-10.8%	5.6%	-31.1%	100%				
cornering speed limit m/s	-17.0%	0.9%	18.0%	0.8%	28.0%	-30.3%	52.4%	-16.6%	100%			
Judgment Jx	11.9%	11.3%	11.2%	11.2%	11.2%	11.1%	10.9%	10.9%	10.9%	100%		
Judgment Jy	5.3%	4.5%	4.6%	4.6%	4.7%	4.6%	4.5%	4.4%	4.4%	93.2%	100%	
Judgment Jz	8.9%	8.3%	8.3%	8.3%	8.3%	8.2%	8.1%	8.0%	8.0%	92.5%	97.0%	100%

Fig. 10. Correlation matrix of the considered parameters

The subjective investigations were conducted mainly between 10:00 and 20:00 and mainly involved women (63% of the interviewees). Almost 40% of the interviewees are young people aged between 18 and 25, and over 75% are under the age of 35, mainly composed of students of first and second-grade schools. The movements are mainly short-lived, 88% with travel times of less than 15' (Fig. 11).

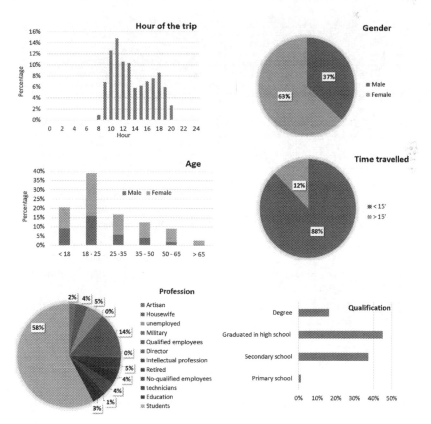

Fig. 11. Descriptive statistics of the surveys

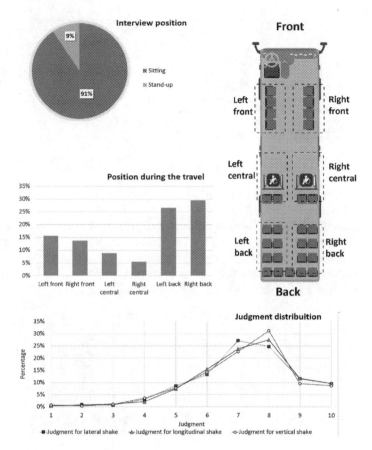

Fig. 12. Positions during interviews and judgment distribution

During the journey, 55% of the interviewed were positioned in the back of the bus. The passengers during the interview were 91% standing, and only 9% were sitting, In 75% of cases, the judgments are above 7. Judgments 7 and 8 exceed 55% (Fig. 12). These results clearly show that most of passengers rate the comfort on board along the three acceleration axes in the same manner, thus they seldom distinguishing among braking/acceleration actions, characteristic of the route and vertical vibrations mainly related to the pavement roughness.

Figure 13 shows that 1) the difference between couple of judgments is never greater than 4, 2) the 55% makes the same judgment and 3) approximately 88% differ only by one point.

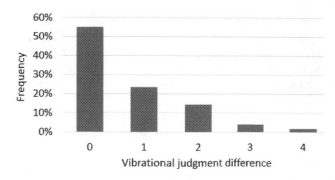

Fig. 13. Vibrational judgment difference between the component x, y, and z for each interview

Finally, it is interesting to observe the differences in judgments according to gender and age (Fig. 14a). Females tend to give a decreasing judgment with age while males show an opposite trend. Another trend observed in the group of interviews, decidedly marked in the female population, is a correlation between the average opinion expressed and the peak traffic hours (Fig. 14b).

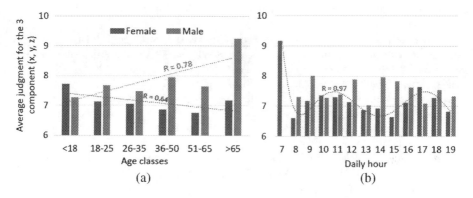

Fig. 14. a) On the left: average judgment vs. age classes; b) average judgment vs. daily hour

4   Conclusions and Remarks

The survey highlights how the perception of vibrational comfort on board in public transport can be particularly complex. A multiplicity of physical and subjective parameters can modify passenger perception. Objective measurements, such as the three distinct acceleration components, the speed, and the characteristics of the track, are felt very differently depending on the sex, age, and position inside the vehicle during the journey.

Trivial, predictably high correlated, have been obtained between the x, y, z acceleration components, and between the judgments Jx, Jy, and Jz. Users tend to judge the travel experience overall without discerning the three components. The interviewees attribute values very similar to the three components (lateral, longitudinal, and vertical ones) even in the presence of significant variability of the road condition and in the presence of considerable difference in the levels of the three components. The difference between couple of judgments of each acceleration component differs only by one point for the 88% of the interviewed.

The results generally show weak correlations between the selected parameters and passenger judgments. Conversely, travel speeds have significant correlation values. There is a moderate inverse correlation between the vibrational level and the age of the passengers. The younger age groups tend to have more severe judgments, attributable to their higher demand for comfort. Another trend observed in the group of interviews, particularly in the female population, is a relationship between the average opinion expressed and the peak traffic hours. The presence of preferential lanes increases the onboard comfort quality in terms of speed regularity, without private cars interferences.

These results are a preliminary step in the authors' agenda, and thus, further research is suggested. It has been shown how many objective parameters can affect the comfort. In addition, passengers rated the perceived comfort along the three axes. Therefore, an advanced econometric model may be calibrated to examine the impact of objective measurements on the overall judgment. In this way, a gradual comfort scale may be perfectioned building on [1]. It can be part of a real-time dashboard, which shows to the bus driver when driving in comfortable/uncomfortable conditions, thus also improving the measurement of the service quality [37].

Acknowledgments. This study was supported by the MIUR (Ministry of Education, Universities and Research [Italy]) through a project entitled WEAKI TRANSIT: WEAK-demand areas Innovative TRANsport Shared services for Italian Towns (Project protocol: 20174ARRHT_004; CUP Code: F74I19001290001), financed with the PRIN 2017 (Research Projects of National Relevance) program. We authorize the MIUR to reproduce and distribute reprints for Governmental purposes, notwithstanding any copyright notations thereon. Any opinions, findings, and conclusions or recommendations expressed in this material are those of the authors and do not necessarily reflect the views of the MIUR.

This work also has been partially supported by the MIUR within the Smart City framework (project: PON04a2_00381 "CAGLIARI2020"). The authors are grateful for the CTM SpA, which made its data available for this study. The views expressed herein are those of the authors and are not necessarily those of the Italian bus operator.

References

1. Barabino, B., Coni, M., Olivo, A., Pungillo, G., Rassu, N.: Standing passenger comfort: a new scale for evaluating the real-time driving style of bus transit services. IEEE Trans. Intell. Transp. Syst. **20**(12) (2019) https://doi.org/10.1109/tits.2019.292180

2. Shen, X., Feng, S., Li, Z., Hu, B.: Analysis of bus passenger comfort perception based on passenger load factor and in-vehicle time. SpringerPlus **5**(1), 1–10 (2016). https://doi.org/10.1186/s40064-016-1694-7

3. Barabino, B., Cabras, N.A., Conversano, C., Olivo, A.: An integrated approach to select key quality indicators in transit services. Soc. Indic. Res. **149**, 1045–1080 (2020). https://doi.org/10.1007/s11205-020-02284-0

On-Board Comfort of Different Age Passengers   671

4. Rassu, N., et al.: Real-time evaluation of the on-board comfort of standing passenger in bus transit services. In: 26th ITS World Congress, Singapore, 21–25 October 2019
5. Maternini, G., Cadei, M.: A comfort scale for standing bus passengers in relation to certain road characteristics. Transp. Lett. Int. J. Transp. Res. **6**(3), 136–141 (2014). https://doi.org/10.1179/1942787514Y.0000000020
6. Af Wahlberg, A.E.: Short-term effects of training in economical driving passenger comfort and driver acceleration behavior. Int. J. Ind. Ergon. **36**, 151–163 (2006)
7. Nassiri, P., Koohpaei, A., Zeraati, H., Shalkouhi, P.J.: Train passengers comfort with regard to whole-body, vibration. Journal of Low-Frequency Noise Vibration and Active Control **30**(2), 125–136 (2011). https://doi.org/10.1260/0263-0923.30.2.125
8. Hoberock, L.L.: A survey of longitudinal acceleration comfort studies in ground transportation vehicles. J. Dyn. Syst. Meas. Contr. **99**(2), 76–84 (1977)
9. Oborne, J.: Vibration and passenger comfort. Appl. Ergon. **8**(2), 97–101 (1977). https://doi.org/10.1016/0003-6870(77)90060-6
10. Lam, F.M.H., Lau, R.W.K., Chung, R.C.K., Pang, M.Y.C.: The effect of whole-body vibration on balance, mobility and falls in older adults: a systematic review and meta-analysis. Maturitas **72**(3), 206–213 (2012). https://doi.org/10.1016/j.maturitas.2012.04.009
11. Merriman, H., Jackson, K.: The effects of whole-body vibration training in aging adults: a systematic review. J. Geriatr. Phys. Ther. **32**(3), 134–145 (2009)
12. Zhao, H., Guo, L., Zeng, X.: Evaluation of bus vibration comfort based on passenger crowdsourcing mode. Math. Prob. Eng. **2016**. Article n. 2132454 (2016). https://doi.org/10.1155/2016/2132454
13. Eboli, L., Mazzulla, G., Pungillo, G.: Measuring bus comfort levels by using acceleration instantaneous values. Transp. Res. Procedia **18**, 27–34 (2016). https://doi.org/10.1016/j.trpro.2016.12.004
14. Bodini, I., Lancini, M., Pasinetti, S., Vetturi D.: Techniques for on-board vibrational passenger comfort monitoring in public transport. In: 12th IMEKO TC10 Workshop on Technical Diagnostics New Perspectives in Measurements, Tools, and Techniques for Industrial Applications 6–7 June 2013, Florence, Italy
15. Castellanos, J.C., Fruett, F.: Embedded system to evaluate the passenger comfort in public transportation based on dynamical vehicle behavior with user's feedback. Measurement **47**, 442–451 (2014)
16. Zhang, Y., Liu, J., Qian, X., Qiu, A., Zhang, F.: An automatic road network construction method using massive GPS trajectory data. Int. J. Geo-Inf. **6**, 400 (2017). https://doi.org/10.3390/ijgi6120400. https://www.mdpi.com/journal/ijgi
17. Biagioni, J., Eriksson, J.: Map inference in the face of noise and disparity. In: Proceedings of the 20th International Conference on Advances in Geographic Information Systems, Redondo Beach, CA, USA, 6–9 November 2012, pp. 79–88 (2012)
18. Ahmed, M., Wenk, C.: Constructing street networks from GPS trajectories. In: Epstein, L., Ferragina, P. (eds.) ESA 2012. LNCS, vol. 7501, pp. 60–71. Springer, Heidelberg (2012). https://doi.org/10.1007/978-3-642-33090-2_7
19. Cao, L., Krumm, J.: From GPS traces to a routable road map. In: Proceedings of the 17th ACM SIGSPATIAL International Conference on Advances in Geographic Information Systems, Seattle, WA, USA, 4–6 November 2009, pp. 3–12 (2009)
20. Karagiorgou, S., Pfoser, D.: On vehicle tracking data-based road network generation. In: Proceedings of the 20th International Conference on Advances in Geographic Information Systems, Redondo Beach, CA, USA, 6–9 November 2012, pp. 89–98 (2012)
21. Fathi, A., Krumm, J.: Detecting road intersections from GPS traces. In: Fabrikant, S.I., Reichenbacher, T., van Kreveld, M., Schlieder, C. (eds.) GIScience 2010. LNCS, vol. 6292, pp. 56–69. Springer, Heidelberg (2010). https://doi.org/10.1007/978-3-642-15300-6_5

22. Li, H., Kulik, L., Ramamohanarao, K.: Robust inferences of travel paths from GPS trajectories. Int. J. Geogr. Inf. Sci. **29**, 2194–2222 (2015)
23. Qiu, J., Wang, R.: Inferring road maps from sparsely sampled GPS traces. J. Locat. Based Serv. **10**, 111–124 (2016)
24. Ahmed, M., Karagiorgou, S., Pfoser, D., Wenk, C.: A comparison and evaluation of map construction algorithms using vehicle tracking data. Geoinformatica **19**(3), 601–632 (2014). https://doi.org/10.1007/s10707-014-0222-6
25. Davics, J., Beresford, A.R., Hopper, A.: Scalable, distributed, real-time map generation. IEEE Pervasive Comput. **5**, 47–54 (2006)
26. Kuntzsch, C., Sester, M., Brenner, C.: Generative models for road network reconstruction. Int. J. Geogr. Inf. Sci. **30**, 1012–1039 (2016)
27. Ekpenyong, F., Palmer-Brown, D., Brimicombe, A.: Extracting road information from recorded GPS data using a snap-drift neural network. Neurocomputing **73**, 24–36 (2009)
28. Transportation—Logistics and Services. European Standard EN 13816: Public passenger transport –Service quality definition, targeting, and measurement, EN 13816 (2002)
29. Coni, M., Garau, C., Pinna, F.: How has Cagliari changed its citizens in smart citizens? Exploring the influence of ITS technology on urban social interactions. In: Gervasi, O., et al. (eds.) ICCSA 2018. LNCS, vol. 10962, pp. 573–588. Springer, Cham (2018). https://doi.org/10.1007/978-3-319-95168-3_39
30. Tilocca, P., et al.: Managing data and rethinking applications in an innovative mid-sized bus fleet. Transp. Res. Procedia **25**, 1904–1924 (2017)
31. Naddeo, A., Cappetti, N., Califano, R., Vallone, M.: The role of expectation in comfort perception. In; 6th International Conference on Applied Human Factors and Ergonomics (AHFE 2015) and the Affiliated Conferences, AHFE 2015, Procedia Manufacturing vol. 3, 4784–4791 (2015)
32. Coni, M.: Livelli di Rumore e Vibrazioni Indotte all' Interno di un Mezzo da Due Diversi Tipi di Pavimentazione Stradale. Le Strade **1301**, 289–295 (1994)
33. Coni, M.: Analisi Sperimentale e Simulazione Numerica del Campo Acustico e Vibrazionale di un Mezzo per il Trasporto Pubblico Urbano. Ph.D. dissertation, National Library Rome and Florence (1995)
34. Mechanical vibration and shock - Evaluation of human exposure to whole-body vibration, International Standard ISO 2631, 2nd edn. (1997)
35. Coni, M.: Analisi Sperimentale e Simulazione Numerica del Campo Acustico e Vibrazionale di un Mezzo per il Trasporto Pubblico Urbano
36. Zeeman, A., Booysen, M.J.: Combining speed and acceleration to detect reckless driving in the informal public transport industry. In: Intelligent Transportation Systems-(ITSC), 16th International IEEE Conference on. IEEE, pp. 756–761 (2013)
37. Wahlstrom, J., Skog, I., Handel, P.: Risk assessment of vehicle cornering events in GNSS data-driven insurance telematics. In: IEEE 17th International Conference on Intelligent Transportation Systems (ITSC), October 2014, pp. 3132–3137 (2014)
38. Barabino, B.: Automatic recognition of 'low-quality' vehicles and bus stops in bus services. Public Transp. **10**(2), 257–289 (2018)

Vulnerable Users and Public Transport Service: Analysis on Expected and Perceived Quality Data

Francesca Maltinti[1]([✉]) [iD], Nicoletta Rassu[1] [iD], Mauro Coni[1] [iD],
Chiara Garau[1] [iD], Francesco Pinna[1] [iD], Roberto Devoto[1] [iD],
and Benedetto Barabino[2] [iD]

[1] Department of Civil and Environmental Engineering and Architecture
(DICAAR), University of Cagliari, via Marengo 3, 09123 Cagliari, Italy
{maltinti,nicoletta.rassu,mconi,cgarau,fpinna,
devotor}@unica.it
[2] Department of Civil, Environmental, Architectural Engineering
and Mathematics (DICATAM), University of Brescia,
via Branze 43, 25123 Brescia, Italy
benedetto.barabino@unibs.it

Abstract. Today's cities are meeting places, economic and social development centers, where all citizens should have the opportunity to live and move, according to adequate quality of life standards. However, this does not always correspond to reality in particular for the most vulnerable categories of the population. So, UN's 2030 Agenda underlines the need to make cities inclusive and accessible by means, for instance, a suitable transport system for all, and in particular for vulnerable people as older people.

A lot of studies presented interesting contributes on how older people choose to move and initiatives taken to address their public transport requirements, but no attention has been given to evaluate expected and perceived quality of public transport system, particularly referring to older people. So, the aim of this study is to highlight which should be the most important attributes of a public transport service (PTS) for over 65 years old passengers and if the local PTS satisfy their desires. By an intercept on board survey in the metropolitan area of Cagliari, it has been shown that, for all users, PTS appears qualitatively adequate with respect to each attribute analysed and vulnerable customers are more satisfied than all.

Keywords: Accessibility · Public transport service · Older people · Cagliari

1 Introduction

Today's cities are meeting places, economic and social development centers, where all citizens should have the opportunity to live and move, according to adequate quality of life standards in line with the current smart paradigm cities. However, this does not always correspond to reality not only because cities continue to develop in a chaotic and differentiated way, with large development gaps and services offered between the

© Springer Nature Switzerland AG 2020
O. Gervasi et al. (Eds.): ICCSA 2020, LNCS 12255, pp. 673–689, 2020.
https://doi.org/10.1007/978-3-030-58820-5_49

city center and the periphery, but also because the most vulnerable categories of the population are often excluded from this development (such as people with disabilities, the elderly people who risk being marginalized with the consequent worsening of their condition of disadvantage and exclusion).

In addition, as evidenced by UN's 2030 Agenda[1], by 2030 it is expected that almost 60% of the world population will live in urban areas and, in particular the goal n.11 underlines the need to "make cities and human settlements inclusive, safe, resilient and sustainable" [1].

Specifically, this means that States and in particular local governments will have to face important challenges and propose appropriate policies to "provide access to safe, affordable, accessible and sustainable transport systems for all, [...] by expanding public transport, with special attention to the needs of those in vulnerable situations, women, children, persons with disabilities and older persons" [1].

The proposal of this paper fits into this framework, aimed at reorganizing the city in a smart way, by analyzing the quality expected and perceived of a public transportation system to make urban environments more sustainable, more inclusive and more accessible for all. Indeed, today, public transport plays a key role in urban space accessibility and provides the opportunity to access to several urban services to all categories of users, including the most disadvantaged such as elderly people.

In Europe, life expectancy is increasing as a result of improved quality of life and medical discoveries and it is known that aging is accompanied by changes of physiological performances as reduced flexibility and strength, impairment of visual and auditive perception, increased vulnerability to bone fracture, etc. which can influence mobility of older people [2]. Mollenkopf and Flaschenträger [3] find that "older persons suffer from the tighter and more aggressive traffic".

Other studies conducted in America [4–7], Canada [8–10], Australia [11], the Netherlands [12] and United Kingdom [13], observe that private car is the most preferred elderly transport mode, but in these last two Countries the percentage of car use decreases with increasing age. However, transport facilities represent a very important opportunity for elderly to avoid dependency on private transport and to travel to do shopping, to reach health care center, retirement recreation [14] or to visit retail services as food shops, banks, post office, chemists, etc. Also, older people, who are usually retired, can maintain social bonds thanks to public transport which allows independence, freedom of movement and choice [15] and [16].

But, what does older people think about public transport? What they need?

Metz [17] draws elderly's perfect journey using public transport: it should involve a short and safe walk to the bus stop, a brief and sheltered wait, punctuality, a safe and comfortable journey and a bus stop near to the final destination.

Fatima and Moridpour [18] examine the situation in Melbourne and the reason because elderly don't use public transportation and prefer private car. Often, older

---

[1] The UN's 2030 Agenda for Sustainable Development has 17 Sustainable Development Goals (SDGs) at its core, is about making people's lives better (https://ec.europa.eu/sustainable-development/about_en).

adults may be not able to walk to the bus stop or to climb the stairs, or to pay for transportation services and, also, they did not feel confident in crowded interchanges.

Borges [19] estimates that 10–20% of European citizens still find barriers and reduced accessibility on public transport, nevertheless Marsden et al. [20] and Koffman et al. [21] observe that road crossing and bus stop facilities represent the main aspects which can dissuading older people from using public transport. Shrestha et al. [22] find that various initiatives have been carried out or are underway to address older people's public transport requirements in many national and international policies.

All previous studies presented interesting contributes on how older people choose to move and initiatives taken to address their public transport requirements. However, to the best of our knowledge, no attention has been given to evaluate expected and perceived quality of public transport system, particularly referring to older people.

This paper covers this gap by analyzing data collected during a survey campaign carried out in July 2019 on board of the buses of CTM, that is the name of the public transport company of Cagliari. The aim of this study is to highlight which are the most important attributes of a public transport service (PTS) for over 65 years old passengers and if the local PTS satisfy their expectations.

The paper is structured in six sections including this introduction. Section 2 describes public transport service of Cagliari metropolitan area. Section 3 presents the questionnaire submitted to do the survey. Section 4 describes the methodology adopted to build a gradual evaluation on quality of public transport service from elderly viewpoint. Results are reported in Sect. 5. Finally, Sect. 6 provides the conclusions and research perspectives.

2 Public Transport Service in Cagliari Metropolitan Area

Fig. 1. Metropolitan city of Cagliari

The Metropolitan City of Cagliari (consisting of 17 municipalities including the city of Cagliari) in 2017 counts 431,038 inhabitants (see Fig. 1). Starting from 2011, the Metropolitan City of Cagliari assumed a new strategic plan to improve local public transport network, which led the CTM to become the 2nd public transport in Italy in 2013 [23]. This plan was developed with the University of Cagliari and provided using of Intelligent Transportation Systems (ITSs)'s technologies, improving routes and fleet buses, forbidding traffic cars in the historical center and promoting places and pedestrian areas, developing a network of cycle paths, supporting the use of car-sharing, carpooling, bike sharing, electric mobility and completing and integrating tramway network. These actions produced different and important improvements in the area. First of all, citizen started to modify their behavior walking, running, cycling, using the public transport service, so living the city in a completely different way. But it is not all. Coni et al. [24] identify and analyze further benefits for private traffic, for public traffic, for safety and for users. They find a reduction in inter-municipal private traffic (of 8,2%) and in intra-municipal private traffic (of 9,1%), in reducing of travel time (an average of 20%) and an increase of commercial speed on the main roads of the city. Passengers on public transport increased of 23% in 5 years and traffic safety also improved: accident rate decreased by 32% in 7 years. Also, the Automatic Vehicle Location system on buses produced an improvement of punctuality and information of the public transport service for users [25]. Thanks to these efforts, all CTM's routes have the service quality certified according to European Norms [26].

Currently, CTM manages 30 Bus lines, 1 electric bus line, a fleet of 276 buses and a network of 432 km long by the support of ITSs.

CTM is adapting the stops to allow and facilitate access on busses to people with disabilities. Several stops are equipped with a manual platform for getting on and off the bus. All buses are equipped with low floor, handrails, priority seating facilities, wheelchairs space and real time audible and visual information.

Another CTM service that meets the difficulties of disadvantaged passengers is the Amico Bus: it is a "door to door" and on-call bus service, funded by the Autonomous Region of Sardinia, and it integrates the ordinary public transport offer [27].

3   The Survey

The data examined in this paper were collected during a survey conducted in July 2019 on CTM fleet. Sampling was carried out by 8 observers, who carried out surveys during weekdays in three consecutive weeks. The survey campaign was conducted on 26 outward and return routes for a total of 198 rides.

The questionnaire administered to users was organized into four sections but for quality analysis the authors examined just two:

1. General data;
2. Data related to the quality of service in turn divided into Expected and Perceived.

The questions were formulated in closed mode. This solution allows, during the processing phase, to analyze the collected data appropriately aggregating the responses obtained by passengers. The type of closed response guarantees clarity in the answers and simplify analysis process. In addition, with this type of survey, the interlocutor is facilitated in filling in the questionnaire since he does not have to think about how to write the answers.

Section General Data reported information on observers (identification code, date and time), line (name, number of vehicle, direction, stop of getting on) interviewed (gender, age, educational qualification, residence, profession and position during the interview).

This paper reports the analysis on data related to the quality of service, referred to quality expected (or desired) and quality perceived.

More precisely, the part dealing with the quality included 2 sets of 23 questions each (see Fig. 2), evaluated on a 1 to 10 scale (1 = the worst; 10 = the best). The first set was designed to show the importance given to the attributes investigated. The questions, referred to the urban public transport in general, were formulated as follows: "On a scale from 1 to 10, how important would you consider to be the (name the attribute) within the urban public transport system as a whole?" The second set of questions was aimed at discovering the degree of perceived satisfaction toward the attributes analyzed at bus line level. The questions were formulated as follows: "On a scale from 1 to 10, how satisfied are you of the (name the attribute) with reference to the (name the urban bus route where the interview was held)?" The difference between importance and perceived satisfaction provided the gap score, that is, the degree of criticality as perceived by the average rider using the system within the Cagliari's metropolitan area. As already mentioned, our scale ranged from 1 to 10 (10 points scale), despite the majority of applications adopting a 5 or 7 Likert scale. The motivating reason to adopt a 1 to 10 scale is its adoption in the Italian scholastic evaluation method. Thus, the authors assume that, for the interviewed passengers, it is easier to provide ratings from 1 to 10, rather than the 1 to 5 or 1 to 7. Nevertheless, Dawes [28] pointed out the similar reliability of different scales from a statistical viewpoint, even if more options tend to lead to somewhat lower scores. However, the choice of a 1–10 scale does not influence the generality of the method, which is effective using any scale range.

During the investigation campaign, 754 questionnaires were administered and acquired.

On a scale from 1 to 10, how important would you consider to be the following attributes within the urban public transport system as a whole?		On a scale from 1 to 10, how satisfied are you of the following attributes with reference to this urban bus route?	
Nl	Low noise levels produced by vehicles	**Nl**	Low noise levels produced by vehicles
Cv	Cleaning of vehicles	**Cv**	Cleaning of vehicles
Pb	Ease to find a seat on board	**Pb**	Ease to find a seat on board
Ss	Stop status (cleaning, seats, bus shelter)	**Ss**	Stop status (cleaning, seats, bus shelter)
P	Punctuality and regularity of service	**P**	Punctuality and regularity of service
Gi	General information presence	**Gi**	General information presence
Ut	Update on timetable and frequency during stops	**Ut**	Update on timetable and frequency during stops
UtA	Update on timetable and frequency by App	**UtA**	Update on timetable and frequency by App
Ur	Update on ride during stops	**Ur**	Update on ride during stops
UrA	Update on ride by App	**UrA**	Update on ride by App
Fi	Information on fares	**Fi**	Information on fares
S	Presence of safety information	**S**	Presence of safety information
F	Frequency	**F**	Frequency
Tt	Travel time	**Tt**	Travel time
Eb	Ease of buying tickets / passes	**Eb**	Ease of buying tickets / passes
Ev	Ease of validating ticket	**Ev**	Ease of validating ticket
Dsa	Driver's driving style (acceleration and braking)	**Dsa**	Driver's driving style (acceleration and braking)
Dsc	Driver's driving style (Left and right curves)	**Dsc**	Driver's driving style (Left and right curves)
Dsj	Driving style of the drivers (jerks along the route)	**Dsj**	Driving style of the drivers (jerks along the route)
C	Courtesy of employees (drivers, call centers, administrative staff)	**C**	Courtesy of employees (drivers, call centers, administrative staff)
A	Appearance of staff (uniform, identification card)	**A**	Appearance of staff (uniform, identification card)
Cs	Conditions of supports to stand	**Cs**	Conditions of supports to stand
H	Hazard prevention (fire extinguisher, hammer, interior lighting)	**H**	Hazard prevention (fire extinguisher, hammer, interior lighting)

(left column marked *Quality EXPECTED*, right column marked *Quality PERCEIVED*)

Fig. 2. Full list of quality characteristics

4 Methodology

In this section, a simple framework for analyzing quality of transport service is presented. Figure 3 shows the four levels on which the quality of transport service analysis was organized: 1. Data collection; 2. Selection of significant attribute for over 65 years old users; 3. Analysis on expected and perceived data for all users and for over 65 years old users; 4. Comparison of results.

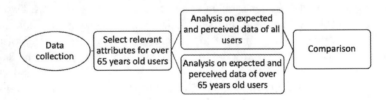

Fig. 3. The proposed framework for analyzing quality of transport service

Data were collected by the questionnaire described in Sect. 3. It was administered to passengers on board. Users had to express a judgment on 23 transport service characteristics assessing them on the basis of the importance they gave to each of them and referring on the specific line they were using. Their evaluations have been collected and reordered in a spreadsheet, separating Expected/Desired data from Perceived data.

In literature, there is a lack of methodologies to objectively determining a set of key significant quality indicators for monitoring the public transport quality. Just Barabino et al. [29] propose a robust methodology for identifying and selecting key quality indicators using both data collected through international surveys and Monte Carlo simulation methods. The attributes reported in the questionnaire correspond to these indicators.

For this study, the authors selected only 18 of the 23 transport service characteristics: 1. Low noise levels produced by vehicles (Nl), 2. Cleaning of vehicles (Cv), 3. Ease to find a seat on board (Pb), 4. Stop status (cleaning, seats, bus shelter) (Ss), 5. Punctuality and regularity of service (P), 6. General information presence (Gi), 7. Update on timetable and frequency during stops (Ut), 8. Update on ride during stops (Ur), 9. Information on fares (Fi), 10. Presence of safety information (S), 11. Frequency (F), 12. Travel time (Tt), 13. Ease of buying tickets/passes (Eb), 14. Ease of validating ticket (Ev), 15. Courtesy of employees (drivers, call centers, administrative staff) (C), 16. Appearance of staff (uniform, identification card) (A), 17. Conditions of supports to stand (Cs) and 18. Hazard prevention (fire extinguisher, hammer, interior lighting) (H).

Elderly's answers on the *Update on timetable and frequency by App* and *Update on ride by App* attributes were less than 30%, so these items were excluded from the study because they were irrelevant.

While *Driver's driving style (acceleration and braking)*, *Driver's driving style (Left and right curves)* and *Driving style of the drivers (jerks along the route)* attributes were not considered because they were analyzed in another work.

First of all, expected data of all users were examined to highlight if the chosen attributes were fundamental requirements for passengers. The number of answers for each score and each attribute were counted; the higher the number of responses on the highest ratings, for a given characteristic, the greater the importance the user gives to that characteristic.

Then to establish an order of priority among characteristics, weights of every characteristics have been determined, on the basis of users' responses and the degree of preference.

Let

Nc_{ji} be the number of times that the characteristic j has received i-th judgment; the score of preference of the j-th travel characteristic Sc_j is given by the following expression:

$$Sc_j = \sum_i \left[Nc_{j,i} * (i) \right] \tag{1}$$

So, the weight of the j-th characteristic is given by the incidence that the score of preference of the j-th travel characteristic has on the total:

$$W_j = \frac{Sc_j}{\sum_j Sc_j} \tag{2}$$

The same analysis was conducted on perceived data of all users and results were compared with expected data, in order to understand whether the offer of the transport service corresponds to user expectations or not. The authors applied SERVQUAL methodology to investigate the difference between qualitative perceptions and expectations. The SERVQUAL methodology was introduced by Parasuraman et al. [30–32] and represents the most widely applied methodology to measure customers' perceived quality across the service industry. Moreover, it was recently applied in public transport [33]. The gap between perceived (P) and expected (E) quality was calculated for each attribute. This allows assessing the qualitative difference between what is actually observed and what would represent an "ideal" of service. The vast majority of studies adopting this methodology have produced negative gaps (P < E), because of the general inadequacy in meeting customers' expectations or the less than satisfactory degree of perceived quality. Such outcome is not surprising, given the high expectations normally held by the final users of a service and the not always linear relation between satisfaction and service performance [34].

The same procedure was repeated on expected and perceived data selecting only judgments of over 65 years old people.

Lastly, SERVQUAL gaps obtained considering all users' responses and selecting only over 65 years old users' ones were compared to draw conclusions.

5   Analysis on Expected and Perceived Quality Data

In this section, the authors specifically examine the answers of sample related to expected and perceived quality expressed by the eighteen selected attributes.

These judgments represent the degree of preference and were elaborated in order to determine weights that users assigned to each features of the travel in order to establish a priority scale between them.

5.1   General Users

First, the responses of all users were investigated. The analysis has produced results showed in Fig. 4 where how many users gave that judgment to a specific attribute are reported.

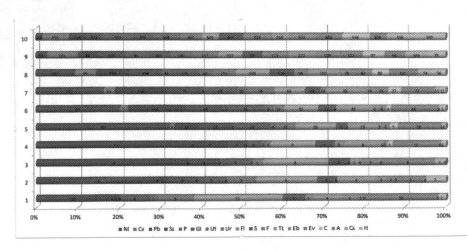

Fig. 4. Users responses on travel characteristics (expected)

Figure 4 shows that users assigned higher scores (between 8 to 10) to all chosen attributes. This result expresses the importance that sample entrusts to those characteristics of the public transport. In other words, this means that all users have a great expectation on public travel service.

On the basis of these responses and the degree of preference, weights of every characteristics have been determined.

Results are shown in Fig. 5. Looking at the obtained results, users assigned a higher weight to Punctuality and regularity of service (P), followed by Frequency (F) and Hazard prevention (H). So, these are more important travel service characteristics for surveyed people. At the last three position, there are Information on fares (Fi), Appearance of staff (A) and Low noise levels (Nl).

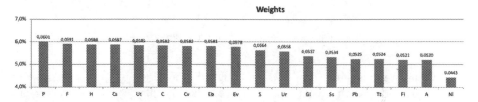

Fig. 5. Weights of characteristics of travel service (expected)

The same analysis was conducted on perceived data, that is on users' judgments related to the ride where they were. Findings are shown in Fig. 6.

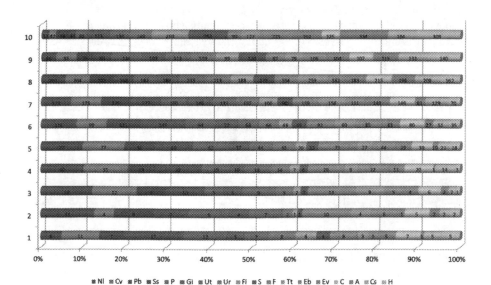

Fig. 6. Users responses on travel characteristics (perceived)

In this case, most of responses are concentrated in high ratings (between 6 and 10) for all attributes, but it is also true that all attributes received low degree of preference (between 1 and 5).

Starting from these responses and calculating weights of every characteristics, results are shown in Fig. 7:

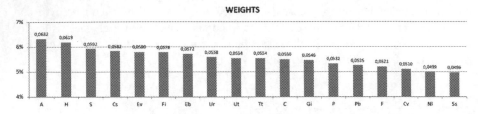

Fig. 7. Weights of characteristics of travel service (perceived)

Looking at the obtained results, users assigned a higher weight to Appearance of staff (A), Hazard prevention (H) and Presence of safety information (S). At the last three position, there are: Cleaning of vehicles (Cv), Low noise levels (Nl), Stop status (Ss).

5.2 Vulnerable Users

The authors applied the same analysis to expected and perceived data related to vulnerable users, considering passengers over 65 years old.

The analysis on expected data has produced results showed in following Fig. 8: the majority of users over 65 years old assigned highest score to all chosen attributes, so they express a great expectation on public travel service.

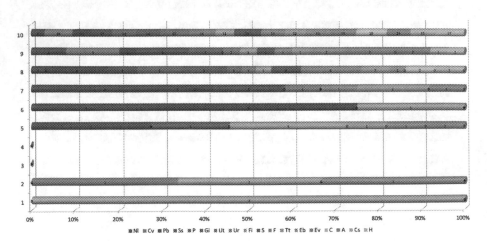

Fig. 8. Vulnerable users' responses on travel characteristics (expected)

Weights

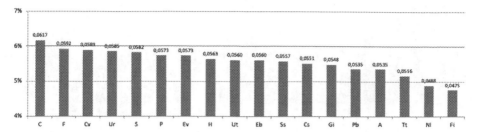

Fig. 9. Weights of characteristics of travel service for vulnerable users (expected)

Looking at weights (Fig. 9) vulnerable users gave a great importance to Courtesy (C) and to Frequency (F), followed by Cleaning of vehicles (Cv). The least important attribute is Information on fares (Fi) preceded by Low noise levels (Nl) and Travel time (Tt).

While, the analysis on perceived data has produced results showed in Fig. 10.

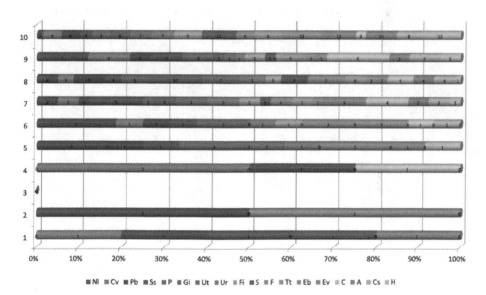

Nl Cv Pb Ss P Gi Ut Ur Fi S F Tt Eb Ev C A Cs H

Fig. 10. Vulnerable users' responses on travel characteristics (perceived)

Vulnerable users assign higher scores (between 7 to 10) to all chosen attributes. So, it means that they are satisfied by transport service. Looking at weights (Fig. 11) it can be notice that Ease of buying and validation tickets/passes (Eb, Ev) and Hazard prevention (H) are the characteristics which obtain higher scores. Conversely, Ease to find a seat on board (Pb), Stop status (Ss) and Low noise levels produced by vehicles (Nl) are at the end of the ranking.

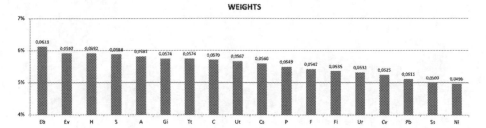

Fig. 11. Weights of characteristics of travel service for vulnerable users (perceived)

5.3 Comparison

Results on data analysis are summarized in Table 1. First four columns of data report average scores for each attribute. It can be notice that the overall average result indicates a substantial lack of inefficiencies, with an average perceived quality along rides investigated of 7,76 for general users and of 8,42 for over 65 years old users (up against expectations as high as 9,04 for general users and 9,31 for vulnerable users). Elderly customer's evaluations, both on perceived and expected quality, are always higher than those of the rest of all users. These outcomes show the particularly high qualitative standards demanded by public transport users in Cagliari, a feature which might imply increased difficulties in the provision of a service able to duly accommodate needs and requirements. Surprisingly enough, no single attribute registers particular criticism, as testified by average scores consistently higher than 6.5.

Next the gaps were computed to investigate the difference between qualitative perceptions and expectations. Results for each attribute are illustrated in the sixth and seventh column of Table 1.

Table 1. Average and SERVQUAL gap scores of attributes

Attributes	Quality perceived (P)		Quality expected (E)		General users	Vulnerable users	Zcal P-E
	General users	Vulnerable users	General users	Vulnerable users	P-E	P-E	
Nl	6,96	7,05	7,22	7,45	−0,25	−0,44	0,19
Cv	7,04	7,84	9,41	9,84	−2,37	−1,90	−0,82
Pb	7,28	8,06	8,51	8,95	−1,24	−1,25	0,01
Ss	6,86	7,47	8,64	9,32	−1,78	−1,75	−0,06
P	7,37	8,21	9,74	9,58	−2,40	−1,30	−2,82
Gi	7,83	8,58	8,74	9,16	−1,17	−0,55	−1,64
Ut	7,69	8,47	9,50	9,89	−1,83	−0,85	−1,52
Ur	7,80	8,39	9,06	9,30	−1,30	−1,75	1,09
Fi	8,35	8,94	8,51	7,95	−0,45	0,05	−1,03

(*continued*)

Table 1. (*continued*)

Attributes	Quality perceived (P)		Quality expected (E)		General users P-E	Vulnerable users P-E	Zcal P-E
	General users	Vulnerable users	General users	Vulnerable users			
S	8,43	8,79	9,18	9,74	−0,95	−0,90	−0,10
F	7,22	7,70	9,59	9,40	−2,38	−1,70	−1,52
Tt	7,75	9,06	8,60	9,11	−0,85	−0,05	−2,12
Eb	7,93	9,16	9,49	9,37	−1,53	−0,20	−2,53
Ev	8,03	8,84	9,40	9,58	−1,36	−0,70	−2,52
C	7,65	8,10	9,48	9,80	−1,82	−1,70	−0,35
A	8,81	8,68	8,47	9,44	0,34	−0,25	1,58
Cs	8,11	8,83	9,59	9,72	−1,47	−0,80	−2,81
H	8,65	9,33	9,61	9,94	−0,97	−0,55	−1,37

As happens in the most SERVQUAL applications, Table 1 emphasizes the negative gaps between perceptions and expectations/importance. However, the presence of negative gaps is heavily influenced by the users' expectations, with different attributes scoring more than 8 in the 1 to 10 scale. Furthermore, the gap P-E, even if negative, derives from the difference of high average scores. The gap is positive for Appearance of staff (A), for general users, and Information on fares (Fi), for elderly users. For these two attributes, perceived quality exceeds desired one. Comparing P-E gaps obtained considering all users' responses and selecting only over 65 years old users' one, it can be noticed that vulnerable customers are more satisfied of public transport service than all. In general, these results let the authors believe that urban public transport within the Cagliari's metropolitan area can be described as qualitatively adequate with respect to each attribute analysed.

Finally, to investigate if the gaps statistically differ between these segments, a statistical significance analysis of a two-sample z-test between their means was also conducted at the 95% significance level, which corresponds a critical value (Zc) of 1,645. The calculated values (Zcal) are shown in the last column of Table 1. It can be noticed that only for six attributes (P, Gi, Tt; Eb, Ev and Cs) the observed value is greater than the critical one. Therefore, only for these six attributes, there is a significant difference between the evaluations of the sample made up only by the elderly and the total sample. Conversely, for the remaining attributes, the evaluations may be indifferently taken from the two segments.

6 Conclusions

The main purpose of this article is to analyze the quality expected and perceived of a public transportation system in particular referring to over 65 years old customers' viewpoint. Indeed, they belong to the category of vulnerable users who more often than others may have difficulty in moving and accessing to urban spaces. The study can be useful to public transport companies to identify what are the expectations and needs of vulnerable users in order to make the service more functioning, efficient and accessible to this category of customers. The purpose fits in the literature and in general objective of UN's 2030 Agenda which both underlines the need to make cities smart [35], sustainable [36], inclusive and accessible by means, for instance, a suitable public transport system for all.

The data examined in this paper were collected during a survey conducted in July 2019 on board of the buses of CTM, the public transport company of Cagliari. The study highlighted which are the most important attributes of a public transport service (PTS) for all users and over 65 years old passengers, and if the local PTS satisfy their expectations. The data analysis showed that, for all users, the most important features that the public transport service should offer are Punctuality and regularity of service (P), followed by Frequency (F) and Hazard prevention (H); while for elderly customers they are Courtesy (C) and Frequency (F), followed by Cleaning of vehicles (Cv).

The investigation on the degree of perceived satisfaction toward the attributes was conducted at bus route level. Appearance of staff (A), Hazard prevention (H) and Presence of safety information (S) attributes obtained higher scores for all users. While over 65 years old customers appreciated a lot Ease of buying and validation tickets/passes (Eb, Ev) and Hazard prevention (H).

The authors applied SERVQUAL methodology to investigate the difference between qualitative perceptions (P) and expectations (E). Gaps P-E are all negative (except for two attributes): as a rule, this means that public transport service doesn't meet users' expectations. But these results are heavily influenced by the users' expectations, with different attributes scoring more than 8. Furthermore, gap is calculated on high average ratings that pass the score of 6.5. Indeed, the overall average result indicates a substantial lack of inefficiencies, with an average perceived quality along rides investigated of 7,76 for general users and of 8,42 for over 65 years old users.

All that said the analysis let the authors believe that urban public transport within the Cagliari's metropolitan area can be described as qualitatively adequate with respect to each attribute analyzed.

Comparing P-E gaps obtained considering all users' responses and selecting only over 65 years old users' one, it can be noticed that vulnerable customers are more satisfied of public transport service than all.

However, if the CTM wanted to further improve, this analysis suggests that its management policy should focus on Punctuality (P), Frequency (F) and Vehicles Cleaning (Cv).

In a future research, safety and security concern could be explored. Older people are more vulnerable to injuries and they take longer to recover than younger people. So, safety on board represent a crucial issue for over 65 years old passengers. Safety on board is strictly correlated to driver behavior, hence expected and perceived safety requirements could be investigated by data on driver's driving style related to accelerations and brakings, right and left curves and vertical jolts. This data could be matched and compared with objective safety requisites measuring longitudinal and transversal accelerations, decelerations and speed, by means of a GPS on bus, to set safety and comfort threshold as in [37].

Acknowledgments. This study is supported by the MIUR (Ministry of Education, Universities and Research [Italy]) through two project entitled: the SMART CITY framework (project: PON04a2_00381 "CAGLIARI2020") and WEAKI TRANSIT: WEAK-demand areas Innovative TRANsport Shared services for Italian Towns (Project protocol: 20174ARRHT_004; CUP Code: F74I19001290001), financed with the PRIN 2017 (Research Projects of National Relevance) programme. We authorize the MIUR to reproduce and distribute reprints for Governmental purposes, notwithstanding any copyright notations thereon. Any opinions, findings and conclusions or recommendations expressed in this material are those of the authors, and do not necessarily reflect the views of the MIUR. Moreover, the authors are grateful CTM SpA, which made its data available for this study.

Author Contributions. Conceptualization, all; methodology and formal analysis, Francesca Maltinti, Nicoletta Rassu, Benedetto Barabino; introduction and literary review Francesca Maltinti and Chiara Garau; writing-original draft preparation, Francesca Maltinti; writing-review and editing Francesca Maltinti, Benedetto Barabino and Mauro Coni; visualization, all. All authors have read and agreed to the published version of the manuscript.

References

1. An official website of the European Union. https://ec.europa.eu/sustainable-development/goal11_en. Accessed 18 Feb 2020
2. Gewalt, S.: Wirtschaftsfaktor Alter - Körperliche Veränderungen verstehen, Angebot anpassen. RKW Kompetenzzentrum, Frankfurt (2011)
3. Mollenkopf, H., Flaschenträger, P.: Erhaltung von Mobilität im Alter, Bundesministerium für Familie, Senioren, Frauen und Jugend (Hrsg.), Stuttgart (2001)
4. Collia, D.V., Sharp, J., Giesbrecht, L.: The 2001 national household travel survey: a look into the travel patterns of older Americans. J. Saf. Res. **34**(4), 461–470 (2003). https://doi.org/10.1016/j.jsr.2003.10.001
5. Kim, S., Ulfarsson, G.F.: Travel mode choice of the elderly: effects of personal, household, neighborhood, and trip characteristics. J. Transp. Res. Board **1894**(1), 117–126 (2004). https://doi.org/10.3141/1894-13
6. Hess, D.B.: Access to public transit and its influence on ridership for older adults in two US cities. J. Transp. Land Use **2**(1), 3–27 (2009). https://doi.org/10.5198/jtlu.v2i1.11
7. Kim, S.: Assessing mobility in an aging society: personal and built environment factors associated with older people's subjective transportation deficiency in the US. Transp. Res. Part F Traffic Psychol. Behav. **14**(5), 422–429 (2011). https://doi.org/10.1016/j.trf.2011.04.011
8. Newbold, K.B., Scott, D.M., Spinney, J.E.L., Kanaroglou, P., Paez, A.: Travel behavior within Canadas older population: a cohort analysis. J. Transp. Geogr. **13**(1), 340–351 (2005). https://doi.org/10.1016/j.jtrangeo.2004.07.007
9. Mercado, R., Paez, A.: Determinants of distance traveled with a focus on the elderly: a multilevel analysis in the Hamilton CMA Canada. J. Transp. Geogr. **17**(1), 65–76 (2009). https://doi.org/10.1016/j.jtrangeo.2008.04.012
10. Paez, A., Scott, D., Potoglou, P., Kanarogou, P.: Elderly mobility: demographic and spatial analysis of trip making in the Hamilton CMA, Canada. Urban Stud. **44**(1), 123–146 (2007). http://orca.cf.ac.uk/id/eprint/37320
11. Currie, G., Delbosc, A.: Exploring public transport usage trends in an ageing population. Transportation **37**(1), 151–164 (2009). https://doi.org/10.1007/s11116-009-9224-x

12. Schwanen, T., Dijst, M., Dieleman, F.M.: Leisure trips of senior citizens: determinants of modal choice. Tijdschrift voor Economische en Sociale Geografie **92**(3), 347–360 (2001). https://doi.org/10.1111/1467-9663.00161

13. Raeside, H., Li, R., Chen, T., McQuaid, R.: Population ageing, gender and the transportation system. Res. Transp. Econ. **34**(1), 39–47 (2012). https://doi.org/10.1016/j.retrec.2011.12.007

14. Fobker, S., Grotz, R.: Everyday mobility of elderly people in different urban settings: the example of the city of Bonn, Germany. Urban Stud. **43**(1), 99–118 (2006)

15. Davey, J.A.: Older people and transport: coping without a car. Ageing Soc. **27**(1), 49–65 (2007). https://doi.org/10.1017/S0144686X06005332

16. Gabriel, Z., Bowling, A.: Quality of life from the perspectives of older people. Ageing Soc. **24**(1), 675–691 (2004). https://doi.org/10.1017/S0144686X03001582

17. Metz, D.: Transport policy for an ageing population. Transp. Rev. **23**(4), 375–386 (2003). https://doi.org/10.1080/0144164032000048573

18. Fatima, K., Moridpour, S.: Measuring public transport accessibility for elderly. In: Proceedings of 6th International Conference on Traffic and Logistic Engineering (ICTLE 2018), Les Ulis (2019). https://doi.org/10.1145/3321619.3321651

19. Borges, I.: The added value of accessible public transport for all in the context of demographic ageing. In: Proceedings of XXIII World Road Congress, Paris (2012)

20. Marsden, G., Jopson, A., Cattan, M., Woodward, J.: Transport and older people: integrating transport planning tools with user needs. In: Proceedings of 11th World Conference on Transport Research, Leeds (2007)

21. Koffman, D., Richard, R., Pfeiffer, A., Chapman, S.: Funding the Public Transportation Needs of an Aging Population. American Public Transportation Association, San Francisco (2010)

22. Shrestha, B.P., Millonig, A., Hounsell, N.B., McDonald, M.: Review of public transport needs of older people in European context. J. Popul. Ageing **10**(4), 343–361 (2016). https://doi.org/10.1007/s12062-016-9168-9

23. CTM homepage. https://www.ctmcagliari.it/notizia.php?id=606. Accessed 05 Mar 2020

24. Coni, M., Garau, C., Pinna, F.: How has Cagliari changed its citizens in smart citizens? Exploring the influence of ITS technology on urban social interactions. In: Gervasi, O., et al. (eds.) ICCSA 2018. LNCS, vol. 10962, pp. 573–588. Springer, Cham (2018). https://doi.org/10.1007/978-3-319-95168-3_39

25. Tilocca, P., et al.: Managing data and rethinking applications in an innovative mid-sized bus fleet. Transp. Res. Procedia **25**, 1904–1924 (2017). https://doi.org/10.1016/j.trpro.2017.05.184

26. Barabino, B.: Automatic recognition of "low-quality" vehicles and bus stops in bus services. Public Transp. **10**(2), 257–289 (2018). https://doi.org/10.1007/s12469-018-0180-8

27. CTM homepage. https://www.ctmcagliari.it.. Accessed 15 Dec 2019

28. Dawes, J.: Do data characteristics change according to the number of scale points used? Int. J. Market Res. **50**(1), 61–77 (2008)

29. Barabino, B., Cabras, N.A., Conversano, C., Olivo, A.: An integrated approach to select key quality indicators in transit services. Soc. Ind. Res. **149**, 1045–1080 (2020). https://doi.org/10.1007/s11205-020-02284-0

30. Parasuraman, A., Zeithaml, V.A.L., Berry, L.: A conceptual model of service quality and its implication for future research. J. Market. **49**(4), 41–50 (1985). https://doi.org/10.2307/1251430

31. Parasuraman, A., Zeithaml, V.A., Berry, L.L.: SERVQUAL: a multiple-item scale for measuring customer perceptions of service quality. J. Retail. **64**(1), 12–40 (1988)

32. Parasuraman, A., Berry, L.L., Zeithaml, V.A.: Refinement and reassessment of the SERVQUAL scale. J. Retail. **67**(4), 420–450 (1991)

33. Barabino, B., Deiana, E., Tilocca, P.: Measuring service quality in urban bus transport: a modified SERVQUAL approach. I. J. Qual. Serv. Sci. **4**(3), 238–252 (2012). https://doi.org/10.1108/17566691211269567

34. Friman, M., Fellesson, M.: Service supply and customer satisfaction in public transportation: the quality paradox. J. Public Transp. **12**(4), 57–69 (2009). https://doi.org/10.5038/2375-0901.12.4.4

35. Dembski, F., Wössner, U., Letzgus, M., Ruddat, M., Yamu, C.: Urban digital twins for smart cities and citizens: the case study of Herrenberg, Germany. Sustainability **12**(6), 2307 (2020). https://doi.org/10.3390/su12062307

36. Garau, C., Desogus, G., Zamperlin, P.: Governing technology-based urbanism: degeneration to technocracy or development to progressive planning? In: Aurigi, A., Willis, K.S. (eds.) The Routledge Companion to Smart Cities, Routledge, pp. 157–173 (2020). https://doi.org/10.4324/9781315178387

37. Barabino, B., Coni, M., Olivo, A., Pungillo, G., Rassu, N.: Standing passenger comfort: a new scale for evaluating the real-time driving style of bus transit services. IEEE Trans. Intell. Transp. Syst. **20**(12), 4665–4678 (2019). https://doi.org/10.1109/tits.2019.2921807

Accessibility to Local Public Transport in Cagliari with Focus on the Elderly

Rassu Nicoletta[1]([⊠]) [iD], Francesca Maltinti[1] [iD], Mauro Coni[1] [iD],
Chiara Garau[1] [iD], Benedetto Barabino[2] [iD], Francesco Pinna[1] [iD],
and Roberto Devoto[1] [iD]

[1] Department of Civil and Environmental Engineering
and Architecture (DICAAR), University of Cagliari,
via Marengo 2, 09123 Cagliari, Italy
{nicoletta.rassu,maltinti,mconi,cgarau,fpinna,
devotor}@unica.it
[2] Department of Civil, Environmental, Architectural
Engineering and Mathematics (DICATAM), University of Brescia,
Via Brianze 43, 25123 Brescia, Italy
benedetto.barabino@unibs.it

Abstract. The principle that inspired the authors in the preparation of this study is the concept of "*expanded accessibility*" in terms of usability of spaces, places and services, for their users. From here, in the face of the periodic survey work carried out on local public transport vehicles managed by the transport company of the Municipality of Cagliari, the characteristics of the overall sample have been designated. The data sample is analyzed with focus on elderly people. Some statements are reported to show how much and how these passenger use public transport and related technological services. Finally this segment of demand is compared with the complementary one (under 65 years). The outcomes show that the key elements that distinguish the two segments concern multimodality and technological services.

Keywords: Elderly · Public transport · Travel behavior · Accessibility

1 Introduction

Accessible transport and the guarantee of movement are the passport for a daily life characterized by independence for all age groups. Mobility means having transport services, or the set of network infrastructures, means and operating procedures (e.g. ticket offices, information etc.), both in spatial and temporal scale as well as information; knowing how to use them, being able to do it and having the means to pay for them are the attributes that distinguish its accessibility [1].

Accessible transport practices are promoted through the series of International Conferences on Mobility and Transport for the Elderly and Disabled (COMOTRED), supported by the US Research Board since 1978. This initiative is recognized as the world's leading forum for the exchange of results of policy research and approaches [2].

© Springer Nature Switzerland AG 2020
O. Gervasi et al. (Eds.): ICCSA 2020, LNCS 12255, pp. 690–705, 2020.
https://doi.org/10.1007/978-3-030-58820-5_50

The growing progress in medicine and the improvement of the standard of living have had a positive impact on people's life expectancy, which has increased worldwide. The natural aging process is accompanied by physiological and customary changes that are reflected in the mobility choices [3]. With age, older people tend to make shorter and fewer trips than other age groups [4].

They begin to walk more and use public transport. In 2008 a survey claimed that after 55 years of age, the use of the car constantly decreases, while for those 75 years old and more, walking and public transport become a valid alternatives [5]. In support of this, the authors believe that in addition to the physiological changes typical of age, there is also a social reason: the end of full-time work, i.e. one of the main reasons for systematic moves.

However, due to the same dynamics, the improvement in health and income levels also had as a downside a more active, more independent and more "*mobile*" population [6] also in terms of car ownership and use [7, 8]. While studies highlight the importance of mobility of older people for their social inclusion [9] and for a good quality of life [10, 11], there is no lack of concerns about the implications that such mobility can have on society both in terms of congestion [12, 13], safety and environment.

In fact, in order to maintain their active lifestyle it is necessary to guarantee them access to public transport. This would allow elderly to continue using goods and services when they are no longer able to drive or simply as an alternative to using a private vehicle [3]. In this regard, it is therefore essential that public transport structures are functional to provide acceptable levels of mobility specific to their needs [14].

A concrete answer in this sense is given by the new Intelligent Transportation Systems applied to the public transport system. ITS play a leading role in that they characterize transport in an innovative and sustainable way, for a better use of urban space and time, optimizing transport network, both in terms of capacity and travel time reliability [15, 16], with inevitable positive externalities on the quality of life of people [17].

These are the premises of the study conducted by the authors who sees the city of Cagliari as a reference scenario and its public transport system as a setting in which the users of the service move. Thanks to the new strategic plan of 2011, developed in partnership between the Municipality of Cagliari, the University of Cagliari and the CTM (i.e. the Public Transport Company), the public transport system has undergone important interventions aimed at improving its efficiency in terms of travel times, punctuality and its service quality [17–19].

The investments on the local public transport network and digital infrastructures in 5 years (2010 ÷ 2015) generated an increase in the flow of passengers by 23%. Among these interventions the creation of friendly applications and devices, attracted new users, especially among the younger ones. Coni et al. [17], concluded that all the interventions implemented by the public administration through ITS and urban policies towards sustainable mobility, have improved the quality of the environment and, consequently, in the quality of life of their citizens. The citizens, in fact, manages part of the movements, some systematic, using more sustainable modes like public transport, walking and cycling. It is in this context that the study conducted by the authors fits.

This paper investigates some characteristics on travel behavior of the 65 years old segment using data collected by an intercept on-board survey of passengers of CTM.

First, the authors examined some characteristics of users in general. Subsequently, the analysis focused on weak users, meaning the over 65 years segment, with the aim of discover their characteristics. Their travel behavior and the rate of use of technological services are examined in order to highlight, impediments to accessing the service in its complexity, if any The latter could be brought to the attention of the service operator that could convey them in order to make the service more efficient. Once the data were acquired, they are analyzed using by descriptive statistics.

The remainder of this paper is organized as follows. Section 2 presents the context analysis with the nature of the investigation carried out, with particular reference to the section of the questionnaire. The section dedicated to the methodology concludes this section. Section 3 shows the results of the analysis of the general characteristics and travel behavior for both the whole sample and the segment of the elderly. Finally, Sect. 4 provides conclusions and draw future perspectives.

2   Data and Method

The study was conducted on CTM, the public transport company of Cagliari. Cagliari is the most important and densely populated town in Sardinia (Italy). It has 154.108 inhabitants, and it is the 26th town more populous of Italy. Its metropolitan area counts 431.038 inhabitants. Starting from 2011, Cagliari and its 17 municipalities adopted a new strategic plan to improve local public transport network. This plan was developed with the University of Cagliari and provided using of ITS, improving lines and fleet buses, forbidding traffic cars in the historical center and promoting places and pedestrian areas, developing a network of cycle paths, supporting the use of car-sharing, carpooling bike sharing, electric mobility and completing and integrating tramway network [17]. Currently, CTM operates public transportation by 271 vehicles (i.e., buses and trolleys) and serves approximately 40.8 million trips a year. Moreover, these vehicles travel over 12.4 million km per year along 34 routes [20]. Its routes operate in a heterogeneous context including residential areas, large industrial sites, shopping centers, entertainment activities and service companies. Moreover, since 2011, CTM makes a bi-annual intercept survey, designed to elicit socio-demographic, travel behavior and customer satisfaction information [21].

CTM has a control room which coordinates and monitors all buses on the road in real time and the information points. Users can download an App where they can buy tickets, check the real time of bus arrivals, find the path to reach a destination or the routes list as well as other information about specific services or about changes in the services. On CTM Website, it is possible to find information about the company, routes, tickets and transport pass, the path to reach a destination, statistics, traffic and other information about specific services. Every bus stop is equipped with intelligent bus-stop sign which provides the time of bus arrivals in real time [17, 18].

2.1   The Survey

The survey was conducted in July 2019. The sampling was carried out by 8 total observers, four out of these observers were surveyors of CTM and 4 were technicians from the DICAAr (Department of Civil Engineering, Environment and Architecture). They who carried out the surveys during the weekdays in three consecutive weeks, for a total of 10 days.

CTM collected data for this experimentation on a pool of 26 routes, which are representative of the general bus network regarding passengers, lengths (6 ÷ 18 km), vehicle types (7 ÷ 18 m) and capacities (24 ÷ 170 passengers). A total of 198 trips was investigated.

The questionnaire administered to passengers is organized into four sections, only the first two contain the data useful for the purposes of the current study:

- The first section is general and reports on contextual information, including the date, time, route investigated and a question regarding the passengers' agreement to participate in the survey;
- The second section deals with socio-demographic attributes, including gender, age, educational qualifications, employment, car availability and reason for using the bus and trip-related attributes, including trip purpose, in-vehicle time, other transit systems used, and bus use frequency;
- The third and fourth sections deal respectively with the quality of the service and the fare evasion.

All questions were formulated in closed form (i.e. see Fig. 2). This solution allows, during the processing phase, to be able to analyze the collected data, appropriately aggregating the responses of passengers. Therefore, the type of closed response enforces the dual need to clarity responses and simplify the process. Furthermore, this type of question structure does not worry the interlocutor since he/she does not have to think about how to formulate the answer, since the latter is contained among the proposed options [22].

2.2 Methodology

The method of analysis is represented in Fig. 1.

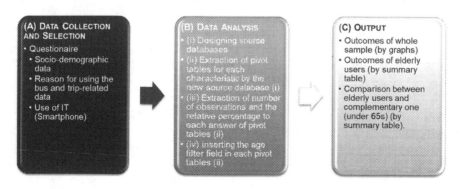

Fig. 1. Method of analysis

(A) Data Collection and Selection

During the survey campaign, 754 questionnaires were administered and acquired. Collected data were loaded into a database. According to the purpose of the work, the data analyzed concern:

- Socio-demographic characteristics: gender, age, residence, education and profession;
- Travel behavior: travel purpose, frequency of use, how he/she traveled (sitting or standing) and in what position of the bus, travel ticket, use and type of other transport operators, ownership of private vehicle and why to choose of bus for the trip (Fig. 2);
- Info mobility use: smartphone ownership, the utilization rate of the App, the travel ticket purchase via App and the info-channel (Fig. 2).

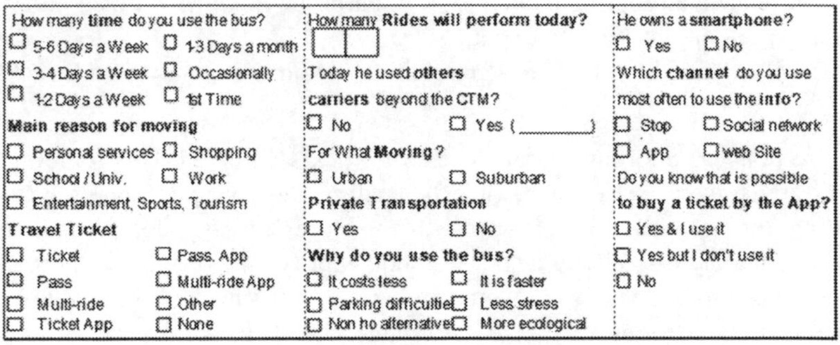
How many **time** do you use the bus?
☐ 5-6 Days a Week ☐ 1-3 Days a month
☐ 3-4 Days a Week ☐ Occasionally
☐ 1-2 Days a Week ☐ 1st Time
Main reason for moving
☐ Personal services ☐ Shopping
☐ School / Univ. ☐ Work
☐ Entertainment, Sports, Tourism
Travel Ticket
☐ Ticket ☐ Pass. App
☐ Pass ☐ Multi-ride App
☐ Multi-ride ☐ Other
☐ Ticket App ☐ None

How many **Rides will perform today?**
Today he used **others carriers** beyond the CTM?
☐ No ☐ Yes (________)
For What **Moving**?
☐ Urban ☐ Suburban
Private Transportation
☐ Yes ☐ No
Why do you use the bus?
☐ It costs less ☐ It is faster
☐ Parking difficultie ☐ Less stress
☐ Non ho alternative ☐ More ecological

He owns a **smartphone**?
☐ Yes ☐ No
Which **channel** do you use most often to use the **info**?
☐ Stop ☐ Social network
☐ App ☐ web Site
Do you know that is possible **to buy a ticket by the App?**
☐ Yes & I use it
☐ Yes but I don't use it
☐ No

Fig. 2. Travel behavior data and info mobility use

(B) Data Analysis

The method used to process the data is as follows. The questionnaire responses were uploaded into a database with dimensions $i \times j$ (755×94). Columns j contain the characteristics, rows i contain the answers of the sample.

It should be noted that the questionnaire had sections that were not taken into consideration in the present study, as they are not necessary for our current analysis. The sections rejected regard the quality and fare evasion. Therefore, (*i*) the source database for our processing has $i \times y$ dimensions (with $y < j$), where y indicates the number of characteristics analyzed. The latter are those described in section (A).

The data analysis (*ii*) was done by extracting a pivot table for each characteristic y from the new source database. For each pivot table (iii) and for each answer the number of observations b and the relative percentage p were extracted. Each pivot report was sorted in descending order of the number of observations b. The comparison between the elderly and the remaining segment was made (*iv*) using the pivots created, by inserting the age filter field in each of them. Proceeding in this way the value fields of number of observations b and percentage p were automatically updated.

The data were analyzed through descriptive statistics.

(C) Output

The results of the analysis are shown first for the whole sample. For these, it was preferred to analyze each attribute by a graph that contained the answers given. The results on the elderly were reported in a summary sheet, where for each characteristic the results of this segment and of its complementary (under 65 years) were reported. For the main characteristics that had comparable answers, the two samples (over and under 65 years) were examined through a statistical significance analysis of the proportions at a significance level of 95%, which corresponds to a value critical (Z_c) of 1,96.

3 Results and Discussion

This section reports the results of the analysis. It is divided into two parts: the first discusses the results related to the overall sample; the second one comments the results related to the elderly, both individually but also comparing them with the complementary segment.

3.1 Overall Users

General Data

The first 7 queries of the questionnaire asked for general user information. The analysis of the answers has given following results.

The gender distribution of the interviewees shows that female sex is the most frequent class (63% of the sample). Looking at the age, most of the users are young people aged between 18 and 25 (39%) and younger (21%). The 17% is between 26 and 35 years old and the 12% among 36 and 50 years old. The remaining 12% is over 51 years old (Fig. 3 – left side).

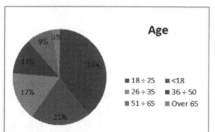
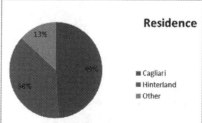

Fig. 3. Age and residence

About 49% of the sample resides in the city center, 38% in the hinterland and 13% in the neighboring municipalities (Fig. 3 – right side).

The whole sample (~99%) has a middle school certificate (Fig. 4 – left side). Out of these, 45% have a diploma and 16% have a degree. Half of sample that has a middle school license (53%) is still in a school age (<18) or are students undergraduate (Fig. 4 – right side).

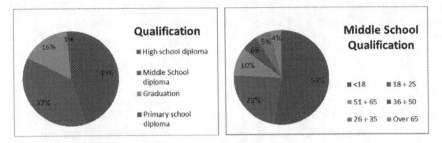

Fig. 4. Qualification and middle school qualification by age

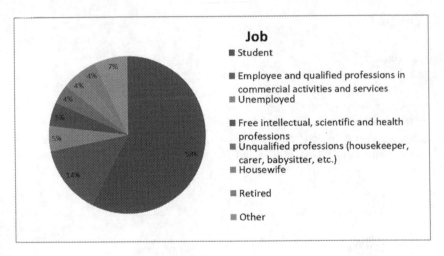

Fig. 5. Job

Confirming the above, Fig. 5 shows that students are the category most represented (58%), percentage that rises to 88% if the analysis is restricted to the age group under 25 years of age. Then there are employees (14%) followed by the unemployed and freelancers, with the same percentage (5%) and unqualified professions, housewives and retirees (4%). The remaining categories were merged into a single class called Other (7%).

The 91% of the sample interviewed was seated and the remaining 8% was standing. The major part of the sample (56%) stayed in the rear area of the bus while 29% was in the front. Only 14% was in the center of the bus.

Travel Behavior

The 80% of the sample uses public transport respectively for leisure and sport (35%), for work (23%) and to reach high schools and universities (22%). The remaining 20% uses public transport for personal services (18%) and for shopping (2%) (Fig. 6).

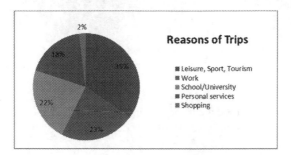

Fig. 6. Reasons of trips

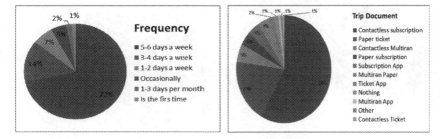

Fig. 7. Frequency and trip document

The analysis showed that the sample is highly represented by regular passenger who use the service regularly during the week and the day (Fig. 7). Specifically, left side of Fig. 7 shows that 86% of sampled passengers travel from 3 to 6 days during the week, respectively 72% between 5–6 days and 14% between 3–4 days and from 1 to 4 daily journeys. Analyzing trip document (Fig. 7 right side), it can be noticed an attitude to the use of a travel pass in various forms: 58% of passengers uses the contactless subscription and 8% uses the other solutions, both on paper and via the app, both in the same percentages (4% each one). The 19% use paper ticket (single) and 5% use the contactless multi-ride. The remaining solutions are shown in Fig. 7.

Another interesting aspect is the result on intermodality with other public transport operators (Fig. 8). Only the 16% of sample uses other operators. Out of these: 72% of passengers use the regional transport operator (ARST) both in Bus mode (46%) and in Metro - Tramway mode (27%) and 24% use FdS. 76% of passengers use other operators to suburban journeys and the 24% for urban journeys.

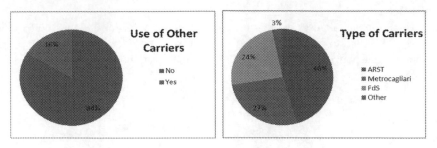

Fig. 8. Use and type of other carriers

The motivation for the modal choice of collective transport was examined in relation to the possession of the private car, in order to detect the motivation of the choice. This is shown in Fig. 9.

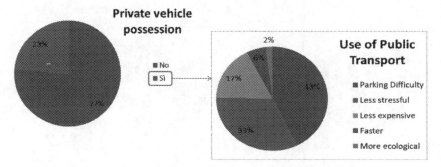

Fig. 9. Reasons of using public transport

As shown in Fig. 9, 77% of the sample does not have a private vehicle, therefore, it is clear that for these users the choice of public transport is a real necessity. For the remaining part of the sample, the public transport is preferred to private car for reasons related to: the traffic component, which is manifested by the difficulty in finding parking, especially in the city center, and with the greater speed of movement compared to the private vehicle (48%). Furthermore 33% of user find it less stressful 17% of the sample chooses it because it is less expensive and finally a minority (2%) motivates the choice in an ecological way.

Looking at data on the possession of a smartphone and the use of the App (Fig. 10), almost all the sample interviewed owns a smartphone.

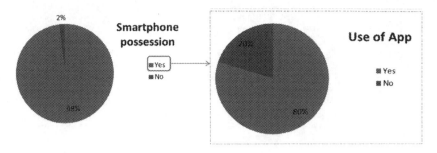

Fig. 10. Media possession and usage

Out of these, 80% have downloaded and use the CTM application and must of them use it primarily as an information channel (94%). For those who do not use it, the information on the transport service is taken in order: by the website and by information panel at the stop. Furthermore, as regards the knowledge of the possibility to purchasing the travel pass through the application, 71% of users who have downloaded the app, knows the service but do not use it, 21% use it and 8% does not know this possibility. The percentages change slightly if the field extends to the whole sample.

3.2 Elderly Users

This part shows the results on the sampled demand of elderly. In order to highlight any impediments and/or limits to the use of public transport in terms of accessibility and/or technological services, the results of the analysis on this demand segment are compared to those of the complementary segment.

The outcomes are shown in Table 1 in which for each attribute (first column) the results of weak users (Over 65s) and complementary users are reported respectively. The results of statistical test are reported in column 4 (Z_{calc})[1].

Table 1. Typical traveler form - elderly and complementary users

Characteristic	Type Traveler (>65 years)	Type Traveler (<65 years)	Z_{calc}
Gender	*Females (80%)* *Males (20%)*	*Females (63%)* *Males (37%)*	1,58
Residence	*Cagliari (55%)* *Hinterland (35%)* *Other (10%)*	*Cagliari (49%)* *Hinterland (38%)* *Other (13%)*	*n.c.*
Profession	*Retired (70%)* *Housewife (25%)* *Education, training and research specialist (5%)*	*Student (59%)* *Employee and qualified professions in commercial activities and services (14%)* *Unemployed (5%)* *Freelance professional of intellectual, scientific and health professions (5%)* *Other (16%)*	*n.c.*

(continued)

---

[1] "*n.c.*": "not calculated" refers to the characteristics where Z_{calc} is not been calculated.

Table 1. (*continued*)

Characteristic	Type Traveler (>65 years)	Type Traveler (<65 years)	Z_{calc}
Location on board and where	*Sitting (95%)* *Standing (5%)* *Rear (45%)* *Central (30%)* *Front (25%)*	*Sitting 90%* *Standing (10%)* *Rear (56%)* *Front (30%)* *Central (14%)*	*n.c.*
Reason	*Personal Services (88%)* *Leisure, Sport, Tourism (6%)* *Shopping (6%)*	*Leisure, Sport, Tourism (35%)* *Job and School/University (each one 23%)* *Personal Services (16%)* *Shopping (2%)*	*n.c.*
Frequency of use	*5–6 days a week (72%)* *3–4 days a week (11%)* *Occasionally (11%)* *It's the first time (6%)*	*5–6 days a week (72%)* *3–4 days a week (14%)* *1–2 days a week (7%)* *Other (7%)*	*n.c.*
Rides	*2 (39%)* *4 (22%)* *6/8/3 (11%)* *1 (6%)*	*2 (40%)* *4 (24%)* *3/1 (11%)* *6/5 (5%)* *Other (4%)*	*n.c.*
Travel ticket	*Contactless subscription (66%)* *Multi-rides Contactless (17%)* *Paper ticket (17%)*	*Contactless subscription (58%)* *Paper ticket (19%)* *Multi-rides Contactless (5%)* *Other (18%)*	*n.c.*
Use of other carriers	*No 100%*	*No 83%* *Yes 17%*	*1.90*
Type of carriers	–	Composition of the 17% of users that using other carriers: *ARST (46%)* *Metrocagliari (27%)* *FdS (24%)* *Other (4%)*	*n.c.*
Moving with another mode	–	*Suburban (76%)* *Urban (24%)*	*n.c.*
Private vehicle ownership	*No (89%)* *Yes (11%)*	*No (76%)* *Yes (24%)*	*1.25*
Use of the bus	For car owners only: *Parking Difficulty (50%)* *Less stressful (50%)*	For car owners only: *Parking Difficulty (43%)* *Less stressful (32%)* *Less expensive (17%)* *(Other 8%)*	*n.c.*
Smartphone possession	*Yes (79%)* *No (21%)*	*Yes (99%)* *No (1%)*	*6.01*
Use of app	*No (87%)* *Yes (13%)*	*Yes (81%)* *No (19%)*	– *7.31*
Info channel	For those who DO NOT use the APP: *Bus stop (81%)* *WEB site (19%)*	For those who DO NOT use the APP: *Bus stop (65%)* *WEB site (32%)* *Other (3%)*	*n.c.*
Purchase with app	For the users of the APP: *Yes but I don't use it (100%)*	For the users of the APP: *Yes but I don't use it (71%)* *Yes and I use it (21%)* *No (8%)*	*0.91*

The results on the gender of users over 65 confirmed a dominance of women over the male component, to a greater extent than the complementary demand (80% vs. 63%). This is in line with the Dutch study [6] in which there is a greater propensity by older women to use public transport and to walk compared to the male gender who instead uses the car more often.

The 55% lives in Cagliari and 35% in the Hinterland. Considering the age group, it is natural that it is represented by retired with whom housewives stand out (25%). The 95% of the sample interviewed occupied a seat, preferring the rear and central area of the vehicle.

The 89% use the bus for personal services and the rest for leisure and shopping to the same extent. These reasons are in line with those found in a survey conducted in Germany [5] in which it emerged that the main purposes of the movements of the elderly were shopping and leisure. The study cited further states that in favor of these results: access to healthcare facilities, grocery stores, post offices and other cultural, social and leisure facilities (including libraries, leisure centers, non-food stores, city centers and places of worship) were considered as elements of relevance in a review of the accessibility planning of local transport [23, 24].

To sum up, most of the sample uses the public transport service almost daily: between 3–6 days/week (83%). Of these, most make multiple trips per day (2/4).

Turning to the travel pass, 83% use a contactless travel pass both in the subscription form (66%) and in the multi-journey (17%).

Nobody uses other operators. This aspect confirms the aptitude of older people to travel for shorter distances [6]. The authors believe that the shortness of the journey is closely connected with the main reasons for the trip given by the elderly population. In fact, it is assumed that the trips for leisure and purchases have destinations that do not require a long journey in the sense of plurality of carriers.

The use of travel by public transport is the only alternative available for 89% of passengers without a private car. Conversely, it is worth noting that the owners of a private vehicle use the bus owing to the difficulty in finding a parking space or stress due to traffic congestion in the same percentages (50%).

Lastly, regarding the technology available to users and on the information channels, it has been ascertained that the 79% of the sample owns a smartphone. Only 13% use the CTM app and no one makes the purchase through the app despite knowing the service. The information channel for the majority who do not use the app is the bus stop and the website.

The results of the statistical test, reported in the fourth column, show the Z_{calc} values lower than the critical value for four observed characteristics. These are: gender, use of other operators, private vehicle ownership and knowledge and use of the purchase service via app. This allows us to conclude that the two samples have no statistical significance with respect to the observed characteristics. Conversely, for the possession of the smartphone and the use of the app, the test result returned Z_{calc} values higher than the critical value. In this case it is concluded that the two samples have a high statistical significance.

Continuing the comparison between the two macro demand segments, considering the almost daily frequency, both can be considered as regular users. Given the difference in the age group and socio-demographic differences in employment, differences in travel motivation for the trip are implicit.

In both cases, the percentage of users who do not own a private car is high (89% vs. 76%), greater for those over 65 and less for the rest. Considering that in the latter class there are minors, the percentage drops by 5 percentage points if they are removed from the segment.

However, the key elements that distinguish the two segments concern multimodality and technological services. The difference between the two samples, for the second category, is also supported by a high statistical significance of the test. For the former, instead, the value of $Z_{calc} = 1.90$ is at the limit for a significance level of 95%.

As for the first point, it is stated that elderly passengers use collective transport limited to the CTM network. In fact, since there are no users from suburban areas, there is no recourse to the combined use of other carriers. An element that could justify this result could be due to the fact that for the elderly, given their age, they do not move anymore for work and/or study. Systematic trips home/work-study often requires the use of multiple carriers to reach the destination.

Another substantial element of difference is the ownership of the smartphone and the services connected to it. The 21% of the over 65 category does not have a smartphone against 1% of the complementary category.

Restricting the analysis to the owners of the smartphone only, only 13% of the elderly downloaded the transport operator application's (vs. 81%). The service is used only to acquire information but not to buy the travel ticket despite they know this option.

4 Conclusions

Growing progress in medicine and the improvement in the quality of life have had a positive impact on people's life expectancy, which has increased worldwide. We find ourselves in front of a more active elderly population, who moves more and even in the absence of full-time work commitment, maintains its independence in carrying out its activities that are attributable to leisure and shopping. The natural aging process is accompanied by physiological and customary changes that are reflected in the mobility choices. The elderly walks more and uses public transport. The study proposed by the authors focuses on the behavior of these users.

On the basis of the periodic quality survey carried out by the public transport company of the Municipality of Cagliari (CTM) on its vehicles, 754 questionnaires were collected. From these data, socio-demographic characteristics and travel behavior were investigated. The analysis was done using descriptive statistics.

By the data provided by the CTM, the sample of the elderly is 3%. This result is not surprising as the survey was motivated by business needs and aimed to evaluate the service quality. Hence, despite the limited sample size, the authors wanted to analyze the behavior of over 65 years who, especially for some characteristics, showed specificities that deserve further study.

The results for both the overall sample and the share of demand of elderly showed that the users are systematic. However, the study found that the use of multimodality and technological services are the discriminating elements between the two samples. The difference in this sense is not only qualitative but was also supported by the statistical test of significance. In fact, the test result showed that the difference between the two groups (over and under 65 years) is statistically significant.

As for the intermodality, the elderly do not use other operators but limit themselves to using public transport on the local network. This confirms that the elderly make shorter trips, an option that is probably also due to the reasons for the movement that distinguish this age group. Most elderly have a smartphone, but only 13% use the app as an information channel only.

As regards the actions to be suggested to the Company, nothing can be added about intermodality, as none of the elderly use it. If this aspect will be confirmed by a more detailed investigation, it would confirm their habits on the use of public transport for short and short-term trips. So, in this sense, there is no glimpse of a policy to suggest to the companies involved in order to acquire this demand segment as well.

Conversely, as for technological services, there are some elements that could facilitate the use of the services by increasing its accessibility. In this regard, a distinction must be made between:

- Network consultation services, timetables and route interrogation services;
- The purchase service.

While for the first category it would be enough to enhance advertising, for example on board vehicles, for the second category the purchase service should be facilitated. It is known that the elderly, especially in these latitudes, are rather hostile to credit card purchases. Therefore, a solution to be able to use the subscription service through the app, could be to make it possible to upload credit directly to the sales network (e.g., Tobacconists, newsagents). This would facilitate the purchase service and would probably allow the spread of the use of the app, even for the category of users over 65 years.

To conclude, the authors confirm their interest in deepening the study on this segment of users. In this regard, a new targeted investigation could be set up precisely on the elderly. In fact, it would be interesting to understand, in the context of the Municipality of Cagliari (with a temperate climate, with investments in structures for pedestrian and cycle paths), what their real travel habits are, what their travel behavior is as well as their modal choices. This could be a starting point for future studies.

Acknowledgements. This study is supported by the MIUR (Ministry of Education, Universities and Research [Italy]) through two project entitled: the SMART CITY framework (project: PON04a2_00381 "CAGLIARI2020") and WEAKI TRANSIT: WEAK-demand areas Innovative TRANsport Shared services for Italian Towns (Project protocol: 20174ARRHT_004; CUP Code: F74I19001290001), financed with the PRIN 2017 (Research Projects of National Relevance) programme. We authorize the MIUR to reproduce and distribute reprints for Governmental purposes, notwithstanding any copyright notations thereon. Any opinions, findings and conclusions or recommendations expressed in this material are those of the authors, and do not necessarily reflect the views of the MIUR. Moreover, the authors are grateful CTM SpA, which made its data available for this study.

Author Contributions. Conceptualization, all; methodology and formal analysis, Nicoletta Rassu, Francesca Maltinti, Benedetto Barabino and Mauro Coni; introduction and literary review Nicoletta Rassu, Francesca Maltinti and Benedetto Barabino; writing-original draft preparation, Nicoletta Rassu; writing-review and editing Nicoletta Rassu, Benedetto Barabino and Francesca Maltinti; visualization, all. All authors have read and agreed to the published version of the manuscript.

References

1. Ling Suen, S., Mitchell, C.G.B.: Accessible Transportation and Mobility. TRB Transportation in the New Millennium (2000)
2. Ashford, N., Bell, W.: Mobility for the Elderly and Handicapped. Loughborough University of Technology, Loughborough, England (1978)
3. Shrestha, B.P., Millonig, A., Hounsell, N.B., McDonald, M.: Review of public transport needs of older people in european context. J. Population Ageing **10**(4), 343–361 (2016). https://doi.org/10.1007/s12062-016-9168-9
4. Collia, D.V., Sharp, J., Giesbrecht, L.: The 2001 national household travel survey: a look into the travel patterns of older Americans. J. Saf. Res. **34**(4), 461–470 (2003)
5. MiD: Mobilität in Deutschland 2008. Bundesministeriums für Verkehr, Bau- und Stadtentwicklung (BMVBS), Germany (2008). http://www.mobilitaet-in-deutschland.de
6. Böcker, L., van Amen, P., Helbich, M.: Elderly travel frequencies and transport mode choices in Greater Rotterdam, the Netherlands. Transportation **44**(4), 831–852 (2016). https://doi.org/10.1007/s11116-016-9680-z
7. Marrattoli, R.A., De Leon, C.F.M., Glass, T.A., Williams, C.S., Cooney, L.M., Berkman, L.F.: Consequences of driving cessation: decreased out-of-home activity levels. J. Gerontol. Ser. B **55**(6), 334–340 (2000)
8. Arentze, T.A., Timmermans, H.J.P., Jorritsma, P., OldeKalter, M.J., Schoenmakers, A.: More gray hair- but for whom? Scenario-based simulations of elderly activity travel patterns in 2020. Transportation **35**, 613–627 (2008). https://doi.org/10.1007/s11116-008-9170-z
9. Ravulaparthy, S.K., Goulias, K.G., Yoon, S.Y., Polydoropoulou, A.: Transport mobility, activity and subjective well-being. In: Roorda, M., Miller, E. (eds.) Travel Behaviour Research: Current Foundations, Future Prospect. Lulu Publishers, Raleigh (2013)
10. Delbosc, A., Currie, G.: Exploring the relative influences of transport disadvantage and social exclusion on well-being. Trans. Policy **18**(4), 555–562 (2011)
11. Haustein, S., Siren, A.K.: Seniors' unmet mobility needs—how important is a driving licence? J. Transp. Geogr. **41**, 45–52 (2014)
12. Rosenbloom, S.: Sustainability and automobility among the elderly: an international assessment. Transportation **28**, 375–408 (2001)
13. Banister, D., Bowling, A.: Quality of life for the elderly: the transport dimension. Transp. Policy **11**(2), 105–115 (2004)
14. Gilhooly, M.L.M., et al.: Transport and ageing: Extending quality of life via public and private transport. ESCR report L48025025, Brunel University Research Archive (2002)

15. Torrisi, V., Ignaccolo, M., Inturri, G.: Analysis of road urban transport network capacity through a dynamic assignment model: validation of different measurement methods. Transp. Res. Procedia **27**, 1026–1033 (2017)
16. Torrisi, V., Ignaccolo, M., Inturri, G.: Estimating travel time reliability in urban areas through a dynamic simulation model. Transp. Res. Procedia **27**, 857–864 (2017)
17. Coni, M., Garau, C., Pinna, F.: How has cagliari changed its citizens in smart citizens? Exploring the influence of its technology on urban social interactions. In: Gervasi, O., et al. (eds.) ICCSA 2018. LNCS, vol. 10962, pp. 573–588. Springer, Cham (2018). https://doi.org/10.1007/978-3-319-95168-3_39
18. Tilocca, P., et al.: Managing data and rethinking applications in an innovative mid-sized bus fleet. Transp. Res. Procedia **25**, 1904–1924 (2017)
19. Barabino, B.: Automatic recognition of 'low-quality' vehicles and bus stops in bus services. Public Transp. **10**(2), 257–289 (2018). https://doi.org/10.1007/s12469-018-0180-8
20. CTM 2020: Carta della mobilità 2019–2020, Cagliari, Italy. Accessed December 2019. http://www.ctmcagliari.it/
21. Barabino, B., Deiana, E., Tilocca, P.: Urban transport management and customer perceived quality: a case study in the metropolitan area of Cagliari, Italy. Theoret. Empirical Res. Urban Manage. **6**(1), 19–32 (2011)
22. Devoto, R., Rassu, N.: L.C. & Tourism analysis of users of international low cost flights from Cagliari-Elmas airport. In: 18th Air Transport Research Society (ATRS), World Conference 2014, Bordeaux, France, 27–30 June 2012
23. Help the Aged: Travel, Access and Older People: A Review of Local Transport Accessibility Planning (2006)
24. Help the Aged: Travel, access and older people: A review of local transport accessibility planning. A report for Help the Aged by Helen Lesowiec. London: Help the Aged (2006b)

Beyond Architectural Barriers: Building a Bridge Between Disability and Universal Design

Francesco Pinna[✉] [ID], Chiara Garau [ID], Francesca Maltinti [ID], and Mauro Coni [ID]

Department of Civil and Environmental Engineering and Architecture (DICAAR), University of Cagliari, 09129 Cagliari, Italy
{fpinna, cgarau, maltinti, mconi}@unica.it

Abstract. The paper is focused on the evolution of the concept of accessibility, by considering data of the World Health Organization (WHO) and of the Istat (Italian statistical institute). From these data it emerges that the population (worldwide and in Italy) dealing with disability represents an important share of the total. These disabilities are linked not only with disease, but also with other situation due to age, size, language, culture, job, etc. For this reason, this paper analyses how the way of seeing and dealing disability is changed over time, starting from the Italian Standard evolution. Then the action of the WHO is analyzed. The two WHO focus points are: i) disability is a health condition in an unfavorable environment; ii) disability is not a problem of a minority group within a community, but an experience that everyone, in their lifetime, can experience. All of these analyses underlined the importance of the environment influence on life of every person. Finally, the concept of Universal design UD is investigated, highlighting the importance of recognizing and understanding that human beings will have different steps in their abilities throughout their life. The originality of this research is the shifting of the attention also to people normally served by poor services, such as people of small stature, the elderly, pregnant women, parents with children in strollers, people who speak different languages and more.

Keywords: Accessibility · Disability · Universal design · World Health Organization · Architectural barriers

Notes: This paper is the result of the joint work of the authors. 'Introduction' 'Evolution of accessibility as a function of disability: the regulatory apparatus in Italy', 'New scenarios after COVID-19' era and 'Discussion and Conclusions' were written jointly by the authors. Francesco Pinna wrote the 'Evolution of accessibility as a function of disability: the universal design with its definition and its principles'. Chiara Garau wrote the 'Evolution of accessibility as a function of disability: the action of the World Health Organization (WHO)'.

© Springer Nature Switzerland AG 2020
O. Gervasi et al. (Eds.): ICCSA 2020, LNCS 12255, pp. 706–721, 2020.
https://doi.org/10.1007/978-3-030-58820-5_51

1 Introduction

Accessibility, disability and universal design are now outdated concepts, that over the past few years changed their declination and interrelation, thanks to many international associations, whose work was reworked in its entirety by the World Health Organization (WHO) [1–3].

In particular, this change considered the methodological, technical and cultural approach, in relation to problems concerning accessibility and its relationship with disability [4, 5]. To understand this evolution, the authors begin to analyze the definitions of disability and accessibility, while for that one of universal design UD, see paragraph 4. The disability is defined by WHO as a functional impairment, activity limitation, or participation restriction that reflects the interaction between body and society [6].

Accessibility can instead be related to the concept of individual freedom, because there is a limitation for the human being to freedom of movement, knowledge of things and the usability of services where there is inaccessibility [7]. This condition, may be also influenced by the surrounding context and by the effect that endogenous (e.g. one's own abilities) and exogenous (e.g. interference with traffic) phenomena can have on accessibility [8, 9].

The evaluation of accessibility in urban spaces is often evaluated through the calculation of indices, based on infrastructural aspects subjective perceptions [10–12]. However, the design parameters are based on the "standard user" as an agile person with good vision, hearing, and mobility. These design parameters do not meet the needs of the growing disabled population.

To understand the extension of the problem it is useful to give some numbers. The WHO data indicates that approximately 15% of the global population have a disability [13, 14].

In Italy, according to the latest Istat Report of 2019 [15], people with serious limitations in their usual activities are 3,100,000 (5.2% of the population); between these, about 50% belong to the age group >75 years (about 1 in 5 seniors). Approximately 600,000 citizens are deprived of aid services and only 19.2% say they are satisfied with their lives, against 44.5% of the rest of the population. Taking in account some specific aspects, the data are no less worrying with reference to the opportunities for life and socialization.

As for health and independence, 61% of people with serious limitations are in bad health, compared to 0.6% of the rest of the population and there are 1,400,000 non-autonomous elderly people with disabilities. As for education, there are 272 thousand pupils with disabilities who study in schools that only in 31.5% of cases are without physical barriers and, indeed, only in 17.5% of cases are without sensory and perceptive barriers. As for employment, only 31.3% of people with serious limitations are employed (57.8% in the rest of the population) and, of these, 65.4% are satisfied with their jobs (75.9% in the rest of the population). Finally, in participating in cultural and sporting activities, only 9.3% attend museums, theaters, etc. and only 9.1% play sports (respectively 30.8% and 36.6% in the rest of the population).

This picture is certainly disconcerting and strengthens the need for modern and, above all, effective interventions to make sure that disadvantaged people can have a life, as far as possible, with the same opportunities and possibilities as those who do not has problems.

Today this idea has difficulty to be applied and often not for the lack of adequate Standards and Acts. In fact, the regulatory apparatus on architectural barriers is often formally applied, without taking into account unwritten but common-sense elementary rules. Even worse, the set of rules is often applied as an obligation, without having a full knowledge of the whole and the complexity of the issues that are being dealt with.

It appears evident the need to clarify what is at the basis of the removal of architectural barriers, specifying how the solution of these are not only technical solutions, but, more importantly, leads to practical, economic and socio-cultural benefits closely linked to the achievement of accessibility. This approach, seen as a process, and not as an outcome, is extremely tied to the concept of healthy city [16–18] which can also benefit from new transport solutions and emerging technologies [19–22].

In fact, both the public space and the spaces inside the buildings must have adequate accessibility, necessary not only for disabled people but also for the entire community, becoming the characteristic sign of the modernity of a society [23]. In this regard, it results fundamental to adopt inclusive approaches by involving key stakeholders and capturing citizens' preferences from a multiple criteria perspective [24–26].

Starting from these assumptions, the paper is organized as follows. Firstly, a background is given to clarify the evolution of the regulatory apparatus in Italy in relation to the main key concepts of accessibility and disability. Then, the authors analyse the action of the World Health Organization (WHO) in order to underline how it is changed the point of view on deficit, disability and handicap. Finally, the UD with its definition and its principles is analysed with also the new scenarios opened after the COVID-19 era. The paper concludes with a discussion on the findings emerged and on possible future developments on the research in this field.

2   Evolution of Accessibility as a Function of Disability: The Regulatory Apparatus in Italy

In Italy, the set of rules relating to the elimination and overcoming of architectural barriers is always characterized by the distinction between: 1) buildings and public-private spaces open to the public; 2) buildings and private spaces.

The first regulatory action was the law 30/03/1971 No. 118 (in Italian called *Conversione in legge del D.L. 30 gennaio 1971 n° 5, e nuove forme dei mutilati ed invalidi civili*). However, it only concerned public offices or offices open to the public and school, pre-school or social interest institutions, all of them newly constructed. In implementation of this law, the D.P.R. No. 384/1978, now repealed by Presidential Decree 503/1996.

Only in 1986 was the problem tackled again, providing for a ban on approving construction and renovation projects in compliance with the technical standards relating to the removal of architectural barriers and establishing that all buildings in contrast with these provisions could not benefit from public contributions or subsidies.

The discipline of architectural barriers in private construction was born, instead, with the Law 09/01/1989 No. 13 (in Italian called *Disposizioni per favorire il superamento e l'eliminazione delle barriere architettoniche negli edifici privati*) and the relative Implementation Regulation adopted with Decree of the Ministry of Public Works 14/06/1989 No. 236. In this law the problem was faced with a different logic since attention is focused on prevention rather than on the amnesty of buildings. That is, compliance with the technical requirements of the Implementing Regulation is imposed on both new and renovated buildings.

What was still partially excluded from the scope of the legislation were the renovations and extraordinary maintenance works, the restoration and conservative restoration.

Law 05/02/1992 No. 104 (in Italian called *Legge quadro per l'assistenza, l'integrazione e i diritti delle persone handicappate*) was issued, in order to deal with every possible aspect of the handicap. The art. 24 of this law recalls all the current legislation on the removal and overcoming of architectural barriers, referring no longer to new or existing buildings but also to the concept of "building works". This law briefly extends the scope of application not only to the renovation of entire buildings, but also to smaller renovations. Furthermore, this law provides for penalties for technicians for works realized in compliance with the regulations.

Therefore, the discipline of architectural barriers in private construction in the nineties was more up to date and coherent with EU guidelines than that relating to public buildings.

The Presidential Decree 24/07/1996 No. 503 (in Italian called *Regolamento recante norme per l'eliminazione delle barriere architettoniche negli edifici, spazi e servizi pubblici*) intervened to modify this situation. It gave new more specific provisions for public spaces and buildings and, at the same time, extended the requirements of Ministerial Decree 236/1989 to these categories. In particular, the projects of public spaces and urbanization works with prevalently pedestrian use have to include at least an accessible path capable of allowing the use of services, social relations and environmental use also for people with reduced or impeded motor skills or sensory.

Finally, Law No. 67 of 01/03/2006 (in Italian called *Misure per la tutela giudiziaria delle persone con disabilità vittime di discriminazioni*) establishes measures for the judicial protection of people with disabilities who are victims of discrimination. This condition occurs "when an apparently neutral provision, criterion, practice, act, pact or behavior puts a person with a disability at a disadvantage compared to other people".

Italy, with Law No. 18 of 03/03/2009, ratified and enforced the United Nations Convention on the Rights of Persons with Disabilities, adopted by the UN General Assembly on 13 December 2006 and entered into force May 3, 2008 [27].

In all international laws, as well as in Italy, the legislative requirements regarding the removal of architectural barriers do not constitute a constraint but are configured as an added value aimed at a better quality of the work as it is more enjoyable and certainly safer. It is also evident that it is necessary not to design "dedicated" solutions only for disabled people but to have all users as users of these interventions, thus obtaining generalized benefits.

However, this regulatory process has not been able to completely eliminate the discrimination related to the technical solutions identified. A clear example of this is

Law 13/1989 which sets three quality levels that can be reached by design without barriers: accessibility, visitability and adaptability.

Accessibility expresses the highest level as it allows the total use of the structure in the immediate term. The visitability represents a level of accessibility limited to a more or less extended part of the structure which allows, in any case, any type of fundamental relationship also to the person with reduced or impeded motor or sensory capacity. Adaptability represents a reduced level of quality, potentially susceptible to transformation into an accessibility level, thus placing itself as a deferred accessibility.

In practice, adaptability means the possibility of modifying the built space over time at limited costs, in order to make it completely and easily usable even by people with reduced or impeded motor or sensory capacity.

However, these three levels are now outdated, also because they continue to maintain a clear distinction in the use of space between "able-bodied" users and users with reduced or impeded motor or sensory capacity. Beyond accessibility, in fact, visibility does not make the space totally usable, but identifies special solutions for special people, thus maintaining discrimination, even if hidden by the given possibility. Adaptability is, instead, a subtle form of discrimination as it allows to create spaces that are not accessible but that can be transformed at a reduced cost; this discrimination is evident, first of all, because it provides that the achievement of full accessibility is at the expense of disadvantaged people and not, in some way, of the community and, secondly, that this possibility is strictly linked to the economic capacity of those who must intervene: the costs, in fact, become limited if someone can afford them, otherwise they are always and in any case inaccessible.

Finally, going beyond the regulatory process, it is necessary to make a very important consideration on the public space: this often has characteristics not comparable with those of private spaces, especially when the intervention concerns the oldest urban fabric and areas with more altimetric trends handled. In any case, cities are believed to have a good degree of adaptability to removal of architectural barriers.

3   Evolution of Accessibility as a Function of Disability: The Action of the World Health Organization (WHO)

The action of the WHO has developed over time, identifying three fundamental evolutionary phases. The first is responsible for the historical definition of the handicap of 1980, contained within the "International Classification of Impairments, Disabilities, and Handicaps" [28]. It distinguished three levels:

- Impairments (I code), concerned with abnormalities of body structure and appearance and with organ or system function) resulting from any cause; in principle, impairments represent disturbances at the organ level.
- Disabilities (D code), reflecting the consequences of impairment in terms of functional performance and activity by the individual; disabilities thus represent disturbances at the level of the person.

- Handicaps (H code), concerned with the disadvantages experienced by the individual as a result of impairments and disabilities; handicaps thus reflect interaction with and adaptation to the individual's surroundings.

The second phase starts in 1999, when WHO published the new International Classification of Functioning and Disability: ICIDH-2 [29], where two of the three main concepts that characterize a morbidity process are redefined:

- its externalization: impairment
- objectification: no more disabilities but personal activities
- the social consequences: no more handicaps or disadvantages but different social participation

More precisely:

- with personal activities we consider the limitations of nature, duration and quality that a person undergoes in his/her activities, at any level of complexity, due to a structural or functional impairment. Based on this definition, each person is disabled.
- with social participation we consider the restrictions of nature, duration and quality that a person suffers in all areas or aspects of his/her life due to the interaction between impairments, activities and contextual factors.

In the new WHO classification, the term "handicap" is definitively shelved because the handicap is a relative and not absolute fact, as opposed to the deficit. For example, blindness cannot be denied and is therefore absolute; the disadvantage (handicap) is related to living and working conditions, therefore to the reality in which the blind person is placed. The handicap is therefore a meeting between the individual and the situation. It is a reducible or (unfortunately) increasing disadvantage.

The third phase was born in 2001, with the International Classification of Functioning, Disability and Health (ICF) [30]. It defines an innovative, multidisciplinary and universal approach classification tool.

The ICF describes the state of health of people in relation to their existential areas (social, family, work) in order to catch the difficulties that in the socio-cultural context can cause disabilities. It therefore describes not people, but their situations of daily life in relation to their environmental context and highlights the individual not only as a person with diseases or disabilities, but, above all, highlighting their uniqueness and globality.

In summary, there are two innovative aspects of the ICF classification. The first is related to the extensive analysis of the health status of individuals and places the correlation between health and the environment, defining disability as a health condition in an unfavorable environment. Previously with the other classifications (ICD and ICIDH), terms such as illness, impairment and handicap were largely used, mainly in the negative sense, with reference to situations of deficit. The new concept of disability is instead based on elements such as universalism, the integrated approach and the multidimensional model of functioning and disability.

The second aspect is based on the concept that disability is not a problem of a minority group within a community, but an experience that everyone, in their lifetime, can experience. WHO, through the ICF, proposes a model of universal disability, applicable to any person, able-bodied or disabled as each person can be in a precarious environmental context. This can cause disability regardless of whether the cause of the discomfort is physical, psychic or sensory in nature. What matters is to intervene in the social context by building material and immaterial infrastructures that reduce disability.

Disability is therefore not only a deficit, lack, deprivation on an organic or psychic level, but it is a condition that goes beyond limitation, which overcomes mental and architectural barriers [31]. Disability is a universal condition [32] and therefore it is not only applicable to the person who is in a wheelchair, who does not see or hear. Therefore, the evaluation of the influence of the environment on the life of individuals becomes important: society, the family and the working context can influence the state of health, decrease our ability to perform tasks that are required and put us in a difficult situation.

4 Evolution of Accessibility as a Function of Disability: The Universal Design with Its Definition and Its Principles

The definition of Universal Design (UD) is changed over time, just as there are numerous ways to define it (inclusive design [33, 34], design for all, life span design, etc.) [23]. Its first definition focused on usability issues: "The design of products and environments to be usable by all people, to the greatest extent possible, without the need for adaptation or specialized design" [36]. Today, the meaning includes broader issues of social inclusion. The new definition states that UD is "a process that enables and empowers a diverse population by improving human performance, health and wellness, and social participation" [37: p. 56]. The general principle is that UD is useful to have a life easier, healthier, and friendlier for all.

UD improves the quality of life for a wide range of individuals and puts people with disabilities on an equal playing field. It does not substitute for assistive technology, but benefits people with functional limitations and society as a whole, supporting people in being more self-reliant and socially engaged. For businesses and government, it reduces the economic burden of special programs and services designed to assist individual citizens, clients, or customers.

From this point of view, UD should be considered a process rather than an end state.

Starting from these assumptions, the UD is the design of products and environments to be usable by all people, to the greatest extent possible, without the need for adaptation or specialized design [38]. Table 1 shows the principles of UD and their related guidelines.

The principles of UD address only universally usable design, while the practice of design involves more than considerations for usability. Designers must also incorporate other considerations, such as economic, engineering, cultural, gender and environmental concerns, into design processes. These principles offer designers guidance to better integrate features that meet the needs of as many users as possible.

Table 1. The principles of Universal Design and its Guidelines [39]

Principles	Guidelines
Equitable use	1a. Provide the same means of use for all users: identical whenever possible; equivalent when not 1b. Avoid segregating or stigmatizing any users 1c. Allow provisions for privacy, security and safety that are equally available to all users 1d. Make the design appealing to all users
Flexibility in use	2a. Provide choice in methods of use 2b. Accommodate right or left-handed access and use 2c. Adapt to user's accuracy and precision 2d. Provide adaptability to the user's pace
Simple and intuitive use	3a. Eliminate unnecessary complexity 3b. Be consistent with user expectations and intuition 3c. Accommodate a wide range of literacy and language skills 3d. Arrange information consistent with its importance 3e. Provide effective prompting and feedback during and after task completion
Perceptible information	4a. Use different modes (e.g., pictorial, verbal, tactile) for redundant presentation of essential information 4b. Provide adequate contrast between essential information and its surroundings 4c. Maximize legibility of essential information 4d. Differentiate elements in ways that can be described (in order to make it easy to give instructions or directions) 4e. Provide compatibility with a variety of techniques or devices used by people with sensory limitations
Tolerance for error	5a. Arrange elements to minimize hazards and errors: most used elements, most accessible; hazardous elements eliminated, isolated or shielded 5b. Provide warnings of hazards and errors 5c. Provide fail-safe features 5d. Discourage unconscious actions in tasks that require vigilance
Low physical effort	6a. Allow users to maintain neutral body position 6b. Use reasonable operating forces 6c. Minimize repetitive actions 6d. Minimize sustained physical effort
Size and space for approach and use	7a. Provide a clear line of sight to important elements for any seated or standing user 7b. Make reach to all components comfortable for any seated or standing user 7c. Accommodate variations in hand and grip size 7d. Provide adequate space for the use of assistive devices or personal assistance

To update these principles, eight goals of UD were developed, specifying the concept of UD, resulting in human performance, health and well-being and social participation, and addressing contextual and cultural issues.

In middle and low-income countries, one barrier to adoption of UD is the fact that it is often perceived as idealistic, expensive, or an imposition of Western values. This fact can be overcame considering that design strategies will differ or be adapted in different places and by different cultures. In fact, it is important that UD strategies also concern cultural values associated with social, economic, and physical context.

Table 2 shows the eight goals [37].

Table 2. The eight goals of Universal Design

	Goals	
1	Body fit	Adapting to a wide range of body sizes and abilities
2	Comfort	Keeping needs within desirable limits of body function
3	Awareness	Ensuring that critical information for use is easily perceived
4	Understanding	Using methods of operation and use intuitive, clear, and unambiguous
5	Wellness	Contributing to health promotion, avoidance of disease, and prevention of injury
6	Social integration	Treating all groups with dignity and respect
7	Personalization	Incorporating opportunities for choice and the expression of individual preferences
8	Cultural appropriateness	Respecting and reinforcing cultural values and the social, economic and environmental context of any design project

The principles of UD bring with them the concept of Universal Abilities. The aim is to recognize and understand that human beings will have different steps in their abilities throughout their life. This takes us to think that there are no distinctions between citizens with or without disabilities, highlighting what is usable and safe for all. This leads to shifting attention also to people normally served by poor services, such as people of small stature, the elderly, pregnant women, parents with children in strollers, people who speak different languages and more.

The comprehension of disability is, from this point of view, very useful: the knowledge of the basic characteristics of different disabilities and the consequent barriers is critical towards understanding individual needs and how to address them when designing the built environment. There are many types of disabilities, that, for ease of reading, can be divided in these classes [40: p. 11]:

Physical Disabilities: involve limited mobility (to walk, move, stand for long periods or to carry objects) or stamina, or restricted skill (to bend, dress, feed oneself, or to use everyday objects).

Visual Disabilities: involve complete blindness, limited or residual sight, but also a loss of visual clarity/acuity or a decrease in the size of the visual field.

Auditory Disabilities: involve people having partial or no hearing (persons who are deaf, deafened or hard of hearing). The difference can be various: for someone, the loudness of the sound will determine whether it is heard, for others, it depends on the type of sound (e.g., consonants versus vowels, or the intonation). In other cases, individuals may also become confused by certain sounds due to excessive background noises.

Situational Disabilities: involve people with difficulties caused by age, size, language or culture. In specific settings involve persons who are situationally disabled. Other types are people with small children, carrying heavy objects, or people with temporary accident injuries.

Mental Health Disabilities: they are very numerous and different and overlap with other types of disabilities, including emotional disabilities. Some common mental health disabilities include bipolar disorder, psychosis, schizophrenia, anxiety, attention deficit, mood and eating disorders. In addition, mental health is often influenced by external factors, such as where people live, their individual environments, genetics, income and education levels, and people's relationships with friends and family.

Emotional Disabilities: their causes are very varied and common forms are depression, anxiety or stress, that can be hidden or apparent. They may appear as indifference or mood swings.

Intellectual, Developmental and Learning Disabilities: cognitive impairment can vary widely, from severe intellectual disabilities, to the inability to remember, to the absence or impairment of specific cognitive functions (language, autism). A particularly complex disability is autism. Children and adults with autism have difficulties in verbal and nonverbal communication, social interactions, and leisure or play activities.

Therefore, disabilities are many and extremely different and this is certainly a complication for whom are choosing the best solutions. In fact, the removal of architectural barriers is not exclusively a problem for the categories of extreme hardship: the numerical increase of the elderly population (with their numerous degenerative diseases), the number of people affected from injury (forced for a certain period to undergo limitations in their usual mobility), pregnant women, but also parents and grandparents with prams or strollers, workers moving loads or even only people who go to shopping with a trolley makes it clear that remove barriers is a way of generating a city for everyone.

This issue is central to UD, which sets the criteria for a design inclusive and valid for all.

In fact, often, thinking to solve one problem, another determines. This is because a sectoral vision can determine a consequence on someone with problems different from one considered. An example is the substantial difference that the intervention has towards visually impaired people or people in wheelchairs: for the first, a perfectly connected infrastructure, with no elevation continuity, will be an absolute perceptive barrier, for the latter the altitude difference is an absolute physical barrier. But a soil roughness, not carefully evaluated or not limited in reasonable portions from a functional and dimensional point of view, can also be a barrier.

It must therefore be concluded that the sub-categories of the various disabilities are many as well as the answers to be given to the disabilities present in our society are innumerable. There is never a valid solution in the exact measure for everyone.

However, following COVID-19 pandemic some reflections emerged which will be described in the following paragraph.

5   New Scenarios After COVID-19 Era

The global situation linked to the COVID-19 pandemic highlighted the presence of elements of discrimination that were previously difficult to identify, above all because some behaviours, action methodologies or information and education systems, created to combat the pandemic, could become commonplace. The COVID-19 has emphasized the higher risk for people with disabilities or chronic illnesses, especially in low and middle-income countries. In order to overtake this problem, people with disabilities must be included in all plans to manage the current COVID-19 coronavirus outbreak. This implies that the information provided by governments and institutions both to prevent infection and to know how to act in case of illness must be available in accessible formats, including sign language, video captioning, the use of alternative text in images and graphics displayed digitally, and easy-to-read versions. Secondly, it is necessary to face the problem in accessing health services and hygiene products, as well as to consider reasonable accommodation measures to allow people with disabilities to study or work from home and, if that is not possible, to ensure they receive enough education or a paid leave to guarantee their income. Similarly, the decision of many States to introduce confinement measures to fight the pandemic should be adapted to the needs of specific groups to ensure their well-being. For example, people who need home assistance should keep receiving it and, in the case of people with psychosocial disabilities, they cannot be required to live in total isolation [41].

These goals are achieved, by considering the following points:

- ensuring public health information and communication around COVID-19 is fully accessible.
- any supporting documents on COVID-19 should be fully accessible to people with disabilities. All agencies should publish and share their information on COVID19 in accessible formats, including in which shared materials are accessible online for people using screen reader software, and presentation materials accessible using universal design elemental and additional formats, such as the use of sign languages, Easy Read, plain language, captioned media, Braille, augmentative and alternative communication, and other accessible means.
- the WHO COVID-19 Disability Briefing will became the basis for any indications or advice.
- the collaboration with representative organisations of people with disabilities to distribute fully accessible public health information should be active [42].

From this point of view, the International Disability Alliance (IDA) compiled a list of the main barriers that people with disabilities face in this emergency situation along with some practical solutions and recommendations [43] (Table 3).

Table 3. International disability alliance key recommendations

	Key Recommendations
1	People with disabilities must receive information about infection mitigating tips, public restriction plans, and the services offered, in a diversity of accessible formats with use of accessible technologies
2	Additional protective measures must be taken for people with certain types of impairment
3	All preparedness and response plans must be inclusive of and accessible to women with disabilities
4	No disability-based institutionalization and abandonment is acceptable
5	During quarantine, support services, personal assistance, physical and communication accessibility must be ensured
6	Measures of public restrictions must consider persons with disabilities on an equal basis with others
7	Persons with disabilities in need of health services due to COVID19 cannot be deprioritized on the ground of their disability
8	Organizations of Persons with Disabilities can and should play a key role in raising awareness of persons with disabilities and their families
9	Organizations of Persons with Disabilities can and should play a key role in advocating for disability-inclusive response to the COVID19 crisis

6 Discussion and Conclusions

In this paper the authors have analyzed the national and international evolution of the issues concerning what, in an elementary way, has always been called removal of the architectural barriers. Analyzes have shown the overcoming of this concept, which has always been linked, above all, to physical disability.

UD, on the other hand, has shown that the handicap is not linked, as traditionally thought, to the deficit, but that it depends strictly on the environment in which the human being is forced to live. This implies that it is necessary to extend the concept of disability to all citizens because each of them will happen to be in conditions of disability, temporarily (due to fractures, surgical operations, etc.) or definitively, by age, by social status, etc.

In this regard and in accordance with WBDG Accessible Committee [35], the analysis of the principles and goals of UD highlights some issues (such as aging in place, sustainability, workplace design, public spaces, and social justice). The following considerations can be made on these issues.

Aging in Place: many people want to age where they currently live. A research [44] on adults over the age of 65 showed that almost 90% want to remain in their own home for as long as they are able and 80% plans to live permanently in their current residence. Aging in place offers numerous social and financial benefits and promotes keys to successful aging such as life satisfaction, health, and self-esteem. Another research [45] describes factors that often prevent older adults from aging in place (such as land organization for car use, lack of access to transportation, etc.). Others who remain in their homes with barriers that endanger their safety and limit their ability to participate in the community due to the costs of the necessary renovations.

To remain in their own homes while aging, people need housing designs that can be adapted to wider range of health conditions than usual. So, it is necessary to adopt UD features for aging in place. This includes a no-step entry, bathrooms on an accessible floor level, a sleeping space on an accessible level, good lighting, efficient space planning, and other features that reduce effort and accommodate short-term and chronic disabilities.

Sustainability: Sustainable products used in buildings need to be designed not only for people with limited function in order to comply with accessibility laws, but also for the broader population or they will not be effective in practice. Due to their novelty, they often present usability issues to end users. Acceptance of innovative sustainable products can be enhanced through UD.

Workplace: UD is a basic consideration when designing workplace environments for several reasons: 21.3 million (nearly 65%) of American adults with disabilities in working-age (16–64 years old) live with a chronic condition that inhibits their capacity to maintain employment [46]. Good design of the workplace can help increase participation of people with disabilities in the workforce and can help to ensure that fewer accommodations will be needed if an employee has a disability. Additionally, achieving the highest level of usability in the workplace environment increases overall task efficiency, productivity, employee morale, and general safety.

Public Spaces: they include facilities open to the public such as stores, restaurants, amusement parks, parks and other recreation facilities, street rights-of-way, and transportation systems. Public arrangements are a critical domain for UD because they are characterized by participation activities, such as civic affairs, employment, recreation, education, and community mobility.

Social Justice: although initially focused on disability rights, UD can focus on any civil rights issue because design for diversity is concerned with social justice for all. Thus, UD should give attention to supporting access to housing, education, healthcare, transportation, and other resources in society for all those groups that have been excluded from full participation. UD is particularly appropriate in the context of design for low-income minority groups, which often have higher rates of disability than the general population.

These issues represent only some aspects on which great attention has never been paid and on which the authors intend to focus their research in the future.

In addition, the analysis led the authors to reflect on the concept of accessibility in cases where problems related to disability are being treated. In fact, this concept is widely used in its meaning of possibility of accessing a place, a service, a good, etc.

A classic example of this is accessibility linked to transport infrastructure problems, material and immaterial links between areas, or more generally, to problems related to ease of movement rather than full usability.

With this work, the authors argue that for problems related to disability it is preferable to use the term "usability" instead of accessibility, which makes more evident the character of a device, a service, a resource or an environment to be easily usable by any type of user.

Acknowledgements. This study was also supported by the MIUR (Ministry of Education, Universities and Research [Italy]) through a project entitled WEAKI TRANSIT: WEAK-demand areas Innovative TRANsport Shared services for Italian Towns (Project protocol: 20174ARRHT_004: CUP Code: F74I19001290001), financed with the PRIN 2017 (Research Projects of National Relevance) programme. We authorize the MIUR to reproduce and distribute reprints for Governmental purposes, notwithstanding any copyright notations thereon. Any opinions, findings and conclusions or recommendations expressed in this material are those of the authors, and do not necessarily reflect the views of the MIUR.

References

1. Iwarsson, S., Ståhl, A.: Accessibility, usability and universal design—positioning and definition of concepts describing person-environment relationships. Disabil. Rehabil. **25**(2), 57–66 (2003)
2. Lid, I.M.: Universal design and disability: an interdisciplinary perspective. Disabil. Rehabil. **36**(16), 1344–1349 (2014)
3. Thomas, E.V., Warren-Findlow, J., Reeve, C.L., Webb, J.B., Laditka, S.B., Quinlan, M.M.: Universal design for measurement: centering the experiences of individuals with disabilities within health measurement research. Eval. Health Prof. (2020). https://doi.org/10.1177/0163278719900530
4. Brown, S.C.: Methodological paradigms that shape disability research. In: Handbook of Disability Studies, pp. 145–170 (2001)
5. Hamraie, A.: Building Access: Universal Design and the Politics of Disability. University of Minnesota Press, Minneapolis (2017)
6. World Health Organization: World report on disability 2011. World Health Organization, viewed 27 February 2020 (2011). https://apps.who.int/iris/bitstream/handle/10665/44575/9789240685215_eng.pdf
7. Soltani, S.H.K., Sham, M., Awang, M., Yaman, R.: Accessibility for disabled in public transportation terminal. Procedia Soc. Behav. Sci. **35**, 89–96 (2012)
8. Torrisi, V., Ignaccolo, M., Inturri, G.: Analysis of road urban transport network capacity through a dynamic assignment model: validation of different measurement methods. Transp. Res. Procedia **27**, 1026–1033 (2017). https://doi.org/10.1016/j.trpro.2017.12.135
9. Torrisi, V., Ignaccolo, M., Inturri, G.: Estimating travel time reliability in urban areas through a dynamic simulation model. Transp. Res. Procedia **27**, 857–864 (2017). https://doi.org/10.1016/j.trpro.2017.12.134
10. Ignaccolo, M., Inturri, G., Giuffrida, N., Le Pira, M., Torrisi, V., Calabrò, G.: A step towards walkable environments: spatial analysis of pedestrian compatibility in an urban context. Europ. Transp.\Trasporti Europei **76**(6), 1–12 (2020)

11. Ignaccolo, C., Giuffrida, N., Torrisi, V.: The queensway of New York city. a proposal for sustainable mobility in queens. In: Town and Infrastructure Planning for Safety and Urban Quality, pp. 69–76 (2018). https://doi.org/10.1201/9781351173360-12
12. Ignaccolo, M., Inturri, G., Cocuzza, E., Giuffrida, N., Torrisi, V.: Framework for the evaluation of the quality of pedestrian routes for the sustainability of port-city shared areas. In: Coastal Cities and Their Sustainable Future III. WIT Transactions on The Built Environment, vol. 188. WIT Press (2019). ISSN 1743-3509. https://doi.org/10.2495/cc190021
13. World Bank: Disability inclusion (2018). http://www.worldbank.org/en/topic/disability. Accessed 12 Feb 2020
14. World Health Organization: Disabilities and rehabilitation: World report on disability (2018). https://www.who.int/disabilities/world_report/2011/report/en/. Accessed 12 February 2020
15. Istat, Conoscere il mondo della disabilità: persone, relazioni e istituzioni, published 03 December 2019. ISBN: 978-88-458-2005-2
16. WTO Regional Office for Europe UN City. http://www.euro.who.int/en/health-topics/environment-and-health/urban-health/who-european-healthy-cities-network/what-is-a-healthy-city. Accessed 12 Feb 2020
17. Mouton, M., et al.: Towards 'smart cities' as 'healthy cities': health equity in a digital age. Can. J. Public Health 110(3), 331–334 (2019). https://doi.org/10.17269/s41997-019-00177-5
18. Zhao, J.: Exploration and practices of China's urban development models. In: Towards Sustainable Cities in China, pp. 15–36. Springer, New York (2011). https://doi.org/10.1007/978-1-4419-8243-8_2
19. Torrisi, V., Ignaccolo, M., Inturri, G.: Innovative transport systems to promote sustainable mobility: developing the model architecture of a traffic control and supervisor system. In: Gervasi, O., et al. (eds.) ICCSA 2018. LNCS, vol. 10962, pp. 622–638. Springer, Cham (2018). https://doi.org/10.1007/978-3-319-95168-3_42
20. Torrisi, V., Ignaccolo, M., Inturri, G.: Toward a sustainable mobility through a dynamic real-time traffic monitoring, estimation and forecasting system: The RE.S.E.T. project. In: Town and Infrastructure Planning for Safety and Urban Quality - Proceedings of the 23rd International Conference on Living and Walking in Cities, LWC 2017, pp. 241–247 (2018). https://doi.org/10.1201/9781351173360-32
21. Campisi, T., Torrisi, V., Ignaccolo, M., Inturri, G., Tesoriere, G.: University propensity assessment to car sharing services using mixed survey data: the Italian case study of Enna city. Transp. Res. Procedia 47, 433–440 (2020). https://doi.org/10.1016/j.trpro.2020.03.155
22. Torrisi, V., Ignaccolo, M., Inturri, G., Giuffrida, N.: Combining sensor traffic and simulation data to measure urban road network reliability. In: International Conference on Traffic and Transport Engineering (ICTTE) Proceedings, Belgrade, November 2016, p. 1004 (2016)
23. Goldsmith, S.: Designing for the Disabled: the New Paradigm. Routledge, London (2012)
24. Ignaccolo, M., Inturri, G., García-Melón, M., Giuffrida, N., Le Pira, M., Torrisi, V.: Combining Analytic Hierarchy Process (AHP) with role-playing games for stakeholder engagement in complex transport decisions. Transp. Res. Procedia 27, 500–507 (2017). https://doi.org/10.1016/j.trpro.2017.12.069
25. Ignaccolo, M., Inturri, G., Giuffrida, N., Le Pira, M., Torrisi, V.: Structuring transport decision-making problems through stakeholder engagement: the case of Catania metro accessibility. Trans. Infrastruct. Syst. 919–926 (2017). https://doi.org/10.1201/9781315281896-118
26. Ignaccolo, M., Inturri, G., Giuffrida, N., Pira, M.L., Torrisi, V.: Public engagement for designing new transport services: investigating citizen preferences from a multiple criteria perspective. Transp. Res. Procedia 37, 91–98 (2019). https://doi.org/10.1016/j.trpro.2018.12.170

27. United Nations: Convention on the rights of persons with disabilities United Nations, New York (2006). https://www.un.org/disabilities/convention/conventionfull.shtml. Accessed 27 Feb 2020

28. https://apps.who.int/iris/bitstream/handle/10665/41003/9241541261_eng.pdf;jsessionid= 416E3E6F33938894F6093BE9FEB22256?sequence=1

29. World Health Organization: The International Classification of Functioning and Disability: ICIDH-2. Geneva (1999)

30. World Health Organization: The International Classification of Functioning, Disability and Health (ICF). WHO, Geneva (2001). http://www.who.int/classifications/icf/en/. Accessed 27 Feb 2020

31. Conway, M.A.: Embodying the law: negotiating disability identity and civil rights. Law Imagining Differ. **75**, 43–78 (2018)

32. Sone, E.M., Hoza, M.: Re-engaging cultural perspectives on disability discourse: an analysis of the Bakossi and isiXhosa oral traditions. Southern Afr. J. Folklore Stud. **27**(1), 10–29 (2017)

33. Coleman, R.: The case for inclusive design e an overview. In: 12th Triennial Congress. International Ergonomics Association and the Human Factors Association of Canada, Toronto, Canada (1994)

34. John Clarkson, P., Coleman, R.: History of inclusive design in the UK. Appl. Ergon. (2013). https://doi.org/10.1016/j.apergo.2013.03.002

35. WBDG Accessible Committee (Jordana L. Maisel, PhD and Molly Ranahan). Beyond Accessibility to Universal Design, Center for Inclusive Design and Environmental Access (IDeA) (2017). https://www.wbdg.org/design-objectives/accessible/beyond-accessibility-universal-design. Accessed 27 Feb 2020

36. Mace, R.L., Hardie, G.J., Plaice, J.P.: Accessible environments. Towards universal design, In: Preiser, W., et al. (Hg.): Design Interventions. Towards a More Humane Architecture, New York (1991)

37. Steinfeld, E., Maisel, J.L.: Universal Design: Creating Inclusive Environments. Wiley, New Jersey (2012)

38. AA. VV. Design for Independence and Dignity for Everyone: Vision, Hearing, Communication, Mobility, Cognition. Alberta Editor (2008)

39. The Principles of Universal Design, Version 2.0 by The Center for Universal Design. North Carolina State University, 01 Apr 1997

40. Markham Accessibility Design Guidelines, Town of Markham Development Services Commission

41. The impact of COVID-19 on persons with disabilities. https://bridgingthegap-project.eu/the-impact-of-covid-19-on-people-with-disabilities/

42. Accessibility Campaign - COVID19. http://www.internationaldisabilityalliance.org/acessibility-campaign

43. Toward a Disability-Inclusive COVID19 Response: 10 recommendations from the International Disability Alliance. http://www.internationaldisabilityalliance.org/content/covid-19-and-disability-movement

44. Anderson, G.O.: Loneliness among older adults: a national survey of adults 45+. AARP Research, Washington, DC, September 2010. https://doi.org/10.26419/res.00064.001

45. Aging in Place: A State Survey of Livability Policies and Practices, by Nicholas Farber, Douglas Shinkle (National Conference of State Legislatures), Jana Lynott, Wendy Fox-Grage, Rodney Harrell (Public Policy Institute), December, 2011

46. Waldrop, J., Stern, S.M.: Disability Status 2000. vol. 8, 2 edn., U.S. Department of Commerce, Economics and Statistics Administration, U.S. Census Bureau (2003)

Extended Accessibility and Cultural Heritage: A New Approach to Fruition and Conservation

Francesco Pinna$^{(\boxtimes)}$ ⓘ, Mattia Cogoni, Andrea Pinna ⓘ,
Giovanni Battista Cocco ⓘ, and Caterina Giannattasio ⓘ

Department of Civil and Environmental Engineering and Architecture
(DICAAR), University of Cagliari, 09129 Cagliari, Italy
{fpinna, gbcocco, cgiannatt}@unica.it,
mattia90cogoni@gmail.com, pinnandreal6@gmail.com

Abstract. The theme of accessibility has assumed considerable importance for the fruition of cultural heritage, evolving into the more extensive and sensitive concept of "extended accessibility". In this way it is possible to overcome the concept of "architectural barrier" intended in the reductive sense of physical obstacle, giving the same importance to all those barriers that are still neglected or even ignored today, such as psycho - cognitive, sensory and communicative ones.

Therefore, designing the extended accessibility means putting the human being with all his/her needs and requirements at the centre of attention. From this point of view, five main declinations can be identified, physical, cognitive, alternative accessibility, sensoriality and visibility catalysts, each of which has a fundamental role for the usability and enhancement of cultural sites. For each declination, a case study was analysed in which the topic was addressed by proposing different solutions able to give a concrete answer to these various problems.

Finally, a case study has been examined, the Nuragic Sanctuary of Santa Vittoria di Serri, highlighting the main problems in terms of accessibility and studying a series of solutions that could improve the usability of the archaeological area.

What has been analysed clearly highlights how there is no contrast between accessibility and usability and protection of cultural heritage, but how these aspects can coexist and indeed contribute to the improvement of the cultural opportunities.

Keywords: Cultural heritage · Extended accessibility · Disability · Universal design · Architectural barriers

1 Introduction

In the last twenty years, the theme of accessibility has assumed a considerable importance for the fruition of cultural heritage, becoming the basis of any good project for the valorisation and preservation of places of memory [1].

Improving accessibility has its own complexity, but, above all, it implies a change of mentality and attitude towards the heterogeneity of the users, with the acquisition of

© Springer Nature Switzerland AG 2020
O. Gervasi et al. (Eds.): ICCSA 2020, LNCS 12255, pp. 722–738, 2020.
https://doi.org/10.1007/978-3-030-58820-5_52

a broader point of view that can meet to the diversity of users [2: p. 1]. The concept of accessibility thus evolves into the more extensive and sensitive concept of "extended accessibility", which highlights the intent to overcome the concept of "architectural barrier" intended in the reductive sense of physical obstacle, giving the same importance to all those barriers still neglected or even ignored today, such as psychological, cognitive, sensory and communicative ones.

Therefore, designing extended accessibility means to put human beings with all their needs and requirements at the centre of attention. Only in this way it will be possible to eliminate solutions dedicated exclusively to people with disabilities, in favour of inclusive solutions, designed for an expanded user, according to the principles of "Universal Design" [1, 3, 4].

In the paper authors analyse the five main declinations that make up the extended accessibility, i.e. physical, cognitive, alternative accessibility, sensoriality and visibility catalysts, highlighting their fundamental role that each of them has for usability and enhancement of cultural heritage and presenting an illustrative example of intervention for each declination. Finally, a case study is analysed, the Nuragic Sanctuary of Santa Vittoria di Serri, highlighting its main problems in terms of accessibility and proposing a series of useful solutions to improve the usability of the archaeological area.

2 Declinations of Accessibility

The fruition represents today the main objective of any activity of enhancement and protection of the cultural heritage. To ensure extended accessibility in places of culture is therefore a priority task. For this reason, accessibility is rightfully placed within any good preservation and enhancement project, representing a fundamental point of heritage conservation.

The concept of extended accessibility is here divided into five main areas of intervention, which all have the aim to ensure the full enjoyment of cultural heritage for the whole population.

First of all, physical accessibility; in fact, sites of cultural interest are often formed by architectural works that are expressed through the quality of the space and therefore the user's direct experience becomes a fundamental factor for understanding and enjoying these sites [1: p. 9].

To ensure full usability, the physical accessibility must always be accompanied by the cognitive accessibility, which deals with communication barriers, more imperceptible than physical ones but no less strong [5]. The lack of communication, especially for users who reveal a specific need, is what still further moves people away from cultural sites, contrasting what should be the priority goal of enhancement, that is to attract the largest number of users to cultural heritage [4, 6].

In turn, cognitive accessibility is closely linked to the theme of sensoriality. The involvement of all the senses in a balanced way is an essential aspect to guarantee a pleasant perception of space and everything around us. When it comes to extended usability, the theme of sensoriality should be of considerable importance, while actually it is unfortunately one of the most neglected aspects, inclusive solutions continue to be few, and sensory barriers are still the most numerous.

It is important to specify that in any case accessibility is not always fully obtainable, in particular the physical one that has to deal with numerous limits due to different factors, including in particular those related to conservation, but also to the morphology of the sites and architectural and spatial characteristics of each cultural building. Therefore, where the accessibility of the structures is not fully achievable, "compensatory" forms of usability must be provided, which guarantee at least the unsubstantial accessibility [7]. Therefore, the fourth line of action is the so-called "alternative accessibility", which allows to overcome architectural barriers thanks to new digital technologies which allow to enhance the visit of sites or even to enjoy a virtual visit to users who do not have the necessary skills for the direct visit. Alternative accessibility is also not limited to overcome problems related to physical barriers, but can also improve cognitive and sensory barriers, thanks to tools able to show virtual additions to the existing state [8].

The last line of action concerns the visibility catalysts which, with the help of digital environments, in particular websites, social networks and video games, allow to establish a relationship between people and cultural heritage and to reach an extended and heterogeneous audience.

Therefore, we can say that accessibility requires universal design, which knows how to manage the different intervention features, showing the same attention to all types of barriers, inviting an inclusive design that is truly suitable for everyone. Furthermore, overcoming all architectural barriers is a real civil conquest, as it makes possible safer and comfortable environments, not only for users with disabilities, but for anyone.

2.1 Physical Accessibility

Sites of cultural interest are often made up of architectural structures that express themselves through the quality of the space; therefore, the direct experience of the users becomes a fundamental factor to understand and enjoy these sites. Ensuring physical accessibility represents an important step forward for people with disabilities, and also for those who may find him/herself in temporary conditions of reduced mobility.

Unfortunately, the issue of physical accessibility has collided with conservation for a long time. The interventions aimed to ensure accessibility were often considered too invasive and even incompatible with the protection of cultural heritage. This hostility always led to the adoption of temporary solutions, which have caused undoubtedly greater aesthetic damage than permanent, more detailed and careful solutions [1: p. 9]. Furthermore, time has shown how an unused asset "dies" quickly, because the limited accessibility of the sites often causes poor maintenance.

In the last thirty years, the world's cultural heritage has seen an extraordinary increase in tourist pressure, leading to an inevitable evolution of the concepts of usability and accessibility. All the architectural assets that form the cultural heritage are often characterized by architectural barriers and each visitor can have different skills and different interests. For these reasons, such a consistent heritage combined with an equally high number of visitors gives a complexity often underestimated to the theme of accessibility. Overcoming architectural barriers can no longer be considered a simple "compliance to standards" based on pre-packaged solutions, often inconsistent and inconspicuous, but must become a methodological path based on targeted research activities capable to offer extensible and adaptable solutions to the typological multiplicity of cultural heritage [1: p. 10]. In summary, any intervention aimed to improve the accessibility of these sites must be able to reconcile the needs of conservation and protection with the need to overcome architectural barriers, responding to technical-design problems, to problems related to the users' characteristics and finally to problems represented by the protection measures.

In 2007, the Italian Ministry for heritage, cultural activities and tourism, in collaboration with Universities and many other stakeholders, edited the "Guidelines for overcoming architectural barriers in places of cultural interest", a synergistic document addressed to all those will have to face the issue of accessibility [5: p. 159]. Here, the meaning of the term "architectural barrier" has been significantly expanded, as it must not only take into account the classic physical obstacles but must include elements of various nature. Too long paths, the lack of orientation measures, the absence of handrails, the lack of seats, and all those elements that could constitute an inconvenience or discomfort are therefore considered architectural barriers. This type of approach is called "Universal Design" as it allows to design spaces that can be used by everyone, thus introducing the concept of "Extended Use" which brings together the multiplicity of individual characteristics of people, aiming to achieve inclusive solutions valid for everyone [1].

An emblematic case is the archaeological site of Pompeii. Here, in recent years, the considerable tourist pressure, combined with the evolution of the concept of accessibility, has revealed the need for new interventions in order to adapt the site. In 2010, the research "Accessible Pompeii. Guidelines for the extended fruition of the archaeological site" was carried on by the Science and Technology Centre of the University of Naples "Federico II". The area was divided into four sectors and each of them has been studied by a different operating group, aiming at relating conservation with the overcoming of architectural barriers, in order to ensure the best conditions of safety and comfort. The result was a series of projects aimed to improve the accessibility of Pompeii, ensuring an extended usability [9].

Fig. 1. Pompeii. Project "Pompeiifor all". Accessible path through the site area.

Fig. 2. Pompeii. Project "Pompeii for all". Solution for overcoming the carriage stones along the site visit routes. (https://www.lifegate. it/persone/news/pompei-per-tutti-inaugurato-itinerario-disabili)

In 2014, the proposal to improve the physical accessibility of Pompeii also came from the Ministry for Cultural Heritage and Activities (Ministero per i Beni e le Attività Culturali MiBACT). Thus the "Pompeii for all" project was born, from the collaboration of multidisciplinary teams, with the aim to study and realize simple solutions capable of solving complex problems, responding to the needs of all visitors. The case was particularly complex, as it still presents itself as a real city, with all the morphological and material problems that derive from it. An alive and dead city at the same time, as it stops in time but walked every day by visitors [10]. Despite everything, thanks to in-depth archaeological studies at the base of a complex and extensive project, "Pompeii for all" has created 3.5 km of accessible paths that, starting from the access doors, accompanyall the users to homes and public spaces, giving organicity to the visit and respecting the urban organization of the ancient city (Fig. 1 and 2).

2.2 Cognitive Accessibility

As said, physical accessibility must be the basis of any enhancement project. Personal experience, that is the possibility to "enter" in sites of culture, is undoubtedly very important, but it is not always sufficient to fully understand and enjoy the cultural heritage, especially for less expert users. Addressing the issue of accessibility therefore means taking into account all the needs of an "extended user", considering not only the physical barriers, linked to motor skills, but also the communication barriers, paying particular attention to people with mental and cognitive disabilities [5: p. 153]. The world of cognitive disabilities is particularly large, as it includes learning difficulties, autism, comprehension problems, down syndrome, etc.

The communication barriers, however, do not concern only the disabled people, but also children, who from this point of view represent a "particular" audience, and people who simply feel inadequate and not capable to understand high cultural level matters. People with cognitive difficulties cannot be considered a homogeneous "category", and therefore there are no solutions that can satisfy everyone's needs in the same way. In some cases, it may be sufficient to create information systems set up with a high level of understanding. In more serious cases, "other" aspects must be considered, for example by offering a new experience, which does not necessarily have to lead to learning, but which can still stimulate curiosity, creativity and involvement [4]. The task must be to communicate and transmit information in a clear, simple and widely accessible way, interpreting user requests, listening to the needs of the public and learning to understand the needs and expectations of that group of population more "distant" from the cultural institution. Eliminating the immaterial obstacles will allow to respond qualitatively and quantitatively to the expectations of all citizens. To achieve this, however, a real paradigm change is required. When organizing any exhibition, one should ask why people should visit it. The answer can only be given through the sharing of the interests of all potential users, who must therefore be involved both in the design phases and during the management of the environments, continually re-modelling them on the basis of customer satisfaction, in order to guarantee always a full experiential fruition [6].

The Rocca Aldobrandesca case study presents a significative model of cognitive accessibility. It is located in the highest part of the historic centre of Arcidosso, on the slopes of Mount Amiata, (Grosseto). Its musealization is part of the decades-long collaboration between the University of Florence and the Municipality of Arcidosso. The Rocca is one of the few cases in which considerable importance has been given to interactive design, with the aim of minimizing communication barriers.

The first step was to analyse the socio-economic and managerial context, trying to understand the interests and the needs of the potential users thanks to various preliminary surveys. These activities allowed to develop communication strategies based on documented and non-hypothetical critical issues and needs.

Subsequently, an interactive museum project was started, always based on the collaboration between designers and users (residents, tourists, students, etc.), during which a series of tools, closely linked to cognitive accessibility, were studied to understand the results of archaeological research. The obtained solutions were tested in the temporary exhibition organized by the University of Florence and the Municipality of Arcidosso in December 2011, with the aim of testing their effectiveness and collecting further suggestions from as many users as possible.

Once this experimentation was concluded, the final visit routes were designed and implemented. The museum space is today a true interactive communication organism, where the visitors can "interrogate" the archaeological and architectural buildings based on their interests and their level of competence [11] (Fig. 3 and 4).

Fig. 3. Arcidosso. Rocca Aldobrandesca. Visit route of the Rocca. Bronze architectural-stratigraphic model located in piazza Cavallotti. (https://www.tripadvisor.com/LocationPhotoDirectLink-g1050424-d8608144-i380103351-Aldobrandesca_Fortress-Arcidosso_Province_of_Grosseto_Tuscany.html)

Fig. 4. Arcidosso. Rocca Aldobrandesca. Museum itinerary. (https://www.facebook.com/locoarcidosso/photos/a.975996452427318/2473041362722812/?type=3)

2.3   The Sensory Perception

The five senses represent the "windows" that people use to collect information from the outside world. Actually, the sense organs are not independent, but interact with each other and with the whole organism, as a sophisticated mechanism for collecting information [12]. Therefore, the sensation is nothing more than a response to external stimuli, which allows people to build their own "image" of the objects and places that surround them. One of the factors that most complicates this type of sensory exploration is represented by synaesthesia, that is the simultaneous action of multiple senses, which, although autonomous, do not always work in a detached way [13: p. 1]. The involvement of all the senses in a balanced way becomes an essential aspect to ensure a pleasant perception of space and everything around us.

For this reason, the theme of sensoriality should have a considerable importance for the usability of cultural heritage, while in reality it is unfortunately one of the most neglected aspects. In addition, for people with sensory disabilities, the right to accessibility is not yet recognized and protected, as in the case of physical disabilities. Therefore, the places equipped with suitable measures to allow these people the opportunity to enjoy and understand the cultural heritage are still few.

In the first place, there are certainly the visual barriers, since almost all sites of cultural interest require sight as an organ of sense indispensable for their understanding, thus compromising their fruition in case of blindness or low vision [2: p. 17]. This sensorial barrier is closely linked to the cultural assumption that "art is vision" and that the "do not touch" rule reigns in museums. In fact, human beings have five senses, two of which allow them to recognize and perceive objects: sight and touch. This makes immediately clear that touch is the only way to "replace" sight.

This argument is strong but thorny at the same time, as it collides with the theme of heritage protection. Therefore, it will be necessary to distinguish what would not suffer any damage from the objects for which the enforcement of the "do not touch" rule is instead rightful. These objects can still be reproduced with tactile copies [6: p. 78]. Furthermore, touch is also able to exclusively capture many interesting qualities of objects and places. When someone touches something, one can perceive its shape, temperature, consistency, softness, roughness and many other sensations that could not be understood with other senses. This is not only valid only for the blind, but also for people with no visual handicap, who have already forgotten the tactile approach in the relationship with things, and do not understand its wonderful resources [6]. Therefore, in order to remove these sensorial barriers, all museums and sites should make possible for visitors to handle real objects and finds, but also reproductions, tactile maps, braille tags and bas-reliefs.

The problems related to people with hearing impairments are equally important. Unfortunately, this issue is still poorly addressed despite the difficulties that can occur during a visit. Furthermore, deafness is not clearly visible like other disabilities, and this means that they often go unnoticed and that their needs are neglected. The deaf people do not have access to the audio guides, they cannot use the normal guided tours and, when a guide who knows the sign language is present, they must remain particularly focused on the explanation, losing the opportunity to enjoy the view of the artworks and the sites. In order to break down these barriers, solutions able to guarantee an independent visit for deaf people should be found, such as panels, cards and captions that explain the finds with particularly accurate texts, but above all "videoguides", i.e. videos that illustrate, through sign language and subtitles, cultural sites and historical and artistic works [14].

Also, another important sense is the sense of smell, often ignored and forgotten, which represents the first filter between mankind and the outside world and is considered the most spontaneous of the five senses. The sense of smell creates in our minds the most immediate and profound impression of places and things, and contributes to creating an immersive and totalizing environment, capable to create an emotionally original experience [13: p. 2]. The potential of this sense is still underestimated and ignored today. Only in some, mostly temporary, exhibitions, the aesthetic aspect has been enriched with smells and perfumes, capable of creating engaging atmospheres, releasing memories and creating appeal.

Also, we have to remember that, in addition to the sensory barriers, there are many other problems indirectly related to the world of sensory (i.e. autism, daltonism, etc.) [15], and, in conclusion, we can say that if all the senses were treated with the same importance, the lack of one of them would not definitively preclude access to cultural heritage.

The MAV (Virtual Archaeological Museum) of Ercolano is one of the first cases in Italy that combine multisensory with the accessibility of cultural heritage.

The MAV represents a modern, technological and digital "smart museum" with over seventy multimedia installations which, through scenographic reconstructions, holograms and visual interfaces, produce a virtual and interactive path that is a journey back in time [16].

The "In all senses" project of 2018 and 2019 has the task to combine the advantages offered by new technologies with the potential of multisensory, offering an engaging and, above all, original cognitive experience, and removing the sensorial barriers that characterize these sites.

The aim is to guarantee sensory knowledge to "live" Pompeii and Ercolano in a dimension never done before, capable of actively involving the five senses. In addition to "seeing", it will be possible to "listen", through the virtual guides stories of Pompeii and Ercolano and thanks to the audio speakers placed along the way, simulating the voices of the people, the city's ancient noises and even the flow of water to the *calidarium*'s pool. It will be possible to "touch" through interactive devices, such as large touch screens, which give the visitor the opportunity to "clean" the walls from the ash, personally rediscovering the ancient frescoes (Fig. 5).

Fig. 5. MAV Ercolano. Thanks to large touch screens, visitors discover the frescoes by "cleaning" the walls from the ash. (https://www.pompei.it/scavi-ercolano/mav.htm)

The sense of smell will be involved thanks to special perfume machines, managed by software capable of reconstructing and emanating the characteristic essences of the sites, in particular the scents of the gardens, the ancient smells of the peristyle of the villas, typical of the Roman house, and the scent of rose petals that inebriates the rooms of the *calidarium*.

Finally, it will be possible to "taste" thanks to the workshops dedicated to the nutrition history of the ancient Rome [17].

The visit ends with the reconstruction of the eruption of Vesuvius that destroyed these cities, with a spectacular 5D projection, also created thanks to sophisticated immersive systems, which involves visitors with sound effects, vibrations, flashes and lights in an enveloping experience very different from the classic three-dimensional visualizations.

2.4 Alternative Accessibility

As said before, physical, cognitive and sensorial accessibility have a great importance for the enhancement of cultural heritage. But accessibility is not always fully achievable, especially in cases where it is necessary to combine the practical reasons of contemporary use with those of conservation and protection of cultural heritage [18].

The limits that prevent complete physical accessibility are due to various factors, including, in particular, morphology of the sites and architectural and spatial characteristics of the buildings [19: p. 1256].

To the numerous limits due to the physical-constructive characteristics of the sites must be added the problems related to conservation, since in some cases physical accessibility could represent a danger for the protection of certain cultural heritage.

Where the physical accessibility is not allowed or prosecutable, other forms of usability must be provided, to overcome architectural barriers in an alternative way, i.e. by offering the possibility to virtually visit these sites using new digital technologies [7]. These modern technologies also have many other potentials, such as the possibility of "seeing" beyond the state of fact, making possible to show the history of buildings and settlements as a real time machine, describing chronologically and culturally distant situations [8: p. 411].

Furthermore, digital environments offer a fruition in a contemporary interactive and captivating key, capable of evoking great interest in visitors, particularly in the new generations, proving a powerful means capable to approach and, therefore, to educate population to culture. In this way, alternative accessibility, in addition to the overcoming of the limits of physical accessibility, integrates and enhances the cognitive and sensorial accessibility, guaranteeing a free and expanded use of cultural heritage, and configuring itself as a tool capable to "rejuvenate" the enhancement system, bringing it to move with the times [20: p. 65].

The main technologies able to meet these needs are: Augmented Reality, where the normal reality perceived by our senses is superimposed with artificial and virtual information; Virtual Reality, which generates virtual spaces within which the user can move freely, thanks to special VR viewers; and, at last, the Automatic Recognition Systems which, thanks to simple two-dimensional barcodes readable through the tablet and smartphone camera, allow to view in-depth and easily updated information.

Favouring alternative accessibility was the enhancement strategy of the Faragola site, where, in 2003, the University of Foggia unearthed an extensive and articulated rural settlement from the Roman and late Antiquity time.

The research process ended with the creation of the Time Machine, a complex prototype that involved a group of experts from different sectors, who dedicated themselves to carrying out specific tasks: drafting documents; digital documentation; creation of models in computer graphics; concept creation and project management [21]. The goal was to narrate the entire life of the site from the origins, creating imaginary dimensions capable to provide information that could not have been understood in the state of fact. The Time Machine, thanks to the powerful 3D modelling and virtual reality technologies, offers the opportunity to virtually visit the site, moving freely in the various environments and moving through time, experiencing the various life stages of the site and discovering the enormous changes that a multi-layered archaeological site has undergone throughout history [8] (Fig. 6).

Fig. 6. Time Machine for the site of Faragola. Virtual visit of the Villa in the 400 A.D. [21].

2.5 Visibility Catalysts

As said before, technology, through modern digital tools, is contributing to the enhancement of cultural heritage, integrating physical accessibility, strengthening cognitive accessibility and offering innovative, increasingly immersive and engaging experiences to visitors. Technology makes another important tool available to cultural sites, the Digital Environments, useful to spread knowledge of heritage through the Internet. These environments represent real visibility catalysts, capable to reach a wide and heterogeneous public.

Visibility, still underestimated by most cultural organizations, represents one of the most important aspects for the enhancement of heritage, as it is closely linked to cultural activities and tourism. Poor visibility means poor accessibility and usability, as users who seek information remotely will never express a cultural demand about certain tourist destinations if those destinations are unable to "get to them". Digital environments can therefore play an incisive role in promoting and extending the cultural offer, ensuring an international visibility of the heritage. The ones that best meet this need are certainly the websites, followed by social media and video games, which represent the new frontier of digital communication at the service of culture.

The websites offer the opportunity to discover the cultural realities of the area and represent an important support for the organization of a possible visit. This aspect is remarkably important, as users increasingly tend to plan their visits in advance, for example according to their time available. Programming can even become indispensable for people with special needs, such as the people with a disability, the elderly and families with children, who hardly visit a site without having first acquired some information about its characteristics and the difficulties that could be encountered. The websites must provide detailed and exhaustive information of two different types: the cultural characteristics of the place and the general characteristics on the organization and management of the visit, as well as the conditions of accessibility and usability of the site [10: p. 450].

Planning the visit is therefore the main function of a website, but not the only one. Photos, videos and, in particular, virtual tours, increasingly popular in cultural web portals, offer a stimulating anticipation of the visit, aimed to increase the interest, and give the opportunity to virtually visit the site for people who, for various reasons, cannot do it physically, contributing in an alternative way to its enhancement [22].

Another important digital environment is represented by social media, considered "dynamic sites", as they allow continuous interaction between network and users, who can comment, write articles, upload images and more. Thanks to them, the "one to many" monologue of web 1.0 has been replaced by a "many to many" dialogue typical of web 2.0. These platforms are also widespread, thanks above all to the mobile web and smartphones, with which users are connected practically 24 h on social networks [23]. These characteristics have attracted the curiosity and interest of cultural institutions, which begin to feel the need to "be social". Thanks to social media, cultural sites have the opportunity to share their most interesting, creative and up-to-date content online. At the same time, users can participate, comment and even create content, interacting with the cultural institutions of which they are supporters [24].

In 2016, the MiBACT recognized cultural value to a new digital environment: video games. Furthermore, the EU Decision, about the European Year of Heritage 2018 in May 2017, contains a strong reference to the need for a greater connection between the artistic heritage and the younger generations [25: p. 11]. It is therefore essential to reflect on the relationship between video games and learning experiences related to art and culture. Video games can become an excellent tool for the enhancement and dissemination of our immense historical and cultural heritage, as they combine playful intent and didactic intent, and allow to get there easily to new generations.

From this point of view, a particularly interesting case is the famous video game Assassin's Creed, which gave the places where it was set, for example in Monteriggioni (Italy), a remarkable visibility, superior to what any promotional activity could guarantee. The number of tourists, mainly young people, who arrive every year in Monteriggioni from all over the world, attracted exclusively by the suggestions created by the video game, is surprising. A new form of tourism was born, defined as "Game

Tourism" or "Videogame Tourism", which prompts players from all over the world to go to the places where their favourite games have been set. The potential of this phenomenon must be immediately understood and made an integral part of tourism strategies at national and local level. One of the few cultural realities that has seized this occasion is the National Archaeological Museum of Naples, with the video game "Father and son", made with the specific aim to make the heritage of Naples known to the whole world [26].

#MuseoWeek is one of the first projects that sees art and social networks as protagonists, with the aim to sensitize the public to art. This initiative, launched in 2014, in the days from 24 to 30 March, has scheduled the "Week of European Museums", during which museum institutions and users will meet virtually on twitter.

The intent was to exploit the ability of social networks to act as a direct link between users and institutions, offering special access to thousands of museums and galleries and starting up interesting debates on culture. People who have visited at least one museum during this week is invited to share their experience on social media, expressing their opinions, so that they can compare themselves with other users and especially with the staff of the institutions. The museums social media managers therefore had the task to manage the initiative by interacting with users and with museums across Europe.

The week was divided into several themed days, with the aim to direct and guide the various conversations on specific topics, proposing a different hashtag every day: #DayInTheLife, #MuseumMastermind, #MuseumMemories, #BehindTheArt, #AskTheCurator, #MuseumSelfies and finally #GetCreative, which closed this week inviting culture fans to imagine and describe their ideal museum [27].

With 104 thousand tweets analysed, tweeted by almost 58 thousand users, #MuseumWeek has been able to connect the public with museum institutions, artworks, history and science, in an engaging and interactive way. An unexpected international success, which has encouraged to repeat the event also in the following years. The #MuseumWeek is progressively growing year after year. The event has therefore evolved considerably over time, always maintaining the same great goal, to make culture available to everyone and to offer art lovers additional reasons to visit their favourite collections [28].

3   Access to Use: Proposals to Improve the Physical and Cognitive Accessibility for the Nuragic Sanctuary of Santa Vittoria di Serri

The Nuragic Sanctuary of Santa Vittoria is located on the western end of the Giara di Serri, in Sardinia, in a point of wide visual domain. Serri has a great cultural heritage with evidence dating back to the Nuragic Civilization (18th–3rd century B.C.), of which the main expression is the Sanctuary of Santa Vittoria [29: p. 292]. The elements that attest its importance are manifold: the extraordinary location; the large extension, fully protected in accordance with the Italian Heritage Protection Law, equal to about 22 hectares, of which currently only 3.5 are excavated and can be visited; the quantity and type of religious buildings, a sort of anthology of the sacred architecture of Nuragic Sardinia; the exceptional nature of the archaeological finds; the continuity of the cult during the historical periods, testified both by the finds and by the reuse of the structures [30]. From an architectural point of view, the Sanctuary presents all the main characteristics of the sanctuary areas: the presence of circular structures with seats better defined as "Meeting huts"; templar areas used for water worship; differentiation and variety of architectures present in the sanctuary complex; presence of collective structures such as rotundas, stepped basins and squares [29: p. 276]. This Sanctuary was discovered by the archaeologist Taramelli A. in 1907, and the first excavation was started two years later in 1909 [31: p. 14]. The numerous studies on the discovery of the site, published in the first thirty years of the 1900s, allowed the world to know this archaeological site, which soon became a particularly attractive place for scholars and enthusiasts, who came from all over the world to admire the archaeological remains brought to light after millennia. This moment of splendour was followed by a long period of "abandonment" from the point of view both of accessibility and of enhancement, marking a setback in the site growth. For several decades the Sanctuary counted a negligible number of visitors compared to its potential. This shows that the extraordinary nature of a site emerges only if accompanied by the right enhancement actions, capable to attract the greatest number of visitors, and good usability, aimed to respond to the needs of an expanded user.

Archive research, site inspections carried out at different times of the year and interviews addressed to site users, have allowed to understand the main accessibility problems of the area. One of the most evident is the entrance building, that cannot guarantee the necessary reception functions in this site. Also, the paths are made with a stone ballast recently covered with a compacted ground finish. These routes present evident problems in terms of physical accessibility: excessive lengths, difference in height, uneven surfaces, absence of rest areas and shelters.

Another problem is the directional signs, which are fundamental for the usability of the sites, particularly in large archaeological areas, but in Santa Vittoria are deficient and inadequate, so that they compromise the visitor orientation. Also, the information panels are excessive, causing a dispersion of information, making the site difficult to read and understand. This aspect is aggravated by the fact that panels are not arranged along the visit route, but near the structures, often resulting unreachable.

The poor physical-cognitive accessibility of the Sanctuary does not allow the visitor to live and fully understand the nature of the site. There is a poor perception of the place, which does not allow archaeological remains, naturally elusive, to communicate and transmit intelligible information. This shows how the enhancement of the site requires a much broader perspective, which integrates the tools of research and archaeological conservation with those of the architectural project, giving this term the broader meanings that it underlies. The question on which architecture is called to answer is that of the interpretation/presentation of the site to visitors, to which is added the fundamental aspect concerning the intervention quality [32, 33].

Starting from this assumption, an attempt was made to study a series of mediation systems, aimed to solve the main problems of the case study, but which can be extended to similar cases, resulting useful and valid for a broader number of sites.

Near the entrance to the archaeological area, a compacted ground square has been designed, which integrates with the territorial context ensuring a homogeneous surface that can be easily walked. In the square there is the new entrance building, consisting of a semi hypogeum architecture, in continuity with the territory, which integrates with the landscape by exploiting the particularity of the topography. The roof of the new building, consisting of a narrow and long plate, becomes a square conceived as a panoramic viewpoint, from which visitors can scan into the ruins in the distance, establishing a first contact with them. The large plate is holed by the ramp which allows access to the internal rooms, positioned at a lower level of the countryside. These environments are delimited by a pure transparent volume, which helps to limit the visual impact of the architecture and guarantees the visual continuity of the landscape. Inside it houses the reception services at the Sanctuary and a large room that has the function of transmitting to the visitor all the information necessary to understand the site, enhancing the visit experience thanks to three-dimensional reproductions of the most important finds found on the site and through interactive systems capable of transmitting all the information necessary to prepare people for the visit, creating a combination of indirect devices and direct knowledge of the archaeological remains (Fig. 7).

In reference to the principle, one could also mention the fact that architecture, as always, maintains its organizing aptitude, with which it confronts itself, revealing the opportunities of the site and the comprehension of places. Indeed, in this case, the building is partially underground not to express the reasons for its "camouflage", but rather to show the visitor that one of the greatest preciousness of the context lies in the ability to dig deep into the ground, as happened, for example, for the holy well of Santa Vittoria. In this sense, the water line is not only a clear reference to the context, but it is also an element able to physically and emotionally guide the visitor.

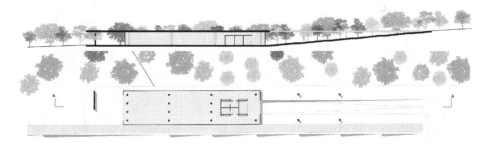

Fig. 7. Project for the new entrance building to the Sanctuary (Architectures for archaeology. Studies for physical and cognitive accessibility for the Sanctuary of Santa Vittoria di Serri. Master degree thesis by Mattia Cogoni)

The Sanctuary paths that guide visitors from the new building to the nuragic architectures, built in compacted ground, have been hierarchized taking into account the visitors flow and the impact of the intervention. There are: a "main path", which from the entrance square leads to the western area of the site; "visit routes", which lead to the main areas of the Sanctuary; "footpaths", which from the visit path lead to the various nuragic architectures. There are connecting ramps with adjustable feet, in order to solve critical points. All paths are equipped with guide curbs that allow blind people to visit autonomously and where necessary they take on the double function of system holder curb, which allows to equip the entire area reducing the impact of the intervention.

All the intersection between paths have a tactile paving made with the use of cobblestones, which characterizes the area and also helps blind people to perceive the intersection. These points are also equipped with directional signs, which indicate to the visitor the area accessible from any direction and the length of the respective path, always ensuring orientation. At the ends of the paths, near the architectures, there is an area for tourists involved in a guided tour, in which there is an information panel that contains information designed to ensure maximum understanding of the archaeological remains for all users (Fig. 8).

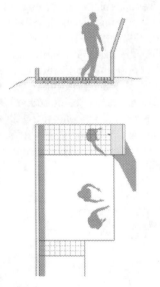

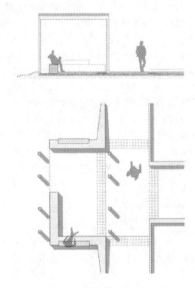

Fig. 8. Project for information and rest areas to welcome tourists during the guided tour.

Fig. 9. Project of shelter for rest areas. (Architectures for archaeology. Studies for physical and cognitive accessibility for the Sanctuary of Santa Vittoria di Serri. Master degree thesis by Mattia Cogoni)

Along the paths there are several rest areas, which allow visitors to rest, enjoying the shade offered by the area vegetation. Also, in this case there is the tactile paving that characterizes the area and helps blind people to perceive its presence. Finally, at the intersection between the main path and the visit path, which represents the midpoint of the site, there is a pergola that incorporates the shapes and horizontality of the entrance building. This volume represents the "entrance door" of the western area of the Sanctuary and offers a shelter for visitors (Fig. 9).

References

1. Agostiano, M., Baracco, L., Caprara, G., Pane, A., Virdia, E.: Linee Guida per il superamento delle barriere architettoniche nei luoghi di interesse culturale. Gangemi Editore, Roma (2008)
2. Miglietta, A.M.: Il museo accessibile: barriere, azioni e riflessioni (2017)
3. Steinfeld, E., Maisel, J.L.: Universal Design: Creating Inclusive Environments. Wiley, New Jersey (2012)
4. The Principles of Universal Design, Version 2.0 by The Center for Universal Design. North Carolina State University, 01 April 1997
5. Agostiano, M.: L'accessibilità come strumento strategico del ministero dei beni culturali per la tutela e valorizzazione delle aree archeologiche. In: Picone, R. (ed.) POMPEI ACCESSIBILE Per una fruizione ampliata del sito archeologico. L'ERMA di BRET-SCHNEIDER, Roma (2013)
6. Cetorelli, G., Guido, M.R.: Quaderni della valorizzazione: Il patrimonio culturale per tutti. Fruibilità, riconoscibilità, accessibilità. Proposte, interventi, itinerari per l'accoglienza ai beni storico-artistici e alle strutture turistiche. Fast Edit, Acquaviva Picena (2017)
7. Murru, S.: Accessibilità e fortificazioni. In: Giannattasio, C., Grillo, S.M., Murru, S. (eds.) Il sistema di torri costiere in Sardegna. L'ERMA di BRETSCHNEIDER, Roma (2017)
8. De Felice, G., Sibilano, M.G.: Strategie di documentazione per la ricerca e la comunicazione archeologica. Il caso di Faragola. In: Digitalización 3d del patrimonio arqueológico II (2009)
9. Fabbrocino, G., Saitto, V.: I dispositivi per l'accessibilità nell'area di porta marina. In: Picone, R. (ed.) POMPEI ACCESSIBILE Per una fruizione ampliata del sito archeologico. L'ERMA di BRETSCHNEIDER, Roma (2013)
10. Agostiano, M., Pane, A.: Indirizzi operativi per una fruizione ampliata del sito archeologico di Pompei. In: Picone, R. (ed.) POMPEI ACCESSIBILE Per una fruizione ampliata del sito archeologico. L'ERMA di BRETSCHNEIDER, Roma (2013)
11. Nucciotti, M.: Una musealizzazione interattiva 'unplugged': archeologia pubblica alla rocca aldobrandesca di Arcidosso. In: Dionisio, G., Jasink, A.M. (eds.) MUSINT 2 Nuove esperienze di ricerca e didattica nella museologia interattiva. Firenze University Press (2016)
12. I cinque sensi per la scienza. https://www.lifegate.it/persone/stile-di-vita/i_cinque_sensi_per_la_scienza
13. Lucibello, S.: Verso un'Architettura Sensoriale (2010)
14. Progetto MAPS (Musei Accessibili per le Persone Sorde). http://annoeuropeo2018.beniculturali.it/eventi/progetto-maps-musei-accessibili-le-persone-sorde/
15. La sensorialità nello spettro autistico, disponibile su. http://www.gfrvitale.altervista.org/index.php/pr-i-s-m-a/20-autismo/545-la-sensorialita-nello-spettro-autistico
16. Il museo MAV. https://www.museomav.it/museo/
17. MAV 4.0 – Uno smart museo 5D. http://www.museincampania.com/mav-4-0-uno-smart-museo-5d-per-tutti-i-sen-si/
18. Bartolomucci, C., Giannattasio, C.: Il conflitto tra accessibilità e fruizione nel progetto di conservazione (2009)
19. Giannattasio, C., Pinna, A., Pintus, V., Pirisino, S.: Accessibilità integrata per architetture inaccessibili. I castelli della Sardegna (XIV-XV sec.). In: Marotta, A., Spal-lone, R. (eds.) Defensive Architecture of the Mediterranean, vol. IX. Politecnico di Torino (2018)
20. Peripimeno, M.: Sistemi 'leggeri' di valorizzazione e musealizzazione (l'esperienza LIAAM). In: Forgione, A., Redi, F. (eds.) VI congresso nazionale di archeologia medievale. All'Insegna del Giglio, l'Aquila (2012)

738   F. Pinna et al.

21. De Felice, G.: Una macchina del tempo per l'archeologia, Metodologie e tecnologie per la ricerca e la fruizione virtuale del sito di Faragola. Edipuglia, Bari (2012)
22. Convegno: "La cultura del web, il web per la cultura". https://www.beniculturali.it/mibac/export/MiBAC/sito-MiBAC/Contenuti/Mi-bacUnif/Comunicati/visualizza_asset.html_1271558599.html
23. Didattica e turismo 2.0. Nuove tecnologie per la divulgazione del patrimonio culturale. http://storiaefuturo.eu/didattica-e-turismo-2-0-nuove-tecnologie-per-la-divulga-zione-del-patrimonio-culturale/
24. Progetto #svegliamuseo. http://www.svegliamuseo.com/it/
25. Lampis A.: Ambienti digitali e musei: esperienze e prospettive in Italia. In: Luigini, A., Panciroli, C. (eds.) Ambienti digitali per l'educazione all'arte e al patrimonio (2018)
26. Videogiochi per il turismo culturale. https://www.tuomuseo.it/gaming/videogiochi-per-il-turismo-culturale/
27. #MuseumWeek: il museo in 140 caratteri. https://www.wired.it/internet/social-network/2014/04/01/museumwe-ek-il-museo-140-caratteri-cosi-ti-racconto-larte-un-tweet/
28. #MuseumWeek. https://www.beniculturalionline.it/event.php?n=1653
29. Porcedda, F.: Modelli di insediamento di Preistoria e Protostoria nel Sarcidano e nella Marmilla Orientale (Sardegna, Italia). Granada: Università di Granada (2019)
30. Canu, N.: Gli interventi della Soprintendenza per i beni archeologici per le province di Sassari e Nuoro a Santa Vittoria. Ricerche d'archivio. In: Canu, N., Cicilloni, R. (eds.) Il Santuario di Santa Vittoria di Serri, tra archeologia del passato e archeologia del futuro. Edizioni Quasar, Roma (2015)
31. Casagrande, M.: Storia di una scoperta, le prime esplorazioni a Santa Vittoria di Serri. In: Canu, N., Cicilloni, R. (eds.) Il Santuario di Santa Vittoria di Serri, tra archeologia del passato e archeologia del futuro. Edizioni Quasar, Roma (2015)
32. Casadei, C.: L'integrazione nel paesaggio. In: Rassegna di architettura e urbanistica. vol. 151. Architettura e archeologia. Quodlibet (2017)
33. Lagunes, M.M.: Architettura per l'archeologia. In: Rassegna di architettura e urbanistica. vol. 151. Architettura e archeologia. Quodlibet (2017)

International Workshop on Virtual and Augmented Reality and Applications (VRA 2020)

Wearable Device for Immersive Virtual Reality Control and Application in Upper Limbs Motor Rehabilitation

Mateus Michelin Jurioli[1] , Alexandre Fonseca Brandao[2,3] ,
Bárbara Cristina Silva Guedes Martins[3,4] , Eduardo do Valle Simões[1],
and Cláudeo Fabino Motta Toledo[1(✉)]

[1] Instite of Mathematics and Computer Science, USP, Butanta, Brazil
mateus.jurioli@gmail.com, claudio@icmc.usp.br
[2] Physics Institute Gleb Wataghim, IFGW, UNICAMP, Rio de Janerio, Brazil
[3] Brazilian Institute of Neuroscience and Neurotechnology, BRAINN, UNICAMP,
Sao Paulo, Brazil
[4] School of Medical Sciences, FCM, UNICAMP, Sao Paulo, Brazil

Abstract. Virtual Reality (VR) has been used in several areas such as video games, technical training, movies and teaching. VR-based interventions have also been applied for motor rehabilitation, e.g., to help the patient recovery from disabilities provoked by stroke, cognitive deficit or musculoskeletal problem. VR combined with wearable tracking devices creates new possibilities to apply immersive approaches during motor rehabilitation. This can enhance the health care making it more interesting and pleasant for patients as well as more effective for physicians and physiotherapists. However, the costs related to this technology may be impracticable for a wide application by public health system. Therefore, this paper introduces preliminary results for a low-cost wearable device, which is integrated to VR environments aiming to provide a better quality rehabilitation process for most patient with motor disabilities.

Keywords: Virtual reality · Rehabilitation · Wearable device · Immersive environment

1 Introduction

Virtual Reality (VR) is a new technology that is expanding year by year. In the 1950s the VR emerged as a promising innovation for entertainment. Nowadays, it is used in several areas such as video games, technical training, movies and teaching [2,10,11,33]. VR is also applied in clinical interventions for rehabilitation processes. There are applications in motor recovery therapies [15,17,29,31,32], such as those used to help patients recovering from disabilities caused by stroke, cognitive impairment or musculoskeletal problems. One of the reasons for using VR environment to stimulate, e.g., a post stroke's brain is the immersion level of the surroundings, making the procedures look like a day-to-day activity [15].

© Springer Nature Switzerland AG 2020
O. Gervasi et al. (Eds.): ICCSA 2020, LNCS 12255, pp. 741–756, 2020.
https://doi.org/10.1007/978-3-030-58820-5_53

The stroke is the third leading cause of disability worldwide [37]. To reduce stroke's side-effects and prevent serious sequelae, the rehabilitation process must start as soon as possible after a stroke event. The rehabilitation is conducted mainly through physiotherapy and occupational therapy sessions [20]. The authors [28] describe that repetitive motions during the physiotherapy sessions can help the rehabilitation process, but to keep the patient motivated while doing all repetitions is a challenging process.

VR interaction usually relies on controllers with buttons and joysticks, or visual-based controllers such as Kinect. These type of controllers are not always adaptable to a patient with a low movement of her/his arm. Thus, a tailor-made wearable device can become necessary to control better the objects within the virtual environment. The combination of VR with wearable tracking devices creates new possibilities for therapists, when using immersive approaches during motor rehabilitation. This approach can enhance health care, making it more interest and pleasant for patients as well as more effective for physiotherapists.

However, the costs related to this technology may be impracticable for a wide application by public health systems. Therefore, the present paper reports the preliminary results achieved by a research project where a low-cost virtual reality (VR) device has been developed. The device will help stroke patients and therapists to improve the motor rehabilitation process. The proposed device has two main parts: software and hardware. The first one includes the VR environment itself, which means everything that the patient will see in the smart-phone with the VR headset. The second part is the wearable device that will track the patient's motion and send them to the smart-phone.

The aim is to make available a more immersive treatment for patients as well as affordable for public health systems, without compromising the quality of the rehabilitation process. To pursue such a goal, we integrate the VR environment into a wearable device that controls interactive parts of the virtual space. We use a VR headset for smart-phones with a wearable device customized for reaching such a goal. The integration of the VR headset (with a smartphone) and the wearable device becomes this framework portable and easy to set up and handle. As everything developed must be low cost, we design the VR environments to run on a wide variety of smartphone models.

2   Related Works

In recent years, interventions using VR have found applications in complementary therapy for more traditional neurorehabilitation methods [1,17,21,26,31, 32,35]. However, the effectiveness of using VR as a tool for rehabilitation is still a topic raising discussion among therapist [29]. In this scenario, the treatment within a virtual environment is based on the Mirror Neuron System (MNS), which is a group of neurons that can replicate the functions of other neurons [3,23]. The Mirror neurons, when stimulated by VR, may accelerate the reorganization and functional recovery in post-stroke patients [4].

The authors [14] show that using VR as a complement to conventional reha-bilitation achieved better results than just the conventional ones. The study used a control group, under only traditional recovery, and an experimental group under traditional and VR rehabilitation. The focus of such research was in upper limb rehab, aiming to get a better evaluation of both treatments. One of the con-ventional approaches for upper limb rehabilitation is the exoskeleton robot. This kind of robot helps the user to make movements almost without applying any force. A compilation of exoskeleton devices to assist in rehabilitation is presented by [18]. The use of VR with these prototypes is also evaluated by [8,27]. These devices have many advantages, but also two main issues: a high cost and low mobility for patients. The present paper tries to introduce a device able to fill such a gap.

The study conducted in [6] shows the effectiveness of VR training in motor performance and cognitive recovery of post-stroke patients. The proposed solu-tion is the BTs-Nirvana, a high-cost device. The results reported that VR pro-motes better results than conventional rehabilitation protocols.

The study in [1] show a smart glove (FlexiForce and FlexSensors 2.2) with inertial measure unity (IMU) to control a VR world for rehabilitation purpose. The smart glove provides the finger's flexion and force, and in other words, this device could help in the patient hand's rehabilitation.

The author in [5] show an IMU's sensor as an evaluation system for measuring the degree of shoulder joint movement. In the study, the author evaluates the IMU in comparison with traditional protractor evaluation. The results concluded that the sensor is precise and can be used to assess the range of motion of the patient shoulder.

The work in [7] presents a device to control a virtual reality environment for lower limbs. The device has a sonar with a gyroscope/accelerometer to track the position of the leg, used for gesture control. A VR city was developed to facilitate the patient immersion during the treatment.

The VR-based procedures in stroke patients show relevant improvement in their upper limb performance as reported by [29] and [21], when compared against traditional treatments. The study in [35] indicates that VR can help, when associated with a conventional rehabilitation process, once the visual feed-back from VR becomes the process more enjoyable and attractive for patients. The engagement in the rehabilitation process can be enhanced using the VR [22]. A recent scoping review about the VR applications in rehabilitation is provided by [9] and [30].

The authors in [19] report that VR technology is progressing year-by-year, becoming a useful tool to improve the recovery of the patient's cognitive function. It is described the improvements achieved in the cognitive domains of patients that used the VR as an auxiliary treatment. These improvements are based on the results reported from eight clinical studies. In the study made by [16], the VR therapy was used with functional electrical stimulation (FES) to evaluate the benefit of the VR in the rehabilitation of upper limbs. The authors in [16] concludes that the VR stimulation associated with FES presented better results than FES alone.

3   VR Device

The development of this device has taken place in collaboration with an experienced therapist and meets the need for rehabilitation procedures defined by them. The main objective of the device is to translate the movement of the patient's arm into the virtual environment, amplifying or decreasing her/his sensitivity based on the rehabilitation process.

One of the requests for the device was that the therapist could move the user's hand without interfering with the tracking system. This requirement meant that a visual-based tracking system became almost impossible since there was overlap between the therapist and the patient's arms. The device and the related software are required to perform all the functionalities without the user pressing a single button.

Based on such requirements, this project proposes a device that tracks the arm using a spherical coordinate system. In other words, the device tracks a point such as P1 in Fig. 1(a), based on another fixed point P0, using two angles and a fixed value. The set value r is the distance between the point P0 and P1, while the angle ϕ is the angle between Z-axis and the vector $\overrightarrow{P0P1}$. The second angle φ is between the X-axis and the projection of the vector $\overrightarrow{P0P1}$ in the XY-plane, as P1 can see it in Fig. 1(b).

To apply this use of a spherical coordinate system in the real world, we included an Inertial Measurement Unit (IMU) in the patient's arm between her/his wrist and elbow as shown by Fig. 1(b). In this situation, P0 is set to the elbow while P1 in the wrist. This layout means that the device is tracking the wrist's angles concerning the elbow joint.

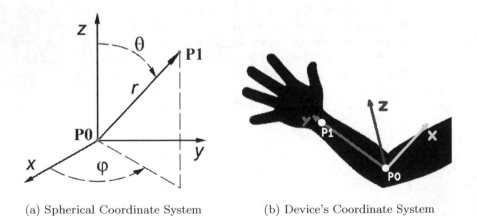

(a) Spherical Coordinate System   (b) Device's Coordinate System

Fig. 1. Coordinate system

3.1   Device's Hardware

Arduino Nano microcontroller was used with one IMU (MPU-6050) and a Bluetooth module (HC-05) to develop the device. The microcontroller, powered by a 9 V battery, and all other components by the microcontroller. The current total cost is around $11.00.

The IMU sensor is responsible for getting the gyroscope, accelerometer and magnetometer data. The MPU-6065 uses the Digital Motion Processor (DMP) to fuse this data and reduce the errors of each one of the sensors. A quaternion Q returns the result of this fusion, which is given by Eq. 1 to describe the orientation of an object in a 3D space.

$$Q = q_0 + q_1 i + q_2 j + q_3 k = (q_0, q_1, q_2, q_3) \tag{1}$$

The quaternion is sent to the Arduino Nano and translated to the Euler angles (roll ϕ, pitch θ, yaw ψ) using the formula below:

$$\begin{bmatrix} \phi \\ \theta \\ \psi \end{bmatrix} = \begin{bmatrix} \arctan \frac{2(q_0 q_1 + q_2 q_3)}{1 - 2(q_1^2 + q_2^2)} \\ \arcsin(2(q_0 q_2 - q_3 q_1)) \\ \arctan \frac{2(q_0 q_3 + q_1 q_2)}{1 - 2(q_2^2 + q_3^2)} \end{bmatrix} \tag{2}$$

These angles represent the angles of the patient's wrist in relation to the elbows. The first angle (ϕ) is the rotation in the X-axis, the second angle is the rotation in the (θ) Y-axis, and the third one (ψ) the rotation in the Z-axis. We define the axes X, Y, Z in Fig. 1(b).

After the data is processed, it is sent to the smartphone (via Bluetooth module) and allows you to control the VR environment. The devices present a switch to power on and a button to reset the centre position of the VR environment as it will explain in Sect. 4.1.

3.2   Device's Encapsulation

As a device to be used by the therapist in the rehabilitation processes, it has to be simple, practical and versatile to reach all the complexity of each patient treatment. Thus, we encapsulate the device in a 3D printed box made using ABS (Acrylonitrile Butadiene Styrene) plastic, including another space to store the battery. We also used Velcro tape to wrap everything in the patient's arm as presented in Fig. 2.

4   Jigsaw Puzzle

The main focus of the software was to assist therapist and patients, based on the type of movements done by the patients following the therapist commands. The device is evaluated in a real-world situation through a VR jigsaw puzzle. The software for such game was made using the Unity3D engine [36]. We use a smartphone with a headset to simulate the immersive environment, and the

(a) Disassembled device

(b) Device mounted in the patient's arm

Fig. 2. Proposed device

3D puzzle must be able to run in low-cost smartphone models. At this step of our research project, the software can run from any smartphone with quad-core processor, 1.3 GHz and 2 GB of RAM.

4.1 Puzzle Settings

The jigsaw puzzle presents a few settings as shown by Fig. 3. The therapist can use these settings to optimize the VR experience during the recovery process. The parameter settings implemented until now are level of sensitivity, the number of pieces in the puzzle, in which arm the patient will hold the device, hitbox and image selection.

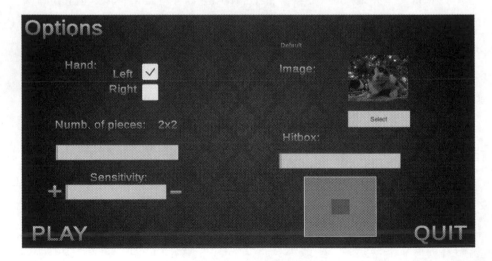

Fig. 3. Puzzle setting screen

The parameter level of sensitivity represents how the real motion will be translated into the VR environment. It is a number that can be set by the therapist between 200 to 2000. If the sensitivity is set in 200, this means that a small motion in the real-world will be translated as a larger one in the puzzle. On the other hand, this effect is less amplified when higher values for sensitivity are set. The therapist also sets the number of pieces that the patient will assemble to complete the full image. Now the value is limited to cut the image from 2×2 to 4×4 pieces, but it can be expanded based on the type of treatment.

The software works with one patient arm being used in the VR environment to control every interaction with the puzzle. Thus, the therapist must set whether the patient will move the puzzle pieces using the left or right hand. The precision reached by the user when catching and placing the pieces is another relevant feature that needs to be approached. Based on this demand, a hitbox sliding bar was implemented on the menu. The hitbox tells us how near to the centre of the piece the user must be closed enough to pick the piece up as well as to place it in the right position.

For instance, the orange square in Fig. 3 represents one piece, and the red square (hitbox) is where the user needs to go to pick the piece up. Once the user is holding the piece, she/he needs to put it in the right position. This position has the same hitbox as the piece; in other words, the user needs to get inside the area of the hitbox to put the piece in place. Figure 4 illustrates the hitbox when the user is catching and placing the piece.

The hitbox is not visible for the user, but the hitbox sliding bar in Fig. 3 gives the therapists the ability to control the size of the hitbox to fit the patient's necessities. Thus, the therapist can adjust the hitbox, becoming more or less challenging to pick up or to position the pieces as illustrated in Fig. 5.

The patient's motivation is an essential part of the rehabilitation process. Because of this, the puzzle was developed to accept different images, including personal ones from the patient.

4.2 Puzzle's Gameplay

After the therapist settings, the software initializes the protocol for device calibration. The calibration will evaluate and remove possible errors lead by noises when the device is not moving. If the sensor is not moving (spatial displacement), its output should be zero, but the sensor may present some noise. Moreover, the calibration protocol compiles all the noises and removes them. The VR's headset can be placed in the patient while the calibration is happening. Figure 6 shows the calibration processes screen.

After the calibration, the therapist can start the Jigsaw puzzle by pressing the red button on the device. At this point, the device will consider the real world's position as the centre of the virtual environment. The patient will need to have some space in the real environment to move the arm for all directions (up, down, left and right).

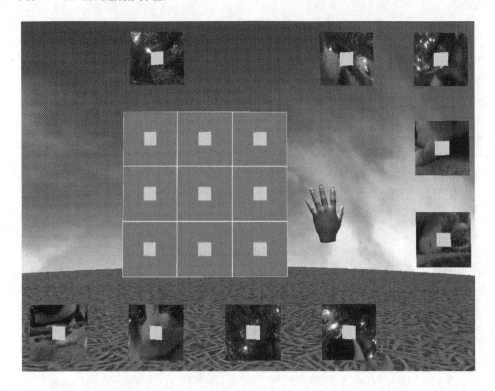

Fig. 4. Hitbox

(a) High precision - small hitbox

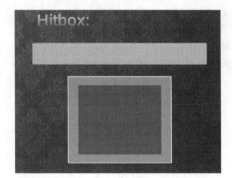

(b) Low precision - large hitbox

Fig. 5. Hitbox settings

Once the game started, the user only has to complete the virtual puzzle. When the user gets the piece, the software helps him to find the right position of the piece showing a red square in the respective area (Fig. 7). A full picture will be also shown in the upper right corner to help the patient finding the image.

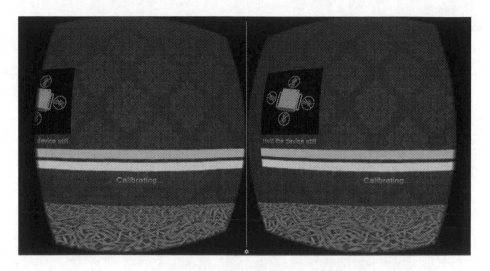

Fig. 6. Calibration screen

Fig. 7. Jigsaw Puzzle

4.3 Puzzle Data

The relevant data processed by the software is stored during the patient gameplay to evaluate his/her rehabilitation process. The data stored is the time that the patient needs to complete the puzzle, all the hand position the patient moved in the environment and all the settings the therapist put to start the VR environment. These data allows quantifying the movements performed by the patient during the execution of the puzzle.

5   Experimental Evaluation

The experimental evaluation was conducted with healthy volunteers at this stage of the project, and it was separated into two parts. First, the device is evaluated by itself before being used by the volunteers. Next, the volunteers will handle the device, play the game and report their remarks by answering a questionnaire.

5.1   Device's Evaluation

The device was submitted to a few tests before experimental procedures with volunteers. These tests evaluated the device's precision and the device's robustness.

Precision: To measure the accuracy, the device was left still for 3 min, and the data collected was evaluated. All the relevant data gathered is shown in Table 1. As expected, there is a minimum and acceptable deviation near zero degrees in the position setting.

Table 1. Device stability within a non-movement situation

Results	Max. deviation	Min. deviation	Standard deviation
Roll	0.038°	−0.351°	0.024°
Pitch	0.788°	−0.641°	0.253°
Yaw	0.027°	−0.022°	0.009°

The standard deviation must be around zero; otherwise, the user will start to notice hand movement over time. Thus, the maximum and minimum values in Table 1 need to be close to zero to achieve excellent accuracy without a spike in the movement.

Robustness: The device robustness is the reliability of the hardware, such as the precision of the movements after a long period using it. The device was in a non-movement stage for 1 h, after this time, the errors were evaluated as it can be seen in Table 2:

Table 2. Device's reliability in a long run

Results	Max. deviation	Min. deviation	Standard deviation
Roll	0.037°	−0.338°	0.028°
Pitch	0.672°	−0.596°	0.249°
Yaw	0.024°	−0.024°	0.011°

Comparing Table 1 and Table 2, we conclude that the device presented the same precision over time, without drifting in any angle for the long run. Next, the device was put in a zero position and moved 90° in roll, 90° in pitch and 90° in yaw, and returned to the point zero. After repeating this procedure five times, the device stayed still for 10 s, and the difference to the initial position was evaluated, as shown in Table 3:

Table 3. Device's precision in repetitive tasks

Results	Averages differences
Roll	0.186°
Pitch	−1.272°
Yaw	0.088°

The differences on average must be as close to zero as possible to get a better tracking device. There was a discrepancy in the average difference when comparing the pitch against row and yaw. This average difference is explained by how the DMP calculates the error. However, the pitch angle (rotation in Y-axis) is not used and relevant in the experiment, since such angle stands for the supination and pronation of the arm.

5.2 Evaluation with Volunteers

Volunteers evaluated the device taking into account the device delay, the VR motion sickness effects, level of sensitivity when solving the puzzle, and the overall evaluation of their experience. The volunteers were healthy adults with an undergraduate degree, and ranging from 28 to 50 years old.

Delay: The device's delay is the difference in time between moving the device and its respective arm motion simulation within the VR environment. For the delay evaluation, the volunteers were a total of 16 healthy subjects and five therapists. They answered some questions about how the delay affected their puzzle experience. In the 16 healthy subject group, the device's delay harmed the movements of the puzzle pieces for eight healthy subjects, there was delay but without compromising the movements for six subjects, and the delay was not observed by two subjects. On the other hand, all five therapists answered that there was a noticed delay for a healthy person, but it is not noticeable for a patient with post-stroke movement disability. Based on these reports, the delay problem must be better evaluated through a real situation with post-stroke patients. After such evaluation, we can decide whether it is or not a real problem when using the device.

Motion Sickness: The motion sickness occurs when there is a conflict between what the body is feeling, and the eyes see. For instance, the body is moving, but the eyes are seeing a still image, which can produce a motion sickness in a person [12,25]. In virtual reality devices, the motion sickness can happen when there is delay from the Virtual reality screen to the head movement, a drop in the number of screen frames per second happens, or some sensors data conflict resulting in a false screen image [13].

The 16 healthy volunteers helped us to evaluate this motion sickness based on two criteria: discomfort using the VR (headache, stomach awareness or nausea) and disorientation or instability. In this group, a total of 14 subjects evaluates that the VR experience did not lead to any discomfort; the other two said that they could not assess this point. Regarding disorientation, all subjects agree that there was no such sensation.

Level of Sensitivity: The 16 volunteers were submitted to a test in sensitivity variation. In other words, eight volunteers tested the 3×3 puzzle with minimal sensitivity (wide arm movement); the other eight volunteers tested the same 3×3 puzzle, but with maximum sensitivity, (restricted arm movement). The average time to complete the task is shown in Table 4.

Table 4. Average time to complete the puzzle

	Averages time(sec.)	Standard deviation(sec.)
Minimum sensitivity	133.162	28.668
Maximum sensitivity	107.535	13.344

The average time got higher in minimum sensitivity because of the wider range of motion needed to reach the pieces. In the other hand, the high standard deviation shows that there was a discrepancy the time between the users. One of the possible evaluation is the initial adaptation of some users when using the device. In the minimum sensitivity, there are volunteers that needed more few minutes to get used to the device and the virtual reality environment.

Overall Evaluation: The 16 subjects answered a questionnaire with a few questions about the software. Each volunteer solves the jigsaw puzzle once from 3×3 setup. The question and answers can be seen in Table 5.

Table 5. Volunteers evaluation of the Virtual reality puzzle

	Strongly agree	Agree	Neutral	Disagree	Strongly disagree
It's a easy game	11	5	0	0	0
It's a intuitive game	10	6	0	0	0
It's a fun game	5	7	4	0	0
It's a immersive game	10	4	2	0	0

The results show that for a healthy person, the game can be considered secure, intuitive and immersive. On the other hand, the game was not considered a fun game for most of the subjects. This impression can mean that for a healthy subject, the game is too easy or monotonous in a certain way. Based on this feedback, a future work to improve the variations of arm exercise will be considered to make the interactive surrounds more fun. All these questions will be reevaluated with patients in the next phase of this project.

6   Conclusion and Future Works

The present paper introduced a low-cost virtual reality (VR) device to help patients and therapists during the motor rehabilitation process, where some preliminary results are reported. The current device costs around $11.00 and it can run on quad-core smartphones with only 2 GB of RAM.

The device presented few issues such as the delay noticed by the volunteers. However, the therapists evaluated that such level of delay will not be a problem for patients. As next step of this project, the device will be evaluated with patients during their motor rehabilitation procedures.

The device showed a very accurate precision for the application. Regarding the test of robustness, the device presented a consistent result for all aspects under evaluation. It means that the DMP used in the IMU was consistent and correct all possible errors in the long run.

The volunteers well evaluated the software as a whole, but it needs to be tested in a real situation with post-stroke patients. This will allow us to find more specific issues in the software.

As future works, the software and the device's hardware will be optimized to improve performance and include some changes in its functioning, such as a vibration sensor for user's feedback from the virtual world. One of the possibles complements is to use a second device between the shoulder (P0) and elbow (P1) to get depth as a new degree of freedom within the virtual environment. This new degree of freedom can improve the interaction with the virtual world. For instance, it can allow to achieve some object far away, stimulating the elbow extension of the patient.

Another possible software improvement is to make the environment more realistic, changing the surroundings for more daily ones such as chicken, parks or bedrooms environments. This can make the patients experience more immersive as well as improve their motivation.

Acknowledgments. This research was partially supported by Capes (from Portuguese, *Coordenação de Aperfeiçoamento de Pessoal de Nível Superior*) and FAPESP (Sao Paulo Research Foundation, Brazil). FAPESP process: 2015/03695-5 (grant related to author: A.F.B). The development of the proposed device is the result of a research collaboration between the Center for Research in Mathematics Science Applied to Industry - CeMEAI (from Portuguese, *Centro de Pesquisa em Ciências Matemáticas Aplicadas à Industria* (http://cepid.fapesp.br/en/centro/15/) - FAPESP

Process: 2013/07375-0) and the Brazilian Research Institute of Neuroscience and Neurotechnology - BRAINN (http://cepid.fapesp.br/en/centro/11/) (FAPESP Process: 2013/07559-3), both are Research, Innovation and Dissemination Centres (RIDC) funded by FAPESP.

References

1. Ricardo, A., Postolache, O., Girão, P.S.: Physical rehabilitation based on smart wearable and virtual reality serious game. In: 2019 IEEE International Instrumentation and Measurement Technology Conference (I2MTC). IEEE (2019)
2. Alfaro, L., et al.: Virtual reality full immersion techniques for enhancing workers performance, 20 years later: a review and a reformulation. In: Virtual Reality 10.10 (2019). https://doi.org/10.1007/978-0-387-35086-8_34
3. Cameirão, M.S., et al.: Neurorehabilitation using the virtual reality based rehabilitation gaming system: methodology, design, psychometrics, usability and validation. J. Neuroengineering Rehabil. 7(1), 48 (2010). https://doi.org/10.1186/1743-0003-7-48
4. Carvalho, D., et al.: The mirror neuron system in post-stroke rehabilitation. Int. Archieves Med. 6(1), 41 (2013)
5. Cui, J., Yeh, S.-C., Lee, S.-H.: Wearable sensors integrated with virtual reality: a self-guided healthcare system measuring shoulder joint mobility for frozen shoulder. J. Heathc. Eng. 2019, 1 (2019)
6. De Luca, R., et al.: Effects of virtual reality-based training with BTs-Nirvana on functional recovery in stroke patients: preliminary considerations. Int. J. Neurosci. 128(9), 791–796 (2018)
7. Dias, D.R.C., Alvarenga, I.C., Guimarães, M.P., Trevelin, L.C., Castellano, G., Brandão, A.F.: eStreet: Virtual reality and wearable devices applied to rehabilitation. In: Gervasi, O., et al. (eds.) ICCSA 2018. LNCS, vol. 10963, pp. 775–789. Springer, Cham (2018). https://doi.org/10.1007/978-3-319-95171-3_60
8. Frisoli, A., et al.: Arm rehabilitation with a robotic exoskeleleton in Virtual Reality. In: 2007 IEEE 10th International Conference on Rehabilitation Robotics. IEEE (2007)
9. Glegg, S.M.N., Levac, D.E.: Barriers, facilitators and interventions to support virtual reality implementation in rehabilitation: a scoping review. PMR 10(11), 1237–1251 (2018)
10. Guo, L.: Application Research of Virtual Reality Technology in Film and TV Creation (2019)
11. Huang, K.-T., et al.: Augmented versus virtual reality in education: an exploratory study examining science knowledge retention when using augmented reality/virtual reality mobile applications. Cyberpsychol. Behav. Soc. Networking 22(2), 105–110 (2019)
12. Johnson, D.M.: Introduction to and Review of Simulator Sickness Research (2005)
13. LaViola, J.J.: A discussion of cybersickness in virtual environments. SIGCHI Bull. 32(1), 47–56 (2000). https://doi.org/10.1145/333329.333344
14. Kiper, P., et al.: Virtual reality for upper limb rehabilitation in subacute and chronic stroke: a randomized controlled trial. Archieves Phys. Med. Rehabil. 99(5), 834–842 (2018)
15. Laver, KE., et al.: Virtual reality for stroke rehabilitation. In: Cochrane database of systematic reviews, vol. 11 (2017)

16. Lee, S.H., et al.: Virtual reality rehabilitation with functional electrical stimulation improves upper extremity function in patients with chronic stroke: a pilot randomized controlled study. Archieves Phys. Med. Rehabil. **99**(8), 1447–1453 (2018)

17. Levin, M.F., Weiss, P.L., Keshner, E.A.: Emergence of virtual reality as a tool for upper limb rehabilitation: incorporation of motor control and motor learning principles. Phys. Therapy **95**(3), 415–425 (2015)

18. Lo, H.S., Xie, S.Q.: Exoskeleton robots for upper-limb rehabilitation: state of the art and future prospects. Med. Eng. Phys. **34**(3), 261–268 (2012)

19. Maggio, M.G., et al.: Virtual reality and cognitive rehabilitation in people with stroke: an overview. J. Neurosci. Nurs. **51**(2), 101–105 (2019)

20. Maulden, S.A., et al.: Timing of initiation of rehabilitation after stroke. Arch. Phys. Med. Rehabil. **86**(12), 34–40 (2005)

21. Piron, L., et al.: Exercises for paretic upper limb after stroke: a combined virtual-reality and telemedicine approach. J. Rehabil. Med. **41**(12), 1016–1020 (2009)

22. Qiao, Y., Yang, S.: Healthcare design based on virtual reality technology: enhance the user's engagement in the rehabilitation process. In: International Conference on Applied Human Factors and Ergonomics. Springer, Cham (2019). https://doi.org/10.1007/978-3-030-20476-1_41

23. Rajmohan, V., Mohandas, E.: Mirror neuron system. Ind. J. Psychiatry **49**(1), 66 (2007)

24. Rathore, S.S., Hinn, A.R., Cooper, L.S., Tyroler, H.A., Rosamond, W.D.: Characterization of incident stroke signs and symptoms: findings from the atherosclerosis risk in communities study. Stroke **33**(11), 2718–2721 (2002)

25. Reason, J.T., Brand, J.J.: Motion Sickness. Academic Press, New York (1975)

26. Rose, F.D., Barbara, M.B., Rizzo, A.A.: Virtual reality in brain damage rehabilitation. Cyberpsychol. Behav. **8**(3), 241–262 (2005)

27. Secco, E.L., Tadesse, A.M.: A wearable exoskeleton for hand kinesthetic feedback in virtual reality. In: O'Hare, G.M.P., O'Grady, M.J., O'Donoghue, J., Henn, P. (eds.) MobiHealth 2019. LNICST, vol. 320, pp. 186–200. Springer, Cham (2020). https://doi.org/10.1007/978-3-030-49289-2_15

28. Shin, J.-H., Ryu, H., Jang, S.H.: A task-specific interactive game-based virtual reality rehabilitation system for patients with stroke: a usability test and two clinical experiments. J. Neuroengineering Rehabil. **11**(1), 32 (2014)

29. da Silva Cameirão, M., et al.: Virtual reality based rehabilitation speeds up functional recovery of the upper extremities after stroke: a randomized controlled pilot study in the acute phase of stroke using the rehabilitation gaming system. Restorative Neurol. Neurosci. **29**(5), 287–298 (2011)

30. Soares, A.V., et al.: The use of Virtual Reality for upper limb rehabilitation of hemiparetic Stroke patients. Fisioterapia em Movimento **27**(3), 309–317 (2014)

31. Sveistrup, H.: Motor rehabilitation using virtual reality. J. Neuroengineering Rehabil. **1**(1), 10 (2004)

32. Schultheis, M., Rizzo, A.: The application of virtual reality technology in rehabilitation. Rehabil. Psychol. **46**, 296–311 (2001). https://doi.org/10.1037/0090-5550.46.3.296

33. Sweetser, P., Rogalewicz, Z., Li, Q.: Understanding enjoyment in VR games with GameFlow. In: 25th ACM Symposium on Virtual Reality Software and Technology (2019)

34. Thilarajah, S., Clark, R.A., Williams, G.: Wearable sensors and Mobile Health (mHealth) technologies to assess and promote physical activity in stroke: a narrative review. Brain Impairment **17**(1), 34–42 (2016)

35. Turolla, A., et al.: Virtual reality for the rehabilitation of the upper limb motor function after stroke: a prospective controlled trial. J. Neuroengineering Rehabil. **10**(1), 85 (2013). https://doi.org/10.1186/1743-0003-10-85
36. Unity. https://unity3d.com, Accessed 20 Jan 2020
37. World Health Organization. https://www.who.int/, Accessed 12 Feb 2020

Biomechanics Sensor Node for Virtual Reality: A Wearable Device Applied to Gait Recovery for Neurofunctional Rehabilitation

Alexandre Fonseca Brandão[1,2,3] , Diego Roberto Colombo Dias[2,4(✉)] ,
Sávyo Toledo Machado Reis[4] , Clovis Magri Cabreira[7] ,
Maria Cecilia Moraes Frade[5] , Thomas Beltrame[2,5] ,
Marcelo de Paiva Guimarães[5,6] , and Gabriela Castellano[1,2]

[1] Institute of Physics Gleb Wataghin, University of Campinas, Campinas, SP, Brazil
{abrandao,gabriela}@ifi.unicamp.br
[2] Brazilian Institute of Neuroscience and Neurotechnology, University of Campinas,
Campinas, SP 13083887, Brazil
beltramethomas@gmail.com
[3] Institute for Bioengineering of Catalonia - IBEC, Barcelona, Spain
[4] Universidade Federal de São João del-Rei, São João del-Rei, MG, Brazil
diegodias@ufsj.edu.br, savyomachado@gmail.com
[5] Universidade Federal de São Paulo, São Paulo, SP, Brazil
mariaceciliafrade@gmail.com, marcelodepaiva@gmail.com
[6] Centro Universitário Campo Limpo Paulista - UNIFACCAMP,
Campo Limpo Paulista, Brazil
[7] Center for Research and Development in Telecommunications (CPqD),
Campinas, SP, Brazil
cmagri@cpqd.com.br

Abstract. In several segments of the health areas, sensing has become a trend. Sensors allow data quantification for use in decision making or even to predict the clinical evolution of a given treatment, such as in rehabilitation therapies to restore patients' motor and cognitive functions. This paper presents the Biomechanics Sensor Node (BSN), composed of an inertial measurement unit (IMU), developed to infer input information and control virtual environments. We also present a software solution, which integrates the BSN data with Unity Editor, one of the most used game engine nowadays. This asset allows Unity-developed virtual reality applications to use BSN a secure interaction device. Thus, during rehabilitation sessions, the patient receives visual stimuli from the virtual environment, controlled by the BSN device, while the therapist has access to the information about the movements performed in the therapy.

Keywords: Wearable sensors · Stationary gait · Virtual reality · Human computer-interaction · Neurofunctional rehabilitation

© Springer Nature Switzerland AG 2020
O. Gervasi et al. (Eds.): ICCSA 2020, LNCS 12255, pp. 757–770, 2020.
https://doi.org/10.1007/978-3-030-58820-5_54

1   Introduction

With the advancement of technology, virtual reality (VR) has been growing and becoming ever more present. Nowadays, we are using VR in areas as education, health therapies, and entertainment industries. The term "virtual reality" was coined in 1989 by Jaron Lanier. VR technologies aim to recreate the sensation of reality to the subject, leading him/her to experience the interaction with a virtual environment (VE) as a momentary reality [25].

A natural way to interact with this virtual environment is required for a completely immersive experience. There must be a way of interacting with it, and in most cases, a navigation device is responsible for mediating this communication with VE.

Nowadays, devices such as Kinect allow the user to move through a VE [37]. Such devices are still quite limited in terms of user freedom, precision, and complexity of movement control. These restrictions give rise to a scenario favorable to the creation of new solutions that aim to optimize the immersion of the user. Other examples of devices are the wearable sensors fixed in different parts of the user's body, which can capture patterns of movement. A problem with this sort of device is that they present excessive battery consumption, requiring continuous recharging, which can become a negative point in the user experience. Low energy technologies have been developed to mitigate this problem, resulting in so-called low energy devices.

With the virtual environment integrated with wearable devices, it is possible to develop solutions for a wide range of healthcare applications. These include the prevention of muscular atrophy (sarcopenia), neurological recovery from diseases such as stroke, Parkinson's [20], Alzheimer's [8], and respiratory rehabilitation, such as Chronic Obstructive Pulmonary Disease (COPD) [33]. Among vascular diseases, stroke represents the leading cause of long-term disability. The increasing proportion of survivors from this disease is associated with an increase in patients who persist with neurological deficit. Indeed, more than half of the survivors remain with a severe disability affecting functional independence in daily life activities [17,24].

For this reason, rehabilitation programs based on VR [25] have been highlighted as an alternative and complementary therapy for motor recovery [15,18,19,23,30]. VR can stimulate various sensory systems of the human body, including the visual and auditory systems, which facilitate the input and output of information to the brain. Therefore, VR systems can be used in conjunction with other therapeutic interventions to increase the complexity of tasks during the rehabilitation process [1,7,16,27,28,32]. This complement is particularly important when considering the potential increase in the number of patients with stroke and neurodegenerative diseases in the future.

Every VR interface must be composed of immersion and interaction devices. Regarding interaction devices, we can highlight the use of inertial devices as a means of body tracking, which is not new, but still lacks specific solutions for healthcare. Foxlin [11], a few years ago, came up with a walking tracking solution called NavShoe. The solution consisted of an inertial sensor attached to the shoelace of one of the user's feet, connected to a PDA (wireless). Tregillus and Folmer [29] presented a walking solution in VE using the smartphone's sensors. Wittman et al. [35] studied the feasibility of an unsupervised arm therapy for self-directed rehabilitation therapy in patients' homes using an inertial measurement unit (IMU)-based VR system (ArmeoSenso) in their homes for six weeks. These solutions have been using inertial sensors for tracking virtual environments. However, in most of them, the prototypes are focused on one group of members (upper or lower).

Given these considerations, this paper presents a Biomechanics Sensor Node (BSN), which is a wearable device developed by our group. BSN contains gyro, accelerometer, and compass sensors, which are combined to associate user movement with input commands to control virtual reality applications. We also present a Unity Asset which integrates the BSN data with VR applications. We also present a Unity Asset[1] which integrates the BSN data with VR applications.

This article is organized as follows: Sect. 2 presents the material and methods used to create the BSN device. Section 3 shows our case study results. Section 4 presents the discussions, and lastly, Sect. 5 presents the conclusions.

2   Materials and Methods

For the construction of the BSN device, previous results [9, 12], also developed by our group, were used. These are the GestureMaps (non-immersive) application, presented in Sect. 2.1, and the e-Street (immersive) application, presented in Sect. 2.2. Finally, in Sect. 2.3, we present the main contribution of this paper, the actual development of the BSN device.

2.1   GestureMaps

GestureMaps is a mixed VR application [5], where the user can navigate the virtual maps of Google Street View using stationary gait movements. This movement is identified through a gesture recognition sensor, Kinect type, which translates the stationary gait into an input for the VR system, allowing user navigation (output) through the virtual environment. In this case, a hip and knee flexion movement is required from the user. A distance of at least ten centimeters from the foot relative to the floor is required to ensure displacement in the virtual environment. Figure 1 shows an example of the use of GestureMaps [12].

---

[1] The Asset is an item (e.g., source code, a 3D model, an audio file or an image) that facilitates to create Unity applications. An asset can be used to build diverse applications. Unity is a cross-platform engine that is used to develop games on multiple platforms.

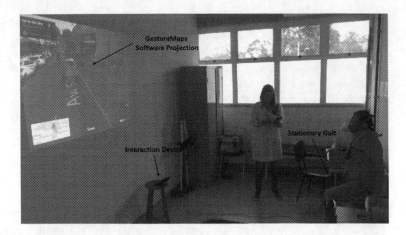

Fig. 1. Example of use of GestureMaps. The subject uses stationary gait to navigate the virtual environment.

2.2   e-Street and Interaction Device: Ultrasound Sensor and Arduino-Based

A virtual city (called e-Street) was created to develop an immersive version of GestureMaps in a Unity 3D environment to simulate navigation, street cross-ing, and spatial orientation. This virtual urban environment reproduces traffic situations, with autonomous cars that circulate in the e-Street.

An interaction device was constructed from ultrasound sensors and an Arduino to translate the stationary gait movements into input for the e-Street software. From actions that reach displacements of three centimeters (or more) of the ultrasound sensors, it is possible to start navigation in the urban virtual environment by the user [9]. An Arduino (UNO) microcontroller, two sonars (HC-SR04), and one Bluetooth module (HC-05) were used to create the BSN wearable device. Figure 2 represents the e-Street software interface and interac-tion device.

2.3   Biomechanics Sensor Node - BSN

The BSN device was developed due to the imprecision and clumsiness of the ultrasound sensors used for interaction with the e-Street environment. To inter-act more precisely with a virtual environment, an ergonomic bracelet that could be attached to the wrist or ankle was designed to be used to track the user's movements.

From inertial sensors, the connection between the bracelet (BSN) and the VR software (e-Street - Unity 3D) is possible. The Unity 3D (motor engine) proved very suitable for the development of the solution (e-Street + BSN). Besides, this game engine also has support for exporting the applications to the mobile environment, which is essential since smartphones can be used with the BSN.

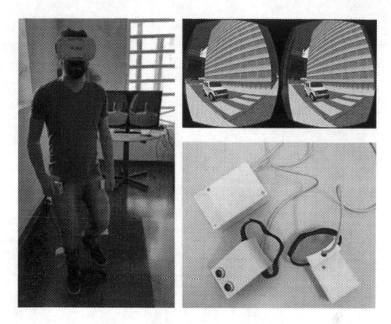

Fig. 2. e-Street interface (upper right corner) and interaction device (lower right corner).

Next, the development of the asset was carried out, bringing together all the functions implemented in the BSN. In this way, the communication module and the BSN sensors were configured correctly, according to the information pertinent to the communication protocol (Table 1).

Table 1. Gestural interaction devices comparative.

Gestural interaction devices				
Device	Sensor	Gesture recognition	Movement required	Controlled software
Kinect	Infrared	Computer vision	Stationary gait	GestureMaps
Arduino-based	Ultrasonic	Spatial displacement on the Y axis	Foot up and down (Y-axis)	e-Street
BSN	IMU	Three-dimensional spatial displacement	Stationary gait	e-Street

The BSN device is also prepared to send the raw data to the Internet of Things - IoT DoJot platform [10], which is a Brazilian open-source platform (developed by CPqD – https://www.cpqd.com.br/). These quantitative data can be compared with qualitative data, relative to the clinical evolution of the patient, and thus be related to the proposed motor and neurofunctional rehabilitation treatment. Figure 3 presents the BSN connection with the IoT platform. The flowchart shows the communication between the BSN device, the e-Street software (Unity 3D), and the DoJoT platform (IoT).

Fig. 3. Communication between BSN, Android/Unity and Dojot.

3   Results

3.1   BSN Communication and Data Collection Service

The communication occurs through four phases: scanning of devices compatible with BLE technology; BSN identification in the list of found devices and connection requests; sending of calibration command with BSN, and reading the BSN sensor data.

The service responsible for collecting BSN data is named Data Collection Service. In this category of services, it is possible to find the step information and battery status, which is essential for future applications.

Regarding the available services for reading the information that is Notify type, they send information to the recipients only when the data is updated. Thus, it is possible to subscribe to these services to get constant data feedback. This subscription becomes interesting in the process of tracking members since applications can create a history of user movement in space.

For the first step execution, we use a scan function through a Unity script, which verifies the presence of nearby connected devices that support the BLE protocol. The device must be switched on and in standby mode, waiting for new connections. The identification of this Bluetooth connection occurs with the blue color of the light-emitting diode (LED), which uses the RGB (red, green, and blue) system.

In the second step, the identification (ID) of the device of interest was made using its name or media access control (MAC) address. Then your ID is represented on the bracelet by a white LED. Thus, an information exchange with the armband is allowed. If the pairing process occurs without problems, the LED will turn green.

In the third step, the calibration command is sent to the BSN, a BLE package consisting of two elements: service and characteristic. If no shipping problems occur, the LED turns orange, returning to the green color again after the calibration process. Finally, in the fourth step, the information available in the BSN is read, getting for each data a Service UUID, and a Characteristic UUID.

3.2 BSN Asset

Knowing that the *Asset* to be developed has all the bracelet manipulation features, it includes both functions, the configuration service, and the data collection service. The functions that compose the *Asset* are: FindBSN, ConnectBSN, CalibrateBSN, ReceiveQuaternions, ReceiveRawData, ReceiveEuler, ReceiveRotationMatrix, ReceiveCompass, ReceiveGravityVector, ReceiveBatteryStatus, and ReceiveSteps.

Since the developed solution must allow the connection between a mobile device and BSN, we have proposed some functions for this purpose. FindBSN and ConnectBSN are responsible for this task; they are described by Algorithm 1 and Algorithm 2, respectively. The first one tracks all devices that support BLE technology and identifies the BSN among them. The second makes the connection itself with the armband, where after the function call, the device is available for future instructions.

Algorithm 1: FindBSN function pseudocode

Result: Find BSN

1 **begin**
2   FoundDeviceList.DeviceAddressList ← List¡DeviceObject¿();
3   initializeBLE();
4   discoveredDevices ← scanForPeripherals();
5   **foreach** *DeviceObject d ∈ discoveredDevices* **do**
6   **if** *d.name = "BSN"* **then**
7   FoundDeviceList.DeviceAddressList.Add(d);

Algorithm 2: ConnectBSN function pseudocode

Result: BSN connection established

1 **begin**
2   **foreach** *DeviceObject d ∈ FoundDeviceList.DeviceAddressList* **do**
3   bsn ← d;
4   connectToPeripheral(bsn);

3.3   BSN Calibration

With the connection between the BSN and a mobile device (smartphone), it is possible to perform the calibration function. Thus, through the function CalibrateBSN described in Algorithm 3, the smartphone sends the calibration command to the BSN, a set of bytes using service and characteristic corresponding to the calibration command.

Algorithm 3: CalibrateBSN function pseudocode

Result: Starting BSN calibration

1 **begin**
2   serviceWriteUUID ← "XXXX";
3   characteristicCalibrationUUID ← "XXXX";
4   calibrateBytes ← { bytes };
5   sendBytesBSN(calibrateBytes, bsnDevice.Address, serviceWriteUUID, characteristicCalibrationUUID);

3.4   BSN Data Reading

BSN data reading occurs by a service containing a standard UUID, which is used by all the read functions present in the Asset. Thus, to consult the information present in the armband, the Characteristic UUID must be equal to the information UUID that one wishes to obtain.

Algorithm 4 presents the ReceiveSteps function. The step data are obtained using the Characteristic UUID equivalent to the step information. The result of the ReceiveSteps function is a set of bytes, converted to the uint16_t format an unsigned integer of 16 bits size. With the bytes duly converted, we have the number of steps counted by the BSN.

Algorithm 4: ReceiveSteps function pseudocode

Output: steps

1 **begin**
2   serviceReadUUID ← "XXXX";
3   characteristicReadStepUUID ← "XXXX";
4   stepBytes ← subscribeCharacteristicWithDeviceAddress(bsnDevice.Address, serviceReadUUID, characteristicReadStepUUID);
5   steps ← convertToUInt16(stepBytes)

Algorithm 5 presents the pseudocode of the ReceiveQuaternions function. The registration function results in a set of bytes that contains the components W, X, Y, and Z of the quaternion vector. Thus, the byte set is converted to an int32_t data pattern to obtain the actual data of the four components. Finally, the function groups all the components and returns Q, the quaternion vector obtained from the BSN.

Algorithm 5: ReceiveQuaternions function pseudocode

Output: Q

1 **begin**
2   serviceReadUUID ← "XXXX";
3   characteristicReadQuaternionsUUID ← "XXXX";
4   qByte ← subscribeCharacteristicWithDeviceAddress(bsnDevice.Address, serviceReadUUID, characteristicReadQuaternionsUUID);
5   qw, qx, qy, qz ← convertToInt32(quaternionsByte);
6   Q ← {qW,qx,qy,qz};

We create the ReceiveRawData function, to obtain the raw data of the BSN device. Algorithm 6 presents the use of the Characteristic UUID equivalent to the data information sensor. Thus, we convert the resulting bytes (that contains the X, Y, and Z components of the accelerometer, gyroscope and compass sensors) to the int16_t standard data, the default used by the BSN for this data set. Finally, the function groups the elements of each sensor into an R vector, returning a composite list of the vectors of each sensor.

Algorithm 6: ReceiveRawData function pseudocode

Output: R

1 **begin**
2   serviceReadUUID ← "XXXX";
3   characteristicReadRawDataUUID ← "XXXX";
4   rawDataByte ← subscribeCharacteristicWithDeviceAddress(bsnDevice.Address, serviceReadUUID, characteristicReadRawDataUUID);
5   acelX, acelY, acelZ, gyroX, gyroY, gyroZ, compX, compY, compZ ← convertToInt16(rawDataByte);
6   accelerometer ← {acelX, acelY, acelZ};
7   gyroscope ← {gyroX, gyroY, gyroZ};
8   compass ← {compX, compY, compZ};
9   R ← {accelerometer, gyroscope, compass };

To illustrate the behavior of the Asset developed, Fig. 4, we describe the process of obtaining the steps given by the user, showing all the actions (steps) performed as input.

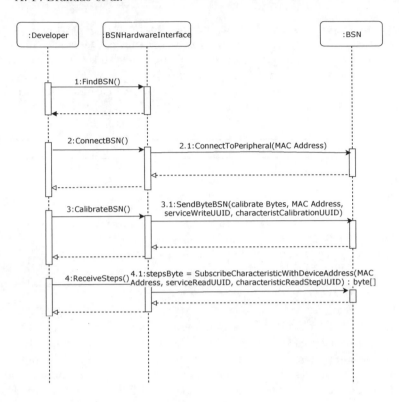

Fig. 4. BSN sequence diagram.

The first command (step 1 of the diagram) is responsible for identifying the BSN among nearby devices that support BLE technology. In this step, the BSN has the LED on blue.

After the second method call (step 2 of the diagram), the bracelet emits a pink light, signaling that there has been a connection request. In this step, the device performs the process of matching and applying filters to the sensors.

Once the pairing process is complete, the BSN LED turns green. At this stage, the bracelet enters in standby mode, waiting for commands from the paired smartphone. In this way, we represent any input sent with the calibration command.

After sending the calibration command (step 3 of the diagram) to the device, the bracelet emits an orange light, which corresponds to the calibration process. At this point, it is necessary to perform three equal movements, with a pause of two seconds between them, so that the bracelet registers the movement correctly. After the calibration process occurs, the LED turns green again.

Finally, the method responsible for receiving the steps (step 4 of the diagram) counts the steps. With the calibrated BSN, we add the value one to the step counter with each step complete.

4   Discussion

Wearables are becoming very popular and accessible due to reduced costs [14], allowing patients to obtain personal biological data daily. The smaller sensor sizes, associated with low power wireless communication, are allowing users/patients to use such devices imperceptibly, with data acquisition performed throughout the day.

The use of this type of technology is finding more and more applications in health sciences, which will lead us to a deeper understanding of disease development through the analysis of the collected data [2]. Biological data obtained from wearables has the potential to allow providing more objective and effective treatments for patients with neurofunctional disorders.

With the advancement in the use of miniature sensors and mobile devices and with the high computational power of data processing, studies with wearable devices in the area of rehabilitation are becoming ever more feasible and have great potential to motivate patients in the process of physical recovery [3,36] and be used in the neuroscience field [6].

Regarding the present study, because the BSN has the form of a bracelet, this device can become part of the patient's dressing room. Thus, it will not cause discomfort and will still collect data in real-time during treatment due to remote BLE communication. Other studies have presented interaction devices, based on Inertial Measurement Unity (IMU), aimed at health applications. Such as the instrumented trail-making task (iTMT) developed for the prevention of fragility [38]; and the ArmeoSenso, which connects with the virtual environment and allows the control of a virtual arm, offering elbow flexion and extension stimuli [35]. These can be used for monitoring rehabilitation patients in hospitals and at home [13].

Our BSN device uses an IMU (such as gesture recognition sensor) to calibrate a specific motion and convert it into input for virtual reality systems. Other commercial IMU-based motion analysis systems, such as Werium [34] and SWORD health [26], serve as inspiration for the next stages of development of our BSN device. The idea is to expand its functionality to gather a range of motion information and integrate it with kinematic analysis software such as RehabGesture [4], also developed by our team.

From the identification of the movements through the BSN device, it was possible to integrate it with the e-Street VR software allowing the user to navigate in the virtual city. The outcome of this integration is expected to be an e-Health solution, with applications in several fields such as rehabilitation, motor learning, and fall prevention.

Due to the motor requirements of the lower limb muscles and the cognitive requirements needed for spatial orientation during software control, this solution finds application in fall prevention therapies in the elderly and the recovery of gait movements after stroke.

However, studies have also pointed out the need to increase the number of multicenter and randomized clinical trials with a representative sample of the population, to highlight the full potential of VR as a complement to rehabilitation therapy and to consolidate the efficacy of treatment in medium and long-term [21,22,31].

5   Conclusions

In this article, we present the proposal and design of a BSN device by the lack of tools that can track the upper and lower limbs and the results of our initial solutions using Arduino. Our BSN allows up to 8 devices to be scanned at the same time, enabling multiple body parts to be tracked, lower, and upper limbs.

We also presented an Asset, which is a set of functionalities for the Unity game engine. It facilitates the development of virtual reality applications integrated with our BSN device. Using this solution, the developers can quickly perform actions such as connection, calibration, and capture of raw data.

The Unity development solution is also a significant contribution since the interface between developer and device should be simple and easy. With Unity Asset built, you can connect, calibrate, capture raw data, and allow sensor fusion and motion composition. The result of our BSN device is a universal and customizable tool, providing calibration of steady-gait-related movements as well as their interaction with VR environments.

The next step is the use of the BSN device for control of an avatar to simulate Activities of Daily Living (ADLs), through virtual limbs and objects control, for interaction with other individuals/patients in a multiuser virtual environment, or for sports simulation for improving skills and techniques. The limitations of the study refer to the need for testing with neurological patients in rehabilitation clinics and hospitals, expected as future work.

Funding. FAPESP (Sao Paulo Research Foundation, Brazil) grant number 2015/03695-5 (grant related to author: A.F.B.). The EMBRAPII (Brazilian Agency for Research and Industrial Innovation) and SEBRAE made a financial contribution to the development of BSN.

References

1. Aşkın, A., Atar, E., Koçyiğit, H., Tosun, A.: Effects of kinect-based virtual reality game training on upper extremity motor recovery in chronic stroke. Somatosens. Mot. Res. **35**(1), 25–32 (2018)
2. Beltrame, T., Amelard, R., Wong, A., Hughson, R.L.: Extracting aerobic system dynamics during unsupervised activities of daily living using wearable sensor machine learning models. J. Appl. Physiol. **124**(2), 473–481 (2017)
3. Bernhard, F.P., Sartor, J., Bettecken, K., Hobert, M.A., Arnold, C., Weber, Y.G., Poli, S., Margraf, N.G., Schlenstedt, C., Hansen, C., et al.: Wearables for gait and balance assessment in the neurological ward-study design and first results of a prospective cross-sectional feasibility study with 384 inpatients. BMC Neurol. **18**(1), 114 (2018)

4. Brandao, A.F., Dias, D.R., Castellano, G., Parizotto, N.A., Trevelin, L.C.: Rehabgesture: an alternative tool for measuring human movement. Telemedicine e-Health **22**(7), 584–589 (2016)
5. Brandão, A.F., Dias, D.R.C., Guimarães, M.P., Trevelin, L.C., Parizotto, N.A., Castellano, G.: Gesturecollection for motor and cognitive stimuli: virtual reality and e-health prospects. J. Health Inform. **10**(1), 9–16 (2018)
6. Byrom, B., McCarthy, M., Schueler, P., Muehlhausen, W.: Brain monitoring devices in neuroscience clinical research: the potential of remote monitoring using sensors, wearables, and mobile devices. Clin. Pharmacol. Ther. **104**, 59–71 (2018)
7. Cameirao, M.S., i Badia, S.B., Duarte, E., Frisoli, A., Verschure, P.F.: The combined impact of virtual reality neurorehabilitation and its interfaces on upper extremity functional recovery in patients with chronic stroke. Stroke **43**(10), 2720–2728 (2012)
8. Cushman, L.A., Stein, K., Duffy, C.J.: Detecting navigational deficits in cognitive aging and alzheimer disease using virtual reality. Neurology **71**(12), 888–895 (2008)
9. Dias, D.R.C., Alvarenga, I.C., Guimarães, M.P., Trevelin, L.C., Castellano, G., Brandão, A.F.: eStreet: virtual reality and wearable devices applied to rehabilitation. In: Gervasi, O., Murgante, B., Misra, S., Stankova, E., Torre, C.M., Rocha, A.M.A.C., Taniar, D., Apduhan, B.O., Tarantino, E., Ryu, Y. (eds.) ICCSA 2018. LNCS, vol. 10963, pp. 775–789. Springer, Cham (2018). https://doi.org/10.1007/978-3-319-95171-3_60
10. dojot: dojot documentation (2019). https://dojotdocs.readthedocs.io/en/latest/. Accessed Dec 2019
11. Foxlin, E.: Pedestrian tracking with shoe-mounted inertial sensors. IEEE Comput. Graph. Appl. **6**, 38–46 (2005)
12. Frade, M.C., dos Reis, I.M., Basso-Vanelli, R.P., Brandão, A.F., Jamami, M.: Reproducibility and validity of the 6-minute stationary walk test associated with virtual reality in subjects with COPD. Respiratory care, pp. respcare-06237 (2019). https://doi.org/10.4187/respcare.06237
13. Hadjidj, A., Bouabdallah, A., Challal, Y.: Rehabilitation supervision using wireless sensor networks. In: 2011 IEEE International Symposium on a World of Wireless, Mobile and Multimedia Networks (WoWMoM), pp. 1–3. IEEE (2011)
14. Hsu, Y.L., Yang, S.C., Chang, H.C., Lai, H.C.: Human daily and sport activity recognition using a wearable inertial sensor network. IEEE Access **6**, 31715–31728 (2018)
15. Laver, K.E., George, S., Thomas, S., Deutsch, J.E., Crotty, M.: Virtual reality for stroke rehabilitation. Cochrane Database Syst. Rev. (2) (2015)
16. Lloréns, R., Noé, E., Colomer, C., Alcañiz, M.: Effectiveness, usability, and cost-benefit of a virtual reality-based telerehabilitation program for balance recovery after stroke: a randomized controlled trial. Arch. Phys. Med. Rehabil. **96**(3), 418–425 (2015)
17. Nichols-Larsen, D.S., Clark, P., Zeringue, A., Greenspan, A., Blanton, S.: Factors influencing stroke survivors' quality of life during subacute recovery. Stroke **36**(7), 1480–1484 (2005)
18. Piron, L., et al.: Exercises for paretic upper limb after stroke: a combined virtual-reality and telemedicine approach. J. Rehabil. Med. **41**(12), 1016–1020 (2009)
19. Rose, F.D., Brooks, B.M., Rizzo, A.A.: Virtual reality in brain damage rehabilitation. Cyberpsychol. Behav. **8**(3), 241–262 (2005)

20. dos Santos Mendes, F.A., et al.: Motor learning, retention and transfer after virtual-reality-based training in parkinson's disease-effect of motor and cognitive demands of games: a longitudinal, controlled clinical study. Physiotherapy **98**(3), 217–223 (2012)

21. Saposnik, G., et al.: Efficacy and safety of non-immersive virtual reality exercising in stroke rehabilitation (EVREST): a randomised, multicentre, single-blind, controlled trial. Lancet Neurol. **15**(10), 1019–1027 (2016)

22. Schuster-Amft, C., et al.: Effect of a four-week virtual reality-based training versus conventional therapy on upper limb motor function after stroke: a multicenter parallel group randomized trial. PLoS ONE **13**(10), e0204455 (2018)

23. Shin, J.H., Ryu, H., Jang, S.H.: A task-specific interactive game-based virtual reality rehabilitation system for patients with stroke: a usability test and two clinical experiments. J. Neuroeng. Rehab. **11**(1), 32 (2014)

24. Statements, A.S.: Heart disease and stroke statistics 2013 update. Circulation **127**(1), e6 (2013)

25. Steuer, J.: Defining virtual reality: dimensions determining telepresence. J. Commun. **42**(4), 73–93 (1992)

26. SwordHealth: Reinventing Physical Threapy (2019). https://swordhealth.com/. Accessed Feb 2019

27. Tieri, G., Morone, G., Paolucci, S., Iosa, M.: Virtual reality in cognitive and motor rehabilitation: facts, fiction and fallacies. Expert Rev. Med. Dev. **15**(2), 107–117 (2018)

28. Tobler-Ammann, B.C., et al.: Exergames encouraging exploration of hemineglected space in stroke patients with visuospatial neglect: a feasibility study. JMIR Serious Games **5**(3), e17 (2017)

29. Tregillus, S., Folmer, E.: VR-step: walking-in-place using inertial sensing for hands free navigation in mobile VR environments. In: Proceedings of the 2016 CHI Conference on Human Factors in Computing Systems, pp. 1250–1255. ACM (2016)

30. Turolla, A., et al.: Virtual reality for the rehabilitation of the upper limb motor function after stroke: a prospective controlled trial. J. Neuroeng. Rehab. **10**(1), 85 (2013)

31. Vanbellingen, T., Filius, S.J., Nyffeler, T., van Wegen, E.E.: Usability of videogame-based dexterity training in the early rehabilitation phase of stroke patients: a pilot study. Front. Neurol. **8**, 654 (2017)

32. Wade, E., Winstein, C.J.: Virtual reality and robotics for stroke rehabilitation: where do we go from here? Top. Stroke Rehab. **18**(6), 685–700 (2011)

33. Wardini, R., et al.: Using a virtual game system to innovate pulmonary rehabilitation: safety, adherence and enjoyment in severe chronic obstructive pulmonary disease. Can. Respir. J. **20**(5), 357–361 (2013)

34. Werium: INICIO - Werium Solutions (2019). http://www.weriumsolutions.com/. Accessed Feb 2019

35. Wittmann, F., et al.: Self-directed arm therapy at home after stroke with a sensor-based virtual reality training system. J. Neuroeng. Rehab. **13**(1), 75 (2016)

36. Zago, M., et al.: Gait evaluation using inertial measurement units in subjects with parkinson's disease. J. Electromyogr. Kinesiol. (2018)

37. Zhang, Z.: Microsoft kinect sensor and its effect. IEEE Multimed. **19**(2), 4–10 (2012)

38. Zhou, H., Razjouyan, J., Halder, D., Naik, A.D., Kunik, M.E., Najafi, B.: Instrumented trail-making task: application of wearable sensor to determine physical frailty phenotypes. Gerontology **65**, 186–197 (2018)

Dynamic Adaptive Communication Strategy for Fully Immersive, Interactive and Collaborative Virtual Reality Applications

Adjeryan Cartaxo Freitas[1] (iD), Diego Roberto Colombo Dias[2] (iD),
Alexandre Fonseca Brandão[3] (iD), Rita de Fátima Rodrigues
Guimarães[1,4] (iD), and Marcelo de Paiva Guimarães[1,5(✉)] (iD)

[1] Computer Science Master Program (Unifaccamp),
Campo Limpo Paulista, Brazil
adjeryance@gmail.com, rita.guimaraes@gmail.com,
marcelodepaiva@gmail.com
[2] Computer Science Department (UFSJ), São João Del Rei, Brazil
diegocolombo.dias@gmail.com
[3] Institito de Física Gleb Wataghin (UNICAMP), Campinas, Brazil
abrandao@ifi.unicamp.br
[4] Applied Linguistics (Institute of Language Studies/Unicamp), Campinas,
Brazil
[5] Núcleo de Ensino a Distância (UAB/Reitoria), UNIFESP, São Paulo, Brazil

Abstract. An online meeting allows people with a common purpose to discuss ideas, goals, and objectives, regardless of national and international boundaries. Using internet technologies, users can communicate with others at remote locations without leaving their offices. However, internet communication can show considerable variation in terms of packet loss, time variation, and delay. This paper presents a strategy for dynamically adapting communication between fully immersive, interactive, and collaborative virtual reality applications. Our strategy is implemented based on the optimal path forest classifier, allowing us to analyze the network communication and to provide parameters for the application communication library to perform dynamic adaptation. We also present the GClassifier tool, which is used to implement this strategy, and some test results.

Keywords: Virtual reality · Network · Communication adversity · Classifier

1 Introduction

Fully immersive, interactive, and collaborative virtual reality applications allow users to interact and navigate in synthetic worlds (i.e., both real and virtual) while solving a single task. They also include multi-projection applications (e.g., cave automatic virtual environments (CAVEs) and power walls). These systems are composed of diverse virtual reality environments that are connected remotely with each other over the internet. In the early years, these applications were executed using high-end super-computers; however, due to advances in computer hardware and software, the graphic cluster has become the default architecture used for these applications [1–4].

© Springer Nature Switzerland AG 2020
O. Gervasi et al. (Eds.): ICCSA 2020, LNCS 12255, pp. 771–783, 2020.
https://doi.org/10.1007/978-3-030-58820-5_55

Each instance of the application has a local graphic cluster that renders multiple views of the same visual dataset in real time, and each cluster may be composed of different types of nodes (e.g., rendering nodes, a file server node, input nodes, and a master node to manage the environment), while intra-cluster communication uses a local area network (LAN) to handle data from multiple nodes in real time using a master/slave architecture to run a local environment. Inter-cluster communication is achieved by using a peer-to-peer approach to connect the remote environments, and an intelligent network service is required to interconnect these resources. One of the development challenges of these environments is to provide efficient communication and synchronization that can guarantee intra- and inter-cluster datalock (i.e. ensuring data coherence between processes) and framelock (i.e. maintaining the coherence of scenes).

A dynamic network protocol (e.g., Transmission Control Protocol (TCP), Datagram Protocol (UDP) or Stream Control Transmission Protocol (SCTP)) can be used to implement inter-cluster communication (via a wide area network or WAN), allowing for adaptation of communication and synchronization according to the situation that is faced. Inter-cluster communication uses LANs that can be considered close to perfect. A fully collaborative virtual reality application may generate large communication datasets, since the frame rate must be above 60 frames per second (fps) to give a good stereoscopic view. Although there are several sniffers that can assist in network analysis, such as TCPdump[1], Ngrep[2], and Snort[3], there is a lack of tools that can classify the data collected in this way. Sniffers do not take advantage of the human cognitive capacity of learning and pattern recognition, and the network administrator typically performs a manual analysis of a massive amount of data. Some efforts have already made using approaches such as support vector machines (SVMs) [5] and artificial neural networks [6], although these require considerable computational time for large datasets, especially in the training phase [7].

This paper presents a strategy for analyzing packet loss variables (packets lost in the connections between nodes), time variation (average time for packet delivery between nodes), and delay (delay in packet delivery between nodes). This allows a communication library to perform dynamic adaptation, which is used to implement fully immersive, interactive, and collaborative virtual reality applications. This forms the main contribution of this work, which proposed a powerful real-time solution for network adversity analysis. We use a supervised pattern recognition technique based on the optimum path forest (OPF) [8] to classify the adversity variables. Based on the requirements of fully immersive, interactive, and collaborative virtual reality applications, a dataset was manually classified into several adversity classes. The resulting set associated with a specific description was used to train the classifier. We tested our approach using a dataset from a traffic simulation, and compared the predicted classes with the adversity classes initially defined. We also compared the captured data using a network tool to provide adaptation parameters for the communication libraries. Also in

---

[1] https://www.tcpdump.org/manpages/tcpdump.1.html.

[2] http://ngrep.sourceforge.net/usage.html.

[3] https://www.snort.org/.

this paper, we present a graphical tool called GClassifier, which can be used to automate the training and classification tasks via a friendly interface.

This paper is organized as follows. In Sect. 2, we discuss the features of fully immersive, interactive, and virtual reality applications. Section 3 explains the details of the GClassifier tool used to implement our strategy. Section 4 presents some test results. Finally, Sect. 5 contains the conclusion of this paper.

2 Fully Immersive, Interactive and Collaborative Virtual Reality Applications

Fully immersive, interactive, and collaborative virtual reality applications allow remote users to share a space at the same time. Their main features are immersion, interactivity, involvement, and collaboration. Immersion provides the user with the perception of being physically present inside the simulated world, and can be achieved, for instance, using 3D stereoscopic displays and motion tracking devices. Interactivity is associated with the responsiveness of the simulated environment to user actions, while involvement is related to the user's engagement with the virtual environment. Collaboration in a virtual reality environment [9, 10] allows groups to work together on the execution of a single task. In this paper, we focus on virtual reality systems that accommodate participants that are connected remotely.

Today, it is possible to create high-quality virtual reality applications using high-level tools such as Unity 3D[4] and Ogre3D[5], which allow sophisticated synthetic environments to be built. However, to enable collaboration, it is necessary to consider that during navigation and interaction, users perform actions that are transmitted over the network [11], and the remote site will receive updates caused by these actions after a certain amount of delay [12]. This problem has led to the use of low-level application programming interfaces (APIs) (e.g., sockets over TCP/UDP, PVM[6], and MPI[7]) to facilitate information exchanges and synchronization. Thus, the applications running on top of these lower-level APIs become limited by factors such as network performance. Input and output devices (e.g., motion tracking, audio, and graphics rendering) may also cause additional latency in these applications, although this is beyond the scope of the present paper.

The graphics clusters used by fully collaborative virtual reality applications give multiple views of the same visual dataset. The nodes in each local cluster access the entire dataset, and then independently determine how much of the dataset is visible given the assigned viewing frustum, based on the local user view, and render only that part. The challenge is to provide a coherent, seamless, and continuous display using the isolated, distributed visual nodes in each local environment. In these applications, data ranging from the view frustum to geometric primitives or even avatar positions are

---

[4] https://unity.com/.

[5] https://www.ogre3d.org/.

[6] http://pvm-plus-plus.sourceforge.net/.

[7] https://www.open-mpi.org/.

continuously sent between nodes, and rendering must be synchronized between the intra- and inter-cluster nodes.

Despite the existence of libraries that can assist in the development of cluster applications, a method has not yet been proposed for maintaining quality data exchanges in an inter-cluster scenario, and this is a promising line of research.

3   GClassifier

Figure 1 depicts the strategy workflow, which includes training, testing, and a run-time network evaluation, to allow the library to adapt the communication to meet the requirements of the application. The process starts by defining the network require-ments of the full, immersive, interactive, and collaborative virtual reality applications. The classes and their features are then (manually) defined. Next, the training set is automatically created, by capturing data using a network simulator (e.g., Network Emulation or NetEm)[8]. This dataset is saved and used for the internal classification of the ensemble. Finally, it is ready to be used directly at runtime by the library to adapt the network communication. The library must be tailored to capture packets, trigger the classification and adapt the communication during runtime (e.g., to choose another network protocol, change the network topology used, and/or perform data buffering if the bandwidth is not sufficient).

Fig. 1. Steps in the proposed strategy for network communication adaptation at application runtime

Figure 2 illustrates the architecture of the software developed here. The GClassifier tool is used to implement this scheme. The main idea is to check the underlying com-munication in terms of packet loss, time delay, and time variation, and the system was coded using the Java language. GClassifier provides a graphical interface that allows the network administrator to fill in the parameters to be used during the training (e.g., physical network card, percentage packet loss and network delay) and test phases (e.g., number of captured packets). It uses charts to represent the results of network com-munication analysis. The core of our strategy is the OPF framework, which allows the user to build classifiers by changing their modules (e.g., the adjacency relation, proto-type estimation methodology, and path-cost function). It also supports multi-classes and

---

[8] http://man7.org/linux/man-pages/man8/tc-netem.8.html.

can handle some degree of overlap between classes [8]. Our solution is based on a supervised classifier that uses a complete graph as an adjacency relation. The training set is interpreted as the nodes of a graph in which the arcs are defined by a given adjacency relation and weighted by the distance function (fmax, which assigns the maximum arc weight along the path). It contains samples from different classes, each of which has a set of features and a distance function that are used to measure their dissimilarity in the feature space. The OPF aims to assign a correct class label to each new sample (prototype), and these compete among themselves to conquer the remaining samples. This process results in optimum path trees. The classes were defined manually based on the network requirements for fully immersive, interactive, and collaborative virtual reality applications. To build the training set, we added values for delay and packet loss for outgoing packets from a specific network interface using the traffic control tool NetEm, and used the ping tool to test the reachability of each node.

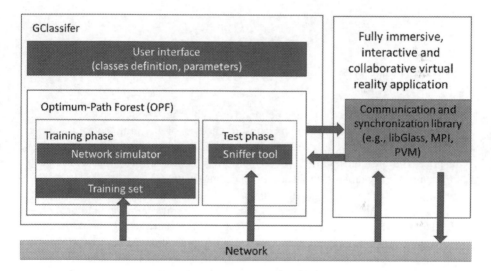

Fig. 2. Architecture of the GClassifier tool

Figure 3 shows an example of the results of a reachability test using the ping tool. The ping results are compared with the optimum path tree, and the tree that matches the sample is associated with the class (rotuled). The communication application library can then gather packets from the network communication, and classify and mitigate the existing adversities.

According to Chen [13], the user experience of a desktop collaborative virtual reality environment is affected when the network latency is greater than 200 ms and/or packet loss is more than 60%. Jitter is the most harmful effect, since it is necessary to maintain a constant speed for the delivery rate of packets; however, this can be mitigated using buffering techniques [14].

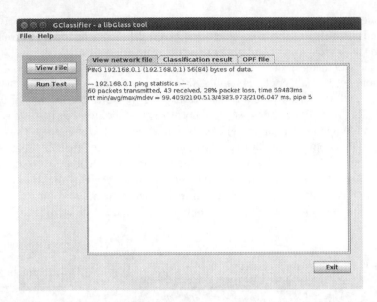

Fig. 3. Example from GClassifier showing the results of a node reachability test

Table 1 lists the range of values defined for each input variable (packet loss, time variation, and delay) and shows the consequences (not harmful, harmful, or very harmful). These values were based on a systematic review performed by Singhal and Zyda [15]. The attributes shown in the table were based on the minimum expected requirements for a graphics application (rendering) with 60 fps, in which the information for each frame is transmitted in one message, resulting in 60 messages per second. The three attributes considered are packet loss, time variation, and delay. Ling et al. [16] reported that delays of up to 200 ms are detrimental for collaborative applications. This also applies to virtual reality applications, due to the real-time interactions between users, and since environmental elements are updated based on each user's actions and reactions. Chen [13] found that packet loss is altered in an

Table 1. Range of values defined for each input variable

	Packet loss	Time variation	Delay
Not harmful	0–3%	0–5 ms	0–60 ms
Harmful	2–6%	4–10 ms	55–200 ms
Very harmful	5–20%	9–100 ms	190–600 ms

environment where the application achieves at least 40 status updates per second. These results allowed us to define the parameters for each OPF class. These values can be changed according to specific requirements; for example, a stereoscopic application requires more fps than a non-stereoscopic one.

Each input variable is used to measure a certain problem associated with network communication, and is related to the network communication adversity. Table 2 shows a combination of 27 classes that are used to define the type of dynamic adaptation

Table 2. Classes of adversity in network communication

Class	Packet loss	Time variation	Delay	Class	Packet loss	Time variation	Delay
1	Not harmful	Not harmful	Not harmful	15	Harmful	Harmful	Very harmful
2	Not harmful	Not harmful	Harmful	16	Harmful	Very Harmful	Not harmful
3	Not harmful	Not harmful	Very harmful	17	Harmful	Very Harmful	Harmful
4	Not harmful	Harmful	Not harmful	18	Harmful	Very Harmful	Very harmful
5	Not harmful	Harmful	Harmful	19	Very harmful	Not harmful	Not harmful
6	Not harmful	Harmful	Very harmful	20	Very harmful	Not harmful	Harmful
7	Not harmful	Very harmful	Not harmful	21	Very harmful	Not harmful	Very harmful
8	Not harmful	Very harmful	Harmful	22	Very harmful	Harmful	Not harmful
9	Not harmful	Very harmful	Very harmful	23	Very harmful	Harmful	Harmful
10	Harmful	Not harmful	Not harmful	24	Very harmful	Harmful	Very harmful
11	Harmful	Not harmful	Harmful	25	Very harmful	Very harmful	Not harmful
12	Harmful	Not harmful	Very harmful	26	Very harmful	Very harmful	Harmful
13	Harmful	Harmful	Not harmful	27	Very harmful	Very harmful	Very harmful
14	Harmful	Harmful	Harmful				

required from the communication library. The most representative instance of each class in the training set was chosen to be in the border region between the classes. Each class is expected to have an associated action from the communication library. This allows the master nodes of each local cluster to regulate its sending rate based on the class defined in a unified approach.

After the training and testing phases, the GClassifier is ready to classify new data using the categories of network communication adversity shown in Table 2. The application communication library can then mitigate the connection issues by applying the following actions:

- Altering the communication protocol: This refers to the set of rules used by computers to exchange messages with each other. TCP is often the default protocol, although in case of adversity, it can be combined with UDP; for example, TCP can be used for critical packets while UDP is used for status update packets. The library could also switch to SCTP, which is a reliable transport protocol that operates over an unreliable and unconnected packet service, such as Internet Protocol (IP).
- Buffering data: Buffers can be used to reduce packet loss as they can compensate for bursts of traffic in which routers cannot handle message forwarding at a given instant [17]. Buffers can also be used to reduce the variability of sender nodes and to transform a variable receiving rate into a constant rate. For example, environmental state update packets can be buffered by a sender node in order to maintain a constant frame rate.
- Changing the network packet size: The use of large packets means that the sender needs to preallocate buffers that are large enough to send and receive the maximum possible size, while the use of small packets will involve more messages requesting to send data.
- Predicting packets: When the adversities are related to packet loss, the communication library can apply a linear prediction model in which future packet signals are estimated using a linear function based on previous samples. A latency compensation method can be used to reduce network latency. One example of a technique that can be adopted is dead reckoning, which performs extrapolation based upon the data received.

Our approach suggests solutions based on the classes identified by the classifier, and considers the actions required to mitigate these adversities. For example, if packet loss is "not harmful", time variation is "very harmful", and delay is "harmful", the communication library may try to mitigate these issues using TCP combined with UDP.

4   Tests

GClassifier automates the training, classification, and visualization of results, and the configuration of the tests is carried out via its interface. The interface contains parameters such as the classes of adversities, and parameters to be passed to NetEm (e.g., the number of packets sent and the delay). We performed 10 tests. Figure 4 illustrates the results of Test 3, in which 60 packets were sent and a delay of 6 ms, a

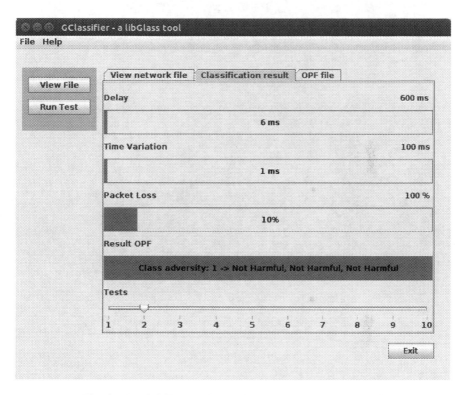

Fig. 4. Reachability test in which no problems were detected

time variation of 1 ms, and a packet loss of 10% were simulated using NetEm.

GClassifer defined this scenario as Class 1 (delay not harmful, time variation not harmful and packet loss not harmful). No adversity was found when a reachability test was executed.

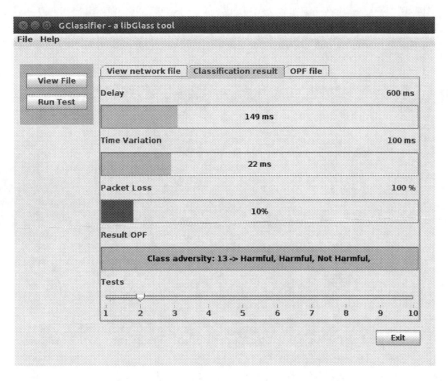

Fig. 5. Reachability test in which a problem was detected

Figure 5 illustrates the results of Test 8, in which a harmful level of adversity was found. This was classified as Class 13. During this test, 60 packets were sent, and a delay of 149 ms, a time variation of 1 ms, and a packet loss of 10% were simulated using NetEm.

The results of Test 3 are shown in Fig. 6. This scenario was classified as Class 27. During this test, 60 packets were sent, and a delay of 501 ms, a time variation of 87 ms, and a packet loss of 60% were simulated using NetEm.

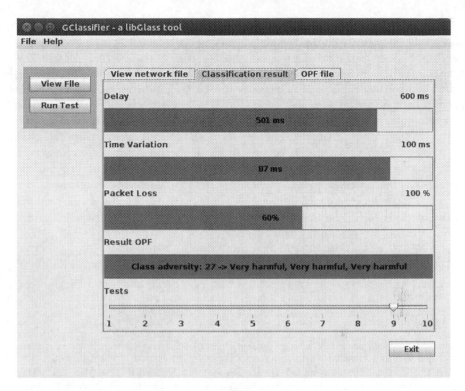

Fig. 6. Reachability test in which a serious problem was detected

5 Conclusion

Fully immersive, interactive, and collaborative virtual reality applications aim to use human sensory perception to send information to users' brains, to help them to solve a given task within a computer-generated environment. The developers of these applications need to overcome many barriers in terms of combining different hardware and software to achieve a sense of presence.

In recent years, due to the advances in computer hardware, software, and networking, these applications have been developed using graphics clusters, which require a knowledge of diverse areas such as computer graphics, human-computer interfaces, distributed systems, and computer networking. Communication within these applications is typically implemented using high-level functionality on top of the low-level primitives that are available (e.g., BSD sockets, PVM, and MPI). One example of a high-level library is libGlass[9], which is tailored for fully immersive applications based on intra-cluster communication. This library offers primitives that can maintain synchronicity and coherence over the data, and provide datalock and framelock.

---

[9] http://libglass.sourceforge.net/.

Currently, the most common solutions are based on computer graphics clusters, with each environment implementing its own. These exchange data and carry out synchronization using inter-cluster communication over the internet. This makes it necessary to conform to strict timing dependencies, meaning that network communication is likely to experience bottlenecks caused by problems such as packet loss, delay, and time variation. We created a strategy to analyze the variables of packet loss, time variation, and delay to allow dynamic adaptation of communication within fully immersive, interactive, and collaborative virtual reality applications. Our strategy was based on the use of a supervised pattern recognition technique called OPF to classify these variables into 27 classes of adversities. To train our classifier, we used data collected by the simulator NetEm. The GClassifier tool automates the training and test phases. The results can be used directly by any library to adapt network communication in the appropriate way, for example, by changing the buffer size and/or the protocol used. In future, we plan to test other pattern recognition techniques.

Acknowledgments. This study was financed in part by the Coordenação de Aperfeiçoamento de Pessoal de Nível Superior - Brasil (CAPES) - Finance Code 001.

References

1. Kuhlen, T.W., Hentschel, B.: Quo vadis cave: does immersive visualization still matter? IEEE Comput. Graph. Appl. **34**, 14–21 (2014). https://doi.org/10.1109/MCG.2014.97
2. Tredinnick, R., Boettcher, B., Smith, S., Solovy, S., Ponto, K.: Uni-CAVE: A Unity3D plugin for non-head mounted VR display systems. In: 2017 IEEE Virtual Reality (VR). pp. 393–394 (2017). https://doi.org/10.1109/VR.2017.7892342
3. Chung, H., Andrews, C., North, C.: A survey of software frameworks for cluster-based large high-resolution displays. IEEE Trans. Vis. Comput. Graph. **20**, 1158–1177 (2014). https://doi.org/10.1109/TVCG.2013.272
4. Luo, L., Mo, J., Chen, H.: Multi-channel visual reality system based on computer cluster. In: 2017 24th International Conference on Mechatronics and Machine Vision in Practice (M2VIP). pp. 1–6 (2017). https://doi.org/10.1109/M2VIP.2017.8211453
5. Boser, B.E., Guyon, I.M., Vapnik, V.N.: A training algorithm for optimal margin classifiers. In: Proceedings of the Fifth Annual Workshop on Computational Learning Theory. pp. 144–152. Association for Computing Machinery, New York, NY, USA (1992). https://doi.org/10.1145/130385.130401
6. Aggarwal, C.C.: Neural Networks and Deep Learning: A Textbook. Springer, Cham (2018)
7. Papa, J.P., Falcão, A.X., Victor, H.C.: Efficient supervised optimum-path forest classification for large datasets. Pattern Recogn. **45**, 512–520 (2012). https://doi.org/10.1016/j.patcog.2011.07.013
8. Papa, J.P., Falcão, A.X., Suzuki, C.T.N.: Supervised pattern classification based on optimum-path forest. Int J Imag Syst Tech. **19**, 120–131 (2009). https://doi.org/10.1002/ima.20188
9. Nguyen, T.T.H., Duval, T.: A survey of communication and awareness in collaborative virtual environments. In: 2014 International Workshop on Collaborative Virtual Environments (3DCVE). pp. 1–8 (2014). https://doi.org/10.1109/3DCVE.2014.7160928

10. Bente, G., Rüggenberg, S., Krämer, N.C., Eschenburg, F.: Avatar-mediated networking: increasing social presence and interpersonal trust in net-based collaborations. Hum. Commun. Res. **34**, 287–318 (2008). https://doi.org/10.1111/j.1468-2958.2008.00322.x
11. Shirmohammadi, S., Georganas, N.D.: An end-to-end communication architecture for collaborative virtual environments. Comput. Net. **35**, 351–367 (2001). https://doi.org/10. 1016/S1389-1286(00)00186-9
12. Gutwin, C., Benford, S., Dyck, J., Fraser, M., Vaghi, I., Greenhalgh, C.: Revealing delay in collaborative environments. In: Proceedings of the SIGCHI Conference on Human Factors in Computing Systems. pp. 503–510. Association for Computing Machinery, New York, NY, USA (2004). https://doi.org/10.1145/985692.985756
13. Ling, C.: Effects of network characteristics on task performance in a desktop CVE system. In: 19th International Conference on Advanced Information Networking and Applications (AINA 2005) (AINA papers). vol. 1, pp. 821–826 (2005). https://doi.org/10.1109/AINA. 2005.171
14. Anthes, C., Haffegee, A., Heinzlreiter, P., Volkert, J.: A scalable network architecture for closely coupled collaboration. Comput. Inf. **24**, 31–51 (2012)
15. Singhal, S., Zyda, M.: Networked Virtual Environments: Design and Implementation. Addison-Wesley Reading, Boston (1999)
16. Chen Ling, X.X., Chen Gen-Cai, C.C.: An effective communication architecture for collaborative virtual systems. In: International Conference on Communication Technology Proceedings, ICCT 2003. vol. 2, pp. 1598–1602 (2003). https://doi.org/10.1109/ICCT.2003. 1209833
17. Sequeira, L., Fernández-Navajas, J., Casadesus, L., Saldana, J., Quintana, I., Ruiz-Mas, J.: The influence of the buffer size in packet loss for competing multimedia and bursty traffic. In: 2013 International Symposium on Performance Evaluation of Computer and Telecommunication Systems (SPECTS). pp. 134–141 (2013)

An Immersive Open Source Environment Using Godot

Francesca Santucci[1], Federico Frenguelli[1], Alessandro De Angelis[1],
Ilaria Cuccaro[3], Damiano Perri[2(✉)] ⓘ, and Marco Simonetti[2] ⓘ

[1] Evonove SrL, Perugia, Italy
[2] Department of Mathematics and Computer Science,
University of Florence, Florence, Italy
damiano.perri@gmail.com
[3] Department of Mathematics and Computer Science,
University of Perugia, Perugia, Italy

Abstract. We present a sample implementation of a Virtual and Augmented Reality immersive environment based on Free and Libre Open Source Hardware and Software and the HTC Vive system, used to enhance the immersive experience of the user and to track her/his movements.

The sense of immersion has increased and stimulated using a footplate and a Tibetan bridge, connected to the virtual world as Augmented Reality applications and implemented through an Arduino board, thereby adopting a low cost, open source hardware and software approach.

The proposed architecture is relatively affordable from the cost point of view, easy to implement, configure and adapt to different contexts. It can be of great help for organizing laboratory classes for young students to afford the implementation of virtual worlds and Augmented Reality applications.

Keywords: Virtual reality · Augmented Reality · Immersive environments · Free and libre open source software · Godot · Blender · Arduino

1 Introduction

The importance of virtual reality grows with the spread of digital technologies in various areas of life. The year 2020 will remain sadly etched in our minds and memories for having deprived us, in various forms, of cherished affections and our lifestyles. In a few months we have seen the use of technology grow disproportionately.

Virtual reality can allow us to explore new forms of communication and distance education, becoming one of the most promising areas for the future, allowing new forms of teaching, capable of bridging the physical distance and giving a new strength to online education.

In a virtual world, the system follows and simulates our movements through images and sounds that give us the illusion that we are moving and acting in

ⓒ Springer Nature Switzerland AG 2020
O. Gervasi et al. (Eds.): ICCSA 2020, LNCS 12255, pp. 784–798, 2020.
https://doi.org/10.1007/978-3-030-58820-5_56

a synthetic world. These sensations become much deeper and more suggestive when we are able to visit the world with immersive devices, like the HTC Vive system, consisting of a base station, hand motion controllers and a Head Mounted Display.

The emotional involvement during a virtual reality experience depends on the quality of the stimulus that involves the player. Suppose that a player is moved by a series of bodies that will change his point of view, so that the player could have the feeling to be moved. To create a more immersive experience, we may add some stimuli (like a vibration system) that are able to move the player in reality.

The purpose of the project is to develop, with *open source* tools and software, an interactive virtual reality experience that allows the player to do a charming and attractive experience, using objects mapped in the virtual world with which the player can interact. In our case we implemented a footplate that is moved by an Arduino system and a Tibetan bridge oscillating along the x-axis. The implemented system represents a low cost, open source and easily reproducible case study, that allows young students to experience the immersive learning.

The paper is organized as follows: in Sect. 2 a review of publication related the paper keywords is carried out, in Sect. 3 the architecture of the system is described, in Sect. 4 the virtual world implemented on Godot and in Blender is described. The Sect. 6 presents some conclusions and a description of future works.

2   Related Works

Since the construction of the first virtual reality viewer in the 1970s, considerable progress has been made year after year. The improvements we are seeing are both hardware and software. The cost of the viewers is decreasing and many new applications are being developed. The sectors where virtual reality finds profitable application are: entertainment, tourism, manufacturing industry, e-commerce, medicine, teaching [1], and troubleshooting (for example in companies).

In the medical field, it is possible to help patients suffering from brain trauma through tele-rehabilitation. An example is in the work described in [2] where a Virtual Reality application based on X3D is presented that allows to stimulate the patient's brain with simple but concrete exercises, such as cross a street at a pedestrian crossing with traffic lights or calling and taking an elevator.

Thanks to modern information technology it is possible for a therapist to dynamically control the patient's status via remote connection, analyze the outcome of practices, and to program new types of exercises. Tele-rehabilitation increase the demand of calculations to be carried out and of data stored on a central repository. To this purpose cloud systems integrated with high performance systems are increasingly important solutions to provide the necessary computing resources. This approach makes it possible to optimize costs and easily afford future development and upgrade plans in relation to the number of users currently using the system and estimating how many will use it in the near future [3].

Teaching is an area where it is possible to use virtual reality (VR) technologies in a productive manner as students adapt and assimilate the explained notions more quickly. This is explained by the increased brain stimulation they receive when immersed in a virtual world, which is a completely different type of experience respect to simply read a text in a book. An example can be found in [4] where the quality of the study of the planets of the solar system improves the use of Virtual Reality.

The use of input devices that integrate the user's movements to the scenarios presented and that allow an increasingly fluid navigation within the network, are of particular importance for the purpose of a deep learning [5]. Furthermore, interconnected environments where huge quantities of personal information flows continuously require the integration of high security protocols [7] and suitably tested performing hardware [8]. For the purpose of secure access to user accounts, the integration with specific devices and deep learning systems for the recognition of facial features [10] or passwords recognized through the movement of the lips [9] is very promising.

In order to make the study environment more likely to real spaces and make it more informative, photos taken from ImageNet[1] have been inserted together with rendered images: through the metadata inserted in it [6], the user also experiences an Augmented Reality environment, which allows him to greatly expand his knowledge.

3   The Architecture of the System

The project consists in a virtual reality experience in which the player can move and interact with the objects available in the environment.

The project was designed thinking about of the real available space. For this reason the experience consists in a circular path: the player will start the game at one edge of the real room, he has to reach a footplate (that is placed both in the virtual and in the real worlds), shown in Fig. 1, get on it and press a button in the virtual world that will activate its movement. When the footplate is activated, in real world it starts to vibrate while, in virtual world, the player is moved to the upper floor. Upstairs there is a path where the player can move and walk until it reaches the bridge. The bridge is able to detect the collision with the player so when he starts to walk over it some forces are applied to the bridge to simulate the behavior of a suspended bridge in the vacuum. The path to be followed by the player is circular in the real world and developed upwards in the virtual world. This technique is designed to solve room spacing's issue and to give the player the feeling of walk a long way.

---

[1] ImageNet is an image database organized according to the WordNet hierarchy (currently only the nouns), in which each node of the hierarchy is depicted by hundreds and thousands of images. it can be found at the URL: http://www.image-net.org.

Fig. 1. The footplate and the button in the initial scene of the virtual environment.

It is fascinating how the virtual reality can influence the player sensation in the same way of real world. Even if the player knows that all system is virtual and not real, when he has to jump in a vacuum he fells scared and does not want to jump.

The aim that our project would reach is to mislead the player's feelings. For this reason we made a path developed upwards in which there is a suspended Tibetan bridge, shown in Fig. 2. Furthermore we add a wooden footplate that is present both in virtual and real world and its position is mapped in the same point. In this way when the player reaches the footplate in virtual world he will reach it in real world too.

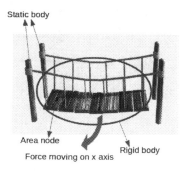

Fig. 2. The Tibetan bridge.

Under the footplate we added some vibration motors, shown in Fig. 3, used to mislead the perception of the player. When the player goes on it and presses the button in the virtual world, the motors will be activated. In this way in the real world the player is affected by some vibrations that give him some feelings of instability while in the virtual world he is moved upstairs, ready to start exploring the virtual world.

Fig. 3. The Arduino board installed on the real footplate.

The development of software for virtual reality requires specialized software and hardware. In fact, virtual reality requires a high frame rate to be able to move smoothly and naturally within a virtual space. This is a core requirement not only for experiencing an enjoyable 3D world, but also in order to prevent the so called *"simulation sickness"*, which might cause dizziness, headaches or even nausea.

First of all, a headset is needed. Our project was developed to work with **HTC Vive**. This is a virtual reality headset developed by **HTC** and **Valve**. The headset uses *room scale tracking technology*, allowing the user to move in 3D space and use motion-tracked handheld controllers to interact with the environment. The kit that HTC Vive offers is composed by different components. We use the following:

- *Headset:* is a device that uses two OLED panels, one per eye, each having a display resolution of 1080 × 1200 (2160 × 1200 combined pixels). It has a refresh rate of 90 Hz and 110° field of view. The device includes a front-facing camera that allows the user to observe their surroundings without removing their headset. The software can also use the camera to identify any static or moving objects in the room; this functionality can be used as part of *Chaperone* safety system which will automatically display a virtual wall or a feed from the camera to safely guide users from obstacles or real-world walls.
- *Controllers:* represent the hands of the player. They have multiple input methods including a track pad, grip buttons, and a dual-stage trigger and a use per change of about 6 h.
- *Base stations:* Also known as the Lighthouse tracking system are two black boxes that create a 360° virtual space. The base stations emit timed infrared pulses at 60 pulses per second that are then picked up by the headset and controllers with sub-millimeter precision.
- *Trackers:* Are some motion tracking accessory. They are designed to be attached to physical accessories and controllers, so that they can be tracked via the Lighthouse system. In our project we attach trackers to the player's feet. In this way we do not have to implement the teleport system [11].

The minimum system requirements that the computer must have to work with HTC Vive are at least:

- the following **hardware**: processor Intel Core i5-4590 or AMD FX 8350; GPU NVIDIA GeForce GTX 970 or AMD Readeon RX 290; memory 4 GB RAM; video output HDMI 1.4, DisplayPort 1.2; 1 x USB 2.0
- and the following **software**: Operating System: Windows 7 SP1, Windows 8.1 or later, Windows 10. [12];

To create a virtual reality experience many software can be used, like Unity 3D, Unreal Engine and Godot. Each software is a game engine and the main difference between them is that Godot is *open source* and does not impose any rules or payments when the game is published.

Probably, to develop a virtual reality experience Unreal Engine and Unity offer a better support and stability, but for the purpose of our project we decided to use Godot. Godot is a free open source project developed by a community of volunteers. It provides a huge set of common tools and a fully integrated game development environment.

The main component of Godot are the *Nodes* that can perform a variety of specialized functions. Each node has a name and some editable properties. It can receive a callback to process every frame, can be extended and can be added to another node as child. A group of nodes organized hierarchically composed a *Scene*. Basically in Godot, running a game means running a scene. A project can contain several scenes, but for start the game, one of them must be selected as the main scene.

The main goal that comes with instancing scenes is that it works as an excellent design language. When making games with Godot the recommended approach is to think about the scenes in a natural way: imagine all the visible elements in your game, write down them in a diagram and start creating a scene for each of them. This approach dismiss the most common design pattern (like Model-View-Controller) used in another game engine.

To have the ability to detect the collisions, Godot offers a *collision system* that allows to build up complex interactions between a variety of objects that compose the game. Each one of these objects could be of four different kinds of physics bodies. Each one reacts in different way to the Godot's physics engine and for this reason it is important to understand what kind of bodies we need. To be able to detect and respond to collisions a *physics body* has to be associated to a *collision shape* that defines the object collision bounds. In this way it is able to detect the contact with other objects.

To interact with headset components and setup a virtual environment a new architecture was introduced in Godot called *ARVRServer*. On top of this architecture, specific implementations are available as interfaces, most of which are plugins based on *GDNative*. GDNative offers a way to integrate features and functions defined inside some external libraries or external modules that must have a C-compatible binary interface. Otherwise these modules or libraries cannot be used inside Godot. Through GDNative we can register symbols, functions names and structures of some dynamic libraries and load them at runtime. These symbols, functions and structure are made available in Godot through a Native Script. Once ARVRServer architecture is added in game project, every time

Godot starts, each available interface will make itself known to the server. In this way we can interact with all the headset components.

ARVRServer plays an important role because through it we can bind code to interact with *SteamVR*. This is a virtual reality hardware and software that makes possible execute a virtual reality experience and communicate with the headset components. So ARVRServer represent a middle-layer between SteamVR and Godot. All available headset components that SteamVR detects are made available in Godot thanks to ARVRServer interfaces.

To interact with Arduino we use a plugin based on GDNative called *GDSercomm*. It is a GDNative module that allows a serial port communication between Arduino and Godot. Arduino is an open source hardware and software company, project and user community that designs and produces single-board micro-controllers kits for building digital devices. We used it to implement the vibration system under the wooden footplate.

To create the game environment like footplate, bridge and other objects with which the player can interact we use Blender. It is a free and open source 3D creation suite and supports the entire 3D pipeline - modeling, rigging, animation, simulation, rendering, composting and motion tracking, even video editing and game creation.

4   The Virtual World Made on Godot and Blender

To create a game with Godot the recommended approach is to think about the scenes that compose the project in a naturally way. So we started to imagine all the visible elements with which the player should interact, write down them in a diagram and creating for each one a Scene (Fig. 4).

Our final diagram is shown in the Fig. 5.

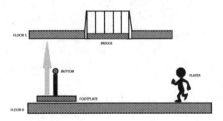

Fig. 4. Diagram with all visible elements

The 4 basic elements that composed our game are:

- **Environment**: composed by the first floor and second floor;
- **Player**: is composed by hands, feet, camera and an arrow that indicates the teleport end point;
- **Footplate** and **Button**;
- **Tibetan bridge**.

Each of these elements has one or more Mesh assign to it. A Mesh is a collection of vertices, edges and faces that defines the shape of a polyhedral object.

To create the meshes we use Blender. It is a versatile and complete software, based on algorithms capable of reproducing the behavior of light in a realistic way. In addition to providing a great variety of features for modeling, lighting and rendering, the program allows a rather simple export of the models within a Godot Engine scene. In order to be displayed correctly, it is important to export the meshes created in Blender in one of the following files supported by Godot: DAE, GLTF, OBJ and ESCN.

The first mesh that we create was the footplate, able to move the observer in the upper floor. This consists of a rectangular table to which we apply a wood texture. Blender provides options to improve some effects related to opacity and color, once the object is hit by light. A similar method has been used for the construction of the Tibetan bridge because also in this case we started modeling from simple cubes and cylinders.

For the Player's hands and feet we download some free assets while, for the first and second floor, we use the basic mesh that Godot makes available.

Once all the meshes were exported in Godot we started to organized them in different scenes to better handle each game's component behavior. A **Scene** is a group of nodes organized hierarchically while a **Node** represents the core component of Godot and it can perform a variety of specialized functions. Another important aspect that we have to take in mind in game development is the ability to detect some collisions through the objects; for this reason Godot provides four basic types of physical bodies able to detect and respond to collisions:

- **Area**: provides detection and influence. It can detect when objects overlap and can emit signals when bodies enter or exit.
- **StaticBody**: is not moved by the physics engine, it participates to collision detection but does not move in response to the collision.
- **RigidBody**: implements simulated physics, we do not control it directly, but we apply forces to it (such as gravity, impulse, etc.) and the physical motor calculates the resulting movement.
- **KinematicBody**: It is not influenced by physics. This type of physic body is useful for moving objects that do not require advanced physics. It must be controlled by the user.

To better understand these information we have to take in mind that each element that we mention before performs a specific role in the game. For this reason we have to use specific nodes in order to obtain the desired behavior.

For example, because the Environment is not intended to move, the elements that compose this scene are StaticBody. Each StaticBody wraps the mesh instance and the collision shape.

The Footplate is a KinematicBody because it has to move the player in the upper floor. This behavior is obtained using the `move_and_slide` function that translates the footplate along the y axis and it stops once it reaches the upper floor. The Bridge is a RigidBody and we apply a rotation impulse to it when the Player walks over it.

The most complex Scene is represented by the Player. Basically it is a RigidBody but, because of it has to work in virtual reality environment, it has to implement some specifics nodes like:

– **ARVROrigin**: is a special node within the AR/VR system that maps the physical location of the center of our tracking space to the virtual location within our game world.
– **ARVRCamera**: is a camera node with a few overrules for AR/VR applied, such as location tracking.
– **ARVRController one for each hand and foot**: is a spatial node representing a spatially-tracked controller. In our project it wraps the hands' and feet's mesh instances and their collision shapes.

The structure of the Player is showed in the above image.

Fig. 5. Player structure tree.

Most of the elements that compose our scenes contains a **CollisionShape** node. It defines the object's collision bounds that is used to detect contact with other objects. In base of the shape of the object that it has to wrap we could use some basic types or create new complex collision shape in Godot. It is important to know that is possible to create some complex collision shape inside other external software - like Blender - and import them in Godot.

One of the most powerful collision features that Godot provides is the collision layer system. It allows to build up complex interactions between a variety of objects. The key concepts are **layers** and **masks**. The **collision_layer** describes the layers that the object appears in. The **collision_mask** describes what layers the body will scan for collisions. Keeping track of what layer you are using could be difficult so Godot provides the possibility to rename the layer (Fig. 6).

In our project we have the following collision situation:

In our project we have the following collision situation:

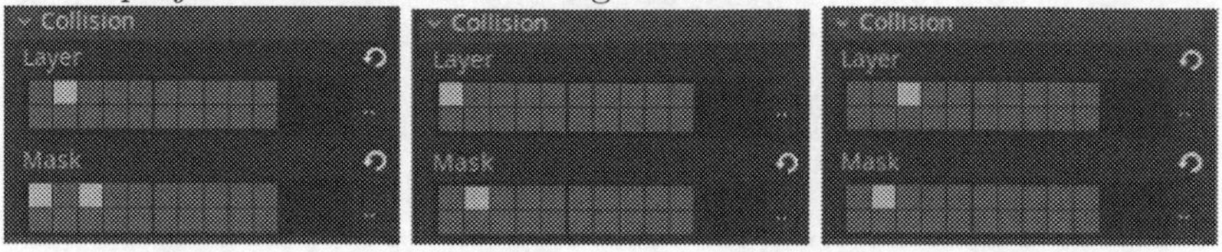

Fig. 6. 1:Player collision 2:Footplate collision 3:Bridge collision

The platform and the environment's floors appear in layer 1 and checks for collisions with player (layer 2). The player appears in layer 2 and checks for collisions with environment (layer 1) and bridge (layer 3). The bridge appears in layer 3 and checks for collisions with player (layer 2).

In order to obtain the desired behavior from Footplate, Bridge and Player we attach to them a **GDScript**. It is a high-level, dynamically typed programming language used to create content. It uses a syntax similar to Python (blocks are indent-based and many keywords are similar). Its goal is to be optimized for and tightly integrated with Godot Engine, allowing great flexibility for content creation and integration.

First of all we combined all the scenes created in the Main scene. We chose it as the main scene that Godot runs when it starts. Also the Main scene has a script attached to it because, when we start the game we have to check the availability of the ARVRServer and its devices. The following code shows how we check the state of ARVRServer and its interfaces.

Listing 1.1. The code used to configure the Main scene.

```
extends Spatial

func _ready():
  var interface = ARVRServer.find_interface("OpenVR")
  if interface and interface.initialize():
    # turn to ARVR mode
    get_viewport().arvr = true

    # keep linear color space, not needed with the GLES2 renderer
    get_viewport().keep_3d_linear = true

    # make sure vsync is disabled or we'll be limited to 60fps
    OS.vsync_enabled = false

    # up our physics to 90fps to get in sync with our rendering
    Engine.target_fps = 90
```

From the code we can see that the Main scene is a Spatial node. Most of 3D game objects inherit from Spatial because it allows to move, scale, rotate and show/hide its children in a 3D project.

The function _ready() is called only once when the node is created. In it is possible to initialize variables, load nodes, materials and all the things that we need to start a scene.

In our case we try to find *OpenVR* interface because, if it is available we initialize the virtual environment and sets the frame per second to 90 to avoid the user sickness.

Once all the interfaces are ready the game starts and all the scenes that we create are visible in the virtual world.

To handle the collision between the Player and the Footplate we attach to the Player the following script:

Listing 1.2. The code used to configure the Player scene.

```
extends RigidBody

var collision
var new_position
var leftfoot
var rightfoot
var positionl
var positionr
var camera
var position
var changel = false
var changer = false

func _ready():
  leftfoot = get_node("PlayerOrigin/LeftFootController/LeftFootArea")
  positionl = leftfoot.get_translation()
  rightfoot = get_node("PlayerOrigin/RightFootController/RightFootArea")
  positionr = rightfoot.get_translation()
  camera = get_node("PlayerOrigin")
  position = camera.get_translation()
  collision = get_node("PlayerCollisionShape")
  new_position = collision.get_translation()

func _process(delta):
  positionl = leftfoot.get_translation()
  positionr = rightfoot.get_translation()
  position = camera.get_translation()
  if changel:
    new_position = collision.set_translation(position)
  elif changer:
    new_position = collision.set_translation(position)

func _on_LeftFootArea_body_entered(body):
  if body.get_name() == "BottomFloor" or body.get_name() == "UpperFloor1":
    if positionl != new_position or positionr != new_position:
      changel = true


func _on_RightFootArea_body_entered(body):
  if body.get_name() == "BottomFloor" or body.get_name() == "UpperFloor1":
    if positionl != new_position or positionr != new_position:
      changer = true


func _on_LeftFootArea_body_exited(body):
  if body.get_name() == "BottomFloor" or body.get_name() == "UpperFloor1":
    changel = false


func _on_RightFootArea_body_exited(body):
  if body.get_name() == "BottomFloor" or body.get_name() == "UpperFloor1":
    changer = false
```

First of all we initialize the controllers with which the Player will interact with the virtual world components. The hands can triggers - thank to the collision shape attached to them - if there are some objects that the Player can press or hold. The feet controllers are useful to handle the movements of the Player. In fact, thank to these we can update the position of the Player in the virtual world every time he walks.

The _process() is a special function that updates object data every delta frames. We use it to update the position of the player every time he moved in the space.

The other functions that are in the script are used to handle specific signals emitted by some Area nodes.

To handle the Player teleport we attach to LeftHandController node another script that create an arrow that became visible each time the trigger button of controller is clicked. This arrow show the end point to which the Player will be moved.

Very interesting is how we connect virtual Footplate with the real one. The connection between the Godot footplate node and Arduino was setup by a special GDNative module called **GDSercomm**. It is a module that allows a serial communication between Godot and Arduino, in other words it provides an API from them. It presents some methods like:

- **list_ports()**: to get all the available ports;
- **open()**: to open a communication, flush() - to update the buffer;
- **get_available()**: return the available reading bytes;
- **write()**: write a string in the buffer.

All these function are contained in Sercomm, a C library.

Listing 1.3. Some pieces of code used to configure the vibration motors from Godot.

```
func _ready():
  timer.connect("timeout", self, "_on_timer_timeout")
  timer_setup()
  upperFloor = get_node("../Environment/UpperFloor1")
  stopping = int(upperFloor.get_translation().y)
  print("ports ", PORT.list_ports())
  var ports = PORT.list_ports();
  PORT.open(ports[0], 9600, 1000)
  PORT.flush()
  print("get_available ", PORT.get_available())

[ ]

func _move_platform_with_button():
  player.set_translation(Vector3(1.7,0,0.8))
  origin.set_translation(Vector3(-1.7,0,-0.8))
  camera.set_translation(Vector3(-1.7,0,-0.8))
  timer.stop()
  is_platform_moving = true
  platform_moved = true
  area_mesh_instance.visible = false
  PORT.write("h")
  PORT.flush()
```

In the _ready() function - in the last rows of code - we establish a connection with Arduino port.

The _move_platform_with_button() function is called when the Player press the button near the Footplate in virtual world. When it is pressed the player is moved upstairs and a string is send to Arduino. In this way we activate the vibration motors that are under the real footplate. To stop it we check if the virtual footplate reaches the upper floor and eventually we stop the translation in the y axis and send a string to Arduino to stop the vibration of the motors.

Listing 1.4. The code used to stop the vibration motors from Godot.

```
func _physics_process(delta):
  if is_platform_moving:
    # makes the platform move
    vel.y = force * delta
    move_and_slide(vel, pos)
    h = self.get_translation().y
    # platform stops
    if h >= stopping + 0.3:
      force = 0
      PORT.write("1")
      PORT.flush()
```

The _physic_process() is used when one needs a framerate-independent deltatime between frames (Fig. 7).

In the end, to handle the rotation of the Bridge when the Player walk over it, we use this script that checks when the **LeftFootArea** or **Right-FootArea** collide with one bridge's board and when it occurs we apply an apply_torque_impulse() to each peace of Bridge the Player touches.

Listing 1.5. The code used to move the bridge when the plyer walk over it.

```
func _on_Board_area_entered(area):
  if area.get_name() == "RightFootArea" or area.get_name() == "
      LeftFootArea":
    timer.start()
    $Boards.apply_torque_impulse(Vector3(0.02, 0.0, 0.0))
```

The final result that we reach is showed in the following image.

Fig. 7. Final result.

5   The Vibration Footplate and Arduino

To make the user to feel the footplate moving under his feet we placed in the real environment a wooden footplate, hacked using an `Arduino Uno` board and two `vibration motors`.

Using the Arduino IDE we uploaded the code shown in listing 1.6 into the board which initialize and handle the serial communication.

In the setup function we initialize the serial communication at 9600 bps and wait until the serial port is ready to communicate, then we configure the pin 8 to behave as output. The loop function does what the name suggests, loops consecutively and reads from the serial, when it receives the "h" character Arduino will set a 3.3 V to the pin 8 starting the vibration motors, in contrary when it receives the "l" character Arduino set a 0 V to the pin 8 which stops the vibration motors.

Listing 1.6. The code used to configure the Arduino board for vibrating the real footplate.

```
int incomingByte = 0;

void setup() {
  Serial.begin(9600);

  while(!Serial){
    ;
  }

  pinMode(8, OUTPUT);
}

void loop() {
  if(Serial.available() > 0) {
    incomingByte = Serial.read();

    if(incomingByte == 'h') {
        digitalWrite(8, HIGH);
    }
    else if (incomingByte == 'l') {
      digitalWrite(8, LOW);
    }
  }
}
```

6   Conclusions and Future Works

The project's purpose is to create an immersive VR experience from the design to the implementation. Through this project we tested the Godot's efficiency for VR games. We obtained good performances both in physics simulations and graphics quality.

In the beginning we created the virtual world space that has the same measurements as the real space in which the player moves, controlled by the HTC Vive system. In this way the player can move in the virtual space without colliding with the room walls. In our case the simulation room was small so it was important to develop a circular and upwards path.

In the experimental phase we faced issues to setup the proper player interactions with other objects. A wrong layers collision setup could compromise the interaction behaviour of the objects or of the player.

The current project was presenting only a footplate as an interactive object. Our goal is to add more interactive objects, we could for example introduce a fan fixed on the ceiling. The fan will be activated with the vibration motors placed under the wooden footplate, to simulate the wind effect.

Furthermore the vibration system can be applied to other static objects.

References

1. Yildirim, G., Elban, M., Yildirim, S.: Analysis of use of virtual reality technologies in history education: a case study. EDU **4**(2), 62–69 (2018)
2. Gervasi, O., Magni, R., Zampolini, M.: Nu!RehaVR: Virtual reality in neuro tele-rehabilitation of patients with traumatic brain injury and stroke. Virtual Reality **14**(2), 131–141 (2010). https://doi.org/10.1007/s10055-009-0149-7
3. Mariotti, M., Gervasi, O., Vella, F., Cuzzocrea, A., Costantini, A.: Strategies and systems towards grids and clouds integration: a DBMS-based solution. Future Gener. Comput. Syst. **88**, 718–729 (2018). https://doi.org/10.1016/j.future.2017.02.047
4. Hussein, M., Nätterdal, C.: The benefits of virtual reality in education: A comparison study. (Bachelor of Science Thesis in Software Engineering and Management Student essay), Chlamers University of Technology, University of Gothenburg, Göteborg, Sweden (2015)
5. Franzoni, V., Gervasi, O.: Guidelines for web usability and accessibility on the Nintendo Wii. In: Gavrilova, M.L., Tan, C.J.K. (eds.) Transactions on Computational Science VI. LNCS, vol. 5730, pp. 19–40. Springer, Heidelberg (2009). https://doi.org/10.1007/978-3-642-10649-1_2
6. Krizhevsky, A., Sutskever, I., Hinton, G.: Imagenet classification with deep convolutional neural networks. In: 25th International Conference on Advance in Neural Information Processing System, pp. 1106–1114 (2012)
7. Gervasi, O., Russo, D., Vella, F.: The AES implantation based on OpenCL for Multi/many core architecture. In: 2010 International Conference on Computational Science and Its Applications, Fukuoka, ICCSA 2010, Washington, DC, USA, IEEE Computer Society (2010). https://doi.org/10.1109/ICCSA.2010.44
8. Vella, F., Neri, I., Gervasi, O., Tasso, S.: A simulation framework for scheduling performance evaluation on CPU-GPU heterogeneous system. In: Murgante, B., et al. (eds.) ICCSA 2012. LNCS, vol. 7336, pp. 457–469. Springer, Heidelberg (2012). https://doi.org/10.1007/978-3-642-31128-4_34
9. Gervasi, O., Magni, R., Ferri, M.: A method for predicting words by interpreting labial movements. In: Gervasi, O., et al. (eds.) ICCSA 2016. LNCS, vol. 9787, pp. 450–464. Springer, Cham (2016). https://doi.org/10.1007/978-3-319-42108-7_34
10. Riganelli, M., Franzoni, V., Gervasi, O., Tasso, S.: EmEx, a tool for automated emotive face recognition using convolutional neural networks. In: Gervasi, O., et al. (eds.) ICCSA 2017. LNCS, vol. 10406, pp. 692–704. Springer, Cham (2017). https://doi.org/10.1007/978-3-319-62398-6_49
11. HTC Vive. https://www.vive.com/eu/, https://en.wikipedia.org/wiki/HTC_Vive
12. Vive - What are the system requirements? https://www.vive.com/us/support/vive/category_howto/what-are-the-system-requirements.html

Teaching Math with the Help of Virtual Reality

Marco Simonetti[1]([⊠]) [iD], Damiano Perri[1] [iD], Natale Amato[2] [iD],
and Osvaldo Gervasi[3] [iD]

[1] Department of Mathematics and Computer Science,
University of Florence, Florence, Italy
m.simonetti@unifi.it
[2] University of Bari, Bari, Italy
[3] Department of Mathematics and Computer Science,
University of Perugia, Perugia, Italy

Abstract. In this work we introduce a learning system based on VR
(Virtual Reality) for studying analytical-geometric structures that are
part of the curriculum in mathematics and physics high school classes.

We believe that an immersive study environment has several advantages over traditional two-dimensional environments (such as a book or
the simple screen of a PC or tablet), such as the spatial understanding of the concepts exposed, more peripheral awareness and moreover
an evident decreasing in the information dispersion phenomenon. This
does not mean that our teaching approach is a substitute for traditional
approaches, but it can serve as a robust tool to support learning. In the
first phase of our research we have sought to understand which mathematical objects and which tools to use to enhance the teaching of mathematics, in order to demonstrate that the use of VR techniques significantly increase the level of understanding of the mathematical subject
being studied by the students.

The system which provides for the integration of two machine levels, hardware and software, was subsequently tested by a representative
sample of students who then provided feedback through a questionnaire.

Keywords: Virtual Reality · Unity3D · Blender

1 Introduction

Much progress has been made in the field of VR since it was first introduced in
the early 1970s. In many fields it has found countless applications such as entertainment [1], teaching [2], tourism [3,4], manufacturing [5,6], networking and
communications [7,8], microelectronic and high performances hardware industries [9,10], e-commerce [11], medicine [12,13].

Today, we have reached a certain maturity in VR technologies. In this work
we will focus on the areas concerning simple VR and AR (Augmented Reality)
experiences in the teaching of mathematics.

© Springer Nature Switzerland AG 2020
O. Gervasi et al. (Eds.): ICCSA 2020, LNCS 12255, pp. 799–809, 2020.
https://doi.org/10.1007/978-3-030-58820-5_57

During our work, we were guided by a specific goal: the possibility of giving a real and visual form to the abstract objects of mathematics.

This represents a further development in the visual representation of mathematical concepts, which in the course of history has evolved from the primitive use representations of simple counting objects, such as the tally sticks, through the elegant structures of the symbolic algebra of the seventeenth century, to the imposing constructions of mathematical analysis and modern geometry, to get to the current and amazing views of numerical analysis through computer graphics.

In this context, we set out to investigate the possibility of extending students' understanding of the concept of link between an algebraic-set structure and its geometric representation on an orthogonal Cartesian space (function).

In the first phase of the work, our attention was directed to a limited number of functions, that are used in senior high-school classes, such as the representation of trajectories in the Cartesian plane and simply surfaces in the three-dimensional space.

The very first proposed functions are as follows:

- $y = \sin x$

    The **sine function** is well known to students who are currently using it to solve analytical and geometric problems. It is also commonly used in physics to model periodic phenomena such as sound and light waves or changes in average temperature during the day or the year [14]. As showed in Fig. 1

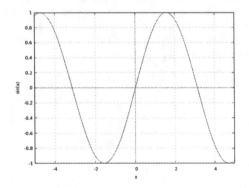

Fig. 1. Sinewave

- $z = x^2 - y^2$

    This function is a classic example of a **saddle surface** that it is a smooth surface containing one or more saddle points.

    Saddle surfaces have negative Gaussian curvature which distinguish them from convex/elliptical surfaces which have positive Gaussian curvature and are very important in the study of non-Euclidean geometry and in the theory of general relativity [15]. As showed in Fig. 2

- $z = xy$

   This function is an example of **hyperbolic paraboloid** [15]. As showed in Fig. 2

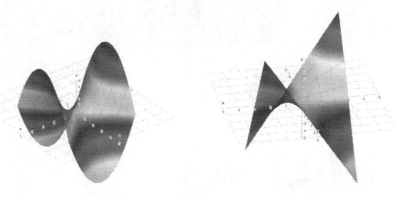

Fig. 2. Saddle Surface (*left*) and Hyperbolic Paraboloid (*right*) Real and Imaginary part respectively of the function f(z) = z^2

- $z = \ln(x^2 + y^2)$

   This function is an example of **bi-dimensional logarithm**, useful to describe astrophysical objects. As showed in Fig. 3

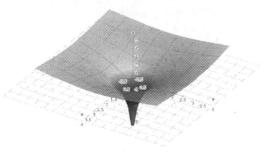

Fig. 3. Bi-dimensional Natural Logarithm

- $z = \dfrac{\sin(x^2 + y^2)}{x^2 + y^2}$

   This function is an example of **bi-dimensional dumped sine**, useful to describe objects in fluid dynamics, electronics and telecommunications. As showed in Fig. 4

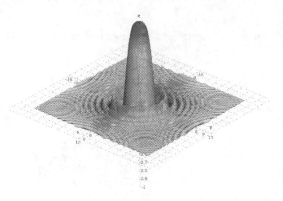

Fig. 4. Dumped Sine

2 Related Works

Stimulating multiple sensory dimensions during the learning process of a concept or idea makes the learning more effective, because our mind needs to experience the reality that surrounds it through multiple experiential levels. For example, through looking, listening and touching build a complex conceptual structure that bears and strengthens our knowledge [16,17]. This multi-sensorial learning is also important in special-need situations (autism, dyslexia).

An immersive study environment has several advantages over traditional two-dimensional environments (such as a book or the simple screen of a PC or tablet), as it gives the spatial understanding of the concepts exposed, more peripheral awareness or more useful information bandwidth and decreasing in the information dispersion phenomenon [18]. Several works have been proposed to achieve the purpose, especially in the natural sciences: chemistry [19], biology [20], physiology [21], physics [22].

The idea may therefore be to create digital environments to enhance skills, knowledge and competences in math, which in turn can decrease anxiety and improve results [23].

Mathematics can be considered one of the most difficult subjects for many students. A recent study asks questions about traditional way of learning and recommends more active and attractive learning approaches [24].

Studies have shown that immersion in a digital environment can improve education in several ways, because, as mentioned earlier, multiple perspectives are activated [25]; this fact has a significant value in all areas of mathematics [26].

In several works it has been seen that despite the mathematical simplicity of the concept of a function [27], many students find it difficult to relate its analytical form to the relative graph, as if the intermediate layers existing between the set concept and the analytic-geometric one prevented a clear understanding of the link [28,29].

It has recently been proven that the use of software capable of explicitly representing the analytic-geometric link existing in the functions can help students develop a positive mindset towards mathematics itself, in terms of attitude, motivation, interest and competence [30], but we believe that new researches need to be done to grasp the profound implications that exist.

3 The Architecture of the System

We have created two different user experiences. One uses VR, while the other uses AR. In both cases the graphic engine used is the same, Unity3D. This software allows the composition of virtual environments starting from basic elements called Assets which the scene is composed with. It also takes care of rendering, real-time lighting calculation and user interaction management. The fundamental tools that have been used are the following:

- the game objects, i.e. the basic elements that make up the scene you want the user to view.
- the scripts, code files written in C# language through which you can execute predefined tasks, such as managing the appearance of objects on the displayed area, or the camera movement as a key on the keyboard is pressed.
- the colliders, that prevent intersection or collision between the character that the user is controlling and the objects in the scene

The shapes are generated with two C# scripts that allow for the modelling of any mathematical function in two or three dimensions. The first script generates the vertices. The second script receives in input a list of vertices and then generates a three-dimensional figure. Let us suppose we want to render a three-dimensional function, for example: $f(z) = x*y$. As we all know, a standard mathematical function like this is defined in the continuum space, so if we wanted it to be visually represented we would need an infinite number of points: the aim is therefore to make the image as plausible as possible in a discreet environment, by appropriately choosing the points to be drawn. To do that, it must be chosen a well-defined length along the X, Y and Z axis, and the number of points (i.e. the number of vertices) that compose the graph must be predetermined. In other words, we need to define a grid of points that will define the level of maximum detail we want to achieve. In addition, we must bear in mind that the greater the level of detail, the more calculations the user's device will have to perform in order to display the object on the screen. Defining a grid of points is equivalent to defining a sampling rate. This is the same as when you are processing an electronic signal (e.g. an audio signal) and want to convert it from a continuous signal to its discrete representation. If the number of samples is too low, we can in fact obtain Aliasing, obtaining an inaccurate representation of the mathematical function we want to show. It is possible to run the program already with the code just described. However, this requires recalculating all forms at runtime each time. To improve performance, we have therefore saved the forms generated with Unity3D inside the filesystem so that they can directly be reloaded at program start, with no need to recalculate all objects from the beginning. We then processed the shapes with Blender, a software designed to process models and three-dimensional objects, in order to reduce polygonal complexity without changing their information content. In other words, the complexity of the figures in terms of vertices has been reduced but an user who observed them would not notice any difference. This is possible using Blender, a software made to process models and three-dimensional objects. Finally, we have included them again in the Unity3D project.

The VR environment is generated and compiled by WebGL technology. This means that the application is compatible with all devices (computers or smartphones) on the market since the environment is usable through a web browser. The graphic quality of the scene adapts according to the computational power of the device, while remaining undemanding in terms of hardware requirements. The scene can be observed through a virtual reality viewer, such as HTC Vive, or through a normal computer monitor. The user has the possibility to move around the virtual environment using mouse and keyboard. Inside the environment are visible three-dimensional geometric shapes that support the learning of mathematical functions that are otherwise difficult to draw. The AR environment uses the Vuforia framework. The program created is an apk, installable on Android smartphones with 7.0+ operating system. Vuforia is an SDK that allows you to analyze the video stream recorded in real time by the phone camera. Vuforia allows you to create a database of markers (called Vumark). These have manually been associated to the game objects of the scene. When one of the markers present in the database is framed by the camera of the user's device,

Fig. 5. VR example

Vuforia tells Unity to show on the scene (and then on the user's screen) the game object associated with the framed Vumark. Moreover, this SDK manages the spatial orientation of the object according to the user's position with respect to the Vumark. If we frame a Vumark and move around it, the object associated with it will rotate as well, allowing us to appreciate it in a realistic way.

4   The Virtual World Made on Unity3D, Blender and Vuforia

In this example, we want to represent a three-dimensional function within a virtual world created with Unity3D. The creation of the figures is done through two scripts.

First of all we define the resolution, that is the level of detail, that the figure must have.

If for instance we set a resolution equal to 100, then we will have a matrix of 100×100 points. In this way we will scroll the variable X and the variable Y along the grid. Then we define the step, i.e. how much space must elapse between one point and the next. The step variable has been fixed at 0.1f. By means of a nested double "for cycle", where the first takes care of the X variable and the second the Z variable, we can calculate the Y value in the grid.

The code we made allows us to obtain the list of points that make up the figure. The next step is to calculate the list of triangles. Triangles are a fundamental element in computer graphics. They specify how the points are interconnected to each other and how they should be represented on screen.

Each "game object" and its figure have an associated script of this type. The difference among the various scripts therefore remains in their ability to calculate the getY function. Every time it is necessary to change the graph to be represented, it is sufficient to specify how to calculate Y to obtain the change of the figure shown; in all cases, the only thing to be done would be to scan the grid (in our example a 100×100 matrix) and recalculate the correct values. A fundamental divergence from this is in the case of two-dimensional functions, like the periodic sine function which is mentioned in Chap. 2. In that case only one "for cycle" was sufficient and a depth fixed at 0.05f. In this way we can represent a two-dimensional function as if it were a tube, which allows us to observe it better when we move around it.

The next step is the generation of the three-dimensional mesh from the vertices and triangles calculated in the previous step. To do this, a generic script has been created, which can be recalled from all the codes present in the Unity3D project. Since a three-dimensional object has been generated inside the program, it is necessary to calculate how the light should behave in order to make it visible to the user's camera.

The hard work would therefore seem how to light the object in the right way: that means that it is necessary to calculate a light intensity value for each polygon which makes up the entire object structure.

This calculation, which can be complex, is carried out very quickly in Unity3D. The calculation is carried out in two phases. At the beginning, a call to a function integrated in the Unity libraries doubles up triangles in the figure, so each of them has got a "specular twin" (i.e. a mirror image), with the normal straight line to the surface with opposite direction to its homologous, so that flow of incident light can correctly be obtained.

Finally, a mesh object is created and vertices, normals and triangles are assigned to it. At the end of this operation the figure (also called mesh) is ready to be shown on screen.

We have then split the work in two different sections, involving Virtual Reality and Augmented Reality respectively. In the first case a room, has been created, and inside the room the three-dimensional figures have been positioned, as shown in Fig. 5.

The project has then been compiled in WebGL in order to be easily used by a web browser and not have any dependence on a specific operating system (Windows, Linux, Android, iOS, etc.). As far as the use with augmented reality is concerned, Vuforia software has been used instead. Vuforia is a framework that integrates within Unity3D. Vuforia allows you to create projects that use augmented reality by providing all the functions essential for operation on mobile phones.

In particular we focused on smartphones with Android operating system.

5   Conclusions and Future Works

In the first phase of our research we tried to understand which mathematical objects and which tools to use to enhance mathematical teaching, having sensed that the use of VR techniques significantly increases the level of understanding of the subject studied by the students.

We would like to expand our research towards the field of immersive learning, in particular those applications that allow the user to be immersed in virtual worlds that increase brain stimulation during the learning phase.

Our approach aims to give the student a wider environment of objects to study and focus on, by selecting among them those of greatest interest and didactic utility. Furthermore, we find it interesting to know the degree of absorption and empathic response of students to the system: sensations, disturbances, emotions. Students' feedback will be valuable in order to further enhance the experience and make the AR and VR environments more interactive and attractive.

That's why the next step we are considering is to allow high school students to evaluate the quality of the work done by filling out a questionnaire.

If the number of students is high enough, we can draw objective conclusions and understand how much virtual reality can impact their perception of mathematics. We are therefore going to select a statistically significant and representative sample, homogeneous by social and cultural level, in order to obtain a set of coherent and indicative answers.

As regards generating functions, the current system is able to display objects that are only statically compiled at compiling-time: for the future we intend to design a dynamic system for the generation of mathematical functions that allows the mathematics teacher to draw randomly any three-dimensional or two-dimensional graph without the need to print a new Vumark every time.

What we want to achieve is a dynamic platform that allows us to understand how the choice of a function and a complete immersive experience in the mathematical object itself (including its specific characteristics and properties) impacts students' learning.

References

1. Franzoni, V., Gervasi, O.: Guidelines for web usability and accessibility on the Nintendo Wii. In: Gavrilova, M.L., Tan, C.J.K. (eds.) Transactions on Computational Science VI. LNCS, vol. 5730, pp. 19–40. Springer, Heidelberg (2009). https://doi.org/10.1007/978-3-642-10649-1_2

2. Yildirim, G., Elban, M., Yildirim, S.: Analysis of use of virtual reality technologies in history education: a case study. Asian J. Educ. Train. **4**, 62–69 (2018). https://doi.org/10.20448/journal.522.2018.42.62.69

3. Williams, P., Perry Hobson, J.S.: Virtual reality and tourism: fact or fantasy? Tour. Manag. **16**(6), 423–427 (1995). ISSN 0261–5177. https://doi.org/10.1016/0261-5177(95)00050-X. http://www.sciencedirect.com/science/article/pii/026151779500050X

4. Yung, R., Khoo-Lattimore, C.: New realities: a systematic literature review on virtual reality and augmented reality in tourism research. Curr. Issues Tour. **22**(17), 2056–2081 (2019). https://doi.org/10.1080/13683500.2017.1417359

5. Doil, F., et al.: Augmented reality for manufacturing planning. In: Proceedings of the Workshop on Virtual Environments 2003. EGVE 2003, Zurich, Switzerland, pp. 71–76. Association for Computing Machinery (2003). ISBN 1581136862. https://doi.org/10.1145/769953.769962

6. Mujber, T.S., Szecsi, T., Hashmi, M.S.J.: Virtual reality applications in manufacturing process simulation. J. Mater. Process. Tech. **155–156**, 1834–1838 (2004). Proceedings of the International Conference on Advances in Materials and Processing Technologies: Part 2, pp. 1834–1838. ISSN 0924–0136. https://doi.org/10.1016/j.jmatprotec.2004.04.401. http://www.sciencedirect.com/science/article/pii/S0924013604005618

7. Lazar, A.A., et al.: Exploiting virtual reality for network management. In: Proceedings of the Singapore ICCS/ISITA 1992, vol. 3, pp. 979–983 (1992). https://doi.org/10.1109/ICCS.1992.255116

8. Taylor, R.M., et al.: VRPN: a device-independent, network-transparent VR peripheral system. In: Proceedings of the ACM Symposium on Virtual Reality Software and Technology. VRST 2001, Bani, Alberta, Canada, pp. 55–61. Association for Computing Machinery (2001). ISBN 1581134274. https://doi.org/10.1145/505008.505019

9. Gervasi, O., Russo, D., Vella, F.: The AES implantation based on OpenCL for Multi/many core architecture. In: 2010 International Conference on Computational Science and Its Applications, pp. 129–134 (2010). https://doi.org/10.1109/ICCSA.2010.44

10. Vella, F., Neri, I., Gervasi, O., Tasso, S.: A simulation framework for scheduling performance evaluation on CPU-GPU heterogeneous system. In: Murgante, B., et al. (eds.) ICCSA 2012. LNCS, vol. 7336, pp. 457–469. Springer, Heidelberg (2012). https://doi.org/10.1007/978-3-642-31128-4_34

11. Papadopoulou, P.: Applying virtual reality for trust-building ecommerce environments. Virtual Reality 11, 107–127 (2007). https://doi.org/10.1007/s10055-006-0059-x

12. Gervasi, O., Magni, R., Zampolini, M.: Nu!RehaVR: virtual reality in neuro telerehabilitation of patients with traumatic brain injury and stroke. Virtual Reality 14, 131–141 (2010). https://doi.org/10.1007/s10055-009-0149-7

13. Bin, S., Masood, S., Jung, Y.: Chapter twenty - virtual and augmented reality in medicine. In: Biomedical Information Technology (Second edn). Feng, D.D. (ed.). Biomedical Engineering. Academic Press, pp. 673–686. ISBN 978-0-12-816034-3 (2020). https://doi.org/10.1016/B978-0-12-816034-3.00020-1. http://www.sciencedirect.com/science/article/pii/B9780128160343000201

14. BoyerUta, C.B., Merzbach, C.: A History of Mathematics, 3rd edn., p. 189. Wiley, New York (2011)

15. Creighton Buck, R.: Advanced Calculus, 3rd edn., p. 160. Waveland Press, Long Grove (2003)

16. Meehan, M., et al.: Physiological measures of presence in stressful virtual environments. ACM Trans. Graph. (TOG) 21(3), 645–652 (2002)

17. Raja, D., et al.: Exploring the benefits of immersion in abstract information visualization. In: Proceedings of Immersive Projection Technology Workshop, pp. 61–69 (2004)

18. Bowman, D.A., McMahan, R.P.: Virtual reality: how much immersion is enough? Computer 40(7), 36–43 (2007)

19. Georgiou, J., Dimitropoulos, K., Manitsaris, A.: A virtual reality laboratory for distance education in chemistry. Int. J. Soc. Sci. 2(1), 34–41 (2007)

20. Tan, S., Waugh, R.: Use of virtual-reality in teaching and learning molecular biology. In: Cai, Y. (ed.) 3D Immersive and Interactive Learning, pp. 17–43. Springer, Singapore (2013). https://doi.org/10.1007/978-981-4021-90-6_2

21. Ryan, J., et al.: A virtual reality electrocardiography teaching tool. In: Proceedings of the Second International Conference, Biomedical Engineering, Innsbruck, pp. 250–253 (2004)

22. Savage, C., et al.: Teaching physics using virtual reality. In: AIP Conference Proceedings, vol. 1263, no. 1, pp. 126–129. American Institute of Physics (2010)

23. Chang, H., Beilock, S.L.: The math anxiety-math performance link and its relation to individual and environmental factors: a review of current behavioral and psychophysiological research. Curr. Opin. Behav. Sci. 10, 33–38 (2016). Neurosci. Educ. ISSN 2352–1546. https://doi.org/10.1016/j.cobeha.2016.04.011. http://www.sciencedirect.com/science/article/pii/S2352154616300882

24. Freeman, S., et al.: Active learning increases student performance in science, engineering, and mathematics. Proc. Nat. Acad. Sci. 111(23), pp. 8410–8415 (2014). ISSN 0027–8424. https://www.pnas.org/content/111/23/8410.full.pdf. https://www.pnas.org/content/111/23/8410

25. Dede, C.: Immersive interfaces for engagement and learning. Science 323(5910), pp. 66–69 (2009). ISSN 0036–8075. 1167311. https://science.sciencemag.org/content/323/5910/66.full.pdf. https://science.sciencemag.org/content/323/5910/66

26. Pasqualotti, A., dal Sasso Freitas, C.M.: MAT3D: a virtual reality modeling language environment for the teaching and learning of mathematics. Cyber Psychol. Behav. 5(5), 409–422 (2002)

27. Akkoç, H., Tall, D.: The simplicity, complexity and complication of the function concept. In: PME Conference, vol. 2., pp. 2–025 (2002)
28. Breidenbach, D., et al.: Development of the process conception of function. Educ. Stud. Math. **23**(3), 247–285 (1992). https://doi.org/10.1007/BF02309532
29. Akkoç, H., Tall, D.: The function concept: comprehension and complication. Proc. Br. Soc. Res. Learn. Math. **23**(1), 1–6 (2003)
30. King, A.: Using Desmos to draw in mathematics. Aust. Math. Teacher **73**(2), 33–37 (2017)

A Virtual Reality Simulator to Assist in Memory Management Lectures

Luiz Felipe Santos Freitas[1] , Alex Sandro Rodrigues Ancioto[1] ,
Rita de Fátima Rodrigues Guimarães[1,2] ,
Valéria Farinazzo Martins[3] , Diego Roberto Colombo Dias[4] ,
and Marcelo de Paiva Guimarães[1,5(✉)]

[1] Computer Science Master Program, Unifaccamp,
Campo Limpo Paulista, Brazil
luiz.freitas@ifms.edu.br, alexancioto@gmail.com,
rita.guimaraes@gmail.com, marcelodepaiva@gmail.com
[2] Applied Linguistics (Institute of Language Studies/Unicamp),
Campinas, Brazil
[3] Faculty of Computing and Informatics, Mackenzie Presbyterian University,
São Paulo, Brazil
valfarinazzo@hotmail.com
[4] Computer Science Department (UFSJ), São João del Rei, Brazil
diegocolombo.dias@gmail.com
[5] Núcleo de Ensino a Distância (UAB/Reitoria), UNIFESP, São Paulo, Brazil

Abstract. Virtual reality technology can assist the teaching-learning process via concrete concepts that follow a sequence of steps to accomplish a task in a three-dimensional space, as proven in the literature (e.g., operating a vehicle or disaster relief simulation). However, it is not clear whether virtual reality can also enhance situations involving concepts that are not inherently related to a three-dimensional space, such as the execution of a computer algorithm. This paper presents an immersive and interactive virtual reality simulator that can aid in the teaching of the memory management functionality of operating systems, including single, fixed and dynamic contiguous techniques, and the non-contiguous technique of paging. Learners are immersed inside a computer motherboard to learn memory management functionality of operating systems. They use a head-mounted display such as 3D virtual reality headsets and can interact with the environment using eye-gaze tracking and a joystick. We also present a case study in which 80 students were divided into two groups to evaluate the simulator. Our results indicate that using our simulator is a more effective approach for teaching memory management concepts than expositive classes. The functionality and usability tests results highlighted the positive aspects of the simulator and improvements that could be made.

Keywords: Computer science · Learning environment · Virtual reality · Memory management · Operating system

© Springer Nature Switzerland AG 2020
O. Gervasi et al. (Eds.): ICCSA 2020, LNCS 12255, pp. 810–825, 2020.
https://doi.org/10.1007/978-3-030-58820-5_58

1 Introduction

Virtual reality has the potential to immerse a learner into situations that would otherwise be difficult (e.g., driving a car [1], a flight simulator [2], arthroscopic training [3], sports training, and education [4]) or would not be feasible (e.g., visiting the interior of a volcano in eruption [5] or navigating within a macromolecular system [6]). It can modify traditional teaching-learning processes, resulting in practical, interactive and fun learning experiences. The scientific literature shows that virtual reality can enhance the learning experience via concrete situations in which learners follow a sequence of steps to accomplish a task (i.e., actions that can be experienced through the senses). Examples include designing a house [7], rehabilitation training [8], welding training [9], operating a vehicle remotely [10] and manipulation of three-dimensional (3D) geometric objects [11, 12]. These examples have in common the fact that they require maneuvers in 3D space, and are experiences involving problems and context that are identical to those in the real world [13]. However, there is also teaching-learning content that is not related to a 3D space, such as the execution of algorithms (i.e., things that do not have a physical existence).

The ability to grasp and manipulate abstract ideas is a vital element of computer science [14, 15]. For example, students need to master abstract concepts that are intrinsic to algorithm design. We study the use of virtual reality in the teaching of memory management in operating system courses; this involves abstract content, and is mandatory in many computer science, information systems and computer engineering curricula. Memory management is one of the most essential functions of an operating system, and is responsible for allocating and managing the computer's main memory [16–18]. All software instructions, data and control instructions are stored in some form of memory. The memory management function monitors the status of each memory position, i.e. whether it is allocated or free, with the aim of achieving effective and efficient use of the main memory. The quantity of memory and the allocation technique used vary according with the type of computer (e.g., supercomputer, desktop, mobile, smart card).

The main memory techniques can be contiguous, meaning that the running process is loaded entirely in memory, or non-contiguous, meaning that the process can be partially loaded [16–18]. Traditionally, a memory management lecturer will follow a textbook, prepare and exhibit slides, and present some theoretical (teacher-centered) exercises [13]. Practical exercises are assigned as homework or projects, and are executed using a real operating system or a simulator based on command-line programs or a two-dimensional (2D) front-end.

This paper presents an immersive and interactive 3D memory management simulator for both contiguous and non-contiguous memory allocation techniques for operating systems. The simulator runs on commodity devices such as desktops and head-mounted displays (HMD) (e.g., Google Cardboard, 3D VR Headsets). Learners can study allocation techniques in situations involving exploration, discovery, observation and the construction of knowledge. The allocation algorithms are visualized and explored using metaphors in the form of 3D elements (e.g., colored boxes). These elements can also represent items within the computer (e.g., processor and controller devices). The simulator can visualize single, static and dynamic contiguous techniques, and non-contiguous paging techniques [16–18].

A key goal of this virtual reality simulator is to promote a (student-centered) discovery approach that gives students the opportunity to enhance their learning and understanding of memory management content via self-study, by means of scenario simulations involving immersion, interactivity and involvement. The simulator offers practical experience of concepts related to memory management. This paper also presents a case study conducted with 80 students, who were randomly assigned into two groups to perform a learning evaluation. Forty of these students formed an experimental group, and were engaged in an introductory memory management lesson using the simulator, while the remainder of the students formed a control group and received instruction in an expositive class. Following the introductory memory management lesson, a post-test was conducted, and a statistical test was performed on the scores of both groups. We hypothesize that memory management concepts can be better assimilated by undergraduate students when the learning process is supported by virtual reality. The students who used the simulator also underwent a functionality and usability test.

The contribution of this paper is three-fold:

- We present an immersive and interactive memory management environment that can assist in memory management classes;
- A new teaching approach based on a virtual reality simulator is validated, rather than simply using the traditional approach to teaching memory management;
- We investigate the use of virtual reality to teach concepts that are not inherently associated with a 3D space.

The remainder of the paper is organized as follows: Sect. 2 discusses prior work related to this research; Sect. 3 describes the methodology used to create and evaluate the simulator; Sect. 4 presents the simulator; Sect. 5 reports on a case study involving our simulator; And Sect. 6 presents the conclusion and suggestions for future work.

2   Related Work

Several efforts have been made towards facilitating the processes of teaching and learning about operating systems. The typical educational approach to assisting these classes is to use project tools such as MINIX [19], GeekOS [20] and ICS OS [21]. This approach allows students to modify the operating system code directly, requiring them to master the programs written in C, C++ and in many cases assembly language.

An alternative approach is to adopt simulators that are based on command line programs or a 2D interface. SOsim [22] is one example that illustrates concepts such as multiprogramming, scheduling, processes, and virtual memory management. This tool uses a 2D matrix to represent processes stored in memory, introducing concepts and techniques using a dynamic and animated 2D interface. Ontko, Reeder and Tanenbaum presented a set of four simulators (scheduling, deadlocking, memory management and file system) called Modern Operating System Simulators (MOSS) [23]. These are based on a command line interface with some graphic elements, and their execution and use are not trivial.

Lopes et al. proposed the Memory Simulator for Teaching of Operating Systems (SIME) [24], which involves a 2D graphical representation of memory management. The student chooses a topic such as memory allocation (contiguous, overlay, static partition, dynamic partition, virtual paged memory) or strategy (first fit, best fit, worst fit, swapping), and the simulator illustrates this. RCOS.java [25] is a 2D java application that simulates a multi-tasking operating system running on simulated hardware. This tool demonstrates the general principles of operating systems (e.g., process and disk management) through controlled animation.

Moreno et al. [26] presented a memory management simulator called MNEME, which uses a 2D interface to assist to teach memory hierarchy and includes topics such as multithreading, hyperpaging, direct and reverse mapping, translation lookaside buffering with levels, age paging control, data loading from server and the definition of an eviction policy. However, it does not simulate memory allocation algorithms. Putchal and Bryant [27] proposed a tutoring system called Synchron-ITS to demonstrate concepts associated with process synchronization and shared memory management. This tool offers a 2D visualization of real-world data from a running Linux operating system, using high-level diagram models and source code examples, enabling students to see the connections between abstract models of synchronization. These authors plan in future work to enable visualizations of the synchronization data structures and algorithms in a 3D representation. ESORV [28] is a process-scheduling simulator based on virtual reality technology that allows students to learn algorithms while navigating inside a computer motherboard and interacting with its components. However, it does not cover the topic of memory management.

Although these simulators aim to assist in courses on operating systems, none of them offer an immersive and interactive learning environment to aid in the teaching of memory management. Moreover, only ESORV offers a 3D interface. The solution presented here is different from the abovementioned approaches in that we address the daunting problem of teaching memory management concepts using virtual reality in a fully immersive and interactive environment. As a result, students are able to take advantage of widely used technologies, thereby improving their learning and understanding. We also present and discuss the results obtained from a case study.

3   Methodology

The simulator was developed using a prototyping technique that was divided into four phases [29]. Phases I, II and III were iterative, and in each of these, a new functionality was identified and incorporated into the system. Phase IV was performed only once. Details of each phase are presented below:

- Requirements (phase I): This task aimed to elicit the requirements for the simulator. We selected 10 teachers of operating systems to fill out a questionnaire which covered the following topics: teacher profile (e.g., age, sex, education); operational systems classes (e.g., topics covered, theoretical/practical classes, educational tools adopted); virtual reality technology (e.g., knowledge, devices, experience in class); and memory management subject (e.g., topics covered, students difficulties).

The results confirmed the existence of a research gap in terms of developing a simulator. We then elicited the relevant requirements.

- Design (phase II): This involved the following basic elements [30]: mechanics, which defined the logic involved (e.g., rules, interaction with the simulator); aesthetics, which were related to the look and feel of the simulator (e.g., metaphors to represent allocation techniques, 3D models, audio, textures, colors); a story that determined the navigation within the environment (e.g., linear or nonlinear navigation, memory management content); and the technology used to create the simulator (e.g., game engine or 3D modeling tool).
- Implementation (phase III): In this step, the simulator was coded and other elements were also created (e.g., 3D models, textures and sounds.
- Evaluation (phase IV): Eighty students were randomly assigned into two groups. The 40 students in the experimental group engaged in an introductory memory management lesson using the virtual reality simulator, while the students in the control group received instruction via an expositive lecture. After this introductory lesson on memory management, a post-test was conducted, and a statistical test was performed on the scores of both groups. We discuss the data analysis and findings of our study below.

4   The Virtual Reality Memory Management Simulator

The main purpose of the simulator was to assist students in learning about the allocation of main memory and in improving their understanding of the advantages and disadvantages of each allocation technique. It was designed so that new techniques could be added easily, requiring only a new routine to allocate the memory according to the new technique. The simulator was developed based on the Unity game engine [31], which is used to create games for desktop platforms, mobile devices, browser-based applications and consoles. Unity projects are exported to diverse platforms natively (e.g. Android, Linux, and Windows). During the simulation, each student can enter into a virtual motherboard and visualize, manipulate and exploit the memory management in real time, pursuing the course objectives at their own pace.

The process of development of the simulator started by using the requirements, drawn from a survey of 10 teachers of operating systems (we were not included). Of these, four teachers (40%) had more than five years of experience of teaching operating systems, five (50%) had between one and five years, and one (10%) had less than one year. All respondents used didactic resources such as transparencies, projectors and acrylic boards. Two (20%) used a simulator, and one (10%) used an open source operating system (Linux). Eight (80%) had just theoretical lectures in their undergraduate course. Seven (70%) reported a lack of educational resources for practical lectures. This lack of innovative material for practical classes motivated us to try and bridge this gap by using an immersive and interactive virtual reality tool to foster learning. The following requirements were identified:

- Environmental requirements (related to the physical environment in which the simulator is deployed):

- Students should be seated in a safe and secure place in order to avoid possible falls, since once the HMD is deployed, the user loses sight the real physical space, and consequently loses cognitive balance;
- Students should not make sudden movements with their heads, in order to reduce sickness or dizziness.
- Functional requirements (related to the functionalities of the simulator):
  - The memory is allocated to a process during its creation;
  - An allocation technique is chosen when the simulation starts. If another technique is chosen, the simulation should be restarted. The user is free to choose any allocation technique;
  - Any process can be finalized during the simulation, and the memory allocated must be released. If the operating system process is finalized, all other processes are also finalized;
  - The first process started by the user must be the operating system. Following this, the user can start other processes.
  - A process is allocated only when enough memory is available;
  - Visual and audio messages should be provided to help users during navigation and interaction, for example, an alert insufficient memory to allocate the process;
  - User should be able to visualize the process control block (PCB) to see details of the process;
  - All elements of the simulation should be represented as 3D elements;
  - The simulation must include contiguous and non-contiguous allocation algorithms.
- Non-functional requirements (related to how the simulator should behave and the constraints on its behavior):
  - New techniques should be able to be added in future;
  - It must support fully immersive visualization, interaction and navigation;
  - It must have versions for both desktop and HMDs (multiplatform);
  - It should be easy to use;
  - It should use clear metaphors to represent the abstract concepts in a 3D environment;
  - Each allocation technique must be simulated in isolation.

The simulator was designed to improve the student's empirical skills as they are learning the allocating algorithms. For example, the teacher can formulate a hypothesis about an algorithm and ask the students to run experiments to support or disprove it. Figure 1 depicts the flow chart for operation of the simulator. After initialization, the user chooses a memory allocation technique or the exit option, and the simulation starts. Soon after this, the user starts to navigate and interact with the simulated environment. Users can perform actions such as creating or deleting processes, or visualizing a PCB. They can use a joystick or eye-gaze tracking to interact with the environment. During creation of a process, spaces memory are associated with colors, and audio and visual messages are presented to users according to the allocation technique chosen initially. Users can also interact with the motherboard elements, such as the processor and device controllers, and visual and audio messages describing their operation are presented.

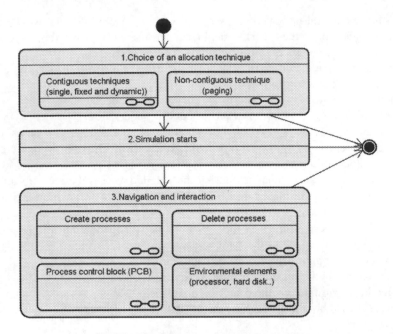

Fig. 1. Flow chart for simulator operation

Figure 2 depicts the simulated motherboard. If the student selects a motherboard element, a realistic computer-generated voice offers an explanation of it, such as "This is the CPU, which performs most of the processing inside the computer". When the help option is chosen, a video clip explains how the simulator works. Figures 2, 3, 4, 5 and 6 have a white point which is the position where the user is looking. This allows the user to interact with an object, triggering an animation for example. This is known as gaze.

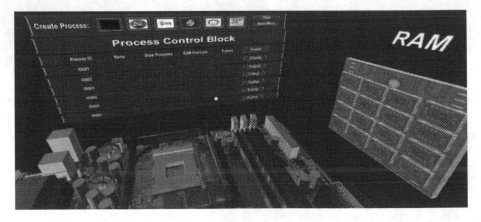

Fig. 2. Memory management simulator

Figure 3(a) depicts a learner visualizing the content of a process control block (PCB), which is a data structure that contains information (e.g., process identification and size) used to manage the process. PCBs differ between processes, and store all the necessary information to represent each one. This data structure stores information about how much memory is used by the schema and what type of memories are used (e.g., page tables, limit registers or segment tables). Figure 3(b) shows a student from Group 2 using a 3D VR Headsets with Bluetooth Remote to run the memory management simulator. The student's face was blurred.

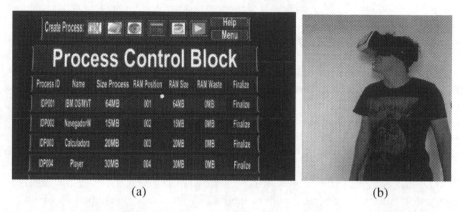

(a)   (b)

Fig. 3. (a) A student visualizes the content of a PCB; (b) A student running the 3D simulation.

Figure 4 depicts the execution of the simulator in a 3D VR Headsets, with a different point of view for the left and right eyes.

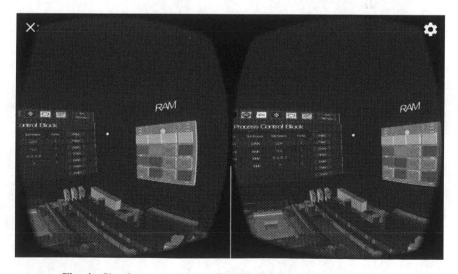

Fig. 4. Simulator running in a 3D VR Headsets (left and right eyes)

In order to illustrate the algorithms, we define metaphors for each situation. This allows us to cover subjects that students normally cannot see or touch but which they need to comprehend in order to understand how memory management works. Woollard [32] argues that these metaphors play an important role in teaching computing and analyzing diverse aspects of their use, and identifies a need for determining the effectiveness and efficiency of particular metaphoric strategies.

The solution adopted here to represent the allocation algorithms was to manipulate dynamic elements based on the student's actions. For example, colored boxes represent the memory area according to the allocation technique chosen. We extended the criteria defined by Mackinlay [33], which were defined to codify a 2D image, in order to create expressiveness, which determines whether the metaphor expresses the desired information, and effectiveness, which determines whether the metaphor explores the human visual system in an effective way. Oberhauser and Lecon [34] proposed an approach that could also be added to this simulator in the future. They created multiple metaphors for visualizing software code structures (e.g., packages and dependencies between classes) in a 3D environment. Their solution has switchable and customizable metaphors, such as visuals (space, terrestrial); groupings (solar systems, glass bubbles or tree-lined cities); connections (pipes, light rays); labels; and background sounds. This is an interesting approach, but it is not common to discuss code details when allocation techniques are being explained (programming would be a prerequisite).

All allocation algorithms implemented here were converted to visual representations using metaphors. Figure 5 depicts the paging allocation technique, in which the address space is broken into blocks of the same size, called pages, and the main memory is divided into small fixed-sized blocks of (physical) memory, called frames. When a process is created, the memory space is represented, and an audio recording explains what is happening. In this case, the user created four processes, and four frames were allocated for the IDP001 process (operating system – shown in orange); four for the IDP002 process (Winamp application - shown in blue); four for the IDP003 process (Napster application – shown in black); and four for the IDP004 process (ICQ application - shown in pink). Memory spaces shown in brown are free spaces. Details about each process can be visualized in the PCB, including the table page.

Fig. 5. Paging allocation (non-contiguous technique).

Figure 6 depicts the static partitioned memory allocation technique, in which the memory is divided into a number of separate fixed areas, each of which can hold one process. Each partition may contain unused space (internal fragmentation).

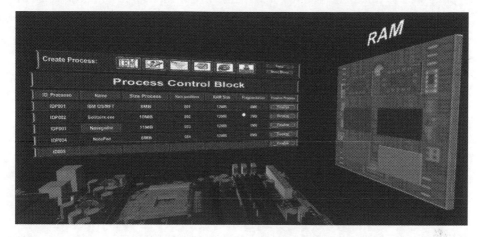

Fig. 6. Static partitioned memory allocation (contiguous technique).

This simulator enables the user to navigate through the motherboard and to observe the memory management technique chosen from various angles with a good spatial view and intuitive interactions, promoting a discovery approach. This solution makes it possible, combining abstract and concrete data in the same virtual reality environment side by side, helping users to understand the links between them.

5 Case Study

An understanding of the students' needs, both in terms of their preferences in the immersive environment and their learning styles, is a key aspect of a successful 3D simulator. In order to validate and improve our simulator, we carried out two randomized experiments: a learning evaluation and a usability evaluation. The study took place in the Federal Institute of Mato Grosso located in the city of Campo Grande, Brazil, with Computer Science degree students. The tests using the simulator were taught in classrooms with one 3D VR Headsets with Bluetooth Remote per student.

5.1 Learning Evaluation

We carried out a learning experiment to evaluate the benefits of using our 3D simulator to teach memory management. We set out to answer the following research question:

Research question: Is our 3D simulator a more effective approach in teaching memory management than an expositive lecture (traditional approach)?

This research question was used as the basis to formulate our hypotheses. Throughout this section, we refer to the approach based on the expositive class as Expositive and that based on the simulator as Simulator.

Hypothesis Formulation: The research question was formalized to allow statistical tests be carried out.

- Null hypothesis (H0): there is no significant difference in efficiency between the two teaching strategies (measured in terms of the student's scores), which can be formalized as follows: H0 = μExpositive = μSimulator.
- Alternative hypothesis, H1: there is a significant difference in efficiency between the two teaching strategies, which can be formalized as follows: H1 = μExpostive ! = μSimulator.

The experiment was broken down into four steps. These steps are listed in chronological order in Table 1.

Table 1. I Stages of learning evaluation

Step	Description	Time
Student profile	All students answered a student profile questionnaire (e.g., age, sex, knowledge of operating systems)	15 min
Division of class	The students were randomly divided into two groups of 40 students.	Free
Learning phase	Group 1: this group went to the laboratory and was taught via an expositive class Group 2: this group went to the laboratory and was taught with the 3D simulator	30 min
Scored test	All students answered twelve questions about memory management	15 min

From the results of the pre-test questionnaire, it was possible to determine the user's profile: all students (100%) had no knowledge of the concepts of operating systems – 38.75% were female; students were between 16 and 53 years old, and half of the users were between 17 and 19 years old.

The class was divided randomly into two groups of 40 (Groups 1 and 2), and we started the lecture (30 min). Group 1 undertook the expositive lecture, and Group 2 used the 3D simulator on an individual basis. Table 2 shows the scores of the students in Groups 1 and 2 in the test (on a scale from zero to 12). The average score for Group 1 was 6.875, and for Group 2 it was 10.425. As shown in Table 2, the 3D simulator lecture method seems to be a more effective approach to introducing students to memory management concepts, and most subjects retained the information imparted to them and performed well on the test.

Table 2. Summary of the scores obtained by Groups 1 and 2 (on a scale of zero to 12)

	Group 1: Expositive class	Group 2: 3D simulator
Median	7	11
Mean	6.875	10.425
Std	3.30	1.48
Max	12	12
Min	2	7

The std for the Group 1 was 3.30, while that for Group 2 was 1.48. The p-value for both was $3.4 * 10^{-8}$ (significance level 0.05). The null hypothesis was rejected since the tests were significant; that is, the change in the student's scores was not random. The results seem to indicate that using the 3D simulator to teach memory management simulator can be an effective approach. Moreover, the teacher who carried out the test reported that the experiment motivated the students, including those who did not usually pay attention during the expositive lecture. The students did not have difficulty interacting with and navigating in the 3D simulator.

5.2 Functionality and Usability Test

After Group 2 had completed the educational test, they also filled out a questionnaire with 12 questions about simulator functionalities and their usability (15 min). The Likert scale [35] was adopted (Strongly disagree, Disagree, Neither agree nor disagree, Agree, Strongly agree). Table 3 gives details of the questionnaire and the results obtained in terms of the user experience, navigation dynamics, and potential execution errors. None of the students left comments (positive, negative or suggestions) about the simulator.

Table 3. System utilization experiences - Group 2

	Strongly disagree	Disagree	Neither agree nor disagree	Agree	Strongly agree
1. The simulator has a pleasant and understandable graphical interface	0.0%	7.5%	12.5%	35.0%	45.0%
2. It is easy to understand what to do in the simulator	0.0%	5.0%	5.0%	27.5%	62.5%
3. The simulator interface is very intuitive	0.0%	5.0%	25.0%	20.0%	50.0%
4. It was easy to learn how to use the simulator	0.0%	5.0%	2.5%	27.5%	65.0%
5. The performance of the simulation was good	0.0%	0.0%	0.0%	20.0%	80.0%

(*continued*)

Table 3. (*continued*)

	Strongly disagree	Disagree	Neither agree nor disagree	Agree	Strongly agree
6. The audio messages worked correctly and were informative	0.0%	0.0%	5.0	17.5%	77.5%
7. When a process is created, it is possible to visualize its memory allocation	0.0%	0.0%	0.0%	17.5%	82.5%
8. It is easy to interact with the elements in the simulator	0.0%	15.0%	2.5%	30.0%	52.5%
9. The video clip that explains how the simulator works is easy to understand and informative	0.0%	2.5%	0.0%	20.0%	77.5%
10. I did not feel discomfort when using the simulator	2.5%	7.5%	2.5%	7.5%	80.0%
11. I felt that I was navigating inside a computer	0.0%	5.0%	0.0%	42.5%	52.5%
12. The simulator helped me to understand memory allocation techniques	0.0%	0.0%	0.0%	17.5%	82.5%
Comments on the simulator (positive or negative aspects, suggestions)					
None of the students left comments					

6 Conclusions

Until recently, the use of virtual reality simulators in an educational context has encountered barriers in terms of the high price of the equipment and a lack of available software. However, technological advances have changed this scenario, allowing teachers to adopt this technology at an affordable cost, for example using mobile devices.

We believe that virtual reality has the potential to provide a myriad of benefits to the learning process, including for subjects that are not inherently related to a 3D space, such as the execution of a memory allocation algorithm. However, to evaluate these benefits, further research is still needed.

This research presents an immersive and interactive simulator for memory allocation. It uses metaphors to represent the execution of the algorithms and the hardware elements. Suitable metaphors were important in increasing the user's perception of directedness, enclosure, engagement, navigation and presence in the motherboard environment. The simulator provided the students with an almost tangible picture of all the concepts and hardware elements involved. Audio media was also used to support this understanding.

An experiment was conducted, and the results showed that the experimental group using the simulator performed significantly better than the control group in terms of achievement in memory management learning. The immersive and interactive simulator environment was able not only to deepen students' memory of the subject, but also to compensate for the shortcomings of a traditional expositive class. We suggest that virtual reality simulators can be used to teach concepts associated with memory management. We also conducted a usability test to evaluate the simulator, and the results highlighted the positive aspects of the simulator and improvements that could be made.

In future, we plan to improve the simulator by adding new allocation techniques and creating better 3D models. We also plan to conduct experiments in multi-projection environments such as systems similar to the CAVE (Cave automatic virtual environment).

Acknowledgments. This study was financed in part by the Coordenação de Aperfeiçoamento de Pessoal de Nível Superior - Brasil (CAPES) - Finance Code 001.

References

1. Ihemedu-Steinke, Q.C., Erbach, R., Halady, P., Meixner, G., Weber, M.: Virtual reality driving simulator based on head-mounted displays. In: Meixner, G., Müller, C. (eds.) Automotive User Interfaces. HIS, pp. 401–428. Springer, Cham (2017). https://doi.org/10.1007/978-3-319-49448-7_15
2. Oberhauser, M., Dreyer, D.: A virtual reality flight simulator for human factors engineer-ing. Cogn. Tech. Work **19**(2–3), 263–277 (2017). https://doi.org/10.1007/s10111-017-0421-7
3. Karahan, M., Kerkhoffs, G.M.M.J., Randelli, P., Tuijthof, G.J.M. (eds.): Effective Training of Arthroscopic Skills. Springer, Heidelberg (2015). https://doi.org/10.1007/978-3-662-44943-1
4. Staurset, E.M., Prasolova-Førland, E.: Creating a smart virtual reality simulator for sports training and education. In: Uskov, V.L., Howlett, R.J., Jain, L.C. (eds.) Smart Education and e-Learning 2016. SIST, vol. 59, pp. 423–433. Springer, Cham (2016). https://doi.org/10.1007/978-3-319-39690-3_38
5. Boudreaux, H., et al.: V-volcano: addressing students' misconceptions in earth sciences learning through virtual reality simulations. In: Bebis, G., et al. (eds.) ISVC 2009. LNCS, vol. 5875, pp. 1009–1018. Springer, Heidelberg (2009). https://doi.org/10.1007/978-3-642-10331-5_94
6. Salvadori, A., Frate, G.D., Pagliai, M., Mancini, G., Barone, V.: Immersive virtual reality in computational chemistry: applications to the analysis of QM and MM data. Int. J. Quantum Chem. **116**(22), 1731–1746 (2016)
7. Wang, X., Schnabel, M.A. (eds.): Mixed Reality in Architecture, Design, and Construction. Springer, Dordrecht (2009). https://doi.org/10.1007/978-1-4020-9088-2
8. Zheng, J., Shi, P., Yu, H.: A virtual reality rehabilitation training system based on upper limb exoskeleton robot. In: 2018 10th International Conference on Intelligent Human-Machine Systems and Cybernetics (IHMSC), vol. 1, pp. 220–223 (2018)
9. Xie, B., Zhou, Q., Yu, L.: A real-time welding training system base on virtual reality. In: 2015 IEEE Virtual Reality (VR), pp. 309–310 (2015)

10. Chin, C.S., Kamsani, N.B., Zhong, X.H., Cui, R., Yang, C.: Unity3D serious game engine for high fidelity virtual reality training of remotely-operated vehicle pilot. In: 2018 10th International Conference on Modelling, Identification and Control (ICMIC) (2018)

11. Hwang, W.-Y., Hu, S.-S.: Analysis of peer learning behaviors using multiple representations in virtual reality and their impacts on geometry problem solving. Comput. Educ. **62**, 308–319 (2013)

12. Kaufmann, H., Schmalstieg, D., Wagner, M.: Construct3D: a virtual reality application for mathematics and geometry education. Educ. Inf. Technol. **5**(4), 263–276 (2000). https://doi.org/10.1023/A:1012049406877

13. Liu, D., Dede, C., Huang, R., Richards, J. (eds.): Virtual, Augmented, and Mixed Realities in Education. SCI. Springer, Singapore (2017). https://doi.org/10.1007/978-981-10-5490-7

14. Dijkstra, E.W.: The humble programmer. Commun. ACM **15**(10), 859–866 (1972)

15. Statter, D., Armoni, M.: Teaching abstract thinking in introduction to computer science for 7th graders. In: Proceedings of the 11th Workshop in Primary and Secondary Computing Education, New York, NY, USA, pp. 80–83 (2016)

16. Tanenbaum, A.S., Bos, H.: Modern Operating Systems, 4th edn. Pearson, Boston (2014)

17. Stallings, W.: Operating Systems: Internals and Design Principles, 9th edn. Pearson, New York (2017)

18. Silberschatz, A., Gagne, G., Galvin, P.B.: Operating System Concepts, Enhanced eText, 10th edn (2018)

19. Du, W., Shang, M., Xu, H.: A novel approach for computer security education using Minix instructional operating system. Comput. Secur. **25**(3), 190–200 (2006)

20. Hovemeyer, D., Hollingsworth, J.K., Bhattacharjee, B.: Running on the bare metal with GeekOS. In: Proceedings of the 35th SIGCSE Technical Symposium on Computer Science Education, New York, NY, USA, pp. 315–319 (2004)

21. Hermocilla, J.A.C.: ICS-OS: a kernel programming approach to teaching operating system concepts. Philippine Inf. Technol. J. **2**(2), 25–30 (2009)

22. Maia, L.P., Machado, F.B., Pacheco Jr, A.C.: A constructivist framework for operating systems education: a pedagogic proposal using the SOsim. In: Proceedings of the 10th Annual SIGCSE Conference on Innovation and Technology in Computer Science Education, New York, NY, USA, pp. 218–222 (2005)

23. Ontko, R., Reeder, A., Tanenbaum, A.S.: Modern Operating Systems Simulators (MOSS). http://www.ontko.com/moss/. Accessed Jan 2020

24. Lopes, Á.R., Souza, D.A., Carvalho, J.R.B., Silva, W.O., Sousa, V.L.P.: SIME: memory simulator for the teaching of operating systems. In: 2012 International Symposium on Computers in Education (SIIE), pp. 1–5 (2012)

25. Jones, D.: RCOS. Java: an animated operating system for computer science education. In: Proceedings of the 1st Conference on Integrating Technology into Computer Science Education, New York, NY, USA, p. 233 (1996)

26. Moreno, L., González, E.J., Popescu, B., Toledo, J., Torres, J., Gonzalez, C.: MNEME: a memory hierarchy simulator for an engineering computer architecture course. Comput. Appl. Eng. Educ. **19**(2), 358–364 (2011)

27. Putchala, M.K., Bryant, A.R.: Synchron-ITS: an interactive tutoring system to teach process synchronization and shared memory concepts in an operating systems course. In: 2016 International Conference on Collaboration Technologies and Systems (CTS), pp. 180–187 (2016)

28. Guimarães, M.P., Scamati, V., Neto, M.P., Martins, V.F., Dias, D.R.C., Brega, J.R.F.: A process-scheduling simulator based on virtual reality technology. In: 2016 IEEE/ACS 13th International Conference of Computer Systems and Applications (AICCSA), pp. 1–6 (2016)

29. Smith, M.F.: Software Prototyping: Adoption, Practice, and Management. McGraw-Hill Book Co Ltd, London; New York (1991)
30. Kalmpourtzis, G.: Educational Game Design Fundamentals: A Journey to Creating Intrinsically Motivating Learning Experiences, 1 edn. CRC Press (2018)
31. Unity, Unity. https://unity3d.com
32. Woollard, W.J.: The rôle of metaphor in the teaching of computing; towards a taxonomy of pedagogic content knowledge, Ph.D. University of Southampton (2004)
33. Mackinlay, J.: Automating the design of graphical presentations of relational information. ACM Trans. Graph. **5**(2), 110–141 (1986)
34. Oberhauser, R., Lecon, C.: Virtual reality flythrough of program code structures. In: Proceedings of the Virtual Reality International Conference - Laval Virtual 2017, New York, NY, USA, pp. 10:1–10:4 (2017)
35. Likert, R.: A technique for the measurement of attitudes. Arch. Psychol. **22**(140), 55 (1932)

Motivational Evaluation of a Virtual Reality Simulator to Teach Disk-Scheduling Algorithms for Solid-State Drives (SSDs)

Alex Sandro Rodrigues Ancioto[1] (ID), Luiz Felipe Santos Freitas[1] (ID),
Diego Roberto Colombo Dias[2] (ID), Valéria Farinazzo Martins[3] (ID),
Alexandre Fonseca Brandão[4] (ID),
and Marcelo de Paiva Guimarães[1,5(✉)] (ID)

[1] Computer Science Master Program, UNIFACCAMP,
Campo Limpo Paulista, Brazil
alexancioto@gmail.com, luiz.freitas@ifms.edu.br,
marcelodepaiva@gmail.com
[2] Computer Science Department (UFSJ), São João del Rei, Brazil
diegocolombo.dias@gmail.com
[3] Faculty of Computing and Informatics, Mackenzie Presbyterian University,
São Paulo, Brazil
valfarinazzo@hotmail.com
[4] Institito de Física Gleb Wataghin (UNICAMP), Campinas, Brazil
abrandao@ifi.unicamp.br
[5] Núcleo de Ensino a Distância (UAB/Reitoria), UNIFESP, São Paulo, Brazil

Abstract. The literature already shows diverse gains in the adoption of virtual reality environments, such as the possibility of safely repeating experiments without increasing the costs. However, it is unclear the advantages of the adoption of two-dimensional (2D) simulators in comparison to three-dimensional (3D) simulators based on virtual reality. We present a motivational analysis of a virtual reality simulator for teaching disk-scheduling algorithms for solid-state drives (SSDs). For this, we developed a fully immersive and interactive simulator. A case study was carried out with 38 students in which it compared the simulator being executed in a 2D environment (desktop) with a 3D environment (Google Cardboard). The results indicate a motivational increase in the 3D environment in some aspects.

Keywords: SSD · Scheduling algorithms · Virtual reality · Simulation

1 Introduction

Computer science major demands innovative training strategies able to adapt to all technological changes that are happening. For example, in order to improve factors such as resistance against mechanical shocks, energy consumption, and performance, in recent years it has become common to adopt solid-state drives (SSDs) instead of the traditional hard disk drives (HDDs) as computer non-volatile storage devices [1, 2].

© Springer Nature Switzerland AG 2020
O. Gervasi et al. (Eds.): ICCSA 2020, LNCS 12255, pp. 826–836, 2020.
https://doi.org/10.1007/978-3-030-58820-5_59

The Operating Systems class, which is essential for any computer science major, should treat the specific disk-scheduling algorithms for SSDs to take full advantage of them. Learning these algorithms SSDs is a challenging task for students, who must learn how the hardware works as well as reorder the input/output (I/O) requests. Operating System classes are traditionally taught using conventional material such as slideshows and blackboards and, rarely, bi-dimensional (2D) or command line simulators [3–6]. This way, the virtual reality simulators are a possibility as new instructional resources.

Virtual reality allows users to be immersed in virtual worlds in real time and interact with the three-dimensional (3D) objects [7]. This technology has proven to be effective in many teaching situations, especially in which users manipulate real objects, such as driving a car [8–11] or riding a motorcycle [12, 13]. However, there are still barriers to be overcome, especially when referring to abstract subjects, which are not directly related to a 3D space, as is the case of the disk-scheduling algorithms for SSDs. Virtual reality simulators can be a feasible option to assist in teaching these algorithms since it allows, for example, the conversion of abstract content into concrete elements, the execution of a task rather than just an observation, the simulation of unreal situations, and free simulation replay without cost increase [14–16]. Moreover, the use of a virtual reality simulator can generate motivational stimuli [17–19], which are important for sustaining learners' curiosities and interests and for creating an effective motivational environment.

This paper aims to present a motivational analysis of a simulator for teaching disk-scheduling algorithms for SSDs. For this, we developed a fully immersive and interactive simulator. It supports disk-scheduling algorithms for SSDs such as NOOP [20] and Parallel Issue Queuing (PIQ) [20], and it also shows the hardware architecture details of an SSD. A case study was carried out with 38 students in which it compared the same simulator being executed in a 2D environment (desktop) with a 3D environment (Google Cardboard). The results indicate a motivational increase in the 3D environment in some aspects.

The remainder of the paper is organized as follows: Sect. 2 explains the disk-scheduling simulator's architecture and provides details of its implementation. Section 3 presents the motivational aspects evaluation. Section 4 shows the experiment setup. Section 5 presents the results, and Sect. 6 shows conclusions and plans for future works.

2 Disk-Scheduling Simulator

SSDs are built using flash microcontrollers to enhance their reliability as well as their speed without mechanical elements [21–24]. They have specific disk-scheduling algorithms which are different from those traditionally used to manage the I/O requests for HDDs. SSDs tend to be adopted by the computers as an efficient storage device solution, and this requires specific computer science skills and expertise to design improvements.

The main purpose of the virtual reality SSD simulator developed is to assist students in learning about the main disk-scheduling algorithms and the hardware details, understanding their advantages and disadvantages. This simulator takes the students to a place where they cannot physically go. It was designed to add new disk-scheduling algorithms easily, requiring only a new routine associated with the 3D models to be added. The simulator was developed using the Unity[1] game engine, which is used to develop games for desktop platforms, mobile devices, browser-based applications, and consoles. During the simulation, each student enters in a laboratory room and visualizes, manipulates, and exploits the algorithms and the associated hardware, pursuing the lecture objectives at their own pace. There is a bench for each algorithm.

For now, the following disk-scheduling algorithms are available [20]:

- NOOP: this algorithm schedules the I/O requests in the order of first in, first out (FIFO).
- PIQ: it orders the I/O requests without conflicts into the same batch and I/O requests with conflicts into different batches. This design allows the multiple I/O requests in one batch to be fulfilled simultaneously by exploiting the SSD parallelism.

The algorithm execution can be visualized in a 3D model. We create metaphors to represent all elements involved in the simulation. For example, the I/O requests are represented as animated cubes. The simulator presents the following features:

- Immersion: it supports hardware, such as head mounted displays (HMDs) (i.e., Google Cardboard, Samsung Gear VR), that allows the users to be isolated from the rest of the world.
- Interaction: it refers to the capacity of the students to move within the virtual world and to interact with the objects, for example, pressing a button. The simulator supports interactions via remote control, joystick, keyboard, and mouse. Interaction contributes to users' feeling of immersion.
- Navigation: it refers to the possibility of the user getting from one location in the environment to another. In the simulator the student can move from one bench to another. Each bench depicts the simulation of an algorithm. Animations are presented when the avatar gets closer. It also displays messages and/or allows students to listen to descriptions of the current activity.

Figure 1 depicts the bench which simulates the NOOP algorithm. The student can visualize the pending queue (reading (R) and writing (W) requisitions) and hardware elements such as host interface, flash translation layer (FTL), and the flash controller. The animation occurs according with the pending queue and the algorithm simulated.

---

[1] https://unity3d.com/.

Fig. 1. Bench for simulation of the NOOP disk-scheduling algorithm.

Figure 2 depicts the algorithm PIQ running in a Google Cardboard (left and right eyes). During our tests, we interacted using a joystick with Bluetooth connection. The simulation represents the separation of the I/O requests into batches where there is no conflict in each batch. After the separation, the request batches are proposed to group requests without conflicts into batches. The conflict detection is based on the location vectors of I/O requests, considering the waiting and outstanding requests in the I/O queue.

Fig. 2. Bench for the PIQ scheduling algorithm (left and right eyes).

3   Motivational Evaluation

The evaluation aimed to compare students' motivation when using the 3D version of the simulator (Google Cardboard) and the 2D (desktop). We created a questionnaire (Table 1) based on the based on the ARCS motivation model [25], which considers the following factors [26]:

- Attention: it refers to the learners' interest in the activity performed. It is essential to get and keep the learners' interest and attention.
- Relevance: it refers to increasing students' interest by connecting their prior experience to the content provided.
- Confidence: when the students believe that they can meet the objectives and that the cost (time or effort) is adequate, their motivation increases.
- Satisfaction: it refers to how much the students are proud and satisfied of what they have achieved during the learning process.

The questionnaire (Table 1) was also created based on level two of the model proposed by Kirkpatrick [27]. This model aims to analyze and evaluate the results of training and educational programs according to four levels. His model also allows identification of the criteria that influence each level. As you move from one level to another, the process becomes more complex and time-consuming, but it delivers more valuable results. In our research, we focus on the first level. The levels are [27]:

- Reaction: it aims to evaluate how the students liked the training, if they found it favorable, engaging, useful, and easy to apply.
- Learning: it aims to determine which expertise, knowledge, or mindsets the students have developed and that these are directly attributable to the training.
- Behavior: it refers in how they apply what they have learned during the activity after completing the training.
- Results: it aims to verify if the targeted outcomes occur as a result of the training.

Table 1 shows the questionnaire created based on the ARCS and Kirkpatrick models to perform the motivational evaluation of our disk-scheduling simulator. These questions were analyzed according with each category. The categories were rated using the Likert scale [28].

Table 1. Motivational questionnaire

Questions	Categories
ARC model [25, 26]	
1. The simulator interface design is attractive	Attention
2. The simulator graphical interface is pleasant	Attention
3. The simulator teaches surprising or unexpected content	Satisfaction
4. The simulator content is relevant to my goals	Relevance
5. The simulator stimulated my interest in knowing more about the subject presented	Relevance

(*continued*)

Table 1. (*continued*)

Questions	Categories
6. The simulator presents abstract content in a practical way	Confidence
7. I felt that I was making progress while using the simulator	Satisfaction
8. The simulator kept me motivated to continue using it	Attention
9. I would like to use this simulator again	Confidence
Training model [27]	
10. I can remember the content presented by the simulator	Learning
11. I can understand the content presented by the simulator	Learning
12. I can apply the content presented by the simulator	Learning

4   Experimental Setup

This section describes the randomized experiment we carried out to evaluate the motivation of using a simulator to assist the learning of disk-scheduling algorithms for SSDs. The study took place in the second semester of 2018 at the Federal Institute of São Paulo, located in the city of Pirituba, Brazil, in Computer Science courses. Formally, we set out to answer the following research question:

Research question: Is a 3D simulator a better motivator to teach disk-scheduling algorithms than a 2D simulator?

The aforementioned research question outlines the issue that this study is intended to investigate. Throughout the rest of the paper, we refer to the approach based on desktop (2D interface) as DESKTOP and the immersive (3D interface) approach as HMD.

To evaluate our conjecture, 38 subjects were assigned to the two different treatments at random: 19 subjects were assigned to DESKTOP, and 19 subjects were assigned to HMD. The main dependent variable is the scores of the subjects in the questionnaire. More specifically, this dependent variable is defined in terms of rating each question.

The experiment was broken down into four steps. These steps are listed in chronological order in Table 2.

Table 2. Motivational evaluation stages

Step	Description	Time
Division of class	The students were divided into two groups of nineteen (19) students randomly	Free
Simulator	Group 1: this group went to the laboratory and was taught with the DESKTOP simulator. The tests were taught in classrooms with one desktop per student Group 2: this group went to the laboratory and was taught with the HMD simulator. The tests were taught in classrooms with one Google Cardboard per student	10 min
Test	All students answered the questionnaire	15 min

5 Results and Discussion

The Likert scale [28] has been adopted (1-Strongly disagree, 2-Disagree, 3-Neither agree nor disagree, 4-Agree, 5-Strongly agree). Table 3 depicts the results obtained. In general, the results were better for the HMD and the standard deviation was lower, indicating that its use can improve the learning process.

Table 3. Motivational evaluation results

	DESKTOP	HMD
Median	3.71	3.76
Mean	3.62	3.82
Std	0.29	0.25
Max	3.95	4.37
Min	3.21	3.42

Figure 3 depicts the results obtained (DESKTOP X HMD). The HMD simulator received the highest grade from most of the students.

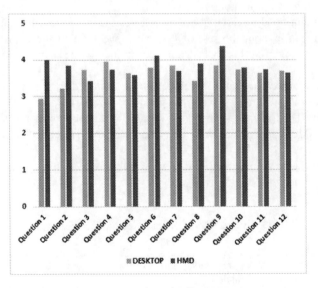

Fig. 3. Motivational evaluation (DESKTOP X HMD)

HMD received the best grades in 7 questions, while DESKTOP was better in 5 questions. According to the categories presented in the questionnaire (Table 1), the results obtained were:

- Attention (questions 1, 2, and 8): the HMD version was better evaluated in all questions. However, it can be observed that the simulator interface, mainly the desktop version, requires improvements. For example, the hardware elements modeled must be improved.
- Satisfaction (questions 3 and 7): Although the grades were similar, the DESKTOP version was better evaluated in both questions. We believe that these results are related to the quality of the 3D model, which should be improved.
- Relevance (questions 4 and 5): the grades were again better for the DESKTOP. These questions are related to student interest in the subject; it was expected that the HMD solution would receive the better grade because virtual reality immerses the student in what he/she is learning. However, this category requires computational experience of the students because it treats their involvement with the content. Thus, we believe that the simulator presented is a tool that can increase this interest, showing the content in practice.
- Confidence (questions 6 and 9): In both questions HMD received higher grades. This result could be because the HMD solution is a novelty to most of the students, and the algorithm animations run in real time and can be seen from different points of view.
- Learning (questions 10, 11, and 12): HMD received higher grades in questions 10 and 11, and DESKTOP was better in question 12. Virtual reality simulators seem to be the natural next step for the evolution of education because of their pillars (immersion, interaction, and imagination). Although the results indicate higher grades to the HMD environment, we understand that further investigation is necessary.

Table 4 depicts the simulator approach that had the better performance according to the questionnaire categories.

Table 4. Categories results

Categories	Best performance
Attention	HMD
Satisfaction	DESKTOP
Relevance	DESKTOP
Confidence	HMD
Learning	Similar

6 Conclusions

Creating a motivational environment for learners is one of the goals of an educational institution, which aim to create a modern and successful teaching/learning process. In recent years, there is growing interest in using simulators based on virtual reality technology to facilitate the teaching/learning process in diverse areas. However, it is not clear their efficiency considering some aspects, for example, learning, motivation, and confidence when compared with traditional simulators such as 2D and command line based. This paper aimed to investigate the motivation aspect, comparing the same simulator in two versions (2D and 3D interface) for teaching disk-scheduling algorithms for SSDs.

SSDs are being increasingly adopted as a storage solution. These devices work differently when compared with magnetic disks. Therefore, the Operating System class needs updated content considering this new scenario. The simulator developed can help students understand how SSDs work, including the algorithms and the hardware involved. For now, NOOP and PIQ algorithms are available, but it has the flexibility to incorporate additional algorithms and other features, such as details about the I/O controllers.

Motivational evaluation is very important for choosing material to assist the class because it can make the learning process more engaging. The results presented indicate that motivation increases in the 3D environment in some aspects; it also shows that further investigation is necessary. It was also noticed that the 3D version kept the student focused in his/her class. During the test, the HMD group showed higher levels of participation.

In the future, we plan to improve the simulator by adding new algorithms and investigating collaborative enterprise learning needs and data analytics. We also plan to improve the 3D models and conduct experiments to determine the simulator's effect on student learning.

Acknowledgments. This study was financed in part by the Coordenação de Aperfeiçoamento de Pessoal de Nível Superior - Brasil (CAPES) - Finance Code 001.

References

1. Lai, W., Fan, Y., Meng, X.: Scan and join optimization by exploiting internal parallelism of flash-based solid state drives. In: Wang, J., Xiong, H., Ishikawa, Y., Xu, J., Zhou, J. (eds.) WAIM 2013. LNCS, vol. 7923, pp. 381–392. Springer, Heidelberg (2013). https://doi.org/10.1007/978-3-642-38562-9_39
2. Liang, J., Xu, Y., Sun, D., Wu, S.: Improving read performance of SSDs via balanced redirected read. In: 2016 IEEE International Conference on Networking, Architecture and Storage (NAS), Long Beach, CA, pp. 1–10
3. Lopes, Á.R., de Souza, D.A., de Carvalho, J.R.B., Silva, W.O., de Sousa, V.L.P.: SIME: Memory simulator for the teaching of operating systems. In: International Symposium on Computers in Education (SIIE), Andorra la Vella, pp. 1–5 (2012)
4. Putchala, M.K., Bryant, A.R.: Synchron-ITS: an interactive tutoring system to teach process synchronization and shared memory concepts in an operating systems course. In: International Conference on Collaboration Technologies and Systems (CTS), Orlando, FL, pp. 180–187 (2016)
5. Moreno, L., González, E.J., Popescu, B., Toledo, J., Torres, J., Gonzalez, C.: MNEME: a memory hierarchy simulator for an engineering computer architecture course. Comput. Appl. Eng. Educ. **19**, 358–364 (2011)
6. Jones, D.: RCOS.java: an animated operating system for computer science education. In: Proceedings of the 1st Conference on Integrating Technology into Computer Science Education (ITiCSE 1996). ACM, New York, pp. 233 (1996)

7. Liu, D., Dede, C., Huang, R., Richards, J. (eds.): Virtual, Augmented, and Mixed Realities in Education. SCI. Springer, Singapore (2017). https://doi.org/10.1007/978-981-10-5490-7

8. Ali, A., Elnaggarz, A., Reichardtz, D., Abdennadher, S.: Gamified virtual reality driving simulator for asserting driving behaviors. In: 1st International Conference on Game, Game Art, and Gamification (ICGGAG), Jakarta, pp. 1–6 (2016)

9. Lindemann, P.,Rigoll, G.: A diminished reality simulation for driver-car interaction with transparent cockpits. In; IEEE Virtual Reality (VR), Los Angeles, CA, pp. 305–306 (2017)

10. Kodama, R., Koge, M., Taguchi, S., Kajimoto, H.: COMS-VR: mobile virtual reality entertainment system using electric car and head-mounted display. In; IEEE Symposium on 3D User Interfaces (3DUI), Los Angeles, CA, pp. 130–133 (2017)

11. Sun, D., Liu, X.: Driving self-learning system based on the virtual reality. In: 3rd IEEE International Conference on Computer and Communications (ICCC), Chengdu, pp. 2544–2548 (2017)

12. Hsu, C.C., Chen, Y.L., Chou, W.C., Huang S.H., Chang, K.K.: Motorcycle riding safety education with virtual reality. In: 2018 IEEE International Conference on Artificial Intelligence and Virtual Reality (AIVR), Taichung, Taiwan, pp. 216–218 (2018)

13. Tetsuro, O.: Design and evaluation of HUD for motorcycle using immersive simulator. In: SIGGRAPH Asia 2015 Head-Up Displays and their Applications (SA 2015), 2 p. ACM, New York, Article 5, (2015)

14. Callaghan, M., Eguíluz, A. G., McLaughlin, G., McShane, N.: Opportunities and challenges in virtual reality for remote and virtual laboratories. In: Proceedings of 2015 12th International Conference on Remote Engineering and Virtual Instrumentation (REV), Bangkok, pp. 235–237 (2015)

15. Tham, J., Duin, A.H., Gee, L., Ernst, N., Abdelqader, B., McGrath, M.: Understanding virtual reality: presence, embodiment, and professional practice. IEEE Trans. Prof. Commun. **61**(2), 178–195 (2018)

16. Ray, A.B., Deb, S.: Smartphone based virtual reality systems in classroom teaching — a study on the effects of learning outcome. In: 2016 IEEE Eighth International Conference on Technology for Education (T4E), Mumbai, pp. 68–71 (2016)

17. Dicheva, D., Irwin, K., Dichev, C.: Motivational factors in educational gamification. In: IEEE 18th International Conference on Advanced Learning Technologies (ICALT), Mumbai, pp. 408–410 (2018)

18. Hamzah, W.A.F.W., Ali, N.H., Saman, M.Y.M., Yusoff, M.H., Yacob, A.: Enhancement of the ARCS model for gamification of learning. In: 3rd International Conference on User Science and Engineering (i-USEr), Shah Alam, pp. 287–291 (2014)

19. Di Serio, Á., Ibáñez, M.B., Kloos, C.D.: Impact of an augmented reality system on students' motivation for a visual art course. Comput. Educ. **68**, 586–596 (2013)

20. Gao, C., Shi, L. Zhao, M. Xue, C.J., Wu, K., Sha, E.H.: Exploiting parallelism in I/O scheduling for access conflict minimization in flash-based solid state drives. In: 30th Symposium on Mass Storage Systems and Technologies (MSST), Santa Clara, CA, pp. 1–11 (2014)

21. Mao, B., Wu, S.: Exploiting request characteristics and internal parallelism to improve SSD performance. In: 33rd IEEE International Conference on Computer Design (ICCD), New York, NY, pp. 447–450 (2015)

22. Mao, B., Wu, S., Duan, L.: Improving the SSD performance by exploiting request characteristics and internal parallelism. IEEE Trans. Comput. Aided Design Integr. Circ. Syst. **37**(2), 472–484 (2018)

23. Dirik, C., Jacob, B.: The performance of PC solid-state disks (SSDs) as a function of bandwidth, concurrency, device architecture, and system organization. SIGARCH Comput. Archit. News **37**(3), 279–289 (2009)

24. Chen, F., Koufaty, D.A., Zhang, X.: Understanding intrinsic characteristics and system implications of flash memory based solid state drives. In: Proceedings of the Eleventh International Joint Conference on Measurement and Modeling of Computer Systems (SIGMETRICS 2009). ACM, New York, pp. 181–192 (2009)
25. Keller, J.M.: Development and use of the ARCS model of instructional design. J. Instruct. Dev. **10**, 2 (1987)
26. Keller, J.M.: Motivational Design for Learning and Performance: The ARCS model approach. Springer, New York (2010). https://doi.org/10.1007/978-1-4419-1250-3
27. Kirkpatrick, J.D., Kirkpatrick, W.K.: Kirkpatrick's Four Levels of Training Evaluation, Association for Talent Development, 1 edn, 200 p. (2016)
28. Likert, R.: A Technique for the Measurement of Attitudes. Archives of Psychology, pp. 1–55 (1932)

New Package in *Maxima* to Build Axonometric Projections from $\mathbb{R}^4$ to $\mathbb{R}^3$ and Visualize Objects Immersed in $\mathbb{R}^4$

Emanuel E. Sobrino[1]([⊠]) [iD], Robert Ipanaqué[1]([⊠]) [iD], Ricardo Velezmoro[1]([⊠]) [iD], and Josel A. Mechato[2]([⊠]) [iD]

[1] Universidad Nacional de Piura, Urb. Miraflores s/n, Castilla, Piura, Peru
enrique1995_26xd@hotmail.com, {ripanaquec,rvelezmorol}@unp.edu.pe
[2] Universidad Privada Antenor Orrego,
Av. Los Tallanes Zona Los Ejidos s/n Piura, Trujillo, Peru
jmechatod1@upao.edu.pe

Abstract. The human being has the need to represent the objects that surround him. But the world around us constitutes a three-dimensional reality and the formats in which it is represented are two-dimensional. Then the problem arises of representing on paper, which has two dimensions, any object immersed in a space that has three dimensions. In response to the problem, the Descriptive Geometry and the Representation Systems are born. The representation systems are a set of operations that allow make projections of objects immersed in three-dimensional space on a plane that is usually the role of drawing. A class of these systems are those obtained from axonometric projections of $\mathbb{R}^3$ to $\mathbb{R}^2$ based on Pohlke's theorem and widely used in the vast majority of scientific texts. In this paper it is proposed to build axonometric projections from $\mathbb{R}^4$ to $\mathbb{R}^3$ to obtain projections of objects immersed in the four-dimensional space on a 3D hyperplane. To visualize the results, a new package encoded in the *Maxima* open source software will be used.

Keywords: Pohlke theorem · Representation systems · Axonometric projections · Plot objetcs in $\mathbb{R}^4$

1 Introduction

The concept of multidimensionality becomes interesting, in the modern world, in the Victorian era [15]. It is at this time, exactly in 1884, that the English ecclesiastic Edwin Abbott [9] publishes the novel Flatland [1] in which themes of profound mathematical significance, related to the n-dimensional Euclidean-spaces (n from one to four) that are still difficult to assimilate in the current era, are described in a simple and enjoyable way. With the appearance of the first programmable electromechanical computers between the years 1930 and 1940 [3] and its subsequent development it becomes possible to venture into the visualization of objects of the tetradimensional Euclidean space and the first

© Springer Nature Switzerland AG 2020
O. Gervasi et al. (Eds.): ICCSA 2020, LNCS 12255, pp. 837–851, 2020.
https://doi.org/10.1007/978-3-030-58820-5_60

investigations are developed [4,8]. From these investigations many more have been carried out [12,16,18–21,23].

The foregoing paragraph indicates that the human being has the need to represent the objects that surround him or those he imagines or projects, to make them known to others. But the world around us constitutes a three-dimensional reality and the formats in which it is represented are two-dimensional. Then the problem arises of representing on paper, whose dimension is two, any object that is immersed in a three-dimensional space. In response to the problem, Descriptive Geometry and Representation Systems are born [10]. A class of these systems are those obtained from axonometric projections of $\mathbb{R}^3$ to $\mathbb{R}^2$ based on the geometric statement of the painter and professor of descriptive geometry, of German nationality, Karl Wilhelm Pohlke. Such a statement is fundamental to axonometric projections and is known as Pohlke's theorem. Pohlke formulated this theorem in 1853 and published it in 1860, without demonstration, in the first part of his textbook on descriptive geometry. The first elementary rigorous proof was given by H. A. Schwarz in 1864, at that time a student of Pohlke [7]. The most common of the axonometric projections is the one that considers three coincident segments at one point (all belonging to the same plane) such that two segments form an angle of ninety sexagesimal degrees and the third forms an angle of one hundred thirtyfive sexagesimal degrees with each of the first two segments [6].

In this paper it is proposed to build axonometric projections from $\mathbb{R}^4$ to $\mathbb{R}^3$ to obtain projections of objects immersed in the four-dimensional space on a 3D hyperplane. The limitation for this proposal to be understood as a natural extension of what is established in Pohlke's theorem is that there are no three-dimensional "screens", since all current computer screens are flat. However, the advantages offered by the *Maxima* v.5.43.0 will be used to simulate the visualization of objects immersed in $\mathbb{R}^3$ [17].

The structure of this paper is as follows: Sect. 2 introduce the Pohlke's theorem, some concepts of planar geometric projections, axonometry and the construction of axonometric projections from $\mathbb{R}^3$ to $\mathbb{R}^2$ and from $\mathbb{R}^4$ to $\mathbb{R}^3$. Then, Sect. 3 introduces the new *Maxima* package, R4projections, and describes the commands implemented within. Finally, Sect. 4 closes with the conclusions and recommendations.

2   Preliminaries

2.1   The Pohlke's Theorem

Theorem 1. Three lines of any length that originate from a point on a plane at different angles can always be considered as a parallel (biased) projection of three lines of the same length perpendicular to each other [13].

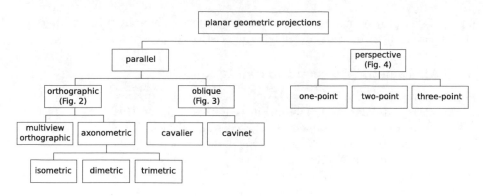

Fig. 1. Classification of projections [2].

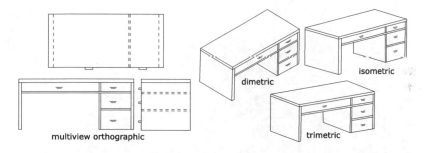

Fig. 2. Pictorial effects of orthographic projections [2].

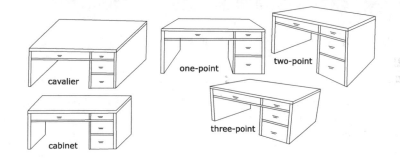

Fig. 3. Pictorial effects of oblique and perspective projections [2].

2.2   Concepts of Planar Geometric Projections

We will understand by *projection*[1] both the mapping of a three-dimensional space in a two-dimensional subspace and the image resulting from applying such a mapping to an object. Planar geometric projections can be classified

---

[1] This paper will work only with linear projections, specifically with axonometric projections.

into parallel projections or perspective projections; which in turn admit other classifications according to certain characteristics (Figs. 1, 2 and 3) [2].

2.3   Axonometric Projections from $\mathbb{R}^3$ to $\mathbb{R}^2$

Given a projection, by Pohlke's theorem, it is possible to select the projections of the coordinate axes as shown in Fig. 4, for example. In this way the $\bar{O}\bar{X}\bar{Y}\bar{Z}$ system will have been obtained as a projection of the $OXYZ$ system (Fig. 4). So, the image $\bar{P}$ of a point $P = (x, y, z)$ is determining by the four steps, starting a point $\bar{O}$: 1) go x in $\bar{X}$-direction, then 2) go y in $\bar{Y}$-direction, then 3) go z in $\bar{Z}$-direction and 4) mark the point as $\bar{P}$ (Fig. 4, right). It is worth mentioning that it is recommended to multiply the values x, y, z by factors

$$0 < v_x, v_y, v_z \leq 1 \tag{1}$$

in order to obtain a better representation [2].

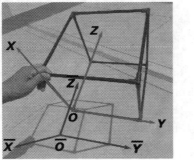 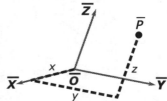

Fig. 4. Pohlke's theorem.

Figure 4 (right) shows a projection for which the arrangement of $\bar{X}, \bar{Y}, \bar{Z}$ axes is not the most common. Next, the analytical expressions of a projection that is the most common in most mathematical texts will be established (Fig. 5, left). To do this, the coordinate system generated by $\{O; \boldsymbol{i}, \boldsymbol{j}, \boldsymbol{k}\}$, with axes: OX, OY, OZ, will be projected on the coordinate system generated by $\{O'; \boldsymbol{e}_1, \boldsymbol{e}_2\}$, with axes: $O'X', O'Y'$ [11].

Let's define the projection $\mathbf{p} : \mathbb{R}^3 \to \mathbb{R}^2$ (Fig. 5) for which it is true that

$$\mathbf{p}(\boldsymbol{i}) = -\frac{1}{\sqrt{2}}(\boldsymbol{e}_1 + \boldsymbol{e}_2) = \left(-\frac{1}{\sqrt{2}}, -\frac{1}{\sqrt{2}}\right),$$
$$\mathbf{p}(\boldsymbol{j}) = \boldsymbol{e}_1 = (1, 0),$$
$$\mathbf{p}(\boldsymbol{k}) = \boldsymbol{e}_2 = (0, 1).$$

Let $P = (x, y, z)$ be an arbitrary point of $\mathbb{R}^3$ then, considering a result of linear algebra,

$$\mathbf{p}(P) = \mathbf{p}(x, y, z) = \begin{pmatrix} -\frac{1}{\sqrt{2}} & 1 & 0 \\ -\frac{1}{\sqrt{2}} & 0 & 1 \end{pmatrix} \begin{pmatrix} x \\ y \\ z \end{pmatrix}. \tag{2}$$

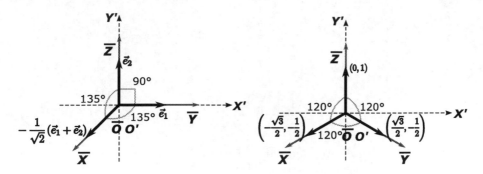

Fig. 5. Scheme to obtain the analytical expressions of two axonometric projection: dimetric (left) and isometric (right).

Equation (2) indicates that the point $P = (x, y, z)$ projects onto the point $P' = \left(-\frac{x}{\sqrt{2}} + y, -\frac{x}{\sqrt{2}} + z\right)$. This projection is called a dimetric projection.

Thus, for example, if another common axonometric projection is considered (Fig. 5, right), it is obtained

$$\mathbf{p}(x, y, z) = \begin{pmatrix} -\frac{\sqrt{3}}{2} & \frac{\sqrt{3}}{2} & 0 \\ -\frac{1}{2} & -\frac{1}{2} & 1 \end{pmatrix} \begin{pmatrix} x \\ y \\ z \end{pmatrix}. \tag{3}$$

This projection is called a isometric projection.

Next, the graphs of the projections of some mathematical objects will be shown. First, when applying a dimetric axometric projection (Fig. 6) and then when applying an isometric axonometric projection (Fig. 7). Note that, in the case of the axonometric projection, according to (1), $v_x = \frac{3}{5}$, $v_y = v_z = 1$; while for the other case, $v_x = v_y = v_z = 1$.

The analytical expressions of a projection $\mathbf{p}$ allow to obtain projections of mathematical objects from $\mathbb{R}^3$ to $\mathbb{R}^2$, according to the choice of $\bar{X}, \bar{Y}, \bar{Z}$ axes.

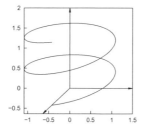
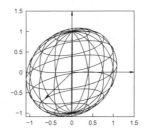

Fig. 6. Dimetric axonometric projection of a circular helix (left) as well as the u-parameter and v-parameter curves of a sphere (right).

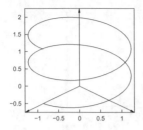 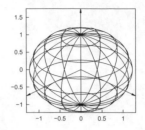

Fig. 7. Isometric axonometric projection of a circular helix (left) as well as the u-parameter and v-parameter curves of a sphere (right).

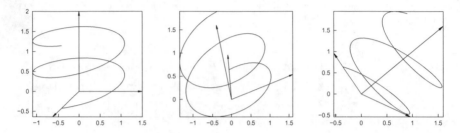

Fig. 8. Simulation of some rotations of the projection of the curve $\alpha(t) = (\cos(t), \sin(t), \frac{t}{8})$. The center and right figures exemplify trimetric axonometric projections.

However, all projections obtained lack movement in $\mathbb{R}^3$ but it is possible to simulate such movement using the product

$$R = R_z(\gamma)\,R_y(\beta)\,R_x(\alpha)\,,$$

which serves to represent a rotation around the z, y and x axes. Figure 8 was obtained after applying rotations to the coordinate functions of the helix

$$\alpha(t) = \left(\cos(t), \sin(t), \frac{t}{8}\right),\ 0 < t < 4\pi,$$

starting from the dimetric axonometric projection.

2.4   Axonometric Projections from $\mathbb{R}^4$ to $\mathbb{R}^3$

Pohlke's theorem was enunciated for projections of $\mathbb{R}^3$ on $\mathbb{R}^2$; however, it is possible to expand it naturally for projections of $\mathbb{R}^4$ on $\mathbb{R}^3$ [6,14,22]. For example, taking into account that the projection of the OX axis of Fig. 9 (right) is on the prolongation of the diagonal of a square (Fig. 9, left) it is possible to extend this idea to project the $OXYZW$ system on the $\bar{O}\bar{X}\bar{Y}\bar{Z}\bar{W}$ system, choosing the axes as shown in Fig. 9 (right). Note that the projection of the OX axis is chosen such that it rests on the prolongation of the diagonal of a cube, in addition

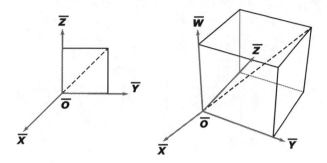

Fig. 9. The most common 2D axonometric projection (left) and a simile 3D axono-metric projection (right).

$\sphericalangle\, \bar{Y}\bar{Z} = \sphericalangle\, \bar{Y}\bar{W} = \sphericalangle\, \bar{Z}\bar{W} = 90°$ and $\sphericalangle\, \bar{X}\bar{Y} = \sphericalangle\, \bar{X}\bar{Z} = \sphericalangle\, \bar{X}\bar{W} \approx 125°15'51.803''$. To find the analytical expressions of this projection, the coordinate system generated by $\{O; \boldsymbol{i}, \boldsymbol{j}, \boldsymbol{k}, \boldsymbol{l}\}$, with axes: OX, OY, OZ, OW, will be projected on the coordinate system generated by $\{O'; \boldsymbol{e}_1, \boldsymbol{e}_2, \boldsymbol{e}_3\}$, with axes: $O'X'$, $O'Y'$, $O'Z'$.

Let's define the projection $\mathbf{p} : \mathbb{R}^4 \to \mathbb{R}^3$ (Fig. 10) for which it is true that

$$\mathbf{p}\,(\boldsymbol{i}) = -\frac{1}{\sqrt{3}}\,(\boldsymbol{e}_1 + \boldsymbol{e}_2 + \boldsymbol{e}_3) = \left(-\frac{1}{\sqrt{3}}, -\frac{1}{\sqrt{3}}, -\frac{1}{\sqrt{3}}\right),$$
$$\mathbf{p}\,(\boldsymbol{j}) = \boldsymbol{e}_1 = (1, 0, 0),$$
$$\mathbf{p}\,(\boldsymbol{k}) = \boldsymbol{e}_2 = (0, 1, 0),$$
$$\mathbf{p}\,(\boldsymbol{l}) = \boldsymbol{e}_3 = (0, 0, 1).$$

Let $P(x, y, z, w)$ be an arbitrary point of $\mathbb{R}^4$ then

$$\mathbf{p}(P) = \mathbf{p}(x, y, z, w) = \begin{pmatrix} -\frac{1}{\sqrt{3}} & 1 & 0 & 0 \\ -\frac{1}{\sqrt{3}} & 0 & 1 & 0 \\ -\frac{1}{\sqrt{3}} & 0 & 0 & 1 \end{pmatrix} \begin{pmatrix} x \\ y \\ z \\ w \end{pmatrix}. \tag{4}$$

Equation (4) indicates that the point $P = (x, y, z, w)$ projects onto the point $P' = \left(-\frac{x}{\sqrt{3}} + y, -\frac{x}{\sqrt{3}} + z, -\frac{x}{\sqrt{3}} + w\right)$.

Another example is obtained extend the projection defined in (3). Figure 11 (left) shows that the origin of the $\bar{O}\bar{X}\bar{Y}\bar{Z}$ system is located on the centroid of an equilateral triangle and the axes start from the centroid towards the vertices of the triangle. In the same way, it is possible to locate the origin of the $\bar{O}\bar{X}\bar{Y}\bar{Z}\bar{W}$ system on the centroid of an equilateral tetrahedron and the axes that start from the centroid towards the vertices of the tetrahedron (Fig. 11, right). In this way the projection

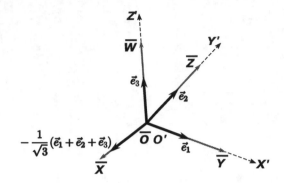

Fig. 10. Scheme to obtain the analytical expressions of a 3D axonometric projection.

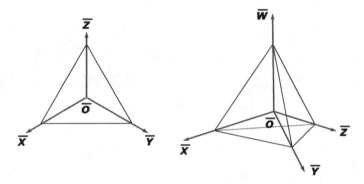

Fig. 11. Another common 2D axonometric projection (left) and a simile 3D axonometric projection (right).

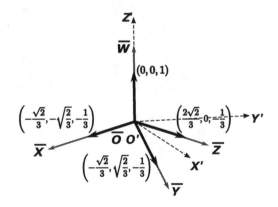

Fig. 12. Scheme to obtain the analytical expressions of another 3D axonometric projection.

$$\mathbf{p}(x, y, z, w) = \begin{pmatrix} -\frac{\sqrt{2}}{3} & -\frac{\sqrt{2}}{3} & \frac{2\sqrt{2}}{3} & 0 \\ -\sqrt{\frac{2}{3}} & \sqrt{\frac{2}{3}} & 0 & 0 \\ -\frac{1}{3} & -\frac{1}{3} & -\frac{1}{3} & 1 \end{pmatrix} \begin{pmatrix} x \\ y \\ z \\ w \end{pmatrix}. \tag{5}$$

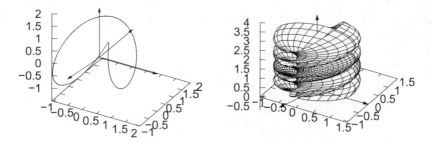

Fig. 13. Projection of the curve β (left) as well as the surface S (right) according to (4).

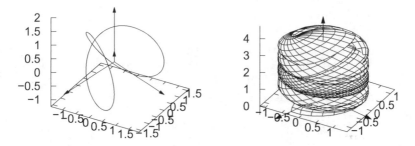

Fig. 14. Projection of the curve β (left) as well as the surface S (right) according to (5).

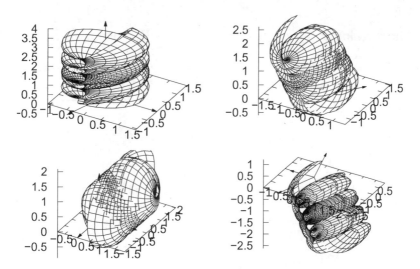

Fig. 15. Simulation of some rotations of the projection of the surface $S(u, v) = \left(\cos(u)\cos(v), \sin(u)\cos(v), \sin(v), \frac{u+v}{8}\right)$.

is obtained (Fig. 12). Here the angles formed by the axes, taken two by two, measure approximately $161°33'54.1842''$.

Figure 13 shows the graphs of the curve

$$\beta(t) = (\cos(t), \sin(t), \cos(2t), \sin(2t)), \quad 0 < t < 2\pi,$$

(left) and of the surface

$$S(u, v) = \left(\cos(u)\cos(v), \sin(u)\cos(v), \sin(v), \frac{u+v}{8} \right), \quad 0 < u, v < 4\pi,$$

(right) projected according to (4), while Fig. 14 shows the same graphs but projected according to (5). Note that, in the case of the projection according to (4), expanding the indications of (1), $v_x = \frac{3}{5}$, $v_y = v_z = v_w = 1$; while in the case of the projection according to (5), $v_x = v_y = v_z = v_w = 1$.

The analytical expressions of a projection $\mathbf{p}$ allow to obtain projections of mathematical objects from $\mathbb{R}^4$ to $\mathbb{R}^3$, according to the choice of $\bar{X}, \bar{Y}, \bar{Z}, \bar{W}$ axes. However, all projections obtained lack movement in $\mathbb{R}^4$ but it is possible to simulate such movement using the product

$$R = R_{zw}(\psi)\, R_{yw}(\varphi)\, R_{yz}(\delta)\, R_{xw}(\gamma)\, R_{xz}(\beta)\, R_{xy}(\alpha),$$

which serves to represent a rotation around the zw, yw, yz, xw, xz and xy planes. Figure 15 was obtained after applying rotations to the coordinate functions of the surface $S(u, v) = \left(\cos(u)\cos(v), \sin(u)\cos(v), \sin(v), \frac{u+v}{8}\right), 0 < u, v < 4\pi$.

3   The Package `R4projections`: Some Illustrative Examples

This section describes some examples of the application of this package. First, the package is loaded:

```
load(R4projections);
```

The two main functions incorporated in this package are:

draw4d, complexplot, plot4d.

With the **draw4d** function it is possible to visualize the plotting of the projections of points, lines, vectors, explicit functions, parametric curves, parametric surfaces and complex surfaces.

Next, a random list of points is plotted and then they are linked by a line.

```
p:create_list(map(random,[10,15,20,10]),k,1,10)$
draw4d( points(p) );
```

See Fig. 16 (left).

```
draw4d( points_joined=true,points(p) );
```

See Fig. 16 *(right)*.

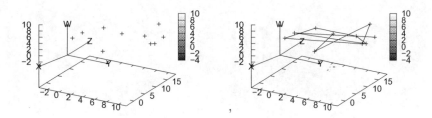

,

Fig. 16. Projections of points and lines from $\mathbb{R}^4$.

The following code allows obtaining the plotting of a set of vectors.

```
draw4d(  head_length=0.03,head_angle=10,
    vector([0,1/2,0,sqrt(3)/2],[-1/2,0,sqrt(3)/2,0]),
    vector([-1,0,0,0],[-1/2,0,0,-sqrt(3)/2]),
    vector([0,1/2,-sqrt(3)/2,0],[1,0,0,0])  )$
```

See Fig. 17.

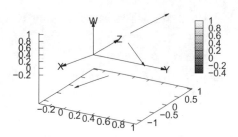

Fig. 17. Projections of vectors from $\mathbb{R}^4$.

To plotting one or more curves we would have to type the following code.

```
draw4d(  proportional_axes=xy,xyplane=-1.25,nticks=100,
    parametric(cos(t-1)*cos(t)^2,cos(t-1)*cos(t)*sin(t),
        cos(t-1)*sin(t),-sin(t-1),t,0,2*%pi)  )$
```

See Fig. 18 *(left)*.

```
draw4d(  proportional_axes=xy,xyplane=-1.25,nticks=100,
    parametric(cos(t-1)*cos(t)^2,cos(t-1)*cos(t)*sin(t),
        cos(t-1)*sin(t),-sin(t-1),t,0,2*%pi),
    parametric(cos(t)^2*cos(2*t),cos(t)*sin(t)*cos(2*t),
        cos(t)*sin(2*t),sin(t),t,0,2*%pi)  )$
```

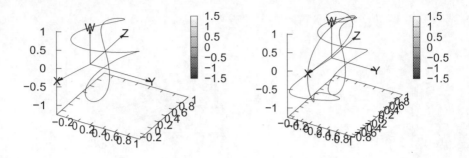

Fig. 18. Projections of curves from $\mathbb{R}^4$.

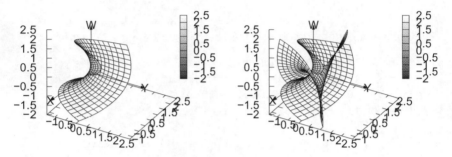

Fig. 19. Projections of surfaces from $\mathbb{R}^4$.

See Fig. 18 (right).

The `parametric_surface` function affected by the `draw4d` function allows to plotting one or more surfaces given in parametric form.

```
draw4d( proportional_axes=xy,xyplane=-1.25,nticks=100,
    parametric_surface(u+v,u^2-v^2,u*v,u-v,u,-1,1,v,-1,1)  )$
```

See Fig. 19 (left).

```
draw4d( proportional_axes=xy,xyplane=-1.25,nticks=100,
    parametric_surface(u+v,u^2-v^2,u*v,u-v,u,-1,1,v,-1,1),
    parametric_surface(u^2-v^2,u,v,2*u*v,u,-1,1,v,-1,1)  )$
```

See Fig. 19 (right).

Thanks to the isomorphism that exists between $\mathbb{C}$ and $\mathbb{R}^2$, as well as between $\mathbb{C}^2$ and $\mathbb{R}^4$, it is possible to obtain the graphs of complex functions such as $F(z) = z^2$ and $F(z) = \Gamma(z)$.

```
complexplot( z^2,[z,-1-%i,1+%i],[plot_format,openmath] )$
```

See Fig. 20 (left).

```
complexplot( gamma(z),[z,-3-3*%i,3+3*%i],[plot_format,openmath] )$
```

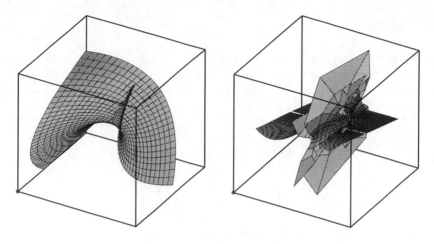

Fig. 20. Projections of complexes surfaces from $\mathbb{C}^2$.

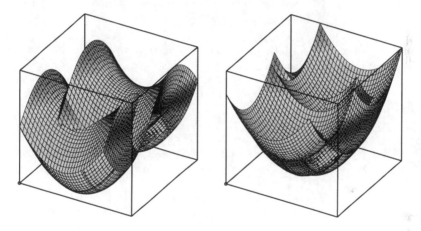

Fig. 21. Projections of solids from $\mathbb{R}^4$.

See Fig. 20 (right).

Finally the plotting of two solids are shown (Fig. 21).

```
plot4d(
      [u,v,w,u^2+v^2+w^2],[u,-1,1],[v,-1,1],[w,-1,1],
      [plot_format,openmath]
)$
```

See Fig. 20 (left).

```
plot4d(
      [u,v,w,u^2+v^2-w^2],[u,-1,1],[v,-1,1],[w,-1,1],
      [plot_format,openmath]
)$
```

See Fig. 20 (right).

4   Conclusions

In this paper, axonometric projections from $\mathbb{R}^4$ to $\mathbb{R}^3$ are constructed to obtain projections of objects immersed in four-dimensional space on a 3D hyperplane. These constructions are made as an extension of the construction of the axonometric projections from $\mathbb{R}^3$ to $\mathbb{R}^2$, which are based on the Pohlke theorem. Here is the natural extent of two of the most common projections from $\mathbb{R}^3$ to $\mathbb{R}^2$. Taking as a reference the diagonal of a square, for one, and the centroid of an equilateral triangle, for the other, it is possible to extend them two projections from $\mathbb{R}^4$ to $\mathbb{R}^3$ for which the diagonal of a cube and the centroid of a tetrahedron, respectively. Of course, it is possible to build countless of these projections. To simulate rotations in $\mathbb{R}^4$, in the same way as for $\mathbb{R}^3$, the six matrices associated with rotations around the six coordinate planes are used. In addition, the new *Maxima* package is described: R4projections. This package incorporates functions to plotting: points, lines, vectors, curves, surfaces, complex surfaces and solids; immersed in $\mathbb{R}^4$. Several illustrative examples, aimed to show the good performance of the package, are also given.

Acknowledgements. The authors would like to thank to the reviewers for their valuable comments and suggestions.

References

1. Abbott, E.: Flatland: A Romance of Many Dimensions. Seely & Co, London (1884)
2. Carlbom, I., Paciorek, J.: Planar geometric projections and viewing transformations. ACM Comput. Surv. **10**(4), 465–502 (1978)
3. Clements, A.: History of the Computer. http://www.cengage.com/resource_uploads/downloads/1111987041_374938.pdf. Accessed 10 Feb 2020
4. Hoffmann, C., Zhou, J.: Visualization of Surfaces in Four-Dimensional Space. https://pdfs.semanticscholar.org/4fd8/0d8a71878ec50e3a5fb48a98cd0e0bdc2091.pdf. Accessed 10 Feb 2020
5. Lehmann, C.: Analytic Geometry (Sixth printing). Wiley, New York (1947)
6. Lindgren, C.E., Slaby, S.M.: Four Dimensional Descriptive Geometry. McGraw-Hill, New York (1968)
7. Manfrin, R.: A proof of Pohlke's theorem with an analytic determination of the reference trihedron. J. Geom. Graph. **22**(2), 195–205 (2017)
8. Noll, A.: A computer technique for displaying n-dimensional hyperobjects. Commun. ACM **10**, 469–473 (1967)
9. O'Connor, J., Robertson, E.: Edwin Abbott Abbott. http://www-groups.dcs.st-and.ac.uk/~history/Biographies/Abbott.html. Accessed 10 Feb 2020
10. Rodríguez, J., Álvarez, V.: Geometría descriptiva: Sistema de perspectiva axonométrica (Seventh Edition, vol. 3). S. A. Donostiarra, España (2012)
11. Rovenski, V.: Geometry of Curves and Surfaces with MAPLE. Birkhäuser, Boston (2000)
12. Sakai, Y., Hashimoto, S.: Interactive four-dimensional space visualization using five-dimensional homogeneous processing for intuitive understanding. Inf. Media Technol. **2**(1), 574–591 (2007)

13. Schwarz, H.A.: Elementarer Beweis des Pohlkeschen Fundamentalsatzes der Axonometrie. Crelle's J. **63**, 309–3014 (1864)
14. Schreiber, P.: Generalized descriptive geometry. J. Geom. Graph. **6**(1), 37–59 (2002)
15. Swisher, C.: Victorian England. Greenhaven Press, San Diego (2000)
16. Velezmoro, R., Ipanaqué, R., Mechato, J.A.: A mathematica package for visualizing objects inmersed in $\mathbb{R}^4$. In: Misra, S., et al. (eds.) ICCSA 2019. LNCS, vol. 11624, pp. 479–493. Springer, Cham (2019). https://doi.org/10.1007/978-3-030-24311-1_35
17. Villate, J.: Maxima 5.42.0 Manual. http://maxima.sourceforge.net/docs/manual/maxima.html. Accessed 17 Feb 2020
18. Volkert, K.: On models for visualizing four-dimensional figures. Math. Intell. **39**(2), 27–35 (2017)
19. Wang, W., et al.: Interactive exploration of 4D geometry with volumetric halos. In: Pacific Graphics Short Papers, pp. 1–6. The Eurographics Association (2013)
20. Wuyts, G.: Wugi's QBComplex. http://home.scarlet.be/wugi/qbComplex.html. Accessed 11 Feb 2020
21. Xiaoqi, Y.: New Directions in Four-Dimensional Mathematical Visualization. School of Computer Engineering, Game Lab (2015)
22. Zachariáš, S., Velichová, D.: Projection from 4D to 3D. J. Geom. Graph. **4**(1), 55–69 (2000)
23. Zhou, J.: Visualization of Four Dimensional Space and Its Applications. D. Phil. Thesis, Department of Computer Science Technical Reports. Paper 922 (1991)

International Workshop on Advanced and Computational Methods for Earth Science Applications (WACM4ES 2020)

Dam Break and Human Disaster: Córrego do Feijão, Brumadinho, MG

Pedro Benedito Casagrande[1]([✉]) [iD], Maria Giovana Parisi[3] [iD],
Ana Clara Mourão Moura[2] [iD], Lourdes Manresa Camargos[3] [iD],
Camila Marques Zyngier[2] [iD], Viviane da Silva Borges Barbosa[4] [iD],
Danilo Marques de Magalhães[3] [iD],
and Gilberto Rodrigues da Silva[4] [iD]

[1] Escola de Engenharia and Instituto de Geociências, Universidade Federal de
Minas Gerais (UFMG), Av. Antônio Carlos 6627, Belo Horizonte, Brazil
pcasagrande@demin.ufmg.br
[2] Escola de Arquitetura, Universidade Federal de Minas Gerais (UFMG),
Rua Paraíba 697, Belo Horizonte, Brazil
anaclara@ufmg.br, camila.zynger@gmail.com
[3] Instituto de Geociências, Universidade Federal de Minas Gerais (UFMG),
Av. Antônio Carlos 6627, Belo Horizonte, Brazil
{mgparizzi18,danilommagalhaes}@gmail.com,
loumcamargos@hotmail.com
[4] Escola de Engenharia, Universidade Federal de Minas Gerais (UFMG),
Av. Antônio Carlos 6627, Belo Horizonte, Brazil
{vborges,grsilva}@demin.ufmg.br

Abstract. The study area was surrounding Córrego do Feijão Mine, located in
the city of Brumadinho/MG, Brazil. From this proposal, we present the analysis
of the effect of disruption of one of the tailings dams of the Córrego do Feijão
Mine, which took place in January 2019, under the responsibility of Vale S.A.
The rupture culminated in mud flow. A study and characterization of the area
was made, to understand the flow of the waters, and consequently, the mud. In
addition, it was possible to obtain information on the land use of the area before
and after the break using remote sensing (Sentinel-2A) supervised image classification. Through a spatial and temporal analysis, it was estimated that the mud
reached a total of 2.48 km^2, being the class of robust vegetation the most
affected by the disaster in numerical terms. The typology of anthropic areas,
despite being the smallest area hit by mud, was the one that suffered the greatest
impact. The importance of an analysis of the elements that belong in the area of
study and how they behave, in order to avoid and mitigate situations of vulnerability is considered very important. Finally, it is emphasized the relevance of
a spatial planning studies that considers the integrated planning between the
juxtaposition of human activities, social and spatial relations and their various
impacts on the landscape.

Keywords: Territorial planning · Córrego do Feijão Mine · Dam break

O. Gervasi et al. (Eds.): ICCSA 2020, LNCS 12255, pp. 855–863, 2020.
https://doi.org/10.1007/978-3-030-58820-5_61

1 Introduction

In the mining sector, space has limitations of choices and alternatives, since the ore location is not where has the best facilities for human activity, it occurs in a specific geological context.

In this sense, mining dams are highly known for generating high environmental impact and landscape transformation, and their management is the target of direct criticism from society (Duarte 2008) [1]. As large anthropic structures are, the possibility of some event cannot be ruled out, even if it has a value close to zero. In this way the risk should be minimized as much as possible and, according to Bowles et al. (1998) [2], one of the premises for this is security, which includes protecting the population that lives with this type of infrastructure.

It is well known that within all the anthropic activities that generate more expressive impacts, mining stands out. Mining affects the territory where it is carried out (Cetem 2014) [3] and, consequently, the leasing of its elements (infrastructure and operation) should contemplate the socio-environmental issues within the watershed in which it is inserted. The elements present downstream should be considered mainly, since in any disaster that may occur, the tendency is that the elements linked to the movement of materials move from the highest quota point to the lowest quota, in general, following the same path of the water flow network.

In this sense, the watershed is considered as a preferential cutout of environmental analysis and planning, as it is a system in which all actions adopted are reflected in its spatial set. Thus, the use of a water network as an analysis unit is relevant, since the watershed, connected to the water network, is a cell in which it is possible to understand the interrelationships existing between the elements and processes of the landscape, being then the hydrographic network, or part of it, is defined as an element of high importance for the study of environmental problems (Botelho 1999) [4].

The present study uses as spatial clipping of the Ferro Carvão Stream in the Paraopeba River, watershed directly affected by the rupture of one of the dams of the Córrego do Feijão Mine, in Brumadinho (MG).

2 Satellite Images

The use of satellite images for digital image processing applications is a very successful technology in data collection for data collection and monitoring of events on a global and local scale (Meneses and Almeida 2012) [5]. This is because the data collection presented is distant from the object under study, because it is not performed *in loco* (Jensen 2009) [6] and there is a possibility of understanding the phenomenon under study on a temporal scale.

It is well known that satellite images, in digital or analog form, are very important and useful for urban planning and land use, as they allow the evaluation of changes in the landscape of a region and during a given period, for example, recording coverage plant at any moment. Another importance is its periodicity of imagery, which is short, enabling the analysis of the phenomenon in whatever its spatial modification (Machado 2002) [7].

The images used was Sentinel-2A, belonging to the Copernicus program of the European Space Agency. This type of image collects data that allows to detect small movements and changes in the terrain, useful for monitoring vegetation, water bodies and structures (ESA 2017) [8]. The images of this satellite are captured in bands of different wavelengths (Table 1), with a spatial resolution of 10 m (red, green and blue).

Table 1. Spatial resolution of the bands Red, Green, Blue and Near Infrared of Sentinel-2A Images. Source: The authors, modified from ESA (2017).

Band number	Central wavelength (μm)	Spatial resolution (m)
Band - 2 (Blue)	0,490	10
Band - 3 (Green)	0,560	10
Band - 4 (Red)	0,665	10

The combination of Bands RGB (Red, Green and Blue) is the most used among the color models (Meneses and Almeida 2012) [5]. This system stands out for the great freedom it presents to the analyst to explore the possible combinations of three colors with three bands in order to obtain the color image of better contrast. Figure 1 demonstrates the conversion of a digital image into the process of forming a colored composition in the RGB standard.

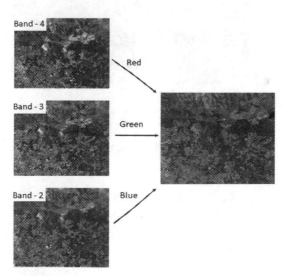

Fig. 1. Combination of Red Bands, Green, Blue to Generate True Color Image. (Color figure online) Source: The authors

Each element of the Earth's surface has a spectral signature that is related to the relative intensity with which the body reflects or emits electromagnetic waves at different lengths, in response to the action of sunlight on its surface. That means, a part of sunlight is absorbed by the body, another part is scattered, and the remaining part is reflected. This reflected part is captured by the satellite. These interactions are dependent on the physical and chemical characteristics of the target on which the incidence of light occurs.

In this case study, based on the composition with the specified bands, supervised classification of satellite images in the study area was made, with the use of classifiers per region that use, in addition to the spectral information of each pixel, the information of conformation or spatial arrangement. This involves the relationship between pixels and their neighbors and seeks to simulate the behavior of a photo interpretation, recognizing homogeneous areas of images, based on the spectral and spatial properties of the images (Santos et al. 2010) [9]. By comparing one pixel to other pixels of known identity, you can group those whose spectral reflectance are similar in more or less homogeneous classes (Santos et al. 2010) [9]. This activity need the use of geoprocessing software to visualize the images and to select the samples of the structural that in analyze.

3   Methodology

The work consisted of the elaboration of supervised classification of satellite images in order to obtain the final temporal and spatial analysis, following the subsequent methodological steps, present in the flowchart of Fig. 2 and described below:

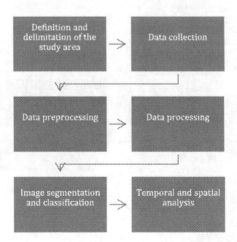

Fig. 2. Flowchart of methodological procedures. Source: The authors

On January 25th of 2019, there was a rupture of one of the dams of the Córrego do Feijão Mine in Brumadinho (MG), under the responsibility of the company Vale S.A. With the disruption, 12 million cubic meters of wet iron ore tailings leaked and went through the bed of the Ferro Carvão Stream, reaching the locality of Córrego do Feijão and later the city of Brumadinho.

The area is located within the municipality of Brumadinho (Fig. 3), Minas Gerais, and is 32.4 km² long. The watershed of Ferro Carvão Stream is inserted in the Paraopeba River basin, in the São Francisco Hydrographic Region.

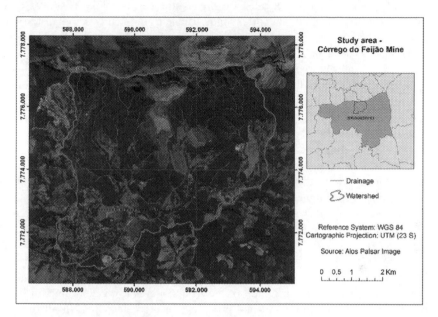

Fig. 3. Location of the study area. The watershed that the Córrego do Feijão mine is inserted, Brumadinho/Brazil. Source: The authors

Image processing has been done by acquisition of the satellite images for the area, from two dates, one of the pre-break (24/09/2018) and another related to the post-breakup (01/02/2019). The processing with an interactive classification of images was performed in the *ArcMap 10.7* software, in which the spectral characteristics of the pixel are considered. The processing of the images is a combination of Bands RGB (Red, Green and Blue), for the conversion of a digital image into the process of forming a colored composition in the RGB standard.

This technic requires sample areas, of each type of class. These samples are the training areas, which are obtained by selecting previous samples of each type of class. This step is done by the operator of the program and it is a visual selection, based on elements such as tonality/color, shape and texture of the pixels of each image. The classification was divided differently for each of the two images. In the image corresponding to the pre-rupture of the dam, four classes of land use and occupation were defined: robust vegetation, no vegetation, mining area and other anthropized areas. In the image corresponding to the post rupture of the dam, five classes of land use and occupation were highlighted: robust vegetation, no vegetation, mining area, tailings and other anthropized areas. Urban areas, roads, agriculture and pastures were grouped in the class for 'other anthropized areas'.

4   Characterization of the Area and Consequences of the Event

The area of this case study is located on the southern axis of the fragment of the metropolis of Belo Horizonte that corresponds to one of the main vectors of territorial expansion, composed of the municipality of Brumadinho, in which the Córrego do Feijão Mine is located. In this space there are several urban, environmental and economic conflicts – related to mining mainly – which often operate without articulation.

Thus, the interest in redirecting the use of space as an economic instrument for capital production generates the phenomenon of large open-air mining and the lack of planning of the territory by the public authorities, with fragility in the definition of areas appropriate for each type of activity, some of them conflicting. Therefore, the action of the State must become a fundamental instrument in the management of the territory in order to organize and plan the same.

Mining, at the study site, tends to occur in places with high topography, since in the local geological constitution of this mineral province iron deposits are located in lithologies that are in higher topography (Faria 2012) [10]. This situation may cause, if there is a disaster with the infrastructure of mines, the movement of the material from the higher local topographic point to the local topographic low, thus, there is a greater need for the Public Power to know its territory well and avoid possible overlap of urban, environmental and economic interests. An important way to solve the use of municipal space could be the adoption of environmental conservation units in impact amortization spaces, thus environmental protection instruments could fulfill functions that would enable the control of space use (Costa 2006) [11].

The rupture of the dam allowed the tailings mud to flow by the surface water determined by the differences of altitudes. The dam was located in a large section of the area and with a greater slope than other adjacent areas (Fig. 4), moving through the path of the Ferro Carvão Stream, reaching the locality of Córrego do Feijão and later the city of Brumadinho. All the structures that where across the path of the mud has been destroyed, such as the cafeteria and the administrative office of the mine. The rural local community was also directly reached by the mud (Fig. 5).

The classification of images also allows us to extract information about the territory of analysis. By classifying satellite images from the study site, information on the use and occupation of the soil of the watershed was extracted before and after the rupture of one of the dams of the Córrego do Feijão Mine (Fig. 5).

It was possible to calculate the areas representing the classes of land use and occupation before and after the rupture of the dam. Additional information was obtained from the area affected by mud for each type of land use and occupation, as well as the total area affected by mining tailings.

Table 2 shows that the most mud-affected class was robust vegetation, representing a total of 0.94 km^2, followed by the mining area, with 0.87 km^2. The anthropized area, which for this analysis represents urban areas, rural residences, roads and agriculture, was hit by mud in an area of 0.66 km^2. Despite being the least achieved class of use and occupation in numerical terms, it is the typology that has suffered the greatest impacts, since it directly affected people and animals.

Slope map (%) and hypsometric map (m) of watershed in Brumadinho

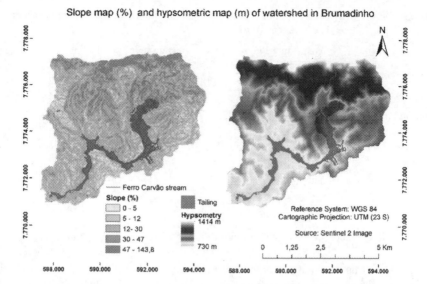

Fig. 4. Slope (left) and Hypsometric (right) maps. Source: The authors

Use and Occupation of Watershed Soil in Brumadinho -
Pre-rupture and post-rupture of the tailings dam

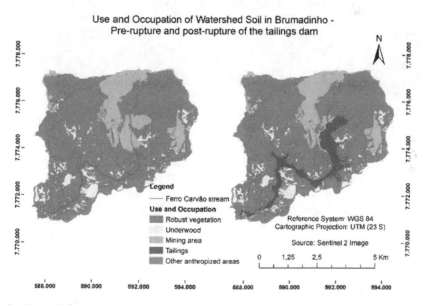

Fig. 5. Use and Occupation of the soil of watershed in Brumadinho - Previous (left) and Post Breakup (right). Source: The authors

It is important to highlight that this analysis is limited to the watershed area of immediate influence, delimited to the study. It is known that after the mud hit the Valley of the Ferro Carvão Stream and adjacent streams, this was towards the

Table 2. Estimated areas corresponding to the use and occupation of the soil and areas affected by the tailings. Source: The authors.

Land use and occupation	Area (km^2) Pre-breakup	Post-breakup area (km^2)	Tailings-stricken area (km^2)
Robust vegetation	21,71	20,77	0,94
No vegetation	1,87	1,87	0,00
Other anthropized areas	4,34	3,67	0,66
Mining area	4,77	3,90	0,87
Reject	0,00	2,48	–
Total	32,69	32,69	2,48

Paraopeba River and the city of Brumadinho, reaching new areas and causing other impacts.

The study makes a temporal and spatial analysis of the study area, taking into consideration the hydrographic watershed directly affected by the rupture. It is also sought to understand how the dynamics and distribution of mud had been determined by the spatial organization of the watershed, according to its hypsometric, slope, drainage, urban occupation. This allowed the characterization of the types of use and occupation of the most vulnerable sites when reached by the mud-flow.

5   Conclusion

Currently, with remote sensing techniques it is possible to characterize areas vulnerable to a certain risk, in this case the rupture of a dam. Access to satellite images is free, and you can use free software (*QGIS*, e.g.) to perform the same process presented here. The images already have a good temporal resolution, which means the possibility of monitoring changes in soil coverage by any user who makes use of geoinformation technologies. Similarly, access to topographic data is also free, which favors users from devising three-dimensional modeling to understand the territory. Studies of this nature are possible for any public administration.

We highlight a broader perspective, that nature is treated as a subject, that is entitled, and not as an object to be explored (Calgaro et al. 2016) [12]. Thus, activities related to man must contemplate the geographical space that has the greatest affinity to be allocated and not how it is currently carried out, where the project is first elaborated and then becomes the physical means for it to adhere to the enterprise.

Finally, we note the demand for attention to the subject relationship and nature in order to consider that nature is the main element taken into account when there are human interventions and not that the determining object is the activity to be developed by man, and the profit to be achieved, as usually occurs.

Acknowledgments. The authors would like to thank the CNPq support through the project "Geodesign and Parametric Modeling of Territorial Occupation: Geoprocessing for the proposal of a Master Plan for the Landscape for the Quadrilátero Ferrífero-MG", Process 401066/2016-9, Edital Universal 01/2016 and FAPEMIG PPM-00368-18.

References

1. Duarte, A.P.: Classificação das barragens de contenção de rejeitos de mineração e de resíduos industriais no estado de minas gerais em relação ao potencial de risco - Dissertação de mestrado em Saneamento, Meio Ambiente e Recursos Hídricos, EE/UFMG. 114p. (2008)
2. Bowles, D.S., Anderson, L.R., Glover, T.F.: The practice of dam safety risk assessment and management: its roots, its branches, and its fruit. In: USCOLD Annual Meeting and Lecture, Buffalo, New York, p. 18. (1998)
3. CETEM/MCTI: Recursos minerais e comunidade: impactos humanos, socioambientais e econômicos. In: Fernandes, F.R.C., Alamino, R.D.C.J., Araújo, E.R. (eds.). Rio de Janeiro (RJ), 392 p. (2014)
4. Botelho, M.H.C.: Águas de Chuva: Engenharia das Águas Pluviais nas Cidades, 2nd edn., p. 237. Edgard Blücher, São Paulo (1998)
5. Meneses, P.R., Almeida, T.: Introdução ao Processamento de Imagens de Sensoriamento Remoto. Brasília: Editoras UnB - CNPq. 266p. (2012)
6. Jensen, J.R.: Sensoriamento Remoto do Ambiente: Uma Perspectiva em Recursos Terrestres. In: Tradução: José Carlos Neves Epiphanio (coordenador), vol. 14, pp. 511–572. Parêntese, São José dos Campos (SP) (2009)
7. Machado, S.A.: Sensores de alta resolução espacial. Trabalho apresentado à disciplina de Sistemas e Sensores Avançados para Observação da Terra. Programa de Pós-Graduação em Sensoriamento Remoto. Instituto Nacional de Pesquisas Espaciais, São José dos Campos (SP) (2002)
8. Esa 2017. https://sentinel.esa.int/web/sentinel/sentinel-data-access
9. Santos, A.R., Peluzio, T.M.O., Saito, N.S.: SPRING 5.1.2: passo a passo: aplicações práticas. CAUFRES, Alegre, 153p. (2010)
10. Faria, D.M.C.P.: Análises de la capacidad del turismo en el desarrollo económico regional: el caso de Inhotim y Brumadinho. Tese de doutorado – Universidad de Alicante, Departamento de Análisis Económico Aplicado/Universidade Federal de Minas Gerais, Centro de Desenvolvimento e Planejamento Regional. Alicante/Belo Horizonte. 362p. (2012)
11. Costa, H.S.M.: Mercado imobiliário, Estado e natureza na produção do espaço metropolitano. Novas periferias metropolitanas. A expansão metropolitana em Belo Horizonte: dinâmica e especificidades no Eixo Sul, pp. 101–124. Editora C/ Arte, Belo Horizonte (2006)
12. Calgaro, C., Gardelin, L. D., Santos, S. A.: O novo constitucionalismo Latino-Americano e o risco ecológico: a restauração e a reparação do dano ambiental. Revista Contribuciones a las Ciencias Sociales, julio-septiembre (2016)

Self-organizing-Map Analysis of InSAR Time Series for the Early Warning of Structural Safety in Urban Areas

Augusto Montisci$^{(\boxtimes)}$ ⓘ and Maria Cristina Porcu ⓘ

University of Cagliari, Cagliari, Italy

Abstract. Among the many causes of collapse of civil structures, those related to the downfall of foundations are crucial for their likely catastrophic consequences. Interferometric synthetic aperture radar (InSAR) techniques may help monitoring the time evolution of ground displacements affecting engineered structures in large urban areas. Artificial neural networks can be exploited to analyze the huge amount of data that is collected over long periods of time on very dense grid of geographical points. The paper presents a neural network-based analysis tool, able to evidence similarities among time series acquired in different points and times. This tool could support an early-warning system, aiming to forecast critical events in urban areas. The implemented procedure is tested on a dataset of InSAR time series recorded over an area of the city of London.

Keywords: Remote sensing · Collapse prevention · Early warning in urban areas · InSAR time-series · Artificial neural network · Autoencoding · Ground settlements · Structural safety

1 Introduction

The health monitoring of civil structures generally entails performance assessment and structural damage detection, which are typically achieved through in-situ sensing campaigns [1–6]. When very big structures (dams, viaducts, aqueducts) or blocks of many buildings (in urban areas) need to be monitored, classical in-situ techniques may become expensive and even impractical. In these cases, remote sensing based on InSAR techniques can be very useful for reveling signs of distress characterizing a structure or an infrastructure during its life span [7–10].

Such techniques can help to monitor long-term ground displacements, the most critical of which can put the foundations' stability of structures and infrastructures at risk [11–14].

This study aims to provide a data analysis procedure, which can be used as a tool to forecast incoming phenomena of foundation downfalls and subsidence in large urban areas. For this purpose, an artificial neural network-based algorithm is implemented to process InSAR data in real-time to obtain an automatized alert system. A database of ground displacement time-series recorded over a long period of time (more than four years) at a high-density grid of geographical points within the city of London, is adopted to test the method.

© Springer Nature Switzerland AG 2020
O. Gervasi et al. (Eds.): ICCSA 2020, LNCS 12255, pp. 864–876, 2020.
https://doi.org/10.1007/978-3-030-58820-5_62

It can be noted that neural network-based methods have been already applied to the civil engineering field [15, 16], while early-warning systems have been developed to forecast different kinds of risk [17–21]. However, there is a lack of systematic automatized procedures to analyze InSAR-recorded time-series of ground displacements in urban areas, able to provide failure risk early-warning systems.

Based on clustering subsets of sequences through a neural network learning, the method presented in this paper leads to identify similarities among time series acquired in different points and times. The assumption is that critical events, such as downfalls and subsidence, are preceded by typical behaviors of the ground. Therefore, based on similarities with previous records, a monitoring system able to foresee incoming critical events can be developed. The paper aims to demonstrate the suitability of the approach to detect such similarities, while the detection of actual critical cases is beyond the scope of this work.

2   The Early-Warning Method

A Self Organizing Map (SOM [22]) is a kind of artificial neural network [23, 24] that is trained through Unsupervised Learning (UL) [25]. Unlike the more popular supervised learning (Multi-Layer Perceptrons, Support vector machines, Radial basis functions), where the neural network is adapted in order to associate training input patterns to corresponding desired outputs, the UL is based on finding unknown features of the input data distribution, such as principal directions [26] or presence of clusters [27]. Thus, unlike in the supervised learning, in the UL it is not possible to define an error since no target is defined. An internal updating rule is defined instead, which tends to "imitate" the inputs of the training set. It is worth to note that some operations are mandatory in both supervised and unsupervised learning as, for instance, splitting the dataset into Training, Validation and Test sets. In this work, the SOMs are used to cluster the time sequences of displacements, in order to highlight similarities between on-line recorded data and pre-selected sequences exhibiting critical behaviors.

A flowchart of the method is provided in Fig. 1. In some phases of the process the intervention of the Operator is foreseen. Anyway, it is limited only to the selection of the set of examples, without prejudicing the unsupervised learning paradigm.

The method follows three separated branches: Sequences selection, Training and Monitoring. In the Sequence-selection phase, a subset of time sequences is selected for the successive phase of Training. This selection aims to reduce the number of training examples, by increasing the relevance of critical behaviors. A ranking of the time sequences is preliminary obtained, based on a given feature that can be, for instance, the range of values or the instantaneous rate. Only the sequences that are above a fixed position in the ranking are kept for the Training phase (ranking-based selection). During the Sequence-selection phase, the Operator establishes the feature for the ranking and the threshold for the selection. The selected sequences are thus stored into the database. The obtained subset is furtherly reduced before the Training (cluster-based selection), by using a SOM which clusters the subset of sequences. The Operator selects some clusters of interest, and the sequences belonging to these clusters form the final Training set, which is stored into the Database.

The Training phase consists in clustering the time windows extracted from the sequences. Once the Operator has set the window duration, the training is processed automatically. Let N be the number of samples of each sequence and W the samples of a window, then $F = N - W + 1$ is the number of windows for each sequence. The number of sequences of the Training set multiplied by F gives the set of patterns that are clustered by a new SOM network, which will be used as alarm generator in the Monitoring phase. The clusters containing windows associated to critical events are labelled as "warning". Both the trained SOM and the list of warning clusters are stored into the Database.

The Monitoring phase generates early warnings of potential critical events in the area under control. For each of the monitored points in the area, a window covering the last W samples of the recorded time-sequence, is extracted. All these patterns (last windows of the time series) are fed to the previously trained SOM, which assigns them to the different clusters. The Monitoring phase can follow two distinct paths. In the first one (Procedure 1), an alarm is generated for all the windows falling in "warning" clusters, and the corresponding points are highlighted in the city map. The criterion to label as "warning" a cluster is established by the Operator. In the alternative path (Procedure 2), a specific event represented by a noticeable window is chosen by the Operator, and the cluster which this window belongs to is labelled as "warning". Again, the windows of the monitoring set that fall in the "warning" cluster, make the corresponding geographical points be marked in the city map as "warning points".

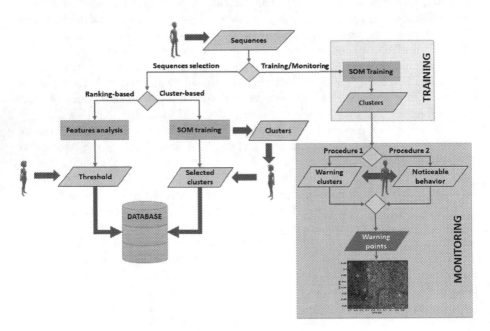

Fig. 1. Flowchart of the method

3   Applying the Method to a Database of Sequences (London)

A database of displacement time-histories recorded by means of InSAR remote sensing at 228701 geographical points of a large area of the city of London (see Fig. 2) and elaborated through the multitemporal technique MT-InSAR was considered to test the method described in Sect. 2. The same geographical area and InSAR time-histories have been used in [8, 9], to which the reader may refer for more details about the data. The displacements were recorded from April 2011 to December 2015 at irregular time-intervals. Four instances of time-histories taken from the database are plotted in Fig. 3. Three of them show a behavior that may require attention, while the last one is a normal trend of ground displacements.

By means of linear splines, the sequences were divided into regular time intervals and collected in a matrix of 228701 rows and 81 columns, these latter corresponding to the samples.

A subset of sequences was initially selected through the ranking-based criterion, assuming the range of values in the sequence as parameter for the ranking. A lower bound of the positions in this ranking was set and the sequences overcoming this bound were kept as the first skimmed subset. This subset was made up by 57176 sequences. The cluster-based criterion was then applied to this subset. A SOM network, with 10 × 10 outputs, was trained to obtain a clustering of the subset. The clusters of interest were finally selected based on their behavior, and the sequences belonging to them formed the training set of the early warning system. The final training set contained 5960 sequences.

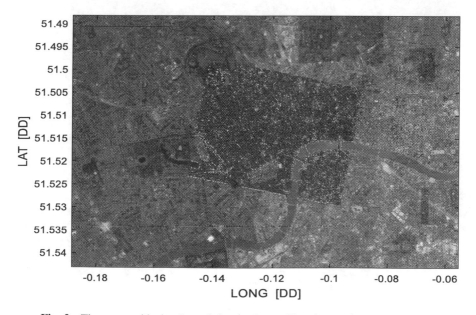

Fig. 2. The geographical points of the database of London, scale 1:50000 [8, 9].

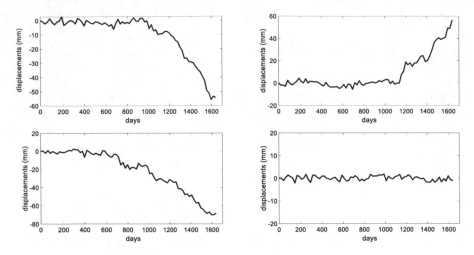

Fig. 3. Some sequences of displacements taken from the database of London

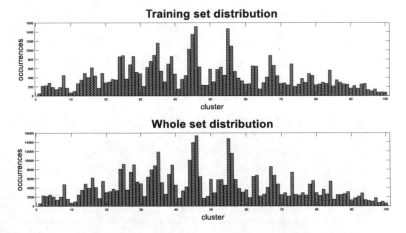

Fig. 4. Histogram of the clusters' incidence in the training subset and in the entire set.

A new SOM network, with 100 outputs, was trained on sequences' windows of 10 samples. It is worth to note that each sequence gave rise to $81 - 10 + 1 = 72$ windows, so that the dataset for the training consisted of $5960 \times 72 = 429120$ windows. A 10% of this dataset was considered as training set, while the remaining part was adopted as validation set. Figure 4 shows how the windows are distributed among the clusters in the training and validation sets, respectively. A comparison between the two histograms highlights the capability of the SOM network, trained over the training set, to represent the whole distribution.

The trained SOM was ready to generate warnings over the last (most recent) windows of all the sequences of the monitored area. This could be done by applying Procedure 1 (warning clusters) or Procedure 2 (noticeable behavior).

3.1   Monitoring Through Procedure 1

According to Procedure 1, an analysis of the clusters obtained by applying the SOM network to the patterns of the Training set, was preliminarily made. The analysis was based on a density-contour-plot of points related to each cluster. Based on this analysis criterion, most of the clusters have been found to be of very little interest to the goal of the procedure, due to the homogeneous distribution of the involved points in the area (an instance of a non-significant cluster is provided in Fig. 5).

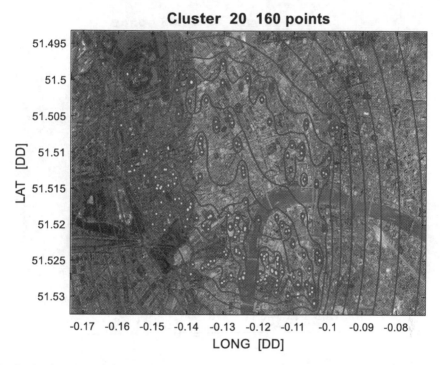

Fig. 5. An instance of the density distribution of the geographical points relevant to a non-significant cluster (Procedure 1).

Only two clusters were selected to the phase of monitoring, namely Cluster 46 and Cluster 10. The first one (see Fig. 6) was labelled as "warning" due to the high concentration of points on specific areas (yellow clouds of points). Such areas were found to lay along the path of the cross-rail twin tunnels that were under excavation during the period of acquisition of the data. The effects of these excavations on adjacent buildings were studied in [8, 9]. The second "warning" cluster was chosen due to the low number of involved points (see Fig. 7a), which is related to a rare and for this reason a possible anomalous behavior. Figure 7b shows the average trend and the upper and lower envelopes of the cluster.

It is to note that the criteria adopted herein to select the "warning" clusters in Procedure 1 are just some of the possible criteria that may be chosen by the Operator, who could also, for instance, base his decision on the examination of the average trend and the range of the displacements in the cluster. An examination of all the possible criteria that could be adopted is beyond the scope of this work, the aim of which is to demonstrate the attitude of the approach to reveal similarities between recorded and current time series. In this example, therefore, the choice of the critical clusters was made for the sole purpose of showing the functionality of the proposed method.

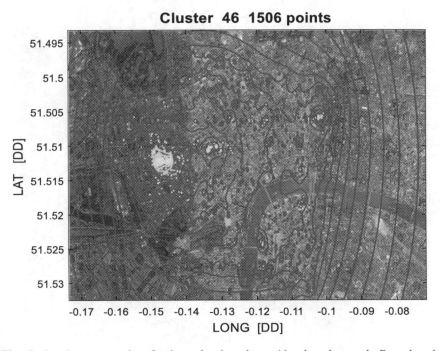

Fig. 6. Density-contour-plot of points related to cluster 46, selected to apply Procedure 1.

The trained SOM was then recalled on the windows to be monitored. Those that fell within the selected clusters made the points to which they belong be labelled as "warning". In Fig. 8 are displayed the geographical points associated to Cluster 46. The monitoring procedure evidenced that the swarm of points with analogous behavior is propagating over a larger area. The nature of this behavior is to be investigated after the training phase, when the cluster is defined. Since large clusters are characterized by dispersed behaviors, the kind and the likely severity of the phenomenon should be evaluated through in-situ inspections. Once this phenomenon has been classified as "critical", Procedure 1 is able to provide information about its ongoing spatial evolution.

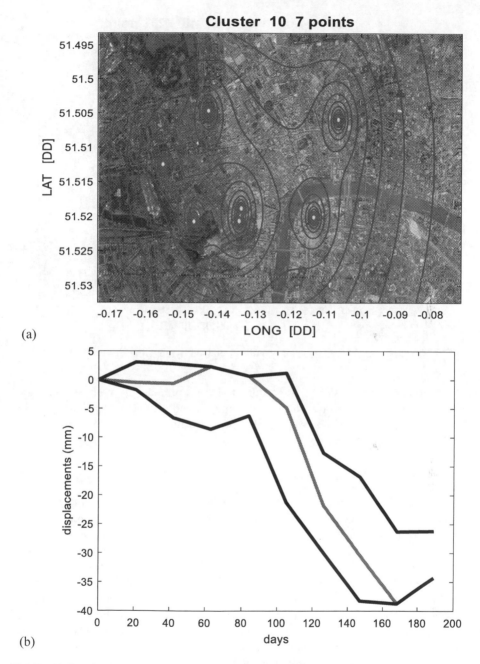

Fig. 7. (a) Density-contour-plot of points related to Cluster 10, selected to apply Procedure 1; (b) prototype (in red), upper and lower envelopes (in black) of the cluster (Color figure online).

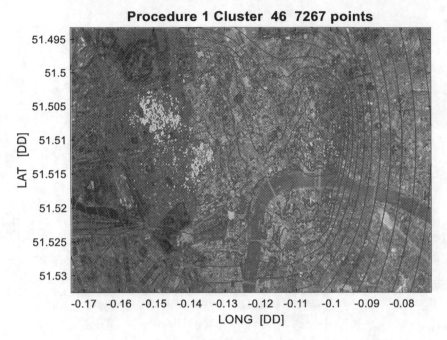

Fig. 8. Density-contour-plot of points obtained by applying Procedure 1.

When applied to Cluster 10, Procedure 1 did not provide any point. In this case, very few points belong to the cluster (see Fig. 7a) and a rather anomalous behavior characterizes the cluster (Fig. 7b). Therefore, it is reasonable that a similar behavior is not detected in the monitoring period.

3.2   Monitoring Through Procedure 2

By following Procedure 2, a window was selected due to its noticeable behavior, namely the one plotted in red in Fig. 9a. In Fig. 9b is evidenced the relevant geographical point. In this case, the cluster which this noticeable window belongs to was considered as a "warning cluster" in the monitoring phase. The monitoring was then carried out by following the same steps followed in Procedure 1. The geographical points labelled as "warning" according to Procedure 2 are plotted in Fig. 10a. It can be noted that only 6 points were found, which confirms the anomaly of the considered behavior. The windows belonging to these points are plotted in Fig. 10b (in blue) together with the selected noticeable window (in red). The comparison between the reference window and the windows detected though Procedure 2 shows the good ability of the method to find similarities of behavior.

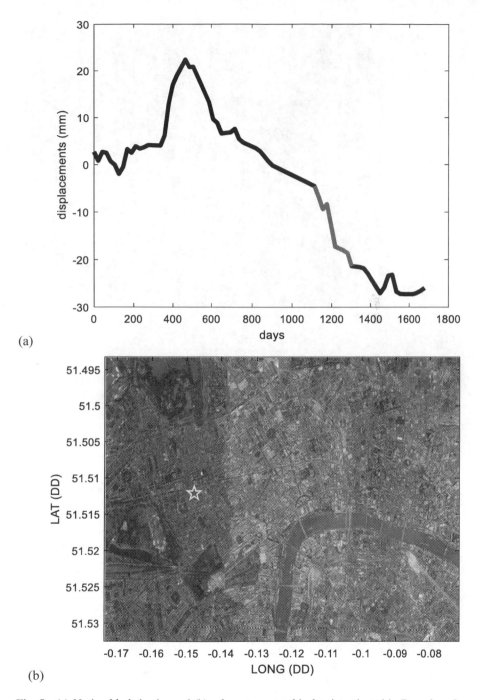

(a)

(b)

Fig. 9. (a) Noticeable behavior and (b) relevant geographical point selected in Procedure 2.

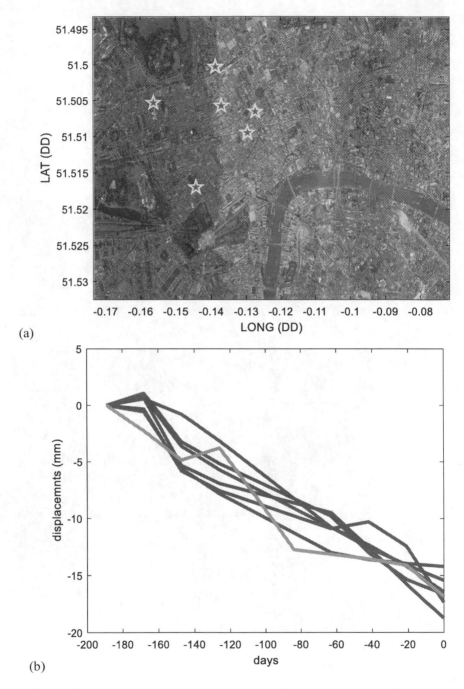

(a)

(b)

Fig. 10. (a) Warning points obtained with Procedure 2; (b) reference window (red) and warning windows (blue) (Color figure online).

4   Conclusions

The paper presents a method to analyze big data relevant to time-series of displacements recorded through InSAR techniques in urban areas. The method highlights similitudes among displacement sequences by means of a self-organizing-map neural network. Based on the similitude between recent time-series and critical events occurred in the past, incoming critical behaviors can be forecasted.

A dataset of displacements time-series, recorded at a very dense grid of geographical points in a large area of London, is taken as a case-study to test the method. Rate and range of displacements are assumed as target features in the application. The method presented in the paper is a preliminary tool that can form the basis for the development of an automatized early-warning procedure to forecast critical events relevant to ground displacements that may affect the stability of engineered structures in large urban areas. The method is assumed to be used by expert operators, who can select the more appropriate time-window duration and decide which target features are more suitable to forecast specific alarm behaviors. The correct framing of the events labelled as "warning" should be directed to successive in situ inspections and expert analysis.

Acknowledgements. Dr. Pietro Milillo of Jet Propulsion Laboratory, CALTECH (Pasadena, USA) is gratefully acknowledged for giving the database used in this paper and precious suggestions.

References

1. Chen, C.H. (ed.): Ultrasonic and advanced methods for nondestructive testing and material characterization. World Scientific Publishing, Singapore (2007)
2. Porcu, M.C., Pieczonka, L., Frau, A., Staszewski, W.J., Aymerich, F.: Assessing the scaling subtraction method for impact damage detection in composite plates. J. Nondestruct. Eval. **36**(2), 1–16 (2017). https://doi.org/10.1007/s10921-017-0413-9
3. Porcu, M.C., Patteri, D.M., Melis, S., Aymerich, F.: Effectiveness of the FRF curvature technique for structural health monitoring. Constr. Build. Mat. **226**, 173–187 (2019)
4. Frau, A., Pieczonka, L., Porcu, M.C., Staszewski, W.J., Aymerich, F.: Analysis of elastic nonlinearity for impact damage detection in composite laminates. J. Phys: Conf. Ser. **628**(1), 012103 (2015)
5. Loi, G., Porcu, M.C., Pieczonka, L., Staszewski, W.J., Aymerich, F.: Scaling subtraction method for damage detection in composite beams. Procedia Structural Integrity **24**, 118–126 (2019)
6. Floris, I., Sales, S., Calderon, P.A., Adam, J.M.: Measurement uncertainty of multicore optical fiber sensors used to sense curvature and bending direction. Measurement **132**, 35–46 (2019)
7. Milillo, P., Porcu, M. C., Lundgren, P., Soccodato, F., Salzer, J., Fielding, E., Biondi, F.: The ongoing destabilization of the Mosul dam as observed by synthetic aperture radar interferometry. In: 2017 IEEE International Geoscience and Remote Sensing Symposium (IGARSS). pp. 6279–6282 (2017)

8. Milillo, P., Giardina, G., DeJong, M., Perissin, D., Milillo, G.: Multi-temporal InSAR structural damage assessment: the London crossrail case study. Remote Sens. **10**(2), 287 (2018)

9. Giardina, G., Milillo, P., DeJong, M.J., Perissin, D., Milillo, G.: Evaluation of InSAR monitoring data for post-tunnelling settlement damage assessment. Struct. Control Hlth. **26** (2), e2285 (2019)

10. Milillo, P., Giardina, G., Perissin, D., Milillo, G., Coletta, A., Terranova, C.: Pre-Collapse space geodetic observations of critical infrastructure: the Morandi bridge, Genoa, Italy. Remote Sens. **11**(12), 1403 (2019)

11. Raucoules, D., Colesanti, C., Carnec, C.: Use of SAR interferometry for detecting and assessing ground subsidence. Comptes Rendus Geosci. **339**(5), 289–302 (2007)

12. Kontogianni, V., Pytharouli, S., Stiros, S.: Ground subsidence, quaternary faults and vulnerability of utilities and transportation networks in Thessaly, Greece. Environ. Geol. **52** (6), 1085–1095 (2007)

13. Kong, T.B., Komoo, I.: Urban geology: case study of Kuala Lumpur. Eng. Geol. **28**(1–2), 71–94 (1990)

14. Cubrinovski, M., Robinson, K., Taylor, M., Hughes, M., Orense, R.: Lateral spreading and its impacts in urban areas in the 2010–2011 Christchurch earthquakes, New Zeland. J. Geol. Geophys. **55**(3), 255–269 (2012)

15. Monjezi, M., Hasanipanah, M., Khandelwal, M.: Evaluation and prediction of blast-induced ground vibration at Shur river dam, Iran, by artificial neural network. Neural Comput. Appl. **22**(7–8), 1637–1643 (2013)

16. Ghaboussi, J., Joghataie, A.: Active control of structures using neural networks. J. Eng. Mech. **121**(4), 555–567 (1995)

17. Rainieri, C., Fabbrocino, G., Cosenza, E.: Integrated seismic early warning and structural health monitoring of critical civil infrastructures in seismically prone areas. Struct. Hlth. Monitor. **10**(3), 291–308 (2011)

18. Carcangiu, S., Fanni, A., Pegoraro, P.A., Sias, G., Sulis, S.: Forecasting-aided monitoring for the distribution system state estimation. Complexity (2020)

19. Cannas, B., et al.: Towards an automatic filament detector with a Faster R-CNN on MAST-U. Fusion Eng. Des. **146**, 374–377 (2019)

20. Secci, R., Laura Foddis, M., Mazzella, A., Montisci, A., Uras, G.: Artificial neural networks and Kriging method for slope geomechanical characterization. In: Lollino, G., Giordan, D., Crosta, Giovanni B., Corominas, J., Azzam, R., Wasowski, J., Sciarra, N. (eds.) Engineering Geology for Society and Territory - Volume 2, pp. 1357–1361. Springer, Cham (2015). https://doi.org/10.1007/978-3-319-09057-3_239

21. Carcangiu, S., Montisci, A.: A Locally recurrent neural network-based approach for the early fault detection. In: IEEE 4th International Forum on Research & Technology for Society and Industry (RTSI), pp. 1–6. Palermo (2018)

22. Kohonen, T.: Self-organized formation of topologically correct feature maps. Biol. Cybern. **43**(1), 59–69 (1982)

23. Da Silva, I.N., Spatti, D.H., Flauzino, R.A., Liboni, L.H.B., dos Reis Alves, S.F.: Artificial neural networks. Springer International Publishing, Cham (2017)

24. Wang, J.: Artificial neural networks versus natural neural networks: a connectionist paradigm for preference assessment. Decis. Support Syst. **11**(5), 415–429 (1994)

25. Hebb, D.O.: The organization of behavior: a neuropsychological theory. Science Eds (1962)

26. Sanger, T.D.: Optimal unsupervised learning in a single-layer linear feedforward neural network. Neural Networks **2**(6), 459–473 (1989)

27. Maass, W.: On the computational power of winner-take-all. Neural Comput. **12**(11), 2519–2535 (2000)

Artificial Neural Networks Based Approach for Identification of Unknown Pollution Sources in Aquifers

Maria Laura Foddis🆔 and Augusto Montisci(✉)🆔

University of Cagliari, Cagliari, Italy
augusto.montisci@unica.it

Abstract. This work focuses on groundwater resources contaminations identification. The problem of identifying an unknown pollution source in polluted aquifers, based on known contaminant concentrations measurement in the studied areas, is part of the broader group of issues, called inverse problems. In this field, often pollution may result from contaminations whose origins are generated in different times and places where these contaminations have been actually found. To address such scenarios, it is necessary to develop specific techniques that allow to identify time and space features of unknown contaminant sources. The characterization of the contaminant source is of utmost importance for the planning of subsurface remediation in the polluted site. In this work, such identification is solved as an inverse problem in two stages. Firstly a Multi Layer Perceptron neural network is trained on a set of numerical simulations, and then the case under study is reconstructed by inverting the neural model.

Keywords: Artificial neural networks inversion · Inverse problems · Groundwater pollution source identification, groundwater modelling

1 Introduction

Only a small percentage of water present on earth is useful for human use and 98% of this water is represented by water reserves contained in aquifers. These reserves are the most important water resources used for agriculture, drinking and industrial purposes. However, groundwater is exposed to man-made pollution. One of the major issues for groundwater specialists is the effective management of the groundwater quality because contamination of groundwater may prevent its use. Due to increased pollution phenomena, groundwater has become increasingly vulnerable and its sustainable management is nowadays extremely important to protect global health (Foddis 2011; Smith et al. 2016; WHO 2017).

When groundwater is polluted the restauration of the quality and the removal of pollutants are a very slow, hence, lengthy, and, sometimes, practically impossible task. This implies the need to develop effective monitoring and pollution forecasting methods, which can support the protection of key zones, especially in those areas where the geological characteristics of the soil allow relatively easy penetration of

© Springer Nature Switzerland AG 2020
O. Gervasi et al. (Eds.): ICCSA 2020, LNCS 12255, pp. 877–890, 2020.
https://doi.org/10.1007/978-3-030-58820-5_63

anthropogenic pollution into the groundwater. Consequently, a sensible management and monitoring aimed at protecting the groundwater quality and at safeguarding the groundwater resources from contaminations have a vital importance for life support systems.

In the field of groundwater resources contaminations, it should be underlined that in some cases, pollution may be the consequence of contaminations whose origins are generated in different times and places from where these contaminations have been detected. To tackle such situations, the development of techniques that allow one to identify the features and the behaviour in time and space of these unknown pollution sources is compulsory.

In addition, the determination of the initial conditions of pollution at the contaminant source level is of considerable interest in the framework of the implementation of the European Union Directive 2004/35/EC: this directive concerns environmental liability with regard to the prevention and compensation of environmental damages, based on the "polluter-payer" principle.

In general, the problem of determining the unknown model parameters is usually identified in hydrogeology as "inverse problem" (Carrera et al. 2005). Solving the inverse problem, in hydrogeology, is the main goal of modelling groundwater flow and contaminant transport. In order to reach the solution of the inverse problem, in this work we propose the use of a new methodology based on the application of the Artificial Neural Networks (ANN) (Carcangiu et al. 2016, 2019; Yaman et al. 2013).

Over the past decades, ANNs have become increasingly popular as a problem-solving tool and have been extensively used as a forecasting tool in many disciplines. Many recent studies have focused on the use of ANNs to examine their suitability to model environmental processes, such as, soil geomechanical characterization (Secci et al. 2015), the effect of climate parameters with respect to groundwater levels (Jei-houni et al. 2019), the rainfall-runoff prediction (Tanty and Desmukh 2015), the prediction of processes in hydrologic cycle (Nourani et al. 2014), the prediction of nitrate concentration in groundwater (Ostad-Ali-Askari et al. 2016; Foddis et al. 2015b, 2017, 2019; Mousavi and Amiri 2012; Sathish Kumar 2013), the prediction of zonal transmissivity (Ajmera 2008) and the simulation of contaminant transport in porous media (Nourani et al. 2018, 2017a, 2017b).

Few authors investigated the feasibility of solving the inverse problems linked with hydrogeological phenomena by using ANNs. Among these, in Zio (1997), an ANN is trained to identify the value of the dispersion coefficient in a simple analytic contaminant transport model; in Fanni et al. (2002), an ANN is used to locate a pollutant source; in Rajanayaka et al. (2002), a hybrid approach based on a combination of two types of ANN model is applied to estimate hydrogeological parameters; in Mahar and Datta (2000) an ANNs is used to identify the location and duration of groundwater pollution sources under transient flow and transport conditions; in Scintu (2004), ANNs are trained to predict the coordinates of the pollutant source and the time the pollution occurred; in Singh and Datta (2007, 2004a, 2004b) ANNs are used to identify unknown pollution sources feature taking into account also cases where the concentration observation data were partially missing; in Foddis et al. (2013) are used for locating the source of a contamination event in time and space; in Foddis et al. (2015a) are used to determine the profile of the pollutant source on the basis of a set of measurements in monitoring wells.

The purpose of this work is to demonstrate the feasibility of using the ANNs to define the behaviour of un unknown pollution sources. To this end, a theoretical scenario has been considered that consists of an accidental spill of a pollutant that caused the contamination of a shallow aquifer. The proposed ANN-based inverse problem-solving method can be summarised in two main steps. In the first step, an ANN is trained to solve the direct problem. After the training, the ANN generalization capability is exploited to estimate the contaminant concentration in pumping wells corresponding to a new pollution source. In the second step, the trained ANN is inverted in order to solve the inverse problem. In the following paragraph the methodology is deeply described.

2 Method Description

2.1 Training of the Neural Network Model

As highlighted in the previous section, ANNs have been widely used for the characterization of geological systems. The main advantage of this approach is that it is possible to study the behavior of the system without having an analytical model of it. Many different neural networks techniques are proposed in literature, depending on the specific problem at hand.

In particular, the Multi Layer Perceptrons (MLPs) ANNs used in this work, can be trained to imitate the system under study, seen as a dynamic input-output system. To this end, a suitable number of input-output pairs have to be generated to form the training set, and then the ANN is trained to associate the corresponding patterns. In this study, the Neural Network Toolbox of Matlab has been used.

The MLP is structured in layers of neurons (Fig. 1), the first being the Input Layer, and the last one the Output Layer. These are the only mandatory layers of the MLP. The intermediate layers (Hidden Layers) are the seat of the nonlinearity of the network, and they represent the degrees of freedom. In general, MLPs could have whichever number of layers, but it has been demonstrated that an MLP with only one hidden layer is a universal approximator (Cybenko 1989). For this reason, in this paper, the MLPs are considered having only one hidden layer without further specification. MLPs have the twofold advantage of using transcendent functions and of determining the parameters by means of examples. This second property makes it possible to develop a model of the system without an analytical formalization but simply based on a suitable set of input/output pairs of example patterns.

The features of the developed ANN depend on the nature of the analyzed problems and there are no theoretical guidelines for determining the best way out. The model is specific to the system under consideration and it cannot be built a priori.

The training of the ANN consists in applying a learning rule that modifies the weights of the connections based on the difference between the calculated and the desired output of the network. The aim of the training is to make the ANN able to

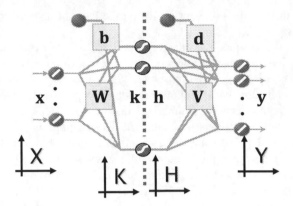

Fig. 1. Algebraic structure of the MLP neural network

generalize the acquired information, i.e. to give the correct output even for examples not included in the training set.

This aspect is crucial for the application described in this work, where the aim is to reconstruct the input by inverting the trained ANN.

2.2   Neural Network Model Inversion

The trained neural network has inside it all the required information to make a model of the input-output relationship. We can leverage on such information to solve the inverse problem, which consists in determining the contaminant source that correspond to a given evolution of the contaminant concentration in the pumping wells. To this end, let's consider the equations system that represents the algebraic input-output relation implemented by the neural network:

$$\begin{array}{ll} a) \\ b) \\ c) \end{array} \left\{ \begin{array}{l} \mathbf{W} \cdot x + \mathbf{b} = k \\ h = \sigma(k) \\ \mathbf{V} \cdot h + \mathbf{d} = y \end{array} \right. \tag{1}$$

where capital letters represent matrices and lower case letters represent vectors, more in details x and y are the input and the output vectors respectively, k and h are auxiliary variables that respectively represent the input and the output of the hidden layer, $\mathbf{W}$ is the weights matrix of the first layer of connections and $\mathbf{b}$ is the corresponding bias vector, $\mathbf{V}$ is the weights matrix of the second layer of connections and $\mathbf{d}$ is the corresponding bias vector, and finally $\sigma(\cdot)$ is the monotonic nonlinear activation function of the hidden layer. From (1) it can be seen that the first and the third equations are linear, while the nonlinearity of the network is due the second equation, which is a set of decoupled invertible equations.

To handle the inversion problem, it is convenient to define the geometrical spaces where the single variables are described. Let's indicate with $\mathbf{X}$ the space where the input of the network is defined, $\mathbf{K}$ the input space of the hidden layer, $\mathbf{H}$ the output space of the hidden layer, and finally $\mathbf{Y}$ the output space of the whole neural network.

In Fig. 1, the defined parameters and variables are represented.

The objective of the inversion problem is to find the input vector $\mathbf{x}^*$ corresponding to a given output vector $\mathbf{y}^*$, namely the source of contaminant which corresponds to a given (measured) contaminant concentration time series at the pumping wells.

According to the precision and the sensitivity of the trained neural network, the target output $\mathbf{y}^*$ has to be assigned with a suitable margin. If the network is highly sensitive, a small deviation of the output could cause a large displacement of the inverted solution. On the other hand, if the model is not precise, a large margin has to be considered. Let's assume now that a proper margin has been determined, which combines the two conflicting requirements. Therefore, the inverse problem can be formulated as:

$$\text{find } \mathbf{x}^* \ni \mathbf{y}^* - \varepsilon \leq \mathrm{NN}(\mathbf{x}^*) \leq \mathbf{y}^* + \varepsilon \tag{2}$$

where $\mathbf{y} = \mathrm{NN}(\mathbf{x})$ is the output of the neural network calculated for the input vector $\mathbf{x}$, and ε is the tolerance of the output. The constraints in (2) are linear, and they can be globally expressed in the following simplified notation:

$$\mathbf{A} \cdot \mathbf{y} \leq \mathbf{a} \tag{3}$$

where $\mathbf{A}$ is the matrix of the coefficients and $\mathbf{a}$ is the constant term vector.

According to (1.c), the (3) can be reported in the space $\mathbf{H}$:

$$\mathbf{A} \cdot (\mathbf{V} \cdot \boldsymbol{h} + \mathbf{d}) \leq \mathbf{a} \tag{4}$$

At the same time, the vector $\boldsymbol{h}$ is the output of a saturating function (sigmoid), therefore, to be inverted its components must be within the interval of feasibility. Furthermore, a saturated value of the sigmoidal function makes the inversion undetermined, therefore the bounds of the $\boldsymbol{h}$ are assigned with a certain margin η:

$$\mathbf{h}_{min} - \eta \leq \boldsymbol{h} \leq \mathbf{h}_{max} - \eta \tag{5}$$

Both (4) and (5) are linear constraints, therefore for sake of simplicity we will merge them into a unique linear inequalities system:

$$\mathbf{C} \cdot \boldsymbol{h} \leq \mathbf{c} \tag{6}$$

where $\mathbf{C}$ is the matrix of the coefficients and $\mathbf{c}$ is the constant term vector.

The inequality (6) represents the first check-point in inverting the target $\mathbf{y}^*$. In fact, in order to continue in backpropagating the target, the linear domain represented in (6) must be not empty. Well-known Linear Programming algorithms can be used to perform this check and, in case the domain is not empty, they return a feasible point of the domain. The possibility to find feasible points strictly depends on how the neural network has been trained. If the training set surrounds the target point, it is likely that the target can be obtained as the interpolation, although nonlinear, of the training set. In the present problem, the input-output relationship is nonlinear, therefore the training set could not have the proper characteristics at the first try. Nonetheless, resorting to the inversion procedure, it is possible to generate new training examples that are more and more close to the target point, so that this is a feasible output of the network, and then the domain (6) is not empty.

Such feasible point can be translated from the space **H** to the space **K** by using the Eq. (1.b). Provided that the activation function of the hidden neurons is monotonic, the point k, in the space **K**, corresponding to the feasible point is unique. The vector k, together with the bias b, plays the role of constant term in the linear equation system (1.a). Depending on the structure of the neural network, the (1.a) could be underdetermined (the hidden neurons are less than the input neurons), determined (equal number of neurons in the input and in the hidden layer), overdetermined (the input neurons are less than the hidden neurons). In most part of cases, the third case occurs, as the number of hidden neurons is directly connected to the degrees of freedom of the neural network. This occurred also in the present study, therefore it will be assumed as working hypothesis.

In the case of the coefficients matrix **W** in (1.a) is full-rank, the unique vector x which minimizes the minimum squared error can be assumed as solution of the system. This vector is the solution of the following linear equation system:

$$\mathbf{W}^T\mathbf{W} \cdot x = \mathbf{W}^T(k - \mathbf{b}) \tag{7}$$

The Eq. (7) is obtained by the (1.a) by multiplying per the transposal of the coefficients matrix, and it has equal number of unknowns and equations. By assuming that **W** is full-rank, the coefficients matrix $[\mathbf{W}^T\mathbf{W}]$ is invertible, and then the solution can be determined as:

$$x = [\mathbf{W}^T\mathbf{W}]^{-1} \cdot \mathbf{W}^T(k - \mathbf{b}) \tag{8}$$

The vector x is the first proposal of the inversion problem solution $\mathbf{x}^*$. In general, the solution x of the (8) cannot match perfectly the vector k, as the system is overdetermined. If the neural network is well-trained, we know that a vector k^* obtainable from $\mathbf{x}^*$ exists, but in case the hidden layer has more neurons of the output layer, there are infinite solutions of the Eq. (1.c), while if the neural network is well trained, the solution $\mathbf{x}^*$ of the inverse problem must be unique. In practice, one needs to find the intersection between the domain (6), which in the space **K** writes:

$$\mathbf{C} \cdot \sigma(k) \leq \mathbf{c} \tag{9}$$

and the subspace of **K** generated by x by means of (1.a). Several procedures are available to find such intersection, which in terms of x writes:

$$\mathbf{C} \cdot \sigma(\mathbf{W} \cdot x + \mathbf{b}) \leq \mathbf{c} \tag{10}$$

In this study, a simple first-order approach has been applied, which approximates the left-side hand of (10) with a linear function:

$$\mathbf{C} \cdot \sigma(\hat{x}) + \mathbf{C} \cdot \mathbf{diag}[\sigma'(\hat{x})] \cdot \mathbf{W} \cdot dx \leq \mathbf{c} \tag{11}$$

where $\sigma'(\hat{x})$ is the derivative of the activation function calculated in the current point, and dx is the increment of the variable. The (11) is used to seek iteratively one point of the domain (10), which will be a solution $\mathbf{x}^*$ of the inverse problem.

Remarks. In general, some trials are needed to obtain the required precision. This is mainly due to the fact that the training set at the beginning is not properly surrounding the target point, and then the trained neural network is not enough precise around that point. As a consequence, even if the output error of the neural network is within the margins, the uncertainty on the inverted solution $\mathbf{x}^*$ could be unacceptable. In this case, the pair $[\mathbf{x}^*, NN(\mathbf{x}^*)]$ can be added to the training set and the neural network trained again. By iterating this procedure, the training set becomes more and more focused on the target point, and then more precise in approximating the input-output relationship around that region.

A second remark concerns the sensitivity of the input with respect to the output. The forward robustness of the network, which is an advantage when the neural model is used for the solution of the direct problem, is a drawback when one is interested to solve the inverse problem, especially when the problem at hand is the parameter identification, like in the present application. In fact, the forward robustness implies that a wide range of inputs yields the same output, which means in the present study that the configuration of the contaminant source has large margins of uncertainty. A complete analysis of these aspects is beyond the scope of this work, and then it will be a topic for future works.

3   Case Study

The performance of the proposed methodology has been evaluated by defining the behavior in time and space of the unknown punctual pollution source of a generic phreatic aquifer.

3.1   Groundwater Flow and Contaminant Transport Numerical Model

The data set of the input/output pairs of example patterns was been constructed through a coherent number of hydrogeological scenarios, based on a 3D model of the domain developed by Aswed (2008). The input patterns were made of the pollution source features in terms of the injection rates in the four hydrogeological layers. The output patterns were contaminant concentration observation data at 45 pumping wells. Sources and pumping wells are related by a bi-univocal relationship, meaning that any specific profile of pumping wells corresponds to one specific contaminant source behavior.

The numerical model represents a contaminated zone enclosed within a 3D domain of 6 km width, 20 km length, and about 110 m depth. The aquifer domain was discretized by using a 3D triangular prismatic grid with 25,388 nodes and 45,460 elements. According to the estimated geometry of the cross-sections (the landfill site was divided into eight zones by soil type) the domain is discretized into ten layers. The contaminant source is located in the first four layers having thicknesses, respectively, of 16 m, 4 m, 5 m, and 5 m from the top to the bottom. The volume of contaminated aquifer has been estimated in about 230–1,300 m^3 and the surface contaminant infiltration is about 7–37 m^2 assuming that the pollution depth is 35 m (Aswed 2008).

The 3D flux and contaminant transport numerical model used for constructing the patterns was calibrated using measured data of CCl4 concentration that were collected over 12 years (1992–2004) and simulations were performed for 1970 to 2024 (Vigouroux 1983; Aswed 2008).

To calculate the contaminant concentration in each pumping well we resort to the numerical simulation software TRACES (Transport or RadioActiver Elements in the Subsurface) developed by Hoteit and Ackerer (2003), that combines the mixed hybrid finite elements and discontinuous finite elements to solve the hydrodynamic state and mass transfer in the porous media.

The set of 292 input/output pairs of example patterns has been made derived from a random set of pollution sources behavior, and the corresponding contaminant concentration in pumping wells have been calculated by using TRACES.

The example patterns obtained with TRACES consist of 584 matrices of contaminant concentrations:

- 292 matrices corresponding to the features of the pollution sources. These has dimensions [11 520 × 4] where 11 520 represents the time (days) and 4 represents the layers in the source location.
- 292 matrices corresponding to contaminant concentration in the monitoring wells. These has dimensions of [4 000 × 45]; where 4 000 represents the values of contaminant concentration measured each 5 days (for a total time of simulation of 20.000 days) and 45 represents the monitoring wells in the domain. In this case it was taken only one value of contaminant concentration in monitoring wells each five days, for computational needs and this time step could not be increased, due to numerical criterion.

The 292 input matrices and 292 output matrices have been reorganized to form two matrices which describe the whole training set: one for the input and one for the output. Input and output matrices were too large to be processed through the ANN, so a data pre-processing has been performed in order to drastically reduce their dimension.

3.2 Training of the Neural Network Model

The system under study is the numerical model described in Sect. 3.1. The target was constructed by assuming a concentration of contaminant in the 4 layers under the origin for a period of 20 000 days (about 54 years). A homogeneous concentration is assumed in each layer, and also it is assumed that the concentration decays exponentially with the time. In this sense, the evolution of the source is completely described by 8 parameters, corresponding to 2 parameters of the exponential trend associated to each layer.

By means of the software TRACES, the propagation of the contaminant in the underground of the modeled area has been simulated for a period of time of 20 000 days with a time step of 5 days. The curve of the concentration has been then extracted in correspondence of the 45 pumping wells of the model (see Sect. 3.1).

In Fig. 2, the time diagram of the contaminant concentration in a well is reported. It looks like a Maxwell-Boltzmann curve, which can be assumed to approximate it. Such curve can be completely described with 3 parameters (occurrence of the max, maximum value and full width at half maximum), which can be used as features to describe the single curve. Nonetheless, the reconstruction of the time diagrams at the wells is not an objective of this study, therefore any set of features which univocally identify the curves of the dataset could be properly used. By comparing several curves obtained in the simulation it has been found that only 2 parameters, day of occurrence and averaged concentration, are sufficient to identify univocally the behavior at the wells. Taking into account that 45 pumping wells are foreseen in the case study, the pattern which represents the behavior of the wells in a single case consists of 90 components. This number should be strongly reduced to suitably train the neural network.

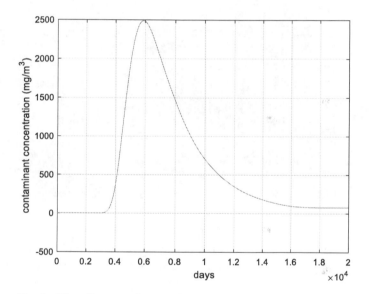

Fig. 2. Time diagram of contaminant measured at the pumping well

A training set of 292 examples has been created to train the neural network. To this end, a random set of sources has been created, and the corresponding evolutions have been calculated by means of TRACES. In the real cases, the creation of the training set is performed in a blind way, because only the measurements at the pumping wells are available. Therefore, it is possible that some outliers are included in the set, which could negatively affect the training. Such examples have to be detected and removed by the database. In order to reduce the volume of the data, the Principal Component Analysis has been applied to the 292 examples. As it is well known, the covariance matrix eigenvalues give a measure of the variance along each principal component, therefore it is possible to select a subset of components with a chosen variance. By dropping a fraction of variance of the distribution equal to 10^{-6}, the 90 components have been reduced to 6. On the basis of the distribution of these features, it is possible to detect outliers, if there are any. In Fig. 3 the outliers detection method is shown. The first feature of the example No. 193 and the second feature of the example No. 51 are much different from the other ones, which implies that in normalizing the features the dynamic is lost, and the feature will be completely useless for the model. As a consequence, these examples have to be removed by the training set, and new examples have to be generated. A good strategy to define additional examples is to perform a convex combination of the examples whose output is near the target.

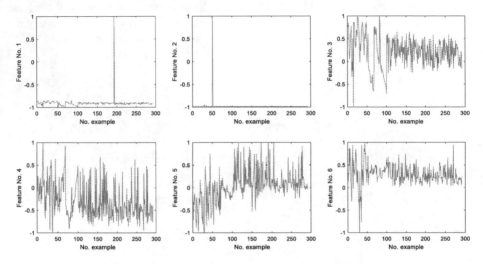

Fig. 3. Outliers detection by means of analysis of the features

The absence of outliers facilitates the training of the network. Several trainings, with different number of hidden neurons have been performed, in order to guarantee a good precision in reproducing the training set and in approximating the validation set. Finally, the structure assumed for the inversion has an 8-30-6 layout. In all the cases a number of epochs less than 100 have been sufficient to stabilize the value of the performance.

3.3 Neural Network Model Inversion

The inversion algorithm described in Sect. 2.2 has been applied to the trained neural network. An example belonging to the test set has been considered. The output domain (Eq. (2)) is defined as a neighborhood with margin 10^{-2} of the target to be inverted. This margin has been assumed on the basis of the error observed in the training set. In case no solution is found, this margin could be relaxed. The target vector and the margin completely define the feasibility domain of the output, according to Eq. (3). By means of the Eqs. (4) and (5), this domain is translated in the space **H**, then in the space **K** (Eq. (1.b)), and finally in the input space (Eq. (8)). By resorting to the Eq. (11), the solution has been iteratively modified in order to fulfil the constraints (2). The sought solution is the time diagram of the pollutant concentration in the four underground layers. As the validation set has been created by running the FEM model, the exact solution is available for comparison. In the Fig. 4 the actual source is compared with that one obtained with the inversion procedure.

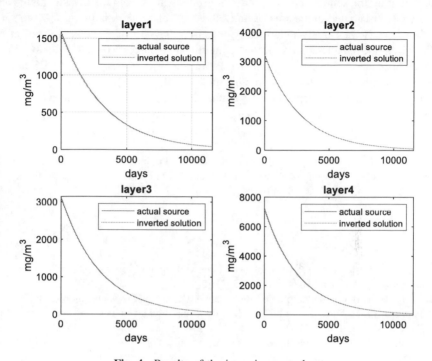

Fig. 4. Results of the inversion procedure

All the cases of training, validation and test sets assume by hypothesis an exponential trend in the source, and the neural model has been structured as a consequence. More specifically, the inputs of the neural network are the amplitude and the exponential coefficient of an exponential curve. For this reason, the exponential trend of the inverted solution is a result easy to obtain. To better evaluate the performance of the inversion it could be more meaningful to evaluate the percentage error of the inverted solution with respect to the exact one. In Table 1 this comparison is reported.

Table 1.

Solutions	Layer 1		Layer 2		Layer 3		Layer 4	
	Amp.	Coeff. $\times 10^{-3}$	Amp.	Coeff. $\times 10^{-3}$	Amp.	Coeff. $\times 10^{-3}$	Amp.	Coeff. $\times 10^{-3}$
Sought	1561	−3.10	3190	−3.59	3100	−3.38	7150	−3.76
Inverted	1590	−3.09	3213	−3.57	3139	−3.38	7270	−3.75
Err%	1.84	0.45	0.72	0.66	1.24	0.13	1.67	0.24

4   Conclusion

In this paper, a neural network-based method is proposed to solve the inverse problem of determining the source of contaminant of groundwaters from the measurements on a set of wells distributed in the area of interest. A neural network is first trained to solve the direct problem, namely determining the time diagram of the contaminant at the wells given the characteristics of the contaminant source. To this end, a suitable number of scenarios have been simulated by means of the software TRACES and the corresponding time evolution of contaminant concentration at the wells is determined. Successively, a scenario represented by time diagrams measured at the wells is presented to the previously trained neural network, and the corresponding input is determined. This input represents the solution of the inverse problem.

Acknowledgements. Authors would like to thank Prof. Philippe Ackerer from Laboratory of HYdrology and GEochemistry of Strasbourg (LHyGes - UMR 7517) of Strasbourg (France) for allowing the use of the TRACES software.

References

Ajmera, T.K., Rastogi, A.K.: Artificial neural network application on estimation of aquifer transmissivity. J. Spatial Hydrol. **8**(2), 15–31 (2008)

Aswed, T.: Modélisation de la pollution de la nappe d'alsace par solvants chlores. Ph.D. thesis, Université Louis Pasteur, Institut de Mécanique des Fluides et des Solides, UMR-CNRS 7507, Strasbourg, France (2008)

Carcangiu, S., Cardelli, E., Faba, A., Fanni, A., Montisci, A., Quondam, S.: Moving vector hysteron model identification based on neural network inversion. In: 2016 IEEE 2nd International Forum on Research and Technologies for Society and Industry Leveraging a Better Tomorrow, RTSI 2016, art. no. 7740638 (2016)

Carcangiu, S., Fanni, A., Montisci, A.: Electric capacitance tomography for nondestructive testing of standing trees. Int. J. Numer. Model. **32**, e2252 (2019). https://doi.org/10.1002/jnm.2252

Carrera, J., Alcolea, A., Medina, A., Hidalgo, J., Slooten, J.: Inverse problem in hydrogeology. Hydrogeol. J. **13**, 206–222 (2005)

Cybenko, G.: Approximation by superposition of a sigmoid function. Math. Control Signals Syst. **2**, 303–314 (1989)

Directive 2004/35/CE European Parliament and of the Council of 21 April 2004 on environmental liability with regard to the prevention and remedying of environmental damage. Official Journal of the European Communities L 143/56, 30 April 2004

Fanni, A., Uras, G., Usai, M., Zedda, M.K.: Neural Network for monitoring. Groundwater. In: Fifth International Conference on Hidroinformatics, Cardiff, UK, 1–5 July 2002, pp. 687–692 (2002)

Foddis, M.L.: Application of artificial neural networks in hydrogeology: identification of unknown pollution sources in contaminated aquifers. Ph.D. thesis, University of Cagliari and University of Strasbourg (2011)

Foddis, M.L., Ackerer, P., Montisci, A., Uras, G.: Ann-based approach for the estimation aquifer pollutant source behaviour, water science and technology. Water Sci. Technol.: Water Supply **15**(6), 1285–1294 (2015a)

Foddis, M.L., Matzeu, A., Montisci, A., Uras, G.: Application of three different methods to evaluate the nitrate pollution of groundwater in the Arborea plain (Sardinia - Italy). Rendiconti Online Società Geologica Italiana **35**, 136–139 (2015b)

Foddis, M.L., Ackerer, P., Montisci, A., Uras, G.: Polluted aquifer inverse problem solution using artificial neural networks. AQUA Mundi **Am07054**, 015–021 (2013)

Foddis, M.L., Montisci, A., Trablesi, F., Uras, G.: An ANN-MLP based approach for the estimation of nitrate contamination. Water Sci. Technol.: Water Supply **19**(7), 1911–1917 (2019)

Foddis, M.L., Matzeu, A., Montisci, A., Uras, G.: The Arborea plain (Sardinia-Italy) nitrate pollution evaluation. Italian J. Eng. Geol. Environ. (Specialissue1), 67–76 (2017)

Hoteit, H., Acherer, P.: TRACES user's guide V 1.00. Institut mécanique des fluides et des solides de Strasbourg (2003)

Jeihouni, E., Eslamian, S., Mohammadi, M., Zareian, M.J.: Simulation of groundwater level fluctuations in response to main climate parameters using a wavelet–ANN hybrid technique for the Shabestar Plain, Iran. Environ. Earth Sci. **78**(10), 293 (2019)

Mahar, P.S., Datta, B.: Identification of pollution sources in transient groundwater systems. Water Resour. Manag. **14**, 209–227 (2000)

Mousavi, S.F., Amiri, M.J.: Modelling nitrate concentration of groundwater using adaptive neural-based fuzzy inference system. Soil Water Resour. **7**(2), 73–83 (2012)

Nourani, V., Mousavi, S., Sadikoglu, F.: Conjunction of artificial intelligence-meshless methods for contaminant transport modeling in porous media: an experimental case study. J. Hydroinformatics **20**(5), 1163–1179 (2018)

Nourani, V., Mousavi, S., Dabrowska, D., Sadikoglu, F.: Conjunction of radial basis function interpolator and artificial intelligence models for time-space modeling of contaminant transport in porous media. J. Hydrol. **548**, 569–587 (2017a)

Nourani, V., Mousavi, S., Sadikoglu, F., Singh, V.P.: Experimental and AI-based numerical modeling of contaminant transport in porous media. J. Contam. Hydrol. **205**, 78–95 (2017b)

Nourani, V., Hosseini, B.A., Adamowski, J., Kisi, O.: Applications of hybrid wavelet–artificial intelligence models in hydrology. J. Hydrol. **514**, 358–377 (2014)

Ostad-Ali-Askari, K., Shayannejad, M., Ghorbanizadeh-Kharazi, H.: Artificial neural network for modeling nitrate pollution of groundwater in marginal area of Zayandeh-rood River, Isfahan, Iran. KSCE J. Civil Eng. **21**(1), 134–140 (2016)

Rajanayaka, C., Samarasinghe, S., Kulasiri, D.: Solving the inverse problem in stochastic groundwater modelling with artificial neural networks. In: Rizzoli, A.E., Jakeman, A.J. (eds.) Integrated Assessment and Decision Support. International Environmental Modelling and Software Society, Manno, Switzerland, vol. 2 (2002)

Sathish Kumar, S., Mageshkumar, P., Santhanam, H., Stalin John, M.R., Amal Raj, S.: A new logic-based model to predict nitrates in groundwater using Artificial Neural Network (ANN). Pollution Res. **32**(3), 635–641 (2013)

Scintu, C.: Reti neurali artificiali: una applicazione nello studio di acquiferi contaminati. Ph.D. thesis, University of Cagliari, Italy (2004)

Secci, R., Laura Foddis, M., Mazzella, A., Montisci, A., Uras, G.: Artificial neural networks and kriging method for slope geomechanical characterization. In: Lollino, G., et al. (eds.) Engineering Geology for Society and Territory - Volume 2, pp. 1357–1361. Springer, Cham (2015). https://doi.org/10.1007/978-3-319-09057-3_239

Singh, R.M., Datta, B.: Artificial neural network modeling for identification of unknown pollution sources in groundwater with partially missing concentration observation data. Water Resour. Manag. **21**(3), 557–572 (2007). https://doi.org/10.1007/s11269-006-9029-z

Singh, R.M., Datta, B.: Groundwater pollution source and simultaneous parameter estimation using pattern matching by artificial neural network. Environ. Forensics **5**(3), 143–153 (2004)

Singh, R.M., Datta, B., Jain, A.: Identification of unknown groundwater pollution sources using artificial neural networks. J. Water Resour. Plann. Manag. **130**(6), 506–514 (2004)

Smith, M., Cross, K., Paden, M., Laben, P.: Spring - managing groundwater sustainably. IUCN (2016). ISBN 978-2-8317-1789-0

Tanty, R., Desmukh, T.S.: Application of artificial neural network in hydrology-a review. Int. J. Eng. Tech. Res. **4**(6), 184–188 (2015)

Vigouroux, P., Vançon, J.P., Drogue, C.: Conception d'un model de propagation de pollution en nappe aquifer-Exemple d'application à la nappe du Rhin. J. Hydrol. **64**(1–4), 267–279 (1983)

World Health Organization (WHO): Protecting Groundwater for Health - Understanding the drinking-water catchment (2017)

Yaman, F., Yakhno, V., Potthast, R.: A survey on inverse problems for applied sciences. Math. Problems Eng. (2013). https://doi.org/10.1155/2013/976837

Zio, E.: Approaching the inverse problem of parameter estimation in groundwater models by means of artificial neural networks. Progress Nuclear Energy **31**(3), 303–315 (1997)

Geophysical Modelling of a Sedimentary Portion of the White Volta Basin (Ghana)

Giulio Vignoli[1,2(✉)] 🆔, Elikplim Abla Dzikunoo[3] 🆔,
Flemming Jørgensen[4] 🆔, Sandow Mark Yidana[3],
Bruce Banoeng-Yakubo[3], and Peng Bai[1]

[1] University of Cagliari, Cagliari, Italy
gvignoli@unica.it
[2] GEUS, Aarhus, Denmark
[3] University of Ghana, Accra, Ghana
[4] Central Denmark Region, Viborg, Denmark

Abstract. This research deals with the essential steps carried out during the processing and inversion of the airborne time-domain electromagnetic (TEM) data used within the framework of the GhanAqua project – aiming at the groundwater development for sustainable agriculture in the White Volta basin in Ghana.

The processing of pre-existing airborne TEM data has been performed with the state-of-the-art methodologies. In this respect, (1) the minimum possible gate-dependent lateral stacking between adjacent soundings has been performed for the preparation of the data; (2) a 1D nonlinear forward modelling has been used for the inversion of the stacked data; (3) even if the forward modelling was 1D, the data have been inverted by spatially constraining the adjacent models (in a pseudo-2/3D fashion). We adopted an iterative approach in which the processing and inversion parameters, and the type of stabilizer utilized, have been decided after an a-posteriori analysis. Hence, after every inversion, the results have been discussed with the geologists (1) to assess, at least qualitatively, the uncertainty of the solution features and (2) to, as much as possible, include prior geological knowledge into the geophysical analysis.

The new geophysical insights detected geological features that might be interpreted as glacial paleovalleys. If confirmed, those structures can have a significant impact in terms of their socio-economic relevance (i.e. as groundwater reservoirs); as well as from a scientific point of view (as they would require rethinking the stratigraphy of the area). In addition, these kind of Sturtian glacial evidences in West Africa could support the Snowball Earth hypothesis.

Keywords: Airborne transient electromagnetics · Sparse regularization · Conductivity depth image · Snowball earth · Paleovalleys

1 The Area and the Data

The investigated area is a sedimentary part of the White Volta basin (Fig. 1), with special focus on the project area: the Nasia Catchment – located in the north-eastern part of Ghana, between latitudes 9°55'N and 10°40'N, and longitude 1°05'W and 0°15'E.

© Springer Nature Switzerland AG 2020
O. Gervasi et al. (Eds.): ICCSA 2020, LNCS 12255, pp. 891–902, 2020.
https://doi.org/10.1007/978-3-030-58820-5_64

Large portions of Ghana have been studied by using several airborne geophysical methodologies during the European Union sponsored, Mining Sector Support Programme, from 2005 to 2010. These data include three regional surveys performed by Fugro Airborne Surveys and consisting of: a magnetic and gamma-ray spectrometry survey (line-spacing 500 m, alt. 120 m); a gravity survey (line-spacing 5000 m, alt.

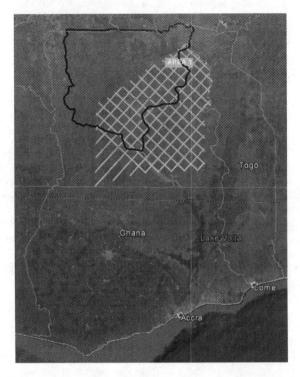

Fig. 1. Map of Ghana with the White Volta basin (within the black frame) together with the flight lines considered in the present research.

860 m); and a magnetic and TEM survey (line-spacing 20000 m). In addition, several higher resolution TEM surveys were performed, in which the line-spacing was significantly smaller (200 m). In Fig. 1, the flight-lines from the TEM surveys that have been considered in the present study are shown in grey. Hence, in this research, by the kind concession of the Ghana Geological Survey Authority (GGSA), and within the framework of the Memorandum of Understanding, signed on 23/03/2015 between the University of Ghana (UoG) and GGSA, we had the chance to work on part of the available regional dataset and on the high-resolution measurements collected over an area (Area 1) partially overlapping the Nasia catchment (Fig. 1). The airborne TEM data were collected by using a GEOTEM 20-channel multicoil system, with a transmitter area of 231 m^2 and 6 turns, at a nominal height of 120 m. The receiver was ~ 130 m behind the center of the transmitting loop. The pulse width was 4066 μs, and the off-time 15834 μs. The nominal transmitter current was 560 A. During the

surveys all three components (X, Y, Z) were recorded. More details about the specifications of the data collection can be found in [1, 2].

The contractor supplied the raw data together with the associated Conductivity Depth Images [3]. Conductivity Depth Imaging (CDI) is a very effective tool for the detection of potential mineral targets. In fact, CDI provides a direct and fast translation of the measured data into electrical resistivity parameters with very high lateral resolution and with no need for a proper inversion or complex forward modelling of the underlying physical system [4]. However, since the GhanAqua project aims at the reconstruction of the geology and, in turn, of the hydrogeology, of the area, it was crucial to verify alternative approaches capable of retrieving relatively small resistivity variations while preserving the spatial coherence of the subsurface features. Thus, it has been necessary to verify the performances of an actual inversion of the data via a 1D nonlinear forward modelling code, spatially constraining the adjacent 1D resistivity models.

The raw data supplied by the contractor as the final deliverable were B-field data; besides the benefits discussed in [5], the choice of B-field has some additional advantages in terms of signal-to-noise ratio; in fact, the B-field is associated with data integration over time, that corresponds to some sort of data stacking in time. Moreover, to have a fair comparison between the CDIs and the inversion results (in order to properly assess what can be gained by a geomodelling-oriented processing and inversion), the original B-field data (and not the dB/dt measurements) have been re-processed and utilized.

1.1 The First Processing Step: Lateral Stacking

Clearly, the data stacking can (should) be performed, not only in time (by considering the B-field measurements), but also in the other "direction", that is, spatially, along the line of flight. In the workflow implemented in this research, a moving window with a varying width depending on the considered time-gate has been used in a fashion similar to the one detailed, for example, in [10, 11] (in the latter, the stacking width is frequency-dependent). Hence, we used (i) a narrower stacking width for the early gates and (ii) a wider one for late gates. This allowed a maximization of the lateral resolution at shallow layers (early gates), and an increase of the robustness of the signal at depth (late gates) where, in any case, a larger spatial footprint is due to the physics of the method. In practice, the size of the window for the Z-component of the B-field was chosen to increase linearly from around 8 s, for the first gate (4.5 ms), to approximately 20 s, for the 11th gate (11.563 ms), and to remain constant for the last four gates. Only the Z and X components have been processed (using the same settings). Out of the 20 measured channels, after the lateral stacking, 15 channels have been used for the Z-component, and 12 for the X-component. The large number of channels that could be used demonstrate once again the very good quality of the data collected in the first place by Fugro. A sample of processed measurements is shown in Fig. 2.

The source waveform is quite stable in shape, whereas the same is not always true for the amplitude (Fig. 3). Even within the same flight, variations significantly larger than 10 A may occur, and they can be much larger if different flights are considered (while the nominal current is 560 A, the actual current peak can vary from 539 to 566 A

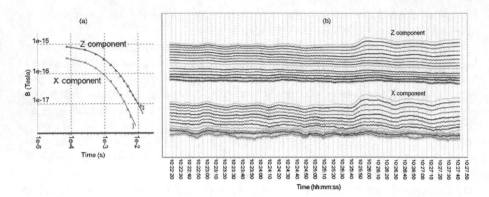

Fig. 2. (a) Example of the Z- and X-component records; the vertical bars represent the stacked data with their uncertainty; the solid lines show the calculated responses from the inversion model (not shown). (b) A sample of the B-field measurements obtained after the application of the spatial stacking procedure (moving window with gate-dependent width).

from flight to flight.). In any case, this variability has been properly taken into account during the inversion.

2   The Inversion

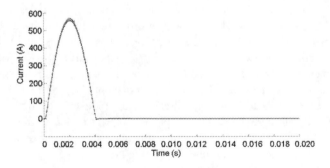

Fig. 3. Example of waveforms for the flight 71 in the Area 1.

Currently, 1D forward modelling algorithms which incorporate all the characteristics of the instrument's transfer function are efficient and popular choices [6]. However, 2D forward modelling codes [7], and even 3D [8] approaches, are becoming more and more frequently used. In this respect, there are many examples in literature which discuss the advantages of inversion schemes based on 1D or 2–3D forward modelling (e.g. [9, 12, 13]). The choice of a specific forward modelling is largely determined by the computational resources available. In fact, even with 1D algorithms, days, or even weeks, might be necessary to invert large airborne datasets. Thus, for practical reasons, here, a 1D inversion approach has been used.

The inversion scheme employed includes different kinds of regularization to cope with the inherent ill-posedness of the problem. Testing different inversion approaches (each incorporating different prior information) allowed the implementation of an iterative geological-geophysical strategy for the inclusion of the geological knowledge into the inversion process and, to some extent, for the qualitative estimation of the uncertainty (Fig. 4). Even if the forward modelling used is 1D, the adjacent resistivity models were mutually constrained. In this way, it was possible to ensure some degree of lateral coherence between the neighboring 1D models and, also, within each individual 1D model. Thus, the regularization acted in both vertical and horizontal directions. The lateral and vertical constraints have been defined via the regularization term in the objective function minimized during the inversion. Several inversions were performed by using (i) minimum gradient support (MGS), (ii) L1-norm (MGN-L1), and (iii) minimum gradient L2-norm (MGN) regularizations, with different weights for the stabilizer.

So, the considered objective function $P_s(d_{obs}, m, \alpha)$ consists of the sum of the data misfit term, $\phi(d_{obs})$, and the stabilizer, $s(m)$ – with m being the resistivity model to be reconstructed and d_{obs} the observed data:

$$P_s(d_{obs}, m, \alpha) = \phi(d_{obs}) + \alpha s(m); \tag{1}$$

the factor α controls the importance/weight of the prior information (i.e. $s(m)$) with respect to the data. The data misfit $\phi(d_{obs})$ has been chosen equal to the $\frac{1}{N}\sqrt{\sum_{i=1}^{N}\left(\frac{d_{obs}-d_{calc}}{\sigma_d}\right)_i^2}$, in which: σ_d is an estimation of the uncertainty in the measurement, d_{calc} is the response calculated from m, and N is the number of measurements. α is chosen a-posteriori in order to get $\phi(d_{obs}) \sim 1$. Clearly, the (unique and stable) selected solution m depends on the choice of the stabilizing term $s(m)$ [14–19]. In this study, three different kinds of $s(m)$ have been tested:

- minimum gradient norm (MGN), $s_{MGN}(m) = \left\|\frac{\Delta m}{\sigma_m}\right\|_{L2}$;

- minimum gradient L1-norm (MGN-L1), $s_{MGN-L1}(m) = \left\|\frac{\Delta m}{\sigma_m}\right\|_{L1}$;

- minimum gradient support (MGS), $s_{MGS}(m) = \sum_{k=1}^{M}\frac{\left(\frac{\Delta m}{\sigma_m}\right)_k^2}{\left(\frac{\Delta m}{\sigma_m}\right)_k^2 + 1}$, in which, M is the number of model parameters.

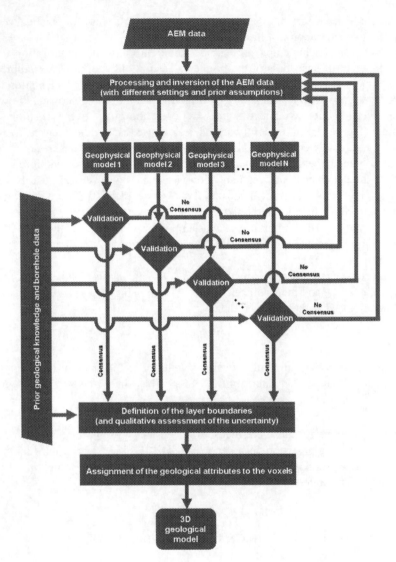

Fig. 4. The flowchart describing the iterative process between geologists and geophysicists aiming at the development of the geomodel integrating all the diverse pieces of knowledge (geophysical, but also prior geological information, wells, etc.) into a coherent picture.

3   The Results

The first, very evident, difference obtained through the new reprocessing and inversion workflow is clear when we compare the original CDIs against the new inversions (see, for example, Fig. 5 and Fig. 6).

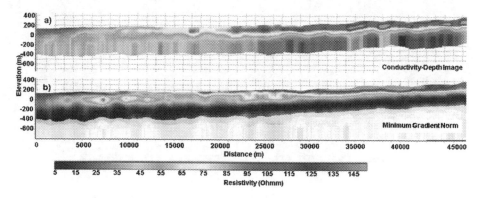

Fig. 5. Comparison between the original CDI (a) and one of the new (Minimum Gradient Norm) results (b).

In particular, as expected, the CDI results are generally characterized by higher lateral variability, since every individual B-field curve is mapped into the associated 1D resistivity model independently, whereas the MGN regularization (as it minimizes, the vertical and lateral variations of the resistivity model) imposes some degree of spatial coherence. Considering, for example, Fig. 5a, as discussed in detail in the recent [20], CDI's lateral heterogeneity is evident not only in the shallow, right, portion of the section, where resistive inclusions are evident, but, also, at depth, along the flight line, where spurious lateral oscillations of the electrical properties are visible. On the other hand, the MGN result in the same figure (Fig. 5b) is laterally more consistent. Despite the lateral coherence of the MGN result, the reconstruction of resistive heterogeneities – at a distance of approximately 10 km, well-separated from the resistive superficial unit by an evident conductive formation (very differently from what is retrieved by the CDI) – is not prevented.

These might appear as minor details, but not when a quantitative geological modelling needs to be performed. This is the case every time a geomodel needs to capture the essential geological features to be included in a subsequent effective hydrogeological simulation. In this respect, it is worth mentioning the interesting resistive features embedded into the conductive surroundings and located between 20 and 30 km: they have been interpreted as possible glacial paleovalleys. The impacts of these possible geological structures are not only interesting in the scientific sense – as their existence would require rediscussing the current regional stratigraphy and support the occurrence of Sturtian glaciation in the West Africa craton (compatible with the Neoproterozoic Snowball Earth hypothesis) – but also from a hydrogeological point of view since they can act as good groundwater reservoirs and they would definitely play a big role as preferential paths for the groundwater modelling.

The MGN-L1 regularization (an example is shown in Fig. 6b) provides results, again, significantly different from the corresponding CDI sections (Fig. 6a), and, at the same time, quite blocky. This is, indeed, not surprising as the L1-norm favors the retrieval of sparse solutions [21].

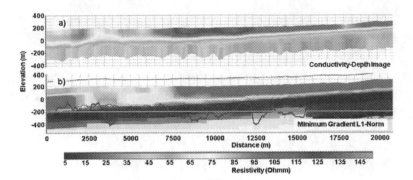

Fig. 6. Comparison between the original CDI (a) and one of the new Minimum Gradient L1-norm results (b).

Similar conclusions can be drawn by using the MGS regularization. In this respect, Fig. 7 shows a comparison between the (more standard) MGN and the MGS solutions [22].

Clearly, during the iterative geophysical-geological interpretation (Fig. 4), only the inversion results characterized by similar levels of data misfits have been considered and compared.

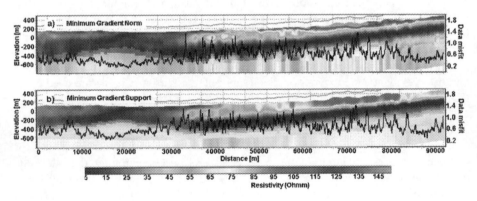

Fig. 7. Comparison between a smooth (MGN) solution (a) and a sharp (MGS) result (b). The black lines show the data misfits.

For example, the solutions in Fig. 7 can be considered equivalent from a purely geophysical point of view (but, definitely, not in their possible geological interpretations) as the misfits between the calculated and observed data (black lines in panels (a) and (b) in Fig. 7) are comparable.

Not only the variability with respect to different regularization strategies, but also the sensitivity with respect to the possible choices of the σ_m values (in particular for the horizontal components of the model variation) when using the same stabilizer had to be tested. In this regard, for example, Fig. 8 and Fig. 9 demonstrate the effects of two

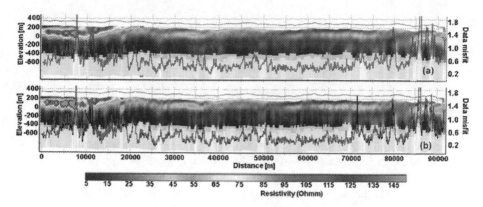

Fig. 8. Comparison between two smooth (MGN) solutions with different lateral constraints: tighter for (a) than for (b). The red line – panel (a) – represents the data misfit for the tighter case (for convenience, it is shown also in panel (b)); the black line is the data misfit for the solution in the panel (b).

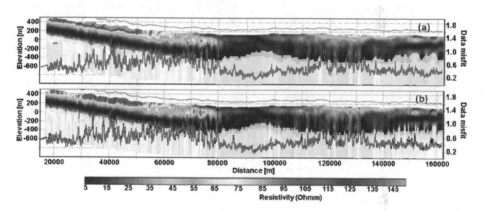

Fig. 9. Comparison between two smooth (MGN) solutions with different lateral constraints: tighter for (a) than for (b). The red line – panel (a) – represents the data misfit for the tighter case (for convenience, it is shown also in panel (b)); the black line is the data misfit for the solution in the panel (b).

different weights for the horizontal constraints. Again, by merely considering the geophysical data, it would not be possible to decide which one is the best as the data misfit associated with the two significantly different models are largely overlapping (black and red lines in Fig. 8b and Fig. 9b).

Concerning all the inversion results, it is worth noting the considerable depth of investigation (indicated as a white mask, for example, in both panels of Fig. 9); generally, the geophysical model parameters could be considered sensitive to the data down to the remarkable depth of ∼500 m. This, not only, demonstrates, once more, the quality of the original data, but, also, confirms that the survey was designed for deep exploration and not for high-resolution shallow investigations. Therefore, the new inversions provide important insights on the geological settings and highlight resistive, relatively shallow structures, possibly relevant as groundwater resources.

4 Conclusions

This research is intended to further elaborate on the recent results discussed in [20]. In [20], Dzikunoo et al. discuss the stratigraphic interpretation of reprocessed airborne electromagnetic data in the Nasia basin in Northern Ghana; here, we show some of the geophysical inversions performed in the sedimentary portion of the White Volta basin that were partially used for the construction of the geomodel of the Nasia basin.

In particular, we show how ill-posed the inversion problem is (considering the finite number of noisy measurements); we demonstrate how solutions, characterized by similar level of compatibility with the observed data, can be significantly different (with potentially large consequences in terms of subsequent geological interpretation). We used that large number of geophysical models for the effective implementation of the flowchart in Fig. 4. Thus, since the different geophysical results are fitting the data equally well, from a mere geophysical perspective, they should be all considered satisfactory. For this reason, the contribution of the geologists (with their "prejudices" about the possible geological structures) is fundamental. From an epistemological point of view, the geophysics has been used to falsify some of the geological alternatives - i.e. those that were not fitting also the geophysical data [23]. In the same line of reasoning, the multiple retrieved geophysical models have been used to assess (at least in a qualitative way) the uncertainty of the inferred structures. Definitely, a more systematic way to investigate the model space could be implemented through stochastic inversion of the data. Unfortunately, this was still found unpractical due to the high computational cost of these kinds of approaches.

This study shows also that, though Conductivity Depth Imaging is an extremely valuable tool for mineral exploration, most likely, for quantitative geological modelling, different approaches (including dedicated processing and inversion strategies) can be beneficial.

Furthermore, the present work demonstrates that the large amounts of geophysical data, originally collected for mineral exploration purposes can be effectively used for (hydro)geological mapping. This might be relevant every time groundwater mapping is a priority, but the large costs of the geophysical data acquisitions prevent any significant initiative.

References

1. Fugro airborne surveys: Airborne geophysical survey of the Volta River Basin and Keta Basin logistics and processing report Geotem areas 1 to 8. Job. N. 06401 (2008)
2. Fugro airborne surveys: Airborne geophysical survey of the Volta River Basin and Keta Basin logistics and processing report Geotem regional survey. Job. N. 06401 (2008)
3. Macnae, J.C., Smith, R., Polzer, B.D., Lamontagne, Y., Klinkert, P.S.: Conductivity-depth imaging of airborne electromagnetic step-response data. Geophysics **56**, 102–114 (1991)
4. Christiansen, A.V., Auken, E., Kirkegaard, C., Schamper, C., Vignoli, G.: An efficient hybrid scheme for fast and accurate inversion of airborne transient electromagnetic data. Explor. Geophys. **47**(4), 323–330 (2016)
5. Smith, R., Annan, P.: The use of B-field measurements in airborne time-domain system: Part I. benefits of B-field versus dB/dt data. Explor. Geophys. **29**, 24–29 (1998)
6. Auken, E., et al.: An overview of a highly versatile forward and stable inverse algorithm for airborne, groundbased and borehole electromagnetic and electric data. Explor. Geophys. **46**(3), 223–235 (2015). https://doi.org/10.1071/eg13097
7. Wilson, G.A., Raiche, A., Sugeng, F.: 2.5D inversion of airborne electromagnetic data. Explor. Geophys. **37**, 363–371 (2006)
8. Cox, L.H., Wilson, G.A., Zhdanov, M.S.: 3D inversion of airborne electromagnetic data using a moving footprint. Explor. Geophys. **41**, 250–259 (2013)
9. Ley-Cooper, A.Y., et al.: Airborne electromagnetic modelling options and their consequences in target definition. Explor. Geophys. **46**, 74–84 (2014). https://doi.org/10.1071/eg14045
10. Auken, E., Christiansen, A.V., Westergaard, J.H., Kirkegaard, C., Foged, N., Viezzoli, A.: An integrated processing scheme for high-resolution airborne electromagnetic surveys, the SkyTEM system. Explor. Geophys. **40**, 184–192 (2009)
11. Vignoli, G., Gervasio, I., Brancatelli, G., Boaga, J., Della Vedova, B., Cassiani, G.: Frequency-dependent multi-offset phase analysis of surface waves: an example of high-resolution characterization of a riparian aquifer. Geophys. Pros. **64**, 102–111 (2015)
12. Viezzoli, A., Munday, T., Auken, E., Christiansen, A.V.: Accurate quasi 3D versus practical full 3D inversion of AEM data – the Bookpurnong case study. Preview **149**, 23–31 (2010). https://doi.org/10.1071/PVv2010n149p23
13. Commer, M., Hordt, A., Helwig, S., Scholl, C.: Threedimensional inversion of time-domain EM data with highly constrained model complexities. In: 20 Kolloquium Elektromagnetische Tiefenforschung, pp. 114–123 (2003)
14. Zhdanov, M.S., Vignoli, G., Ueda, T.: Sharp boundary inversion in crosswell travel-time tomography. J. Geophys. Eng. **3**(2), 122–134 (2006)
15. Ley-Cooper, A.Y., et al.: Airborne electromagnetic modelling options and their consequences in target definition. Explor. Geophys. **46**(1), 74–84 (2015)
16. Vignoli, G., Sapia, V., Menghini, A., Viezzoli, A.: Examples of improved inversion of different airborne electromagnetic datasets via sharp regularization. J. Environ. Eng. Geophys. **22**(1), 51–61 (2017)
17. Pagliara, G., Vignoli, G.: Focusing inversion techniques applied to electrical resistance tomography in an experimental tank. In: XI International Congress of the International Association for Mathematical Geology, Liège, Belgium (2006)
18. Vignoli, G., Zanzi, L.: Focusing inversion technique applied to radar tomographic data. In: Near Surface – 11th European Meeting of Environmental and Engineering Geophysics, European Association of Geoscientists & Engineers, Palermo (2005)

19. Vignoli, G., Deiana, R., Cassiani, G.: Focused inversion of vertical radar profile (VRP) traveltime data. Geophysics **77**(1), H9–H18 (2012)
20. Dzikunoo, E.A., Vignoli, G., Jørgensen, F., Yidana, S.M., Banoeng-Yakubo, B.: New regional stratigraphic insights from a 3D geological model of the Nasia sub-basin, Ghana, developed for hydrogeological purposes and based on reprocessed B-field data originally collected for mineral exploration. Solid Earth **11**, 349–361 (2020)
21. Utsugi, M.: 3-D inversion of magnetic data based on the L1–L2 norm regularization. Earth Planets Space **71**(1), 1–19 (2019). https://doi.org/10.1186/s40623-019-1052-4
22. Vignoli, G., Fiandaca, G., Christiansen, A.V., Kirkegaard, C., Auken, E.: Sharp spatially constrained inversion with applications to transient electromagnetic data. Geophys. Prospect. **63**(1), 243–255 (2015). https://doi.org/10.1111/1365-2478.12185
23. Tarantola, A.: Popper, Bayes and the inverse problem. Nat. Phys. **2**, 492 (2006). https://doi.org/10.1038/nphys375

A Fast and Efficient Picking Algorithm for Earthquake Early Warning Application Based on the Variance Piecewise Constant Models

Nicoletta D'Angelo[1]([✉]) [iD], Giada Adelfio[1,2] [iD], Antonino D'Alessandro[2] [iD], and Marcello Chiodi[1,2] [iD]

[1] Dipartimento di Scienze Economiche, Aziendali e Statistiche, Università degli Studi di Palermo, Palermo, Italy
nicoletta.dangelo@unipa.it
[2] Istituto Nazionale di Geofisica e Vulcanologia, Rome, Italy

Abstract. An earthquake warning system, or earthquake early warning system, is a system of accelerometers, seismometers, communication, computers, and alarms that is devised for notifying adjoining regions of a substantial earthquake while it is in progress. This is not the same as earthquake prediction, which is currently incapable of producing decisive event warnings. The implementation of efficient and computationally simple picking algorithm is necessary for this purpose, as well as automatic picking of seismic phases for seismic surveillance and routine earthquake location for fast hypocenter determination. In this paper, a picking method, based on the detection of signals changes in variance, is proposed, taking advantage of a generalized linear model formulation of the investigated problem. An application to simulated data is provided.

Keywords: Earthquake Early Warning · Picking · Change-points

1 Introduction

The term "Earthquake Early Warning" (EEW) is used to describe real-time earthquake information systems that have the potential to provide a warning before significant ground shaking. Warning times range from a few seconds to a little more than a minute and are primarily a function of the distance of the user from the earthquake epicentre. In EEW system, generally, two approaches could be followed, called an onsite and regional warning. The principle of onsite or single-station warning [7] is to detect seismic energy at a single location and provide warning of coming ground shaking at the same location, i.e., detect the P-wave and predict the peak shaking. The regional warning makes use of a seismic network and typically combines information derived by several stations. Generally speaking, the EEW systems first detects earthquakes, in particular, P-wave first arrival and then transmits a useful warning. Given that the strongest

© Springer Nature Switzerland AG 2020
O. Gervasi et al. (Eds.): ICCSA 2020, LNCS 12255, pp. 903–913, 2020.
https://doi.org/10.1007/978-3-030-58820-5_65

ground shaking usually arrives at the time of, or after, the S-wave arrival, using the P-wave to provide warning has the potential to increase the warning time everywhere, to reduce the radius of the blind zone, and to potentially provide a warning at the epicentre. It is therefore important for a robust EEW system, the implementation of efficient and computationally simple picking algorithm. Automatic picking of seismic phases is also important in seismic surveillance and routine earthquake location for fast hypocenter determination. To be suitable for both application, a false alarm must be avoided and time picking must be as accurate as possible.

In this work, we propose a new automatic picking algorithm suitable for the implementation of EEW and in seismic surveillance. The algorithm, based on changes in variance, is tested on synthetic seismograms.

This paper is structured as follows: first, in Sect. 2, an overview about the most widespread automatic picking algorithms is reported; secondly, the description of the proposed methodology is reported in Sect. 3; finally, in Sect. 4, the variance piecewise constant models are applied to seismic waveforms; the last section is devoted to conclusions and final remarks.

2   Automated Seismogram Onset Time Determination

For correct early warning, it is fundamental to recognize early the beginning of a seismogram employing fast and robust algorithms. This is important because the algorithm must run in real-time and false alarm or lost event should be avoided. First arrival times on seismograms coincides with the arrival of the first P-wave. The time of the phase-detection $\hat{T}_i$ at a station i interpreted as the first P-phase arrival time, which is, of course, afflicted with an error ϵ_i. $\hat{T}_i$ may be written as:

$$\hat{T}_i = T_0 + t_i + \epsilon_i,$$

where T_0 is the source time and t_i is the travel time of a P-wave to station i. The coincidence trigger detects an event, if for any combination of a minimum number of stations (typically three or four) the condition

$$|\hat{T}_i - \hat{T}_j| \le \epsilon$$

is met. ϵ is the maximum allowed difference between trigger times at neighbouring stations. This coincidence trigger works satisfying for local networks, where the number of stations and the aperture of the network is not large. For regional and global networks this simple event detection algorithm has to be modified.

[12, Chapter 16] review the most widespread automatic picking algorithms and analyze their properties. Here we report a brief overview. It is also worth to notice that comparative works among different pickers have been carried out in literature [4,11,19].

[5,6] introduce the concept of characteristic function (CF), where the 'character' of the seismic trace is specified. The CF is obtained by one or several non-linear transformations of the seismogram and should increase abruptly at

the arrival time of a seismic wave. In addition to the calculation of the CF the next steps of a picking algorithm are the estimation of the arrival time from the CF and the quality estimation.

The Allen picker is a fast and robust algorithm, which also accounts for automatic quality assessment. However, as this algorithm is amplitude based only, it might miss emergent P-onsets. A comparative study by [11] shows that this algorithm tends to pick somewhat early compared to what an analyst would pick.

Another widely used picking algorithm is the one proposed by [8]. This algorithm is frequently applied, e.g. by 'Programmable Interactive Toolbox for Seismological Analysis' (PITSA, [17]) and the picking system MannekenPix [4].

In contrast to Allen's squared envelope function, this CF is sensitive to changes in amplitude, frequency as well as in phase.

The Baer and Kradolfer picker is also very fast and robust and quite user-friendly, as this algorithm only needs 4 input parameters. A shortcoming of this algorithm is the missing automated quality assessment. Several comparative studies [4,11,19] show how this picking algorithm tends to be somewhat late compared to manual P-picks.

When an earthquake signal occurs, the statistical properties of a seismogram change abruptly. Therefore, the measurement of statistical properties in a moving window are suitable for the determination of a CF and subsequent estimation of arrival times. The statistical properties of the seismogram might be characterized by its distribution density function and by parameters like variance, skewness and kurtosis. The latter two are parameters of higher order statistics (HOS) and are defined by [10].

Though just amplitude-based, higher order statistics are quite sensitive even to emergent P-onsets. In combination with a sophisticated picking algorithm (e.g. [11]), which exploits the entire information provided by the determined CF, it yields excellent results. If precisely tuned, the automated quality assessment proposed by [11] gives similar weights as the analysts. However, choosing the parameters for this sophisticated algorithm is quite difficult and needs a great experience.

The so called autoregressive-Akaike-Information-Criterion-piker (AR-AIC) proposed by [19] is based on the work by [2,3,13] and [21].

A longer time series is divided into two locally stationary segments each modelled by an autoregressive (AR) process. The first segment represents noise, the second segment contains the signal. After estimating the two sets of AR parameters, two prediction errors are computed and then the minimum of the two-model Akaike-Information-Criterion (AIC) indicates the arrival time.

The AR-AIC picker is a highly more sophisticated algorithm based on information theory. The algorithm is computationally quite expensive and hence much slower than the other reviewed pickers.

3 Variance Piecewise Constant Models

[1] considers the case of changepoint detection procedure for changes in variation, assuming that the variance function can be described by a piecewise constant function with segments delimited by unknown changepoints.

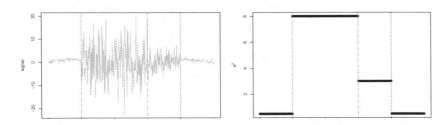

Fig. 1. An example of simulated signal and its corresponding variance with jump points

Let y_i be the outcome and x_i be the observed sample, for $i = 1, 2, \ldots, n$ occasions. Let us assume that $y_i = \mu_i + \epsilon_i$, where μ_i is for instance a sinusoidal function representing the observed signal and $\epsilon_i \sim N(0, \sigma_i^2)$ is an error temr. In this context, σ_i^2 is a variance function approximated by a piecewise constant regression function with $K_0 + 1$ segments. An example is shown in Fig. 1. For simplicity, the model for changes in variance after the k^*th observation is

$$y_i = \begin{cases} \mu_i + \lambda \epsilon_i & 1 \leq i \leq k^* \\ \mu_i + \tilde{\lambda} \epsilon_i & k^* \leq i \leq n \end{cases}$$

with λ, $\tilde{\lambda}$, and k^* unknown and

$$\begin{cases} H_0 : & \lambda = \tilde{\lambda} \\ H_1 : & \lambda \neq \tilde{\lambda} \end{cases}$$

Taking advantage of a generalized linear model formulation of the investigated problem, the test for stepwise changes in variance of a sequence of Gaussian random variables may be transformed equivalently to the case of testing for changes in mean of the squared residuals from an estimated linear model that accounts for the mean behaviour of the observed signal. The estimation of the mean signal $\hat{\mu}$ can be carried out by using a common smoothing procedure, e.g., fitting a cubic smoothing spline to the data. Following a suggestion in [20], a gamma generalized linear model (GLM) is fitted with a log-link function, with response given by the squared studentized residuals $s_i = (y_i - \hat{y}_i)^2 / w_i$, with $\hat{y} = \hat{\mu}$ and weights $w_i = 1 - h_i$, where h_i is the ith diagonal element of the hat matrix H. According to this approach, testing H_0 against H_1 means that we are looking for a change in the mean of the residuals from a fitted linear model.

The proposed approach can be considered as a wider version of the *cumSeg* models proposed in [16] for independent normally distributed observations with constant variance and piecewise constant means to detect multiple changepoints in the mean of the gene expression levels in genomic sequences by the least squares approach. The authors assume that the datum $y_i, \forall i$ is defined as the sum of the signal μ_i and noise $\epsilon_i \sim N(0, \sigma_i^2)$ and that μ_i is approximated by a piecewise constant regression function with $K_0 + 1$ segments, that is:

$$y_i = \beta_1 + \delta_1 I(x_i > \psi_1) + \ldots + \delta_{K_0} I(x_i > \psi_{K_0}) + \epsilon_i.$$

Here, $I(\cdot)$ is the indicator function, such that $I(x) = 1$ is x is true, ψ represents the K_0 locations of the changes on the observed phenomenon, β_1 is the mean level for $x_i < \psi_1$, and δ is the vector of the differences in the mean levels at the change points. The authors proceed to take the cumulative sums of the jump-points model to get a convenient modelling expression that faces the discontinuities at the changepoints ψ_k assuming a piecewise linear or segmented relationship. Therefore, looking for changes in variance, the model is specified as

$$g(\theta_i) = \beta_1 x_i + \delta_1 (x_i - \psi_1)_+ + \ldots + \delta_{K_0} (x_i - \psi_{K_0})_+ \tag{1}$$

where $\theta_i = E[\sum_j^i s_j]$ and it has the advantage of an efficient estimating approach via the algorithm discussed in [14, 15], fitting iteratively the generalized linear model:

$$g(\theta_i) = \beta_1 x_i + \sum_k \delta_k \tilde{U}_{ik} + \sum_k \gamma_k \tilde{V}_{ik}^-, \tag{2}$$

where $\tilde{U}_{ik} = (x_i - \tilde{\psi}_k)_+$, $\tilde{V}_{ik}^- = -I(x_i > \tilde{\psi}_k)$. The parameters β_1 and δ are the same of Eq. (1), while the γ are the working coefficients useful for the estimation procedure [15]. At each step the working model in Eq. (2) is fitted and new estimates of the changepoints are obtained via

$$\hat{\psi}_k = \tilde{\psi}_k + \frac{\hat{\gamma}_k}{\hat{\delta}_k}$$

iterating the process up to convergence. $K^*(< K)$ values are returned, producing the fitted model

$$g(\hat{\theta}_i^*) = \hat{\beta}_1 + \hat{\delta} V_{i1} + \ldots + \hat{\delta}_{K^*} V_{iK^*},$$

where $V_{ik} = I(x_i > \hat{\psi}_k)$ for $k = 1, 2, \ldots, K^*$ and the squared residuals are modelled as the response of a gamma GLM with logarithmic link function. Selecting the number of significant changepoints means selecting the significant variables among $V_1, \ldots, V_k$, where K^* is the number of estimated changepoints from model (1). The author solves the model selection problem by using the *lars* algorithm by [9]. Thus, the fitted optimal model with $\hat{K} \leq K^*$ changepoints is selected by the generalized Bayesian Information Criterion (BIC_{C_n}), defined by:

$$BIC_{C_n} = -2 \log L + edf \log(n) C_n$$

where L is the likelihood function, *edf* is the actual model dimension quantified by the number of estimated parameters (including the intercept, the δ and ψ vectors), and C_n is a known constant.

4   Application to Seismic Waveforms

The choice of C_n. The first issue concerns the value of C_n to used in the BIC_{C_n} criterion to select the changepoints. Therefore, by simulation, we assess the performance of different specifications of C_n. Assuming for simplicity $x_i = i$, $i = 1, \ldots, 700$, the true variance used for the simulations is $\sigma_i^2 = 0.5 + 10I(i > 175)$, while the true mean is not specified, as the mean behaviour of the signal is assumed to be unknown. We consider BIC_{C_n} with different values of C_n and we report the results in Table 1.

Table 1. Empirical means and Mean Squared Error values of the detected number of changepoints over 500 runs and for $K_0 = 1$

	C_n			
	1	$\log(n)$	$\log\log(n)$	$2\log\log(n)$
Mean	0.94	0.96	0.96	0.94
mse	0.12	0.07	0.04	0.06

Among the different examined specifications of C_n, simulations reveal that $C_n = \log\log n$ has the best performance. Thus, we use this value for the provided analysis.

The Simulated Signals. To test the performance of the algorithm, a dataset consisting of 100 waveforms over 60 s is simulated. The changepoints are three, equal to 10, 12, and 22 s. The first changepoint represents the arrival of the first P-wave, the second one represents the arrival time of the fist S-wave and the last one corresponds to the end of the seismic event [18].

The simulated dataset is shown in Fig. 2. Each signal has the same changepoints but different variances corresponding to each phase.

First, the algorithm is applied to the entire dataset. For each waveform, we obtain a different set of changepoints, estimated along with the signal. We report the output of the procedure applied to the first waveform of the dataset in Fig. 3.

The dashed red lines are placed in correspondence of the changepoints estimated through the algorithm. As we may notice, the proposed algorithm succeeds in the identification of the arrival of both the P-wave and S-wave. The straight lines are three changepoints closer to the true values (10, 12 and 22 s), and therefore they represent the changepoints, among all the estimated ones, that a further algorithm should pick as the three relevant changepoints.

In Table 2 the summary statistics of the three relevant changepoints estimated along the whole dataset are reported. We may see that the mean values are close to the true values and that the smallest mean squared error is the one of the first changepoint, that is, the arrival of the first P-wave. Indeed, the estimates of the other two changepoints are less precise. This effect can be related to the occurrence of the first changepoint in correspondence of the most abrupt change in variation of the signal, making it easier to detect.

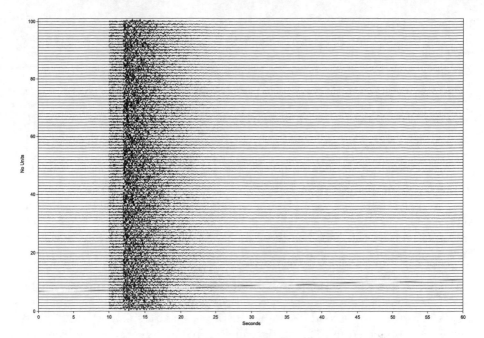

Fig. 2. Simulated dataset of 100 signals

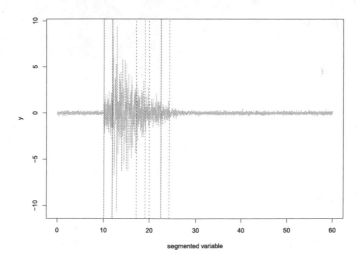

Fig. 3. Changepoints detection in the first seismic waveform of the simulated dataset (Color figure online)

Table 2. Empirical means and Mean Squared Error values of the three relevant change-points over the 100 waveforms of the simulated dataset, obtained through the application of the algorithm

	ψ_1	ψ_2	ψ_3
Mean	9.90	11.79	22.09
mse	0.03	0.44	0.46

Simulated Trend. Then, to test the performance of the algorithm in different settings, further analysis is proposed.

The analyses are carried out assuming underlying trends equal to $\mu_1 = \sin \pi x$ and $\mu_2 = 0.4 \sin 100\pi x$, where x in equally spaced in the range $[1 : 6000]$. These are superimposed and added to the simulated signals. In Fig. 4 (left panel) the first waveform of the simulated dataset is shown, together with the simulated trends, plotted in red. Therefore, the algorithm can account for a mean behaviour of the observed signal, without any loss of precision. In particular, two different models are considered to take into account the mean behaviour of the signal. The first is linear and the second is obtained fitting a smooth spline with 100 knots. These are represented in Fig. 4 (right panel) in red and green, respectively.

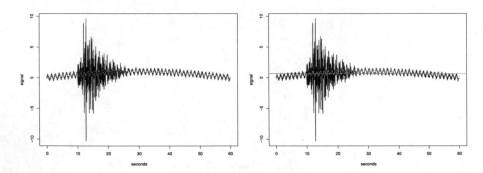

Fig. 4. Simulated data with trend (on the left) and two mean behaviours estimated to take into account the trend (on the right), byb a linear model in red and by splines in green, respectively. (Color figure online)

In Table 3 the results of the application along with the whole dataset, to which the mean behaviour is added, are shown.

We may notice that the estimates of the relevant changepoints are more precise when taking into account the mean behaviour of the signal through a smooth spline, rather than ignoring it. Indeed, as we may notice from Table 3, the mean values are closer to the true changepoints and the Mean Square Error Values are smaller.

Table 3. Empirical means and Mean Squared Error values of the three relevant change-points estimated through the application of the algorithm to the original simulated data plus the trend

		ψ_1	ψ_2	ψ_3
linear	Mean	9.91	11.94	21.97
	mse	0.10	0.34	0.58
spline	Mean	9.90	11.75	22.08
	mse	0.03	0.15	0.47

Post Selection. Finally, we propose a further algorithm to detect, among the estimated changepoints, the three ones corresponding to the arrival of the first P-wave, the arrival of the first S-wave and the end of the seismic event. In particular, we compare the ratio between the variances of subsequent phases of the signal and select only the biggest three. As far as the first algorithm, we fit a smoothing spline to account for the mean behaviour of the signal (see Fig. 5 and Table 4). Of course, the post-selection adds uncertainty to the estimates obtained through the application of the algorithm, so the Mean Squared Error values obtained are the sum of the Mean Squared Errors from the true values plus the uncertainty due to the post-selection. Therefore, as the Mean Squared Error value referred to the first changepoint is equal to the one of the proposed procedure, this means that the first changepoint is always correctly selected by the post-selection algorithm.

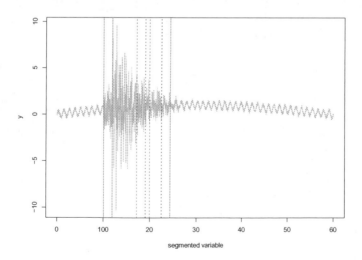

Fig. 5. Results of the algorithm applied to the simulated data with the trend estimated through a smoothing spline with 100 knots. Changepoints estimated by the algorithm are the red dashed lines while the those estimated by the post selection are in green. (Color figure online)

Table 4. Empirical means and Mean Squared Error values of the three relevant change-points over the 100 waveforms of the simulated dataset, with the added trend, obtained through the application of the algorithm and the post-selection approach.

	ψ_1	ψ_2	ψ_3
Mean	9.90	12.29	21.39
mse	0.03	2.75	6.13

Overall, we may conclude that the algorithm succeeds most of the times in picking the first relevant changepoints, that is the one corresponding to the arrival of the first P-wave. Concerning the second changepoint, that is the one corresponding to the arrival of the first S-wave, this is more easily detected if the mean behaviour of the underlying trend is taken into account through a smoothing spline with the right choice of the number of knots. Indeed, some preliminary analyses, not reported here for brevity, show that a smoothing spline with too many knots tends to overfit the signal, hiding that variation of the signal that could make clearer the detection of the changepoints. Finally, we see that in all the considered setting, the last relevant changepoint, that corresponds to the end of the seismic event, is the most difficult to detect. This may related to the less abrupt change in variation at the end of the signal and, therefore, both the proposed algorithms and the post-selection one can not be accurate in this case.

5   Conclusions and Future Work

The proposed approach is a highly sophisticated algorithm based on changes in variation.

All the analysis carried out in the present work account for simulated data, showing that the proposed algorithm accounts for unknown trends of the signals. Future work will deal with real data, depending on the different characteristics of the analysed region that may affect the observed waveforms. Moreover, taking into account the trend of the signal, by fitting splines, is important to remove all those changes in the waveform that are not attributable to the seismic event.

Moreover, in future work, we will perform comparison between the proposed method and the other already existing algorithms, as the Allen picker, Baer and Kradolfer picker, higher order statistics and AR-AIC picker, to asses their general performance, also in terms of computational efficiency and robustness.

References

1. Adelfio, G.: Change-point detection for variance piecewise constant models. Commun. Stat. Simul. Computat. **41**(4), 437–448 (2012)
2. Akaike, H.: Markovian representation of stochastic processes by canonical variables. SIAM J. Control **13**(1), 162–173 (1975)

3. Akaike, H.: Autoregressive model fitting for control. In: Parzen, E., Tanabe, K., Kitagawa, G. (eds.) Selected Papers of Hirotugu Akaike. SSS, pp. 153–170. Springer, New York (1998). https://doi.org/10.1007/978-1-4612-1694-0_12

4. Aldersons, F.: Toward Three-dimensional Crustal Structure of the Dead Sea Region From Local Earthquake Tomography (2004)

5. Allen, R.: Automatic phase pickers: their present use and future prospects. Bull. Seismol. Soc. Am. **72**(6B), S225–S242 (1982)

6. Allen, R.V.: Automatic earthquake recognition and timing from single traces. Bull. Seismol. Soc. Am. **68**(5), 1521–1532 (1978)

7. Allen, R.M., Gasparini, P., Kamigaichi, O., Bose, M.: The status of earthquake early warning around the world: an introductory overview. Seismol. Res. Lett. **80**(5), 682–693 (2009)

8. Baer, M., Kradolfer, U.: An automatic phase picker for local and teleseismic events. Bull. Seismol. Soc. Am. **77**(4), 1437–1445 (1987)

9. Efron, B., Hastie, T., Johnstone, I., Tibshirani, R., et al.: Least angle regression. Ann. Stat. **32**(2), 407–499 (2004)

10. Hartung, J., Elpelt, B., Klösener, K.H.: Statistik: Lehr-und Handbuch der angewandten Statistik. Walter de Gruyter GmbH & Co KG (2014)

11. Küperkoch, L., Meier, T., Lee, J., Friederich, W., Group, E.W.: Automated determination of p-phase arrival times at regional and local distances using higher order statistics. Geophys. J. Int. **181**(2), 1159–1170 (2010)

12. Küperkoch, L., Meier, T., Diehl, T.: Automated event and phase identification. In: New Manual of Seismological Observatory Practice 2 (NMSOP-2), pp. 1–52 (2012)

13. Morita, Y.: Automatic detection of onset time of seismic waves and its confidence interval using the autoregressive model fitting. Earthquake **37**, 281–293 (1984)

14. Muggeo, V.: Segmented: an R package to fit regression models with broken-line relationships. R NEWS **8**(1), 20–25 (2008)

15. Muggeo, V.M.: Estimating regression models with unknown break-points. Statist. Med. **22**(19), 3055–3071 (2003)

16. Muggeo, V.M., Adelfio, G.: Efficient change point detection for genomic sequences of continuous measurements. Bioinformatics **27**(2), 161–166 (2011)

17. Scherbaum, F., Johnson, J., Rietbrock, A.: Programmable Interactive Toolbox for Seismological Analysis (1999)

18. Schmidt, H., Tango, G.: Efficient global matrix approach to the computation of synthetic seismograms. Geophys. J. Int. **84**(2), 331–359 (1986)

19. Sleeman, R., Van Eck, T.: Robust automatic p-phase picking: an on-line implementation in the analysis of broadband seismogram recordings. Phys. Earth Planetary Interiors **113**(1–4), 265–275 (1999)

20. Smyth, G.K., Huele, A.F., Verbyla, A.P.: Exact and approximate REML for heteroscedastic regression. Stat. Model. **1**(3), 161–175 (2001)

21. Takanami, T., Kitagawa, G.: A new efficient procedure for the estimation of onset times of seismic waves. J. Phys. Earth **36**(6), 267–290 (1988)

The Stress Field in the Northern Apulia (Southern Italy), as Deduced from Microearthquake Focal Mechanisms: New Insight from Local Seismic Monitoring

Marilena Filippucci[✉], Pierpaolo Pierri, Salvatore de Lorenzo, and Andrea Tallarico

Università degli Studi di Bari Aldo Moro, Dipartimento di Scienze della Terra e Geoambientali, Campus Universitario, via E. Orabona n°4, 70125 Bari, Italy
marilena.filippucci@uniba.it

Abstract. The historical seismicity catalogs report that the Gargano area (Apulia region, southern Italy) has been site of medium to high magnitude earthquakes. Instrumental seismicity suffers of the poor coverage of the seismic stations of the RSN (National Seismic Network). To improve the seismological monitoring of the area, in 2013 the OTRIONS seismic network (OSN), managed by the University of Bari - Italy, in cooperation with INGV (National Institute of Geophysics and Volcanology), was installed. In this study, focal mechanisms of single and composite events have been computed using 118 micro-earthquakes occurred in this area. We subdivided the dataset into subsets according to their location and depth, distinguishing between the Promontory zone and the Apulian foredeep. High quality focal mechanisms and low-misfit stress tensor inversion were obtained for three groups of events. To better constrain the stress tensor we included also focal mechanism solutions obtained in previous studies. In the southwestern Apulian foredeep zone, a normal fault kinematics is inferred, normal to the Apennine stress direction; in the Promontory zone, the fault kinematics indicate inverse fault mechanisms striking in NE-SW direction. Differently from previous analyses, the stress orientations inferred in this study agree with those inferred in the World Stress Map.

Keywords: Gargano promontory (Southern Italy) · Focal mechanisms · Stress tensor inversion · Microseismicity · OTRIONS seismic network

1 Introduction

The Apulia region (southern Italy) is presently characterized by low to moderate seismicity, as shown by the instrumental observations, while the historical catalogues report 15 earthquakes with $M_w > 5.5$ striking the Gargano promontory and surrounding area since 1361 (Rovida et al. 2019) (Fig. 1). The historical San Severo earthquake, occurred in 1627, is the most energetic earthquake in the area (Del Gaudio et al. 2007), even if the identification of the causative fault is still an open question. On the contrary, both the recent 2002 San Giuliano di Puglia earthquake and the 1893

© Springer Nature Switzerland AG 2020
O. Gervasi et al. (Eds.): ICCSA 2020, LNCS 12255, pp. 914–927, 2020.
https://doi.org/10.1007/978-3-030-58820-5_66

Mattinata earthquake are related to the activity along the E-W trending South Gargano fault line (Borre et al. 2003). In fact, it is generally accepted that the Molise earthquake is due to the reactivation of E-W striking faults (Di Bucci and Mazzoli 2003; Valensise et al. 2004) whose surface expression is probably represented by the E-W Mattinata fault (Fig. 1) in the Gargano Promontory (Tondi et al. 2005).

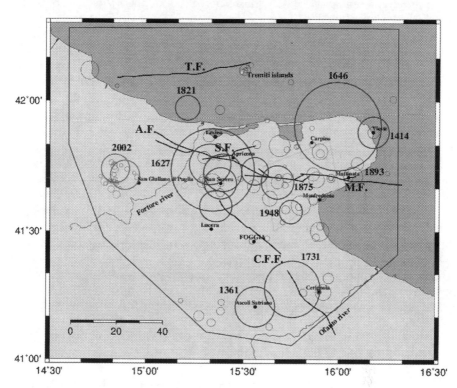

Fig. 1. Seismicity of northern Apulia extracted in the blue polygonal area from the CPTI2015 version 2.0 catalogue (Rovida et al. 2019). Circles represent focal volumes according to Bath and Duda (1964) formula: thicker ones correspond to events with $M_w \geq 5.5$: blue, green and red ones correspond to events occurred between 1361–1983, 1984–1999, 2000–2017, respectively. Noteworthy fault systems, proposed as possible seismogenic structures by authors cited in brackets, are shown with red lines: A.F. = Apricena fault (Patacca and Scandone, 2004), C.F. F. = Cerignola - Foggia fault (Patacca and Scandone, 2001), M.F. = Mattinata fault (Valensise et al., 2004), S.F. = Sannicandro Garganico - Apricena fault (Salvi et al., 1999), T.F. = Tremiti fault (Favali et al. 1993). The study area is marked by green line. (Color figure online)

Analyzing 10 years of seismicity (1995–2004), Milano et al. (2005) concluded that the E-W striking fault system in the Gargano Promontory presents a dextral slipping in response to a NW-SE compression, affecting the deeper layers of the crust, since the foci depths concentrate between 15 and 25 km. This behavior is interpreted as a geodynamic process consisting of the eastward rollback of the Adriatic foreland respect to the Apulian foreland that, causing a northeastward propagation of the thrust front of

Northern Apennines faster than that of Southern Apennines, determines the active dextral strike-slip tectonics on both the Gargano Promontory (Milano et al. 2005) and on the Tremiti Islands (Doglioni et al. 1994).

By analyzing the instrumental seismicity occurred between 1985 and 2004, Del Gaudio et al. (2007) tried to identify the seismogenic structures responsible of both the 1627 San Severo earthquake and the seismicity of the northern Apulia. The authors distinguished between foreland and foredeep regions: the first one is characterized by a regional stress combining NW compression and NE extension, so that seismogenic structures should be strike–slip faults (N-S sinistral or E-W dextral faults), with a slight transpressive character; the second one is characterized by transtensive mechanisms with NW oriented normal faults, similar to the dominant NE extension of the Apennine chain.

In the Gargano area, the local seismic network OTRIONS (hereafter OSN) revealed an intense seismic activity never recorded before, with magnitude less than that of the Apennine Chain.

In this paper we propose an evaluation of the stress field regime in the Gargano promontory, through a focal mechanism analysis of microearthquakes recorded by the OSN seismic network. We investigate the lateral and depth dependence of the stress field in the Gargano Promontory fault zone. Since about the 80% of the recorded earthquakes have magnitude smaller than 2, we carried out a preliminary manual refined picking of seismograms. Focal mechanisms for both the single and the composite event, were computed from the inversion of P wave polarities. Several tests were carried out by inverting different combinations of data. Finally, based on the obtained results and other observational evidence, a possible stress accumulation mechanism of the Gargano Promontory is proposed.

2   Data from the OTRIONS Seismic Network

The dataset considered in this paper is described by de Lorenzo et al. (2017). It consists of about 400 earthquakes localized in the Gargano Promontory and surrounding areas, occurring over a period of approximately 15 months (from April 2013 to July 2014). The events were recorded mainly by OSN and sporadically integrated by some stations belonging to the national seismic network of the INGV. Over 93% of the considered events were not detected by the INGV Earthquakes National Center (CNT). The maximum epicentral distances do not exceed 25 km and the magnitudes range from 0.1 to 1.7.

The considered earthquakes can be grouped into three categories according to the depth and geographical position of their hypocenter. Following the work of Filippucci et al. (2019a), we have analyzed the G1 group of events (blue circles in Fig. 2) among the events that fall within the area with the greatest surface heat flow density (ZSW area in Filippucci et al. 2019a), the G3 group of events (red circles in Fig. 2) that fall into the area with the lowest surface heat flow in the Gargano Promontory (ZNE area in Filippucci et al. 2019a) and a group of events (G2 group, yellow circles in Fig. 2) which fall into a "transition zone" between the ZSW and ZNE areas.

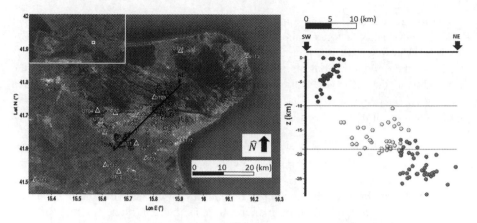

Fig. 2. Geographical map of the Gargano Promontory and depth distribution of earthquake foci along the black profile (SW-NE). The blue, red, yellow circles are the epicentres of the earthquakes of the group G1, G2, G3 respectively. The stations of the OTRIONS seismic network are reported as white triangles. (Color figure online)

Group G1. It consists of 38 events located in the area bounded between the Apulian foredeep and the Gargano foreland. The foci depth is rather shallow, between about 1 and 10 km, with an average depth of 3.8 km. The magnitudes are very small, ranging between 0.7 and 1.5 (average magnitude 1.0).

Group G2. It consists of 35 events with epicenters belonging to an area between the shallower (G1 group) and the deeper (G3 group) earthquakes. The foci depth ranges between 10 and 20 km with an average of 16.5 km. The magnitudes vary between 0.1 and 1.6 with an average of 0.8.

Group G3. It consists of 45 earthquakes which occurred inside the Gargano Promontory. The hypocentral depths range between 17 and 28 km, with an average of about 22 km. The magnitudes range between 0.3 and 1.7 (average magnitude 0.9).

The three identified groups of events were then used to derive the fault plane solutions of the Gargano micro-earthquakes as a function of the depth by moving along the SW-NE direction.

3   Single and Composite Fault Plane Solutions

The fault plane solutions were calculated using the FPFIT code (Reasenberg and Oppenheimer 1985). The velocity model used for the computation of the azimuths and the take-off angles is the same as that used for the location of events (de Lorenzo et al. 2017). We examined 118 earthquakes, 966 P-wave were picked, and 648 P-polarities were recognized. We discarded all the events for which less than 6 polarities were available allowing the inference of the fault plane solutions only for 58 micro-earthquakes. The remaining 60 events, characterized by a number of P polarities less than 6, were however used in the determination of the composite focal mechanism.

From the focal mechanism solutions, we selected the solutions based on the two FPFIT output quality factors Q_f and Q_p. All focal mechanisms with one or both quality factors C were rejected. Another useful parameter in the FPFIT inversion output is STDR, i.e. the station distribution ratio, that ranges inside {0.0,1.0} and sensitive to the distribution of the data on the focal sphere, relative to the radiation pattern. When STDR < 0.5 it means that a relatively large number of data fall too close to nodal planes; such a solution is less robust than one for which STDR > 0.5 and then it was rejected.

As discussed by Imanishi et al. (2011), P wave first-motion polarity alone cannot constrain the mechanism of earthquakes by using only few data. Since most of the events have magnitude less than 2, the number of P wave polarities ranges between 6 and 12. Although this is a high number of P polarities for events with this small size, it remains a low number for the purpose of constraining the fault plane solution. In order to better constrain to the FPFIT inversion, we attributed a weight to the polarity datum which varies from 0 to 2 (following the weighting of the picking used by SAC software). The attribution of the weights to the polarity data used in the FPFIT inversion lowers the misfit. The best fit solution of each event was determined by minimizing the residual between the observed and theoretical amplitudes, where a grid search approach was applied for strike, dip, and slip angles at 5° intervals. The next step was to obtain the composite focal mechanism for each identified group of events; the use of P polarities of grouped events allows to increase the coverage of the focal sphere under the hypothesis that the events of each group are attributable to an ideal single structure.

Group G1. For this group a total of 149 P-polarities was recognized among 264 identified P-wave arrival times. As concerns the single event solutions, 10 focal mechanism solutions were determined and 9 of them are constrained by data. Following the diagram of Zoback (1992), 3 of the 9 single focal mechanisms are of unknown (U) fault type and were discarded. The remaining 6 fault plane solutions are listed in Table 1 and plotted in Fig. 3 (locations in Appendix).

The composite focal mechanism was then obtained by performing two different inversions: the first by considering the polarity data of all the 38 earthquakes of the group; the second by considering only the 9 best single solutions. The results of the 2 obtained composite focal mechanism are very similar to each other (Table 4) and are classified as normal fault (NF) type (Fig. 3).

Group G2. For this group a total of 214 P-polarities was recognized among 298 P-wave arrival times. As concerns the single event solutions, 20 focal mechanism solutions were determined, with rather stable solutions. Three of these events were discarded because of the quality factors of type C, two events were discarded since STDR < 0.5. As a result of this data selection, 15 single focal mechanism solutions were finally classified as thrust fault (TF) type and one NF type (Table 2 and Fig. 3, locations in Appendix).

The composite focal mechanism, obtained using all the available 214 polarities of the 35 events, is of the TF type and it remains stable also considering only the 15 best solution events (Table 4, Fig. 3).

Group G3. For this group a total of 404 P-polarities was recognized among 285 P-wave arrival times. As concerns the single event solutions, 28 focal mechanisms were determined. After the data selection by the quality factors and the STDR criterion, 13 single focal mechanism solutions were constrained with the majority of the events of TF type and only few solutions classified as strike-slip (SS), NF type and 4 of the U type, which were rejected (Table 3 and Fig. 3, locations in Appendix).

When computing the composite fault plane solutions both using all the available polarities and also limiting the inversion to the best solution events (Table 4), the fault plane solution is quite stable, and classified as TF type (Fig. 3).

Table 1. List of fault plane solutions of the events of group G1. For each event the identification number (Id), strike φ, dip δ and rake λ of the 2 nodal planes, the trend and plunge of the P and T axes, the STDR, the quality factors (Q_f and Q_p) and the fault type (FT) are reported.

G1 (Id)	φ_1	δ_1	λ_1	φ_2	δ_2	λ_2	Trend P	Plunge P	Trend T	Plunge T	STDR	Q_f	Q_p	FT
8	260	85	-30	353	60	-174	212	24	310	17	0.87	A	B	SS
11	45	55	-90	225	35	-90	315	80	135	10	0.85	A	B	NF
13	40	60	-80	201	31	-107	335	73	123	14	0.62	A	B	NF
15	40	65	-140	290	54	-31	260	45	163	6	0.63	A	B	NS
24	55	70	-140	309	53	-25	278	42	178	11	0.71	A	B	NS
34	75	65	-120	309	38	-43	302	59	186	15	0.71	A	A	NF

Table 2. As the Table 1 for the events of group G2.

G2 (Id)	φ_1	δ_1	λ_1	φ_2	δ_2	λ_2	Trend P	Plunge P	Trend T	Plunge T	STDR	Q_f	Q_p	FT
2	125	65	100	282	27	70	208	19	55	68	0.84	A	B	TF
7	125	65	110	264	32	54	200	18	69	64	0.80	A	B	TF
11	115	60	120	246	41	49	184	10	74	62	0.78	A	B	TF
13	150	20	140	278	77	74	21	31	169	55	0.65	A	A	TF
17	145	45	100	311	46	80	48	0	141	83	0.63	A	A	TF
19	135	40	130	267	61	62	17	11	130	63	0.71	A	B	TF
20	110	25	150	228	78	68	335	29	112	52	0.83	A	B	TF
22	50	25	80	241	65	95	328	20	160	69	0.80	A	A	TF
23	90	45	110	243	48	71	346	2	83	76	0.75	A	B	TF
25	340	10	100	150	80	88	241	35	58	55	0.83	A	B	TF
30	140	20	130	278	75	77	19	29	170	58	0.77	A	B	TF
31	190	10	-90	10	80	-90	280	55	100	35	0.80	A	B	NF
32	40	60	90	220	30	90	130	15	310	75	0.71	A	B	TF
33	355	55	90	175	35	90	85	10	265	80	0.71	A	B	TF
34	160	40	110	315	53	74	56	7	173	76	0.71	A	A	TF

Table 3. As the Table 1 for the events of group G3.

G3 (Id)	φ_1	δ_1	λ_1	φ_2	δ_2	λ_2	Trend P	Plunge P	Trend T	Plunge T	STDR	Q_f	Q_p	FT
5	150	40	130	282	61	62	32	11	145	63	0.62	A	A	TF
9	30	20	120	178	73	80	277	27	73	61	0.88	A	B	TF
12	75	40	70	280	53	106	359	7	242	76	0.50	A	A	TF
14	115	45	140	236	63	53	352	10	97	55	0.83	A	B	TF
19	155	50	90	335	40	90	245	5	65	85	0.70	A	B	TF
24	80	45	130	210	57	57	323	7	66	62	0.80	A	B	TF
35	140	45	100	306	46	80	43	0	136	83	0.69	A	A	TF
41	100	60	70	316	36	121	204	13	329	68	0.61	A	A	TF
44	120	35	130	254	64	66	2	16	125	63	0.72	A	B	TF

We analyzed the effect of the velocity model on focal mechanism solutions; by using the Calcagnile and Panza (1980) velocity model retrieved for the Apulian lithosphere, used in the paper of Del Gaudio et al. (2007), we inferred some small variations, of the P and T-axes orientations, with respect to the above described results, only for few events of G1 group. This may be due to the shallow foci depth which gives rise to different values of take-off angles. No difference is obtained for G2 and G3 groups.

Table 4. List of composite fault plane solutions. The number of events (N_{ev}) used for the composite solution, the number of polarities (N_{pol}), strike φ, dip δ and rake λ of the 2 nodal planes, the trend and plunge of the P and T axes, the STDR, the quality factors (Q_f and Q_p) and the fault type (FT) are reported.

	N_{ev}	N_{Pol}	φ_1	δ_1	λ_1	φ_2	δ_2	λ_2	Trend P	Plunge P	Trend T	Plunge T	STDR	Q_f	Q_p	FT
G1	38	149	50	55	-130	286	51	-47	261	58	167	2	0.61	C	A	NF
	9	56	55	50	-120	277	48	-59	258	67	166	1	0.60	C	A	NF
G2	35	214	95	40	110	250	53	74	351	7	108	76	0.72	C	B	TF
	15	120	115	50	120	253	48	59	184	1	92	67	0.71	C	A	TF
G3	45	285	70	55	60	295	45	126	181	6	283	65	0.53	C	A	TF
	13	110	100	45	120	241	52	63	349	4	89	69	0.75	C	B	TF

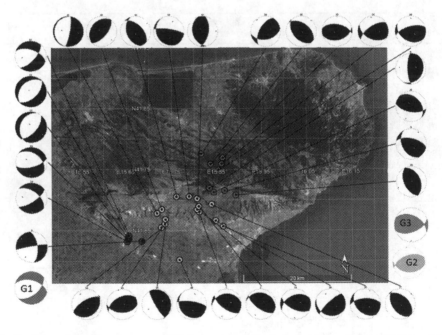

Fig. 3. Map of the Gargano area with the accepted focal mechanism solutions. Colors of the beach ball correspond to the single event focal mechanism (black), composite focal mechanism for the G1 group (blue), composite focal mechanism for the G2 group (yellow), composite focal mechanism for the G3 group (red). (Color figure online)

4 Stress Field in the Gargano Area

We performed the stress inversion of the available focal mechanisms by using the FMSI (Focal Mechanism Stress Inversion) package by Gephart (1990). This inversion scheme provides accurate estimates of the stress tensor since it resolves four of the six independent components of the stress tensor. This method allows to obtain the three eigenvectors, i.e. the maximum, the minimum and the intermediate compressive principal stress axis directions (σ_1, σ_3 and σ_2), and one dimensionless parameter $R = (\sigma_2 - \sigma_1)/(\sigma_3 - \sigma_1)$ which, combining the magnitudes of the principal stresses, constrains the shape of the stress ellipsoid. The R value ranges from $R = 0$ ($\sigma_2 = \sigma_1$) to $R = 1$ ($\sigma_2 = \sigma_3$).

The inversion uses the dataset of fault orientation to determine the best-fitting values of the four stress parameters.

To better constrain the stress values obtained by the FMSI inversion, to each fault plane solution a weight was assigned. After several tests, we assigned to each datum the weigh $W = \sum W_i$ (the weights W_i are detailed in Table 5) that decreases with decreasing the quality factors and that increases with increasing the number of polarities.

Table 5. Weighting criteria assigned to the fault plane solution in the FMSI inversion.

	Qf=A, Qp=A	Qf=B, Qp=B	Npol=6	Npol={7,8}	Npol={9,10}	Npol≥11
W_i; $i=\{$ Qf, Qp , Npol $\}$	3	2	0	1	2	3

We applied the two acceptance criteria of the stress solutions as proposed by Lu et al. (1997). The first criterion requires that the 95% confidence regions of the maximum and minimum principal directions must not overlap to consider as acceptable the solution. The second criterion, which account for the degree of heterogeneity of the investigated medium, requires that the misfit angle has not to exceed 6°. Only if these criteria hold, the stress solution can be considered homogeneous and acceptable.

The stress tensor inversion was applied to all three groups of events, defined in the preceding section and the results are listed and plotted in Fig. 4 and described below.

G1 Group. The stress field was inferred from the inversion of the 9 best constrained fault plane solutions. The 95% confidence regions of the solution are very narrow and the misfit = 3.86° indicates homogeneity of the medium. The axis of maximum compression σ_1, that is subvertical (vertical lithostatic stress orientation, S_v), together with the intermediate stress axis σ_2 (maximum horizontal compression orientation, S_{Hmax}) and the minimum stress axis σ_3 (minimum horizontal compression orientation, S_{hmin}) indicate a normal faulting kinematics. $R = 0.15$ is very low and indicates that in the first 10 km of depth, in the southwestern Gargano, σ_1 and σ_2 have similar values, greater than σ_3 (Fig. 4).

G2 Group. The stress field was inferred from the inversion of the 15 best fault plane solutions. The 95% confidence regions of the solution don't overlap and the very low misfit = 3.03° indicate homogeneity of the medium. The subvertical axis of minimum compression σ_3 (S_v) and the sub-horizontal stress axes σ_1 (S_{Hmax}) and σ_2 (S_{hmin}) indicate a thrust faulting kinematics. R = 0.3 indicates that deeper in the crust, moving toward the northeastern Gargano, the kinematics changes and s_1 and s_2 begin to differ from each other but are still greater than s_3 (Fig. 4).

G3 Group. The stress field was inferred from the inversion of 13 fault plane solutions. The 95% confidence regions of the solution don't overlap and the misfit = 4.91° indicates homogeneity of the deeper layers of the crust continuing toward northwestern in the Gargano. The subvertical axis of minimum compression σ_3 (S_v) and the sub-horizontal stress axes σ_1 (S_{Hmax}) and σ_2 (S_{hmin}) indicate a thrust faulting kinematics, like that of G2 group. R = 0.45 indicates that σ_2 has an intermediate value between σ_1 and σ_3 (Fig. 4).

G2-G3 Group. We used the events of G2 and G3 groups, that brought similar results in terms of tectonic kinematics and output parameters, to obtain a unique stress field solution. Also in this case, the 95% confidence regions of the solution don't overlap. The misfit = 5.72° represents the higher value among the considered groups, indicating a lower degree of homogeneity at depth between 15 and 25 km. The R = 0.35 is intermediate between the results of G2 and G3 groups, taken individually (Fig. 4). If we try to assemble the groups in order to include the G1 group, the results of the FMSI inversion fall outside the criteria of acceptability indicating a great heterogeneity of the focal mechanism data. In fact, if we unify the groups G1-G2, for a total of 24 focal mechanism solutions, the misfit is 6.64°; if we unify all the groups G1-G2-G3, for a total of 37 events, the misfit is 7.67°. Both the assemblages result in a misfit greater than the reference threshold of acceptability of 6°; therefore they have been both rejected.

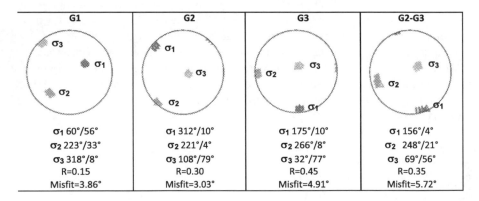

Fig. 4. Results of the FMSI inversion for the three considered event groups (G1, G2 and G3) and for the merged group G2–G3. Angles of trend/plunge of the principal stress axes ($\sigma 1$, $\sigma 2$, $\sigma 3$) within 95% confidence area, the R value and the misfit angle are indicated for each group.

5 Discussion and Conclusions

In previous works, the lateral dependence of microearthquake foci depths (Filippucci et al. 2019a), of the coda quality factor attenuation (Filippucci et al. 2019b) and of resistivity (Tripaldi 2020) was observed. Therefore, we can hypothesize that stress field exhibits the same dependence. The focal mechanism solutions show clear variation among the considered groups: for G1 group the kinematics is normal faulting, whereas for G2 and G3 groups the kinematics is thrust faulting (Fig. 3). The composite mechanism results, obtained for the three groups separately, indicate that the solutions are stable and confirm that the kinematics of faulting changes abruptly, i.e. in few tenths of kilometers, from normal to thrust (Fig. 3). This change corresponds also to the foci deepening (Fig. 2).

The stress field results also show an abrupt change in the horizontal maximum stress direction S_{Hmax}, since it passes from normal faulting NE-SW S_{Hmax} oriented for G1 group, to a reverse faulting NW-SE S_{Hmax} oriented for the G2 and G3 groups. This indicates a clockwise rotation of S_{Hmax} moving deeper and toward the northeastern sector of the Gargano Promontory. By considering the groups G2 and G3 together, the maximum horizontal stress S_{Hmax} is oriented in an intermediate angle between the two groups taken separately.

Previous studies of focal mechanisms and stress field in this area have been proposed. Frepoli and Amato (2000), by grouping the seismicity of a broader area including the Gargano Promontory, found a normal faulting kinematics with the horizontal maximum stress oriented as for the Apennine stress (plunge/trend: $\sigma_1 = 73/130$, $\sigma_2 = 17/310$, $\sigma_3 = 0/40$). Milano et al. (2005), by analyzing the seismicity of a more restricted area (including the Gargano Promontory), found a strike-slip kinematics with an oblique (normal/strike-slip) component and the stress solution indicates normal faulting ($\sigma_1 = 63/260$ and $\sigma_3 = 30/39$). Instead, Del Gaudio et al. (2007), from the analysis of $M_L > 1.6$ seismicity, found focal mechanisms of strike-slip kinematics with a slight normal component in the southwestern zone and a slight inverse component in the northeastern promontory. Overall, they obtained a unique strike-slip stress field solution ($\sigma_1 = 12/321$, $\sigma_2 = 55/69$, $\sigma_3 = 32/224$) for the area of the Gargano Promontory. Our results for G2 and G3 groups disagree with those found by Del Gaudio et al. (2007) regarding the faulting kinematics. In fact, the strike-slip component is completely absent in our solutions. However, our results confirm the orientation of S_{Hmax} stress component found by Del Gaudio et al. (2007). This discrepancy may indicate the heterogeneity of the whole fault system. Our results do not agree with those of Milano et al. (2005) and of Frepoli and Amato (2000) in any of the areas covered by the three groups.

Considering G1 group, the kinematics is normal faulting, as characteristics of the Apennine chain, but S_{Hmax} is normal to that of the Apennine stress orientation. This result was obtained with few events and needs further investigations since, in the area covered by G1 group, the available seismic catalogues are lacking. As concern G2 and

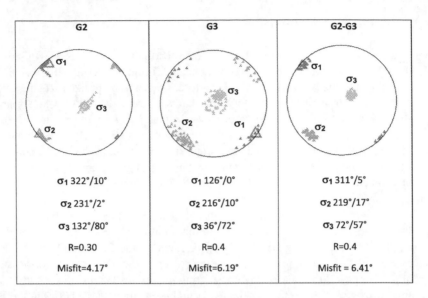

Fig. 5. Results of the FMSI inversion for the considered groups of events including the events of the dataset of Del Gaudio et al. (2007) which belong to each group. Angles of trend/plunge of the principal stress axes σ_1, σ_2, σ_3) within 95% confidence area, the R value and the misfit angle are indicated for each group

G3 groups, our results, in terms of trend and plunge of S_{Hmax}, agree with the Italian Stress Map (Montone and Mariucci 2016) even if we use a different event dataset covering a part of the Gargano Promontory, otherwise lacking information.

In order to check our results, a further inference of the stress orientation was done by adding the events of Del Gaudio et al. (2007) to our dataset. We selected only the events that fall in the volume of each group, separately. None of the events used by Del Gaudio et al. (2007) falls within the volume defined by G1 group while 4 events fall into the G2 group and 4 events into the G3 group. So, we repeated the stress inversion for the G2, G3 and for the combined G2-G3 groups (results in Fig. 5). Even if the heterogeneity of the focal mechanisms of each group increases (the misfit angle increases respect to that in Fig. 4), the results of thrust faulting are confirmed. The integration of our data with the focal mechanisms of Del Gaudio et al. (2007) indicates a slight heterogeneity of preexisting faults in the Gargano area but confirm the NW-SE thrust faulting.

The fault strike orientations in the Gargano area as inferred in this work and in the World Stress Map (WSM, Heidbach et al. 2018) disagree with the image of the surface traces of faults inferred in the area (Doglioni et al. 1994; Chilovi et al. 2000; Brankman and Aydin 2004; Patacca and Scandone 2004), indicating that the deep present-day micro-seismicity occurs on structures that are perpendicular to the mapped fault lines and to which the contractional tectonic evolution of the Gargano Promontory is attributed (Bertotti et al. 1999; Brankman and Aydin 2004; Billi et al. 2007). The disagreement between the present-day tectonic regime, as also recently sketched by Roselli et al. (2018), and the surface tectonic lines has been investigated by Billi et al.

(2007) who considered, as present-day kinematics, the normal fault regime found by Milano et al. (2005). Results however don't agree both with our study and with the WSM. So further geodynamical investigations are needed. The only way to better constrain the issues arising from this study is to pile up further events through the seismic monitoring of the Gargano area with a dense and modern seismometer array.

Acknowledgements. Figures were obtained by employing the GMT freeware package by Wessel and Smith (1998) and by the Google Earth Pro, Google, Inc. California.

Appendix

Locations of events of G1, G2 and G3groups, plotted in Fig. 3. For each event the id. number (Id), the origin (Date and Time, N Lat, E Lon and Depth), the magnitude (Ml), the residual (RMS), the horizontal and vertical errors (ERZ, ERH), the number of recording stations (Nstat), the number of recognized polarities (Npol) are reported.

G1 (Id)	Date	Time	N Lat (°)	E Lon (°)	Depth (km)	M_l	RMS (s)	ERH (km)	ERZ (km)	N_{stat}	N_{pol}
8	2013-06-28	07:02:42	41.63	15.68	3.8	0.9	0.17	0.9	1.1	8	6
11	2013-07-05	11:09:26	41.64	15.65	4.3	1.4	0.14	0.6	0.6	9	6
13	2013-07-22	12:25:47	41.64	15.65	4.6	1.5	0.16	0.6	0.8	9	6
15	2013-08-08	09:13:04	41.64	15.66	3.9	1.4	0.12	0.5	1.0	8	7
24	2013-11-25	10:12:21	41.63	15.65	4.6	1.4	0.20	0.5	1.4	9	7
34	2014-06-13	12:10:03	41.64	15.66	4.8	1.2	0.17	0.8	1.0	7	6

G2 (Id)	Date	Time	N Lat (°)	E Lon (°)	Depth (km)	M_l	RMS (s)	ERH (km)	ERZ (km)	N_{stat}	N_{pol}
2	2013-04-25	08:58:33	41.69	15.81	18.4	0.9	0.09	0.7	0.5	8	7
7	2013-06-25	10:02:38	41.69	15.81	18.9	1.6	0.10	0.4	0.4	11	10
11	2013-09-13	00:41:26	41.68	15.81	18.3	1.4	0.10	0.4	0.4	12	11
13	2013-09-21	03:17:42	41.71	15.79	18.5	0.4	0.09	0.5	0.4	9	8
17	2013-10-27	00:25:05	41.69	15.84	17.7	0.6	0.13	0.6	0.6	10	6
19	2013-12-08	13:13:33	41.66	15.86	12.7	0.7	0.11	0.5	0.6	9	7
20	2013-12-09	21:29:22	41.67	15.85	17.5	0.6	0.07	0.4	0.4	9	9
22	2014-01-23	14:20:49	41.66	15.73	17.9	0.7	0.07	0.3	0.3	10	9
23	2014-01-25	15:19:04	41.66	15.73	17.9	1.6	0.07	0.3	0.3	10	10
25	2014-03-03	22:40:11	41.67	15.74	19.9	0.8	0.07	0.3	0.3	11	9
30	2014-05-15	03:50:48	41.60	15.77	13.4	1.1	0.11	0.3	0.5	12	6
31	2014-06-03	01:59:42	41.68	15.72	14.5	0.1	0.07	0.3	0.4	8	6
32	2014-06-18	12:10:01	41.69	15.73	14.5	0.7	0.20	0.1	0.1	8	6
33	2014-07-05	13:25:17	41.70	15.81	14.2	0.9	0.51	1.8	2.1	11	9
34	2014-07-09	20:20:12	41.71	15.76	18.8	0.8	0.62	3.0	3.0	9	7

G3 (Id)	Date	Time	N Lat (°)	E Lon (°)	Depth (km)	M_l	RMS (s)	ERH (km)	ERZ (km)	N_{stat}	N_{pol}
5	2013-06-20	06:40:22	41.71	15.82	18.6	1.4	0.11	0.6	0.5	9	7
9	2013-08-04	20:08:32	41.72	15.88	19.7	0.5	0.09	0.6	0.5	8	6
12	2013-09-11	19:08:27	41.79	15.87	23.5	1.7	0.15	0.9	0.8	11	11
14	2013-10-09	02:27:56	41.70	15.86	23.9	1.0	0.12	0.7	0.6	10	6
19	2013-11-04	18:30:40	41.77	15.84	23.3	1.3	0.12	0.7	0.5	10	6
24	2013-11-23	15:03:08	41.71	15.87	22.8	1.6	0.13	0.8	0.5	12	9
35	2014-03-10	01:03:02	41.79	15.82	24.2	1.4	0.14	0.8	0.6	13	9
41	2014-04-12	03:10:02	41.72	15.88	23.1	0.8	0.20	0.9	0.7	14	12
44	2014-07-11	10:38:28	41.79	15.87	25.1	1.3	0.23	1.2	0.8	12	7

References

Bath, M., Duda, S.J.: Earthquake volume, fault plane area, seismic energy, strain, deformation and related quantities. Ann. Geofis. **17**(3), 353–368 (1964). https://doi.org/10.4401/ag-5213

Bertotti, G., Casolari, E., Picotti, V.: The Gargano Promontory, a contractional belt. Terra Nova **11**, 168–173 (1999). https://doi.org/10.1046/j.1365-3121.1999.00243.x

Billi, A., Gambini, R., Nicolai, C., Storti, F.: Neogene-Quaternary intraforeland transpression along a Mesozoic platform-basin margin: the Gargano fault system, Adria, Italy. Geosphere **3** (1), 1–15 (2007). https://doi.org/10.1130/GES00057.1

Borre, K., et al.: The COST project in Italy: analysis and monitoring of seismogenic faults in the Gargano and Norcia areas (central-southern Apennines, Italy). J. Geodyn. **36**(1–2), 3–18 (2003). https://doi.org/10.1016/S0264-3707(03)00035-8

Brankman, C.M., Aydin, A.: Uplift and contractional deformation along a segmented strike-slip fault system: the Gargano Promontory, southern Italy. J. Struct. Geol. **26**, 807–824 (2004). https://doi.org/10.1016/j.jsg.2003.08.018

Calcagnile, G., Panza, G.F.: The main characteristics of the lithosphere-asthenosphere system in Italy and surroundings regions. Pure. appl. Geophys. **119**(4), 865–879 (1980). https://doi.org/10.1007/BF01131263

Chilovi, C., De Feyter, A.J., Pompucci, A.: Wrench zone reactivation in the Adriatic block: the example of the Mattinata fault system (SE Italy). Boll. Soc. Geol. It. **119**, 3–8 (2000)

de Lorenzo, S., Michele, M., Emolo, A., Tallarico, A.: A 1D P-wave velocity model of the Gargano promontory (southeastern Italy). J. Seismol. **21**(4), 909–919 (2017). https://doi.org/10.1007/s10950-017-9643-7

Del Gaudio, V., Pierri, P., Frepoli, A., Calcagnile, G., Venisti, N., Cimini, G.: A critical revision of the seismicity of northern Apulia (Adriatic microplate - Southern Italy) and implications for the identification of seismogenic structures. Tectonophysics **436**(1–4), 9–35 (2007). https://doi.org/10.1016/j.tecto.2007.02.013

Di Bucci, D., Mazzoli, S.: The October-November 2002 Molise seismic sequence (southern Italy): an expression of Adria intraplate deformation. J. Geol. Soc. Lond. **160**(4), 503–506 (2003)

Doglioni, C., Mongelli, F., Pieri, P.: The Puglia uplift (SE Italy): an anomaly in the foreland or the Apenninic subduction due to buckling or a thick continental lithosphere. Tectonics **13**(5), 1309–1321 (1994). https://doi.org/10.1029/94TC01501

Favali, P., Funiciello, R., Mattietti, G., Mele, G., Salvini, F.: An active margin across the Adriatic Sea (central Mediterranean Sea). Tectonophysics **219**, 109–117 (1993). https://doi.org/10.1016/0040-1951(93)90290-Z

Filippucci, M., Tallarico, A., Dragoni, M., de Lorenzo, S.: Relationship between depth of seismicity and heat flow: the case of the Gargano area (Italy). Pure. appl. Geophys. **176**(6), 2383–2394 (2019a). https://doi.org/10.1007/s00024-019-02107-5

Filippucci, M., Del Pezzo, E., de Lorenzo, S., Tallarico, A.: 2D kernel-based imaging of coda-Q space variations in the Gargano Promontory (Southern Italy). Phys. Earth Planet. Int. **297**, 106313 (2019b). https://doi.org/10.1016/j.pepi.2019.106313

Frepoli, A., Amato, A.: Spatial variation in stresses in peninsular Italy and Sicily from background seismicity. Tectonophysics **317**(1–2), 109–124 (2000). https://doi.org/10.1016/S0040-1951(99)00265-6

Gephart, J.W.: FMSI: a FORTRAN program for inverting fault/slickenside and earthquake focal mechanism data to obtain the regional stress tensor. Comput. Geosci. **16**, 953–989 (1990). https://doi.org/10.1016/0098-3004(90)90105-3

Heidbach, O., et al.: The World Stress Map database release 2016: crustal stress pattern across scales. Tectonophysics **744**, 484–498 (2018). https://doi.org/10.1016/j.tecto.2018.07.007

Imanishi, K., et al.: Depth-dependent stress field in and around the Atotsugawa fault, central Japan, deduced from microearthquake focal mechanisms: evidence for localized aseismic deformation in the downward extension of the fault. J. Geophys. Res. **116**, B01305 (2011). https://doi.org/10.1029/2010JB007900

Lu, Z., Wyss, M., Pulpan, H.: Details of stress directions in the Alaska subduction zone from fault plane solutions. J. Geophys. Res. **102**(B3), 5385–5402 (1997). https://doi.org/10.1029/96JB03666

Milano, G., Di Giovambattista, R., Ventura, G.: Seismic constraints on the present-day kinematics of the Gargano foreland, Italy, at the transition zone between the southern and northern Apennine belts. Geophys. Res. Lett. **32**, L24308 (2005). https://doi.org/10.1029/2005GL024604

Montone, P., Mariucci, M.T.: The new release of the Italian contemporary stress map. Geophys. J. Int. **205**(3), 1525–1531 (2016). https://doi.org/10.1093/gji/ggw100

Patacca, E., Scandone, P.: Identificazione e valutazione di strutture sismogenetiche. Rapporto tecnico, Convenzione ENEA - Dipartimento di Scienze della Terra Università di Pisa, Italy (2001)

Patacca, E., Scandone, P.: The 1627 Gargano earthquake (Southern Italy): identification and characterization of the causative fault. J. Seismol. **8**(2), 259–273 (2004). https://doi.org/10.1023/B:JOSE.0000021393.77543.1E

Reasenberg, P., Oppenheimer, D.: FPFIT, FPPLOT and FPPAGE: FORTRAN computer programs for calculating and displaying earthquake fault-plane solutions. USGS Open-File Rep., 85–739 (1985). https://doi.org/10.3133/ofr85739

Roselli, P., Marzocchi, W., Mariucci, M.T., Montone, P.: Earthquake focal mechanism forecasting in Italy for PSHA purposes. Geophys. J. Int. **212**(1), 491–508 (2018). https://doi.org/10.1093/gji/ggx383

Rovida, A., Locati, M., Camassi, R., Lolli, B., Gasperini, P.: Catalogo Parametrico dei Terremoti Italiani (CPTI15), versione 2.0. Istituto Nazionale di Geofisica e Vulcanologia (INGV) (2019). https://doi.org/10.13127/CPTI/CPTI15.2

Salvi, S., et al.: A multidisciplinary approach to earthquake research: implementation of a geochemical geographic information system for the Gargano site, Southern Italy. Nat. Haz. **20**, 255–278 (1999). https://doi.org/10.1023/A:1008105621134

Tondi, E., Piccardi, L., Cacon, S., Kontny, B., Cello, G.: Structural and time constraints for dextral shear along the seismogenic Mattinata Fault (Gargano, southern Italy). J. Geodyn. **40**(2–3), 134–152 (2005). https://doi.org/10.1016/j.jog.2005.07.003

Tripaldi, S.: Electrical signatures of a permeable zone in carbonates hosting local geothermal manifestations: insights for the deep fluid flow in the Gargano area (south-eastern Italy). Boll. Geof. Teor. Appl. **61**(2), 219–232 (2020). https://doi.org/10.4430/bgta0312

Valensise, G., Pantosti, D., Basili, R.: Seismology and tectonic setting of the 2002 Molise, Italy, Earthquake. Earthq. Spectra **20**, 23–37 (2004). https://doi.org/10.1193/1.1756136

Wessel, P., Smith, W.H.F.: New, improved version of Generic Mapping Tools released. Eos, Trans. Am. Geophys. Un. **79**(47), 579 (1998). https://doi.org/10.1029/98EO00426

Zoback, M.L.: First and second order patterns of stress in the lithosphere: the World Stress Map Project. J. Geophys. Res. **97**, 11703–11728 (1992). https://doi.org/10.1029/92JB00132

Integrated Vibration Analysis for Historical Dome Structures: A Complementary Approach Based on Conventional Geophysical Methods and Remote Sensing Techniques

Luca Piroddi$^{(\boxtimes)}$ ⓘ and Sergio Vincenzo Calcina ⓘ

Department of Civil Engineering, Environmental Engineering and Architecture
DICAAR, University of Cagliari, via Marengo 2, 09123 Cagliari, Italy
lucapiroddi@yahoo.it

Abstract. The paper presents a study based on integrated non-destructive sensing methods aimed at defining the experimental vibration properties of a historical dome by using environmental microtremor measurements only. The integrated approach consists in the use of both contact and remote sensors to acquire ambient vibration data. The measurements of vibration were carried out with a high-sensitive tri-axial seismometer (Tromino) and a coherent radar system (Image By Interferometry System, IBIS-S). Five asynchronous velocimetric stations were arranged over a profile on the external side of the structure to acquire ambient vibration time-series on radial, tangential and vertical directions. In order to detect the displacements of the internal surface of the dome, the radar interferometer was positioned inside the church using three station points of measure along the main axis of the structure, with different geometric configurations for each station. With this technique, synchronous signals coming from the structure were simultaneously acquired and analyzed. Both seismic time-series and microwave signals were processed to derive the experimental vibration properties of the structure, mainly concerning the dynamic behavior of the circular dome. In addition, to evaluate the capabilities of the radar system in the indoor configuration, a Finite Element model of the structure was built, and the experimental results were compared to the numerical outputs.

Keywords: Ground-based radar interferometry · Ambient vibration tests · Non-destructive measurements · Microwave systems · Cultural heritage · Finite element modeling

1 Introduction

In the last decades, advances in ground-based radar interferometry systems have allowed the diffusion of microwave sensors to measure remotely the vibration of slender structures [1]. Many authors have proposed researches based on the use of radar sensors to measure displacement time-series on different kinds of structures, such as modern skyscrapers [2], concrete and earth dams [3, 4], bridges [5, 6], stay-cables of stay-cabled bridges [7–9], bell towers and historical structures [6, 10–17] and other

© Springer Nature Switzerland AG 2020
O. Gervasi et al. (Eds.): ICCSA 2020, LNCS 12255, pp. 928–943, 2020.
https://doi.org/10.1007/978-3-030-58820-5_67

civil infrastructures [18]. Terrestrial remote sensing techniques have been widely applied in many geological and environmental studies for the monitoring of unstable slopes [19], landslides [20, 21], mines [22], sinkholes [23] and underground cavities [24]. Main structural studies were focused on the use of terrestrial remote sensing to perform static [25] and dynamic tests [26]. In both cases, ground-based radar remote sensing provides results in good agreement with conventional techniques based on the use of contact arrays and standard devices to measure the displacements of targets [1].

In this paper an integrated non-destructive approach based on the use of contact seismic sensors and a microwave remote system is presented. The studied structure is the historical church of "Beata Vergine Assunta", in the small village of Guasila (southern Sardinia, Italy). The experimental frequency response of its ancient dome is derived from output-only measurements of ambient vibration. In order to identify most favorable operative conditions, the terrestrial coherent radar system was positioned inside the church with different geometric configurations. The tri-axial velocity sensor was installed on the outside surface of the structure in four station points, including a ground station. The comparison between microtremor traces and microwave signals allowed the identification of the main experimental vibration properties of the structure. Finally, a numerical simulation has been proposed to better interpret the experimental results obtained using both direct sensors and no-contact systems.

1.1 The Surveyed Structure

The church of the "Beata Vergine Assunta" is a central plan building located on the top of a hill dominating the rural village of Guasila. The current structure was designed in 1839 by the architect Gaetano Cima (Cagliari, 1805–1878), following the aesthetic canon of neoclassical architecture [27]. It was decided to demolish a pre-existent church, and the new structure was realized in the years from 1842 to 1852 in the middle of the urban center, in the historical sub-region of *Trexenta*. Eight large pillars divide the central main aisle from the side chapels each one communicating with two lateral paths from the main entrance to the sacristy at the rear of the church.

The pillars support the central dome of the structure with four arches and a drum. The dome, with a circular opening on the top, was closed by a cylindrical lantern later. A monumental pronaos with six columns in Doric style and two lateral pillars, surmounted by a triangular tympanum, decorates the main façade of the church. The ancient bell tower is the unique part still existing of the previous Baroque church.

Over the eastern side of the church, five buttresses were subsequently built to content lateral loads of the structure. On this side, a tall reinforced concrete retaining wall was realized, to constrain foundation terrains on the natural slope of the hill, few meters from the church. The design of the temple is clearly inspired by the shape of the Pantheon in Rome (Italy) and the eurythmic proportions of the design are probably suggested by the studies of the great Italian architect Palladio. In Fig. 1 different images of the church of Guasila are shown. Since the construction time, several problems of stability have been described (e.g. in the technical reports of architect Cima) [28]. The problems were even attributed to the low technical qualities of the materials used to build the structure, mainly consisting of local stone, marl and sandstone, characterized by weak degree of compaction and lithification [28]. Recently, the structure has been studied in the framework of a restoration and diagnostic project based on multidisciplinary approaches [28–30]. In these studies, minero-petrographic analyses, geometric-architectural surveys, structural surveys, geotechnical and geophysical investigations were carried to implement the knowledge concerning the structural health state of the church.

2   Methods and Materials

Vibration data were acquired by means of two different measurement tools and were integrated to build a better detailed model of the experimental frequency response of the structure. Some images of the two instruments used for the dynamic surveys are shown in Fig. 2:

- Tromino 3D velocimeter (Fig. 2a);
- IBIS-S Ground-based radar interferometer (Fig. 2b).

Fig. 1. Church of Beata Vergine Assunta of Guasila (Sardinia, Italy): (a) historical image of the church (postcard of the first decade of '900, "Collezione Colombini"; (b) image from the square in front of the main façade of the church; (c) aerial perspective view of the structure.

Fig. 2. Images of the instruments used for the dynamic surveys: (a) Tri-axial velocity sensor placed in the seismic station [TR05] in correspondence of the cylindrical lantern; (b) Ground-based microwave interferometer during the acquisition in correspondence to the central station [ST03].

2.1   Microtremor Spectral Analyses

Standard Spectral Ratios (SSR) method [31] has been used to analyze microtremor seismic data. This processing technique uses a reference station to filter ambient vibration data in order to isolate the contributions depending on the natural modes of vibration of the structure by the other components of microtremor. The assumption of linear dynamic behavior of the structures underlies this method. Through the SSR approach, the experimental frequency response of a dynamic system can be derived, along each component of the motion, in agreement with the following equation:

$$SSR(f) = \frac{|H_i(f)|}{|H_{ref}(f)|} \tag{1}$$

where $|H_i(f)|$ and $|H_{ref}(f)|$ indicate the amplitude spectra related to the i-th station and to the reference station, respectively.

Many authors propose the Standard Spectral Ratios method as both expeditious and effective technique. The method provides a reliable estimation of the experimental vibration properties of different types of structures, such as civil structures, ancient towers, earthquake damaged buildings and concrete dams [12, 32–34].

Fig. 3. Spatial distribution of the asynchronous microtremor stations (yellow rectangles) placed at the base of the structure and on it. The blue orthogonal axes indicate the local reference system utilized for the survey. (Color figure online)

An ambient vibration survey was carried out asynchronously acquiring micro-tremor time-series on five stations. Figure 3 shows the scheme of acquisition for the measurements. In order to identify the natural frequencies that mainly characterize the experimental dynamic behavior of the circular dome in the global complex system of the structure, SSRs were derived by monitoring three different reference stations.

This instrumental configuration aimed to put in evidence the vibration frequencies characterized by maximum amplitudes on the dome along three orthogonal directions, identified as Radial, Tangential and Vertical directions (with regards to the dome geometry in correspondence to the sensor configurations). The first reference site was chosen in correspondence to the lowest station [TR01], placed at the ground surface, in the lateral parvis to the structure. This spatial position was identified in order to acquire reference signals minimally affected by the vibration of the elements of the church. Other reference stations were [TR02] and [TR03], placed on the outside bearing wall of the structure and at the base of the circular dome. These reference stations were used to highlight the different behavior of remaining parts of the structure. Directional analyses of microtremor was performed in order to detect directional components of the structural motion. The duration of the acquisition for each measurement of microtremor was 20 min. Sampling frequency was 512 Hz.

2.2   Ground-Based Radar Interferometry: Basic Working Principles

Terrestrial remote sensing allows the measurements of the displacements without any direct array of sensors (e.g. velocity seismic sensors or accelerometers) installed on the structure. The displacements of different points are derived by reflected or backscattered electromagnetic signals which come back from the reflectors to the radar antenna.

The radar sensor generates microwave signals by means of the Stepped Frequency Continuous Wave (SF-CW) technique. This method uses high resolution signals [35, 36] characterized by stepped frequency waveforms over time (Fig. 4a). The displacements of the targets illuminated by the radar beam derived from the interferometric analysis [37]. The method allows to obtain time series of displacement looking at the phase shift measured between different backscattered or reflected signals coming from the same range bin.

The component of the displacement vector along the radar Line Of Sight $d_{LOS}(t)$ derives from the phase-shift $\Delta\varphi(t)$ according to the following equation:

$$d_{LOS}(t) = \frac{\lambda}{4\pi}\Delta\phi(t) \tag{2}$$

where λ is the wavelength of the signal. Interferometric processing can be used only when the sensor is based on a coherent radar system, capable to detect the phase of the received signals. Although the Eq. (2) provides a first estimation of the displacements achieved by the radar system [38], it represents a good approximation for most engineering applications.

Minimum amplitude of displacement that can be measured by means of this technique depends on the range resolution (δR) of the radar interferometer. This feature provides the capability of the radar to resolve separately two targets along the Line Of Sight of the system and depends on the signal bandwidth (B) according to the following equation:

$$\delta R = \frac{c}{2B} \tag{3}$$

where c indicates the speed of light.

For a radar system operating in *Ku* band (with central frequency of 17 GHz and wavelength λ equal to 1.76 cm) a phase variation of 1° corresponds to a displacement of 20 μm [39].

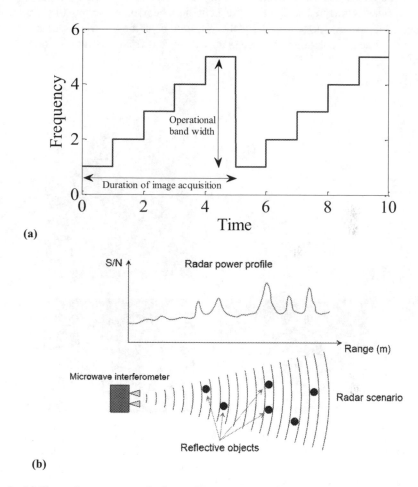

(a)

(b)

Fig. 4. (a) Illustrative spectrum of a Stepped Frequency Continuous Wave signal; (b) Schematic one-dimensional Radar Power Profile.

The microwave sensor used for the survey was the IBIS-S system (Image By Interferometry Survey, by IDS). This sensor is a coherent radar system without synthetic aperture that cannot detect the Direction Of Arrival of the reflected signals (no-DOA radar interferometer). For simple geometries, this limitation can be partially overcome by illuminating the same target element from different antenna positions. The antenna of a radar sensor is characterized by a lateral attenuation of emitted signal, with respect to the maximum axial signal, which is expressed by the azimuthal and vertical beamwidth. For the sensor used in the survey, azimuthal beamwidth has values of 17° considering a decay of the intensity of -3 dB and of $34°$ at -10 dB, while vertical beamwidth is $15°$ at -3 dB and $45°$ at -10 dB. A typical spatial scenario sampled by this radar sensor is plotted in Fig. 4 jointly with the Radar Power Profile, which shows maximum amplitudes of the backscattered signals along the range distance in correspondence to the reflective objects indicated with black circles in the schematic plan view of the scenario. However, this system does not allow the estimation of the contribution of different targets positioned at the same distance (same range bin) from the radar station.

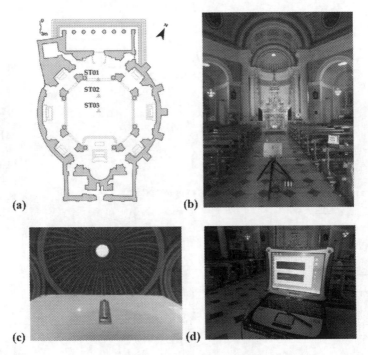

Fig. 5. Some images of the interferometric survey: (a) spatial distribution of the microwave interferometer stations (yellow triangles); (b) IBIS-S sensor during the survey, [ST02] station; (c) investigated scenario, [ST03] station; (d) experimental radar power profile and displacements time-series plotted in real time. (Color figure online)

The microwave survey was carried out using different configurations. The measurements were performed inside the church by means of three positions of the radar interferometer, indicated in Fig. 5a with yellow triangles ([**ST01**], [**ST02**] and [**ST03**]). In order to assess the most favorable operative conditions to perform the radar survey, different configurations of measure were tested for each acquisition position (by modifying the inclination angle of the sensor head). Some images of the radar survey

Table 1. Interferometric radar stations: geometric acquisition layout.

Ground-based radar station ID	Configuration	Vertical inclination degree [°]	Duration [s]
[ST01]	A	85	1,200
	B	70	1,200
	C	40	1,200
[ST02]	A	70	1,200
	B	45	1,200
[ST03]	A	80	1,200
	B	65	1,200

are shown in Fig. 5. The geometric features of acquisition are reported in Table 1. Each radar station is considered in order to collect the information about a projected component of the true displacement along the Line Of Sight (LOS) direction. Combining all data, the real displacement vector can be estimated.

3 Experimental Results

3.1 Microtremor Seismic Survey

The standard spectral ratios of experimental time series, computed for the three reference stations, are reported in Fig. 6 and in Fig. 7. Starting from the analysis of the SSRs referred to the **[TR01]** station, located at the base of the structure (ground level), and looking at the vertical spectral ratios, the frequency peak with maximum amplitude is detected at the **[TR05]** microtremor station, located on the top of the dome, at a value of 7.4 Hz (Fig. 7a). The amplification effect related to this frequency is probably due to a structural vibration mode that mainly involves the body of the dome of the church, with maximum deformations along the vertical direction. In fact, this peak is not clearly visible in the horizontal components of spectral ratios, computed for the same station point (Fig. 6).

Furthermore, it is totally absent in the vertical spectral ratios, calculated for the stations positioned in the other levels of church. First two natural frequencies of vibration of the structure are recognizable at 4.0 Hz and at 4.6 Hz. These frequency peaks are clearly identified in all SSRs. The frequency peak at 4.0 Hz shows the maximum amplification along the radial component of displacement, but it is also present, although with lower amplitude, in both Tangential and Vertical components of the motion. Conversely, the frequency peak at 4.6 Hz mainly characterizes the horizontal Tangential spectral ratio and it does not show any substantial amplification along the vertical component (Fig. 7a).

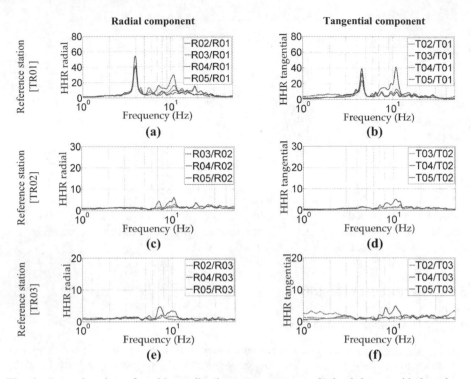

Fig. 6. Spectral ratios of ambient vibration measurements obtained by considering three different reference stations. Radial (a, c, e) and tangential (b, d, f) horizontal components of motion.

The frequency peak at 10.8 Hz is affected by significant amplitude in all components of the motion with maximum amplitude measured along both vertical and tangential spectral ratios. The spectra, filtered by means of the signal recorded at **[TR02]** station, highlight amplitude peaks at frequencies higher than 7 Hz. Probably, the first natural frequencies of vibration of the structure (4.0 Hz, 4.6 Hz) are not significantly amplified at the upper level of the church. The vertical spectral ratios clearly show the frequency peak centered at 7.4 Hz in agreement with the spectral ratios computed by the station installed at the ground level, evidencing that probably the parts of the structure between the first two reference stations, **[TR01]** and **[TR02]**, do not affect much this frequency amplification.

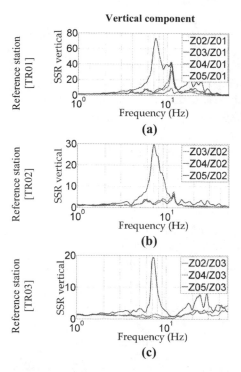

Fig. 7. Spectral ratios of ambient vibration measurements obtained by considering three different reference stations. Vertical components of motion.

3.2   Interferometric Radar Survey

In order to investigate the vibration response of the structure under operational conditions, different dynamic surveys were carried out using the IBIS-S radar interferometer. The radar survey was performed on 14 February 2020, with intense wind acting on the external side of the structure. Several geometric configurations of the radar sensor were tested with the non-trivial purpose to explore the operative capabilities of the remote sensor during the dynamic surveys, performed in indoor experimental conditions of a complex but known scenario. The position of the radar and the tilt of the antenna were modified in order to identify the most favorable geometries of acquisition. Microwave data were acquired using a sampling rate of 100 Hz over time windows of 20 min. The range resolution and the maximum range were set equal to 0.75 m and 50 m, respectively. In Fig. 8 the one-dimensional radar power profile, calculated for the configuration B in the station [ST01], Table 1, is plotted. This location, settled to mainly illuminate the internal surface of the circular dome from different distances, was chosen for the preliminary analysis and the comparison with seismic data. The radar power profile that corresponds to this set of measurements is characterized by significant amplitudes of backscattered electromagnetic signals in correspondence to the range bins 29 (21.75 m, average distance from the radar system), 32 (24 m), 33 (24.75 m) and 35 (26.25 m), with a high Signal to Noise Ratio (SNR). There are also other range bins that show high amplitude SNR peaks. However, these signals do not correspond to any clearly identified structural element of the church and were discarded for the analysis. Further measurements were performed installing the sensor in correspondence to the stations **[ST02]** and **[ST03]**. The results obtained for these sets of measurements are not discussed here, but were considered to derive more information about the experimental vibration properties of the structure. The radar power profiles show different range bins characterized by intense amplitude of the backscattered signals. These signals are probably due to the presence of many lateral backscatterers, corresponding to the architectonical elements that are present on the internal walls of the structure. In addition, the curvature of the surface of the dome does not represent a single backscatterer but can be considered like as a continuous distribution of reflective points, positioned at increasing distances from the radar sensor. This feature is confirmed by the comparison among the amplitude spectra, derived from different range bins that correspond to reflective points on the structure. The radar bins with SNR higher than 40 were selected for the displacement and the frequency analyses.

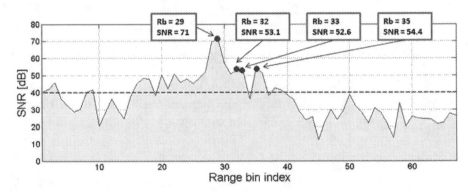

Fig. 8. Radar Power Profile corresponding to the measurement performed through the configuration B in the radar station [ST01]: blue circles indicate the range bins selected for the spectral analysis. (Color figure online)

Figure 9 shows the Power Spectral Densities functions derived from the signals corresponding to the range bins 32, 33 and 35, selected from the radar scenario of **[ST01]** station, configuration **B**. Two clear harmonic components are shown in all selected spectra. The first frequency peak recognized by the interferometric survey is centered at 7.68 Hz. This frequency peak is very close to the vibration frequency of 7.4 Hz, detected by means of the SSRs of microtremor, calculated for the vertical component of the structure motion (with different reference stations). This frequency component is characterized by high amplification in correspondence to the measurement taken on the dome of the church (**[TR05]**, lantern). This frequency can be interpreted as a natural frequency associated to a structural vibration mode that mainly involves the dome of the church. In fact, this experimental vibration mode is characterized by prevalent deformations along the vertical component of the signals.

The second frequency peak, shown by the graph in Fig. 9, is localized at 15.34 Hz. However, this frequency component was not detected by means of the microtremor measurements. All Power Spectral Density (PSD) functions, derived from the dynamic microwave surveys, do not show any frequency peaks related to the first and to the second vibration modes of the structure (4.0 Hz and 4.5 Hz). This phenomenon could be due to the low amplitude deformation associated with these vibration modes in the LOS direction of the radar.

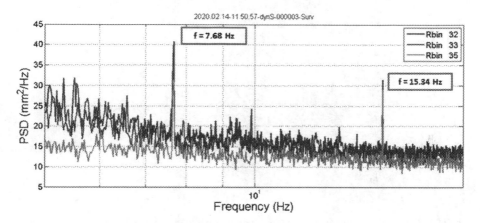

Fig. 9. Power spectral density functions derived from the range bins 32, 33 and 35, selected from the radar scenario corresponding to the station [ST01], configuration B.

4   Numerical Results

A three-dimensional preliminary Finite Element (FE) model of the main central body of the church was realized to compare the experimental results with the outputs of the numerical simulation and to better evaluate the correspondence between the synthetic dynamic response of the model and the interferometric radar results.

The dynamic simulation was performed using the software Autodesk Inventor. The geometry of the structure was simplified and the discrete model was built using 145,814 nodes and 85,525 elements. The eight central pillars that support the upper part of the structure and the central circular dome were included in the model. Furthermore, lateral structural elements were inserted in order to simulate the horizontal constraint action due to the chapels of the church. The material properties (density and elastic modulus), were assigned in agreement with the scientific literature and taking into account specific analyses done on the samples of building materials [31].

Preliminary results highlight that the dynamic behavior of the model shows a vibration mode characterized by significant deformations along the vertical direction (Fig. 10). The deformations corresponding to this natural mode (frequency of 7.16 Hz) mainly regard the circular dome and the upper part of the model. The preliminary numerical outputs show a good agreement with the experimental results.

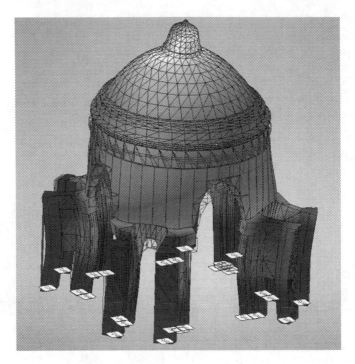

Fig. 10. Preliminary numerical dynamic analysis: synthetic mode shape with maximum deformations detected in the top of the structure.

5   Conclusion

Thanks to the integration of non-destructive methods based on conventional velocity sensors and terrestrial remote sensing systems, the experimental dynamic study of a historical structure was proposed. The complementary approach was utilized to perform the dynamic characterization of the dome of the church of "Beata Vergine Assunta" in Guasila. Spectral analyses of microtremor were used to derive the main vibration properties of the structure starting from five asynchronous stations of environmental noise. Microtremor spectra showed high amplification effects at frequencies of 4.0 Hz, 4.6 Hz and 7.4 Hz for the radial, tangential and vertical components of the motion. Ground-based radar interferometry surveys were performed inside the structure. Interferometric results show that the experimental datasets contain the contribution of a natural mode of vibration, that mainly characterizes the upper part of the structure (circular dome) at the frequency of 7.68 Hz. Preliminary numerical outputs derived from the Finite Element analysis show a good agreement with the experimental results of the surveys. Future studies will be performed to improve the analysis of the interferometric data and to implement a more detailed Finite Element simulation.

Acknowledgements. The authors are grateful to Don Alessandro Guiso, for permission to carry out the surveys on the church of "Beata Vergine Assunta" in the village of Guasila, to Mr. Luigi Noli and Mr. Mario Sitzia for their fundamental technical support provided during the measurements.

References

1. Pieraccini, M., Miccinesi, L.: Ground-based radar interferometry: a bibliographic review. Remote Sens. **11**, 1029 (2019)
2. Zhou, L., et al.: Monitoring and analysis of dynamic characteristics of super high-rise buildings using GB-RAR: a case study of the WGC under construction, China. Appl. Sci. **10** (3), 808 (2020)
3. Bukenya, P., Moyo, P., Beushausen, H., Oosthuizen, C.: Health monitoring of concrete dams: a literature review. J. Civil Struct. Health Monitor. **4**, 235–244 (2014). https://doi.org/ 10.1007/s13349-014-0079-2
4. Di Pasquale, A., Nico, G., Pitullo, A., Prezioso, G.: Monitoring strategies of earth dams by ground-based radar interferometry: how to extract useful information for seismic risk assessment. Sensors **18**(1), 244 (2018)
5. Stabile, T.A., Perrone, A., Gallipoli, M.R., Ditommaso, R., Ponzo, F.C.: Dynamic survey of the Musmeci bridge by joint application of ground-based microwave radar interferometry and ambient noise standard spectral ratio techniques. IEEE Geosci. Remote Sens. Lett. **10**(4), 870–874 (2013)
6. Marchisio, M., et al.: Applications of new technologies of ground-based interferometric radar to the study of cultural heritage buildings. In: Near Surface 2008, EAGE 14th European Meeting of Environmental and Engineering Geophysics, pp. 1–4. EAGE, Houten, The Netherlands (2008)
7. Cunha, A., Caetano, E.: Dynamic measurements on stay cables of cable-stayed bridges using an interferometry laser system. Exp. Techn. **23**(3), 38–43 (1999). https://doi.org/10.1111/j. 1747-1567.1999.tb01570.x
8. Gentile, C.: Deflection measurement on vibrating stay cables by non-contact microwave interferometer. NDT&E Int. **43**, 231–240 (2010)
9. Gentile, C.: Application of microwave remote sensing to dynamic testing of stay-cables. Remote Sens. **2**(1), 36–51 (2010)
10. Atzeni, C., Bicci, A., Dei, D., Fratini, M., Pieraccini, M.: Remote survey of the Leaning Tower of Pisa by interferometric sensing. IEEE Geosci. Remote Sens. Lett. **7**, 185–189 (2010)
11. Calcina, S.V., Piroddi, L., Ranieri, G.: Interferometric radar applications for the monitoring of vibrations of cultural heritage buildings and comparison with 3D velocimeter. In: Proceedings of the 33rd EARSeL Symposium 2013, Italy, pp. 141–155. EARSeL, Münster, Germany (2013)
12. Calcina, S.V., Piroddi, L., Ranieri, G.: Vibration analysis of historic bell towers by means of contact and remote sensing measurements. Nondestr. Test. Eval. **31**(4), 331–359 (2016)
13. Marchisio, M., Piroddi, L., Ranieri, G., Calcina, S.V., Farina, P.: Comparison of natural and artificial forcing to study the dynamic behaviour of bell towers in low wind context by means of ground-based radar interferometry: the case of the Leaning Tower in Pisa. J. Geophys. Eng. **11**(5), 055004 (2014)
14. Pieraccini, M., Fratini, M., Dei, D., Atzeni, C.: Structural testing of Historical Heritage Site Towers by microwave remote sensing. J. Cult. Heritage **10**, 174–182 (2009)

15. Pieraccini, M., Dei, D., Betti, M., Bartoli, G., Tucci, G., Guardini, N.: Dynamic identification of historic masonry towers through an expeditious and no-contact approach: application to the "Torre del Mangia" in Siena (Italy). J. Cult. Heritage 15, 275–282 (2014)
16. Calcina, S.V., Piroddi, L., Ranieri, G.: Fast dynamic control of damaged historical buildings: a new useful approach for structural health monitoring after an earthquake. ISRN Civil Eng. 2013, 1–6 (2013). (article ID 527604)
17. Fratini, M., Pieraccini, M., Atzeni, C., Betti, M., Bartoli, G.: Assessment of vibration reduction on the Baptistery of San Giovanni in Florence (Italy) after vehicular traffic block. J. Cult. Heritage 12, 323–328 (2011)
18. Luzi, G., Crosetto, M., Fernández, E.: Radar interferometry for monitoring the vibration characteristics of buildings and civil structures: recent case studies in Spain. Sensors 17(4), 669 (2017). https://doi.org/10.3390/s17040669
19. Noferini, L., Pieraccini, M., Luzi, G., Mecatti, D., Macaluso, G., Atzeni, C.: Ground-based radar interferometry for monitoring unstable slopes. In: Proceedings of the 2006 International Geoscience and Remote Sensing Symposium (IGARSS 2006), pp. 4088–4091. IEEE, New York (2006)
20. Lombardi, L., et al.: The Calatabiano landslide (southern Italy): preliminary GB-InSAR monitoring data and remote 3D mapping. Landslides 14, 685–696 (2017). https://doi.org/10.1007/s10346-016-0767-6
21. Pieraccini, M., et al.: Landslide monitoring by ground-based radar interferometry: a field test in Valdarno (Italy). Int. J. Remote Sens. 24(6), 1385–1391 (2003)
22. Carlà, T., Farina, P., Intrieri, E., Ketizmend, H., Casagli, N.: Integration of ground-based radar and satellite InSAR data for the analysis of an unexpected slope failure in an open-pit mine. Eng. Geol. 235, 39–52 (2018)
23. Intrieri, E., et al.: Sinkhole monitoring and early warning: an experimental and successful GB-InSAR application. Geomorphology 241, 304–314 (2015)
24. Calcina, S.V., Piroddi, L., Ranieri, G., Trogu, A.: Terrestrial remote sensing and microtremor measurements for the study of the vibrations of a rock mass with large underground cavities. Rendiconti Online della Società Geologica Italiana 35, 46–49 (2015)
25. Dei, D., Mecatti, D., Pieraccini, M.: Static testing of a bridge using an interferometric radar: the case study of "Ponte degli Alpini", Belluno, Italy. Sci. World J. 2013, 7 (2013). (article ID 504958)
26. Pieraccini, M.: Monitoring of civil infrastructures by interferometric radar: a review. Sci. World J. 2013, 8 (2013). (article ID 786961)
27. Naitza, S.: Architettura dal tardo '600 al classicismo purista, collana "Storia dell'arte in Sardegna". Ilisso edizioni, Nuoro (1992)
28. Grillo, S.M., Pilia, E., Vacca, G.: Integrated study of the Beata Vergine Assunta dome with structure from motion and diagnostic approaches. In: International Archives of the Photogrammetry, Remote Sensing & Spatial Information Sciences, vol. XLII-2/W11, pp. 579–585. ISPRS, Hannover (2019)
29. Sanjust, P., Mistretta, F., Pilia, E.: The Pantheon of Gaetano Cima in Guasila. Interdisciplinary studies for its structural conservation. TEMA: Technol. Eng. Mater. Archit. 5(2), 158–169 (2019)
30. Mistretta, F., Sanjust, P.: Il santuario della Beata Vergine Assunta in Guasila. Storia, analisi e prospettive future per la conservazione. CG Creazioni grafiche, Guasila, Italy (2018)
31. Borcherdt, R.D.: Effects of local geology on ground motion near San Francisco Bay. Bull. Seismol. Soc. Am. 60, 29–61 (1970)
32. Calcina, S.V., Eltrudis, L., Piroddi, L., Ranieri, G.: Ambient vibration tests of an arch dam with different reservoir water levels: experimental results and comparison with finite element modelling. Sci. World J. 2014, 1–12 (2014). (article ID 692709)

33. Castellaro, S., Padrón, L.A., Mulargia, F.: The different response of apparently identical structures: a far-field lesson from the Mirandola 20th May 2012 earthquake. Bull. Earthq. Eng. **12**(5), 2481–2493 (2013). https://doi.org/10.1007/s10518-013-9505-9
34. Gallipoli, M.R., Mucciarelli, M., Castro, R.R., Monachesi, G., Contri, P.: Structure, soil–structure response and effects of damage based on observations of horizontal-to-vertical spectral ratios of microtremors. Soil Dyn. Earthq. Eng. **24**, 487–495 (2004)
35. Taylor, J.D.: Ultra-Wideband Radar Technology. CRC Press, Boca Raton (2001)
36. Wehner, D.R.: High-Resolution Radar, 2nd edn. Artech House, Norwood (1995)
37. Henderson, F.M., Lewis, A.J.: Manual of Remote Sensing. Principles and Applications of Imaging Radar, 3rd edn. Wiley, New York (1998)
38. Luzi, G., Monserrat, O., Crosetto, M.: Real aperture radar interferometry as a tool for buildings vibration monitoring: limits and potentials from an experimental study. In: Proceedings of the 10th International Conference on Vibration Measurements by Laser and Noncontact Techniques – AIVELA 2012, pp. 309–317. American Institute of Physics, College Park (2013)
39. Luzi, G., Crosetto, M.: Building monitoring using a ground-based radar. In: Beer, M., Kougioumtzoglou, I.A., Patelli, E., Au, S.K. (eds.) Encyclopedia of Earthquake Engineering. Springer, Berlin (2015)

Geophysical and Remote Sensing Techniques for Evaluating Historical Stratigraphy and Assessing the Conservation Status of Defensive Structures Heritage: Preliminary Results from the Military Buildings at San Filippo Bastion, Cagliari, Italy

Luca Piroddi[1]([⊠]) [ID], Sergio Vincenzo Calcina[1] [ID],
Donatella Rita Fiorino[1] [ID], Silvana Grillo[2] [ID], Antonio Trogu[1] [ID],
and Giulio Vignoli[1,3] [ID]

[1] Department of Civil Engineering, Environmental Engineering
and Architecture, DICAAR, UniCA, Cagliari, Italy
lucapiroddi@yahoo.it
[2] Department of Chemical and Geological Sciences, DSCG,
UniCA, Cagliari, Italy
[3] Geological Survey of Denmark and Greenland GEUS, Aarhus, Denmark

Abstract. This paper describes the preliminary results of integrated non-destructive surveys for the diagnosis of the materials and for the analysis of the underground structures of an historical building. The studied structure was built in the center of Cagliari, Italy. A single channel 200 MHz Ground Penetrating Radar (GPR) survey was carried out in order to provide the 3D reconstruction of the buried structures localized under the floor level of two rooms of the structure. Two 3D models of the underground environments were derived from orthogonal radar profiles. In addition, active Infrared Thermography (IRT) and Multispectral Imaging techniques (MSI) were utilized to perform the non-invasive inspection of the conditions of the surface materials. IRT images were processed via the Principal Component Analysis (PCA) technique. The reflective patterns of the GPR maps allowed to locate several buried anomalies. IRT data and MSI images have provided a fundamental support to enhance discontinuities and defects of the investigated surfaces.

Keywords: Historical architecture · Ground Penetrating Radar · Active Infrared Thermography · Multispectral Imaging · Integrated diagnostic methods

1 Introduction

Nowadays, both geophysical methods and non-destructive techniques are considered essential tools for the analysis of the integrity status of valuable historical structures. The increasing interest towards the restoration and the rehabilitation of ancient structures and monumental buildings has encouraged the use of these techniques for the diagnosis of the materials properties and the identification of defects, degradation, past

© Springer Nature Switzerland AG 2020
O. Gervasi et al. (Eds.): ICCSA 2020, LNCS 12255, pp. 944–959, 2020.
https://doi.org/10.1007/978-3-030-58820-5_68

interventions and pre-existing underground structures [1]. Several geophysical techniques were utilized to explore buried and external structures, such as foundations of historical buildings [2], ancient bridges [3], underground water systems and aqueducts [4], archaeological remains [5–8] and military architectures [9]. Geophysical surveys were performed to study the experimental dynamic behavior of historical structures [10–13] and ancient artificial urban caves [14]. Over the time, even miniaturized systems, so-called micro-geophysical methods, were improved to characterize construction materials, ancient walls, frescoes and historical artworks [15–18].

In this framework, the preliminary results of the integrated non-invasive surveys carried out within a monumental structure in the historical center of Cagliari (southern Sardinia, Italy) are discussed. Ground Penetrating Radar (GPR) surveys, Infrared Thermography (IRT) and Multispectral (MS) measurements have been applied. The surveyed structure is the "*Bastione di San Filippo*", constructed by the Piedmont Corps Engineers in the early 1700s, as a defensive reinforcement to the northwest of the city. The research has preliminary investigated the historical stratifications, the metamorphoses and changes in the uses of the spaces of the Bastion, closely related to the life of the military facility and uses, including the Royal Bakery dating back to 1823. At present, the Bastion houses the military library and the Military Red Cross, and it is a listed building since 2014 (Fig. 1.a). The structure comprises several buildings, belonging from different chronological phases. The most interesting structures are the two rectangular vaulted rooms - once used as a casemate - and other connected internal environments (Fig. 1.b–1.c) [19, 20].

The study has been carried out within the General Agreement signed in September 2018 by the University of Cagliari and the Italian Ministry of Defence [21].

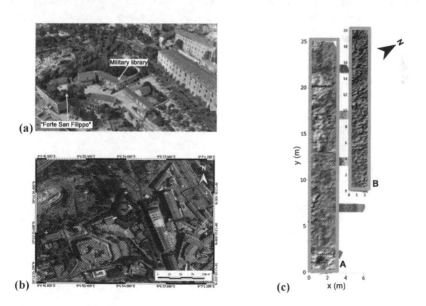

Fig. 1. Bastion of "*San Filippo*": (a) 3D image of the "*Forte San Filippo*" and the structure of the military library; (b) aerial image of the surveyed structure (red polygon); (c) schematic plan of the A and B rooms overlapped by the GPR maps. (Color figure online)

2   Materials and Methods

2.1   Ground Penetrating Radar: General Principles and Data Collection

GPR methods include different geophysical techniques based on the use of transmitted and/or reflected high-frequency microwave pulses. Generally, a transmitter generates the electromagnetic signals that, in turns, are collected by a receiving unit. The GPR techniques comprise different layouts of acquisition. In particular, transmitter and receiver can be separated (bistatic configuration) or can be the same antenna (monostatic configuration). The electromagnetic (EM) signals recorded at the receiver antenna permit to estimate both electrical and magnetic properties of the investigated materials. The velocity of the electromagnetic pulses travelling through materials with low-magnetic susceptibility depends on both the relative dielectric permettivity (ε_r) and the relative magnetic permittivity (μ_r) of the medium, according to the following equation [22]:

$$v = \frac{c}{\sqrt{\varepsilon_r \mu_r}} \tag{1}$$

The attenuation of the radar signals decreases as the frequency decreases (and/or when the electrical conductivity increases). Therefore, this parameter directly affects the depth of investigation of the GPR survey and both vertical and horizontal spatial resolution. It is possible to estimate the resolution of the radar survey starting from the wavelength of the electromagnetic signal. As a rule of thumb, the spatial resolution corresponds to about one-quarter of the wavelength of the signal.

The radar antenna is designed to transmit microwave signals over a specific bandwidth of frequencies with maximum power in correspondence to a central frequency. The spectral position of the maximum power peak of the transmitted waveform is inversely proportional to the duration of the radar pulse [20]. The bandwidth of the emitted signal is equal to the peak frequency of the amplitude monochromatic spectrum.

Ground Penetrating Radar survey was carried out using the IDS, Fast Wave DAD system controlled by K2 Fast Wave software, acquisition unit operating in monostatic configuration with a central frequency of 200 MHz. The GPR survey allowed the investigation of the rooms indicated with the letters A and B in Fig. 1.c, by covering, in a relative short time (five hours) an area of 120 m^2. The time of acquisition was set to 110 ns in order to investigate down to a theoretical depth of investigation of around 5 m. The survey consisted of parallel radar profiles with a line-spacing of 0.5 m along the x-direction (short side of the room, Fig. 1.c). Additional radar profiles were acquired along the perpendicular direction with the same spatial interval (y-direction of Fig. 1.c) in order to create a regular grid. The horizontal distance along each radar profile was measured through the use of spatial markers in correspondence to pre-established positions of the antenna. The frequency band of the radar probe was chosen to meet the best compromise between a significant depth of investigation and a suitable spatial resolution of the radar survey. The geometry of acquisition was designed in order to assure both a suitable spatial coverage and a significant lateral resolution.

The radar data were processed through Reflexw package (by Sandmeier®). The processing flow was composed of de-wow, move start time, background removal, gain, band pass, time-to-depth conversion. 3D reconstruction of the GPR anomalies was done via the analysis of the spatial coherence of the reflected and the diffracted signals in the depth interval between the floor surface and about 2.9 m depth. The three-dimensional reconstruction inferred from the radar data allowed imaging the spatial extension of the electromagnetic anomalies in both vertical and horizontal directions.

2.2   Infrared Thermography (IRT): General Principles and Data Collection

The Infrared Thermography (IRT) technique is a completely non-destructive methodology consisting of active and passive measurements of the infrared radiation emitted by the studied object. During the IRT data collection, a digital infrared camera is utilized to acquire the signals in the frequency band of the thermal-infrared, where the bodies at common environmental temperatures have the maximum of EM emission. From the acquired data, it is possible to obtain a reliable estimation of the main physical properties of the materials; in particular, both the thermal properties (e.g. conductivity, diffusivity, effusivity and specific heat) and spectral properties (emissivity, absorption, reflection and transmission coefficients) of the material can be assessed [23]. These physical properties are indirectly connected to medium characteristics such as porosity, superficial roughness and moisture. In turns, these inferred features of the medium can be very helpful in the assessment of the defects, degradation status and water content of the materials and potentially their spatial distributions.

The active IRT was carried out via a digital thermal camera (FLIR System AB model P30 PAL). The measurements were acquired indoor with three different points of view. Hence, the collected IRT data can be considered not affected significantly by the external weather conditions.

The *Principal Component Analysis* (PCA) was performed to process the infrared (IR) time-lapse thermal data. This procedure is a widely used linear projection technique which was implemented to map the original $(m \times p)$ matrix A into a second $(s \times p)$ matrix A_p characterized by $s < p$. Basically, the matrix A is projected on a new system of principal axis, according to the following general relationship:

$$A_p = U^T A \tag{2}$$

where the columns of the matrix U include the projection vectors that maximize the variance in the projected A_p. Therefore, this numerical technique highlights the uncorrelated projected distributions included in the data. The principal axes correspond to orthogonal eigenvectors of the square scatter matrix S $(m \times m)$. PCA is usually performed via the *Singular Value Decomposition* (SVD).

In particular, the scatter matrix can be derived as follows:

$$S = UDU^T = [U_s U_n] \begin{bmatrix} D_s & 0 \\ 0 & D_n \end{bmatrix} [U_s U_n]^T, \tag{3}$$

where the matrix U represents the modal matrix, or the eigenvector matrix, and D is the diagonal matrix corresponding to the eigenvalues of the scatter matrix.

The PCA of the IR thermographic data is suitable to enhance the visibility of defects in thermal infrared data and to improve the interpretation of the experimental IR images [24]. In the present study, the PCA of the IR data was performed by using a MATLAB® tool.

In parallel to the PCA approach and aiming at a wider support to experimental data interpretation, time dependent IRT datasets were also processed with other statistical approaches - like the regression models - aiming at further detecting the main features in the data by compacting the dynamic behavior into few images [25–28].

2.3   Multispectral Analysis: Methodology and Acquisition

Multispectral remote sensing applied to cultural heritage targets includes a family of techniques which investigate the surface finishes by means of their responses to extremely high frequency electromagnetic waves. Depending on frequency ranges used for energizing and sensing the artifacts we can choose transmission or reflection experimental configurations, also depending on the thickness of investigated objects. In particular, reflectometry, in the bands ranging from ultraviolet to near-infrared, can be used to highlights finishes defects and can enhance readability of drawings and paintings (sometimes even evidencing drawings completely invisible to eyes) by overcoming the shielding of exterior paintings layers and dirt patinas [16, 29–34].

In order to perform the multispectral survey, a modified digital single-lens reflex (DSLR) camera (original model NIKON D750) was used after removing the internal visible region passband filter: Five narrow EM bands from ultraviolet (UV) to near-infrared (NIR) were separately acquired with different exposure setups [17, 31–34]. In fact, the three colors channels of the standard sensors in many digital cameras are sensitive to an EM spectrum wider than visible spectrum. This additional portion of the recorded spectrum is generally filtered out though a bandpass filter installed by default by the manufacturer. Removing this filter (or substituting it with alternative filters - impacting other frequency bands – which can be added even in the external optics bodies) allows the users to acquire images over other ranges compatible with the full spectrum of the recording sensor (Fig. 2). The camera setup parameters were remotely controlled with the commercial acquisition software package Nikon Camera Control Pro 2. To make more uniform the target lighting, artificial halogen lights were utilized, and the contribution of natural light was highly reduced as the data were collected indoor.

The external bandpass EM filters, mounted over the optics, were:

- an UV bandpass filtering configuration, with acquisition in the range 320–390 nm;
- a visible bandpass filter with a window in the range 390–700 nm, to record images at visible wavelengths;
- an IR high pass filter at 720 nm;
- an IR high pass filter at 850 nm;
- an IR high pass filter at 950 nm.

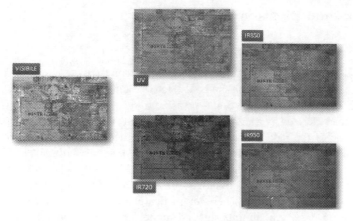

Fig. 2. Raw data example acquired within multispectral survey.

Multispectral images were processed with a Multi Images Stacking (MIS) algorithm [31–33]. The results enhanced low-visible details related to artifacts contents or connected to the conditions of the target. With this technique, photographic acquisitions are done with different and variable camera exposure set-up, obtaining one RGB raw image for each chosen exposure; the recorded raw images are converted to 16 bit grayscale images and stacked together to generate an image which maintains a high level of detail optimized from each exposure acquisition (Fig. 3). This procedure is repeated for each spectral family of acquisitions (each EM passband filter).

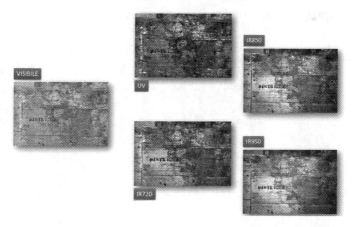

Fig. 3. Stacked images after the application of Multi Images Stacking (MIS) algorithm.

3 Results and Discussion

3.1 GPR Results

The results of the GPR survey show a relatively complex patterns of anomalies with different sizes and shapes in both the investigated rooms. From the horizontal slices at different depth in Fig. 4 and Fig. 5, it is possible to detect several high-amplitude signal reflections characterized by a significant spatial (both vertical and horizontal) coherence. The amplitude of the radar signals decreases as the depth increases. In particular, the slices regarding the location A are characterized by five intense GPR shallow anomalies. with horizontal sizes ranging between 1.5 m and 4.5 m. Despite a theoretical depth of around 5 m, the actual survey volume goes from 0 m to 2.9 m depth, under which the signal-to-noise ratio is too low. These anomalies can be classified accordingly to their three-dimensional shape, their intensity and shape. The GPR anomalies, indicated with the symbols A1, A2 and A3 (red rectangles), form one group. They are characterized by intense signals with significant spatial continuity. The horizontal extension of the A1 anomaly increases with depth and reaches its maximum at about 2.5 m. The A2 anomaly is detected at 20 m along the y-direction of the local reference system and covers a surface of about 6 m^2. The anomaly A3 has an area of about 2 m^2 at the surface and has its maximum horizontal extension between 1 m and 2 m. The nature of these highly reflective patterns is not clearly identified. However, the anomalies highlight the presence of a marked heterogeneity in the distribution of the electrical and the magnetic properties of the subsurface materials. The high-amplitude anomalies A1 and A2 could be generated by the presence of outcrops of the underground bedrock or by buried artificial structures related to the construction of the fortifications (in this respect, a preliminary hypothesis to be verified is that A1 and A3 might be buttress of a portion of one of the several successions of defense walls of the city).

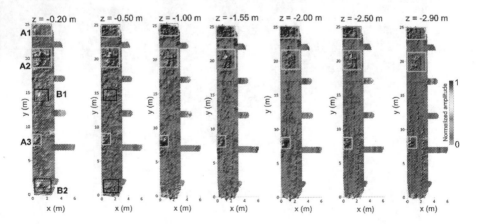

Fig. 4. GPR survey, room A: horizontal slices localized at a depth comprised between 0.2 m and 2.9 m. (Color figure online)

The geological units of the site mainly consist of limestone and superficial soils. Even other materials, used in the past to realize the embankment, can be locally observed. A second class of GPR anomalies includes relatively little reflective bodies, characterized by a smaller vertical extension; they are indicated with the letters B1 and B2 (blue rectangles) in Fig. 4. In particular, B2 shows its maximum amplitude at a depth between 0.1 and 0.5 m.

The GPR survey carried out in the room B highlights a more complex distribution of the electromagnetic signals. As we can see in Fig. 5, the pattern of anomalies is characterized by lower amplitude of the signals. The few detected anomalies of strong amplitude are localized in the depth interval: 0.5 to 1.5 m.

In particular, in the interval, in the y-direction, ranging from 15 m to 20 m, two GPR anomalies pop up. This set of anomalies are included inside the red rectangles indicated with the symbols D1 and D2 (but viseable also at $z = -0.2$ and $z = -1.55$). In the slices related to a depth of 0.20 m and 0.50 m two anomalies, indicated with the symbols C1 and C2, are visible. These bodies progressively vanish as depth increases. The GPR anomalies C3 and C4 appear at a depth of about 0.80 m from the surface of the pavement of the room B and reach a maximum vertical development equal to 1 m.

Based on the preliminary analysis, the nature of these reflective bodies is strongly uncertain and needs of further analyses. In this room, the GPR maps show also a higher frequency distribution of spatial features with minor amplitude, which can be interpreted as a higher noise level possibly masking significant anomalies or also as the EM response of preparatory works and rubbles accumulations for the hill profile flattening and pavement foundations.

However, the GPR results allow the identification of few interesting areas of significant amplitude to focus on during future investigations.

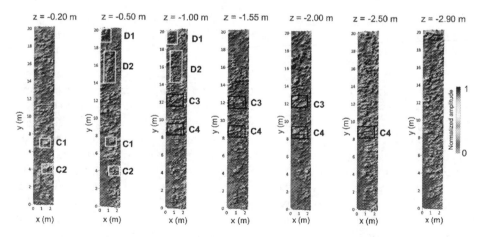

Fig. 5. GPR survey, room B: horizontal slices localized at depth comprised between 0.2 m and 2.9 m.

3.2   Description of IRT Results

The active IRT survey was performed to study the surfaces of the walls of the buildings in the study area. In particular, the investigation was performed to identify the main defects on the plasters of the internal walls, to assess the moisture content and patterns and other phenomena of degradation potentially correlated to different thermal properties of the construction materials. The images plotted in Fig. 6 show the IRT raw data.

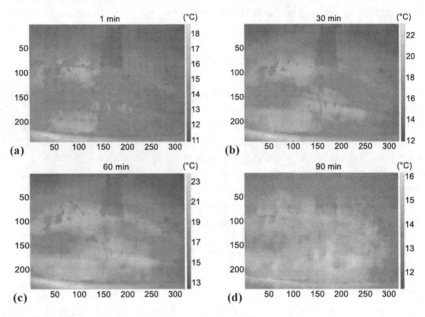

Fig. 6. Infrared Thermography: raw data acquired in correspondence to the position n.1, during heating and cooling phases. The color scale indicates the temperature of the surveyed surface. (Color figure online)

The preliminary analyses of the results highlight the presence of different thermal responses of the surveyed materials. These heterogeneous zones correspond to different stains with chromatic changes that could be attributed to the diffusion of biological colonization, dirt with varying moisture content and mold. Localized cracks, detachments and zones with loose adherence of the construction materials could be identified through the IRT inspection. The zones with loose adhesion of mortar usually result in higher temperatures due to the air filling the space between the wall and the detached surface thermally isolating the shallow layers from the deeper portions of the medium [35]. Thermal anomalies clearly show that the physicals properties of the materials are highly depending on the state of integrity. The warmer anomalies in the thermograms are usually related to high emissivity values. The presence of the main low-temperature anomalies can be justified by humid materials (characterized by a higher thermal capacity) and/or t by differences in emissivity and roughness. The time-lapse approach and parametric analysis of temperatures variation can help the interpretation of IRT results.

The PCA highlights different types of thermal response for each specific analyzed areal sector of the surveyed surface. In this respect, Fig. 7 shows some PCA results of dynamic IRT data in terms of the autovectors (blue curve on the right column): along their directions, the dataset is progressively projected with the associated scores for each pixel shown in the panels on the left (eigenvalues).

In Fig. 7, the first (in terms of statistical representativity) three (independent) autovectors are plotted. Qualitatively, they have opposite behaviors:

i)   the first principal component describes the mean dynamic during the experiment, with a heating energization followed by the natural cooling phase and the scores image showing how much each pixel responds to this sequence;

ii) the second principal component concerns the mean residual dynamic with respect to the first principal component projection, and has opposite trends, with a cooling phase followed by a heating one;

iii) the third principal component has also a first cooling stage followed by a heating phase, but shows a mean behavior which is no anymore pseudo-linear but rather curved.

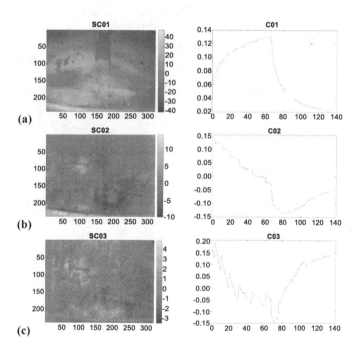

Fig. 7. PCA results of IRT survey for the first acquisition dataset, in terms of eigenvectors (blue curves on the right) and scores matrices (images on le left): first (a), second (b) and third (c) principal component results. (Color figure online)

The first two scores images have ranges of variability evidencing that the first component is one order of magnitude more meaningful in terms of the time-lapse representativity.

Principal components following the third have less variance differences from each preceding one, maintaining a spatial coherence of the scores images up to the sixth principal component, but continuing to show the same order of magnitude as the second one up to, at least, the eighth, substantially being the last two investigated random noise maps.

First component image is strongly influenced by the energization geometries and by properties of the exposed surfaces (e.g. material/emissivity, surface displacement and roughness), while these effects are not so evident in the others. Some radiometric artifacts due to optics are also fully included in the first component image like vignetting effects on the borders of the image.

Further detailed analysis of PCA is extending the interpretation to the first six principal components projections. More in depth analyses are in progress to map in detail the features of the materials and to correlate the thermal behavior of the different homogenous zones to the nature and the origin of the thermal anomalies.

Looking at the time-lapse dataset, PCA can be integrated by the analytical approaches based on data regression. In the cases the regression model can describe and summarize the experimental behavior, outputs maintain a physical meaning of the maps like, for instance, in the case of Intercept Temperature (T_0) and Thermal Gradient (TG or dT/dt) in Fig. 8. The two maps in Fig. 8 are qualitatively very similar but in-depth analysis allow to give significant sparks for the thermal behavior classification of the inspected pixels.

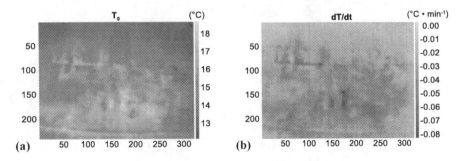

Fig. 8. Results of cooling dataset linear regression: (a) Intercept Temperature (T_0) and (b) Thermal Gradient (dT/dt).

Their joint analysis provides evidences of different behavior of heat flux diffusion towards the inner parts of the wall (Fig. 9). Scatter diagram in Fig. 9.a confirms that T_0 and TG maps are strongly correlated but composite RGB image in Fig. 9.b suggests some interesting features: this map has been produced normalizing T_0 and TG matrices and putting normalized T_0 matrix on red channel, normalized TG matrix on green channel, and a flat 255-value matrix on blue channel. In the composite RGB image, blue pixels imply that a small thermal dynamic was recorded (small T_0 and TG values) while white regions are indicative of the opposite behavior (high T_0 and TG values).

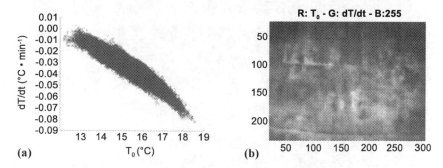

Fig. 9. Results comparison of the correlations between the two thermal indices obtained by the cooling dataset linear regression: (a) Scatter diagram (dT/dt versus T_0) and (b) RGB composite image (R: T_0; G: dT/dt; B: 255). (Color figure online)

Purple-dominating areas, corresponding to high T_0 and common TG values, identify patterns of anomalously high energization due to the geometries of IR lamps emitting lobes: in fact, in these pixels the high temperature reached at the end of the heating phase doesn't correspond to high TG during the cooling phase. Conversely, white patterns are more suspicious of defects such as plaster detachments and air bubbles because to a high temperature reached at the end of the heating phase corresponds a quick cooling stage. Some blue areas correspond to exposed surfaces without the most external plasters, while some others are the signature of the same vignetting feature observed in the scores map related to the first principal component of the full thermal cycle analysis.

3.3 Multispectral Results

Multispectral data were collected across the walls of the most Eastern room of the military complex with controlled and artificial illumination conditions. Inspected surfaces present signs, drawings and paintings over two different materials: wooden tables and plastered walls with paintings outcropping in some areas characterized by missing external finishes. Acquisition points were set at about 1.5 m from the targets.

The multispectral observations made possible to read parts of writings in the wooden tables hidden by dirt and even scraped regions (Fig. 10); so, the longer wavelengths (lambda > 850 nm and >950) of the NIR signals sensed the traces of the inks penetrated the wooden medium. The difference in contrast of the two images is partially due to the narrower band associated to 950 nm high-pass filter acquisition which implies a lower quantity of energy reaching the sensor.

Other EM bands were more effective in evidencing and differentiating elements of varying conditions, such as scrapes or grooves. On the other targets, during the multispectral survey, MIS technique allowed enhancement other writings and a drawing

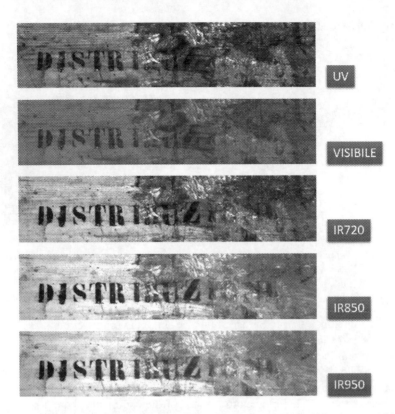

Fig. 10. Detail of stacked multispectral images focusing on an old writing over a table of the recycled wooden coating of part of the walls: at IR850 and partially at IR950 high pass band, the original writing "DISTRIBUZIONE" (distribution, in Italian) is readable, while it is not, when higher frequencies are used (in particular within the visible frequency range and even worse with UV data).

over the same type of wooden support and some paintings that were realized in an intermediate plaster which was only partially visible because it was somewhere crashed down and otherwhere covered by thick opaque layers of other finishes.

The multispectral imaging was not able to penetrate these most superficial opaque layers but allowed to record different spectral responses of the exposed paintings elements. In particular, a big difference between the historically exposed and some close surfaces was detected for wide extensions: the second surfaces were probably exposed only in recent times, as it was inferable by the features and the borders of their crashed elements. This different response could be due to different moisture conditions and also to different oxidation stage.

4 Conclusion

The complementary use of Ground Penetrating Radar surveys, Infrared Thermography and Multispectral Imaging techniques allowed to define an integrated fully non-invasive diagnostic protocol for historical buildings. The methodological approach was designed to perform a reliable analysis of the integrity status of the materials (internal surfaces and wall paintings) and to inspect underground structures. Two internal environments of an ancient building in the historical centre of Cagliari were explored through a GPR survey. The sectors characterized by significant amplitude of the reflected signals were identified. The origin of the main GPR anomalies was strongly uncertain and suggested future further analyses. Infrared Thermographic survey allowed to map degradation phenomena and shallow stains on the surfaces of the internal walls of the building. Multispectral imaging was utilized to improve the readability of old writings on wooden supports.

Acknowledgements. Authors would like to thank also Luigi Noli and Mario Sitzia from University of Cagliari for their invaluable technical support. This research was performed with the fundamental help of the students of the degree in Architecture. Moreover, this work would not be possible without the support of the in charge local authorities of *Comando Militare Esercito "Sardegna"*. Authors thank all of them for their contribution.

References

1. Cataldo, R., De Donno, A., De Nunzio, G., Leucci, G., Nuzzo, L., Siviero, S.: Integrated methods for analysis of deterioration of cultural heritage: the Crypt of "Cattedrale di Otranto". J. Cult. Heritage **6**(1), 29–38 (2005)
2. Abu-Zeid, N., Botteon, D., Cocco, G., Santarato, G.: Non-invasive characterisation of ancient foundations in Venice using the electrical resistivity imaging technique. NDT&E Int. **39**, 67–75 (2006)
3. Solla, M., Lorenzo, H., Rial, F.I., Novo, A.: Ground-penetrating radar for the structural evaluation of masonry bridges: results and interpretational tools. Constr. Build. Mater. **29**, 458–465 (2012)
4. Trogu, A., Ranieri, G., Calcina, S.V., Piroddi, L.: The ancient Roman aqueduct of Karales (Cagliari, Sardinia, Italy): applicability of geophysics methods to finding the underground remains. Archaeol. Prospect. **21**(3), 157–168 (2014)
5. Casas, A., et al.: Non-invasive geophysical surveys in search of the Roman Temple of Augustus under the Cathedral of Tarragona (Catalonia, Spain): a case study. Surv. Geophys. **39**, 1107–1124 (2018). https://doi.org/10.1007/s10712-018-9470-6
6. Piga, C., Piroddi, L., Pompianu, F., Ranieri, G., Stocco, S., Trogu, A.: Integrated geophysical and aerial sensing methods for archaeology: a case history in the Punic Site of Villamar (Sardinia, Italy). Remote Sens. **6**(11), 10986–11012 (2014)
7. Piroddi, L., Loddo, F., Calcina, S.V., Trogu, A., Cogoni, M., Ranieri, G.: Integrated geophysical survey to reconstruct historical landscape in Undug areas of the Roman ancient town of Nora, Cagliari, Italy. In: 2018 Metrology for Archaeology and Cultural Heritage, pp. 244–248. IEEE, New York (2018)

8. Piroddi, L., Calcina, S.V., Trogu, A., Ranieri, G.: Automated resistivity profiling (ARP) to explore wide archaeological areas: the prehistoric site of Mont'e Prama, Sardinia, Italy. Remote Sens. **12**, 461 (2020). https://doi.org/10.3390/rs12030461
9. Pirinu, A., Balia, R., Piroddi, L., Trogu, A., Utzeri, M., Vignoli, G.: Deepening the knowledge of military architecture in an urban context through digital representations integrated with geophysical surveys. The city walls of Cagliari (Italy). In: 2018 Metrology for Archaeology and Cultural Heritage, pp. 211–215. IEEE, New York (2018)
10. Calcina, S.V., Piroddi, L., Ranieri, G.: Fast dynamic control of damaged historical buildings: a new useful approach for Structural Health Monitoring after an earthquake. ISRN Civil Eng. **2013**, 1–6 (2013)
11. Calcina, S.V., Piroddi, L., Ranieri, G.: Vibration analysis of historic bell towers by means of contact and remote sensing measurements. Nondestr. Test. Eval. **31**(4), 331–359 (2016)
12. Marchisio, M., Piroddi, L., Ranieri, G., Calcina, S.V., Farina, P.: Comparison of natural and artificial forcing to study the dynamic behavior of bell towers in low wind context by means of ground-based radar interferometry: the case of the Leaning Tower in Pisa. J. Geophys. Eng. **11**(5), 055004 (2014)
13. Piroddi, L., Calcina, S.V.: Integrated vibration analysis for historical dome structures: a complementary approach based on conventional geophysical methods and remote sensing techniques. In: Gervasi, O., et al. (eds.) ICCSA 2020. LNCS, vol. 12249–12255, pp. 928–943. Springer, Heidelberg (2020, in press)
14. Calcina, S.V., Piroddi, L., Ranieri, G., Trogu, A.: Terrestrial remote sensing and microtremor measurements for the study of the vibrations of a rock mass with large underground cavities. Rendiconti Online della Società Geologica Italiana **35**(2015), 46–49 (2015). https://doi.org/10.3301/ROL.2015.60
15. Cosentino, P.L., Capizzi, P., Fiandaca, G., Martorana, R., Messina, P.: Advances in microgeophysics for engineering and cultural heritage. J. Earth Sci. **20**(3), 626–639 (2009). https://doi.org/10.1007/s12583-009-0052-x
16. Cosentino, A., Gil, M., Ribeiro, M., Di Mauro, R.: Technical photography for mural paintings: the newly discovered frescoes in Aci Sant'Antonio (Sicily, Italy). Cons. Patrim. **20**, 23–33 (2014)
17. Piroddi, L., Vignoli, G., Trogu, A., Deidda, G.P.: Non-destructive diagnostics of architectonic elements in San Giuseppe Calasanzio's church in Cagliari: a test-case for micro-geophysical methods within the framework of holistic/integrated protocols for artefact knowledge. In: 2018 IEEE International Conference on Metrology for Archaeology and Cultural Heritage, pp. 17–21. IEEE, New York (2018)
18. Ranieri, G., et al.: Method and system for activating and controlling a water-repelling process in walls. European Patent EP3040490B1, priority 2014-12-30, grant 2017
19. Fiorino, D.R., Pirinu, A.: Interdisciplinary contribution to the protection plan of the fortified old town of Cagliari (Italy). Int. J. Heritage Archit. **1**(2), 163–174 (2017)
20. Fiorino, D.R., Santoni, V.: Scenari di riconversione del Bastione di San Filippo a Cagliari. Proposte progettuali per un Distretto dell'Arte (Perspectives for the reconversion of the San Filippo Bastion in Cagliari. New design proposals for an Art District). In: Damiani, G., Fiorino, D.R. (eds.) Military Landscapes, pp. 125–136. Skira, Milan (2017)
21. Fiorino, D.R., Iannotti, P., Mellano, P.: Il riuso delle aree militari in Italia: esperienze di ricerca e didattica per le caserme di Bolzano e Cagliari in Il patrimonio culturale in mutamento. Le sfide dell'uso. In: 35° Convegno Internazionale Scienza e Beni Culturali, pp. 749–760. Edizioni Arcadia Ricerche, Marghera Venezia, Italy (2019)
22. Davis, J.L., Annan, A.P.: Ground-penetrating radar for high-resolution mapping of soil and rock stratigraphy. Geophys. Prospect. **37**, 531–551 (1989)

23. Avdelidis, N.P., Moropoulou, A.: Applications of infrared thermography for the investiga-tion of historic structures. J. Cult. Heritage **5**, 119–127 (2004)
24. Martinetti, S., Grinzato, E., Bison, P.G., Bozzi, E., Cimenti, M.: Statistical analysis of IR thermographic sequences by PCA. Infrared Phys. Technol. **46**, 85–91 (2004)
25. Piroddi, L., Ranieri, G.: Night thermal gradient: a new potential tool for earthquake precursors studies. An application to the seismic area of L'Aquila (central Italy). IEEE J. Sel. Top. Appl. Earth Observ. Remote Sens. **5**(1), 307–312 (2011)
26. Piroddi, L., Ranieri, G., Freund, F., Trogu, A.: Geology, tectonics and topography underlined by L'Aquila earthquake TIR precursors. Geophys. J. Int. **197**(3), 1532–1536 (2014)
27. Piroddi, L.: From high temporal resolution to enhanced radiometric resolution: Night Thermal Gradient results. In: International GeoHazard Research Society (IGRS) 2014 Symposium at NASA Ames Research Center, 10 December 2014, Moffett Field, California, USA (invited speech) (2014)
28. Piroddi, L.: From high temporal resolution to synthetically enhanced radiometric resolution: insights from Night Thermal Gradient results. Eur. Phys. J. Spec. Top. (2020, in press). (Freund, F., Kamer, Y., Ouillon, G., Scoville, J., Sornette, D. (eds.) ISSN: 1951-6355 (Print Edition), ISSN: 1951-6401 (Electronic Edition))
29. Lerma, J.L.: Automatic plotting of architectural facades with multispectral images. J. Surv. Eng. **131**(3), 73–77 (2005)
30. Remondino, F., Rizzi, A.: Reality-based 3D documentation of natural and cultural heritage sites-techniques, problems, and examples. Appl. Geomat. **2**(3), 85–100 (2010)
31. Cogoni, M.: Nuove tecnologie non distruttive per lo studio e il restauro dei beni monumentali: applicazioni termografiche e multispettrali nell'ipogeo di San Salvatore di Sinis in Cabras. Master degree thesis in Conservazione dei beni architettonici e ambientali, academic year 2014/15
32. Piroddi, L., Ranieri, G., Cogoni, M., Trogu, A., Loddo, F.: Time and spectral multiresolution remote sensing for the study of ancient wall drawings at San Salvatore hypogeum, Italy. In: Proceedings of the 22nd European Meeting of Environmental and Engineering Geophysics, Near Surface Geoscience 2016, pp. 1–5. EAGE, Houten (2016)
33. Trogu, A., Cogoni, M., Ranieri, G., Piroddi, L., Loddo, F.: Invisible but not lost. The recovery of the wall drawings of the hypogeum of San Salvatore di Sinis (Sardinia, Italy). In: Proceedings of 24th Annual Meeting of the European Association of Archaeologists, vol. 1, p. 489. Edicions de la Universitat de Barcelona, Barcelona (2018)
34. Piroddi, L., Calcina, S.V., Trogu, A., Vignoli, G.: Towards the definition of a low-cost toolbox for qualitative inspection of painted historical vaults by means of modified DSLR cameras, open source programs and signal processing techniques. In: Gervasi, O., et al. (eds.) ICCSA 2020. LNCS, vol. 12249–12255, pp. 971–991. Springer, Heidelberg (2020, in press)
35. Menezes, A., Glória Gomes, M., Flores-Colen, I.: In-situ assessment of physical performance and degradation analysis of rendering walls. Constr. Build. Mater. **75**, 283–292 (2015)

Application of Non-invasive Measurements in the Recent Studies of the Scrovegni Chapel: Results and Considerations

Rita Deiana$^{(\boxtimes)}$ (iD)

Department of Cultural Heritage, University of Padova, 35139 Padova, Italy
rita.deiana@unipd.it

Abstract. The Scrovegni Chapel is known all over the world for the famous frescoes made by Giotto that decorate its interior. The building stands on the remains of the Roman amphitheater of Padua, in a unique, highly scenic position. Many unsolved doubts about the origins of this building and its link with the Roman amphitheater affect the Chapel. The evident structural and decorative in-homogeneities visible between the various parts of the building (e.g., the nave, the apse, the sacristy, the hypogeum and the walls under the roof), pose numerous doubts about the transformations that must have affected it over the centuries, probably changing its original shape. This work reports some examples of recent applications of ground-penetrating radar (GPR), electrical resistivity tomography (ERT), IR thermography, and multispectral imaging to the study of the Scrovegni Chapel. The results of the multidisciplinary project, of which these measurements are part, demonstrate that the integrated approach represents the basic condition for the right interpretation and comprehension of the results of non-invasive approach, mostly in complex archaeological and historical context as well as that of the Scrovegni Chapel.

Keywords: Geophysical methods · Non-invasive measurements · Scrovegni Chapel

1 Introduction

The use of geophysical methods for non-invasive identification of buried targets and the determination of the extension of the archaeological sites before their excavation is well known for decades [1–5]. Many examples of case-histories, in the recent scientific literature, show the usefulness of the application of a single geophysical method or a combination of different techniques in Cultural Heritage studies [6, 7]. The most common geophysical measurements adopted for archaeological investigations are based on magnetic, ground-penetrating radar (GPR), electrical resistivity tomography (ERT), electro-magnetic induction (EMI), or frequency domain electro-magnetic (FDEM) techniques. However, the possibility of the application of this broad range of methods, in particular contexts, such as urban surveys or indoor measurements, due to the noise and logistical constraints, is drastically restricted, often reducing it to the use more or less only the GPR technique [8].

© Springer Nature Switzerland AG 2020
O. Gervasi et al. (Eds.): ICCSA 2020, LNCS 12255, pp. 960–970, 2020.
https://doi.org/10.1007/978-3-030-58820-5_69

Closely related to these restrictions, and relatively more recent, are the developments of micro-geophysics measurements as a part of non-invasive diagnostic methods, useful for the analysis of historic buildings and their decorative systems [9–13]. In this case, non-invasive measurements can provide information on the nature and condition of the inner parts of the buildings, or of their decorations. This information is essential to correctly design and implement all interventions aimed at safeguarding, protecting, monitoring, and conserving the historical-artistic and archaeological heritage. In general, the common feature of all these techniques, regardless of scale and context, is the possibility of identifying the presence of anomalies/targets of interest in a non-invasive manner. In this sense, an example of the potential and advantages deriving from combined use of non-invasive techniques is offered by the recent studies conducted on the Scrovegni Chapel and the area of the Roman amphitheater of Padua, hosting this famous building (Fig. 1). The application of non-invasive techniques, at different scales of investigation and for different purposes, provided, in fact, in this context new useful information about the transformations that must have affected the Chapel over the centuries.

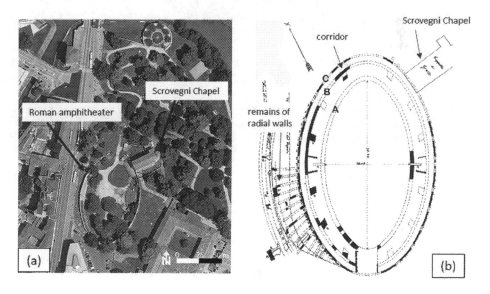

Fig. 1. (a) Location and link between the Scrovegni Chapel and Roman amphitheater of Padova (Google Earth modified); (b) Reconstruction of Roman amphitheater of Padova and distribution of its remains at the beginning of the nineteenth century (Brunelli Bonetti reconstruction modified)

The geophysical and, most in general, the non-invasive measurements carried out in this specific context, were a part of a multidisciplinary project, involving a number of experts in archaeology, history of art of the University of Padova, restorers of the Italian High Institute for Conservation and Restoration (ISCR), the local Superintendence (Soprintendenza archeologia, belle arti e paesaggio per l'area metropolitana di Venezia e le province di Belluno, Padova e Treviso) and the Municipality of Padova.

Thanks to this project, new integrated studies were made in synergy with the humanistic and technical-scientific support, aiming at the collection of new data about the Scrovegni Chapel [14]. The project demonstrated the importance of the contribution of non-invasive methods for the study of multi-layered historical sites. At the same time, it stressed that, especially in complex contexts, the contribution of archival documents and all the information available on the interventions carried out on the structure is necessary for a correct analysis and reading of the results of non-direct measurements.

The Scrovegni Chapel stands on the north-eastern sector of the Roman amphitheater of Padova (Fig. 1a). In particular, the building is not right-oriented E-W. Still, the south-western façade of the Chapel and the corresponding wall of the hypogeum, set on one elliptical wall of the amphitheater (Fig. 1b). The absence of documentation about the first centuries of the building's life has played and still plays a substantial role in understanding the events that have affected this location. Think, for example, of the particular position and orientation of the building, the role, and genesis of the hypogeum. Historical documents do not explicitly mention this underground space. Until today there is no agreement on the function of the so-called hypogeum of the Scrovegni Chapel and on the reasons that led to the construction of the Chapel only partially above it.

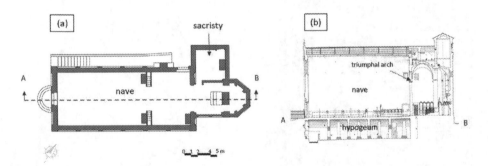

Fig. 2. (a) Plan of the Scrovegni Chapel, (b) Longitudinal section of the Scrovegni Chapel

The orientation of the building does not correspond with that of the radial walls of the Roman amphitheater (Fig. 1b), as documented by the archaeological excavations made between the end of the nineteenth century and the 2013 [15]. The current floor level of the hypogeum (Fig. 2b) would also presuppose that the radial walls of the Roman amphitheater and its foundations, found below in other parts of the Roman structure [15], have been demolished in this part, in 1300, to build the hypogeum. The asymmetric plan of the Chapel, by the presence of the sacristy on the northern side (Fig. 2a), also raises doubts about the possible demolition or non-realization of a southern part of a hypothetical transept of which the sacristy would represent one of the two parts.

2   Geophysical Measurements in the Roman Amphitheater

In order to analyze the link between the Scrovegni Chapel and the Roman amphitheater, also verifying the presence of buried remains of demolished parts of the Chapel, a series of GPR and ERT measurements were collected outside of the Chapel (Figs. 3, 4).

In particular, a GPR mapping was performed in the space in front of the SW facade of the Chapel (Fig. 3a), using an IDS RIS MF Hi-Mod GPR system with a dual-frequency 400–900 MHz antenna, making parallel lines every 0.3 m in the NW-SE direction. The collected data were post-processed using the ReflexW software, carrying out the start times correction, the mean-dewow filtering, the gain application, and the background removal for each GPR section.

Fig. 3. (a) Location of GPR measurements (Google Earth modified), (b) Time slice of GPR iso-amplitude at −1 m depth, (c) Historical photo (1944) of the interventions to protect the Scrovegni Chapel during the II World War (SABAP VE-MET); (d) Old postal card showing the Scrovegni Chapel (before the collapse of its porch in 1817) and Foscari-Gradenigo Palace (Padua Municipal Archives)

GPR sections were after interpolated to obtain a pseudo-volume of the investigated area, extracting the maps of the iso-amplitudes of the reflected signal at different depths. Figure 3b shows, in particular, the map of the iso-amplitudes of the reflected GPR signal referring to the pseudo-depth of 1 m, obtained assuming an average signal of transit speed of 0.1 m/ns.

Two old images found in the historical archives (Fig. 3c and d) helped in the interpretation of some of the anomalies identified in the GPR time slice (Fig. 3b). The photo in Fig. 3c, found in the historical archives of the local Superintendence (Soprintendenza archeologia, belle arti e paesaggio per l'area metropolitana di Venezia e le province di Belluno, Padova e Treviso- SABAP), taken during the intervention for the protection of the Scrovegni Chapel in the II World War, shows a big trench in front of the SW façade of the building (Fig. 3c). Probably this trench, although filled, generated the GPR anomaly here detected, as the lateral anomalies probably due to the buried remains of the ancient porch, collapsed in the nineteenth century, showed in the old postal card found in the historical archives of the Municipality of Padova (Fig. 3d).

Also, two ERT lines (L1 and L2 in Fig. 4) were carried out in the space outside the Chapel, in the area of the Roman amphitheater, to study the link between the Scrovegni building with the Roman structure and to identify the presence of possible underground structures, as hypothesized by several scholars [16, 17]. Both ERT lines were made with the use of an IRIS Syscal pro-72 resistivity-meter using 48 stain steel electrodes.

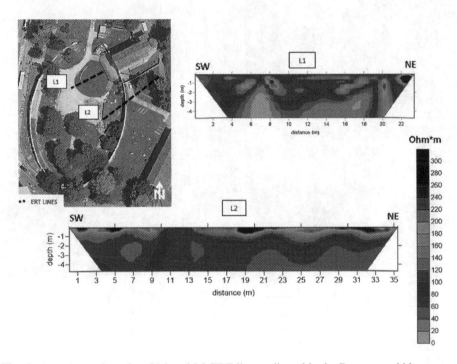

Fig. 4. Location and results of L1 and L2 ERT lines collected in the Roman amphitheater area

An electrode spacing of 0.5 m was adopted, for a total length of 23.5 m of a single line, and a corresponding investigation depth of about 5 m. The L2 tomography was carried out in roll-along mode, by performing two consecutive acquisitions, overlapping 24 channels, for a total length of 35.5 m, maintaining the same depth of investigation of about 5 m.

The results of the two ERT lines are shown in the images L1 and L2 in Fig. 4. The L1 line highlights the presence of some anomalies, which, due to their shape and type, could indicate the presence of buried structures related to the Roman amphitheater. The L2 line surely intercepts in the SW side, a part of the radial walls of the amphitheater and a known underground corridor. At the same time, it would seem to exclude in its NE side the presence of remains of foundations of a hypothetic demolished part of the Chapel transept.

3 Non-invasive Measurements Inside the Scrovegni Chapel

The large amount of data collected as part of the multidisciplinary project on the Scrovegni Chapel does not allow, given the limited purposes of this contribution, to account for the actual large number of non-invasive measurements realized to support this study also inside the building.

Therefore, only two examples of IR thermography and Multispectral Imaging for the analysis and understanding of the transformations of the internal structure of the Chapel during the centuries will be here discussed. The main feature of these two investigation methods lies in the possibility of acquiring data relating to the presence of anomalies in the structures without direct contact with the surfaces to be investigated. The absence of contact with the investigation surfaces represents the necessary condition for having the possibility of acquiring data on structures (e.g., walls) on which there is an extremely delicate and fragile decorative apparatus (e.g., frescoes) [18–24]. Although therefore these techniques do not allow in general to obtain detailed information on the deeper internal structure of the investigated system and in general arise with different purposes, the application in this context highlights some potential not yet fully exploited.

The use of IR thermography, inside the Scrovegni Chapel, has allowed us to discuss some of the hypotheses put forward by some scholars on its original distribution and partition of the space (Fig. 5).

Starting, for example, from what hypothesized by Laura Jacobus [25], about the existence of a partition and a pulpit necessarily clamped to the inner northern and southern walls of the nave, some thermographic IR measurements were made to verifying the actual existence of any anomalies of interest on the two walls. IR thermograms were acquired with a Flir T620BX/45° thermal imaging camera without artificial surface heating. The thermal measurements were repeated in different periods of the year, trying to identify the natural optimal seasonal thermal gradient to highlight possible anomalies in the walls.

Two thermal IR frames of the acquisitions made in January in the period of a maximum natural thermal gradient are shown in Figs. 5a and 5b. These thermal images evidencing other known hidden anomalies under the frescoes in the southern wall [26] made it possible to exclude the presence of any other anomaly compatible with traces of the presence of old structures. Even Multispectral Imaging, using a NIKON D800 FR modified camera by Profilocolore company, with an IR 850 nm band filter, confirmed the absence of structural interventions on the entire frescoed walls, except the traces of the insertion of the two small lateral wall screens in the nave (Fig. 6).

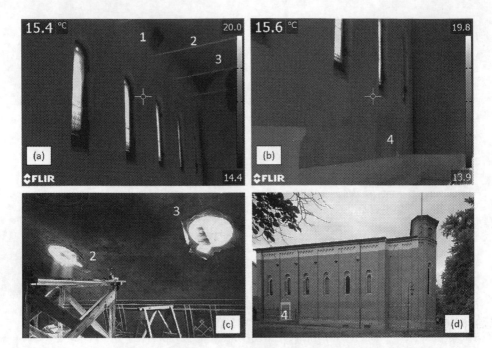

Fig. 5. (a) Thermal IR image of the upper part of the internal southern wall of the Scrovegni Chapel, (b) Thermal IR image of the lower part of the internal southern wall of the Scrovegni Chapel, (c) Historical photo of the interventions to protect the Scrovegni Chapel during the II World War (SABAP VE-MET); (d) Image of the external southern side of the Scrovegni Chapel with a visible walled door

Multispectral Imaging also allowed identifying the most likely original position of the wooden Cross painted by Giotto in the triumphal arch that connects the nave with the apse in the Chapel (Fig. 7e).

The wooden Cross was undoubtedly part of the Giotto's narration inside the Chapel. Multispectral images taken in the both opposite sides of the triumphal arch (Figs. 7a, b) show the presence of two specular anomalies (Figs. 7c, d).

These anomalies could apparently correspond to the positions of the holes for the insertion of a wooden beam supporting the Giotto's Cross, just between the two lateral funeral scenes (in Italian so-called "coretti") with funeral lanterns (Fig. 7e) and to face precisely the Cross painted in the opposite south side of the nave (Fig. 7f).

Fig. 6. (a) VIS and (c) IR filtered image (850 nm) of the wall screen insertion in the southern wall of the Scrovegni Chapel, (b) VIS and (d) IR filtered image (850 nm) of the wall screen insertion in the northern wall of the Scrovegni Chapel

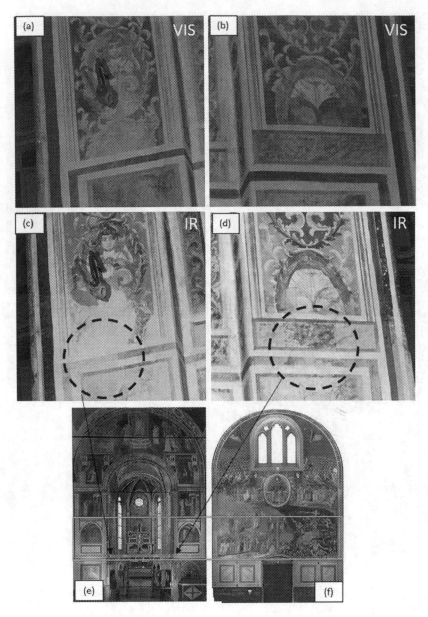

Fig. 7. (a) VIS and (c) IR filtered image (850 nm) showing an anomaly in the north side of the triumphal arch of the Scrovegni Chapel, (b) VIS (d) IR filtered image (850 nm) showing an anomaly in the south side of the triumphal arch of the Scrovegni Chapel; (e) hypothesis of the Giotto's Cross position in the triumphal arch; (f) position of the Cross in the Resurrection southern wall fresco

4 Conclusions

The results of the application of non-invasive methods from the field scale to the small one for the study of the Scrovegni Chapel in the Roman amphitheater of Padova demonstrated the high potential and additional value offered by these non-direct measurements. At the same time, these studies demonstrated that only by the synergy given by the multidisciplinary approach, involving humanistic and technical scientific worlds and only thanks to the dialogue between these experts from different disciplines, non-invasive data could be correctly interpreted, thus offering a real and useful contribution, fundamental in the complex field of Cultural Heritage studies.

Acknowledgments. The author wish to thank the University of Padova, the Municipality of Padova, the local Superintendence (Soprintendenza archeologia, belle arti e paesaggio per l'area metropolitana di Venezia e le province di Belluno, Padova e Treviso), and the Italian High Institute for Conservation and Restoration (ISCR), as partners of the research protocol "Metodologie integrate per lo studio di edifici storici affrescati: il caso della Cappella Scrovegni a Padova". This project was funded by the University of Padova, grant CPDA141049.

References

1. Clark, A.: Seeing Beneath the Soil. Prospecting Methods in Archaeology. B.T. Batsford Ltd., London (1990)
2. Schmidt, A.: Geophysical Data in Archaeology: A Guide to Good Practice. Oxbow Books, Oxford (2001)
3. Witten, A.: Handbook of Geophysics in Archaeology. Equinox Publishing, Sheffield (2006)
4. Campana, S., Piro, S.: Seeing the Unseen. Geophysics and Landscape Archaeology. Taylor & Francis Group, Milton (2009)
5. Sala, R., Garcia, E., Tamba, R.: Archaeological Geophysics - From Basics to New Perspectives. In: Archaeology, New Approaches in Theory and Techniques, Imma Ollich-Castanyer, IntechOpen (2012). https://doi.org/10.5772/45619
6. Sala, R., Tamba, R., Garcia, E.: Application of geophysical methods to cultural heritage. Elements **12**(1), 19–25 (2012). https://doi.org/10.2113/gselements.12.1.19
7. Cozzolino, M., Di Giovanni, E., Mauriello, P., Piro, S., Zamuner, D.: Geophysical methods for cultural heritage. Geophysical Methods for Cultural Heritage Management. SG, pp. 9–66. Springer, Cham (2018). https://doi.org/10.1007/978-3-319-74790-3_3
8. Casas, A., et al.: Non-invasive geophysical surveys in search of the Roman Temple of Augustus under the Cathedral of Tarragona (Catalonia, Spain): a case study. Surv. Geophys. **39**(6), 1107–1124 (2018). https://doi.org/10.1007/s10712-018-9470-6
9. Ranieri, G., Deiana, R., Piga, C.: Non-contact micro-geophysical measurements in the study of wall structures. Environ. Semeiot. **1**, 154–176 (2008). https://doi.org/10.3383/es.1.2.1
10. Cosentino, P., Capizzi, P., Fiandaca, G., Martorana, R., Messina, P.: Advances in microgeophysics for engineering and cultural heritage. J. Earth Sci. **20**, 626–639 (2009)
11. Perez-Gracia, V., Di Capua, D., Gonzalez-Drigo, R., Caselles, O., Beneit, L., Salinas, V.: GPR resolution in Cultural Heritage applications. In: Proceedings of the 13th International Conference on Ground Penetrating Radar (GPR 2010), pp. 1–5 (2010)

12. Cosentino, P., Capizzi, P., Martorana, R., Messina, P., Schiavone, S.: From geophysics to microgeophysics for engineering and cultural heritage. Int. J. Geophys. **2011**, 8 (2011). https://doi.org/10.1155/2011/428412
13. Martinho, E., Dionísio, A.: Main geophysical techniques used for non-destructive evaluation in cultural built heritage: a review. J. Geophys. Eng. **11**(5), 053001 (2014). https://doi.org/10.1088/1742-2132/11/5/053001
14. Deiana, R.: La cappella degli Scrovegni nell'anfiteatro romano di Padova: nuove ricerche e questioni irrisolte. Padova University Press, Padova (2018)
15. Bressan, M., Fagan, M.: Padova, anfiteatro romano. Gli scavi 2013: risultati scientifici, questioni aperte. In: Notizie di Archeologia del Veneto, 2/2013, pp. 28–37 (2015)
16. Zampieri G.: La cappella degli Scrovegni in Padova. Il sito e l'area archeologica, Skira, Milano (2004)
17. Bressan, M.: L'anfiteatro romano di Padova. Uno studio degli ambienti sotterranei. In: Atti della Giornata di Studi Livio, Padova e l'universo veneto nel bimillenario della morte dello storico (2017)
18. Carlomagno, G., Di Maio, R., Meola, C., Roberti, N.: Infrared thermography and geophysical techniques in cultural heritage conservation. Quant. InfraRed Thermogr. J. **2**(1), 5–24 (2005). https://doi.org/10.3166/qirt.2.5-24
19. Mercuri, F., Cicero, C., Orazi, N., Paoloni, S., Marinelli, M., Zammit, U.: Infrared thermography applied to the study of cultural heritage. Int. J. Thermophys. **36**(5), 1189–1194 (2014). https://doi.org/10.1007/s10765-014-1645-x
20. Moropoulou, A., Avdelidis, N., Karoglou, M., Delegou, E., Alexakis, E.: Multispectral applications of infrared thermography in the diagnosis and protection of built cultural heritage. Appl. Sci. **8**, 284 (2018). https://doi.org/10.3390/app8020284
21. Sarawade, A., Charniya, N.: Infrared thermography and its applications: a review, pp. 280–285 (2018). https://doi.org/10.1109/cesys.2018.8723875
22. Glavaš, H., Hadzima-Nyarko, M., Haničar Buljan, I., Barić, T.: Locating hidden elements in walls of cultural heritage buildings by using infrared thermography. Buildings **9**, 32 (2019). https://doi.org/10.3390/buildings9020032
23. Brusco, N., Capeleto, S., Fedel, M., et al.: A system for 3D modeling frescoed historical buildings with multispectral texture information. Mach. Vis. Appl. **17**, 373–393 (2006). https://doi.org/10.1007/s00138-006-0026-2
24. Asscher, Y., et al.: Combining multispectral images with X-ray fluorescence to quantify the distribution of pigments in the frigidarium of the Sarno Baths, Pompeii. J. Cult. Heritage (2019). https://doi.org/10.1016/j.culher.2019.04.014
25. Jacobus L.: Giotto and the Arena Chapel. Art, Architecture and Experience. Brepols, London (2008)
26. Grinzato, E., Bressan, C., Marinetti, S., Bison, P., Bonacina, C.: Monitoring of the Scrovegni Chapel by IR thermography: Giotto at infrared. Infrared Phys. Technol. **43**(3), 165–169 (2002). https://doi.org/10.1016/S1350-4495(02)00136-6

Towards the Definition of a Low-Cost Toolbox for Qualitative Inspection of Painted Historical Vaults by Means of Modified DSLR Cameras, Open Source Programs and Signal Processing Techniques

Luca Piroddi[1]([⊠]) [iD], Sergio Vincenzo Calcina[1] [iD], Antonio Trogu[1] [iD], and Giulio Vignoli[1,2] [iD]

[1] Department of Civil Engineering, Environmental Engineering and Architecture, DICAAR-UniCA, Cagliari, Italy
lucapiroddi@yahoo.it
[2] Geological Survey of Denmark and Greenland GEUS, Aarhus, Denmark

Abstract. Historical architecture is a primary element containing the identity values of a society. The wide diffusion of many ancient buildings gathering part of these values on painting walls over territories often characterized by poor technological or economic resources brings to consider the development of low-cost protocols to inspect valued surfaces and to give the authorities in charge of preservation and restoration adequate technical information. Here we present the preliminary results of a recent application of remote sensing micro-geophysical techniques to typical architectural targets such as vaults. A modified commercial Digital Single-Lens Reflex (DSLR) camera was used to acquire multispectral datasets on portions of a painted vault. Multispectral datasets were used raw or after the application of a pre-processing step with a Multi Images Stacking (MIS) algorithm. Multispectral images were then processed with spatial wavelet decomposition, histogram enhancing, thresholds application, image fusion, false colors compositing and Principal Component Analysis (PCA) techniques. Software used have been GNU Image Manipulation Program (GIMP) and Mathworks MATLAB (which can be substituted for the processing steps proposed by the built-in functions of GNU OCTAVE open-source software). Processed images were able to highlight features on vault paintings revealing details of the surface or its very shallow layers which were impossible or very difficult to distinguish in raw data. In fact, they emphasized low-visible details, differences in apparently similar finishes or pigments, cracks and probably details of surface preparation.

Keywords: Multispectral analysis · Digital image processing · PCA · Cultural heritage · Historical architecture · Painted walls inspection · Low cost diagnostics

© Springer Nature Switzerland AG 2020
O. Gervasi et al. (Eds.): ICCSA 2020, LNCS 12255, pp. 971–991, 2020.
https://doi.org/10.1007/978-3-030-58820-5_70

1   Introduction

In this paper, we present a recent multispectral survey carried out within a monumental building in the historical center of Cagliari, Italy: the church of San Giuseppe Calasanzio (Fig. 1a). Built between XVII and XVIII centuries in a baroque style, like other Italian churches of the Piarists' Order [1], together with the adjacent college. The church has a barrel-vaulted nave with three chapels intercommunicating on the sides and a deep presbytery, covered with a dome on an octagonal drum from which it is possible to laterally reach the sacristy and the building of the college (Fig. 1b); The complex is currently close because of long-lasting and incomplete restoration works with a general state of decay of the inner finishes. At ground level, the vault of the sacristy, indicated with red region in Fig. 1b and geometrically reconstructed in Fig. 2, has painting finishes with pictures of religious themes on the inner side, with decayed parts (Fig. 3a, b). First floor level over the sacristy is communicating with the college.

(a)   (b)

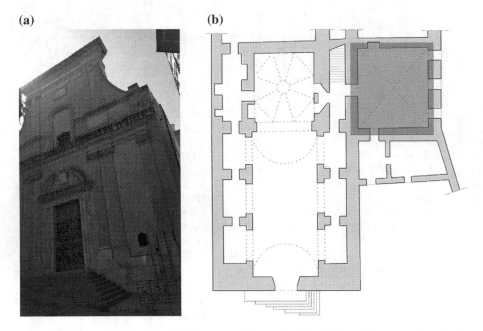

Fig. 1. Façade of the church of San Giuseppe Calasanzio (a) and plan of the ground level of the church with the connected sacristy indicated with a red region (b). (Color figure online)

Fig. 2. 3D model of the inner surface of the sacristy vault, reconstructed with Structure from Motion techniques.

Instrumental miniaturization has recently focused the interest of geophysical community to the application of micro-geophysics to also architectural elements [2–16].

The growing attention of our society to cultural heritage assets made possible an extension of traditional disciplinary limits to new methods and technology which, even with strong contribution from consolidated geophysical techniques, are developing aiming to resolve specific issues linked to the new diagnostic targets [17, 18].

In this context, an important role is being played by remote sensing techniques. Nowadays, remote sensing methods are an evolving research field taking advantage of the knowledge contamination from many specializations related to surveys and technology [19].

The most immediate demand for historical architecture documentation is the reconstruction of detailed and reliable 3D models of the monuments or their elements, that can be achieved with geomatic technologies such as photogrammetry through image-based modelling and Terrestrial Laser Scanner [20–26]. Structural analysis of cultural heritage assets is also possible by means of motion video magnification [27] or other photogrammetric techniques [28].

The experimental dynamic behavior of valuable historical slender structures, such as bridges, bell towers or other structures with one dimension prevailing on the others, can be assessed with ground-based remote sensing instruments simultaneously measuring structural vibrations of multiple backscattering points by means of Real Aperture Radar (RAR) interferometry [29–33].

Based on the radar interferometry, even slow movements of more complex building elements or parts of historical centers and Cultural Heritage sites are monitored using satellite Synthetic Aperture Radar [34–37].

Another emerging remote sensing technique in the field of Cultural Heritage inspection is the so called Teraherz (THz) technology, which, based on the recording of

(a)

(b)

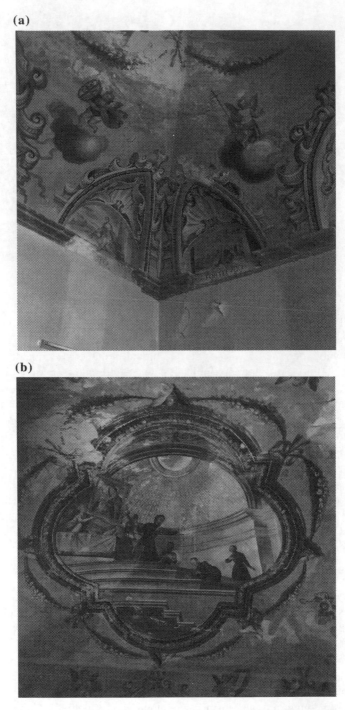

Fig. 3. Details of the sacristy vault paintings on a corner at the set level **(a)** and in the middle at the keystone level **(b)**.

electromagnetic (EM) waves of that bands, is used on various kinds of archaeological or historical items allowing, under specific experimental setups, to image studies bodies at various depths [38, 39].

Thermal infrared acquisitions allow the assessment of various issues linked to monuments studies, like detection of moisture presence, cracks, voids and anomalous elements in historical walls [21, 40–45]. The application of infrared thermography to small objects reliably identified hidden defects or invisible restoration works [38, 46–49].

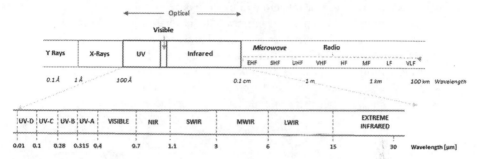

Fig. 4. Schematic representation of the most important EM bands for remote sensing applications [50, 51]. The bands involved in this study are highlighted in yellow. (Color figure online)

Multispectral (MS) remote sensing mostly investigates the surface finishes through their interaction with the radiation from a range of wavelengths, both visible and invisible to the human eye, across the EM spectrum. Acquisition setup include camera, light sources, and filters parameters.

Multispectral images are usually composed by different monochrome images collected by filtering the electromagnetic signals reflected and/or emitted by the objects through narrow spectral bands (Fig. 4). In most cases, the images are acquired:

- at the spectral interval of the ultraviolet light, at wavelengths lower than 400 nm;
- at the visible frequencies, corresponding to the wavelength interval comprised between about 400 nm and 700 nm;
- and at several frequency bands of the infrared signals, typically in the spectral bands of
  - Near Infrared (NIR), between 700 nm and 1100 nm,
  - Short Wavelength Infrared (SWIR), between 1100 and 3000 nm,
  - Mid Wavelength Infrared (MWIR), from 3000 nm to 6000 nm,
  - Long Wavelength Infrared (LWIR), from 6000 to 15000 nm,
  - and Far/Extreme Infrared (TIR), from 15000 nm to 1000000 nm.

These EM bands sensing is also known as optical remote sensing and is sensitive to a wide range of applications [19].

We have already mentioned THz and thermographic techniques, which often constitute part of the multispectral protocols extended to all or most parts of the optical remote sensing bands [38, 45, 49].

Over the time, the multispectral analysis has been improved to study paintings, frescoes and historical documents [52]. Advances in this field of study allow the identification of the kind of material utilized by the artists and the detection of overlays, drawing additions, defects and past pictures not clearly readable by means of the visible light. Depending on the comparison of the energizing and the recorded spectrum, we can distinguish fluorescence or reflectometric surveys.

The most common experimental configurations are based on recording the reflection of a natural or artificial energizing flux, in bands from ultraviolet (UV) to near-infrared (NIR), (Fig. 5). Their use allows to study the most superficial layers of paintings and writings [53–57]. As predictable, the penetration depth of the different signals mainly depends on their wavelength. As shown in the scheme of Fig. 5, the investigation depth increases as the frequency of the electromagnetic wave decreases.

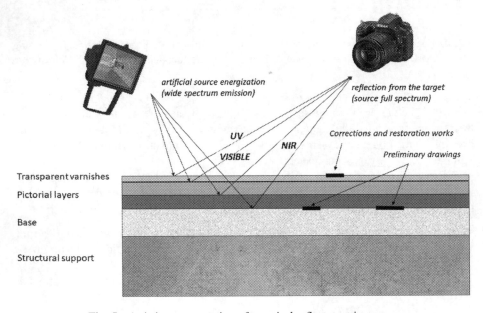

Fig. 5. Artistic representation of a typical reflectometric survey.

MS surveys are characterized by several parameters that influence the quality and the features of the experimental images. In the scientific literature different resolutions are defined. In particular, the spatial resolution indicates the size of a single pixel of the acquired data. The spectral resolution describes the width of the spectral bands that the sensor is suitable to record. The radiometric resolution defines the ability of the sensor to differentiate among small variations in the sensor incoming EM signal. In addition, the time resolution represents the time interval between two consecutive acquisitions [19].

In November and December 2017, the complex of San Giuseppe Calasanzio was the object of geophysical measurements as a preliminary step to develop a diagnostic protocol for the integrated knowledge of historical architectonic elements [11].

To test the usefulness of multispectral reflectometric methods for the inspection of precious inaccessible surfaces, this proximal sensing technique was applied to the sacristy painted vault. A set of low-cost hardware constitutes the acquisition instrumental fleet. Some processing steps are developed and proposed that can be easily implemented with open-source tools. Their preliminary application to the multispectral datasets is described to verify potentialities in detail enhancing, joint information retrieving and rough differentiation of apparently very similar pigments.

2 Data Acquisition and Preprocessing

2.1 Data Acquisition

The multispectral images were collected in raw format using a digital single-lens reflex (DSLR) camera, Nikon D750, modified by removal of the internal bandpass EM original filter. This, permanent, operation allows the camera sensor to receive and record EM energy for a spectrum wider than the only visible band for which it was designed. To perform the multispectral over multiple narrower bands, five external optical filters were mounted, one by one, over the camera lenses (Fig. 6):

- an UV bandpass filter, with acquisition in the range 320–390 nm;
- a visible bandpass filter, in the range 390–700 nm;
- an IR high pass filter at 720 nm;
- an IR high pass filter at 850 nm;
- an IR high pass filter at 950 nm.

The camera setup was remotely controlled with a commercial acquisition software package distributed by the same manufacturer, the Nikon Camera Control Pro 2 (Fig. 7a). Raw images had been acquired at a resolution of 6016 by 4016 pixels, with the following acquisition setup:

- Bit range: 14 bit
- F-stop: f/8
- Sensitivity: ISO-800
- Focal distance: 42 mm
- Exposition time: variable

To make more uniform the target lighting and to guarantee an energization over the camera recording bands, four artificial halogen lights were utilized (960 W, in total), and natural light was reduced as much as possible.

The MS datasets were collected shots through four shots across the painted vault of the sacristy (Fig. 7b): the camera was positioned approximately at one meter from ground, with direction mostly perpendicular to the vault inspected regions.

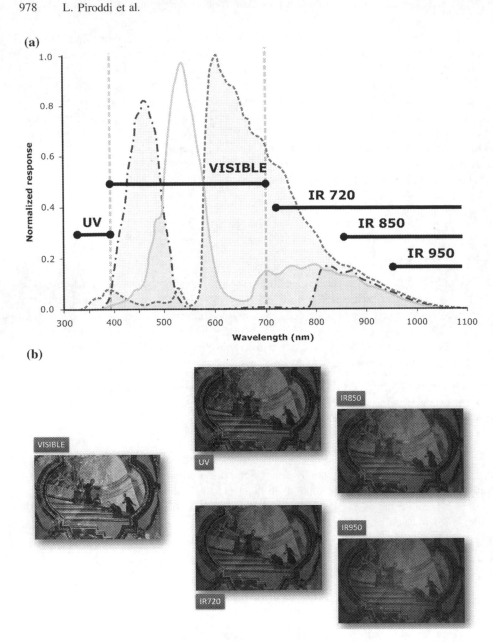

Fig. 6. (a) Representation of multispectral bands configurations (black lines indicate the fives EM filters), plotted over the sensitivity curves of the three RGB channels of a camera, the Nikon D200, similar to the one used during MS acquisition (RGB channels sensitivity from [42]. (b) Raw data example acquired within the multispectral survey.

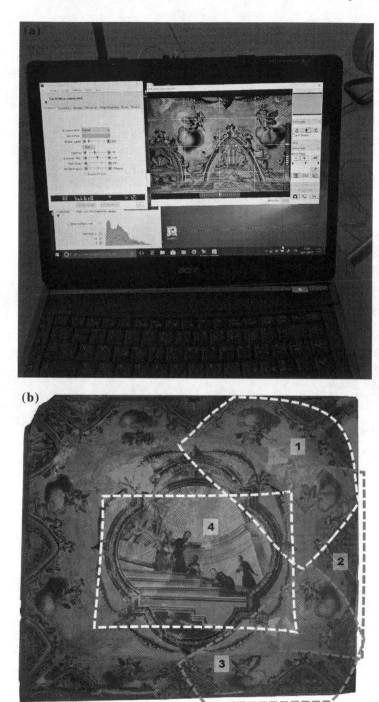

Fig. 7. (a) Setting up parameters and data preview through the acquisition software environment (courtesy F. Mura). (b) Regions of the painted vault surveyed by the four MS shots.

2.2 Pre-processing

Preliminarily to most processing steps, acquires datasets have been pre-processed with a Multi-Image Stacking (MIS) approach [45, 55–57]. Following this technique, raw MS images are acquired setting multiple camera exposition times for each combination of the other acquisition parameters (shot, optical filters, camera and light setups). Each RGB image, recorder with the given exposure, is then converted to a 16 bit grayscale image and then stacked with others at varying exposition time to produce an image (representative of the full stack images) which maintains a high level of details, optimized over each region of expositions (Fig. 8). This procedure is repeated for each spectral gathering of acquisitions (each EM passband filter) and for each shot, using free image conversion and common mathematical processing tools.

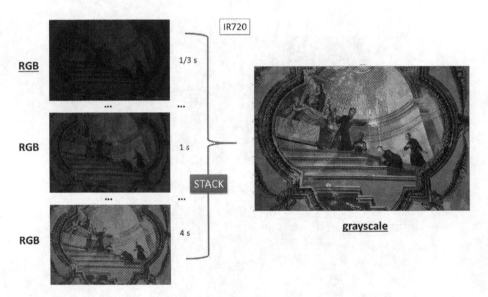

Fig. 8. The Multi Images Stacking (MIS) procedure: raw data (at varying exposure times of acquisition) on the left are the input to produce the stacked grayscale image on the right.

3 Data Processing

MS data are essentially images that can be processed as images or matrices with most common software tools for image editing (like GIMP, GNU Image Manipulation Program, or Photoshop by Adobe) and mathematical processing (like GNU Octave or MATLAB, MATrix LABoratory, by MathWorks).

The processing proposed in this study are feasible with both free and proprietary software, even though they are realized through GIMP and MATLAB.

3.1 Digital Image Processing and Spatial Filtering

One set of the processing steps implemented to enhance the qualitative interpretation of the MS datasets include most common functions in image editing, such as histogram enhancing, contrast magnification, color tuning, image fusion techniques, and others [58].

Furthermore, spatial signals in stacked grayscale images are evidenced using the Wavelet Decompose function [56], which is now included in the standard distribution of GIMP. The workflow for this processing step, illustrated in Fig. 9, can be summarized in:

- image spatial wavelet decomposition (6 levels), regional field removing (−1 level);
- histogram enhancing, contrast and brightness calibration, curve levels adjustments;
- merging of resulting high spatial frequency levels.

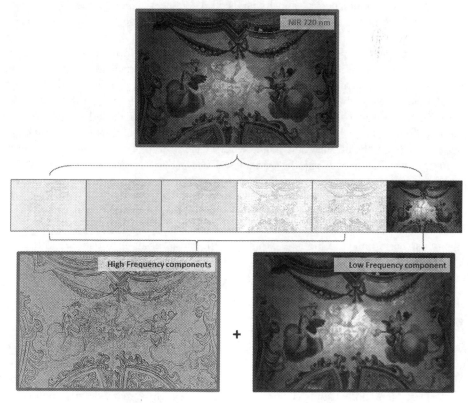

Fig. 9. Spatial wavelet decomposition of a stacked NIR image (bordered with violet) into low (red) and high (cyan) frequency components, with the application of histogram enhancing and grain fusion over high frequency levels. (Color figure online)

Finally, spectral dimension of experimental datasets can be explored, inside image editing environment, using popular tools like RGB channel combination or levels merging with the possibility to set up many parameters.

3.2   Principal Component Analysis of the MS Datasets

The second set of experimented processing steps was realized inside less user friendly but more powerful and flexible platforms, like the mathematical programming environments which however maintain a certain easy to use with respect to programming languages.

Most of the processing developed inside GIMP can be repeated even inside MATLAB environment, and some were, but with a little bigger difficulty due to the substantial absence of a graphical interface to tune many of the processing parameters. At least for beginners. Nevertheless, mathematical processing platforms flexibly allow to implement most complex processing like Principal Component Analysis, which is quite common in multispectral and hyperspectral remote sensing protocols so much that is available in specialized environmental remote sensing software (e.g. the open source SNAP by ESA).

The Principal Component Analysis (PCA) is a linear transformation implemented with the purpose to reduce multidimensional data in a few dimensions data set. The principle at the base of this technique considers that in many cases the data show correlations between their different dimensions. Through the PCA, the data are projected in a new set of axes. The new reference system is composed by the fewest possible dimensions. Therefore, this procedure consists of a coordinate transformation that allows to plot the original data in a new reference system of orthogonal axes with a minimum correlation between the variables. The first axis, derived from the PCA process, is oriented in the direction of the most variation, the second, in the direction of the new-most variation, etc. In order to calculate the new set of axes, the eigenvalues-eigenvectors decomposition is utilized. The eigenvectors are unit vectors pointing in the direction of the new axes of the reference system. The axis with the highest eigenvalue corresponds to the axis explaining the most variation of data set [59].

4   Results

4.1   Digital Image Processing and Spatial Filtering

Various sets of digital image processing were applied to the sample datasets, revealing great potentialities on their use to have a quick access to interpretable data through free software of generalist use. Images in Fig. 10 and their magnification in Fig. 11 show how is possible to quite simply obtain enhanced images where many details previously unrecognizable are revealed and interpretation of the inspected surfaces is aided.

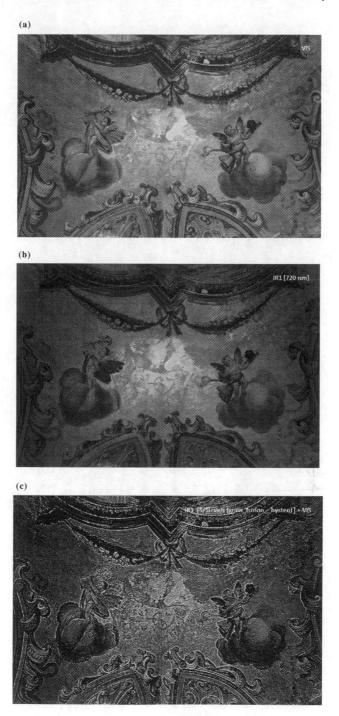

Fig. 10. Example of Digital Image Processing results on shot 1 dataset: visible (**a**) and NIR 720 nm (**b**) stacked data on the top images, and enhanced image (**c**) obtained by visible merging with the isolated and emphasized high spatial frequency signals of NIR image, on the bottom.

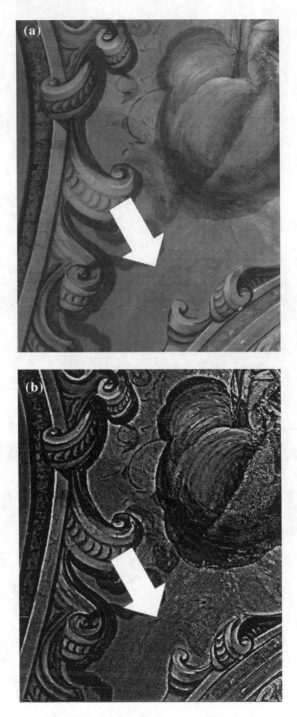

Fig. 11. Enlarged example of Digital Image Processing results on shot 1 dataset, at the bottom corner on the left: visible **(a)** and enhanced image **(b)**, showing a larger amount of details recognizable in the latter and the possibility to read painted subjects previously erroneously interpretable as noise or dirt on the paints.

Global view of Fig. 10 allows to evaluate the great quantity of informative data that appear to the watcher in terms of color lost drawings, minor cracks, surface roughness, to name some. Looking at a sample magnification, in Fig. 11, it is possible to notice a lot of the features of the original paints, revealing many details of leaves and decorations or evidencing an element previously imperceptible like the tape indicated by the white arrow.

4.2   Principal Component Analysis of the MS Datasets

Principal Component Analyses were applied to the four shots MS data, both raw, stacked and their combination. Here are presented some results from the processing of mixed datasets, with raw RGB visible images converted to bit depth homogeneous to grayscale UV and NIR data. In these conditions, we have input multidimensional matrices consisting in three layers for each acquisition at visible band for varying exposure times, plus one stacked UV layer and three stacked NIR layers (720, 850 and 950 nm filters). The layers identities are the vector base to which the eigenvectors proposed by the PCA are projected in the coordinates contained in the coefficient vectors matrix. For each eigenvector or Principal Component (PC), the dataset has a new coordinate per pixel, the eigenvalue or score matrix, consisting in the eigenvalues of the PCA transformation.

Fig. 12.   Visible band raw image of the shot 4.

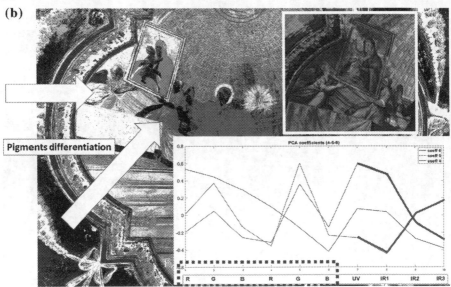

Fig. 13. PCA results on the shot 4 multispectral dataset: **(a)** 6-th principal component scores with the application of a visualization threshold aiming at contrast enhancement; **(b)** RGB false color combination of three principal components scores (R #4, G #5, B #6) with the superimposition of their coefficients (eigenvectors) plots: the white arrows indicate two angels' vests with quite similar color at visible wavelength but very different on PC5 (green) and PC6 (blue) projections. (Color figure online)

Figure 12 shows an RGB visible image acquired for shot 4. Figure 13 reports some results for the MS mixed dataset of the same shot. Figure 13a is the map of the 6-th PC score matrix, to which a threshold definition is applied to enhance the image contrast: many high frequency spatial features are evidenced, with respect to the RGB visible image, that can be reconducted to a subsurface roughness potentially related even to preparatory works. Figure 13b is an RGB false color combination of three principal components scores (R: PC #4; G: PC #5; B: PC #6) used here to differentiate two pigments with almost the same color, indicated by the white arrows. In the same figure, the coefficients of the three used PCs are plotted over part of the RGB false color image: the plot evidence that PC5 and PC6 have almost the same behavior over the original RBG axes constituted by two RGB acquisitions at visible band, but differ each other a lot for original coordinates corresponding to UV, NIR1 (720 nm) and NIR3 (950 nm) acquisitions. As a graphical validation we can see, in the map on the same figure, that the two angels' vests on the left of the image are represented with different behavior, being PC5 (green) prevalent for one and PC6 (blue) for the other. Despite of this, they are very similar in the visible band image (reported also inside Fig. 13b in the white bordered square on the top-right).

5   Conclusion

The paper presents a first approach towards the definition of a low-cost toolbox for qualitative inspection of valued painted surfaces. Most of the elements (low-cost modified DLSR cameras, pre-processing algorithms, digital image elaboration commands, signal processing techniques) were already existing before this application and are proposed here with the aim of a possible flexible integration in the context of the (qualitative) analysis of valued historical surfaced. The low-cost approach is essential to give a useful set of hardware and software tools which could be applied even to case studies of historical importance but with minor budget availability.

Processed images were able to highlight features on the vault paintings revealing details of the surface or its very shallow layers which were impossible or very difficult to distinguish in raw data. In fact, they emphasized low-visible details, differences in apparently similar finishes or pigments, cracks and probably details of surface preparation.

Acknowledgements. The authors gratefully acknowledge the essential help of L. Noli and M. Sitzia during data acquisition and instrumental setup. They also would like to thank F. Mura for the photo of Fig. 7.a. Finally, a special thanks to prof. D.R. Fiorino and the local prefecture for permitting the access to the San Giuseppe monumental structure.

References

1. Fiorino, D.R., Bagnolo, V., Grillo, S., Nonne, S., Schirru, M.: Integrated sciences for heritage reuse: interdisciplinary studies on the piarist college of San Giuseppe in Cagliari (Italy). Int. J. Heritage Archit. **1**(4), 517–537 (2017)

2. Arosio, D., Hojat, A., Munda, S., Zanzi, L.: High-frequency GPR investigations in Saint Vigilius Cathedral, Trento. In: 24th European Meeting of Environmental and Engineering Geophysics, Houten, The Netherlands, pp. 1–5. EAGE (2018)

3. Binda, L., Lualdi, M., Saisi, A., Zanzi, L.: Radar investigation as a complementary tool for the diagnosis of historic masonry buildings. Int. J. Mater. Struct. Integr. 5(1), 1–25 (2011)

4. Capizzi, P., Cosentino, P.L.: Electromagnetic and ultrasonic investigations on a Roman marble slab. J. Geophys. Eng. 8(3), S117–S125 (2011)

5. Cardarelli, E., De Donno, G., Scatigno, C., Oliveti, I., Martinez, M.P., Prieto-Taboada, N.: Geophysical and geochemical techniques to assess the origin of rising damp of a Roman building (Ostia Antica archaeological site). Microchem. J. 129, 49–57 (2016)

6. Cosentino, P.L., Capizzi, P., Fiandaca, G., Martorana, R., Messina, P.: Advances in microgeophysics for engineering and cultural heritage. J. Earth Sci. 20(3), 626–639 (2009)

7. Cosentino, P.L., Fiandaca, G., Messina, P., Martorana, R., Capizzi, P., Amoroz, I.R.: Method for detecting a sonic imprint of a three-dimensional object and related apparatus. U. S. Patent No. 8,166,820, 1 May 2012

8. Deiana, R., Leucci, G., Martorana, R.: New perspectives on geophysics for archaeology: a special issue. Surv. Geophys. 39(6), 1035–1038 (2018)

9. Martinho, E., Dionísio, A.: Main geophysical techniques used for non-destructive evaluation in cultural built heritage: a review. J. Geophys. Eng. 11(5), 053001 (2014)

10. Pirinu, A., Balia, R., Piroddi, L., Trogu, A., Utzeri, M., Vignoli, G.: Deepening the knowledge of military architecture in an urban context through digital representations integrated with geophysical surveys. the city walls of Cagliari (Italy). In: 2018 Metrology for Archaeology and Cultural Heritage, New York, USA, pp. 211–215. IEEE (2018)

11. Piroddi, L., Vignoli, G., Trogu, A., Deidda, G.P.: Non-destructive diagnostics of architectonic elements in San Giuseppe Calasanzio's Church in Cagliari: a test-case for micro-geophysical methods within the framework of holistic/integrated protocols for artefact knowledge. In: 2018 IEEE International Conference on Metrology for Archaeology and Cultural Heritage, pp. 17–21, New York, USA. IEEE (2018)

12. Ranieri, G., et al.: Method and system for activating and controlling a water-repelling process in walls. European Patent EP3040490B1, priority 2014-12-30, grant 2017 (2014)

13. Ranieri, G., Trogu, A., Loddo, F., Piroddi, L., Cogoni, M.: Digital museum from integrated 3D aerial photogrammetry, laser scanner and geophysics data. In: Proceedings of 24th European Meeting of Environmental and Engineering Geophysics, September 2018, Houten, The Netherlands, pp. 1–5. EAGE (2018)

14. Sambuelli, L., Comina, C., Catanzariti, G., Barsuglia, F., Morelli, G., Porcelli, F.: The third KV62 radar scan: searching for hidden chambers adjacent to Tutankhamun's tomb. J. Cult. Herit. 39, 288–296 (2019)

15. Tsourlos, P.I., Tsokas, G.N.: Non-destructive electrical resistivity tomography survey at the south walls of the Acropolis of Athens. Archaeol. Prospect. 18(3), 173–186 (2011)

16. Valluzzi, M.R., Lorenzoni, F., Deiana, R., Taffarel, S., Modena, C.: Non-destructive investigations for structural qualification of the Sarno Baths Pompeii. J. Cult. Herit. 40, 280–287 (2019)

17. Piro, S., et al.: Geophysics and cultural heritage: a living field of research for Italian geophysicists. First Break 33(8), 43–54 (2015)

18. Porcelli, F., et al.: Integrated geophysics and geomatics surveys in the valley of the kings. Sensors 20(6), 1552 (2020)

19. Lillesand, T., Kiefer, R.W., Chipman, J.: Remote Sensing and Image Interpretation. Wiley, Hoboken (2015)

20. Bernardini, F., et al.: Early Roman military fortifications and the origin of Trieste, Italy. Proc. Natl. Acad. Sci. 112(13), E1520–E1529 (2015)

21. Costanzo, A., Minasi, M., Casula, G., Musacchio, M., Buongiorno, M.F.: Combined use of terrestrial laser scanning and IR thermography applied to a historical building. Sensors **15**(1), 194–213 (2015)
22. Fiorino, D.R., Giannattasio, C., Grillo, S., Pintus, V., Porcu, M., Quaquero, E., Vacca, G.: The management of the restoration site. Diagnostic techniques, problems and perspectives. In: GEORES 2019 2nd International Conference on "Cultural Heritage: challenges, new perspectives and technology innovation". Springer, Heidelberg (2019)
23. Salonia, P., Scolastico, S., Pozzi, A., Marcolongo, A., Messina, T.L.: Multi-scale cultural heritage survey: quick digital photogrammetric systems. J. Cult. Herit. **10**, e59–e64 (2009)
24. Shi, R., Xu, M., Zhu, L.: New techniques of remote sensing in the university of architecture and planning. In: 2009 IEEE International Geoscience and Remote Sensing Symposium, New York, vol. 2, p. II-642. IEEE (2009)
25. Xu, Z., Wu, L., Shen, Y., Li, F., Wang, Q., Wang, R.: Tridimensional reconstruction applied to cultural heritage with the use of camera-equipped UAV and terrestrial laser scanner. Remote Sens. **6**(11), 10413–10434 (2014)
26. Yastikli, N.: Documentation of cultural heritage using digital photogrammetry and laser scanning. J. Cult. Herit. **8**(4), 423–427 (2007)
27. Fioriti, V., Roselli, I., Tatì, A., Romano, R., De Canio, G.: Motion magnification analysis applied to the dynamic identification of historic constructions. IOP Conf. Ser. Mater. Sci. Eng. **364**(1), 012001 (2018). IOP Publishing
28. Mistretta, F., Sanna, G., Stochino, F., Vacca, G.: Structure from motion point clouds for structural monitoring. Remote Sens. **11**(16), 1940 (2019)
29. Calcina, S.V., Piroddi, L., Ranieri, G.: Fast dynamic control of damaged historical buildings: a new useful approach for Structural Health Monitoring after an earthquake. ISRN Civ. Eng. **2013**, 1–6 (2013). Article ID 527604
30. Calcina, S.V., Piroddi, L., Ranieri, G.: Vibration analysis of historic bell towers by means of contact and remote sensing measurements. Nondestruct. Test. Eval. **31**(4), 331–359 (2016)
31. Marchisio, M., et al.: Applications of new technologies of ground-based interferometric radar to the study of cultural heritage buildings. In: 14th European Meeting of Environmental and Engineering Geophysics, Houten, The Netherlands, pp. 1–4, EAGE (2008)
32. Marchisio, M., Piroddi, L., Ranieri, G., Calcina, S.V., Farina, P.: Comparison of natural and artificial forcing to study the dynamic behaviour of bell towers in low wind context by means of ground-based radar interferometry: the case of the Leaning Tower in Pisa. J. Geophys. Eng. **11**(5), 055004 (2014)
33. Piroddi, L., Calcina, S.V.: Integrated vibration analysis for historical dome structures: a complementary approach based on conventional geophysical methods and remote sensing techniques. In: Gervasi, O. (eds.) ICCSA 2020, LNCS, vol. 12255, pp. 928–943. Springer, Heidelberg (2020)
34. Cigna, F., Lasaponara, R., Masini, N., Milillo, P., Tapete, D.: Persistent scatterer interferometry processing of COSMO-SkyMed StripMap HIMAGE time series to depict deformation of the historic centre of Rome, Italy. Remote Sens. **6**(12), 12593–12618 (2014)
35. Milillo, P., Giardina, G., DeJong, M.J., Perissin, D., Milillo, G.: Multi-temporal InSAR structural damage assessment: The London crossrail case study. Remote Sens. **10**(2), 287 (2018)
36. Tapete, D., Casagli, N., Luzi, G., Fanti, R., Gigli, G., Leva, D.: Integrating radar and laser-based remote sensing techniques for monitoring structural deformation of archaeological monuments. J. Archaeol. Sci. **40**(1), 176–189 (2013)

37. Mazzanti, P., Brunetti, A., Scarascia Mugnozza, G.: Mode TinSAR: an ESA incubation project dedicated to the terrestrial SAR interferometry. In: Proceedings of "Fringe 2011 Workshop", Frascati, Italy, 19–23 September 2011, ESA SP-697, January 2012

38. Bendada, A., Sfarra, S., Ibarra, C., Akhloufi, M., Pradere, C., Maldague, X.: Subsurface imaging for panel paintings inspection: a comparative study of the ultraviolet, the visible, the infrared and the terahertz spectra. Opto-Electron. Rev. 23(1), 90–101 (2015)

39. Cosentino, A.: Terahertz and cultural heritage science: examination of art and archaeology. Technologies 4(1), 6 (2016)

40. Avdelidis, N.P., Moropoulou, A.: Applications of infrared thermography for the investigation of historic structures. J. Cult. Herit. 5(1), 119–127 (2004)

41. Carlomagno, G.M., Di Maio, R., Meola, C., Roberti, N.: Infrared thermography and geophysical techniques in cultural heritage conservation. Quant. InfraRed Thermogr. J. 2(1), 5–24 (2005)

42. Arndt, R.W.: Square pulse thermography in frequency domain as adaptation of pulsed phase thermography for qualitative and quantitative applications in cultural heritage and civil engineering. Infrared Phys. Technol. 53(4), 246–253 (2010)

43. Sfarra, S., Marcucci, E., Ambrosini, D., Paoletti, D.: Infrared exploration of the architectural heritage: from passive infrared thermography to hybrid infrared thermography (HIRT) approach. Materiales de Construcción 66(323), 094, 1–16 (2016)

44. Perilli, S., Sfarra, S., Ambrosini, D., Paoletti, D., Mai, S., Scozzafava, M., Yao, Y.: Combined experimental and computational approach for defect detection in precious walls built in indoor environments. Int. J. Therm. Sci. 129, 29–46 (2018)

45. Piroddi, L., Calcina, S.V., Fiorino, D.R., Grillo, S., Trogu, A., Vignoli, G.: Geophysical and remote sensing techniques for evaluating historical stratigraphy and assessing the conservation status of defensive structures heritage: preliminary results from the military buildings at San Filippo bastion, Cagliari, Italy. In: Gervasi, O., et al. ICCSA 2020, LNCS, vol. 12255, pp. 944–959. Springer, Heidelberg (2020)

46. Mercuri, F., Zammit, U., Orazi, N., Paoloni, S., Marinelli, M., Scudieri, F.: Active infrared thermography applied to the investigation of art and historic artefacts. J. Therm. Anal. Calorim. 104(2), 475 (2011)

47. Orazi, N., et al.: Thermographic analysis of bronze sculptures. Stud. Conserv. 61(4), 236–244 (2016)

48. Di Tuccio, M.C., Ludwig, N., Gargano, M., Bernardi, A.: Thermographic inspection of cracks in the mixed materials statue: Ratto delle Sabine. Herit. Sci. 3(1), 1–8 (2015). https://doi.org/10.1186/s40494-015-0041-6

49. Peeters, J., et al.: IR Reflectography and active thermography on artworks: the added value of the 1.5–3 µm Band. App. Sci. 8(1), 50 (2018)

50. Stillman, G.E., Van Valkenburg, M.E.: Reference Data for Engineers: Radio, Electronics. Computers and Communications. Elsevier, Amsterdam (2001)

51. Verhoeven, G.: Basics of photography for cultural heritage imaging. In: Stylianidis, E., Remondino, F. (eds.) 3D Recording, Documentation and Management of Cultural Heritage, pp. 127–251. Whittles Publishing, Dunbeath (2016)

52. Marengo, E., et al.: Development of a technique based on multi-spectral imaging for monitoring the conservation of cultural heritage objects. Anal. Chim. Acta 706, 229–237 (2011)

53. Lerma, J.L.: Automatic plotting of architectural facades with multispectral images. J. Surv. Eng. 131(3), 73–77 (2005)

54. Remondino, F., Rizzi, A.: Reality-based 3D documentation of natural and cultural heritage sites—techniques, problems, and examples. Appl. Geomat. 2(3), 85–100 (2010)Cogoni, M.: Nuove tecnologie non distruttive per lo studio e il restauro dei beni monumenta-li:

applicazioni termografiche e multispettrali nell'ipogeo di San Salvatore di Sinis in Cabras. M.Sc. thesis, academic year 2014/15

56. Piroddi, L., Ranieri, G., Cogoni, M., Trogu, A., Loddo, F.: Time and spectral multiresolution remote sensing for the study of ancient wall drawings at San Salvatore hypogeum, Italy". In: Proceedings of the 22nd European Meeting of Environmental and Engineering Geophysics, Near Surface Geoscience 2016, Houten, The Netherlands, pp. 1–5. EAGE (2016)

57. Trogu, A., Cogoni, M., Ranieri, G., Piroddi, L., Loddo, F.: Invisible but not lost. The recovery of the wall drawings of the hypogeum of San Salvatore di Sinis (Sardinia, Italy). In: Proceedings of 24th Annual Meeting of the European Association of Archaeologists, vol. 1, p. 489. Edicions de la Universitat de Barcelona, Barcelona (2018)

58. Whitt, P.: Beginning Photo Retouching and Restoration using GIMP. Apress, New York (2014)

59. Wallisch, P.: Principal components analysis. In: Wallisch, P., Lusignan, M.E., Benayoun, M. D., Baker, T.I., Dickey, A.S., Hatsopoulos, N.G. (eds.) MATLAB for Neuroscientists, pp. 305–315. Academic Press, Cambridge (2014)

International Workshop on High Performance and Pervasive Computing (WHPPC 2020)

Support Vector Machine for Path Loss Predictions in Urban Environment

Robert O. Abolade[1], Solomon O. Famakinde[2], Segun I. Popoola[3,4(✉)],
Olasunkanmi F. Oseni[1], Aderemi A. Atayero[3], and Sanjay Misra[3]

[1] Department of Electronic and Electrical Engineering,
Ladoke Akintola University of Technology, Ogbomoso, Nigeria
[2] Department of Electronic and Computer Engineering, Lagos State University,
Epe, Nigeria
[3] IoT-Enabled Smart and Connected Communities (SmartCU) Cluster,
Covenant University, Ota, Nigeria
segun.popoola@covenantuniversity.edu.ng
[4] Department of Engineering, Manchester Metropolitan University,
Manchester M1 5GD, UK

Abstract. Path Loss (PL) propagation models are important for accurate radio network design and planning. In this paper, we propose a new radio propagation model for PL predictions in urban environment using Support Vector Machine (SVM). Field measurement campaigns are conducted in urban environment to obtain mobile network and path loss information of radio signals transmitted at 900, 1800 and 2100 MHz frequencies. SVM model is trained with field measurement data to predict path loss in urban propagation environment. Performance of SVM model is evaluated using Mean Absolute Error (MAE), Mean Square Error (MSE), Root Mean Square Error (RMSE) and Standard Error Deviation (SED). Results show that SVM achieve MAE, MSE, RMSE and SED of 7.953 dB, 99.966 dB, 9.998 dB and 9.940 dB respectively. SVM model outperforms existing empirical models (Okumura-Hata, COST 231, ECC-33 and Egli) with relatively low prediction error.

Keywords: Support vector machine · Path loss · Radio propagation · Radio network planning · Machine learning

1 Introduction

Over the years, the use of mobile communication systems has continued to grow, rapidly leading to increase in network capacity [1–3]. In a bid to design an efficient wireless communications system, the random nature of the propagation channel poses a great challenge for efficient design of mobile network engineer [4–6]. Path Loss (PL) is the attenuation of radio signal power between transmitting and receiving station due to reflection, refraction and diffraction among other propagation mechanisms [7,8]. For accurate radio network design and planning, PL propagation models are important because they have effect on signal coverage and network

© Springer Nature Switzerland AG 2020
O. Gervasi et al. (Eds.): ICCSA 2020, LNCS 12255, pp. 995–1006, 2020.
https://doi.org/10.1007/978-3-030-58820-5_71

interference [9]. Since network engineer has no control of the terrain, it is imperative to deployed accurate PL prediction model for efficient cellular communication system. PL prediction models are mathematical formulas used to characterize radio wave propagation as a function of distance, transmission frequency, antenna height and other conditions [10–14]. Radio propagation environments are categorized into rural, suburban, and urban with different and unique geographical features [7]. In previous works, Hata, COST 231, and Standard Propagation Model (SPM) models have been proposed for radio network planning at 1800 MHz [15–19]. However, signal attenuation and PL is determined by the nature of the terrain features such as high building, foliage and trees [20, 21].

In previous works, Artificial Neural Network (ANN), Adaptive Neuro-Fuzzy Inference System (ANFIS) and Extreme Learning Machine (ELM) have been used to solve PL prediction problem [22]. Support Vector Machine is an algorithm than can be used to distinguish between two-groups or classes (classification) and also to obtain mathematical model for data prediction (regression) in a network. Support Vector Machine (SVM) was proposed for PL predictions in [23]. The results show that SVM gave lower computational complexity compared to that obtained using Multilayer Perceptron (MLP) neural network. The Laplacian kernel was the best among the investigated kernels. Also, the SVM algorithm using Laplacian kernel and MLP had similar performance. The authors in [24] proposed regularization of non-linear path with a modified Huber loss for the SVM. The result show that the algorithm can compute the nonlinear regularization path. SVM-based modeling technique of cabin PL prediction was also proposed in [25]. The measured path loss values points were trained inside the cabin which was used to predict the PL values of the un-measured points. The results show that modelling system is better than the curve fitting system. The authors in [26] proposed nonlinear regularization path algorithm for a class of machines learning that have quadratic penalty, which is also known as quadratic SVM loss. A nonlinear path algorithm was developed using approximation technique. The developed algorithm gave better result over conventional method. Some research activities have been carried employing machine learning in PL prediction mainly in developed countries but not in Nigeria.

In this paper, a new radio propagation model is proposed for path loss predictions in urban environment using SVM. Field measurement campaigns are conducted in urban environment to obtain mobile network and path loss information of radio signals transmitted at 900, 1800 and 2100 MHz frequencies. SVM model is trained with field measurement data to predict path loss in urban propagation environment.

2   Materials and Method

2.1   Radio Signal Measurement and Data Collection

Extensive field measurement campaign was conducted within Canaan-land, Ota, Ogun State, Nigeria. Most of these physical structures have considerable heights such that they obstruct line of sight and produce non-line of sight signal paths in wireless communication channel at radio frequencies. Information about the geographic location and the altitude of the radio transmitters are presented in Table 1.

Table 1. Geographic locations of base station transmitters

BTS ID	Longitude	Latitude	Altitude (m)
A2GS1	3.162867	6.675068	50
A2GS2	3.162867	6.675068	50
A2GS3	3.162867	6.675068	50
A3GS1	3.162867	6.675068	50
A3GS2	3.162867	6.675068	50
A3GS3	3.162867	6.675068	50
E2GS1	3.164015	6.675253	52
E2GS3	3.164015	6.675253	52
E3GS1	3.164015	6.675253	52
E3GS3	3.164015	6.675253	52
M2GS1	3.163930	6.675245	52
M2GS3	3.163930	6.675245	52
M3GS1	3.163930	6.675245	52
M3GS3	3.163930	6.675245	52

A drive test experimental setup was designed for the field measurement campaign. The equipment, devices, and tools that constitute the experimental setup include: six commercial transceivers with fourteen (14) directional antennas, two mobile receivers, a Global Positioning System (GPS) receiver, a radio signal measurement software that runs on a Personal Computer (PC), and a motor vehicle. Ericsson RBS 2216, Ericsson RBS 2116, and Ericsson RBS 6201 base station transceivers were used for radio signal transmission at 900, 1800, and 2100 MHz respectively. Sectorial antennas of 13 dBi gain, 120° horizontally polarized sector panel were used to radiate electromagnetic signals which emanate from Ericsson RBS 2216 transmitters. 18 dBi gain, 65° vertically polarized antennas were used for radio wave transmission at 1710–1880 MHz frequency range. 17 dBi gain, 90° vertically polarized antennas were utilized for radio propagation at 2090–2290 frequency range. Two Sony Ericsson w995 mobile phones, with processing speed of 369 MHz and a removable Li-Po 930 mAh battery each, were used for radio signal reception at 900, 1800, and 2100 MHz. A Universal Serial Board (USB) magnet mount GPS receiver, BU-353-S4, was used to track mobile receiver's location at a given time. A 64-bit Windows Operating System (OS), 4 GB Random Access Memory (RAM) laptop with Intel® Core™ i5, M520 @2.40 GHz central processing capacity was used for data logging and storage.

When planning the drive test measurement survey, the area covered was initially scanned to ensure that there was no interference. The Broadcast Control Channel (BCCH) single frequency channel was obtained during each survey. There are two contiguous unused channels of a clearance of 200 kHz on either side of the measured signal so as to ensure that the measured frequency is clean. Radio signal measurements were conducted along 14 drive test survey routes in order to adequately represent the wireless channel characteristics of a typical urban propagation environment. Received Signal Strength (RSS) from respective transmitters were measured, recorded, and stored as the mobile receivers are driven along each survey route using TEMS^{TM} Investigation software developed by InfoVista®. The amount of radio signal power transmitted by each of the transmitters was 43 dB and the selected mobile receiver has a minimum sensitivity of -100 dBm.

The empirical measurements covered six (6) commercial transceivers with fourteen (14) directional antennas namely: A2GS1, A2GS2, A2GS3, A3GS1, AW3GS2, A3GS3, E2GS1, E2GS3, E3GS1, E3GS3, M2GS1, M2GS3, M3GS1, and M3GS3. Radio signal transmission and reception were performed at 900, 1800, and 2100 MHz operating frequencies, as expected of GSM, Digital Cellular System (DCS), and UMTS wireless systems respectively, in the directions of the base station antennas. Continuous measurement of the RSS, longitude, latitude, elevation, altitude, frequency and clutter height were recorded.

2.2   Data Pre-processing

Data collected through drive test (i.e. RSS, Longitude, Latitude, Elevation, and Frequency) were exported from TEMS Investigation software developed by Info-Vista into a spreadsheet file format. Mapping and location analysis of RSS data collected at 900, 1800, 2100 MHz radio frequencies were performed using Map-Info Pro^{TM}, produced by Pitney Bowes. Appropriate data filtering and sorting were performed using Microsoft Excel 2013 to remove data instance duplicates. The whole experimental field measurement process was accurately represented in ATOLL v3.1 radio network planning software produced by Forsk. Separation distances between base station transmitters and mobile receivers were computed for all data instances using ATOLL software.

The complete filtered and sorted data with nine variables (longitude, latitude, elevation, altitude, frequency, clutter height, distance, RSS, and PL) were randomly classified into 75% of training dataset and 25% of testing dataset for path loss model development and evaluation.

2.3   Development of SVM Model for PL Predictions

SVM was established and developed for learning theory. Moreover, excellent performances were gotten in regression and time series prediction applications with the aid of SVM regression, otherwise termed as Support Vector Regression (SVR) [27,28]. SVM consist of kernel methods which refer to a class of algorithms intended for pattern analysis. However, kernels have various conditions upon which they depend on.

Most influencing input variable attributes were selected using 10-fold validation approach. CFS Subset Evaluator and Greedy Stepwise methods were used to search and evaluate the influence of seven independent attributes on a dependent variable (path loss). These algorithms were implemented in a Java-based machine learning software, WEKA, produced at the University of Waikato, New Zealand. Furthermore, SVM-based PL model was developed by SMOreg regression algorithm. Model parameters and kernel evaluations were obtained for PL predictions in heterogeneous urban environment.

The performance and prediction accuracy of the empirical and SVM-based PL model was evaluated using Mean Absolute Error (MAE), Mean Square Error (MSE), Root Mean Square Error (RMSE) and Standard Error Deviation (SED) with respect to PL values in both training data and testing data, respectively. MAE, MSE, RMSE and SED were calculated using Eqs. (1)–(4) respectively [29,30]:

$$MAE = \frac{1}{k}\sum_{i=1}^{k}(PL_{m,i} - PL_{p,i}), \tag{1}$$

$$MSE = \frac{1}{k}\sum_{i=1}^{k}(PL_{m,i} - PL_{p,i})^2, \tag{2}$$

$$RMSE = \sqrt{\frac{1}{k}\sum_{i=1}^{k}(PL_{m,i} - PL_{p,i})^2}, \tag{3}$$

$$SED = \sqrt{\frac{1}{k}\sum_{i=1}^{k}(|PL_{m,i} - PL_{p,i}|) - MAE}, \tag{4}$$

where PL_m is the measured PL; PL_p is the predicted PL; and k is the number of samples in the dataset. Empirical models such as; Hata, COST 231, ECC-33 and Egli which are commonly used were employed for PL prediction based on the distance input vector provided in training and testing data sets.

3   Results and Discussion

The results obtained in this work are presented in this section. The data instances from field measurement campaign were collected and analyzed for model development. Information about the results obtained during data collection are presented in Table 2. A total of 123,985 raw data instances were logged with an average of 8,856 data instances per antenna. The remaining 18,865 unique data instances were curated for model development and evaluation after the duplicate has been removed. The mean number of unique data instances available along the survey routes of each of the fourteen sectors is 1,348. 75% of the complete RSS dataset (i.e. 14,142 unique data instances) was used for model training. The remaining 25% (i.e. 4,714 unique data instances) was used for model evaluation and testing.

Model was trained using 10-fold cross validation technique instead of dataset splitting approach. The parameters of SVM-based PL model are presented in Table 3.

Table 2. Quantitative summary of field measurement data

BTS ID	Raw data	Duplicates	Filtered data
A2GS1	2284	1626	658
A2GS2	3918	3168	750
A2GS3	4838	3388	1450
A3GS1	5551	4632	919
A3GS2	8139	7414	725
A3GS3	11555	9687	1868
E2GS1	11028	9067	1961
E2GS3	6591	4837	1754
E3GS1	24371	22274	2097
E3GS3	18319	15828	2491
M2GS1	4228	3439	789
M2GS3	6597	5052	1545
M3GS1	4123	3734	389
M3GS3	12443	10974	1469
Total	123985	105120	18865

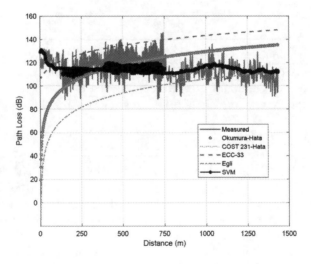

Fig. 1. Training results for path loss predictions at 900 MHz

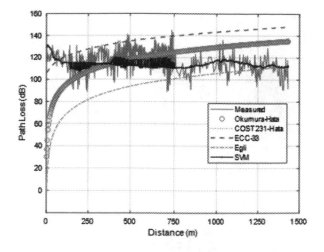

Fig. 2. Training results for path loss predictions at 1800 MHz

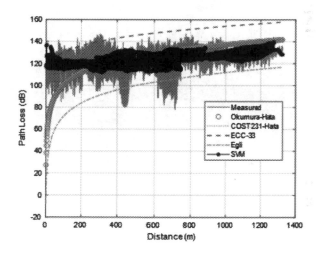

Fig. 3. Training results for path loss predictions at 2100 MHz

The developed SVM-based model and empirical models such as Okumura-Hata, COST 231, ECC-33 and Egli models were compared to the measured PL values for training and testing datasets to evaluate the prediction accuracy and generalization ability of the model. The results of the predicted model at 900, 1800 and 2100 MHz relative to the measured PL values in both training and testing datasets are graphically represented in Figs. 1, 2, 3, 4, 5 and 6 respectively.

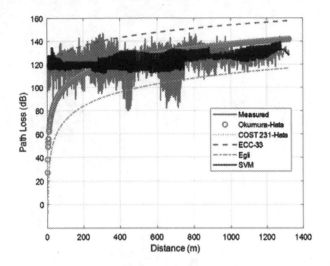

Fig. 4. Testing results for path loss predictions at 900 MHz

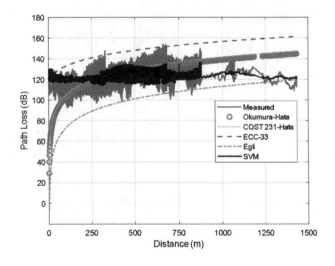

Fig. 5. Testing results for path loss predictions at 1800 MHz

Egli model produced the highest prediction error with MAE, MSE, RMSE, and SED of 27.000 dB, 969.657 dB, 31.139 dB, and 16.384 dB, respectively when compared to the measured PL values in training dataset. The performance evaluation results of the empirical models and SVM PL model based on the training data are presented in Table 4. The performance evaluation results of the empirical models and SVM PL model based on the testing data are presented in Table 5. The generalization ability demonstrated by SVM-based PL model (MAE, MSE, RMSE, SED of 7.933 dB, 98.773 dB, 9.938 dB, and 9.878 dB

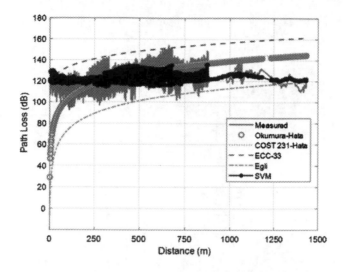

Fig. 6. Testing results for path loss predictions at 2100 MHz

Table 3. SVM model parameters

Attribute (normalized)	Weight
Constant	0.4487
Longitude	0.1939
Latitude	−0.2789
Elevation	−0.2531
Altitude	0.4655
Frequency	0.1207
Clutter height	−0.0149
Distance	0.1413

respectively) is much relatively better than those of all the empirical models. Egli model demonstrated the least generalization ability with MAE, MSE, RMSE, and SED of 27.044 dB, 974.318 dB, 31.214 dB, and 16.429 dB, respectively when compared to the measured PL values in testing dataset.

The prediction outputs of the developed SVM-based model, and popular empirical models (i.e. Okumura-Hata, COST 231, ECC-33, and Egli) were compared to the measured path loss values in both training and testing datasets to evaluate the prediction accuracy and generalization ability of the path loss models. The prediction error produced by SVM-based path loss model (MAE, MSE, RMSE, and SED values of 7.953 dB, 99.966 dB, 9.998 dB, and 9.940 dB respectively) is much relatively lower than those of all the empirical models.

Table 4. Performance of SVM and empirical PL models on training dataset

Model	MAE (dB)	MSE (dB)	RMSE (dB)	SED (dB)
Okumura-Hata	11.51	236.93	15.393	15.391
COST 231	11.778	241.055	15.526	15.374
ECC-33	21.884	609.75	24.693	11.948
Egli	27	969.657	31.139	16.384
SVM	7.953	99.966	9.998	9.94

Table 5. Performance of SVM and empirical PL models on testing dataset

Model	MAE (dB)	MSE (dB)	RMSE (dB)	SED (dB)
Okumura-Hata	11.507	237.888	15.424	15.424
COST 231	11.765	241.847	15.551	15.409
ECC-33	21.831	607.061	24.639	11.896
Egli	27.044	974.318	31.214	16.429
SVM	7.933	98.773	9.938	9.878

Egli model produced the highest prediction error with MAE, MSE, RMSE, and SED values of 27.000 dB, 969.657 dB, 31.139 dB, and 16.384 dB, respectively when compared to the measured path loss values in training dataset.

4   Conclusion

In this paper, SVM model was developed for path loss predictions in urban propagation environment. Field measurement campaigns were conducted to obtain RSS values and path loss values at varying longitude, latitude, altitude, elevation, clutter height, distance, and available radio frequencies (900, 1800, and 2100 MHz) within Canaaland, Ota, Ogun State, Nigeria. SVM model was trained with the network parameters to predict path loss. The performance of SVM model was compared with empirical models (Hata, COST 231, ECC-33, and Egli). Results from experimentation showed that SVM model gave the best output with MAE, MSE, RMSE, SED of 7.953 dB, 99.966 dB, 9.998 dB, 9.940 dB respectively. Comparative analysis showed that SVM model achieved high prediction accuracy with better generalization ability.

Acknowledgement. This work was carried out under the IoT-Enabled Smart and Connected Communities (*SmartCU*) research cluster of the Department of Electrical and Information Engineering, Covenant University, Ota, Nigeria. The research was fully sponsored by Covenant University Centre for Research, Innovation and Development (CUCRID), Covenant University, Ota, Nigeria.

References

1. Berezdivin, R., Breinig, R., Topp, R.: Next-generation wireless communications concepts and technologies. IEEE Commun. Mag. **40**, 108–116 (2002)
2. Ghosh, A., Ratasuk, R., Mondal, B., Mangalvedhe, N., Thomas, T.: LTE-advanced: next-generation wireless broadband technology. IEEE Wirel. Commun. **17**, 10–22 (2010)
3. Wang, C.-X., Haider, F., Gao, X., You, X.-H., Yang, Y., Yuan, D., et al.: Cellular architecture and key technologies for 5G wireless communication networks. IEEE Commun. Mag. **52**, 122–130 (2014)
4. Laiho, J., Wacker, A., Novosad, T. (eds.): Radio Network Planning and Optimisation for UMTS, vol. 2. Wiley, New York (2002)
5. Mishra, A.R. (eds.): Advanced Cellular Network Planning and Optimisation: 2G/2.5G/3G... Evolution to 4G. Wiley, New York (2007)
6. Mishra, A.R. (eds.): Fundamentals of Network Planning and Optimisation 2G/3G/4G: Evolution to 5G. Wiley, New York (2018)
7. Rappaport, T.S.: Wireless Communications: Principles and Practice, vol. 2. Prentice Hall PTR, New Jersey (1996)
8. Tse, D., Viswanath, P.: Fundamentals of Wireless Communication. Cambridge University Press, Cambridge (2005)
9. Nawrocki, M., Aghvami, H., Dohler, M.: Understanding UMTS Radio Network Modelling, Planning and Automated Optimisation: Theory and Practice. Wiley, New York (2006)
10. Oseni, O.F., Popoola, S.I., Abolade, R.O., Adegbola, O.A.: Comparative analysis of received signal strength prediction models for radio network planning of GSM 900 MHz in Ilorin, Nigeria. Int. J. Innov. Technol. Exploring Eng. **4**, 45–50 (2014)
11. Obot, A., Simeon, O., Afolayan, J.: Comparative analysis of path loss prediction models for urban macrocellular environments. Niger. J. Technol. **30**, 50–59 (2011)
12. Popoola, S.I., Atayero, A.A., Popoola, O.A.: Comparative assessment of data obtained using empirical models for path loss predictions in a university campus environment. Data Brief **18**, 380–393 (2018)
13. Faruk, N., Ayeni, A., Adediran, Y.: Characterization of propagation path loss at VHF/UHF bands for Ilorin city, Nigeria. Niger. J. Technol. **32**, 253–265 (2013)
14. Salman, M.A., Popoola, S.I., Faruk, N., Surajudeen-Bakinde, N., Oloyede, A.A., Olawoyin, L.A.: Adaptive neuro-fuzzy model for path loss prediction in the VHF band. In: International Conference on Computing Networking and Informatics (ICCNI) 2017, pp. 1–6 (2017)
15. Al Salameh, M.S., Al-Zu'bi, M.M.: Prediction of radiowave propagation for wireless cellular networks in Jordan. In: 2015 7th International Conference on Knowledge and Smart Technology (KST), pp. 149–154 (2015)
16. Faruk, N., Ayeni, A., Adediran, Y.A.: On the study of empirical path loss models for accurate prediction of TV signal for secondary users. Prog. Electromagn. Res. **49**, 155–176 (2013)
17. Ibhaze, A.E., Ajose, S.O., Atayero, A.A.-A., Idachaba, F.E.: Developing smart cities through optimal wireless mobile network. In: IEEE International Conference on Emerging Technologies and Innovative Business Practices for the Transformation of Societies (EmergiTech) 2016, pp. 118–123 (2016)
18. Nimavat, V.D., Kulkarni, G.: Simulation and performance evaluation of GSM propagation channel under the urban, suburban and rural environments. In: 2012 International Conference on Communication, Information & Computing Technology (ICCICT), pp. 1–5 (2012)

19. Rath, H.K., Verma, S., Simha, A., Karandikar, A.: Path loss model for Indian terrain-empirical approach. In: Twenty Second National Conference on Communication (NCC) 2016, pp. 1–6 (2016)
20. Oseni, O.F., Popoola, S.I., Enumah, H., Gordian, A.: Radio frequency optimization of mobile networks in Abeokuta, Nigeria for improved quality of service. Int. J. Res. Eng. Technol. **3**, 174–180 (2014)
21. Mitra, A., Reddy, B.: Handbook on Radio propagation for tropical and subtropical countries (1987)
22. Goldberg, D.E., Holland, J.H.: Genetic algorithms and machine learning. Mach. Learn. **3**, 95–99 (1988)
23. Benmus, T.A., Abboud, R., Shatter, M.K.: Neural network approach to model the propagation path loss for great Tripoli area at 900, 1800, and 2100 MHz bands. In: 2015 16th International Conference on Sciences and Techniques of Automatic Control and Computer Engineering (STA), pp. 793–798 ((2015)
24. Ostlin, E., Zepernick, H.-J., Suzuki, H.: Macrocell path-loss prediction using artificial neural networks. IEEE Trans. Veh. Technol. **59**, 2735–2747 (2010)
25. DalkiliÇ, T.E., Hanci, B.Y., Apaydin, A.: Fuzzy adaptive neural network approach to path loss prediction in urban areas at GSM-900 band. Turkish J. Electri. Eng. Comput. Sci. **18**, 1077–1094 (2010)
26. Ayadi, M., Zineb, A.B., Tabbane, S.: A UHF path loss model using learning machine for heterogeneous networks. IEEE Trans. Antennas Propag. **65**, 3675–3683 (2017)
27. Stitson, M., Gammerman, A., Vapnik, V., Vovk, V., Watkins, C., Weston, J.: Support vector regression with ANOVA decomposition kernels. In: Soentpiet, R., (ed.) Advances in Kernel Methods–Support Vector Learning, pp. 285–292 (1999)
28. Müller, K.-R., Smola, A.J., Rätsch, G., Schölkopf, B., Kohlmorgen, J., Vapnik, V.: Predicting time series with support vector machines. In: Gerstner, W., Germond, A., Hasler, M., Nicoud, J.-D. (eds.) ICANN 1997. LNCS, vol. 1327, pp. 999–1004. Springer, Heidelberg (1997). https://doi.org/10.1007/BFb0020283
29. Faruk, N., Popoola, S.I., Surajudeen-Bakinde, N.T., Oloyede, A.A., Abdulkarim, A., Olawoyin, L.A., et al.: Path loss predictions in the VHF and UHF bands within urban environments: experimental investigation of empirical, heuristics and geospatial models. IEEE Access **7**, 77293–77307 (2019)
30. Popoola, S.I., Jefia, A., Atayero, A.A., Kingsley, O., Faruk, N., Oseni, O.F., et al.: Determination of neural network parameters for path loss prediction in very high frequency wireless channel. IEEE Access **7**, 150462–150483 (2019)

Correction to: Leveraging Underwater Cultural Heritage (UCH) Potential for Smart and Sustainable Development in Mediterranean Islands

Dionisia Koutsi and Anastasia Stratigea [iD]

Correction to:
**Chapter "Leveraging Underwater Cultural Heritage
(UCH) Potential for Smart and Sustainable Development
in Mediterranean Islands" in: O. Gervasi et al. (Eds.):**
Computational Science and Its Applications – ICCSA 2020,
LNCS 12255, https://doi.org/10.1007/978-3-030-58820-5_19

In an older version of this paper, the first author's surname "Koutsi" was placed before their first name "Dionisia". This has been corrected.

The updated version of this chapter can be found at
https://doi.org/10.1007/978-3-030-58820-5_19

© Springer Nature Switzerland AG 2021
O. Gervasi et al. (Eds.): ICCSA 2020, LNCS 12255, p. C1, 2021.
https://doi.org/10.1007/978-3-030-58820-5_72

Author Index

Printed in the United States
by Baker & Taylor Publisher Services